DISPUTE RESOLUTION

ASPEN PUBLISHERS

DISPUTE RESOLUTION

Negotiation, Mediation, and Other Processes

Fifth Edition

STEPHEN B. GOLDBERG

Professor of Law, *Emeritus*
Northwestern University

FRANK E.A. SANDER

Bussey Professor, *Emeritus*
Harvard University

NANCY H. ROGERS

Dean and Michael E. Moritz Chair in Alternative Dispute Resolution
The Ohio State University Moritz College of Law

SARAH RUDOLPH COLE

Squire, Sanders & Dempsey Designated Professor of Law
The Ohio State University Moritz College of Law

Wolters Kluwer
Law & Business

AUSTIN BOSTON CHICAGO NEW YORK THE NETHERLANDS

Aspen Publishers
Attn: Permissions Department
76 Ninth Avenue, 7th Floor
New York, NY 10011-5201

To contact Customer Care, e-mail customer.care@aspenpublishers.com, call 1-800-234-1660, fax 1-800-901-9075, or mail correspondence to:

Aspen Publishers
Attn: Order Department
PO Box 990
Frederick, MD 21705

Printed in the United States of America.

1 2 3 4 5 6 7 8 9 0

ISBN 978-0-7355-6403-9

Library of Congress Cataloging-in-Publication Data

Dispute resolution : negotiation, mediation, and other processes / Stephen B. Goldberg . . . [et al.]. — 5th ed.
p. cm.
ISBN 978-0-7355-6403-9 (hardcover : alk. paper)
1. Dispute resolution (Law) — United States. I. Goldberg, Stephen B.

KF9084.G65 2007
347.73′9 — dc22 2007008582

About Wolters Kluwer Law & Business

Wolters Kluwer Law & Business is a leading provider of research information and workflow solutions in key specialty areas. The strengths of the individual brands of Aspen Publishers, CCH, Kluwer Law International and Loislaw are aligned within Wolters Kluwer Law & Business to provide comprehensive, in-depth solutions and expert-authored content for the legal, professional and education markets.

CCH was founded in 1913 and has served more than four generations of business professionals and their clients. The CCH products in the Wolters Kluwer Law & Business group are highly regarded electronic and print resources for legal, securities, antitrust and trade regulation, government contracting, banking, pension, payroll, employment and labor, and healthcare reimbursement and compliance professionals.

Aspen Publishers is a leading information provider for attorneys, business professionals and law students. Written by preeminent authorities, Aspen products offer analytical and practical information in a range of specialty practice areas from securities law and intellectual property to mergers and acquisitions and pension/benefits. Aspen's trusted legal education resources provide professors and students with high-quality, up-to-date and effective resources for successful instruction and study in all areas of the law.

Kluwer Law International supplies the global business community with comprehensive English-language international legal information. Legal practitioners, corporate counsel and business executives around the world rely on the Kluwer Law International journals, loose-leafs, books and electronic products for authoritative information in many areas of international legal practice.

Loislaw is a premier provider of digitized legal content to small law firm practitioners of various specializations. Loislaw provides attorneys with the ability to quickly and efficiently find the necessary legal information they need, when and where they need it, by facilitating access to primary law as well as state-specific law, records, forms and treatises.

Wolters Kluwer Law & Business, a unit of Wolters Kluwer, is headquartered in New York and Riverwoods, Illinois. Wolters Kluwer is a leading multinational publisher and information services company.

To Jeanne Brett, Valerie, Gillian, Amanda, Benjamin, Myranda Goldberg,
Emily, Alison, Tom, and Ernie Sander,
Doug, Jill, and Kim Rogers, Lynne and Kevin Robbins, and
Doug, Samuel, and Joshua Cole,

With undisputed gratitude

Summary of Contents

Contents

Preface

This fifth edition appears only four years after the fourth, reflecting the rapid pace of developments in this burgeoning field. Our goal has been to reflect these new developments, both legal and empirical. We have refined the strong points of the prior edition. Chapter 1 provides a broad overview of the dispute resolution landscape, followed by a thorough exploration of each of the primary processes (negotiation, mediation, and arbitration). Next comes a chapter that deals with some hybrids and that challenges the reader to assimilate and apply the information learned to a variety of settings, ranging from representing parties in mediation to designing effective systems for resolving disputes. To the existing areas of subject matter application (courts, family, public policy, and international) we have added a new chapter that deals with the emerging subject of exporting some of our most successful techniques to other countries, and in turn importing some of their proven institutions to help solve our own disputes. A concluding chapter focuses on the future of ADR from a policy perspective, and responds to a question that our students frequently ask: "Can I earn a living in ADR?"

We have also expanded the number of simulations and questions because of our conviction that these represent excellent ways for students to gain an understanding of the various processes. A number of the simulations are keyed to available videotapes, so that students can first do the simulations themselves and then see how they are handled by experienced dispute resolvers—a sequence that we have found particularly instructive.

There are various ways in which this book can be employed in teaching ADR. It can be used in a basic course—first, by looking to the text and excerpts as a basis for a conceptual discussion of the legal and policy issues. A second approach would be to organize class discussion around the questions that are sprinkled through each chapter. Quite obviously, these two approaches can be combined.

A considerably different approach looks to the book as background reading for simulations. Such simulations are used to acquaint the student with various dispute resolution processes by having the student watch or engage in the simulations as, for example, a negotiator, a mediator, or an arbitrator. This approach, too, can be combined with any of the others. The Teacher's Manual contains our suggestions for various ways of presenting such a basic overview course.

Of course, the book can also be used for more specialized offerings, such as an advanced seminar in conflict resolution.

We begin each chapter with an introductory note designed to orient the student to the main themes of the text and excerpts that follow. The excerpts have been selected from what we view as the most interesting and important materials in each area of dispute resolution; they are supplemented by extensive Notes and comments.

In general, footnotes and other references have been omitted from the excerpts; footnotes that have not been omitted retain their original numbering. Our own footnotes are indicated by asterisks. Most chapters also contain a series of questions designed to raise some of the important issues suggested by the materials and conclude with a list of references. Included in these lists are the books and articles cited in the chapter, as well as materials that we recommend for additional reading. Items from which excerpts are drawn are not necessarily included in these lists. A cumulative compendium of references is found in the back of the book.

We have followed standard conventions in the use of ellipses. In excerpts that use an outline format, we have not included ellipses where an interruption of the numbered or lettered sequence of material indicates an omission.

This book is primarily intended for law students and lawyers. We hope that others will also find it useful, but it seems important to stress that is not intended as a book on the philosophical or sociological aspects of conflict. Others have performed this task far better than we could.

We gratefully acknowledge the receipt of funding for the work that led to this book from the Ohio State University Moritz College of Law.

We also wish to record our appreciation to the many people who have provided valuable assistance, most particularly Chris Carlson, Sonya Cook, Melissa Cryder, Sharon Flower, Robika Garner, Eric Grasha, Art Greenbaum, Philip Harter, Emily Haynes, Deborah Laufer, Trina Lott, Craig McEwen, Kristen Noga, Mary Ellen O'Connell, Gene Orza, Jeff Senger, Deborah Smith, Erik Stock, Lawrence Susskind, Peter Swire, Cathy Thompson, Barbara Underwood, Marilyn Uzuner, and Detlev Vagts. In addition, we are especially grateful to Melody Davies and her Aspen colleagues without whom this book would not have appeared when it did. Last but not least, we want to acknowledge our gratitude to the countless students who have helped to sharpen our thinking about ADR.

S.B.G.
F.E.A.S.
N.H.R.
S.R.C.

January 2007

Acknowledgments

The authors gratefully acknowledge the permissions granted to reproduce the following materials.

AARON, Marjorie Corman, and David P. HOFFER (1997) "Decision Analysis as a Method of Evaluating the Trial Alternative," in Dwight Golann, *Mediating Legal Disputes: Effective Strategies for Lawyers and Mediators.* Reprinted by permission.

ALFINI, James J., and Eric R. GALTON, eds. (1998) *ADR Personalities and Practice Tips.* ABA Section of Dispute Resolution. Reprinted by permission.

AMERICAN BAR ASSOCIATION (2006) Model Rules of Professional Conduct 1.6, 1.12, 2.4, and 4.1. ©2006 by the American Bar Association. Reprinted with permission. Copies of ABA *Model Rules of Professional Conduct,* 2006 Edition are available from Service Center, American Bar Association, 321 North Clark Street, Chicago, IL 60610, 1-800-285-2221.

——— (2005) Model Standards of Conduct for Mediators. Copyright © 2005 by the American Bar Association. Reprinted with permission.

——— (2001) Model Standards of Practice for Family and Divorce Mediation. Copyright © 2001 by the American Bar Association. Reprinted with permission

BRAZIL, Wayne (1999) "Comparing Structures for the Delivery of ADR Services by Courts: Critical Values and Concerns." 14 *Ohio St. J. Disp. Resol.* Reprinted by permission.

BRETT, Jeanne M., Stephen B. GOLDBERG, and William L. URY (1994) "Managing Conflict: The Strategy of Dispute Systems Design." 6 *Bus. Wk. Executive Briefing Service.* Adapted with permission of McGraw-Hill, Inc.

BÜHRING-UHLE, Christian (1996) *Arbitration and Mediation in International Business.* Reprinted by permission.

CARTER, Jimmy (1982) *Keeping Faith: Memoirs of a President.* Copyright © 1982 by Jimmy Carter. Used by permission of Bantam Books, a division of Bantam Doubleday Dell Publishing Group, Inc. A new paperback edition of *Keeping Faith* was published in 1995 by the University of Arkansas Press.

CENTER FOR DISPUTE SETTLEMENT and THE INSTITUTE OF JUDICIAL ADMINISTRATION (1992) National Standards for Court-Connected Mediation Programs. Reprinted by permission.

CHERNICK, Richard, Helen J. BENDIX, and Robert C. BARRETT (1997) *Private Judging: Privatizing Civil Justice.* Reprinted by permission.

COLE, Sarah (2005) "Mediator Certification: Has the Time Come?" 11 *Disp. Resol. Mag.* 7 (Spring). © 2005 by the American Bar Association. Reprinted by permission.

——— (2006) "Unauthorized Practice of Law Charges: A Risk for Lawyers Representing Clients in Mediation and Arbitration in a Multijurisdictional Practice Environment," 13 *Disp. Resol. Mag.* 26 (Fall). © 2006 by the American Bar Association. Reprinted by permission.

COSTANTINO, C., and C. MERCHANT (1996) *Designing Conflict Management Systems.* San Francisco: Jossey-Bass. Reprinted by permission.

CPR INSTITUTE FOR DISPUTE RESOLUTION *Dispute Resolution Clauses and Rule 4.5.4 CPR-Georgetown Rules.* Reprinted by permission of the CPR Institute for Dispute Resolution.

CROUCH, Richard E. (1982) "The Dark Side of Mediation: Still Unexplored," *Alternative Means of Family Dispute Resolution* 339. This article first appeared in *Family Advocate,* a publication of the ABA Family Law Section. Reprinted by permission.

DEZALAY, Yves, and Bryant G. GARTH (1996) *Dealing in Virtue: International Commercial Arbitration and the Construction of a Transnational Legal Order.* Reprinted by permission.

FISHER, Roger, and William URY (1981, 1991) *Getting to Yes.* Copyright © 1981, 1991 by Roger Fisher and William Ury. Reprinted by permission of Houghton Mifflin Company. All rights reserved.

FISS, Owen (1984) "Against Settlement," 93 *Yale Law Journal* 1075. Reprinted by permission of the Yale Law Journal Company and Fred B. Rothman & Company.

FOLBERG, Jay (1983) "Divorce Mediation—Promises and Problems," paper prepared for Midwinter Meeting of ABA Section of Family Law, St. Thomas. Reprinted by permission.

GOLDBERG, Stephen B., Jeanne M. BRETT, and William L. URY (1991) "Designing an Effective Dispute Resolution System." Adapted from S.B. Goldberg, J.M. Brett, W.L. Ury, "Designing an Effective Dispute Resolution System," in *Donovan Leisure Newton & Irvine Practice Book,* J. Wilkinson, editor. Copyright © 1991 by John Wiley & Sons, Inc. Used with permission.

GOLDBERG, Stephen B., Eric D. GREEN, and Frank E.A. SANDER (1989) "Litigation, Arbitration or Mediation: A Dialogue," *A.B.A.J.* Reprinted with permission from the June 1989 Issue of the *ABA Journal, The Lawyer's Magazine,* published by the American Bar Association.

GOLDSTONE, Richard (2006) "The South African Truth and Reconciliation Commission: Is It Relevant to the US?" 12 *Disp. Resol. Mag.* 19-21 (Spring). Reprinted by permission.

GRAY, Erika B. (1992) "One Approach to Diagnostic Assesement of Civil Cases: The Individual Case-Screening Conference." Reprinted from the Summer 1992 issue of *The Court Manager* with the permission of the National Association for Court Management.

GUZMAN, Andrew, and Beth A. SIMMONS (2002) "To Settle or Empanel? An Empirical Analysis of Litigation and Settlement at the World Trade Organizations," 31 *J. Legal Stud.* 205. Reprinted by permission.

HAMILTON, Michael, and Dominic BRYAN (2007) "Deepening Democracy? Dispute System Design and the Mediation of Contested Parades in Northern Ireland," 22 *Ohio St. J. Disp. Resol.* 133. Reprinted by permission.

HARTER, Philip (1982) "Negotiating Regulations: A Cure for Malaise," 71 *Geo L.J.* 1. Reprinted with permission.

HARTER, Philip J. (2000) "Assessing the Assessors," 9 *N.Y.U. Envtl. L.J.* 32. Reprinted by permission.

HAYNES, John (1981) *Divorce Mediation: A Practical Guide for Therapists and Counselors.* Reprinted by permission of John Haynes, President, Haynes Mediation Associates, New York.

HOUCK, Stephen D. (1988) "Complex Commercial Arbitration: Designing a Process to Suit the Case," 43 *Arb. J.* 3. Reprinted from The Arbitration Journal, a quarterly magazine published by the American Arbitration Association.

KNEBEL, Fletcher, and Gerald S. CLAY (1987) *Before You Sue.* Copyright © 1987 by Fletcher Knebel and Gerald S. Clay. Reprinted by permission.

LAX, David A., and James K. SEBENIUS (1986) *The Manager as Negotiator.* Copyright © 1986 by David A. Lax and James K. Sebenius. Reprinted by permission of The Free Press, a division of Simon & Schuster.

McEWEN, Craig (1998) *Note on Mediation Research.* Printed by permission.

McEWEN, Craig, and Nancy ROGERS (1994) "Bring the Lawyers into Divorce Mediation," ABA *Disp. Resol. Mag.*, Vol. 1, No. 2 (Summer). Reprinted by permission of the American Bar Association.

McGOVERN, Francis (1986) "Toward a Functional Approach for Managing Complex Litigation," 53 *University of Chicago Law Review* 440. Reprinted by permission.

MELTSNER, Michael, and Philip G. SCHRAG (1973) "Negotiating Tactics for Legal Services Lawyers." Reprinted with permission from 7 *Clearinghouse Rev.* 259 (1973). Copyright © 1973, National Clearinghouse for Legal Services, Inc.

MNOOKIN, Robert, Scott PEPPET, and Andrew TULUMELLO (1996) "The Tension Between Empathy and Assertiveness," 12 *Neg. J.* 217. Reprinted by permission of Plenum Publishing Corp.

NATIONAL CONFERENCE OF COMMISSIONERS OF UNIFORM STATE LAWS (1994) Uniform Arbitration Act. Copyright © 1994 by the National Conference of Commissioners on Uniform State Laws. Reprinted with permission.

——— (2000) Revised Uniform Arbitration Act. Copyright © 2000 by the National Conference of Commissioners on Uniform State Laws. Reprinted with permission.

——— (2003) Uniform Mediation Act. Copyright © 2003 by the National Conference of Commissioners on Uniform State Laws. Reprinted with permission.

PEARSON, Jessica (1994) "Family Mediation," in *National Symposium on Court-Connected Dispute Resolution Research: A Report on Current Research Findings—Implications for Courts and Future Research Needs* 51-77. Reprinted by permission of the State Justice Institute.

RAIFFA, Howard (1982) *The Art and Science of Negotiation.* Reprinted by permission of Harvard University Press. Copyright © 1982 by the President and Fellows of Harvard College.

RIMELSPACH, René L. (2002) "Mediating Family Disputes in a World with Domestic Violence: How to Devise a Safe and Effective Court-Connected Mediation Program," 17 *Ohio St. J. Disp. Resol.* 95. Reprinted with permission.

RISKIN, Leonard (1991) "The Represented Client in a Settlement Conference: The Lessons of *G. Heileman Brewing Co. v. Joseph Oat Corp.*," 69 *Wash. U.L.Q.* 1059. Reprinted by permission.

ROGERS, Nancy, and Richard SALEM (1987) *A Student's Guide to Mediation and the Law.* Copyright © by Matthew Bender and Company, Inc. Reprinted by permission.

RUBIN, Jeffrey, and Frank SANDER (1981) "Culture, Negotiation, and the Eye of the Beholder," 7 *Neg. J.* 249. Reprinted by permission.

——— (1988) "When Should We Use Agents," 4 *Neg. J.* 395. Reprinted by permission.

SANDER, Frank E.A., H. William ALLEN, and Deborah HENSLER (1996) "Judicial (Mis) Use of ADR," 27 *U. Toledo L. Rev.* 885. Reprinted by permission of the University of Toledo Law School.

SANDER, Frank E.A., and Stephen B. GOLDBERG (1994) "Fitting the Forum to the Fuss: A User-Friendly Guide to Selecting an ADR Procedure," 10 *Neg. J.* 49. Reprinted by permission.

SANDER, Frank, and Jeffrey RUBIN (1988) "The Janus Quality of Negotiation," 4 *Neg. J.* 109. Reprinted by permission.

SHERMAN, Edward (1993) "Court-Mandated Alternative Dispute Resolution: What Form of Participation Should Be Required?" Originally appeared in Vol. 46, No. 5 of the *SMU Law Review.* Reprinted with permission from the *SMU Law Review* and the Southern Methodist University School of Law.

SINGER, Linda (1994) *Settling Disputes.* Reprinted by permission.

SOCIETY OF PROFESSIONALS IN DISPUTE RESOLUTION (1990) *Mandated Participation and Settlement Coercion: Dispute Resolution as it Relates to the Courts.* This publication was funded by a grant from the National Institute for Dispute Resolution. Reprinted by permission.

SOCIETY OF PROFESSIONALS IN DISPUTE RESOLUTION (1989) *Report of the SPIDR Commission on Qualifications.* This publication was funded by a grant from the National Institute for Dispute Resolution. Reprinted by permission.

SUSSKIND, Lawrence, and Jeffrey CRUIKSHANK (1987) *Breaking the Impasse.* Copyright © 1987 by Basic Books, Inc. Reprinted by permission of Basic Books, a division of HarperCollins Publishers.

SUSSKIND, Lawrence, Sarah McKEARNAN, and Jennifer THOMAS-LARMER (1999). *The Consensus Building Handbook.* Reprinted by permission.

URY, William (1991) *Getting Past No.* Copyright © 1991 by William Ury. Used by permission of Bantam Books, a division of Random House, Inc.

WHITE, James (1980) "Machiavelli and the Bar: Ethical Limitations on Lying in Negotiation," *American Bar Foundation Research Journal* 926. Reprinted with permission from 1980 American Bar Foundation Research Journal.

WHITE, James (1984) "The Pros and Cons of 'Getting to Yes,'" 34 *Journal of Legal Education* 115. Copyright © 1984 by AALS. Reprinted by permission of the Journal of Legal Education.

The authors acknowledge further the permissions granted to reproduce the following exercises.

Alpha-Beta Robotic Negoatition. Adapted with permission from a simulation created by Thomas N. Gladwin, Director of the International Business Negotiation Program, Leonard N. Stern School of Business, New York University.

Bryan v. Oakdale. Reprinted by permission of the Harvard Program on Negotiation.

Caroline's Donut Shop. Reprinted by permission of Cheryl B. McDonald, Pepperdine University School of Law, and Nancy Rogers, Ohio State University Law School.

The Daily Bugle. Reprinted by permission.

DONS. Reprinted by permission of the Harvard Program on Negotiation.

The Halfway House. Adapted with permission of the authors.

Little v. Jenks. Reprinted by permission of the Harvard Program on Negotiation.

Medical Malpractice Claim. Reprinted by permission.

The Neighborhood Spat. Adapted with permission from ROGERS, Nancy, and Richard SALEM (1987) Teacher's Guide to *A Student's Guide to Mediation and the Law.*

Perfect Packaging and 5-Year-Old-Girl. Mediation Center for Dispute Resolution and the Dispute Resolution Institute of Hamline University School of Law. Reprinted by permission.

Pepulator Pricing. Copyright © 1986 by the President and Fellows of Harvard College. All rights reserved. Reprinted with permission.

Prosando v. High-Tech. Copyright © 1994 by the CPR Institute for Dispute Resolution. Reprinted by permission.

Rapid Printing v. Scott Computers. Reprinted by permission of the authors.

The Red Devil Dog Restaurant Lease. Reprinted by permission.

Texoil. Reprinted by permission.

Too Old to Rock and Roll. Reprinted by permission.

World Oil Co. v. Northeast Shipbuilding. Adapted with permission of National Institute for Trial Advocacy.

The authors also want to thank Carole L. Hinchcliff, Associate Director, The Ohio State University Moritz Law Library, for her work in preparing "A Guide to Selected Resources" (Appendix I).

PART I

OVERVIEW

Chapter 1

Disputing Procedures

A. THE PROCESSES

The most common form of dispute resolution is negotiation. Compared to processes using neutral "third parties," negotiation has the advantage of allowing the parties themselves to control the process and the solution. If the parties cannot settle the dispute themselves and bring in a third party, they cede some control over the process but not necessarily over the solution. In fact, a critical distinguishing factor among the third-party processes is whether the neutral has power to impose a solution or simply to assist the disputants in arriving at their own solution. The most common example of the latter is mediation; the former is commonly called adjudication, whether performed by a court or by a private adjudicator known as an arbitrator.

Elements of these three primary processes—negotiation, mediation, and adjudication—have been combined in a number of ways in a rich variety of "hybrid" dispute resolution processes. For example, an adjudication-like presentation of proofs and arguments is combined with negotiation in the minitrial; arbitration is combined with court adjudication in a procedure known as rent-a-judge or private judging; and mediation is combined with arbitration in med-arb. Other well-known hybrid processes are the ombudsman (which involves a mediator-investigator), the neutral expert, the early neutral evaluator, and the summary jury trial. Some characteristics of these processes are summarized in Table 1-1 and Table 1-2. Further details concerning these hybrids are discussed in Chapter 5.

Distinguishing among the processes is more complex than this simple description suggests, however, because of variations in application. For example, although parties to mediation usually control the outcome, they may lose some of that control if the mediator is authorized to make a recommendation to the court in the event of impasse.

Moreover, control over outcome is only one significant criterion for differentiating among third-party processes. Others distinguish among processes on the basis of whether the parties, as opposed to only their lawyers, participate in a significant way (cf. Rifkin and Sawyer, 1982; Lind et al., 1990). They point to the positive impact of the parties' participation on their satisfaction with their experience in the justice system.

Another cut at differentiating various processes appears in Ury, Brett, and Goldberg (1988), a pathbreaking book that opened up the new field of dispute system design—ways of analyzing and providing a systematic mechanism for dealing with a stream of disputes in a particular setting (e.g., claims against an insurance

Table 1-1
"Primary" Dispute Resolution Processes

Characteristics	*Adjudication*	*Arbitration* *	*Mediation*	*Negotiation*
Voluntary/Involuntary	Involuntary	Voluntary	Voluntary†	Voluntary
Binding/Nonbinding	Binding; subject to appeal	Binding, subject to review on limited grounds	If agreement, enforceable as contract; sometimes agreement embodied in court decree	If agreement, enforceable as contract
Third party	Imposed, third-party neutral decision-maker, generally with no specialized expertise in dispute subject	Party-selected third-party decision-maker, often with specialized subject expertise	Party-selected outside facilitator	No third-party facilitator
Degree of formality	Formalized and highly structured by predetermined, rigid rules	Procedurally less formal; procedural rules and substantive law may be set by parties	Usually informal, unstructured	Usually informal, unstructured
Nature of proceeding	Opportunity to present proofs and arguments	Opportunity for each party to present proofs and arguments	Unbounded presentation of evidence, arguments and interests	Unbounded presentation of evidence, arguments and interests
Outcome	Principled decision, supported by reasoned opinion	Sometimes principled decision supported by reasoned opinion; sometimes compromise without opinion	Mutually acceptable agreement sought	Mutually acceptable agreement sought
Private/Public	Public	Private, unless judicial review sought	Private†	Private

* Court-annexed arbitration is involuntary, nonbinding, and public.
† In some jurisdictions, mediation is mandatory for certain kinds of cases or if a court so orders. In such cases mediation may not be private.

Table 1-2
"Hybrid" Dispute Resolution Processes

Characteristics	*Private Judging*	*Neutral Expert Fact-Finding*	*MiniTrial*	*Ombudsman*	*Summary Jury Trial*
Voluntary/ Involuntary	Voluntary	Voluntary or involuntary under FRE 706	Voluntary	Voluntary	Voluntary or involuntary
Binding/ Nonbinding	Binding, subject to appeal	Nonbinding but results may be admissible	Nonbinding; if agreement, enforceable as contract	Nonbinding	Nonbinding; if agreement, enforceable as contract
Third party	Party-selected third-party decision-maker, may have to be former judge or lawyer	Third-party neutral with specialized subject matter expertise; may be selected by the parties or the court	Party-selected neutral advisor, sometimes with specialized subject expertise	Third-party selected by institution	Mock jury impaneled by court
Degree of formality	Statutory procedure but highly flexible as to timing, place and procedures	Informal	Less formal than adjudication; procedural rules may be set by parties	Informal	Procedural rules fixed; less formal than adjudication
Nature of proceeding	Opportunity to present proofs and arguments	Investigatory	Opportunity to present summary proofs and arguments	Investigatory	Opportunity to present summary proofs and arguments
Outcome	Principled decision, sometimes supported by findings of fact and conclusions of law	Report or testimony	Mutually acceptable agreement sought	Report	Advisory verdict to facilitate settlement
Private/Public	Private, unless judicial enforcement sought	Private, unless disclosed in court	Usually private	Private	Usually public

company, employer-employee disputes, or claims arising out of a mass tort). (See Chapter 5 for further discussion of this topic.)

Ury, Brett, and Goldberg (1988) distinguish among processes based on whether the aim is to reconcile the disputants' underlying interests, determine who is right, or determine who is more powerful. Reconciling interests typically occurs during negotiation processes, and involves "probing for deep-seated concerns, devising creative solutions and making trade-offs" (ibid. 6). The prototypical rights-focused procedure is adjudication. Power procedures include strikes, wars and "power-based negotiation, typified by an exchange of threats" (ibid. 8). Ury, Brett, and Goldberg suggest that dispute resolution designers might juxtapose various kinds of processes but should keep in mind that, "in general, reconciling interests is less costly than determining who is right, which in turn is less costly than determining who is more powerful" (ibid. 15).

B. SOURCES AND GOALS OF THE ALTERNATIVE DISPUTE RESOLUTION MOVEMENT

The broad-based advocacy over the past two decades for increased use of mediation, arbitration, and related processes is often called the alternative dispute resolution movement. These movement years merit study because the issues raised by institutionalization of dispute resolution processes have their roots in the hopes of ADR movement supporters and in the early critiques of their aspirations.*

Even before there was an ADR movement, methods other than litigation were used for resolving disputes. Some claims were not "voiced" at all for fear of alienating the offender, and those that were raised often were resolved by a host of indigenous mechanisms such as the ward boss, the village priest, and the family friend (Felstiner et al., 1980-1981). Even if a case was ultimately filed in court, it was likely to be resolved by a process other than litigation.

Negotiation has long been the most popular method for resolving differences— even after the filing of litigation. In fact, only about a tenth of the civil cases filed in U.S. courts are disposed of by trial and another fifth by some sort of pretrial adjudication (Kritzer, 1986).† Arbitration has been used throughout the world for centuries, and its use has been favored by law in most American jurisdictions for more than 60 years. Mediation by respected community members was a central means of conflict management in small-scale societies across the world and commonplace in this country within cohesive immigrant or religious groups as early as colonial New England (Auerbach, 1983; Merry and Milner, 1993; Nader

*A brief note on terminology. If ADR stands for alternative dispute resolution, what is it alternative to? The court system? But, since most disputes are disposed of by negotiation and other noncourt processes, perhaps these processes are the norm. Or should the acronym be AMDR for "alternative" (in the sense of various) methods of dispute resolution, including courts? Or, as some contend, ADR should stand for "appropriate dispute resolution." Yet another option is simply to use DR for all the different dispute resolution methods.

†Indeed, more recent studies concerning "the Vanishing Trial" suggest that the proportion of cases in court that are disposed of by full trial is closer to 4 percent (Galanter, 2004; Symposium on Vanishing Trial, 2006).

and Todd, 1978). Professional mediators came on the scene for collective bargaining disputes in a few settings early in the century and more broadly in the 1940s (Aaron et al., 1977). In addition, as long as 50 years ago, a few courts encouraged use of mediation (calling it "conciliation") in minor criminal or family disputes (Galanter, 1986).

Interest increased substantially in the 1970s in what were called for the first time "alternative" methods of dispute resolution, a reference to the use of these processes in place of litigation. Different proponents of ADR sought to achieve different goals, not all of which were consistent. One part of the movement, responding to the civil rights strife of the 1960s and 1970s, saw ADR as a means of bringing together different racial groups. At approximately the same time, the courts became involved in ADR. At the 1976 Pound Conference, leading jurists and lawyers expressed concern about increased expense and delay for parties in a crowded justice system (Levin and Wheeler, 1979). A task force resulting from the conference was intrigued with Professor Frank Sander's vision of a court that was not simply a courthouse but a dispute resolution center where the grievant, with the aid of a screening clerk, would be directed to the process (or sequence of processes) most appropriate to a particular type of case (Sander, 1976). The task force recommended public funding of pilot programs using mediation and arbitration, and the American Bar Association's new committee on dispute resolution encouraged creation of three model "multidoor courthouses" (Levin and Wheeler, 1979; Ray, 1985).

While courts and litigators focused on a variety of dispute resolution processes to reduce the courts' and parties' costs, other ADR advocates saw mediation as a means to serve different interests. They wrote longingly about "warmer" ways of disputing (Smith, 1978) in the informal tribal "moots" or neighborhood elder conciliations (Nader and Todd, 1978; Danzig, 1973). Commentators expressed hope that expanded use of informal methods would result in resolutions more suited to the parties' needs, reduced reliance on laws and lawyers, rebirth of local communities, transformation of long-term relationships, and relief for nonparties affected by conflict, such as the children of divorcing couples (cf. Shonholtz, 1984; Merry and Milner, 1993; Bush and Folger, 2005).

Reflecting these goals, the San Francisco Community Boards program was launched in 1976 to strengthen urban neighborhood ties and find an alternative to the public justice system. Eschewing the courts, lawyers, and adversarial process, the Boards program developed a mediation program and a widely acclaimed training program for volunteer mediators. However, researchers found no evidence that the Boards program achieved the desired neighborhood changes. Further, even with a $500,000 annual budget, the Boards mediated only around 100 cases per year (Merry and Milner, 1993).

In the late 1970s applicants for funding of dispute resolution programs followed the time-honored method of announcing that all these aims — from reducing caseloads to strengthening communities — could be accomplished through their efforts. Not surprisingly, only a few years after the establishment of the first "neighborhood justice centers" offering mediation of criminal and small civil disputes, researchers announced that only a portion of their goals had been realized. The parties found mediation less expensive and were satisfied with its fairness, but few people took advantage of mediation services, thus producing no significant effects on court caseloads or savings in public funds (Cook, Roehl, and Sheppard, 1980; Tomasic, 1982).

With a recognition that all hopes could not be realized in each program, the late 1980s were characterized by efforts to establish priorities among the sometimes competing justifications for dispute resolution:

- To lower court caseloads and expenses,
- To reduce the parties' expenses and time,
- To provide speedy settlement of those disputes that were disruptive of the community or the lives of the parties' families,
- To improve public satisfaction with the justice system,
- To encourage resolutions that were suited to the parties' needs,
- To increase voluntary compliance with resolutions,
- To restore the influence of neighborhood and community values and the cohesiveness of communities,
- To provide accessible forums to people with disputes, and
- To teach the public to try more effective processes than violence or litigation for settling disputes.

Differences in priorities among these justifications led some, for example, to favor local neighborhood-based dispute resolution programs over court-run programs, to advocate funding for mediation over processes that resembled trials for similar disputes, or to favor free dispute resolution services over services for a fee. These differing weights to various values persist, leading to arguments over the shape of current public policy toward dispute resolution.

In the 1980s, client groups began their own advocacy. The insurance industry funded experiments to reduce the parties' litigation expenses. Corporate counsel supported efforts by the nonprofit CPR Institute for Dispute Resolution (now renamed the International Institute of Conflict Prevention and Resolution) to institutionalize dispute resolution practices among businesses and their lawyers. These efforts placed high priority on the needs of the parties themselves, their access to faster and less costly resolutions, and procedures less disruptive of business relationships. The period produced increased use of private adjudicators, such as arbitrators and retired judges, and experimentation with a "minitrial" process and mediation in a business context.

Another development of the 1980s was the emergence of commentary critical of the ADR movement. Yale law professor Owen Fiss led the charge with allegations that the justice system would suffer as the result of publicly supported settlement facilitation:

> [The courts'] job is not to maximize the ends of private parties, nor simply to secure the peace, but to explicate and give force to the values embodied in authoritative texts such as the Constitution and statutes: to interpret those values and to bring reality into accord with them. This duty is not discharged when the parties settle (Fiss, 1984).

In addition to this commentary, social scientists and legal scholars began to report research that challenged every premise of the movement's call for public support. Was there truly a "litigation crisis" (Galanter, 1983; Daniels, 1984)? Did ADR processes merely provide more hospitable procedures or did they change outcomes (Greatbatch and Dingwall, 1989)? Did "community" mediation programs have any impact on the host neighborhood (Merry and Milner, 1993)? Were there cost savings or reductions in court delay as the result of ADR (Esser, 1989)*? Critics of the movement argued that the burden of persuasion should be on those advocating change to demonstrate that the gains in terms of the courts, community, parties, and quality of life exceeded the harm they forewarned for the justice system.

During this period, lawmakers who supported ADR added statutory provisions to ensure the fairness of ADR outcomes; to provide guidelines for excluding certain cases from dispute resolution programs, including those involving important public policies; and to require evaluation of the programs as a prerequisite to future funding.

As the 1990s came to an end, the focus of statutes and commentary shifted from experimentation to institutionalization. For example, in the Alternative Dispute Resolution Act of 1998, Congress directed every federal district court to establish its own ADR program by local rule, and required the litigants in each case to consider the use of ADR at an appropriate stage in the litigation. State court systems, too, have been increasingly insisting that parties participate in various pre-adjudication processes. Sophisticated business clients are also demanding greater use of ADR. Pressure from these two critical sources — the courts and the clients — is forcing the legal profession to learn new tools that will equip it better to handle the increasing number and complexity of disputes in the years ahead.

As the new century began, efforts were launched to establish consensus regarding competing goals for public policy related to mediation. One prominent initiative produced the Uniform Mediation Act (Appendix E), which creates a privilege to encourage the effective use of mediation. At the same time, the Act tempers the impulse to support mediation use with measures designed to protect the parties from certain pressures to settle or efforts to mislead them. The Act also recognizes the need for the use of evidence from the mediation within the justice system. In its first five years, eight states and the District of Columbia have enacted the Uniform Mediation Act, which is a decent enactment pace as uniform acts go. But it is still too early to predict whether this, or various other standards initiatives (see Appendices G and H) will produce consensus on the right public policy path among competing goals for mediation and among varied views regarding the appropriate relationship between mediation and the justice system.

C. APPLICATIONS

In addition to their use in such traditional areas as business and the family, dispute resolution processes have been used, at least on an experimental basis, in toxic tort, farmer-lender, and doctor-patient — in fact, for almost every kind of dispute.

As a result, lawyering increasingly calls for expertise in dispute resolution. Lawyers negotiating business contracts now consider clauses requiring participation in a range of dispute resolution processes, not simply arbitration, for disputes

*A subsequent preliminary study of the increased use of ADR in the federal courts can be found in Kakalik et al., 1997. See also pp. 153-158, 401-402.

arising under the contracts. In other contexts, lawyers help their clients design appropriate processes. They also represent clients or act as neutrals within these processes.

Enthusiasm for dispute resolution has led to changes in court procedures. For example, the District of Columbia Superior Court "multidoor" staff recommends cases for different dispute resolution procedural tracks, and in other jurisdictions judges are authorized to refer cases to dispute resolution processes. In a number of states, mediation has become the initial court procedure for contested child custody and visitation cases. Appellate parties and their lawyers are sometimes called by court officials for a telephonic mediation. The Hawaii Supreme Court reaches beyond court dockets, providing mediators for public policy disputes not yet in litigation (NIDR, 1987).

Dispute resolution processes have also become part of administrative practice. In 1990, Congress passed two statutes designed to increase the use of ADR by federal agencies — the Administrative Dispute Resolution Act, which explicitly authorizes and encourages administrative agencies to use a wide variety of ADR techniques, and the Negotiated Rulemaking Act, similarly authorizing and encouraging the agencies to use negotiated rulemaking in lieu of traditional adversarial rulemaking under the Administrative Procedure Act (see p. 523).* In 1991, President Bush issued Executive Order 12778, which suggested that ADR can contribute to the prompt, fair, and efficient resolution of claims for and against the government. This Order was followed by one issued by President Clinton (No. 12988) in 1996, which went further and urged government counsel to make reasonable attempts to resolve a dispute through the use of ADR before proceeding to trial. It also provided for suitable training of litigation counsel in ADR. In May 1998, President Clinton established an interagency committee to facilitate agency use of ADR techniques. Under state legislation, agency dispute resolution procedures are often specially designed for particular categories of cases.

Dispute resolution processes are thriving as well outside the legal system. Hundreds of schools now have peer mediation programs, some stationing "fuss buster" mediators on playgrounds to handle arguments (cf. Davis, 1986). The number of independent nonprofit dispute resolution programs, mostly serving pro se parties, grew dramatically during the last 15 years. Traditional dispute resolution providers, such as the nonprofit American Arbitration Association and a number of religious institutions, have watched their caseloads expand in recent years (Beer, 1986), and many new providers — some of them for-profit — have appeared. In areas of traditional use of dispute resolution, the participants have tried new methods. For instance, grievance mediation, in which mediation and advisory arbitration are provided in a single procedure, has been successfully used in place of conventional labor arbitration.

These dispute resolution efforts outside the legal system are sometimes stimulated by changes in law, thus presenting policy issues of particular interest to lawyers. In New York, for example, hospitals are required by law to provide mediation for arguments over orders not to resuscitate a patient (N.Y. Public Health Law §2972).

It is difficult to gauge the effects of these new applications of dispute resolution on the practice of law, the justice system, and the pattern of disputing (Bush, 1989; Florida State Symposium Issue, 1991). One development that seems to

*Both these statutes were renewed in 1996.

hold promise for fundamental change in all these contexts has been the renewed interest in negotiation as the principal means of dispute resolution, evidenced by the innovative research and theory included in the next chapter and by the development of such techniques as "collaborative lawyering" (p. 361), where a lawyer limits his or her services to forms of dispute resolution other than litigation. Also encouraging is the growth in courses in professional schools and elsewhere (ABA, 2000; Florida Law Review, 1998). Another notable development underscoring the growing professionalization of the dispute resolution field is the greater attention now paid to ethical issues. Although it is still too soon to tell, these developments may improve the practice of negotiation such that more disputes will be resolved by negotiation with less need for third-party involvement. As ensuing chapters point out, third-party involvement, however well-intentioned and designed, creates problems that are not present when a dispute is resolved exclusively by the involved parties.

D. CONCERNS

The institutionalization of dispute resolution processes is occurring rapidly, so there is often little time to reflect on the serious issues raised by the changes. As you study dispute resolution processes, consider the following questions:

- If the alternatives to adjudication have all the advantages claimed for them, why are they not more widely used? Are there aspects of the legal system that deter the use of alternatives? Or does the lack of demand for alternatives demonstrate that the alternatives movement is primarily a result of self-interest on the part of dispute resolution providers rather than an expression of the need for alternative dispute resolution processes?
- Apart from the promise of monetary savings for the parties and courts, what are the benefits of settlement for the parties and for the public system?
- Is there a danger that mediation, with its emphasis on accommodation and compromise, will deter large-scale structural changes in political and societal institutions that only court adjudication can accomplish and that it will thus serve the interests of the powerful against the disadvantaged?
- Is there an adequate empirical basis for the claimed advantages of the dispute resolution processes? How, for example, can one adequately measure the asserted advantages of mediation over adjudication? Is it possible to develop a sophisticated cost-benefit analysis of alternative processes?
- Can we develop a satisfactory taxonomy of dispute resolution processes, matching disputes to appropriate dispute resolution processes?
- Is there a danger that in our preoccupation with finding the "appropriate" dispute resolution process we will lose sight of the need for fair outcomes?
- Can the alternatives movement survive success? If dispute resolution processes become widely used, will they suffer from the woes common to other heavily used institutions — increasing costs and delays, bureaucratization, and perfunctory performance?

- If the courts refer parties to private dispute resolution practitioners, how can they assure a high quality of service? Should there be regulation of the practice of dispute resolution similar to that of the practice of law? Will regulation hasten the bureaucratization of dispute resolution? In such cases of court referral to private providers, who should pay for the service — the court or the disputants? Will this new source of income for private providers threaten the integrity of the referral process?
- Is there a risk that the wealthy will desert the courts if the courts encourage those who can afford to hire private dispute resolvers?
- If public funds are insufficient to fund dispute resolution services for all kinds of cases, what kinds of cases should receive the highest priority? For example, should highest priority be given to those cases in which the court is most likely to realize savings? Those in which the litigation disrupts the lives of others than the parties? Those in which the parties have continuing relationships?
- In light of the prominent place of the courts and the fact that they provide litigation services for a nominal fee, should the courts integrate a wide variety of dispute resolution services into processes they offer? If so, how should this be done?

References

AARON, Benjamin, Beatrice BURGOON, Donald CULLEN, Dana EISCHEN, Mark KAHN, Charles REHMUS, and Jacob SEIDENBERG, eds. (1977) *The Railway Labor Act at Fifty.* Washington, D.C.: National Mediation Board.

AMERICAN BAR ASSOCIATION SECTION OF DISPUTE RESOLUTION (2000) *ABA Directory of Law School Alternative Dispute Resolution Courses and Programs.* Washington, D.C.: ABA.

AUERBACH, Jerold S. (1983) *Justice Without Law?* New York: Oxford.

BEER, Jennifer (1986) *Peacemaking in Your Neighborhood: Reflections on an Experiment in Community Mediation.* Philadelphia: New Society Publishers.

BOK, Derek C. (1983) "A Flawed System of Law Practice and Training," 33 *J. Legal Educ.* 530.

BRUNET, Edward, Charles B. CRAVER, and Ellen E. DEASON (2006) *Alternative Dispute Resolution: The Advocate's Perspective* (3d ed.). LexisNexis.

BUSH, Robert Baruch (1989) "Efficiency and Protection, or Empowerment and Recognition? The Mediator's Role and Ethical Standards in Mediation," 41 *Fla. L. Rev.* 253.

BUSH, Robert Baruch, and Joseph P. FOLGER (2005) *The Promise of Mediation* (2d ed.). San Francisco: Jossey-Bass.

CAPELLETTI, Mauro, ed. (1978) *Access to Justice.* 4 vols. Alphen aan den Rijn: Sijthoff and Noordhoff.

COOK, Royer, Janice ROEHL, and David SHEPPARD (1980) *Neighborhood Justice Centers Field Test.* Washington, D.C.: U.S. Department of Justice, National Institute of Justice.

DANIELS, Stephen (1984) "Ladders and Bushes: The Problem of Caseloads and Studying Court Activities Over Time," *Am. B. Found. Res. J.* 751.

DANZIG, Richard (1973) "Towards the Creation of a Complementary, Decentralized System of Criminal Justice," 26 *Stan. L. Rev.* 1.

DAVIS, Albie (1986) "Dispute Resolution at an Early Age," 2 *Neg. J.* 287.

ENGEL, David M. (1983) "Cases, Conflict and Accommodation: Patterns of Interaction in a Small Community," *Am. B. Found. Res. J.* 803.

ESSER, John (1989) "Evaluations of Dispute Processing: We Do Not Know What We Think and We Do Not Think What We Know," 66 *Den. U. L. Rev.* 499.

FELSTINER, William F. (1974) "Influences of Social Organization on Dispute Processing," 9 *Law & Socy. Rev.* 63.

FELSTINER, William F., Richard L. ABEL, and Austin SARAT (1980-1981) "The Emergence and Transformation of Disputes: Naming, Blaming, Claiming," 15 *Law & Socy. Rev.* 631.

FISS, Owen (1984) "Against Settlement," 93 *Yale L.J.* 1073.

FLORIDA LAW REVIEW (1998) Symposium Issue, Vol. 50 (Sept.).

FLORIDA STATE UNIVERSITY LAW REVIEW (1991) Symposium Issue, Vol. 19 (Summer).

FOLBERG, Jay, Dwight GOLANN, Lisa KLOPPENBERG, and Thomas STIPANOWICH (2005) *Resolving Disputes: Theory, Practice, and Law.* New York: Aspen.

FULLER, Lon (1963) "Collective Bargaining and the Arbitrator," 1963 *Wis. L. Rev.* 1.

——— (1971) "Mediation: Its Forms and Functions," 44 *S. Cal. L. Rev.* 305.

——— (1978) "The Forms and Limits of Adjudication," 92 *Harv. L. Rev.* 353.

GALANTER, Marc (1983) "Reading the Landscape of Disputes: What We Know and Don't Know (and Think We Know) About Our Allegedly Contentious and Litigious Society," 31 *UCLA L. Rev.* 4.

——— (1986) "The Emergence of the Judge as a Mediator in Civil Cases," 69 *Judicature* 257.

——— (2004) "The Vanishing Trial: An Examination of Trials and Related Matters in Federal and State Courts," 1 *J. Empirical Legal Stud.* 459.

GREATBATCH, David, and Robert DINGWALL (1989) "Selective Facilitation: Some Preliminary Observations on a Strategy Used by Divorce Mediators," 23 *Law & Socy. Rev.* 613.

HINCHCLIFF, Carole (1991) *Dispute Resolution: A Selective Bibliography.* Washington, D.C.: ABA.

KAKALIK, James S., Terrence DUNWORTH, Laural A. HILL, Daniel McCAFFREY, Marian OSHIRO, Nicholas M. PACE, and Mary A. VIANA (1997) *Implementation of The Civil Justice Reform Act in Pilot and Comparison Districts.* Santa Monica: Rand Inst. for Civil Justice.

KRITZER, Herbert (1986) "Adjudication to Settlement: Shading in the Gray," 70 *Judicature* 161.

——— (1991) *Let's Make a Deal.* Madison: University of Wisconsin Press.

LEVIN, A. Leo, and Russell WHEELER, eds. (1979) *The Pound Conference: Perspectives on Justice in the Future.* St. Paul: West.

LIND, E. Allen, Robert MACCOUN, Patricia EBENER, William FELSTINER, Deborah HENSLER, Judith RESNIK, and Tom TYLER (1990) "In the Eye of the Beholder: Tort Litigants' Evaluations of Their Experiences in the Civil Justice System," 24 *Law & Socy. Rev.* 953.

MARKS, Jonathan M., Earl JOHNSON, Jr., and Peter L. SZANTON (1984) *Dispute Resolution in America: Processes in Evolution.* Washington, D.C.: National Institute for Dispute Resolution.

McGILLIS, Daniel (1997) *Community Mediation Programs: Developments and Challenges.* Washington, D.C.: U.S. Department of Justice, National Institute of Justice.

MENKEL-MEADOW, Carrie J., Lela P. LOVE, Andrea K. SCHNEIDER, and Jean R. STERNLIGHT (2005) *Dispute Resolution: Beyond the Adversarial Model.* New York: Aspen.

MERRY, Sally (1990) *Getting Justice and Getting Even: Legal Consciousness of Working-Class Americans.* Chicago: University of Chicago Press.

MERRY, Sally, and Neil MILNER (1993) *Popular Justice, Social Transformation and the Ideology of Community: Perspectives on Community Mediation.* Ann Arbor: University of Michigan Press.

MILLER, Richard E., and Austin SARAT (1980-1981) "Grievances, Claims, and Disputes: Assessing the Adversary Culture," 15 *Law & Socy. Rev.* 525.

MOFFITT, M., and R. BORDONE, eds. *Handbook of Dispute Resolution.* (2005) San Francisco: Jossey-Bass.

NADER, Laura (1979) "Disputing Without the Force of Law," 88 *Yale L.J.* 998.

NADER, Laura, and Harry TODD (1978) *The Disputing Process: Law in Ten Societies.* New York: Columbia University Press.

NATIONAL INSTITUTE FOR DISPUTE RESOLUTION (1987) "Statewide Offices of Mediation: Experiments in Public Policy," *Forum* (Dec.).

RAU, Alan, Edward F. SHERMAN, and Scott R. PEPPET (2002) *Processes of Dispute Resolution: The Role of Lawyers* (3d ed.). New York: Foundation Press.

RAY, Larry (1985) "The Multi-Door Courthouse Idea: Building the Courthouse of the Future . . . Today," 1 *Ohio St. J. Disp. Resol.* 7.

RIFKIN, Janet, and Joanne SAWYER (1982) "Alternative Dispute Resolution: From a Legal Services Perspective," *NLADA Briefcase* 20 (Fall).

RISKIN, Leonard L., James E. WESTBROOK, Chris GUTHRIE, Timothy J. HEINSZ, Richard C. REUBEN, and Jennifer K. ROBBENNOLT (2005) *Dispute Resolution and Lawyers* (3d ed.). St. Paul, Minn.: West.

SALEM, Richard (1985) "The Alternative Dispute Resolution Movement: An Overview," 40 *Arbitration J.* 3 (Sept.).

SANDER, Frank E. A. (1976) "Varieties of Dispute Processing," 70 *F.R.D.* 111.

——— (1985) "Alternative Methods of Dispute Resolution: An Overview," 37 *U. Fla. L. Rev.* 1.

SANDER, Frank E. A., and Frederick E. SNYDER (1979) *Alternative Methods of Dispute Settlement—A Selected Bibliography.* Washington, D.C.: ABA.

SHONHOLTZ, Ray (1984) "Neighborhood Justice Systems: Work, Structure, and Guiding Principles," 5 *Mediation Q.* 3 (Sept.).

SINGER, Linda (1994) *Settling Disputes* (2d ed.). Boulder: Westview Press.

SMITH, David (1978) "A Warmer Way of Disputing: Mediation and Conciliation," 26 *Am. J. Com. L.* 365.

STONE, Katherine V.W. (2000) *Private Justice: The Law of Alternative Dispute Resolution.* New York: Foundation Press.

SYMPOSIUM ON VANISHING TRIAL (2006) *J Disp. Resol.* No. 1.

TOMASIC, Roman (1982) "Mediation as an Alternative to Adjudication: Rhetoric and Reality in the Neighborhood Justice Movement." In Roman TOMASIC and Malcolm FEELEY, eds. (1983) *Neighborhood Justice: Assessment of an Emerging Idea.* New York: Longman.

TRACHTE-HUBER, E. Wendy, and Steven K. HUBER (1996) *Alternative Dispute Resolution.* Cincinnati: Anderson.

URY, William, Jeanne BRETT, and Stephen GOLDBERG (1988) *Getting Disputes Resolved: Designing Systems to Cut the Costs of Conflict.* San Francisco: Jossey-Bass.

WARE, Stephen J. (2001) *Alternative Dispute Resolution.* St. Paul: West.

PART II

PROCESSES

Chapter 2
Negotiation

Negotiation — communication for the purpose of persuasion — is the preeminent mode of dispute resolution. We negotiate with our friends about where to eat dinner, with our spouses about who will do the household chores, with our children about what time they will go to bed. For most lawyers negotiation is a major part of their professional duties. Of those disputes that come into a lawyer's office, the vast majority are resolved by negotiation rather than litigation. Lawyers also spend substantial amounts of time negotiating a wide variety of contracts and other transactional arrangements.

Many beginning negotiators, as well as some who are quite experienced, use a negotiating strategy known as distributional or competitive. Assume, for example, that you are buying property on behalf of a client. If you are like many negotiators, you will make an initial offer that is considerably less than your client is ultimately willing to pay. You will disparage the value of the property, move your offer up gradually, and pay only as much as you believe you must to avoid losing the property. If the seller seeks to add issues to the negotiation, such as time of payment or, in an international transaction, the currency in which payment is to be made, you will say that you are willing to discuss those issues after a price has been agreed on, but not before.

If you are using a competitive strategy, you will typically seek whatever tactical advantages are available. You may, for example, schedule the negotiation to take place in your office, be certain to outnumber the other side, and act tough — especially against a patsy.

If this is an accurate description of how you approach — or would like to approach — negotiations, you will not lack for advice on improving your negotiating style. A sizeable body of literature exists that gives advice — at both the strategic and tactical levels — on how to win as much as you can in negotiations. A good example of such advice at the tactical level follows. Though addressed specifically to legal services lawyers, it would appear equally relevant for other attorneys as well.

M. MELTSNER AND P. SCHRAG, NEGOTIATING TACTICS FOR LEGAL SERVICES LAWYERS

7 Clearinghouse Rev. 259 (1973)

This article catalogues several successful negotiating tactics. Of course, not every tactic described is appropriate for every negotiation; the use of each depends on the particular case and especially upon the perceived relative strengths of the parties during the bargaining process. In general, a party who appears to himself and to his adversary to be strongly desirous of negotiations is less able to use the more powerful tactics set forth. Even the attorney who must negotiate from a position of perceived weakness should be familiar with the tactics that may be used against him, so that he may defend himself as best he can.

This list of tactics is not intended to endorse the *propriety* of every one of them, but there can be no doubt of their *efficacy* in appropriate situations. All of these techniques are commonly used by lawyers, and the attorney who chooses to abjure one because it is ethically dubious should at least learn to recognize and to understand the device so that he can defend against it. The more "tricky" of these ploys are used most commonly in urban centers, where lawyers are not likely to be negotiating repeatedly with the same adverse attorneys who will eventually recognize their favorite tactics. Lawyers who have to deal with each other in case after case are more likely to conduct an open, straightforward discussion than those who may never negotiate with each other again.

I. Preparatory Tactics

1. *Arrange to negotiate on your own turf.* Whenever possible, insist that the meeting be held in your office or in another setting where you will feel more comfortable than your adversary, and where he will be at a psychological disadvantage because he has had to come to you. . . .

Some neighborhood poverty lawyers who negotiate with attorneys for banks, realty corporations, and other large firms have added a new twist to the "home base" tactic by attempting to maneuver their adversaries into entering the ghetto, sometimes for the first time in their lives. Their fears for their physical safety and their shock at viewing local housing conditions may reduce their bargaining effectiveness. . . .

2. *Balance or slightly outnumber the other side.* Attempt to ascertain or estimate the number of persons the other side is bringing to the meeting, and do your best to ensure that your side is represented by at least the same number of persons, and possibly one additional person. In a bargaining session where two negotiate against one, or three against two, the side with fewer representatives is usually at a disadvantage in that it will tire more readily and will be less able to control the flow of discussion. There is also a tendency in a bargaining situation to reach a compromise evenly balanced among the views of all participants, even if two of the participants are on one side and one on the other, so the active presence of additional bargainers materially affects the outcome. On the other hand, an adversary who feels cornered because he is substantially outnumbered may feel too insecure to bargain seriously. Be prepared therefore to justify the presence of additional representatives on the ground that they have technical expertise necessary to successful completion of the settlement.

3. *Time the negotiations to advantage.* When one side wants to get the discussion over with quickly, it usually loses. If you perceive that your adversary is anxious to settle quickly (or to avoid protracted discussion because his client is only paying a set fee), arrange to negotiate when you can spend a lot of time at it (e.g., when you have a whole day clear), when your adversary is pressed for time, or when one of you has so little time that, after enough discussion to whet your adversary's appetite, negotiations must be adjourned for a week or two. You may find that under

these conditions, your adversary makes major concessions to avoid further loss of time. . . .

4. *Know the facts thoroughly.* Unless he is deliberately unprepared so that the negotiations will be delayed, an unprepared lawyer is usually at a severe disadvantage. He will constantly have to apologize for his ignorance, and his apologies often create a subtle pressure to concede points as to which his adversary is better informed. In addition, an unprepared lawyer may feel inner pressure to compromise because he does not wish to reveal his ignorance by participation in an extended discussion.

5. *Lock yourself in.* This is a risky but powerful prenegotiation tactic and should be used only with the greatest care. In cases that have attracted public attention, an attorney can increase his bargaining power by announcing publicly a position from which he will not retreat so that his adversary knows that he will lose face if he does in fact retreat. Then the attorney can convincingly say that aspect of his position is nonnegotiable. Attorneys who use this tactic sometimes have their bluff called, and may, in fact, have to make a concession and then explain the retreat to their clients.

6. *Designate one of your demands a "precondition."* If the other side wants to talk (e.g., if it requested the negotiations), a lawyer can often improve the chances of a favorable outcome by calling one of his demands a "precondition" to negotiations. If the precondition is met, he starts out with a psychological advantage, a substantive gain, and fewer items which are subject to compromise in the discussions that follow. Even if the precondition pertains only to action during the negotiations themselves, for example, that neither party will speak to the press until their conclusion, the temporary resolution of certain issues is likely to set a pattern for the eventual settlement.

II. Initial Tactics

7. *When it is in your interest, make the other side tender the first offer.* The party making the first offer suffers the disadvantage of conceding that it really wants to settle. Furthermore, it may make an offer that actually concedes more than the other side thought it could get at the end of the negotiating process. The attorney who receives such a surprising offer will declare his shock that so little is being tendered, and will demand much more. One surprisingly successful technique for evoking the first offer is to remain silent. Few people can tolerate more than a few seconds of silence during a negotiation; most feel compelled to say something to break the ice. Or you might simply say to your adversary, "Why don't you start by giving us an idea of your position." There are situations, however, where by making the first offer a party advantageously sets the agenda for the entire discussion. The negotiations may never leave the questions raised initially; other questions, which may be the weakest from your point of view, will fall into place as part of a general wrap-up of the deal.

8. *Make your first demand very high.* Outrageously unreasonable demands become more justifiable after substantial discussion. Even if an initially high demand is rejected, it makes a subsequent demand that is almost as high appear to be a more reasonable compromise. The negotiator who opens with a reasonable compromise is likely to be pushed to a worse settlement than he could have obtained by harder bargaining. Nevertheless, some demands are too outrageous

to make. They will encourage your adversary to believe that you are not seriously interested in bargaining despite your protestations to the contrary.

9. *Place your major demands at the beginning of the agenda.* There seem to be "honeymoon" periods, in which negotiators make compromises more freely, at the outset of negotiations and at their conclusion. By forcing your adversary to deal at the outset, when he wants most to compromise, with the items of greatest interest to you, or at the end, when he has invested many hours or weeks of time in negotiating and wants a return on his investment, you can improve your client's position.

10. *Make the other side make the first compromise.* There is a psychological advantage in benefitting from the first concession. Studies indicate that losers generally make the first concessions in negotiating a dispute.

III. Tactics Generally

11. *Use two negotiators who play different roles.* The famous "Mutt and Jeff" technique, in which police use one friendly and one nasty interrogator to extract a statement from a reluctant defendant, works well in negotiation. Two lawyers for the same side feign an internal dispute concerning their position; one takes the hard line, offering almost no compromise, while the other appears to desire to make small concessions, and occasionally he prevails. Lawyers adverse to such a team frequently grasp at the marginal concessions because they seem substantial in relation to the position of the hard-liner.

12. *Invoke law or justice.* To a surprising extent, lawyers are impressed with the citation of authority, and laymen tend to be overwhelmed by a reference to a case or statute. If your adversary seems to react to it, quote or advert to legal authority as often as possible, particularly if you can assert that the position you urge is legally compelled, or that the one he desires is either legally prohibited or at least troublesome. If the other side seems to desire an end to the discussions more than you do, lengthy analytical discussion of cases and statutes is also a good way to kill time without disclosing any facts about your client's case. If the law is not on your side, avoid using it. Instead, invoke more general principles of justice, or whatever other kind of authority (e.g., public pressure) seems to support your position.

13. *Be tough — especially against a patsy.* "Unfortunately, when one party is conciliatory and the other cantankerous, the imbalance usually favors the competitive player in the short run."

14. *Appear irrational where it seems helpful.* This is a dangerous but often successful tactic. An adversary who is himself an expert negotiator can be thrown off base considerably by a lawyer who does not seem to play the same game, for example, one who seems to behave irrationally. Premier Nikita Krushchev significantly increased the deterrent power of the relatively small Soviet nuclear force by banging his shoe on the table at the United Nations in 1960; he gave the impression of being somewhat imbalanced — a man who might unleash nuclear weapons upon even a slight provocation.

15. *Raise some of your demands as the negotiations progress.* The conventional model of negotiation contemplates both sides lowering their demands until a compromise is finally reached. But the highly successful negotiator backtracks; he raises one of his

demands for every two concessions he makes and occasionally reopens for further discussion topics that everyone thought had been settled and laid aside. This tactic not only reduces the aggregate concession he makes, but it makes the other side want to finish the negotiation quickly before he stiffens his position any more or retracts the concessions he had made. The party who desires to finish quickly has two strikes against him.

16. *Claim that you do not have authority to compromise.* You can make a topic non-negotiable by persuading your adversary that you do not have, and cannot obtain, the authority to go beyond a certain point. The freshman negotiator sometimes makes the mistake of trying to impress the other side with his authority; the expert modestly explains that he has very little authority, and that his client is adamant. (Of course, the client's supposed adamancy stops just at the point of the minimum concessions the lawyer thinks he need make.) The lawyer should not bring his client with him to the negotiation unless he has a clear understanding of why he is doing so; he exposes himself to the real danger that his adversary will go over his head to the client himself, and he gives up the power to invoke his client's instructions as a reason for refusing to agree to a particular demand.

17. *Clear the agreement with your client before signing it.* Before you reach final agreement, you will want to consult with your client. Checking with the client is not only an obligation that you owe to him, it is an important bargaining tactic. It enables you to delay the proceedings while you check, and it gives you a chance to consider any errors you might have made before you sign.

18. *Make your adversary feel good.* Never gloat over the terms of a settlement. Not only is such behavior boorish, but it may provoke an adversary to reopen negotiations or to adopt a different and stronger negotiating posture the next time you deal with him. . . .

19. *After agreement has been reached, have your client reject it and raise his demands.* This is the most ethically dubious of the tactics listed, but there will be occasions where a lawyer will have to defend against it or even employ it. After laboring for hours, days, or weeks to work out a settlement, a negotiator is likely to be dismayed by the prospect of the agreement falling through. As a result, his adversary may be able to obtain last minute concessions. Such a strategy can boomerang; it may so anger an adversary that he simply refuses to bargain, even though bargaining is still in his interest, or he may fight fire with fire by increasing his own demands.

20. *Promptly reduce the agreement to writing yourself.* . . . Quite often the terms that have been agreed upon will be subject to differing interpretations, some of which favor your side, some of which favor your adversary's side. You should, therefore, volunteer to undertake the labor of drafting the agreement. By doing so, you can choose language which reflects your interpretation of the terms agreed upon. . . . If you draft the document, the other side should be given an opportunity to correct it and to discuss any language not faithfully incorporating the agreement that has been reached. But many lawyers are not thorough editors, so the opportunity to write the first draft becomes the power to choose critically important language. If an adversary writes the first draft, you should be prepared to go over it line by line and, if necessary, to rewrite every word.

An excellent example of a thoughtful, analytical approach to both the strategic and tactical aspects of distributional bargaining is contained in the following excerpt.

H. RAIFFA, THE ART AND SCIENCE OF NEGOTIATION

33-44, 126-130 (1982)

Two-party bargaining can be divided into two types: distributive and integrative. In the distributive case one single issue, such as money, is under contention and the parties have almost strictly opposing interests on that issue: the more you get, the less the other party gets, and—with some exceptions and provisos—you want as much as you can get. Of course, if you are too greedy or if your adversary is too greedy, or if you both are too greedy, you will both fail to come to an agreement that would mean profits for both of you (that is why I speak of "almost" strictly opposing interests). . . .

Two disputants bargain over a price; one wants the price to be high, whereas the other wants it low. One wants to maximize the agreed-upon price, the other to minimize it. Usually the maximizer can be viewed as a seller and the minimizer as a buyer. This interpretation is extremely narrow: the ex-wife who is arguing over alimony in a divorce case does not want to view herself as a seller, and the plaintiff who is suing a negligent party doesn't think of himself as a seller. But still, for the most part, you will not go too far astray if you think of the prototypical problem [herein] as the problem of a seller and a buyer haggling over a single price.

Sometimes the single commodity in contention may be something like time instead of money. The contractor wants more time, the "contractee" less time. . . . Or the disputed commodity may be a particular amount of effort or attention, or the number of days of someone's vacation, or the percentage of a harvest, and so on. The important thing to remember is that in distributive bargaining only one issue is being negotiated.

We will begin with a very special case, whose strategic elements will reappear in more complicated variations. There are two negotiators, each monolithic; they are engaged in a one-time bargaining situation with no anticipated repetitions with each other; they come to the bargaining table with no former "favors" they have to repay, and this bargain is not linked with others that they are worrying about; there is a single issue (money) under contention; they can break off negotiations and not arrive at an agreement; neither party must get a proposed contract ratified by others; breaking off negotiations is their only threat; there is no formal time constraint (such as a strike deadline); agreements made are legally binding; negotiations are private; and each expects the other to be "appropriately honorable." Finally, the parties do not use the services of an intervenor. . . .

3. Elmtree House

The following case study is mostly make-believe; one might speak of it as an "armchair" case. It involves a colleague of mine—I'll call him Steve—who, as a professor of business, was quite knowledgeable about finance but not a practitioner of the art and science of negotiation.

Steve was on the governing board of Elmtree House, a halfway house for young men and women ages eighteen to twenty-five who needed the support of a sympathetic group and professional guidance to ease their transition from mental institutions back to society. Many of the residents had had nervous breakdowns, or were borderline schizophrenics, or were recovering from unfortunate experiences with drugs. Located on the outskirts of Boston in the industrial city of Somerville, Elmtree House accommodated about twenty residents. The neighborhood was in a transition stage; some said that it would deteriorate further, others that it was on the way up. In any case, it did not provide an ideal recuperative setting because of its agitated atmosphere. Although the house was small and quite run down, the lot itself was extensive, consisting of a full acre of ground. Its once-magnificent stand of elm trees had succumbed to disease.

The governing board, through a subcommittee, had once investigated the possibility of moving Elmtree from Somerville to a quieter, semi-residential community. Other suitable houses were located in the nearby cities of Brookline, Medford, and Allston, but the financial aspects were prohibitive and the idea of moving was reluctantly dropped.

Some months later, a Mr. Wilson approached Elmtree's director, Mrs. Peters, who lived in the house with her husband and child. Wilson indicated that his firm, a combined architectural and developmental contractor, might be interested in buying the Elmtree property. This was out of the blue. No public announcement had ever been made that Elmtree House was interested in a move. Mrs. Peters responded that the thought had never occurred to her, but that if the price were right, the governing board might just consider it. Wilson gave Mrs. Peters his card and said that he would like to pursue the topic further if there were a chance for a deal.

The governing board asked Steve to follow up on this promising lead. The other board members were prominent individuals in clinical psychology, medicine, vocational guidance, and the clergy; none besides Steve had any feeling for business negotiations of this kind, and since they fully trusted Steve, they essentially gave him carte blanche to negotiate. Of course, no legal transaction could be consummated without the board's formal approval.

Steve sought my advice on how he should approach Mr. Wilson, and we decided that an informal phone call was in order. Steve accepted an invitation to discuss possibilities over cocktails at a nearby hotel. He decided not to talk about any money matters at that first meeting—just to sound out Wilson and find out what he might have in mind. He insisted, I think rightly, on paying his own bill. I assured him that he also did rightly in not even hinting to Wilson that the governing board was looking for other locations.

Based on that first meeting, as well as on some probing into Wilson's business affiliations, Steve ascertained that Wilson was a legitimate businessman of decent reputation. Steve thought that Wilson's company wanted the Elmtree property as a possible site for a condominium. Wilson wished to talk money matters right away, but Steve needed a couple of weeks to prepare for negotiations. He used the excuse that he needed the approval of the governing board before he could proceed to serious negotiations.

During the next twelve days, Steve did a number of things. First, he tried to ascertain Elmtree's *reservation price* or walkaway price—that is, the minimum price that Elmtree House, the seller, could accept. The reservation price was difficult to determine, since it depended on the availability of alternative sites to relocate. Steve learned that of the other sites that had previously been located, the one in Brookline was no longer available but the other two, in Medford and in Allston, were still possibilities—for the right price. Steve talked with the owners of those sites and found out that the Medford property could be had for about $175,000 and the Allston property for about $235,000.

Steve decided that Elmtree House would need at least $220,000 before a move to Medford could be undertaken and that it would need $275,000 to justify a move to Allston. These figures took into account the cost of moving, minor repairs, insurance, and a small sum for risk aversion. The Allston site (needing $275,000) was much better than the Medford site (needing $220,000), which in turn was better than the site at Elmtree. So Steve decided that his reservation price would be $220,000. He would take nothing less, and hope to get more—possibly enough more to justify the Allston alternative. This bit of research took about six hours, or a couple of evenings' work.

Meanwhile Steve's wife, Mary, contacted several realtors looking for alternate properties. There were a few nibbles, but nothing definite turned up.

What next?

Steve next investigated what Elmtree House would bring if sold on the open market. By examining the sale prices of houses in the vicinity and by talking to local realtors and real estate experts, he learned that the Elmtree property was probably worth only about $125,000. He felt that if sold without Wilson in the picture, the house would go for between $110,000 and $145,000 (with probability one-half), and it was just as likely to go below $110,000 as above $145,000. How disappointing! This took another four hours of research time.

What next?

What was the story from Wilson's perspective? It was difficult for us to make judgments about the buyer's *reservation price*—that is, the maximum price that Wilson would be willing to offer before he definitely would break off negotiations, not temporarily for strategic purposes, but permanently. Neither Steve nor I had any expertise in the matter. We went for advice to a number of real estate experts (some at the Harvard Business School) and we also queried two contractors in the Boston area. Our experts did not agree with one another, but they all took our question about reservation price seriously, and we were convinced that they understood our problem. A lot, we were told, depended on the intention of the developers. How high a structure would they be permitted to build on the site? Were they buying up other land as well? Steve found out that the answer to the latter question was yes. The matter turned out to be much more involved than Steve or I had imagined it would be. After ten hours of his time and five hours of my time, we decided that we were hopelessly vague about our assessment of Wilson's reservation price. Figure 1 shows Steve's assessed probability density function—all things considered—of Wilson's *RP* (reservation price). As of two days before the start of real negotiations, Steve would have bet even money that Wilson's *RP* lay in the interval from $250,000 (the lower quartile) to $475,000 (the upper quartile).

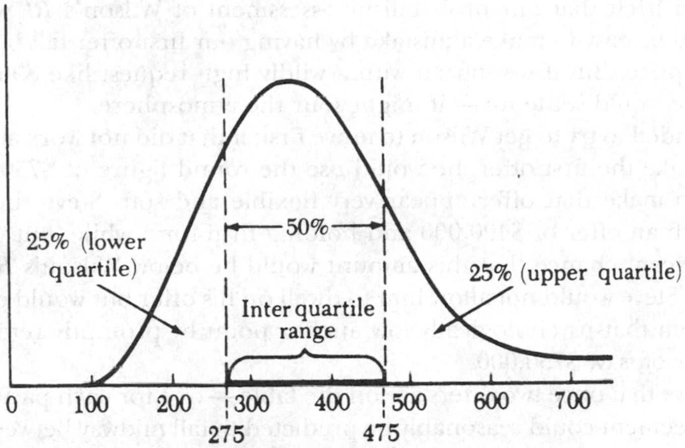

Figure 1
Steve's probability assessment of Wilson's reservation price for Elmtree House. (Vertical scale is such that the area under the probability density function is 1.00.)

After all this preparation, Steve and I discussed his negotiation strategy. It had already been decided that the meeting would be at a hotel suite to which Wilson's company had access. Steve and I had no objection to this venue; the dining room of Elmtree House would have been too hectic, and his own university office inappropriate.

Feeling that he needed someone at the discussions to advise him on legal details, Steve decided to invite Harry Jones, a Boston lawyer and former member of Elmtree House's governing board. Jones agreed to participate, and Steve reserved two hours to brief him prior to the meeting.[5]

We also thought it might be a good idea for Steve to bring along Mrs. Peters. She was the person who was most knowledgeable about Elmtree House, and perhaps an appeal to Wilson's social conscience might help. It was agreed that Steve alone would talk about money matters. Mrs. Peters would be coached to talk about the important social role of halfway houses and to argue that it did not make sense for Elmtree House to move unless there would be substantial improvement in the surrounding amenities: "You know how hard it is on kids to move from one neighborhood to another. Just think how severe the effects will be on the young residents of Elmtree House." Mrs. Peters actually did have conflicting feelings about moving, and it would be easy for her to marshal arguments against a move.

What should be Steve's opening gambit? Who should start the bidding first? If Wilson insisted that Steve make the first offer, what should that be? If Wilson opened with *x* thousand dollars, what should Steve's counteroffer be? How far could this be planned in advance? Were there any obvious traps to be avoided?

5. One colleague of mine suggested that bringing a lawyer to the initial negotiations might have hurt Steve's cause: it indicated too much of a desire to do business and to settle details.

Steve and I felt that our probabilistic assessment of Wilson's *RP* was so broad that it would be easy to make a mistake by having our first offer fall below his true reservation price. But if we started with a wildly high request like $900,000—way over what we would settle for—it might sour the atmosphere.

Steve decided to try to get Wilson to move first; if that did not work and if he were forced to make the first offer, he would use the round figure of $750,000, but he would try to make that offer appear very flexible and soft. Steve thought about opening with an offer of $400,000 and holding firm for a while, but we felt there was a 40 percent chance that this amount would be below Wilson's *RP*. If Wilson moved first, Steve would not allow him to dwell on his offer but would quickly try to get away from that psychologically low anchor point by promptly retorting with a counteroffer of, say, $750,000.

I told Steve that once two offers are on the table—one for each party—the final point of agreement could reasonably be predicted to fall midway between those two extremes. So if Wilson offered $200,000 and if Steve came back with $400,000, a reasonable bet would be a settlement of $300,000—provided, of course, that that midway figure fell within the potential zone of agreement, the range between Steve's (the seller's) true *RP* and Wilson's (the buyer's) true *RP*. For starters, Steve thought that it would be nice if he could get $350,000 from Wilson, but, of course, Steve realized that his own *RP* was still $220,000.

We talked about the role of time. Should Steve be willing to walk away from the bargaining table if Wilson's most recent offer was above $220,000? I reminded Steve that there is no objective formula for this. He would be confronted with a standard decision problem under uncertainty, and his assessment of Wilson's *RP* could be better evaluated after sounding out Wilson than it could be with present information. The danger in breaking off negotiations—and a lot depends on how they're broken off—was that Wilson might have other opportunities to pursue at the same time.

As it turned out, the first round of negotiations was, in Steve's eyes, a disaster, and afterward he wasn't even sure that there would be a second round. Mrs. Peters performed admirably, but to no avail; it seemed unlikely that Wilson would raise his offer to Elmtree's reservation price. After preliminary pleasantries and some posturing, Wilson said, "Tell me the bare minimum you would accept from us, and I'll see if I can throw in something extra." Steve expected that gambit, and instead of outright misrepresentation he responded, "Why don't you tell us the very maximum that you are willing to pay, and we'll see if we can shave off a bit." Luckily, Wilson was amused at that response. He finally made his opening offer at $125,000, but first bolstered it with a lot of facts about what other property was selling for in that section of Somerville. Steve immediately responded that Elmtree House could always sell their property for more money than Wilson was offering, and that they did not have the faintest intention of moving. They would consider moving only if they could relocate in a much more tranquil environment where real estate values were high. Steve claimed that the trouble of moving could be justified only by a sale price of about $600,000, and Mrs. Peters concurred.[6] Steve chose that $600,000 figure keeping in mind that the mid-point between $150,000 and $600,000 was

6. A student of mine suggested that during negotiations, obvious modifications could have been made to the exterior of Elmtree House to give the impression that the residents indeed had no intention of moving.

above his aspiration level of $350,000. Wilson retorted that prices like that were out of the question. The two sides jockeyed around a bit and decided to break off, with hints that they might each do a bit more homework.

Steve and I talked about how we should reassess our judgmental distribution of Wilson's *RP*. Steve had the definite impression that the $600,000 figure was really well above Wilson's *RP*, but I reminded him that Wilson was an expert and that if his *RP* were above $600,000 he would want to lead Steve to think otherwise. We decided to wait a week and then have Steve tell Wilson that Elmtree's board would be willing to come down to $500,000.[7]

Two days later, however, Steve received a call from Wilson, who said that his conscience was bothering him. He had had a dream about Mrs. Peters and the social good she was bringing to this world, and this had persuaded him that, even though it did not make business sense, he should increase his offer to $250,000. Steve could not contain himself and blurted out his first mistake: "Now that's more like it!" But then he regained his composure and said that he thought that he could get Elmtree's board to come down to $475,000. They agreed to meet again in a couple of days for what would hopefully be a final round of bargaining.

Following this phone conversation with Wilson, Steve told me that he had inadvertently led Wilson to believe that his $250,000 offer would suffice; but Steve also felt that his offer of $475,000 was coming close to Wilson's *RP*, because this seemed to be the only reason for Wilson's reference to a "final round of bargaining." We talked further about strategy and we revised some probabilistic assessments.

Over the next two days there was more jockeying between the two sides, and Wilson successively yielded from $250,000 to $275,000 to $290,000 and finally to a *firm last offer* of $300,000, whereas Steve went from $475,000 to $425,000 to $400,000, and then—painfully when Wilson sat fixedly at $300,000, inched down to $350,000. Steve finally broke off by saying that he would have to contact key members of the governing board to see if he could possibly break the $350,000 barrier.

Now, $300,000 not only pierced Steve's *RP* of $220,000 (needed for the Medford move), but also would make it possible for Elmtree House to buy the more desirable Allston property. It had at that point become a question of "gravy." I asked Steve whether he thought Wilson would go over $300,000 and he responded that although it would take some face-saving maneuver, he thought Wilson could be moved up. The problem was, he felt, that if Wilson were involved in other deals and if one of these should turn out badly, Wilson might well decide to wash his hands of Elmtree.

Steve did two things next. He first asked Harry Jones to put in place all but the very final touches on a legal agreement for acquiring the Allston property. Jones reported the next day that all was in order but that it was going to cost $20,000 more than anticipated to do some necessary repair work on the house in order to meet Allston's fire standards. Still, $300,000 would meet those needs. Second, Steve worked with Mrs. Peters to find out what an extra $25,000 or $50,000 would mean to Elmtree House. Mrs. Peters said that half of any extra money should

7. A colleague to whom I recounted this story thought that our assessment of Wilson's *RP* should have been updated during the breaks in the negotiations by going back to the experts we had consulted initially; Steve should have been more aware of information he might have obtained from Wilson that the experts could have used to reassess Wilson's *RP*.

definitely go into the Financial Aid Fund for prospective residents who could not quite afford Elmtree House, and that it could also be used to purchase items on her little list of "necessary luxuries": a color television set, an upright piano, new mattresses and dishes, repair of broken furniture, a large freezer so that she could buy meat in bulk, and so on. Her "little list" became increasingly long as her enthusiasm mounted — but \$10,000 to \$20,000 would suffice to make a fair dent in it, and as Mrs. Peters talked she became even more excited about those fringes than about the move to Allston. She was all for holding out for \$350,000.

The next day Steve called Wilson and explained to him that the members of Elmtree's board were divided about accepting \$300,000 (that was actually true). "Would it be possible for your company to yield a bit and do, for free, the equivalent of \$30,000 or \$40,000 worth of repair work on Elmtree's new property if our deal with you goes through? In that case, we could go with the \$300,000 offer." Wilson responded that he was delighted that the board was smart enough to accept his magnanimous offer of \$300,000. Steve was speechless. Wilson then explained that his company had a firm policy not to entangle itself with side deals involving free contract work. He didn't blame Steve for trying, but his suggestion was out of the question.

"Well then," Steve responded, "it would surely help us if your company could make a tax-free gift to Elmtree House of, say, \$40,000, for Elmtree's Financial Aid Fund for needy residents."

"Now that's an idea! Forty grand is too high, but I'll ask our lawyers if we can contribute twenty grand."

"Twenty-five?"

"Okay — twenty-five."

It turned out that for legal reasons Wilson's company paid a straight \$325,000 to Elmtree House, but Wilson had succeeded in finding a good face-saving reason for breaking his "firm last offer" of \$300,000.

Lest readers think erroneously that it's always wise to bargain tough, I might suggest another perfectly plausible version of this story: Wilson might have backed out of the deal suddenly, at the time when he made his firm last offer of \$300,000 and Steve demanded \$350,000. An alternative venture competitive with the Elmtree deal might have turned out magnificently profitable for Wilson.

4. Analytical Models and Empirical Results

With Elmtree House as a basis, we can now simplify and abstract. Later we will begin building up the complexities.

Consider the case in which two bargainers must jointly decide on a determinate value of some continuous variable (like money) that they can mutually adjust. One bargainer wants the value to be high — the higher the better — whereas the other bargainer wants the value to be low — the lower the better. We could label these agents "high aspirer" and "low aspirer," but for our purposes "buyer" and "seller" will be sufficient, even though the context we'll be dealing with is much broader than that consisting of simple business transactions in which there is an actual seller and buyer.

To simplify matters, let's assume that each bargaining agent is monolithic: he or she does not have to convince the members of some constituency that they should ratify the agreement. Let's also assume that the bargaining agents are primarily concerned about this deal only, that linkages to similar problems over repetitive plays, or linkages to other outstanding problems, are minimal—or, better yet, are nil. Setting precedents, cashing credits for past favors, and log-rolling between problems are not appropriate concerns. Time is a more troublesome matter. . . .

A CHECKLIST FOR NEGOTIATORS

Suppose that *you* represent one of two parties that have to negotiate the price of a commodity, the value of a firm, a wage rate, an out-of-court settlement, or the date of a proposed marriage. Based on the discussion of the preceding chapters, what are the things that you will want to keep in mind? Think of yourself for the moment as the seller—or maximizer, if you will—who wants the final contract value to be high rather than low. Your adversary, the buyer (or minimizer), is seeking a low contract value. Assume that you are your own boss and that your side is monolithic, that you do not necessarily have to come to any agreement, that contracts once agreed upon are secure, that negotiations are nonstrident, and that the only threat the parties can make is the threat not to settle.

Preparing for Negotiations

First, *know yourself.* Think about what you need, want, aspire to. Consider what will happen to you if no deal is struck. Search diligently for competing and substitute alternatives. Analyze (or at least think about) your other alternatives, and, all things considered, assign a certainty-equivalent value to your best alternative to a negotiated agreement; this is your subjective evaluation of the no-agreement state. Assess your reservation price for each round of negotiations. Your reservation price—which is based on the value you have placed on the no-agreement state—is the absolute minimum value that you (as the maximizer) would be willing to settle for. Any lesser value would be worse than the no-agreement state; you would walk away from the bargaining rather than settle for a value less than this minimum. Amass your arguments for the negotiations: facts, data, arguments, rationalizations, including arguments about what is fair and how an arbitrator might settle the dispute.

Second, *know your adversaries.* Consider what will happen to them (or he or she, as the case may be) if no deal is struck. Speculate about their alternatives. Examine your perceptions of their reservation price; think about the uncertainties in these perceptions (and, if it is natural to you, encode them into probabilistic assessments). Investigate their credentials, their legitimacy, their integrity. Investigate how they have negotiated in the past.

Third, give thought to the *negotiating conventions* in each context. How open should you be? Can you believe what your adversaries will say? Is it customary to withhold unfavorable information? What number of iterations in the negotiation dance is respectable or customary? Can negotiations be done in stages? If so, what is your reservation value for each upcoming stage? How will each stage of the negotiations affect your continuing relations with your adversaries?

Fourth, consider the *logistics* of the situation. Who should negotiate? Should roles be assigned to the negotiators on your side? Do you need professional assistance, such as representation by a skilled negotiator? Where should negotiations take place, and when? If they will be of an international nature, in what language should the negotiations be conducted, and who should supply the translators?

Fifth, remember that *simulated role playing* can be of value in preparing your strategy. Try to find someone to play the role of your adversaries and give careful thought to what their tactics might be. Arrange for simulated negotiations.

Sixth, iterate and set your *aspiration levels*. Giving consideration to all the above points, what contract value should you strive for? It's easy to say "the more the better," but it's helpful to have some target level that is a reasonable distance from your bottom-line, walkaway price. Your aspiration level might well shift during negotiations, but your reservation price should remain firmer; it too could shift, however, if the other side provides information enabling you to reassess your other opportunities or the value you place on an agreement.

Opening Gambits

Who should make the first concrete offer? Beware of opening so conservatively that your offer falls well within your adversaries' acceptance region. Beware of opening with so extreme a value that you hurt the ambience of negotiations; also, if you are too extreme you will have to make disproportionately large concessions. If you open first, and if your adversaries are ill prepared, you might influence their perception of their own reservation price by your opening offer: your opening offer anchors their thinking about the value of the venture to themselves. Be aware of this anchoring phenomenon if the situation is reversed.

Gauge your reaction to an extreme first offer. Don't get locked in by talking about your adversaries' extreme offer; don't let their offer be the vantage point for subsequent modifications. The best strategy in this case is to either break off negotiations until they modify their offer, or quickly counter with an offer of your own. When two offers are on the table, the midpoint is a natural focal point, so think about this when you make an initial counteroffer. Compare the midpoint of the two offers with your aspiration level.

Protect your integrity. Try to avoid disclosing information (such as your reservation price) as an alternative to giving false information. Use phrases like "This is what I would like to get" rather than "This is what I *must* get," when your "must" value is not really a must.

The Negotiation Dance

The pattern of concessions. The most common pattern of concessions (for a maximizer) is monotone decreasing—that is, the intervals between your decreasing offers become successively smaller, signaling that you are approaching your limit (which does not necessarily have to be your reservation price; it could be your readjusted aspiration level). The number of concessions that you should be prepared to make depends on the context. Your concessions should be paced and linked to those of your adversary.

Reassessing perceptions. During the negotiations, reassess your perceptions about your adversaries' reservation price. Remember that they might want you to infer that their reservation price is lower than it really is. Conversely, you might want them to believe that your reservation price is higher than it really is. How aggressive should you be in this game of deception? Again, it depends on norms, on the extent to which you guard your integrity, on whether you will be continuing relations with your adversaries, on your (probabilistic) perceptions of their reactions, on your attitudes toward risk, on how you empathize with the needs of the other side, and on what you think is "fair."

Your adversaries may have information that is relevant to an evaluation of your own reservation price; part of your negotiating strategy may be to ferret out some of this information. But be careful of possible deceptions on their part, such as selective disclosure of information.

As you go along, reassess your aspiration levels. This is hard to do analytically, but you should nevertheless keep such reassessment in mind. Your adversaries are doing the same.

End Play

Making commitments. For sincere or possibly insincere reasons, you might want to signal that some value is as far as you can or will go. How can you convince your adversaries that you really mean it? That your stance is not merely a bargaining ploy? For example, you might threaten to break off negotiations, leaving it somewhat vague as to whether negotiations could start up again; or you might make statements that limit your further flexibility.

Breaking a commitment gracefully. How can you disengage from a commitment that didn't work? You can get new instructions from the interests you represent. You can add new issues. . . . You can get new information. You can be replaced by a new negotiator for your side. And so on.

Helping your adversaries to break a commitment gracefully. It may be to your advantage to let your adversaries disengage from an agreement without too much loss of face. You could, for example, imply that the situation has changed when it really hasn't. Or you might imply that they were not well organized to begin with and it's reasonable for them to change their mind. Conversely, if you would like to free yourself from a commitment, you might want to give your adversaries the opportunity to help you.

In the abstract, these games of deception may sound somewhat immoral. But in concrete situations they do not seem so at all. In the case of Elmtree House, it seemed quite proper and natural for Steve to engage in such behavior—for example, by suggesting that Wilson's company donate some construction work or make a contribution to a scholarship fund. These ploys were designed to provide Wilson with a face-saving means of breaking his absolute top, irrevocable offer.

A commitment is really not a commitment if both sides realize that it can be easily broken. So it may be necessary in some contexts to escalate the rhetoric in order to achieve "real commitment" or a "real-real commitment." This is akin to the situation described in the Sorensen Chevrolet case: the lawyer for the plaintiff offered a rock-bottom price of $350,000; on the steps of the courthouse a new lawyer for the plaintiff offered the rock-rock-bottom price of $300,000. Maybe in the judge's chamber the plaintiff herself might have overruled her lawyers and offered the REAL FINAL offer of $250,000.

Introducing an intervenor. If you suspect that your latest rejected offer is well within your adversaries' acceptance region and if you refuse to move still lower toward your own reservation price, you might have to give up and break off negotiations. Before doing that, you might suggest bringing in a mediator or even an arbitrator. Both you and your adversaries might be willing to disclose more confidential information to an intervenor than to each other.

Broadening the domain of negotiation. In the end, there may be no zone of agreement, or—because of stated commitments—there may be no way of achieving a solution even if there is one. But if the domain of negotiation is enlarged to include more complicated exchanges (for example, contingency arrangements) or to include additional issues, then a mutually profitable contract may be possible and desirable for both parties.

A final word of advice; don't gloat about how well you have done. After settling a merger for $7 million, don't tell your future partners that your reservation price was only $4 million; that won't make them feel good. You might be tempted to lie for their benefit and make a vague claim to a reservation price of about $6.5 million—but lies, even beneficial ones, generate their own complications. Some confidential information should remain confidential even after the fact.*

Questions

2.1 Suppose that a bride-to-be and her fiancé disagree about the date of their proposed marriage. She wants the wedding to take place in June, but knowing that her fiancé wants a fall wedding, she proposes April, hoping for a favorable compromise. Her fiancé, who wants a September wedding, but also anticipating a compromise, proposes October. They settle for July, which is midway between April and October. Is this a satisfactory approach to negotiating a resolution of their disagreement regarding the appropriate date of their marriage? Why? Is your answer generalizable to negotiation in other contexts?

2.2 Raiffa refers (p. 30) to the "negotiation dance," the pattern of offer and counteroffer by which negotiators seek to close the gap between their opening positions in order to reach agreement. Raiffa also makes various suggestions for succeeding in this process. Occasionally, however, a negotiator will say to an opposing negotiator: "I have too much respect for you to go through a negotiation dance with you. Instead, I want to deal with you in a completely candid and ethical manner. Accordingly, I am going to tell you the minimum price that my client has authorized me to accept. If your client is willing to pay that price, we have a deal. If not, we don't and there's no point wasting each other's time talking about it." Assuming that the negotiator is being honest in stating the client's position, what is your view of this approach to negotiation?

*Professor Raiffa, together with John Richardson and David Metcalfe, recently published a broad-ranging revision of *The Art and Science of Negotiation,* entitled *Negotiation Analysis: The Science and Art of Collaborative Decision Making.* The new book puts forth Professor Raiffa's latest thinking about the negotiation process, and covers a wide range of related topics, including risk and uncertainty, fair division, and the role of third parties.

Note: Principled Negotiation

A different approach to negotiation is described by Roger Fisher and William Ury in their widely read book, *Getting to Yes.* This approach has variously been characterized as "principled," "integrative," "problem-solving," "interests-based," "win-win," or "cooperative." The five basic elements of this approach, according to Fisher and Ury, are these:

1. *Separate the people from the problem.* The negotiators should attack the problem, not each other.
2. *Focus on interests not positions.* Your positions are what you want. Your interests are why you want them. Focusing on interests may uncover the existence of mutual or complementary interests that will make agreement possible. One interest that Fisher and Ury suggest is typically important to both negotiators is that of maintaining a good long-term relationship between them. This relationship is of much less concern to those who follow a competitive strategy and is often a casualty of such a strategy.
3. *Invent options for mutual gain.* Negotiating need not be a competitive game in which each negotiator seeks to gain the biggest slice of a fixed pie. To the contrary, there may be bargaining outcomes that will advance the interests of both negotiators. One well-known example involves the two children who are trying to decide which of them should get the only orange in the house. After some frustrating negotiations, they decide to divide the orange in half. If they had realized that one child wanted to squeeze the orange for its juice, and the other wanted to grate the rind to flavor a cake, an agreement that maximized the interests of each would have become apparent.
4. *Insist on using objective criteria.* There are some negotiations, or at least some issues, that are not susceptible to a "win win" approach. The price of something can be such an issue, since each dollar I give you is one dollar less for me. To minimize the risk of either inefficient haggling or a failure to reach agreement on such issues, Fisher and Ury suggest that the parties focus on objective criteria to govern the outcome. Thus, instead of negotiating over the price of a used car, one party might look to the blue book value, the other to the depreciated cost. Even if they cannot agree on which standard should control, focusing on objective criteria may narrow the range of disagreement.
5. *Know your best alternative to a negotiated agreement (BATNA).* The reason you negotiate with someone is to produce better results than you could obtain without negotiating with that person. If you are unaware of what results you could obtain if the negotiations are unsuccessful, you run the risk of entering into an agreement that you would be better off rejecting or rejecting an agreement that you would be better off entering into. For example, it would be unwise to agree to buy a car from a friend for $6,000 without knowing how much a similar car would cost you elsewhere. The latter figure is your BATNA.

   You should also know as much as possible about the other party's BATNA. If your friend does not sell the car to you, how much will it command elsewhere? Knowing the answer to this question might substantially affect the amount of your offer. It may be difficult to determine the other party's BATNA, but the value of this information is often sufficiently great that you should be willing to devote considerable effort to determining it. At the very least, you should ask questions of the other party designed to aid you in determining the other party's BATNA.*

Question

2.3 An alert reader of *Getting to Yes* suggested that negotiators must concern themselves not only with the BATNA, but also with the WATNA (the worst alternative to a negotiated agreement). Do you agree? What would be a good example of the relevance of the WATNA in a specific negotiation?

The concepts of principled negotiation, as set out by Fisher and Ury, have gained many converts and are widely espoused. Still, this approach has been criticized on both the tactical and strategic levels. At the tactical level, it has been suggested that a Fisher and Ury "principled negotiator" would be incapable of standing up to a negotiator who followed the precepts of Meltsner and Schrag. In an excerpt from *Getting Past No* (1991), William Ury offers tactical advice for dealing with a Meltsner and Schrag "tough" negotiator. Are you persuaded that following this advice would enable you to deal with such a negotiator?

W. URY, GETTING PAST NO†

(Draft ed. 1990)

PROBLEM PEOPLE, PROBLEM SITUATIONS

Suppose that you have just made the sale of the year. The negotiation with the client was long and hard, but it will double your sales total for the year. Having announced the deal triumphantly to your associates and made the necessary arrangements with manufacturing, you bring in the agreement for the client to sign. He stops you and says: "Now that we've agreed on what you'll provide us, we'd be happy to go ahead as long as you give us a 10% discount." You are stunned. . .

Common sense tells us that anyone can be difficult to deal with at times. Faced with high pressure jobs, deadlines, and limited resources, it is a wonder that people can deal as reasonably and respectfully with each other as they do. Even if the other person is reasonable most of the time, there comes a point in many negotiations when he isn't — when he simply digs in or launches into a string of threats.

Often, in order to protect yourself against an unreasonable person, you find yourself forced to play his game. You dig in; you issue counterthreats; you attack him back. But is there any way you can get him to play *your* game — to engage with you in problem-solving negotiation? How can you, in effect, change the game in order to reach a satisfactory agreement efficiently and amicably?

* Students should not be content with this summary and are strongly urged to read *Getting to Yes* in its entirety.

† The final version of *Getting Past No* was published under the title, *Getting Past No: Dealing with Difficult People* (1991).

In order to answer this question, we need first to understand the problem we are up against — the other side's behavior and our normal reactions to it. We must further understand their underlying motivations and why our normal reactions just reinforce their behavior. Only then can we formulate a sound approach.

The Problem

The problem is first the other side's behavior, and second, the fact that our normal reactions do not deal effectively with it.

THREE KINDS OF BEHAVIOR

In his efforts to win, the other person usually resorts to three kinds of behavior:

Stonewalling

Stonewalling — refusing to budge from one's position or refusing to negotiate at all — works by convincing you that the other person has no flexibility and that it is useless to try to reach any outcome other than his announced position. Stonewalling can take the form of a *fait accompli:* "What's done is done. It can't be changed." Or a resort to company policy: "I can't do anything about it. It's company policy." Or a reference to a previous commitment: "I told the membership that I would resign as union negotiator before I would accept any less than an 8% raise." Or an excuse for endless delay: "We'll get back to you." Or a final declaration: "You can take it or leave it!" Any other suggestion on your part is met with a NO.

Attacks

Attacks are pressure tactics designed to intimidate you and make you feel so uncomfortable that you ultimately give in to the other side's demands. Perhaps the most common form of attack is to threaten you with dire consequences unless you accept their position: "Do it or else!" The other person may also attack your proposal ("Your figures are way out of line!"), your credibility ("You haven't been in this job long, have you?"), or your status and authority ("We want to talk to the real decision-maker."). An attacker will insult, badger, and bully you until he gets his way.

Tricks

A trick takes advantage of your expectations of truth-telling and good faith so that you come to accept the other side's position. One kind of trick is manipulating the data — using false, phony, or confusing figures. Another is the "no authority" ploy in which the other person misleads you into believing that he has the authority to decide the issue, only to inform you after you have used up all your flexibility that in fact someone else must decide. Tricks lure you under false pretenses into giving in.

COMMON REACTIONS

What can you do when confronted with difficult behavior? Wanting to negotiate in a problem-solving fashion, you may try to reason with the unreasonable person. But he will tend to hear whatever reasons you give for changing his mind as positional arguments designed to pressure him into giving in. He will hear whatever compromise proposals you make either as tricks intended to take him in or as confirming evidence that his tactics have worked. He sees the problem-solving game as *your* game. If he agrees to cooperate, he will have "given in" to you. Naturally then, he continues and even intensifies his stonewalling, attacks, and tricks. In frustration then, you turn to one of the three normal reactions to this kind of behavior: acting difficult yourself, giving in, or breaking off the relationship.

Act Difficult

Your first temptation is probably to get into the ring and fight back on the same terms. "Fight fire with fire" and "give them a taste of their own medicine" are adages that come to mind. When someone attacks you, your instinctive reaction is to attack them back.

More rationally, you may hope that, by showing them that two can play the same game, you will bring them to their senses and open the way for negotiation. In some cases, particularly if you are dealing with someone who wants an agreement but is simply hoping to get a better deal, you may succeed.

In most cases, however, this strategy will simply land you in a futile and costly confrontation. You merely give the other person the justification he seeks for his unreasonable behavior. He will say to himself: "Ah, I knew that you were out to get me. This proves it." He becomes even more fearful, hostile, and rigid. Escalation often follows in the form of a verbal showdown, a corporate jungle fight, a lawsuit, or a war. . . .

Yet another problem with responding in kind is that the kind of people who stonewall, attack, or use tricks are usually very good at it. They may actually be hoping that you are going to attack them back for you are then on their turf, playing the game the way they like to play it. If you are in the tiger's cage, it may not be wise to pick a fight.

Give In

The opposite of acting difficult is to give in. You may feel so uncomfortable that you just want to get it over with, or that you have no choice but to concede. You may decide that it is not worth getting into a fight or that, in fact, the other side has a point. Or maybe you feel that giving in will allay their suspicions, thus creating a better relationship.

Sometimes this may be the most sensible course. If a fight is far more costly than the matter is worth, you may be wise to let it go. If someone has a gun against your head, you probably ought to hand over your wallet.

Usually, however, giving in results in an unsatisfactory outcome. You feel "had." Moreover, it rewards the other side for bad behavior and gives you a reputation for weakness that he — and others — may try to exploit in the future. Just as giving in to a child's temper tantrum only reinforces this behavior pattern, so giving in to an angry person only encourages angry outbursts in the future. Your boss' or client's terrible temper may appear to be a personality trait, not a tactic to get a better deal, but think about it. He developed that personality as a child because he learned that, when he threw a tantrum, he got what he wanted from his parents. A temper can be controlled—he doesn't throw a tantrum in front of *his* boss, just in front of you when he wants something.

People are intimidated and appease the unreasonable person, often under the illusion that, if they give in just this one last time, they will get him off their back and they will never have to deal with him again. Wrong. Usually, that person comes back for further concessions if only because he knows that he can get you to give in. As Heywood Broun once put it, an appeaser believes that if you keep on throwing steaks to a tiger, the tiger will become a vegetarian.

Break Off

A third course of action is to break off relations. Cease contact with the difficult person or organization. Don't do business with them. If it's a marriage, get a divorce. If it's a job, resign. If the problem is a neighbor, move away from the neighborhood. If you are involved in a joint venture, dissolve it.

At times, avoidance is a perfectly appropriate strategy. Sometimes it is better to end a personal or business relationship if continuing it means being taken advantage of or getting into a fight again and again. Sometimes too, breaking off reminds the other side of the stake they have in the relationship and leads them to act more reasonably.

Usually, however, the costs — both financial and emotional — of breaking off the relationship are high: a lost client, a career setback, a broken family. Breaking off is often a hasty reaction which people come to regret later. We all know people who take a job or enter a personal relationship, become frustrated by their boss or partner, and then leave without giving it a chance. Often, they misinterpret the other person's behavior and do not try to work it out. A pattern of breaking off relationships means you never get anywhere—you are always starting over.

What is more, the option is often not a genuine one. The costs of disengaging from the relationship may be so high that you feel you have little choice but to deal with the person or organization who is being difficult. Finally, as with giving in, breaking off can signal weakness. It can lead others to seek to exploit you further, knowing that you will not stand your ground. . . .

Each of the three normal reactions is an understandable response to difficult behavior, but none is usually satisfactory. To figure out a better approach, we must first understand what drives the behavior and why the normal reactions fail to work.

Analysis

Why Don't People Want to Cooperate?

We are often led to believe that stonewalling, attacks, and tricks are just part of the other person's basic nature, with the implication that we can do little to change the difficult behavior. Notwithstanding the strong relationship between behavior and personality, you can affect behavior if you can deal successfully with the underlying motivations. People resisting cooperation are typically driven by a varying mix of four motivations:

They Are Afraid

Many people with whom one negotiates feel fearful, insecure, and suspicious. Seeing the world as "eat or be eaten," they take rigid positions to protect themselves and are quick to overreact. Behind their verbal fireworks and angry outbursts lie a fear of losing authority or status, a fear of losing control, or a fear of losing their job. Feeling as they do, they do not make fine differences between negotiating in good faith and using deceit; they will tend to use any tactics that promise to help them defend themselves against you, the hostile threat.

They Don't Know Better

Often people use stonewalling, attacks, or tricks not because they are by nature unreasonable or difficult, but simply because they know no other way to negotiate. The conventional way when the going gets tough is to turn rigid, to attack vigorously, or to resort to ruses. That is usually what we learn in childhood from fights in the sandbox or from watching our parents quarrel. Not knowing how to engage in problem-solving negotiation, the only alternative people see to unreasonable tactics is to give in — and they don't want to do that.

They Don't See What's in It for Them

Even if the other person is aware of the possibility of cooperative negotiation, he may spurn it because he does not see how his interests can be met in this fashion. *Why* should he cooperate?

They Think They Can Win

Often people are motivated by greed, hunger for power, or simple opportunism. They are guided by the precept that "What is mine is mine. What is yours is negotiable." Why share the pie fairly when they can make away with the lion's share? If the client believes he can get a 10% discount by trapping you, why shouldn't he use the tactic? Why should people cooperate when they think they can win? . . .

The Method

What method will . . . enable you to break through the other person's resistance and engage him in problem-solving negotiation? A careful study of successful negotiation practice reveals such a method, which may be called *breakthrough negotiation.* The breakthrough method can be distilled into five basic steps. The first step enables you to avoid reacting in the normal way. The second defuses the other person's fears, the third educates him, the fourth entices him, and the fifth impresses him that he cannot win easily. The method is indirect and step by step.

The very first step of the method is not to react to the other person's tactics. A NO or an attack can stun you into submission or into a counterattack, which is exactly what the other side wants. Short of breaking off the relationship, how can you stop reacting? An indirect approach is to detach yourself mentally from the negotiation and suspend your reaction, preferably by taking a break. Imagine yourself standing on a balcony looking down on your situation. On the balcony, you can recognize the other side's tactics, remember what your real interests are, and, if you have time, prepare thoroughly for the negotiation. You are thus able to regain control over yourself, frustrating their attempt to throw you off balance. The first step, in short, is: *Go to the Balcony.*

Before you can negotiate, however, you must defuse their fears and suspicions. Short of giving in, how can you disarm them? They expect you to attack or to resist; they are ready for that. So act indirectly and do the opposite of what they expect. The opposite of pushing against someone is to draw him into a friendly interaction; in other words, step to his side. Listen to him and acknowledge his point, and agree with him whenever you can. Acknowledge the person himself—his competence, his authority, and his status. In this way, you create a climate for problem-solving negotiation. The second step then is: *Step to Their Side.*

The next step is to change the game. Instead of rejecting your opponent's position—which usually only reinforces it—direct his attention to the problem of meeting each side's interests. Take whatever he says and reframe it as an attempt to deal with the problem. Ask problem-solving questions, such as "Why is it that you want that?" or "What would you do if you were in my shoes?" or "What if we were to . . . ?" Rather than trying to teach him yourself, let the problem be his teacher. Reframe his tactics, too: Go around stone walls, deflect attacks, and expose tricks. To change the game, change the frame. The third step is: *Don't Reject . . . Reframe.*

Now at last you can negotiate, but you still have to entice them to agreement. Not yet convinced of the benefits, people stall. You may be tempted to push and insist, but this will likely lead them only to harden and resist. The indirect alternative is to "build them a golden bridge to retreat across," as one ancient Chinese strategist put it. Think of yourself as a mediator. Bridge the gap between their interests and yours. Make the outcome appear as a victory for them—or at least a way out with honor. Build on their ideas. Make it easy and convenient for them to agree. The fourth step is: *Build Them a Golden Bridge.*

If your opponent still resists and thinks he can win without negotiating, you must educate him to the contrary. You must make it hard for him to say no. You could use threats and force, but these often backfire; if you push him into a corner, he will likely lash out, throwing even more resources into the fight against you. Instead, educate him about the costs of not agreeing. Ask reality-testing questions, warn rather than threaten, and demonstrate your BATNA. Use it only if necessary and minimize his resistance by exercising restraint and reassuring him that your goal is mutual satisfaction, not victory. Make sure he knows the golden bridge is always open. In short, use power to bring him to his senses, not his knees. The final step then is: *Bring Them to Their Senses, Not Their Knees.*

These five steps deal progressively with each major barrier to problem-solving negotiation. Going to the balcony deals with your own reaction; acknowledging the other person defuses his fears; reframing changes the game to problem-solving negotiation; building him a golden bridge entices him with the benefits of agreement; and using power to bring him to his senses impresses him that it is not worth trying to exploit you.

Consider a simple example. A sales executive was responsible for the New York garment industry which is known for a peculiar negotiating style characterized by frequent insults, invective, and threats. She sent a young and inexperienced account executive to pay a visit on a client. The client gave her the full treatment, shouting and swearing and going so far as to threaten to throw her out of a sixth-floor window. The account executive came back to her boss in tears.

So the boss called the client herself. The client gave her the same dressing down — personal insults, curses and the like. She listened patiently, holding the phone away from her ear, until he took a pause for breath. Then she said in a calm voice: "Now I just want to let you know one thing. You can continue to shout and swear at me as long as you like. Because I can take it. I've been married!" There was a dead silence at the other end of the phone and then she heard: "Hey, I like that . . . I can do business with you." She then proceeded to ask him what the problem was and together they came up with a solution that satisfied them both.

What was the sales executive doing? She didn't appease the customer nor did she counterattack — those were the direct reactions he expected. Instead, she went to her mental balcony and collected her thoughts. She then disarmed him by surprising him and acknowledging the ploy, making it OK for him to swear and shout. Once she had created a climate for negotiation, she began to ask problem-solving questions, letting the problem be his teacher. Together they were able to build him a golden bridge. She didn't score a win over him; instead she won him over. . . .

A fundamental criticism of Fisher and Ury's *Getting to Yes* has been that, wholly apart from its value at the tactical level, it provides guidance only in those negotiations in which mutual gains are possible, and ignores those in which any gains for one negotiator are realized at the expense of the other. This criticism is forcefully stated in James White's review of *Getting to Yes.*

J. WHITE, THE PROS AND CONS OF "GETTING TO YES"

34 J. Legal Educ. 115-117 (1984)

Getting to Yes is a puzzling book. On the one hand it offers a forceful and persuasive criticism of much traditional negotiating behavior. It suggests a variety of negotiating techniques that are both clever and likely to facilitate effective negotiation. On the other hand, the authors seem to deny the existence of a significant part of the negotiation process, and to oversimplify or explain away many of the most troublesome problems inherent in the art and practice of negotiation. The book is frequently naive, occasionally self-righteous, but often helpful. . . .

The book's thesis is well summarized by the following passage:

> Behind opposed positions lie shared and compatible interests, as well as conflicting ones. We tend to assume that because the other side's positions are opposed to ours, their

> interests must also be opposed. If we have an interest in defending ourselves, then they must want to attack us. If we have an interest in minimizing the rent, then their interest must be to maximize it. In many negotiations, however, a close examination of the underlying interests will reveal the existence of many more interests that are shared or compatible than ones that are opposed [p. 43].

This point is useful for all who teach or think about negotiation. The tendency of those deeply involved in negotiation or its teaching is probably to exaggerate the importance of negotiation on issues where the parties are diametrically opposed and to ignore situations where the parties' interests are compatible. By emphasizing that fact, and by making a clear articulation of the importance of cooperation, imagination, and the search for alternative solutions, the authors teach helpful lessons. The book therefore provides worthwhile reading for every professional negotiator and will make sound instruction for every tyro.

Unfortunately the book's emphasis upon mutually profitable adjustment, on the "problem solving" aspect of bargaining, is also the book's weakness. It is a weakness because emphasis of this aspect of bargaining is done to almost total exclusion of the other aspect of bargaining, "distributional bargaining," where one for me is minus one for you. . . .

Students of negotiation have long distinguished between that aspect of bargaining in which modification of the parties' positions can produce benefits for one without significant cost to the other, and on the other hand, cases where benefits to one come only at significant cost to the other. They have variously described the former as "exploring for mutual profitable adjustments," "the efficiency aspect of bargaining," or "problem solving." The other has been characterized as "distributional bargaining" or "share bargaining." Thus some would describe a typical negotiation as one in which the parties initially begin by cooperative or efficiency bargaining, in which each gains something with each new adjustment without the other losing any significant benefit. Eventually, however, one comes to bargaining in which added benefits to one impose corresponding significant costs on the other. For example, in a labor contract one might engage in cooperative bargaining by the modification of a medical plan so that the employer could engage a less expensive medical insurance provider, yet one that offered improved services. Each side gains by that change from the old contract. Ultimately parties in a labor negotiation will come to a raw economic exchange in which additional wage dollars for the employees will be dollars subtracted from the corporate profits, dollars that cannot be paid in dividends to the shareholders.

One can concede the authors' thesis (that too many negotiators are incapable of engaging in problem solving or in finding adequate options for mutual gain), yet still maintain that the most demanding aspect of nearly every negotiation is the distributional one in which one seeks more at the expense of the other. My principal criticism of the book is that it seems to overlook the ultimate hard bargaining. Had the authors stated that they were dividing the negotiation process in two and were dealing with only part of it, that omission would be excusable. That is not what they have done. Rather they seem to assume that a clever negotiator can make any negotiation into problem solving and thus completely avoid the difficult distribution. . . . To my mind this is naive. By so distorting reality, they detract from their powerful and central thesis.

Chapter 5, entitled "Insist on Objective Criteria," is a particularly naive misperception or rejection of the guts of distributive negotiation. Here, as elsewhere, the authors draw a stark distinction between a negotiator who simply takes a position without explanation and sticks to it as a matter of "will," and the negotiator who is reasonable and insists upon "objective criteria." Of course the world is hardly as simple as the authors suggest. Every party who takes a position will have some rationale for that position; every able negotiator rationalizes every position that he takes. Rarely will an effective negotiator simply assert "X" as his price and insist that the other party meet it.

The suggestion that one can find objective criteria (as opposed to persuasive rationalizations) seems quite inaccurate. . . . One who could sell his automobile to a particular person for $6,000 could not necessarily sell it for more than $5,000 to another person, not because of principle, but because of the need of the seller to sell and the differential need of the two buyers to buy. To say that there are objective criteria that call for a $5,000 or $6,000 price, or in the case of a personal injury suit for a million dollars or an $800,000 judgment, is to ignore the true dynamics of the situation and to exaggerate the power of objective criteria. . . .

In short, the authors' suggestion in Chapter 5 that one can avoid "contests of will" and thereby eliminate the exercise of raw power is at best naive and at worst misleading. Their suggestion that the parties look to objective criteria to strengthen their cases is a useful technique used by every able negotiator. Occasionally it may do what they suggest: give an obvious answer on which all can agree. Most of the time it will do no more than give the superficial appearance of reasonableness and honesty to one party's position. . . .

One might argue that, contrary to White's criticism, some of the basic principles of *Getting to Yes* are applicable to the distributive or value-claiming aspects of bargaining. For example, the objective of focusing on your BATNA is not to create value but to avoid entering into an agreement that is distributionally less satisfactory than you could obtain elsewhere. Similarly, the reason for focusing on objective criteria is to avoid inefficient haggling in the distributional stages of a negotiation. Thus, to the extent that White's criticism is valid, it may not be that Fisher and Ury do not deal with the distributive aspects of bargaining, but rather that they do not do so explicitly. As for White's criticism that focusing on objective criteria is of little value, Fisher and Ury have this to say:

R. FISHER, W. URY, AND B. PATTON, GETTING TO YES

(2d ed. 1991)

In most negotiations there will be no one "right" or "fairest" answer; people will advance different standards by which to judge what is fair. Yet using external standards improves on haggling in three ways: An outcome informed even by conflicting standards of fairness and community practice is likely to be wiser than an arbitrary result. Using standards reduces the costs of "backing down"—it is easier to agree to follow a principle or independent standard than to give in to the other side's positional demands. And finally, unlike arbitrary positions, some standards are more persuasive than others.

In a negotiation between a young associate and a Wall Street law firm over salary, for example, it would be absurd for the hiring partner to say, "I don't suppose you think you are any smar[illegible] you the same salary I made when I started out forty y[illegible] young [illegible] point out the impact of inflation over [illegible] current salaries. If the partner proposed using the current salaries for [illegible] Dayton or Des Moines, the young lawyer [illegible] the average salary for young lawyers in similarly prestigious Manhattan firms as a more appropriate standard.

Usually one standard will be more persuasive than another to the extent that it is more directly on point, more widely accepted, and more immediately relevant in terms of time, place, and circumstances.

Agreement on the "best" standard is not necessary. Differences in values, culture, experience, and perceptions may well lead parties to disagree about the relative merits of different standards. If it were necessary to agree on which standard was "best," settling a negotiation might not be possible. But agreement on criteria is not necessary. Criteria are just one tool that may help the parties find an agreement better for both than no agreement. Using external standards often helps narrow the range of disagreement and may help expand the area of potential agreement. When standards have been refined to the point that it is difficult to argue persuasively that one standard is more applicable than another, the parties can explore tradeoffs or resort to fair procedures to settle the remaining differences. They can flip a coin, use an arbitrator, or even split the difference.

According to some negotiation scholars, while Fisher and Ury may focus overmuch on the problem-solving or integrative aspects of bargaining, White's attention is too focused on the distributive aspects. David Lax and James Sebenius attempt a broader view of the negotiation process, one that seeks to encompass both integrative and distributive aspects.

D. LAX AND J. SEBENIUS, THE MANAGER AS NEGOTIATOR*

29-41, 158-166, 91-105 (1986)

THE NEGOTIATOR'S DILEMMA: CREATING AND CLAIMING VALUE

. . . That negotiation includes cooperation and competition, common and conflicting interests, is nothing new. In fact, it is typically understood that these elements are both present and can be disentangled. Deep down, however, some people believe that the elements of conflict are illusory, that meaningful communication will erase any such unfortunate misperceptions. Others see mainly competition and take the cooperative pieces to be minimal. Some overtly acknowledge the reality of each aspect but direct all their attention to one of them and wish, pretend, or act as if the other does not exist. Still others hold to a more balanced view that accepts both elements as significant but seeks to treat them separately. [A]ll these approaches are flawed.

A deeper analysis shows that the competitive and cooperative elements are inextricably entwined. In practice, they cannot be separated. This bonding is fundamentally important to the analysis, structuring, and conduct of negotiation. There is a central, inescapable tension between cooperative moves to create value jointly and competitive moves to gain individual advantage. This tension affects virtually all tactical and strategic choice. Analysts must come to grips with it; negotiators must manage it. Neither denial nor discomfort will make it disappear.

WARRING CONCEPTIONS OF NEGOTIATION

Negotiators and analysts tend to fall into two groups that are guided by warring conceptions of the bargaining process. In the left-hand corner are the "value creators," and in the right-hand corner are the "value claimers."

Value Creators

Value creators tend to believe that, above all, successful negotiators must be inventive and cooperative enough to devise an agreement that yields considerable gain to each party, relative to no-agreement possibilities. Some speak about the need for replacing the "win-lose" image of negotiation with "win-win" negotiation, from which all parties presumably derive great value. For example, suppose that the mayor of a southern city learns when negotiating with the city's police union that, compared to the union, she places relatively greater weight on wage reductions than on the composition of a civilian review board. She may find that offering changes in the composition of the board for previously unattainable wage reductions may create benefit for both parties compared to the otherwise likely agreement with higher wages and with the current civilian review board composition. . . .

We create value by finding *joint gains* for all negotiating parties. A joint gain represents an improvement from each party's point of view; one's gain need not be another's loss. An extremely simple example makes the point. Say that two young boys each have three pieces of fruit. Willy, who hates bananas and loves pears, has a banana and two oranges. Sam, who hates pears and loves bananas, has a pear and two apples. The first move is easy: they trade banana for pear and are both happier. But after making this deal, they realize that they can do still better. Though each has a taste both for apples and oranges, a second piece of the same fruit is less desirable than the first. So they also swap an apple for an orange. The banana-pear exchange represents an improvement over the no-trade alternative; the apple-orange transaction that leaves each with three different kinds of fruit improves the original agreement—is a joint gain—for both boys.

The economist's analogy is simple: creativity has expanded the size of the pie under negotiation. Value creators see the essence of negotiating as expanding the pie, as pursuing joint gains. This is aided by openness, clear communication, sharing information, creativity, an attitude of joint problem solving, and cultivating common interests.

Value Claimers

Value claimers, on the other hand, tend to see this drive for joint gain as naive and weak-minded. For them, negotiation is hard, tough bargaining. The object of negotiation is to convince the other guy that he wants what you have to offer much more than you want what he has; moreover, you have all the time in the world while he is up against pressing deadlines. To "win" at negotiating—and thus make the other fellow "lose"—one must start high, concede slowly, exaggerate the value of concessions, minimize the benefits of the other's concessions, conceal information, argue forcefully on behalf of principles that imply favorable settlements, make commitments to accept only highly favorable agreements, and be willing to outwait the other fellow. . . .

At the heart of this adversarial approach is an image of a negotiation with a winner and a loser: "We are dividing a pie of fixed size and every slice I give to you is a slice I do not get; thus, I need to *claim* as much of the value as possible by giving you as little as possible."

A FUNDAMENTAL TENSION OF NEGOTIATION

Both of these images of negotiation are incomplete and inadequate. Value creating and value claiming are linked parts of negotiation. Both processes are present. No matter how much creative problem solving enlarges the pie, it must still be divided; value that has been created must be claimed. And, if the pie is not enlarged, there will be less to divide; there is more value to be claimed if one has helped create it first. An essential tension in negotiation exists between cooperative moves to create value and competitive moves to claim it. . . .

THE TENSION AT THE TACTICAL LEVEL

The tension between cooperative moves to create value and competitive moves to claim it is greatly exacerbated by the interaction of the tactics used either to create or claim value.

First, tactics for claiming value (which we will call "claiming tactics") can impede its creation. Exaggerating the value of concessions and minimizing the benefit of others' concessions presents a distorted picture of one's relative preferences; thus, mutually beneficial trades may not be discovered. Making threats or commitments to highly favorable outcomes surely impedes hearing and understanding others' interests. Concealing information may also cause one to leave joint gains on the table. In fact, excessive use of tactics for claiming value may well sour the parties' relationship and reduce the trust between them. Such tactics may also evoke a variety of unhelpful interests. Conflict may escalate and make joint prospects less appealing and settlement less likely.

Tension for the competition of elements.

Value Creators — both gains the goal — Depends on the revealing of what is of value to each. Lopsided, influenced

Value claimers — Win-Lose what you win I lose... is competitive — Narrow-minded.

Sec[illegible]o tactics for claiming value. Revea[illegible] is risky. If the mayor states that s[illegible]ons than to civilian review board[illegible]nd by saying that the union memb[illegible] but would be willing to give in a li[illegible]nsate them handsomely by comp[illegible] a negotiator would accept positi[illegible]ond issue can be exploited: "So, y[illegible]ss the merits of the second issue.'[illegible]often be taken as a sign that its pr[illegible]essions. Thus, such offers somet[illegible]erests can be held hostage in exc[illegible]divorcing husband and wife may b[illegible]e husband may "suddenly" develo[illegible]s on alimony in return for giving[illegible]

In [illegible]ons not to be open and coope[illegible] to claim value. Moves to claim value thus tend to drive out moves to create it. Yet, if both choose to claim value, by being dishonest or less than forthcoming about preferences, beliefs, or minimum requirements, they may miss mutually beneficial terms for agreement.

Indeed, the structure of many bargaining situations suggests that negotiators will tend to leave joint gains on the table or even reach impasses when mutually acceptable agreements are available. . . .

THE NEGOTIATOR'S DILEMMA

. . . Consider two negotiators (. . . named Ward and Stone) each of whom can choose between two negotiating styles: creating value (being open, sharing information about preferences and beliefs, not being misleading about minimum requirements, and so forth) and claiming value (being cagey and misleading about preferences, beliefs, and minimum requirements; making commitments and threats, and so forth). Each has the same two options for any tactical choice. If both choose to create value, they each receive a good outcome, which we will call GOOD for each. If Ward chooses to create value and Stone chooses to claim value, then Stone does even better than if he had chosen to create value — rank this outcome GREAT for Stone — but Ward does much worse — rank this outcome TERRIBLE for him. Similarly, if Stone is the creative one and Ward is the claimer, then Ward does well — rank this outcome for him as GREAT — while Stone's outcome is TERRIBLE. If both claim, they fail to find joint gains and come up with a mediocre outcome, which we call MEDIOCRE for both. Figure 2.1 summarizes the outcomes for each choice. In each box, Ward's payoff is in the lower left corner and Stone's is in the upper right. Thus, when Ward claims and Stone creates, Ward's outcome is GREAT while Stone's is TERRIBLE.

Now, if Ward were going to create, Stone would prefer the GREAT outcome obtained by claiming to the GOOD outcome he could have obtained by creating; so, Stone should claim. If, on the other hand, Ward were going to claim, Stone

Ward's Choice		Stone's Choice: Create	Stone's Choice: Claim
	Create	GOOD GOOD	GREAT TERRIBLE
	Claim	TERRIBLE GREAT	MEDIOCRE MEDIOCRE

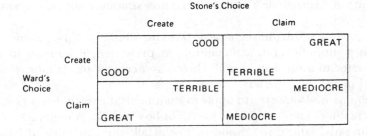

The lower left entry in each cell is Ward's outcome; the second entry is Stone's.

Figure 2.1
The Negotiator's Dilemma

would prefer the MEDIOCRE outcome from claiming to the TERRIBLE outcome he would receive from creating. In fact, no matter what Ward does, it seems that Stone would be better off trying to claim value!

Similarly, Ward should also prefer to claim. By symmetric reasoning, if Stone chooses to create, Ward prefers the GREAT outcome he gets by claiming to the GOOD outcome he gets from creating. If Stone claims, Ward prefers the MEDIOCRE outcome he gets from claiming to the TERRIBLE outcome he gets from creating.

Both negotiators choose to claim. They land in the lower right-hand box and receive MEDIOCRE outcomes. They leave joint gains on the table, since both would prefer the GOOD outcomes they could have received had they both chosen to create value and ended up in the upper left-hand box.

This is the crux of the Negotiator's Dilemma. Individually rational decisions to emphasize claiming tactics by being cagey and misleading lead to a mutually undesirable outcome. As described, this situation has the structure of the famous "Prisoner's Dilemma."* In such situations, the motivation to protect oneself and employ tactics for claiming value is compelling. Because tactics for claiming value impede creation, we expect negotiators in many settings to leave joint gains on the table. And, over time, this inexorable pull towards claiming tactics is insidious: negotiators will "learn" to become value claimers. A negotiator inclined towards sharing information and constructing creative, mutually desirable agreements, after being skewered in several encounters with experienced value-claimers, may bitterly come to alter his strategy to a more self-protective, value-claiming stance. . . .

* [The "Prisoner's Dilemma," a well-known bargaining game, is based on a hypothetical incident in which two suspects are taken into custody, charged with a serious crime, and separated so that they cannot communicate. The district attorney interviews them separately, telling each that if neither confesses to the crime of which they are suspected, each will be prosecuted on a lesser charge and receive a one-year sentence. If they both confess, each will receive an eight-year sentence. If one confesses, but the other does not, the confessor will receive only a three-month sentence, while the other will receive a ten-year sentence.

The dilemma for each prisoner is whether to not confess, trusting the other prisoner to do the same, so that each will receive a one-year sentence, a "good" outcome (see Figure 2.1), or to confess, risking a "mediocre" outcome (eight years) if the other prisoner also confesses, but hoping for a "great" outcome (three months) if the other prisoner does not confess. — EDS.]

TAKING THE NEGOTIATOR'S DILEMMA METAPHOR SERIOUSLY BUT NOT LITERALLY

The Negotiator's Dilemma characterizes the whole of a negotiation. Yet the Dilemma is a simplification, a metaphor. As presented, it appears to condemn each negotiator to a once-and-for-all choice as a creator or claimer; clearly there are many choices along the way.

The dilemma is also meant to apply to each tactical choice. Even here, the line between "creating" and "claiming" need not be clear-cut. A negotiator can reveal information early, late, throughout, or not at all; she can mislead by omission, commission, or be straight. She may discover a new option for mutual benefit, a joint gain, but present it in such a way that it emphasizes only agreements highly favorable to her. She may offer a creative proposal or hold back because it conveys sensitive information about tradeoffs or minimal requirements. Yet at a basic enough level, tactical choices embody the creating-claiming tension, even if they contain elements of both.

Thus, we take the Negotiator's Dilemma seriously, even though we do not take the matrix representation literally. The tension it reflects between cooperative impulses to create value and competitive impulses to claim it is inherent in the large and in the small. The essence of effective negotiation involves managing this tension, creating while claiming value. . . .

[The authors suggest three approaches to manage the tension between creating and claiming value: (1) Assume that there is no potential to create value and that all negotiation consists of claiming. They reject this approach with the comment that "stubborn battles over small pies typically offer little for all." (2) Assume that there is no claiming and that all negotiation consists of creatively searching for joint gains (the "win-win" philosophy). They reject this approach also, pointing out its vulnerability to exploitation by properly disguised claiming tactics. (3) The third approach — conditional openness — is discussed in some detail, beginning with a description of a Prisoner's Dilemma experiment conducted by Robert Axelrod (1984).]

Axelrod asked a number of specialists from a broad sweep of related disciplines to submit computer programs to participate in a tournament of repeated plays of the Prisoner's Dilemma. Each program would be pitted against every other program for a large number of plays of the Prisoner's Dilemma; each program or "strategy" would be rated according to the total number of points obtained against the strategies of all its opponents. The strategies range from the simple — RANDOM which flipped a coin to decide whether to cooperate or defect and TIT-FOR-TAT which cooperated on the first play and in subsequent rounds merely repeated its opponent's immediately previous move — to many devilishly exploitative schemes, including some that calculated the rate at which the opponent defected and then defected just a little bit more frequently.

Axelrod's synthesis of his results is intriguing. First, the strategies that did well were "nice": they did not defect first. Second, they were "provocable" in that they punished a defection by defecting, at least on the next round. Third, they were "forgiving" in that after punishing a defection they gave the opponent the opportunity to resume cooperation. Thus, unlike other strategies that were less nice or forgiving, they did not become locked, after a defection, in a long series of mutual recriminations. Fourth, they were clear or "not too clever." Eliciting continued cooperation is sufficiently tricky that moves whose intentions were difficult to decipher tended to result in unproductive defections. Such strategies performed well because they were able to elicit cooperation and avoid gross exploitation. We call these strategies "conditionally open." The simplest of the submitted conditionally open strategies, TIT-FOR-TAT, actually won the tournament. . . .

Axelrod's results suggest the elements of a strategy for managing the tension between creating and claiming value. A negotiator can attempt to divide the process into a number of small steps and to view each step as a round in a repeated Prisoner's Dilemma. He can attempt to be conditionally open, warily seeking mutual cooperation, ready to punish or claim value when his counterpart does so, but ultimately forgiving of transgressions. The attempt to create value is linked to an implicit threat to claim vigorously if the counterpart does, but also to the assurance that a repentant claimer will be allowed to return to good graces. Thus, both can avoid condemnation to endless mutual recriminations. Throughout the process, the negotiator may be better off if his moves are not mysterious.

The Negotiator's Dilemma and the Prisoner's Dilemma are analogies to negotiation and as simplifications cannot be taken literally. In negotiation, one seeks ways of eliciting cooperation without becoming vulnerable to claiming tactics. In Axelrod's experiments, certain strategies were able to elicit this sort of cooperation. What characteristics were responsible? Can some negotiations in which these characteristics are not fully present be modified to exhibit them? In what ways do negotiations differ from Axelrod's game that make it easier to elicit cooperation?

What Characteristics of the Repeated Prisoner's Dilemma Experiment, and Potentially Negotiation, Enable This Sort of Cooperation?

Repetition. Players cooperate when they know that their current actions can affect their future payoffs, when they believe that a defection now will lead to sufficient defection by their opponent to make the initial move undesirable. Thus, when the repetition is about to end—as in the last play, of the Prisoner's Dilemma—defections are likely.

In negotiations, repetition take many forms. A negotiation can be broken into many stages by several means: for example, by separating issues, by writing a number of drafts, or by taking several meetings to reach agreement. Or, two actors may have to deal with each other on many matters over a long period; consider two managers who both expect to remain in the same company for a long time and will need each other's cooperation. Or, the repetition may come solely through linkage: although an individual may never negotiate with the same person again, his reputation as honest and reliable can circulate through the closely knit circle they inhabit. For example, a movie producer who is believed in the film-making community to have cheated some of his investors by creative accounting may have difficulty raising money from other backers.

But, not all negotiation involves meaningful repetition. There do exist important one-shot deals. And, at the end of many rounds of a negotiation, parties may not expect to have significant continued dealings with each other. Finally, whether or not there are to be more dealings can be a tactical choice. For example, Ralph may exploit trust and convenient legalities to fleece his long-time partner while setting in motion steps to dissolve their partnership. [T]herefore common and suggested tactics for cliciting cooperation essentially involve enhancing the likelihood of repetition. And, many tactics for claiming value involve moves to eliminate meaningful repetition. . . .

Is It Easier to Elicit Cooperation in Negotiation Than in the Prisoner's Dilemma?

Apart from its characteristic payoffs, the Prisoner's Dilemma has two notable features: the players cannot communicate nor can they make binding commitments to choose in a particular way. If the players could do both, they could ensure cooperation. By contrast, negotiators *can* discuss future intentions. Moreover, they can sometimes credibly commit to cooperate or threaten to punish unless the other behaves appropriately. Even the partial ability to take these actions in negotiation can improve the likelihood of cooperation over that in the stylized version of the repeated Prisoner's Dilemma.

By their close ties to the Negotiator's Dilemma, Robert Axelrod's findings for maximizing one's results in the Prisoner's Dilemma suggest a potent strategy for managing the tension between creating and claiming: be nice but provocable, forgiving, and not too cute. Looking behind this advice, however, we see that repetition, detection of claiming, and the relationship of payoffs within and among rounds of the Negotiator's Dilemma affect a negotiator's ability to elicit sufficient cooperation without making himself vulnerable. The greater ability in certain settings to communicate and make binding commitments can also affect this objective. The next sections discuss tactics and approaches that manipulate all these factors to elicit mutual cooperation or, by eliciting the cooperation of another, to claim the lion's share of the gains so created.

Making Creating Value Seem Better Than Claiming It

If negotiators come to see cooperative moves as better than competitive ones, then the tension between creating and claiming can diminish. A variety of tactics aim at improving the expected payoffs from moves to create value relative to claiming actions.

Choice of Negotiating Philosophy. For example, instead of inviting others to announce their *positions* on the issues first, which could highlight distributive concerns and put everyone's credibility at stake, a negotiator might announce that she is only interested in a careful explanation of everyone's underlying *interests.* Or a session can be billed as "brainstorming," only to invent options, and with no criticism allowed. Such emphases may help create an ethos in which creative moves are the obvious and desirable choice.

Breaking Up the Process and Channeling It Toward Cooperation. Because many negotiations involve a series of tactical choices, in effect, they take place in several steps. General discussions are followed by offers and counteroffers that are accompanied by principled justifications. The offers and counteroffers are interspersed with attempts to devise joint gains, to persuade, to make commitments, and so on. In tactical choices, negotiators face much the same dilemma at each step. They try to build "momentum" and trust by establishing a pleasant environment, making visible concessions on a few issues early in the negotiations to show good faith. A strong dose of the appropriate cooperative attitudes early on may spill over to later phases so the negotiators can tackle the "hard" issues in a manner that facilitates jointly desirable agreements. Thus, negotiators create and highlight repetition that might otherwise have gone unnoticed in order to induce cooperative behavior.

Of course, settling the easy issues first to build momentum may eliminate potential for creating value by trades or logrolling between those issues and the remaining "hard" ones. . . . When previously settled issues cannot easily be reopened, potential joint gain or even agreement itself may be foregone. On the other hand, to the extent that such tactics forestall claiming and allow for learning and ingenuity, the joint value created by more cooperative and trusting negotiators may more than offset this loss of potential joint value. The desirability of such tactics thus depends on one's assessment of the nature of the issues and the effect of such tactics on the other's attitudes.

Invoking Repeated Dealings. Embedding a negotiation in a series of repeated dealings can induce interests in trust and the relationship. It may also set expectations and precedents for cooperation. Since egregious claiming [illegible] often be detected before the end of one of a series of negotiations, it may be mitigated. (Of course, if one party feels it can [illegible] to advantage [illegible] remain secret, it may use the extended interaction for [illegible] exploitation.) . . .

When the negotiation is in fact one of [illegible] repeated [illegible], negotiators may be able to mitigate claiming [illegible] by agreeing initially on a principle for division of gains. [illegible] partners of an investment bank may have agreed many years ago on [illegible] dividing profits in subsequent years, they need not bargain to divide the [illegible] their full energies could go to creating value. Such dividing rules, [illegible] much of an organization's structure, may evolve as an intended or unintended [illegible] of prior divisions. And those rules, like other agreements, can come up for renegotiation. . . .

Making Cooperative Norms Salient. Negotiators often try to make norms for "appropriate" behavior more salient, in effect to penalize blatant claiming tactics. ("What is going on? We're engineers. Let's deal with this difference rationally." "Look, we're in this together. It's not fair to be selfish. We've got to find a better solution, one that works for *all* of us.") . . .

Socialization. Over time, with repeated dealings and reinforcement of cooperative norms, negotiators' values can change so that egregious and even overt claiming tactics simply become undesirable. For example, the socialization of recruits into an organization may cause many to see that grossly competitive moves, which might seem appropriate in dealings with those outside the organization, are completely inappropriate in dealings within it. . . .

Interests: The Measure of Negotiation . . .

[According to Lax and Sebenius, if negotiators want to create value, they will often succeed by focusing not on their similarities, but their differences. They state:]

1. When contemplating the potential gains from agreement, begin with a careful inventory of all the ways that the parties differ from one another — not how they are alike.

2. The basic principle underlying the realization of joint gains from differences is to match what one side finds or expects to be relatively costless with what the other finds or expects to be most valuable, and vice versa. . . .

DIFFERENCES OF INTEREST IMPLY EXCHANGES

If a vegetarian with some meat bargains with a carnivore who owns some vegetables, it is precisely the *difference* in their known preferences that can facilitate reaching an agreement. No one would counsel the vegetarian to persuade the carnivore of the zucchini's succulent taste. More complicated negotiations may concern several items. Although the parties may have opposing preferences on the settlement of each issue, they may feel most strongly about different issues. An overall agreement can reflect these different preferences by resolving the issues of relati… of that side. A package or "horse … whole, all prefer it to no agreem…

Trad…

. . . C… effects of a settlement; another… uestion; thus, both might profit b… nmediate issue. One side may be … uiet accommodation for a particul… een vegetables and meat, form ar… d results, or the intrinsic versus … y crafted agreements can often d…

Trading on Differences
① Vegetarian has meat.
Carnivore has veggies.
Trade is mutually
beneficial because
of explicit differences.
② singer and owner
fee plus % ticket sales

PROBABILITY DIFFERENCES SUGGEST CONTINGENT AGREEMENTS

At the heart of the sale of an investment property may be the buyer's belief that its price will rise and the seller's conviction that it will drop. The deal is facilitated by differences in belief about what will happen. . . . Take the case of a singer at impasse with the owner of an auditorium over payment for a proposed concert. Since the singer expected the house to be filled while the owner projected only a half-capacity crowd, a contingent arrangement was ultimately agreed to in which the performer got a modest fixed fee plus a set percentage of the ticket receipts. Since the expected value of this agreement was greater to the performer than its expected cost to the owner, given their very different projections of attendance, the concert went ahead with both sides feeling better off and willing to accept whatever happened. . . .

DIFFERENCES IN RISK AVERSION LEAD TO RISK-SHARING SCHEMES

Suppose that two people agree on the probabilities of an uncertain prospect. Even so, they may still react differently to taking the risks involved. In such cases, they may devise a variety of ways to share the risk. In general, such mechanisms should shift more of the risk to the party who is less risk-averse than the other. For example, suppose that Mr. Broussard, a single, fairly wealthy, middle-aged accountant, and Ms. Armitage, a younger, less-well-off lawyer with significant family responsibilities, are planning to buy and operate a business together. The younger, more risk-averse Ms. Armitage may prefer to take a larger but fixed salary while Mr. Broussard may prefer a smaller set salary but much larger share of any profits. Though they may expect the same total amount of money to be paid in compensation, both parties are better off than had they, say, both chosen either fixed salaries or large contingent payments. . . .

DOVETAILING OTHER DIFFERENCES

. . . Generally, . . . good negotiators can find ways to make use of many more differences — in the participants' criteria for success, in attitudes toward precedent and principle, in constituencies, in personal and organizational situations, in ideology, in conceptions of fairness, and so on. By this discussion, we hardly intend to produce an exhaustive enumeration, but instead, to convey the sense that differences are as varied as negotiators. If recognized, this truth carries a profoundly optimistic message for the process of creating value. . . .

Question

2.4 Axelrod's experiments (pp. 48-49) in which Tit-for-Tat turned out to be the most successful strategy in repeated plays of a Prisoner's Dilemma game were performed on a computer. Are there problems in using this strategy in face-to-face negotiations that are not present in a computer game? What are they? Would you nonetheless support Tit-forTat as a sound strategy for managing the tension between creating and claiming value?

What do we know about how lawyers actually negotiate? In a much discussed study (Williams, 1983), Professor Gerald Williams surveyed 1,000 lawyers in the Phoenix area in 1976 (and later did some follow-up studies in other cities). He asked each lawyer to think about a recent negotiation, and then rate the opposing lawyer on a number of scales (including one involving word associations such as "caring," "hostile," and "timid"). Finally, he asked the lawyers to locate the opponent on an effectiveness scale ranging from nine (highly effective) to one (ineffective).

When Williams collated the data, he found that the rated opponents fell into two broad clusters that he called "cooperative" and "competitive." When each of these was associated with the effectiveness scale, four groups evolved:

- Effective cooperative
- Ineffective cooperative
- Effective competitive
- Ineffective competitive

By far, the largest group was *effective cooperative*. Very few people fell into the *ineffective cooperative* category. And the last two groups were roughly equal and relatively small in size.

Some of the conclusions Williams drew from this experiment were:

1. Most of us by nature are either cooperatives or competitives, and our primary goal should be to move to the effective end of our category. (What do you think that might involve for the *ineffective competitive*? For the *ineffective cooperative*?)

2. But the most skilled negotiators are versatile, and move readily from *effective competitive* to *effective cooperative*, or vice versa, depending upon the particular problem and circumstances, including the orientation of their opponent.

Because many questions were raised about the methodology of the study, Professor Andrea Schneider (2002) recently sought to replicate Williams' study. But she made a number of changes: (1) Because the original study had included very few women and minorities, a more representative sample was used; (2) In light of the evolving terminology in the field, the basic polar opposites in Williams' study (cooperative and competitive) were changed to "problem solving" and "adversarial." In addition, the list of associational adjectives was modified.

Her results are generally consistent with the earlier Williams study. They show again the pervasiveness of the problem-solving effective negotiator and should destroy once and for all "the myth of the effective hard bargainer" (p. 196). Of course it must be remembered that her study, too, does not describe what lawyers actually do, but rather it depicts the negotiating styles of a group of lawyers as seen by their opponents.

R. MNOOKIN, S. PEPPET, AND A. TULUMELLO, THE TENSION BETWEEN EMPATHY AND ASSERTIVENESS

12 Neg. J. 217-228 (1996)

. . . [B]y assertiveness, we mean the capacity to express and advocate for one's own interests. By empathy, we mean the capacity to demonstrate an accurate, nonjudgmental understanding of another person's concerns and perspective.

Empathy and assertiveness are in "tension" because many negotiators implicitly assume that these two sets of skills represent polar opposites along a single continuum and that each is incompatible with the other. Some worry, for example, that to listen or empathize too much signals weakness or agreement; they perceive empathy to be incompatible with assertion. Others are concerned that if they advocate too strongly they will upset or anger their counterpart; they believe that assertion undermines empathy. Many negotiators fall somewhere in between. Not needing to dominate but preferring not to surrender control, they are unsure how much to assert. Or, open to understanding the other side but also wanting to secure the best possible outcome, they do not know how much to empathize. In short, many negotiators feel stuck. We propose that empathy and assertiveness do not represent polar opposites along a single dimension and that rather they should be conceptualized as two independent dimensions of negotiation behavior.

EMPATHY

For purposes of negotiation, we define empathy as the process of demonstrating an accurate, nonjudgmental understanding of the other side's needs, interests, and positions. There are two components to this definition. The first involves a skill psychologists call *perspective-taking*— trying to see the world through the other negotiator's eyes. The second is the nonjudgmental *expression* of the other person's viewpoint in a way that is open to correction. . . .

Defined in this way, empathy requires neither sympathy nor agreement. Sympathy is "feeling for" someone — it refers to an affective response to the other person's predicament. For us, empathy does not require people to have sympathy for others' plight. . . . Instead, it simply requires the expression of how the world looks to that person.

The benefits of empathy relate to the integrative and distributive aspects of bargaining. Consider first the potential benefits of understanding (but not yet demonstrating) the other side's viewpoint. Skilled negotiators often can "see through" another person's statements to find hidden interests or feelings, even when they are inchoate in the other's mind. Perspective-taking thus facilitates value-creation by enabling a negotiator to craft arguments, proposals, or trade-offs that reflect another's interests and that may create the basis for trade.

Perspective-taking also facilitates distributive moves. To the extent we understand another negotiator, we will better predict their goals, expectations, and strategic choices. This enables good perspective-takers to gain a strategic advantage — analogous, perhaps, to playing a game of chess with advance knowledge of the other side's moves. It may also mean that good perspective-takers will more easily see through bluffing or other gambits based on artifice. Research confirms that negotiators with higher perspective-taking ability negotiate agreements of higher value than those with lower perspective-taking ability.

The capacity to *demonstrate* our understanding of the other side's viewpoint — to reflect back how they see the world — confers additional benefits. Negotiators in both personal and business disputes typically have a deep need to tell their story and to feel that it has been understood. Meeting this need, therefore, can dramatically shift the tone of a relationship. . . .

Another important benefit of expressing our understanding is that this process may help correct interpersonal misperception. . . .

Finally, empathy inspires openness in others and may itself be persuasive. . . .

ASSERTIVENESS

By assertiveness, we mean the ability to express and advocate for one's own needs, interests, and positions. The underlying skills include identifying one's own interests, speaking (making arguments, explaining), and even listening. Assertiveness also presupposes the self-esteem or belief that one's interests are valid and that it is legitimate to satisfy them. . . .

We can relate the benefits of assertiveness to the integrative and distributive aspects of bargaining. It is well established that assertion confers distributive benefits — assertive negotiators tend to get more of what they want. Less well

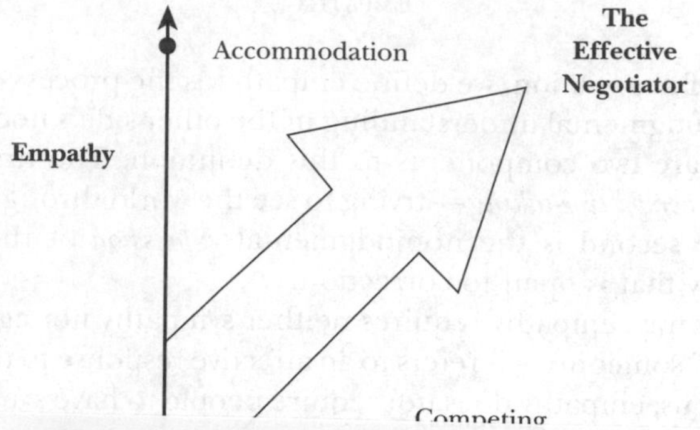

Risk Averse
The least RA side should bear the risk.
Empathy — invites openness and may bring about persuasiveness.
Fig. 3

understood is the … ss contributes to value-creation be … 's interests that joint gains may b … ommercial negotiations between … ict arises in the context of a long … ssert their interests, both may su …

Assertiveness … Assertive negotiators who voice … r of exploitation than those who d … ip difficulties as they occur — rat … tiating interpersonal adjustmen …

Negotiation Styles: Competing, Accommodating, and Avoiding

Our claim that empathy and assertiveness represent different dimensions can be illuminated by considering three common negotiation "styles." These are *competing, accommodating* and *avoiding*, each of which represents a different suboptimal combination of empathy and assertiveness. . . . A *competitive* style consists of substantial assertion but little empathy. . . . *Accommodating* consists of substantial empathy, but little assertion. . . . An *avoiding* style consists of low levels of empathy and assertiveness. . . . Figure 3 . . . measures empathy along the vertical analysis and assertiveness along the horizontal axis. [The authors point out that the use of both empathy and assertion is valuable to negotiators who use any of these styles.]

The Effective Negotiator

. . . If both negotiators can skillfully empathize and assert, the pair can work toward a beneficial solution that exploits the opportunities for value-creation and manages distributive issues.

Even if one's counterpart is *not* so skilled, however, we believe that a negotiator is most effective if she leads the way by successfully combining empathy and assertiveness. . . . This often means agreeing to listen and empathize for a period on the condition that the other side agrees to try to do so later in the negotiation, and also discussing explicitly that a demonstrated understanding of the other's views should not be interpreted as agreement. In this way, a negotiation can sometimes evolve toward problem-solving even if it begins less productively.

In all events, our claim is that the effective negotiator should be able to draw upon his own well-developed empathy and assertiveness skills no matter what the orientation of the other side.

The tension between empathy and assertiveness, along with the tension between creating and claiming and the tension between principal and agent, are the primary focus of the book *Beyond Winning—Negotiating to Create Value in Deals and Disputes* (2000) by these same three authors. The book focuses particularly on the role of lawyers in negotiation, and the opportunities they present for problem solving and value creation.

Managing the tension between empathy and assertiveness is one aspect of the emotional issues that arise in negotiation. Another is posed by the challenge of handling a *difficult negotiation*—that is, a negotiation that is fraught with intense feelings on both sides, such as firing an ineffective but angry employee, or saying "no" to a troubled, disorganized colleague who keeps asking you at 5 PM to help her complete her assigned work. This topic is addressed in an important book, *Difficult Conversations,* by Douglas Stone, Bruce Patton, and Sheila Heen (1999). The key, according to the authors, is to sort out three different conversations: (1) The "what happened?" conversation, which seeks to separate how each side sees the situation, distinguishing between the *impact* on the listener ("you made me very angry") and the *intent* of the speaker; (2) the "feelings" conversation, which explores how each side feels about the matter being discussed; and (3) the "identity" conversation, which attempts to relate the experienced feelings to the participants' self-perception or identity.

During the "what happened?" conversation, the authors advise that the speaker can achieve agreement more readily by minimizing the role of blame and avoiding the temptation to attribute intent, particularly malicious intent, to the other person. On attributing intent, they warn:

> The easiest and most common way of expressing [blame] is with an accusatory question: "How come you wanted to hurt me?" . . . [This may seem as if] we are sharing our hurt, frustration, anger, or confusion. . . . [But to our opponents it appears as if] we are trying to provoke, accuse, or malign them. . . . We should not be surprised, then, that they try to defend themselves, or attack back . . . (p. 49).

Instead, the authors counsel, "say what the other person did, tell them what its impact was on you, and explain your assumption about their intentions, taking care to label it as a hypothesis that you are checking rather than asserting it to be true" (p. 54).

Often, the "feelings conversation" is omitted in favor of blaming or avoidance. The authors suggest speaking directly about one's own feelings while acknowledging the expressed feelings of the other person in the conversation. An easy way, they say, is to begin the statement with "I feel . . ." and to respond to feelings by asking more: "Before I give you a sense of what's going on with me, tell me more about your feeling that I talk down to you" (pp. 105-06).

The internal "identity conversation" may disrupt the concentration needed to conduct an emotional conversation effectively. People often react in ways that are counter-productive when something in the conversation challenges their basic feelings about being competent, a "good person," and "worthy of love." For example, an individual calmly begins a conversation with a supervisor to secure permission to do something, and the supervisor responds that the employee has not performed the job effectively. Now, the employee may become absorbed with the threat to her self-image as a talented professional and unable to carry on the first conversation effectively.

It would hardly be possible to compile a chapter on negotiation without treating the subject of negotiating power. After all, negotiating power is generally thought to be one of the determinative factors in the outcome of many negotiations. Indeed, some commentators would suggest that ultimately all negotiation outcomes are a function of power. Yet most attempts to define negotiating power have been unsuccessful. In the following excerpt, Lax and Sebenius attempt a new approach to negotiating power, one that focuses less on defining it than on analyzing the ways in which various sources of supposed power may affect outcome. Based on that analysis, the authors seek a clearer understanding of the components of negotiating power.

D. LAX AND J. SEBENIUS, THE MANAGER AS NEGOTIATOR*

249-257 (1986)

What about "negotiating power"? . . . The concept is notoriously slippery. Seeking to understand the sources of power has mired many in plausible but incorrect generalizations.

Consider a few common notions of what gives power.

"One party has power if it can inflict harm on another, especially if it can inflict 'more' harm than it will suffer." Yet the United States' unquestioned capacity for the nuclear annihilation of North Vietnam did not yield Vietnamese submission before or during the peace talks.

"Having more resources gives one power." But, if a rich person's child is kidnapped, having much accessible money may not help in the negotiation; that person may merely pay more.

"Having someone in your debt gives power." The borrower who owes the bank $450,000, is six months behind on house payments, and has a very sick wife may think he has problems, but it may be his banker who is really in trouble.

"Being rational and persuasive gives one power." Yet a bargainer who refuses to listen to an eminently reasonable argument and "irrationally" insists on having his demands met "or else" will sometimes succeed.

"Having full authority and control over one's organization is power." Yet the union leader who can line his people up behind almost any agreement may get a less favorable settlement than the leader whose flexibility is limited by a powerful, militant faction.

In each of these cases, the supposedly "powerful" party's interests do not appear to have been advanced. The common generalizations do not quite work.

Attempts to define power often lead into tautological quicksand. For example, one widely cited definition reads, "*A* has power over *B* to the extent that he can get *B* to do something that he would not otherwise do." In other words, if *A* has power over *B*, he can get an extremely good deal in negotiations with *B*. But how can we tell that *A* is more powerful? Well, he got a good outcome from *B*. Power defined this way and negotiated outcomes themselves cannot be distinguished. . . .

ASSOCIATING POWER WITH FAVORABLE CHANGES IN THE BARGAINING SET

We observe that the things thought to give "power" seem to succeed when they advantageously change perceptions of the bargaining set and to fail when they do not. We argue that "power" is associated with the ability to favorably change the bargaining set.

What "a favorable change in the bargaining set" means is a bit trickier than it may seem at first blush. Given his current situation, a negotiator can assess a probability distribution over the possible outcomes. If a new tactic were employed, the likelihoods of different outcomes would change; thus he has a revised probability distribution of outcomes given the new tactic. If he prefers the revised probability distribution to the original, we say that he has favorably changed the bargaining set. While this change need not guarantee him a more favorable outcome, he thinks it more likely. . . .

INTERPRETING SOME COMMON IDEAS OF POWER

With this focus on the bargaining set, let us return to some of the supposed sources of power and see when they succeed and fail.

The United States' capacity for nuclear attack did not determine Vietnamese choices because the threat to do so was not credible; having the capacity without the credible threat of using it did not change Vietnamese perceptions of their alternatives to agreement on preferred American terms, and hence, the way they saw the bargaining set. The ability to inflict harm may also fail to influence bargaining if it goes unnoticed or cannot be communicated; the hornet flying toward you may not move out of your path even though you explain that you will kill it if it stings you. And, the capacity for harm can fail if what *seems* harmful in fact is not. The threat to kill someone who aspires to martyrdom may not lead to cooperation. And, inflicting harm often fails to yield desired outcomes when it provokes conflict escalation.

In these cases, the ability to harm failed because the moves did not advantageously change the bargaining set, because they were not credible, not communicated or not actually harmful, or because they brought in harmful new interests that swamped what was originally at stake.

This is not to deny the effect of the ability to harm another on bargaining. To take but one example, countless managers have paid countless millions of dollars in "greenmail." Say that a corporate raider buys a large block of the firm's stock and credibly threatens to acquire a controlling share and dismember the firm unless his shares are purchased from him at an inflated price. The firm's managers often grant his demands. His threat has shifted their perceptions of their no-agreement alternatives—if they do not respond, they may lose their jobs following the acquisition. The implicit threats of firing, of the withdrawal of college tuition, of physical harm if money is not handed over, and the like, when credible and known, frequently change the bargaining range in "favorable" ways.

By the same token, the available wealth of the kidnapped child's rich parents unfavorably changes the bargaining set relative to having less accessible money. The government could seek favorably to change the bargaining range if it immediately impounded the parents' assets the moment the kidnapping became known. Of course, more resources can certainly lead to favorable changes in the bargaining set. An executive with considerable resources may gain others' cooperation because they hope that she will reward them in future encounters; she may never do so, but the potential reward shapes the others' perceptions of the current bargaining set. (And greater resources may translate into greater capacity to impose sanctions.)

The negotiation between the banker and her strapped borrower over rescheduling the loan is trickier. Because she can foreclose and ruin the borrower's valued credit rating, his no-agreement alternatives are undesirable. In contrast, if the borrower feels certain that he will lose his rating anyway, his no-agreement alternatives would be unchanged by the banker's action and he may feel less cooperative about repayment.

But this looks only at the foreclosure's effect on the borrower and not on the banker. If foreclosing is quite costly for the banker, her no-agreement alternative (foreclosure) will be much worse than in the case where it is not costly. Our guess would be that this condition would be reflected in an easier negotiated repayment schedule. In short, having someone in one's debt need not give "power." What matters here are the parties' perceptions of their no-agreement alternatives.

In our earlier example, the "irrational" person effectively removed from consideration an unfavorable part of the bargaining set by successfully refusing to hear about or discuss it. But, forsaking rational discussion may mean missing the possibility of agreement at all if the "irrational" person commits to a point that is outside the bargaining set. Possibilities for expanding the bargaining set by rational problem solving are foregone. Moreover, such behavior may unfavorably alter the bargaining set by bringing in new interests (e.g., appropriate behavior, revenge) that swamp the original interests at stake.

Similarly, not having full authority and control over his organization helped the union leader; his militant faction made it impossible to accept certain agreements, thus eliminating them from the bargaining set. In other circumstances, on the other hand, having full authority and control over one's organization is associated with "power." The executive whose firm always delivers on his promises may be able to expand the perceived bargaining set in many encounters. . . .

Normative Conformity

Claims that one's position is right, legitimate, and principled can carry weight in negotiation. For some people, acting in such a manner has intrinsic value and improves potential agreements that are normatively "correct." And pressing for positions that arguably are principled or legitimate may impose costs on other parties who would go against them. As anthropologist P. H. Gulliver wrote:

> Even if negotiators themselves are unimpressed by normative conformity—and the evidence does not support so gross a conclusion—they are often constrained to conform, or at least to conform more than they otherwise might, because they need to appear to accept and adhere to the rules, standards, and values of their society.

To the extent that such constraints are effective, they limit the bargaining set in a way favorable to the person who invoked the principle.

Moreover, to the extent that such principles derive from the larger society, arguments about them can escape the implication that one party is stronger and the other weaker. Recourse to external standards is one way to avoid attributions of weakness and loss of face, ingredients that can worsen the bargaining set from the standpoint of all parties.

Often people discuss principle as if it were a question of right versus might. To us, the real question involves how invoking it does or does not change perceptions of the bargaining set. Strong evidence that norms can have this effect comes from observing the extent to which people employ them, genuinely or cynically. . . .

Analyzing "power" in and of itself has often proved to be a sterile exercise. However, directly focusing on factors that can change perceptions of the bargaining set and the ways that such changes influence outcomes seems more fruitful for both theory and practice. By no means is this different approach likely to be a panacea; the bargaining range is a subjective concept and the relationship between alterations in it and eventual agreements is hardly certain.

Questions

2.5 One context in which the United States often seems to have little bargaining power is when it seeks to negotiate the release of hostages, particularly those seized by Middle Eastern terrorists. What, following Lax's and Sebenius's analysis, is the reason for the U.S. lack of power in these negotiations? And, more important, what might the United States do to improve its bargaining power?

2.6 What is the relationship between bargaining power and the strategic and tactical approach that a negotiator should adopt? Should a conclusion that you have greater bargaining power than the other negotiator lead you to adopt a competitive, value-claiming approach? What about the reverse case where you believe you are the less powerful party? What approaches might you utilize in that situation? See Adler and Silverstein (2000).

To this point, we have not distinguished between negotiation over the terms of a relationship that is about to be created (deal-making) and negotiation to settle a dispute arising out of past events (dispute settlement). In the Note on The Janus Quality of Negotiation, we point out the tendency of deal-making negotiation to look forward and focus on interests and the tendency of dispute settlement to look backward and focus on rights. We also suggest the interplay between the two types of negotiation, as deal-making negotiation leads to agreements that create rights that may later form the norms for dispute settlement negotiation. Most important, some disputes arising out of an agreement can best be resolved by formulating a new agreement, thereby converting dispute settlement negotiation into deal-making negotiation.

*Note: The Janus Quality of Negotiation — Deal-Making and Dispute Settlement**

It is by now standard advice to negotiators to prepare adequately — by exploring in advance interests, options, and alternatives. Only rarely, however, do parties prepare by trying to understand the kind of negotiation they are in: either a negotiation over the terms of a relationship that is about to be created or a negotiated settlement of a dispute arising out of past events (cf. Eisenberg, 1976).†

We here explore some differences between negotiation over entry into a relationship (what we will refer to as deal-making negotiation, or DMN) and negotiation over resolving a dispute arising out of past events (what we will refer to as dispute settlement negotiation, or DSN).

By definition, deal-making negotiation arises when parties embark upon a deal. The thrust of deal-making — and hence of the negotiations that lead to the deal — is forward looking. The parties typically have come together in order to reach agreement and anticipate a future relationship under the umbrella of the deal that has been struck. By contrast, dispute settlement negotiation is a backward-looking transaction because dispute settlement, in the sense the term is used here, means a dispute arising out of past events.

Note that although the distinction between DMN and DSN is fairly clear, there is often a symbiotic interplay between the two. A DMN creates rights that may later form the norms of DSN. Conversely, some disputes arising under an agreement can best be resolved by creating a new relationship (or formulating a new agreement) between the parties, thereby turning a DSN into a new deal.

What are some of the practical implications of these distinctions?

1. DSN looks more to rights (established by law or under a previously made deal); parties in a DSN pay attention to what they feel entitled to. In contrast, DMN

* This note has been adapted from Sander and Rubin (1988).

† For a more detailed analysis of deal-making negotiations, focusing particularly on the pre-negotation stages, see Lax and Sebenius (2006).

looks more to interests because there often aren't any "rights" governing a deal that has not yet been struck. This distinction is attenuated by the symbiotic relationship point made above. That is, in a typical DSN one can look forward by creating a new deal or backward to the rights established under the agreement or by law. This is a particular problem for lawyers, who are all too prone in cases of dispute settlement to look backward to the legal rights of the disputants (i.e., the court outcome) rather than see the case as an opportunity for a new agreement that meets the future needs of the parties and downplays their rights under the present agreement.

Theoretically, negotiations over interests (as in DMN) should be easier to move to agreement than negotiations over rights (as in DSN). Interests can be satisfied in multiple ways, by devising creative options for joint gain, and thus tend to be non-zero sum in nature; rights, although they need not be construed as zero sum, are typically so interpreted by protagonists: Either I win or you win—but not both.

2. In both DMN and DSN the best alternative to a negotiated agreement (or BATNA) may be unclear. In DSN, one party may "lump it," declining to press its claim any further if it has been rejected by the other party. Or if the disputing parties have a relationship preceding the events giving rise to the dispute, the BATNA for each may simply be to abandon that relationship. Alternatively, the dispute may be taken to court, where the outcome may or may not be reasonably predictable. In DMN, the alternative may be even more unclear. If *A* doesn't sell his house to *B*, *A* may not sell his house at all. Or *A* may sell it to *P* or *Q*.

   Where, then, should agreement be easier to reach? Quite possibly in DSN, where there may be fewer options away from the table than in DMN. Offsetting this, however, is the fact that if adjudication is the BATNA, the parties' assessments of their likelihood of prevailing in adjudication may vary widely, thus leading each to value a proposed agreement differently. In either event, the likelihood is that whatever agreement is reached through DMN will have a better chance of taking root because it is more likely to satisfy the interests of each than is typically rights-oriented DSN.

3. Another consequence is that in DSN there is more likely to be an adversarial flavor to the proceedings. In the words of Lax and Sebenius (1986), DSN is often about the "claiming" of resources that are in dispute. DMN, in contrast, is often concerned with "creating" opportunities that make negotiated settlement an attractive outcome.
4. The mode of discourse and the external frames of reference are also likely to be quite different in the two types of negotiation. In DMN, the parties have wide-ranging opportunities to explore each other's interests and options. The mode of discourse will therefore tend to be informal, reasonably friendly, and focused on a frame of reference that lies in the future: What happens to us if we should reach agreement? The focus of activity is devising an agreement that you are ready to "live with" later on.

   In contrast, DSN is characterized by a more formal, less friendly mode of discourse. And the frame of reference, as we earlier observed, is in the past—usually including a canvass of all the sins of commission and omission that have led the disputants into their present quandary.

Table 2-1
Summary of Differences Between DMN and DSN

DSN	*DMN*
Looks backward	Looks forward
Focuses on claiming	Focuses on creating
Focuses on rights	Focuses on interests
BATNA sometimes unclear	BATNA frequently unclear
Adversarial style	Joint problem solving style

Table 2-1 summarizes the key differences between making a deal as compared with settling a dispute. We acknowledge the possibility of oversimplification in our tendency to portray DMN as the "good guy" and DSN as the "bad." Still, we do think that the advantages of DMN are great when it is feasible. There will, however, be many situations in which disputes cannot be resolved by formulating a new agreement, so that if settlement is possible it must be through DSN. Even in those situations, however, Ury, Brett, and Goldberg (1988) assert that wise negotiators can often reach agreement by forgoing an adversarial style that focuses on rights in favor of a problem-solving approach that focuses on interests.

Ultimately, the distinction between DMN and DSN blurs by the realization that negotiation takes place along a temporal continuum: what starts out as pure DMN — as the parties contemplate the attractiveness of entering into a negotiating relationship — is inevitably followed by that very relationship and by the attendant possibility that disputes will arise that, in turn, will have to be settled through DSN. Beyond that lies the possibility that DSN foreshadows the reaching of a new agreement through DMN. Thus the reflective negotiator would do well to understand that he or she will eventually come to know both faces of the negotiation process.

It is common for lawyers to negotiate on behalf of their clients, and there are often substantial advantages in their doing so. However, as pointed out by Rubin and Sander in the next excerpt, there may also be risks involved for the client who turns negotiations over to her attorney, rather than negotiating herself. Thus, attorney and client should consider carefully whether negotiations on behalf of the client should be carried out by the attorney, the client, or both.

J. RUBIN AND F. SANDER, WHEN SHOULD WE USE AGENTS? DIRECT VS. REPRESENTATIVE NEGOTIATION

4 Neg. J. 395, 396-400 (1988)

. . . One of the primary reasons that principals choose to negotiate through agents is that the latter possess expertise that makes agreement — particularly favorable agreement — more likely. This expertise is likely to be of three different stripes:

Substantive knowledge. A tax attorney or accountant knows things about the current tax code that make it more likely that negotiations with an IRS auditor will benefit the client as much as possible. Similarly, a divorce lawyer, an engineering consultant, and a real estate agent may have substantive knowledge in a rather narrow domain of expertise, and this expertise may redound to the client's benefit.

Process expertise. Quite apart from the specific expertise they may have in particular content areas, agents may have skill at the negotiation *process*, per se, thereby enhancing the prospects of a favorable agreement. . . .

Specific influences. A Washington lobbyist is paid to know the "right" people, to have access to the "corridors of power" that the principals themselves are unlikely to possess. Such "pull" can certainly help immensely, and is yet another form of expertise that agents may possess, although the lure of this "access" often outweighs in promise the special benefits that are confirmed in reality. . . .

Note also that principals may not always know what expertise they need. Thus, a person who has a dispute that seems headed for the courts may automatically seek out a litigator, not realizing that the vast preponderance of cases are settled by negotiation, requiring very different skills that the litigator may not possess. So, although agents do indeed possess different forms of expertise that may enhance the prospects of a favorable settlement, clients do not necessarily know what they need; it's a bit like the problem of looking up the proper spelling of a word in the dictionary when you haven't got a clue about how to spell the word in question.

Detachment

Another important reason for using an agent to do the actual negotiation is that the principals may be too emotionally entangled in the subject of the dispute. A classic example is divorce. A husband and wife, caught in the throes of a bitter fight over the end of their marriage, may benefit from the "buffering" that agents can provide. Rather than confront each other with the depth of their anger and bitterness, the principals may do far better by communicating only *indirectly*, via their respective representatives. Stated most generally, when the negotiating climate is adversarial—when the disputants are confrontational rather than collaborative—it may be wiser to manage the conflict through intermediaries than run the risk of an impasse or explosion resulting from direct exchange.

Sometimes, however, it is the *agents* who are too intensely entangled. What is needed then is the detachment and rationality that only the principals can bring to the exchange. For example, lawyers may get too caught up in the adversary game and lose sight of the underlying problem that is dividing the principals (e.g., how to resolve a dispute about the quality of goods delivered as part of a long-term supply contract). The lawyers may be more concerned about who would win in court, while the clients simply want to get their derailed relationship back on track. Hence the thrust of some modern dispute resolution mechanisms (such as the mini-trial) is precisely to take the dispute *out* of the hands of the technicians and give it back to the primary parties.

Note, however, that the very "detachment" we are touting as a virtue of negotiation through agents can also be a liability. For example, in some interpersonal negotiations, apology and reconciliation may be an important ingredient of any resolution. Surrogates who are primarily technicians may not be able to bring to bear these empathic qualities.

Tactical Flexibility

The use of agents allows various gambits to be played out by the principals in an effort to ratchet as much as possible from the other side. For example, if a seller asserts that the bottom line is $100,000, the buyer can try to haggle, albeit at the risk of losing the deal. If the buyer employs an agent, however, the agent can profess willingness to pay that sum but plead lack of authority, thereby gaining valuable time and opportunity for fuller consideration of the situation together with the principal. . . .

Conversely, an agent may be used in order to push the other side in tough, even obnoxious, fashion, making it possible — in the best tradition of the "good cop bad cop" ploy — for the client to intercede at last, and seem the essence of sweet reason in comparison with the agent. . . .

Note that the tactical flexibility conferred by representative negotiations presupposes a competitive negotiating climate, a zero-sum contest in which each negotiator wishes to outsmart the other. . . . To repeat, the assumption behind this line of analysis is that effective negotiation requires some measure of artifice and duplicity, and that this is often best accomplished through the use of some sort of foil or alter ego — in the form of the agent. But the converse is not necessarily true: Where the negotiation is conducted in a problem-solving manner, agents may still be helpful, not because they resort to strategic ruses, but because they can help articulate interests, options, and alternatives. Four heads are clearly better than two, for example, when it comes to brainstorming about possible ways of reconciling the parties' interests.

Offsetting — indeed, typically *more* than offsetting — the three above apparent virtues of representative negotiation are several sources of difficulty. Each is sufficiently important and potentially problematic that we believe caution is necessary before entering into negotiation through agents.

[One source of difficulty, according to Rubin and Sander, is that representative negotiations involve more people than do direct negotiations. They state:]

. . . For instance, a message intended by a client may not be the message transmitted by that client's agent to the other party. Or the message received by that agent from the other party may be very different from the one that that agent (either deliberately or inadvertently) manages to convey to his or her client. . . .

Different dynamics will characterize the negotiation depending on whether it is between clients, between lawyers, or with both present. If just the clients are there, the dealings will be more direct and forthright, and issues of authority and ratification disappear. With just the lawyers present, there may be less direct factual information, but concomitantly more candor about delicate topics. Suppose, for example, that an aging soprano seeks to persuade an opera company to sign her for the lead role in an upcoming opera. If she is not present, the opera's agent may try to lower the price, contending that the singer is past her prime. Such candor is not recommended if the singer is present at the negotiation!

Problems of "Ownership" and Conflicting Interests

In theory, it is clear that the principal calls the shots. Imagine, however, an agent who is intent on . . . searching for objective criteria and a fair outcome. Suppose the client simply wants the best possible outcome, perhaps because it is a one-shot deal not involving a future relationship with the other party. What if the agent (a lawyer, perhaps) *does* care about his future relationship with the other *agent*, and wants to be remembered as a fair and scrupulous bargainer? How *should* this conflict get resolved and how, in the absence of explicit discussion, *will* it be resolved, if at all? Conversely, the client, because of a valuable long-term relationship, may want to maintain good relations with the other side. But if the client simply looks for an agent who is renowned for an ability to pull out all the stops, the client's overall objectives may suffer as the result of an overzealous advocate.

This issue may arise in a number of contexts. Suppose that, in the course of a dispute settlement negotiation, a lawyer who is intent on getting the best possible deal for a client turns down an offer that was within the client's acceptable range. Is this proper behavior by the agent? The Model Rules of Professional Conduct for attorneys explicitly require (see Rules 1.2(a), 1.4) that every offer must be communicated to the principal, and perhaps a failure to do so might lead to a successful malpractice action against the attorney if the deal finally fell through. . . .

Differing goals and standards of agent and principal may create conflicting pulls. For example, the buyer's agent may be compensated as a percentage of the purchase price, thus creating an incentive to have the price as high as possible. The buyer, of course, wants the lowest possible price. Similarly, where a lawyer is paid by the hour, there may be an incentive to draw out the negotiation, whereas the client prefers an expeditious negotiation at the lowest possible cost.

While these are not insoluble problems, to be sure, they do constitute yet another example of the difficulties that may arise as one moves to representative negotiations. Although in theory the principals are in command, once agents have been introduced the chemistry changes, and new actors—with agenda, incentives, and constraints of their own—are part of the picture. Short of an abrupt firing of the agents, principals may find themselves less in control of the situation once agents have come on the scene.

Questions

2.7 As Rubin and Sander note (p. 64), someone who is involved in a dispute may engage an attorney to negotiate in his behalf because of the attorney's legal knowledge. Is there any risk that the attorney's viewing the dispute based on that knowledge may work to the client's disadvantage in the negotiations?

2.8 In each of the following situations, identify which of these choices you would prefer and why: (1) the clients negotiating without lawyers present, (2) the lawyer accompanying the client to the negotiation, (3) the lawyers negotiating without the clients present.

a. Negotiations between builder and architect concerning responsibility for a collapsed floor in a construction project that is still in progress;

b. Negotiations between employer and discharged employee, when the two are brother and sister (see pp. 116-137);
c. Negotiations concerning child custody and support between parties to a divorce involving allegations of spousal violence and;
d. Negotiations between insurance companies regarding responsibility for damages occurring in a four-party automobile accident.

2.9 You are a senior partner in a well-established law firm with its main office in Chicago and other offices in major cities worldwide. A wealthy Middle Eastern oil magnate, who has been represented in all his European dealings for many years by your London office, has requested the Chicago office to represent him in forthcoming negotiations concerning his planned purchase of a little-known painting presently owned by Art Chicago, a recently formed museum that is attempting to interest children in Chicago in fine art. In briefing you for these negotiations, your client tells you that he has been advised by his art experts that the painting, previously attributed to a comparatively obscure French artist, was instead the work of Gauguin. His instructions to you are that under no circumstances may you reveal this fact to Art Chicago since it increases the market value of the painting by millions of dollars.

You are now preparing for negotiations in which Art Chicago will be represented by its general counsel, a recent law school graduate. What, if any, difficulties do your client's instructions create for you? How will you resolve those difficulties? (You may want to read through p. 81 before answering this question.)

2.10 What are the advantages and disadvantages of dispute resolution by negotiation as compared to adjudication? Are there circumstances (for example, particular types of disputes or relationships between the parties) in which adjudication is a preferable mode of dispute resolution?

2.11 Plaintiff's new Chevrolet was totally destroyed when it was struck by a vehicle owned and operated by Jones Chevrolet Dealers, Inc. Plaintiff, who was uninjured in the accident, has brought suit against Jones for $16,000, the cost of his car. Attorneys for the plaintiff and for Jones have been attempting to negotiate a settlement without success. Plaintiff's attorney concedes that her client was partially at fault, but no more than 25 percent. She argues that under the comparative negligence standard in effect in this jurisdiction, the least plaintiff would expect at trial is a $12,000 judgment. Since the cost of trial to her client would be approximately $1,000, she has offered to settle for $11,000. Defendant's attorney, contending that plaintiff was 50 percent at fault, has offered $8,000 in settlement. The offers have been rejected, and the case is set for trial next week. Do you have any suggestions for settlement that might be acceptable to both parties?

2.12 Approximately 30 days ago you paid $50,000 to acquire a franchise for a Best Burger restaurant. The franchise payment is nonrefundable and limited to a specific location — the vacant lot owned by you on the northeast corner of a busy intersection. The franchise is transferable only with the approval of Best Burger. Partners, however, can be added at your discretion.

You have recently learned that Sam Smith, a well-to-do lawyer who lives across the street from you and whose children play with your children, has bought the lot across the intersection from your lot; he is planning to put in a Burger Master restaurant for which he has recently acquired a franchise. You estimate that if yours were to be the only restaurant located at the intersection, you would enjoy profits of $75,000 per year. On the other hand, if there is competition from a Burger Master restaurant, you would expect to lose at least $25,000 annually. You have every reason to suppose that Smith's franchise cost approximately the same as yours, and that his profit and loss outlook is approximately the same as yours.

Smith has asked for a meeting to see if together you can reach an agreement on how to deal with the situation. What approach will you take in the negotiations? What result will you seek, and how will you go about attaining it?

2.13 Some commentators assert that men and women negotiate differently, while others are skeptical (see pp. 143-145).

On the basis of extensive interviews with women negotiators, the authors of a recent book (Kolb and Williams, 2000) point out that often the primary negotiation across the table is significantly affected by a parallel "shadow" negotiation in which the negotiator comes to grips with her self-concept and her image of her negotiation strengths (or weaknesses). In order to have an effective across-the-table negotiation style, each negotiator must first skillfully manage this "shadow" negotiation. This entails a mastery of the issues in the case, but equally important is the development of a confident, self-assured persona. In your negotiating experience, have you observed gender differences in negotiation strategy or tactics? Compare the issues raised by intercultural negotiations, which are dealt with in Chapter 11.

In another recent book (Babcock and Laschever, 2003), the authors examined why women often receive considerably lower salaries than do men with similar background and education. Relying on surveys and their own empirical studies of women's behavior during negotiations, the authors concluded that women dislike negotiating and avoid it when possible. For example, the authors found that women will pay as much as $1,353 more for a car to avoid negotiating over the price. The authors found that because of these fears and a collective pessimism about the likelihood of success if negotiations occur, women also often ask for less during salary negotiations and consequently receive, on average, 30 percent less than do men. The authors emphasize that women's apprehensions about negotiation significantly affect their lifetime earning potential. For example, the authors contend that by failing to negotiate a first salary, women will forfeit more than half a million dollars by age 60. Like Kolb and Williams, Babcock and Laschever hope to change the way women negotiate by identifying the adverse consequences associated with their reluctance to do so.

The ethical obligations of the attorney engaged in negotiation is an exceedingly difficult issue for a number of reasons, many of which are explored by James White in his provocative article, which follows. As White notes, in many situations the very essence of negotiation consists of attempting to deceive the other party about, for example, the most one party will pay to obtain a desired outcome. That being so, the question is not whether a negotiator may mislead her opponent but on what subjects and by what means. It is difficult to obtain general agreement on ethical standards for answering such questions and equally difficult, in view of the privacy in which most negotiations are conducted, to enforce agreed-upon standards.

Perhaps in recognition of these difficulties, the American Bar Association Model Code of Professional Responsibility for many years dealt only tangentially with the lawyer's negotiating behavior. In 1980, however, an attempt was made to draft model rules imposing on the lawyer-negotiator explicit ethical obligations concerning fairness and truthfulness. These draft rules are discussed in White's article. Subsequently, in 1983, final rules were promulgated. Carefully compare those rules, which follow White's article, with the draft rules.

J. WHITE, MACHIAVELLI AND THE BAR: ETHICAL LIMITATIONS ON LYING IN NEGOTIATION

Am. B. Found. Research J. 926, 926-935, 938 (1980)

... The difficulty of proposing acceptable rules concerning truthfulness in negotiation is presented by several circumstances. First, negotiation is nonpublic behavior. If one negotiator lies to another, only by happenstance will the other discover the lie. If the settlement is concluded by negotiation, there will be no trial, no public testimony by conflicting witnesses, and thus no opportunity to examine the truthfulness of assertions made during the negotiation. Consequently, in negotiation, more than in other contexts, ethical norms can probably be violated with greater confidence that there will be no discovery and punishment. Whether one is likely to be caught for violating an ethical standard says nothing about the merit of the standard. However, if the low probability of punishment means that many lawyers will violate the standard, the standard becomes even more difficult for the honest lawyer to follow, for by doing so he may be forfeiting a significant advantage for his client to others who do not follow the rules.

[A] second difficulty in drafting ethical norms for negotiators ... is the almost galactic scope of disputes that are subject to resolution by negotiation. One who conceives of negotiation as an alternative to a lawsuit has only scratched the surface. Negotiation is also the process by which one deals with the opposing side in war, with terrorists, with labor or management in a labor agreement, with buyers and sellers of goods, services, and real estate, with lessors, with governmental agencies, and with one's clients, acquaintances, and family. By limiting his consideration to negotiations in which a lawyer is involved in his professional role, one eliminates some of the most difficult cases but is left with a rather large and irregular universe of disputes. Surely society would tolerate and indeed expect different forms of behavior on the one hand from one assigned to negotiate with terrorists and on the other from one who is negotiating with the citizens on behalf of a governmental agency. The difference between those two cases illustrates the less drastic distinctions that may be called for by differences between other negotiating situations. Performance that is standard in one negotiating arena may be gauche, conceivably unethical, in another. More than almost any other form of lawyer behavior, the process of negotiation is varied; it differs from place to place and from subject matter to subject matter. It calls, therefore, either for quite different rules in different contexts or for rules stated only at a very high level of generality.

A final complication in drafting rules about truthfulness arises out of the paradoxical nature of the negotiator's responsibility. On the one hand the negotiator must be fair and truthful; on the other he must mislead his opponent. Like the poker player, a negotiator hopes that his opponent will overestimate the value of his hand. Like the poker player, in a variety of ways he must facilitate his opponent's inaccurate assessment. The critical difference between those who are successful negotiators and those who are not lies in this capacity both to mislead and not to be misled.

Some experienced negotiators will deny the accuracy of this assertion, but they will be wrong. I submit that a careful examination of the behavior of even the most forthright, honest, and trustworthy negotiators will show them actively engaged in misleading their opponents about their true positions. That is true of both the plaintiff and the defendant in a lawsuit. It is true of both labor and management in a collective bargaining agreement. It is true as well of both the buyer and the seller in a wide variety of sales transactions. To conceal one's true position, to mislead an opponent about one's true settling point, is the essence of negotiation.

Of course there are limits on acceptable deceptive behavior in negotiation, but there is the paradox. How can one be "fair" but also mislead? Can we ask the negotiator to mislead, but fairly, like the soldier who must kill, but humanely?

Truthtelling in General

The obligation to behave truthfully in negotiation is embodied in the requirement of [proposed] Rule 4.2(a) that directs the lawyer to "be fair in dealing with other participants." . . .

The comment on fairness under Rule 4.2 makes explicit what is implicit in the rule itself by the following sentence: "Fairness in negotiation implies that representations by or on behalf of one party to the other party be truthful." Standing alone that statement is too broad. Even the Comments contemplate activities such as puffing which, in the broadest sense, are untruthful. It seems quite unlikely that the drafters intend or can realistically hope to outlaw a variety of other nontruthful behavior in negotiations. Below we will consider some examples, but for the time being we will consider the complexity of the task.

Pious and generalized assertions that the negotiator must be "honest" or that the lawyer must use "candor" are not helpful. They are at too high a level of generality, and they fail to appreciate the fact that truth and truthful behavior at one time in one set of circumstances with one set of negotiators may be untruthful in another circumstance with other negotiators. There is no general principle waiting somewhere to be discovered as Judge Alvin B. Rubin seems to suggest in his article on lawyer's ethics.[10] Rather, mostly we are doing what he says we are not doing, namely, hunting for the rules of the game as the game is played in that particular circumstance.

The definition of truth is in part a function of the substance of the negotiation. Because of the policies that lie behind the securities and exchange laws and the

10. Rubin [(1975: 589)] states his position as follows: "The lawyer must act honestly and in good faith. Another lawyer, or a layman, who deals with a lawyer should not need to exercise the same degree of caution that he would if trading for reputedly antique copper jugs in an oriental bazaar. It is inherent in the concept of an ethic, as a principle of good conduct, that it is morally binding on the conscience of the professional, and not merely a rule of the game adopted because other players observe (or fail to adopt) the same rule."

demands that Congress has made that information be provided to those who buy and sell, one suspects that lawyers engaged in SEC work have a higher standard of truthfulness than do those whose agreements and negotiations will not affect public buying and selling of assets. Conversely, where the thing to be bought and sold is in fact a lawsuit in which two professional traders conclude the deal, truth means something else. Here truth and candor call for a smaller amount of disclosure, permit greater distortion, and allow the other professional to suffer from his own ignorance and sloth in a way that would not be acceptable in the SEC case. In his article Rubin recognizes that there are such different perceptions among members of the bar engaged in different kinds of practice, and he suggests that there should not be such differences. Why not? Why is it so clear that one's responsibility for truth ought not be a function of the policy, the consequences, and the skill and expectations of the opponent?

Apart from the kinds of differences in truthfulness and candor which arise from the subject matter of the negotiation, one suspects that there are other differences attributable to regional and ethnic differences among negotiators. Although I have only anecdotal data to support this idea, it seems plausible that one's expectation concerning truth and candor might be different in a small, homogeneous community from what it would be in a large, heterogeneous community of lawyers. For one thing, all of the lawyers in the small and homogeneous community will share a common ethnic and environmental background. Each will have been subjected to the same kind of training about what kinds of lies are appropriate and what are not appropriate.

Moreover, the costs of conformity to ethical norms are less in a small community. Because the community is small, it will be easy to know those who do not conform to the standards and to protect oneself against that small number. Conversely, in the large and heterogeneous community, one will not have confidence either about the norms that have been learned by the opposing negotiator or about his conformance to those norms. . . .

If the Comments or the body of the Model Rules are to refer to truthfulness, they should be understood to mean not an absolute but a relative truth as it is defined in context. That context in turn should be determined by the subject matter of the negotiation and, to a lesser extent, by the region and the background of the negotiators. Of course, such a flexible standard does not resolve the difficulties that arise when negotiators of different experience meet one another. I despair of solving that problem by the promulgation of rules, for to do so would require the drafters of these rules to do something that they obviously could not wish to do. That is, unless they wish to rely on the norms in the various subcultures in the bar to flesh out the rules, they will have to draft an extensive and complex body of rules.

FIVE CASES

Although it is not necessary to draft such a set of rules, it is probably important to give more than the simple disclaimer about the impossibility of defining the appropriate limits of puffing that the drafters have given in the current Comments. To test these limits, consider five cases. Easiest is the question that arises when one misrepresents his true opinion about the meaning of a case or a statute. Presumably such a misrepresentation is accepted lawyer behavior both in and out of court and is not intended to be precluded by the requirement that the lawyer be "truthful." In writing his briefs, arguing his case, and attempting to persuade the opposing party in negotiation, it is the lawyer's right and probably his responsibility to argue for plausible interpretations of cases and statutes which favor his client's interest, even in circumstances where privately he has advised his client that those are not his true interpretations of the cases and statutes.

A second form of distortion that the Comments plainly envision as permissible is distortion concerning the value of one's case or of the other subject matter involved in the negotiation. Thus the Comments make explicit reference to "puffery." Presumably they are attempting to draw the same line that one draws in commercial law between express warranties and "mere puffing" under section 2-313 of the Uniform Commercial Code. While this line is not easy to draw, it generally means that the seller of a product has the right to make general statements concerning the value of his product without having the law treat those statements as warranties and without having liability if they turn out to be inaccurate estimates of the value. As the statements descend toward greater and greater particularity, as the ignorance of the person receiving the statements increases, the courts are likely to find them to be not puffing but express warranties. By the same token a lawyer could make assertions about his case or about the subject matter of his negotiation in general terms, and if those proved to be inaccurate, they would not be a violation of the ethical standards. Presumably such statements are not violations of the ethical standards even when they conflict with the lawyer's dispassionate analysis of the value of his case.

A third case is related to puffing but different from it. This is the use of the so-called false demand. It is a standard negotiating technique in collective bargaining negotiation and in some other multiple-issue negotiations for one side to include a series of demands about which it cares little or not at all. The purpose of including these demands is to increase one's supply of negotiating currency. One hopes to convince the other party that one or more of these false demands is important and thus successfully to trade it for some significant concession. The assertion of and argument for a false demand involves the same kind of distortion that is involved in puffing or in arguing the merits of cases or statutes that are not really controlling. The proponent of a false demand implicitly or explicitly states his interest in the demand and his estimation of it. Such behavior is untruthful in the broadest sense; yet at least in collective bargaining negotiation its use is a standard part of the process and is not thought to be inappropriate by any experienced bargainer.

Two final examples may be more troublesome. The first involves the response of a lawyer to a question from the other side. Assume that the defendant has instructed his lawyer to accept any settlement offer under $100,000. Having received that instruction, how does the defendant's lawyer respond to the plaintiff's question, "I think $90,000 will settle this case. Will your client give $90,000?" Do you see the dilemma that question poses for the defense lawyer? It calls for information that would not have to be disclosed. A truthful answer to it concludes the negotiation and dashes any possibility of negotiating a lower settlement even in circumstances in which the plaintiff might be willing to accept half of $90,000. Even a moment's hesitation in response to the question may be a nonverbal communication to a clever plaintiff's lawyer that the defendant has given such authority. Yet a negative response is a lie.

It is no answer that a clever lawyer will answer all such questions about authority by refusing to answer them, nor is it an answer that some lawyers will be clever enough to tell their clients not to grant them authority to accept a given sum until the final stages in negotiation. Most of us are not that careful or that clever. Few will routinely refuse to answer such questions in cases in which the client has granted a much lower limit than that discussed by the other party, for in that case an honest answer about the absence of authority is a quick and effective method of changing the opponent's settling point, and it is one that few of us will [forgo] when our authority is far below that requested by the other party. Thus despite the fact that a clever negotiator can avoid having to lie or to reveal his settling point, many lawyers, perhaps most, will sometime be forced by such a question either to lie or to reveal that they have been granted such authority by saying so or by their silence in response to a direct question. Is it fair to lie in such a case?

Before one examines the possible justifications for a lie in that circumstance, consider a final example recently suggested to me by a lawyer in practice. There the lawyer represented three persons who had been charged with shoplifting. Having satisfied himself that there was no significant conflict of interest, the defense lawyer told the prosecutor that two of the three would plead guilty only if the case was dismissed against the third. Previously those two had told the defense counsel that they would plead guilty irrespective of what the third did, and the third had said that he wished to go to trial unless the charges were dropped. Thus the defense lawyer lied to the prosecutor by stating that the two would plead only if the third were allowed to go free. Can the lie be justified in this case?[21]

How does one distinguish the cases where truthfulness is not required and those where it is required? Why do the first three cases seem easy? I suggest they are easy cases because the rules of the game are explicit and well developed in those areas. Everyone expects a lawyer to distort the value of his own case, of his own facts and arguments, and to deprecate those of his opponent. No one is surprised by that, and the system accepts and expects that behavior. To a lesser extent the same is true of the false demand procedure in labor-management negotiations where the ploy is sufficiently widely used to be explicitly identified in the literature. A layman might say that this behavior falls within the ambit of "exaggeration," a form of behavior that while not necessarily respected is not regarded as morally reprehensible in our society.

The last two cases are more difficult. In one the lawyer lies about his authority; in the other he lies about the intention of his clients. It would be more difficult to justify the lies in those cases by arguing that the rules of the game explicitly permit that sort of behavior. Some might say that the rules of the game provide for such distortion, but I suspect that many lawyers would say that such lies are out of bounds and are not part of the rules of the game. Can the lie about authority be justified on the ground that the question itself was improper? Put another way, if I have a right to keep certain information to myself, and if any behavior but a lie will reveal that information to the other side, am I justified in lying? I think not. Particularly in the case in which there are other avenues open to the respondent, should we not ask

21. Consider a variation on the last case. Assume that the defense lawyer did not say explicitly that the two would plead only if the third were allowed to go free but simply said, "If you drop the charges against one, the other two will plead guilty." In that case the lie is not explicit but surely the inference which the defense lawyer wishes the prosecutor to draw is the same. Should that change the outcome?

him to take those avenues? That is, the careful negotiator here can turn aside all such questions and by doing so avoid any inference from his failure to answer such questions.

What makes the last case a close one? Conceivably it is the idea that one accused by the state is entitled to greater leeway in making his case. Possibly one can argue that there is no injury to the state when such a person, particularly an innocent person, goes free. Is it conceivable that the act can be justified on the ground that it is part of the game in this context, that prosecutors as well as defense lawyers routinely misstate what they, their witnesses, and their clients can and will do? None of these arguments seems persuasive. Justice is not served by freeing a guilty person. The system does not necessarily achieve better results by trading two guilty pleas for a dismissal. Perhaps its justification has its roots in the same idea that formerly held that a misrepresentation of one's state of mind was not actionable for it was not a misrepresentation of fact.

In a sense rules governing these cases may simply arise from a recognition by the law of its limited power to shape human behavior. By tolerating exaggeration and puffing in the sales transaction, by refusing to make misstatement of one's intention actionable, the law may simply have recognized the bounds of its control over human behavior. Having said that, one is still left with the question, Are the lies permissible in the last two cases? My general conclusion is that they are not, but I am not nearly as comfortable with that conclusion as I am with the conclusion about the first three cases.

Taken together, the five foregoing cases show me that we do not and cannot intend that a negotiator be "truthful" in the broadest sense of that term. At the minimum we allow him some deviation from truthfulness in asserting his true opinion about cases, statutes, or the value of the subject of the negotiation in other respects. In addition some of us are likely to allow him to lie in response to certain questions that are regarded as out of bounds, and possibly to lie in circumstances where his interest is great and the injury seems small. It would be unfortunate, therefore, for the rule that requires "fairness" to be interpreted to require that a negotiator be truthful in every respect and in all of his dealings. It should be read to allow at least those kinds of untruthfulness that are implicitly and explicitly recognized as acceptable in his forum, a forum defined both by the subject matter and by the participants. . . .

Conclusion

To draft effective legislation is difficult; to draft effective ethical rules is close to impossible. Such drafters must walk the narrow line between being too general and too specific. If their rules are too general, they will have no influence on any behavior and give little guidance even to those who wish to follow the rules. If they are too specific, they omit certain areas or conflict with appropriate rules for problems not foreseen but apparently covered.

There are other, more formidable obstacles. These drafters are essentially powerless. They draft the rules, but the American Bar Association must pass them, and the rules must then be adopted by various courts or other agencies in the states. Finally the enforcement of the rules is left to a hodgepodge of bar committees and grievance agencies of varied will and capacity. Thus the drafters are far removed from and have little control over those who ultimately will enact and enforce the rules. For that reason, even more than most legislators, drafters of ethical rules have limited power to influence behavior. This weakness presents a final dilemma and one they have not always faced as well as they should, namely, to make the appropriate trade-off between what is "right" and what can be done. To enact stern and righteous rules in Chicago will not fool the people in Keokuk. The public will not believe them, and the bar will not follow them. What level of violation of the rules can the bar accept without the rules as a whole becoming a mockery? I do not know and the drafters can only guess. Because of the danger presented if the norms are widely and routinely violated, the drafters should err on the conservative side and must sometimes reject better and more desirable rules for poorer ones simply because the violation of the higher standard would cast all the rules in doubt.

ABA, MODEL RULES OF PROFESSIONAL CONDUCT

(1983, as amended 2001-2002)

RULE 4.1 TRUTHFULNESS IN STATEMENTS TO OTHERS

In the course of representing a client a lawyer shall not knowingly:

(a) make a false statement of material fact or law to a third person; or
(b) fail to disclose a material fact to a third person when disclosure is necessary to avoid assisting a criminal or fraudulent act by a client, unless disclosure is prohibited by Rule 1.6 [dealing with lawyer-client confidentiality].

COMMENT

Misrepresentation

A lawyer is required to be truthful when dealing with others on a client's behalf, but generally has no affirmative duty to inform an opposing party of relevant facts. A misrepresentation can occur if the lawyer incorporates or affirms a statement of another person that the lawyer knows is false. Misrepresentations can also occur by partially true but misleading statements or omissions that are the equivalent of affirmative false statements. For dishonest conduct that does not amount to a false statement or for misrepresentations by a lawyer other than in the course of representing a client, see Rule 8.4.

Statements of Fact

This Rule refers to statements of fact. Whether a particular statement should be regarded as one of fact can depend on the circumstances. Under generally accepted conventions in negotiation, certain types of statements ordinarily are not taken as statements of material fact. Estimates of price or value placed on the subject of a transaction and a party's intentions as to an acceptable settlement of a claim are ordinarily in this category, and so is the existence of an undisclosed principal except where nondisclosure of the principal would constitute fraud. Lawyers should be mindful of their obligations under applicable law to avoid criminal and tortious misrepresentation.

Crime or Fraud by Client

Under Rule 1.2(d), a lawyer is prohibited from counseling or assisting a client in conduct that the lawyer knows is criminal or fraudulent. Paragraph (b) states a specific application of the principle set forth in Rule 1.2(d) and addresses the situation where a client's crime or fraud takes the form of a lie or misrepresentation. Ordinarily, a lawyer can avoid assisting a client's crime or fraud by withdrawing from the representation. Sometimes it may be necessary for the lawyer to give notice of the fact of withdrawal and to disaffirm an opinion, document, affirmation or the like. In extreme cases, substantive law may require a lawyer to disclose information relating to the representation to avoid being deemed to have assisted the client's crime or fraud. If the lawyer can avoid assisting a client's crime or fraud only by disclosing this information, then under paragraph (b) the lawyer is required to do so, unless the disclosure is prohibited by Rule 1.6.

Rule 1.6 Confidentiality of Information

(a) A lawyer shall not reveal information relating to the representation of a client unless the client gives informed consent, the disclosure is impliedly authorized in order to carry out the representation or the disclosure is permitted by paragraph (b).

(b) A lawyer may reveal information relating to the representation of a client to the extent the lawyer reasonably believes necessary:

(1) to prevent reasonably certain death or substantial bodily harm;

(2) to prevent the client from committing a crime or fraud that is reasonably certain to result in substantial injury to the financial interests or property of another and in furtherance of which the client has used or is using the lawyer's services;

(3) to prevent, mitigate or rectify substantial injury to the financial interests or property of another that is reasonably certain to result or has resulted from the client's commission of a crime or fraud in furtherance of which the client has used the lawyer's services;

(4) to secure legal advice about the lawyer's compliance with these Rules;

(5) to establish a claim or defense on behalf of the lawyer in a controversy between the lawyer and the client, to establish a defense to a criminal charge or civil claim against the lawyer based upon conduct in which the client was involved, or to respond to allegations in any proceeding concerning the lawyer's representation of the client; or

(6) to comply with other law or a court order.

A lawyer must be concerned not only with the ethical implications of what she says—or does not say—in negotiations, but with the legal implications as well. The latter topic is treated by Professor Shell in the following article.

G. SHELL, WHEN IS IT LEGAL TO LIE IN NEGOTIATIONS?

Sloan Mgmt. Rev. 93, 94-96 (Spring 1991)

The elements of common law fraud are deceptively simple. A statement is fraudulent when the speaker makes a knowing misrepresentation of a material fact on which the victim reasonably relies and which causes damages. . . .

Knowing

The common law definition of fraud requires that the speaker have a particular state of mind with respect to the fact he misrepresents: the statement must be made "knowingly." This generally means that the speaker knows what he says is false. One way of getting around fraud, therefore, might be for the speaker to avoid contact with information that would lead to a "knowing" state of mind. For example, a company president might suspect that his company is in poor financial health, but he does not yet "know" it because he has not seen the latest quarterly reports. When his advisers ask to set up a meeting to discuss these reports, he tells them to hold off. He is about to go into negotiations with an important supplier and would like to be able to say, honestly, that so far as he knows the company is paying its bills. Does this get the president off the hook? No. The courts have stretched the definition of "knowing" to include statements that are "reckless," that is, those made with a conscious disregard for their truth. Thus, when the information that will give the speaker the truth is close at hand and he deliberately turns away in order to maintain a convenient state of ignorance, the law will treat him as if he spoke with full knowledge that his statements were false. . . .

Misrepresentation

In general, the law requires the speaker to make a positive misstatement before it will attach liability for fraud. Thus, a basic rule for commercial negotiators is to "be silent and be safe." As a practical matter, of course, silence is difficult to maintain if one's bargaining opponent is an astute questioner. In the face of inconvenient questions, negotiators are often forced to resort to verbal feints and dodges such as, "I don't know about that," or, when pressed, "That is not a subject I am at liberty to discuss."

There are circumstances when such dodges will not do, and it may be fraudulent to keep your peace about an issue. When does a negotiator have a duty to frankly disclose matters that may hurt his bargaining position? Under recent cases, the law imposes affirmative disclosure duties in the following four circumstances:

1. *When the nondisclosing party makes a partial disclosure that is or becomes misleading in light of all the facts.* If you say your company is profitable, you may have a duty to disclose whether you used questionable accounting techniques to arrive at that

statement. If you show a loss in the next quarter and negotiations are still ongoing, you may be required to disclose the loss. One way to avoid this is to make no statements on delicate subjects in the first place. Then you have no duty to correct or update yourself.

2. *When the parties stand in a fiduciary relationship to one another.* In negotiations involving trustees and beneficiaries, parties must be completely frank and cannot rely on the "be silent and be safe" rubric. Note, however, that courts have recently broadened the notion of a "fiduciary" to include banks, franchisors, and other commercial players who deal with business partners on a somewhat-less-than-arm's-length basis. In short, it is becoming increasingly risky to withhold important information in negotiations with parties who depend on you for their commercial well-being.

3. *When the nondisclosing party has "superior information" vital to the transaction that is not accessible to the other side.* This is a slippery exception, but the best test is one of conscience. Indeed, courts often state that the legal test of disclosure is whether "equity or good conscience" requires that the fact be revealed. Would you feel cheated if the other side didn't tell you about the hidden fact? Or would you secretly kick yourself for not having found it out yourself? If the former, you should consult an attorney. A recent case applying this exception held that an employer owed a duty to a prospective employee to disclose contingency plans for shutting down the project for which the employee was hired. In general, sellers have a greater duty than buyers to disclose things they know about their own property. Thus, a home seller must disclose termite infestation in her home. But an oil company need not disclose the existence of oil on a farmer's land when negotiating a purchase.

4. *When special transactions are at issue, such as insurance contracts.* Insurers must fully disclose the scope of coverage, and insureds must fully disclose their insurance risk. If you apply for a life insurance policy and do not disclose your heart condition, you have committed fraud.

If none of these four exceptions applies, you are not likely to be found liable for common law fraud based on a nondisclosure. Beware of special statutory modifications of the common law rules, however. For example, if the sale of your company involves a purchase or sale of securities, state and federal antifraud rules may impose a stiffer duty of disclosure than may apply under the common law. . . .

Material

Most people lie about something during negotiations. Often they seek to deceive others by making initial demands that far exceed their true needs or desires. Sometimes they mislead others about their reservation price or "bottom line." Of course, demands and reservation prices may not be "facts." One may have only a vague idea of what one really wants or is willing to pay for something. Hence, a statement that an asking price is too high may not be a true misrepresentation as much as a statement of preference. Suppose, however, that a negotiator has been given authority by a seller to peddle an item for any price greater than $10,000. Is it fraud for the negotiator to reject an offer of $12,000 and state that the deal cannot be closed at that price? In fact, the deal could be closed for that price so there has been a knowing misrepresentation of fact. The question is whether this fact is material in a legal sense. It is not. . . .

Demands and reservation prices are not, as a matter of law, material to a deal. . . .

Some experienced negotiators may be surprised to learn, however, that there are legal problems when negotiators try to embellish their refusals to accept a particular price with supporting lies. Lies about "other offers" are classic problem cases of this sort. For example, take the following relatively older but still leading case from Massachusetts. A commercial landlord bought a building and proceeded to negotiate a new lease with a toy shop tenant when the tenant's lease expired. The proprietor of the toy shop bargained hard and refused to pay the landlord's demand for a $10,000 increase in rent. The landlord then told the shop owner that he had another tenant willing to pay the amount and threatened the current tenant with immediate eviction if he did not promptly agree to the new rate. The tenant paid, but learned several years later that the threat had been a bluff; there was no other tenant. The tenant sued successfully for fraud.

In a more recent case, this time from Oklahoma, a real estate agent was held liable for fraud, including *punitive* damages, when she pressured a buyer into closing on a home with a story that a rival buyer (the contractor who built the house) was willing to pay the asking price and would do so later that same day. In these cases, the made-up offer was a lie; it concerned an objective fact (either someone had made an offer or they had not), and the courts ruled that the lie could be material given all the circumstances.

Questions

2.14 You are a writer who owns and works at a beautiful house in a part of town that is not yet extensively developed. You purchased the house for $125,000, and six months ago it was appraised at $200,000. Recently, you learned that the property at the end of the road has been purchased by a paramilitary group, the Blue Berets. Though they have not yet taken possession, your inquiries have turned up the fact that their daytime activities will be regulated by amplified bugle calls every 30 to 60 minutes. Since this will obviously interfere with your work, you list your house with a realtor. You are soon contacted by a couple, both of whom work nights, who tell you that they are interested in the house primarily because of the quiet neighborhood. What do you say to them? Suppose that you are the attorney for the writer. Would that affect what you say?

2.15 Assume the same facts as in question 2.14, except that the Blue Berets, instead of taking possession of the property, sold it to the Conservation Foundation. You are now contacted by an elderly couple who have recently immigrated to the United States and speak little English. They begin negotiations by offering $300,000 for the house. Assuming you are the writer who owns the home, what do you do? Now assume that you are the attorney for the writer. How would that affect your response?

2.16 You are the attorney for the company president whom Shell describes as having "deliberately turn[ed] away in order to maintain a convenient state of ignorance" about the financial health of his company. The company president tells you about this just before the two of you enter negotiations with the "important supplier." Are you required by Rule 4.1 to disclose the president's fraud to the supplier?

2.17 Would it be fraudulent for the writer in question 2.14 to fail to disclose the forthcoming taking of possession and bugle calls by the Blue Berets? If so, and the writer learned of the Blue Berets' purchase from you, his attorney, would you violate Rule 4.1 by nondisclosure?

2.18 In the example given by Shell in which the seller authorized his agent to accept any price over $10,000, suppose that the buyer's agent had asked her, "Are you authorized to accept $11,000?" Would it be fraudulent for the seller's agent to say "No"? If the seller's agent were an attorney, would saying "no" violate Rule 4.1? Could the attorney-agent respond to the question in a manner that would avoid both the risks of fraud and of a Rule 4.1 violation, while at the same time protecting the seller's bargaining position?

2.19 Recently, dissatisfaction has been expressed by some concerning the minimalist approach of Rule 4.1. See, e.g., Alfini (1999). What kind of changes might be considered to make the provision more meaningful?

For a wide-ranging collection of articles on negotiation ethics, see Menkel-Meadow and Wheeler (2004).

R. MNOOKIN, WHY NEGOTIATIONS FAIL: AN EXPLORATION OF BARRIERS TO THE RESOLUTION OF CONFLICT

8 Ohio St. J. on Dis. Res. 235, 238-246, 248-249 (1993)

Conflict is inevitable, but efficient and fair resolution is not. Conflicts can persist even though there may be any number of possible resolutions that would better serve the interests of the parties. . . . In our everyday personal and professional lives, we have all witnessed disputes where the absence of a resolution imposes substantial and avoidable costs on all parties. Moreover, many resolutions that are achieved—whether through negotiation or imposition—conspicuously fail to satisfy the economist's criterion of Pareto efficiency. . . .

Why is it that under circumstances where there are resolutions that better serve disputants, negotiations often fail to achieve efficient resolutions? In other words, what are the barriers to the negotiated resolution of conflict?

A. STRATEGIC BARRIERS

The first barrier to the negotiated resolution of conflict is inherent in a central characteristic of negotiation. Negotiation can be metaphorically compared to making a pie and then dividing it up. The process of conflict resolution affects both the size of the pie, and who gets what size slice.

The disputants' behavior may affect the size of the pie in a variety of ways. On the one hand, spending on avoidable legal fees and other process costs shrinks the pie. On the other hand, negotiators can together "create value" and make the pie bigger by discovering resolutions in which each party contributes special complementary skills that can be combined in a synergistic way, or by exploiting differences in relative preferences that permit trades that make both parties better off. . . .

Negotiation also involves issues concerning the distribution of benefits, and, with respect to pure distribution, both parties cannot be made better off at the same time. Given a pie of fixed size, a larger slice for you means a smaller one for me.

Because bargaining typically entails both efficiency issues (that is, how big the pie can be made) and distributive issues (that is, who gets what size slice), negotiation involves an inherent tension — one that David Lax and James Sebenius have dubbed the "negotiator's dilemma." In order to create value, it is critically important that options be created in light of both parties' underlying interests and preferences. This suggests the importance of openness and disclosure, so that a variety of options can be analyzed and compared from the perspective of all concerned. However, when it comes to the distributive aspects of bargaining, full disclosure — particularly if unreciprocated by the other side — can often lead to outcomes in which the more open party receives a comparatively smaller slice. To put it another way, unreciprocated approaches to creating value leave their maker vulnerable to claiming tactics. On the other hand, focusing on the distributive aspects of bargaining can often lead to unnecessary deadlocks and, more fundamentally, a failure to discover options or alternatives that make both sides better off. . . .

Even when both parties know all the relevant information, and that potential gains may result from a negotiated deal, strategic bargaining over how to divide the pie can still lead to deadlock (with no deal at all) or protracted and expensive bargaining, thus shrinking the pie. For example, suppose Nancy has a house for sale for which she has a reservation price of $245,000. I am willing to pay up to $295,000 for the house. Any deal within a bargaining range from $245,000 to $295,000 would make both of us better off than no sale at all. Suppose we each know the other's reservation price. Will there be a deal? Not necessarily. If we disagree about how the $50,000 "surplus" should be divided (each wanting all or most of it), our negotiation may end in a deadlock. We might engage in hardball negotiation tactics in which each tried to persuade the other that he or she was committed to walking away from a beneficial deal, rather than accept less than $40,000 of the surplus. Nancy might claim that she won't take a nickel less than $285,000, or even $294,999 for that matter. Indeed, she might go so far as to give a power of attorney to an agent to sell only at that price, and then leave town in order to make her commitment credible. Of course, I could play the same type of game and the result would then be that no deal is made and that we are both worse off. In this case, the obvious tension between the distribution of the $50,000 and the value creating possibilities inherent in any sale within the bargaining range may result in no deal.

Strategic behavior — which may be rational for a self-interested party concerned with maximizing the size of his or her own slice — can often lead to inefficient outcomes. Those subjected to claiming tactics often respond in kind, and the net result typically is to push up the cost of the dispute resolution process. . . . Parties may be tempted to engage in strategic behavior, hoping to get more. Often all they do is shrink the size of the pie. Those experienced in the civil litigation process see this all the time. One or both sides often attempt to use pre-trial discovery as leverage to force the other side into agreeing to a more favorable settlement. Often the net result, however, is simply that both sides spend unnecessary money on the dispute resolution process.

B. THE PRINCIPAL/AGENT PROBLEM

The second barrier is suggested by recent work relating to transaction cost economics, and is sometimes called the "principal/agent" problem. . . . The basic problem is that the incentives for an agent (whether it be a lawyer, employee, or officer) negotiating on behalf of a party to a dispute may induce behavior that fails to serve the interests of the principal itself. The relevant research suggests that it is no simple matter—whether by contract or custom—to align perfectly the incentives for an agent with the interests of the principal. This divergence may act as a barrier to efficient resolution of conflict.

Litigation is fraught with principal/agent problems. In civil litigation, for example—particularly where the lawyers on both sides are being paid by the hour—there is very little incentive for the opposing lawyers to cooperate, particularly if the clients have the capacity to pay for trench warfare and are angry to boot. Commentators have suggested that this is one reason many cases settle on the courthouse steps, and not before: for the lawyers, a late settlement may avoid the possible embarrassment of an extreme outcome, while at the same time providing substantial fees. . . .

C. COGNITIVE BARRIERS

The third barrier is a by-product of the way the human mind processes information, deals with risks and uncertainties, and makes inferences and judgments. Research by cognitive psychologists during the last fifteen years suggests several ways in which human reasoning often departs from that suggested by theories of rational judgment and decision making. . . .

Suppose everyone attending this evening's lecture is offered the following happy choice: At the end of my lecture you can exit at the north end of the hall or the south end. If you choose the north exit, you will be handed an envelope in which there will be a crisp new twenty dollar bill. Instead, if you choose the south exit, you will be given a sealed envelope randomly pulled from a bin. One quarter of these envelopes contain a $100 bill, but three quarters are empty. In other words, you can have a sure gain of $20 if you go out the north door, or you can instead gamble by choosing the south door where you will have a 25% chance of winning $100 and a 75% chance of winning nothing. Which would you choose? A great deal of experimental work suggests that the overwhelming majority of you would choose the sure gain of $20, even though the "expected value" of the second alternative, $25, is slightly more. This is a well known phenomenon called "risk aversion." The principle is that most people will take a sure thing over a gamble, even where the gamble may have a somewhat higher "expected" payoff.

Daniel Kahneman and Amos Tversky have advanced our understanding of behavior under uncertainty with a remarkable discovery. They suggest that, in order to avoid what would otherwise be a sure loss, many people will gamble, even if the expected loss from the gamble is larger. Their basic idea can be illustrated by changing my hypothetical. Although you didn't know this when you were invited to this lecture, it is not free. At the end of the lecture, the doors are going to be locked. If you go out the north door, you'll be required to *pay* $20 as an exit fee.

If you go out the south door, you'll participate in a lottery by drawing an envelope. Three quarters of the time you're going to be let out for free, but one quarter of the time you're going to be required to pay $100. Rest assured all the money is going to the Dean's fund — a very good cause. What do you choose? There's a great deal of empirical research, based on the initial work of Kahneman and Tversky, suggesting that the majority of this audience would choose the south exit — i.e., most of you would gamble to avoid having to lose $20 for sure. Kahneman and Tversky call this "loss aversion."

Now think of these two examples together. Risk aversion suggests that most of you would not gamble for a gain, even though the expected value of $25 exceeds the sure thing of $20. On the other hand, most of you would gamble to avoid a sure loss, even though, on the average, the loss of going out the south door is higher. Experimental evidence suggests that the proportion of people who will gamble to avoid a loss is much greater than those who would gamble to realize a gain.

Loss aversion can act as a cognitive barrier to the negotiated resolution of conflict for a variety of reasons. For example, both sides may fight on in a dispute in the hope that they may avoid any losses, even though the continuation of the dispute involves a gamble in which the loss may end up being far greater. Loss aversion may explain Lyndon Johnson's decision, in 1965, to commit additional troops to Vietnam as an attempt to avoid the sure loss attendant to withdrawal, and as a gamble that there might be some way in the future to avoid any loss at all. Similarly, negotiators may, in some circumstances, be adverse to offering a concession in circumstances where they view the concession as a sure loss. Indeed, the notion of rights or entitlements may be associated with a more extreme form of loss aversion that Kahneman and Tversky call "enhanced loss aversion," because losses "compounded by outrage are much less acceptable than losses that are caused by misfortune or by legitimate actions of others."

One of the most striking features of loss aversion is that whether something is viewed as a gain or loss — and what kind of gain or loss it is considered — depends upon a reference point, and the choice of a reference point is sometimes manipulable. Once again, a simple example suggested by Kahneman and Tversky can illustrate.

Suppose you and a friend decide to go to Cleveland for a big night out on the town. You've made reservations at an elegant restaurant that will cost $100 a couple. In addition, you've bought two superb seats — at $50 each — to hear the Cleveland orchestra. You set off for Cleveland, thinking you have your symphony tickets and $100, but no credit cards.

Imagine that you park your car in Cleveland and make a horrifying discovery — you've lost the tickets. Assume that you cannot be admitted to the symphony without tickets. Also imagine that someone is standing in front of the Symphony Hall offering to sell two tickets for $100. You have a choice. You can use the $100 you intended for the fancy dinner to buy the tickets to hear the concert, or you can skip the concert and simply go to dinner. What would you do?

Consider a second hypothetical. After you park your car, you look in your wallet and you realize to your horror that the $100 is gone, but the tickets are there. In front of the Symphony Hall is a person holding a small sign indicating she would like to buy two tickets for $100. What do you do? Do you sell the tickets and go to dinner? Or do you instead skip dinner and simply go to the concert?

Experimental research suggests that in the first example many more people will skip the symphony and simply go out to dinner, while in the second example, the proportions are nearly reversed; most people would skip dinner and go to the concert. The way we keep our mental accounts is such that, in the first instance, to buy the tickets a second time would somehow be to overspend our ticket budget. And, yet, an economist would point out that the two situations are essentially identical because there is a ready and efficient market in which you can convert tickets to money or money to tickets.

The purpose of the hypotheticals is to suggest that whether or not an event is framed as a loss can often affect behavior. This powerful idea concerning "framing" has important implications for the resolution of disputes to which I will return later.

D. "REACTIVE DEVALUATION" OF COMPROMISES AND CONCESSIONS

The final barrier I wish to discuss is "reactive devaluation," and is an example of a social/psychological barrier that arises from the dynamics of the negotiation process and the inferences that negotiators draw from their interactions. My Stanford colleague, psychology Professor Lee Ross, and his students have done experimental work to suggest that, especially between adversaries, when one side offers a particular concession or proposes a particular exchange of compromises, the other side may diminish the attractiveness of that offer or proposed exchange simply because it originated with a perceived opponent. The basic notion is a familiar one, especially for lawyers. How often have you had a client indicate to you in the midst of litigation, "If only we could settle this case for $7,000. I'd love to put this whole matter behind me." Lo and behold, the next day, the other side's attorney calls and offers to settle for $7,000. You excitedly call your client and say, "Guess what—the other side has just offered to settle this case for $7,000." You expect to hear jubilation on the other end of the phone, but instead there is silence. Finally, your client says, "Obviously they must know something we don't know. If $7,000 is a good settlement for them, it can't be a good settlement for us."

Both in laboratory and field settings, Ross and his colleagues have marshalled interesting evidence for "reactive devaluation." They have demonstrated that a given compromise proposal is rated less positively when proposed by someone on the other side than when proposed by a neutral or an ally. They also demonstrated that a concession that is actually offered is rated lower than a concession that is withheld, and that a compromise is rated less highly after it has been put on the table by the other side than it was beforehand. . . .

III. OVERCOMING STRATEGIC BARRIERS: THE ROLES OF NEGOTIATORS AND MEDIATORS

The study of barriers can do more than simply help us understand why negotiations sometimes fail when they should not. It can also contribute to our understanding of how to overcome these barriers. Let me illustrate this by using the preceding analysis of four barriers briefly to explore the role of mediators, and to suggest why neutrals can often facilitate the efficient resolution of disputes by overcoming these specific barriers.

First, let us consider the strategic barrier. To the extent that a neutral third party is trusted by both sides, the neutral may be able to induce the parties to reveal information about their underlying interests, needs, priorities, and aspirations that they would not disclose to their adversary. This information may permit a trusted mediator to help the parties enlarge the pie in circumstances where the parties acting alone could not. Moreover, a mediator can foster a problem-solving atmosphere and lessen the temptation on the part of each side to engage in strategic behavior. A skilled mediator can often get parties to move beyond political posturing and recriminations about past wrongs and to instead consider possible gains from a fair resolution of the dispute.

A mediator also can help overcome barriers posed by principal/agent problems. A mediator may bring clients themselves to the table, and help them understand their shared interest in minimizing legal fees and costs in circumstances where the lawyers themselves might not be doing so. In circumstances where a middle manager is acting to prevent a settlement that might benefit the company, but might be harmful to the manager's own career, an astute mediator can sometimes bring another company representative to the table who does not have a personal stake in the outcome.

A mediator can also promote dispute resolution by helping overcome cognitive barriers. Through a variety of processes, a mediator can often help each side understand the power of the case from the other side's perspective. Moreover, by reframing the dispute and suggesting a resolution that avoids blame and stresses the positive aspects of a resolution, a mediator may be able to lessen the effects of loss aversion. . . . By emphasizing the potential gains to both sides of the resolution and deemphasizing the losses that the resolution is going to entail, mediators (and lawyers) often facilitate resolution.

With respect to the fourth barrier, reactive devaluation, mediators can play an important and quite obvious role. Reactive devaluation can often be sidestepped if the source of a proposal is a neutral—not one of the parties. Indeed, one of the trade secrets of mediators is that after talking separately to each side about what might or might not be acceptable, the mediator takes responsibility for making a proposal. This helps both parties avoid reactive devaluation by allowing them to accept as sensible a proposal that they might have rejected if it had come directly from their adversary. . . .

In addition to the barriers discussed by Mnookin, it has been suggested that negotiators fail to reach agreement or at least optimal agreement due to some or all of the following factors:

1. Failure of adequate preparation (fact gathering and analysis as well as strategic planning)
2. Failure of effective communication
3. Emotionalism

4. Extrinsic factors such as linkages to other disputes or preexisting commitments
5. Different perceptions of alternatives to agreement
   a. Different information
   b. Different assessments of the same information*
6. Constituency pressures
7. Stakes not suited to compromise, such as intensely held personal values that are not likely to be conceded voluntarily, or where a party's economic survival is threatened
8. Different attitudes toward risk
9. Different attitudes toward the desirability of a prompt settlement
10. No zone of agreement

When reading the next chapter, consider which of these failures to reach agreement might be overcome by the involvement of a mediator.

EXERCISE 2.1: TEXOIL†

Texoil, a large petroleum refining company, owns some service stations outright. For the most part, however, it contracts with individual service station owners to provide them with all their requirements of gasoline, oil, tires, batteries, and accessories. One of the independent service station owners, who has been under contract with Texoil since the station was built, has recently put the station up for sale. In addition to notifying Texoil of the planned sale, the owner notified all the other major oil companies. The owner also put ads in the local newspapers, as well as in a national professional journal of service station owners. The ad said that the owner was selling for family reasons.

The service station, which has the rather exotic name "Port of Call Service Station," is located on one of the main routes leading to the Port of Los Angeles. Nearby are numerous shopping centers, as well as some light industry. There are also two other service stations approximately one mile away.

The owner of the service station has never been willing to have any employee other than his spouse. They have kept the station open from 6:00 A.M. to 8:00 P.M. every day of the year. Their annual income, including wages, has been approximately $75,000 (before taxes).

(Confidential information for both parties is contained in the Teacher's Manual.)

*A dramatic demonstration of this proposition can be found in Rosenthal (1974), which describes the wide range of predicted jury verdicts given by different personal injury lawyers and insurance claim adjusters to the same factual situation. In one case, for example, predicted jury verdicts ranged from $2,000 to $30,000. There is also evidence that a negotiator's perception of the fair value of an item subject to negotiation varies according to the negotiator's position. Thus, sellers tend to value an object being sold more highly than do buyers (Raiffa, 1982: 93-94).

†This exercise has been adapted and translated by Professor Stephen B. Goldberg from an exercise created by Henri Le Cloarec and copyrighted by Mobil France.

EXERCISE 2.2: NAM CHOI v. AUSTIN UNIVERSITY MEDICAL SCHOOL*

Ted Nam Choi is the 23-year-old son of Cambodian immigrants who came to the United States in 1979. After graduating from Vernon Valley Community College, Nam Choi was admitted to Austin University Medical School under its affirmative action program, even though he had lower MCAT (Medical College Aptitude Test) scores than most Austin students. In view of the prestige of Austin University Medical School, one of the best in the United States, Nam Choi was thrilled to be admitted.

In December of Nam Choi's first year, however, he became aware of a difficulty in dealing with multiple choice examinations, and, by the end of the first year, he had failed five of fifteen courses. Although the Austin Medical School guidelines provide for dismissal after two course failures, the dean, on the recommendation of the Student-Faculty Affirmative Action Committee, allowed Nam Choi to repeat the first-year program.

During the summer, Nam Choi underwent neuropsychological evaluations at the request and expense of Austin Medical School. The difficulties identified by the psychologists impair Nam Choi's ability to answer multiple choice questions. They discovered that even when he understands a subject fully and is capable of discussing it intelligently, he tends to "freeze" when forced to respond to a multiple choice question about that subject. (The psychologists suspect that this psychological blank is due to the life-or-death multiple choices that Nam Choi had to make as a child living through the fighting in Cambodia.)

Unfortunately for Nam Choi, American medical school examinations, as well as the medical boards which each student must pass in order to practice in the United States, are nearly all of the multiple choice type. (The exams are so designed in order to test the student's comprehension of a large body of knowledge and capacity to make diagnostic choices.)

Nam Choi began his second exposure to the first-year program with the assistance of counseling, tutors, notetakers, and taped lectures. At the end of the year, he again failed three courses, Pharmacology, Biology, and Biochemistry. At the request of the Student-Faculty Affirmative Action Committee, the dean allowed him to take make-up exams in these courses. He failed all for the third time. Nam Choi was then dismissed from Austin Medical School.

Following an unavailing complaint with the U.S. Department of Education Office for Civil Rights, Nam Choi filed a civil action alleging that the Austin University Medical School dismissal constituted discrimination on the basis of handicap. Section 504 of the Rehabilitation Act of 1973 provides that

> [no] otherwise qualified individual with handicaps in the United States . . . shall, solely by reason of her or his handicap, be excluded from participation in, be denied the benefits of, or be subjected to discrimination under any program or activity receiving Federal financial assistance. . . .

*This exercise has been adapted from an exercise developed by Thomas O Patrick, Lecturer in Law, College of Law, West Virginia University, and is used with his permission.

It is undisputed that Austin University Medical School receives substantial federal financial assistance and that it is subject to the provisions of §504.

(Confidential information for each attorney is contained in the Teacher's Manual.)

EXERCISE 2.3: STAR

Three months ago, the once-popular rock group Sarren, Trace, Arthurs, and Robin (STAR) regrouped for their first performance together in 13 years. Following the well-received benefit concert, Robin revealed that he has decided to work with the group once again, primarily because Sarren has kicked his drug habit and is now serious about making music. The four have already started recording a new album and are now on a major concert tour.

"We're gonna make a fantastic album," insisted 45-year-old David Sarren, standing backstage after a recent concert. "We're gonna really show them what we can do!"

"Everybody's together again," Robin, 41, said as he relaxed with Steven Trace in his dressing room between shows. "Can't be STAR if you don't have Sarren. . . ." He glanced over at the 42-year-old Trace, who added, "It feels like we're a band again."

Sarren spent eight months in a Texas jail last year following drug and illegal weapon convictions. During that time he successfully overcame his addiction to cocaine. He was released seven months ago. "We got David back almost from the dead," said Graham Arthurs, 45. "This first year has been the big test for him, and so far he's passed with flying colors."

Last month in L.A. the group began a recording that, if all goes as planned, will become the second STAR studio album. The group's only previous studio album was released 15 years ago. Attempts to record a follow-up ended abruptly when Neal Robin, upset by arguing within the group, walked out and, as Sarren once put it, "never came back."

One hitch in the group's plans has come for Helene Heffen, president of Heffen Records. Six weeks ago, Robin signed an exclusive two-album, two-year recording contract with Heffen Records, and Heffen doesn't want him appearing on a STAR CD unless it comes out on the Heffen label. Sarren, Trace, and Arthurs are signed to exclusive contracts with Pacific, each of which has three albums and three years remaining, and Paul Pack, president of Pacific, wants any STAR CD to be released by Pacific. According to Pack, since three of the four are under Pacific contracts, "It only makes sense to have a CD on the Pacific label."

Heffen's response, when she learned of Pack's statement, was that "if Sarren, Trace and Arthurs want to make a CD with Neal Robin, that CD can only be made for me. I will not allow Neal Robin to make a CD for anybody else while he's under exclusive contract to me and owes me two albums."

"I don't know how it's all going to work out," said Robin, "but I'm sure that the companies will figure it out. It's not my problem. We're gonna make an album anyway. No one can stop us from doing what we want. And then when it's done, it's done. Whatever happens to it after that, that's a business deal."

A few days ago, representatives of Pacific Records and Heffen Records agreed to discuss the STAR problem. Their meeting is scheduled for next week.

(Confidential information for each representative is contained in the Teacher's Manual.)

EXERCISE 2.4: PEPULATOR PRICING*

The pepulator market is entirely controlled by two giants of the industry: Pulsar Pepulator and Consolidated Pepulator Co. Each company currently has 50 percent of the entire market for pepulators. Both companies currently sell their pepulators at a unit price of $20. As long as they sell at the same unit price, each company can expect to retain its market share. But if one company sells at a lower price than the other, it will expand its market share and increase its profits at the expense of the other company. However, both firms are very large and neither can realistically expect to put the other out of business by undercutting the other's price for a few months.

You are a member of the board of one of these two companies. Each month for the next eight months you will be asked to set that month's price for your firm's pepulators. Your goal is to maximize your firm's profits. You are entirely indifferent to the profits of the other firm. The stockholders of your company care only about your firm's profits and do not consider market share per se or the profits of the other firm to be relevant.

Market research has revealed that the monthly profits of your firm will depend on the price you set and the price of your competitor. However, uncontrollable market forces render it unprofitable for either firm to raise its price above $30. The exact price-to-profit matrix that each firm faces appears in Figure 2-1.

Remember that your goal is to maximize *your own firm's* annual profits. By state law your price choice is limited to a multiple of $10.

Consolidated Pepulator

		$30	**$20**	**$10**
		$11,000,000	$18,000,000	$15,000,000
	$30	$11,000,000	$2,000,000	$2,000,000
		$2,000,000	$8,000,000	$15,000,000
Pulsar Pepulator	**$20**	$18,000,000	$8,000,000	$3,000,000
		$2,000,000	$3,000,000	$5,000,000
	$10	$15,000,000	$15,000,000	$5,000,000

NOTE: Pulsar's payoff is at the lower left of each cell; Consolidated's is at the upper right in each cell.

Figure 2-1

* This case was created for the Harvard Negotiation Project by Roger Fisher based on a payoff matrix created by Mark Drooks.

(*Note:* Antitrust laws should *not* be taken into consideration in negotiating this exercise. You may regard those laws as temporarily suspended.)

SCORE SHEET

Month	*Price Chosen*		*Profit for Month*		*Cumul. Total Profit*	
	Pulsar	*Consol.*	*Pulsar*	*Consol.*	*Pulsar*	*Consol.*
1						
2						
3						
4						
5						
6						
7						
8						

EXERCISE 2.5: TOO OLD TO ROCK AND ROLL*

Seattle SuperTheater (SST) is a private theater company that stages six productions a year. In the past decade, seven of its productions have moved on to Broadway, more than any other regional theater.

Each year SST produces one musical. This year's musical will be STORMIN' — a new rock musical set at a military medical unit in Saudi Arabia during the Gulf War. Those who have seen the script describe it as "a rock & roll M*A*S*H in the desert." They say it has the potential to be a big commercial hit, but you never can tell in show business.

The three lead roles, two romantic leads and the unit commander, were cast. The romantic leads are two newcomers, and the unit commander, Colonel Plotter, was Tiny Turner, one of the biggest rock stars of the seventies. But yesterday disaster struck, and Turner pulled out, citing "artistic differences with the director." A new Colonel must be found, soon.

Interest at SST quickly focused on Jerry McCarthy, former lead singer of the Bootlegs (one of the biggest, most influential bands of the sixties) and the Ailerons (in the seventies). Jerry has played at SST twice, five and twelve years ago, and got good notices. Jerry is the right age for the role — one of the very few active big name rockers who is, and the only one with a track record at SST. Recently, however, *Rolling Stone* (which is not alone) has started calling Jerry "too old to rock and roll." Jerry's old records with the Bootlegs still sell well, but the concert offers have become few and far between.

SST has 4,000 seats, and has scheduled 16 performances of STORMIN'. Ticket prices average $40, and have risen 33 percent in the past five years. Average attendance at SST is believed to be about 85 percent to 90 percent of capacity over the past five years. About half of these are pre-sold season tickets, and the rest are bought as single tickets by the general public.

While SST fees are confidential, most people know that when Jerry played in *Jesus Christ Superstar* five years ago, the fee was $40,000 for 16 shows in a featured

* This exercise was adapted by Kenneth S. Gallant and Mary Beth Lagenaur, University of Idaho, from an exercise created by Norbert Jacker, DePaul University College of Law. Used with permission.

(i.e., not quite starring) role. Twelve years ago, as the star of *Tommy,* Jerry received $60,000 for 15 shows. In the past 12 years, fees for stars of musical comedies have quadrupled. In the past five years alone they have doubled.

Although it is difficult to generalize, a lead role like the Colonel might generate a fee twice that of a featured role. A name star in a lead role might expect to get twice what a lesser name would get. Word on the street has it that each of the newcomers in STORMIN' is getting $90,000 for the 16 shows.

(Confidential information for Jerry McCarthy, the SST director of STORMIN', and the attorneys for each, is in the Teacher's Manual.)

EXERCISE 2.6: COLONIAL CONFECTIONERS, INC.

Colonial Confectioners, Inc. presently operates a candy factory in a one-story building on the edge of downtown Salem. The factory was built about the turn of the century, and has been in continuous operation since then. Approximately two weeks ago, Tom Rampal, the 75-year-old president and chief executive officer of Colonial, received a phone call from an attorney named Lawrence about a client who was interested in purchasing Colonial. Rampal told Lawrence that he would be interested in whatever Lawrence had to say, but that he was about to leave the country for a long-planned vacation with his wife. Accordingly he directed Lawrence to contact his attorney, J. M. Cublier, to discuss Lawrence's proposition. Lawrence did so, and the two attorneys are to meet tomorrow.

(Confidential information for each attorney is contained in the Teacher's Manual.)

EXERCISE 2.7: RAPID PRINTING CO. v. SCOTT COMPUTERS, INC.*

Rapid Printing Co. specializes in business forms, journals, and reports. Its gross income for fiscal year 1997 was approximately $1.75 million. Scott Computers, Inc. manufactures, sells, and leases computers and associated software. Its gross income for fiscal 1997 was approximately $340 million.

Beginning in February 1997, Dee Williams, Rapid's vice president for operations, and June Robertson, a Scott salesperson, had a series of meetings to discuss Williams's plan to develop a system of remote computerized composition through portable terminals placed at Rapid's customers' locations. On February 15, 1997, Williams sent out letters to several companies, including Scott, requesting proposals for a computer system with capacity for remote computerized composition (Appendix A). With such a system, customers could transmit data directly to Rapid in typeset-ready format, enabling Rapid to perform its composition functions

*This exercise was prepared by Stephen B. Goldberg, Northwestern University Law School, Chicago, Illinois, and Jeanne M. Brett, Kellogg Graduate School of Management, Northwestern University, Evanston, Illinois. Technical advice about the use of computers in the printing industry was provided by James Mason, Kellogg Graduate School of Management, Executive Masters Program. The exercise was prepared for an American Arbitration Association Task Force on Teaching Dispute Resolution in law and business schools.

faster and more accurately than its competitors, none of which possessed such a computer system.[1] These meetings concluded with the March 17, 1997 signing of a five-year contract between Scott and Rapid, pursuant to which Scott was to lease and install the hardware and operating programs necessary for the Rapid system (Appendix B).

In July 1997, the Scott hardware was fully installed at Rapid. It soon developed, however, that the system was incapable of computerized composition because it lacked an appropriate application program.[2] At that point, a dispute developed between Rapid and Scott concerning whose responsibility it was to provide an application program. According to Rapid, June Robertson had promised Williams that Scott would provide Rapid with Print-Rite, a Scott application program for the computer industry, at no cost if Rapid would lease Scott hardware. Robertson denied having promised to provide Print-Rite, asserting that when she sought to interest Williams in leasing Print-Rite, he said he was not interested, since he planned to program the new system himself. Scott took the position that it had fully performed its obligations under the lease and demanded that Rapid begin making payments. Rapid refused to do so.

In April 1998, Rapid brought suit against Scott, claiming that Scott had defrauded Rapid and had breached its contract with Rapid by promising Print-Rite and not making it available. Rapid sought $5 million in damages from Scott, claiming that it lost profits in that amount as a result of the failure of the new system to operate as planned (Appendix C). Scott has prepared, but not yet filed, a counterclaim against Rapid for approximately $500,000, the amount due it under the contract.

It is Scott's policy to attempt to resolve all disputes short of litigation. Pursuant to that policy, Scott initiated the meeting that is about to take place. Present at that meeting will be S. S. Scott, president and CEO of Scott Computers; B. R. Brown, president and chairman of the board of Rapid Printing; Gil Santina, Scott's attorney; and Lane Christian, Rapid's attorney.

For purposes of this exercise, it is now May 1998.

(Confidential information for each attorney and each principal is contained in the Teacher's Manual.)

1. The composition of documents, particularly those with many graphics, charts, and tables, has until recently been a largely manual operation. Computerized composition systems allow graphic and type composition to be designed and edited directly on a terminal. The data representing the document are stored in the mainframe computer. These data are then output to a phototypesetter, which transforms the data into a high-resolution image, which is printed on special paper, which can then be photographed, or in some models the image is transferred directly to film. The film is then used in the conventional manner to make plates for the printing machines.

2. The world of data processing is divided into two parts, hardware and software. Hardware is the physical equipment, consisting of a computer and its peripheral devices. Software consists of the computer programs used to operate the hardware.

There are two types of computer programs. Operating programs direct the hardware and interface between the more specific task-oriented application programs and the hardware. Application programs are written to direct the computer to perform specific user-oriented functions, such as the preparation of invoices and inventory records.

APPENDIX A

Rapid Printing Co.

February 15, 1997

Ms. June Robertson
Scott Computers
324 Lawrence Ave.
Lawrence, Illiana 60611

Dear Ms. Robertson:

As we discussed last week, Rapid Printing Co. is desirous of purchasing a computer system which will have capabilities for computerized composition and typesetting, including remote composition through terminals at customers' locations.
In particular, we want:

1	mainframe computer with 4MB memory
2	tape drives
1	internal multiplex channel for the tape subsystem
1	input/output control device
1	diskette read/write device
1	line printer, 300 LPM
1	expanded character set
1	letter quality printer, 200 CPS
6	CRT terminals
6	keyboards
6	modems
1	synch/asynch interface
1	phototypesetter
1	typesetter-mainframe interface

Please provide me, at your earliest convenience, with an itemized proposal. I look forward to your proposal.

Sincerely,

/s/ Dee Williams
Vice President, Operations
Rapid Printing Co.
2001 North Sheffield
Deerfield, Illiana

APPENDIX B

Rapid Printing Co.
2001 North Sheffield
Deerfield, Illiana

Scott Computers, Inc.
Lease and Service Agreement

Scott Computers, Inc., on acceptance of this contract by means of a signature in the Acceptance Block of this contract, shall provide the customer with the products and services described herein subject to the following terms and conditions.

EQUIPMENT SCHEDULE

Item No.	*Description*	*Number of Units*	*Total Monthly Maintenance Charge*	*Total Monthly Equipment Charge*
S-104	30/85 processor with CRT console 4MB memory	01	$ 924	$4,200
S-127	Tape drive	02	142	380
S-128	Multiplex channel for tape subsystem	01	52	221
S-141	Input/Output control device	01	75	205
S-151	Diskette read/write	01	54	212
S-161	Line printer, 300 LPM	01	187	272
S-162	Expanded characterset	01	9	38
S-165	Letter printer, 200 CPS	01	32	102
S-170	CRT terminals	06	194	886
S-171	Keyboard	06	25	112
S-181	Modem	06	32	148
S-185	Synch/Asynch interface	01	—	9
R-2071	Phototypesetter	01	270	1,230
R-2078	Typesetter-mainframe DMA interface	01	54	246
Subtotals			2,050	8,261
Less 25% new customer discount				2,065
TOTALS			$2,050	$6,196

PROGRAM PRODUCTS

Item No.	*Description*	*Monthly Charge*
2274	OS/IV operating system	$ 75
2281	OS/IV operating editor	50
2221	OS/IV Cobol	60
X341	OS/IV typesetter-driver	85
TOTAL		$270

1. DEFINITIONS

The following terms shall have the meanings set forth below whenever they are used in this Agreement including the preceding page.

(a) "Documentation" means the then-current, generally distributed, standard visually readable materials published by Scott Computers for customer use with units of Equipment or Programming Aids.
(b) "Equipment" means all the units of Equipment listed on the Equipment Schedule of this Agreement as modified by any supplement.
(c) "Programming Aids" means the software programs that Scott Computers announces and generally distributes for the Equipment while this Agreement is in effect.
(d) "Monthly Equipment Charges" means the monthly charges the Customer is obligated to pay hereunder for the use of the units of Equipment whether those charges are designated by Scott Computers as Monthly Rent or 5 Year Lease Charges.
(e) "Products" means the Equipment, Documentation, and Programming Aids described herein.
(f) "Software Correction" service means corrections, if any, to Programming Aids issued from a Scott Computers location and transmitted to the Customer without a separate charge.
(g) "Services" means Equipment Maintenance services and Software Correction service described herein.
(h) "Site" means the room or rooms within which each unit of Equipment is to be installed, at the addresses designated herein.

2. TERM OF AGREEMENT

This Agreement shall become effective on the date it is accepted by Scott Computers. It shall continue in effect for an initial term of five (5) years starting from the date specified in Section 5(b) for commencement of Monthly Equipment Charges for the first unit of Equipment installed under this Agreement, which is listed in the Equipment Schedule on the effective date of this Agreement. This Agreement shall continue in effect after the initial term until terminated or canceled in accordance with the provisions of Section 7.

3. EQUIPMENT MAINTENANCE SERVICE

(a) Scott Computers shall provide preventive and remedial maintenance service to maintain the Equipment in satisfactory operating condition. Scott Computers shall determine the frequency and the duration of preventive maintenance.
(b) Payment of the Base Monthly Maintenance Charges shall entitle the Customer to on-call remedial maintenance service between the hours of

7 A.M. and 6 P.M., five (5) days per week, Monday through Friday, excluding holidays.

4. PROGRAMMING AIDS AND DOCUMENTATION

(a) Scott Computers shall furnish to the Customer, while this Agreement is in effect, one copy of such Programming Aids and Documentation as are then available, subject to Scott Computers' then prevailing terms, conditions, and charges.
(b) Scott Computers hereby grants to the Customer, while this Agreement is in effect, a personal, non-transferable and non-exclusive license to use the Programming Aids and Documentation designated by Scott Computers as proprietary only on the Equipment and at the Site.
(c) The Customer may modify any Programming Aid or Documentation for its own use and at its own responsibility and expense to meet its specific requirements. Any portion of the Programming Aids or Documentation included in such modification shall be subject to the same conditions and limitations as have been designated herein for the original Programming Aids or Documentation.
(d) Scott Computers shall provide information to the Customer in respect to the appropriate use of the Programming Aids in Customer's operations; however, the Customer assumes responsibility for the supervision, management, and control of the Programming Aids.

5. CHARGES

(a) The Customer shall pay all charges within thirty (30) days after date of invoice.
(b) Monthly Equipment Charges and Base Monthly Maintenance Charges will commence, as to each unit of Equipment, on the date such unit of Equipment is installed and ready for use as certified by Scott Computers, and will be invoiced monthly in advance. The charges do not include, and the Customer assumes the cost of: (1) operating supplies; (2) painting or refinishing the Equipment; (3) movement of any unit of Equipment or part thereof; and (4) repair of damage to the Equipment, including replacement of parts, resulting from the fault of the Customer or causes reasonably within the Customer's control.

6. WARRANTY

(a) Scott Computers warrants that the Equipment, when installed, shall be free from defects in material and workmanship.
(b) Scott Computers further warrants that, under normal use and service, the Equipment shall remain in satisfactory operating condition.

(c) Scott Computers' sole and exclusive liability under these warranties shall be that Scott Computer, at its option, either: (1) adjusts or repairs as promptly as is possible the defective parts or units of Equipment claimed to cause unsatisfactory operation of the Equipment; or (2) replaces such defective parts or units of Equipment at no additional cost to the Customer.
(d) Scott Computers' warranties, with respect to any unit of Equipment furnished hereunder, shall extend only to the Customer and may not be altered or extended.

7. EXTENSIONS, CANCELLATION AND REPOSSESSION

(a) Either party may on thirty (30) days' prior written notice cancel any unit of Equipment at the end of the initial term of this Agreement.
(b) If at any time during the term of this Agreement, the Customer fails to make payments due hereunder within thirty (30) days of the date on which those payments are due, the entire amount owed to Scott Computers under this Agreement shall immediately become due.

8. LIMITATION OF LIABILITY

(a) Except as herein expressly stated, there are no warranties, express or implied, by operation of law or otherwise, of the products or services furnished hereunder. Scott Computers disclaims any implied warranty of merchantability or fitness for a particular purpose. In no event shall Scott Computers be liable for any incidental, indirect, special, or consequential damages in connection with or arising out of this agreement or the existence, furnishing, functioning or the Customer's use of any products or services provided for in this agreement. The Customer's sole and exclusive remedy for liability of any kind, including negligence, with respect to the products and services furnished hereunder, shall be limited to the remedies provided in Section 6 of this agreement.
(b) The Customer further agrees that Scott Computers shall not be liable for: (1) any loss of use, revenue or profit; (2) any claim, demand or action against the Customer by any third party.

9. GENERAL PROVISIONS

(a) This Agreement constitutes the entire agreement between the parties with respect to the subject matter hereof and shall supersede all previous proposals, both oral and written, negotiations, representations, commitments, writings, agreements, and all other communications between the parties. It may not be released, discharged, changed or modified except by an instrument in writing signed by a duly authorized representative of each of the parties. The term of this Agreement shall prevail notwithstanding any variance with the terms and conditions of any order submitted by the Customer.

Scott Computers, Inc. Acceptance by	Customer Rapid Printing Co.
Slade Gorton	*Dee Williams*
Signature	Signature
Vice President, Sales	*Vice President, Operations*
Title	Title
March 17, 1997	*March 17, 1997*
Date	Date

APPENDIX C

UNITED STATES DISTRICT COURT FOR THE
EASTERN DISTRICT OF ILLIANA

Rapid Printing Co., an
Illiana Corporation,
Plaintiff,
vs.
Scott Computers, Inc.
a foreign corporation,
Defendant

No. 98C 4722

COMPLAINT FOR DECLARATORY JUDGMENT AND OTHER RELIEF

Now comes the plaintiff, Rapid Printing Co., by its counsel, Christian, Ingrid and O'Berne, and for its Complaint against defendant, Scott Computers, Inc., states as follows:

1. Rapid Printing Co. ("Rapid"), is a corporation organized under the laws of the State of Illiana and having its principal place of business in Deerfield, Illiana. Rapid is in the business of providing printing services.

2. Scott Computers, Inc., ("Scott") is a corporation organized under the laws of the State of Delmarva and having its principal place of business in Ames. It manufactures computer systems and is engaged in the business of providing by sale or lease to its customers computer systems and support therefor.

3. Prior to February 1997, Rapid was desirous of acquiring an integrated computer system that would provide it with certain specified typesetting and remote access functions.

4. On or about February 1, 1997, representatives of Rapid met with representatives of Scott to discuss Rapid's computer requirements.

5. At that meeting and thereafter, Scott, through its agents, represented that it had a program known as Print-Rite, which fit the requirements of Rapid; more specifically, Scott represented to Rapid that Print-Rite was capable of performing the computerized composition and typesetting functions required by Rapid. Scott further represented that if Rapid leased hardware from Scott, it would provide Rapid with Print-Rite at no charge.

6. The representations made by Scott were relied upon by Rapid, and were material to Rapid's decision to purchase a computer system from Scott.

7. On or about March 17, 1997, in reliance on the aforesaid representations of Scott, which Rapid believed to be true, Rapid entered into a written lease agreement with respect to the computer system.

8. In May 1997, Scott began delivering to Rapid computer equipment.

9. The aforesaid representations of fact by Scott were knowingly false and untrue when made to Rapid in that Scott never intended to provide Rapid with a system that met Rapid's requirements.

10. Scott made the aforesaid false representations to Rapid for the purpose of inducing Rapid to enter into the lease agreement.

11. On Scott's failure to meet Rapid's requirements, Rapid repeatedly requested that Scott fulfill its representations as aforesaid, but Scott failed and refused to do so.

12. The aforesaid lease agreements, and any and all modifications thereof, were executed by Rapid based upon Rapid's belief and reliance upon the untrue and material representations made by Scott, as aforesaid.

13. The aforesaid lease agreements and any and all modifications thereof, having resulted from the fraudulent representations of Scott, are voidable at the option of Rapid.

14. By this complaint and by repeated communications from counsel for Rapid to various officers and representatives of Scott, defendant is and was advised that the plaintiff declares said lease agreement void and of no further effect.

15. In reliance on the representations of Scott, and to prepare its premises and facilities for the delivery and installation of the computer system, Rapid incurred expenses for material and labor in the amount of $150,000.

16. As a direct and proximate result of Scott's false representations, Rapid suffered a substantial loss of business in that it lost customers, sales, and profits, and further suffered a loss of its business reputation and goodwill, all in the amount of $5,000,000.

WHEREFORE, plaintiff prays that this Court enter judgment declaring the written agreement between the parties hereto be null and void, and award judgment against the defendant in the amount of $5,150,000, plus punitive damages and costs and attorneys' fees incurred in connection with this action.

Respectfully submitted,

/s/ Lane J. Christian
Attorney for Plaintiff

Lane J. Christian
Christian, Ingrid & O'Berne
222 Fountain Place
Deerfield, Illiana 84210

April 15, 1998

EXERCISE 2.8: FG&T TOWER*

Forrest, Gleason & Tewksbury (FG&T) is a 200-member law firm in the major metropolitan center of Clydesdale. The firm has been quite profitable in recent years and contemplates hiring 15 to 20 entry-level attorneys each year for the next three to five years.

Clydesdale is located on the shore of a large lake, and the firm has recently relocated its offices to a newly built lake-front tower. The managing partner of the firm, F. L. Forrest, has been approached by the developers of the office tower

*This exercise was developed for the Northwestern University Law School Negotiation Workshop by Rand Boyers, Northwestern University Law School, Class of 1986.

about the possibility of the firm purchasing the building. The developers have told Forrest, however, that they must have the firm's decision within a week or they will offer the building to one of the other major tenants.

It is certain that the firm can obtain a sizeable loan to finance the purchase. It is uncertain, however, whether Forrest can get the necessary approval of a majority of the seven-person Executive Committee. The deal would provide two major benefits. First, the building would be named FG&T Tower, which would create a high level of name recognition for the firm. Second, once the currently soft real estate market firms up, renting space in the building could be highly profitable for the firm.

While these benefits appear convincing, it is likely that some partners will object to the deal because as long as the real estate market remains soft, the payments on the loan necessary to purchase the building will drain partnership earnings, thus providing less partnership income to the partners. Furthermore, some partners believe that owning a building might detract from the firm's current high standing in the community. Law firms, they say, should provide only legal services, not office space. Thus, there is little doubt that the decision of the Executive Committee will be a close one.

There are seven members of the Executive Committee. Except for Forrest, who is a permanent member, all of the others were elected by the entire partnership and serve three-year terms. Neither Forrest nor any other member of the Executive Committee can be removed from the committee prior to the expiration of their terms, except by a majority of the partners at a general partnership meeting. Nor may the chair of the Executive Committee be removed from that position, except at a general partnership meeting. The committee is chaired by Forrest who, in addition to being managing partner, is also chair of the powerful Hiring and Promotions Committee, and head of the Corporate Department. For purposes of this meeting, Forrest has the proxy to vote on behalf of Glenn Gleason, another senior member of the Executive Committee who is involved in litigation outside the country and cannot be reached. Both Forrest and Gleason strongly support purchase of the building.

Andy Aldrich is a young partner whose great ability as a litigator has led to Aldrich's being the head of the Litigation Department at a comparatively young age. Blair Barrister is a partner in the Tax Department.

Chris Carlisle is a senior real estate partner who has been with the firm since its formation in 1963. Over the years, Carlisle has produced a lot of income for the firm and is bitter at never having been made a named partner or even selected for a position of committee or department leadership. (All of those positions are selected by the managing partner with the advice and consent of the Executive Committee.)

Dana Douglas is a middle-level litigation partner. Douglas contributes a lot of time and money to organizations providing legal assistance to minorities and has been actively campaigning for the immediate institution in the firm of an affirmative action plan. (The firm presently has nine minority associates and one minority, partner, Douglas.)

Erin Edwards, also a litigation partner, is the youngest and newest member of the Executive Committee. Edwards's career has been meteoric. Edwards made partner in only five years and is the youngest person ever to serve on the Executive Committee.

Forrest has called a special meeting of the Executive Committee to make a decision about purchasing the building. The partnership agreement permits a special meeting of the Executive Committee to discuss an issue that demands immediate attention. However, the agreement requires that the issue be resolved by the end of the meeting. Other issues *may* be discussed and even voted on, but the principal issue for which the meeting was called *must* be resolved. Such resolution will be determined by majority vote. The chair of the Executive Committee has the power to decide the order in which motions are to be voted on, but a motion that is made and seconded must be voted on by the close of the meeting. All voting will be done by secret ballot and no member of the committee may abstain. Once a motion has been voted on, it cannot be reconsidered except on a motion made by a committee member on the prevailing side of the motion, and approved by a majority of the committee.

Once a meeting of the Executive Committee has begun, no recesses or adjournments are allowed until all motions that have been made and seconded are decided. Nor, once a meeting of the Executive Committee has begun, may any members of the Executive Committee engage in private meetings or caucuses, as such behavior is regarded as inappropriate.

(Confidential information for Aldrich, Barrister, Carlisle, Douglas, Edwards, and Forrest is in the Teacher's Manual.)

EXERCISE 2.9: MEDICAL MALPRACTICE CLAIM*

A medical malpractice suit was filed by plaintiff, a jazz pianist, against a physician who injected her hand with a drug called AR-21. Lawyers for the parties have stipulated that plaintiff sought treatment from defendant for arthritic pain in the hand and that defendant administered AR-21 at the first office visit. They further agree that plaintiff returned, complaining of numbness, and that defendant advised plaintiff to let the drug wear off. After several weeks of treatment by another medical professional, the numbness did subside. AR-21 is a new drug for arthritic pain that is used by about 10 percent of physicians treating arthritis. In the complaint, plaintiff alleged negligence and battery, and sought $20,000 for the cost of therapy, $60,000 for income lost as the result of missed performances, $420,000 for pain and suffering, and $500,000 in punitive damages. Defendant's medical malpractice insurance lapsed prior to plaintiff's treatment.

Plaintiff changed lawyers after six months of litigation, and the new lawyer arranged a negotiation session with defense counsel. The lawyers have agreed to have their clients available in case they decide to ask them to participate in the negotiations (see pp. 357-360) and have stipulated that the settlement discussions will not be admissible at trial.

(Confidential information for each attorney is in the Teacher's Manual.)

*This role play was adapted, with permission, from the facts of *Tape I. Dispute Negotiation: The Thompson v. Decker Medical Malpractice Claim,* in *The Dispute Resolution and Lawyers Videotape Series* (West, 1991). Copyright © 1991 by the Curators of the University of Missouri. That tape was based upon Robert M. Ackerman, "The Case of the Weary Hand: A Negotiation Exercise for Torts," in Leonard L. Riskin and James E. Westbrook, *Instructor's Manual for Dispute Resolution and Lawyers* 287 (West, 1987).

EXERCISE 2.10: THE DONS NEGOTIATION*

General Instructions

The year is 2021 and the AIDS virus has been completely obliterated. Researchers at The Johns Hopkins University discovered a vaccine as well as a serum which cures the disease in mid-course. All children are now vaccinated for the disease shortly after birth. There has not been a case of AIDS reported in the United States since the serum was developed 18 years ago.

Five years ago, however, scientists discovered a new lethal virus, Dysfunction of the Nervous Systems, DONS. The disease can *only* be transmitted through either vaginal or anal intercourse. Unlike AIDS, it cannot be transmitted through blood transfusions. All persons who have contracted DONS have died from it within a range of four to six years. DONS can be detected in the bloodstream of the individual one to four months after entering the body, and there are highly accurate home testing kits. Thus far, there is no cure for DONS, and the only preventive measures available are abstention from sexual activity or the use of condoms.

On November 1, 2019, Chris Wilson engaged in unprotected sexual intercourse with her boyfriend of six months and contracted the DONS virus. On March 16, 2020, Chris tested positive for the virus. Upset and disillusioned, she denied that she had the disease for a period of several months.

Chris attended a social function in early June, however, where she met Pat Stevens. The two eventually became involved in a relationship and on August 2, 2020, they had sexual intercourse for the first time while staying at Chris's ranch in Montana. It was the first time in four and one-half years that Pat had engaged in intercourse.

Chris felt that Pat was a great support for her. She was able to tell Pat about the depression she felt over her youngest child Annie, who has leukemia. She told Pat that she was worried that she would not be able to meet the expenses of Annie's treatment since the insurance policy had reached its maximum, and the cost of her treatment was approximately $200,000 per year. She told Pat that it had taken her five years to save $600,000, which she had set aside for Annie's expenses. Pat thought that Chris's deep depression was simply related to the cancer-stricken child, and he tried to be as supportive as possible.

The relationship lasted for four months, during which the two had numerous sexual relations without using condoms. Chris, still in denial about contracting the virus, did not care that she may have been infecting her new boyfriend with the deadly DONS disease. Later, she didn't disclose it because it seemed the damage was probably done in all events. The relationship deteriorated, and on September 13, 2020, the two stopped dating. Their last sexual encounter was on September 2, 2020.

On January 2, 2021, Pat received a letter from Chris confessing that she had the DONS virus. In the letter, Chris told Pat that she had known she had the

* This case was created for the Harvard Negotiation Research Project by Nevan Elam and was revised by Whitney Fox. It was further revised by Bob Bordone & Jonathan Cohen of the Harvard Negotiation Research Project. Copies are available at a reasonable cost from the Program on Negotiation Clearinghouse, Pound Hall 500, Harvard Law School, Cambridge, MA 02138. Tel.: (617) 495-1684. This case may not be reproduced, revised, or translated in whole or part by any means without written permission from the Director of the Clearinghouse. Please help to preserve its usefulness by keeping it confidential. The fees charged for the use of Clearinghouse materials help to subsidize their distribution.

disease before their relationship, but that she was unable to tell Pat while they were dating. In the letter, Chris suggested that Pat be tested for DONS and expressed the hope that he would test negative. The next day, Pat purchased a home testing kit but unfortunately tested positive for the virus. Pat spent the next month in a troubled emotional state, and on February 9, 2021, he wrote to Chris and told her that he planned to sue her for the cost of treatment and other damages. Chris responded on February 20, 2021, stating that the lawsuit would not be necessary. She suggested that their lawyers negotiate an agreeable settlement.

(Confidential information for both parties is contained in the Teacher's Manual.)

References

ADLER, Robert S., and Elliot M. SILVERSTEIN (2000) "When David Meets Goliath: Dealing with Power Differentials in Negotiation," 5 *Harv. Neg. L. Rev.* 1.

ALFINI, James (1999) "Settlement Ethics and Lawyering in ADR Proceedings: A Proposal to Revise Rule 4.1," 19 *N. Ill. U. L. Rev.* 225.

AXELROD, Robert (1984) *The Evolution of Cooperation.* New York: Basic Books.

BABCOCK, Linda, and Sara LASCHEVER (2003) *Women Don't Ask: Negotiation and the Gender Divide.* Princeton, N.J.: Princeton University Press.

BASTRESS, Robert F., and Joseph D. HARBAUGH (1990) *Interviewing, Counselling, and Negotiating.* Boston: Little, Brown.

BRESLIN, J. William, and Jeffrey Z. RUBIN, eds. (1991) *Negotiation Theory and Practice.* Cambridge, Mass.: Program on Negotiation.

BRETT, Jeanne M. (1991) "Negotiating Group Decisions," 7 *Neg. J.* 291.

CONDLIN, Robert J. (1992) "Bargaining in the Dark: The Normative Incoherence of Lawyer Dispute Bargaining Role," 51 *Md. L. Rev.* 1.

EISENBERG, Melvin (1976) "Private Ordering Through Negotiation: Dispute Settlement and Rulemaking," 89 *Harv. L. Rev.* 637.

FISHER, Roger, and William URY (1981) *Getting to Yes.* New York: Penguin.

FISHER, Roger, William URY, and Bruce PATTON (1991) *Getting to Yes: Negotiating Agreement Without Giving In* (2d ed.). Boston: Houghton Mifflin.

GIFFORD, Donald G. (1989) *Legal Negotiation.* St. Paul, Minn.: West.

GENN, Hazel (1987) *Hard Bargaining: Out of Court Settlement in Personal Injury Actions.* Oxford: Clarendon Press.

HUBER, Peter (1984) "Competition, Conglomerates, and the Evolution of Cooperation," 93 *Yale L.J.* 1147.

KOLB, Deborah, and Judith WILLIAMS (2000) *The Shadow Negotiation: How Women Can Master the Hidden Agendas That Determine Bargaining Success.* New York: Simon & Schuster.

KOROBKIN, Russell (2002) *Negotiation Theory and Strategy.* New York: Aspen.

KRITZER, Herbert M. (1991) *Let's Make a Deal.* Madison: University of Wisconsin Press.

LAX, David A., and James K. SEBENIUS (1986) *The Manager as Negotiator.* New York: Free Press.

——— (2006) *3-D Negotiation.* Boston: Harvard Business School Press.

LEWICKI, Roy J., Joseph LITTERER, David M. SAUNDERS, and John W. MINTON (1993) *Negotiation* (2d ed.). Homewood, Ill.: Richard D. Irwin.

LOWENTHAL, Gary T. (1988) "The Bar's Failure to Require Truthful Bargaining by Lawyers," 2 *Geo. J. Legal Ethics* 411.

MELTSNER, Michael, and Philip G. SCHRAG (1973) "Negotiating Tactics for Legal Services Lawyers," 7 *Clearinghouse Rev.* 259.
MENKEL-MEADOW, Carrie, and Michael WHEELER (2004) *What's Fair—Ethics for Negotiators.* San Francisco: Jossey-Bass.
MNOOKIN, Robert H. (1993) "Why Negotiations Fail: An Exploration of Barriers to the Resolution of Conflict," 8 *Ohio St. J. Disp. Resol.* 235.
——— (1994) "Cooperation and Conflict Between Litigators," 12 *Alternatives* 125.
MNOOKIN, Robert H., and Ronald J. GILSON (1994) "Disputing Through Agents: Cooperation and Conflict Between Lawyers in Litigation," 94 *Colum. L. Rev.* 509.
MNOOKIN, Robert H., and Lawrence SUSSKIND, eds. (1999) *Negotiating on Behalf of Others.* Thousand Oaks: Sage.
MNOOKIN, Robert H., Scott PEPPET, and Andrew TULUMELLO (1996) "The Tension Between Empathy and Assertiveness," 12 *Neg. J.* 217.
——— (2000) *Beyond Winning: Negotiating to Create Value in Deals and Disputes.* Cambridge, Mass.: Harvard University Press.
MURNIGHAN, J. Keith (1991) *The Dynamics of Bargaining Games.* Englewood Cliffs, N.J.: Prentice-Hall.
NEALE, Margaret A., and Max H. BAZERMAN (1991) *Cognition and Rationality in Negotiation.* New York: Free Press.
NEGOTIATOR'S FIELDBOOK (2006) (A. K. Schneider and Christopher Honeyman, eds.) Washington, D.C.: ABA Section Disp. Res.
RAIFFA, Howard (1982) *The Art and Science of Negotiation.* Cambridge, Mass.: Harvard University Press.
RAIFFA, Howard, with John RICHARDSON and David METCALFE (2002) *Negotiation Analysis: The Science and Art of Collaborative Decision Making.* Cambridge, Mass.: Harvard University Press.
ROSENTHAL, Douglas (1974) *Lawyer and Client: Who's in Charge.* New York: Russell Sage.
RUBIN, Alvin B. (1975) "A Causerie on Lawyers' Ethics in Negotiation," 35 *La. L. Rev.* 577.
RUBIN, Jeffrey Z., and Frank E. A. SANDER (1988) "When Should We Use Agents? Direct vs. Representative Negotiation," 4 *Neg. J.* 395.
SANDER, Frank E. A., and Jeffrey Z. RUBIN (1988) "The Janus Quality of Negotiations: Dealmaking and Dispute Settlement," 4 *Neg. J.* 109.
SCHELLING, Thomas C. (1984) *Choice and Consequence.* Cambridge, Mass.: Harvard University Press.
SCHNEIDER, Andrea K. (2002) "Shattering Negotiation Myths: Empirical Evidence on the Effectiveness of Negotiation Style," 7 *Harv. Neg. L. Rev.* 143.
SCHNEIDER, A. K., and Christopher HONEYMAN, eds. (2006) *Negotiator's Fieldbook.* Washington, D.C.: ABA Section of Dispute Resolution.
SHELL, G. Richard (1991) "When Is It Legal to Lie in Negotiations?" *Sloan Mgmt. Rev.* 93 (Spring).
——— Richard (1999) *Bargaining for Advantage.* New York: Viking.
STONE, Douglas, Bruce PATTON, and Sheila HEEN (1999) *Difficult Conversations.* New York: Viking.
THOMPSON, Leigh (2001) *The Mind and Heart of the Negotiator* (2d ed.). Upper Saddle River, N.J.: Prentice-Hall.
URY, William (1991) *Getting Past No: Negotiating with Difficult People.* New York: Bantam Books.
URY, William, Jeanne M. BRETT, and Stephen B. GOLDBERG (1988) *Getting Disputes Resolved: Designing Systems to Cut the Costs of Conflict.* San Francisco: Jossey-Bass.
WETLAUFER, Gerald B. (1990) "The Ethics of Lying in Negotiations," 75 *Iowa L. Rev.* 1219.
WHITE, James (1980) "Machiavelli and the Bar: Ethical Limitations on Lying in Negotiation," *Am. B. Found. Res. J.* 926.
——— (1984) "The Pros and Cons of 'Getting to Yes,'" 34 *J. Legal Educ.* 115.
WILLIAMS, Gerald (1983) *Legal Negotiation and Settlement.* St. Paul: West.

Chapter 3
Mediation

Mediation is negotiation carried out with the assistance of a third party. The mediator, in contrast to the arbitrator or judge, has no power to impose an outcome on disputing parties.

Despite the lack of "teeth" in the mediation process, the involvement of a mediator alters the dynamics of negotiations. Depending on what seems to be impeding agreement (see pp. 86-87) the mediator may attempt to

- Encourage exchanges of information,
- Provide new information,
- Help the parties to understand each other's views,
- Let them know that their concerns are understood,
- Promote a productive level of emotional expression,
- Deal with differences in perceptions and interests between negotiators and constituents (including lawyer and client),
- Help negotiators realistically assess alternatives to settlement,
- Encourage flexibility,
- Shift the focus from the past to the future,
- Stimulate the parties to suggest creative settlements,
- Learn (often in separate sessions with each party) about those interests the parties are reluctant to disclose to each other, and
- Invent solutions that meet the fundamental interests of all parties.

Section A focuses on the mediation techniques that are employed in these efforts.

Some contend that the mediator changes not only the dynamics of negotiations but also the outcome. Hence they raise questions about the impact of the change. Which parties tend to gain power? Which lose? Mediation does not always result in settlement. Is the overall picture a cost-effective one for the parties? For the courts? What is the impact of mediation on the effectiveness of the justice system and the role of law? The debate over whether the public system should encourage the use of mediation by funding mediation programs, providing court referrals to increase participation, guaranteeing immunity from liability for mediators, or other means is the topic of Section B. Section C presents social science assessments of mediation. Section D focuses on how publicly supported mediation should be regulated. This is followed by Section E on professional ethics and the lawyer-mediator.

A. THE PRACTICE OF MEDIATION

Mediators' strategies vary widely. Some mediators attempt to focus the negotiations on satisfying the vital interests of each party; others focus on legal rights, sometimes providing a neutral assessment of the outcome in court or arbitration. Some encourage the active participation of both lawyers and clients; others exclude either clients or lawyers from the sessions. Some mediators endeavor to maintain neutrality; others deliberately become advocates of a particular outcome or protectors of non-parties' interests (cf. Smith, 1985).

Despite differences in approach or emphasis, experienced mediators tend to employ similar practices. In the readings that follow, Richard Salem and Nancy Rogers divide common practices into stages that include premediation or "getting to the table," the opening of mediation, the parties' opening presentations, mediated negotiations, and reaching agreement. Roger Fisher and William Ury highlight a technique they call the "one-text procedure."

This is followed by a fictitious mediation case study in which Fletcher Knebel and Gerald Clay describe the emotions of the disputants, their gradual movement toward settlement, seeming impasse, and ultimate resolution. One of the techniques used by the mediator in that case was to encourage an apology, and we discuss that technique in a note on the role of apology in dispute resolution. This is followed by notes about dealing with impasse and dealing with cultural and gender-based differences in the context of mediation.

In most contexts, the mediator and parties assume that the aim of mediation is settlement, though certainly not settlement at any cost. The parties may seek a mediator in intercultural disputes, however, with a primary aim of promoting understanding (pp. 145-146), and parties may engage mediators for public policy disputes with the hope of narrowing issues and organizing the debate (pp. 513-525). Some commentators view mediation in all contexts as valuable primarily to enhance the parties' "self-determination and party interaction or engagement" (Bush and Folger, 2005:95) and to help the parties' communication so that they understand and appreciate each other's perspectives:

> [T]he mediation process contains within it a unique potential for transforming people—engendering moral growth—by helping them wrestle with difficult circumstances and bridge human differences, in the very midst of conflict. This transformative potential stems from mediation's capacity to generate two important effects, empowerment and recognition. In simplest terms, *empowerment* means the restoration to individuals of a sense of their own value and strength and their own capacity to handle life's problems. *Recognition* means the evocation in individuals of acknowledgment and empathy for the situation and problems of others. When both of these processes are held central in the practice of mediation, parties are helped to use conflicts as opportunities for moral growth, and the transformative potential of mediation is realized [Bush and Folger, 2005:22].

The varying levels of priority given to settlement and other goals for mediation underlie disagreements about appropriate mediator approaches and techniques. Some of these disagreements are reflected in the excerpts that follow.

N. ROGERS AND R. SALEM, A STUDENT'S GUIDE TO MEDIATION AND THE LAW

7-39 (1987)

There is no "best" way to mediate a dispute. Mediation techniques vary with the parties, the conflict and the mediation program. Private sector labor mediation, for example, tends to reflect the competitive and positional nature of traditional collective bargaining negotiating and the mediator will spend considerable time working separately (caucusing) with the parties. Child custody mediation typically is a more cooperative process, at times bordering on counseling, and the mediator spends more time working with the parties together. In insurance claims mediation, where there generally is a single issue and the parties are unlikely to have a continuing relationship, mediators often expedite settlements by offering an opinion on the value of the case. While most mediation is conducted with a single mediator, some community-based programs use two-person teams. In high-volume, court- and prosecutor-affiliated programs, mediations often are concluded in less than 30 minutes, while environmental mediations may take months. . . .

Mediation is usually a by-product of failure — the inability of disputants to work out their own differences. Each party typically comes to mediation locked into a position that the other(s) will not accept. The parties distrust each other and may be angry, frustrated, discouraged or hurt. Their inability to reach a settlement may be due as much to the emotions of the case as to facts. . . .

The process experienced mediators use is simple, even in complex disputes. . . . The parties are provided a forum where they can vent their feelings while telling their "stories" so that they feel heard and understood. The mediator thus enables them to approach their conflict with clear heads and greater objectivity. They are then encouraged to disclose information they have not disclosed before, listen to things they have not heard before, open their minds to ideas they have not considered and generate ideas that may not have previously occurred to them. . . .

Mediators traditionally enter disputes with little authority, so their ability to help bring about settlements . . . depends, in part, upon the willingness of the parties to accept the mediator. Mediators typically gain this acceptance by earning the parties' trust, a process that begins with the mediator's first interaction with the disputants and continues until mediation is concluded.

Trust is attained and maintained when the mediator is perceived by the disputants as an individual who understands and cares about the parties and their disputes, has the skills to guide them to a negotiated settlement, treats them impartially, is honest, will protect each party from being hurt during mediation by the other's aggressiveness or their own perceived inadequacies, and has no interests that conflict with helping to bring about a resolution which is in the parties' best interest. Only when trust has been established can the parties be expected to be candid with the mediator, disclose their real interests and value the mediator's reactions. . . .

Effective mediators play a number of roles and use a variety of techniques, but none is more important than being a skilled listener. Careful listening may provide mediators with an understanding of the dispute, but . . . "understanding has limited utility unless the mediator can somehow convey to the parties the fact that he knows the essence of the problem. At that point and only then can he expect to be accorded confidence and respect." Mediators often convey this understanding through empathic or active listening.

Empathic listening means listening for how the parties feel as well as to what they are saying, and providing verbal and nonverbal (eye contact, facial expression, body position) feedback that lets them know the mediator understands and cares about both. An empathic mediator conveys respect to the parties, doesn't register approval or disapproval of what is being said, refrains from providing unsolicited advice and does not interrupt.

Especially in disputes where emotions run high, an empathic mediator may be the first person really to listen to what the parties have to say. When parties feel somebody is listening to them, they are more inclined to be candid and to listen to the other side of the story. As they listen, doubts tend to creep into their minds about the validity of their own assumptions and positions. Hence the parties are likely to become receptive to exploring alternatives.

While this process is sequential, in that each step leads to the next, it is also cyclical and self-reinforcing. That is, the higher the level of trust, the more information is likely to be shared. This in turn increases understanding, further raises trust levels and enhances the flow of more information and understanding. . . .

For convenience of discussion, the mediation can be divided into five stages: (A) pre-mediation or "getting to the table," (B) the opening of mediation, (C) the parties' opening presentations, (D) mediated negotiations and (E) agreement.

[A] Getting to the Table

Those who are convinced that mediation usually benefits all parties may find it disconcerting that getting the parties to agree to mediation can be the most difficult part of the process. . . .

[The authors discuss the means by which parties arrive at mediation: (1) contact with a mediator or mediation center that, in turn, contacts the other party; (2) referral of both parties by a prosecutor or court, sometimes accompanied by pressure to mediate; (3) mediator instigation; (4) legal compulsion to mediate. Compelled mediation, as well as pressure to mediate, raises issues that are discussed at pp. 404-426.]

[B] The Opening of Mediation

The mediator's opening statement varies to fit the parties and the dispute. It may be lengthy and detailed in child custody cases, as it lays the foundation for a series of mediation sessions that can span weeks or months. In insurance or commercial matters, where the parties are typically represented by others and will have no continuing relationship, the opening may be brief, dealing primarily with mediation rules, confidentiality issues and the impartiality of the mediator. In labor negotiations, where the parties typically know the process and may even know the mediator, a lengthy explanation of the rules may be unnecessary and the mediator may use a casual approach, even humor, to establish rapport.

In an interpersonal dispute, where two parties have a continuing relationship and are embroiled in a dispute that has left them emotionally distraught and distrustful, the mediator may use the following approach: After greeting and seating them, the mediator spends as much time as necessary demystifying the process. Mediation and its rules are carefully explained with emphasis on the informal and consensual nature of the process, the mediator's impartiality and the responsibility of the parties to find their own solutions. The parties are assured ample uninterrupted time to tell their stories. The limits of confidentiality may be explained, and the parties are informed that the mediator may want to meet with them alone ("caucus") as well as together in order to help bring about a settlement. At the same time, they are assured that during caucuses they will have an opportunity to discuss things they may not want to say in the presence of the other disputant. The mediator may congratulate the parties for attempting to work out their differences amicably and hold out the likelihood, based on prior experience, that the dispute can be resolved in a comparatively short time. Questions are encouraged and the mediator uses them to confirm that the parties understand the path on which they are embarking and that they agree to abide by its rules. The mediator tries to make the parties as comfortable and secure as possible. . . .

[C] The Parties' Opening Presentations

Typically, the parties are given "uninterrupted" time to describe the dispute at the conclusion of the mediator's opening. The initiator of the complaint usually begins, although the decision on who speaks first may vary, depending upon the nature of the dispute, the temperament of the parties or the policy of the mediation program. Sometimes the parties resolve the dispute after hearing each other's opening statements with minimal direction from the mediator. . . .

When the parties come to the table distraught or angry, a straight-forward presentation may not be forthcoming. Aware that people may need to deal with their feelings before they can discuss the situation clearly, some mediators provide a controlled forum for a limited venting of feelings early in the process on the theory that the expression and acknowledgment of hurts and frustrations helps to humanize the conflict, surface underlying issues that must be addressed in order to resolve the dispute and facilitate a rational discussion. . . .

The mediator typically uses the opening presentations to:

- Learn as much as possible about the parties' interests and priorities and determine whether underlying conflicts must be addressed to resolve the immediate dispute . . . ,
- Close the gap between the facts and the parties' differing perceptions of them. Frequently this occurs without the third party's intervention, but the mediator may reinforce the process ("Then you are saying, Mr. Wilson, you are not upset with the construction of the garage in Ms. Christopher's back yard, but only object to the workmen starting at 6 A.M. when you are still asleep.").
- Demonstrate positive aspects of the relationship and the goals the disputants have in common ("As I understand it from what you both said, you have been

doing business together since 1979, this relationship has been of financial benefit to both your companies, and you both would like to find a way to resolve this matter so you can keep doing business together. Is that correct?").

- Encourage and model negotiating behaviors more likely to produce settlements ("Mr. Shade, we agreed at the outset not to interrupt. You'll have as much time as you need when she is done."). . . .

[D] Mediated Negotiations

[1] Cooperative vs. Competitive Bargaining

Mediators try to prevent disputants from locking themselves into positions before they have either listened to the other party or given full thought to their own interests and needs. . . . The sooner parties declare their positions, the more likely they are to argue for them and the more difficult it becomes for them to change their minds without losing face. For that reason, mediators may avoid asking parties to express positions until after the opening presentations, and when they do, they use an approach that will produce a range of alternatives ("What do you think are some ways to settle this matter?" rather than "How much do you need to settle?").

[2] Ordering the Issues

A rational order for discussing the issues may emerge or the mediator may propose one. It often provides negotiating momentum to start with issues on which consensus appears likely. . . .

Conversely, the mediator may decide to deal with an overriding issue before any others are addressed. . . .

[3] Identifying Alternatives

Even when the parties want to settle, they usually have to work hard to identify acceptable alternatives. Potential solutions may occur to the mediator, but mediators tend to withhold them until the parties have had ample time to suggest their own ideas because the parties have more information, are better able to find an acceptable solution and are more likely to stick with a solution of their own making. . . .

When disputants are unable or unwilling to come up with their own solutions, even with discreet prompting from the mediator, the mediator may suggest alternatives. This may first be done in separate meetings with the parties. In this private setting the mediator may be able to determine what is inhibiting the flow of ideas at the table and what might be an acceptable solution. By floating ideas in caucus, the mediator avoids putting the parties in the awkward position of rejecting the mediator's proposal in front of the other disputant. At times a party will accept a mediator's suggestion, while the same proposal would be rejected if it came from the other disputant (see p. 86).

[4] OTHER MEDIATOR APPROACHES TO AVOID IMPASSE

If the parties remain in a competitive negotiating posture despite the mediator's efforts to create a cooperative environment, the mediator may have to de-emphasize the role of "empathic listener" and move into other roles. As an "agent of reality," for example, the mediator might ask a party in caucus about a reluctance to make any concessions. The mediator might ask, "Even if you are awarded the full amount in court, how long will it take until you have the money in your pocket?" The mediator might note that the other party had already made several concessions and firmly counsel that "unless you show some flexibility, it doesn't appear we will reach a settlement. . . ."

[5] HOLDING CAUCUSES

Caucuses are private meetings the mediator conducts with each party during the course of mediation. They are used to: provide an opportunity for a party to vent and cool down when emotions flare; encourage candor and get to the root of the dispute; clarify an issue; spend time alone with a party to build trust; provide time to review the issues and alternatives; encourage movement when a party is unyielding; help a party determine if a position is realistic; remind a party of the consequences of not reaching agreement; get information that may help generate or shape new alternatives; check whether a party has thought through the potential consequences of a probable agreement or separate one party from the threatening or intimidating conduct of the other. Before concluding the caucus, the mediator asks whether there is any information from that meeting which should not be disclosed to the other party. To maintain credibility, the mediator usually caucuses with all parties before bringing them back together in joint session. . . .

[E] AGREEMENT

As negotiations progress, the mediator summarizes areas of agreement to motivate the parties toward a final settlement. If the parties move to common positions, the mediator typically helps draft the agreement. . . .

The mediated agreement may be verbal or written. It may be executed on the spot or held pending review by counsel. It may be a private agreement or incorporated into a consent judgment in pending litigation. There may be an enforcement clause that provides for monitoring by the mediator or another party and specifies what the parties will do if they believe the agreement has been violated. . . .

When the parties fail to agree on all issues, the mediator may try to salvage the positive result of mediation. The parties may be able to stipulate certain facts, cooperate in discovery or agree to another way to resolve the dispute. They may have learned to negotiate better and may, in fact, settle unresolved issues themselves later.

R. FISHER AND W. URY, GETTING TO YES

118-122 (1981)

Consider the One-Text Procedure

You will probably call in a third party only if your own efforts to shift the game from positional bargaining to principled negotiation have failed. The problem you face may be illustrated by a simple story of a negotiation between a husband and wife who plan to build a new house.

The wife is thinking of a two-story house with a chimney and a bay window. The husband is thinking of a modern ranch-style house, with a den and a garage with a lot of storage space. In the process of negotiating, each asks the other a number of questions, like "What are your views on the living room?" and "Do you really insist on having it your way?" Through answering such questions, two separate plans become more and more fixed. They each ask an architect to prepare first a sketch and then more detailed plans, ever more firmly digging themselves into their respective positions. In response to the wife's demand for some flexibility, the husband agrees to reduce the length of the garage by one foot. In response to his insistence on a concession, the wife agrees to give up a back porch which she says she had always wanted, but which did not even appear on her plan. Each argues in support of one plan and against the other. In the process, feelings are hurt and communication becomes difficult. Neither side wants to make a concession since it will likely lead only to requests for more concessions.

This is a classic case of positional bargaining. If you cannot change the process to one of seeking a solution on the merits, perhaps a third party can. More easily than one of those directly involved, a mediator can separate the people from the problem and direct the discussion to interests and options. Further, he or she can often suggest some impartial basis for resolving differences. A third party can also separate inventing from decision-making, reduce the number of decisions required to reach agreement, and help the parties know what they will get when they do decide. One process designed to enable a third party to do all this is known as the *one-text procedure.*

In the house-designing negotiation between husband and wife, an independent architect is called in and shown the latest plans reflecting the present positions of the husband and the wife. Not all third parties will behave wisely. One architect, for example, might ask the parties for clarification of their positions, press them for a long series of concessions, and make them even more emotionally attached to their particular solutions. But an architect using the one-text procedure would behave differently. Rather than ask about their positions he asks about their interests: not how big a bay window the wife wants, but why she wants it. "Is it for morning sun or afternoon sun? Is it to look out or look in?" He would ask the husband, "Why do you want a garage? What things do you need to store? What do you expect to do in your den? Read? Look at television? Entertain friends? When will you use the den? During the day? Weekends? Evenings?" And so forth.

The architect makes clear he is not asking either spouse to give up a position. Rather, he is exploring the possibility that he might be able to make a recommendation to them — but even that is uncertain. At this stage he is just trying to learn all he can about their needs and interests.

Afterwards, the architect develops a list of interests and needs of the two spouses ("morning sun, open fireplace, comfortable place to read, room for a shop, storage for snowblower and medium-sized car," and so on). He asks each spouse in turn to criticize the list and suggest improvements on it. It is hard to make concessions, but it is easy to criticize.

A few days later the architect returns with a rough floor plan. "Personally, I am dissatisfied with it, but before working on it further I thought I would get your criticisms." The husband might say, "What's wrong with it? Well, for one thing, the bathroom is too far from the bedroom. I don't see enough room for my books. And where would overnight guests sleep?" The wife, too, is asked for her criticism of the first sketch.

A short time later the architect comes back with a second sketch, again asking for criticism. "I've tried to deal with the bathroom problem and the book problem, and also with the idea of using the den as a spare bedroom. What do you think about this?" As the plan takes shape, each spouse will tend to raise those issues most important to him or to her, not trivial details. Without conceding anything, the wife, for example, will want to make sure that the architect fully understands her major needs. No one's ego, not even that of the architect, is committed to any draft. Inventing the best possible reconciliation of their interests within the financial constraints is separated from making decisions and is free of the fear of making an overhasty commitment. Husband and wife do not have to abandon their positions, but they now sit side by side, at least figuratively, jointly critiquing the plans as they take shape and helping the architect prepare a recommendation he may later present to them.

And so it goes, through a third plan, a fourth, and a fifth. Finally, when he feels he can improve it no further, the architect says, "This is the best I can do. I have tried to reconcile your various interests as best I could. Many of the issues I have resolved using standard architectural and engineering solutions, precedent, and the best professional judgment I can bring to bear. Here it is. I recommend you accept this plan."

Each spouse now has only one decision to make: yes or no. In making their decisions they know exactly what they are going to get. And a yes answer can be made contingent on the other side's also saying yes. The one-text procedure not only shifts the game away from positional bargaining, it greatly simplifies the process both of inventing options and of deciding jointly on one. . . .

The one-text procedure is a great help for two-party negotiations involving a mediator. It is almost essential for large multilateral negotiations. One hundred and fifty nations, for example, cannot constructively discuss a hundred and fifty different proposals. Nor can they make concessions contingent upon mutual concessions by everybody else. They need some way to simplify the process of decision-making. The one-text procedure serves that purpose.

Question

3.1 Based on mediator observations, Chris Honeyman (1990) argues that effective mediators have expertise in the subject matter of the dispute. Others disagree. The District of Columbia Superior Court matched the mediator's substantive expertise and the substantive nature of the case. The court's research indicates that matching does not improve settlement rates, but that mediators prefer to handle cases within their areas of expertise.* Research in four Ohio counties also shows no significantly higher settlement rates when the mediator had substantive expertise. At the same time, mediators with substantive expertise were more likely to evaluate the merits of the case, and the lawyers rated mediators with substantive expertise as more competent (Wissler, 1997). Recently proposed mediator certification programs focus on training, education, and mediation experience, not substantive expertise (Cole, 2005). Should substantive expertise be a part of a mediator's qualifications to serve in a court-connected program?

F. KNEBEL AND G. CLAY, BEFORE YOU SUE†

87-133 (1987)

[Six weeks ago, Rosemary Wofford was discharged by her brother, Stephen Holloway, the owner of Holloway Interiors, from her position as manager of Holloway Interiors' Princeton, New Jersey store. Contending that the discharge violated her employment contract, Wofford went to attorney Mara Bianchi for advice. At her urging, she agreed to mediation, and she and Bianchi are about to meet with Holloway and his attorney, Pat Cavanaugh. The four of them have just seated themselves in the room where the mediation will take place.]

. . . The mediator walks in a moment later. Seymour F. Weinstein is a large friendly man with a craggy face that no one would call handsome. . . . Weinstein shucks his jacket, hangs it over the chair at the end of the table, and gestures toward the seats on either side of him. "No protocol here. Let's have Mr. Holloway on one side with his lawyer and Mrs. Wofford and her attorney on the other side. Take your pick."

When the contending pairs have seated themselves after some hesitation over location, Weinstein begins. "First, . . . as to the style here. Everything's informal. No taking of oaths, no rules of evidence, no testifying and cross-examination. None of that courtroom routine. In no way is this a trial. This is a discussion. . . . Unless you object, I'll use first names and please call me Seymour. For that matter, you're welcome to use my nickname, Cy. . . .

Bianchi concludes by noting that her client has reduced her request for damages to $500,000, down from the original $750,000 as set out in the first letter to her brother. "We wanted to enter these talks in a spirit of cooperation." However, the new figure is completely justified, she contends, when one considers lost salary and bonuses of almost four years plus compensation for the severe injury done to Wofford's professional career. The sum, she says, does not include any punitive damages that might be obtained in a court action.

"Thank you." Weinstein turns to Wofford. "Do you have anything to add?"

"I certainly do. Mara says I was disheartened when Stephen fired me. Disheartened! I was crushed. I had worked ten and eleven hours a day in that store." She speaks with heat and color rises in her cheeks. "I spent plenty of damn Sundays in the place too. I gave that shop everything I had and I boosted profits when friends said it couldn't be done. And then to be fired out of hand, not a word of warning — "

*Telephone interview, Melinda Ostermeyer, Director, Multidoor Division, District of Columbia Supreme Court, October 10, 1991.

†With the permission of the authors, some names and pronouns have been changed in this excerpt.

"That's not true!" Holloway shouts.

Weinstein raises a palm like a traffic policeman. "Hold it. Remember our rule. You'll have your turn. . . . Go ahead, Rosemary."

"No word of warning, no apology, no nothing. Just bang, not even a thank-you, ma'am. God, the way he treated me, you'd think we were back in the Middle Ages with master and serf or something."

"Anything else?"

"Yes. I'm here because Mara thought it might work. But I'm putting everyone on notice. If I don't get a decent settlement for what happened, I intend to sue."

"Both sides reserve the right to go to litigation," says Weinstein. "That's part of the agreement here. . . . All right, Pat, let's hear how you and your client look at this matter."

"Cy, we think Mrs. Wofford has no cause at all for action." Cavanaugh shrugs and throws open her hands, a gesture of gentle innocence rudely wronged. "Here's a sister who goes to work for her brother. She changes the chain's image, hurts sales in other stores and so she doesn't work out, and he lets her go. That's all there is to it. So what's the big deal? This kind of thing, as unfortunate as it may be for the person let out, happens thousands of times every day in this country. That's the common sense view of this matter. As for the law, it's squarely on our side." . . .

Cavanaugh then expands on her position paper's contention that far from owing his sister $750,000—"or the five hundred thousand they've so quickly come down to"—Holloway should be paid $200,000 to recompense him for the slump in revenues caused by Rosemary's damage to the chain's image. . . .

"Okay, I think I have the picture from both sides," says Weinstein. "Let's take a ten-minute break and then I'll caucus with the complainants. So Pat and Stephen, if you want to take a stroll, plan on being back here at eleven o'clock when I'll confer with you two."

Weinstein solicits legal arguments by counsel at the outset. Law professor Dwight Golann defends this practice:

> First, parties experience the psychological benefit of listening to their counsel . . . argue their case to their opponents. Second, both the lawyers and the parties hear a direct, unvarnished summary of the strengths of the other side's case. . . . Third, the experience of arguing facilitates the rest of the process by focusing the participants on the facts of the controversy and on the legal principles that should be applied. Fourth, when you ask each side to begin by presenting the facts and legal principles in a controlled manner, the implied message is that rational discussion—not making offers and demands—is the right way to negotiate. Fifth, preparing for an argument forces each side to assess its theories and key facts in light of the discovery to date (Golann, 1996:45-46).

What are the potential disadvantages of this approach?

Rosemary Wofford and Mara Bianchi make use of the lavatories, then chat for a few minutes until Seymour Weinstein beckons them back into the conference room.

He asks them to sit on either side of him while he takes his seat at the end of the long oak table.

Weinstein opens with a request. "Do you mind," he asks Bianchi, "if I speak directly to Rosemary?"

"Not at all," Mara replies. "Thanks for asking, but no need to go through me. This is her show." . . .

"Could you tell me exactly what took place when he dismissed you?"

"Yes, you ought to know that." She is eager to talk about the episode. "It'll tell you a great deal about Stephen. . . . I had just opened the store at nine-thirty on a Monday morning when he called from New York. He said—and I remember very clearly his first words—he said, 'Rosemary, it has become clear that we can no longer work together. I'm requesting that you leave our employ as of the close of business this Friday.'

"It was like being hit on the forehead with a mallet. I couldn't say a thing for a time, but when I got myself together, I asked him why and he said my actions had 'cheapened' the Holloway Interiors name. . . .

"I was so shook, I wasn't even angry, just kind of numb. I couldn't figure it. I did say that we had a five-year contract, in case he'd forgotten. Oh, he knew about that, but he said I had 'breached' the contract by my actions in buying 'less than high-quality merchandise.' When he used the word 'breached,' I got the idea that he had talked to a lawyer before calling me.

"Of course, I was in a state of shock. . . . I burst out crying and was a mess for the rest of the day. I remember that I called Stephen back about ten-thirty and asked him if he didn't have any more to say to me. I meant, you know, as family. After all, he had just fired his sister without so much as a single 'I'm sorry' or anything. He just said that our merchandising ideas were too far apart and that I did not share his goals for the company. Nothing personal, no apology, no sorry, just zap like that.

"Seymour, I've never been so hurt in my life. Not just the dismissal, but that my own brother would do it that way, cold and unfeeling. God, even in the big anonymous corporations, the personnel officer tries to be decent when he has to kick somebody out."

Weinstein takes a pocket-size notebook from his hip pocket and jots down a note. "I understand how you felt. I'm wondering now how you'd feel if your brother apologized at this late date for the manner, if not the reasons, for firing you?"

"I'd feel like he was putting me on—if he ever could bring himself to do it. Or I'd figure he was trying to get some advantage in these sessions here." . . .

Weinstein draws her out some more on her ideas about working in the future. They chat for some time and she concludes by voicing a fervent hope that she can get another challenging job in the home furnishings field where she wants to make a career for the next fifteen years or so.

"But of course after the way Stephen has been talking about me in the industry," she says, "that's going to be hard. Believe me, he's not giving his sister any ringing endorsement."

"What if we could get a pledge from him that he would not say anything belittling or disparaging about you from now on? Would that be a major point with you?"

She brightens. "Indeed it would."

"What if we could get him to write a good reference for you?"

"Oh, la-la, that'll be the day." She tosses her head with a mocking laugh. "You get that, Seymour, and I'll recommend you for sainthood."

"Nice idea, but wrong religion. Besides, I look strange enough without a halo. . . . Just two more questions, Rosemary, and remember that what we say in this room stays right here. How old are you?"

"Fifty-three."

"Lastly. If you could wave a fairy's wand and waft yourself into the best of all possible situations, what would it be? What would you consider an ideal life for yourself from now on?"

. . . She tilts her head as she reflects. . . . "I'd like my own home furnishings shop that I could run as I wish. I've got a lot of ideas and I think I could make a success of it, maybe build my own chain in a few years. And no snob appeal stuff, either." She laughs. "Well, not much, anyway."

Weinstein turns to Mara Bianchi on his left. "Mara, now that we've got most all the facts at hand, I'd like to explore your client's position with you. Let me think out loud here just a bit. You check me if I misstate anywhere."

"Shoot."

The mediator takes ten minutes to sum up the highlights of the case, stressing the contract and dismissal, . . . the degree to which Holloway Interiors suffered a tarnishing of its image, and how much harm had been done to Wofford's career by her discharge.

"To start with, Mara, I can't see five hundred thousand dollar damages here. Oh, sure, you might get one jury out of a hundred to go up that much, but look at the average jury, no. You're way too high. And let me tell you why I think so." He glances at Rosemary as well as her attorney.

"First off, age is a factor here. Rosemary, you have about fifteen good career years ahead of you, maybe one or two more. Now unfortunately . . . as healthy as you appear, you are at that stage of life where things can happen to you, although not as much as at my age, thank God. So, even if we concede that the discharge injured your career, it's not as though you had thirty working years ahead of you.

"Second, Mara, has Mrs. Wofford's career in home furnishings actually been hurt all that much? We don't really know, do we, because she hasn't returned to the job market yet? My guess is that a woman with her credentials and background—she boosted earnings in a difficult situation—would get a job with relative ease."

"But one of comparative executive responsibility?" asks Bianchi quickly. "That's the question here."

"I quickly realize that." Weinstein nods. "But we haven't tested that, have we? So we just have to take the common sense view that in today's employment picture, [a] capable woman with know-how and friends in the industry could make a fairly decent connection for herself." He hesitates. "What's the big grin for, Mara?"

"Your comment," the lawyer replies. "Cy, in one sentence, you've just stated what in litigation would require reams of case citations and pretrial statements and hours of argument without ever arriving at a definite conclusion."

Weinstein talks some more about Wofford's current economic situation. "What I'm getting around to is this," he says at last. "What if I could get a pledge out of

Holloway, one that would be written into any final agreement, that henceforth he would say nothing disparaging about his sister?"

Mediator Weinstein questions Wofford concerning her future employment plans and concerns. He asks whether a pledge not to belittle her would meet her concerns about getting a job. The question fits into a mediator orientation that law professor Leonard Riskin has labeled "broad" and "facilitative." By "broad," Professor Riskin refers to mediator action that focuses the parties beyond the possible legal action. By "facilitative," the mediator assumes party choice once the mediator "clarif[ies] and . . . enhance[s] communication . . . in order to help them decide what to do" (Riskin, 1996:24).

A few moments later, Weinstein states to Wofford's lawyer that he cannot "see" $500,000 in damages. The statement about damages falls within Riskin's definitions of "narrow" and "evaluative" mediation in that the mediator guides the parties to view settlement in terms of the likely outcome of litigation and provides an assessment of that outcome (Riskin, 1996:26).

Was it appropriate for Weinstein to give an evaluation? If so, should the evaluation have been done differently? Commentators disagree:

Law professor Dwight Golann: "Properly performed, a neutral evaluation can be a major force in producing an agreement. Recourse to this strategy assumes, however, that the impasse is based in large part on a disagreement about the merits and that a less extreme approach will not be effective. [T]here is a real danger that a poorly performed or badly timed evaluation will derail the entire settlement process" (Golann, 1996:53).

Law professor Lela Love: "[T]he evaluative tasks . . . not only divert the mediator away from facilitation, but also can compromise the mediator's neutrality . . . because the mediator will be favoring one side in his or her judgment. . . . With an evaluator, disputants . . . are in a competitive mind-set seeking to capture the evaluator's favor and win the case. . . . If it is acceptable or customary for mediators to give opinions on likely court outcomes or the merits of particular legal claims or defenses, then only lawyers and substantive experts will be competent to mediate. . . . So-called 'evaluative mediation' pulls mediation away from creativity and into an adversarial frame" (Love, 1997:939-941, 945).

Law professor Robert A. Baruch Bush: "Why focus mediation practice solely on the objective of speedily and cheaply reaching a settlement—or reaching a good, creative, fair or optimal settlement? If these were the only valued products of mediation, it might make sense for mediators to focus on arm twisting, case evaluation, deal-making or problem-solving. But the evidence suggests that there are other products of the process that parties value equally or even more highly [including a sense of empowerment and a recognition of the other persons and their perspectives]" (Bush 1996a:29).

Marjorie Aaron, formerly executive director, Harvard Program on Negotiation: "[T]he mediation community has been somewhat coy on the issue of mediators providing evaluation of legal disputes. [M]ainstream writings of mediator techniques . . . commonly describe and approve of behaviors such as 'probing for difficult questions,' 'reality testing,' or 'providing a dose of reality.' These implicitly recognize that impasse is often caused by the parties' failure to analyze and evaluate the alternatives in a rigorous and realistic way. . . . In practice, a tough question seldom leads to an epiphany in an overzealous, overcommitted trial counsel or client. Moreover, thinking of a mediator's obligations to provide feedback on the parties' analysis as limited to hard questions, reality testing, and scattered pieces of feedback leads to sloppy practice—it relieves the mediator of responsibility for thinking through a comprehensive analysis with the parties" (Aaron and Hoffer, 1996:269-270).

"Of course, that would be a big step forward," says Bianchi. "Wouldn't you agree, Rosemary?"

"Oh, yes. That would help. Definitely."

"But in money terms? If I could get you a nondisparagement pledge, would you be willing to reduce your demands?"

"I could recommend that, assuming it was a straight good-faith promise without any cute hedging. What's your reaction, Rosemary?"

"I'm inclined to follow your advice. Sure, if Stephen made an honest promise like that, I'd be willing to cut down on the money."

"How much? Would you authorize me to tell the other side that you'd drop to four hundred thousand with that kind of promise?"

Bianchi looks questioningly at Rosemary.

"What do you think?" she asks in response.

"I'd say yes, provided we approve the proposed wording."

"Okay then, on that condition." Rosemary nods. "I want to see just what he'd promise."

Weinstein grasps the edge of the table. "All right, that'll permit me to take something concrete to the caucus with the other side. If we can get a comparable measure of movement from them, I'd say we'd done a good morning's work. We'll see. . . . And Rosemary, I'm going to try for that letter of recommendation."

"Good luck." She shakes her head. "As I said, that'll put you up there with the other workers of miracles."

In the caucus with Stephen Holloway and his attorney, Weinstein . . . starts off in a cheerful, upbeat manner.

"I'm happy to tell you that we already have some major yielding from the other side, provided they can get a promise from you people, a quite reasonable promise in my view."

"What do they want?" Cavanaugh is promptly suspicious.

"A simple pledge from your client that he would not at any time disparage or comment negatively on Rosemary Wofford's abilities as a home furnishings executive."

"And what's the major yielding?" asks Cavanaugh.

"They'll reduce their demands to four hundred thousand dollars. In short, you're getting a hundred thousand for a promise not to do what you probably wouldn't do anyway. I call that a bargain."

"I'm certainly willing to make that promise," Holloway says quickly.

"Good, that's our first movement." Weinstein plucks at his shirt sleeves. "Now I'd like to get to know something about you, Stephen." . . .

What advantages did Weinstein gain by starting with the pledge when neither party made this demand?

Holloway responds with some eagerness and soon he's rattling on about his business. . . . It is a good fifteen minutes before he finishes and Weinstein turns to Cavanaugh for a discussion of legal points. After a few exchanges, Weinstein says that he thinks their request for $200,000 damages from Wofford "just doesn't belong in this ballpark."

"My hunch is, Pat, that you just tossed that in as an extra bargaining chip," says Weinstein. "Could we start off by disposing of that? You must realize that under the circumstances—a quite valid contract broken, for one thing—no court in the country would ask Rosemary to pay you a dollar, let alone two hundred thousand of them."

Cavanaugh chews on her lip. "In light of the other side's full-scale retreat from their original asking price, I think I can recommend to Stephen that we not insist on that figure. Stephen?"

"You're in charge of the dollars and cents, Pat. You're the expert, not me."

Cavanaugh beams as she spreads her arms. "Now Cy, what more could a lawyer ask of her client?" She bows to Holloway. "I'm putting you up for the Wise-Man-of-the-Year Award."

"May I take it then that you've withdrawn the request?" asks Weinstein.

"Subject to reactivation should we go to litigation, of course."

"Of course. That's always understood here." Weinstein leans across the table. "All right; now let's talk real money. If I could guarantee prompt acceptance, what would you offer Rosemary at this moment? What'll you pay to walk out of here right now with an agreement in your pocket?"

Cavanaugh nods with a grin. "I figured you'd ask that, Cy, at just about this time." She glances at her wristwatch. "Eleven forty-five A.M. And in just about that way. As a matter of fact, Stephen and I discussed the situation last night." She lists the expenses they'd face if they prepared for trial, legal and auxiliary costs, charges against the business for Stephen's lost time and energy, the embarrassment of sister fighting brother, the risk of Holloway Interiors being damaged by some unforeseen testimony.

"In light of everything," Cavanaugh concludes, "and not for an instant admitting any blame on our part, but solely to get rid of a nuisance complaint that has some unsavory potential to it, we are willing to make a walk-away offer of fifty thousand dollars."

"Would that include a written pledge not to denigrate Rosemary in any way?"

"From my standpoint, yes." Cavanaugh looks at Holloway. "Stephen?"

"Absolutely." Holloway nods emphatically.

"What about a letter of recommendation for Rosemary?"

Holloway shakes his head just as emphatically. "Absolutely not."

Weinstein sighs. "That may cause problems." He rises, looks from Cavanaugh to Holloway, then stretches. "Still, I think we're making progress." He's in a good mood as he puts on his jacket. "Let's get the others in here for a minute."

Weinstein summons Wofford and Bianchi and they all stand in the conference room. "I just want to tell all of you that our work is paying off. Stephen Holloway has put a solid fifty thousand dollar offer on the table along with a promise to give a written pledge not to disparage Rosemary Wofford in any way. He has also withdrawn his demand for two hundred thousand. Mrs. Wofford, on her part, has reduced her asking sum to four hundred from five hundred thousand. So after three hours' work, we've squeezed the difference between you down to three hundred and fifty thousand—or just half of what it was when we walked in here."

He looks about the room. "So I consider that real headway. If we can do as well this afternoon, we might even wrap this thing up in a couple of days. So now let's break for lunch and be back here at one-fifteen." . . .

Weinstein notes the changes in the parties' positions, but generally makes little use of two common mediator techniques: summarization and explicit ordering of the issues. In research on small claims mediation, communications professor Victor Wall and researcher Marcia Dewhurst state that frequent summarization correlates with higher settlement rates:

> A third party's summarizing . . . has six beneficial effects. First, simply by controlling the floor and the topic, the mediator exerts control. . . . Second, . . . the mediator determines both the way in which those issues are discussed and the range of resolution possibilities. . . Third, the perception that one's ideas are being understood as a result . . . might well be associated with how satisfied disputants are with the mediator and the mediation process. Fourth, . . . mediator [summaries] often highlight points of agreement. . . . Fifth, . . . a mediator may remove from the disputants some of the psychological burden of initiating concessions. . . . Sixth, . . . the mediator can encourage parties to think about the relative costs and advantages of reaching an agreement . . . (Wall and Dewhurst, 1991:67).

Would you expect summarization to have similar benefits if used in the context of mediation of business disputes?

Mediators often use summarization to move to a forward-looking agenda after the parties conclude their versions of past events. Mediator Karl Slaikeu gives this example:

> As I listened to each of you in our private meetings, I took notes on significant themes that you each want to address. With your permission [granted ahead of time by each party], I can summarize them now as a possible agenda for our meeting. First, you both expressed a desire to get closure on that unpleasant telephone interaction that occurred last week. Second, there is the issue of job descriptions—what should they be? Third, there is the issue of budget cuts, and what to do about them. Would either of you like to add to the list, or correct anything? [Assist parties in completing the agenda.] Should we start with the first item? (Slaikeu, 1996:138-139.)

If Weinstein decided to summarize and list the issues, what should he say? What are the advantages and disadvantages of doing so under the facts of this mediation?

When Weinstein returns, Wofford says that after consulting with Bianchi she has decided to reduce her monetary demand by $25,000 and is now asking "only" $375,000. . . . "That isn't as much reduction as I'd hoped," he says. "I don't think either you or Mara has yet made a realistic forecast of what you could expect to get from a jury. From my experience with juries, only a rare, rare one would award you that much in this kind of case."

They discuss the figure for a good half hour before Bianchi says: "Of course, Cy, if Stephen Holloway will give his sister a good letter of recommendation, we would consider that equivalent to a bit of money."

"How much would the letter be worth? Is it a hundred thousand dollar letter?" Weinstein bores in.

"It might be." Bianchi eyes the ceiling. "All depends on what the letter says, how strong the recommendation is."

"Okay, I'll try the other side again now. Send in Stephen and Pat, please."

The mediator radiates confidence and pleasure as he greets the home furnishings executive and his lawyer. "Once more, I can report progress." He talks in broad generalities for a few minutes. "So, while their monetary concession is a modest one, twenty-five thousand, bringing their total demand down to three hundred and seventy-five thousand, they've also dropped an especially revealing hint." Weinstein has learned the value of suspense in his dealings.

"A hint?" Cavanaugh snaps at the bait. "What's the revealing hint?"

Weinstein leans forward, lowering his voice as if about to convey a secret: "I got the clear impression that one of Rosemary's major goals in these sessions is to come away with a strong letter of recommendation from you, Stephen. She wants to go back to work as a manager or executive in home furnishings and a letter from a person of your stature would be worth a great deal to her."

"Worth how much?" asks Cavanaugh quickly.

"No, no," says Stephen Holloway just as quickly. "I don't intend to trade a letter of recommendation for some reduction in her demands for money. It's a matter of integrity. She either deserves a recommendation or she doesn't and money doesn't enter the equation." . . .

They discuss Wofford's business talents and the possibilities of a letter of recommendation for a solid hour without nearing a consensus. It becomes apparent that Cavanaugh is quite willing to trade a letter for a substantial reduction in Wofford's money demands, but her client adamantly refuses to let his sister "buy a recommendation from me." . . .

Weinstein looks at his wristwatch. A few minutes before five. He risks a shot.

"Look, we're right up against quitting time and I'm beginning to wonder just how much good faith bargaining we've got here. The other side made a modest concession this afternoon. You've made none at all. I'd like to ask a blunt question: Stephen, do you want an agreement to come out of these sessions?"

"Yes, I do." He says it with emphasis. "I do not want my company taken to court." He glances at Cavanaugh. "But that doesn't mean, on the other hand, that I'm willing to give away Holloway Interiors just to stay out of court. Oh no. I'll fight if I have to. Any agreement here has to be fair."

"Right." The mediator opens his palms once more. "But what are you giving me to take back to the other side? This afternoon you haven't budged an inch."

Holloway gets up and beckons Cavanaugh. "Pardon us, just a minute, Mr. Weinstein." The two confer in whispers at the end of the table while the mediator reflects that Holloway is the only participant who has yet to call him "Seymour" or "Cy." He thinks that of the two disputants, he prefers Wofford by a wide margin, but no sooner does he become conscious of the thought than he bans it. He knows from experience that he can never afford to take sides, that to do so might influence his behavior subconsciously and thus hamper chances of an agreement.

What caused Weinstein to prefer Wofford "by a wide margin"? Consider community mediator Jennifer Beer's suggestion as to one common source of bias:

> Mediators may be drawn to disputants who talk easily, cooperate with the mediation process, show willingness to compromise or apologize . . . (Beer et al., 1982:55).

"Cy," says Cavanaugh when the two return to their places. "As a token of our hope to get an agreement, we've decided to raise our offer to sixty-five thousand."

"Good." It is much less than Weinstein expected, but at this late hour he'll take anything. "And how about a letter? Will you at least consider one, Stephen?"

Holloway pulls at his chin as he thinks. "I'll do this, I'll promise to think it over this evening. I want to review in my own mind just what her talents are." . . .

Mediator Seymour Weinstein has a brisk businesslike air when the battling brother and sister and their lawyers meet him at 10 A.M. to begin the second day of mediation. He summarizes the situation in his customary optimistic vein, then faces Holloway.

"Can you tell us what you've decided about the letter of recommendation, Stephen?"

The president of Holloway Interiors, cool, controlled, and precise of speech, nods with a tight smile. Today he is wearing a different three-piece suit, this one of a pale blue summerweight material as elegantly tailored as yesterday's. "I've come to the conclusion that it would be a mistake to give a letter of recommendation priority here. My main concern is to clear the decks of Mrs. Wofford's totally unjustified claim for damages. I consider that claim outrageous in any amount. I dismissed her because she defied orders. No business can operate with that kind of insubordination."

"Stephen — " Mara Bianchi begins.

"No." Holloway cuts off Wofford's lawyer. "Let me finish. We have offered sixty-five thousand dollars to get rid of this matter. Even that I feel is a kind of blackmail." His temper is rising. "She threatens to sue me and the only way I can protect myself is to shell out money to buy her off. That's the trouble with our legal system. The innocent get hauled into court and then have to pay blackmail or else spend weeks and months mired in a swamp of legal actions."

"Stephen!" Wofford shouts. "Damn it, you broke a contract when you fired me."

Weinstein raises a hand. "Rosemary, please. You've given your word not to interrupt." He takes command. "Now I think it's unfortunate that we've slipped back into accusations. I thought you two got all of that out of your systems yesterday." He continues in similar vein, trying to pacify the combatants, for several minutes. "The fact is," he concludes, "that you've both told us in straightforward terms that you want to reach an agreement here. I believe that you do. So please, humor me by throwing all those angry charges overboard. We'll make progress if you both keep your eyes on the goal — a written agreement that will dispose of this matter."

Should Weinstein have intervened earlier in this emotional exchange? Consider mediator Christopher Moore's advice:

> Venting [emotions] in joint session has value only if it provides a productive physiological release for one or more parties without damaging the delicate relationship between disputants, or if it serves to educate a party about the source or intensity of emotion around a particular issue. When venting is conducted to punish another party, it will probably result in a deterioration of the relationship of the parties. When this occurs, the mediator should encourage the party to hold a caucus . . . (Moore, 1996:168).

"My client made the last move here, Cy," says Pat Cavanaugh when the mediator finishes. "Last evening he offered sixty-five thousand to walk away from this. We'd like to know, does Mrs. Wofford accept?" The lawyer fixes her gaze on Wofford.

"I most decidedly do not. Do you need an explanation?"

"We can skip that, Rosemary," says Weinstein. "Now I'd like to caucus with you and Mara. My last session was with Stephen. So could you two please leave now. I'll get back to you in a half hour or so."

When seated with Mara Bianchi and Rosemary Wofford, Weinstein cautions them against discouragement. "My hunch is that a letter of recommendation is still possible. You'll note that Stephen used the word 'priority.' He won't give the letter 'priority' because he first wants to clear up the money question. But he stopped short of saying he'd never write a letter."

"He just reverted to type," says Wofford caustically. "He started blowing his top again. He knows he's in the wrong and that's his way of defending himself."

Weinstein remains silent for a few moments while he toys with his notebook and fountain pen. "Rosemary, yesterday you gave a graphic description of the time your brother discharged you. I got the impression that it was the manner of the act, rather than the act itself, that hurt you the most. Am I right about that?"

"Absolutely." She taps the table. "Oh, of course, I thought he had no reason on earth to fire me and I resented it — deeply. But it was the rude, really cruel way that he did it." Suddenly she is blinking back a tear and dabbing at her eyes with a handkerchief. "I just can't imagine me treating him that way. . . . Well, so much for family."

As the mediator jots something in his notebook, she asks: "Why do you ask, Seymour?"

"I'm just not sure myself." He pauses, gazes upward. "I just happened to think of what you said yesterday. I suppose it's that I find the road to an agreement is always smoother if I can get a good fix on the psychology and character of both parties. Businesspeople come in here to mediate money matters, but actually there are often personal differences that trouble them as much as the money. Cash becomes merely a measurement in settling a lot of other things." . . .

They talk some more and then Weinstein says that he gave considerable thought the previous night to their $375,000 offer and concluded that in light of Holloway's increased offer of $65,000, "they could do much better." He takes some papers from the inner breast pocket of his jacket, which hangs on the chair behind him. "I happened to have these statistics from another contract mediation I did last month." He spreads the papers on the table and invites attention to them. "These are average and mean jury awards in contract disputes correlated on this graph here with the original demands of the plaintiffs."

As they study the scrawled numbers and inspect the graph, Seymour says that although the data are confusing, it would appear that the great bulk of jury awards for cases in which the plaintiffs asked damages in the range of Rosemary's demands fell far below the asking prices. "Of course, you get a few million-plus awards in there that throw the averages out of whack. But certainly, a look at these figures gives little hope that you'd get three seventy-five from a jury."

"Can I tell you something in confidence, Cy?" asks Bianchi.

"Of course. As I said at the outset, nothing said in confidence goes to the other party—at least not through me."

"I told Rosemary the day she brought her problem to me that I thought the case was worth in the neighborhood of two hundred thousand, that she'd get about that from a jury or a settlement on the eve of trial or at mediation, for that matter."

"Are you telling me that you'd take two hundred thousand to end this case?"

Bianchi laughs. "Hey, Cy, you close in as fast as a boxer. . . . Would we call it quits for two hundred thousand? I can't tell you that. Depends. We would promise utmost consideration. Now that's strictly between us."

"And for the record?" Weinstein cocks his head as he waits.

"Last evening before we quit, Stephen and Pat raised their offer to sixty-five thousand. Rosemary and I discussed the whole situation this morning at breakfast. We feel that their fifteen thousand dollar increase, while completely unsatisfactory—paltry stuff, really—does show intent to bridge the gap between us. In return, we're willing to reduce our demand for damages by fifty thousand. So Rosemary authorizes you to tell Stephen and Pat that we now ask only three hundred and twenty-five thousand."

The mediator nods and gets up quickly. "Thanks. Would you please send in the other side. I hope to keep this momentum going until there's no gap at all between you."

But Weinstein's hope founders shortly before noon. He tries many of the tools in the mediator's bag, but can fetch Stephen Holloway no higher than $75,000. This $10,000 increase arouses neither excitement nor gratitude in Rosemary Wofford and she refuses, under Bianchi's advice, to reduce her demand to less than $315,000. . . .

Weinstein, dejected, plans to sneak off for lunch by himself. He is putting on his rumpled jacket when an idea strikes. God, why hadn't he thought of that before?

He turns to Bianchi and her client. "By the way, would you two mind if I lunched with Pat and Stephen? I've got a hunch that just might take us somewhere."

"Not at all," says Wofford. . . .

"Okay with me, Cy," says Bianchi.

"Come on." Weinstein steps between Holloway and Cavanaugh and takes the arm of each. "Be my guest. . . . I've got something I want to try out on you." . . .

"Okay," says Cavanaugh after a time, "what did you want to try out on us?" . . .

"Let me ask you a direct question." Weinstein levels a finger at Holloway, swings it toward Bianchi. "If, by making one single move—you could get the kind of agreement in this mediation that would satisfy you completely, would you make that move?"

"What move are you thinking of?" Stephen is intrigued.

Weinstein lays a hand on Holloway's arm. "You have the chance to wind up these negotiations and get the kind of settlement you want by performing one simple, but difficult act. Nobody has so indicated from the other side, but I'd stake my mediator's fee on it. You do the right thing and this case might just fall in your lap."

"And the right thing is?" Now Holloway's voice reflects some of Cavanaugh's skepticism.

"Apologize to your sister for the way you fired her."

Color flares in Stephen's face. "I'll be damned if—" he begins in anger.

"No. Hear me out." Weinstein holds up his hand. "This woman, your sister, hurts deep down inside her because of the manner in which you fired her. Not the business reasons, mind you. Those nicked her pride, but she can live with them. What came like a knife slash was the sudden peremptory and naked way you did it—"

Cavanaugh cuts in. "Cy, let me—"

"No," says Weinstein, "both of you listen now for a while. I'm trying to save you a couple of hundred grand, so let me finish. I've got a lot to say."

The mediator says he has come to the conclusion that the *manner* of Rosemary's discharge is the crux of the case, that although Rosemary probably doesn't know this herself, it becomes obvious to anyone who listens closely to her. "You heard her yesterday. She said she was 'crushed' after all her work to be fired out of hand, no warning."

Actually, Weinstein surmises aloud, if Holloway had broken the dismissal news to his sister gently, explained it with kindness in some detail and offered to help her get another job, she would never have gone to a lawyer and they wouldn't be here today. Cy says that Stephen has said nothing to cast the manner of firing in another light, so he assumes Rosemary's account is substantially correct.

"Am I right about that, Stephen?"

"Well, I intended to make it easy on her," he replies, "But it just didn't come out that way. I have, frankly, a very hard time with that sort of thing. I'm no good at applying, you know, social ointments, as it were." . . .

They sit in silence for a time, then Seymour says: "Stephen, you said you 'intended to make it easy' on your sister that day you called her from the city. Doesn't that mean you regret the way you discharged her?"

"Well, yes, I wish I'd had the words to tell her in a different way. I told you how bad I am at that kind of thing."

"So if you do regret it, why not go the extra step and apologize to Rosemary for the way you did it?"

"You mean today?" The chief of Holloway Interiors looks stricken.

"Sure, why not? I can tell you one thing." Cy leans forward and focuses his gaze on Stephen. "If you can make a sincere apology to your sister—sincere now, no faking—it'll go a long way toward wrapping up this case the way you want. That woman is crying for a sign of your affection." . . .

Holloway looks at Cavanaugh. "What do you think, Pat?"

"As a fellow guest at this chic hot dog luncheon, I shouldn't fault anything our host says. As your lawyer, I am attracted by Cy's prediction that if you apologize, you may get what you want out of this case. I have no idea whether he's right. But hell, what would you be risking? I don't see how you and Rosemary could make your relationship any worse than it is."

Stephen sits in quiet struggle, his thoughts of the trauma of confrontation written in his pained expression.

"Okay," he says at last. "I'll do it. You two go on together. I want to walk by myself and plan just what to say." . . .

When Wofford and Holloway finally appear, Bianchi clocks the entire dialogue at one hour two minutes. Brother and sister stand quietly with the three lawyers. Holloway wears an ambiguous smile, but seems no more relaxed than he did earlier. Wofford may have been crying. Her eyes look strained and she holds a handkerchief in her hand.

"Well?" It is Weinstein who speaks but the other attorneys appear just as impatient for the news.

"I apologized to Rosemary for the brusque way I discharged her, she's forgiven me and we're ready to resume the mediation." Holloway apparently does not care to amplify.

When Seymour looks inquiringly at Wofford, she says: "We didn't do any negotiating, if that's what you're wondering."

"All right then. Let's go back to work." The mediator leads the group up to the eleventh floor and back to the mediation room. They all take their original seats.

"Now," says Weinstein, "I'll need some more information on just where you stand. We can't mediate blindfolded in total darkness. Without going into details, could one of you please outline what you discussed, decided, or whatever?"

Holloway nods to Wofford. "You do it, will you?"

"Well, I'm not sure what to say." She looks down at her lap. "Stephen apologized to me in a very sweet way. I know it was hard for him, but he did it, saying that you had suggested it." She glances at Weinstein. "Did you talk at all about the matter before us?" Weinstein asks.

Holloway answers this time. "Just that Rosemary said maybe our trouble was partially her fault because she never really liked the idea of aiming a business solely toward the affluent. I don't understand that attitude at all, but she does feel that way, so I guess it was a mistake for her to take the Princeton store in the first place."

Rosemary sighs. "Yeah, there were mistakes on both sides." She looks at Cy. "But that doesn't change the fact that I was bounced without cause and that my career has been damaged and that the law has been violated or at least bent the hell out of shape." She says this last sharply.

"All right then," says the mediator. "Can I assume two things then? One, that the emotional charge between you has been somewhat defused. Two, that otherwise the status of this case remains where it was when we adjourned for lunch."

Holloway nods. "Yes, I'd say that's a fair summation. Maybe I should add this though. If any of you have gotten the idea that I don't appreciate Rosemary's business talents, you're wrong. I think that she's very good at what she does and that with a different company with different goals, she'd make a fine executive."

"Thanks," says Wofford. "Of course, there's never been any question about Stephen's ability. His success speaks for itself. . . . I won't quarrel with either of your assumptions, Seymour. You stated the situation just about right."

"Okay, and when we quit for lunch," says Weinstein, "we had collapsed the gap between the parties to two hundred and forty thousand dollars. That is, Stephen had offered seventy-five thousand to settle, but Rosemary was asking three hundred and fifteen thousand. . . . Now, going back to our regular mediation sessions, I'd like some time with Mara and Rosemary. So, Pat, if you and your client could step outside for a few minutes, please."

"I think we can make some real headway now," says Weinstein when he again has placed Wofford on his right and Bianchi on his left. "This morning Stephen flatly refused to write a recommendation for you, Rosemary, but in light of what he's said about your talents just now, I see no reason why he wouldn't change his mind. What do you think?"

"Yes, I think he might give me a decent letter now."

"All right then." A yellow pad rests in the center of the table and Weinstein draws the legal-size notepaper to him. "Let's draft a statement for him to sign that will be as strong as you want. I think it ought to admit the differences that led to your leaving Holloway Interiors—since everyone of any consequence in the trade knows it anyway—but otherwise give you a big send-off. Okay with you, Mara?"

Both Bianchi and her client agree, so the three set to work devising a recommendation. Each writes out several paragraphs, they discuss the differences, and then Mara draws up a draft that Rosemary approves. As perfected after some twenty minutes of work, it reads:

> To Whom It May Concern:
>
> I highly recommend Rosemary Wofford for an executive or managerial post in the field of home furnishings. She has exhibited extraordinary talent in our company, is ambitious, and plans to continue her career elsewhere.
>
> While it is no secret in the industry that she has left Holloway Interiors, I want to say that our disagreement over policy in no way reflects on her wide-ranging abilities.
>
> Sincerely,
>
> Stephen Holloway
> President, Holloway Interiors

"All right now," says Weinstein, "how much are you willing to give to get that letter? Is this a one hundred and fifty thousand dollar letter?"

"Not in my book." Bianchi shakes her head. "I'd be willing to make some concession, but come down to one sixty-five in our demand? No."

"I don't know, Mara." Wofford frowns. "Why not come down that far? With that letter and a hundred and sixty-five thousand dollars, I'd be all set. I'd take me a good vacation and then hit the job market with lots of confidence."

"I'm thinking of our bargaining position," Bianchi replies. "Let's not come down so fast. I'd call it a hundred-grand letter. So we'd reduce our price to two hundred and fifteen thousand dollars."

"Why not round it off?" asks Weinstein quickly. "Tell 'em you want two hundred thousand and the letter."

"Fine with me," says Wofford.

"Okay. I'll buy that," Bianchi adds.

Weinstein folds the long yellow paper on which the letter has been written. "Good." He rises. "Please send the others in. I'll see what we can do with this. I'll get back to you in a half hour or so."

Weinstein waits until Holloway and Cavanaugh are seated, then hands Holloway the folded paper. "If you're willing to sign that, Stephen, it'll save you an awful lot of money."

Holloway slowly reads the letter, looks at the mediator, and taps his fingers on the table. "You know I told you this morning that I wasn't ready to give my sister a letter of recommendation."

"I didn't forget," Weinstein's eyes lock with Holloway's. "But everyone felt that circumstances had changed markedly since your talk with Rosemary. Haven't they?"

"Yes, they have." Holloway places the letter on the table, takes a ballpoint pen from the breast pocket of his jacket, and rapidly scrawls his name under "Sincerely." He says, "There," and starts to hand the paper to Weinstein. "Wait a minute." He scratches out "wide-ranging" in the last line and writes in "superior" so that the final phrase reads: ". . . I want to say that our disagreement over policy in no way reflects on her superior abilities."

"That should be all right with Rosemary," says Holloway. " 'Wide-ranging' doesn't sound like me. Let me keep this. I'll have it typed up on Holloway Interiors stationery and mail it to her."

"Hold it, not so fast." Attorney Cavanaugh raises a hand. "Let's find out first how much they'll come down in return for that letter."

Holloway inspects his coat sleeve, brushes a speck of lint from it. "I don't want this mixed up with money. Rosemary is entitled to the letter. She does have superior abilities and as her brother, I intend to say so."

"Damn it, as your attorney, I can't allow you to throw away a bargaining advantage like that. That's worth a lot of money."

"Allow me or not, as you please." Stephen's tone has frost on it. "The fact is, I've already agreed to it. I'm not going back on my word. . . ."

After a few moments of silence, Weinstein says: "I hear you, Stephen. However, your sister also has already acted. She is now asking only two hundred thousand to settle this matter."

Again Holloway looks Weinstein full in the eyes. "And I'm offering only seventy-five thousand. On your next shuttle, please inform Rosemary and her lawyer that I won't budge from that position. My lawyer informs me that my sister, not I, broke the contract, so I'd be entirely within my rights to refuse to pay anything at all. I'm offering seventy-five thousand only to avoid the tedium of a court trial and the scandalous loss of time involved. . . ."

"Stephen, Stephen," Weinstein admonishes. "That contract is your weakest point under the law. It is very, very doubtful that any jury would conclude that

Rosemary, rather than you, breached that written contract. You're standing on awfully slippery ground there. I'm sure your attorney will concur."

"I've told him that his legal grounds are not solid," says Cavanaugh, "and that juries tend to favor the subordinate in cases like this. I haven't changed my mind."

Weinstein again centers his eyes on Holloway. "Stephen?"

"I will not go a penny above seventy-five thousand." He clenches his jaws. . . .

"You must realize," says Weinstein slowly, "what that means, Stephen. Your sister most certainly will file suit and your life for the next several years will be dominated and harassed by a legal action that will cost you a great deal of money and which, in the end, as your lawyer has indicated, you have little hope of winning outright."

"I'll take that risk. I will not pay a cent more." Holloway sets himself in granite. "I know I'm right."

"In that event . . ." Weinstein slaps the table and gets to his feet. He slips quickly into his jacket and pockets his ballpoint pen. "That's it, the end of the road." . . .

Is Weinstein pressuring Holloway to settle, or is he merely setting forth alternatives? Some commentators would characterize these intensive inquiries as "pressure tactics" but would not necessarily oppose the use of them. Psychology professors Kenneth Kressel and Dean Pruitt summarize important considerations:

Views on "pressure tactics": "A prevailing ideology, especially in community and family mediation, views [pressure] tactics as alien to good mediation. Instead, so this view goes, the mediator's principal tools are reason and compassion" (Kressel and Pruitt, 1989:418).

Prevailing practices regarding "pressure tactics": "Ideology notwithstanding, the research . . shows that most mediators regard pressure tactics as an essential ingredient of their kit bag . . ." (Kressel and Pruitt, 1989:418-419).

Research on the effectiveness of "pressure tactics": "[In the labor context, while] pressure tactics had a positive relationship with general settlement under a few circumstances, the prevailing association was negative. Pressure tactics had even more dubious effects when the measure of outcome was the parties' relationship with one another" (Kressel and Pruitt, 1989:420).

Are "pressure tactics" inappropriate?

"If you will stay here a moment," says Weinstein brusquely, "I'll fetch the others and we'll lay this thing to rest as quickly as we can." . . .

Thwarted, Weinstein stalks to the door, places his hand on the doorknob, pauses, straightens, stands immobile for a curiously long time, then suddenly whirls about toward the surprised pair.

"Well, I'll be damned!" He marches back to his chair, whips off his jacket, and hangs it on the back of his chair again. "Sit down." His craggy face has a glow. "Now why didn't I think of this an hour ago?"

Holloway and Cavanaugh ease back into their seats. At first baffled, they quickly surrender to curiosity. Cavanaugh, however, has a small smile as she tilts her head. What, she seems to be asking, is this shrewd old dude up to this time?

"How many ways to skin a cat?" asks Weinstein. "Is it nine? No, that's lives. There's more than one way to skin . . ." He talks with a rush of excitement. "Anyway, I got this flash at the doorway, what if . . . All right, slow down, Seymour, and let's backtrack here." He levels a finger at Holloway. "Stephen, am I not correct that you think highly of your sister's business abilities? You said so in the letter of recommendation and you also praised her talents to us. Right?"

"I wasn't just being generous," Stephen replies. "She's excellent at business. It's just that she and I . . ."

Weinstein ends the demurrer with a sweep of his arm. "And it's also true, as you know, that Rosemary is very anxious to get back to work. Indeed, she'd like to open her own shop and go after the business that's a price level or two below the one you aim at. Let me ask you, Stephen, is there any reason a home furnishings shop aimed at the upper middle class shouldn't make money if properly run?"

"None at all. It's not my bag, but lots of shops make good money targeting the economic slice below my customers."

"Do you think Rosemary could make good money doing that?"

"No question," says Holloway emphatically. "She's got the head for it and the necessary drive as well."

"How much profit should a store like that make?"

"On sales? I'd say twenty percent after taxes."

"Does Holloway Interiors make that much?"

"No. To maintain our reputation for excellence with elegance costs money. We net around twelve percent after taxes."

"How much in start-up costs to open a store aimed at the people we're talking about?"

Holloway reflects with a finger at his lips. "Depending on the location, I'd say between a million and a million-two, including everything. That's renting, not buying your floor space."

"Would you invest in a store like that?"

"That depends on who's running . . ." Holloway checks himself, looks at Weinstein with dawning recognition. "Oh, I see what you mean." He gathers his brows in concentration.

"And why not?" Weinstein spreads an expansive smile. "You and Rosemary are back on speaking terms. You admire her ability. She certainly admires yours. She borrows the money with your credit guaranteeing the loan. Maybe she puts up some money, whatever she has. You leave her alone to run her own show. You don't make your investment public. She expands the business as she goes along and you both get fat on the way. It's regular movie script stuff. Writes itself."

"Hey, Cy," says Cavanaugh. "Let the man catch his breath."

"Yes, I . . . Well, I never thought along those lines." Holloway pauses, frowns. "It takes a bit of getting used to."

"Take all day, the night too." Weinstein has caught fire with the idea. "We can recess the mediation while you think it over. This project has legs, Stephen. This time you get Cavanaugh and Bianchi to draw up a tight agreement between you and Rosemary. Lots of ways to go. You could make it a corporation with you owning most of the stock and Rosemary owning some and she taking a stipulated salary and a bonus arrangement. But she runs the thing. All you have to do is rake in the money and give Rosemary advice if she asks for it."

"It does have some attractive features." Stephen is pondering. "I would like to insist on at least eighty percent ownership. I don't know whether she'd — "

"Stephen," Cavanaugh interrupts, "are you sure you want to go into business with this lady? We have plenty of grief with her as it is."

"I'm thinking, Pat. Rosemary could reach a market that's been undercultivated."

"And now you and Rosemary are on a more normal footing." Seymour bulls ahead. "Oh sure, you're not pals, you're still keeping your distance, but you trust each other's ability and each other's drive to succeed. Those are often better trusting points for the long haul than affection. Also you know you're not going to cheat each other. It's not like doing business with a stranger."

"I'm listening." Holloway's mind, it's apparent, is also working at a fast clip. "What about this frightful case, Rosemary's demand for money?"

"In my thinking," says the mediator, "you'd wipe out everything but this new project. Nobody pays anybody anything. You don't write any letters or sign any statements. You two just agree to go into business together. Case closed."

"We kiss and make up and live happily ever after, huh?" says Holloway with a splash of acid.

"Forget your sibling feelings for a minute. Think about business." Weinstein leans closer to Holloway. "Why not let me put this up to Rosemary? Let me tell her that while you haven't said yes, you haven't said no either. Let's see if she has any liking for the deal."

"All right, let's find that out," says Holloway. "After all, if she isn't interested, there's no use us wasting time on it, is there?" But the possibility lights up his eyes.

"Done." Weinstein stands up. He's supercharged now. "Send in Rosemary and Mara, will you? Then I'll get back to you as soon as she gives me the word."

Should Weinstein have suggested a means to settle? Consider the following divergent viewpoints on this issue.

Law professor Robert Baruch Bush and communications professor Joseph Folger: "[In a transformative approach to mediation,] [m]ediators consciously try to avoid shaping issues, proposals, or terms for settlement, or even pushing for the achievement of settlement at all. Instead, they encourage parties to define problems and find solutions for themselves, and they endorse and support the parties' own efforts to do so" (Bush and Folger, 2005:101).

Psychology professors Kenneth Kressel and Dean Pruitt: "Despite a persistent ideology that mediators ought to refrain from pushing their own ideas, it is quite evident that they are often a primary source of settlement proposals and that they are not at all shy about playing such a role. Thus, Pearson and Thoennes report that in divorce mediation the mediator was the source of most of the proposed solutions. . . . Studies of both labor mediation . . . and judicial mediation . . . identify forceful suggestion-making as a central dimension of mediator behavior" (Kressel and Pruitt, 1989:394, 417).

Should Weinstein have made this proposal, if he had thought of it, on the first day?

Labor mediator Walter Maggiolo: "The mediator, by careful listening and constant evaluation of the positions taken by the parties, translates their thoughts into suggestions and advances them at the appropriate moment when each party is prepared to accept them. . . . If a suggestion is made too soon, it may be rejected out of hand. . . . In order for a mediator's suggestion to have the greatest weight, it must be made at a time when the parties have reached a stage in their negotiations at which they will be most receptive. One of the prerequisites to receptivity is that the parties must have been conditioned to accept the less perfect because it may lead to an agreement, rather than to insist on the perfect which only continues the impasse" (Maggiolo, 1985:142, 159-160).

"What happened to Stephen?" asks Wofford as she walks in. "He looks like somebody just handed him a million dollars."

"Maybe you did." Weinstein grins. He finds it hard to contain himself. "Or better yet, maybe you will — and get as much yourself."

"Okay, Cy," says Mara Bianchi. "No more suspense, please."

"Oh, but I love suspense." He waits until they're seated. "Rosemary, if you could get a million dollars worth of financing tomorrow, could you open up the kind of store you want to run?"

"Let's see. If I scratched, I might scrape up fifty or sixty thousand of my own." She sighs. "So, yes. A million is just about the size of the lottery I'd have to win."

"How about a bank loan?" Weinstein is enjoying this.

"With my collateral and track record? Let's not fantasize, Seymour."

"If I could get you the million, how soon could you get under way on the project?"

"First thing next week." She pauses. "Hey, what is this?" Suspecting, she asks: "For God's sake, Seymour, don't tell me that Stephen wants to back me in business now?"

Seymour glows with his project. "He didn't say yes and he didn't say no. What he did say was that I should find out first whether Rosemary would consider it."

"Well, of all the . . ." She sinks back in her chair. "I don't know. I have to give this some head power." She taps her temples.

"Was this your idea, Cy?" asks Bianchi.

"Yep. Hit me like a flash. Why are we in here fighting over who gives how much to whom, I thought, when these two fast-track business types can join forces and make themselves a pile?"

"And just what did Stephen say?"

"I told you. But I swear he's hot for the idea. He's willing to co-sign for a million at the bank. You should see his eyes light up."

Wofford raises a hand like a traffic cop. "Hold it. The caution light is on. He's thinking about control, I'll bet. No way would I do that. I worked for him once, remember."

"I don't think so." Weinstein shakes his head. "He didn't object when I said you ought to have control, he to advise only if you asked him. You'd get a fixed salary, but you'd both put the profits back into the business for a few years. I think I could get him to agree in writing to your control. Don't forget, Rosemary, your brother is a good businessman and he likes money. He knows how good you are and he knows how much you could make with stores aiming at the upper-middle folks."

"Stores?" Wofford laughs with mock hysteria. "God, I haven't got one yet and the man is already multiplying me into a chain."

"Right. A chain it could become with Stephen's guarantee for a bank loan and your ideas, work, and talent." . . .

"No question, the proposal tempts me," says Wofford. "Do you see any reason why not, Mara?"

"None in sight." The attorney shares Weinstein's enthusiasm. "We'll just make sure we have an unmistakable agreement on your sole control. Then we want to insist that Stephen spell out just how he sees the arrangement. No ambiguities this time around."

Like a batter before the pitch, Wofford takes a deep breath. "All right. If Stephen gives the right answers, I'll go."

"Great. That's it then. . . . You two stay here and I'll call in the other side." Weinstein bows to Wofford with a smile. "Pardon, your partner and his attorney."

Seats are shuffled as Holloway and Cavanaugh return to the room. Weinstein waits until everyone has the place he or she occupied when the first joint session began.

"Stephen," he says, "Rosemary is willing to start up a joint business venture with you, she borrowing roughly a million with you as the guarantor. But only on one important condition. Why don't you state it in your own words, Rosemary."

"Yes." She addresses her brother. "Stephen, I think this is an exciting idea that has a lot of promise for both of us. But I'm not interested unless I can run my own show. Are you willing to give me control?"

"Yes." He is serious, unsmiling. "I would want you to keep me informed at least on a monthly basis and I'd hope that if you needed advice, you'd feel free to call on me."

"Would you be willing to put that in writing?" She asks this gently, yet with insistence.

"Yes, of course. I assume all this and everything else connected with a deal would be put in careful legal language and that our lawyers would set up the necessary framework."

"I'm considering two agreements," says Weinstein. "One when we finish here today that seals the arrangement in plain but explicit English and then a second one in a few weeks in which Pat and Mara spell it all out in proper legal terms."

"Okay, if Stephen's willing, I am." She looks at her brother with a touch of shyness.

"I'm willing," Holloway responds.

"All right." Weinstein beams on brother and sister. "Could you please seal that with a handshake?"

Stephen arises and puts out his hand. Rosemary, standing, reaches out and grasps it.

"It's a deal," he says as he shakes.

"Deal," she says. . . .

Bianchi, the self-appointed timer, looks at her wristwatch. "Six-fifty-six. Cy, you wrapped this one up in slightly less than sixteen hours, including lunches."

The two lawyers talk about drafting the formal papers for the new enterprise, then Weinstein invites all hands for a celebratory drink. Brother and sister walk out together.

The Costs

In reaching an agreement with her brother, ending all existing legal differences between them, Rosemary Wofford has added a sixteen-hour bill from her attorney of $2,400. She must also pay $1,200, half of Weinstein's fee for the mediation. She must add another $650, the American Arbitration Association's charge per party for arranging the mediation and providing the meeting place. So her expenses have grown by $4,250 and now stand at $7,550.

Since the cost of drafting the legal agreement for the joint home furnishings venture will be charged against start-up costs, Rosemary Wofford has thus closed out the contract and discharge dispute with Stephen Holloway at a final cost to her of $7,550. It has been six weeks and four days since she walked into lawyer Bianchi's office with intent to sue her brother for breach of contract.

[The authors then describe the costs of a similar family business dispute that ended after a four-day trial some four years after the plaintiff contacted a lawyer. The clients eventually paid their attorneys and experts (also in 1987 dollars) $61,324.50 (Knebel and Clay, 1987:219-220).]

Question

3.2 Turn to Appendix H, Model Standards of Conduct for Mediators, Standard I(a). Consider whether the mediator in the Knebel and Clay excerpt satisfied Standard I(a)'s requirement that the parties' consent to the mediation process be informed.

Note: The Role of Apology in Dispute Resolution

The first lesson of dispute resolution that many of us learn as children is the importance of apologizing. This is, however, a lesson that is soon forgotten, or at least little used, in American dispute resolution. Kenny Hegland (1982:69) makes this point nicely:

> In my first year Contracts class, I wished to review various doctrines we had recently studied. I put the following:
>
> > In a long term installment contract, seller promises buyer to deliver widgets at the rate of 1,000 a month. The first two deliveries are perfect. However, in the third month seller delivers only 990 widgets. Buyer becomes so incensed that he rejects deliveries and refuses to pay for the widgets already delivered.
>
> After stating the problem, I asked, "If you were Seller, what would you say?" What I was looking for was a discussion of the various common law theories which would force the buyer to pay for the widgets delivered and those which would throw buyer into breach for

cancelling the remaining deliveries. In short, I wanted the class to come up with the legal doctrines which would allow Seller to crush Buyer.

After asking the question, I looked around the room for a volunteer. As is so often the case with first year students, I found that they were all either writing in their notebooks or inspecting their shoes. There was, however, one eager face, that of an eight year old son of one of my students. It seems that he was suffering through Contracts due to his mother's sin of failing to find a sitter. Suddenly he raised his hand. Such behavior, even from an eight year old, must be rewarded.

"OK," I said, "What would you say if you were the seller?"

"I'd say, 'I'm sorry.' "

Many mediators have had one or more experiences similar to that described in the excerpt from *Before You Sue*, in which an apology was the key to a settlement that might otherwise not have been attainable. At times, the injured party wants above all an admission by the other party that he or she did wrong; no more is necessary to achieve a settlement. At other times, an apology of itself is insufficient to resolve a dispute but will so reduce tension and ease the relationship between the parties that the issues separating them are resolved with dispatch. Furthermore, to the extent that the dispute has occurred in the context of an ongoing relationship, the apology is valuable in repairing whatever harm to the relationship has resulted from the dispute. In this respect, the apology serves one of the goals of mediation — the repair of frayed relationships.

With the increasing role of mediation and other nonadjudicative techniques of dispute resolution, one would expect the use of the apology to bulk increasingly large. Indeed, in Japan, where rights-based dispute resolution is less well entrenched, apology plays a central role in the resolution of disputes (Wagatsuma and Rosett, 1986). For example, following the 1982 Japan Air Lines crash in Tokyo Bay, its president promptly visited all the families of the crash victims to offer apologies and compensation. No lawsuits were filed. Formal apologies of this nature are common in Japan and often result in dispute resolution without recourse to litigation.

There are several obstacles to a greater use of apology as a dispute resolution technique in the United States. Initially, while in Japan filing a lawsuit is accompanied by shame, here it is the apology that is often seen as demeaning. Hence apologies are hard to extract — often harder than money. (Sometimes in a neighborhood dispute, mediators manage to get the respondent to apologize as part of the final rapprochement, but usually only after the parties' claims and counterclaims have been heard and resolved.)

Reluctance to apologize may also be the product of rules of evidence that treat an apology as an admission of fault that can be used to prove wrongdoing. Thus it is commonplace for insurance companies and attorneys to advise policyholders against expressing sympathy for a person injured by the policyholder, for fear such an expression will be treated as an admission of guilt.

It is possible that the view of an apology as demeaning the person who gives it will diminish with an increased emphasis on accommodative dispute settlement. Perhaps state legislatures, motivated by a desire to encourage settlement and so decrease court congestion, will also take steps to eliminate the use of an apology or an expression of sympathy as an admission of wrongdoing in subsequent litigation. In December 1986, Massachusetts enacted a law (Chapter 652) providing that "gestures expressing sympathy or a general sense of benevolence relating to the pain, suffering or death of a person involved in an accident" would not be admissible into evidence as an admission of liability. Although this provision does not encompass apologies, one can readily envision an extension in that direction. Additionally, if an apology is offered as part of the settlement process, it would be inadmissible under common law rules excluding from evidence even admissions of liability made during settlement negotiations.

One American corporation is said to have coupled an initially supportive approach with hard-nosed litigation tactics in a novel effort to reduce claims. According to the *Wall Street Journal* (November 7, 1986), following a 1985 airport crash that killed 137 people, Delta Air Lines dispatched employees to be with every family to help with minor matters — such as looking for a briefcase lost in the crash — and with serious matters — such as funerals. If someone just wanted to talk, a Delta employee was there as a "friend."

Subsequently, according to the *Journal*, many victims found it difficult to sue their "friend." Far fewer suits were filed against Delta than might have been expected based on the results of other accidents — only 65 out of a possible 152. For those who filed suit, however, the *Journal* reports, Delta's attorneys showed them "just how painful a lawsuit can be." According to the attorney for one plaintiff, Delta and its insurance carriers used information obtained from grieving family members in subsequent settlement negotiations. For instance, the attorney alleges, a distraught family member had told a sympathetic adjuster that the victim, a married man, had been having an extramarital affair. "They threw it back at us in settlement talks and really took us by surprise," said the lawyer, adding that victims should be cautioned that anything they say may be used against them in a suit. One may hope that this peculiarly American twist on a well-entrenched Japanese practice will not become commonplace.

Putting aside Delta's use of apologies, in what types of disputes might an apology be most useful in bringing about an amicable resolution? Are there disputes in which an apology might be of little or no use? If an apology is to be made for dispute resolution purposes, when should it take place? See generally Levi (1997).

Note: Dealing with Impasse

Mediator Cy Weinstein broke an impasse (pp. 132-137) by presenting an idea that was carefully tailored to the interests expressed by the parties. Experienced mediators have a mental cache of these impasse-breaking techniques. The mediator analyzes why the parties have not reached agreement and selects the technique most likely to overcome that barrier. Some techniques merely return to the mediation basics — encouraging expression of emotions, reality testing, summarizing to emphasize progress, reframing, and so forth — that Rogers and Salem (1987) discussed (pp. 109-113). A few additional ideas include:

Turning positions to interests: "The mediator turns the conversation from positions to interests. 'I imagine you could hold the line in that way, and it is possible, of course, that the other side will come around. However, before testing that, let me ask a few questions. What are the interests behind the position you have stated? Put another way, what are you trying to accomplish, or what are you trying to honor, by taking this position?' The objective here, of course, is to transfer talk from the positions back up to matters of the heart" (Slaikeu, 1996:151).

Ask for priorities: "Parties who assert that every item in a negotiation is of equal significance are either posturing for position or lack a clear idea of their own interests or aspirations. Some things *are* more important than others. People make choices by how they act, if not by what they say. A mediator must look for a party's priorities, even if the party does not explicitly rank them for her" (Stulberg, 1987:97).

Question positions: Mediator George W. Taylor suggests creating doubts about expressed positions: "I have found it helpful to say, 'You are certainly right on the basis of the facts you have used, but did you realize this new fact which has just been brought out? [H]ow does it fit in with your analysis?' " (Maggiolo, 1985:93).

Search again for hidden issues:

- "Look for clues that a hidden issue is present: for example, an unusual display of emotion, irrational arguments, or a good past relationship among the parties.
- Ask explicitly about whether such an issue exists.
- Approach these issues first in the privacy of the caucus where people are more likely to be candid; consider sounding out the lawyers away from their clients.
- Do not be discouraged by an initial brush-off; instead, raise the issue again once your relationships with the participants are stronger.
- After you have identified a hidden issue or opportunity, encourage each side to address it in its settlement proposal.
- Conduct private or joint brainstorming sessions to develop options.
- If necessary, construct, float, and advocate for imaginative solutions yourself" (Golann, 1996:57).

Bring additional people to the table: Slaikeu suggests that the mediator may be able to solicit new ideas simply by adding an attorney or other person to each side (Slaikeu, 1996:154).

Emphasize the unpleasantness of continuing the dispute: "What happens if the parties don't resolve their problem? People begrudgingly alter their life-styles to deal with the nagging problem. Morale plummets, people brood, and performance deteriorates; annoyance festers and resentment builds. The problem persists; it never evaporates or modulates into something else. These can be the real consequences of living with an unresolved problem. The mediator must ask the parties: Do you prefer this possible state of affairs over that envisioned in the proposed settlement terms? If not, then change your position and develop acceptable solutions; if yes, there will be no mediated agreement" (Stulberg, 1987:104).

Emphasize the advantages of resolving the dispute immediately: "I have found that emphasizing the advantages of resolving the dispute is an even more powerful motivator than emphasizing the disadvantages of continuing the dispute. I will often ask the parties, late in the mediation, when a potential agreement is under consideration, 'How would you like to walk away from here today with this matter completely behind you?' " (Personal interview with Stephen Goldberg.)

Role reversal: "Sometimes a party will change her position or better appreciate a particular demand of the other party if the mediator gets her to analyze the negotiating issue from the other party's viewpoint. . . . Parties become less resistant to settlement as they confront the reality of relinquishing control over their fate to those other forces. A mediator uses a time constraint to chasten parties so they will take responsibility for managing their future" (Stulberg, 1987:100).

Decision analysis: Negotiators sometimes use a decision tree, based on likelihoods of success at various stages in litigation, to assess their own settlement positions. The use of decision analysis is discussed in Chapter 5 (see pp. 363-369).

Questions

3.3 Review the list of obstacles to a negotiated agreement set out at the end of Chapter 2 (pp. 86-87). What were the obstacles to settlement by Holloway and Wofford? What techniques and skills did the mediator employ to overcome these obstacles?

3.4 What would have been gained or lost if Holloway's and Wofford's attorneys had not accompanied them? What would have been gained or lost if the attorneys had attended the sessions without their clients?

3.5 In contrast to Weinstein's approach to mediation, many divorce mediators conduct all sessions with both parties present. Are there reasons to avoid caucuses?

3.6 Suppose Holloway and Wofford agreed that Weinstein could make a binding decision on their failure to reach agreement. Would either party have been as frank in separate sessions with Weinstein? If so, would Wofford have been hurt by her lawyer's statement that she had assessed the case at only $200,000? See the materials on "med-arb" in Chapter 5 (pp. 307-309). What are the advantages and disadvantages of encouraging judges to mediate cases on their own dockets? (See Wall, Schiller, and Ebert, 1984.)

3.7 Mediator Seymour Weinstein was a lawyer, but mediators are drawn from a variety of professions. Was Weinstein's background in law an advantage or disadvantage in the Wofford-Holloway mediation?

3.8 Does Rosemary Wofford use the approach to negotiation described by Carol Gilligan and Trina Grillo (pp. 143-145)? Would she fare better in litigation?

3.9 What is the likely cause of the impasse in each of the following scenarios? What should the mediator do next?

a. After introductory remarks by the mediator, Sandy Kaler angrily relates that a dentist, Dr. Molly Breel, filled a cavity and then recommended that she have caps placed on her teeth, which were yellowed by years of smoking. Kaler readily agreed, paying $400. A week after Breel capped Kaler's teeth, the teeth caps turned green. Two weeks later, Kaler scheduled this mediation and asked for $3,000 to have the teeth repaired by another dentist. Breel responds that she had warned Kaler not to smoke again and argues that any discoloration only could have been caused by smoking. Breel then offers to remove or replace the caps for an extra $400. Kaler admits telling Breel that she had stopped smoking but said that Breel had not told her that smoking would turn the caps green. She repeats her $3,000 demand. Breel then offers to remove the caps without a charge, just to get the matter behind her. With her voice rising, Kaler says that she had called the receptionist the day that her teeth turned color to ask that the caps be removed without a charge and that Breel had not returned the call. She adds angrily that she would never let Breel touch her teeth again. In separate caucuses, Breel tells the mediator that she fears referral to another dentist because of the effect on her reputation, and Kaler tells the mediator that she has felt so embarrassed by her green teeth that she feels that someone should pay.

b. Samantha and Lawrence separate and agree to try to settle all significant issues through mediation before filing for a dissolution of their marriage. All financial issues are resolved first, and they meet with their lawyers and the mediator to discuss the living arrangements for their eight-year-old daughter, Phoebe. Lawrence suggests that Phoebe live with Samantha weekdays and with him on weekends. Samantha responds that she would agree to such an arrangement only if Lawrence would agree that his girlfriend would not be staying with Lawrence on the weekends. At that, Lawrence accuses Samantha of having an affair with a married neighbor, and Samantha bursts into tears. Lawrence's lawyer suggests that it was time to focus on parenting with the marriage over and that the issue of girlfriends and boyfriends should not be a part of any arrangements for Phoebe. Samantha and Lawrence calm down, but Samantha insists that Phoebe not be exposed to Lawrence's girlfriend living in his apartment, assuring Lawrence that she would agree to a reciprocal condition for the time that Phoebe stayed with her. Lawrence flatly refuses to agree to the condition.

c. Sixteen-year-old Jason Bole, through his parents, sues the city for damages. All agree that a city police officer who was pursuing a fleeing suspect accidentally shot Jason while Jason was mowing a neighbor's lawn. The bullet cannot safely be removed from Jason's back. The chief of police and the officer expressed consternation about the error and apologized publicly. Lawyers for the plaintiff and the city have been negotiating for months in an effort to settle pending litigation. The city believes that the doctrine of sovereign immunity protects the city from liability. Lawyers for Jason argue that sovereign immunity will not preclude liability because the city recklessly failed to train and supervise police in the use of firearms. The lawyers also disagree on how the jury will assess the differing expert testimony regarding the prognosis for Jason's future. When they begin the mediation, Jason's lawyer demands $2 million. Lawyers for the city say that they would pay $40,000, an amount that they think would cover attorney's fees for Jason's lawyer. In a caucus, the city's lawyer indicates that they would pay $100,000 if this amount would fully settle the matter, but that a higher offer would require city council approval and that approval was unlikely. Jason's lawyer indicates in caucus a willingness to spread payments over a long period and a willingness to reduce the total amount to $1 million but says that he would take the matter to trial if $1 million was not acceptable to the city.

3.10 Consider the following problems. In which would reference to mediation serve the client's interests? Why or why not?

a. Your client seeks to open a nonprofit group home for developmentally disabled adults in a residential neighborhood. Eight neighborhood residents have retained a lawyer to oppose your client's request for a variance from zoning requirements. Vocal opposition generally delays approval, with your client making mortgage payments for an empty house in the meantime. Therefore, the client is willing to pay for the mediation if you think it is likely to lead to settlement.

b. Your client is a shy woman involved in a bitter custody battle with her husband over three young children. She believes that her husband does not really want custody but is using her desire to have them as a bargaining chip to secure a reduction in her demand for half the marital assets. She also suspects that he has more assets than have been revealed to date.

c. Your client, a corporation, is seeking damages against the construction company that built the leaky roof on its corporate headquarters. Lawyers for the construction company seem uninterested in negotiations. The construction company is in financial difficulty and may be trying to delay the seemingly inevitable payments.

d. You are the city attorney. The city council excluded a group of citizens wearing swastika armbands from council chambers. The citizen group filed suit in federal court arguing that the council's actions violated first amendment rights. The council has announced publicly that it will exclude those wearing racist symbols unless ordered by a court to do otherwise.

3.11 Although mediators typically work alone, in some situations mediators with different qualifications or of different sexes work together as a team. What are the advantages and disadvantages of co-mediation? Does its value depend on the type of dispute involved?

3.12 Some commentators suggest that the way to resolve the debate about whether it is appropriate for the mediator to evaluate is to leave that choice to the parties (Riskin, 1996:39-40; Stark, 1997). Law professor Joseph Stulberg suggests the difficulty of that response:

> Consider the situation in which Party A or her lawyer indicates that she prefers a mediator with an evaluative-narrow orientation, and Party B or her lawyer indicates that she prefers a mediator whose orientation is facilitative-broad. If one assumes that the parties are ordered to appear in mediation, how should the parties proceed? (Stulberg, 1997:993).

How do you respond to Professor Stulberg's question?

Note: Dealing with Differences

Mediators can play key roles in bridging cultural differences. The mediator is in a position to improve communications and promote understanding of others' values by using traditional mediation techniques. For example, the mediator helps one person, perhaps an older person, understand the perspective of a younger person by asking the younger person to explain why he feels a certain way. If these persons are still on different wavelengths, the mediator next may ask the older person to state what she heard the younger person say and then inquire whether the younger person believes that this synopsis captured his view. This patient approach also leads each to feel assured that the expressed viewpoint is appreciated by the other. The mediator also may increase use of summarization, being careful to use language all will understand. Alternatively, the mediator may shuttle more often among the parties, trying to avoid miscues about negotiating moves that might lead to defensive negotiation and thus the potential loss of joint gains among negotiating parties (see Brett et al., 1996, p. 557).

Just as the mediator's contributions may be especially significant in the face of cultural differences, in some instances these differences may render conventional mediation approaches ineffective. For example, the use of a mediator who encourages expression of emotions may seem risky when the conflict is between members of groups with a history of intergroup violence (see Morrow and Wilson, 1993). People with a tradition against sharing problems with strangers may find mediation by neutral professionals unattractive (Folger, 1991).

Differences also affect communications between the parties and the mediator. Cultural and gender-based stereotypes may block a disputing party's trust of the mediator, lead to misunderstandings of the mediator's actions, spark statements that make even veteran mediators reach into their reserves to avoid becoming emotional, and pose personal and professional dilemmas for the mediators. Mediator Pat Williams provides this example:

> Smith, a white male student, called the university mediation office to complain about "reverse racial discrimination" that had resulted in an African-American student being hired for the library job he wanted. Mediator Matley assured Smith that a mediation process was available in which he could discuss his complaint with a representative of the library personnel office. When Smith walked into the mediation room a week later, Matley, an African-American woman, introduced herself. Smith briefly lost his composure, and then said, "It will be difficult for you to be objective, won't it?" Matley replied, "No" and explained the mediation process. Later in the session, Smith interrupted the other disputant, and Matley turned to look directly at Smith, saying firmly, "Here are your options: either you can abide by the requirement that no one interrupts or I can terminate this proceeding and you are on your own." Later Smith filed a complaint against Matley, claiming that she had spoken abusively to him during the session. Matley responded, "All I did was act professionally and firmly. He must think that women should be soft-spoken and demure. I was raised to be assertive and professionally trained to speak directly." Afterwards, she wondered, "Should I have spoken less forcefully? The women Smith knows would not have spoken so bluntly except in anger. Also, his reaction to my skin color may have caused him to view me as even more threatening. Still, I don't like changing my style to accommodate his stereotypes."*

What, if any, cultural or gender-based stereotypes appear in this vignette? Should the mediator have acted any differently?

Suppose instead that misunderstandings arise because of differences among the parties. Here a mediator is well situated to improve communications. As discussed above, the mediator may restate important points to avoid misinterpretation, ask each disputant to explain how a statement is intended or heard, or operate a shuttle-style of diplomacy.

Some contend that differences in negotiation approaches may lead to bargaining imbalances — not simply misunderstanding (Woods, 1985; Delgado, 1988; Lerman,

*Interview with Pat Williams, OmbudsOffice, Ohio State University, September 12, 1991.

1984). For example, law professor Trina Grillo suggests that women negotiating with men may be disadvantaged in mediation:

> Carol Gilligan describes two different, gendered modes of thought. The female mode is characterized by an "ethic of care" which emphasizes nurturance, connection with others, and contextual thinking. The male mode is characterized by an "ethic of justice" which emphasizes individualism, the use of rules to resolve moral dilemmas, and equality. Under Gilligan's view, the male mode leads one to strive for individualism and autonomy, while the female mode leads one to strive for connection with and caring for others. . . . If she is easily persuaded to be cooperative, but [the other party] is not, she can only lose. If it is indeed her disposition to be caring and focused on relationships, . . . the language of relationship, caring, and cooperation will be appealing to her and make her vulnerable. . . . In short, in mediation such a woman may be encouraged to repeat exactly those behaviors that have proven hazardous to her in the past (Grillo, 1991).

Not all commentators believe that women are at a negotiating disadvantage, and research does not substantiate it (Kressel and Pruitt, 1989; Kelly and Gigy, 1989; Thoennes, Pearson, and Bell, 1991; Burton et al., 1991, regarding negotiating approaches of lawyers; Craver, 1990; Pearson, 1991. But see Emery and Jackson, 1989; Babcock and Laschever, 2003).

Question

3.13* Eastern Ulster University in Northern Ireland has 15,000 full-time students, three-quarters of whom are Protestant, one-quarter of whom are Catholic, and a few of whom are Travelers (a common Irish word used for the Roma peoples who are among those historically called gypsies). In the last 24 hours, the chairperson of the Department of Education received the following memos from advanced students and from a professor in the department.

Memo
TO: Department Chairperson
FROM: Students
RE: Events of the Past Week in Advanced Teaching Methods 306

According to the syllabus that the class received at the beginning of Advanced Teaching Methods 306, the past week of class was to have been devoted to the teaching of Irish history. However, some of the students in the class believe that the majority of the information and examples presented by Professor Smythe have had a Protestant bias and that, in fact, misleading and erroneous information has been presented on the role of Catholics and Travelers in the history of Ireland. When a student raised her hand and requested a more multicultural, balanced, and accurate exchange of information, Professor Smythe became visibly angry. He

*This fictional account was written by Laura Williams and Nancy Rogers.

said that a Protestant focus would be more interesting to this class. He denied that any of the information presented on the roles of Catholics and Travelers was inaccurate. Several students heard him say under his breath that he was ''sick of this multicultural nonsense.'' Despite Professor Smythe's obvious misgivings, he asked for a show of hands from those students who wanted a more multicultural perspective. Twenty-three of the 35 students raised their hands. Professor Smythe then asked the students what they meant by a ''more multicultural'' exchange of information. After each student comment, Professor Smythe interrupted and gave his opposing viewpoint. He stated that Protestants have been made to feel ashamed of their own history, often feeling silenced when they attempt to present a Protestant viewpoint in these ''politically correct'' times. Eventually, the discussion disintegrated into a shouting match between Professor Smythe and several students. Class meets again in four days, and we all dread returning to this angry environment.

We believed that the incident that occurred in Advanced Teaching Methods 306 is symptomatic of a larger problem in this department, but also that any attempt to broaden the perspective is looked on with hostility and derision by the department. We believe that these concerns must be addressed by the department immediately. We request a public forum open to all 20 faculty and 80 students in this department to discuss the concerns raised above.

Memo

TO: Chairperson of the Department of Education
FROM: Carl Smythe
RE: Recent Incident in Advanced Teaching Methods 306

I have read the students' memo about the incident that occurred in my Advanced Teaching Methods class. I was berated in class, accused of being culturally insensitive and inaccurate in my teaching about Irish history. Several aggressive students turned a discussion about students' concerns into a shouting match. Out of sheer frustration, I lost my composure. I believe that I am being unfairly attacked, and I need your support. I am not culturally insensitive, hostile to Catholics and Travelers, or only able to see the Protestant perspective. I do believe that the Protestant perspective is an important one to teach and understand and believe that I should not be required to sacrifice historical accuracy to be perceived as culturally sensitive. I would like to meet with you. I would be willing to

```
meet with students also, but only if you can ensure a calm,
intellectual exchange of ideas and not a free-for-all.
```

The chairperson of the Department of Education wants your help in responding to these memos. She wants to avoid escalation of hostility and alienation and in fact to reduce it, to get the class going again, to make progress toward better multicultural understanding, to increase the appreciation that each participant in this conflict has of the others' legitimate concerns, and to let faculty feel that they are respected and supported as scholars.

a. What are the barriers to achieving the chairperson's goals? What techniques can be used to overcome these barriers?
b. What are the possible problems that might occur if the department holds an open forum? What is likely to occur if the chairperson declines to hold the open forum?
c. Assuming that an open forum will be held, how should the facilitator for the open forum be selected? What traits should be sought in a facilitator?
d. How should the ground rules and process used in the forum differ from a typical mediation session as described in Rogers and Salem (1987) (pp. 110-111).
e. How would your answers change if the incident occurred at a university in Chicago and concerned racial and ethnic issues?

B. PUBLIC ENCOURAGEMENT OF MEDIATION

Public encouragement of mediation expanded rapidly over the last twenty years. Currently, millions of dollars of public monies are allocated to fund mediation programs. Disputing parties are commonly required by law to participate in mediation. Further, mediation is often sheltered by laws that protect mediators from liability and subpoena and that encourage the use of mediation by offering confidentiality and expedited case processing.

Critics of the growing public support of mediation do not suggest that the state should prevent parties from engaging a mediator if they wish to do so, but they do question the wisdom of using public resources and lawmaking authority to encourage mediation. The excerpts that follow raise some of the arguments for and against public support. They provide a taste of the more complex real debate concerning not only mediation but also other processes of dispute resolution.*

1. The Parties' Satisfaction with the Process and Result

Psychologist Tom R. Tyler: "Perhaps the most striking aspect of alternative dispute resolution programs to emerge from evaluations is their general

*The quotations in this section have been assembled to highlight a variety of viewpoints relating to mediation or other nonbinding forms of dispute resolution. The brief excerpts may not reflect the broader views of the writers. The full articles or books are referenced at the end of the chapter.

popularity. People typically seem satisfied with informal dispute resolution efforts, often more so than with traditional adjudication, and generally feel committed to decisions reached in them" (Tyler, 1989:436).

Anthropologist Sally Merry and Sociologist Susan Silbey: "[D]espite . . . evidence that disputants are satisfied with [alternative dispute resolution mechanisms], there continue to be relatively few people who seek them out without a justice system referral. . . . The argument that after ten years of experimentation and discussion of alternative dispute resolution, citizens do not use alternatives because they are unaware of them, is . . . unconvincing. . . . We would like to suggest a further explanation: citizens do not use alternatives voluntarily to the extent hoped for by proponents of [alternative dispute resolution mechanisms] because by the time a conflict is serious enough to warrant an outsider's intervention, disputants do not want what alternatives have to offer. At this point, the grievant wants vindication, protection of his or her rights (as he or she perceives them), an advocate to help in the battle, or a third party who will uncover the 'truth' and declare the other party wrong" (Merry and Silbey, 1984:152-153).

Law Professor Leonard Riskin: "Mediation offers some clear advantages over adversary processing: it is cheaper, faster, and potentially more hospitable to unique solutions that take more fully into account nonmaterial interests of the disputants. It can educate the parties about each other's needs and those of their community. Thus, it can help them learn to work together and to see that through cooperation both can make positive gains. One reason for these advantages is that mediation is less hemmed-in by rules of procedure or substantive law and certain assumptions that dominate the adversary process. [I]n mediation . . . the ultimate authority resides with the disputants. The conflict is seen as unique and therefore less subject to solution by application of some general principle. The case is neither to be governed by a precedent nor to set one. Thus, . . . whatever a party deems relevant is relevant" (Riskin, 1983:34).

Law professor Marc Galanter: "The argument that settlement is 'more responsive to parties' needs than adjudication' implies that settlement does more than maximize party preferences and satisfaction. . . . It asserts that good negotiation can achieve the satisfaction of parties' needs. It is not clear how far its proponents would assert that, holding case characteristics equal, the settlements negotiated by the negotiators who populate the world today actually achieve such results to a greater degree than cases that are adjudicated. [It would be difficult to mount such a showing.] Settlements are not intrinsically good or bad, any more than adjudication is good or bad. Settlements do not share any generic traits that commend us to avoid them per se or promote them" (Galanter, 1988:67-68, 82-83).

2. *The Role of the Law and the Role of the Community*

Law professor Owen Fiss: "The dispute-resolution story makes settlement appear as a perfect substitute for judgment . . . by trivializing the remedial dimensions of a lawsuit, and also by reducing the social function of the lawsuit to one of resolving private disputes: In that story, settlement appears to achieve exactly the same purpose as judgment—peace between the parties—but at considerably less expense to society. . . . In my view, however, the purpose of adjudication should be understood in broader terms. Adjudication uses public resources. [The court's job] is not to maximize the ends of private parties, nor simply to secure the peace, but to explicate and give force to the values embodied in authoritative texts such as the Constitution and statutes: to interpret those values and to bring reality into accord with them. . . . A settlement will . . . deprive a court of the occasion . . . to render an interpretation" (Fiss, 1984:1085).

U.S. Magistrate Wayne Brazil: "This concern [of Professor Fiss] would be triggered by [the court's settlement conference] program if its principal purpose and effect were to increase significantly the overall settlement rate and thus to reduce appreciably the opportunities for judges and juries to contribute to the evolution of legal norms, to determine what the facts underlying given disputes are, and to apply the relevant norms to those facts. I am aware of no evidence, however, that the court's settlement program has a significant impact on overall settlement rates. [A] significant commitment of judicial resources to the settlement process represents a greater rather than a lesser involvement by the public in the process by which disputes are resolved and in the enforcement of the basic rules of our society" (Brazil, 1990:316-317).

U.S. Court of Appeals Judge Harry T. Edwards: "A subtle variation on this problem of private application of public standards is the acceptance by many ADR advocates of the 'broken-telephone' theory of dispute resolution that suggests that disputes are simply 'failures to communicate' and will therefore yield to 'repair service by the expert "facilitator."' . . . One essential function of law is to reflect the public resolution of such unreconcilable differences; lawmakers are forced to choose among these differing visions of the public good. A potential danger of ADR is that disputants who seek only understanding and reconciliation may treat as irrelevant the choices made by our lawmakers and may, as a result, ignore public values reflected in rules of law" (Edwards, 1986:678-679).

Anthropologist Laura Nader: "[Through discourse about ADR, a] movement to control litigation was being constructed to replace justice and rights talk with what I call harmony ideology, the belief that harmony in the guise of compromise or agreement is ipso facto better than an adversary posture. In any period of history, harmony ideology is accompanied by an intolerance for conflict. The intention to prevent the expression of discord rather than to deal with its cause takes on prominence" (Nader, 1993:3).

Mediator Jennifer Beer: "There is always tension between the community's need to work out more amicable future interactions between members and the community's obligation to run a just and predictable system where behavior beyond set limits is consistently and publicly condemned. The school building has been spray painted several times this summer and the windows broken. Is it more important to punish all vandals equally or to stop the vandalism and pay for the clean-up? Two families are harassing each other and up the street more households are getting involved. Maybe they should be urged to talk things out. Maybe they should both be fined. Those involved have to negotiate with the community about which outcome is more desirable: justice or good relations. . . . Mediation is biased toward regaining harmony. The community advocating mediation is choosing a process which favors stability and good relations" (Beer, 1986:195, 197-198).

Law professor Robert A. Baruch Bush: "Through the recognition fostered in mediation, individuals will gain greater capacity to understand and communicate more effectively with others. Their increased capacity in both of these dimensions will both motivate and enable individuals to identify larger issues themselves, form coalitions, and bargain more effectively for social change. . . . When individuals develop a more positive view of the other party, through the recognition process that occurs in mediation, this positive view is carried over and applied to whatever 'group' that party is seen as part of. Moreover, the individual who has acquired the more positive view carries this view back and spreads it within his/her own social network, where it influences others as well. The combination of these carry-over and carry-back effects leads to a multiplier effect. [T]his theory suggests that the kind of change produced at the individual level, through a transformative approach to mediation, can lead to social change as well" (Bush, 1996a:732-733).

Law professor Timothy Terrell: "While advocates of ADR suggest that legalistic litigation is antithetical to our sense of community, I will contend that our community is legalistic, that law may constitute our only modern sense of community. If so, individual rights are more important than repose, and the implicit assumptions of ADR are seriously flawed" (Terrell, 1987:542).

3. Equal Justice

Legal historian Jerold Auerbach: "Alternatives are designed to provide a safety valve, to siphon discontent from courts. . . . They may deflect energy from political organization by groups of people with common grievances; or discourage effective litigation strategies that could provide substantial benefits. They may, in the end, create a two-track justice system that dispenses informal 'justice' to poor people with 'small' claims and 'minor' disputes" (Auerbach, 1983:144).

Law professor Richard Abel: "[O]nly within the legal system can advocates even hope to pursue the ideal of equal justice in a society riven by inequalities of class, race and gender and dominated by the power of capital and state. Formal law cannot eliminate substantive social inequalities, but it can limit their influence. Law is the sole arena within which unequals can hope to achieve justice. Only equals can risk a confrontation within the informal processes of the economy and the polity. Certainly advocates can imagine, and should strive for, a society that has overcome the inequalities that presently divide us; in such a society, informal processes could play a more prominent role. But until that millennium comes, formality is the best, often the only, defense against power" (Abel, 1985:383).

Former legal services lawyer, now law professor, William Simon: "Formal systems tend to be more difficult for people without special training or experience to participate in. [The formal] procedures can also subvert conflict and induce acquiescence. They can do so by convincing the disadvantaged that their losses are the result of a fair contest . . . , by making disadvantaged litigants feel incompetent and by making litigants feel dependent on professional helpers" (Simon, 1985:386, 388).

Law professor Jay Folberg and Mediator Alison Taylor: "The question of fairness in the outcome of a dispute should be asked equally of all forms of dispute resolution, including bargained agreements and litigation. Many disputes resolved outside of mediation are the result of unequal bargaining power due to different levels of experience, patterns of dominance, different propensities for risk avoidance, the greater emotional needs of one disputant, or psychological obstacles in the path to settlement. Should the matter proceed to litigation, the same items may skew the fairness of the outcome in court as in the bargaining phase—and in addition there may be unequal resources to bear the costs of litigation, different levels of sophistication in choosing the best attorneys, and just plain luck as to which judge is assigned to make a decision" (Folberg and Taylor, 1984:246-247).

Law professor Richard Delgado: "In some settings, persons feel free to act in prejudiced fashion; in others, they do not. The principal feature that suppresses prejudice is the certainty that prejudice, if displayed, will be remarked and punished—that it will not be tolerated but will result in active condemnation. . . . These social science insights shed light on the ability of different dispute resolution forums to minimize bias. The formalities of court trial are calculated to check prejudice. The trappings of formality—the flags, black robes, the rituals—remind the participants that trials are occasions on which the higher values of the American Creed are to preponderate, rather than the less noble values we embrace during times of intimacy. Equality of status is sought to be preserved—each party is represented by a lawyer and has a prescribed time and manner of speaking. Counsel direct their arguments not toward each other but toward a neutral judge or jury. Adjudication avoids the unstructured, unchecked, low-visibility types of interaction that, according to social scientists, foster prejudice. . . . When ADR cannot avoid dealing with sharply contested claims, its structureless setting and absence of formal rules increase the likelihood of an outcome colored by prejudice, with the result that the haves once again come out ahead" (Delgado, 1988:153-154).

Sociologist Craig McEwen: "Comparisons of mediation and adjudication often assume incorrectly that parties in mediation do not have the benefit of legal advice and representation while those in litigation do. Thus, these studies confuse two issues: the consequences of being unrepresented and the effects of using mediation. It will be difficult to assess the equity issue until research reflects the role of legal representation in both" (Rogers and McEwen, 1991:18).

4. The Effect on the Courts

U.S. Court of Appeals Judge Harry T. Edwards: "An important second issue in any discussion of proposals for alternative dispute resolution is the problem of court congestion. . . . It is true that, by almost any measure, the pervasiveness of law and the impact of legal institutions have increased rapidly in the last two decades. The number of cases filed in state courts has risen steadily and filings in federal courts have mushroomed. . . . Despite that dramatic increase in filing, however, the number of district court judges has grown almost proportionally. . . . At the federal appellate level, the caseload problem is more troubling. Between 1960 and 1980 the number of appeals filed in federal courts of appeals increased fourfold, while the number of judges only doubled. And, Supreme Court filings are now more than twice what they were in 1960. . . . I continue to believe that 'it is dangerous for courts to erect procedural roadblocks or limit the development of substantive law in certain disfavored areas in the hope of making more manageable their case loads.' [Still, trials are delayed and litigation] may be too expensive for most parties. These are compelling reasons for us to consider some alternatives to our existing court system. . . . So long as we remain committed to the 'rule of law' and continue to seek equal justice for all persons, I am convinced that the ADR experiment is one we must pursue" (Edwards, 1985:433-435, 443-444).

U.S. Court of Appeals Judge Richard Posner: ". . . I am not persuaded that making settlement cheaper to the parties is the solution to the caseload crisis. I would prefer to make the parties bear a larger fraction of the total costs of trial, including the queueing costs that trials impose on other parties. A recent study found that the average out-of-pocket cost to the federal government of certain tort cases tried by jury is $15,028 — and this excludes the queueing costs. But the fee for filing a case in federal district court is only $60. More realistic filing fees would be a simpler as well as more efficacious method of dealing with the caseload crisis than new ways of inducing people to settle lawsuits before trial. . . . Although court-annexed arbitration has the effect of increasing the filing fees for small claims, it does so in rather a sneaky fashion" (Posner, 1986:392-393).

Question

3.14 In which of the following situations is it appropriate for the public system to encourage the use of mediation through funding, referral, or other means?

a. A low-income housing resident has filed a class action against federal housing authorities in an attempt to keep them from cutting off federal subsidies to the housing development. The housing development owner has violated federal regulations, and the federal government has already sustained substantial losses. The residents say that they will have no place to live if the development is closed and that they are willing to operate the development themselves if the government will fund their cooperative venture. The case would be mediated by a state "public policy" mediation program.

b. Two large corporations are scheduled to begin a three-month patent trial. Settlement discussions have been unproductive. The lawyer for the defendant corporation, who advised the corporation originally that its product did not infringe the plaintiff's patent, refuses to recommend an offer over $50,000. The lawyer for the plaintiff corporation has demanded $2 million. One corporation is headquartered in Alaska; the other in Florida. The case would be mediated by a lawyer-mediator appointed and paid by the court.

c. McGovern alleges that Johnson mugged him but was apprehended by a police officer before taking his wallet. Johnson counters that McGovern walked up to him in front of a bar and started a fight. McGovern and Johnson had not seen each other before the incident and have not seen each other since. McGovern suffered broken ribs and is worried about his medical bills. The case would be mediated by a community mediation program with connections to the prosecutor.

d. Brian Masters, a 14-year-old, has missed 30 days of school. Brian says that his working mother asks him to stay home to take care of his little sister whenever his sister is sick and cannot attend the day care center. Brian's mother says that this accounts for only 10 of the 30 days. The school is prepared to recommend truancy charges against Brian if the matter is not resolved in a juvenile court prefiling mediation program.

e. Stover bought two tires from Jenner's, a local gas station. He was offered retreads but decided to buy new ones instead. Recently, when he had a flat, the service attendant at the station to which he brought the tire told him that the tires were used. When Stover confronted Jenner with this information, Jenner became angry and vigorously denied the accusation. Stover talked to another neighbor who had a similar experience with Jenner.

Stover does not have a lawyer (the amount in controversy did not seem to warrant the investment) and does not realize that treble damages would be available if he could prove his allegations. The mediation program is staffed by nonlawyer mediators who are unlikely to know about the treble damage statute.

f. Sanford is a shy woman working on an otherwise all-male construction crew. The crew supervisor often comes over to her and yells at her, probably just because he enjoys seeing Sanford cower or begin to cry. Sanford tries to stick it out because she hopes to become a supervisor herself for one of the company crews. However, she becomes distraught and consults a lawyer about filing a claim. The lawyer advises Sanford that the law is unsettled in her jurisdiction on the issue of whether the supervisor's shouting constitutes sexual harassment. The lawyer adds that, in light of the unsettled legal issue, a public interest law firm would probably represent her without charge. On the lawyer's advice, she files a claim with the relevant state civil rights agency to exhaust administrative remedies. The agency has a mediation program.

C. SOCIAL SCIENCE ASSESSMENTS OF MEDIATION

The views expressed by the commentators in the foregoing policy dialogue rest on assumptions about how people behave and how institutions operate. The same is true of the advice on mediation techniques quoted in the first section of this chapter. How accurate are these assumptions? In this section, we provide highlights of several recent studies of mediation that bear on policy and practice issues discussed earlier in the chapter. Although pertinent, the results in these studies come with a special caveat: social scientists caution against giving undue weight to findings from any individual study. They suggest that accumulated studies provide a better basis for policy and strategy decisions. In the last note, sociologist Craig McEwen synthesizes findings from multiple studies of mediation. His list of findings with broad research support is short; much remains to be done in terms of establishing or refuting the assumptions made by commentators.

We refer to the four recent studies reported below as the "private," "state civil court," "small claims court," and "federal court" mediation studies. In the "private" mediation study, Jeanne M. Brett, Zoe I. Barsness, and Stephen B. Goldberg examined 449 disputes handled by private dispute resolution providers (Brett et al., 1996). In the "state civil court" mediation study, Roselle Wissler, in cooperation with the Ohio State University College of Law Database Project, studied 650 medium to large civil disputes mediated by court-appointed volunteer mediators in four Ohio counties (Wissler, 1997). Wissler later reported on expanded research with data from 1,700 mediated civil cases in nine Ohio courts (Wissler, 2002). In the "small claims court" mediation study, Michele Hermann, Gary LaFree, Christine Rack, and Mary Beth West investigated the results in 600 small claims cases in New Mexico, 280 of which were mediated (Hermann et al., 1993). In the "federal court" mediation study, researchers from the RAND Corporation analyzed 1,200 federal district court cases, half of which were mediated by volunteer or paid private mediators (Kakalik et al., 1996).

Satisfaction with mediation in public and private sectors: The vast majority of mediation participants expressed satisfaction with the process, the neutral, and the outcome — whether the mediator was a paid private provider or a court-appointed volunteer. Parties compelled to mediate by a contract clause or court order were as satisfied or almost as satisfied as those who agreed to participate at the outset of the mediation.

The private mediation study compared responses of participants in mediation with responses by participants in arbitration. Parties whose disputes were mediated were overwhelmingly pleased with the process, the neutral, the outcome, and the implementation — more so than participants whose cases were arbitrated.

In the state civil court study, 96 percent of the parties whose cases were mediated by court-appointed volunteer mediators rated the mediator as neutral and even-handed. Ninety-two percent would recommend mediation to a friend or colleague who had a similar problem. Only 2 percent of the attorneys and 3 percent of the parties said that the state civil court mediation process was unfair.

Relationships: The private mediation study provides support for the view that mediation is more likely to improve relationships than is adjudication. Parties were more likely to state that their relationship had been improved when they used mediation rather than arbitration.

Mediator evaluation: Whether the mediator evaluated the merits of the case, thought so important by some commentators, had only slight effects in the eyes of the parties. In fact, the evaluation was such an insignificant factor for many parties in state civil court mediation that they did not always remember it occurring even when the mediator indicated that an evaluation had been given. The mediator's evaluation did not affect settlement rates in the private setting, though settlement rates increased in the state civil court mediation when the mediator evaluated. In the state civil court mediation, parties expressed higher satisfaction if the mediator evaluated the case. Mediators who evaluated tended not to cut mediation short, as suggested by some commentators; in fact, evaluative mediation lasted longer than nonevaluative mediation.

Mediator recommendations: In contrast to these slight reactions to mediator evaluation, state civil court mediators who recommended a particular settlement met strong adverse reactions. Settlement rates grew substantially—by 24 percent. The parties were less likely to view the mediation process as fair and the mediator as neutral, however, when the mediator recommended a specific settlement.

Mediator qualifications: Mediator qualifications often include hours of mediation training, substantive expertise, and sometimes educational degrees (see pp. 163-175). In the state civil court setting, volunteer mediators had mediation training that ranged from fewer than 6 hours of training in mediation to over 80 hours of training. All had a law degree, but about half did not usually practice in the substantive area at issue in the case. Their legal practice experience varied from a few years to decades. None of these factors affected settlement rates. Mediation training hours also did not affect the parties' satisfaction ratings, but attorneys were more impressed with the competence of mediators with substantive expertise in the legal issues of the dispute. Although Wissler (1997) warns that the assignment of cases to mediators was not random, one would still expect more dramatic results if these typical mediator qualifications were important prerequisites to quality mediation. What mediator traits did affect results or party satisfaction? Of the measured traits of mediators, only experience (having mediated more than 15 cases) even approached a statistically significant relationship with settlement. The research suggests that the task of identifying qualifications for mediators that will affect outcomes or satisfaction is complicated and that common mediation qualification rules and statutes may focus on the wrong attributes.

Outcomes by gender and ethnicity: Commentators raise concerns about whether women and ethnic and racial minorities fare worse in mediation. In the New Mexico small claims court study, women who were claimants achieved the same monetary success (measured by percentage of amounts claimed) in mediation as men. Women who were respondents achieved better monetary success than men. Ethnic minority parties (85 percent Hispanic), however, fared worse monetarily in mediation than white parties unless the co-mediators were both ethnic minorities. Ethnic minority parties also fared worse in litigation, but still did better in litigation than in mediation. Over half of the parties had lawyers, but ethnic minority parties were less likely to be represented by counsel. The researchers warned that they did not distinguish the effects of having legal representation from effects of ethnicity on the results (see McEwen and Rogers, p. 467). At the same time, the differing results reached when mediators had ethnic backgrounds like the parties suggests that the effects of legal representation will not explain all differences. One of the researchers concludes that those running mediation programs should "pay serious attention to the potential impact of power imbalances. . . ." (Hermann, 1994).

Disputant participation: Participation of the actual disputants had a highly significant effect on settlement rates in the state civil court mediation programs. Settlement rates were 23 percent higher if no party critical to the resolution was missing. The parties' satisfaction was higher in the federal courts that encourage their attendance at mediation sessions than in the courts that did not.

System costs: The federal courts spent $130 to $490 for each case mediated. Researchers could not find significant reductions in time to disposition for mediated cases.

Party costs: The parties spent less on private mediation than on private arbitration. Median costs of mediation were $2,750, compared to $11,800 for arbitration. Most parties and lawyers in state civil court mediation believed that mediation either had no effect on their litigation costs or had reduced the costs (see pp. 355-356 regarding costs and timing of mediation vis-à-vis discovery). In contrast, the federal court mediation study found no significant cost savings or increases as a result of mediation when costs were measured by the number of hours lawyers said that they spent in federal court litigation.

The snapshot taken by these four studies: Mediation is well received by participants in a variety of settings, unless the mediator recommends a particular settlement. Disputing parties welcome rather than resent the addition of mediation to the processing of their case. There are indications, however, like the New Mexico study regarding outcomes and the federal courts study regarding party costs, that parties and attorneys may not really know mediation's effects on costs or outcomes.

The commentators' views about what is high-quality mediation were not all borne out by the results in these studies. The results of mediation were about the same for facilitative and evaluative mediators, for mediators who were trained a little and a lot, and for mediators with substantive expertise and without. Parties and attorneys did not react negatively to mediator evaluation; in fact, sometimes they liked it better.

C. McEWEN, NOTE ON MEDIATION RESEARCH

Empirical research about mediation in a variety of contexts indicates that:

- Disputants (and their attorneys) engaged in mediation are very likely to be satisfied with the process and to find it fair. Such judgments about mediation tend to be either comparable to or more favorable than judgments about other processes like trial or negotiation.
- Similar comparisons hold for disputant satisfaction with, and sense of fairness of, the outcomes of mediation, although disputants tend to be less happy with outcomes than with process.
- Where compliance with mediated outcomes has been studied, it appears to be as high or higher than compliance with adjudicated outcomes.
- In most research, settlement rates in mandatory mediation are similar to those in voluntary mediation, although there are occasional findings of lower rates after mandatory referral. Party assessments of the mediation process and outcome are similar in mandatory and voluntary mediation.
- By and large, case type is unrelated to settlement rates or to disputant perceptions of the process.
- Outcomes of mediated agreements are often quite similar to those achieved through negotiation or adjudication, but they are somewhat more likely to include non-monetary arrangements and/or detailed conditions for implementation of the agreement. Like negotiation, mediation often — but not always — leads to somewhat lower monetary settlements than might be awarded after trial.

The very limited evidence we have indicates that when litigants settle through mediation, they often save money. When mediation is another step in the litigation process, it does not increase costs substantially.

- There is no evidence to show that mediation saves courts money, although it may in some instances contribute to avoidance of possible future costs (i.e., of hiring new judges and opening new courtrooms).
- No compelling evidence exists to resolve the debate between those who argue that mediation empowers disputants and those who argue that it harms disadvantaged parties.
- In the mediation process some parties appear to experience pressure to settle or to follow the mediator's values in shaping the terms of a settlement.
- Mediator qualifications such as amount or kind of training and extent of experience show little consistent relationship with such factors as settlement rates or party assessments of the process.

Of course, the implementation of mediation varies widely from one jurisdiction and one subject area to the next. Such differences in the timing of mediation in relation to case filing or the degree and kind of engagement that lawyers have in the process appear to have significant consequences for "time-savings" in mediation and potentially in costs. This variation in implementation also significantly limits the ability to generalize research findings about mediation from one setting to another, and also affects the way one might think about controversial issues such as party awareness of legal rights in the mediation process.

Nonetheless, the research on mediation to date does bear on many of the issues under debate regarding mediation, while leaving others unresolved. Despite the fact that disputants typically choose to invoke courts before arriving at mediation, they tend to find the mediation experience to be a good and "just" one once they enter the process. It is important to note that experience in courts is often seen as just and satisfying as well, although marginally less so in many of the comparisons that exist. Nor does mediation appear to be the weak process some have claimed. In fact, if anything, compliance may be enhanced by the mediation process.

The very strength of the mediation process raises concerns, given evidence that under some circumstances parties may be persuaded by mediators to accept outcomes and that the process itself can create its own momentum and pressures for agreement. Those concerns about pressure are highlighted by the wide variation in training, format, court supervision, and restraint of mediators in mediation programs. The fact that mediated outcomes may differ from those achieved in negotiation or at trial is consistent with the claim that mediation can produce creative outcomes reflective of the needs of parties. At the same time, it highlights the concern that mediation may lead some parties to accept agreements that ignore or compromise their legal rights.

Despite the extensive commentary arguing that mediation harms parties from disadvantaged groups (ethnic minorities, women, consumers, the poor), little empirical evidence exists either to support or to challenge this argument. More important, there may be disagreement about what evidence is appropriate. For critics, empowerment of disadvantaged parties may come only from legal advocacy and defense or expansion of legal rights. For mediation advocates, empowerment of disadvantaged persons may come by encouraging individual involvement and responsibility in disputing and seeking settlement. When definitions of empowerment differ so radically, empirical evidence is not likely to resolve the debate.

The evidence of limited efficiency gains through mediation may speak to inappropriate expectations of it, to the wide variations in the ways mediation is implemented in relation to court processes, and to the difficulties of research on this issue. Many mediation advocates would argue that to involve parties and consider issues in depth, mediation should take longer than perfunctory court hearings or lawyer-to-lawyer negotiation. When mediation operates under time pressures, in contrast, it may not meet party needs and may increase pressures to settle. The speed of mediation may also be a function of highly variable court practices of case management and the rules and timing of mediation referral.

Research about the costs for courts and for parties of varying dispute resolution procedures is fraught with challenges. Measurement and assignment of costs is not straightforward. For example, which court costs count for cases in the regular litigation process and for cases in a court-annexed mediation program? How is volunteer time valued in assessing the costs of a mediation program? Comparisons of costs can be confusing as well. For example, should the costs of non-mediated cases be averaged so as to include the very high expenses of a few tried cases (some of which have been through mediation) as well as the much lower costs of the many settled cases? These are among the dozens of questions that make confident cost comparisons difficult.

Fierce debates among mediators about what "real mediation" is or should be also remain unresolved by mediation research. Some research on civil case mediation suggests, for example, that settlements are more likely when mediators participate actively in mediation and reveal their assessments of the merits of the case. In other settings, mediator approach appears unrelated to settlement. Parties show no reduction in their perceptions of fairness and do not feel pressured to settle, unless the mediator goes so far as to recommend a *particular* settlement. Mediator style and its impacts on parties and cases require considerably more research.

Question

3.15 Empirical evidence fails to shed light on several points disputed by commentators in the policy dialogue on pages 147-152 (see Esser, 1989). Who should bear the burden of persuasion in the policy argument—those who advocate increased public support of mediation or those who oppose it?

D. REGULATING MEDIATION

The growth in public support for mediation indicates that the arguments in its favor have been persuasive. At the same time, the concerns about mediation, discussed in the last section, have spurred efforts to control the quality of mediation.

Some such efforts require no changes in the law. For instance, professional mediation associations promote high quality through consumer education, mediator rosters, continuing education for mediators, ethics codes that are voluntary or enforced by exclusion from membership in the associations, and peer review among mediators (see SPIDR Report, pp. 164-169). However, courts, administrative agencies, and legislators have become increasingly involved in mediation funding and referral, and they are reluctant to rely solely on informal schemes that depend for success on the voluntary compliance of mediators or the watchfulness of consumers or private associations.

This reluctance has led to experimentation with what is called here the "regulation" of mediation. The regulation consists of efforts to enforce standards of quality. The standards of quality underlying enforcement schemes differ from jurisdiction to jurisdiction, though the standards commonly concern fairness, costs, and respect for the justice system (Section D1, infra).

The enforcement schemes (Section D2, infra) reflect a variety of approaches to regulation, which are divided in the discussion below into:

- Entry-level requirements, such as educational qualifications, for mediators;
- Mediator accountability provisions, such as binding codes of ethics, civil liability for mediators, program funding requirements, and occasionally even criminal liability for mediators; and
- Mediation-related procedures, such as expert assistance for the parties, exclusion of some cases from mediation, and judicial review of mediated agreements.

The experimentation has led to an immense new body of law regarding mediation. There are now more than 2,000 state and federal statutes that concern mediation (Cole et al., 2003 & 2006 Supp.). Adding to the statutory complexity, numerous court rules, administrative regulations, and judicial rulings also govern the mediation process. These laws vary in their regulatory approach from one jurisdiction to the next and also by type of case within each jurisdiction.

In 2002, both the American Bar Association and the National Conference of Commissioners on Uniform State Laws approved the Uniform Mediation Act. Eight states and the District of Columbia have adopted the Act. The Act relies on the third type of enforcement scheme set out above—it provides for mediation-related procedures as the means to achieve quality. Specifically, mediator reports to the decision-maker are prohibited. Parties are permitted to have a lawyer or other person accompanying them. In one way, the Act relies on mediator accountability. The mediator must disclose conflicts of interest and, if asked, qualifications to mediate. (Sections 7, 9, 10, Uniform Mediation Act, Appendix E.) Is this the optimal combination of approaches to regulating quality in mediation?

1. *Standards of Quality for Mediation*

One way to begin the task of regulating to achieve quality is to translate the concerns expressed in Section B into legal standards. Drafters may find the translation challenging, however, because people disagree about how fairness and other goals should be defined. A second challenge is to weigh the costs of the regulation against the gain. Ultimately, aims touted by some commentators such as personal reconciliation (p. 108) may be lost in the winnowing process, either because law would be a clumsy mechanism to achieve them or because the goals may not be worth the effort in the eyes of legislators. We discuss the goals and legal standards emerging in the law in this section, and the enforcement mechanisms in the next section.

a. Fairness

If all parties have attorneys, it may be sufficient to define fairness as consent to the result by parties within a process that has integrity. The statutory standards might then relate to lack of coercion to settle (see pp. 406-409) and neutrality of the mediator. In contrast, unrepresented parties may face marked differences in negotiating experience and understanding of their alternatives to settling. To protect these persons, some jurisdictions have developed standards for fairness based on balance in the negotiation process or equivalency in outcomes.

Balanced negotiation process: The concern that imbalances in negotiating power will have harmful effects has been addressed in some jurisdictions through legal standards regarding the process of mediation. In Hawaii, for example, mediators are directed by court standards to "promote fairness" and encourage full disclosure of information between parties (Hawaii Supreme Court Standards for Public and Private Mediators, 1986). The Iowa Supreme Court rules require family mediators to assure a productive dialogue (Rules Governing Standards of Practice for Lawyer-Mediators in Family Disputes, 1986).

One difficulty with these standards is that bargaining imbalances are not easily identified. Negotiating power may be based on differing access to legal expertise, negotiating ability of the parties or their representatives, ability and willingness to take risks, ability to withstand delay in resolution, vulnerability to damage from publicity, willingness and ability to evade collection efforts, and countless other things. Negotiating power can also change over time and from issue to issue, adding to the difficulty of identifying imbalances.

The next problem lies in determining when the extent of the imbalance—if identified accurately—is serious enough to warrant regulation. Is it when the effect in mediation exceeds that in the likely alternative process? If so, this would require use of a comparative standard. We discuss the shortcomings of comparative standards below (p. 162).

Once bargaining imbalances are identified and their extent determined, the next task is to determine what types of bargaining imbalances should be avoided. Those based on lack of access to legal expertise and financial resources seem especially important to avoid, because they fall most frequently on the poor. An Oklahoma court rule reflects this view, stating that if one party has a lawyer and another does not, the party without representation may refuse to participate in the mediation (Oklahoma Supreme Court Rules and Procedures for Dispute Resolution Act, Rule 10). Beyond this, public policy interests do not demand total bargaining parity. For instance, the law does not seek to neutralize a bargaining advantage gained by one party because the other has a criminal record and will therefore be less credible as a witness at trial, or a bargaining advantage held by an AIDS patient because the insurance company defendant is trying to avoid damaging precedent and offers more in settlement than is likely to be awarded after trial (Aiken, 1992).

Equivalent or "fair" outcome: Those who despair at regulating the mediation process often aim instead at regulating outcomes. It has been suggested by commentators that mediated agreements should be consistent with the anticipated outcome at trial or, instead, that mediated agreements should be consistent with the settlement a party would approve after hearing what a lawyer would have recommended (e.g., Maute, 1990). If this latter comparative standard could be embodied in law and enforced, it has the advantage over the former standard of including such considerations as the expense, uncertainty, and emotional stress of litigation and the likelihood of compliance. Unfortunately, these added considerations are often unknown by the judge or mediator who must make the comparison. Further, predicting the lawyer's advice may be so difficult that the standard collapses. In one experiment, a panel of divorce lawyers was asked to assess the quality of settlement agreements. The researchers reported, "Typically, one experienced attorney viewed a visitation arrangement as appropriate while another felt it was only fair and a third scored it as poor" (Thoennes, Pearson, and Bell, 1991:163).

Because of practical problems with comparative standards, some noncomparative measures of mediated agreements are imposed by law. For example, under various statutes or court rules, a mediator complies with the law if the best interests of children are promoted (Cal. Civ. Code §3180(b)) or a judge approves it (Colo. Rev. Stat. §13-22-308). Some of these standards presuppose that law is not the only measure of fairness. "Best interests of the child," for example, could be defined by other standards, though settling on nonlegal criteria may be problematic. The judicial approval requirement has the advantage of dodging, for the moment, the issue of an appropriate criterion for assessing mediated agreements.

b. Costs

Disputants and courts hope that mediation will result in cost savings. Generally, they anticipate savings only if mediation produces a settlement. Further, *early* settlement increases cost savings for both the parties and the courts (see p. 403). Perhaps to encourage cost savings, nonprofit program funding in some jurisdictions is based in part on the number of settlements reached (710 ILCS 20/4 et seq.). A state funding formula that takes the number of settlements into account may make it more difficult to achieve fairness in mediation. A community mediator in such a state may hesitate to terminate an unbalanced mediation, knowing that her program's funding may be affected by the number of settlements it reaches.

c. The Effectiveness of the Justice System

The regulation of mediation reflects the need to maintain public confidence in the justice system and to keep it accessible to persons of all income levels, not just the desire to provide high-quality mediation. For example, to maintain access to the justice system, legislatures and courts sometime place ceilings on mediation fees. Judges may want to require certain mediator qualifications so that the public views court staff members as highly trained professionals even if research does not substantiate the need for the qualifications in terms of the quality of the mediation process. Statutes requiring assessments regarding participant satisfaction may respond as much to the desire to preserve confidence in the courts as to improve the quality of the mediation.

Mediation regulation may also stem from concerns, expressed by critics, that additional settlements resulting from mediation will diminish the courts' role in clarifying the law through judicial precedent, and in deterring undesirable conduct through criminal and civil penalties and trial publicity. Efforts to respond to these critiques are evidenced in procedural standards, such as requirements for judicial review of mediated agreements and standards for selecting cases for mediation referral. For example, two decades of efforts by victim advocates have persuaded lawmakers to increase sanctions for domestic violence (see Chapter 8). Courts are more frequently treating family violence as crimes. Victim advocates fear that these efforts will be undermined by mediated settlements (Lerman, 1984:79-94). Responding to this concern, statutes regarding mediation programs commonly exclude such cases from mediation (e.g., Iowa Code §236.13). Thus concern for deterring family violence has been translated into a standard for selecting cases suitable for mediation.

d. A Word on Comparative Standards

Many of these standards are comparative — for instance, comparing mediated settlements with court judgments. We have discussed the implementation problems, but comparative standards also present conceptual problems. It may not be sensible to aspire to standards based on comparisons of outcomes of mediation and trial. The likely alternative to mediation in a particular situation might not be litigation but unassisted negotiations, arbitration, administrative process, political battle, economic warfare, or simply doing nothing.

Moreover, even if litigation is the likely alternative, the apt comparison is not between ideal mediation and ideal litigation, but between what is likely to occur in each process. For instance, it makes little sense to assume that either mediators or judges advise litigants of their rights or look out for interests of nonparties if this is typically not the case. Without a lawyer, the consumer who seeks redress from a car manufacturer or dealer for a bent car axle may have difficulty both navigating through the court process and negotiating in mediation. Nonetheless, the lack of a lawyer may be less damaging in mediation, where the focus may be less on the parties' legal rights than on whether the defendants can settle for less than litigation costs.

Questions

3.16 Standards for publicly assisted mediated settlements are often higher than for settlements achieved after unassisted negotiations. For unassisted settlements, present laws are usually satisfied if the parties consent to the outcome; no contract defenses (fraud, unconscionability, and so on) are available; the agreement does not contravene public policy; and it is not a special type (custody, class action) requiring court approval. Why should legal standards be different for mediated settlements than for settlements reached without the assistance of a mediator?

3.17 Mr. and Mrs. Thompson purchased a home 2 years ago after saving for 20 years. Both have eighth-grade educations, and Mrs. Thompson works at minimum wage. Mr. Thompson is ill and unable to work. A few months ago, they signed an agreement with a contractor to remodel their kitchen. They also signed a note secured by a mortgage on their home. The contractor did a little work and then, after bilking 100 other families as well, disappeared. The bank that purchased all the notes from the contractor seeks to collect and has threatened, through its law firm, to foreclose on the Thompsons' house. The Thompsons are represented by a legal services attorney who was admitted to the bar a few months ago and is anxious to engage in a first negotiation.

If the case is mediated, what will be the bargaining imbalances? Which bargaining imbalances would lead to unjust results in mediation? Would the results be more just in litigation or in unassisted negotiations?

3.18 In a sexual harassment case, the mediated settlement provides that the alleged harasser will be transferred away from the plant where the plaintiff works, that no one will disclose the settlement, and that the defendant employer will pay the plaintiff $75,000. Assume that the anticipated judgment after trial, set for a year from now, would be $125,000. Are the results equivalent? Is the outcome fair to the parties? Is it harmful to nonparties?

2. *Enforcement Mechanisms*

a. Mediator Qualifications

Legislators and courts have tried to ensure quality in the mediation process through entry requirements for mediators. These mediator qualifications are based on the assumption that education, training, and experience indicate ability and create an inclination to act in a particular way. For example, if a mediator undergoes training in dealing with power imbalances, the assumption is that the mediator will be more likely to intervene effectively in such situations. A mediator who has met training and experience requirements will presumably be more adept at leading parties to settlement. Research substantiates that mediation experience, not education or substantive expertise, increases settlements (Wissler, 1997; Wissler, 2002).

Legislators have not waited for research, however, and qualifications for mediators in publicly supported or referred programs have been imposed by statute in at least 38 states and by court rule in others. The Uniform Mediation Act §9(c) requires mediators to disclose their qualifications at a party's request. Nebraska's adoption of the UMA imposes an obligation on mediators to disclose qualifications, based on the reasoning that consumers might not know when they should request disclosure (Neb. Rev. Stat. §25-2938(c)). The following report, which was adopted by the Society for Professionals in Dispute Resolution (SPIDR), discusses the formal and informal means available to promote quality in dispute resolution and the special considerations inherent in imposing qualifications by law to achieve this goal.

SOCIETY OF PROFESSIONALS IN DISPUTE RESOLUTION, REPORT OF THE SPIDR COMMISSION ON QUALIFICATIONS

(1989)

. . . Rationale

The most commonly discussed purposes of setting criteria for individuals to practice as neutrals are (1) to protect the consumer and (2) to protect the integrity of various dispute resolution processes. Many policy makers and professionals in the field are concerned about individuals with little information about or skill in dispute resolution simply "hanging out a shingle" and offering to mediate or arbitrate anyone's dispute. Further, concerns are being raised about poorly trained and inexperienced neutrals offering training to others. The risks are several — the interests of parties may be harmed by incompetent practice and the public's understanding of what it means to request specific dispute resolution services may become confused, leading to public dissatisfaction with the field and claims that mediation and arbitration are merely a form of second class justice.

Proposals to establish qualifications for neutrals also raise considerable controversy, however. Some of the reaction appears to be anxiety among members of a profession newly faced with regulation. Many substantive concerns also have been raised, particularly about mandatory standards of certification, including: (1) creating inappropriate barriers to entry into the field, thus, (2) hampering the innovative quality of the profession, and (3) limiting the broad dissemination of peacemaking skills in society. Even many of those who are persuaded that there is a need for some mandatory standards are concerned that it may not be possible yet to define and measure competence. . . .

Although current developments in legislating qualifications most frequently apply to disputes referred by courts, these developments are likely to shape the practice of dispute resolution in all sectors. With so many statutory or court-ordered requirements in place, avoidance of the issue is no longer an option. Rather, the question is what are the most appropriate and useful ways to achieve the objectives of policy makers who are concerned about ensuring qualified practice, without the negative consequences of limiting the field.

Policy Options

There is no single way to promote quality in any professional practice. Among the options are [the following]. . . .

A. Free Market

Classically, in the "free market" consumers of a service select any provider they wish, with no regulation of consumer or provider. This situation can be found in much labor arbitration practice and in the mediation of some family, commercial, and environmental disputes. Based on this experience, some assert that the free market is sufficient to ensure quality of practice because the parties will continue to select only those who have provided competent service.

B. DISCLOSURE REQUIREMENTS

A concern raised about the "free market" approach is that many parties, particularly those who do not use dispute resolution services on a regular basis, do not have access to complete information about practicing neutrals. Thus, these parties cannot make the *informed* choice on which the advantages of the free market depend. Consequently, some suggest that disclosure requirements would make a significant contribution to consumer protection. . . .

C. PUBLIC/CONSUMER EDUCATION

Reliance on informed choice also assumes that parties will consider what characteristics of a neutral will serve their best interests. Although some parties are experienced in how dispute resolution processes and neutrals function, others are not. Some public and private agencies consider it their responsibility to conduct educational programs for potential parties or to raise questions to help them think through the implications of a variety of options. . . .

D. "AFTER THE FACT" CONTROLS, [SUCH AS] MALPRACTICE LAWSUITS

The threat of malpractice lawsuits is one method of increasing the likelihood that individuals in any profession will practice in a competent manner. Few malpractice cases have been filed against neutrals to date and few professional standards exist against which to judge whether a particular individual has been guilty of malpractice in a given situation. The increasing tendency to formulate standards of practice may have growing implications for malpractice actions. . . .

E. ROSTERS

An increasingly common means for encouraging the use of dispute resolution services is to establish "rosters" through which parties can obtain the services of a neutral. A roster differs from a dispute resolution program in that the neutrals listed on a roster provide services independently of the organization maintaining the roster. Although organizations that compile rosters vary in the amount of screening that they do, most stand behind the competence of the individuals included on their rosters. Examples of rosters are the lists maintained by the Federal Mediation and Conciliation Service and the American Arbitration Association. . . .

F. VOLUNTARY STANDARDS

Various professional organizations, such as the National Academy of Arbitrators, have adopted their own form of standards through their membership criteria. Another example is the Academy of Family Mediators, which has established detailed membership requirements and criteria to accredit mediators and trainers.

Neutrals participate in these organizations voluntarily; if they choose not to do so they are not barred from practice. If the standards of the organization are explicit, well publicized, and seen as desirable by consumers, however, the consumers' preference for neutrals possessing the "credential" of membership in that organization may serve to increase the use of neutrals with those qualifications.

G. CODES OF PROFESSIONAL ETHICS

One form of voluntary standards is a code of ethics, such as the code developed by the Society of Professionals in Dispute Resolution. Parties have the opportunity to know more about, and possibly value the qualities of, neutrals subscribing to a code of ethics.

H. MANDATORY STANDARDS FOR NEUTRALS

Some suggest that specific standards should be set for who should be allowed to practice as a neutral, in part because parties often do *not* have a free choice of the neutral providing a dispute resolution service. Among those who hold this view there are differences about what criteria are good measures of competent practice. The most common pattern to date is for states to require degrees earned in related professions, such as law, social work, or counseling. The specific degrees required vary. Recent regulations promulgated by the Florida Supreme Court, for example, limit court-referred family mediators to those with one of the following credentials: a master's degree in social work, mental health, behavioral or social sciences; psychiatrists; attorneys; and certified public accountants.

Some states include training requirements; one incorporates experience. In some states, such as Florida, a minimum number of hours of court-approved dispute resolution training is combined with academic degree requirements. . . .

There are different ways of setting standards for neutrals. The least restrictive is some form of certification, which may be performed by a private organization or a public agency. Lack of certification does not bar an individual from practicing. Licensing is more restrictive, performed by a public agency as a condition of practice.

I. MANDATORY STANDARDS FOR PROGRAMS

. . . Some suggest that setting criteria for *programs* offering dispute resolution services, rather than criteria for individual neutrals, might be an effective way to ensure quality of dispute resolution services without limiting the entry of individual neutrals into the field. . . .

J. IMPROVEMENTS IN TRAINING FOR NEUTRALS

Regardless of whether any limitations on entry are established, a strong case can be made for requiring continuing training and evaluation of dispute resolution skills. . . .

Principles

There is no single answer to what constitutes a qualified neutral or which of the policy options described is appropriate to ensure that those who practice are qualified to do so. SPIDR recommends the following central principles:

A. that no single entity (rather, a variety of organizations) should establish qualifications for neutrals;
B. that the greater the degree of choice the parties have over the dispute resolution process, program or neutral, the less mandatory should be the qualification requirements; and
C. that qualification criteria should be based on performance, rather than paper credentials.

A. No Single Entity

1-2. Clearly, the dispute resolution field is a diverse one. Even though there are some skills that are basic, the knowledge and techniques required to practice competently may vary by context, by process, by issue, or by institutional setting. Different criteria also may be relevant to binding arbitration, non-binding arbitration, mediation (where neutrals do not give opinions), and ombudsmanry. . . .

It may be important to avoid policies that would allow any one public or private body to establish uniform criteria for all neutrals, even for a single sector. Such uniformity could restrict the development of different dispute resolution approaches and, if misused, could close the ranks of the profession to particular social or ethnic groups.

Thus, SPIDR recommends:

1. Where criteria for determining minimum competence in different contexts are warranted, they should be established by a variety of agencies working in those contexts. No single entity should be relied on to certify general dispute resolution competence. . . .

B. Degree of Choice

3. . . . The Commission has identified three categories of relative choice by the parties:

a. independent neutrals offering services to the public through a free market, or public or private institutions in which parties have *full choice* of process, program, and neutral;
b. public or private institutions in which parties have a choice of *some,* but not all, of the following: process, program, and neutral; and
c. public or private institutions in which parties have *no choice* of process, program, or neutral.

If one of the purposes of efforts to ensure competent practice is to protect the consumer, different approaches may be appropriate depending on the degree of freedom or ability that the parties have to choose and thus to protect themselves. Thus, SPIDR recommends:

> 3. The extent to which qualifications for neutrals are mandated should vary by the degree of choice the parties have over the dispute resolution process, the program offering dispute resolution services, and the neutral. The greater the degree of choice, the less mandatory should be the requirements.

Based on this general principle, SPIDR suggests three basic strategies corresponding to the degree of choice by the parties: . . .

> 4. No standards or qualifications should be required that would prevent any person from providing dispute resolution services, when parties have free choice of the process, program, *and* individual neutral, provided that the parties are given access to [specified] information about the neutral. . . .
>
> 5. Where courts, public agencies, or private organizations operate programs that do *not* offer the parties a choice of the dispute resolution process, program, or neutral to which the parties must go to engage in that process, standards or qualifications for such programs and neutrals should be set by an appropriate public entity (typically the legislature or its delegee), in accordance with the principles set forth in this document. Information about such standards or qualifications should be made available to the parties.

6. Finally, where the parties have a choice of some — but not all — of the elements of process, program, or neutral, the elucidation of a general standard to govern qualifications is difficult. SPIDR's recommended approach is to require programs offering dispute resolution services to *disclose* their selection criteria but not to tell them what criteria they should use. Thus, when the parties have some, but not complete, choice of process, program, or neutral, SPIDR recommends:

> 6. It is the responsibility of public and private programs offering dispute resolution services to define clearly the services they provide, to establish clear criteria for selecting intervenors and evaluating intervenor performance, to conduct periodic performance evaluations, and to offer [specified] information about the program and the neutral(s) to parties. . . .

C. PERFORMANCE-BASED QUALIFICATIONS

. . . The committee knows of no evidence that formal degrees are necessary to competent performance as a neutral. Indeed, there is impressive evidence that some individuals who do not possess these credentials make excellent dispute resolvers. Furthermore, the requirement of a graduate degree in any discipline clearly creates a significant barrier to the entry of many competent individuals into the profession. . .

> . . . 7. Knowledge acquired in obtaining various degrees can be useful in the practice of dispute resolution. At this time and for the foreseeable future, however, no such degree in itself ensures competence as a neutral. Furthermore, requiring a degree would foreclose

alternative avenues of demonstrating dispute resolution competence. Consequently, no degree should be considered a prerequisite for service as a neutral.

8-10. SPIDR believes that performance criteria (such as neutrality, demonstrated knowledge of relevant practices and procedures, ability to listen and understand, and ability to write a considered opinion for arbitrators) are more useful and appropriate in setting qualifications to practice than is the manner in which one achieves those criteria (such as formal degrees, training, or experience). Thus, SPIDR recommends: . . .

9. Any requirements concerning who can practice as a neutral should be based on performance. In establishing requirements, any certifying bodies or agencies maintaining rosters or lists of "acceptable" neutrals should emphasize the knowledge and skills necessary for competent practice, not the education or other method by which an individual acquired the knowledge or skills.

10. One goal of establishing standards should be to encourage and increase the diversity of practicing neutrals. Consequently, standards should be scrutinized carefully to avoid the exclusion of groups based on race, sex, age, handicap, nationality, religion, or sexual preference.

11. Clearly, if performance criteria are preferred to educational degrees, it is important to identify and measure the characteristics and capabilities that determine competence. While recognizing the difficulty of the task, the Commission believes that it is possible to test for competence and well worth the effort it entails. . . .

As an alternative, experience can be a useful screening tool to identify those who can mediate or arbitrate and those who would benefit from further training. Criteria such as the amount and diversity of prior dispute resolution experience, the complexity of previous cases handled, and the amount and diversity of experience as a negotiator in similar cases all may be useful. Well designed training and apprenticeship programs, with significant personal observation and feedback, also may be able to provide an equivalent of competency testing.

Note

In 1995, SPIDR (now "Association for Conflict Resolution," or ACR) approved a second report on qualifications, stressing the importance of private rosters and certification systems to improve the operation of the marketplace as a check on the quality of mediation. The commission reaffirmed the 1989 commission's view that knowledge about what constitutes "competency" for a mediator and other types of neutrals is "at a nascent stage." The commission also pointed out that desirable abilities for the neutral might vary depending on the aims of the dispute resolution process, the setting, and the parties. Given the lack of empirical evidence to justify some types of qualifications and the contextual variations, the commission recommended against mediator licensure. It also urged those who might impose qualifications not to restrict unnecessarily party choice of mediators and to guard against selection criteria that would reduce the diversity of the mediator pool. In 2004, ACR proposed a mediator certification program for entry-level mediators. This proposal is discussed in the excerpt below.

Questions

3.19 Despite the SPIDR Commission's statements that educational degrees have not been shown to relate to competent performance, a number of statutes still require advanced degrees for mediators in publicly supported programs. What are the costs of imposing degree requirements? Can these be justified as a means of building public confidence in mediation?

3.20 The SPIDR Commission recommends that dispute resolution programs periodically evaluate the dispute resolution skills of their neutrals. Should the evaluation include effectiveness in dealing with power imbalances? How would that effectiveness be determined?

In 2007, the widespread adoption of certification standards for mediators may be on the horizon. The Association for Conflict Resolution (ACR, formerly SPIDR), a major national dispute resolution organization, created a mediator certification program designed to enhance the credentials of its members. Before ACR implemented this program, the ABA Section on Dispute Resolution joined with ACR to study the feasibility of developing a national mediator certification program. In addition, Florida has implemented a revised mediator certification program that requires prospective mediators to accumulate a specified number of points before they may receive certification. The Federal Mediation and Conciliation Service (FMCS) also proposed a new certification system but it was forced to shelve it due to financial considerations.

S. COLE, MEDIATOR CERTIFICATION: HAS THE TIME COME?

11 Disp. Resol. Mag. 7-12 (Spring 2005)

To assess whether this movement toward certification is cause for commendation or for concern, we must first consider the stated goals of certification, along with the related questions of whether, and to whom, those goals are important. Second, if the goals are worthwhile, we should consider the efficacy of the various certification approaches in achieving the goals. This article explores both of these topics, and suggests potential areas of concern regarding each. It ultimately concludes that the organizations should make greater efforts to ensure that there is buy-in regarding the appropriate goals. It further concludes that the certification proposals now on the table may, in fact, be counterproductive, even for achieving the currently stated goals.

Goals of Certification

The goals of mediator certification include (1) protecting consumers from the effect of "bad" mediators, (2) reducing court congestion (assuming that more cases will settle if high-quality mediators handle them), and (3) promoting mediation by, among other things, improving mediator credibility through an external indication of quality (Weckstein, 1996). The ACR Task Force on Mediator Certification stated that a voluntary certification process would also (1) provide uniform verification of a basic level of training, (2) create among mediators a "more solid foundation of competency and professionalism," (3) assist consumers in selecting a mediator, and (4) enable certified mediators to influence the development of the mediation field.

Assessing the Goals

As a general matter, these goals all seem directed at three interrelated and symbiotic objectives: protecting and assisting consumers, improving overall mediator quality, and enhancing the credibility of "good" mediators in the marketplace. The first question, then, is whether these are necessary, or even worthwhile, goals to pursue. Do consumers need greater protection from bad mediators or more help in selecting qualified mediators? Do "good" mediators need or want to enhance their market credibility through certification? In mediation circles, anecdotal tales of bad mediators are common. But is there a consensus on what constitutes a bad mediator, or, conversely, on what characteristics "good" mediators share?

Defining a Quality Mediator

The last question is perhaps the most elusive. For some time, the mediation community has believed that a key component of a good mediation is a quality mediator. But the necessary attributes of a quality mediator are often described in subjective terms that may not easily lend themselves to paper-file-based certification programs. For example, some have suggested that quality mediators must listen actively; identify issues; frame issues so that mediation parties understand them; use clear, neutral language; deal ably with complex factual scenarios; show respect for parties; earn the trust of parties; and separate their own values from the issues before them (Wissler, 2002). Magistrate Judge Wayne Brazil has offered additional characteristics: moral integrity, honesty, sensitivity, sustainable energy and positive spirit, commitment to procedural fairness, and the ability to refrain from forming premature opinions (Brazil, 1999).

All of these characteristics sound good — it is hard to argue against moral integrity and honesty — yet sources for concern remain as we consider certification designed to achieve or promote "quality" mediators. First, notwithstanding the various attributes listed above, it is not wholly clear that there is as yet a widely shared consensus on exactly which attributes, and in what proportions, lead to mediator quality. Is "sensitivity" really necessary, and if so, what exactly does it mean, and how much of it is required? Of course a mediator should "earn the trust of parties," but how is that accomplished, and which mediator attributes facilitate it?

In short, if the goal of certification programs is "separating the wheat from the chaff," more work should be done to determine how to differentiate the two. Until there is a shared consensus of which attributes we should be looking for, it is difficult at best to discuss the specifics of certification programs for assessing whether those attributes are present.

CONSIDERING CONSUMERS

Nor is it clear that consensus within the mediation community as to what constitutes mediator quality is the final answer on that issue. If a goal of mediator certification is to enhance the market credibility (and thus, perhaps, the market value) of "good" mediators, perhaps we should be looking to mediation consumers to ascertain what they think constitutes mediator quality. We could survey various segments of users of mediation services — those who hire mediators for voluntary mediations or those who use court mediators — and ask them what they look for when they hire a mediator or, after they have received mediation services, which factors led them to conclude that a mediator was or was not a quality mediator.

Given that the sole empirical study of parties' assessments of mediator qualifications revealed that parties preferred mediators with experience (Pearson and Thoennes, 1988), we might speculate that the results of such a survey would suggest that experience is a major factor in assessing mediator quality. Perhaps through the consultant jointly hired by ACR and the ABA, a clearer picture of what consumers' interests are will emerge.

Under this approach, market surveys would determine what customers want, and then certification could act as a "seal of approval" that the listed mediators possess those consumer-selected attributes. A program designed along these lines would allow mediation consumers, especially those who currently rely on word of mouth from people they trust, to cast a wider net in their search for a mediator. The certification would lower consumers' search costs, while still ensuring that the mediator they select has the qualities that they, and others in the market for mediation services, have identified as important. . . .

CURRENT CERTIFICATION SYSTEM DESIGN

Even if we assume that the characteristics listed above reflect some shared notion of "quality" that we can use without further investigation, issues still arise with regard to current certification system design. If certification is intended to be a mark of quality, then a certification program should design its standards to assess whether a given applicant possesses the attributes that have been identified as important to quality. Because the attributes themselves are subjective, however, the certification proposals to date have largely relied on proxies for demonstrating quality. That is, rather than attempting to assess the presence of desirable characteristics in a given applicant directly, the proposals look to things like experience, education, and training — things that may suggest that the applicant has the necessary skill set.

But, if the certification programs are going to rely on these indirect metrics, the burden is on the organizations backing the programs to demonstrate the positive correlation between the presence of the indirect attributes and the desired attributes. That is, no one cares (or should care), in the abstract, that a mediator has been trained. It is only if mediator training, at least as a general matter, leads to a higher-quality mediation experience, that questions regarding an applicant's training are relevant. The same is true of education or experience. It is not the existence of those factors per se, but their correlation to mediator quality that makes them relevant.

Linking Training and Quality

To date, however, remarkably little empirical work has been done that demonstrates a strong link between training or education, on the one hand, and mediator quality on the other. I am aware of only one study that has looked at the issue, and that study concluded that the only relevant variable for predicting mediator quality was experience (Pearson and Thoennes, 1988). If that study is correct (and more studies would certainly be welcome), certification programs that impose training or educational requirements seem ill-suited to the task of improving mediator quality, identifying high-quality mediators, or protecting the consumers of mediation services.

In addition to the lack of any empirical evidence supporting a link between training or education and mediator quality, there are also reasons to think that such requirements may in fact be counterproductive. A brief examination of ACR's proposed mediator certification plan shows how such a plan might, in some ways, undermine an effort to ensure mediator quality.

ACR's Proposal

To obtain ACR's proposed certification, an applicant submits a portfolio of experience, training, and education. ACR evaluates the portfolio and then requires that the applicant take a written test to become eligible for placement on the ACR roster. A successful applicant for ACR's roster must have 100 hours of training, 80 of which must be training in mediation process skills. A mediator may satisfy up to 20 of the 100 hours as a trainer or teacher. Applicants must also demonstrate that they have 100 total hours of mediation or co-mediation within the last five years or 500 hours over a lifetime. Successful applicants will also be subject to periodic recertification and decertification for ethical and professional standards violations. In addition, applicants denied placement on the roster are entitled to appeal ACR's decision. Applicants must obtain professional liability insurance, disclose criminal convictions, and provide letters of reference in order to gain and maintain placement on the roster. . . . [Florida has adopted a new plan as well, but bases certification on a "point" system rather than directly examining hours of training and experience and educational degrees obtained.]

Ensuring Diversity

The hour-and-point requirements identified in the ACR proposal may undermine the goal of ensuring high-quality mediation. ACR . . . claims that its proposed voluntary certification process is "designed with heightened attention and respect for all manner of diversity in the broadest sense." While ACR's intent to ensure diversity in the mediation pool is laudable, the goal of ensuring a diverse mediator pool will not be achieved through point systems and testing. Unfortunately, such systems tend to reward those who have sufficient funds to pay for mediation training and advanced degrees. Moreover, members of historically disadvantaged groups are unlikely to be able to satisfy experiential requirements necessary to obtain certification if they do not have the same ability to network as do members of the majority.

In addition, an hours-and-point–centered plan might exclude a number of mediators who would otherwise satisfy the existing view of what constitutes a quality mediator. For example, imagine a man who began his mediation career 20 years ago when there was little formal mediation training available. He mediated frequently for 15 years and then became a professional mediator/trainer. He would not qualify for the certification ACR proposed because he has insufficient training and cannot satisfy the experience requirement (while he could satisfy the 500-hour lifetime experience requirement, he failed to document his mediations). . . .

Adding Holistic Review

One way of ensuring (at least during the period where the mediation community moves toward certification) that quality mediators are capable of obtaining certification would be to maintain existing hour-or-point requirements, but to allow a committee at ACR or another organization to engage in an additional holistic review of an applicant's portfolio. Holistic review, where a committee could deviate from the rigid standards in appropriate cases, might be more successful in protecting a diverse mediator pool and ensuring that mediators who have considerable experience but lack formal training, or those who have considerable training but lack experience, may nevertheless receive certification. While certification programs may be inevitable, they should not undermine diversity nor preclude qualified mediators from continuing to practice their chosen profession.

Evaluating the Written Test

In addition, ACR and the ABA should carefully consider the effectiveness of ACR's proposed written test. According to ACR, the proposed test is designed to test 11 areas of knowledge, including communication; conflict theory; content management and resources; cultural diversity; ethics; history of mediation; models, strategies, and styles; negotiation; process structure; role of third party; and systems and group dynamics. While ACR contemplates that the written test would have to be carefully written and evaluated before it would be promulgated, and that a mediator could engage in self-study to pass the test, there may be little correlation between a mediator's score on the test and whether she is a quality mediator. . . .

Certifying the Trainers

Finally, it may be that the current certification movement is focusing on the wrong audience. To ensure quality mediators, it would seem sensible to focus on those entities *training* the mediators rather than on the mediators alone. Because training appears to be a major component of all certification proposals, if training can be correlated with quality mediation, evaluation of existing training programs, with a focus on ensuring quality in those programs, makes sense. Moreover, because the target audience is much smaller, it might be considerably less expensive to put a trainer certification into place.

The ABA Section on Dispute Resolution clearly contemplated this possibility when it created a task force to address this issue. This task force completed a draft report in October 2002. Among other things, the report recommended that the task force develop "model standards for mediator preparation programs [and] outline one or more model systems of mediator credentialing to recommend to states or to the field, focusing initially on the accreditation of mediator preparation programs." Since ACR's proposal on mediator certification came out, however, the ABA appears to have abandoned the effort to consider credentialing training entities. Because quality mediators are more likely to come out of reputable training institutions, adding trainer certification to the focus of current certification plans would be an excellent idea.

Recommendations

While certification, correctly structured, could provide benefits to the mediation field by protecting the public, promoting mediation, increasing the likelihood that some mediators may have more productive careers, and reducing court congestion, providing certification through points accumulation and written testing is problematic. Moreover, even though the current certification plans are voluntary, the ACR-ABA plan is to explore creation of a national mediator certification program. If certification becomes widespread, it seems likely that certification will be viewed as an essential characteristic of a mediator and that mediators who choose not to pursue certification or who do not meet the proposed standards will not be able to maintain a viable practice.

In an effort to preserve diversity within the mediation field and to avoid precluding qualified mediators from obtaining certification, the national mediator certification effort should add a holistic review to the certification process for mediator applicants whose background strongly suggests that they could be quality mediators. Advocates of national mediator certification should also consider certifying mediator preparation programs. These efforts would be more consistent with the various articulated organizational goals and would be more equitable to existing and future mediators. At the same time, this refocusing might provide a more useful credential for mediators as well as helpful information to consumers that they might utilize when selecting a mediator.

Questions

3.21 Compare Professor Cole's description of ACR's proposed mediator certification plan with SPIDR's policy report on qualifications. In what ways has ACR departed from SPIDR's original vision? Why do you think there has been some movement away from the original policy discussion?

3.22 Should the ABA-ACR joint task force recommend a national mediator certification program? What would the benefits of such a program be? What problems do you foresee in implementing such a program? The ABA Section on Dispute Resolution and ACR recently surveyed 3,100 mediators, who reported that they were generally uncertain about whether a national program was necessary, but that if one were to be implemented, they would find it valuable (http://www.acrnet.org/pdfs/certificationresults2005.pdf). Most mediators responding to the survey believed that certification should focus on entry-level mediators and that an application fee should be between $200 and $300.

b. Holding the Mediator Accountable

Another method to achieve the aims discussed above is to hold the mediator accountable for accepting appropriate cases, managing the bargaining, and achieving an outcome that is acceptable from a public policy standpoint. In the dialogue that follows, a mediator and a professor argue about whether the mediator should be held responsible for the process and outcome of mediation.

Note: The Life of the Mediator—to Be or Not to Be (Accountable)

At a recent meeting of the Letsawldewit Mediation Society, which is composed of both practicing mediators and teachers of mediation, a professor *(P)* and a mediator *(M)* were discussing the day's program.

M: Boy, I've really had it. If I hear one more word about the moral and spiritual uplift of being a mediator, I'm going to find some other line of work. As far as I'm concerned, it's just plain hard work, and I wish these pontificators would begin to address some of the tough issues we all face every day.

P: I agree. But you've got to admit that speech by Larry Susskind (1981) was really interesting. I've believed for a long time that a mediator should be held accountable for an agreement that she mediates, and Susskind is certainly persuasive on that point. As he says, it simply isn't enough to ask whether the parties find the agreement to be acceptable:

> [E]nvironmental mediators ought to accept responsibility for ensuring (1) that the interests of parties not directly involved in negotiations, but with a stake in the outcome, are adequately represented and protected; (2) that agreements are as fair and stable as possible; and (3) that agreements reached are interpreted as intended by the community-at-large and set constructive precedents.
>
> Otherwise, mediation can be used as a device by which the stronger party takes advantage of the weaker, or they both take advantage of others.

My only disagreement with Susskind is that he limits his argument to the mediation of environmental disputes, while I would extend it to mediation in other contexts.

M: I couldn't disagree more. I thought that Josh Stulberg (1981) clearly demonstrated the flaws in Susskind's thesis. As Stulberg noted, determining whether an agreement is fair and optimal even as between the parties at the bargaining table can be an awesome task. Extending that inquiry to include whether the agreement is fair to persons not in the negotiations, about whose desires and interests the mediator may know little or nothing, only compounds this difficulty. Furthermore, as Stulberg asks, who authorized the mediator to decide the fairness of an agreement that is acceptable to the parties?

There's also one point that Stulberg only hints at that I think is crucial. Whatever the theoretical appeal of Susskind's thesis, as a practical matter it just won't work. You've done some mediation, and you know as well as I do that what you're doing as a mediator is helping parties who have been unable to reach agreement on their own. They don't go to a mediator because they want to, but because they have to: they're stuck. I don't know about you but I find it difficult enough to bring parties like that to some agreement they can both live with. Doing that takes about 110 percent of my concentration. I think that if a mediator has to concern himself not only with getting an agreement, but also with whether that agreement is fair, both as between the negotiating parties and others, the practical effect is going to be that mediation will be a far less effective tool for reaching agreement. It's like the baseball player who tries to hit a home run every time he's at bat; it's pretty impressive when he succeeds, but he strikes out a lot, too.

P: I agree with everything you say, but what's the alternative? It seems to me that a mediator cannot escape what she feels to be her ethical responsibility for helping the parties to reach fair agreements by copping out on the grounds that the task is difficult. Take a divorce situation for example: assume that the parties have grossly unequal bargaining power and that they are about to enter into an agreement that is blatantly unfair to absent parties like the children. How can the mediator escape the responsibility that she feels for such an unfair agreement simply because the task is difficult?

M: First of all, I'm not just saying that the task is difficult for the mediator, but that imposing it on her may frustrate the central goal of both negotiation and mediation — to reach an agreement.

Second, you assume the very issue we're discussing. Why do you assume that if the parties reach an agreement the mediator should be regarded as being responsible for what's in it?

P: How can that inference be avoided? The mediator is involved in the negotiations, and the world at large is going to tar her with that agreement. Suppose that the wife takes that agreement to her lawyer, and he tells her that she has been grossly taken advantage of. Isn't the lawyer, and everybody else to whom she shows that agreement, going to say, "How on earth did that mediator let you agree to something like that?"

M: Well, anybody who says that just doesn't understand mediation. The point I'm making is that if the mediator has to spend her time worrying about whether the agreement she's trying to get is going to be unfair, all too often there won't be any agreement to worry about. Then your divorcing parties will be right back in court, which is what they went to mediation to avoid.

P: That may be true, but from my perspective no agreement is better than an unfair agreement.

M: I wonder if we can't reach a compromise on this issue. I'm not opposed to having mediated agreements reviewed for fairness — at least when the mediation is court-ordered — but I am opposed to asking the mediator to perform the review function. What would you think of having the agreement reviewed by a different institution or person than the mediator? That way you avoid the confusion of roles and let each institution play the role that it is best suited to play.

P: Well, that sounds good, but I'm afraid it's just wishful thinking. Again in areas I know something about, such as divorce mediation, the courts are simply not equipped to provide a useful oversight role. They just rubber stamp the agreements the parties arrive at and thus reduce their burgeoning caseloads.

Maybe there isn't an all-or-nothing answer to this question. There may be some areas where there really is no effective other agency to review the agreement, and mediator concern for more than just reaching an agreement is the least bad solution. And then there are other areas where either the situation is not likely to be so extreme as the one I have sketched because the parties are relatively sophisticated or have attorneys, or else there is a competent and capable alternative to having the mediator assume all those tasks. I would certainly agree with you that this solution would be preferable if it could be made effective.

M: You ask the question a couple of times: what's the alternative? I think one alternative is either judicial or administrative review. Now you say, well, they just can't do it. But what you're really saying is they haven't done it. You're proposing what I regard as a fundamental shift in the role of mediator, and I'm saying to you that if you want to make a fundamental shift, let's change how the courts review these agreements. Rather than muddy the mediator's institutional responsibility and role, let's have the courts do what is their proper and appropriate role.

P: I think it's more complicated than that. First of all, as I have said several times, mediators have been doing some of these tasks — perhaps you would say not too effectively, and sometimes at a cost of not getting an agreement — but still they have been doing them. And courts, by and large, have not been doing them. It would take a major reallocation of the kind you well describe to accomplish that shift in responsibility.

But I'm not sure whether even if that could be achieved it would be desirable. There is the question of economy and efficiency. The mediator now learns a great deal about the case and about the impact of a proposed agreement on present parties and absent parties. A judge would have to start all over again to address those issues.

M: Yes, I agree that it's theoretically more efficient to have the mediator act both as a mediator and as a quasi-judge passing on fairness. But once you add this additional task to the mediator's central goal of helping the parties reach agreement, then you run the risk of losing the genius of mediation itself and winding up with no agreement. In the parties' view the mediator's value lies in her commitment to settlement and not to a particular interest. Once a party perceives the mediator to be seeking to further a particular interest, whether present at the bargaining table or not, the mediator becomes just another negotiator. At that point the mediator is part of the problem, not part of the solution (Ross, 1984:51).

P: You know, I think this whole question is rather similar to the question of whether the same person can serve as both mediator and arbitrator in the same dispute. There, too, we are talking about commingling different roles in one person. And while I generally agree with you that that's not desirable, my view there, as well as here, is that, as with the answer to most questions, it depends. It depends on the nature of the case, on the alternatives that are available and on some of the other factors we have already mentioned. Perhaps the question is not as simple as either of us thinks.

M: When you say that it depends on the nature of the case, what are you talking about?

P: Well, the greater the power disparity between the parties, the more important it is that the mediator be held responsible for the fairness of the agreement. I know that I just couldn't sign off on an agreement that was grossly unfair to both a divorcing wife and her absent and unrepresented children.

M: I must admit that I've never been in that situation. I work almost exclusively in the labor-management field. There we don't usually see gross power disparities, and when we do, we figure that's what Congress intended by establishing a system of free collective bargaining. It's up to the workers to protect themselves by organizing into strong unions, and if they can't do it, it's not the mediator's responsibility to protect them.

P: It appears to me that we are each influenced by the fields in which we work. When I mediate it's primarily in family situations, where it is fairly common to find that one of the parties has a considerable power advantage over the other, and there's certainly no congressional policy that says that the financially weaker spouse must suffer the consequences of her weakness.

M: I think we've found something we can agree on. I'm willing to accept — at least outside the labor context — the notion that if there is truly a great power disparity between the parties, the mediator has some responsibility for the content of an agreement that he mediates. If it is so unfair that it offends his conscience, he probably should withdraw rather than be associated with it.

P: When you speak of unfairness, are you looking only to the fairness of the agreement as between the negotiating parties or are you also willing to examine the fairness of the agreement as it impacts on parties not represented in the mediation — the children, for example?

M: I just don't know. I suppose that I might agree to look out for the children, but that's only because if I didn't worry about them and they didn't have separate legal representation, it's unlikely that their interests would be considered by anyone else. On the other hand, who am I to think that I know more about the interests of unrepresented children? I know that I would not object to an agreement that was satisfactory to the parties simply because I thought it might be unfair to some undefined absent third party.

P: Let me push you a little bit on that. Suppose that an employer and an all-white union agree in a dispute that you are mediating that whites will be given preference over blacks in hiring. What would you do?

M: First of all, I'd point out to them that the clause was unlawful and could cause both of them considerable legal trouble. If they still wanted to include it, I'm not sure what I would do. I might decide that the courts would strike it down and that I needn't worry, or I might decide that I just couldn't be associated with such an agreement, and step out of the negotiations. I just don't know. It seems to me, however, that if I were to step out, it would be because of my personal values, not because I felt that as a mediator I had an ethical obligation to do so.

P: That strikes me as the kind of fine academic distinction that you generally accuse me of making. We both seem to agree that it is probably inappropriate for a mediator to be a party to an agreement that discriminates unfairly against absent parties. If you're happier calling that part of her personal value system, that's fine with me.

M: I must say that I'm glad that you are a professor, not a legislator. If your ideas of accountability were imposed by law, I would hate to think of what would happen to mediation!

Note: Mediator Accountability

A number of statutes and court rules make the mediator accountable for the course of mediation. For example, mediators are sometimes required to be certain that parties are informed about legal aspects of their disputes (Iowa Supreme Court Rules Governing Standards of Practice for Lawyer-Mediators in Family Disputes, 2006). Mediators are occasionally directed to terminate the mediation if the dialogue is unproductive, if it appears that one party is unwilling to participate meaningfully, or where it is necessary to protect the parties from harm (Oklahoma Supreme Court Rules and Procedures for Dispute Resolution Act, Appendix A). Under some child custody mediation statutes, mediators must assess or raise the interests of the parties' children (Cal. Civ. Code §3180(b)).

Occasionally, the law specifies the consequences for mediators who breach these duties. For example, a few statutes impose criminal or quasi-criminal penalties for disclosing confidential mediation communications or failing to disclose qualifications (42 U.S.C. §2000g-2; Ga. Code Ann. §8-3-208(a); Minn. Stat. Ann. §572.37). New Hampshire has taken a step toward licensure by creating a board to certify and then discipline "certified marital mediators" according to standards set by that board (N.H. Rev. Stat. Ann. §328-C:4-8). In some instances, public funding for a mediation program may be terminated if mediators employed by that program fail to comply with applicable standards (e.g., N.Y. Jud. Law §849-b).

More frequently, no remedy has been specified for a breach of the mediator's duty. Where no remedy is provided, the laws presumably would be enforced through civil actions, filed by those harmed if the mediator fails to comply. However, there are no reported judgments against mediators and few reports of suits. In the rare cases where mediator negligence is alleged, courts struggle to identify a "mediator" standard of care. *Chang's Imports, Inc. v. Srader*, 216 F. Supp. 2d 325 (S.D.N.Y. 2002). Moreover, mediators are sometimes accorded immunity from liability either by statute (Fla. Stat. Ann. §44.107, Okla. Stat. tit. 12 §1805(E) (liability only if gross negligence) and Iowa Code §679C.115) or, when appointed by the court, as an extension of judicial immunity. The U.S. Court of Appeals for the District of Columbia ruled that court-appointed case evaluators (a term the court says can be used interchangeably with mediators) were entitled to quasi-judicial immunity. *Wagshal v. Foster*, 28 F.3d 1249 (D.C. Cir. 1994). See also *Meyers v. Contra Costa County Department of Social Services*, 812 F.2d 1154 (9th Cir.), cert. denied, 484 U.S. 829 (1987) (court employees acting as conciliators entitled to quasi-judicial immunity). The *Wagshal* court pointed out the similarity of case evaluation to judicial case management and settlement activities and stated that the aggrieved party had adequate remedies without recourse to civil liability. The adequacy of other remedies is questioned by a set of standards. The National Standards for Court-Connected Mediation Programs (Center for Dispute Settlement, 1992) warn against extending immunity to mediators, reasoning that it is inappropriate to deny "recourse to litigants injured by incompetent service," especially if the service is provided for a fee (comments to Standard 14).

If mediators are immune from liability, what relief is available if the mediator makes statements to the judge that might prejudice a party's case or discloses information when confidentiality has been promised? Should relief be available? Should it matter whether the mediator is appointed by a court or charges a fee?*

Questions

3.23 Edith Smith sued Gladys McGuire, the mediator privately retained by Smith and her husband to mediate their child custody and visitation dispute, claiming that she was damaged by McGuire's professional negligence, intentional and negligent infliction of emotional distress, and fraud. In the divorce action, Smith had asserted that her husband had physically and sexually abused their son, and she had sought termination of her husband's custody and visitation rights. Smith claims that McGuire failed to disclose her lack of expertise in child abuse, her acquaintance with Smith's husband through professional seminars, and her friendship with one of the partners of the law firm representing Smith's husband in the divorce action. Further, Smith alleges that McGuire screamed at her, ridiculed her, accused her of lying, stated that she would lose custody of her son if she persisted in believing the child's allegations of abuse, and lied about a doctor's report concerning abuse of the child. The mediation did not result in settlement.

McGuire has moved to dismiss the complaint, arguing that immunity from liability is necessary to encourage professionals to act as mediators. McGuire contends that immunity will not leave aggrieved parties without remedies. A party allegedly harmed by a mediator's action could obtain relief by challenging the validity of the mediated agreement; if there was no agreement, the party would not be harmed.

Smith points out that comparable professionals, such as lawyers and social workers, are not immune from liability for professional misconduct. She suggests that clothing mediators with immunity would leave nonsettling parties without recourse and make it impossible to hold mediators accountable for their actions. Smith also argues that the immunity of judges is irrelevant, since judicial immunity is designed to promote independent decision-making, not negotiation assistance. Although judicial immunity has been applied to judges and their appointees in their capacity as conveners of settlement conferences, immunity is extended to these activities only to assure the freedom they need for decision-making. The immunity should not be extended to persons not officially appointed by the court.

How should the court rule on the issue of immunity? Should the legislature pass a statute granting immunity to mediators? If mediators are immune from liability, is there another effective way to hold mediators accountable? Cf. *Howard v. Drapkin*,

*Another indirect form of mediator quality control comes about through guidelines formulated for Provider Organizations. See Margaret L. Shaw and Elizabeth Plapinger (2001) "Ethical Guidelines—ADR Provider Organizations Should Increase Transparency, Disclosure," *Disp. Resol. Mag.* 14 (Spring). See pp. 296-297 for a discussion of the applicability of these guidelines to arbitrators.

222 Cal. App. 3d 843, 271 Cal. Rptr. 893 (2d Dist. 1990) (regarding a psychologist retained to produce a report for the parties and containing dicta regarding immunity for mediators).

3.24 What should a child custody mediator do to comply with a statutory requirement to terminate mediation whenever "continuation of the process would harm or prejudice . . . the children"? Will compliance with the statute render the mediator less effective? Should the mediator be liable if a child is hurt by a mediated agreement?

c. Required Mediation Procedures

Some states regulate court or agency procedures in an effort to achieve bargaining balances and other aims discussed above (see also the Uniform Mediation Act, Sections 7, 9, 10, Appendix E). For example, Minnesota provides financial planning assistance to farmers engaged in mediation with lenders (Minn. Stat. §583.26; see also Iowa Code §654A.7). California provides funding for domestic violence advocates to attend mediation sessions and affords the victim the right to engage in mediation without entering the same room with or seeing the other party (Cal. Fam. Code §§6303, 10012). Alaska and North Dakota permit the parties to bring legal counsel to child custody mediation sessions, and Alaska allows a peremptory challenge to child custody mediators (Alaska Stat. §25.20.080; N.D. Cent. Code §14-09.1-05). The Uniform Mediation Act affords mediation parties the right to bring an accompanying person and renders ineffective any pre-mediation waiver of this right (Section 10, Appendix E). Maine requires judicial review of mediated agreements (Me. Rev. State Ann. tit. 19A, §251). Under one statute, the agreement may be set aside if the mediator evidences "partiality, corruption, or misconduct" that prejudices a party (Minn. Stat. Ann. §572.36). Under the Uniform Mediation Act, a mediator may not report to the judge or other official who may rule on the dispute. Thus, the mediator cannot pressure settlement by implying that a negative report to the judge might follow if a party resists settlement (Section 7, Appendix E).

Like the laws regarding qualifications and mediator accountability, laws providing for mediation procedures are directed primarily at avoiding bargaining imbalances and ensuring or encouraging fair outcomes. To the extent that they can be used instead of mediator accountability, the procedural rules have several positive features. One advantage, discussed in the dialogue above (pp. 176-180) is that they leave the mediator free to focus on the bargaining. Further, the procedural requirements are less likely to involve the mediator as the party to any disputes about compliance. Instead, disputes would be among parties to the case, either as procedural motions or in the enforcement of the mediated agreement. Often procedural requirements such as provision of expert assistance can be enforced without disturbing the privacy of the mediation session, the topic of Chapter 7.

Questions

3.25 Does judicial review of mediated agreements represent a significant check against unfairness if the judge is not told about the content of negotiations?

3.26 If the parties are represented by counsel at the mediation session and can exercise peremptory challenges to mediators, is there a need for mediator qualifications?

3.27 Identify the standards and enforcement schemes most likely to promote high quality or fairness in mediation. What are the costs, in terms of stifling mediation or turning mediators into bureaucrats, of implementing your scheme?

E. THE LAWYER-MEDIATOR AND PROFESSIONAL RESPONSIBILITY

Lawyers bring legal knowledge and experience to the mediator's role, and their expertise may change the mediation process in several ways. The lawyer-mediator can set out the legal issues in a way that may remove some unevenness in negotiating power between represented and unrepresented parties. The lawyer-mediator can also draft the mediated agreement for review by the parties' independent counsel, so that the participants can avoid the expense of bringing their lawyers to the sessions. Finally, even if the parties bring their lawyers to the mediation session, reality testing about likely litigation results by a lawyer-mediator may be a useful aid to achieving settlement.

Lawyer-mediators who identify themselves as such and make these contributions to evening the bargaining, saving money for the parties, or improving settlement prospects must tread carefully, however, because of ethical restrictions for lawyers. A formidable obstacle is the prohibition against representation of clients whose interests conflict. Lawyers also must avoid violating their duties to preserve reasonable expectations of confidentiality. Ethics authorities have construed these duties regarding conflict of interest and confidentiality* —whether the expectations arise during the mediation process or representation of a mediation party—primarily in the context of two issues:

1. Should a lawyer-mediator give legal information to or draft agreements for unrepresented mediation parties?
2. Under what circumstances should a lawyer-mediator (or that lawyer-mediator's law firm) be permitted (a) to represent or sue any mediation party or (b) to mediate when the lawyer-mediator has previously represented one of the mediation parties?

*Other ethical issues arise from the organization of a mediation practice. For example, lawyers should be certain that their mediation practices comply with prohibitions against "false or misleading" advertising, partnership and fee-splitting with nonlawyers, submitting to control of professional judgment by nonlawyers, and assisting in the unauthorized practice of law. See ABA Model Rules of Professional Conduct 7.1, 5.4, 5.5 and question 3.29, infra. Some jurisdictions still follow the older ABA Model Code of Professional Responsibility, which has comparable provisions. Some mediator practices may constitute the unauthorized practice of law if the mediator is not an attorney. See generally David Hoffman & Natasha Affolder, "Mediation and UPL: Do Mediators Have a Well-Founded Fear of Prosecution?" *Disp. Resol. Mag.* 20 (Winter, 2000); Sarah R. Cole et al., *Mediation: Law, Policy, Practice,* 2d ed., vol. 1, §10:5 (2003 & 2006 Supp.).

At stake as these questions are resolved are a number of competing values: making mediation services broadly available; ensuring fairness in mediation; maintaining public confidence in the loyalty of lawyers and the neutrality of mediators; and preserving confidentiality for both lawyer-client relations and mediation.

1. *The Provision of Legal Information and Drafting Assistance During Mediation Sessions Involving Unrepresented Parties*

A landlord locks out a tenant who is behind on the rent rather than securing a court judgment of eviction. At a mediation regarding past rent, the tenant is intent on reaching settlement but has no idea that a court might award damages for the illegal lockout. The tenant has insufficient funds to hire an attorney, and the local legal assistance organization is itself strapped for funds and is handling only emergencies.* Should the lawyer-mediator remain silent while the parties reach a settlement? Does the lawyer-mediator violate ethical provisions by informing the parties about how a court is likely to rule in the face of evidence of a lockout? Does the lawyer-mediator risk discipline by drafting the settlement agreement to resolve rent issues but to leave open later litigation regarding termination of the tenancy?

Ethical authorities provide no clear answers regarding how the lawyer-mediator can use legal expertise in the tenant lockout example, and those in the field disagree on what the answers should be. Can the lawyer-mediator skirt the conflict of interest quagmire by engaging in some activities that use legal expertise, but avoiding those activities that would be deemed "representing" the parties?† Richard Crouch in the first excerpt below points out how difficult it will be to delineate between activities that do and do not run afoul of the interests ethical codes seek to protect in the context of divorce mediation. In the second excerpt, a bar ethics advisory opinion makes some of these tough decisions, approving some activities by the lawyer-mediator and prohibiting others.

R. CROUCH, THE DARK SIDE OF MEDIATION: STILL UNEXPLORED

In Alternative Means of Family Dispute Resolution 339-357 (ABA 1982)

The popularity of mediation as an answer to some of the very real problems we have with divorce litigation as a dispute resolution process is impossible to deny. Just

*Cf. Nancy H. Rogers and Richard A. Salem, The Lock Out Videotape (1987).

†Avoidance of conflict of interest problems regarding "representation" in the mediation session does not result in a lawyer avoiding all ethical issues, as the next section makes clear. A lawyer may be "practicing law" even if not representing clients. See question 3.29, p. 190. Also, a lawyer is governed by certain aspects of the ethical restrictions even when not practicing law. In 1994, the American Bar Association amended its Model Rules of Professional Conduct to cover the lawyer in the provision of "law-related" services. ABA Model Rules of Professional Conduct 5.7. Although not yet widely adopted by state ethics authorities, the provision may represent a trend toward recognizing that clients do not distinguish representation from related services by lawyers and should be protected in their reliance that the lawyer will act ethically in all respects.

now it is riding the crest of an immense wave of fad appeal, both inside the professions and in the popular media. . . .

So why don't I sprint for the nearest mediation bandwagon? . . .

It's just that I can see glaring ethical problems to which no one yet seems to have any answers that stand up under logical analysis. I see considerable danger of ethics code violations and malpractice liability for lawyers, along with tremendous potential for the exploitation of unsuspecting clients. I go around asking the questions, sincerely and politely, and I am still waiting for the answers. . . .

. . . I wonder about the mediators who unwittingly fall in with, and facilitate, the exploitation of one party. Lawyer-mediators, clever as they are (and I have to admit I have also met some who are none too swift) can be psychologically exploited too. And the problem still exists even if the mediator does perceive what is going on.

A lawyer trying to preserve the mediation climate will at least have to make some extremely subtle judgments about when to alert the other party to overreaching. The bright new ideas of client self-determination and autonomy are consistent with letting one party freely choose to be a victim of exploitation. However, it is both a factual and a philosophical question to decide the degree to which a particular person's choice is free. In the unfathomable subtleties of long-standing marital relationships, a dominant party can even be the one who appears on the surface to be the weaker party, and this can be subtle enough to fool even trained and experienced observers.

The attorney may go to ultimately unwarranted lengths to preserve the tenuous mediation agreement from breaking down. Now insofar as the attorney lets mediation go on, or solves the problem by cutting mediation off, that attorney is probably acting for one of the parties and against the other. This is because in most situations of exploitation, one party benefits and the other loses, by the continuation of mediation.

Also, ignorance of what a court would do with the particular case nearly always operates to the benefit of one party and the detriment of the other, even if they both are ignorant. And the lawyer who sounds the alarm about overreaching, so as to cut mediation off, had better be sure that it really was overreaching and was sufficiently exploitative to warrant this remedy. That is because scuttling the mediation effort not only hurts the party who was dominant at that moment, but costs both of them a lot of wasted time, money and effort.

Also, both the lawyer and the mediation center that he or she works for or takes referrals from has considerable interest in seeing "successful" mediations go through. In mediation the geometrically-projected return business from two satisfied clients who serve as "living advertisements" is a very tempting inducement. It is just what you *don't* get in law practice. Producing a compromise that is not entirely fair (especially when the exploited spouse, unschooled in the ways of courts, does not perceive the unfairness) may appear the preferable alternative in many close cases. . . .

Is Anybody "Represented"?

Next, just what is this nonsense about "representation"? Representation as conceived by the legal profession, and indeed the English language, is something very far removed from what goes on in the mediation context. The lawyer who plays mediator is more like an impartial umpire and discussion leader and is certainly not "representing the interests" of one person against the other as an advocate. . . .

The best mediators and post-mediation lawyers say as clearly as possible that they are not representing anybody in this business. In fact, some of the ethics opinions require them to. These disavowals might not be effective when they are offset by other seductive and confusing generalities that mediation clients customarily hear, but at least they are something.

In my opinion it is not enough to disavow "representation" in just those words. I think clients should also be expressly told that an attorney-client relationship has not been formed and that the "service" they are getting is not what lawyers have traditionally provided to clients. The contract and waiver that they sign should expressly acknowledge that this is a new and experimental product designed to save them money.

We think this waiver is implicit in the mere fact that the couple sought mediation, but I think experience so far shows that the clients usually don't grasp that at all. We assume they knowingly agree to do without all those good things that a lawyer as advisor-advocate traditionally provides. But I think we are letting ourselves be fooled along with them. What most of these clients really seek — and at first think they are getting — is the modern alternative plus the traditional lawyer-client relationship. Thus the waivers we expect absolutely have to be made plain to them.

Many lawyers rationalize their divided loyalties in these matters by saying they serve as a "mere scrivener." This would mean that they simply "put into legal language" what the parties have already agreed to without lawyer help. This sounds nice, but it doesn't hold up. . . . The reason is that actually (if we do decent work) legal language is plain English. The parties themselves could put a separation agreement into language that would be *legal* (i.e., for a court to incorporate into a decree). The only help a drafting lawyer contributes is in the protection or advancement of a contracting party's interests.

This is why the best lawyers taking part in this debate ask "how can you draft anything impartially?" Every slight variation in wording, every comma and period, makes one side's potential future court position better or worse. The most scrupulous practitioners say they will "draft for both" only if each party also has an independent private lawyer. This three-lawyer scheme is ideal on a number of other counts as well — but how great a device is that for saving most people money?

Wearing Many Hats . . .

Everyone agrees that there should be no post-mediation representation by any involved lawyer if the agreement should break down so that it's a contested divorce case. On whether an involved lawyer can do the court representation in an uncontested case, opinion is divided. . . .

Can You Consent?

Of course, lawyer conflict-of-interest questions have long been resolved by resort to the legal principle that no wrong is done to him who consents. However, consent to a waiver this complicated and this far-reaching is something else again. Considering how many lawyers fail to appreciate how much conflict of interest is being consented to — how much is being forfeited — as part of the mediation schemes popular today, it is unlikely that clients appreciate how much protection they are giving up. Truly informed consent to a thing like this may be impossible, but if possible it certainly requires a full explanation of what, in terms of legal ethics, is going on.

The recent ethics opinions carving out a permissible niche for mediation try to cure the conflict-of-interest problem by saying that after taking all the other precautions required a lawyer must stop trying to be "impartial" when he perceives that the conflict is so severe that it just would not be proper to go on like this. . . .

A Perilous Choice

. . . Perceiving when a divorce-related matter is too conflict-ridden to go on with is such a difficult concept that it's almost a joke. It can be downright ridiculous when you consider the background against which this decision will be made.

First, as noted above, the lawyer who's responsible for cutting off the mediation-advice-agreement-divorce process anywhere along the line will have a lot of people to answer to. That lawyer will lose some anticipated fees if not some earned ones. He also will have hurt the clients by telling them they have wasted the time and money invested so far. He isn't likely to get much new business by word-of-mouth advertising from these unsatisfied clients. And if this happens very often he won't get any more referrals from that mediation center either. The pressure to see a "successful" mediation go through is considerable.

That is why sensitive lawyers worry about another point of conflict between modern mediation plans and the ethics rules as we have known them. A lawyer is not supposed to sacrifice his or her independence by becoming subject to the control of lay agencies. It is easy to see how the desire to stay on a mediation referral panel could put enormous pressure on an ordinarily scrupulous lawyer's judgment. The mediation shops do not want a vast number of mediations to be unsuccessfully terminated. . . .

A Possible New Rule

[The author proposes a new rule requiring, inter alia, that there be a written contract containing "all the assumptions and ground rules." This should be orally explained, and the clients should be given three days after signing the contract to revoke it. It should be made clear that no one is receiving legal representation and that the lawyer cannot represent anyone in court. Legal advice should be given only in the presence of both parties, and the mediation should be terminated if there is impermissible overreaching.]

You will notice that this rule not only lets the lawyer try to juggle roles and wear multiple hats, but also does not require independent outside lawyer counsel. If a party wants to get it during the three-day waiting period that is his or her business. The un-waivable waiting periods will make a mediated agreement harder, in some ways, to get than an ordinary separation agreement—but the precautions are ones that can't be blamed on the legal profession's greed, and that don't in fact cost money.

I think this suggested rule, or something like it, is worth trying, because alternative dispute resolution is worth it. Mediation is not the cure-all that the hucksters, the cultists and the happy zealots among the learned professions would have us believe; but it is a worthwhile idea. If mediation lowers the cost of divorce by replacing expensive lawyer hours with significantly less expensive mediator hours, and gives people settlements they are more willing to live with because they can't blame the mistakes on their lawyers, then it will be a noble achievement. . . .

ASSOCIATION OF THE BAR OF THE CITY OF NEW YORK, OPINION NUMBER 80-23

(1980)

We have been asked whether lawyers may ethically participate in a divorce mediation program organized by a non-profit organization. . . .

This Committee recognizes that there are circumstances where it is desirable that parties to a matrimonial dispute be afforded an alternative to the adversarial process with its legal and emotional costs. The Code's recognition that lawyers may serve as mediators (EC 5-20), as well as ethical aspirations which recognize a lawyer's duty to assist the public in recognizing legal problems and aiding those who cannot afford the usual costs of legal assistance (EC 2-1; EC 2-25), make it inconceivable to us that the Code would deny the public the availability of non-adversary legal assistance in the resolution of divorce disputes.

[T]he Committee also recognizes that in some circumstances, the complex and conflicting interests involved in a particular matrimonial dispute, the difficult legal issues involved, the subtle legal ramifications of particular resolutions, and the inequality in bargaining power resulting from differences in the personalities or sophistication of the parties make it virtually impossible to achieve a just result free from later recriminations of bias or malpractice, unless both parties are represented by separate counsel. . . .

Accordingly, to harmonize these various considerations, we have concluded that lawyers may participate in the divorce mediation procedure proposed in the inquiry here, only on the following conditions.

To begin with, the lawyer may *not* participate in the divorce mediation process where it appears that the issues between the parties are of such complexity or difficulty that the parties cannot prudently reach a resolution without the advice of separate and independent legal counsel.

If the lawyer is satisfied that the situation is one in which the parties can intelligently and prudently consent to mediation and the use of an impartial legal adviser, then the lawyer may undertake these roles provided the lawyer observes the following rules:

First, the lawyer must clearly and fully advise the parties of the limitations on his or her role and specifically, of the fact that the lawyer represents neither party and that accordingly, they should not look to the lawyer to protect their individual interests or to keep confidences of one party from the other.

Second, the lawyer must fully and clearly explain the risks of proceeding without separate legal counsel and thereafter proceed only with the consent of the parties and only if the lawyer is satisfied that the parties understand the risks and understand the significance of the fact that the lawyer represents neither party. . . .

Fourth, lawyers may provide impartial legal advice and assist in reducing the parties' agreement to writing only where the lawyer fully explains all pertinent considerations and alternatives and the consequences to each party of choosing the resolution agreed upon.

Fifth, the lawyer may give legal advice only to both parties in the presence of the other.

Sixth, the lawyer must advise the parties of the advantages of seeking independent legal counsel before executing any agreement drafted by the lawyer.

Seventh, the lawyer may not represent either of the parties in any subsequent legal proceedings relating to the divorce. . . .

In 2002, the American Bar Association amended ABA Rule of Professional Conduct 2.4 to state:

> (a) A lawyer serves as a third-party neutral when the lawyer assists two or more persons who are not clients of the lawyer to reach a resolution of a dispute or other matter that has arisen between them. Service as a third-party neutral may include service as an arbitrator, a mediator or in such other capacity as will enable the lawyer to assist the parties to resolve the matter.
>
> (b) A lawyer serving as a third-party neutral shall inform unrepresented parties that the lawyer is not representing them. When the lawyer knows or reasonably should know that a party does not understand the lawyer's role in the matter, the lawyer shall explain the difference between the lawyer's role as a third-party neutral and a lawyer's role as one who represents a client.

COMMENTARY

> [1] Alternative dispute resolution has become a substantial part of the civil justice system. Aside from representing clients in dispute resolution processes, lawyers often serve as third-party neutrals. A third-party neutral is a person, such as a mediator, arbitrator, conciliator or evaluator, who assists the parties, represented or unrepresented, in the resolution of a dispute or in the arrangement of a transaction. Whether a third-party neutral serves primarily as a facilitator, evaluator or decisionmaker depends on the particular process that is either selected by the parties or mandated by a court.
>
> [2] The role of a third-party neutral is not unique to lawyers, although, in some court-connected contexts, only lawyers are allowed to serve in this role or to handle certain types of cases. In performing this role, the lawyer may be subject to court rules or other law that apply either to third-party neutrals generally or to lawyers serving as third-party neutrals. Lawyer-neutrals may also be subject to various codes of ethics, such as the Code of Ethics for Arbitrators in Commercial Disputes prepared by a joint committee of the American Bar Association and the American Arbitration Association or the Model Standards of Conduct for Mediators jointly prepared by the American Bar Association, the American Arbitration Association and the Society of Professionals in Dispute Resolution.

[3] Unlike nonlawyers who serve as third-party neutrals, lawyers serving in this role may experience unique problems as a result of differences between the role of a third-party neutral and a lawyer's service as a client representative. The potential for confusion is significant when the parties are unrepresented in the process. Thus, paragraph (b) requires a lawyer-neutral to inform unrepresented parties that the lawyer is not representing them. For some parties, particularly parties who frequently use dispute-resolution processes, this information will be sufficient. For others, particularly those who are using the process for the first time, more information will be required. Where appropriate, the lawyer should inform unrepresented parties of the important differences between the lawyer's role as third-party neutral and a lawyer's role as a client representative, including the inapplicability of the attorney-client evidentiary privilege. The extent of disclosure required under this paragraph will depend on the particular parties involved and the subject matter of the proceeding, as well as the particular features of the dispute-resolution process selected.

[4] A lawyer who serves as a third-party neutral subsequently may be asked to serve as a lawyer representing a client in the same matter. The conflicts of interest that arise for both the individual lawyer and the lawyer's law firm are addressed in Rule 1.12. . . .

[5] Lawyers who represent clients in alternative dispute-resolution processes are governed by the Rules of Professional Conduct. When the dispute-resolution process takes place before a tribunal, as in binding arbitration, . . . the lawyer's duty of candor is governed by Rule 3.3. Otherwise, the lawyer's duty of candor toward both the third-party neutral and other parties is governed by Rule 4.1 (governing truthfulness in statements to others).

Questions

3.28 Do (1) the New York opinion and (2) ABA Rule of Professional Conduct 2.4 address Crouch's concerns? Do these approaches unnecessarily restrict the lawyer-mediator?

3.29 In 2005, the Oregon bar association issued an opinion regarding ethical problems presented if an attorney and psychologist form a domestic relations mediation service. According to the Oregon opinion, an attorney who acts as a mediator does not *represent* any of the parties. However, the mediator may be engaged in the *practice of law* if any part of the service involves "the application of a general body of legal knowledge to the problem of a specific entity or individual." The opinion states that the drafting of the settlement agreement constitutes the practice of law. Thus, if the mediator gives legal advice or drafts the agreement, a partnership or fee-splitting arrangement with the psychologist would be prohibited by the ethics code. Oregon Bar Association, Formal Opinion 2005-101. Should the Oregon code be amended to permit fee-splitting and partnerships between lawyer and nonlawyer mediators?

2. *Representation of or Advocacy Against a Mediation Participant and Mediation Involving Prior Clients; Imputed Conflicts*

Tough issues arise as courts and bar authorities apply conflict of interest and confidentiality provisions to the other activities of the lawyer-mediator, and then extend these prohibitions to the mediator's law firm (see Menkel-Meadow, 1997). Must the mediator disclose all prior activities related to all participants, including those of the mediator's law firm, before undertaking a mediation? The Uniform Mediation Act §9(a) requires mediators to disclose those conflicts "that a reasonable individual would consider likely to affect the impartiality of the mediator." The UMA and similar requirements might involve extensive conflicts checks in some large firms, which then might permit firm lawyers to mediate only when substantial fees are involved. Can the mediator or the mediator's law firm thereafter represent a mediation party or represent another party in a matter adverse to a mediation party? In the case that follows, the court examines whether a law firm can represent a mediation party on issues related to the dispute mediated by one of its lawyers. A new ABA Rule of Professional Conduct, set out after this case, allows later law firm representation when screening procedures are implemented.

McKENZIE CONSTRUCTION v. ST. CROIX STORAGE CORP.

961 F. Supp. 857 (D. St. Croix 1997)

RESNICK, U.S. Magistrate Judge.

This matter is before the Court on defendants St. Croix Storage Corp. and Sun Storage Partners, L.P.'s motion to disqualify the law firm of Rohn & Cusick as counsel for plaintiffs in this action. . . .

Plaintiff McKenzie Construction is a local lumber retail company who brought this damages action against defendants St. Croix Storage Corp. for conversion of lumber. The Court ordered the matter submitted to mediation and later appointed Attorney Lisa Moorehead as mediator. Mediation was unsuccessful and the parties have resumed preparation for trial.

In seeking to disqualify the firm of Rohn & Cusick, defendants claim that the firm's hiring of Attorney Moorehead, who was the mediator appointed by the Court to settle this case, presents an irreparable conflict of interest in contravention of the rules governing the conduct of mediators and attorneys alike. . . .

The recent case of *Poly Software International, Inc. v. Su*, 880 F. Supp. 1487 (D. Utah 1995), discusses the identical issue presented in the case sub judice. In that case, two parties agreed to mediate a copyright action which they were defending. However, soon after the mediated settlement the parties sued each other. One of the parties retained the mediator as his counsel. The other party moved to disqualify the mediator-turned-attorney in light of his prior status as mediator in the previous action. The District Court disqualified the attorney and his law firm from participating in the litigation and held that an attorney who serves as a mediator cannot subsequently represent anyone in a substantially related matter without consent of the original parties. The court reasoned that mediators routinely receive and preserve confidences in much the same manner as an attorney. The court referred to the Model Rules of Professional Conduct and concluded that where the mediator was privy to confidential information, the applicable ethical rules imposed the same responsibilities as the rules relating to an attorney's subsequent representation of a former client. The court also considered the rule prohibiting judges and other adjudicative officers from representing anyone in connection with a matter in which he or she participated "personally and substantially." Model Rule 1.2.

Likewise, in *Cho v. Superior Court*, 39 Cal. App. 4th 113, 45 Cal. Rptr. 2d 863 (1995), a former judge and his law firm were disqualified from representing a party in an action in which the former judge had participated in settlement conferences. . . . The court cautioned that "no amount of assurances or screening procedures, no 'cone of silence' could ever convince the opposing party that the confidences would not be used to its disadvantage." Id. 45 Cal. Rptr. 2d at 869. The Court concluded that based on the nature of the attorney's prior participation, there is a presumption that confidences were revealed, and the attorney should not have "to engage in subtle evaluation of the extent to which he acquired relevant information in the first representation and of the actual use of that representation." . . .

This Court finds, and many commentators agree, that during mediation parties are encouraged to disclose the strengths and weaknesses of their positions, in an effort to arrive at a settlement. Protection of confidences in such a setting strengthens the incentive of parties to negotiate without fear that the mediator will subsequently use the information against them. Additionally, the rules regulating attorney conduct place the onus on the attorney to "remain conscious of the obligation to preserve confidences and maintain loyalty." . . . It is clear from the record that the parties met to negotiate a settlement. It is undisputed that the mediation lasted at least one hour. It is not unreasonable to assume that in light of the nature and purpose of the proceeding, that confidential information was disclosed by the parties. Notwithstanding Attorney Moorehead's statements to the contrary, the present situation presents such a serious affront to the policy that forms the basis of the rules, that this Court has no choice but to conclude that Attorney Moorehead must be disqualified.

This Court further finds that disqualification of Attorney Moorehead should be imputed to the other members of the firm. The cases and Model Rule 1.10(a)[4] require such disqualification.*

In 2002, the ABA expanded Rule 1.12 dealing with conflicts of interest rules for former judges or arbitrators to extend also to mediators "and other third-party neutrals":

RULE 1.12: FORMER JUDGE, ARBITRATOR MEDIATOR OR OTHER THIRD-PARTY NEUTRAL

(a) Except as stated in paragraph (d), a lawyer shall not represent anyone in connection with a matter in which the lawyer participated personally and substantially as a judge or other adjudicative officer, or law clerk to such a person or as an arbitrator, mediator or

4. The rule states: "While lawyers are associated in a firm, none of them shall knowingly represent a client when any one of them practicing alone would be prohibited from doing so by Rule 1.7, 1.8(c), 1.9 or 2.2."

*The court declined to rule on whether any screening mechanism would be sufficient because the attorney-mediator had contacts with one of the parties after joining the firm.

other third-party neutral, unless all parties to the proceeding give informed consent, confirmed in writing.

(b) A lawyer shall not negotiate for employment with any person who is involved as a party or as lawyer for a party in a matter in which the lawyer is participating personally and substantially as a judge or other adjudicative officer or as an arbitrator, mediator or other third-party neutral. A lawyer serving as a law clerk to a judge; or other adjudicative officer may negotiate for employment with a party or lawyer involved in a matter in which the clerk is participating personally and substantially, but only after the lawyer has notified the judge or other adjudicative officer.

(c) If a lawyer is disqualified by paragraph (a), no lawyer in a firm with which that lawyer is associated may knowingly undertake or continue representation in the matter unless:

(1) the disqualified lawyer is timely screened from any participation in the matter and is apportioned no part of the fee therefrom; and

(2) written notice is promptly given to the parties and any appropriate tribunal to enable them to ascertain compliance with the provisions of this rule.

(d) An arbitrator selected as a partisan of a party in a multimember arbitration panel is not prohibited from subsequently representing that party.

In 2002, a task force recommended the rule below, which differs from the new ABA rule, particularly in providing an assumed "safe harbor" for related representation after a year while still prohibiting representation in the same dispute at any time.

CPR INSTITUTE FOR DISPUTE RESOLUTION—GEORGETOWN COMMISSION ON ETHICS AND STANDARDS IN ALTERNATIVE DISPUTE RESOLUTION—MODEL RULES FOR THE LAWYER NEUTRAL

Rule 4.5.4 Conflicts of Interest

(a) Disqualification of Individual Third Party Neutrals

(1) A lawyer who is serving as a third party neutral shall not, during the course of an ADR proceeding, seek to establish any financial, business, representational, neutral or personal relationship with or acquire an interest in, any party, entity or counsel who is involved in the matter in which the lawyer is participating as a neutral, unless all parties consent after full disclosure.

(2) A lawyer who has served as a third party neutral shall not subsequently represent any party to the ADR proceeding (in which the third party neutral served as neutral) in the same or a substantially related matter, unless all parties consent after full disclosure.

(3) A lawyer who has served as a third party neutral shall not subsequently represent a party adverse to a former ADR party where the lawyer-neutral has acquired information protected by confidentiality under this Rule, without the consent of the former ADR party.

(4) Where the circumstances might reasonably create the appearance that the neutral had been influenced in the ADR process by the anticipation or

expectation of a subsequent relationship or interest, a lawyer who has served as a third party neutral shall not subsequently acquire an interest in or represent a party to the ADR proceeding in a substantially unrelated matter for a period of one year or other reasonable period of time under the circumstances, unless all parties consent after full disclosure.

(b) Imputation of Conflicts to Affiliated Lawyers and Removing Imputation

(1) If a lawyer is disqualified by section (a), no lawyer who is affiliated with that lawyer may knowingly undertake or continue representation in any substantially related or unrelated matter unless the personally disqualified lawyer is adequately screened from any participation in the matter, is apportioned no fee from the matter and timely and adequate notice of the screening has been provided to all affected parties and tribunals, provided that no material confidential information about any of the parties to the ADR proceeding has been communicated by the personally disqualified lawyer to the affiliated lawyer or that lawyer's firm.

. . . (d) If a lawyer serves as a neutral at the request of a court, public agency or other group for a de minimis period and pro bono publico, the firm with which the lawyer is associated is not subject to imputation under 4.5.4(b).

Questions

3.30 ABA Rule of Professional Conduct 1.12 and the CPR rule accept the screening approach, though they differ on when it is appropriate. In contrast, the *Cho* court (discussed in the *McKenzie Construction* case) rejects screening. Which approach is best?* Why? Regarding the CPR rule, why should the pro bono nature of the mediator make any difference?

3.31 Compare ABA Rule 1.12 and the CPR rule. Which takes the better approach? Why?

3. Representation of Clients in Out-of-State Mediation; Unauthorized Practice of Law

As mediation use increases it has become more common for lawyers to represent clients in out-of-state mediations. Unfortunately, many states do not have procedures for permitting out-of-state lawyers to receive *pro hac vice* status so that they may represent clients without fear of an unauthorized-practice-of-law charge. The following excerpt discusses this emerging problem and possible methods for handling the issue in the future:

*Sometimes the standard for determining whether a judge disqualifies a lawyer for conflict of interest differs from the standard for determining what should be provided in the ethics rules regarding conflict of interest. In answering this question, you can set aside for the moment the varying considerations involved with ethics rule-drafting, on the one hand, and judicial disqualification of counsel, on the other hand.

S. COLE, UNAUTHORIZED PRACTICE OF LAW CHARGES: A RISK FOR LAWYERS REPRESENTING CLIENTS IN MEDIATION AND ARBITRATION IN A MULTI-JURISDICTIONAL PRACTICE ENVIRONMENT

13 Disp. Resol. Mag. 26 (Fall 2006)

The increasing prevalence of ADR processes and multi-jurisdictional practice raises the risk that lawyers may face unauthorized practice of law (UPL) charges when they represent clients in arbitration or mediation. UPL statutes, which exist to prohibit lawyers from practicing in jurisdictions where they are not licensed, are designed to protect the public from substandard service offered by unregulated lawyers. Moreover, UPL statutes regulate the legal profession and protect the integrity of the judicial system. As dispute resolution has grown, more and more lawyers represent clients in dispute resolution processes outside the jurisdiction that licensed them. Not surprisingly, opposing counsel in some of these processes allege that an unlicensed lawyer's participation in the ADR process constitutes the unauthorized practice of law. Courts have struggled to come up with a uniform response to such allegations.

Whether representation of a client in a dispute resolution process might be the unauthorized practice of law first arose in the context of arbitration. In a seminal case from California, *Birbrower v. Superior Court,* the California Supreme Court held that two New York lawyers engaged in the unauthorized practice of law when they prepared a California client for an arbitration that would take place in California. Reasoning that negotiation and preparation for arbitration involve strategizing and providing legal advice about California law, the Court concluded that preparation for arbitration was the practice of law. The California legislature repealed the *Birbrower* holding by enacting legislation that permits a lawyer not licensed in California to represent a client in a California arbitration if she submits credentials to the parties and the arbitrator and maintains local counsel.

Despite the passage of this reform legislation, other jurisdictions followed the original *Birbrower* holding. In Ohio, for example, the Supreme Court held that out-of-state lawyers representing clients in arbitration engage in the unauthorized practice of law. In *Disciplinary Counsel v. Alexicole,* the lawyer was charged with the unauthorized practice of law when he provided legal advice to an Ohio client about filing a claim in arbitration for a securities law violation. The Court found that an unlicensed attorney who offers such advice or provides "legal services, including the representation on another's behalf during discovery, settlement negotiations, and pretrial conferences to resolve claims of legal liability," engages in the unauthorized practice of law. Moreover, the Court stated, prohibitions against representation extend not only to arbitration, but also to any "other legal or quasi-legal proceeding, including any terms and conditions of a settlement of any dispute."

* * *

Only two courts have considered whether client representation during a *mediation* could constitute the unauthorized practice of law. In *Fought & Co. v. Steel Engineering,* an out-of-state lawyer worked with a Hawaii lawyer to prepare his client's mediation position statement. In addition, the out-of-state lawyer conducted legal research, analyzed opponents' briefs, and planned an appeal strategy. Unfortunately, in analyzing the UPL claim, the Hawaii Supreme Court failed to discuss separately whether preparation for mediation was a UPL violation. The Court's ultimate holding that the lawyer's combined activities did not constitute the unauthorized practice of law under the Hawaii statute suggests that the Hawaii court would not have found that mediation preparation alone was the unauthorized practice of law.

The Indiana Supreme Court also addressed the question, albeit indirectly. In *In the Matter of John M. Hughes,* the Court found that a lawyer engaged in the unauthorized practice of law when, in addition to appearing for and representing clients in mediation, an out-of-state lawyer represented clients in depositions, was listed on an Indiana law firm's letterhead as "Attorney at Law" without a jurisdictional limitation, and the law firm's answering machine identified the lawyer as a member of the firm. It is unclear from this opinion whether the Indiana court would have found the lawyer liable if the only activities he engaged in were the representation of clients during mediation.

Since the opinions considering whether out-of-state attorneys engage in the unauthorized practice of law when they prepare for or represent clients during mediation offer little guidance, a court confronted with the question would likely turn to the various arbitration decisions for assistance. While the processes differ, the underlying analysis, preparation and participation in both mediation and arbitration rely on the lawyer's legal understanding of the merits of the underlying dispute. Moreover, courts have looked to arbitration precedent in mediation cases for guidance in the past. Thus, it would not be surprising if they were to examine arbitration precedent as an analogy to assist them in understanding the issue as it arises in mediation. In light of the conflict among courts considering this issue in the arbitration context, however, examination of existing arbitration precedent seems unlikely to yield a clear answer.

Policy efforts to resolve this problem have been helpful. The popularity of multijurisdictional practice, together with the increased use of ADR and a growing number of cases involving UPL charges, led the ABA to develop a clearer definition of what practices constitute the unauthorized practice of law. The ABA addressed the question in its August 2000 ABA Report on the Commission on Multijurisdictional Practice, concluding that representing clients in ADR in a foreign jurisdiction is permissible. Model Rule 5.5 states:

Rule 5.5: Unauthorized Practice of Law; Multijurisdictional Practice of Law

(a) A lawyer shall not practice law in a jurisdiction in violation of the regulation of the legal profession in that jurisdiction, or assist another in doing so.

. . .

(c) A lawyer admitted in another United States jurisdiction, and not disbarred or suspended from practice in any jurisdiction, may provide legal services on a temporary basis in this jurisdiction that:

(1) are undertaken in association with a lawyer who is admitted to practice in this jurisdiction and who actively participates in the matter;

(2) are in or reasonably related to a pending or potential proceeding before a tribunal in this or another jurisdiction, if the lawyer, or a person the lawyer is assisting, is authorized by law or order to appear in such proceeding or reasonably expects to be so authorized;

(3) are in or reasonably related to a pending or potential arbitration, mediation, or other alternative dispute resolution proceeding in this or another jurisdiction, if the services arise out of or are reasonably related to the lawyer's practice in a jurisdiction in which the lawyer is admitted to practice and are not services for which the forum requires pro hac vice admission; or

(4) are not within paragraphs (c)(2) or (c)(3) and arise out of or are reasonably related to the lawyer's practice in a jurisdiction in which the lawyer is admitted to practice.

. . .

In drafting a rule that permits lawyers to represent clients in ADR proceedings, the Commission reasoned that knowledge of jurisdictional law is less important in ADR proceedings because state and local law play a lesser role in arbitration and mediation than in litigation. Moreover, the Commission believed, conducting the ADR process in a particular jurisdiction may have nothing to do with a desire to apply that jurisdiction's law. Instead, it may be the most convenient location for multiple parties from different states or it may be the location of the parties' chosen arbitrator or mediator. In those circumstances, the ABA concluded, the state's need to control who practices law in a particular jurisdiction in order to protect citizens from counsel unfamiliar with the jurisdiction's laws is not very strong and should yield to the parties' interests in choosing their own counsel and/or neutral.

The ABA Report has been influential. Since the ABA Report was issued, twenty-five state supreme courts have adopted a rule either identical or similar to Model Rule of Professional Conduct 5.5. Although this is a promising development, lawyers must nevertheless be careful when engaging in multijurisdictional practice since half the states have not yet adopted legislation like Rule 5.5. Rule 5.5 is also limited in its scope. It does not protect, for example, some activities in which an out-of-state lawyer might like to participate, such as an out-of-state advertising campaign. Moreover, lawyers engaged in arbitration practice in states that have yet to adopt Rule 5.5 expose themselves to a significant risk of a UPL finding. In the absence of state efforts to enact legislation overturning these court rulings or amend existing *pro hac vice* rules to include representation in dispute resolution processes, the risk-averse lawyer should refrain from representing parties in jurisdictions where they are not licensed. While it would seem that mediation deserves different treatment than arbitration in this context because knowledge of legal rules is even less important in the typical mediation, the Hawaii and Indiana Supreme Court decisions suggest that a cautious approach to this issue would nevertheless be appropriate.

MEDIATION EXERCISES

The instructions below are for the person who will play the role of mediator. Confidential instructions for those playing the disputing parties will be provided by the instructor from the Teacher's Manual. It is important to stay in your role as you act out the simulations.

EXERCISE 3.1: THE NEIGHBORHOOD SPAT*

You are the mediator in a community mediation center. T. C. Veranda, a 67-year-old retiree, was referred to the center by the police after she filed a complaint

*Adapted with permission from Nancy Rogers and Richard Salem, Teacher's Guide to *A Student's Guide to Mediation and the Law* (1987). New York: Matthew Bender.

against a 19-year-old neighbor, Fran Moran, for spraying paint on a door to her house. No prosecution has been instituted. Before you begin the mediation, think out the approach you will take. What will you explain to the parties about the mediation program procedures (you may make these up)? How will you make them feel at ease? How will you encourage the parties to suggest a number of options for resolving their dispute?

EXERCISE 3.2: A SHORTAGE OF LOW-INCOME HOUSING*

You are the director of a state mediation agency. A local federal judge called last week to say that she had appointed you as the mediator of a pending case and had ordered the parties to meet with you for an hour to discuss whether they should agree to a more extended mediation with you. A copy of the class action complaint filed by the plaintiffs arrived yesterday. The plaintiffs are applicants for or tenants in public housing in Steeltown. They are joined by a group of nonprofit organizations, called the City Coalition for Affordable Housing, who advocate an increase in low-income housing. The defendants are the Steeltown Municipal Housing Authority (SMHA) and the Secretary of the U.S. Department of Housing and Urban Development (HUD). The plaintiffs allege violations of the federal and state fair housing statutes, federal environmental laws, and the fifth and fourteenth amendments to the United States Constitution. The complaint contains the following summary of its extensive requests for relief:

> Plaintiffs seek first to halt the imminent demolition of portions of Christopher and Kingsford Housing Projects, pending a determination of their claims that demolition would violate applicable law and that there is in any event no realistic plan insuring one-for-one replacement housing. They also seek to halt and reverse the SMHA's pattern of causing or permitting housing conditions to deteriorate to the point where it is tantamount to demolition, including the SMHA's failure to properly maintain and rehabilitate and to rent all available units. Finally, plaintiffs seek to bar permanently needless demolition of other SMHA housing units.

You have read in the newspaper about allegations that SMHA has secretly agreed to sell public housing project land to a consortium of business persons for a sports arena. A grand jury is investigating allegations that two SMHA officials accepted bribes in connection with another land sale. Last week, officials from HUD arrived to audit SMHA's books.

Consider your approach to this dispute. What additional preparation will you do? How will you persuade the parties to agree to mediation? What will you do about confidentiality? How do you expect to frame the issues? What is the best order for discussion of the issues?

Conduct the first session and then revise your tentative strategy.

*The authors are grateful to Eric Max, whose mediation work served as a basis for this exercise.

EXERCISE 3.3: THE RED DEVIL DOG RESTAURANT LEASE*

You are an attorney in private practice and have agreed to mediate a dispute between a commercial landlord and a prospective tenant. The referral came from the landlord's lawyer. The landlord will pay for the first two hours of mediation. The prospective tenant, who apparently has no lawyer, has agreed to attend, as long as the landlord does not bring a lawyer. Piecing together information provided by the referring lawyer and the prospective tenant, you surmise that the prospective tenant had agreed to rent the premises to operate a local franchise of the well-known Red Devil Dog Restaurant chain. The lease provides for payment of $1,000 per month plus 3 percent of gross sales for a five-year period. After the landlord made $2,500 in modifications and the tenant moved in boxes of equipment, the news broke that the Red Devil Dog chain had filed for bankruptcy. The prospective tenant then called to cancel the lease, and the landlord responded with a letter demanding $80,000. The mediation has been scheduled in the early evening because the prospective tenant works days as a nurse. Your secretary reports that the prospective tenant sounded angry.

Before you begin the mediation, think out your approach. Do you expect any bargaining imbalances? If so, should your approach change in any way? If the disputing parties are angry, how can you get them to focus on possible solutions?

EXERCISE 3.4: BARRY v. KNIGHT

Sandy Knight and Kellen Barry are neighbors, with adjoining houses on Ocean View Drive in Swamphead. Their relations had been generally good until two weeks ago when Knight, in order to improve the ocean view from Knight's house, trimmed two feet from three hemlocks located near the mutual property line, on property claimed by Barry. Barry demanded that Knight pay $600 to replace the three hemlocks and Knight refused. Mutual friends suggested that they try to resolve the matter through mediation at the North Shore Neighborhood Justice Center, and they agreed to do so.

The mediator is a volunteer at the NSNJC, and the mediation is scheduled for tomorrow evening.

EXERCISE 3.5: SANTARA v. KESSEL

Approximately six months ago, Randy Santara and Brett Kessel set up a home catering business called Ring-and-Serve. After some initial success, the business fell on hard times, and disagreements developed between the partners. Last month, Santara filed a lawsuit for dissolution of the partnership. On the suggestion of the

*Reprinted from Nancy H. Rogers, The Red Devil Dog Lease Mediation Roleplay, in Leonard L. Riskin, *Instructor's Manual for Tape III. Mediation: The Red Devil Dog Lease* (West 1992). Copyright © 1992 by the Curators of the University of Missouri. Reprinted with permission. This exercise is based on Tape III, which was based on Dale A. Whitman, "The Missing Tenant," in Leonard L. Riskin and James E. Westbrook, *Instructor's Manual for Dispute Resolution and Lawyers* (West 1987).

clerk of court, that suit was referred to the Story Neighborhood Justice Center for mediation by a volunteer mediator.

EXERCISE 3.6: BRYAN v. OAKDALE*

Approximately three months ago, an automobile owned by plaintiff D. V. Bryan was damaged when it was driven into a large hole on Andover Street in Oakdale. When the City of Oakdale refused to pay for the cost of repairing the car, Bryan filed suit against the city in Small Claims Court. At the suggestion of the clerk of the Small Claims Court, Bryan and Lee Carnevale, an attorney for the city, will attempt to resolve the dispute by mediation at the Oakdale Neighborhood Justice Center.

EXERCISE 3.7: LITTLE v. JENKS

Approximately one month ago, Sandy Jenks sold a car to Chris Little, a good friend. Little soon became dissatisfied with the car, claiming that it had a faulty exhaust system. Little asked Jenks to take the car back and refund Little's money. When Jenks refused to do so, Little filed suit against Jenks for $1,500. The clerk of court suggested that they try to resolve the dispute by mediation, and they agreed to do so. The case is about to be heard at the Neighborhood Justice Center.

EXERCISE 3.8: THE GRINDER

Industrial Machinery Company, a Denver company, manufactures a complete line of machinery used to produce bricks. One machine, a grinder, grinds clay. The ground clay is then formed into the shape of a brick and placed in a kiln for baking.

In the spring of 1989, Industrial sold a grinder for $170,000 to Better Brick Company (BBC), also a Denver company. Problems immediately arose with the grinder, and those problems still exist. It clogs, ceases to work effectively, and has to be shut down and cleaned on a weekly basis. The cleaning takes several hours. In addition, at least once a month the grinder requires more serious repairs, which render it inoperable for two days. When the grinder is not working, BBC's brick manufacturing process is stalled.

When Industrial sold the grinder to BBC, it extended express warranties that the grinder would operate at a certain minimum speed and down time "would not exceed industry standards." The contract stated that aside from these warranties, no other warranties or representations applied:

> *Entire Agreement.* This Agreement contains the entire agreement and understanding of the parties with respect to the entire subject matter hereof, and there are no representations, inducements, promises or agreements, oral or otherwise, not embodied herein. Any

*This exercise is based on one prepared by the Harvard Program on Negotiation and is used with its permission.

and all prior discussions, negotiations, commitments and understandings relating thereto are merged herein.

When it operates properly, the grinder operates at the minimum speed, but no faster. BBC had expected that the grinder would operate somewhat faster than the minimum speed, as most industrial grinders do. Increased speed in the grinder's operations would enable BBC to produce more bricks each week, because grinders operate somewhat more slowly than the other machinery used to form the bricks. Speed is a relevant concern to BBC because there is great demand for bricks in the region in which it sells, which includes the entire southwestern United States, because of a buoyant economy.

The parties disagree as to the cause of the problems with the grinder. BBC claims that the grinder is defective. Industrial claims that BBC does not process its clay in a manner that comports with industry standards: its machines that sort the clay prior to grinding (the sorters) are very old and do not sort its clay as effectively as the newer sorters which other brick manufacturers use. Therefore, the grinder is forced to handle larger clay particles than grinders typically handle. Industrial's warranties did not include an exception for clay particles the size that BBC uses, but no other brick manufacturer in the United States grinds such large particles.

Industrial's grinder operations manual recommends the use of sorters that eliminate large clay particles. BBC claims it brought this language to the attention of Ray Slick, the Industrial salesman who sold the grinder to BBC, and Slick stated that "large particles are no problem for this baby." Shortly after receiving his commission from this sale, Ray moved to the South Pacific and cannot be found. The parties disagree as to whether Industrial knew about BBC's clay and impliedly warranted that the grinder was fit for the particular purpose for which BBC is using it.

BBC has not yet paid for the grinder. Industrial has demanded that BBC promptly pay it for the grinder or else it will commence suit. BBC likewise has threatened to sue Industrial for breach of contract. BBC claims that because of the problems with the grinder, it has lost sales of approximately 200,000 bricks per month and has lost profits of two cents per brick. In addition, certain large customers of BBC have begun to buy bricks from BBC's competitors because during periods when the grinder is down BBC has not been able to fulfill their demand for bricks. BBC believes that if the grinder problem is not quickly resolved, its lost sales could increase to 100,000 bricks per week. Industrial challenges BBC's calculation of lost sales.

The parties acknowledge that a lawsuit regarding the grinder would involve a number of experts and be very complicated, expensive, and time-consuming. The principals in this dispute are the CEOs of the two companies and their attorneys. Industrial's CEO is Dick Jones and its lawyer is Marcia Kramer. BBC's CEO is Richard Bennington and its lawyer is Jerry ("the Mauler") Johnson, so-called because of his expert use of "scorched-earth" litigation tactics. His motto is "settlement is for wimps."

Richard Bennington heard about mediation in a business law class and suggested its use here. Industrial agreed. You are the mediator selected by the parties.

EXERCISE 3.9: PROSANDO v. HIGH-TECH*

Prosando, a German-Argentine joint venture based in Argentina, is a distributor of office and business equipment. High-Tech is a large, well-established computer manufacturer, with its headquarters in southern California.

In January 2000, Prosando entered into an exclusive five-year distribution contract with High-Tech. Prosando agreed to establish a distribution network for High-Tech's Futura A and B minicomputers throughout South America and to use High-Tech's trademark in doing so.

Immediately after the contract was signed, Prosando ordered 50 Futura A computers. High-Tech, however, refused to ship until its legal department had reviewed the contract. Following that review, in June 2000, High-Tech insisted that it retain the right to sell directly in South America. Prosando reluctantly agreed, and in August 2000, High-Tech shipped 50 Futura A computers to Prosando.

In October 2000, Prosando ordered another 20 Futura A computers, which were delivered in December 2000. In January 2001, High-Tech discontinued the Futura A and introduced the Century series, but refused initially to allow Prosando to distribute that series. According to High-Tech, Prosando's distribution contract was limited to the Futura series. In June 2001 (one and one-half years into the contract), High-Tech agreed to allow Prosando to distribute the Century series. In February 2002, Prosando ordered 18 Century series computers.

In June 2002, without prior warning, High-Tech notified Prosando that the contract would be terminated in 30 days because of Prosando's clear and unequivocal breach of contract. According to High-Tech, Prosando had:

1. Failed to use its best efforts to sell the product within the assigned territory to the total dissatisfaction of the Seller, since Prosando had placed orders for only 88 units of product in 24 months.
2. Failed to establish a "distributor" network on or before June 30, 2001. As of June 2002, Prosando had established a total of four distributors, all in Chile.
3. Failed to submit or negotiate annual purchase commitments.

The relevant provisions of the contract are these:

A. Prosando shall have the sole right (except for High-Tech) to sell High-Tech Futura A and Futura B minicomputers, and any updates thereto (hereafter "the product") within the assigned territory.
B. Prosando shall use its best efforts to sell within the assigned territory.
C. Prosando shall establish a distribution network within the assigned territory to the satisfaction of High-Tech.
D. Prosando shall have its distribution network in place by June 2001. If it fails to do so, High-Tech shall have the right to terminate Prosando's status as

*This exercise was created for the CPR Institute for Dispute Resolution by Cathy Cronin-Harris, Vice President, and Professor Stephen Goldberg as a basis for CPR's 36-minute videotape, *Mediation in Action: Resolving a Complex Business Dispute* (1994). The videotape is available from CPR, 366 Madison Avenue, 14th floor, New York, NY 10017 (212)949-6490, www.cpradr.org.

exclusive South American distributor of the product, and to engage other distributors in addition to Prosando.

E. Prosando must place a noncancellable blanket order for 100 of the product totalling one million U.S. dollars upon execution of this agreement for delivery on or after ________. (Left blank in the contract.)

F. On each calendar year commencing in ________ (left blank in the contract) the parties will agree on the minimum purchase requirements for the subsequent twelve-month period. If agreement is not achieved, either party may terminate this agreement upon prior 90 days' written notice.

G. Upon termination of this Agreement becoming effective: (a) Neither party shall be liable to the other for loss of profits or prospective profits of any kind or nature sustained or arising out of or alleged to have arisen out of such termination.

On receiving High-Tech's June 2002 notice of termination, Prosando continued to sell its remaining High-Tech equipment.

In September 2002, Prosando initiated litigation in the U.S. District Court for the Southern District of California, claiming damages for breach of contract and fraud: $1 million for loss of business reputation; $6 million for lost profits; and actual reliance damages of $3 million expended on the contract (including capitalized loans, leasing of premises, personnel, promoting and advertising the product, travel, etc.), a total of $10 million.

High-Tech denied all allegations and counterclaimed for $126,000 for equipment shipped and not paid for.

At the suggestion of the district court, the parties have agreed to attempt to resolve this dispute through mediation.

EXERCISE 3.10: THE LAST DANCE*

Two years ago, Jackie (who had been a dancer and then a choreographer) was working as an assistant director for a large New York dance company. At that point, Dance Innovation, a smaller New York company, hired her to become its Artistic Director and resident choreographer (when its founder and previous Artistic Director, Peter George, died suddenly). The three-year contract provided that any works she produced as part of her employment were to be considered "work for hire." She could be fired with six months' notice.

The mission of Dance Innovation was to support the work of new choreographers. Jackie brought with her a work in progress that she had been creating (on the side) while at (and with the permission of) her former employer. She completed that work, MOTIF, while at Dance Innovation (and it was produced by the company). She created a second work, CHORALE, during her first year at Dance Innovation (and it was produced by the company). She was working on a third major work, ENSEMBLE (which was to be produced in the upcoming season), when she was fired.

*This exercise was reprinted with the permission of Gary Friedman and the Harvard Program on Negotiation.

Mickey, Dance Innovation's Chairman and Executive Director, sent Jackie a letter notifying her of her dismissal because she was focused almost exclusively on the creation of her own work (rather than devoting attention to her own work *and* supporting the work of new choreographers) and was consistently over budget. He also informed her that, in his mind, ENSEMBLE was virtually completed when Jackie left, needing at most a little final polishing and refinement and that the company is going forward with completing ENSEMBLE which will be the centerpiece of its upcoming season. He further maintained that any works completed by Jackie or that she was working on while employed are exclusively the property of Dance Innovation.

When Jackie received the letter, she had a difficult confrontation with Mickey. Jackie reminded Mickey of the six months' notice provision in her contract. Mickey responded that she should have considered herself on notice for months. Jackie then hired a lawyer. Both Jackie and Mickey will bring their lawyers to the mediation session.

Before you begin the mediation, think through your approach. Do you think that it would be a good idea to hold separate meetings with each "side"?

Additional information for the parties and lawyers is included in the Teacher's Manual.

EXERCISE 3.11: ADA AUDITORIUM DILEMMA[1]

Sidney Student has filed a lawsuit against the Arlington College of Law, a private college, alleging violation of the federal Americans with Disabilities Act (ADA). Pursuant to a new statutory provision, his lawsuit has been scheduled for mediation prior to being scheduled for trial.

Sidney is a former student of the Arlington College of Law. He began his legal education in the fall of 2003, and, as an exceptionally ambitious student, Sidney chose to attend class full-time during both summer terms. Therefore, Sidney was able to meet all of his graduation requirements, including his requirement of attending school for six full-time semesters, one semester early. Sidney graduated from the Arlington College of Law in December 2005.

Because so few students graduated in December 2005, the college chose to hold its graduation ceremony in the law school auditorium. The law building, including the auditorium, was built in the 1950s, and thus, the auditorium is not well equipped to give people who use wheelchairs easy access to the stage. During the graduation ceremony, the graduating students were to be presented with their diplomas on stage. This created a problem for Sidney, who uses a wheelchair, and prompted the Arlington College of Law to explore the accessibility of the auditorium stage.

There are two (2) aisles that lead from the rear of the auditorium to the stage, but one (1) aisle has recently been renovated to include a platform that creates wheelchair-accessible seating in the rear of the auditorium. As a result, the aisle is too narrow for wheelchair access to the auditorium stage. Thus, there is really only one (1) aisle that a person who uses a wheelchair could use to reach the stage, and

1. This exercise was created by Meredith Lobritz and Sarah Cole for use in a Disability Discrimination course.

this aisle has a pitch that is too steep for some people who use wheelchairs. In other words, those using wheelchairs can make it down to the bottom of the ramp, but cannot return up the ramp and out of the auditorium on their own. There is no handrail down the aisle.

Even if a person who uses a wheelchair could make it down the aisle to the front of the auditorium stage, the four-foot-high stage only has stairs—there is no ramp. Building a temporary ramp would be prohibitively expensive and would require storage because it would be so large; moreover, there would not be enough room at the bottom of the stage to create a ramp with an appropriate pitch. Alternative options are also costly. For example, it would cost around $3,000 to rent a lift for the stage, or $10,000 to buy a lift.

There are two (2) doors on the back of the stage, both of which open into a hallway in the law school. Neither door, however, leads directly onto the stage. The first door, located at the back of the left side of the stage, leads into a small closet before the stage that is currently used for storage. There is a corner, around which a person would have to negotiate his or her wheelchair in order to get on stage, and there is also a small lip that rises up at the doorway to the stage and that could prove to be a slight impediment to a person who uses a wheelchair. The second door, located at the back of the right side of the stage, leads to a small flight of steps down to the stage, and, again, there is a small lip that rises up at the doorway to the stage.

After weighing all considerations, the law school administration decided that the best solution for Sidney was to have him receive his diploma in the area immediately beneath the front of the stage. So, when Sidney wheeled his chair down the accessible aisle during the ceremony to receive his diploma, he was unable to get back out of the auditorium due to the steep pitch of the aisle. Sidney was extremely embarrassed, and he had to wait until someone was able to help him back up the aisle. Sidney was also angered because he felt segregated: why should he have to receive his diploma from the area beneath the front of the stage while all other graduating students received their diplomas on stage?

The very next day, Sidney filed this suit, alleging that the Arlington College of Law has failed to comply with the ADA in regards to the auditorium. Sidney is seeking injunctive relief and damages, because he does not want any other people who use wheelchairs to have the same experience that he did.

The federal ADA is codified at 42 U.S.C. §§12101 et seq., and in pertinent part provides:

§12181. Definitions.

(9) **Readily achievable.** The term "readily achievable" means easily accomplishable and able to be carried out without much difficulty or expense. In determining whether an action is readily achievable, factors to be considered include—

(A) the nature and cost of the action needed under this Act;

(B) the overall financial resources of the facility or facilities involved in the action; the number of persons employed at such facility; the effect on expenses and resources, or the impact otherwise of such action upon the operation of the facility; . . .

§12182. Prohibition of discrimination by public accommodations.

(a) **General rule.** No individual shall be discriminated against on the basis of disability in the full and equal enjoyment of the goods, services, facilities, privileges, advantages, or accommodations of any place of public accommodation by any person who owns, leases (or leases to), or operates a place of public accommodation.

(b) **Construction.**

(2) **Specific prohibitions.**

(A) **Discrimination.** For purposes of subsection (a), discrimination includes—

(ii) a failure to make reasonable modifications in policies, practices, or procedures, when such modifications are necessary to afford such goods, services, facilities, privileges, advantages, or accommodations to individuals with disabilities, unless the entity can demonstrate that making such modifications would fundamentally alter the nature of such goods, services, facilities, privileges, advantages, or accommodations;

(iii) a failure to take such steps as may be necessary to ensure that no individual with a disability is excluded, denied services, segregated or otherwise treated differently than other individuals because of the absence of auxiliary aids and services, unless the entity can demonstrate that taking such steps would fundamentally alter the nature of the goods, service, facility, privilege, advantage, or accommodation being offered or would result in an undue burden;

(iv) a failure to remove architectural barriers . . . in existing facilities, . . . where such removal is readily achievable; and

(v) where an entity can demonstrate that the removal of a barrier under clause (iv) is not readily achievable, a failure to make such goods, services, facilities, privileges, advantages, or accommodations available through alternative methods if such methods are readily achievable.

§12188. Enforcement.

(a) **In general.**

(2) Injunctive relief. In the case of violations of . . . 42 USC §12182 (b)(2)(A)(iv) . . . , injunctive relief shall include an order to alter facilities to make such facilities readily accessible to and usable by individuals with disabilities to the extent required by this title. Where appropriate, injunctive relief shall also include requiring the provision of an auxiliary aid or service, modification of a policy, . . . or provision of alternative methods, to the extent required by this title.

The mediation between Sidney, represented by counsel, and the Arlington College of Law, also represented by counsel, is scheduled for today.

EXERCISE 3.12: PATERNAL VISITATION*

Mohammed, a West African man in his mid-thirties living in Columbus, Ohio, recently learned that he is the father of a 2-year-old boy, Na'il. The child's mother, Suzanne, is a 35-year-old African-American woman. Suzanne has three other children, with different fathers. Suzanne and Mohammed have not seen each other for

*This problem was created by Sarah Cole and Amy Wenger.

over two years. When Mohammed learned two months ago that he was the boy's father, he asked Suzanne if he could spend time with him. Suzanne turned him down, in part because Mohammed had refused to have anything to do with Na'il until he was convinced that he was Nail's father. At the same time, Suzanne asked Mohammed to begin making child support payments of $600 per month. Mohammed is a taxi driver who makes approximately $36,000 per year.

Before you begin the mediation, consider the impact that culture may have on this mediation. Do you expect differences in the parties' approaches to mediation or expectations about outcome? If so, how do you think you should handle these issues?

References

AARON, Benjamin, Beatrice BURGOON, Donald CULLEN, Dana EISCHEN, Mark KAHN, Charles REHMUS, and Jacob SEIDENBERG, eds. (1977) *The Railway Labor Act at Fifty.* Washington, D.C.: National Mediation Board.

AARON, Marjorie Corman (1995) "The Value of Decision Analysis in Mediation Practice," 11 *Neg. J.* 123.

AARON, Marjorie Corman, and David P. HOFFER (1996) "Decision Analysis as a Method of Evaluating the Trial Alternative," in D. Golann, *Mediating Legal Disputes: Effective Strategies for Lawyers and Mediators.* New York: Aspen Publishers.

ABA Section of Dispute Resolution (2002) *Report on Mediator Credentialing and Quality Assurance, Discussion Draft,* available at www.abanet.org/dispute/home.html.

ABEL, Richard (1985) "Informalism: A Tactical Equivalent to Law," 19 *Clearinghouse Rev.* 375.

ACR Task Force on Mediator Certification (2004) *Report to ACR Board of Directors,* available at www.ACRnet.org.

AIKEN, Jane (1992) "Settlement of AIDS Cases" (Unpublished manuscript available at Arizona State University College of Law).

ALFINI, James J., Sharon B. PRESS, Jean R. STERNLIGHT, and Joseph B. STULBERG (2006) *Mediation Theory and Practice* (2d ed.). Newark: Matthew Bender/LEXIS.

AUERBACH, Jerold (1983) *Justice Without Law?* New York: Oxford University Press.

BABCOCK, Linda, and Sara LASCHEVER (2003) *Women Don't Ask: Negotiation and the Gender Divide,* Princeton, N.J.: Princeton University Press.

BEER, Jennifer (1986) *Peacemaking in Your Neighborhood.* Philadelphia: New Society Publishers.

BEER, Jennifer, Eileen STIEF, and Charles WALKER (1982) *Peacemaking in Your Neighborhood.* Concordville, PA: Friends Suburban Project.

BRAZIL, Wayne (1990) "A Close Look at Three Court-Sponsored ADR Programs: Why They Exist, How They Operate, What They Deliver, and Whether They Threaten Important Values," *U. Chi. Legal F.* 303.

——— (1999) "Comparing Structures for the Delivery of ADR Services by Courts: Critical Values and Concerns," 14 *Ohio St. J. Disp. Resol.* 715.

BRETT, Jeanne M., Zoe I. BARSNESS, and Stephen B. GOLDBERG (1996) "The Effectiveness of Mediation: An Independent Analysis of Cases Handled by Four Major Service Providers," 12 *Neg. J.* 259.

BURTON, Lloyd, Larry FARMER, Elizabeth GEE, Lorie JOHNSON, and Gerald WILLIAMS (1991) "Feminist Theory, Professional Ethics, and Gender-Related Distinctions in Attorney Negotiating Styles," *J. Disp. Resol.* 199.

BUSH, Robert Baruch (1989) "Efficiency and Protection, or Empowerment and Recognition? The Mediator's Role and Ethical Standards in Mediation," 41 *Fla. L. Rev.* 253.

——— (1994) "Symposium: Dilemmas of Mediation Practice," *J. Disp. Resol.* 1.
——— (1996a) "The Unexplored Possibilities of Community Mediation: A Comment on Merry and Milner," 21 *Law & Soc. Inquiry* 715.
——— (1996b) "What Do We Need a Mediator For?: Mediation's 'Value-Added' for Negotiators," 12 *Ohio St. J. Disp. Resol.* 1.
BUSH, Robert A. Baruch, and Joseph P. FOLGER (2005) *The Promise of Mediation* (2d ed.). San Francisco: Jossey-Bass.
CENTER FOR DISPUTE SETTLEMENT (1991) *Mediation for the Professional: Training Manual.* Washington, D.C.: Center for Dispute Settlement.
——— (1992) *National Standards for Court-Connected Mediation Programs.* Washington, D.C.: Center for Dispute Settlement.
CLOKE, Kenneth (1990) *Mediation: Revenge and the Magic of Forgiveness.* Santa Monica: Center for Dispute Resolution.
——— (2000) *Mediating Dangerously.* San Francisco: Jossey-Bass.
COBB, Sara, and Janet RIFKIN (1991) "Practice and Paradox: Deconstructing Neutrality in Mediation," 16 *Law & Soc. Inquiry* 35 (Winter).
COBEN, James R. and Peter N. THOMPSON (2006) "Disputing Irony: A Systematic Look at Litigation About Mediation," 11 *Harv. Negot. L. Rev.* 43.
COLE, Sarah R. (2005) "Mediator Certification: Has the Time Come?" 11 *Disp. Resol. Mag.* 7.
——— (2006) "Unauthorized Practice of Law Charges: A Risk for Lawyers Representing Clients in Mediation and Arbitration in a Multijurisdictional Practice Environment," 13 *Disp. Resol. Mag.* 26.
COLE, Sarah R., Nancy H. ROGERS, and Craig A. McEWEN (2003 & 2006 Supp.) *Mediation: Law, Policy, Practice* (2d ed.). St. Paul: West.
COLOSI, Thomas (1984) Foreword, *SPIDR, Ethical Issues in Dispute Resolution* 1983 Annual Proceedings xiv.
COOK, Royer, Janice ROEHL, and David SHEPPARD (1980) *Neighborhood Justice Centers Field Test.* Washington, D.C.: U.S. Department of Justice, National Institute of Justice.
CRAVER, Charles (1990) "The Impact of Gender on Clinical Negotiating Achievement," 6 *Ohio St. J. Disp. Resol.* 1.
CROUCH, Richard (1982) "The Dark Side of Mediation: Still Unexplored," in Alternative Means of Family Dispute Resolution (ABA).
DANZIG, Richard (1973) "Toward the Creation of a Complementary, Decentralized System of Criminal Justice," 26 *Stan. L. Rev.* 1.
DELGADO, Richard (1988) "ADR and the Dispossessed: Recent Books About the Deformalization Movement," 13 *Law & Soc. Inquiry* 145.
DOMINGUEZ, David (1994) "Beyond Zero-Sum Games: Multiculturalism as Enriched Law Training for All Students," 44 *J. Legal Educ.* 175.
EDWARDS, Harry (1985) "Hopes and Fears for Alternative Dispute Resolution," 21 *Willamette L. Rev.* 425.
——— (1986) "Alternative Dispute Resolution: Panacea or Anathema?" 99 *Harv. L. Rev.* 668.
ELLIS, Desmond, and Noreen STUCKLESS (1996) *Mediating and Negotiating Marital Conflicts.* Thousand Oaks: Sage Publications.
EMERY, Robert, and Joanne JACKSON (1989) "The Charlottesville Mediation Project: Mediated and Litigated Child Custody Disputes," *Mediation Q.* 3 (Summer).
ESSER, John P. (1989) "Evaluations on Dispute Processing: We Do Not Know What We Think and We Do Not Think What We Know," 66 *Denv. U. L. Rev.* 499.
"Ethics in Dispute Resolution" (2001) *Disp. Resol. Mag.* 3 (Spring).
FAURE, Guy Olivier, and Jeffrey Z. RUBIN (1993) "Lessons for Theory and Research," in *Culture and Negotiation* 209-231, Guy Olivier Faure and Jeffrey Z. Rubin, eds. Newbury Park, CA: Sage Publications.

FISHER, Roger, and William URY (1981) *Getting to Yes: Negotiating Agreement Without Giving In.* Boston: Houghton Mifflin.
FISS, Owen (1984) "Against Settlement," 93 *Yale L.J.* 1073.
FOLBERG, Jay, and Joshua KADISH (1987) "Family Law Mediation," in *Arbitration and Mediation.* Lake Oswego: Oregon State Bar Committee on Continuing Legal Education.
FOLBERG, Jay, and Alison TAYLOR (1984) *Mediation.* San Francisco: Jossey-Bass.
FOLGER, Joseph (1991) "Assessing Community Dispute Resolution Needs," in Karen Grover Duffy, James Grosch, Paul Olczak, eds. *Community Mediation.* New York: Guilford Press.
FREEDMAN, Larry, and Michael PRIGOFF (1986) "Confidentiality in Mediation: The Need for Protection," 2 *Ohio St. J. Disp. Resol.* 37.
FULLER, Lon (1971) "Mediation: Its Forms and Functions," 44 *S. Cal. L. Rev.* 305.
——— (1978) "The Forms and Limits of Adjudication," 92 *Harv. L. Rev.* 353.
GALANTER, Marc (1983) "Reading the Landscape of Disputes: What We Know and Don't Know (and Think We Know) About Our Allegedly Contentious Society," 31 *UCLA L. Rev.* 4.
——— (1986) "The Emergence of the Judge as a Mediator in Civil Cases," 69 *Judicature* 257.
——— (1988) "The Quality of Settlements," *Mo. J. Disp. Resol.* 55.
GANGEL-JACOB, Phyllis (1995) "Some Words of Caution About Divorce Mediation," 23 *Hofstra L. Rev.* 825.
GARTH, Bryant, and Phyllis BERNARD, eds. (2002) *Dispute Resolution Ethics — A Comprehensive Guide.* Washington, D.C.: ABA Section on Dispute Resolution.
GIBSON, Kevin V. (1992) "Confidentiality in Mediation: A Moral Reassessment," *J. Disp. Resol.* 25.
GOLANN, Dwight (1996) *Mediating Legal Disputes: Effective Strategies for Lawyers and Mediators.* New York: Aspen Publishers.
GOLDBERG, Stephen B. (1986) "Meditations of a Mediator," 2 *Neg. J.* 345.
GREATBATCH, David, and Robert DINGWALL (1989) "Selective Facilitation: Some Preliminary Observations on a Strategy Used by Divorce Mediators," 23 *Law & Soc. Rev.* 613.
GREBE, Sarah Childs (1988) "Structured Mediation and Its Variants: What Makes It Unique," in J. Folberg and A. Milne, eds., *Divorce Mediation: Theory and Practice.* New York: Guilford Press.
GREEN, Eric (1986) "A Heretical View of Mediation Privilege," 2 *Ohio St. J. Disp. Resol.* 1.
GRILLO, Trina (1991) "The Mediation Alternative: Process Dangers for Women," 100 *Yale L.J.* 1545.
GUTHRIE, Chris, and James LEVIN (1998) "A 'Party Satisfaction' Perspective on a Comprehensive Mediation Statute," 13 *Ohio St. J. Disp. Resol.* 885.
HAYNES, John M. (1984) "Mediated Negotiations — The Function of the Intake," *Mediation Q.* 3 (December).
——— (1994) *The Fundamentals of Family Mediation.* Albany: State University of New York Press.
HEGLAND, Kenny (1982) "Why Teach Trial Advocacy? An Essay on Never Ask Why," in J. Himmelstein and H. Lesnick, eds., *Humanistic Education in Law.* New York: Columbia University School of Law.
HERMANN, Michele (1994) "New Mexico Research Examines Impact of Gender and Ethnicity in Mediation," *Disp. Resol. Mag.* 10 (Fall).
HERMANN, Michele, Gary LAFREE, Christine RACK, and Mary Beth WEST (1993) *The Metrocourt Project Final Report.* Albuquerque: University of New Mexico Center for the Study and Resolution of Disputes.
HERRMAN, M., ed. (2006) *The Blackwell Handbook of Mediation — Bridging Theory, Practice and Research.* Malden, Mass.: Blackwell Publishing.

HONEYMAN, Christopher (1990) "On Evaluating Mediators," 6 *Neg. J.* 23.
KAGEL, Sam, and Kathy KELLY (1989) *The Anatomy of Mediation.* Washington, D.C.: Bureau of National Affairs.
KAKALIK, James S., Terrence DUNWORTH, Laural A. HILL, Daniel McCAFFREY, Marian OSHIRO, Nicholas M. PACE, and Mary E. VAIANA (1996) *An Evaluation of Mediation and Early Neutral Evaluation Under the Civil Justice Reform Act.* Santa Monica: RAND Corp.
KEILITZ, Susan (1993) *National Symposium on Court-Connected Dispute Resolution Research.* Williamsburg: National Center for State Courts.
KELLY, Joan B. (1995) "Power Imbalance in Divorce and Interpersonal Mediation: Assessment and Intervention," 13 *Mediation Q.* 85.
——— (1996) "A Decade of Divorce Mediation Research: Some Answers and Questions," 34 *Fam. & Conciliation Cts. Rev.* 373.
KELLY, Joan, and Lynn GIGY (1989) "Divorce Mediation: Characteristics of Clients and Outcomes," in Kenneth Kressel and Dean Pruitt, eds., *Mediation Research.* San Francisco: Jossey-Bass.
KNEBEL, F., and G. CLAY, *Before You Sue.* New York: William Morrow & Co.
KOLB, Deborah M., and Associates (1994) *When Talk Works: Profiles of Mediators.* San Francisco: Jossey-Bass.
KOVACH, Kimberly K. (2000) *Mediation: Principles and Practice.* St. Paul: West.
KRESSEL, Kenneth, and Dean G. PRUITT (1989) *Conclusion: A Research Perspective on the Mediation of Social Conflict,* in Kenneth Kressel, Dean G. Pruitt and Associates, *Mediation Research: The Process and Effectiveness of Third-Party Intervention.* San Francisco: Jossey-Bass.
KRIVIS, Jeffrey (2006) *Improvisational Negotiation.* San Francisco: Jossey-Bass.
LERMAN, Lisa (1984) "Mediation of Wife Abuse Cases: The Adverse Impact of Informal Dispute Resolution on Women," 7 *Harv. Womens L.J.* 57.
LEVI, Deborah L. (1997) "The Role of Apology in Mediation," 72 *N.Y.U. L. Rev.* 1165.
LEVINE, Matthew (1984) "Power Imbalances in Dispute Resolution," in Vermont Law School Dispute Resolution Project, *A Study of Barriers to the Use of Alternative Methods of Dispute Resolution.* South Royalton: Vermont Law School.
LEWIS, Michael (1995) "Advocacy in Mediation: One Mediator's View," *Disp. Resol. Mag.* (Fall).
LIND, E. Allen, and Tom R. TYLER (1988) *The Social Psychology of Procedural Justice.* New York: Plenum.
LOVE, Lela P. (1997) "The Top Ten Reasons Why Mediators Should Not Evaluate," 24 *Fla. St. U. L. Rev.* 937.
MAGGIOLO, Walter (1985) *Techniques of Mediation.* New York: Oceana Publications.
MAUTE, Judith (1990) "Mediator Accountability: Responding to Fairness Concerns," *J. Disp. Resol.* 347.
MAYER, Bernard (2004) *Beyond Neutrality: Confronting the Crisis in Conflict Resolution.* San Francisco: Jossey-Bass.
McCRORY, John (1988) "Confidentiality in Mediation of Matrimonial Disputes," 51 *Mod. L. Rev.* 442.
McEWEN, Craig A., and Laura C. WILLIAMS (1998) "Legal Policy and Access to Justice Through Courts and Mediation," 13 *Ohio St. J. Disp. Resol.* 865.
MENKEL-MEADOW, Carrie, ed. (1997) "The Silences of the Restatement of the Law Governing Lawyers: Lawyering as Only Adversary Practice," 10 *Geo. J. Legal Ethics* 631.
——— (2000) *Mediation — Theory, Policy and Practice.* Burlington, VT: Ashgate.
MERRY, Sally, and Susan SILBEY (1984) "What Do Plaintiffs Want? Reexamining the Concept of Dispute," 9 *Just. Sys. J.* 151.
MOORE, Christopher W. (1988) *Techniques to Break Impasse,* in Jay Folberg and Ann Milne, *Divorce Mediation: Theory and Practice.* New York: Guilford Press.

——— (1996) *The Mediation Process* (2d ed.). San Francisco: Jossey-Bass.
MORROW, Duncan, and Derick WILSON (1993) "Three into Two Won't Go? From Mediation to New Relationships in Northern Ireland," *NDR Forum* 13 (Winter).
NADER, Laura (1993) "Controlling Processes in the Practice of Law: Hierarchy and Pacification in the Movement to Re-Form Dispute Ideology," 9 *Ohio St. J. Disp. Resol.* 1.
NADER, Laura, and Harry TODD (1978) *The Disputing Process: Law in Ten Societies.* New York: Columbia University Press.
NEGOTIATION JOURNAL (1993) "Who Really Is a Mediator? A Special Section on the Interim Guidelines," Vol. 9, p. 290.
NIEMIC, Robert J. (1997) *Mediation and Conference Programs in the Federal Courts of Appeals.* Washington, D.C.: Federal Judicial Center.
OH, Heidi M. (1996) Note, "Look Before You Leap: The Failed Promises of Child Custody Mediation," 13 *Prob. L.J.* 157.
OHIO STATE JOURNAL ON DISPUTE RESOLUTION (1986) *Symposium on Critical Issues in Mediation Legislation,* Vol. 2, No. 1.
PEARSON, Jessica (1991) "The Equity of Mediated Divorce Agreements," 9 *Mediation Q.* 179.
PEARSON, Jessica, and Nancy THOENNES (1988) "*Divorce Mediation Results,*" in Jay Folberg and Ann Milne, eds., *Divorce Mediation: Theory and Practice,* 429. New York: Guilford Press.
PIOR, Anne (1993) "What Do the Parties Think? A Follow-Up Study of the Marriage Guidance South Australia (MGSA) Family Mediation Project," 4 *Australian Disp. Resol. J.* 99.
PIPER, Christine (1993) *The Responsible Parent: A Study in Divorce Mediation.* New York: Harvester Wheatsheat.
POSNER, Richard (1986) "The Summary Jury Trial and Other Methods of Alternative Dispute Resolution: Some Cautionary Observations," 53 *U. Chi. L. Rev.* 366.
RISKIN, Leonard (1983) "Mediation and Lawyers," 43 *Ohio St. L.J.* 29.
——— (1993) "Mediator Orientations, Strategies and Techniques," *Alternatives* 111 (Sept.).
——— (1996) "Understanding Mediator's Orientations, Strategies, and Techniques: A Grid for the Perplexed," *Harv. Neg. L. Rev.* 7.
ROGERS, Nancy, and Richard SALEM (1987) *A Student's Guide to Mediation and the Law.* New York: Matthew Bender.
ROSS, Jerome (1984) "Should the Mediator Raise Public Interest Considerations During Negotiations," *SPIDR, Ethical Issues in Dispute Resolution,* 1983 Annual Proceedings 50.
ROTHMAN, Jay (1997) *Resolving Identity-Based Conflict in Nations, Organizations, and Communities.* San Francisco: Jossey-Bass.
SALACUSE, Jeswald W. (1993) "Implications for Practitioners," in Guy Olivier Faure and Jeffrey Z. Rubin, eds. *Culture and Negotiation* 199-208. Newbury Park, CA: Sage Publications.
SALEM, Richard A. (1985) "The Alternative Dispute Resolution Movement: An Overview," 40 *Arb. J.* (Sept.) 3.
SAPOSNEK, Donald T. (1983) *Mediating Child Custody Disputes.* San Francisco: Jossey-Bass.
SAVAGE, Cynthia A. (1996) "Culture and Mediation: A Red Herring," 5 *Am. U. J. Gender & L.* 269.
SIMKIN, William E., and Nicholas A. FIDANDIS (1986) *Mediation and the Dynamics of Collective Bargaining* (2d ed.). Washington, D.C.: Bureau of National Affairs.
SIMON, William (1985) "Legal Informality and Redistributive Politics," 19 *Clearinghouse Rev.* 385.
SINGER, Linda (1990) *Settling Disputes.* Boulder, Colo.: Westview Press.
——— (1994) *Settling Disputes: Conflict Resolution in Business, Families, and the Legal System* (2d ed.). Boulder: Westview Press.
SLAIKEU, Karl A. (1996) *When Push Comes to Shove: A Practical Guide to Mediating Disputes.* San Francisco: Jossey-Bass.

SMITH, William (1985) "Effectiveness of the Biased Mediator," 1 *Neg. J.* 363.
SOCIETY OF PROFESSIONALS IN DISPUTE RESOLUTION (1995) *Ensuring Competence and Quality in Dispute Resolution Practice, Report #2 of the SPIDR Commission on Qualifications.*
——— (1998) *Guidelines for Voluntary Mediation Programs Instituted by Agencies Charged with Enforcing Workplace Rights, Report of the Law and Public Policy Committee.*
STARK, James H. (1997) "The Ethics of Mediation Evaluation: Some Troublesome Questions and Tentative Proposals, From an Evaluative Lawyer Mediator," 38 *S. Tex. L. Rev.* 769.
STULBERG, Joseph (1981) "The Theory and Practice of Mediation: A Reply to Professor Susskind," 6 *Vt. L. Rev.* 85.
——— (1987) *Taking Charge/Managing Conflict.* New York: Lexington Books.
——— (1990) "Tactics of the Mediator," in John H. Wilkinson, ed., *Donovan Leisure Newton & Irvine ADR Practice Book,* 137. New York: John Wiley & Sons.
——— (1998) "Fairness and Mediation," 13 *Ohio St. J. Disp. Resol.* 909.
——— (2005) "Mediation and Justice: What Standards Govern?" 6 *Cardozo J. Conflict Resol.* 213.
SUSSKIND, Lawrence (1981) "Environmental Mediation and the Accountability Problem," 6 *Vt. L. Rev.* 1.
Symposium (2001) "Credentialing Mediators," *Disp. Resol. Mag.* (Fall).
TERRELL, Timothy (1987) "Rights and Wrongs in the Rush to Repose: On Jurisprudential Dangers of Alternative Dispute Resolution," 36 *Emory L.J.* 541.
THOENNES, Nancy, Jessica PEARSON, and Julie BELL (1991) *Evaluation of the Use of Mandatory Divorce Mediation.* Denver: Center for Policy Research.
TOMASIC, Roman (1983) "Mediation as an Alternative to Adjudication: Rhetoric and Reality in the Neighborhood Justice Movement," in Roman Tomasic and Malcolm Feeley, eds. *Neighborhood Justice: Assessment of an Emerging Idea.* New York: Longman Press.
TYLER, Tom (1989) "The Quality of Dispute Resolution Processes and Outcome: Measurement Problems and Possibilities," 66 *U. Denv. L. Rev.* 419.
URY, William, Jeanne BRETT, and Stephen GOLDBERG (1988) *Getting Disputes Resolved.* San Francisco: Jossey-Bass.
WAGATSUMA, Hiroshi, and Arthur ROSETT (1986) "The Implications of Apology: Law and Culture in Japan and the United States," 20 *Law & Soc. Rev.* 461.
WALL, James, Lawrence SCHILLER, and Ronald EBERT (1984) "Should Judges Grease the Slow Wheels of Justice? A Survey on the Effectiveness of Judicial Mediary Techniques," 8 *Am. J. Trial Advoc.* 83.
WALL, Victor D., Jr., and Marcia L. DEWHURST (1991) "Mediator Gender: Communication Differences in Resolved and Unresolved Mediations," 9 *Mediation Q.* 63.
WECKSTEIN, Donald T. (1996) "Mediation Certification: Why and How?" 30 *U.S.F. L. Rev.* 757.
WISSLER, Roselle L. (1996) *Ohio Attorneys' Experience with and Views of Alternative Dispute Resolution Procedures.* Columbus: Supreme Court of Ohio.
——— (1997) *Evaluation of Settlement Week Mediation.* Columbus: Supreme Court of Ohio.
——— (2002) "Court-Connected Mediation in General Civil Cases: What We Know from Empirical Research," 17 *Ohio St. J. Disp. Resol.* 641.
WOODS, Laurie (1985) "Mediation: A Backlash to Women's Progress on Domestic Violence Issues," 19 *Clearinghouse Rev.* 431.
WRIGHT, Martin, and Burt GALAWAY, eds. (1989) *Mediation and Criminal Justice.* London: Sage Publications.

Chapter 4
Arbitration

A. THE PROCESS

Arbitration has been an alternative to litigation for hundreds of years. It was used as early as the thirteenth century by English merchants who preferred to have their disputes resolved according to their own customs (the law merchant) rather than by public law. Commercial arbitration in the United States antedated the American Revolution in New York and several other colonies and is widely used today. Labor arbitration became widespread during the 1940s, and now almost all collective bargaining contracts contain a provision for final and binding arbitration. Additionally, arbitration is used to resolve disputes in the construction industry, disputes between consumers and manufacturers, family disputes, medical malpractice claims, securities disputes, attorney's fee disputes, disputes between nonunionized employees and their employers, community disputes, and civil rights disputes. It is even used to resolve disputes about salaries to be paid to major league baseball players.

Before turning to a more detailed examination of arbitration, it should be noted that in addition to private arbitration, which is typically voluntary but final and binding, a number of jurisdictions have adopted an arbitration procedure that is mandatory for certain types of cases, but does not result in a binding decision. Generally known as *court-ordered* or *court-annexed arbitration,* this procedure is discussed at page 309.

Because arbitration is a private dispute resolution procedure, designed by the parties to serve their particular needs, it cannot be defined or described in a manner that will encompass all arbitration systems. Still, arbitration typically contains the essential elements of court adjudication—proofs and arguments are submitted to a neutral third party who has the power to issue a binding decision. Arbitration differs from court adjudication, however, in that, unless the parties agree otherwise, the only pretrial discovery will be that mandated by the arbitrator. Additionally, the hearing is usually more informal than a court hearing, and the rules of evidence are not strictly applied. Finally, commercial arbitration awards typically contain only the arbitrator's award; commercial arbitrators do not provide reasons for their decisions. This practice is not followed in the labor context or in international commercial arbitration, where arbitrators, like judges, issue reasoned decisions.

Most private arbitration systems provide the following:

- Joint selection and payment of the arbitrator;
- Objective standards on which the arbitrator's decision is to be based (typically the terms of an agreement between parties, the customs of the trade in which they conduct business, the applicable law, or some combination of these); and
- Procedural rules to be applied by the arbitrator.

The theoretical advantages of arbitration over court adjudication are manifold:

- *Expertise of the decision maker.* The arbitrator is selected by the parties, not imposed on them by the courts. Hence, they can choose a decision maker who is expert in the subject matter of their dispute.
- *Finality of the decision.* The courts will nearly always respect a provision that the arbitrator's decision is final and binding. This serves to discourage appeals to the courts and to make provisions for finality meaningful.
- *Privacy of the proceedings.* If the parties wish their proceedings to be shielded from public scrutiny, arbitration—a private forum—is preferable to the courts, which will rarely deny public access.
- *Procedural informality.* Since the parties determine the procedural rules, they can opt for simplicity and informality.
- *Low cost.* Simplified procedures tend to reduce the costs of dispute resolution, as does the typical absence of discovery. Costs also are reduced by lack of opportunity to appeal the arbitrator's decision.
- *Speed.* The same factors that lead to low costs lead to speedy resolution. In addition, the parties need not wait for a trial date to be assigned them but can proceed to arbitration as soon as they and the arbitrator are ready.

These theoretical advantages are not always fully realized. For example, the parties may focus so much on selecting an arbitrator whom they hope will be sympathetic to their position that they do not take advantage of the opportunity to select an arbitrator with expertise in the subject matter of their dispute. Or, the attorneys may be so concerned with copying the procedures of the courts that they lose the advantages of simpler procedures, such as potential reductions in time and cost.

Further, critics charge that some of the purported advantages of arbitration over court adjudication are actually disadvantages. For example, the parties' ability to select the arbitrator is said to encourage arbitrators to search for compromise decisions to avoid antagonizing parties that they hope will select them in future cases. Similarly, the finality of arbitration precludes courts from overturning decisions that are clearly erroneous.

Additionally, arbitration differs from many other alternative dispute resolution (ADR) procedures, such as mediation, in that the neutral, rather than the disputing parties, retains control over the outcome. Thus, the benefits flowing from a mutually agreed-upon resolution by the parties, such as a carefully crafted compromise in which each party gets what it values more, giving up what it values less, cannot realistically be anticipated through arbitration. Nor, because there is no mutually agreed-upon resolution, is the process likely to lead to the high degree of voluntary compliance associated with negotiated or mediated settlements. Some parties have attempted to retain the advantages of both mediation and arbitration through a process known as *med-arb,* in which the mediator, if unsuccessful in resolving the dispute through the agreement of the parties, becomes an arbitrator with power to issue a binding decision. This procedure is discussed at pages 307-309.

Arbitration can be initiated either pursuant to an arbitration provision in an existing contract or on the basis of an ad hoc agreement to arbitrate. Both the Federal Arbitration Act (FAA) and the Uniform Arbitration Act (Appendices B and C), adopted in almost every state, make agreements to arbitrate specifically enforceable. There is a strong public policy in favor of arbitration as a means of relieving court congestion, and both federal and state courts will interpret agreements to arbitrate broadly and exceptions narrowly. Doubts are resolved in favor of coverage. See, e.g., *Shearson/American Express v. McMahon,* 482 U.S. 220 (1987); *United Steelworkers of America v. Warrior & Gulf Navigation Co.,* 363 U.S. 574 (1960); *Madden v. Kaiser Foundation Hospitals,* 17 Cal. 3d 699, 550 P.2d 1178 (1976). Additionally, the FAA displaces state law in the state courts to the extent that state law conflicts with the goals or policies of the Act. See *Volt Information Sciences, Inc. v. Stanford Univ.,* 489 U.S. 468 (1989); *Southland Corp. v. Keating,* 465 U.S. 1 (1984), p. 219.

Arbitration awards are not self-enforcing. Stated otherwise, there is typically no sanction for failing to comply with an arbitrator's award unless that award has been judicially confirmed, in which event failure to comply constitutes contempt of court. Both the FAA and the Uniform Arbitration Act vest courts with jurisdiction to confirm or vacate (refuse to confirm) an arbitration award. Section 10 of the FAA provides that a court may deny confirmation to an arbitrator's award under the following circumstances:*

(a) Where the award was procured by corruption, fraud, or undue means. . . .
(b) Where there was evident partiality or corruption in the arbitrators, or either of them.
(c) Where the arbitrators were guilty of misconduct in refusing to postpone the hearing, on sufficient cause shown, or in refusing to hear evidence pertinent and material to the controversy; or of any other misbehavior by which the rights of any party have been prejudiced.
(d) Where the arbitrators exceeded their powers, or so imperfectly executed them that a mutual, final, and definite award upon the subject matter submitted was not made.

Parties that wish to arbitrate frequently turn either to one of the many for-profit providers of arbitration services; a nonprofit organization such as the American Arbitration Association (AAA) or the Center for Public Resources (CPR); or a government agency, such as the Federal Mediation and Conciliation Service (FMCS). Each of these organizations provides assistance in selecting an arbitrator, administering the arbitration hearing, or, in the case of the AAA, providing procedural rules to govern the conduct of the hearing.

*What if the parties in their submission to arbitration specifically seek to broaden the statutory scope of review? Should this be permitted? See *Kyocera Corp. v. Prudential-Bache Trade Svcs, Inc.,* 341 F.3d 987, 997-1000 (9th Cir. 2003) (en banc), rejecting this approach (discussed at p. 277).

Parties that use the administrative services of the AAA are not obliged to follow AAA procedural rules, but usually do. CPR has developed rules for the nonadministered arbitration of business disputes, in which the arbitrator and the parties' advocates perform most of the functions generally performed by the administering organization.

In order to provide disputing parties with qualified arbitrators, AAA, CPR, FMCS, and many private providers of dispute resolution services maintain arbitration panels composed of approved arbitrators. Commercial arbitrators are apt to be lawyers, business people, professors, or other persons familiar with the business or industry in which a dispute may arise. In the case of labor arbitrators, most have experience in labor law or labor relations. A code of ethics that was jointly promulgated by the AAA and the American Bar Association, revised in 2004, governs commercial arbitrators' conduct (Cole, 2004). There is a separate code for labor arbitrators (Gifford and Hobgood, 1985:413), which was jointly promulgated by the AAA, FMCS, and the National Academy of Arbitrators (a private group comprised of approximately 700 of the country's most respected labor arbitrators).

Some of the advantages and disadvantages of traditional private arbitration compared to litigation are canvassed in the following dialogue.

ARBITRATION OR LITIGATION: A DIALOGUE*

The scene is the law offices of Howland and Smith, a firm with 200 lawyers, including a large litigation section. Jane Garrity, a litigator, and Jim Smith, the firm's ADR specialist, are discussing how to handle a pending case involving one of Howland and Smith's clients, Bramson Ball Bearing Company. Bramson had sold 50,000 ball bearings to Jones Machine Company, a long-time customer, which Jones refused to pay for, claiming they were defective. Bramson denies any defects in the ball bearings and has asked Howland and Smith to bring suit against Jones for $75,000, the amount Jones had agreed to pay.

Smith: Jane, it seems to me this case would be ideal for arbitration. As you know we've got a three- or four-year delay before trial, and Bramson really wants to get its money. If we go to arbitration, we could wind this case up in six or seven months instead of waiting three or four years and then getting a settlement on the courthouse steps or going through litigation and a lengthy appeal. Moreover, there are likely to be difficult technical issues in connection with Jones's claim that the ball bearings were defective. If we go to court, we might have trouble explaining those issues to a judge or jury, but if we go to arbitration, we can choose an arbitrator with technical expertise.

Garrity: You ADR people are always singing the same tune—anything is better than the courts. My experience is that arbitration leaves a lot to be desired. First, it's not that easy to find a competent arbitrator. A lot of them really don't know what they're doing, and in the end they just split the difference.

*This dialogue has been adapted from Goldberg, Green, and Sander, "Litigation, Arbitration or Mediation: A Dialogue," and is reprinted with permission from the June 1989 issue of the *ABA Journal*, published by the American Bar Association.

Smith: I think you're too cynical about our ability to find a good arbitrator. For example, if you contact the American Arbitration Association or the Center for Public Resources they will send both parties a list of proposed arbitrators, with background material on each. Each party can strike one name from the list and rank the others in order of preference. The AAA or CPR will appoint the highest mutual choice. Other dispute resolution organizations follow similar procedures to assist disputing parties in selecting a high-quality arbitrator.

Garrity: That's fine *if* the list of arbitrators they send you has high-quality people on it, but I've heard that's not always so. Then there's no appeal; if you get a bum award, one that's based on a misapplication of the law or is contrary to the weight of the evidence, you're just stuck with it.

Smith: But how important, as a practical matter, is a right of appeal in a case like this? Not only would an appeal add to our costs, but this is a straight breach of contract case with no novel legal issues. The likelihood that an appellate court would reverse the trial court in a case like this is surely not very substantial. From that perspective, it really doesn't matter much whether we're in court or before an arbitrator.

Garrity: Maybe you're right about that, but I think that the knowledge that an appellate court may be reviewing what he does motivates the trial judge to perform to the best of his ability. That's largely missing in arbitration, where there is no meaningful judicial review.

Smith: But if we're careful in selecting the arbitrator, that's much less of a concern. Besides, what we give up in terms of a right to appeal, we gain in finality. You've told me that we have a strong case here, and if we win we won't have to worry about Jones dragging things out by taking an appeal. They could, but the likelihood of success would be so low that it's not probable that they would.

Garrity: Well, I do think that we have a winner, but you never know what an arbitrator or judge, much less a jury, will do to you. That brings me to my next concern about going to arbitration. If I lose a case in court, I can blame the judge. But if we go to arbitration, and I've participated in selecting the arbitrator, I'm likely to get the blame if we lose. So while you praise arbitration because you can pick the arbitrator, that doesn't have much appeal to me.

Smith: Well, if you don't want to select the arbitrator, turn the entire selection procedure over to AAA or CPR. That way you can't be held responsible for who the arbitrator is.

Garrity: That's a possible approach, but I'm not comfortable with turning the selection process completely over to someone else.

Smith: But that's exactly what you do when you go to court! Still, I do have another approach for you. You could pick one arbitrator, the other side could pick one, and those two could agree on a third arbitrator. That would increase costs somewhat, but it would give you some input in selecting the crucial member of the panel. It would also ensure that at least one of the arbitrators is sympathetic to your arguments.

Garrity: No, that's even worse than a single arbitrator. In addition to tripling the costs, a three-person panel more than triples the delays associated with arbitration. It's hard enough to find mutually agreeable hearing dates when you have to work with the schedules of two busy lawyers and one arbitrator—it's almost impossible if you add two more arbitrators. And, speaking of delay, I've heard of cases in which the defendant has tied up an arbitration almost indefinitely by running to court whenever there is some procedural dispute.

Smith: I'm aware of cases like that, too, but they tend to be limited to situations in which arbitration takes place under a preexisting contractual commitment to arbitrate. Those commitments are usually honored, but sometimes when a dispute actually arises, one party sees an advantage in litigation rather than arbitration. In that situation, the reluctant party may resist arbitration in every way it can, including going to court to complain of alleged procedural irregularities in the arbitration. If, however, both parties voluntarily agree to arbitration at the time the dispute arises, neither of them is likely to go to court to block arbitration. In that situation, which is what we will have here if Bramson and Jones agree to arbitrate, a skilled arbitrator can dispose of the case quickly and effectively.

Garrity: That's another problem. Those buzz words "quickly" and "effectively" mean something different to me—namely, that there's no attention paid to the rules of evidence. In arbitration they use the "kitchen sink" approach—everything goes in.

Smith: Well, that's probably an overstatement. There are some arbitrators, particularly those who are lawyers, who are quite strict about what evidence they will admit. If you want an arbitrator like that, you can select one. Alternatively, you can provide that the arbitrator must abide by whatever evidentiary rules you adopt. I just can't emphasize strongly enough that the arbitration format is entirely within the control of the parties. You can make the arbitration as formal or informal, as much or as little like a federal court procedure as you wish. Just because you contact some arbitration agency to select the arbitrator and administer the proceedings doesn't mean you must adopt their rules. That's one of the virtues of arbitration, and I wish that more people would take advantage of it.

Still, I would not advise altering standard arbitration practice in this case. You are right in assuming that the general tendency of arbitrators is not to apply the rules of evidence strictly. As I see it, though, that's a plus for arbitration, not a minus. I've long found the rules of evidence to be a major cause of unnecessarily lengthy trials. Some trial lawyers even say that the rules don't always keep evidence out—they just ensure that it takes longer to get it in, particularly in a jury trial. Surely there are simpler ways of establishing the facts, and that's just what arbitration or a properly run bench trial does—it makes it possible to get to the heart of the matter quickly and without a lot of procedural folderol.

There's one other argument in favor of arbitration that we haven't talked about yet, and that is its privacy. This case involves Jones's complaints about the quality of Bramson's ball bearings, and I doubt that Bramson is very happy at the prospect of Jones spreading those complaints all over the court records, so any newspaper reporter who is interested can write about them. If we go to arbitration, the proceedings will be entirely private, and so will the arbitrator's decision.

Garrity: That's a nice point, but I have still another concern. There's a lot we don't know about this case yet. If we go to arbitration, won't we lose the discovery opportunities we'd have in court?

Smith: Once again, that depends on you and the other party. If you want some discovery, it's important to provide for it in your agreement to arbitrate. If you don't, you may not get any more than the other side will agree to, since many arbitrators will not compel discovery to which either party objects.

My advice on this point would be to provide for only as much discovery as you absolutely need to prepare for trial. One of the things that makes arbitration attractive is that discovery has gotten completely out of hand in court. If we were to go through normal court discovery in this case, say four or five depositions, plus the five or so days you've told me it should take to try it, that could cost Jones as much as $50,000. That just doesn't make sense in a case with a maximum recovery of $75,000. I'm sure that in arbitration, if we could agree on limited discovery—say, two depositions each—and then a skilled arbitrator who didn't waste time by strictly applying the rules of evidence and following formal court room procedures, we could try this case in a maximum of two days at a cost of approximately $20,000. Even adding the arbitrator's fee and an administrative fee for the organization supplying the arbitrator, which together would probably be less than $5,000, we'd still come out way ahead, and we wouldn't have to worry about the costs of an appeal. That's why I think it makes sense to arbitrate this case, not to litigate it. Indeed, I almost think that an attorney who doesn't at least advise his client about the alternatives to litigation for resolving disputes might be guilty of malpractice (see pp. 336-337). So, I think you should raise this possibility with Bramson, and if they are interested, discuss it with Jones's lawyer. You might even be surprised to find him receptive to this idea.

Question

4.1 Are you persuaded that arbitration would be preferable to litigation for resolving this dispute? Why? Is there any ADR procedure other than arbitration that you might suggest for these parties? Why?

As noted in the foregoing dialogue, disputing parties that agree to arbitration rarely take advantage of the opportunity to design a procedure that will best suit their needs. Instead, they typically provide that the procedural rules of the AAA will apply. (You might think about why this is so.) In the following excerpt, attorney Stephen Houck describes an exception to this generalization.

S. HOUCK, COMPLEX COMMERCIAL ARBITRATION: DESIGNING A PROCESS TO SUIT THE CASE

43 Arb. J. 3 (1988)

A recently concluded ad hoc arbitration presents a practical case study in the expeditious resolution of complex commercial disputes. Notwithstanding the complicated factual and legal issues involved (antitrust and patent issues in an intricate worldwide licensing scheme for a sophisticated chemical product), this dispute was definitively resolved within one year of the date on which the parties executed an agreement to arbitrate. Moreover, it was resolved on the basis of a full record developed through broad discovery and a four-week evidentiary hearing before a retired U.S. district court judge. In short, through a variety of features incorporated into the arbitration agreement, the parties obtained the benefits of full-scale federal litigation while avoiding many of its pitfalls (for example, inordinate expense, long delays, and seemingly anomalous monetary damage awards). . . .

Minimizing Risk

The crux of the dispute between the parties [French, English, and American companies] was right of access to the American market. How it was resolved would have a significant impact on corporate marketing plans and strategic decisions affecting resource allocation. The stakes — and gamble inherent in any litigation — were significantly raised by the prospect that damages, and even treble damages amounting to multimillions of dollars, could be assessed against any of the parties.

As a way to minimize risk while still resolving the key issue critical to corporate decision makers, the parties agreed to waive all damages with respect to the specific product in dispute. . . .

Elimination of damages not only minimized the downside potential of an adverse decision for all parties, but also significantly reduced the time necessary for discovery and trial.

Other features of the arbitration agreement that contributed to minimization of risk were the clauses mandating confidentiality, limiting use of materials obtained in discovery to the arbitration, and expressly prohibiting the arbitrators from writing an opinion and making findings of fact. These various clauses increased the likelihood that the impact of the arbitrators' decision would be confined to the issue entrusted to them and would not spill over into other litigation, by collateral estoppel or otherwise.

Minimizing Delay

The critical factor in ensuring timely completion of the arbitration was the agreement's absolute requirement, which could not be altered by the arbitrators, that a decision be rendered within one year of the date of execution. This not only provided a firm, unyielding deadline but required lawyers to make tough cost/benefit decisions during discovery, forcing them to concentrate on essentials and eliminating the excesses sometimes associated with broad discovery in civil litigation.

The arbitration agreement also prescribed dates for certain key events, such as selection of arbitrators, the initial conference with the arbitrators, commencement and conclusion of discovery, trial, and the filing of pretrial briefs and stipulations. While these dates, unlike the deadline for decision, could be extended by the arbitrators or by stipulation, they provided useful guidelines. The arbitrators were given ample means to enforce these guidelines and to prevent any discovery abuses, since the arbitration agreement made the Federal Rules of Civil Procedure, including all its sanctions, applicable to the discovery process.

Discovery was expedited by a unique feature of the agreement, a prohibition on objections during depositions; all objections were expressly reserved until trial. This substantially accelerated the pace of depositions, minimized the burden of litigation on key corporate executives who were deposed, promoted a relatively amicable atmosphere at depositions (especially important because the parties would continue to have commercial relations after the arbitration), and contributed to the virtual elimination of discovery motion practice. Moreover, the few motions that were made were briefed and resolved on an expedited schedule set forth in the arbitration agreement.

Also of vital importance in achieving an expeditious result, particularly at the conclusion of the process, was the agreement's prohibition on both a written decision and an appeal. These features saved months, if not years, in addition to eliminating the uncertainty attendant on any appeal.

Fairness

The advantages realized from minimizing risk and delay would be meaningless if the process were not fair. Moreover, no one would forego the right to appeal unless it was believed that the arbitration was likely to yield a just, rational result. Several features of the arbitration agreement were intended to, and did, instill confidence in the integrity of the process.

The primary means of defining and ensuring a fair process was making the Federal Rules of Civil Procedure applicable to discovery and the Federal Rules of Evidence applicable to the hearing. This not only provided a set of well-defined rules generally regarded as fair, but also a well-developed body of precedents applying those rules. In addition, both the rules and the precedents were familiar to the litigators who would be participating in the arbitration. . . .

Broad discovery is somewhat unusual for an arbitration, but it provided both sides with a full and fair opportunity to develop the facts, eliminated surprise at the hearing, and considerably expedited the hearing itself. The availability of discovery was essential to the perception that the process would eventuate in a just result. Indeed, discovery was a sine qua non to the arbitration itself, involving as it did allegations of conspiracy and willful infringement that would be almost impossible to prove without access to the other side's documents. As noted, the disadvantage most often associated with discovery (undue burden) was avoided by other means.

These discovery and evidentiary rules would have little meaning if improperly or unfairly applied. The procedure devised for selecting the chairperson of the arbitration panel was by agreement of the two party-appointed arbitrators within a prescribed period of time; failing such agreement, the chairperson was to be chosen by the American Arbitration Association from a list of four nominees, two to be proposed by each side. (For more on tripartite arbitration, see Chapter 5 at pp. 306-307.)

Resort to the good offices of the American Arbitration Association was necessary and, perhaps not surprisingly although the parties did not consult with one another, all four nominees were retired U.S. district court judges. Federal trial judges are uniquely qualified by experience and disposition to apply both the Federal Rules of Civil Procedure and the Federal Rules of Evidence. In fact, the judge who ultimately was selected to preside over the arbitration applied the rules in a decisive, evenhanded manner. . . .

Questions

4.2 In order to eliminate the risk to defendants of a multimillion dollar damage finding in the situation described by Houck, plaintiffs agreed to waive all damages. Can you think of means of eliminating that risk that do not require such a waiver by plaintiffs?

4.3 Appliances, Inc., a nationally known manufacturer of major household appliances, is concerned about the unfavorable publicity it has recently received from evidence concerning product performance that has been introduced in product liability suits against it. Appliances, Inc. also is concerned about what it regards as the wholly unjustified amounts of the jury verdicts in some of those cases, verdicts that it believes were based on emotion, not facts. Accordingly, Appliances, Inc. would like to set up a voluntary procedure permitting consumers to elect final and binding arbitration of complaints for damages arising out of allegedly defective products. Appliances, Inc. believes, however, that such an arbitration program will not be used by consumers who have the option of going to court, unless it has the approval of the Consumer's League, a national consumer advocacy group. Students representing, respectively, Appliances, Inc. and the Consumer's League should attempt to negotiate the terms of an arbitration procedure that is satisfactory to both their clients.

4.4 You have been selected as sole arbitrator in a complex commercial dispute. The lawyers have initially asked you to set aside 10 days for the hearing, which surprised you after you reviewed the pre-arbitration filings. But as soon as the hearings started, you began to understand the reason — the attorneys on both sides seem determined to drag out the proceeding. Minor, barely relevant issues are explored at immense length. And much of the initial day was devoted to discovery squabbles. Some gentle efforts by you suggesting the possibility of more accelerated procedures and limited discovery have fallen on deaf ears. At the end of the first day, you contemplate whether you should do anything else — e.g., call a conference with the lawyers. What, if anything, should you do? Does it matter whether the clients are present? If not, should you ask that they attend the next session? Suppose you were the neutral in a three-person board rather than a sole arbitrator (see pp. 306-307)?

B. LEGAL ISSUES IN ARBITRATION

1. Preemption

Congress enacted the Federal Arbitration Act (FAA) in 1925 as a direct response to merchants seeking legislative help to overcome judicial hostility to the enforcement of arbitration agreements. Recognizing its limited power under the Commerce Clause, Congress chose to rely on its power to control federal court jurisdiction; it enacted the FAA as procedural law, applicable only to federal courts. Thirteen years later, in *Erie Railroad Co. v. Tompkins,* 304 U.S. 64 (1938), the Court held that in diversity cases, a federal court should apply federal procedural law, but must apply state substantive law in determining the nature of the parties' rights. As long as courts considered the FAA to be federal procedural law, then, *Erie* presented no bar to its enforceability. In a subsequent case, however, *Bernhardt v. Polygraphic Co. of America,* 350 U.S. 198 (1956), the Court held that the duty to arbitrate did involve substantive law. As a result, it held that, with regard to diversity cases, state laws (rather than federal) regarding arbitration provided the rules of decision, and it thus applied Vermont law to deny a request for arbitration.* In the Court's next examination of this issue, *Prima Paint Corp. v. Flood & Conklin Mfg. Co.,* 388 U.S. 395 (1967), the Court qualified its holding in *Bernhardt* by noting that even in diversity cases, Congress can "prescribe how federal courts are to conduct themselves with respect to subject matter over which Congress plainly has power to legislate." (Id. at 405.) In other words, for disputes involving interstate commerce (such as the one at issue in *Prima Paint*), an area where Congress clearly had the power to regulate, Congress could issue rules governing federal court procedures for resolving the dispute, including rules mandating the enforceability of arbitration clauses, regardless of whether such rules were procedural or substantive. The Court in *Prima Paint,* though, left open the question of the extent to which Congress, in enacting the FAA, had imposed, or constitutionally could impose, such rules on state courts. The Court finally confronted that issue in *Southland Corp. v. Keating,* 465 U.S. 1 (1984).

SOUTHLAND CORP. v. KEATING

465 U.S. 1 (1984)

[Franchisees, whose franchise agreements contain broad arbitration clauses, filed separate actions in the California courts against Southland Corp. for breach of contract and violation of California's Franchise Investment Law. Southland moved to compel arbitration of the claims. To determine whether the action should proceed in court or arbitration, the Court considered whether the Federal Arbitration Act preempted that portion of California's Franchise Investment Law that prohibited franchisees' claims from proceeding in arbitration.]

Chief Justice Burger delivered the opinion of the Court. . . .

III.

The California Franchise Investment Law provides: "Any condition, stipulation or provision purporting to bind any person acquiring any franchise to waive

*The Court avoided addressing the issue presented by the conflict between the Vermont law (under which the arbitration agreement was not enforceable) and the FAA (under which it arguably would have been), by noting that the contract at issue involved neither interstate commerce nor admiralty. The Court noted that because the FAA was strictly limited to those two categories of cases, there was no conflict with Vermont law.

compliance with any provision of this law or any rule or order hereunder is void" (Cal. Corp. Code §31512 (West 1977)). The California Supreme Court interpreted this statute to require judicial consideration of claims brought under the State statute and accordingly refused to enforce the parties' contract to arbitrate such claims. So interpreted the California Franchise Investment Law directly conflicts with §2 of the Federal Arbitration Act and violates the Supremacy Clause.

In enacting §2 of the federal Act, Congress declared a national policy favoring arbitration and withdrew the power of the states to require a judicial forum for the resolution of claims which the contracting parties agreed to resolve by arbitration. . . . We discern only two limitations on the enforceability of arbitration provisions governed by the Federal Arbitration Act: they must be part of a written maritime contract or a contract "evidencing a transaction involving commerce" and such clauses may be revoked upon "grounds as exist at law or in equity for the revocation of any contract." We see nothing in the Act indicating that the broad principle of enforceability is subject to any additional limitations under State law. . . .

The Federal Arbitration Act rests on the authority of Congress to enact substantive rules under the Commerce Clause. . . .

At least since 1824 Congress' authority under the Commerce Clause has been held plenary (*Gibbons v. Ogden*, 22 U.S. 1, 196 (1824)). In the words of Chief Justice Marshall, the authority of Congress is "the power to regulate; that is, to prescribe the rule by which commerce is to be governed" (*Ibid.*) The statements of the Court in *Prima Paint* that the Arbitration Act was an exercise of the Commerce Clause power clearly implied that the substantive rules of the Act were to apply in state as well as federal courts. As Justice Black observed in his dissent, when Congress exercises its authority to enact substantive federal law under the Commerce Clause, it normally creates rules that are enforceable in state as well as federal courts (*Prima Paint*, 388 U.S., at 420). . . .

Although the legislative history is not without ambiguities, there are strong indications that Congress had in mind something more than making arbitration agreements enforceable only in the federal courts. The House Report plainly suggests the more comprehensive objectives: "The purpose of this bill is to make valid and enforceable agreements for arbitration contained in contracts involving interstate commerce or within the jurisdiction or admiralty, or which may be the subject of litigation in the Federal courts" (H.R. Rep. No. 96, 68th Cong., 1st Sess. 1 (1924)). This broader purpose can also be inferred from the reality that Congress would be less likely to address a problem whose impact was confined to federal courts than a problem of large significance in the field of commerce. The Arbitration Act sought to "overcome the rule of equity, that equity will not specifically enforce any arbitration agreement" (Hearing on S. 4214 Before a Subcomm. of the Senate Comm. on the Judiciary, 67th Cong., 4th Sess. 6 (1923)). The House Report accompanying the bill stated: "[t]he need for the law arises from . . . the jealousy of the English courts for their own jurisdiction. . . . This jealousy survived for so lon[g] a period that the principle became firmly embedded in the English common law and was adopted with it by the American courts. The courts have felt that the precedent was too strongly fixed to be overturned without legislative enactment . . ." (H.R. Rep. No. 96, *supra*, 1-2 (1924)).

Surely this makes clear that the House Report contemplated a broad reach of the Act, unencumbered by state law constraints. . . .

Justice O'Connor argues that Congress viewed the Arbitration Act "as a procedural statute, applicable only in federal courts." If it is correct that Congress sought only to create a procedural remedy in the federal courts, there can be no explanation for the express limitation in the Arbitration Act to contracts "involving commerce." 9 U.S.C. §2. . . . On the other hand, Congress would need to call on the Commerce Clause if it intended the Act to apply in state courts. Yet at the same time, its reach would be limited to transactions involving interstate commerce. We therefore view the "involving commerce" requirement in §2, not as an inexplicable limitation on the power of the federal courts, but as a necessary qualification on a statute intended to apply in state and federal courts. Under the interpretation of the Arbitration Act urged by Justice O'Connor, claims brought under the California Franchise Investment Law are not arbitrable when they are raised in state court. Yet it is clear beyond question that if this suit had been brought as a diversity action in a federal district court, the arbitration clause would have been enforceable. The interpretation given to the Arbitration Act by the California Supreme Court would therefore encourage and reward forum shopping. We are unwilling to attribute to Congress the intent, in drawing on the comprehensive powers of the Commerce Clause, to create a right to enforce an arbitration contract and yet make the right dependent for its enforcement on the particular forum in which it is asserted. And since the overwhelming proportion of all civil litigation in this country is in the state courts, we cannot believe Congress intended to limit the Arbitration Act to disputes subject only to federal court jurisdiction. Such an interpretation would frustrate Congressional intent to place "[a]n arbitration agreement . . . upon the same footing as other contracts, where it belongs." H.R. Rep. No. 96, *supra*, 1.

In creating a substantive rule applicable in state as well as federal courts, Congress intended to foreclose state legislative attempts to undercut the enforceability of arbitration agreements. We hold that §31512 of the California Franchise Investment Law violates the Supremacy Clause.

Justice O'Connor with whom Justice Rehnquist joins, dissenting. . . .

II.

The majority opinion decides three issues. First, it holds that §2 creates federal substantive rights that must be enforced by the state courts. Second, though the issue is not raised in this case, the Court states, that §2 substantive rights may not be the basis for invoking federal court jurisdiction under 28 U.S.C. §1331. Third, the Court reads §2 to require state courts to enforce §2 rights using procedures that mimic those specified for federal courts by FAA §§3 and 4. The first of these conclusions is unquestionably wrong as a matter of statutory construction; the second appears to be an attempt to limit the damage done by the first; the third is unnecessary and unwise.

A.

One rarely finds a legislative history as unambiguous as the FAA's. That history establishes conclusively that the 1925 Congress viewed the FAA as a procedural statute, applicable only in federal courts, derived, Congress believed, largely from the federal power to control the jurisdiction of the federal courts. In 1925 Congress emphatically believed arbitration to be a matter of "procedure." At hearings on the Act congressional subcommittees were told: "The theory on which you do this is that you have the right to tell the Federal courts how to proceed." The House Report on the FAA stated: "Whether an agreement for arbitration shall be enforced or not is a question of procedure. . . ." On the floor of the House Congressman Graham assured his fellow members that the FAA "does not involve any new principle of law except to provide a simple method . . . in order to give enforcement. . . . It creates no new legislation, grants no new rights, except a remedy to enforce an agreement in commercial contracts and in admiralty contracts."

Yet another indication that Congress did not intend the FAA to govern state court proceedings is found in the powers Congress relied on in passing the Act. The FAA might have been grounded on Congress's powers to regulate interstate and maritime affairs, since the Act extends only to contracts in those areas. There are, indeed, references in the legislative history to the corresponding federal powers. More numerous, however, are the references to Congress's pre-Erie power to prescribe "general law" applicable in all federal courts. At the congressional hearings, for example: "Congress rests solely upon its power to prescribe the jurisdiction and duties of the Federal courts." . . . Plainly, a power derived from Congress's Article III control over federal court jurisdiction would not by any flight of fancy permit Congress to control proceedings in state courts. The foregoing cannot be dismissed as "ambiguities" in the legislative history. . . .

V.

Today's decision is unfaithful to congressional intent, unnecessary, and, in light of the FAA's antecedents and the intervening contraction of federal power, inexplicable. Although arbitration is a worthy alternative to litigation, today's exercise in judicial revisionism goes too far. I respectfully dissent.

Note

Following *Southland,* the Supreme Court has frequently reiterated that state law, to the extent that it undermines the validity of an arbitration agreement and not other contracts, is preempted. Thus, the FAA preempts state legislation that: (1) required "waiver of the right to sue in court" provisions contained in consumer contracts to appear in larger print (*Doctor's Associates, Inc. v. Casarotto,* 517 U.S. 681 (1996)) and (2) prohibited state courts from using specific performance to enforce arbitration agreements. *Allied-Bruce Terminix Co., Inc. v. Dobson,* 513 U.S. 265 (1995). The Court viewed both state laws as inconsistent with the policy articulated in the Federal Arbitration Act that precludes states from treating arbitration agreements differently than other kinds of contracts.

One troubling aspect of the *Southland* opinion is its surprising interpretation of the FAA's enactment history. As Justice O'Connor emphasized, and most commentators agree, the majority's contention that the FAA was always intended as substantive law is inconsistent with the FAA's legislative history and plain text. Moreover, the majority's FAA analysis creates an interpretive problem that Justice O'Connor mentions, but does not resolve. If the FAA is substantive law, as the majority suggests, must state courts apply not only §2 of the FAA, at issue in *Southland,* but also §§3 and 4? Yet these provisions specify that they apply in federal courts. §3 addresses the issue of court stays in "any suit or proceeding . . . brought in any of the courts of the United States." Section 4 allows a party to move to compel arbitration in "any United States district court." Is it possible to reconcile Chief Justice Burger's majority opinion in *Southland* with the plain language of FAA §§3 and 4? If you were a clerk to a state court judge confronted with a motion to compel arbitration in a case that involved interstate commerce, how would you rule? Would you order the parties to arbitration under §4 of the FAA? Would you rely on §2 and the *Southland* opinion?

Questions

4.5 Numerous state statutes exempt certain kinds of disputes from the coverage of that state's arbitration act. Popular choices for exemption include arbitration agreements involving non-union employer-employee, insured-insurer, personal injury, and real estate disputes (Cole, 2001:786-788) (listing state statutes). Does the FAA, as interpreted in *Southland,* preempt these state statutes? Why do you think states continue to pass such statutes if there is a risk of preemption?

4.6 Stephen Broome conducted an empirical analysis of California unconscionability cases and concluded that California appellate courts are predisposed to finding arbitration agreements unconscionable (Broome, 2006). Would a differential application of unconscionability doctrine be problematic under *Southland* and *Casarotto*?

Note on Application of Preemption Doctrine

Although the Supreme Court is emphatic that federal law preempts state laws that adversely affect the enforceability of arbitration agreements, determining whether the FAA preempts state laws that relate to arbitration is not always an easy task. The FAA provides an incomplete regulatory scheme. While it speaks clearly on the question of enforceability, it contains relatively little guidance on procedural issues in arbitration. For example, the FAA provides no direction on the arbitrator's responsibilities or the arbitrator selection process, and relatively little counsel regarding the preemptive effect of the FAA's standards for judicial review (Hayford and Palmiter, 2002:177-178) (discussing the FAA's "murky sphere" from which little direction can be gleaned). Thus, it is not surprising that the Supreme Court would need to address the extent to which parties could agree to terms governing their arbitration, such as an agreement to abide by state arbitration rules, without triggering FAA preemption. The Supreme Court considered this issue in *Volt Information Sciences, Inc. v. Board of Trustees of the Leland Stanford Junior Univ.*, 489 U.S. 468 (1989). In *Volt,* the parties to a construction contract agreed to use arbitration to resolve all disputes arising out of their contract. The contract also contained a choice of law provision that stated that the laws of the state where the project took place, California, would govern the contract. When a dispute arose, Volt demanded arbitration. Stanford filed suit against Volt and two other contractors and moved to stay the arbitration under California law, which permits a stay of arbitration pending resolution of related litigation between a party to the arbitration agreement and a third party not bound by the agreement. Concluding that the state rules the parties had selected were not preempted, the Court stated:

> The FAA was designed "to overrule the judiciary's long-standing refusal to enforce agreements to arbitrate," and place such agreements "upon the same footing as other contracts. . . ." Accordingly, we have recognized that the FAA does not require parties to arbitrate when they have not agreed to do so, nor does it prevent parties who do agree to arbitrate from excluding certain claims from the scope of their arbitration agreement. It simply requires courts to enforce privately negotiated agreements to arbitrate, like other contracts, in accordance with their terms. . . .
>
> In recognition of Congress' principal purpose of ensuring that private arbitration agreements are enforced according to their terms, we have held that the FAA pre-empts state laws which "require a judicial forum for the resolution of claims which the contracting parties agreed to resolve by arbitration." But it does not follow that the FAA prevents the enforcement of agreements to arbitrate under different rules than those set forth in the Act itself. Indeed, such a result would be quite inimical to the FAA's primary purpose of ensuring that private agreements to arbitrate are enforced according to their terms. Arbitration under the Act is a matter of consent, not coercion, and parties are generally free to structure their arbitration agreements as they see fit. Just as they may limit by contract the issues which they will arbitrate, so too may they specify by contract the rules under which that arbitration will be conducted. Where, as here, the parties have agreed to abide by state rules of arbitration, enforcing those rules according to the terms of the agreement is fully consistent with the goals of the FAA, even if the result is that arbitration is stayed where the Act would otherwise permit it to go forward. By permitting the courts to "rigorously enforce" such agreements according to their terms, we give effect to the contractual rights and expectations of the parties, without doing violence to the policies behind the FAA. The judgment of the Court of Appeals is Affirmed.

Id. at 478-779.

The Court in *Volt* held that the parties' choice of law provision should be enforced even though that meant staying the arbitration until the California court proceeding was concluded. In issuing that holding, the Court explained that parties can agree to application of state rules as long as those rules are generally consistent with the FAA. The Court emphasized that the parties' chosen procedural rules did not undermine the policies that underlie the FAA. Thus, one reading of *Volt* is that the FAA does not preempt procedural rules that are generally pro-arbitration but does preempt substantive law inconsistent with the FAA. The problem then is to assess properly which laws are procedural and which are substantive. After *Volt*, courts typically allowed parties to freely incorporate state arbitration rules or develop their own procedural rules for arbitration where those rules do not impact enforceability and do not undermine the federal policy favoring arbitration.

Questions

4.7 Do you think the parties understood that California arbitration law, which allows a stay of arbitration when litigation has begun against third parties, would apply to their contract?

4.8 What if the parties' choice of law provision requires application of state law that adversely impacts arbitration? In *Mastrobuono v. Shearson Lehman Hutton, Inc.*, 514 U.S. 52 (1995), securities investors signed an agreement with a broker that contained an arbitration agreement and a choice of law provision selecting New York as the governing law. New York law prohibited arbitrators from awarding punitive damages. In a subsequent arbitration, the arbitrator awarded punitive damages to the investors. Should the Court uphold that punitive damages award? Would it matter whether the initial claim was brought in state court or federal court? Following *Mastrobuono,* most courts interpret a choice of law provision as evidencing an intent not to displace the FAA. See, e.g., *Roadway Package System, Inc. v. Kayser,* 257 F.3d 287 (3d Cir. 2001) (citing cases).

Note on Circuit City v. Adams

In 2001, the Supreme Court contemplated the preemption issue again, albeit indirectly. In *Circuit City Stores, Inc. v. Adams,* 532 U.S. 105 (2001), an employee, Saint Clair Adams, filed an employment discrimination lawsuit against Circuit City in state court. Circuit City sought an order in federal court compelling Adams to arbitrate his claims based on the broad arbitration agreement Adams signed at the time he applied for his job. The Court considered whether §1 of the FAA—which excludes from the Act's coverage "contracts of employment of seamen, railroad employees, or any other class of workers engaged in foreign or interstate commerce"—should be interpreted narrowly, exempting from coverage only contracts of employment of transportation workers, or broadly, so that all contracts of employment are beyond the FAA's reach. *Circuit City* addresses the state's role in regulating arbitration. If the §1 exclusion is construed so that the FAA exempts the disputes of all workers in interstate commerce, then the states would have freedom to regulate employment practices without concern about preemption. If the exclusion were construed so that only transportation workers were exempted from the FAA, states would play a very limited role in the regulation of employment arbitration because the FAA would preempt most state efforts to regulate.

In what was essentially a statutory interpretation debate, the Court considered the plain language of §1 of the FAA:

> If . . . there is an argument to be made that arbitration agreements in employment contracts are not covered by the Act, it must be premised on the language of the §1 exclusion provision itself. Respondent, endorsing the reasoning of the Court of Appeals for the Ninth Circuit that the provision excludes all employment contracts, relies on the asserted breadth of the words "contracts of employment of . . . any other class of workers engaged in . . . commerce." Referring to our construction of §2's coverage provision in *Allied-Bruce*—concluding that the words "involving commerce" evidence the congressional intent to regulate to the full extent of its commerce power—respondent contends §1's

interpretation should have a like reach, thus exempting all employment contracts. The two provisions, it is argued, are coterminous; under this view the "involving commerce" provision brings within the FAA's scope all contracts within the Congress' commerce power, and the "engaged in . . . commerce" language in §1 in turn exempts from the FAA all employment contracts falling within that authority.

This reading of §1, however, runs into an immediate and, in our view, insurmountable textual obstacle. Unlike the "involving commerce" language in §2, the words "any other class of workers engaged in . . . commerce" constitute a residual phrase, following, in the same sentence, explicit reference to "seamen" and "railroad employees." Construing the residual phrase to exclude all employment contracts fails to give independent effect to the statute's enumeration of the specific categories of workers which precedes it; there would be no need for Congress to use the phrases "seamen" and "railroad employees" if those same classes of workers were subsumed within the meaning of the "engaged in . . . commerce" residual clause. The wording of §1 calls for the application of the maxim ejusdem generis, the statutory canon that "[w]here general words follow specific words in a statutory enumeration, the general words are construed to embrace only objects similar in nature to those objects enumerated by the preceding specific words." 2A N. Singer, Sutherland on Statutes and Statutory Construction §47.17 (1991). Under this rule of construction the residual clause should be read to give effect to the terms "seamen" and "railroad employees," and should itself be controlled and defined by reference to the enumerated categories of workers which are recited just before it; the interpretation of the clause pressed by respondent fails to produce these results.

The dissenters in the 5–4 decision suggested that the Court should consider the scope of congressional authority to regulate under the commerce power at the time the FAA was enacted:

Times have changed. Judges in the 19th century disfavored private arbitration. The 1925 Act was intended to overcome that attitude, but a number of this Court's cases decided in the last several decades have pushed the pendulum far beyond a neutral attitude and endorsed a policy that strongly favors private arbitration. The strength of that policy preference has been echoed in the recent Court of Appeals opinions on which the Court relies. In a sense, therefore, the Court is standing on its own shoulders when it points to those cases as the basis for its narrow construction of the exclusion in §1. There is little doubt that the Court's interpretation of the Act has given it a scope far beyond the expectations of the Congress that enacted it. . . .

It is not necessarily wrong for the Court to put its own imprint on a statute. But when its refusal to look beyond the raw statutory text enables it to disregard countervailing considerations that were expressed by Members of the enacting Congress and that remain valid today, the Court misuses its authority. As the history of the legislation indicates, the potential disparity in bargaining power between individual employees and large employers was the source of organized labor's opposition to the Act, which it feared would require courts to enforce unfair employment contracts. That same concern . . . underlay Congress' exemption of contracts of employment from mandatory arbitration. When the Court simply ignores the interest of the unrepresented employee, it skews its interpretation with its own policy preferences.

The majority quickly rejected this argument, stating that "[a] variable standard for interpreting common, jurisdictional phrases would contradict our earlier cases and bring instability to statutory interpretation. The Court has declined in past cases to afford significance, in construing the meaning of the statutory jurisdictional provisions 'in commerce' and 'engaged in commerce,' to the circumstance that the statute predated shifts in the Court's Commerce Clause cases."

Note on Class Actions and Arbitration Agreements

In an effort to reduce litigation costs and the negative publicity often associated with class litigation, many businesses and employers are including arbitration clauses in their agreements with customers and employees that either explicitly waive the customer or employee's right to bring a class action in court or that are likely to be interpreted to prohibit class actions. Consumer advocates argue that prohibiting consumers from bringing class actions in court prevents consumers and employees from effectively vindicating their rights in certain categories of claims, especially those involving practices applicable to all members of the class but as to which any consumer has so little at stake that she cannot be expected to pursue her claim.

Consumers challenge class action prohibitions primarily on the ground that it is unconscionable to enforce an arbitration agreement that prohibits class actions. The results of such challenges have been mixed. See *Ting v. AT&T*, 319 F.3d 1126 (9th Cir. 2003) (arbitration agreement that prevents class action is unconscionable); *Powertel, Inc. v. Bexley*, 743 So. 2d 570 (Fla. Dist. Ct. App. 1999) (court did not enforce arbitration agreement received day after lawsuit filed both because it was retroactive and because the clause prohibiting class actions rendered the contract unconscionable); *In re Knepp*, 229 B.R. 821 (N.D. Ala. 1999) (arbitration agreement that interferes with ability to bring class actions is unconscionable). But see *Randolph v. Green Tree Financial Corp.—Alabama*, 244 F.3d 814 (11th Cir. 2001) (agreement authorizing arbitration of Truth in Lending Act claims enforceable even though it precludes class actions).

To avoid precluding parties who have signed arbitration agreements from bringing a class action at all, some courts will order class actions to arbitration. The question then is whether the case will be handled as a class action in arbitration or whether the parties must proceed individually in arbitration (Sternlight, 2000:65). State law may permit consolidation of arbitrations, thus allowing a court to order classwide arbitration (Mottek, 2000). Professor Sternlight suggests that existing federal statutes and traditional contract law should, under certain circumstances, prohibit companies from using arbitration agreements to preclude individual plaintiffs from bringing class actions (Sternlight, 2000:78). Based on the Supreme Court's current attitude toward the enforceability of arbitration agreements, how might a plaintiff, who has signed a broad arbitration agreement, fare if she files a class action in court based on violations of Title VII? Would the court void the arbitration agreement? Would it sever the prohibition on class actions? Would it order the case to arbitration on an individual basis? Or would it order the arbitrator to hear the claims as a class action? Should Congress pass legislation prohibiting the use of arbitration agreements to eliminate the ability to bring class actions? Sternlight suggests that it should (Sternlight, 2000:121).

Should a court ordering parties to participate in arbitration remain involved in the arbitral process? Traditionally, once a court orders parties to arbitration, the court's involvement ceases until the stage where one of the parties requests judicial review of the arbitral award. Should this practice be applied in the classwide arbitration context? Who should make initial determinations regarding certification and notice? What about the rights of absent class members? In the following case, the Supreme Court considered whether an arbitrator could preside over a class action when the arbitration agreement was silent on the issue of class actions.

GREEN TREE FINANCIAL CORP. v. BAZZLE

539 U.S. 444 (2003)

JUSTICE BREYER announced the judgment of the Court and delivered an opinion, in which JUSTICE SCALIA, JUSTICE SOUTER, and JUSTICE GINSBURG join.

This case concerns contracts between a commercial lender and its customers, each of which contains a clause providing for arbitration of all contract-related disputes. The Supreme Court of South Carolina held (1) that the arbitration clauses are silent as to whether arbitration might take the form of class arbitration, and (2) that, in that circumstance, South Carolina law interprets the contracts as permitting class arbitration. We granted certiorari to determine whether this holding is consistent with the Federal Arbitration Act, 9 U.S.C. §1 *et seq.*

We are faced at the outset with a problem concerning the contracts' silence. Are the contracts in fact silent, or do they forbid class arbitration as petitioner Green Tree Financial Corp. contends? Given the South Carolina Supreme Court's holding, it is important to resolve that question. But we cannot do so, not simply because it is a matter of state law, but also because it is a matter for the arbitrator to decide. Because the record suggests that the parties have not yet received an arbitrator's decision on that question of contract interpretation, we vacate the judgment of the South Carolina Supreme Court and remand the case so that this question may be resolved in arbitration.

I

In 1995, respondents Lynn and Burt Bazzle secured a home improvement loan from petitioner Green Tree. The Bazzles and Green Tree entered into a contract, governed by South Carolina law, which included the following arbitration clause:

> ARBITRATION—All disputes, claims, or controversies arising from or relating to this contract or the relationships which result from this contract . . . *shall be resolved by binding arbitration by one arbitrator selected by us with consent of you.*

Respondents Daniel Lackey and George and Florine Buggs entered into loan contracts and security agreements for the purchase of mobile homes with Green Tree. These agreements contained arbitration clauses that were, in all relevant respects, identical to the Bazzles' arbitration clause. (Their contracts substitute the word "you" with the word "Buyer[s]" in the italicized phrase.)

At the time of the loan transactions, Green Tree apparently failed to provide these customers with a legally required form that would have told them that they had a right to name their own lawyers and insurance agents and would have provided space for them to write in those names. The two sets of customers before us now as respondents each filed separate actions in South Carolina state courts, complaining that this failure violated South Carolina law and seeking damages.

In April 1997, the Bazzles asked the court to certify their claims as a class action. Green Tree sought to stay the court proceedings and compel arbitration. On January 5, 1998, the court both (1) certified a class action and (2) entered an order compelling arbitration. Green Tree then selected an arbitrator with the Bazzles' consent. And the arbitrator, administering the proceeding as a class arbitration, eventually awarded the class $10,935,000 in statutory damages, along with attorney's fees. The trial court confirmed the award and Green Tree appealed to the South Carolina of Appeals claiming, among other things, that class arbitration was legally impermissible. [After the court compelled the Lackeys and Buggses to arbitrate, they also proceeded with class arbitration. The arbitrator awarded the class $9,200,000 in statutory damages in addition to attorney's fees. Green Tree appealed this ruling as well.]

The South Carolina Supreme Court withdrew both cases from the Court of Appeals, assumed jurisdiction, and consolidated the proceedings. That court then held that the contracts were silent in respect to class arbitration, that they consequently authorized class arbitration, and that arbitration had properly taken that form. We granted certiorari to consider whether that holding is consistent with the Federal Arbitration Act.

II

The South Carolina Supreme Court's determination that the contracts are silent in respect to class arbitration raises a preliminary question. Green Tree argued there, as it argues here, that the contracts are not silent—that they forbid class arbitration. And we must deal with that argument at the outset, for if it is right, then the South Carolina court's holding is flawed on its own terms; that court neither said nor implied that it would have authorized class arbitration had the parties' arbitration agreement forbidden it.

Whether Green Tree is right about the contracts themselves presents a disputed issue of contract interpretation. THE CHIEF JUSTICE believes that Green Tree is right; indeed, that Green Tree is so clearly right that we should ignore the fact that state law, not federal law, normally governs such matters, and reverse the South Carolina Supreme Court outright. . . . THE CHIEF JUSTICE points out that the contracts say that disputes "shall be resolved . . . by one arbitrator selected by us [Green Tree] with consent of you [Green Tree's customer]." And it finds that class arbitration is clearly inconsistent with this requirement. After all, class arbitration involves an arbitration, not simply between Green Tree and a *named customer,* but also between Green Tree and *other* (represented) customers, all taking place before the arbitrator chosen to arbitrate the initial, *named customer's* dispute.

We do not believe, however, that the contracts' language is as clear as THE CHIEF JUSTICE believes. The class arbitrator *was* "selected by" Green Tree "with consent of" Green Tree's customers, the named plaintiffs. And insofar as the other class members agreed to proceed in class arbitration, they consented as well.

Of course, Green Tree did *not* independently select *this* arbitrator to arbitrate its disputes with the *other* class members. But whether the contracts contain this additional requirement is a question that the literal terms of the contracts do not decide. The contracts simply say (I) "selected by us [Green Tree]." And that is literally what occurred. The contracts do not say (II) "selected by us [Green Tree] to arbitrate this dispute and no other (even identical) dispute with another customer." The question whether (I) in fact implicitly means (II) is the question at issue: Do the contracts forbid class arbitration? Given the broad authority the contracts elsewhere bestow upon the arbitrator (the contracts grant to the arbitrator "all powers," including certain equitable powers "provided by the law and the contract"), the answer to this question is not completely obvious.

At the same time, we cannot automatically accept the South Carolina Supreme Court's resolution of this contract-interpretation question. Under the terms of the parties' contracts, the question—whether the agreement forbids class arbitration—is for the arbitrator to decide. The parties agreed to submit to the arbitrator "[*a*]*ll* disputes, claims, or controversies arising from or relating to this contract or the relationships which result from this contract." And the dispute about what the arbitration contract in each case means (*i.e.*, whether it forbids the use of class arbitration procedures) is a dispute "relating to this contract" and the resulting "relationships." Hence the parties seem to have agreed that an arbitrator, not a judge, would answer the relevant question. And if there is doubt about that matter—about the " 'scope of arbitrable issues' "—we should resolve that doubt " 'in favor of arbitration' " (*Mitsubishi Motors Corp. v. Soler Chrysler-Plymouth, Inc.*, 473 U.S. 614 (1985)).

In certain limited circumstances, courts assume that the parties intended courts, not arbitrators, to decide a particular arbitration-related matter (in the absence of "clea[r] and unmistakabl[e]" evidence to the contrary). *AT&T Technologies, Inc. v. Communications Workers,* 475 U.S. 643, 649 (1986). These limited instances typically involve matters of a kind that "contracting parties would likely have expected a court" to decide. *Howsam v. Dean Witter Reynolds, Inc.,* 537 U.S. 79, 83 (2002). They include certain gateway matters, such as whether the parties have a valid arbitration agreement at all or whether a concededly binding arbitration clause applies to a certain type of controversy.

The question here—whether the contracts forbid class arbitration—does not fall into this narrow exception. It concerns neither the validity of the arbitration clause nor its applicability to the underlying dispute between the parties. Unlike *First Options* (casebook at p. 244), the question is not whether the parties wanted a judge or an arbitrator to decide *whether they agreed to arbitrate a matter.* Rather, the relevant question here is what *kind of arbitration proceeding* the parties agreed to. That question does not concern a state statute or judicial procedures. It concerns contract interpretation and arbitration procedures. Arbitrators are well situated to answer that question. Given these considerations, along with the arbitration contracts' sweeping language concerning the scope of the questions committed to arbitration, this matter of contract interpretation should be for the arbitrator, not the courts, to decide.

III

With respect to this underlying question—whether the arbitration contracts forbid class arbitration—the parties have not yet obtained the arbitration decision that their contracts foresee.

On balance, there is at least a strong likelihood in *Lackey* as well as in *Bazzle* that the arbitrator's decision reflected a court's interpretation of the contracts rather than an arbitrator's interpretation. That being so, we remand the case so that the arbitrator may decide the question of contract interpretation—thereby enforcing the parties' arbitration agreements according to their terms.

The judgment of the South Carolina Supreme Court is vacated, and the case is remanded for further proceedings.

So ordered.

JUSTICE STEVENS, concurring in the judgment and dissenting in part.

The parties agreed that South Carolina law would govern their arbitration agreement. The Supreme Court of South Carolina has held as a matter of state law that class-action arbitrations are permissible if not prohibited by the applicable arbitration agreement, and that the agreement between these parties is silent on the issue. There is nothing in the Federal Arbitration Act that precludes either of these determinations by the Supreme Court of South Carolina.

Arguably the interpretation of the parties' agreement should have been made in the first instance by the arbitrator, rather than the court. Because the decision to conduct a class-action arbitration was correct as a matter of law, and because petitioner has merely challenged the merits of that decision without claiming that it was made by the wrong decisionmaker, there is no need to remand the case to correct that possible error.

Accordingly, I would simply affirm the judgment of the Supreme Court of South Carolina. Were I to adhere to my preferred disposition of the case, however, there would be no controlling judgment of the Court. In order to avoid that outcome, and because JUSTICE BREYER's opinion expresses a view of the case close to my own, I concur in the judgment.

CHIEF JUSTICE REHNQUIST, with whom JUSTICE O'CONNOR and JUSTICE KENNEDY join, dissenting.

The plurality now vacates the judgment of the South Carolina Supreme Court and remands the case for the arbitrator to make this determination. I would reverse because this determination is one for the courts, not for the arbitrator, and the holding of the Supreme Court of South Carolina contravenes the terms of the contract, and is therefore pre-empted by the FAA. . . .

I think that the parties' agreement as to how the arbitrator should be selected is much more akin to the agreement as to what shall be arbitrated, a question for the courts under *First Options*, than it is to "allegations of waiver, delay, or like defenses to arbitrability," which are questions for the arbitrator under *Howsam.*

Under the FAA, "parties are generally free to structure their arbitration agreements as they see fit." (*Volt* at 479 (casebook at p. 227). Here, the parties saw fit to agree that any disputes arising out of the contracts "shall be resolved by binding arbitration by one arbitrator selected by us with consent of you." Each contract expressly defines "us" as petitioner, and "you" as the respondent or respondents named in that specific contract. ("'We' and 'us' means the Seller *above*, its successors and assigns"; "'You' and 'your' means each Buyer *above* and guarantor, jointly and severally" (emphasis added).) Each contract also specifies that it governs all "disputes . . . arising from . . . *this* contract or the relationships which result from *this* contract." These provisions, which the plurality simply ignores, make quite clear that petitioner must select, and each buyer must agree to, a particular arbitrator for disputes between petitioner and that specific buyer.

While the observation of the Supreme Court of South Carolina that the agreement of the parties was silent as to the availability of class-wide arbitration is literally true, the imposition of class-wide arbitration contravenes the just-quoted provision about the selection of an arbitrator. To be sure, the arbitrator that administered the proceedings was "selected by [petitioner] with consent of" the Bazzles, Lackey, and the Buggses. But petitioner had the contractual right to choose an arbitrator for each dispute with the other 3,734 individual class members, and this right was denied when the same arbitrator was foisted upon petitioner to resolve those claims as well. Petitioner may well have chosen different arbitrators for some or all of these other disputes; indeed, it would have been reasonable for petitioner to do so, in order to avoid concentrating all of the risk of substantial damages awards in the hands of a single arbitrator. As petitioner correctly concedes, the FAA does not prohibit parties from choosing to proceed on a class-wide basis. Here, however, the parties simply did not so choose.

. . . Here, the Supreme Court of South Carolina imposed a regime that was contrary to the express agreement of the parties as to how the arbitrator would be chosen. It did not enforce the "agreemen[t] to arbitrate . . . according to [its] terms." *Mastrobuono, supra,* at 54 (internal quotation marks omitted). I would therefore reverse the judgment of the Supreme Court of South Carolina.

Justice Thomas, dissenting.

I continue to believe that the Federal Arbitration Act does not apply to proceedings in state courts. For that reason, the FAA cannot be a ground for pre-empting a state court's interpretation of a private arbitration agreement. Accordingly, I would leave undisturbed the judgment of the Supreme Court of South Carolina.

Questions

4.9 Green Tree may have been caught by surprise when the South Carolina Supreme Court interpreted its customer arbitration agreement to permit class action arbitration. While Chief Justice Rehnquist and two other justices believed that the clause was not silent on its face and, in fact, precluded class action arbitration, the plurality, joined by Justice Stevens, remanded the case to the arbitrator to rule on whether the agreement permits class action arbitration. Following *Bazzle*, are companies like Green Tree more or less likely to modify arbitration agreements that are currently silent on the issue of class action arbitration? Would a court enforce a contractual prohibition on class action arbitration? Or would a prohibition on class claims be ruled unconscionable? The California Supreme Court recently held that an arbitration agreement that precludes class claims is unconscionable if it is in a contract of adhesion that is one-sided and effectively insulates the drafting party from liability that otherwise would be imposed under California law. *See Discover Bank v. Superior Court,* 36 Cal. 4th 148 (Cal. 2005). Although the California Court found that such a prohibition is unconscionable, it did not find that the FAA preempts California law on the question of class action waivers. Despite the *Discover Bank* court's ruling on the preemption question, it is unlikely to be the last court to address the issue of preemption and class action arbitration waivers. The market may also address this question. One of the major arbitral providers, AAA, issued a policy statement that it will not administer arbitrations where the arbitration agreement precludes class claims. JAMS, another major arbitral provider, issued a similar statement but later withdrew it on the ground that the policy created confusion and potentially undermined the neutrality of the arbitration process.

4.10 One of the more intriguing questions, which the *Bazzle* Court does not address, is how an arbitrator should administer a class action arbitration. AAA has a policy governing the administration of class action arbitrations and lists on its website, www.adr.org, the number of class action arbitrations it is currently handling. AAA has a special roster of class action arbitrators. In addition, there are several points during the arbitration process where the arbitrator issues a partial final award. After the partial final award is issued, the parties have 30 days to challenge the award in court. Class certification is one of the arbitrator's determinations that may be challenged in court prior to the arbitration hearing. Even with this new policy, questions remain about the ability of arbitration to handle a class action effectively and fairly. For example, how does a class action arbitration award affect unnamed class members? Will an arbitrator give a prior arbitration award preclusive affect in a subsequent arbitral proceeding involving unnamed class members?

2. *The Revised Uniform Arbitration Act*

In 2000, the National Conference of Commissioners on Uniform State Laws (NCCUSL), in an attempt to bridge the gap in arbitral fairness without triggering preemption, unanimously adopted major revisions to the Uniform Arbitration Act (UAA), the first such revisions since the Act was promulgated in 1955. The UAA had been the law in 49 jurisdictions. Already adopted by 12 states,* and under consideration by a number of other states, the revisions attempt to address arbitral developments created by an extraordinary increase in the use of arbitration and the resulting legal questions (Heinsz, 2001).

The Revised Uniform Arbitration Act (RUAA) (Appendix D), like the Due Process Protocol (see pp. 260-263) before it, tends to judicialize arbitration by increasing the number and type of procedures that parties to an arbitration must utilize. Admitting that its primary objective is to enhance procedural protections in the arbitral process, the drafters emphasize that many of the RUAA's provisions are nonwaivable or nonwaivable until a dispute arises to ensure that "fundamental fairness to the parties will be preserved, particularly in those instances where one party may have significantly less bargaining power than another." (RUAA at i.) Those provisions that cannot be waived until a dispute arises include the right to

*Alaska, Calorado, Hawaii, Nevada, New Jersey, New Mexico, North Carolina, North Dakota, Oklahoma, Oregon, Utah, and Washington have adopted the RUAA.

representation by an attorney at an arbitral proceeding, the right to move the arbitrator to award provisional remedies and interim awards, and the right to move the arbitrator to issue subpoenas for witnesses, records, or to order depositions. (See RUAA sections 4, 8, 17(a), 17(c).) The nonwaivable provisions focus on the parties' ability to waive the court's participation in the arbitral process. Thus, the nonwaivable provisions include those that prohibit parties from: waiving the right to move the court to confirm, vacate, or modify an arbitral award or compel or stay arbitration, the power of the court to award reasonable costs for motions and subsequent judicial proceedings and arbitrator immunity or the arbitrator's right not to testify. (Id. at §4(c).)

Concern about preemption issues prompted RUAA drafters to limit the scope of the Act to the arbitral process itself. (Id. at 14 ("[T]reating arbitration clauses differently from other contractual provisions would raise significant preemption issues under the Federal Arbitration Act.").) Limitations or restrictions of parties' ability to enter into an agreement to arbitrate would, in the view of the drafters, be preempted by the FAA. (Id. at ii.) Although the drafters were less clear about the preemptive impact of the FAA on the provisions governing judicial review of arbitral awards, the drafters, in an earlier draft of the RUAA, nevertheless cautiously approached this issue, eschewing the notion that judicial review of an arbitral award could be granted on grounds other than those articulated in FAA §10. (RUAA draft at 47-52 (February 2000).) For further discussion of the question of whether §10's provisions are default or mandatory rules, see Cole (2000).

The RUAA's focus on governance of arbitration issues was driven by the drafters' belief that the Federal Arbitration Act (FAA) is unlikely to preempt state rules focusing on the workings of the arbitral mechanism. (Id. at iii.) Unlike questions regarding the enforceability of the agreement to arbitrate or the question of arbitral award review, Congress, through the FAA, left the arbitral process largely unregulated. The Supreme Court confirmed this theory in *Volt Information Sciences, Inc. v. Board of Trustees of the Leland Stanford Junior Univ.*, 489 U.S. 468 (1989) (see p. 227) (holding that FAA does not preempt state law principles parties select). Thus, the RUAA's focus on regulating the arbitral process rather than the negotiation of the arbitration agreement makes sense.

Questions

4.11 Imagine that you are a state legislator in a state considering whether to adopt the RUAA. Constituents have identified the following issues as important— the right to receive punitive damages in arbitration, pursue class actions, obtain attorney's fees, and seek meaningful judicial review of the arbitrator's decision. How will you vote on these issues? In light of your knowledge of preemption, how would you draft legislation covering these issues? What about an RUAA provision that prohibited a party from waiving her right to review for manifest disregard of the law, at least until the dispute arises? (For more on judicial review, see pages 284-294.)

4.12 Does the RUAA's judicialization of the arbitral process provide sufficient protection to consumers and employees compelled by pre-dispute arbitration agreements to arbitrate their statutory claims?

3. *Arbitrability*

Courts have long had difficulty determining whether or not a particular claim is arbitrable. According to the Supreme Court, arbitrability addresses whether the parties agreed to arbitrate the merits of a particular claim. While this definition appears straightforward, in fact, courts have been plagued with cases about who decides: (1) whether the parties agreed to arbitrate; (2) whether a particular claim is within the scope of the arbitration clause; and (3) whether the claim is a "procedural arbitrability" claim, in which case an arbitrator hears it, or a "substantive arbitrability" claim, which is for the courts to resolve. To add further complications, the Supreme Court, in 1967, created the "separability" or "severability" doctrine in *Prima Paint Corp. v. Flood & Conklin Mfg. Co.*, 388 U.S. 395 (1967), that permits a court to consider the enforceability of an arbitration clause separately from the remainder of the contract. To understand the current arbitrability jurisprudence, a careful examination of the Court's analysis in *Prima Paint* is necessary.

In that case, Prima Paint and Flood & Conklin (F & C) entered into an agreement to purchase F & C's paint business. As part of the agreement, F & C provided Prima Paint with current customer lists and a covenant not to compete with Prima Paint for six years. The contract contained a broad arbitration clause, covering "any controversy or claim arising out of or relating to this agreement." Shortly after the contract was signed, F & C filed for bankruptcy. As a result, Prima Paint ceased providing F & C with a percentage of receipts from the former F & C customers. When F & C sought to arbitrate the payment dispute, Prima Paint brought suit in federal court for recission of the consulting agreement on the basis of fraudulent inducement. The Court considered whether the issue of fraud in the inducement should be decided by an arbitrator or a court.

The Court concluded that the arbitration agreement may be separated from the "container contract"—i.e., the agreement for the sale of F & C's business that contained the arbitration agreement. Under this separability theory, unless challenges to the formation of a container contract are also levied against the arbitration agreement specifically, the formation issues must be arbitrated. According to the Court, FAA §4, which mandates that a federal court will order the parties to arbitrate "upon being satisfied that the making of the agreement for arbitration . . . is not an issue," compels this conclusion:

> Under §4, with respect to a matter within the jurisdiction of the federal courts save for the existence of an arbitration clause, the federal court is instructed to order arbitration to proceed once it is satisfied that "the making of the agreement for arbitration or the failure to comply (with the arbitration agreement) is not in issue." Accordingly, if the claim is fraud in the inducement of the arbitration clause itself—an issue which goes to the "making" of the agreement to arbitrate—the federal court may proceed to adjudicate it. But the statutory language does not permit the federal court to consider claims of fraud in the inducement of the contract generally. Section 4 does not expressly relate to situations like the present in which a stay is sought of a federal action in order that arbitration may proceed. But it is inconceivable that Congress intended the rule to differ depending upon which party to the arbitration agreement first invokes the assistance of a federal court. We hold, therefore, that in passing upon a §3 application for a stay while the parties arbitrate, a federal court may consider only issues relating to the making and performance of the agreement to arbitrate. In so concluding, we not only honor the

> plain meaning of the statute but also the unmistakably clear congressional purpose that the arbitration procedure, when selected by the parties to a contract, be speedy and not subject to delay and obstruction in the courts.

Does §4 compel the Court's conclusion that an arbitrator should hear contractual validity challenges to a container contract? Section 4 addresses a federal court's role in deciding whether or not to order parties to arbitrate. It does not appear to preclude a federal court's consideration of other issues. Moreover, if a container contract is fraudulently induced, it is probable that every clause within that container contract was fraudulently induced, including the arbitration agreement. Thus, the Court could have held that "the making of the arbitration clause is at issue whenever the making of the agreement containing it is in issue." Can you imagine a factual scenario in which a party fraudulently induced a container contract but not the arbitration agreement?

Questions

4.13 Does the separability doctrine's requirement that arbitrators resolve validity issues seem logical? The dissenters in *Prima Paint* did not think so. They found it "fantastic" that arbitrators, who need not be lawyers, will be entrusted to decide the legal issue of a contract's validity. The dissenters preferred an allocation of responsibility that would allow arbitrators to resolve factual controversies and leave to courts the obligation of making legal determinations regarding validity of the agreement.

4.14 Courts reviewing arbitration agreements often state that the parties' intent should be controlling. Is the separability doctrine consistent with the parties' intent? To answer this question, one might consider whether the parties could be said to have "intended" to enter into two separate contracts — a container contract and an arbitration agreement. Case law suggests that a major issue in arbitration is the problem of ensuring that parties signing arbitration agreements knowingly and voluntarily consent to them. Assuming that parties often do not notice the presence of an arbitration agreement within a larger container contract, can the *Prima Paint* rule possibly be the result the parties intended?

One of the major questions *Prima Paint* did not address is whether a contract that is voidable (i.e., appears legal on its face although illegal means may have been used to obtain consent), such as the one at issue in *Prima Paint,* should be treated differently than a contract that is allegedly void (i.e., illegal on its face). The Supreme Court rejected a distinction between void and voidable contracts and affirmed the validity of the separability doctrine in the following case.

BUCKEYE CHECK CASHING, INC. v. CARDEGNA

126 S. Ct. 1204 (2006)

JUSTICE SCALIA delivered the opinion of the Court.

We decide whether a court or an arbitrator should consider the claim that a contract containing an arbitration provision is void for illegality.

I

[Cardegna and Reuter entered into agreements with Buckeye to receive cash in exchange for a check in the amount of the cash plus a finance charge. The consumers each signed an agreement that contained an arbitration clause requiring them to arbitrate any disputes arising out of their check-cashing relationship. The consumers brought suit in Florida state court, contending that Buckeye charged usurious interest rates and that the contract was illegal under Florida law. Buckeye moved to compel arbitration. The question for the Florida courts was whether the court or an arbitrator should decide whether a contract containing an arbitration clause is illegal on its face. The Florida Supreme Court refused to send the case to arbitration, reasoning that an arbitrator might "breathe life into a contract that not only violates state law, but also is criminal in nature."]

II

A

Challenges to the validity of arbitration agreements "upon such grounds as exist at law or in equity for the revocation of any contract" can be divided into two types. One type challenges specifically the validity of the agreement to arbitrate. The other challenges the contract as a whole, either on a ground that directly affects the entire agreement (*e.g.*, the agreement was fraudulently induced), or on the ground that the illegality of one of the contract's provisions renders the whole contract invalid.[1] Respondents' claim is of this second type. The crux of the complaint is that the contract as a whole (including its arbitration provision) is rendered invalid by the usurious finance charge.

B

Prima Paint and *Southland* answer the question presented here by establishing three propositions. First, as a matter of substantive federal arbitration law, an arbitration provision is severable from the remainder of the contract. Second, unless the challenge is to the arbitration clause itself, the issue of the contract's validity is considered by the arbitrator in the first instance. Third, this arbitration law applies in state as well as federal courts. . . . Applying them to this case, we conclude that because respondents challenge the Agreement, but not specifically its arbitration provisions, those provisions are enforceable apart from the remainder of the

1. The issue of the contract's validity is different from the issue of whether any agreement between the alleged obligor and obligee was ever concluded. Our opinion today addresses only the former, and does not speak to the issue decided in the cases cited by respondents (and by the Florida Supreme Court), which hold that it is for courts to decide whether the alleged obligor ever signed the contract, *Chastain v. Robinson-Humphrey Co.*, 957 F.2d 851 (C.A.11 1992), whether the signor lacked authority to commit the alleged principal, *Sandvik AB v. Advent Int'l Corp.*, 220 F.3d 99 (C.A.3. 2000); *Sphere Drake Ins. Ltd. v. All American Ins. Co.*, 256 F3d 587 (C.A.7 2001), and whether the signor lacked the mental capacity to assent, *Spahr v. Secco*, 330 F.3d 1266 (C.A.10 2003).

contract. The challenge should therefore be considered by an arbitrator, not a court.

In declining to apply *Prima Paint*'s rule of severability, the Florida Supreme Court relied on the distinction between void and voidable contracts. "Florida public policy and contract law," it concluded, permit "no severable, or salvageable, parts of a contract found illegal and void under Florida law." *Prima Paint* makes this conclusion irrelevant. That case rejected application of state severability rules to the arbitration agreement *without discussing* whether the challenge at issue would have rendered the contract void or voidable. Indeed, the opinion expressly disclaimed any need to decide what state-law remedy was available. . . .

C

Respondents assert that *Prima Paint*'s rule of severability does not apply in state court. They argue that *Prima Paint* interpreted only §§3 and 4—two of the FAA's procedural provisions, which appear to apply by their terms only in federal court—but not §2, the only provision that we have applied in state court. This does not accurately describe *Prima Paint.* Although §4, in particular, had much to do with *Prima Paint*'s understanding of the rule of severability, this rule ultimately arises out of §2, the FAA's substantive command that arbitration agreements be treated like all other contracts. The rule of severability establishes how this equal-footing guarantee for "a written [arbitration] provision" is to be implemented. Respondents' reading of *Prima Paint* as establishing nothing more than a federal-court rule of procedure also runs contrary to *Southland*'s understanding of that case. One of the bases for *Southland*'s application of §2 in state court was precisely *Prima Paint*'s "reli[ance] for [its] holding on Congress' broad power to fashion substantive rules under the Commerce Clause." *Southland* itself refused to "believe Congress intended to limit the Arbitration Act to disputes subject only to *federal*-court jurisdiction."

Respondents point to the language of §2 which renders "valid, irrevocable, and enforceable" "a written provision in" or "an agreement in writing to submit to arbitration an existing controversy arising out of" a "contract." Since, respondents argue, the only arbitration agreements to which §2 applies are those involving a "contract," and since an agreement void *ab initio* under state law is not a "contract," there is no "written provision" in or "controversy arising out of" a "contract" to which §2 can apply. This argument echoes Justice Black's dissent in *Prima Paint* "Sections 2 and 3 of the Act assume the existence of a valid contract. They merely provide for enforcement where such a valid contract exists." We do not read "contract" so narrowly. The word appears four times in §2. Its last appearance is in the final clause, which allows a challenge to an arbitration provision "upon such grounds as exist at law or in equity for the revocation of any *contract.*" (Emphasis added.) There can be no doubt that "contract" as used this last time must include contracts that later prove to be void. Otherwise, the grounds for revocation would be limited to those that rendered a contract voidable—which would mean (implausibly) that an arbitration agreement could be challenged as voidable but not as void. Because the sentence's final use of "contract" so obviously includes putative contracts, we will not read the same word earlier in the same sentence to have a more narrow meaning. We note that neither *Prima Paint* nor *Southland* lends support to respondents' reading; as we have discussed, neither case turned on whether the challenge at issue would render the contract voidable or void.

* * *

It is true, as respondents assert, that the *Prima Paint* rule permits a court to enforce an arbitration agreement in a contract that the arbitrator later finds to be void. But it is equally true that respondents' approach permits a court to deny effect to an arbitration provision in a contract that the court later finds to be perfectly enforceable. *Prima Paint* resolved this conundrum—and resolved it in favor of the separate enforceability of arbitration provisions. We reaffirm today that, regardless of whether the challenge is brought in federal or state court, a challenge to the validity of the contract as a whole, and not specifically to the arbitration clause, must go to the arbitrator.

The judgment of the Florida Supreme Court is reversed, and the case is remanded for further proceedings not inconsistent with this opinion.

JUSTICE ALITO took no part in the consideration or decision of this case.

JUSTICE THOMAS, dissenting.

I remain of the view that the Federal Arbitration Act does not apply to proceedings in state courts. Thus, in state-court proceedings, the FAA cannot be the basis for displacing a state law that prohibits enforcement of an arbitration clause contained in a contract that is unenforceable under state law. Accordingly, I would leave undisturbed the judgment of the Florida Supreme Court.

Questions

4.15 Following *Buckeye Check Cashing,* a dispute over whether a void or voidable contract containing an arbitration provision is enforceable is a question for the arbitrator, not the court. The Court also suggested (in footnote 1) that challenges to contract formation are still to be heard by a court. In addition, the Court rejected the consumers' concern that the *Prima Paint* rule allows a court to enforce an arbitration agreement in a contract that the arbitrator later finds to be void, stating that plaintiffs' approach allows a court to deny enforcement of a valid arbitration agreement in a contract that the court later finds enforceable. Does this seem like the right result?

4.16 Unlike the *Prima Paint* Court, the Court in *Buckeye* relied on FAA §2, rather than §§3 and 4, to support its finding that the separability doctrine is valid. The question of whether FAA §§2-4 apply in state court has always been, and continues to be, controversial. But the *Buckeye* Court suggests that §2 may apply in state court, a holding that was possible only because the *Buckeye* case, unlike the *Prima Paint* case, emerged from state court. *Buckeye* does not address the question of whether FAA §§3 and 4 apply in state court. What is the significance of the Court's holding that §2 applies in state court?

Essentially, *Prima Paint* and *Buckege Check Cashing* are decisions that allocate decision-making responsibility between courts and arbitrators. But contractual challenges to container contracts are not the only challenges to arbitration agreements. The Supreme Court has also considered another allocation issue—who should decide whether the parties' agreement to arbitrate is valid.

FIRST OPTIONS OF CHICAGO, INC. v. KAPLAN

514 U.S. 938 (1995)

Justice BREYER delivered the opinion of the Court.

[Several parties, Kaplan, his wife, his wholly owned investment company (MKI) and First Options, were involved in a dispute over a workout agreement that the parties negotiated to compensate First Options, a firm that clears stock trades, for debts Kaplan and MKI incurred during the 1987 stock market crash. Subsequent losses prompted First Options to demand payment. When payment was not forthcoming, First Options filed a motion to compel arbitration. The workout document contained an arbitration clause that was signed by MKI but not by Kaplan. On this basis, Kaplan opposed arbitration. The arbitrators decided they had the power to decide the case and did so, in favor of First Options. The Court here considers whether the courts should decide whether the arbitration panel has jurisdiction over the substance of a dispute.]

[C]onsider [the] three types of disagreement present in this case. First, the Kaplans and First Options disagree about whether the Kaplans are personally liable for MKI's debt to First Options. That disagreement makes up the merits of the dispute. Second, they disagree about whether they agreed to arbitrate the merits. That disagreement is about the arbitrability of the dispute. Third, they disagree about who should have the primary power to decide the second matter. Does that power belong primarily to the arbitrators (because the court reviews their arbitrability decision deferentially) or to the court (because the court makes up its mind about arbitrability independently)? We consider here only this third question.

Although the question is a narrow one, it has a certain practical importance. That is because a party who has not agreed to arbitrate will normally have a right to a court's decision about the merits of its dispute (say, as here, its obligation under a contract). But, where the party has agreed to arbitrate, he or she, in effect, has relinquished much of that right's practical value. The party still can ask a court to review the arbitrator's decision, but the court will set that decision aside only in very unusual circumstances. Hence, who—court or arbitrator—has the primary authority to decide whether a party has agreed to arbitrate can make a critical difference to a party resisting arbitration.

We believe the answer to the "who" question (i.e., the standard-of-review question) is fairly simple. Just as the arbitrability of the merits of a dispute depends upon whether the parties agreed to arbitrate that dispute, so the question "who has the primary power to decide arbitrability" turns upon what the parties agreed about that matter. Did the parties agree to submit the arbitrability question itself to arbitration? If so, then the court's standard for reviewing the arbitrator's decision about that matter should not differ from the standard courts apply when they review any other matter that parties have agreed to arbitrate. That is to say, the court should give considerable leeway to the arbitrator, setting aside his or her decision only in certain narrow circumstances. If, on the other hand, the parties did not agree to submit the arbitrability question itself to arbitration, then the court should decide that question just as it would decide any other question that the parties did not submit to arbitration, namely, independently. These two answers flow inexorably from the fact that arbitration is simply a matter of contract between the parties; it is a way to resolve those disputes — but only those disputes — that the parties have agreed to submit to arbitration.

We agree with First Options, therefore, that a court must defer to an arbitrator's arbitrability decision when the parties submitted that matter to arbitration. Nevertheless, that conclusion does not help First Options win this case. That is because a fair and complete answer to the standard-of-review question requires a word about how a court should decide whether the parties have agreed to submit the arbitrability issue to arbitration. And, that word makes clear that the Kaplans did not agree to arbitrate arbitrability here.

When deciding whether the parties agreed to arbitrate a certain matter (including arbitrability), courts generally (though with a qualification we discuss below) should apply ordinary state-law principles that govern the formation of contracts. The relevant state law here, for example, would require the court to see whether the parties objectively revealed an intent to submit the arbitrability issue to arbitration.

This Court, however, has (as we just said) added an important qualification, applicable when courts decide whether a party has agreed that arbitrators should decide arbitrability: Courts should not assume that the parties agreed to arbitrate arbitrability unless there is "clea[r] and unmistakabl[e]" evidence that they did so. In this manner the law treats silence or ambiguity about the question "who (primarily) should decide arbitrability" differently from the way it treats silence or ambiguity about the question "whether a particular merits-related dispute is arbitrable because it is within the scope of a valid arbitration agreement" — for in respect to this latter question the law reverses the presumption. But, this difference in treatment is understandable. . . .

The latter question arises when the parties have a contract that provides for arbitration of some issues. In such circumstances, the parties likely gave at least some thought to the scope of arbitration. And, given the law's permissive policies in respect to arbitration, one can understand why the law would insist upon clarity before concluding that the parties did not want to arbitrate a related matter. On the other hand, the former question — the "who (primarily) should decide arbitrability" question — is rather arcane. A party often might not focus upon that question or upon the significance of having arbitrators decide the scope of their own powers. And, given the principle that a party can be forced to arbitrate only those issues it specifically has agreed to submit to arbitration, one can understand why courts might hesitate to interpret silence or ambiguity on the "who should decide arbitrability" point as giving the arbitrators that power, for doing so might too often force unwilling parties to arbitrate a matter they reasonably would have thought a judge, not an arbitrator, would decide.

On the record before us, First Options cannot show that the Kaplans clearly agreed to have the arbitrators decide (i.e., to arbitrate) the question of arbitrability. First Options relies on the Kaplans' filing with the arbitrators a written memorandum objecting to the arbitrators' jurisdiction. But merely arguing the arbitrability issue to an arbitrator does not indicate a clear willingness to arbitrate that issue (i.e., a willingness to be effectively bound by the arbitrator's decision on that point). To the contrary, insofar as the Kaplans were forcefully objecting to the arbitrators deciding their dispute with First Options, one naturally would think that they did not want the arbitrators to have binding authority over them. This conclusion draws added support from (1) an obvious explanation for the Kaplans' presence before the arbitrators (i.e., that MKI, Mr. Kaplan's wholly owned firm, was arbitrating workout agreement matters); and (2) Third Circuit law that suggested that the Kaplans might argue arbitrability to the arbitrators without losing their right to independent court review. . . .

We conclude that, because the Kaplans did not clearly agree to submit the question of arbitrability to arbitration, the Court of Appeals was correct in finding that the arbitrability of the Kaplan/First Options dispute was subject to independent review by the courts.

Note on Arbitrability

As mentioned above, arbitrability concerns whether parties agreed to arbitrate the merits of their dispute. *First Options* takes the question one step higher to address the issue of *who decides* whether the parties agreed to arbitrate their dispute. The Court elaborated on the general judicial view that courts, not arbitrators, should make arbitrability determinations, holding that unless the parties clearly and unmistakably agree that arbitrators should resolve arbitrability questions, the courts should decide them. At least two rationales support the *First Options* holding. First, it is appropriate to presumptively assign jurisdictional issues to the courts rather than the arbitrator because an arbitrator has a strong self-interest in finding that a case is arbitrable—i.e., that he will be paid. Second, a party should not be required to arbitrate issues it did not agree to arbitrate. A third rationale, that parties are not likely to consider the arbitrability issue when drafting an agreement and therefore courts, rather than arbitrators, should make arbitrability decisions because that is probably what the parties would have chosen for themselves, seems suspect. Why should we suppose that the parties would have chosen this option? The parties have shown a penchant for private decision-makers. Why should the Court fail to extend that preference to this issue?

Does *First Options* seem consistent with the "healthy federal policy favoring arbitration" that is often cited in cases involving enforcement of an arbitration agreement? Instead of a presumption in favor of arbitrating arbitrability questions, *First Options* suggests that there is a presumption *against* arbitration of arbitrability disputes. In other contexts, such as reviewing an agreement to arbitrate, a state statute requiring the parties to "clearly and unmistakably" agree to arbitrate their claims would be viewed as an inappropriate modification of the traditional contractual requirement that *Southland* preempts. Does *First Options* mark a change in the national federal policy favoring arbitration? Can *First Options* be interpreted to require a clear and unmistakable assent to an adhesion contract? Courts have not extended *First Options*' repudiation of implied waivers outside the arbitrability context.

Is *First Options* consistent with *Prima Paint* and *Buckeye Check Cashing*? In *First Options*, the Court considered who should decide whether the parties agreed to arbitrate a dispute. In *Prima Paint* and *Buckeye Check Cashing*, by contrast, the Court concluded that challenges to the container contract, but not the arbitration clause, should be arbitrated. Had the arbitration clause been challenged, however, both *Prima Paint* and *Buckeye Check Cashing* suggest that a court, not the arbitrator, would resolve the dispute. If one accepts the separability notion as valid, it would seem that the cases can be reconciled—both allow courts to hear challenges to the formation of an agreement to arbitrate.

Other differences among the cases suggest an alternative ground for reconciliation. One important difference between *Prima Paint* and *Buckeye,* on the one hand, and *First Options,* on the other, is that the former cases involved the question of whether a party may enjoin an arbitration while *First Options* concerns the standard of review for an arbitrator's decision, already rendered. In other words, the question for the *Prima Paint* and *Buckeye Check Cashing* Courts was whether the arbitrator should in the first instance decide the question of arbitrability while in *First Options,* the question was to what extent a court should defer to an arbitrator's decision. Whether this distinction makes a difference is not clear, however. Justice Breyer states, in dicta, that the Kaplans could have moved to enjoin the arbitration.

Even if the three decisions are reconcilable, other questions persist. For example, what are the parameters of arbitrability? While the Supreme Court offered a definition of arbitrability in *First Options,* the determining factor for what renders any particular issue arbitrable remains unresolved. The Supreme Court offered guidance on this question in *Howsam v. Dean Witter Reynolds, Inc.*, 123 S. Ct. 588 (2002). At issue in *Howsam* was whether the National Association of Securities Dealers (NASD) statute of limitations, which states that "[n]o dispute, claim or controversy shall be eligible for submission to arbitration under this Code where six (6) years have elapsed from the occurrence or event giving rise to the act or dispute, claim, or controversy," is a jurisdictional prerequisite to arbitration (to be decided by the courts) or a substantive eligibility requirement (to be resolved by arbitrators in the absence of a "clear and unmistakable" agreement to the contrary). The Court concluded that the application of the NASD rule was not a question of arbitrability; instead, it was a procedural issue for the arbitrators to resolve.

> Linguistically speaking, one might call any potentially dispositive gateway question a "question of arbitrability," for its answer will determine whether the underlying controversy will proceed to arbitration on the merits. The Court's case law, however, makes clear that, for purposes of applying the interpretive rule, the phrase "question of arbitrability" has a far more limited scope. The Court has found the phrase applicable in the kind of narrow circumstance where contracting parties would likely have expected a court to have decided the gateway matter, where they are not likely to have thought that they had agreed that an arbitrator would do so, and consequently, where reference of the gateway dispute to the court avoids the risk of forcing parties to arbitrate a matter that they may well not have agreed to arbitrate.
>
> Thus, a gateway dispute about whether the parties are bound by a given arbitration clause raises a "question of arbitrability" for a court to decide. Similarly, a disagreement about whether an arbitration clause in a concededly binding contract applies to a particular type of controversy is for the court.
>
> At the same time the Court has found the phrase "question of arbitrability" not applicable in other kinds of general circumstances where parties would likely expect that an arbitrator would decide the gateway matter. These " 'procedural' questions which grow out of the dispute and bear on its final disposition" are presumptively not for the judge, but for an arbitrator, to decide. So, too, the presumption is that the arbitrator should decide "allegation[s] of waiver, delay, or a like defense to arbitrability." Indeed, the

Revised Uniform Arbitration Act of 2000 (RUAA), seeking to "incorporate the holdings of the vast majority of state courts and the law that has developed under the [Federal Arbitration Act]," states that an "aribitrator shall decide whether a condition precedent to arbitrability has been fulfilled." RUAA §6(c) and comment 2, 7 U.L.A. 12-13 (Supp. 2002). And the comments add that "in the absence of an agreement to the contrary, issues of substantive arbitrability . . . are for a court to decide and issues of procedural arbitrability, i.e., whether prerequisites such as time limits, notice, laches, estoppel, and other conditions precedent to an obligation to arbitrate have been met, are for the arbitrators to decide." Id., §6, comment 2, 7 U.L.A., at 13.

Following this precedent, we find that the applicability of the NASD time limit rule is a matter presumptively for the arbitrator, not for the judge. The time limit rule closely resembles the gateway questions that this Court has found not to be "questions of arbitrability." Such a dispute seems an "aspec[t] of the [controversy] which called the grievance procedures into play" Moreover, the NASD arbitrators, comparatively more expert about the meaning of their own rule, are comparatively better able to interpret and to apply it. In the absence of any statement to the contrary in the arbitration agreement, it is reasonable to infer that the parties intended the agreement to reflect that understanding. And for the law to assume an expectation that aligns (1) decision-maker with (2) comparative expertise will help better to secure a fair and expeditious resolution of the underlying controversy—a goal of arbitration systems and judicial systems alike. We consequently conclude that the NASD's time limit rule falls within the class of gateway procedural disputes that do not present what our cases have called "questions of arbitrability." And the strong pro-court presumption as to the parties' likely intent does not apply.

Does the Court's definition of "questions of arbitrability" satisfy you? What role should party intent play in determining whether an issue is a gateway question for an arbitrator to decide or a "question of arbitrability" for the court? How should party intent be determined if the arbitration agreement fails to address the particular issue now in dispute? For a thorough discussion of *Prima Paint*, *First Options*, and *Howsam*, see Reuben (2003).

C. ARBITRATION OF STATUTORY CLAIMS

As pointed out previously (p. 215), both federal and state courts are authorized to enforce agreements to arbitrate, and there is a strong public policy in favor of doing so. Nonetheless, until fairly recently, courts were reluctant to enforce predispute agreements to arbitrate a claim that was statutorily based, rather than created by contract. This reluctance rested on the courts' view that the legislative intent in creating a statutory right would be frustrated if that right were not effectively enforced, and on the belief that effective enforcement in arbitration was doubtful. Thus, the Supreme Court stated in *Wilko v. Swan*, 346 U.S. 427 (1953), that arbitration proceedings were not suited to cases requiring "subjective findings on the purpose and knowledge of an alleged violator." The Court was also concerned that arbitrators in statutorily based cases must make legal determinations "without judicial instruction on the law" and that an arbitration award "may be made without explanation of [the arbitrator's] reasons and without a complete record of their proceedings." Finally, the Court in *Wilko* noted that the "power to vacate an award is limited" and that "interpretations of the law by the arbitrators, in contrast to manifest disregard, are not subject, in the federal courts, to judicial review for error in interpretation." The Court concluded that in view of these drawbacks to arbitration, the Securities Act claims involved in *Wilko* should not be ordered to arbitration.

In a series of cases beginning in 1985, however, the Supreme Court has taken a strong pro-arbitration position in cases involving statutory claims. The new approach began with *Mitsubishi Motors Corp., Inc. v. Soler Chrysler-Plymouth Inc.*, 473 U.S. 614 (1985), in which the Court upheld an agreement to arbitrate antitrust claims "when that agreement arises from an international transaction" (id. at 624). Then, in *Shearson/American Express, Inc. v. McMahon*, 482 U.S. 220 (1987), the Court upheld an agreement to arbitrate claims arising under the 1934 Exchange Act and the Racketeer Influenced and Corrupt Organizations Act (RICO); and in *Rodriguez de Quijas v. Shearson/American Express, Inc.*, 490 U.S. 477 (1989), the Court reached a similar result with respect to claims arising under the 1933 Securities Act, overruling *Wilko*.

In each of these cases, the Court took the position that while Congress could prohibit the arbitration of statute-based claims, in the absence of clear evidence of such a prohibition in the statute's text or legislative history, arbitration will be barred only on a showing that there exists an inherent conflict between arbitration and the statute's underlying purpose. Arbitration will not be prohibited on the basis of a generalized suspicion of the capacity of arbitration to protect statutory rights. Thus, the Court stated in *Shearson/American Express, Inc. v. McMahon*, 482 U.S. at 232, that:

> In *Mitsubishi*, . . . we recognized that arbitral tribunals are readily capable of handling the factual and legal complications of antitrust claims, notwithstanding the absence of judicial instruction and supervision. Likewise, we have concluded that the streamlined procedures of arbitration do not entail any consequential restriction on substantive rights. Finally, . . . there is no reason to assume at the outset that arbitrators will not follow the law; although judicial scrutiny of arbitration awards necessarily is limited, such review is sufficient to ensure that arbitrators comply with the requirements of the statute.

Despite this strong pro-arbitration bias, doubts remained after *Mitsubishi* and the two *Shearson/American Express* cases whether the Court would compel arbitration of statutory claims outside the commercial context of those cases. Would the Court, for example, compel arbitration of an individual employee's Title VII claim that he had been discharged due to his race? These doubts rested on a line of cases antedating *Mitsubishi* and *Shearson/American Express* that allowed employees with federal statutory claims to press those claims in federal court, even though the claims were previously rejected in arbitration under a collective bargaining contract. *McDonald v. City of West Branch, Mich.*, 466 U.S. 284 (1984); *Barrentine v. Arkansas-Best Freight System, Inc.*, 450 U.S. 728 (1981); *Alexander v. Gardner-Denver Co.*, 415 U.S. 36 (1974).

In *Gilmer v. Interstate/Johnson Lane Corp.*, 500 U.S. 20 (1991), the Court laid most of these doubts to rest. Gilmer had been required by his employer to register with the

New York Stock Exchange (NYSE). His registration application contained an agreement to arbitrate disputes arising out of any termination of employment. When Gilmer was terminated at age 62, he brought suit in federal district court, alleging violation of the Age Discrimination in Employment Act (ADEA). The employer moved to compel arbitration under FAA §4, and the Supreme Court held that arbitration should be compelled.

Gilmer conceded that nothing in the text or legislative history of the ADEA explicitly precluded arbitration. He argued, however, that arbitration was inconsistent with the purposes of the ADEA because of the inadequacy of the arbitration procedures offered by the NYSE. The Court responded:

> Initially, we note that in our recent arbitration cases we have already rejected most of these arguments as insufficient to preclude arbitration of statutory claims. Such generalized attacks on arbitration "res[t] on suspicion of arbitration as a method of weakening the protections afforded in the substantive law to would-be complainants," and as such, they are "far out of step with our current strong endorsement of the federal statutes favoring this method of resolving disputes." Consequently, we address these arguments only briefly.
>
> Gilmer first speculates that arbitration panels will be biased. However, "[w]e decline to indulge the presumption that the parties and arbitral body conducting a proceeding will be unable or unwilling to retain competent, conscientious and impartial arbitrators." In any event, we note that the NYSE arbitration rules, which are applicable to the dispute in this case, provide protections against biased panels. The rules require, for example, that the parties be informed of the employment histories of the arbitrators, and that they be allowed to make further inquiries into the arbitrators' backgrounds. In addition, each party is allowed one peremptory challenge and unlimited challenges for cause. Moreover, the arbitrators are required to disclose "any circumstances which might preclude [them] from rendering an objective and impartial determination." The FAA also protects against bias, by providing that courts may overturn arbitration decisions "[w]here there was evident partiality or corruption in the arbitrators." There has been no showing in this case that those provisions are inadequate to guard against potential bias.
>
> Gilmer also complains that the discovery allowed in arbitration is more limited than in the federal courts, which he contends will make it difficult to prove discrimination. It is unlikely, however, that age discrimination claims require more extensive discovery than other claims that we have found to be arbitrable, such as RICO and antitrust claims. Moreover, there has been no showing in this case that the NYSE discovery provisions, which allow for document production, information requests, depositions, and subpoenas, will prove insufficient to allow ADEA claimants such as Gilmer a fair opportunity to present their claims. Although these procedures might not be as extensive as in the federal courts, by agreeing to arbitrate, a party "trades the procedures and opportunity for review of the courtroom for the simplicity, informality, and expedition of arbitration." Indeed, an important counterweight to the reduced discovery in NYSE arbitration is that arbitrators are not bound by the rules of evidence.
>
> A further alleged deficiency of arbitration is that arbitrators often will not issue written opinions, resulting, Gilmer contends, in a lack of public knowledge of employers' discriminatory policies, an inability to obtain effective appellate review, and a stifling of the development of the law. The NYSE rules, however, do require that all arbitration awards be in writing, and that the awards contain the names of the parties, a summary of the issues in controversy, and a description of the award issued. In addition, the award decisions are made available to the public. Furthermore, judicial

decisions addressing ADEA claims will continue to be issued because it is unlikely that all or even most ADEA claimants will be subject to arbitration agreements. Finally, Gilmer's concerns apply equally to settlements of ADEA claims, which, as noted above, are clearly allowed.[4]

It is also argued that arbitration procedures cannot accurately further the purposes of the ADEA because they do not provide for broad equitable relief and class actions. As the court below noted, however, arbitrators do have the power to fashion equitable relief. . . . But "even if the arbitration could not go forward as a class action or class relief could not be granted by the arbitrator, the fact that the [ADEA] provides for the possibility of bringing a collective action does not mean that individual attempts at conciliation were intended to be barred." Finally, it should be remembered that arbitration agreements will not preclude the EEOC [Equal Employment Opportunity Commission] from bringing actions seeking class-wide and equitable relief.

An additional reason advanced by Gilmer for refusing to enforce arbitration agreements relating to ADEA claims is his contention that there often will be unequal bargaining power between employers and employees. Mere inequality in bargaining power, however, is not a sufficient reason to hold that arbitration agreements are never enforceable in the employment context. Relationships between securities dealers and investors, for example, may involve unequal bargaining power, but we nevertheless held in *Rodriguez de Quijas* and *McMahon* that agreements to arbitrate in that context are enforceable. . . . "Of course, courts should remain attuned to well-supported claims that the agreement to arbitrate resulted from the sort of fraud or overwhelming economic power that would provide grounds 'for the revocation of any contract.'" There is no indication in this case, however, that Gilmer, an experienced businessman, was coerced or defrauded into agreeing to the arbitration clause in his registration application. As with the claimed procedural inadequacies discussed above, this claim of unequal bargaining power is best left for resolution in specific cases. . . .

Justice Stevens, joined by Justice Marshall, dissented.

As this Court previously has noted, authorizing the courts to issue broad injunctive relief is the cornerstone to eliminating discrimination in society. The ADEA, like Title VII, authorizes courts to award broad, class-based injunctive relief to achieve the purposes of the Act. Because commercial arbitration is typically limited to a specific dispute between the particular parties and because the available remedies in arbitral forums generally do not provide for class-wide injunctive relief, I would conclude that an essential purpose of the ADEA is frustrated by compulsory arbitration of employment discrimination claims. Moreover, as Chief Justice Burger explained:

> Plainly, it would not comport with the congressional objectives behind a statute seeking to enforce civil rights protected by Title VII to allow the very forces that had practiced discrimination to contract away the right to enforce civil rights in the courts. For federal courts to defer to arbitral decisions reached by the same combination of forces that had long perpetuated invidious discrimination would have made the foxes guardians of the chickens.

In my opinion the same concerns expressed by Chief Justice Burger with regard to compulsory arbitration of Title VII claims may be said of claims arising under the ADEA. The Court's holding today clearly eviscerates the important role played by an independent judiciary eradicating employment discrimination.

4. Gilmer also contends that judicial review of arbitration decisions is too limited. We have stated, however, that "although judicial scrutiny of arbitration awards necessarily is limited, such review is sufficient to ensure that arbitrators comply with the requirements of the statute" at issue.

Notes

Following *Gilmer,* all the circuits, except the Ninth, held that neither Title VII nor the Civil Rights Act of 1991 barred employers from requiring employees to sign an arbitration agreement as a condition of employment. In 2003 an *en banc* panel of the Ninth Circuit, in *EEOC v. Luce, Forward, Hamilton & Scripps,* 345 F.3d 742 (9th Cir. 2003), joined the remaining circuits by rejecting its previous holding in *Duffield v. Robertson Stephens & Co.,* 144 F.3d 1182 (9th Cir. 1998), and concluded that nothing in the text or legislative history of the Civil Rights Act of 1991 precludes parties from agreeing to arbitrate their statutory employment discrimination claims.

While *Gilmer* approved the use of predispute agreements to arbitrate discrimination claims in the nonunionized workplace, the use of such agreements in the unionized workplace was prohibited by the 1974 Supreme Court decision in *Alexander v. Gardner-Denver,* 415 U.S. 36 (1974). In *Gardner-Denver,* the Court held that an employer may not compel an employee who is union-represented to arbitrate a statutorily-based claim because the employee would be represented in the arbitration by the union, and there would be a potential conflict of interest between the union and the employee. Moreover, the union's agreement to waive access to court that is implicit in its executing the arbitration clause in the collective bargaining agreement cannot be attributed to the individual employee. The *Gardner-Denver* Court thus permitted the employee to bring his Title VII claim in federal court despite the arbitration clause. Did *Gilmer* implicitly overrule the *Gardner-Denver* case? The Fourth Circuit thought so, holding that a unionized employee's statutory claim, based on alleged violations of Title VII and the ADA, could be arbitrated. See *Austin v. Owens-Brockway Glass Container, Inc.,* 78 F.3d 875 (4th Cir.), *cert. denied,* 519 U.S. 980 (1996). The circuits split on this issue and the Supreme Court addressed it in *Wright v. Universal Maritime Service Corp.,* 525 U.S. 70 (1998). In *Wright,* the Court held that a union-negotiated waiver of employees' statutory right to a judicial forum is enforceable only if the right is clearly and unmistakably waived in the collective bargaining agreement.

Should cases like *Gilmer* receive different treatment than those like *Gardner-Denver*? The *Gardner-Denver* Court identified a disparity in interests between the union and the represented employee that it believed precluded arbitration of a statutorily-based claim. The Court's concern was that the union, as labor's exclusive representative, might use its power to bargain to the detriment of the interests of a certain employee or group of employees. In other words, a union might sacrifice individual or protected groups' preferences in order to obtain benefits for the majority. Do you think this might happen? Another possibility exists. It may be that protected groups, better able to organize because of easy identification of similarly-situated individuals, actually have more influence on union decision-making than would the majority. Interest group capture of the union, together with Title VII and the union's duty of fair representation to its members, suggest a strong argument as to why unions do not have a conflict of interest with represented employees during an arbitration. For more on the application of public choice theory to unionized decision-making, see Cole (1997).

The other major concern *Gardner-Denver* raised was that the union's waiver of the right to a judicial forum should not be attributed to the employee. In other words, a union cannot waive a member's right to a judicial forum for a statutory claim because that right belongs to the individual. In *Gilmer,* by contrast, the Court stated that an employee may waive his rights to a judicial forum by signing an arbitration agreement as a condition of employment. What is the difference between the two cases? Imagine employees applying for a job. If the workplace is not unionized, the arbitration agreement may be presented on a take-it-or-leave-it basis—it is not negotiable. In the unionized context, an employee may either begin working under the condition or quit. Because both employees confront the same problem and have the same ability to negotiate the arbitration condition, both agreements should be subject to the same rules governing enforceablity.

Following *Wright,* the question becomes, when does an employee make a clear and unmistakable waiver of her right to bring statutory claims in court? What if the collective bargaining agreement provides that all employees submit all federal causes of action arising out of their employment to arbitration? What if the agreement specifically incorporates statutory anti-discrimination claims into its arbitration clause? Compare *Carson v. Giant Food, Inc.,* 175 F.3d 325 (4th Cir. 1999) (although a clear and unmistakable waiver is possible, it did not exist because general arbitration clause makes no mention of disputes arising under federal law); *Robinson v. Healthtex, Inc.,* No. 99-2023, 2000 U.S. App. LEXIS 11961 (4th Cir. May 30, 2000) (requirements for clear and unmistakable waiver not satisfied); *Rogers v. New York Univ.,* 220 F.3d 73 (2d. Cir. 2000) (both arbitration and nondiscrimination clauses too broad and general to constitute clear and unmistakable waiver); *Bratten v. SSI Servs. Inc.,* 185 F.3d 625 (6th Cir. 1999) (no clear and unmistakable waiver even though agreement contained specific language from Title VII) with *Safrit v. Cone Mills Corp.,* 248 F.3d 306 (4th Cir. 2001) (collective bargaining agreement contains clear and unmistakable waiver of employee's right to bring statutory discrimination claim to court where CBA stated that parties would "abide by all the requirements of Title VII" and that "[u]nresolved grievances arising under this Section are the proper subjects for arbitration").

D. ARBITRATION OF STATUTORY CLAIMS: APPLICATION TO EMPLOYMENT DISPUTES

1. *Repeat v. One-Shot Players*

While *Gilmer* has led to increased interest in the mandatory arbitration of many different types of statutorily-based disputes, its greatest effect has been to encourage a growing number of employers to adopt, or consider adopting, mandatory arbitration procedures for all claims of nonunionized employees. Typically included among the claims for which arbitration is mandatory are those claims based on alleged statutory violations by the employer.

The primary reason for employer interest in mandatory arbitration of statutorily-based claims is undoubtedly the virtual explosion of litigation that has been triggered by the growth in employee protective legislation. In the federal courts alone, the number of suits filed concerning employment grievances grew over 400 percent in the last two decades. Complaints lodged with administrative agencies have risen at a similar rate. In 1993, for example, the EEOC received nearly 90,000 discrimination complaints from employees across the country (Dunlop Commission, 1994:25).

Yet the increased use of employment, consumer, and medical malpractice arbitration is quite controversial. Criticism focuses on the potential unfairness associated with the imposition of arbitration agreements on unsuspecting employees, consumers, and patients. Advocates for these groups view arbitration as a poor substitute for litigation, rife with the opportunity for exploitation of society's most vulnerable citizens. Ultimately, it is the absence of negotiation between employers or businesses on the one hand and employees or consumers on the other that causes arbitration critics to treat arbitration agreements with suspicion. Unlike interactions in the collective bargaining context or among merchants (traditional arbitration users), where all parties are regular participants in negotiation and arbitration, only the employer, or big business, or health provider is a "repeat player" in disputes with employees, consumers, or patients. A repeat player is typically an entity that frequently interacts with a particular institution or engages in certain behaviors, for example, commercial transactions or labor-management negotiations. By contrast, a "one-shot player," the employee, consumer, or patient in arbitration, is an entity or person with limited exposure to negotiating and dispute resolution. For further discussion of repeat player and one-shot player, see Galanter (1974). Critics of pre-dispute arbitration agreements between one-shotters and repeat players view such agreements as problematic because repeat players are thought to have a distinct and systematic advantage in interactions with one-shot players. For example, in employment relationships, repeat players are able to use their experience, knowledge, and economies of scale to gain an advantage in negotiation of the arbitration agreement, the selection of the arbitrator, and the arbitration process (Cole, 1996).

The EEOC, a major critic of pre-dispute arbitration agreements between employers and employees, utilized the repeat player/one-shot player dichotomy to support its policy that such agreements should not be enforced. See Policy Statement on Mandatory Arbitration of Employment Disputes as a Condition of Employment, 133 DLR E-4 (July 11, 1997). In its statement, the EEOC emphasized that the structure of arbitration is biased against the employee. According to the EEOC, the arbitral process provides innumerable benefits to the repeat player employer at the expense of the one-shot employee. For example, the repeat player has systematic advantages both in negotiating the arbitration agreement and in selecting the arbitrator because: (1) it drafts the agreement, garnering the lion's share of the benefits for itself; (2) it has more knowledge both about the process itself and the arbitrators who may preside over hearings; and (3) it has the incentive and opportunity to facilitate informal relationships with those arbitrators. In the EEOC's view, these advantages render the arbitral process irretrievably suspect.

Do you agree with the EEOC's position? Why can't potential plaintiffs obtain sufficient information about arbitrators prior to the arbitration so as to ensure that the arbitrator ultimately selected is unbiased or biased in the employee's favor? Couldn't a group of plaintiff's attorneys develop an accessible shared database of information about prospective arbitrators? Would such an effort make sense? Shouldn't an employee be able to negotiate around an arbitration agreement if he or she is really opposed to it? How successful do you think such negotiations would be? Don't repeat players also have advantages in litigation? Why would the situation be worse in arbitration?

Why does it appear that employees (and the EEOC) are opposed to arbitration? Is the true opponent of arbitration the attorneys who currently represent employees in judicial proceedings? What advantages might arbitration hold for an employee? In answering this question, consider the views of the following commentators. Professor Theodore J. St. Antoine suggests that lower-paid employees might be better off in mandatory arbitration than litigation because they otherwise might not have an opportunity to litigate their case and they might receive a better recovery in arbitration than they would in court:

> Experienced plaintiffs' attorneys have estimated that only about five percent of the individuals with an employment claim who seek help from the private bar are able to obtain counsel. One of the Detroit area's top employment specialists was more precise in a conversation with me. His secretary kept an actual count; he took on only one out of eighty-seven persons who contacted him for possible representation. Now, many of those who are rejected will not have meritorious claims. But others will be workers whose potential dollar recovery will simply not justify the investment of the time and money of a first-rate lawyer in preparing a court action. For those individuals, the cheaper, simpler process of arbitration is the most feasible recourse. It will cost a lawyer far less time and effort to take a case to arbitration; at worst, claimants can represent themselves or be represented by laypersons in this much less formal and intimidating forum. . . .
>
> Even if individual claimants can get to court, mounting empirical evidence indicates most of them will fare less well there than they would before a qualified arbitrator. Several studies show that employees actually win more often in arbitration than in court and, while a successful plaintiff recovers more from a judge and a jury, claimants as a group get more from arbitrators. That was true before the due-process protocol [see p. 260] was adopted, and should be even truer with the protocol in effect.
>
> Most court dockets are heavily backlogged and delay is endemic. That can be devastating for the fired worker without a job or with a much-reduced income. A considerably more conservative judiciary than existed in earlier years may be all too willing to grant summary judgment against those civil-rights plaintiffs who do manage to file suit. Traditional labor arbitrators have had to remain mutually acceptable to unions and employers, and the same is likely to become true for arbitrators in the new employer/individual-employee field as an increasingly savvy plaintiffs' bar develops. There is no comparable check on the lifetime appointees to the federal bench or, as a practical matter, on longtime incumbents of state courts.

St. Antoine (2001).

Most commentators disagree with Professor St. Antoine, suggesting that the courts are a much better place for plaintiffs than is arbitration. Other scholars focus on arbitration itself, evaluating the success of one-shot player employees in obtaining a positive outcome depending on whether they arbitrate against a repeat or one-shot player employer. For example, Professor Lisa Bingham conducted a study of 270 cases consisting of arbitration awards decided in 1993 under the AAA Commercial Arbitration Rules and arbitration awards decided in 1993 and 1994 under the AAA Employment Dispute Rules (Bingham, 1997:206). This study, which reviewed awards rendered prior to the implementation of the Due Process Protocol (see p. 260), revealed that arbitrators award damages to employees less frequently and in lower amounts when the employer is a repeat player (Bingham, 1997:209-210). According to Professor Bingham, in repeat player cases, employees recover only 11 percent of what they demand; while in cases against non-repeat player employers, they recover approximately 48 percent of what they demand (Bingham, 1998:234). Moreover, employees lose significantly more often in cases involving repeat player employers (Bingham, 1997:209). According to the study, employees arbitrating with one-shot player employers win over 70 percent of the time. When arbitrating against repeat player employers, however, they win only 16 percent of the time (Bingham, 1998:234).

Professor Bingham examined the Due Process Protocol's impact on arbitrations between one-shot and repeat players. Her examination offers additional support to the theory that employers have structural advantages in the arbitration process by virtue of their repeat player status (Bingham, 1997:215). Although her study of arbitrations using the Due Process Protocol suggests that the adoption of the protocol lessens the impact of the employer's repeat player status, it certainly does not suggest that the advantage is eliminated. In fact, Professor Bingham reports that only when both the Due Process Protocol and a Personnel Handbook are adopted does the employer's likelihood of success decrease. Bingham could not support her hypothesis that the Due Process Protocol alone reduces the chances of employer success.

A more recent empirical study, conducted by Professor Theodore Eisenberg and Elizabeth Hill, offered additional insight, at least with respect to highly paid employees (Eisenberg and Hill, 2003-2004). According to their study, for highly paid employees (those making more then $60,000 per year), arbitrated outcomes do not differ materially from trial outcomes.

2. *Arbitration of Statutorily-Based Employment Claims*

While commentators and existing empirical studies are highly critical of employer-implemented arbitration schemes, the courts, immediately following *Gilmer,* were generally favorable to mandatory arbitration. Yet today, courts are becoming more receptive to challenges to arbitration on a variety of grounds. The judicial backlash against arbitration agreements, particularly when employees or consumers are involved, has focused on several areas:

- Whether an employee who is being denied the right to sue on the basis of a pre-dispute arbitration agreement knowingly and voluntarily waived the right to sue.
- The fairness of the arbitration procedure to which the employee has agreed, including: (1) allocation of arbitrator's fees and arbitration's costs, (2) arbitration filing fees, and (3) conscionability of the arbitration agreement.
- The impact of arbitration agreements on the EEOC's continuing role in employment discrimination cases.
- The scope of judicial review of the arbitrator's awards.

a. Knowing and Voluntary Waiver of the Right to Sue

While courts often say that a waiver of the right to enforce statutory rights in a judicial forum will not be enforced unless that waiver was knowing and voluntary, they will rarely refuse to enforce an agreement to arbitrate on either of these grounds.

Voluntary

The argument that an agreement to arbitrate should not be enforced because the employee had no practical choice but to accept that agreement or surrender her employment was rejected in *Gilmer* and has rarely been successful since then. Rather, when unequal bargaining power is relied on as a basis for avoiding arbitration, the court's focus is likely to be on the use that the employer made of its greater bargaining power. If it used that power to impose an unfair arbitration procedure, biased against the employee, that may well be grounds for refusing to enforce the agreement to arbitrate.

Knowing

As a general rule, courts have held that an employee who signs a contract containing an arbitration clause has knowingly consented to arbitrate. In *Williams v. Cigna Financial Advisors, Inc.*, 56 F.3d 656 (5th Cir. 1995), for example, Williams signed a U-4 Registration that committed him to adhere to all rules of the NASD. At the time, NASD's Code of Arbitration Procedure did not require arbitration of employment disputes. The rules were later amended, and, according to the court, Williams "consented" to mandatory arbitration when he signed a subsequent U-4 Registration. An even broader interpretation of consent to arbitration appears in *F. J. O'Brien & Associates, Inc. v. Pipkin*, 64 F.3d 257 (7th Cir. 1995). Pipkin signed a contract agreeing to abide by all "requirements" of the National Futures Organization. The court held that "requirements" was defined in two other documents as incorporating a fourth document, the Member Arbitration Rules.

Standards governing consent may change depending on the claims at issue and the consenting party's experience. In *Paul Revere Variable Annuity Ins. Co. v. Zang*, 248 F.3d 1 (1st Cir. 2001), two general managers agreed, as a condition of their employment, to arbitrate all claims arising out of their employment according to NASD rules as they existed at the time of registration and as they "may from time to time be adopted, changed, or amended." When a dispute later arose between the managers and their employer, the managers argued that the arbitration agreement was unenforceable because their consent to it was neither knowing nor voluntary. The First Circuit upheld the arbitration agreement because the case involved employment discrimination claims rather than a contract dispute and the Zang employer neither explicitly agreed to familiarize its employees with the governing regulations nor failed to notify the plaintiffs of the mandatory arbitration provision. Moreover, the court emphasized that the two managers were "professionals" who should be expected to keep up with rule changes.

An exception to this line of cases is *Prudential Insurance Co. of America v. Lai*, 42 F.3d 1299 (9th Cir. 1994), in which the court reversed an order compelling arbitration of Title VII claims because the waiver of statutory remedies was not made knowingly. In that case, the employer did not allow the employees to read the contract before signing it or provide them with a copy of the NASD manual containing the terms of the arbitration agreement, which was incorporated into the contract by reference. Neither the contract nor the NASD manual notified employees that they were required to arbitrate Title VII claims. Thus, at least in the Ninth Circuit, the arbitration agreement itself may need to spell out an employee's claims under protective statutes in order for that agreement to constitute a waiver of the employee's statutory remedies. See also *Nelson v. Cyprus Bagdad Copper Corp.*, 119 F.3d 756 (9th Cir. 1997) (2–1 decision) (provision in employee handbook not effective to provide employee consent); *Rosenberg v. Merrill Lynch, Pierce, Fenner & Smith, Inc.*, 170 F.3d 1, 163 F.3d 73 (1st Cir. 1999) (2–1 decision) (since employer only told employee arbitration was required for claims specified in NYSE rules, but did not give employee a copy of those rules or spell out what they provided, waiver of judicial forum was not "clear and unmistakable" and arbitration clause would not be enforced).

The vast majority of courts considering the issue have rejected the heightened standards proposed in *Lai* and *Rosenberg*. See *Haskins v. Prudential Ins. Co. of America*, 230 F.3d 231 (6th Cir. 2000) (rejecting *Lai* and *Rosenberg*, court holds that employee bound by NASD's U-4 arbitration agreement even though not given copy of NASD arbitration rules); *Seus v. John Nuveen & Co., Inc.*, 146 F.3d 175, 183 n.2 (3d. Cir. 1998) (court expressly disagrees with *Lai* reasoning); *Hart v. Canadian Imperial Bk. of Commerce*, 43 F. Supp. 2d 395, 400 (S.D.N.Y. 1999) (court rejects *Lai*'s knowing and voluntary standard); *Battle v. Prudential Ins. Co. of America*, 973 F. Supp. 861, 866 (D. Minn. 1997) (*Lai* analysis unsound and unsupported by law); *Beauchamp v. Great West Life Assur. Co.*, 918 F. Supp. 1091 (E.D. Mich. 1996) (rejecting *Lai*'s "knowing" standard); but see *walker v. Ryan's Family steak Houses, Inc.*, 400 F.3d 370 (6th Cir. 2005) (knowing and voluntary waiver required). Thus, most plaintiffs will find that a claim based on lack of knowledge or appropriateness of the subject matter for arbitration is unlikely to succeed.

The U.S. Supreme Court held that states may not enact legislation aimed at protecting an unwary party from unknowingly surrendering the right to sue. In *Doctor's Associates, Inc. v. Casarotto*, 517 U.S. 681 (1996), the Court held that the FAA preempted a Montana statute that required that an arbitration clause be printed on the first page in underlined capital letters. "Courts may not . . . invalidate arbitration agreements under state laws applicable only to arbitration provisions. . . . Congress precluded States from singling out arbitration provisions for suspect status, requiring instead that such provisions be placed upon the same footing as other contracts" (id. at 687). While *Casarotto* did not arise in an employment context, there is no reason to suppose that the result would have been otherwise if it had.

Question

4.17 Suppose to protect vulnerable employees by ensuring their waiver of the right to proceed to trial is knowing, a state enacts a statute that provides that an arbitration agreement will be enforceable only if the waiver of the right to trial is clear and unmistakable. Would the statute be desirable? Would it be effective?

b. Fairness of the Arbitration Procedures

From a policy perspective, the issue of fairness of arbitration's procedures has been treated most influentially in two documents—the Dunlop Commission Report and the Due Process Protocol, issued by the Task Force on Alternative Dispute Resolution in Employment—as well as by some recent court decisions. Excerpts from each follow.

COMMISSION ON THE FUTURE OF WORKER-MANAGEMENT RELATIONS, REPORT AND RECOMMENDATIONS

25-33 (1994)

Testimony before the Commission indicated that recent employer experimentation with arbitration has produced programs that range from serious and fair alternatives to litigation, to mechanisms that appear to be of dubious merit for enforcing the public values embedded in our laws.[3] The challenge, then, is how to encourage the creative potential of alternatives to standard court litigation, while ensuring that the legal needs and priorities of a diverse American work force are fairly satisfied. . . .

[T]he Commission believes that development of private arbitration alternatives for workplace disputes must be encouraged. High-quality alternatives to litigation hold the promise of expanding access to public law rights for lower-wage workers. Private arbitration may also allow even the most contentious disputes to be resolved in a manner which permits the complaining employee to raise the dispute without permanently fracturing the employee's working relationship with the employer.

In light of the important social values embodied in public employment law and regulation, however, the Commission believes that a shift to private alternatives must proceed carefully. Significant quality standards should be met by the private arbitration mechanisms developed by individual firms and their employees, to enhance the contributions they make to insuring both protection of and respect for America's workforce. . . .

In specific terms, the Commission recommends the following guide posts for ensuring quality in private arbitration:

Payment of arbitrator. To ensure impartiality of the arbitrator, both the employee and the employer should contribute to the arbitrator's fee. Ideally, the

3. A Wall Street Journal article ("More Law Firms Seek Arbitration for Internal Disputes," Sept. 26, 1994, p. B 13) describes how a number of large law firms are establishing ADR programs in the wake of a $7 million jury verdict against a firm for sexual harassment by one of its partners. One of the programs mentioned was troubling: the arbitrator for an employee's dispute had to be selected from a pool composed of partners in law firms with 50 lawyers or more.

employee contribution should be capped in proportion to the employee's pay, so as to avoid discouraging claims by lower-wage workers.

Awards and remedies. The introduction of a workplace arbitration system should not curb substantive employee protections. This means that private arbitration must offer employees the same array of remedies available to them through litigation in court. Public law arbitrators should be empowered to award whatever relief—including reinstatement, back pay, additional economic damages, punitive awards, injunctive relief, and attorneys' fees—that would be available in court under the law in question.

Final arbitrator ruling. The arbitrator should issue a written opinion spelling out the findings of fact and reasons which led to the decision. This opinion need not correspond in style or length to a court opinion. However, it should set out in understandable terms the basis for the arbitrator's ruling.

Court review. Judicial review of arbitrator rulings must ensure that the arbitration decision reflects an appropriate understanding and interpretation of the relevant legal doctrines. While a reviewing court should defer to an arbitrator's fact findings as long as they have substantial evidentiary basis, the reviewing court's authoritative interpretation of the law should bind arbitrators as much as it now binds administrative agencies and lower courts. For example, if an arbitration decision in regard to a sexual harassment claim fails to grasp and apply the standard set for such claims by the Supreme Court, the reviewing court must overturn the arbitration decision as inconsistent with current law. . . .

TASK FORCE ON ALTERNATIVE DISPUTE RESOLUTION IN EMPLOYMENT, DUE PROCESS PROTOCOL

(1995)*

A Due Process Protocol for Mediation and Arbitration of Statutory Disputes Arising Out of the Employment Relationship

A. PRE- OR POST-DISPUTE ARBITRATION

The Task Force takes no position on the timing of agreements to mediate and/or arbitrate statutory employment disputes, though it agrees that such agreements be knowingly made. The focus of this Protocol is on standards of exemplary due process.

B. RIGHT OF REPRESENTATION

1. Choice of Representative

Employees considering the use of or, in fact, utilizing mediation and/or arbitration procedures should have the right to be represented by a spokesperson

*The Task Force on Alternative Dispute Resolution in Employment was composed of representatives of the American Arbitration Association, American Bar Association, American Civil Liberties Union, Federal Mediation and Conciliation Service, National Academy of Arbitrators, National Employment Lawyers Association, and the Society of Professionals in Dispute Resolution.

of their own choosing. The mediation and arbitration procedure should so specify and should include reference to institutions which might offer assistance, such as bar associations, legal service associations, civil rights organizations, trade unions, etc.

2. Fees for Representation

The amount and method of payment for representation should be determined between the claimant and the representative. We recommend, however, a number of existing systems which provide employer reimbursement of at least a portion of the employee's attorney fees, especially for lower paid employees. The arbitrator should have the authority to provide for fee reimbursement, in whole or in part, as part of the remedy in accordance with applicable law or in the interests of justice. . . .

3. Access to Information

One of the advantages of arbitration is that there is usually less time and money spent in pre-trial discovery. Adequate but limited pre-trial discovery is to be encouraged and employees should have access to all information reasonably relevant to mediation and/or arbitration of their claims. The employees' representative should also have reasonable pre-hearing and hearing access to all such information and documentation.

Necessary pre-hearing depositions consistent with the expedited nature of arbitration should be available.

We also recommend that prior to selection of an arbitrator, each side should be provided with the names, addresses and phone numbers of the representatives of the parties in that arbitrator's six most recent cases to aid them in selection.

C. MEDIATOR AND ARBITRATOR QUALIFICATION

1. Roster Membership

Mediators and arbitrators selected for such cases should have skill in the conduct of hearings, knowledge of the statutory issues at stake in the dispute, and familiarity with the workplace and employment environment. The roster of available mediators and arbitrators should be established on a non-discriminatory basis, diverse by gender, ethnicity, background, experience, etc., to satisfy the parties that their interests and objectives will be respected and fully considered. . . .

2. Training

The creation of a roster containing the foregoing qualifications dictates the development of a training program to educate existing and potential labor and employment mediators and arbitrators as to the statutes, including substantive, procedural and remedial issues to be confronted, and to train experts in the statutes as to employer procedures governing the employment relationship as well as due process and fairness in the conduct and control of arbitration hearings and mediation sessions. . . .

3. *Panel Selection*

Upon request of the parties, the designating agency should utilize a list procedure such as that of the AAA or select a panel composed of an odd number of mediators and arbitrators from its roster or pool. The panel cards for such individuals should be submitted to the parties for their perusal prior to alternate striking of the names on the list, resulting in the designation of the remaining mediator and/or arbitrator.

The selection process could empower the designating agency to appoint a mediator and/or arbitrator if the striking procedure is unacceptable or unsuccessful. As noted above, subject to the consent of the parties, the designating agency should provide the names of the parties and their representatives in recent cases decided by the listed arbitrators.

4. *Conflicts of Interest*

The mediator and arbitrator for a case has a duty to disclose any relationship which might reasonably constitute or be perceived as a conflict of interest. . . .

5. *Authority of the Arbitrator*

The arbitrator should be bound by applicable agreements, statutes, regulations and rules of procedure of the designating agency, including the authority to determine the time and place of the hearing, permit reasonable discovery, issue subpoenas, decide arbitrability issues, preserve order and privacy in the hearings, rule on evidentiary matters, determine the close of the hearing and procedures for post-hearing submissions, and issue an award resolving the submitted dispute.

The arbitrator should be empowered to award whatever relief would be available in court under the law. The arbitrator should issue an opinion and award setting forth a summary of the issues, including the type(s) of dispute(s), the damages and/or other relief requested and awarded, a statement of any other issues resolved, and a statement regarding the disposition of any statutory claim(s).

6. *Compensation of the Mediator and Arbitrator*

Impartiality is best assured by the parties sharing the fees and expenses of the mediator and arbitrator. In cases where the economic condition of a party does not permit equal sharing, the parties should make mutually acceptable arrangements to achieve that goal if at all possible. In the absence of such agreement, the arbitrator should determine allocation of fees. The designating agency, by negotiating the parties' share of costs and collecting such fees, might be able to reduce the bias potential of disparate contributions by forwarding payment to the mediator and/or arbitrator without disclosing the parties' share therein.

D. SCOPE OF REVIEW

The arbitrator's award should be final and binding and the scope of review should be limited.*

A different approach to assuring a fair nonjudicial tribunal for dealing with statutory claims was adopted by the parties to *Cremin v. Merrill Lynch, Pierce, Fenner & Smith, Inc.*, 957 F. Supp. 1460 (N.D. Ill. 1997), a class action alleging sexual discrimination by Merrill Lynch in violation of Title VII. In settlement of that case, the parties agreed that the individual claims of class members would be resolved in a three-step procedure designed by the parties.

Step 1 is to consist of negotiations between Merrill and the claimant. Claims not settled at step 1 are to go to step 2, which is mediation between Merrill and the claimant, with the mediators to be jointly agreed on. Claims not resolved at step 2 go to a step 3 arbitration procedure (referred to by the parties as a "third stage hearing"). If the claim is "complex" (a determination to be made by the mediator), it is to be heard by three arbitrators, all of whom are to be selected by the parties, at least one of whom must be female, and at least two of whom must be knowledgeable in Title VII law. The arbitrators are to follow all applicable law, including the Federal Rules of Evidence, albeit with some exceptions. There are provisions for limited discovery, for written decisions and awards, and for limited judicial review pursuant to the standards of §10 of the FAA.

A similar procedure was adopted in the settlement of another class action sexual discrimination suit, *Martens v. Smith Barney, Inc.*, No. 96 Civ. 3779, 2002 WL 867666 (S.D.N.Y. May 3, 2002). In that procedure all arbitrations are to be heard by three arbitrators, at least one of whom must be female, one must be knowledgeable about alternative dispute resolution, and two must be knowledgeable about employment-related claims.†

COLE v. BURNS INTERNATIONAL SECURITY SERVICES

105 F.3d 1465 (D.C. Cir. 1997)

EDWARDS, Chief Judge.

I. SUMMARY OF OPINION

This case raises important issues regarding whether and to what extent a person can be required, *as a condition of employment*, to (1) waive all rights to a trial by jury in

*The Due Process Protocol has met with substantial approval and adoption. Both the American Arbitration Association and Jams/Endispute adopted it and reserved the right to refuse to administer cases in a dispute resolution system that does not meet the standards of the Due Process Protocol. In August 1997, the NASD, whose arbitration agreement was similar to that at issue in *Gilmer*, proposed, subject to Securities and Exchange Commission (SEC) approval, to require that all arbitration agreements meet standards similar to those of the Due Process Protocol.

The notion of formulating a due process protocol has also spread to other areas, with the recent formulation of such protocols in the consumer and health care fields.

†These settlements represent examples of dispute systems design. See generally Chapter 5, Section B.

a court of competent jurisdiction with respect to any dispute relating to recruitment, employment, or termination, including claims involving laws against discrimination, and (2) sign an agreement providing that, at the employer's option, any such employment disputes must be arbitrated. At its core, this appeal challenges the enforceablity of conditions of employment requiring individuals to arbitrate claims resting on statutory rights. The issues at hand bring into focus the seminal decision of *Gilmer v. Interstate Johnson Lane Corp.*, and call into question the limits of the Supreme Court's holdings in that case.

II. Background

Clinton Cole used to work as a security guard at Union Station in Washington, D.C. for a company called LaSalle and Partners ("LaSalle"). In 1991, Burns Security took over LaSalle's contract to provide security at Union Station and required all LaSalle employees to sign a "Pre-Dispute Resolution Agreement" in order to obtain employment with Burns. . . .

In October 1993, Burns Security fired Cole. After filing charges with the Equal Employment Opportunity Commission, Cole filed the instant complaint in the United States District Court for the District of Columbia, alleging racial discrimination, harassment based on race, retaliation for his writing a letter of complaint regarding sexual harassment of a subordinate employee by another supervisor at Burns, and intentional infliction of emotional distress. Burns moved to compel arbitration of the dispute and to dismiss Cole's complaint pursuant to the terms of the contract.

III. Discussion

B. The Enforceablity of Conditions of Employment Requiring Individual Employees to Arbitrate Claims Resting on Statutory Rights

. . . In order to properly consider the validity of the arbitration agreement in this case, it is crucial to emphasize the distinction between arbitration in the context of collective bargaining and mandatory arbitration of *statutory claims* outside of the context of a union contract. These are vastly different situations, involving very different considerations. Arbitration in collective bargaining has a rich tradition in the United States, and a plethora of case law to support it. Arbitration of statutory claims, however, is the proverbial "new kid on the block," mostly an attempt to reduce the burdens and expenses of formal litigation. And arbitration of statutory claims is hardly legendary, for it is not only a new idea, but it comes in no clear form, and it has many detractors. Not surprisingly, because traditional labor arbitration is so celebrated in the United States, it is easy for the uninitiated to fall prey to the suggestion that the legal precepts governing the enforcement and review of arbitration emanating from collective bargaining should be equally applicable to arbitration of *all* employment disputes. This is a mischievous idea, one that we categorically reject.

1. *The Role of Arbitration: Collective Bargaining and Statutory Claims Distinguished*

Whereas an arbitrator serves as an agent or "alter ego" for the parties to a collective bargaining agreement, an arbitrator who resolves statutory claims serves simply as a private judge. Yet, unlike a judge, an arbitrator is neither publicly chosen nor publicly accountable.

Arbitration of public law issues is also troubling, on a less abstract level, because the structural protections inherent in the collective bargaining context are not duplicated in cases involving mandatory arbitration of individual statutory claims. Unlike the labor case, in which both union and employer are regular participants in the arbitration process, only the employer is a repeat player in cases involving individual statutory claims. As a result, the employer gains some advantage in having superior knowledge with respect to selection of an arbitrator.

Additionally, while a lack of public disclosure of arbitration awards is acceptable in the collective bargaining context, because both employers and unions monitor such decisions and the awards rarely involve issues of concern to persons other than the parties, in the context of individual statutory claims, a lack of public disclosure may systematically favor companies over individuals. Judicial decisions create binding precedent that prevents a recurrence of statutory violations; it is not clear that arbitral decisions have any such preventive effect. The unavailability of arbitral decisions also may prevent potential plaintiffs from locating the information necessary to build a case of intentional misconduct or to establish a pattern or practice of discrimination by particular companies.

Furthermore, as in the instant case, mandatory arbitration agreements in individual employees' contracts often are presented on a take-it-or-leave-it basis; there is no union to negotiate the terms of the arbitration arrangement. . . .

Finally, the competence of arbitrators to analyze and decide purely legal issues in connection with statutory claims has been questioned. Many arbitrators are not lawyers, and they have not traditionally engaged in the same kind of legal analysis performed by judges. . . .

2. *The Validity of the Agreement to Arbitrate in This Case*

The starting point of our analysis is the Supreme Court's decision in *Gilmer*. In that case, the Court held that an employee's agreement to arbitrate employment-related disputes may require him to arbitrate statutory claims under the ADEA because "[b]y agreeing to arbitrate a statutory claim, [an employee] does not forgo the substantive rights afforded by the statute; [he] only submits to their resolution in an arbitral, rather than a judicial, forum." As noted above, the Court emphasized that "so long as the prospective litigant effectively may vindicate [his or her] statutory cause of action in the arbitral forum, the statute will continue to serve both its remedial and deterrent function." . . .

Obviously, *Gilmer* cannot be read as holding that an arbitration agreement is enforceable no matter what rights it waives or what burdens it imposes. Such a holding would be fundamentally at odds with our understanding of the rights accorded to persons protected by public statutes like the ADEA and Title VII. The beneficiaries of public statutes are entitled to the rights and protections provided by the law. Clearly, it would be unlawful for an employer to condition employment on an employee's agreement to give up the right to be free from racial or gender discrimination. . . .

Similarly, an employee cannot be required as a condition of employment to waive access to a neutral forum in which statutory employment discrimination claims may be heard. For example, an employee could not be required to sign an agreement waiving the right to bring Title VII claims in any forum. . . .

We believe that all of the factors addressed in *Gilmer* are satisfied here. In particular, we note that the arbitration arrangement (1) provides for neutral arbitrators, (2) provides for more than minimal discovery, (3) requires a written award, (4) provides for all of the types of relief that would otherwise be available in court, and (5) does not require employees to pay either unreasonable costs *or* any arbitrators' fees or expenses as a condition of access to the arbitration forum. Thus, an employee who is made to use arbitration as a condition of employment "effectively may vindicate [his or her] statutory cause of action in the arbitral forum." . . .

3. The Obligation to Pay Arbitrators' Fees

Although we find that the disputed arbitration agreement is legally valid, there is one point that requires amplification. The arbitration agreement in this case presents an issue not raised by the agreement in *Gilmer:* can an employer condition employment on acceptance of an arbitration agreement that requires the employee to submit his or her statutory claims to arbitration and then requires the employee to pay all or part of the arbitrators' fees? This was not an issue in *Gilmer* (and other like cases), because, under NYSE Rules and NASD Rules, it is standard practice in the securities industry for employers to pay all of the arbitrators' fees. Employees may be required to pay a filing fee, expenses, or an administrative fee, but these expenses are routinely waived in the event of financial hardship.

Thus, in *Gilmer*, the Supreme Court endorsed a system of arbitration in which employees are not required to pay for the arbitrator assigned to hear their statutory claims. There is no reason to think that the Court would have approved arbitration in the absence of this arrangement. Indeed, we are unaware of any situation in American jurisprudence in which a beneficiary of a federal statute has been required to pay for the services of the judge assigned to hear her or his case. Under *Gilmer*, arbitration is supposed to be a reasonable substitute for a judicial forum. Therefore, it would undermine Congress's intent to prevent employees who are seeking to vindicate statutory rights from gaining access to a judicial forum and then require them to pay for the services of an arbitrator when they would never be required to pay for a judge in court.

There is no doubt that parties appearing in federal court may be required to assume the cost of filing fees and other administrative expenses, so any reasonable costs of this sort that accompany arbitration are not problematic.[2] However, if an

2. Even if an employee is not required to pay any portion of an arbitrator's fee, arbitration in a program such as the one administered by AAA is hardly inexpensive. Under the AAA plan, Cole could be required to pay a filing fee of $500.00 (as compared with the $120.00 filing fee that he paid to pursue his claim in District Court), administrative fees of $150.00 per day, room rental fees, and court reporter fees (and, of course, attorneys' fees, if he employs an attorney). The filing fee and other administrative

employee like Cole is required to pay arbitrators' fees ranging from $500 to $1,000 per day *or more,* in addition to administrative and attorneys' fees, is it likely that he will be able to pursue his statutory claims? We think not. . . .

Arbitration will occur in this case only because it has been mandated by the employer as a condition of employment. Absent this requirement, the employee would be free to pursue his claims in court without having to pay for the services of a judge. In such a circumstance—where arbitration has been imposed by the employer and occurs only at the option of the employer—arbitrators' fees should be borne solely by the employer.

Some commentators have suggested that it would be a perversion of the arbitration process to have the arbitrator paid by only one party to the dispute. We fail to appreciate the basis for this concern. If an arbitrator is likely to "lean" in favor of an employer—something we have no reason to suspect—it would be because the employer is a source of future arbitration business, and not because the employer alone pays the arbitrator. It is doubtful that arbitrators care about who pays them, so long as they are paid for their services.

Furthermore, there are several protections against the possibility of arbitrators systematically favoring employers because employers are the source of future business. For one thing, it is unlikely that such corruption would escape the scrutiny of plaintiffs' lawyers or appointing agencies like AAA. Corrupt arbitrators will not survive long in the business. In addition, wise employers and their representatives should see no benefit in currying the favor of corrupt arbitrators, because this will simply invite increased judicial review of arbitral judgments. Finally, if the arbitrators who are assigned to hear and decide statutory claims adhere to the professional and ethical standards set by arbitrators in the context of collective bargaining, there is little reason for concern. In this sense, the rich tradition of arbitration in collective bargaining *does* serve as a valuable model.

In sum, we hold that Cole could not be required to agree to arbitrate his public law claims as a condition of employment if the arbitration agreement required him to pay all or part of the arbitrator's fees and expenses. In light of this holding, we find that the arbitration agreement in this case is valid and enforceable. We do so because we interpret the agreement as requiring Burns Security to pay all of the arbitrator's fees necessary for a full and fair resolution of Cole's statutory claims.

4. Judicial Review

The final issue in this case concerns the scope of judicial review of arbitral awards in cases of this sort, where an employee is compelled as a condition of employment to arbitrate statutory claims. Cole has argued that the arbitration agreement is unconscionable, because any arbitrator's rulings, even as to the meaning of public law under Title VII, will not be subject to judicial review. Cole is wrong on this point.

Judicial review of arbitration awards covering statutory claims is necessarily focused, but that does not mean that meaningful review is unavailable. The FAA

fees imposed by AAA may be reduced or deferred in cases of hardship. See AAA Rule 35. Because Cole has not challenged the administrative fees charged by AAA, we do not address whether the AAA's refusal to waive filing and other administrative fees could preclude enforcement of an arbitration agreement. We assume, for purposes of this case, that employees who would qualify for in forma pauperis status in the federal courts will similarly qualify for a waiver of fees under the AAA Rules.

itself recognizes a number of grounds on which arbitration awards may be vacated. . . .

The Supreme Court has also indicated that arbitration awards can be vacated if they are in "manifest disregard of the law." Although this term has not been defined by the Court, and the circuits have adopted various formulations,[22] we believe that this type of review must be defined by reference to the assumptions underlying the Court's endorsement of arbitration. As discussed above, the strict deference accorded to arbitration decisions in the collective bargaining arena may not be appropriate in statutory cases in which an employee has been forced to resort to arbitration as a condition of employment. Rather, in this statutory context, the "manifest disregard of law" standard must be defined in light of the bases underlying the Court's decisions in *Gilmer*-type cases.

Two assumptions have been central to the Court's decisions in this area. First, the Court has insisted that, " '[b]y agreeing to arbitrate a statutory claim, a party does not forego the substantive rights afforded by the statute; it only submits to their resolution in an arbitral, rather than a judicial, forum.' " Second, the Court has stated repeatedly that, " 'although judicial scrutiny of arbitration awards necessarily is limited, such review is sufficient to ensure that arbitrators comply with the requirements of the statute at issue.' " These twin assumptions regarding the arbitration of statutory claims are valid only if judicial review under the "manifest disregard of the law" standard is sufficiently rigorous to ensure that arbitrators have properly interpreted and applied statutory law.

The value and finality of an employer's arbitration system will not be undermined by focused review of arbitral legal determinations. Most employment discrimination claims are entirely factual in nature and involve well-settled legal principles. . . . As a result, in the vast majority of cases, judicial review of legal determinations to ensure compliance with public law should have no adverse impact on the arbitration process. Nonetheless, there will be some cases in which novel or difficult legal issues are presented demanding judicial judgment. In such cases, the courts are empowered to review an arbitrator's award to ensure that its resolution of public law issues is correct. . . . Because meaningful judicial review of public law issues is available, Cole's agreement to arbitrate is not unconscionable or otherwise unenforceable.

Karen LeCraft HENDERSON, Circuit Judge, concurring in part and dissenting in part:

By conditioning arbitration on the employer's assumption of arbitrator costs, the majority engages in pure judicial fee shifting which finds no support in the FAA, *Gilmer*, or the parties' agreement, not one of which addresses arbitration fee allocation. Yet, relying on this very silence, the majority now declares that the

22. See, e.g., *Advest, Inc. v. McCarthy*, 914 F.2d 6, 8-9 (1st Cir. 1990) (to set aside award for manifest disregard of law, challenger must show award is "(1) unfounded in reason and fact; (2) based on reasoning so palpably faulty that no judge, or group of judges, ever could conceivably have made such a ruling; or (3) mistakenly based on a crucial assumption that is concededly a non-fact."); *Merrill Lynch, Pierce, Fenner & Smith, Inc. v. Jaros*, 70 F.3d 418, 421 (6th Cir. 1995) (award is in manifest disregard of law if "(1) the applicable legal principle is clearly defined and not subject to reasonable debate; and (2) the arbitrators refused to heed that legal principle."); *Health Servs. Mgmt. Corp. v. Hughes*, 975 F.2d 1253, 1267 (7th Cir. 1992) (award is in manifest disregard of law if arbitrator deliberately disregards what he or she knows to be the law).

employer must bear the costs, regardless of the outcome or the merits of the parties' positions, because of the majority's own speculation on what the arbitration costs will be and who will be required to pay them.

Questions

4.18 Paragraph B3 of the Due Process Protocol recommends that prior to the selection of an arbitrator, each side should be provided with information enabling it to contact the representatives of the parties in the arbitrator's six most recent cases. If you were representing the employee, is there any other information that you would like about the arbitrator's prior cases?

4.19 The Due Process Protocol is not limited to the arbitration of statutory disputes arising out of the employment relationship, but applies equally to the mediation of such disputes. What is the value of mediation in a case turning on the interpretation and application of a federal statute?

4.20 The state of Arkabama has a statute that requires all employment disputes to be sent to mediation by a court-appointed mediator prior to such disputes being litigated. The statute also provides that the mediator's fee is to be shared equally by the parties. Does the decision in *Cole* provide a basis for an employee to refuse to pay his share of the mediator's fee?

(1) Arbitration Costs

(a) Arbitrator's Fees

In determining whether an arbitration agreement is unconscionable, courts typically examine the overall fairness of the agreement. Part of the determination of overall fairness turns on whether the agreement requires the plaintiff to pay part of the arbitrator's fees. The *Cole* court suggested that such an arrangement would be unacceptable; the Due Process Protocol, by contrast, suggests that it is appropriate for an employee to pay part of the arbitrator's fees although it recommends that the employer pay for all fees if the employee is "lower paid." The California Supreme Court in *Armendariz v. Foundation Health Psychcare Services, Inc.*, 24 Cal. 4th 83, 102 (Cal. 2000), stated that an arbitration agreement is unenforceable if it requires employees to pay either "unreasonable costs or any arbitrator's fees or expenses as a condition of access to the arbitration forum." See also *Parilla v. IAP Worldwide Svcs., VI, Inc.*, 368 F.3d 269, 283-285 (3d Cir. 2004) ("loser pays" provision in arbitration agreement may be unconscionable); *Maciejewski v. Alpha Systems Lab, Inc.*, No. 6021588, 2002 WL 31888782, unreported (Dec. 30, 2002) (appeals court refuses to enforce agreement requiring arbitration of age and race discrimination claims because requirement that employee pay half of the arbitrators' fees is unconscionable); but see *Zumpano v. Omnipoint Communications,* No. CIV.A.00-CV-595, 2001 WL 43781 (E.D. Pa. Jan. 18, 2001) (arbitration agreement that may require employee to pay part of arbitrator's fees and expenses not per se unconscionable). Twin concerns appear to drive the jurisprudence on this issue.

First, courts hold that the arbitrator's fees and the costs of the arbitration should be proportional to the value of the claim at issue. Second, courts recognize that in court proceedings litigants do not have to pay the judge's fees or high filing fees. See *Irwin v. UBS Paine Webber, Inc.*, 324 F. Supp. 2d, 1103, 1108-1109 (C.D. Cal. 2004) (arbitration fees are unconscionable because more expensive than filing suit in federal court); but see *Rosenberg v. Merrill Lynch, Pierce, Fenner & Smith, Inc.*, 170 F.3d 1 (1st Cir. 1999) (court rejected employee's contention that arbitration agreement was unconscionable because it might subject him to forum fees as high as $3,000 per day); *Bradford v. Rockwell Semiconductor Systems*, 238 F.3d 549 (4th Cir. 2001) (arbitration agreement requiring employee and employer to share arbitration fees and costs is not per se unconscionable; court could conduct case-by-case analysis to determine whether the employee is able to pay the fees and costs and whether litigation costs would deter the employee from bringing a claim in court).

What happens when the parties' agreement is silent on the issue of who bears the costs of the arbitral process? In *Green Tree Financial Corp.-Alabama v. Randolph*, 531 U.S. 79 (2000), the Court considered whether Randolph, who had signed an arbitration agreement when she financed the purchase of a mobile home through Green Tree Financial, was obligated to arbitrate her Truth in Lending Act (TILA) and Equal Credit Opportunity Act claims. The Court concluded that she was, and rejected her argument that the arbitration agreement's silence with respect to payment of filing fees, arbitrators' costs, and other arbitration expenses rendered the agreement unenforceable. The Court stated:

> In determining whether statutory claims may be arbitrated, we first ask whether the parties agreed to submit their claims to arbitration, and then ask whether Congress has evinced an intention to preclude a waiver of judicial remedies for the statutory rights at issue. See *Gilmer*, 111 S. Ct. 1647; *Mitsubishi*, 105 S. Ct. 3346. In this case, it is undisputed that the parties agreed to arbitrate all claims relating to their contract, including claims involving statutory rights. Nor does Randolph contend that the TILA evinces an intention to preclude a waiver of judicial remedies. She contends instead that the arbitration agreement's silence with respect to costs and fees creates a "risk" that she will be required to bear prohibitive arbitration costs if she pursues her claims in an arbitral forum, and thereby forces her to forgo any claims she may have against petitioners. Therefore, she argues, she is unable to vindicate her statutory rights in arbitration.
>
> It may well be that the existence of large arbitration costs could preclude a litigant such as Randolph from effectively vindicating her federal statutory rights in the arbitral forum. But the record does not show that Randolph will bear such costs if she goes to arbitration. Indeed, it contains hardly any information on the matter. As the Court of Appeals recognized, "we lack . . . information about how claimants fare under Green Tree's arbitration clause." The record reveals only the arbitration agreement's silence on the subject, and that fact alone is plainly insufficient to render it unenforceable. The "risk" that Randolph will be saddled with prohibitive costs is too speculative to justify the invalidation of an arbitration agreement.
>
> To invalidate the agreement on that basis would undermine the "liberal federal policy favoring arbitration agreements." *Moses H. Cone Memorial Hospital*, 460 U.S., at 24. We have held that the party seeking to avoid arbitration bears the burden of establishing that Congress intended to preclude arbitration of the statutory claims at issue. See *Gilmer*, supra; *McMahon*, supra. Similarly, we believe that where, as here, a party seeks to invalidate an arbitration agreement on the ground that arbitration would be prohibitively

> expensive, that party bears the burden of showing the likelihood of incurring such costs. Randolph did not meet that burden. How detailed the showing of prohibitive expense must be before the party seeking arbitration must come forward with contrary evidence is a matter we need not discuss; for in this case neither during discovery nor when the case was presented on the merits was there any timely showing at all on the point. The Court of Appeals therefore erred in deciding that the arbitration agreement's silence with respect to costs and fees rendered it unenforceable.[7]

Does it make sense for the Court to wait to rule on the question of whether the allocation of fees was proper until Randolph returns to court, following arbitration, if she contends that the ultimate cost allocation was prohibitively expensive? Does waiting serve the interest of judicial economy?

(b) Arbitration Filing Fees

Allocation of arbitration's filing fees continues to present problems for courts as well. Courts will refuse to enforce an arbitration agreement as unconscionable if the filing fees for the arbitration are excessive. A major case in this area is *Brower v. Gateway 2000, Inc.*, 676 N.Y.S.2d 569 (N.Y. App. Div. 1st Dept. 1998). In that case, a consumer purchasing a computer from Gateway had 30 days following the receipt of the computer to accept or reject the contract of sale. Among other documents accompanying the computer was an arbitration clause that specified the International Chamber of Commerce (ICC) as the arbitral provider. The ICC charged a $4,000 filing fee. The New York Appellate Court held that the filing fees were excessive and the contract was therefore unconscionable. Other courts have determined whether fees are excessive by comparing the amount of fees a plaintiff must pay to the value of the claim at stake. See, for example, *Shankle v. B-G Maintenance Management of Colorado, Inc.*, 163 F.3d 1230 (10th Cir. 1999) (arbitration agreement that requires lower-paid employee to pay half of the arbitrator's fees, which could run anywhere from $1,875 to $5,000, is unenforceable); *Myers v. Terminix Int'l Co.*, 697 N.E.2d 277 (Ohio Cm. Pl. 1998) (arbitration provision in service contract unenforceable because it would require homeowner to pay arbitration filing fee of $2,000 that was hundreds of dollars more than the amount of the underlying dispute). Courts have yet to agree on a formula for assessing when fees become excessive. Thus, allocation of arbitration fees continue to be evaluated on a case-by-case basis.

Questions

4.21 Electronics International, a major electronics retailer with 30,000 employees in the United States, hired Martha Grainger as a sales associate, at the rate of $12 per hour. At the time she began her employment, she signed an arbitration agreement that required her to pay half of the arbitrators' fee, currently

7. We decline to reach respondent's argument that we may affirm the Court of Appeals' conclusion that the arbitration agreement is unenforceable on the alternative ground that the agreement precludes respondent from bringing her claims under the TILA as a class action. [See p. 231.]

$700 per day, and all of the arbitration's filing fee, $400. Martha wants to file a sexual discrimination claim demanding $70,000, but wonders whether these fees and costs can be avoided. Does *Randolph* provide any guidance on the question of whether an employee or consumer should have to shoulder the expense of hiring arbitrators or paying filing fees? What if the Electronics International arbitration agreement stated that "the loser pays" for the arbitrator's fees and the arbitration costs? Is that less problematic? One response to the *Randolph* case came from a major arbitrator provider, the National Arbitration Forum (NAF). Anticipating the need for redistribution of costs in light of *Randolph,* the NAF Code of Procedure shifts in large part the fees for small claims cases involving a dispute between a company and a consumer from employees and consumers to the company or employer. The American Arbitration Association (AAA) subsequently followed suit, capping arbitrator's fees at $375 for consumer cases involving less than $75,000 (the consumer pays half of the fees) and shifting the administrative fees to the business.

4.22 While Judge Edwards requires the employer to pay all the arbitrator's fees as a condition to enforcing an agreement to arbitrate statutorily-based claims, both the Dunlop Commission Report and the Due Process Protocol are concerned that payment solely by the employer creates a risk of arbitrator bias. Are you persuaded that this risk is minimal?

(2) *Conscionability of the Arbitration Agreement*

Another concern that sometimes arises in cases involving mandatory arbitration agreements is whether both parties to the agreement have satisfied their contractual obligations. Perhaps the most egregious example of lack of good faith and fair dealing in forming a contract arose in the following case.

HOOTERS OF AMERICA, INC. v. PHILLIPS

173 F.3d 933 (4th Cir. 1999).

WILKINSON, Chief Judge:

I.

Appellee Annette R. Phillips worked as a bartender at a Hooters restaurant in Myrtle Beach, South Carolina. She was employed since 1989 by appellant Hooters of Myrtle Beach (HOMB). . . . Phillips alleges that in June 1996, Gerald Brooks, a Hooters official and the brother of HOMB's principal owner, sexually harassed her by grabbing and slapping her buttocks. After appealing to her manager for help and being told to "let it go," she quit her job. Phillips then contacted Hooters through an attorney claiming that the attack and the restaurant's failure to address it violated her Title VII rights. Hooters responded that she was required to submit her claims to arbitration according to a binding agreement to arbitrate between the parties.

This agreement arose in 1994 during the implementation of Hooters' alternative dispute resolution program. As part of that program, the company conditioned eligibility for raises, transfers, and promotions upon an employee signing an "Agreement to arbitrate employment-related disputes." The agreement provides that Hooters and the employee each agree to arbitrate all disputes arising out of employment, including "any claim of discrimination, sexual harassment, retaliation, or wrongful discharge, whether arising under federal or state law." The agreement further states that the employee and the company agree to resolve any claims pursuant to the company's rules and procedures for alternative resolution of employment-related disputes, as promulgated by the company from time to time ("the rules"). Company will make available or provide a copy of the rules upon written request of the employee.

The employees of HOMB were initially given a copy of this agreement at an all-staff meeting held on November 20, 1994. HOMB's general manager, Gene Fulcher, told the employees to review the agreement for five days and that they would then be asked to accept or reject the agreement. No employee, however, was given a copy of Hooters' arbitration rules and procedures. Phillips signed the agreement. . . .

In March 1998, the district court denied Hooters' motions to compel arbitration and stay proceedings on the counterclaims. The court found that there was no meeting of the minds on all of the material terms of the agreement and even if there were, Hooters' promise to arbitrate was illusory. In addition, the court found that the arbitration agreement was unconscionable and void for reasons of public policy. Hooters filed this interlocutory appeal, 9 U.S.C. §16. . . .

III.

Hooters argues that Phillips gave her assent to a bilateral agreement to arbitrate. That contract provided for the resolution by arbitration of all employment-related disputes, including claims arising under Title VII. Hooters claims the agreement to arbitrate is valid because Phillips twice signed it voluntarily. Thus, it argues the courts are bound to enforce it and compel arbitration.

We disagree. . . . In this case, the challenge goes to the validity of the arbitration agreement itself. Hooters materially breached the arbitration agreement by promulgating rules so egregiously unfair as to constitute a complete default of its contractual obligation to draft arbitration rules and to do so in good faith. . . .

The Hooters rules when taken as a whole . . . are so one-sided that their only possible purpose is to undermine the neutrality of the proceeding. The rules require the employee to provide the company notice of her claim at the outset, including "the nature of the Claim" and "the specific act(s) or omissions(s) which are the basis of the Claim." Hooters, on the other hand, is not required to file any responsive pleadings or to notice its defenses. Additionally, at the time of filing this notice, the employee must provide the company with a list of all fact witnesses with a brief summary of the facts known to each. The company, however, is not required to reciprocate.

The Hooters rules also provide a mechanism for selecting a panel of three arbitrators that is crafted to ensure a biased decision-maker. The employee and Hooters each select an arbitrator, and the two arbitrators in turn select a third. Good enough, except that the employee's arbitrator and the third arbitrator must be selected from a list of arbitrators created exclusively by Hooters. This gives Hooters control over the entire panel and places no limits whatsoever on whom Hooters can put on the list. Under the rules, Hooters is free to devise lists of partial arbitrators who have existing relationships, financial or familial, with Hooters and its management. In fact, the rules do not even prohibit Hooters from placing its managers themselves on the list. Further, nothing in the rules restricts Hooters from punishing arbitrators who rule against the company by removing them from the list. Given the unrestricted control that one party (Hooters) has over the panel, the selection of an impartial decision-maker would be a surprising result.

Nor is fairness to be found once the proceedings are begun. Although Hooters may expand the scope of arbitration to any matter, "whether related or not to the Employee's Claim," the employee cannot raise "any matter not included in the Notice of Claim." Similarly, Hooters is permitted to move for summary dismissal of employee claims before a hearing is held whereas the employee is not permitted to seek summary judgment. Hooters, but not the employee, may record the arbitration hearing "by audio or videotaping or by verbatim transcription." The rules also grant Hooters the right to bring suit in court to vacate or modify an arbitral award when it can show, by a preponderance of the evidence, that the panel exceeded its authority. No such right is granted to the employee.

In addition, the rules provide that upon 30 days notice Hooters, but not the employee, may cancel the agreement to arbitrate. Moreover, Hooters reserves the right to modify the rules, "in whole or in part," whenever it wishes and "without notice" to the employee. Nothing in the rules even prohibits Hooters from changing the rules in the middle of an arbitration proceeding. . . .

We hold that the promulgation of so many biased rules — especially the scheme whereby one party to the proceeding so controls the arbitral panel — breaches the contract entered into by the parties. The parties agreed to submit their claims to arbitration — a system whereby disputes are fairly resolved by an impartial third party. Hooters by contract took on the obligation of establishing such a system. By creating a sham system unworthy even of the name of arbitration, Hooters completely failed in performing its contractual duty. . . .

IV.

We respect fully the Supreme Court's pronouncement that "questions of arbitrability must be addressed with a healthy regard for the federal policy favoring arbitration." *Moses H. Cone,* 460 U.S. at 24. Our decision should not be misread: We are not holding that the agreement before us is unenforceable because the arbitral proceedings are too abbreviated. An arbitral forum need not replicate the judicial forum. . . .

Nor should our decision be misunderstood as permitting a full-scale assault on the fairness of proceedings before the matter is submitted to arbitration. Generally, objections to the nature of arbitral proceedings are for the arbitrator to decide in the first instance. Only after arbitration may a party then raise such challenges if they meet the narrow grounds set out in 9 U.S.C. §10 for vacating an arbitral award. In the case before us, we only reach the content of the arbitration rules because their promulgation was the duty of one party under the contract. The material breach of this duty warranting rescission is an issue of substantive arbitrability and thus is reviewable before arbitration. This case, however, is the exception that proves the rule: fairness objections should generally be made to the arbitrator, subject only to limited post-arbitration judicial review as set forth in section 10 of the FAA.

By promulgating this system of warped rules, Hooters so skewed the process in its favor that Phillips has been denied arbitration in any meaningful sense of the word. To uphold the promulgation of this aberrational scheme under the heading of arbitration would undermine, not advance, the federal policy favoring alternative dispute resolution. This we refuse to do. The judgment of the district court is affirmed, and the case is remanded for further proceedings consistent with this opinion.

Questions

4.23 What if Hooters contracted with a third party to provide arbitral services? Would an arbitration agreement between an employee and a third-party arbitration-services provider be enforceable? Should it matter if the entity is a for-profit rather than a not-for-profit organization such as the American Arbitration Association? For additional discussion of the third-party neutral's ethical obligations, see Section E of this chapter. What potential problems might there be with such an arrangement? What if the employees did not have to pay any portion of the arbitrator's fees or the costs of the arbitration? Would that make it more likely that a court would enforce the agreement?

4.24 What if the arbitration agreement stated that the employer "shall have the right to select an arbitrator" and "no arbitrator may be selected who shall have provided legal representational services to or for the employer at any time." The arbitration agreement further states that the employee has "knowingly, intelligently and voluntarily" signed it. See *Harold Allen's Mobile Home Factory Outlet, Inc. v. Butler*, 825 So. 2d 779 (Ala. 2002). Does *Hooters* provide guidance in answering this question?

Note on Unconscionability

While employees arguing that their waiver was neither knowing nor voluntary are rarely successful outside the Ninth Circuit, courts have been more receptive to challenges to the conscionability of arbitration agreements. *Gilmer* appeared to give employers license to institute mandatory arbitration agreements. As a result, employers began to adopt more and more restrictive agreements, culminating with agreements like the one at issue in *Hooters.* In response, courts have revived the unconscionability doctrine, appearing increasingly receptive to challenges that arbitration agreements are unconscionable. For example, in *Armendariz v. Foundation Health Psychare Services, Inc.*, 24 Cal. 4th 83 (2000), the California Supreme Court held that a provision mandating that the employee, but not the employer, arbitrate all claims arising from termination, was unconscionable. Judicial receptivity to the unconscionability arguments suggests that courts, at least in the arbitration area, may be stretching the unconscionability definition in order to invalidate arbitration agreements.

Typically, a court requires a party to show both procedural and substantive unconscionability before it will invalidate the agreement. Procedural unconscionability involves the contract formation process. If the agreement results from oppression or unfair surprise, it is procedurally unconscionable. Although oppression results from an inequality of bargaining power "which results in no real negotiation, and an absence of meaningful choice," see *Stirlen v. Supercuts, Inc.*, 51 Cal. App. 4th 1519 (Cal. Ct. App. 1997), the Supreme Court made clear in *Gilmer* that the inequality of bargaining power that exists between employers and employees is not sufficient to render an arbitration agreement unconscionable. The other factor, "unfair surprise," involves "the extent to which the supposedly agreed-upon terms of the bargain are hidden in the prolix printed form drafted by the party seeking to enforce the disputed terms." (*Stirlen*, 51 Cal. App. 4th at 1532.) The typical arbitration agreement, even though drafted by the employer or business, and appearing in small print within an employee handbook, does not rise to the level of procedural unconscionability.

Substantive unconscionability involves the actual terms of the agreement itself. To establish substantive unconscionability, the court requires a party to demonstrate that the terms are so one-sided as to "shock the conscience," or terms "so extreme as to appear unconscionable according to the mores and business practices of the time and place." (*Armendariz*, 80 Cal. Rptr. 2d at 266.) Thus, an arbitration agreement that strips an employee of substantive rights, would rise to the level of substantive unconscionability. *Hooters*, with its limitations on remedies and skewed arbitrator selection process, is an example of substantive unconscionability. Should an employee or consumer have to satisfy both the procedural and substantive unconscionability prongs in order to have an arbitration agreement invalidated? Is it possible to satisfy both prongs of this test? See *Brower v. Gateway 2000, Inc.*, 676 N.Y.S.2d 569, 574 (N.Y. App. Div. 1998) (despite lack of evidence of procedural unconscionability, court holds that excessive filing fees render arbitration agreement unconscionable); see also Broome (2006) (reporting that in California, courts are predisposed to finding arbitration agreements unconscionable). Some courts ignore the two-prong test, failing to mention unconscionability when deciding not to enforce an arbitration agreement because certain terms in the agreement are unfair to the party with less bargaining power. See *Cole v. Burns Int'l Sec. Serv.*, 105 F.3d 1465 (D.C. Cir. 1997) (court invalidates arbitration agreement because it requires employee to bear half the arbitrator's fees; no mention of unconscionability); *Shankle v. B-G Maintenance Management of Colorado, Inc.*, 163 F.3d 1230 (10th Cir. 1999) (same). For a more extensive discussion of unconscionability and pre-dispute arbitration agreements, see Fitzgibbon (2000) (advocating a finding of procedural unconscionability if pre-dispute arbitration agreement signed as condition of employment by lower-paid employee).

Notes and Questions

4.25 On remand from the Supreme Court's *Circuit City Stores Inc. v. Adams* decision interpreting the FAA to include within its scope arbitration agreements in employment contracts (see pp. 229-231), the Ninth Circuit substantively evaluated the arbitration agreement contained in Circuit City's employment application. The Ninth Circuit held that the agreement was unconscionable because it was not negotiable, obligated only the employee, but not the employer, to arbitrate claims, and required the employee to pay half of the arbitration's costs. *Circuit City Stores, Inc. v. Adams*, 279 F.3d 889 (9th Cir. 2002). In another Ninth Circuit case, the court held that inclusion of a 30-day opt-out provision in an arbitration agreement rendered that agreement enforceable because the agreement allows "employees a meaningful choice not to participate in the program." *Circuit City Stores, Inc. v. Ahmed*, 283 F.3d 1198, 1199 (9th Cir. 2002). In response to cases like this and to a recent report from Public Citizen, a consumer advocacy group, contending that arbitration can cost claimants considerably more than litigation, Senators Edward Kennedy and Russ Feingold (a long time champion of the anti-employment arbitration cause) introduced federal legislation designed to amend the FAA to make mandatory arbitration agreements unenforceable.

4.26 Enrand, Inc., an internet start-up company, requires its employees to sign an arbitration agreement on the first day of work. The agreement states that "all workplace disputes will be subject to arbitration. An arbitrator presiding over any workplace dispute may award damages for breach of contract and back pay only." Should such an agreement be enforceable? See *Hooters; Armendariz v. Foundation Health Psychcare Serv., Inc.*, 24 Cal. 4th 83 (Cal. 2000); *Paladino v. Avnet Computer Technologies, Inc.*, 134 F.3d 1054 (11th Cir. 1998). What if the arbitrator could award the same relief as a court except punitive damages?

4.27 Lowrey Petroleum, headquartered in Houston, Texas, mandates that all of its employees sign arbitration agreements as a condition of their employment. The agreement provides that "every claim, dispute or controversy, now existing or hereafter arising, known or unknown, shall be resolved by final and binding arbitration." Two Spanish-speaking employees, who could not read English at the time they began their employment at Lowrey, were recently injured in an explosion. Preferring court to the arbitral forum, they challenge the arbitration agreement on the ground that to enforce it would be unconscionable. What result?

4.28 Paige White began working at Olson Airlines in July 1995. She is a pilot and lives in Chicago, Illinois. She flies on primarily international flights. Olson Airlines is a corporation with headquarters in Chicago, Illinois. On the day she began work, she signed a form indicating receipt of a package of material including a form acknowledging receipt of an employee handbook, an employee handbook, and a form that allowed her to opt out of Olson's arbitration program. The opt-out form stated that failure to turn in a signed opt-out form within 30 days would mean the employee was automatically part of the arbitration program.

During several of her recent flights to Asia, her male co-pilot began making lewd suggestions to her. Among other things, he asked her whether she planned to share her hotel room with anyone once they arrived and whether she wanted to go to a bathhouse with him. He also grabbed and pinched her on several occasions. At the outset, she politely refused his requests and ignored his innuendo and assaults. Yet after enduring several flights during which her co-pilot assaulted and harassed her, she complained to the head of personnel at Olson. Olson did not respond to her claims, telling her to "let it go." Believing she had a good case for a claim of sexual harassment under Title VII, she filed a claim with the EEOC in Chicago. After 180 days, the EEOC issued her a right to sue letter, and she filed suit in district court in Chicago, claiming sexual harassment due to a hostile working environment.

Olson moved to compel arbitration of the claim under 9 U.S.C. §4, citing the arbitration agreement Paige signed during the course of her employment.

Paige does not wish to go to arbitration. She has heard that plaintiffs obtain higher monetary awards in court, and she wants to embarrass the company publicly. She would like to know whether she might successfully challenge the validity of the arbitration agreement. She has told us that she signed the acknowledgment form and received the handbook, but never reviewed it. She also remembers receiving the opt-out form, but she did not realize that she had only 30 days to return it. She never returned it.

The employee handbook, which was 200 pages long, contained, among other provisions, the following:

> **Arbitration Clause:** Employees will resolve any and all claims arising out of their employment with Olson Airlines by final and binding arbitration before a panel of three (3) arbitrators. Such claims include, but are not limited to, the Age Discrimination in Employment Act, Title VII of the Civil Rights Act of 1964, as amended, including the amendments of the Civil Rights Act of 1991.
>
> **Arbitrator Selection Process:** Disputes between employees and Olson Airlines will be resolved by a panel of three arbitrators. The employee will select one arbitrator, and Olson Airlines will select the second arbitrator. The third arbitrator will be selected by the first two appointed arbitrators from a list of Olson employees who have volunteered to act as arbitrators to resolve employment disputes.
>
> **Damages Provisions:** Under this agreement, arbitrators are limited to awarding prevailing plaintiffs compensatory damages only. This agreement expressly prohibits the award of injunctive, equitable or punitive relief.
>
> **Final and Binding:** Arbitration of any dispute brought by an employee against Olson Airlines will result in a final and binding determination of that dispute.

Will Paige be successful in avoiding arbitration of her claims? What are her best arguments?

4.29 Le Chateau, a French restaurant in Columbus, Ohio, recently contacted you and requested that you help them draft a dispute resolution clause that they can include in their employee handbook. Le Chateau has 50 employees. These employees are primarily waiters and waitresses, dishwashers, and cooks. Le Chateau has significant employee turnover and, in the past five years, has been sued twice for race discrimination and once for disability discrimination. All three claims were resolved through the EEOC mediation program. Even though they were resolved early, Le Chateau had significant expenditures for attorneys' fees and for the company time needed to develop a record to support Le Chateau's personnel decisions. Moreover, Le Chateau is afraid that this may be the tip of the iceberg and that, in the future, it will not be able to settle claims through the EEOC mediation process. While not wedded to including an arbitration clause, they have heard that arbitration is cheaper, more efficient, and more confidential than litigation. They would like you to advise them about the propriety of including an arbitration clause and rules governing the arbitration process in their existing employee handbook. Should Le Chateau make use of employment arbitration? What options should it consider? What are consequences of each option from a legal and business perspective? Draft an arbitration agreement for Le Chateau.

c. The Impact of Arbitration Agreements on the EEOC's Continuing Role in Employment Discrimination Cases

One of the questions remaining after *Gilmer* was what impact the existence of an arbitration agreement would have on the EEOC's ability to enforce federal anti-discrimination laws. The *Gilmer* Court acknowledged concern about the effect of its decision on the EEOC's efforts to eradicate workplace discrimination, but concluded that its decision would have a minimal impact on the EEOC for two reasons. First, the EEOC would continue to play a role in discrimination cases because arbitration agreements do not preclude an employee from filing a claim with the EEOC. Second, the existence of an arbitration agreement would have no effect on the EEOC's ability to seek class-wide and injunctive relief on behalf of claimants. Unfortunately, the *Gilmer* decision did not address whether the existence of an arbitration agreement would preclude the EEOC from pursuing monetary relief on behalf of the claimant.

The Supreme Court addressed the issue over 10 years later in *EEOC v. Waffle House, Inc.*

EEOC v. WAFFLE HOUSE, INC.

534 U.S. 279 (2002)

Stevens, Justice delivered the opinion of the Court.

The question presented is whether an agreement between an employer and an employee to arbitrate employment-related disputes bars the Equal Employment Opportunity Commission (EEOC) from pursuing victim-specific judicial relief, such as backpay, reinstatement, and damages, in an enforcement action alleging that the employer has violated Title I of the Americans with Disabilities Act of 1990 (ADA).

[Eric Baker agreed to arbitrate any dispute arising out of his employment at Waffle House. While at work, Baker suffered a seizure. Soon after, he was discharged. Instead of filing a claim in arbitration, Baker filed with the EEOC. The EEOC decided to pursue his case, including a claim for victim-specific relief. The Fourth Circuit rejected the EEOC's claim, authorizing the EEOC to pursue only injunctive or equitable relief on behalf of an employee who had signed an arbitration agreement.]

IV.

The Court of Appeals based its decision on its evaluation of the "competing policies" implemented by the ADA and the FAA, rather than on any language in the text of either the statutes or the arbitration agreement between Baker and respondent. It recognized that the EEOC never agreed to arbitrate its statutory claim and that the EEOC has "independent statutory authority" to vindicate the public interest, but opined that permitting the EEOC to prosecute Baker's claim in court "would significantly trample" the strong federal policy favoring arbitration because Baker had agreed to submit his claim to arbitration. To effectuate this policy, the court distinguished between injunctive and victim-specific relief, and held that the EEOC is barred from obtaining the latter because any public interest served when the EEOC pursues "make whole" relief is outweighed by the policy goals favoring arbitration. Only when the EEOC seeks broad injunctive relief, in the Court of Appeals' view, does the public interest overcome the goals underpinning the FAA. . . .

[The Court of Appeals] simply sought to balance the policy goals of the FAA against the clear language of Title VII and the agreement. While this may be a more coherent approach, it is inconsistent with our recent arbitration cases. The FAA directs courts to place arbitration agreements on equal footing with other contracts, but it "does not require parties to arbitrate when they have not agreed to do so." . . . No one asserts that the EEOC is a party to the contract, or that it agreed to arbitrate its claims. It goes without saying that a contract cannot bind a nonparty. Accordingly, the pro-arbitration policy goals of the FAA do not require the agency to relinquish its statutory authority if it has not agreed to do so.

Even if the policy goals underlying the FAA did necessitate some limit on the EEOC's statutory authority, the line drawn by the Court of Appeals between injunctive and victim-specific relief creates an uncomfortable fit with its avowed purpose of preserving the EEOC's public function while favoring arbitration. For that purpose, the category of victim-specific relief is both overinclusive and underinclusive. For example, it is overinclusive because while punitive damages benefit the individual employee, they also serve an obvious public function in deterring future violations. Punitive damages may often have a greater impact on the behavior of other employers than the threat of an injunction, yet the EEOC is precluded from seeking this form of relief under the Court of Appeals' compromise scheme. And, it is underinclusive because injunctive relief, although seemingly not "victim-specific," can be seen as more closely tied to the employee's injury than to any public interest.

The compromise solution reached by the Court of Appeals turns what is effectively a forum selection clause into a waiver of a nonparty's statutory remedies. But if the federal policy favoring arbitration trumps the plain language of Title VII and the contract, the EEOC should be barred from pursuing any claim outside the arbitral forum. If not, then the statutory language is clear; the EEOC has the authority to pursue victim-specific relief regardless of the forum that the employer and employee have chosen to resolve their disputes. Rather than attempt to split the difference, we are persuaded that, pursuant to Title VII and the ADA, whenever the EEOC chooses from among the many charges filed each year to bring an enforcement action in a particular case, the agency may be seeking to vindicate a public interest, not simply provide make-whole relief for the employee, even when it pursues entirely victim-specific relief. To hold otherwise would undermine the detailed enforcement scheme created by Congress simply to give greater effect to an agreement between private parties that does not even contemplate the EEOC's statutory function.

V.

It is true, as respondent and its *amici* have argued, that Baker's conduct may have the effect of limiting the relief that the EEOC may obtain in court. If, for example, he had failed to mitigate his damages, or had accepted a monetary settlement, any recovery by the EEOC would be limited accordingly. As we have noted, it "goes without saying that the courts can and should preclude double recovery by an individual." *General Telephone*, 446 U.S., at 333.

But no question concerning the validity of his claim or the character of the relief that could be appropriately awarded in either a judicial or an arbitral forum is presented by this record. Baker has not sought arbitration of his claim, nor is there any indication that he has entered into settlement negotiations with respondent. It is an open question whether a settlement or arbitration judgment would affect the validity of the EEOC's claim or the character of relief the EEOC may seek. The only issue before this Court is whether the fact that Baker has signed a mandatory arbitration agreement limits the remedies available to the EEOC. The text of the relevant statutes provides a clear answer to that question. They do not authorize the courts to balance the competing policies of the ADA and the FAA or to second-guess the agency's judgment concerning which of the remedies authorized by law that it shall seek in any given case. . . .

The judgment of the Court of Appeals is reversed, and the case is remanded for further proceedings consistent with this opinion.

Dissent by THOMAS, J., joined by REHNQUIST, C.J. and SCALIA, J.

B.

Not only would it be "inappropriate" for a court to allow the EEOC to obtain victim-specific relief on behalf of Baker, to do so in this case would contravene the "liberal federal policy favoring arbitration agreements" embodied in the FAA.

Under the terms of the FAA, Waffle House's arbitration agreement with Baker is valid and enforceable. The Court reasons, however, that the FAA is not implicated in this case because the EEOC was not a party to the arbitration agreement and "[i]t goes without saying that a contract cannot bind a nonparty." The Court's analysis entirely misses the point. The relevant question here is not whether the EEOC should be bound by Baker's agreement to arbitrate. Rather, it is whether a court should give effect to the arbitration agreement between Waffle House and Baker or whether it should instead allow the EEOC to reduce that arbitration agreement to all but a nullity. I believe that the FAA compels the former course.

By allowing the EEOC to pursue victim-specific relief on behalf of Baker under these circumstances, the Court eviscerates Baker's arbitration agreement with Waffle House and liberates Baker from the consequences of his agreement. Waffle House gains nothing and, if anything, will be worse off in cases where the EEOC brings an enforcement action should it continue to utilize arbitration agreements in the future. This is because it will face the prospect of defending itself in two different forums against two different parties seeking precisely the same relief. It could face the EEOC in court and the employee in an arbitral forum.

The Court does not decide here whether an arbitral judgment would "affect the validity of the EEOC's claim or the character of relief the EEOC may seek" in court. Given the reasoning in the Court's opinion, however, the proverbial handwriting is on the wall. If the EEOC indeed is "the master of its own case," I do not see how an employee's independent decision to pursue arbitral proceedings could affect the validity of the "EEOC's claim" in court. Should this Court in a later case determine that an unfavorable arbitral judgment against an employee precludes the EEOC from seeking similar relief for that employee in court, then the Court's jurisprudence will stand for the following proposition: The EEOC may seek relief for an employee who has signed an arbitration agreement unless that employee decides that he would rather abide by his agreement and arbitrate his claim. Reconciling such a result with the FAA, however, would seem to be an impossible task and would make a mockery of the rationale underlying the Court's holding here: that the EEOC is "the master of its own case."

Assuming that the Court means what it says, an arbitral judgment will not preclude the EEOC's claim for victim-specific relief from going forward, and courts will have to adjust damages awards to avoid double recovery. If an employee, for instance, is able to recover $20,000 through arbitration and a court later concludes in an action brought by the EEOC that the employee is actually entitled to $100,000 in damages, one assumes that a court would only award the EEOC an additional $80,000 to give to the employee. Suppose, however, that the situation is reversed: An arbitrator awards an employee $100,000, but a court later determines that the employee is only entitled to $20,000 in damages. Will the court be required to order the employee to return $80,000 to his employer? I seriously doubt it.

The Court's decision thus places those employers utilizing arbitration agreements at a serious disadvantage. Their employees will be allowed two bites at the apple — one in arbitration and one in litigation conducted by the EEOC — and will be able to benefit from the more favorable of the two rulings. This result, however, discourages the use of arbitration agreements and is thus completely inconsistent with the policies underlying the FAA.

Notes

Victim-specific relief when employee has arbitrated or settled his or her claim: On the issue of monetary relief, the Court acknowledged the lower courts' concern that plaintiffs might obtain double recovery — first through arbitration and then through EEOC-sponsored litigation. The Court made clear that plaintiffs should not be allowed double recovery by obtaining a favorable arbitration award and then receiving money from the EEOC as well. Yet because Baker did not pursue his claim in arbitration, the question remains open whether a settlement or arbitration award would adversely impact the validity of the EEOC's claim or the kind of relief the EEOC might seek. For example, if an employee received an arbitration award for $100,000, with $20,000 allocated for backpay and $80,000 in punitive damages, should the EEOC be permitted to pursue both backpay and punitive damages on the employee's behalf in subsequent litigation with a required offset for sums the employee already received? Or, should the EEOC be barred from bringing a claim because the employee has vindicated her rights in another forum? Another post-*Waffle House* issue might occur as follows: suppose an employee receives $100,000 in arbitration. Should the EEOC nevertheless be allowed to recover additional amounts for victim-specific relief? If it may do so, what should happen if the amount received by the EEOC differs from the amount received by the employee in arbitration? What if, for example, the EEOC recovers only $20,000 of victim-specific relief in court. Should the employee be required to return $80,000 of the arbitration award to the employer? The *Waffle House* dissenters view this as an unlikely possibility. Perhaps the employee should have to return $20,000 to the employer? Subsequent litigation on this issue seems inevitable.

Impact of EEOC settlements on subsequent arbitration: One issue that courts have not addressed is the effect of an EEOC settlement of an employee's claim for victim-specific relief on a subsequent arbitration between the employee and employer. In *Waffle House,* the Court was unequivocal that the EEOC has an independent right to sue and is not bound by the employee's arbitration agreement. Thus, the EEOC should not be precluded from settling claims nor should an employee be barred from arbitrating even after the EEOC has settled a claim on his or her behalf. While an employer will surely introduce the fact of a settlement in a subsequent arbitration (assuming the settlement terms were not confidential), an arbitrator is not bound by the settlement in rendering his or her award. Of course, most arbitrators would consider the existing law barring double recovery on this issue prior to rendering a decision. Thus, a risk of double recovery remains only where an arbitrator ignores or is unaware of existing law.

Will employers abandon arbitration agreements in response to Waffle House? How frequently do these cases arise? The dissent suggests that the EEOC's ability to pursue victim-specific relief will discourage employers from adopting arbitration agreements because the *Waffle House* decision will allow the individual to pursue the employer in the arbitral forum while the EEOC pursues the employer in the judicial forum. The argument that allowing the EEOC to pursue backpay awards on behalf of employees who sign arbitration agreements would discourage employers from adopting arbitration agreements is unsupportable. The EEOC makes "for cause" determinations—i.e., findings that sufficient evidence exists to conclude that the employee was the victim of discrimination—in very few of their cases. In 1994, only 2.69 percent of the cases (1,926 out of 71,563 cases) filed with the EEOC were found to be "for cause" (Selmi, 1996). Moreover, the EEOC does not file suit in all cases in which it enters a "for cause" determination. In 1994, it filed only 347 suits. (Id. at 13.) These numbers suggest that an employee would be extremely imprudent to place substantial hope on making an end-run around his or her arbitration agreement. The likelihood that the EEOC would file a claim on the plaintiff's behalf is extremely low.

Impact on federal policy favoring arbitration: The argument that allowing the EEOC to pursue a claim on behalf of a plaintiff who previously agreed to arbitration would undermine the strong federal policy favoring arbitration is not particularly compelling either. The EEOC's position does not undermine arbitration; instead, it requires parties to use arbitration when they have contracted to do so. It merely contends that because it has independent authority to bring suit against an employer, it should be allowed to do so even when the employee is bound by an arbitration agreement. The EEOC's approach does not interfere with arbitration, it simply works within the arbitral system, allowing the EEOC to recover victim-specific relief only if the employee is unable to recover such relief through arbitration. The dissent's approach, which would prohibit the EEOC from pursuing any monetary relief regardless of whether the individual employee has pursued her claims in arbitration and regardless of what she ultimately recovers, seems to do little to further the federal policy favoring arbitration, but quite a bit to undermine the EEOC's role in eliminating discrimination from the workplace.

Given the stated purpose of the EEOC—to vindicate the public interest in a workplace free from discrimination—the Court's decision not to take away the EEOC's power to punish employers with monetary penalties appears correct. The EEOC clearly views its monetary sanctions as a necessary weapon in its arsenal to create the proper incentives to eradicate discrimination in the workplace. Without monetary penalties, the EEOC's ability to protect the public interest in prohibiting employment discrimination would be impeded. Certainly in a case where the plaintiff makes no attempt to pursue her own remedies, or is limited in the remedies she may recover, no impediment should limit the EEOC's ability to seek monetary damages on her behalf.

d. The Scope of Judicial Review of Arbitration Awards

Traditionally, judicial review of arbitration awards was limited to the statutory grounds outlined in Federal Arbitration Act §10 (see p. 284). Section 10 allows for limited judicial review of arbitral awards, permitting challenges based on procedural irregularities in the arbitration such as corruption, fraud, evident partiality, arbitrator misconduct, and arbitrator misuse of powers. The application of these standards results in few overturned awards. For example, even if the arbitrators' award is inarticulate and unresponsive to the issues, challenging the award on the ground that the arbitrators imperfectly executed their powers will be unsuccessful. *IDS Life Ins. Co. v. Royal Alliance Assoc., Inc.*, 266 F.3d 645 (7th Cir. 2001). In that case, Judge Posner stated that finality in arbitration does not require an award that is "correct or even reasonable." Thus, even when an award suggests the arbitrators were incompetent, it will be upheld.

As the *Cole* case mentions, circuit courts have adopted nonstatutory grounds, such as "manifest disregard of the law," to review arbitration decisions. Other nonstatutory grounds for vacatur include that the award was: completely irrational, in direct conflict with public policy, arbitrary and capricious, or inconsistent with the essence of the parties' underlying contract (Hayford, 1996:764) (all but one circuit adopt one or more of these nonstatutory grounds for reviewing arbitration awards).

The addition of nonstatutory grounds for challenging arbitration awards has not had a significant impact on the finality of such awards. Application of the nonstatutory grounds rarely results in overturning an arbitration award. For example, consider a case in which an arbitrator failed to award attorneys' fees to a successful plaintiff in an ADEA case, even though the Act mandates the award of such fees. See *Di Russa v. Dean Witter Reynolds, Inc.*, 121 F.3d 818 (2d Cir. 1997) (manifest disregard does not exist where failure to show that arbitrators clearly knew of statutory obligation to award attorneys' fees), *cert. denied*, 522 U.S. 1049 (1998). Compare the subsequent Second Circuit case that follows. Can it be reconciled with the prior articulations of the "manifest disregard" doctrine?

HALLIGAN v. PIPER JAFFRAY, INC.

148 F.3d 197 (2d Cir. 1998)

FEINBERG, Circuit Judge.

[Theodore Halligan was hired by the defendant in 1973 as a salesman of equity investments to financial institutions. As a condition of employment, he had to sign a standard form requiring the arbitration of any future disputes. After Tad Piper succeeded his father as CEO of Piper in 1988, Halligan claims that in 1992 he was forced from his job because of his age and despite his continuing high performance. He filed a claim under the ADEA.]

In October 1993, Halligan submitted his ADEA claim, along with other claims, to arbitration before a panel of NASD arbitrators. Before he could complete his own re-direct testimony, however, his health deteriorated and in early 1995 the arbitrators were advised that Halligan was unable to testify further. . . .

During the arbitration hearings, Halligan presented the arbitrators with very strong evidence of age-based discrimination. Piper for its part has conceded throughout that Halligan was "basically qualified." Piper principally contended that Halligan had chosen to retire; it also argued that performance and health issues justified its conduct.

Before leaving Piper in December 1992, Halligan was making nearly $500,000 per year. He ranked fifth out of 25 institutional salesmen. He was ranked first from 1987 through 1991, and had consistently been among Piper's top salesmen. He testified as to repeated discriminatory statements by Tad Piper [and others, which were denied. Halligan also submitted his contemporaneous notes of some of these conversations.] . . .

Piper principally argued that it gave Halligan the options of retiring, agreeing to a new percentage split with Geisness [a younger partner] or being assigned a new group of accounts, and that Halligan agreed to retire in the phone conversation on September 10, 1992. Piper also contended its conduct was justified by concerns over Halligan's performance and health. Halligan had surgery for oral cancer twice (in 1990 and 1991), but returned to work each time after approximately two weeks. Halligan conceded that the surgeries had caused slight speech impairment, but offered various witnesses who testified that Halligan was always able to perform his job. Piper discounted Halligan's objective evidence of performance, arguing that Halligan's accounts had more inherent potential and that the rankings failed to reflect the contributions that other employees had made to Halligan's success. . . .

In March 1996, after extensive hearings, the arbitrators rendered a written award setting forth the claims and defenses of each party, and denying any relief to [Halligan]. The award did not contain any explanation or rationale for the result.

In June 1996, Mrs. Halligan [who succeeded to her husband's claim following his death] petitioned the district court to vacate the award under §10(a) of the Federal Arbitration Act. She argued, among other things, that given the very strong evidence of discrimination and the clear description of the applicable law presented to the arbitrators, the award reflected manifest disregard of the law.

Piper agreed that the law governing the claim was generally not disputed by the parties, but argued in response that it was not the function of the court to review the merits of the decision and that the arbitrators' award was supported by the evidence Piper presented. Piper cross-petitioned the district court to confirm the award.

The district judge refused to vacate the award. She stated in the order of April 14, 1997 that:

> [h]ere, the determination of what constitutes "direct evidence" [of discrimination] . . . is a difficult one to make. In addition, the record . . . does not indicate the Panel's awareness, prior to its determinations, of the standards for burdens of proof. . . . [T]he Panel was faced with the task of evaluating conflicting witness testimony, and where it did not issue a written opinion, I cannot conclude that the panel did in fact disregard the parties' burdens of proof. . . . [C]rediting one witness over another does not constitute manifest disregard of the law [and] this Court's role is not to second-guess the fact-finding done by the Panel. Because there is factual as well as legal support for the Panel's ultimate conclusion, I determine that the Panel did not manifestly disregard the law. . . .

B. Standard of Review of Award

[The court then reviews some of the developments concerning mandatory arbitration as well as the evolution of the "manifest disregard" doctrine.]

C. Application of Standard of Review

We turn now to review of the district court's decision in this case. Mrs. Halligan argued in the district court and repeats to us that the arbitration award reflected manifest disregard of the law. Mrs. Halligan makes a strong case for that proposition. Quite simply, Halligan presented overwhelming evidence that Piper's conduct after Tad Piper became CEO was motivated by age discrimination. Halligan testified to repeated discriminatory statements, and offered contemporaneous notes supporting his version of events, which were in turn backed by the testimony of a witness who saw him making notes. Halligan also presented the testimony of numerous other witnesses who testified that Piper personnel admitted that the company wanted Halligan out. Halligan presented powerful evidence of his performance, in the form of quantitative sales rankings and relevant witness testimony. Notwithstanding Piper's testimony as to Halligan's performance and health, Piper conceded before the arbitrators — and continues to do so — that Halligan's continuing performance was not so unsatisfactory as to justify discharge. Indeed, its principal argument has been that Halligan retired voluntarily. Halligan also made a very strong showing that he did not choose the "option" of quitting but was fired. The strength of Halligan's showing of discriminatory motive is most probative of whether Piper took discriminatory action, i.e., fired him. In addition, the circumstantial evidence surrounding his departure, e.g., his statements to various witnesses about his being "fired," his refusal to write to his clients announcing his "resignation," his retention of counsel, is consistent only with a finding that Halligan was pushed out of his job.

Moreover, this is not a case like *DiRussa* where we refused to find "manifest disregard" because DiRussa had not sufficiently brought the governing law to the attention of the arbitrators. . .

In view of the strong evidence that Halligan was fired because of his age and the agreement of the parties that the arbitrators were correctly advised of the applicable legal principles, we are inclined to hold that they ignored the law or the evidence or both. Moreover, the arbitrators did not explain their award. It is true that we have stated repeatedly that arbitrators have no obligation to do so. But in *Gilmer*, when the Supreme Court ruled that an employee could be forced to assert an ADEA claim in an arbitral forum, the Court did so on the assumptions that the claimant would not forgo the substantive rights afforded by the statute, that the arbitration agreement simply changed the forum for enforcement of those rights and that a claimant could effectively vindicate his or her statutory rights in the arbitration. This case puts those assumptions to the test. The Court also stated in *Gilmer* that "claimed procedural inadequacies" in arbitration "are best left for resolution in specific cases." At least in the circumstances here, we believe that when a reviewing court is inclined to hold that an arbitration panel manifestly disregarded the law, the failure of the arbitrators to explain the award can be taken into account. Having done so, we are left with the firm belief that the arbitrators here manifestly disregarded the law or the evidence or both.

Note

In *Wallace v. Buttar*, 378 F.3d 182 (2d Cir. 2004), the Second Circuit clarified and narrowed the holding in *Halligan*. Emphasizing that vacating an arbitral award is an "extremely rare" occurrence, the court distinguished *Halligan* because of the special circumstances present in the case. In *Halligan*, the arbitral panel dealt with the "unique concerns at issue with employment discrimination claims" and noted that the arbitral panel had provided no written explanation of its factual findings. According to the *Wallace* court, the Second Circuit does not permit vacation of an arbitral award for manifest disregard of the *evidence*; rather, it permits vacation only for manifest disregard of the law. Review of the arbitral award is for the purpose of inferring a ground for the arbitrator's decision from the facts of the case. If the court can discern a ground to support the award, the award should be confirmed.

Note and Questions on Limitations on Judicial Review of Arbitration Awards

As statutory claims are more frequently the subject of arbitrations, courts, like *Cole*, emphasize the importance of ensuring that judicial review is meaningful and that the statutory standards, as well as judicially created standards like "manifest disregard of the law," are applied rigorously. As a result, preemption questions related to judicial review have emerged. For example, preemption may be an issue if a state statute alters the standards of judicial review, as by including review for manifest disregard of the law. Moreover, a federal court's ruling that an alternative standard of review, such as public policy, can be applied may ultimately be overturned should the Supreme Court decide that §10 provides the outer limit of permissible judicial review of arbitration awards. If manifest disregard and other judicially created standards contemplate substantive judicial review of the underlying arbitration award, the question of how broadly §10 may be interpreted becomes quite important.

Courts are not alone in efforts to ensure that judicial review in arbitration is meaningful. Some arbitral repeat players are negotiating among themselves for changes to the arbitral process. The parties are not relying on the arbitral process alone to improve fairness; instead, they rely on the court system as the enforcement mechanism to ensure that efforts to increase quality and fairness in arbitration are achieved. The most prominent method parties have selected to enhance predictability of outcomes is to agree to expanded judicial review of arbitral awards. While some courts have expressed a willingness to adopt the parties' proposed standards for judicial review, other courts have refused. Compare *Gateway Tech., Inc. v. MCI Telecommunications Corp.*, 64 F.3d 993 (5th Cir. 1995) with *Bowen v. Amoco Pipeline Co.*, 254 F.3d 925 (10th Cir. 2001) (parties cannot contractually alter FAA standard for judicial review) and *Kyocera Corp. v. Prudential-Bache Trade Services, Inc.*, 341 F.3d 987 (9th Cir. 2003) (*en banc*) (same). To avoid the legal issues surrounding agreements to expand judicial review, parties might instead agree to have the arbitrator's award reviewed by a panel of appellate arbitrators rather than a district court.

The question of whether, and to what extent, this type of litigant control over the dispute resolution process in the judicial setting is appropriate has been largely ignored. While arbitration and other alternative dispute resolution processes are traditionally private processes in which parties experience substantial autonomy, courts, by contrast, are public institutions, designed to serve a public function. Party attempts to obtain non-traditional exercises of judicial power, then, may jeopardize courts' institutional integrity. Courts need a reliable and consistent framework for evaluating the various requests parties make and determining which they will adopt and which they must deny. Professor Sarah Rudolph Cole has proposed such a test, designed for any request for nontraditional judicial involvement in dispute resolution. First, the court evaluating the request should consider whether Congress granted it the authority to approve the parties' requests. Second, the court must consider whether approval of the parties' request will impermissibly undermine the institutional integrity of the court. Application of this second test may require consideration of the impact on third parties, judicial resources, and the court's institutional stature. If the court finds that it has no authority to approve the parties' request, it should not proceed to step 2 (Cole, 2000:1205–1206).

4.30 Will the two-part test work effectively? Imagine that the parties have agreed that a court will review an arbitral award by treating an arbitration award like a lower court opinion or by rendering a decision with regard only to industry custom, not law. Should a judge enforce such agreements? What impact might that have on the judiciary as a whole? Does the FAA §10 (judicial review provision) allow parties to agree to expand judicial review? What if their standards provide for less judicial review than the FAA provides?

4.31 Assume that the drafters of the Revised Uniform Arbitration Act, in response to cases like *Gateway*, *Kyocera*, and *Bowen*, adopted the following language:

> In addition to other grounds to vacate an award, set forth above [assume grounds to vacate similar to FAA §10(a)], the parties may contract in the arbitration agreement for judicial review of errors of law in the arbitration award. If they have so contracted, the Court shall

vacate the award if the arbitrator has committed an error of law prejudicing the rights of a party.

Should states adopt such a statute? Would federal courts enforce this statute? What are the arguments for and against this statute?

Kyocera, Gateway, and *Bowen* consider whether parties can agree to expand the scope of judicial review of an arbitral award. The following case considers whether parties may limit the court's ability to review an arbitration award under the Federal Arbitration Act on the generally accepted ground of "manifest disregard of the law." The case also considers whether a party may depose an arbitrator.

HOEFT v. MVL GROUP, INC.

343 F.3d 57 (2d Cir. 2003)

B.D. PARKER, JR., Circuit Judge.

[Hoeft and his wife sold their shares in two companies to MVL.] The parties agreed that MVL could defer payment on a part of the purchase price but that the Hoefts would receive a price adjustment [EBITDA] if the value of the companies increased. The amendment [to the purchase contract], which described how this calculation should be made, contained a clause that would require arbitration if the parties could not agree on the amount of the adjustment. The clause stated that:

> the parties were to use their reasonable best efforts to resolve such dispute, and in the event that they are unable to do so such dispute shall be resolved by Steven Sherrill, whose decision in such matters shall be binding and conclusive upon each of the parties hereto and shall not be subject to any type of review or appeal whatsoever.

[A dispute arose over calculation of the EBITDA. Sherrill arbitrated the dispute and issued a $1.4 million arbitration award to the Hoefts. MVL moved to vacate the award on various grounds. The District Court granted MVL's motion on the basis that the arbitrator, Sherrill, manifestly disregarded the law. The District Court also issued an order permitting MVL to depose the arbitrator.]

. . . The in-court deposition of the arbitrator proceeded, with the court supervising. MVL's counsel did not question the arbitrator regarding the allegations of bias or prejudgment. Instead, MVL's counsel questioned the arbitrator regarding his understanding of the calculation of EBITDA under the Amendment and the substance of his decision-making process in calculating Primary Year EBITDA, including the role of GAAP in his calculation. Sherrill testified that he had "disregard[ed] the phrase 'generally accepted accounting principles' " in calculating Primary Year EBITDA and that "the preponderance of evidence suggested that had GAAP been applied, in my determination those two expense items [*i.e.,* the sale-related bonuses and stock option extinguishment costs] would have reduced EBITDA under this calculation." In response to questioning by the Hoefts' counsel, Sherrill testified that in his opinion GAAP provided more than one way to present categories of expenses and was therefore not determinative of EBITDA.

At the close of the deposition, MVL's counsel indicated that he would no longer seek additional discovery. Several days later, MVL's counsel confirmed that "MVL will not be pursuing its arguments of arbitral bias due to prejudgment and that the 'dispute' prerequisite was unmet."

After receiving additional briefing regarding the substantive accounting issues underlying the arbitration award, the District Court denied the Hoefts' petition to confirm the award and granted MVL's motion to vacate it. The District Court concluded that the arbitrator had not exceeded his powers under 9 U.S.C. §10(a)(4), but that he had manifestly disregarded the law in failing to calculate Primary Year EBITDA in accordance with GAAP. Following the entry of judgment, the Hoefts appealed.

Discussion

On appeal, the Hoefts have launched a three-pronged attack on the decision of the District Court. First, they argue that because the Amendment insulated the arbitration award from judicial review, the District Court erred in even considering whether the arbitrator had manifestly disregarded the law. Second, and in the alternative, they argue that the District Court abused its discretion in permitting the arbitrator to be deposed concerning his decision-making process. Third, they argue that the arbitrator neither manifestly disregarded the law nor exceeded his powers.

I. Enforceability of Private Agreements to Preclude Judicial Review of Arbitration Awards.

Under §1(d) of the Amendment, disputes over the calculation of EBITDA were to be "resolved by Steven Sherrill, whose decision in such matters shall be binding and conclusive upon each of the parties hereto and shall not be subject to any type of review or appeal whatsoever." According to the Hoefts, this provision deprived the District Court of the authority to examine the substance of the arbitrator's decision and, thus, to review it for manifest disregard of the law. While the Hoefts did invoke the District Court's jurisdiction in order to obtain a judgment confirming the arbitration award, they contend that there is no contradiction between their petition and their claim that the substance of the arbitrator's decision is unreviewable. The Hoefts rely on the Stock Purchase Agreement and its Amendment as the source of their right to seek confirmation of the award in federal court.

The District Court did not determine whether a private agreement could both authorize a federal court to enter a judgment confirming an arbitral award and divest that court of the authority to review the substance of the award for manifest disregard of the law. Instead, the District Court assumed *arguendo* that parties could agree to eliminate judicial review of an arbitration award, but concluded that §1(d) of the Amendment was not sufficiently clear to indicate the parties' intention to do so.

In urging us to enforce the parties' apparent agreement to insulate the substance of the arbitration award from judicial review, the Hoefts rely on the general principle of freedom of contract and the more specific canon of deference to private agreements to arbitrate. But the freedom to contract, like any freedom, has its limits, and the Hoefts' reliance on the federal policy favoring arbitration overlooks several key assumptions that undergird that policy. It is in part because arbitration awards are subject to minimal judicial review that federal courts voice such strong support for the arbitral process. Arbitration awards are not self-enforcing, a fact that the Hoefts, who petitioned the District Court to confirm the award, cannot deny. Thus, while we have spoken in broad terms of deference to private agreements to arbitrate, we have always done so with an awareness of the confirmation-and-vacatur safety net that hangs below. The FAA prescribes several grounds for vacating arbitration awards that although narrow are nevertheless important. Specifically, §10(a) of the FAA authorizes a district court to vacate an arbitration award:

(1) where the award was procured by corruption, fraud, or undue means;
(2) where there was evident partiality or corruption in the arbitrators, or either of them;
(3) where the arbitrators were guilty of misconduct in refusing to postpone the hearing, upon sufficient cause shown, or in refusing to hear evidence pertinent and material to the controversy; or of any other misbehavior by which the rights of any party have been prejudiced; or
(4) where the arbitrators exceeded their powers, or so imperfectly executed them that a mutual, final, and definite award upon the subject matter submitted was not made.

9 U.S.C. §10(a). The Supreme Court has supplemented the FAA with an additional ground not prescribed in the statute: manifest disregard of the law. The manifest disregard standard together with §10(a) represent a floor for judicial review of arbitration awards below which parties cannot require courts to go, no matter how clear the parties' intentions.

While various courts have enforced private agreements to alter the judicial review to be applied to arbitral awards, as the Hoefts acknowledge, "[m]ost of these cases have involved attempts to *raise* the level of judicial review otherwise available under the FAA." Decisions enforcing agreements to decrease the otherwise applicable level of judicial review are far more scarce. While taking no position on the enforceability of agreements to raise the level of judicial review, we note that there is a fundamental difference between an agreement to increase the scrutiny that courts apply when considering whether to confirm or vacate an arbitration award and an agreement to prevent courts from reviewing the substance of an arbitration award at all.

An agreement that contemplates confirmation but bars all judicial review presents serious concerns. Arbitration agreements are private contracts, but at the end of the process the successful party may obtain a judgment affording resort to the potent public legal remedies available to judgment creditors. In enacting §10(a), Congress impressed limited, but critical, safeguards onto this process, ones that respected the importance and flexibility of private dispute resolution mechanisms, but at the same time barred federal courts from confirming awards tainted by partiality, a lack of elementary procedural fairness, corruption, or similar misconduct. This balance would be eviscerated, and the integrity of the arbitration process could be compromised, if parties could require that awards, flawed for any of these reasons, must nevertheless be blessed by federal courts. Since federal courts are not rubber stamps, parties may not, by private agreement, relieve them of their obligation to review arbitration awards for compliance with §10(a).

The Hoefts contend there is a middle ground. They would draw a distinction between the bases for vacatur enumerated in §10(a), on the one hand, and the judicially created manifest disregard of the law standard, on the other. Thus, the argument goes, we may preclude parties from contracting around §10(a), yet permit them to contract around the manifest disregard standard. Accordingly, the Hoefts urge us to interpret §1(d) of the Amendment as divesting the District Court of the authority to review the arbitration award for manifest disregard of the law, even if it does not divest the court of the authority to review it for corruption, partiality, or the other §10(a) grounds.

But we see no reason to treat manifest disregard of the law differently from the grounds enumerated in §10(a). Through the combination of legislation and common law, narrow standards of reviewing arbitration awards have developed in the courts of this and other Circuits. As the Tenth Circuit held in refusing to enforce a private agreement to expand judicial review of arbitration awards, "in the absence of clear authority to the contrary, parties may not interfere with the judicial process by dictating how the federal courts operate." *Bowen,* 254 F.3d at 936 n.8. Similarly, in a different context the Supreme Court has held that "the mere fact that [a] settlement agreement provides for vacatur" of a judgment does not justify vacatur, *U.S. Bancorp Mortgage Co. v. Bonner Mall P'ship,* 513 U.S. 18, 29, 115 S. Ct. 386, 130 L. Ed. 2d 233 (1994), stating that judicial precedents "are not merely the property of private litigants," *id.* at 26, 115 S. Ct. 386 (citation and quotation marks omitted). The fact that the manifest disregard standard is a product of common law, rather than statute, makes it no less essential to the judicial review of arbitration awards. Just as the Supreme Court held in *Bonner Mall* that private parties may not dictate to a federal court when to vacate another court's judgment, we hold today that private parties may not dictate to a federal court when to enter a judgment enforcing an arbitration award. Judicial standards of review, like judicial precedents, are not the property of private litigants.

Thus, just as a private agreement may vest decision-making authority in an arbitrator, so may it deprive an arbitrator of that authority. Unlike arbitration, however, judicial review is not a creature of contract, and the authority of a federal court to review an arbitration award — or any other matter — does not derive from a private agreement. . . .

II. Deposition of Arbitrator

Before reaching the ultimate question of the correctness of the District Court's vacatur of the arbitration award, we must consider whether the court erred in permitting MVL to depose the arbitrator regarding his decision-making process and in relying on his testimony in deciding to vacate the award. The District Court's decisions to permit the deposition of the arbitrator generally, and to permit questioning regarding his manifest disregard of the law in particular, are reviewed for abuse of discretion.

We begin our analysis with the well-established rule that arbitrators may not be deposed absent "clear evidence of impropriety." The "impropriety" relied on by MVL to support its application to depose Sherrill was the arbitrator's alleged prejudgment of the parties' dispute evidenced by his draft EBITDA calculation in November 2000.

The Hoefts appear to have conceded the permissibility of deposing the arbitrator regarding his alleged prejudgment of the dispute. Regardless, in light of the fact that Sherrill had performed, at the Hoefts' request and prior to the commencement of his role as arbitrator, the very calculation that was the substance of the parties' dispute, the District Court acted within its discretion in permitting MVL's counsel to depose him regarding the allegation of prejudgment. This does not mean, however, that MVL's counsel also should have been permitted to question Sherrill about the substance of his decision-making process. As it turned out, MVL's counsel did not question Sherrill regarding his alleged prejudgment of the EBITDA calculation, and MVL soon withdrew its prejudgment argument.

Thus, the crux of the parties' dispute regarding the deposition of the arbitrator involves the District Court's permitting MVL to examine him regarding his alleged manifest disregard of the law. . . . [T]he Hoefts argue, first, that manifest disregard of the law does not constitute the sort of "impropriety" about which an arbitrator could ever be deposed and, second, that even if manifest disregard were an impropriety, MVL did not present "clear evidence" that the arbitrator had manifestly disregarded the law. We agree with the Hoefts on both points.

While arbitrators may be deposed regarding claims of bias or prejudice, cases are legion in which courts have refused to permit parties to depose arbitrators — or other judicial or quasi-judicial decision-makers — regarding the thought processes underlying their decisions.

An allegation that an arbitrator manifestly disregarded the law, unlike an allegation of bias or prejudgment, necessarily involves . . . the forbidden purpose: inquiring into the arbitrator's decision-making process. A manifest disregard claim involves both objective and subjective components. While the objective component looks to whether the governing law was well defined, the subjective component focuses on the substance of the arbitrator's decision-making process: whether the arbitrator was aware of the governing law, and whether he consciously decided to ignore it. The subjective component of the manifest disregard standard, in particular, may not properly be broached in deposing an arbitrator. That is, the parties to a confirmation or vacatur proceeding may not depose an arbitrator regarding "the knowledge [that he] actually possessed," or whether he "appreciate[d] the existence of a clearly governing legal principle but decide[d] to ignore or pay no attention to it."

A review of the transcript of the arbitrator's deposition makes clear that the bulk of the questioning probed this forbidden terrain. While it may be difficult to prove the subjective prong of the manifest disregard standard without questioning the arbitrator, this fact does not change our result. Permitting depositions of arbitrators regarding their mental processes would make arbitration only the starting point in the dispute resolution process and deprive arbitration awards of the last word on their authors' intentions.

An arbitrator should be free to decide the dispute before him without fear that he will have to explain the basis for his decision, and how he arrived at it, at some later date. If the parties to an arbitration agreement want to know the arbitrator's reasoning, they may request that he include it in his award, as Sherrill did. Once an arbitrator issues an award, however, his role is complete and, like a judge or a jury, he may not be required to answer questions about why he reached a particular result.

Thus, while we do not believe that under the facts presented the District Court abused its discretion in permitting limited, judicially controlled discovery regarding the allegation that the arbitrator had prejudged the dispute, the court should not have permitted MVL's counsel to depose him regarding his decision-making process. The court, therefore, should not have relied on the arbitrator's deposition testimony—which focused exclusively on manifest disregard, not prejudgment—in determining whether he had manifestly disregarded the law in rendering his award.

Conclusion

For these reasons, we reverse the judgment of the District Court vacating the arbitration award and remand with instructions to enter judgment confirming the award, and for further proceedings consistent with this opinion.

Questions

4.32 *Hoeft* suggests that parties may not contract around FAA §10(a) because Congress wanted to protect the integrity of the judicial process by prohibiting courts from confirming tainted awards. What impact should *Hoeft* have on the current debate about parties' ability to expand judicial review of arbitral awards? Does *Hoeft* suggest that the Federal Arbitration Act provides mandatory rules rather than default rules? Do you agree with the *Hoeft* court that parties are also prohibited from contracting around the manifest disregard of the law standard of review, even though it was judicially created? If a state legislature added the manifest disregard standard to its state arbitration act, could a party argue that the FAA preempts the standard? The *Hoeft* case raises the important point that the institutional integrity of the courts (as well as the integrity of the arbitration process) is an independent value that courts should protect. The Supreme Court made this point in the *Bonner Mall* case (casebook, p. 397).

4.33 Should arbitrators be subject to deposition under any circumstances? Do you think that the limitations the *Hoeft* court imposes—that an arbitrator may be asked only questions that would reveal information about the objective components of the arbitrator's decisionmaking—are useful? What information is a party likely to obtain during a deposition if the deposition is limited to objective components of the case? Would such information support a finding that the arbitrator manifestly disregarded the law?

E. ARBITRATION ETHICS

1. *Arbitrator Ethics*

The primary source for guidance regarding arbitrator behavior is the 2004 ABA/AAA Code of Ethics for Arbitrators in Commercial Disputes. The code governs an arbitrator's obligation to disclose conflicts of interest, limit ex parte contacts, maintain confidentiality of the arbitral hearing while ensuring that the hearing proceeds fairly and diligently, and ensure the integrity and fairness of the arbitral process, including decision-making. In general, a rule of reasonableness governs conflicts of interest disclosure. The arbitrator has a duty to use reasonable efforts to conduct a reasonable inquiry regarding conflicts of interest. Like a judge, an arbitrator is not permitted to engage in communications with the parties that would create the appearance of impropriety. Thus, for example, ex parte contacts during an arbitral hearing are prohibited.

In fact, until quite recently, both policy makers and arbitration users largely ignored the issue of an arbitrator's ethical obligations. As one-shot players have begun to participate in arbitration in larger numbers, however, consumer advocates and legislators have paid more attention to these issues. In California, this attention resulted in a controversial and extensive overhauling of state rules governing arbitrator behavior. Critics of mandatory arbitration between one-shot and repeat players appear to be using the opportunity to enhance arbitrators' ethical guidelines as yet another way to improve the procedural protections within the arbitration process. Opponents of the ethics rules have been quick to respond that the new rules are too burdensome and, moreover, are preempted by the FAA. Based on your understanding of the FAA and preemption, do you think ethical rules adopted by statute are preempted?

California's new arbitrator ethics rules purport to create minimum standards of conduct for arbitrators. These standards focus primarily on the arbitrator's obligation to disclose conflicts of interest to the parties, including financial or familial conflicts, as well as past experience. The most controversial new requirement imposes on arbitrators in consumer arbitrations the obligation to disclose:

> Standard 7(b)(12) [A]ny significant past, present, or currently expected financial or professional relationship or affiliation between that dispute resolution provider organization and a party or lawyer in the arbitration.

Ethics Standards for Neutral Arbitrators in Contractual Arbitration, Division VI of the Appendix to the California Rules of Court (eff. January 1, 2003).

Will imposing extensive arbitrator disclosure requirements decrease the perceived problems with consumer arbitration? Does the typical commercial arbitrator have access to arbitral provider organization records sufficient to meet the new disclosure requirements? Might the disclosure requirements have the opposite effect, by making arbitrators aware of relationships that would not otherwise have influenced them? What impact will the new rules have on the finality of arbitration? On parties' interest in bringing motions to disqualify arbitrators?

2. *Ethics of Third-Party Provider Organizations*

The increasing use of arbitration agreements, particularly by employers and businesses in their relationships with employees and consumers, has also focused attention on the character and scope of the ethical obligations of arbitral provider organizations. In May 2002, the CPR-Georgetown Commission on Ethics and Standards of Practice in alternative dispute resolution (ADR) released a set of principles for ADR Provider Organizations—i.e., those organizations that make available neutrals to preside over the variety of available ADR methods. These principles provide, among other things, that ADR Provider Organizations, including arbitral provider organizations, make reasonable efforts to maximize the quality and competence of their services, provide information about their services and organization to potential clients, ensure that they administer ADR processes that are "fundamentally fair and conducted in an impartial manner," provide services of reasonable cost to low-income parties, protect confidentiality by taking "all reasonable steps to protect the level of confidentiality agreed to by the parties, established by the organization or neutral, or set by applicable law or contract," and disclose conflicts of interest "reasonably likely to affect the impartiality or independence" of the Organization or that might create the appearance that the Organization is biased against one party or favorable to another. For a thorough discussion of these rules, see Menkel-Meadow (2001) and Shaw and Plapinger (2001:14).

Principle V, the provision on conflict of interest disclosure, has garnered attention from critics of mandatory arbitration (Palefsky, 2001:19). Principle V states:

> a. The ADR Provider Organization should disclose the existence of any interests or relationships which are reasonably likely to affect the impartiality or independence of the Organization or which might reasonably create the appearance that the Organization is biased against a party or favorable to another, including (i) any financial or other interest by the Organization in the outcome; (ii) any significant financial, business, organizational, professional or other relationship that the Organization has with any of the parties or their counsel, including a contractual stream of referrals, a de facto stream of referrals, or a funding relationship between a party and the organization; or (iii) any other significant source of bias or prejudice concerning the Organization which is reasonably likely to affect impartiality or might reasonably create an appearance of partiality or bias.

The principle requires that an ADR Provider Organization make reasonable efforts to avoid partiality or the appearance of partiality through a process of disclosure to the parties. Although the principle requires that the organization disclose financial interests in the outcome of a dispute, critics suggest that organizations, particularly arbitral provider organizations, will not provide disclosure sufficient to remedy the problems created by a system that is already biased in favor of corporate repeat players. In arbitration particularly, major arbitral providers solicit big businesses, either directly or through an arbitrator on the providers' panel list, to include arbitral provisions in their employment or business contracts and to list the provider as the arbitration organization for disputes that might arise. Does Principle V require that this information be disclosed to parties at the time they select an arbitrator? Critics worry that organizations will interpret the principle narrowly, so that disclosure in this context would not be required even though, in the critics' view, it would create an appearance of bias.

No jurisdiction has adopted the Draft Principles, so they do not have the force of law. Is there any incentive for an organization to represent that it will abide by these rules?

Questions

4.34 Imagine that ABC, an arbitral provider organization located in State X, asks its corporate clients—i.e., those it already provides services to—to join ABC at different levels of membership that range in cost from $5,000 to $50,000. In exchange for becoming a member, ABC will offer special instruction in arbitral and mediation advocacy as well as discounts on fees and services. Is this arrangement ethical? Should this arrangement be disclosed if State X adopts Principle V of the CPR-Georgetown rules?

4.35 ABC Arbitration, which provides arbitration services to corporations and individuals with internet disputes, adopted the CPR-Georgetown Commission on Ethics and Standards of Practice in ADR. It is considering participating in the following activities: (1) submitting an amicus brief on behalf of a party in a major arbitration case in front of the U.S. Supreme Court; or (2) asking ABC arbitrators to identify corporations where they have contacts so that ABC marketing representatives can contact those corporations to seek business and provide training. May ABC engage in these activities? Should ethical rules prevent arbitral organizations like ABC from engaging in these practices?

References

ALLEYNE, Reginald (1996) "Statutory Discrimination Claims: Rights 'Waived' and Lost in the Arbitration Forum," 13 *Hofstra Lab. & Emp. L.J.* 381.

BICKNER, Mei L., Christine VER PLOEG, and Charles FEIGENBAUM (1997) "Developments in Employment Arbitration," 52 *Disp. Resol. J.* 8 (Jan.).

BINGHAM, Lisa B. (1997) "Employment Arbitration: The Repeat Player Effect," 1 *Employee Rts. & Employment Pol'y J.* 189, 206.

——— (1998) "On Repeat Players, Adhesive Contracts, and the Use of Statistics in Judicial Review of Employment Arbitration Awards," 29 *McGeorge L. Rev.* 223, 234.

BOLLER, Harvey R., and Donald J. PETERSON (1998) "Job Discrimination Claims Under Collective Bargaining," 53 *Dis. Resol. J.* 38 (Aug.).

BROOME, Stephen A. (2006) "An Unconscionable Application of the Unconscionability Doctrine: How the California Judiciary Is Circumventing the Federal Arbitration Act," 3 *Hastings Bus. L.J* 39.

BRUNET, Edward, Richard E. SPEIDEL, Jean R. STERNLIGHT, and Stephen J. WARE (2006) *Arbitration Law in America: A Critical Assessment.* New York: Cambridge University Press.

CARBONNEAU, Thomas (1997) *Cases and Materials on Commercial Arbitration.* Yonkers, N.Y.: Juris Publishers.

COLE, Sarah Rudolph (1996) "Incentives and Arbitration: The Case Against Enforcement of Executory Arbitration Agreements Between Employers and Employees," 64 *UMKC L. Rev.* 449.

——— (1997) "A Funny Thing Happened on the Way to the (Alternative) Forum: Reexamining *Alexander v. Gardner-Denver* in the Wake of *Gilmer v. Interstate/Johnson Lane Corp.*," 1997 *B.Y.U. L. Rev.* 591, 600-605.

——— (2000) "Managerial Litigants? The Overlooked Problem of Party Autonomy in Dispute Resolution," 51 *Hastings L.J.* 1199, 1205-1206.

——— (2001) "Uniform Arbitration: 'One Size Fits All' Does Not Fit," 16 *Ohio St. J. Disp. Resol.* 759, 786-788.

——— (2004) "Updating Arbitrator Ethics," 10 *Disp. Resol. Mag.* 24 (summer).

COMMISSION ON THE FUTURE OF WORKER-MANAGEMENT RELATIONS (DUNLOP COMMISSION) (1994) *Report and Recommendations.* Washington, D.C.

COULSON, Robert (1982) *Business Arbitration — What You Need to Know.* New York: American Arbitration Association.

DUNLOP, John T., and Arnold M. ZACK (1997) *Mediation and Arbitration of Employment Disputes.* San Francisco: Jossey-Bass.

EISENBERG, Theodore, and Elizabeth HILL (2003-2004) "Employment Arbitration and Litigation: An Empirical Comparison," 58 *Disp. Resol. J.* 44, 51 (Nov.-Jan.).

EQUAL EMPLOYMENT OPPORTUNITY COMMISSION (1997) "Policy Statement on Mandatory Binding Arbitration of Employment Discrimination Disputes as a Condition of Employment," 52 *Disp. Resol. J.* 11 (Fall).

FITZGIBBON, Susan A. (2000) "Teaching Unconscionability through Agreements to Arbitrate Employment Claims," 44 *St. Louis U. L.J.* 1401.

GALANTER, Marc (1974) "Why the 'Haves' Come Out Ahead: Speculations on the Limits of Legal Change," *9 Law & Soc'y Rev.* 95.

GIFFORD, Courtney D., and William P. HOBGOOD (1985) *Directory of U.S. Labor Arbitrators — A Guide for Finding and Using Arbitrators.* Washington, D.C.: Bureau of National Affairs.

GOLDBERG, Stephen B., Eric D. GREEN, and Frank E. A. SANDER (1989) "Litigation, Arbitration or Mediation: A Dialogue," *ABA Journal* (June).

GORMAN, Robert A. (1995) "The *Gilmer* Decision and the Private Arbitration of Public-Law Disputes," 1995 *U. Ill. L. Rev.* 635.

HARVARD LAW REVIEW (1996) "Developments in the Law–Employment Discrimination," 109 *Harv. L. Rev.* 1568.

HAYFORD, Stephen L. (1996) "Law in Disarray: Judicial Standards for Vacatur of Commercial Arbitration Awards," 30 *Ga. L. Rev.* 731, 764.

HAYFORD, Stephen L., and Alan R. PALMITER (2002) "Arbitration Federalism: A State Role in Commercial Arbitration," 54 *Fla. L. Rev.* 175, 177-178.

HEINSZ, Timothy J. (2001) "The Revised Uniform Arbitration Act: Modernizing, Revising, and Clarifying Arbitration Law," 2001 *J. Disp. Resol.* 1.

HOUCK, Stephen D. (1988) "Complex Commercial Arbitration: Designing a Process to Suit the Case," 43 *Arb. J.* 3.

MACNEIL, Ian R., Richard E. SPEIDEL, and Thomas J. STIPANOWICH (1994) *Federal Arbitration Law — Agreements, Awards, and Remedies Under the Federal Arbitration Act.* Boston: Little, Brown.

MENKEL-MEADOW, Carrie (2001) "Ethics in ADR: The Many 'Cs' of Professional Responsibility and Dispute Resolution," 28 *Fordham Urb. L.J.* 979.

MOTTEK, Jacqueline E. (2000) "The Impact of Mandatory Arbitration Clauses on Class Certification," 69 *U.S.L.W.* 2307.

REUBEN, Richard C. (2003) "Howsam, First Options, and the Demise of Separability: Restoring Access to Justice for Contracts with Arbitration Provisions," 56 *SMU L. Rev.* (forthcoming).

ST. ANTOINE, Theodore J. (2001) "The Changing Role of Labor Arbitration," 76 *Ind. L. J.* 83, 91-93.

SANDER, Frank E. A., and Mark C. FLEMING (1996) "Arbitration of Employment Disputes Under Federal Protective Statutes: How Safe Are Employee Rights?," *Disp. Resol. Mag.* 13 (Spring).

SELMI, Michael (1996) "The Value of the EEOC: Reexamining the Agency's Role in Employment Discrimination Law," 57 *Ohio St. L.J.* 1.

SHAW, Margaret L., and Elizabeth PLAPINGER (2001) "Ethical Guidelines—ADR Provider Organizations Should Increase Transparency, Disclosure," *Disp. Resol. Mag.* 14 (Spring).

STERNLIGHT, Jean R. (2000) "As Mandatory Binding Arbitration Meets the Class Action, Will the Class Action Survive?" 42 *Wm. & Mary L. Rev.* 1, 65.

SYMPOSIUM ON ARBITRATION (1998) *Disp. Resol. Mag.* (Fall).

WILKINSON, John H., ed. (1990) *Donovan Leisure Newton & Irvine ADR Practice Book.* New York: Wiley Law Publications.

WILLNER, Gabriel M., ed. (2005 & Supps.) *Domke on Commercial Arbitration.* Wilmette, Ill.: Callaghan.

Chapter 5

Combining and Applying the Basic Processes

A. INTRODUCTION

Like an architect who designs buildings* a dispute systems designer has a role only if no structure currently exists or if those who use the existing structure find it wanting. Dispute system "design" or "architecture" is born in dissatisfaction with existing processes and flourishes when a new dispute resolution structure offers promise for more closely meeting users' goals. This chapter includes some of the lessons from pioneers in the new "dispute systems design" field, as well as examples of their successes. In many ways, the dispute system field remains in its infancy. Those now entering the field have the opportunity to help develop the principles that will guide the next generation of practitioners.

The dispute systems designer may be a lawyer representing an individual (see Part E) or an expert recommending a new process for a series of cases (see Part C), such as the fishing rights cases discussed in Part F. Alternatively, the designer may work with a variety of affected persons to improve processes for a sector of cases, like e-disputes (see Part F). Sometimes the designer plans new systems for a court, like the multi-door courthouse initiative discussed in Chapter 6. In each situation, the tasks are similar: (1) ascertain goals for the disputing system; (2) establish priorities among those goals; (3) develop a new disputing system better suited to the goals; (4) consult throughout the planning process with clients and others affected by the disputing system; (5) anticipate and plan for potential problems with the new system; and (6) help to implement and re-assess the new system.

Ascertain Goals. The designer's first task is to identify the goals for a system. Often these goals relate to cost, speed, privacy, participation, and level of conflict. This assessment of goals is a precursor to diagnosing how the current processes fall short and whether another system would be a better fit with those goals.

To identify goals, the designer might begin by cataloging dissatisfaction. When users complain that the system is too slow, does not involve the actual disputants, and is costly, the designer hypothesizes that speed to resolution, party participation, and reduction in expense are among key goals. Applying the same principle to the

*The authors are grateful to Christine Merchant, Cathy Costantino, and Robert Mnookin for the analogy to the architect.

representation of a client, when a divorce client worries aloud about how the divorced parents will work together in raising the children, the attentive lawyer understands that preserving parenting relationships is a key goal for that client to achieve in the choice of a dispute resolution process.

Identifying dissatisfaction is only the initial step, however; a designer who fails to understand the key sources of satisfaction with the current system may design a worse system. Maintaining equal access to the justice system, for example, may be a far more important goal than speed and participation, and a structure that favors the wealthy may ultimately be worse than a slow and non-participatory one.

Establish Priorities Among Goals. As these examples suggest, the new design may not meet all goals. To make the best choices in terms of the design structure, the designer should understand priorities among goals. Suppose the users will save money by using mediation only if they do not bring their lawyers to the mediation session. What is more important — their informed consent or saving money? Often these priorities must be set in the midst of the design. Informed consent may matter less than saving money on the process if the parties consider the stakes involved in the dispute to be small.

Develop a New Disputing System Better Suited to the Goals. The designer's next task is to determine whether different systems of dispute resolution fit the users' goals most closely. The designer begins by identifying general principles, such as those described by Goldberg, Brett and Ury (see Part C), including a preference for interest-based processes such as mediation over right-based processes such as arbitration. Then, the designer should reflect on the basic lessons about negotiation, mediation, and arbitration discussed in the last three chapters.

Often, the tailoring of processes to goals tempts the designer to vary the basic processes of negotiation, mediation, arbitration, and litigation. The designer may infuse mediation with a strong dose of reality, changing the process to what has been called "neutral evaluation" or adding a hearing-like portion such as a "mini-trial" or "summary jury trial." Common variations are discussed in Part B; others are added every year.

Consult Throughout the Planning. The designer also should seek input during the planning and implementation from the client and those affected by the processes. An organizational client presents special challenges. Is the client the management of the corporation or the employees? If the client's interests conflict with those of the employees, can the architect afford to ignore them in the design? If a corporation asks for a better system for employee grievances, Merchant and Costantino (see Part C) suggest that the designer may be wise to involve employees as well as management to identify goals and priorities and to consider options for creating a new system that meets needs more broadly. Securing "buy-in" for a new court or public agency system requires understanding the needs of many constituencies, some of whom cannot be reached for consultation. Chapters 6 and 9 address the complex systems of values and decision-making facing the designer in that context.

Anticipate and Plan for Potential Problems with the New System. The dispute system designer also needs expertise in sources of failure. Why do some courts abandon the mediation programs? Why do parties resist participation in the new system? Some of these cautions become more evident after reading later chapters. A partial list of problems that sometimes cause a proposed mediation system to fail might include:

1. *In the midst of a dispute, at least one key party often resists coming to the mediation table.* Therefore, high volume mediation programs typically depend on strong-arm

referrals, pre-dispute mediation contract clauses, or court or public agency directives to participate (see Chapter 6).

2. *Mediation parties settle most often if they trust the process.* Key components of securing that trust include assurance about the mediator's competence (see Chapter 3); how the information will be used (see Chapter 7); whether the mediator has integrity; and perhaps whether the mediator is neutral (see Chapters 3 and 11).
3. *Coercion to settle within mediation fosters resentment and stimulates charges of unfairness over time.* Thus, the pressures that increase settlement rates by, for example, permitting a mediator to threaten the recalcitrant party with disclosure to the judge, may be counter-productive in terms of long-term satisfaction with the process (see Chapter 6).
4. *Negotiation approaches vary by culture.* Techniques that are effective in one setting may not achieve the same results in another (see Chapters 3 and 11).

Help to Implement and Re-assess the New System. Even the best plan may remain on the shelf unless the designer lends a hand at the implementation stage. A small start through a pilot program and an assessment program may serve both to overcome reluctance and to improve the design (see Part C).

This chapter provides more detail on the steps outlined above. Part B explores common combinations of processes. Part C provides more advice on systems design, and Part D on matching process and dispute. Part E narrows the lens to the practicing lawyer and the individual client.

The dispute system designer often creatively challenges conventional wisdom. The designer feeds creativity by learning about successful innovation in a variety of settings. For example, the domestic relations bar has traditionally used an inchoate blend of negotiation and adjudication to solve the problems of clients. Even if this established pattern does not meet clients' needs, is it likely to change? Part F includes a story about domestic relations lawyers who challenged tradition by establishing a new paradigm that puts more emphasis on party control through a changed approach to negotiation.

B. INNOVATIONS IN THE PROCESSES

An initial option for the design elsewhere is to create a new process. The new process might combine elements of the traditional processes—negotiation, mediation, and arbitration—to fit the parties' or the institution's goals. The modified processes described in this section have been used so frequently that lawyers now associate a label, like "mini-trial," with common attributes. The use of these processes spawns legal and policy issues, some of which are examined in this section.

For dispute designers, the processes in this section represent only a start. An effective designer is an innovator at heart and an avid student of new dispute resolutions systems in this nation and elsewhere (see Chapter 11).

1. *Variants of Arbitration*

a. Arbitration of Disputes About Contract Terms and Final Offer Arbitration

Although arbitration is frequently used to resolve disputes about the interpretation or application of an existing contract, it is rarely used to resolve disputes about what the terms of a new contract should be. The reasons for the reluctance to use arbitration in this context are manifold. Parties who have an unresolvable dispute as to their rights under an existing contract must find some adjudicative means to determine those rights, but parties who have an unresolvable dispute concerning what their rights should be under a contract they are seeking to negotiate typically are under no such obligation. If they cannot agree, each is free to seek other parties with whom to negotiate. Hence, they tend to be reluctant to vest a third party with the power to decide what their rights against each other should be. This reluctance is typically overcome only when negotiating parties are required, for any of a number of reasons, to deal exclusively with each other and to reach agreement.

The most widespread use of interest arbitration is in public sector collective bargaining. When a public employer is required by law to negotiate with the union representing its employees, the consequences of a failure to agree—a public employee strike or unilateral employer determination of terms and conditions of employment or both—are sufficiently undesirable that arbitration is sometimes mandated by law. Another context in which interest arbitration is used is in the resolution of salary disputes between major league baseball players and their employers. The baseball players' union and the team owners have agreed that players with under six years of major league service must negotiate their contracts with one team, rather than being free to sell their services to the highest bidder. Since players negotiate the salary portion of their contracts on an individual basis, rather than through collective bargaining, the strike is not a practical option when these negotiations break down. While some players have no option, under these circumstances, but to accept the employer's offer (or not play major league baseball), the labor contract provides for the arbitration of salary disputes for those players with three to six years of service, as well as for a limited number of players with two years of service.

Among the risks associated with the use of arbitration to set contract terms is that availability of arbitration will have a chilling effect on the bargaining process. The parties may avoid making compromises that they might otherwise make because they fear that the arbitrator will split the difference between their final positions. Assume, for example, that the management of baseball team *A* has offered player *B* $400,000 for the coming year, while *B* has demanded $800,000. Management would be willing to go to $600,000, but it fears that if it does and the player stays at $800,000, the arbitrator will split the difference and award the player $700,000. Thus, management will remain firmly at $400,000. The same rationale is likely to affect the player who would be willing to accept $600,000, but does not say so for fear the team will stay at $400,000, and the arbitrator will award $500,000. Thus, the availability of arbitration tends to discourage successful negotiation because each side holds back on concessions that it might otherwise be willing to make.

In order to avoid the chilling effect of conventional arbitration on negotiations, both the major league baseball players' contract and many public sector collective bargaining laws provide for final-offer arbitration. Under final-offer arbitration, the arbitrator may not compromise but must choose the final offer of either one party or the other. This should advance the prospects of successful bargaining. The parties, knowing that the arbitrator cannot compromise, are likely to assume that he will select the more reasonable offer. If each party strives to make its last offer more reasonable than the other party's final offer, the prospects for agreement without resort to arbitration are increased.

To return to the example above, the team that was reluctant to increase its offer from $400,000 to $600,000 because of the risk that the player would stay at $800,000 and the arbitrator would compromise at $700,000, will now be under pressure to move from $400,000 to $600,000. It will fear that if it does not so compromise and the player stays at $800,000, the arbitrator will find $800,000 more reasonable than $400,000 and award $800,000. Similarly, the player will be under pressure to move from $800,000 toward $600,000 for fear that if he does not the arbitrator will find $800,000 unreasonable and award the team's last offer, whatever that may be. To the extent that the availability of final offer arbitration tends to encourage the parties to moderate extreme positions and to move towards each other, it should serve to encourage agreement without resort to arbitration.

The available empirical evidence tends to support the theory that final-offer arbitration has a less chilling effect on negotiation than does conventional arbitration. In those jurisdictions in which conventional arbitration is available after negotiation, arbitration is used approximately twice as often as it is in jurisdictions in which final-offer arbitration is available (Kochan, 1980:288-289).

b. Arbitration Under a "High-Low" Contract

This is essentially adjudication (often in the context of arbitration) with the limits of recovery and loss bounded by agreement of the parties. For example, in a personal injury case in which the plaintiff's demand is for $500,000, the parties may agree in advance of trial that if the jury returns a verdict for the defendant on the issue of liability, the defendant will nonetheless pay the plaintiff a predetermined amount, say $100,000. If the jury's verdict on liability is for the plaintiff, the defendant pays a higher fixed sum, say $300,000. The jury never reaches the issue of damages. The parties retain their rights to appeal on liability issues, but, obviously, waive their appeal rights as to damages.

The principal advantage of arbitration or adjudication under a high-low agreement is that it reduces the risk to both sides by converting a "win-lose" situation into a "partial win-partial lose" situation. The plaintiff is protected against the risk of no return; the defendant is protected against the risk of a staggering liability. A second advantage is that it minimizes the time spent on trying and preparing to try damages. Other advantages include the elimination of appeals based on damages, elimination of compromise verdicts, and the establishment of a cooperative atmosphere that may of itself lead to settlement.

In a variation of this approach the damage issue is also tried, but the parties agree beforehand that if the award falls outside the high-low brackets to which they have agreed, the award will be adjusted to the high or low point. If the award is within the brackets, damages are set at that figure. The disadvantage of this approach is that the parties must try the damage issue. The advantage is that it may be easier to get agreement on the high-low figures because they are not quite as crucial: they determine only the parameters, not necessarily the amount of damages.

c. Tripartite Arbitration

Sometimes parties wish to have three neutral arbitrators, much like an appellate court. Such a process raises no special problems. Occasionally, however, parties provide for a different kind of tripartite panel in which each side names an arbitrator of its choice and then the two party-appointed arbitrators select the neutral chairperson of the three-arbitrator panel. Typically, each party–appointed arbitrator is aligned with the party that appointed her. While parties are free to develop rules to govern the party-appointed and neutral arbitrators' behavior, most tripartite arbitrations anticipate both that the party-appointed arbitrator will be biased in favor of the party who appointed her and that ex parte communications between the party and her arbitrator are permissible, as long as the intention to make such contacts is disclosed to the other arbitrators and the parties.

Parties contract for tripartite arbitration for a variety of reasons. If the party-appointed arbitrator is permitted to have ex parte communications with his party's attorney, critical and evaluative discussions of approach and presentation may benefit the party in developing an effective case. Moreover, during the arbitral hearing, the party-appointed arbitrator may be able to ask questions and elicit answers from the witness that a less knowledgeable or wholly objective arbitrator may overlook.

The value of a party-appointed arbitrator's contributions to the deliberative process depends in large part on the neutral arbitrator's interest in that arbitrator's input. In a complex case that requires specific expertise, a party-appointed arbitrator may provide the neutral arbitrator with useful analysis and commentary on the issues. A neutral arbitrator who is unsure of the outcome may consult extensively with the party-appointed arbitrator in a confidential executive session. In this scenario, a party-appointed arbitrator may be quite valuable because that arbitrator may be able to offer significant input that affects the outcome. A neutral arbitrator confident of the outcome, by contrast, may be less interested in collaboration because the neutral arbitrator will be fairly certain to receive at least one panel member's vote. (See Rogers, 2001.)

Two major disadvantages of tripartite arbitration are time and cost. In a straightforward case where the neutral arbitrator is not interested in input from the party-appointed arbitrators, the expense of a party-appointed arbitrator is wasted. Time is also squandered during a tripartite arbitration if the neutral arbitrator must engage in inefficient negotiations with the panelist most likely to join in his opinion because that panelist is not fully satisfied with the proposed outcome. In addition, the neutral arbitrator may have to abandon his proposed arbitration award in order to gain concurrence from one of his fellow panelists.

Another technical problem may arise. In tripartite arbitration, the partisan arbitrators are named in advance, and sometimes unions and employers appoint important members of their organization as partisan arbitrators. As a result, the partisan arbitrator also may be a necessary witness. The arrangement may be problematic both from a process perspective and because it creates a potential conflict of interest.

To avoid these potential disadvantages, parties considering tripartite arbitration might provide for a screening procedure. Rather than automatically sending cases to tripartite boards, the parties could, by contract, agree that they will evaluate each case as it arises to determine whether the case is appropriate for tripartite arbitration.

Even if the parties use tripartite arbitration efficiently, courts will likely continue to be skeptical of the tripartite arrangement. While acknowledging that parties are free to agree to any form of dispute resolution that they wish, some courts have expressed the opinion that permitting an arbitrator to act as an advocate in the same proceeding may be improper. See, e.g., *Barcon Associates, Inc. v. Tri-County Asphalt Corp.*, 430 A.2d 214 (N.J. 1981) (court will independently review tripartite arbitration process for inappropriate appearance of bias). Nevertheless, courts have difficulty drawing the line between proper partisanship and dishonest behavior and have little legislative or policy guidance on which to draw. The Federal Arbitration Act (FAA) provides virtually no guidance on the issue. While an award may be challenged for "evident partiality," it is more likely that the provision was intended to discourage partisan behavior by neutral arbitrators than partisanship by party-appointed arbitrators. The Code of Ethics for Arbitrators in Commercial Disputes maintains the most comprehensive rules designed to govern party-appointed arbitrators' behavior. Yet these rules do not provide a clear demarcation between proper and improper behavior. For example, Canon VII states, "[n]onneutral arbitrators may be predisposed toward the party who appointed them but in all other respects are obligated to act in good faith and with integrity and fairness. For example, nonneutral arbitrators should not engage in delaying tactics or harassment of any party or witness and should not knowingly make untrue or misleading statements to the other arbitrators." By necessity, the Code also alters the rules on conflicts of interest and disclosure for the party-appointed arbitrator. Even so, the standard governing behavior provides little guidance to either the party-appointed arbitrators or parties that may wish to challenge an award on the basis of partiality.*

Although the line between permissible partisanship and impropriety is not distinct in policy or practice, parties that select tripartite arbitration are typically repeat players in labor or commercial arbitration and are thus quite aware of the risks associated with the process. As parties seek innovative methods for resolving disputes and consider tripartite arbitration in other contexts, courts or legislatures may need to develop clearer guidelines for implementation and judicial evaluation.

d. Med-Arb

In this process, the neutral functions first as a mediator, helping the parties arrive at a mutually acceptable outcome. If mediation fails, the same neutral then serves as an arbitrator, issuing a final and binding decision.

*The Revised Uniform Arbitration Act (see Appendix D) imposes stricter conflict of interest disclosure requirements. The Act imposes the same disclosure obligations on neutral and party-appointed arbitrators. Both arbitrator types must make a reasonable inquiry into potential conflicts and then disclose those conflicts a reasonable person would "consider likely to affect the impartiality of the arbitrator . . ." RUAA §12(a), App. D. An arbitrator who fails to reveal conflicts subjects her award to a vacatur challenge. Id. at §12(d).

The central advantage of med-arb over "pure" mediation followed if necessary by "pure" arbitration, in which different neutrals serve as mediator and arbitrator, is said to be that of efficiency. In the event that mediation fails, the parties need not educate another neutral; the neutral who has been serving as mediator already knows much, if not all, of the information needed to make a decision.

In reality, it is not quite so simple. As Lon Fuller (1962:30) points out, "since the objective of reaching a . . . settlement is different from that of rendering an award . . . , the facts relevant in the two cases are different, or, when they seem the same, are viewed in different aspects." Thus, the mediator turned arbitrator may not be able to issue a decision on the basis of the facts elicited in the mediation stage, but may need to elicit additional evidence or argument. Still, this will be considerably more efficient than starting all over again to select another neutral and educate that neutral from scratch.

Conceding that med-arb has an efficiency advantage over "pure" mediation followed by "pure" arbitration, it nonetheless has some disadvantages. Initially, disputing parties who know that the mediator also has decisional authority are likely to be less candid than they would be with a "pure" mediator about such matters as how they prioritize their interests and the least they will accept to resolve the dispute. They will be unwilling to be candid about these matters because they will fear that if no agreement is reached, the mediator turned arbitrator will use their disclosures against them. For example, a party's disclosure that it would settle for $5,000, rather than the $10,000 it has been demanding, might be used by the mediator turned arbitrator to limit an award in favor of that party to $5,000. Hence, that party will not tell the mediator that, if necessary, it would settle for $5,000. Lacking that information, the mediator may be unable to help the parties reach a settlement at $5,000. In sum, because the med-arb mediator is likely to have less information at his disposal than is the "pure" mediator, he is less likely to obtain mediated settlements.

If, on the other hand, the parties have been candid in the mediation process but no agreement is reached, the mediator turned arbitrator will possess information that he would not have acquired in a purely arbitral role. In the foregoing example, if the claimant disclosed her willingness to accept $5,000, the arbitrator, who is anxious to maintain the good will of both parties for future employment purposes, will find it difficult to ignore that fact in reaching a decision. Even if he does so and concludes independently that the claimant should receive only $5,000, the claimant will suspect that the arbitrator has improperly used information conveyed to him in mediation. Thus, the integrity of both mediation and arbitration is placed at risk when the same person serves as both mediator and arbitrator (Fuller, 1962).

Med-arb is sometimes said to be superior to pure mediation on the grounds that a binding resolution is assured in med-arb. While that is true, the process by which resolution is reached in med-arb may be quite different from the process by which agreement is reached in mediation. In mediation, since the neutral lacks decisional power, the parties' efforts will be directed primarily at developing a resolution of their dispute that is acceptable to each of them. In med-arb, where the neutral has decisional power, each party's primary effort will be to persuade the neutral that it is right. An agreed-upon solution may be more likely in the latter situation than the former, but it is often agreed upon in form only, accepted by the parties (or at least one of them) because the neutral stated that if it were not accepted in mediation, it would be imposed in arbitration.

The different settlement dynamic in med-arb may have two negative consequences in comparison with mediation. Initially, if the parties in med-arb feel that a settlement has been imposed upon them, rather than voluntarily agreed to, they may be less willing to comply with that settlement (see p. 182). Additionally, if the parties focus primarily on persuading the mediator that they are "right" rather than on seeking an accommodation with the other party, they will not improve their ability to resolve disputes without resort to an outside decision-maker. Conversely, there is evidence that participating in mediation with a skilled mediator in an effort to negotiate a resolution and observing how the mediator deals with conflict, asks questions, makes proposals, and seeks alternative solutions improves the parties' ability to resolve disputes even without a mediator (Ury, Brett, and Goldberg, 1988:159). For parties with an ongoing relationship, it may be more important to learn how to reach mutually acceptable accommodations without outside assistance than it is to have a particular dispute resolved promptly and efficiently. Thus, mediation is particularly preferable to med-arb in the context of an ongoing relationship (Goldberg, 1989, 1990).

In an effort to retain the advantages of med-arb while avoiding its disadvantages, some parties have used a variant of med-arb pursuant to which the neutral first acts as a mediator and then as an advisory arbitrator. The neutral is empowered to advise or predict for the parties the likely outcome if they arbitrate but not to serve as arbitrator. If the combination of mediation and advisory arbitration does not lead to resolution, the parties must go to another neutral for final and binding arbitration.

The advantages and disadvantages of this process over standard med-arb are apparent. Since the mediator has no arbitral power, candor in mediation is encouraged, as is the likelihood of a true mediated agreement. The process also serves, as does mediation, the relational advantages of improving the parties' ability to resolve their own disputes. On the other hand, if agreement is not reached and a different neutral must be brought in to arbitrate, the process is likely to be lengthier and more expensive than standard med-arb. A crucial question in gauging the value of this process compared to standard med-arb is thus its success in bringing about settlements without recourse to arbitration.

In the labor context, the available evidence suggests that mediation-advisory arbitration (known in that context as grievance mediation) has been highly successful. Researchers have collected data on approximately 3,000 disputes that have been submitted to grievance mediation and have found that approximately 85 percent of those disputes have been resolved without resort to arbitration.*

e. Court-Annexed Arbitrations

Unlike its voluntary counterpart (see Chapter 4), court-annexed arbitration (COA) is a mandatory, nonbinding form of adjudication, provided for by a statute or court rule in about 33 states and 22 federal district courts (Plapinger and Stienstra, 1996). The program usually extends to a class of cases (such as automobile torts or all money claim cases, with specified exceptions) involving claims below a

*Communication to the authors from Mediation Research and Education Project, Northwestern University, August 1998.

specified jurisdictional amount. Often there is a procedure for judicial exemption from the program for cases that are inappropriate or for voluntary inclusion of cases not covered by the statute. Although there are considerable variations from jurisdiction to jurisdiction, the claims are typically handled in simplified informal hearings before a court-approved arbitrator who is often a volunteer lawyer or retired judge. The arbitrator then renders an award that becomes final after a specified number of days if neither party seeks a trial de novo in court. Sometimes there are disincentives to automatic resort to the de novo remedy in the form of various costs on the petitioner if he does not improve his position in court (or in some jurisdictions do 10 percent better than he did in the arbitration).

Questions

5.1 You represent a property management company that has been negotiating to buy a large downtown office building for approximately six months. All terms of the sale have been agreed on except one: despite numerous concessions by both sides, the parties are at impasse about the sales price. The seller is demanding $200 million; your client is refusing to go above $175 million. Your client is convinced that there is no other building in town that suits its needs as well as this one and is most anxious to buy it. This client is also convinced that its offer is wholly fair and that, as a matter of principle, it ought not increase the amount it is willing to pay. You convey these sentiments to the lawyer for the building owner, and she responds by suggesting that the dispute be submitted to arbitration. What advice would you give to your client regarding this suggestion? If you recommended accepting it, would you propose conventional arbitration or final offer arbitration? How about med-arb?

5.2 You represent an associate professor of sociology at a small mid-western college who is involved in a dispute with one of his colleagues, another associate professor of sociology at the same school, about which of them is entitled to be listed as first author of a book on which they worked together for several years. Each of them claims he did more work than the other and hence is entitled to first authorship. Each of them also asserts that being listed as first author is important for career advancement purposes, since the first author is typically assumed to have made the primary contribution. The two professors have agreed to arbitrate the dispute, but the evidence concerning which of them actually did more work is wholly inconclusive. You have no idea how the arbitration will turn out.

About a week before the scheduled arbitration is to take place, you receive two telephone calls. First, your client calls to tell you that he has been offered a tenured position as a full professor of sociology at a prestigious eastern university. No announcement of this offer has been made, nor will it be announced for several months. Your client also tells you that he still regards his claim as important and wants you to pursue it vigorously.

Later the same day, you receive a call from the attorney representing the other professor. She tells you that she, too, finds the evidence wholly inconclusive. Accordingly, she suggests that, with the assistance of the arbitrator, acting as mediator, you make an effort to resolve the dispute before resorting to arbitration, which she predicts (and you agree) will be both lengthy and expensive. How would you respond to her suggestion?

5.3 In response to the criticisms of med-arb (pp. 308-309), one commentator (Buehring-Uhle, 1991) has proposed the use of a process called "co-med-arb." In this process, one mediator and one arbitrator would jointly conduct a fact-finding hearing followed by mediated settlement discussions in the absence of the arbitrator. If those discussions did not result in an agreement, the arbitrator would issue a decision. What are the strengths and weaknesses of this proposal? How might you cure any weaknesses that you see?

Another response has been arb-med. Here the neutral first hears the case as an arbitrator and renders a decision that is put in a sealed envelope. Then he tries to mediate the case. If he is successful, that ends the matter. If not, the envelope is opened to reveal the premediation arbitration decision. How would you evaluate this variant of med-arb?

5.4 You are the senior partner of the law firm that represents the ABC Manufacturing Company in all labor relations matters, including the negotiation and administration of its collective bargaining agreements. In the last 12 months, your firm represented ABC in over 50 arbitration hearings, prevailing in 36. ABC and the union that represents its employees are now engaged in negotiations for a new collective bargaining agreement. Among the union's proposals is a provision for the mediation of grievances along the lines suggested at page 309. Having done so well at arbitration, the company is reluctant to adopt a different procedure, and requests your advice. How would you respond?

5.5 Usually COA awards are not admissible in a subsequent de novo proceeding. Should they be?

5.6 You represent the defendant doctor in a medical malpractice COA case. The arbitrator awards the plaintiff $16,000. You file a de novo action, resulting in a judgment for plaintiff of $25,000, whereupon, under the applicable local rule, the court imposes attorney's fees and court costs on your client in the amount of $13,000. What arguments might you make against the imposition of such sanctions?

5.7 The state and federal courts of Michigan feature an ADR program called "case evaluation." It calls for a panel of three neutrals to evaluate the case following brief presentation by both sides. The evaluation is then embodied into a court order if all parties accept it. If a party rejects the evaluation, sanctions are authorized where the rejecting party does not improve on the evaluation by at least 10 percent. How would you classify this procedure according to the schema set forth earlier in this section?

5.8 Assume you are hired by the chief justice of a state court system to help her set up a COA program for tort cases. What are the principal design issues you will want to consider? How might you resolve them?

EXERCISE 5.1: SOUTHERN ELECTRIC COMPANY AND PUBLIC UTILITY WORKERS UNION, AFL-CIO*

Southern Electric is a public utility serving four southern and central states. Its 10,000 service, maintenance and clerical employees are represented by the Public Utility Workers Union, AFL-CIO.

*This mediation simulation was developed by Mediation Research & Education Project, Inc., Northwestern University Law School, 357 East Chicago Avenue, Chicago, IL 60611, and is reprinted with permission. A videotape of the mediation is available from Mediation Research & Education Project, Inc.

The collective bargaining agreement, in addition to the typical management rights clause and provision for discipline for just cause, allows the company to establish reasonable rules concerning the conduct of employees. Under the latter provision, the company, for the last four years, has had a rule providing for the discharge of any employee, who, in the course of operating company vehicles, is involved in three preventable accidents in a three-year period. This rule is contained in the employee handbook provided to all employees when they are hired and is posted in areas used by employees with vehicle operating responsibilities. Prior to this case, no employee had reached the three accident-three year level. Nor has the union ever challenged the reasonableness of the three accident-three year rule.

The company has a comprehensive safety program for all drivers, including a 20-hour defensive driving course for employees newly assigned to company vehicles. The safety department conducts these courses; it also investigates all accidents involving company vehicles. Any employee found by the safety department to have been involved in a preventable accident must repeat the defensive driving course.

Joe Doaks has ten years of service with the company. For three years he was a maintenance mechanic in the shop, repairing and maintaining equipment. For the last seven years, he has been a maintenance driver, operating out of a company truck to perform maintenance and repair work on fixed equipment.

Nine months ago, Doaks was involved in an accident while driving a company truck. The official safety department accident report stated that an automobile approaching Doaks's truck, on the opposite side of a two-lane road, had turned left in front of Doaks's truck, that Doaks swerved and braked to avoid colliding with the auto, but hit the right front fender of the auto, causing approximately $500 damage to each vehicle. The report went on to state that Doaks could have avoided the accident had he practiced defensive driving techniques.

The police report stated that Doaks's skid marks indicated he was observing the 25-mile-per-hour speed limit, that the weather was clear, and that visibility was normal. It quoted the driver of the other car as saying that she signaled before she turned in front of Doaks's truck, and quoted Doaks as denying that she had signaled. Neither driver was charged by the police with having violated traffic laws.

Doaks had been involved in two previous accidents while driving company vehicles within the past three years, both of which had been found preventable. One, two years ago, was relatively minor. The other, approximately eighteen months ago, had resulted in an out-of-court settlement by the company of $40,000. After each of these accidents, Doaks repeated the defensive driving course but received no discipline. The union did not file a grievance in either instance.

Based on the safety department's report of the most recent accident and on the previous two preventable accidents, the company discharged Doaks at a meeting at which Doaks had union representation. Within the contract's time limits, he filed a grievance for reinstatement with full back pay. The grievance was not resolved at the first three steps of the grievance procedure and is now scheduled for mediation. If the grievance is not resolved at mediation, the union has the contractual right to demand final and binding arbitration.

(Confidential information for the mediator, the grievant, the union representative, the company maintenance superintendent, and the company industrial relations manager is contained in the Teacher's Manual.)

2. *Minitrial**

In the minitrial, most often used in business disputes, summary presentations are made by attorneys for each party to a panel consisting of a neutral advisor and high-level executives with settlement authority. At the conclusion of the presentations, the executives attempt to negotiate a resolution of their dispute. If they are unable to do so, they may call on the neutral advisor to give a prediction of the likely outcome if the matter is litigated.

The concept underlying the minitrial is that it provides each business executive with a crash course in the merits of the dispute—a brief but firsthand view of the best case that can be put forward by the attorneys for both sides, supplemented, if necessary, by the views of a neutral. Armed with this information, as well as their knowledge of the business relationships of the parties, the executives are equipped to negotiate a resolution of their dispute that makes business sense.

Although the specific procedures of a minitrial may vary depending on the case and the parties' desires, most minitrials contain these key elements:

1. The parties *voluntarily agree* to conduct a minitrial. There is no statutory, regulatory, or (usually) contractual obligation to participate in a minitrial. Parties may terminate the minitrial at any time.

2. The parties negotiate and sign a "protocol" or *procedural agreement* that spells out the steps and timing of the minitrial process. This agreement usually specifies the parties' obligations and responsibilities in the minitrial process, their right to terminate the process, and certain legal matters such as confidentiality of the proceedings and the effect of the process on any pending or future litigation.

3. Prior to the minitrial, the parties *informally exchange key documents,* exhibits, summaries of witnesses' testimony, and short introductory statements in the nature of briefs. The parties may agree to engage in shortened, expedited depositions and other discovery without prejudice to their right to take full discovery later if the minitrial does not settle the case.

4. The *parties select a neutral advisor to preside* over the minitrial. Unlike an arbitrator or judge, the neutral advisor has no authority to make a binding decision but may ask questions that probe the strengths and weaknesses of each party's case. Also, after the minitrial the neutral advisor may be asked by the parties' representatives to advise them on what the likely outcome would be if the case went to trial. Selection of a respected neutral advisor with credibility to the opponent is thus very important: one of the principal goals of the participants if they cannot obtain a favorable settlement in direct negotiations is to persuade the neutral advisor to advise the opponent that it would be better off settling than taking the case to trial.

In most minitrials, the parties select a former judge as the neutral advisor because they believe that a person with prior judicial experience is best able to give them

*The following discussion is taken primarily from Green, Marks, and Olson (1978); Green (1982a); and Green (1982b).

sound advice on likely trial outcomes. In some minitrials, the parties select a nonjudicial expert in the subject matter as the neutral advisor. In other minitrials, the parties dispense with the neutral advisor altogether and rely solely on their business representatives to preside over the minitrial and to conduct the negotiations privately. In still other cases, the parties want the neutral advisor to attempt to mediate a resolution of the dispute. The function the neutral advisor is expected to perform will determine the kind of person best suited for the role. Thus, the most successful neutral advisors have been those who are capable of playing the roles of advisor, mediator, and facilitator as the situation dictates and the parties ultimately determine.

5. At the minitrial itself, the parties' *lawyers make concise, summary presentations of their best case.* Minitrials may last from half a day to three or four days (two days seems typical). Thus, presentations might be limited to from one to six hours for each side, depending on the complexity of the issues. Generally, each party retains complete discretion over how it will use its allotted time. In some cases, the entire presentation is made by the lawyers, similar to an appellate or closing argument. In others, the lawyers call key witnesses to explain parts of the case. Often, key documents are used to explain the case. Quite often, the parties' experts testify on the technical issues. At other minitrials, parties have used movies, views of the scene, and other imaginative devices to communicate the essence of a case in the short time allotted.

At the minitrial, rules of evidence do not apply. Thus, if there is testimony by witnesses, it tends to be in a narrative form under informal questioning by counsel rather than in the question and answer form of trial examination. In most minitrials, time is set aside for rebuttal. This may include an opportunity for questions to opposing counsel, witnesses, and experts, again in an informal, modified cross-examination format. It may also include an open question and answer session in which expert may question expert, lawyer may question lawyer, and client may question client, or any variation of these combinations.

6. Minitrial *presentations are made to high-level representatives of the parties* who have clear settlement authority. Often, the representatives are nonlawyers who have not been involved in creating or trying to resolve the underlying dispute, but who have authority or at least persuasive power over the decision of whether to settle. In cases involving businesses, the party representatives are generally at least one level higher in the corporate hierarchy than the businesspeople who have been involved in the case prior to the minitrial.

At the minitrial, the nonlegal party representatives listen, observe, and ask questions to clarify points, much like a judge or arbitrator would, but they do not sit with or assist the advocates. Immediately after the parties' adversarial presentations on the merits of the case, the nonlegal representatives meet privately and attempt to negotiate a resolution. The theory behind the minitrial is that the party representatives, once they are informed about the merits of the dispute, will be better able than the advocates or lower-level party representatives to appraise their positions and negotiate a mutually beneficial settlement.

7. Most minitrial agreements specify that the entire process, including both any statements made in the course of the minitrial and the opinion of the neutral advisor, is *confidential and inadmissible* in any subsequent proceeding. The parties also agree that the neutral advisor may not testify or consult with any party in that

case. Such agreements, however, face uncertain prospects of enforcement. See page 460.

EXERCISE 5.2: WORLD OIL CO. v. NORTHEAST SHIPBUILDING, INC.*

General Information

World Oil Co. was the sole owner and operator of the Very Large Crude Carrier (VLCC) *J. B. John.* The *J. B. John* was one of only four existing VLCCs, at the time the largest oil tankers in the world. Northeast Shipbuilding, Inc., which had built ships for World for many years, designed and built the *J. B. John* and delivered the ship to World in May 1997. The other three VLCCs also built by Northeast were owned and operated by other tanker companies.

On April 16, 2003, at about 9:45 A.M., while the *J. B. John* was in the English Channel, approximately eight miles off the coast of France, she suffered a complete breakdown of her steering gear and began to drift out of control. Heavy winds and rough seas aggravated the situation and caused the *J. B. John* to drift toward the French shore. The crew of the *J. B. John* attempted to repair the broken steering gear but without success.

At approximately 11:30 A.M., Captain Francis Griffin of the *J. B. John* called for tug assistance. The salvage tug *Superior* responded, and at approximately 4:00 P.M., a tow line was attached from the *J. B. John* to the *Superior.* The *Superior* began towing the *J. B. John* away from shore, but at 4:15 P.M. the tow line parted. Approximately 30 minutes later, the *J. B. John* struck ground, causing leakage of her oil cargo. The vessel grounded again at about 5:30 P.M. Her engine room then flooded, and the French Coast Guard came to lift all hands ashore. At 4:00 A.M. on April 17, the vessel broke in two.

As a result of the grounding, the *J. B. John*'s entire 230,000 tons of crude oil spilled and washed ashore, causing extensive damage to French beaches and shoreline. The government of France, along with residents, businesses, hotels, and tour operators, brought suit in France against World. Under French law, World was strictly liable for the damages resulting from the oil spill. After a trial limited to the issue of damages, World was ordered in April 2006 to pay plaintiffs $1.2 billion.

Since the grounding of the *J. B. John* and continuing through the award of damages, both World Oil and its CEO, Blaine Kelly, were the subject of intensive criticism in the world press. According to the media, World caused irreparable damage to the ecology of the French coastline, altering forever a way of life that had persisted for centuries. Kelly, who throughout the affair had been unwilling to comment on it, was also blasted for demonstrating, according to one paper, "a stunning lack of compassion and insensitivity" to the damage done by World.

In October 2006, World brought suit against Northeast in the U.S. District Court for Ames seeking contribution and indemnification from Northeast. According to World, the *J. B. John* was defectively designed and built by Northeast, causing the ship's grounding and the subsequent oil spill.

*This exercise is adapted from advanced trial advocacy materials developed by the National Institute for Trial Advocacy and from a Center for Public Resources videotape, *Out of Court.*

Contentions of the Parties

The contentions of the parties, drawn from their initial pleadings and responses, are these:

According to World, the *J. B. John* was completely designed and constructed by Northeast. The vessel was designed to carry crude oil across the seas and to withstand the normal rigors of maritime transport, such as heavy winds and high seas. However, on April 16, 2003, on a typical trip across the seas, the *J. B. John*'s steering gear failed. This breakdown was caused by the failure of a flange on the steering gear and of studs holding the flange, which caused hydraulic fluid to leak from the steering gear system. This loss of fluid caused a complete loss of pressure within the system and rendered the steering gear mechanism incapable of turning the ship's rudder. On inspection, it was found that the studs that failed were not spaced equidistantly around the flange that blew open and that the flange itself was not designed to withstand the pressure that existed within the hydraulic steering system. There is also evidence that Northeast Shipbuilding did not use materials that could withstand the pressures that it knew would build up within the steering system, and that Northeast miscalculated the pressure that would in fact build up within the system. Had it not been for the actions of Northeast, the *J. B. John* would never have grounded and spilled its oil. Northeast is liable to World on theories of strict liability, breach of warranty, and negligence. Northeast should thus be required to indemnify World for the $1.2 billion in damages which World has been ordered to pay as a result of the oil spill.

According to Northeast, it built the *J. B. John* according to specifications provided by World, implementing a new design, that of a very large crude oil carrier, in compliance with national and international shipbuilding standards. The materials used in the steering gear were tested, and similar materials had been used previously in steering mechanisms installed in the *J. B. John*'s three sister ships. None of those ships has had difficulty with its steering mechanisms. In brief, Northeast's steering gear was a reasonably safe product that was installed with reasonable care.

Furthermore, according to Northeast, the damages assessed against World resulted from World's own negligence. Initially, Northeast recommended to World, at the time the *J. B. John* was under construction, that an auxiliary steering system be installed, which would have operated if the main steering gear failed, but World failed to accept that recommendation. Additionally, World failed to maintain the steering system properly. This became obvious when the steering gear mechanism was recovered from the ship, and it was found that the studs throughout the system were tightened at different tensions and many were missing washers. Because the damages for which World was held liable were solely the result of its negligence, World is not entitled to contribution or indemnification from Northeast.

A Minitrial

Last month, Judge Mary Kessel, to whom *World v. Northeast* had been assigned, met with counsel for both parties for a status conference pursuant to Rule 16 of the Federal Rules of Civil Procedure. During this conference, it became apparent that each side had a very different view of the facts and had reached quite different conclusions about the relative strengths of its case and the amount of an appropriate settlement. Further, counsel made clear that there was much that needed to be learned through discovery before they would have a complete picture of the case. At the end of this discussion the court "suggested" to the parties that they talk about whether a minitrial might be an effective procedure for attempting to resolve their dispute.

a. Each party having decided that it would like to participate in a minitrial, their general counsel, each accompanied by outside trial counsel, now meet to negotiate the terms of a minitrial procedural agreement.

b. Outside trial counsel now conduct a minitrial pursuant to the terms of the procedural agreement. Also participating in the minitrial will be business representatives, inside counsel, and a neutral advisor (if the agreement provides for a neutral).

(Confidential information for both parties is contained in the Teacher's Manual.)

3. *Summary Jury Trial*

The summary jury trial is an adaptation of the minitrial for cases in which the parties want more direct information about likely jury reaction than they would receive from the prediction of a minitrial neutral advisor. The summary jury trial takes place in court with a judge or magistrate presiding and an advisory jury, drawn from the regular jury pool, in the jury box. The jurors usually are not told that their role is advisory until after they return their verdict. Thus, they are encouraged to treat their decisional task as seriously as would an actual jury.

Lawyers for each party make summary presentations, typically based on material that has been the subject of discovery and would be admissible at trial. The jurors deliberate, return a verdict, and then answer the attorneys' questions about both their verdict and their reaction to particular evidence and arguments. Following the return of the jury's verdict and the questioning of the jury, the lawyers and their principals, whose attendance is mandatory, engage in settlement discussions. If no settlement results, the jury's verdict is not admissible at trial.

While summary jury trials undoubtedly settle some cases that would otherwise go to trial, the frequency with which they do so is unknown (Posner, 1986). Additionally, the process is sufficiently costly in terms of court time that it is generally reserved for cases that are expected to take weeks or months to try. The summary jury trial is particularly useful for those novel or unusual cases in which the jury's verdict is difficult to predict and that difficulty is deterring settlement. (A court's authority to compel a reluctant party to participate in a summary jury trial is discussed at pp. 409-412.)

Questions

5.9 Pipeco, Inc. sued Northwest Power Co. for $15 million damages arising out of Pipeco's contract to supply the piping at Northwest's new generating facility. Pipeco alleges that delays and changes caused by Northwest increased the cost of its work by that amount. The case has been in litigation for nearly three years, and both sides have already spent more than half of the $2 million each expects to pay in legal fees through trial, which is not expected for another year and a half.

The presidents of Pipeco and Northwest, although friendly, have been unable to resolve the case privately. At in-house counsel's suggestion, they held a minitrial. After the minitrial, the neutral advisor informed the executives that at trial Pipeco is likely to recover close to the $15 million claimed and recommended settlement in that range. The parties settled for a $13 million payment to Pipeco.

Subsequently, Northwest petitioned the Public Service Commission (PSC) for a rate increase. Northwest's petition included, as expenses that should be considered in calculating the rate base, the $13 million payment to Pipeco. At a brief hearing before the PSC, at which the neutral advisor's opinion was read into the record by the attorney for Northwest, the requested rate increase was approved.

a. If you represented the Northwest Public Interest Research Group (NWPIRG), a consumer's rights organization challenging the rate increase in court, what arguments would you make concerning these events?

b. If, during the rate increase hearing before the PSC, NWPIRG sought to compel the neutral advisor to testify to the reasons for her opinion and to produce her notes from the minitrial reflecting her impressions of the parties' presentations, how should the hearing officer rule?

5.10 Which of the following cases might be especially suitable for a summary jury trial?

a. A sexual harassment case turning on the credibility of two key witnesses;

b. A series of nine ground water pollution cases against the same defendant growing out of the same transaction and involving difficult questions of law and fact;

c. A product liability case involving an injury to a child by an allegedly defective toy.

4. *Early Neutral Evaluation and "Rights-Based" Mediation*

As the name implies, early neutral evaluation (ENE), pioneered in the U.S. District Court for Northern California and replicated in many other jurisdictions under a variety of labels, calls for an assessment of the case early in its history by an experienced neutral (usually a volunteer attorney selected by the court) on the basis of brief presentations by both sides. If the case does not settle, the assessment is kept confidential, and the evaluator helps the parties to simplify and tailor the case for more expeditious handling in trial. Sometimes the evaluator also assists the parties in monitoring discovery requests.

A great variety of activities pass under the rubric "mediation." It may be useful for systems design purposes to distinguish between rights-based mediation and interest-based mediation, even though in practice that distinction cannot always be clearly drawn because some programs and some mediators blend the two approaches. Where the mediator focuses on the legal rights of the parties, her approach closely resembles that in ENE, although the "assessment" or "evaluation" (see pp. 120-121) provided by the mediator may sometimes be less direct than is the case in ENE.

Interest-based mediation differs markedly from ENE in that the interest-based mediator "facilitates" (see pp. 109-113) and does not offer an evaluation of the relative strength and weakness of each side's case but seeks to help the parties to work out a mutually acceptable integrative solution.

*5. Ombudsman**

In the Scandinavian countries, where the concept originated, the ombudsman is a public official appointed to hear citizen complaints and conduct independent fact-finding investigation, with the goal of correcting abuses of public administration. In the United States, the ombudsman function has developed quite differently.

L. SINGER, SETTLING DISPUTES

99-102 (2d ed. 1994)

Although in the classic Scandinavian model, the ombudsman never works for the institution he or she is supposed to oversee, in this country the ombudsperson concept has appeared most frequently since the late 1960s as part of the management of a public or private organization. Here, the ombudsperson is considered a neutral member of the corporate structure, located outside the normal managerial chain of command and reporting directly to the president of the organization. The person's job is to help resolve work-related disputes through informal counseling, mediation, or, more rarely, investigation and recommendations to management.

Perhaps because of the difficulty in combining these responsibilities with other duties to the same employer, ombudspeople have been used primarily in large corporations and universities. (However, there is no reason smaller companies could not contract with an outside neutral for more flexible, part-time service.) Approximately 200 large corporations, including McDonald's, Control Data, Federal Express, IBM, American Optical Company, AT&T Information Systems, Rockwell International, and the Bank of America, have in-house neutrals. There are an additional 100 ombuds offices in colleges and universities. The Internal Revenue Service also established an ombudsperson to help resolve taxpayers' problems with the IRS. Organizations with multiple locations frequently establish "800" numbers for easy telephone access to their ombudspeople.

According to Mary Rowe, who has served as ombudsperson at the Massachusetts Institute of Technology for close to twenty years, her functions cover a broad range: simply listening to employees' concerns on a confidential basis (often at night on the telephone or at restaurants or other places outside of work) and giving advice on how difficult situations might be dealt with by the people themselves; acting as a go-between for employees and their supervisors; conducting face-to-face mediation; and performing formal investigation and reporting to the university's president. More than nine out of ten corporate neutrals were chosen from within their organizations, generally because they already were seen as natural mediators. In explaining how they can be neutral when they work for the employer who is part of a dispute, these people say that their job is to assure employees of fair process and

*In Swedish, the word *ombudsman* is not gender specific, hence is used to refer to both masculine and feminine occupants of the position. In this country, however, some authors, such as Linda Singer in the excerpt that follows, use the term *ombuds* or *ombudsperson.*

that their loyalty to the employer is satisfied when they settle disputes among employees evenhandedly.

Ombudspeople attempt to assure employees not only that they are neutral but that they will keep all communications confidential and help to protect complaining employees from reprisals. In this regard, virtually all in-house neutrals accept anonymous complaints from employees. When dealing with sensitive areas, such as sexual harassment, experienced neutrals have found many employees embarrassed to have their identities revealed. On the other hand, it may not be practical to try to resolve some types of problems (such as complaints of nonpromotion) without determining the identity of the complainant.

The ombudsman at a Fortune 500 company, with several thousand employees in the Washington, D.C., suburbs, cites two examples typical of the complaints his office deals with daily.

Anne had been a secretary with the corporation for ten years. Her office had twelve secretarial bays, with two secretaries occupying each bay. A new coworker was a chainsmoker. Anne asked her neighbor to refrain from smoking at her desk, but she continued to smoke, to Anne's discomfort and annoyance. Anne complained to her boss, who told her that there were too many smokers in the office to ban smoking. Anne considered resigning.

John was one of fifteen mail clerks with the corporation. It was regular practice in the mail room for packages to be stacked so that access to the fire exit was blocked every afternoon. John considered this practice unsafe but was reluctant to mention it to his supervisor, the office manager, because one month earlier another clerk had been fired for "complaining too much."

At the suggestion of her boss, Anne brought her complaint to the ombudsman, who promptly scheduled a meeting to discuss the company's smoking policy in secretarial bays. Invited were all interested smokers and nonsmokers, together with the management representative responsible for assigning secretaries. Although the smokers recognized that many companies recently had implemented no smoking policies in work areas, they vehemently opposed such a ban. The nonsmokers expressed concerns about their health and discomfort from inhaling smoke on the job. The management representative explained that smokers and nonsmokers sometimes are assigned to the same secretarial bay in order to keep the secretary in close proximity to her boss. After hearing suggestions from the employees, the management representative agreed to take smoking preference into consideration when making secretarial assignments and to reassign those secretaries who requested it. Anne was reassigned to another secretarial bay, where her new neighbor did not smoke.

John took his complaint directly to the ombudsman, requesting absolute confidentiality. The ombudsman listened to his concerns and elicited suggestions for resolving the safety hazard. Next, the ombudsman met with John's supervisor and, without divulging John's identity, informed the office manager that there was concern about the stacking of packages in front of the fire exit. The ombudsman asked the supervisor for suggestions to eliminate the safety hazard and conveyed John's suggestions. The ombudsman and the supervisor then together developed a solution to keep the fire exit clear.

Through dealing with such complaints, neutrals can give managers what Mary Rowe calls "upward feedback" and can act as a bellwether of problems that could burgeon into lawsuits: "Ombuds give management early warning of new problems.

There was sexual harassment in the early to mid-1970s, for example, and fraud and waste issues in the late 1970s. As counselors to managers and workers, ombuds are in an ideal position to detect major problems as they arise." In this sense, these individuals function differently from most mediators. Some ombudspeople believe that their additional role of undertaking independent investigations and recommending changes to management gives them more viability and clout than in-house mediators have and helps to compensate for the possible effect on their credibility of the fact that they are insiders.

Note

Ombuds sometimes advocate for designated groups of persons, such as residents of nursing homes. In 2001, the American Bar Association House of Delegates approved standards to apply to this new role, which they termed the "Advocate Ombuds," as well as those roles described by Singer. The standards, amended by the ABA House of Delegates in 2004, contrast the role of the "Advocate Ombuds" with the "Legislative and Executive Ombuds," who are employed by the government to investigate complaints about government practices, and the "Organizational Ombuds," who are employed by private organizations and described in Singer's excerpt. The ABA standards identify the essence of good practice for all ombuds as "independence, impartiality in conducting inquiries and investigations, and confidentiality." The ABA report suggests that the essence of the ombuds' role should be specified in advance.*

C. DISPUTE SYSTEMS DESIGN

The materials in this section discuss the tasks facing the dispute systems designer. Goldberg, Brett, and Ury present their views on the principles of effective dispute systems design. Costantino and Merchant urge involvement of the stakeholders in designing the system, setting out an approach called "interest-based conflict management design." Those who design often lend a hand in implementation as well, a theme that runs through all of the commentary and the notes following.

S. GOLDBERG, J. BRETT, AND W. URY, DESIGNING AN EFFECTIVE DISPUTE RESOLUTION SYSTEM

Adapted from Donovan Leisure Newton and Irvine ADR Practice Book 38-47 (J. Wilkinson ed. 1991 Supp.)

In 1987, IBM and Fujitsu, in settling a number of disputes arising out of IBM's charge that Fujitsu had improperly used IBM software, agreed to set up a technical facility under the direction of a neutral expert. In that facility, Fujitsu could examine

*Standards for the Establishment and Operation of Ombuds Offices, Amended by the ABA House of Delegates, February 9, 2004. Available at www.abanet.org/adminlaw/ombuds/115.pdf (Harter, 2005).

certain categories of IBM software and choose those it wished to use. IBM was entitled to compensation for any software used by Fujitsu. Disputes about appropriate use were to be resolved by the neutral expert; disputes about compensation were to be resolved by arbitration prior to Fujitsu's use of the software in question.

In 1986, two oil companies that were about to engage in a joint venture agreed that all disputes arising out of the joint venture would be submitted to a partnership committee. Disputes not resolved by the partnership committee were to be referred to two senior executives, one from each company, both uninvolved in the joint venture. The executives' task was to study the problem and, in consultation with their companies, negotiate a settlement. If they were unsuccessful, the dispute was to be sent to final and binding arbitration.

Why did the corporations in those two examples set up elaborate dispute resolution systems? Why didn't Fujitsu and IBM simply agree on a monetary settlement of their disputes? Why didn't the two oil companies simply provide that any dispute between them would be resolved by arbitration?

The answer is clear. More and more companies are realizing that if they are involved in a long-term relationship — buyer-seller, client-service provider, joint venture or market leader-follower (like IBM and Fujitsu) — disputes between them are inevitable. It is not enough to settle one of those disputes, as IBM and Fujitsu might have done, because more are likely to arise. It is not enough to agree on a single dispute resolution procedure, as the oil companies might have done, because a procedure that is satisfactory for one dispute may not be satisfactory for all disputes, and a procedure that is satisfactory at one stage of a dispute may not be satisfactory at another stage of the same dispute.

The task for parties who can reasonably anticipate a stream of disputes between them is to go beyond settling those disputes one at a time and to go beyond selecting one procedure to resolve all disputes. Their goal should be to design a comprehensive and effective dispute resolution system.

Our basic approach to dispute resolution recognizes that in seeking to resolve a dispute parties may focus on interests, rights, or power. An interests-based approach is better than a rights-based or power-based approach because it tends to produce higher satisfaction with outcomes, better relationships, and less recurrence of disputes. The transaction costs of resolving disputes through an interests-based procedure are also less than with a rights-based or power-based procedure.

Despite the general advantages of resolving disputes by procedures that focus on the parties' interests, resolving all disputes in this fashion is not possible. In some disputes, though fewer than often supposed, interests are so opposed that agreement is not possible. In others, the parties' perceptions of who is right or more powerful are so different that they cannot establish a range within which to negotiate a resolution of their competing interests. A procedure may be needed to clarify their rights before an interests-based resolution can succeed. The third-party evaluation in the summary jury trial and early neutral evaluation, as well as that sometimes provided by the neutral in a minitrial, are procedures by which rights information is provided as a precursor to an interests-based negotiation. . . . The task of those designing a dispute resolution system, typically the parties' attorneys, is not to eliminate rights and power procedures but to limit their use to those situations in which they are necessary. It is also to provide low-cost ways to determine rights or power for those disputes that cannot be resolved by focusing on interests alone. Arbitration, for example, is a lower-cost procedure than court for resolving rights disputes.

Diagnosis

Dispute systems design is used in two quite different situations. Parties who are about to enter into a relationship, such as the oil companies' joint venture described earlier, will focus on designing an effective system *before* disputes arise. More often, however, it is not until the existing system becomes distressed, with many disputes being resolved by rights or power battles, that the parties realize that it is in their joint interest to develop a more effective system.

In the latter situation, the designers must begin by diagnosing the existing situation. What kinds of disputes occur, with whom, what dispute resolution procedures are being used, and why? Diagnosis is essential, because changes are unlikely to be successful unless they respond to the needs that have caused the existing system to become distressed.

Design: Six Principles

The six basic principles of dispute systems design are:

1. Prevention
2. Put the focus on interests
3. Build in "loop backs" to negotiation
4. Provide low-cost rights and power backups
5. Arrange procedures in a low-to-high cost sequence
6. Provide the necessary motivation, skills, resources, and environment.

Principle 1: Prevention

When one party to a relationship is considering action that will affect the other, it should at least notify, and ideally consult, the other before taking that action. (*Notification* refers simply to an announcement in advance of the intended action; *consultation* goes further and offers an opportunity to discuss the proposed action before it takes place.) Notification and consultation can prevent disputes that arise through sheer misunderstanding. They can also reduce the anger and kneejerk opposition that often result when decisions are made unilaterally. They also serve to identify points of difference that may be more easily resolved before action is taken than after.

Sophisticated parties seek not only to avoid disputes but also to learn from them. At some manufacturing companies, lawyers and managers regularly analyze consumer complaints to determine what changes in product design might reduce the likelihood of similar disputes in the future. Wise designers build into the system procedures for postdispute analysis and feedback.

Another impportant means of preventing disputes is to deal with the behavior that is producing disputes. This is the approach that the U.S. Navy and Marine Corps have adopted in designing a system to deal with sexual harassment disputes. A central element in that system is sensitizing people to recognize potentially objectionable conduct. To do so, the Navy and Marine corps adopted a simple but powerful metaphor: the stoplight. "Red" behavior is unacceptable; "yellow" is potentially so; "green" is appropriate and encouraged. Examples are given of each to provide guidance in deterring conduct that might be construed as sexual harassment.

PRINCIPLE 2: PUT THE FOCUS ON INTERESTS

Putting the focus on interests is the central tenet of dispute systems design. Effective dispute resolution systems make full use of procedures that can help disputing parties seek an interests-based solution.

In order to encourage the interests-based resolution of disputes, an increasing number of contract clauses explicitly provide for negotiation as the first step in resolving a dispute between competing businesses. These clauses typically designate who will participate in the negotiation, when it must begin and end, and what happens if it is unsuccessful. They often provide for a multistep procedure in which a dispute that is not successfully resolved at one step is then negotiated at a higher step by different negotiators.

Mediation is a valuable means to ensure that interests are thoroughly considered before a dispute turns into a lawsuit. According to former Motorola General Counsel Richard Weise, "Motorola has found mediation to be successful practically every time it's been used. . . . If we can get them into mediation, we are confident that we can find a settlement. The difficulty is getting the other party to agree to mediate."

To use another example, the Southwest Texas Methodist Hospital dispute system includes a mediation clause as a condition of admission. When patients sign into the hospital, they agree to mediate any disputes with the hospital. Should a dispute arise, the agreement offers a face-saving way for both hospital and patient to enter into interests-based dispute resolution.

Brown & Root, a nationwide construction and engineering firm, has established a system for employee disputes that provides multiple opportunities for mediation. To make the process easily accessible, Brown & Root trained employees in interests-based mediation skills and made them available to mediate disputes between other employees and supervisors. While they have no authority over either, they know how to keep negotiations focused on interests. Mediation is also available from "advisors" who serve as ombudsmen for Brown & Root, as well as from many managers who have been trained in mediation skills. The dispute system also provides for mediation by outside neutrals selected through the American Arbitration Association.

PRINCIPLE 3: BUILD IN "LOOP-BACKS" TO NEGOTIATION

Sometimes interests-based negotiations fail because the parties' perceptions of who is right or who is more powerful are so different that, when interests clash, they cannot establish a range within which to negotiate. At the same time, resort to a full-blown rights or power contest would be costly, not only in financial terms but also in relational terms. Thus, the wise designer will build into the system procedures for providing the parties with information about who would prevail in the event of a contest, without the necessity of their actually engaging in such a contest. Because such procedures are designed to encourage the parties to return to negotiation, they are called *loop-back* procedures.

There are a number of "loop-back" procedures that provide information about rights and so encourage successful negotiation. Among such procedures are the minitrial and the summary jury trial. In the former, information about the likely outcome of a court battle is provided by a neutral advisor; in the latter, that information is provided by a mock jury. The key element of all these procedures is that by providing the parties with credible and neutral information about their rights, and so reducing uncertainty about the outcome of a rights contest, they discourage resort to such a contest and encourage a return to interests-based negotiation.

Another device for encouraging parties to turn back from a rights or power contest to negotiation is the *cooling-off period,* a specified time during which the disputants refrain from a rights or power contest. For example, some contracts provide that if the contractually mandated procedures for resolving disputes are unsuccessful, no party may commence litigation for a fixed time period. The hope—and sometimes the contractual requirement—is that during this period renewed efforts at a negotiated settlement will occur.

The claims resolution facilities that have been established in mass tort situations provide an interesting example of a "loop-back." When A. H. Robins, the manufacturer of the Dalkon Shield contraceptive device, sought bankruptcy protection in 1985, it asked the court to create a "closed fund" from which all present and future claimants would receive payments. The judge hired an expert to determine Robins' probable liability, and to develop a mechanism—the claims facility—for disbursing the monies reserved to cover that liability.

The expert and his team established an extensive data base including the 9,000 claims against Robins that had been resolved prior to 1985, and a sampling of the 300,000 cases that were filed subsequently in response to the court's advertising for claims. They developed full medical records for each case in the sample, as well as payment data for settled cases. Using the data from the settled cases, the team developed statistical weights that linked type and severity of medical condition with amount of payment. They then applied these weights to the unsettled cases and estimated Robins' total liability.

The analysis by the claims facility established a schedule of payments for various medical conditions potentially stemming from use of the Dalkon Shield. The claimant is offered statistical information about what he or she would likely receive in a court proceeding. This information can be used to help the parties "loop-back" to negotiations which take into account the unique particulars of the claim.

Experience with the Dalkon Shield and other claims facilities has demonstrated that such a facility needs to provide more than loop-back information about average outcomes to facilitate the resolution of claims. Claimants' willingness to accept facility-generated awards depends on whether or not they feel their circumstances have been considered. Thus, loop-back information is best accompanied by a procedure like mediation that focuses on the interests of the claimant in receiving as much compensation as possible and the interests of the claims facility in equitably distributing its limited assets.

PRINCIPLE 4: PROVIDE LOW-COST RIGHTS AND POWER BACKUPS

In some disputes interests are so opposed that agreement is not possible. Still, resort to a full-blown court battle would have damaging financial and relational consequences. Thus, an effective dispute resolution system will contain procedures for final and binding resolution of disputes through low-cost alternatives to litigation. Among these procedures are conventional arbitration, expedited arbitration, final-offer arbitration and med-arb.

A low-cost, rights-based dispute resolution system grew out of negotiations in the summer and fall of 1990 between creditors of Drexel, Burnham, Lambert (then in bankruptcy); securities fraud claimants against Drexel, whose claims totaled over $25 billion; and the U.S. Securities and Exchange Commission (SEC). The outcome of those negotiations was an agreement to divide Drexel's assets into two parts. One part would go to creditors, and the other part, which ultimately totaled $228 million, would go to securities fraud claimants.

There was also a provision for $15 million to go to the securities fraud claimants to defray the expenses of allocating their portion of the settlement among them. Any unused portion of the $15 million was to be divided among the securities fraud claimants. These claimants, then, had a strong interest in an allocation process that would be fair, inexpensive, and speedy.

Allocating the available funds among the securities fraud claimants in a fair, inexpensive, and speedy manner presented a formidable challenge. There were over 200 claims, some of which were highly complex class claims, brought on behalf of hundreds of small investors; other claims were equally complex actions brought by banks, insurance companies, and other major corporations. Court proceedings, in which lawyers representing each claimant argued the merits of their claim, would likely have consumed a substantial portion of the claimant's recoveries. A creative solution was needed, and with the prompting of the SEC, which selected two dispute systems designers to advise it, a low-cost rights-based dispute resolution system was designed.

This procedure, which was called the Subclass B Plan of Allocation, provided for the claimants to select a five-person Executive Committee from among the lawyers representing them. The SEC also appointed a representative to the Executive Committee — one of the dispute systems designers.

The Subclass B Plan of Allocation called for the Executive Committee to seek negotiated agreements with all claimants. In the event that negotiations were unsuccessful, the SEC representative was available to mediate. Any claims that could not be consensually resolved were to be assigned a value by the Executive Committee. The value of the unsettled claims as well as the value of those that were negotiated were to be presented to the district court for approval. The district court was authorized to submit unresolved claims to a special master for a recommended decision and then to the district court for final decision, or to proceed directly to a district court final decision.

In dispute systems design terms the Subclass B Plan of Allocation provided for negotiations (between the Executive Committee and claimants), mediation (by the SEC representative), an advisory decision (by a special master), and a final and binding decision by the district court. At each step, the focus was on rights (the legal merits of the claim).

While the system developed to deal with the Drexel, Burnham, Lambert securities fraud claims was set up many years after the events giving rise to those claims, some low-cost rights-based systems achieve impressive results because they resolve disputes immediately. The need for high-speed dispute resolution has long been recognized in the construction industry, where many contractors work on the same project, and a dispute involving any of those contractors can interfere with the ability of others to continue working.

One means of providing high-speed dispute resolution is the dispute review board.* Such a board is typically composed of neutral industry experts, jointly selected by the owner(s) and the general contractor at the beginning of a construction project. The dispute review board meets periodically with the parties to preempt disputes and to promptly evaluate disputes if they occur. The board produces written recommendations, which are based on relevant contract provisions, applicable laws and regulations, and the facts of the dispute. While the recommendations of the board are intended to carry great weight for both the owner and the contractor, they are not binding on either party. They are, however, typically admissible as evidence in any subsequent dispute resolution proceeding.

PRINCIPLE 5: ARRANGE PROCEDURES IN A LOW-TO-HIGH COST SEQUENCE

The first four design principles — prevention; put the focus on interests; build in loop-backs to negotiation; provide low-cost rights and power back-ups — suggest a fifth. Create a sequence of procedures that is based on these principles. The following is a menu of procedures to draw on in designing such a sequence:

Prevention Procedures
- Notification and Consultation
- Post-Dispute Analysis and Feedback

Interests-Based Procedures
- Negotiation
- Mediation

Loop-Back Procedures
- Advisory Arbitration
- Mini-Trial
- Summary Jury Trial
- Cooling-Off Period

Low-Cost Back-Up Procedures
- Conventional Arbitration
- Expedited Arbitration
- Med-Arb
- Final Offer Arbitration

*The following discussion of dispute review boards is drawn from Sander and Thorne (1995).

In creating a sequence for resolving disputes that develop despite the use of prevention procedures, the designers might begin with interests-based negotiation, followed by interests-based mediation. A minitrial might be an optional step for significant disputes, and a cooling-off period required for all disputes. One of the low-cost rights procedures might be the final step, except for those disputes for which both parties agree they need a court precedent.

The Federal Deposit Insurance Corporation uses a negotiation-mediation-arbitration ladder in its system for resolving disputes involving controlled entities such as receiverships. Dispute resolution coordinators in regional offices encourage their colleagues to negotiate the resolution of disputes. Disputes that are not resolved can be mediated at two different levels in the organization. Arbitration is reserved for the few disputes that are not resolved. In 1992 and 1993 only two of the more than 300 cases processed through its in-house system went to arbitration.

The state of Florida recently directed its 11 regional planning councils to develop a system for resolving growth management and planning disputes among local governments, regional agencies, and private interests. The regions agreed to a system consisting of four optional steps to be taken prior to commencing litigation: 1) situational assessment by the regional planning council or another neutral; 2) settlement meetings; 3) mediation; and 4) advisory decision-making. The intent is to use the system like a ladder, resolving as many disputes as possible through situation assessments and settlement meetings. The steps are not mandatory, however, and may be used in any sequence that appears to be appropriate for the dispute.

In adding steps to an existing dispute resolution system, it is important to think about the possible impact of the new procedures on those already used. Adding a procedure may lead disputants to treat earlier steps as pro forma. The attractiveness and accessibility of mediation may lead disputants to negotiate less before calling in a mediator. A sequence of procedures, each only slightly more costly than the previous one, may have the paradoxical effect of encouraging use of higher cost procedures. The best means to guard against this is to space procedures sufficiently far apart that increased transaction costs are noticeable.

PRINCIPLE 6: PROVIDE DISPUTANTS WITH THE NECESSARY MOTIVATION, SKILLS, AND RESOURCES

A final principle cuts across all others. Providing appropriate procedures is important, but insufficient if the parties lack the motivation, skills, and resources to use those procedures effectively. . . .

One problem of motivation that must be dealt with by designers seeking to encourage the use of interests-based procedures by parties who previously relied primarily on rights-based procedures such as litigation is that the change will undoubtedly encounter resistance. The resistance is likely to come from three, sometimes overlapping, sources: those who believe rights-based procedures are "better" for the organization; those, typically attorneys, whose role is threatened because their legal knowledge and skills are less called for in interests-based procedures; and those who believe they have been "winning" with rights-based procedures. If not dealt with, this resistance can subtly but effectively discourage the use of the new interests-based procedures.

In dealing with this opposition, the designers can make a variety of arguments. For those who believe that rights-based procedures are "better" for the corporation or that they have been "winning" with rights-based procedures, the designers can point to the costs of rights-based procedures: high legal fees, more recurrence of disputes, and strained, often destroyed, relationships. For example, the general counsel of a corporation that is in frequent litigation with its distributors, and wins most of the lawsuits, should be able to recognize that "winning" lawsuits is not really "better" for the corporation than is resolving disputes with its distributors by reconciling the interests of each.

Those attorneys who oppose the introduction of interests-based procedures because they view their roles or income to be threatened by the adoption of such procedures can sometimes be shown how they can play a legal role in some interests-based procedures. For example, much of the popularity of the minitrial among lawyers is due to the fact that lawyers are given the opportunity to utilize their trial and advocacy skills during a minitrial. It is true, however, that sometimes a new procedure will diminish the role of some individuals who were important in prior procedures, and no equivalent role can be designed for them in the new procedure. In such cases, those advocating the new procedures must be prepared for opposition and try to insure that it does not undermine the motivation of others to adopt and utilize the new procedures.

Even the most carefully designed dispute resolution system may fail in an environment that is hostile to its goals. The greatest challenge to the Navy and Marine Corps dispute system for sexual harassment is a culture that did not find objectionable incidents such as those that occurred at the 1991 Tailhook convention. Recognizing this, the Navy and Marine Corps have built their program on one of their core values, individual accountability, and have adopted the slogan "You are individually accountable. Do not ignore sexual harassment." They have also taken aggressive action to publicize the program and educate personnel. Early retirement of officers involved in or responsible for the Tailhook incident has demonstrated the commitment to change at the highest level. It is thus possible that the environment exists for the prevention and successful resolution of sexual harassment claims.

Motorola's first step in introducing systems design into its corporate law department was to frame the program in terms consistent with Motorola's strategy of "cycle-time reduction." Anticipating resistance to ADR from attorneys who were litigators, the design team stated the program's goal as reducing the "cycle-time" for the resolution of disputes by reducing dependence on litigation. The second step was to have Motorola's CEO sign the CPR Institute for Dispute Resolution ADR pledge [see Chapter 12] and sell the idea of the pledge to the attorneys in the law department. Richard Weise, Motorola's then General Counsel, says of the pledge, "Read it. It does not say that you or your client are sissies. It acknowledges that you are practical cycle-time reducers, who can be approached without worrying that the other guy is giving signs of weakness." By tying its dispute resolution system to the corporate environment, Motorola is maximizing its potential for success.

As a practical matter, it is rare that disputing parties, even those with a distressed dispute resolution system, will agree to a wholesale redesign of that system. Most systems design efforts involve the application of one or two systems design principles. For example, the National Institute for Dispute Resolution (NIDR) sought to encourage the interests-based resolution of environmental disputes by providing assistance in the development of a critical resource—state offices of mediation (Drake, 1989). Similarly, Motorola, Inc. focused on providing motivation, skills, and resources to encourage its lawyers and managers to rely more on interests-based mediation for the resolution of intercorporate disputes (Weise, 1989).

Some designers, however, have had the opportunity to develop a complete dispute resolution system. One such system was designed for a hospital (Slaikeu, 1989), and another for a divorcing couple (Kelly, 1989).

C. COSTANTINO AND C. MERCHANT, DESIGNING CONFLICT MANAGEMENT SYSTEMS

59, 62-65 (1996)

. . . Interest-based conflict management systems design takes the basic DSD principles of power, rights, and interests and applies them in an organizational context. Rather than focusing primarily on dispute resolution methods, interest-based design applies DSD principles to the design intervention itself. This results in balancing and congruity: interest-based methods created through interest-based design is, in a sense, "walking the talk." . . . For example, the hypothetical Aztec Corporation might become alarmed at the number of complaints surfacing that are related to allegedly disparate promotions in certain departments and might as a result choose to require (rights-based design) that these internal concerns be channeled to the Office of the Ombudsperson (an interest-based method) before an employee is allowed to file any formal complaint with the Human Resources Department. If the new procedure is mandated by Aztec management without any input from employees or their representatives, it may be viewed as an attempt to co-opt those who file complaints and may be resisted to the point of public protest. Interest-based conflict management systems design, on the other hand, would create any new procedures by identifying first what the nature of the problem is with the active participation of those affected and interested. Only with such clarification and involvement would a representative design effort proceed to research, discover, and institutionalize appropriate resolution processes. With the OD values of participation, openness, and feedback honored and enacted throughout the design intervention itself, the result is greater acceptance of the problem at hand and the need for action.

By maximizing the ideas and input of all relevant participants, the resultant output—a conflict management system rather than a dispute resolution program—has greater potential to be durable, satisfactory, and actually used. Similar to the theory that there is a higher level of compliance with mediated rather than imposed resolutions because the parties have been an integral part of the process and have "owned" both the process and the resolution, so too with interest-based as opposed to imposed design. As practitioners have witnessed time and time again in organizational settings, stakeholders are more likely to use systems in which they feel they have a stake or have had a hand in creating. The notion of participation in this context is in the design process itself, not merely in the resulting, predetermined dispute resolution product. For example, using an interest-based conflict management systems design model, employees or their representatives at the Aztec Corporation would actively participate in identifying the perceived problem, designing appropriate modifications to the existing complaint procedure and presenting those recommendations to Aztec's senior officials. In other words, Aztec stakeholders would actually be involved in "shuffling the deck" and would not simply be dealt a new hand. . . . Many design practitioners are also mediators or are familiar with mediation as a dispute resolution technique. In significant respects, interest-based conflict management systems design is really the mediation of an entire system. It is the designer acting as a facilitator, providing processes, and otherwise assisting the organization and its stakeholders to work together to fashion their own conflict management system. It is the designer questioning whether system stakeholders and other necessary parties are "at the table," are involved meaningfully in the design from the beginning. Similarly, just as a mediator has no power to impose a decision on the parties, neither does a designer impose a conflict management system on an organization and its stakeholders. However, as in mediation, an interest-based designer can assist an entire system in understanding and accepting its conflict, can guide it through the highly participatory process of discovering consensus about resolution potentials, and, by not imposing a decision, can empower system participants to accept and manage their own conflict not only now but in the future. Just as disputants are more likely to comply with a resolution reached through mediation because they were integral to the process, so too are stakeholders more likely to use and be satisfied with a conflict management system that they have helped to design. . . .

1. *Implementing the Design*

The Egyptian Pharaoh in the movie "Ten Commandments" issues orders and a minion declares, "so let it be written, so let it be done." For dispute systems architects, the design represents only the beginning. Goldberg, Brett, and Ury discuss the educational and persuasive part of implementation. Sometimes, though, the best the architect can achieve is a willingness to try a piece of the design—e.g., a pilot project. Costantino and Merchant suggest that it might be wise to begin with a pilot project for a number of reasons:

> Our preference and that of many other practitioners is the latter—to "think big and act small." Limited testing or a pilot project approach helps to accomplish the following tasks:
>
> - Determine the willingness of disputants to change dispute resolution methods.
> - Make it safer for individuals with a stake in the old system to experiment with new behaviors and rewards.
> - Test the suitability of the design, its fit with the organization and its members.
> - Uncover previously unknown costs, expectations, attitudes, practices, or other restraints to any wide-scale ADR program initiatives.
>
> Pilot testing, where ADR is introduced on a limited, experimental basis in particular programs, affords the design team, the organization's leadership, and its participant stakeholders with the opportunity to test out the reliability of their information, their design, and their planning—with relatively low cost and low risk. The results of a pilot program illuminate how well ADR works (or does not work) in a particular conflict arena. Problems are uncovered in pilots, "bugs" can be worked out, people get motivated (Costantino and Merchant, 1996, p. 152).

2. *Assessing Whether the Design "Works"*

It may seem tempting to "hand off" to a social scientist the messy work of assessing whether a new system better meets the planners' goals. Despite the appeal of this approach, the dispute systems designer could contribute to success by assisting in the management of assessment and re-design as well as in the original design. The overall financial viability of the project may depend on fashioning an affordable approach to assessment. In addition to cost, the procedures used to assess may interfere with the success of the project. As discussed below, the use of a random selection of cases urged by an evaluator may create a political problem for a court program. Those involved in the project will be sensitive to what is being measured and may change their activities to succeed according to these measurements. For example, if management tracks only cost and time to disposition, the mediator bent on success may terminate each mediation quickly. The designer who understands assessment can help to select a process that best serves the goals of the design.

At best, assessment can demonstrate that a project meets its organizers' goals and identify what might be changed to tailor it more closely to these goals. Unfortunately, social scientists find it hard to measure whether some of these goals have been reached. Sociologist Craig A. McEwen comments regarding the assessment of mediation programs for savings in cost, speed to disposition, fairness, and quality:

> Cost and speed may appear less slippery and more amenable to evaluation than fairness and quality issues. Nonetheless, they present recurrent problems both for measurement and in interpreting their implications for policy. Which costs are to be counted? For example, should the cost of the mediation program include the extra time it takes for court clerks to process cases, as well as the funds for new mediation staff and training? Should postjudgment enforcement be included in the cost per case? What is an apt cost comparison? If the comparison is the cost of processing a civil case, does one include the costs of the courthouse, even though these would not be reduced even if cases settled? . . .
>
> Case-processing speed may be more accurately measured. Nonetheless, the faster resolution occasioned by a small mediation program may barely affect the caseload of the court. Further, the mediation program may be initiated at the same time as other events. . . .
>
> Evaluation of quality, fairness, and the effects of mediation on parties may be as important but even harder, and probably more expensive, to achieve. The first issue is how to translate quality into something less murky. Participant perceptions of fair process and fair outcome have proved the most common measure. . . . But assessments of perceived fairness may not be sufficient for those who believe that the participants were not well-informed about the alternatives—what other processes or outcomes might have been. Other measures of fairness have included analysis of results or outcomes by expert panels, studies of well-being of affected parties (children in custody mediation), and compliance rates. Some of these involve extensive and often costly follow-up activities (Cole et al., sec. 6:15, 2003).

McEwen suggests that the planners consider the dilemma presented by random assignment of cases to mediation:

> Researchers will often seek what they call an "experimental" design in program evaluation. They urge a random assignment of eligible (either by mandate or volunteer) cases to

> mediation and to some other process, such as continued litigation. The suggestion of random assignment may seem politically unwise for the administrator who wants to defend use of resources for the "best" cases. However, absent random assignment, skeptics are likely to attribute differences in result to such factors as self-selection (those most likely to settle are picked for or themselves choose mediation) or, in the case of before-and-after studies, to the effect of other changes in law, court organization, or litigant behavior (Cole et al., sec. 6:16, 2003).

The choice of evaluation affects costs, as well as other values, and McEwen notes that an able architect can manage these effectively:

> [I]ndependent evaluators carry more credibility with the skeptic who does not know how to assess the methodology. Contracting with an independent research firm or university therefore makes evaluation results more believable. At the same time, this often costs tens of thousands of dollars. . . . The most significant roles for expertise and independence are in designing the research and interpreting the data that it produces. Data collection, however, may be the most costly part of an evaluation. Thus, if outsiders can assist with the design and interpretation, program staff and volunteers might assist in the data collection. . . . This combination . . . may provide the degree of independence and expertise to make an evaluation effective and credible and lower its costs substantially.
>
> [If the goal is an internal one of improving management], it is less important to establish credibility by employing outside consultants. In fact, for reasons of cost an internally staffed monitoring effort is preferable. Ideally, limited data gathering will be built into the regular record-keeping of a program. For example, reports of each case mediated might include information about length of mediation, kind of dispute, characteristics of the party. . . . To the extent that other programs use comparable methods of data collection, the internal system may provide a basis to compare with other mediation programs (Cole et al., secs. 6:17, 6:18, 2003).

Questions

5.11 Consolidated Printing and Publishing Co. (CPP) is the largest integrated printing and publishing company in the United States, with book, magazine, telephone directory, and catalog divisions. CPP's gross income for the last fiscal year was $1.7 billion. National Computers is a major manufacturer of computers and software for the printing industry. National's gross income for the last fiscal year was $10.1 billion.

Early in 2002, CPP's catalog division entered into a joint venture with National Computers to begin marketing a new process for producing catalogs that was intended to dramatically decrease the time and costs of designing and producing catalogs. CPP's plan was to place personal computers with graphic capabilities with each catalog customer. CPP thought that National's newest graphic arts software was sufficiently user friendly that with minimal training, customers could take over much of the preliminary design and layout of their own catalogs, then communicate directly with CPP graphic arts personnel via a computer and voice hookup to make refinements, thereby eliminating several design steps.

CPP anticipated that the new technology would free graphic arts personnel from routine catalog layout and allow them to service many more customers. The new technology would also reduce the time involved in catalog production, thus allowing CPP customers to have later submission deadlines than with traditional catalog printing methods. As a result, CPP customers could have their most current products shown in their catalogs and could modify those catalogs at the last minute to reflect any changes in materials, prices, etc.

National's role in the venture was to provide computers, software, and the service support for each. This would include installation of the computers and training the customers to use the graphic arts software. CPP's role was to market the idea and then provide customer support throughout the catalog design and layout process.

Customer response to the new system was strong. Within 60 days of introducing the new system, CPP and National had one-year contracts with five moderate to large customers for their catalogs: F. F. Dean (camping equipment), Baggs (women's clothing), Williams-Mendecino (cooking supplies), KidsKraft (toys), and Trigano (sportswear).

While Baggs and Trigano, whose catalog design departments were already using computers, adapted easily to the new system, the other customers had problems from the very beginning. Not only did their designers have difficulty laying out their catalogs, but they were also plagued by apparent computer malfunctions. As a result, they turned for assistance to National's training staff, with whom they had previously worked and, with somewhat less frequency, to CPP's graphic design personnel.

National's training personnel were hard pressed to keep up with subsequent training commitments and had made no provision for follow-up at sites of customers already trained. National's service personnel made a number of repair calls, then concluded that the problems were not with the hardware or the software, but with the customers' designers, whose inability to use the computers as they had been trained led them to decide that the computers were malfunctioning. National, as a result, began billing these customers for extraordinary support. When customers complained to National's director of customer support, they were advised to review their contracts, none of which provided for ongoing training. Customers who complained were also told that their complaints about the computers' malfunctioning were without basis and that Baggs and Trigano, which had the same equipment, were having no problems.

CPP's graphic arts personnel made a strenuous effort to respond to customers' requests for on-line assistance with preliminary layout and use of the graphics program but were soon overwhelmed by their number. CPP, too, began billing customers for graphic art support of catalog layout that the customers' layout staff was supposed to do on their own. When customers complained about the CPP billing, the director of CPP's graphic arts department explained that the contract price was based on the assumption that initial page layout would be done by the customer on the computer. As a result, the contract provided less time with a graphic artist than conventional methods of catalog design. The customer's failure to provide the initial page layouts had greatly increased the use of CPP's graphic designers. The additional graphic design time was appropriately billed to the customer. The director added that the extra charges were company policy. Complaints taken to the head of the catalog division were met with the same response. The original sales representatives were sympathetic but explained that since Baggs and Trigano were having no unusual problems with the new system, CPP believed that the problems were attributable to the customers, not the system.

The upshot of these difficulties was that each of the three complaining customers returned to conventional catalog production, but at the cost of having their 2002 Christmas catalogs published well after their target dates and after publication of their competitors' catalogs. Since two-thirds to three-quarters of catalog sales and profits are accounted for by Christmas sales, the losses to each of the three customers were great. Each notified CPP and National that it was canceling its contract with them and bringing suit to recover all amounts expended by it in setting up the new system, as well as for lost profits resulting from delayed catalog production. CPP and National, in turn, counterclaimed against the three companies for the amounts owing them under the contracts.

Information about the new system and Trigano's and Baggs's success with it spread quickly throughout the catalog sales industry. Unfortunately, news of the problems that F. F. Dean, KidsKraft, and Williams-Mendecino had with the software, and the subsequent lawsuits, also spread quickly. As a result, CPP's sales representatives began encountering significant skepticism when introducing the new system to potential customers. In a meeting of CPP's and National's joint venture team to decide what to do about the flagging sales of the new system, it was decided to hire a dispute systems design consultant. The consultant was to work with National's training and service personnel and CPP's sales representatives and graphic designers to design a dispute resolution system for use by CPP/National and new customers.

Assume that you are a dispute systems designer and that you were contacted by the CPP/National joint venture team for this project. What advice would you give?

5.12 George Washington High School has a student population of 2,000. It is one of three high schools in Riverwood, a large suburb of a major city. Over the past three years, the school district has experienced the kind of problems that confront many high schools today: vandalism, truancy, theft of school property, and declining test scores. There has been a drastic rise in the use of drugs and alcohol on school grounds. In addition, the school district has been subjected to an increasing amount of litigation by parents on behalf of children who have been suspended for various infractions of rules.

Most recently, Washington High has had two controversies that have aggravated the school's situation:

1. The administration backed the school newspaper's faculty advisor when she refused to publish an article in the paper because she considered it obscene. The student editors resigned and took their case to the student government, from whom they expected support. After a closed meeting with the principal, the student government decided to take no stand on the issue.
2. A prominent student was suspended after repeatedly defying a certain teacher's authority and disrupting his classes. She is a very bright student with a large following among the student "intelligentsia" and some faculty members. Her parents have now filed suit against the school for depriving their daughter of her right to an education.

The district superintendent has been deluged with phone calls due to the recent incidents. The press has reported the lawsuit, something the superintendent had hoped could be avoided. He has decided steps must be taken immediately to develop some form of dispute resolution procedure, and he has requested that you, as a dispute resolution consultant, design a procedure that will handle student problems quickly, fairly, and openly. He would like you to recommend the type of procedure that you think would be most appropriate and to consider all the relevant details of that procedure (including, e.g., number of steps, who should participate at each step, right to representation, and provision for outside review). How do you respond?*

5.13 Bob and Alice have agreed that they will have joint legal and physical custody of their three minor children (Mary, 15; John, 13; Josh, 12) upon their divorce, but they have been unable to agree on who will have primary physical custody should either of them move out of town. Neither plans to move at present, but there are job and relationship possibilities on both sides that could result in one of them wanting to move later. Design a dispute resolution clause for Bob and Alice's separation agreement that covers this eventuality.

D. SELECTION OF THE PROCESS

1. *Lawyers*

As the use of ADR spreads, and as more courts encourage its use, it becomes increasingly likely that the lawyer's duty to discuss ADR options with a client will become mandatory (Cochran, 1993; Breger, 2000). Indeed, it is at least arguable that such a duty is already contained in Model Rule 1.4(b) of the Model Rules of Professional Conduct. That rule states:

> A lawyer shall explain a matter to the extent reasonably necessary to permit the client to make informed decisions regarding the representation.

Some courts have held that the duty to explain a matter to the client includes the duty to communicate settlement offers made by other parties, and the advantages and disadvantages of settlement. (See Cole et al., 2001.) From there, it would appear but a short step to hold that the duty also requires the lawyer to discuss the advantages and disadvantages of pursuing settlement through ADR.

In addition, a number of jurisdictions have taken the first explicit step toward imposing on lawyers an obligation to discuss ADR with their clients. Both Colorado and Hawaii have amended their Model Rules of Professional Conduct to provide:

> In a matter involving or expected to involve litigation, a lawyer should advise the client of alternative forms of dispute resolution which might reasonably be pursued to attempt to resolve the legal dispute or to reach the legal objective sought.

*This question is based on a simulation developed by the Center for Community Justice, Washington, D.C. Instructions for using it as a simulation are contained in the Teacher's Manual.

In New Jersey, where ADR is known as Complementary Dispute Resolution, Supreme Court Rule 1:40-1 states:

> Lawyers should become familiar with available CDR programs and inform their clients of them.

The Texas Supreme Court has adopted a lawyer's creed, a portion of which reads:

> I will advise my client regarding the availability of mediation, arbitration, and other alternative means of resolving and settling disputes.

Regardless of whether a lawyer is required to advise clients of the availability of dispute resolution options other than litigation, it is hardly debatable that a good lawyer will do so. As Professor Sander has stated, "How would we feel about a doctor who suggested surgery without exploring other choices?" Attorney Michael Prigoff, who has argued against the imposition of an ethical duty to discuss ADR with clients, nonetheless conceded, "In my practice, I discuss ADR options in depth with every litigation client" (Sander and Prigoff, 1990).

In discussing ADR with a client, the skilled attorney will not merely lay out the ADR options, but will discuss with the client the characteristics of each of those options. The lawyer and the client should then determine what the client wants in a dispute resolution procedure, and which dispute resolution procedure — including court — is most likely to attain those objectives. Making that determination is the subject of the following article.

F. SANDER AND S. GOLDBERG, FITTING THE FORUM TO THE FUSS: A USER-FRIENDLY GUIDE TO SELECTING AN ADR PROCEDURE

10 Neg. J. 49 (1994)

Mary Stone has worked for the past two years as an accounting manager at the Smith Corporation, a manufacturer of menswear. She is one of only two women in the Accounting Department.

Stone is an attractive single woman of 32. The fact that she is somewhat overweight has made her the object of various jokes around the office, some of them of an explicit sexual nature. Sometimes she will find a crude cartoon on her desk when she arrives in the morning (e.g., a recent one depicted a couple in bed, with the caption "Fat girls are best."); at other times she hears whispered comments about her as she passes by. Although this objectionable behavior has been going on for about four months, it has really got to Stone recently. Last week, she discussed the situation with the director of the Department of Human Resources, who urged her to see the sexual harassment counselor, Jane Willard. Willard promised to send around to the accounting department a reminder about the company's policies on sexual harassment.

Stone has now come to see you, an attorney who specializes in sexual harassment cases. Mindful of the recent emphasis on various ways of resolving disputes outside the courts, you wonder whether this case might be suitable for alternative dispute resolution (ADR).

What sort of questions should be considered in making this determination? [In the casebook text replaced by this article] we . . . identified such factors as the nature of the case, the relationship between the parties, the relief sought by the plaintiff, and the size and complexity of the claim. We suggested, for example, that if a dispute involves a run-of-the-mill tort claim that raises no novel legal questions, then some simple form of adjudication, such as arbitration, might be used, but that a novel claim raising significant legal questions that need judicial elaboration should go to court. Similarly, if the disputants have an ongoing relationship that has broken down, then mediation may be strongly indicated because of its capacity to deal with that issue.

That analysis, which was implicitly from a public policy perspective, considered which procedure would be best for *all* those with an interest in the dispute, not which procedure would be preferred by each individual disputant. In this article, we examine the suitability of various dispute resolution processes from the perspective of the parties to the dispute, and then from the public-interest perspective. We use this two-step approach because we believe that doing so provides a more realistic view of the manner in which decisions regarding the choice of dispute resolution procedure are made.

The initial determination regarding the choice of dispute resolution procedure will be made by each attorney in consultation with his or her client. In these consultations, both court and various types of ADR will, and perhaps must, be considered. Next, the attorneys will discuss with each other the decision each has reached with the client, and will seek to agree upon a procedure. If they do not agree, the complaining party will be free to take the dispute to court. Then, if the court has an ADR program, as is increasingly common, court personnel will decide if the dispute is suitable for some aspect of that program. If the court's ADR program is optional, the parties will be free to reject the court's recommendation; if that program is mandatory, the court will order the parties into some type of ADR.

As counsel for the disputing parties consider which dispute resolution procedure is appropriate for their clients, they face two basic questions: First, what are the client's goals, and what dispute resolution procedure is most likely to achieve those goals? Second, if the client is amenable to settlement, what are the impediments to settlement, and what ADR procedure is most likely to overcome those impediments?

When the decision regarding an appropriate dispute resolution procedure is made from a public perspective, the second question is similar to the kind of analysis an attorney should give to any client; the first question, however, is more complex. Initially, court personnel or public agencies making a recommendation regarding appropriate procedures for resolving a dispute must consider the goals of all parties to the dispute. Furthermore, they must consider the public interest in that dispute. While a private settlement may serve the interests of all parties to the dispute, the public interest may lie in public adjudication (e.g., because of a need for judicial interpretation of a newly enacted statute). . . .

Client Goals

In the hypothetical case with which we began this article, how do you, as Stone's attorney, prepare for your initial interview with your client? Is she eager to remain at the company (perhaps because alternative employment opportunities are scarce) and hence wants to resolve this situation with the least disruption and fuss? Or is she so angry that she is determined to have some outside neutral pronounce her "right," and thus vindicate her position?

Answers to questions like these are critical in determining what dispute resolution procedure is appropriate in this case. The fact that Stone has decided to come to an attorney indicates that she is dissatisfied with the present posture of the dispute. But should she file a lawsuit or seek some other way of resolving the problem? If she has an emotional need for vindication, she will have to resort to some form of adjudication, either in court or—if the company is willing—through private means, such as arbitration or private judging. . . . If Stone wants public vindication, however, or a binding precedent, only court will do.

A form of third-party vindication is available through the minitrial, the summary jury trial, and early neutral evaluation, since in each of these processes a neutral third party evaluates the contentions of the parties. Because these processes are both abbreviated and nonbinding, however, they will not always satisfy a client's desire for vindication.

If Stone wants the opinion of a neutral concerning the merits of her claim less for vindication than as a means of convincing the company that she has a strong claim, and is entitled to a reasonable settlement, then any of the nonbinding evaluative procedures (minitrial, summary jury trial, neutral evaluation) has promise. Choosing among these options will depend on such factors as the client's other goals and the extent to which each procedure is likely to overcome the barriers to settlement, factors that are discussed later in this article.

What if there were other employees with similar complaints of sexual harassment? In that case Stone might again want some formal declaration concerning the illegality of the conduct in question, which then could be used as a precedent in other cases. The company, viewing the problem from its vantage point, might have a similar preference for some type of reasoned adjudication (probably via a court decision, but possibly through arbitration or private judging).

But suppose instead that Stone is eager to keep her job and simply wants the annoying conduct to stop. Perhaps a transfer will accomplish that goal. If the company is willing to meet her halfway, it may be desirable to involve a mediator who can help facilitate this kind of solution in a quiet, confidential manner.

Of course, client goals may change as time passes, conditions change, and feelings wax or wane. Stone may start out bent on vengeance via public vindication and damages. But, as she considers giving up a job she finds satisfying, except for the harassment, her priority may shift from vindication and damages to retaining her job, if she can be assured that the employer has taken steps to protect her from harassment, and perhaps also to protect potential future victims.

These, then, are some of the considerations that lawyers and clients must examine with regard to processes that might meet client objectives. The value of various procedures in meeting specific client objectives is set forth in Table 1.

An important point to note is that the values assigned to each procedure in Table 1 (as well as in Table 2, which follows) are not based on empirical research but rather upon our own experience, combined with the views of other dispute resolution professionals. Moreover, the numerical values assigned to each procedure are not intended to be taken literally, but rather as a shorthand expression of the extent to which each procedure satisfies a particular objective.

Table 1
Extent to Which Dispute Resolution Procedures Satisfy Client Objectives

	Procedures					
	Nonbinding				*Binding*	
Objectives	*Mediation*	*Minitrial*	*Summary Jury Trial*	*Early Neutral Evaluation*	*Arbitration, Private Judging*	*Court*
Minimize Costs	3	2	2	3	1	0
Speed	3	2	2	3	1	0
Privacy[a]	3	3	2	2	3	0
Maintain/ Improve Relationship[b]	3	2	2	1	1	0
Vindication[c]	0	1	1	1	2	3
Neutral Opinion[d]	0	3	3	3	3	3
Precedent[e]	0	0	0	0	2	3
Maximizing/ Minimizing Recovery	0	1	1	1	2	3

0 = Unlikely to satisfy objective
1 = Satisfies objective somewhat
2 = Satisfies objective substantially
3 = Satisfies objective very substantially

a. We believe that a summary jury trial and a neutral evaluation offer less privacy than the other ADR processes, in which the neutral is selected by the parties. In the summary jury trial, a judge or magistrate, as well as a jury, is present; in neutral evaluation, the neutral will typically be a court-appointed attorney. If, however, the neutral evaluator is selected by the parties, neutral evaluation will offer as much privacy as the other ADR processes. Conversely, if a mediator, minitrial neutral, or arbitrator were imposed by the court, that procedure would receive a lower privacy rating.

b. We have given early neutral evaluation a lower rating than the summary jury trial or the minitrial for the capacity to maintain relationships. While all three procedures are relatively brief and thus do little harm to the relationship, the summary jury trial and the minitrial typically involve negotiations between the principals, and such negotiations sometimes have the potential of mending a frayed relationship. If a particular early neutral evaluation were to involve negotiations between the principals, it would receive the same rating as the summary jury trial or the minitrial.

c. Since a need for vindication may be satisfied by an apology, mediation that results in an apology can satisfy the need for vindication. However, in our experience, apologies rarely occur in mediation [see pp. 159-162 of the casebook].

d. We have assigned the same ranking to all the procedures that provide any kind of neutral evaluation. But if one were to take account of the basis for making the evaluation, the procedures that provide for a full presentation of the evidence and arguments (namely, court and arbitration) would receive a higher score. A neutral evaluation which follows a full presentation of evidence and argument is likely to be given greater weight by the parties than is a neutral opinion based upon a more truncated presentation.

e. Although mediation normally seeks to provide a solution to the specific dispute, the parties could also agree on a new rule for future cases and thus obviate the need for a formal precedent.

If, for example, the client's goals are to maintain the relationship and receive a neutral opinion while also maximizing privacy, adding the numerical scores would lead to the following result: mediation 6; minitrial 8; summary jury trial 7; early neutral evaluation 6; arbitration 7; and court 3. One could not, however, conclude from these scores that the minitrial is the preferred procedure. Our analysis of the capacity of each procedure to meet various goals is not that precise. The most that one could conclude at this point in the analysis would be that some ADR procedure is preferable to court.

The next step in the analysis is to list the client's goals in order of priority. If the client is primarily interested in a prompt and inexpensive resolution of the dispute that also maintains or improves the parties' relationship—which is typical of *most* clients in *most* business disputes—mediation is the preferred procedure. Mediation is the only procedure to receive maximum scores on each of these dimensions—cost, speed, and maintain or improve the relationship—as well as on assuring privacy, another interest which is present in many business disputes. It is only when the client's primary interests consist of establishing a precedent, being vindicated, or maximizing (or minimizing) recovery that procedures other than mediation are more likely to be satisfactory.

It should be clear from this discussion that our evaluation is based on assumptions concerning how ADR procedures are typically structured. If the procedures are structured differently, by court order or party design, the extent to which they will satisfy client goals will also differ. For example, mediation will generally cost the parties less and be faster than a summary jury trial or the minitrial, which require preparing to present evidence and arguments in a structured setting, but that is not always the case. Some parties will provide for a comparatively simple minitrial, with a minimum of preparation, while others will participate in a lengthy, somewhat formal mediation that will be expensive and time-consuming. Similarly, we have assumed that mediation is a process distinct from neutral evaluation, and have set the point values in Table 1 accordingly. But some mediators also perform evaluative functions, and some neutral evaluators attempt to mediate. Hence, Table 1 should be understood only as a general guide, subject to modification if the procedures involved differ from the norms on which the table was based.

A related point is that the processes listed in Tables 1 and 2 are discussed more or less in isolation. Often however, it is possible to blend or link different processes (e.g., mediation and evaluation) to develop a hybrid process. Indeed, Tables 1 and 2 can be used as a guide for designing a process that promises to achieve the client's objectives and, where settlement is sought, that is likely to overcome the envisioned impediments.

One final point concerning client goals: Some contend that ADR should be avoided altogether when one party will be sure to win if the matter is litigated. We disagree. First, the likely loser may be persuaded, through the use of one of the evaluative ADR procedures, to concede, thus sparing both parties the costs of litigation. An agreed-upon outcome is also more likely to be fully complied with than a court order. Alternatively, the likely loser may offer, in ADR, a settlement that is better in non-monetary terms than what could be achieved in litigation; such a settlement preserves, and often enhances, the parties' relationship. Thus, the prospect of a victory in litigation is not reason enough for avoiding ADR.

Impediments to Settlement and Ways of Overcoming Them

In some circumstances, a settlement is not in the client's interest. For example, the client may want a binding precedent or may want to impress other potential litigants with its firmness and the consequent costs of asserting claims against it. Alternatively, the client may be in a situation in which there are no relational concerns; the only issue is whether it must pay out money; there is no pre-judgment interest; and the cost of contesting the claim is less than the interest earned on the money. In these and a small number of other situations, settlement will not be in the client's interest.

Still, a satisfactory settlement typically is in the client's interest. It is the inability to obtain such a settlement, in fact, that impels the client to seek the advice of counsel in the first place. The lawyer must consider not only what the client wants but also why the parties have been unable to settle their dispute, and then must find a dispute resolution procedure that is likely to overcome the impediments to settlement. Note, however, that, even though it may initially appear that the parties seek a settlement, sometimes an examination of the impediments to settlement reveals that at least one party wants something that settlement cannot provide (e.g., public vindication or a ruling that establishes an enforceable precedent).

The impediments to settlement, along with the likelihood that various ADR processes will overcome them, are set out in Table 2.

POOR COMMUNICATION

The relationship between the parties and/or their lawyers may be so poor that they cannot effectively communicate. Neither party believes the other, and each searches for hidden daggers in all proposals put forth by the other. An inability to communicate clearly and effectively, which impedes successful negotiations, is often, but not always, the result of a poor relationship. If, for example, the parties come from different cultural backgrounds, they may have great difficulty understanding and appreciating each other's concerns. Or, if there has been a long history of antagonism between the key players, all efforts to communicate are likely to be hampered by that antagonism.

Mediation is of great value in such situations. By controlling communications between the parties — keeping them physically apart, if necessary, and acting as a kind of translator — the mediator can literally "separate the people from the problem." (See Fisher, Ury and Patton, 1991.) In addition, the mediator may encourage a discussion of the factors leading to the dispute, and to the parties' inability to resolve the dispute on their own. How to improve the relationship, and thereby prevent future disputes, or at least to resolve them more easily, may also be considered.

To the extent that procedures such as the minitrial, the summary jury trial, and neutral evaluation permit the parties to address themselves to a neutral third party, rather than each other, these procedures are also somewhat useful in overcoming

Table 2
Likelihood that the ADR Procedure Will Overcome Impediments to Settlement

	Procedures			
Impediment	*Mediation*	*Minitrial*	*Summary Jury Trial*	*Early Neutral Evaluation*
Poor Communication	3	1	1	1
Need to Express Emotions	3	1	1	1
Different View of Facts	2	2	2	2
Different View of Law	2	3	3	3
Important Principle	1	0	0	0
Constituent Pressure*	3	2	2	2
Linkage	2	1	1	1
Multiple Parties	2	1	1	1
Different Lawyer-Client Interests	2	1	1	1
Jackpot Syndrome	0	1	1	1

0 = Unlikely to overcome impediment
1 = Sometimes useful in overcoming impediment
2 = Often useful in overcoming impediment
3 = Most likely to be useful in overcoming impediment

*The values assigned to procedures other than mediation for their capacity to overcome the impediment of constituent pressure assume that the neutral does not have mediation authority. If the neutral does, those procedures should be assigned the same value as mediation.

communications difficulties. However, unless the neutral in these processes plays both an evaluative and a mediatory role, which is typically not the case, these procedures are rated lower than mediation.

THE NEED TO EXPRESS EMOTIONS

At times, no settlement can be achieved until the parties have had the opportunity to express their views to each other about the dispute and each other's conduct. Such venting, combined with the feeling that one has been heard by the other party, has long been recognized as a necessary first step in resolving family and neighborhood disputes. Business disputes are no different. After all, they do not take place between disembodied corporations but between the people who manage those corporations, and who may have as much need to vent as anyone else involved in a dispute.

Mediation is clearly the preferred procedure when venting is necessary. By providing an informal atmosphere that encourages full participation by the disputants themselves, as well as by their lawyers, and by the presence of a neutral who can control the venting process, mediation can create a safe harbor for the parties to express their views fully. Some venting is possible in the evaluative ADR procedures; however, since their focus is on presenting evidence and argument concerning the rights of the parties, they are less hospitable to expressions of feelings.

DIFFERENT VIEWS OF FACTS

Did the defendant engage in the conduct that forms the basis of the plaintiff's complaint? Whose version of the facts is the finder of fact likely to believe? The greater the parties' disagreement on these matters, the more difficult settlement is likely to be.

Frequently, a skilled mediator can persuade the parties to put aside their factual dispute while at the same time agreeing on a mutually acceptable resolution of the dispute. If, however, the determination of disputed facts is essential to a resolution of the case, then some form of adjudication is required, such as a decision by a court, an arbitrator, or a private judge. A summary jury trial, neutral evaluation or minitrial, though not rendering a binding decision, may also aid in overcoming the impediment of conflicting evaluations of the facts by providing a neutral assessment of the case.

DIFFERENT VIEWS OF LEGAL OUTCOME IF SETTLEMENT IS NOT REACHED

Disputants often agree on the facts but disagree on their legal implications. The plaintiff asserts that, on the basis of the agreed-upon facts, he has a 90 percent likelihood of success in court; the defendant, with equal fervor, asserts that she has a 90 percent chance of success. While there may be a legitimate dispute over the likely outcome, both these estimates cannot be right.

Here, too, a mediator can often persuade the parties to resolve their dispute without determining which of their positions is "right." If not, a nonbinding appraisal of the likely outcome by an experienced neutral may be helpful in bringing about a settlement. An early neutral evaluation, a minitrial, or summary jury trial can provide such an appraisal.

ISSUES OF PRINCIPLE

If each of the disputing parties is deeply attached to some "fundamental" principle that must be abandoned or compromised in order to resolve the dispute, then resolution is likely to be difficult. Two examples: a suit challenging the right of neo-Nazis to march in a town where many Holocaust survivors live; and a suit by a religious group objecting to the withdrawal of life support systems from a comatose patient.

In view of the intensity of feelings in cases such as these, it is unlikely that evaluative techniques will be helpful in reaching a settlement. A mediator, however, may be able to find a creative way of reconciling (or bypassing) the seemingly conflicting values of the disputants by searching for a compromise that satisfies their differing interests. For example, in the neo-Nazi right-to-march dispute, the mediator might learn that the primary interest of the neo-Nazis is that of exercising their right to free speech, while the primary interest of the Holocaust survivors is not being confronted with disturbing reminders of the experiences they have suffered. Under these circumstances, mediation might lead to an agreement to allow the march, but to restrict its route to a part of town in which no Holocaust survivors live. To be sure, the parties might reach the same solution, on their own, but this is unlikely when emotions are high, the parties' relationship is terrible, and they must deal directly with each other, rather than through a mediator.

CONSTITUENCY PRESSURES

If one or more of the negotiators represents an institution or group, constituency pressures may impede agreement in two ways: different elements within the institution or group may have different interests in the dispute, or the negotiator may have staked her political or job future on attaining a certain result.

A mediator might deal with the first problem by mediating among the different parties that make up the organization, hoping to come up with a position that meets the divergent concerns. Such a technique is common in labor-management negotiations, where different groups of employees may have conflicting goals. Similarly, in an inter-corporate dispute, the production department of Corporation A may have one idea of what constitutes an acceptable settlement, the sales department may have another, and the finance department may have yet another. However united the corporation may appear to its opponent, a settlement proposal that affects different departments in a disparate fashion may reveal an underlying disunity that can be resolved only by mediation.

The mediator can solve the second problem — a negotiator's investment in a particular solution — by serving as a scapegoat, allowing the representative to blame the unsatisfactory outcome on the pressure exerted by the mediator. The other nonbinding processes can serve a similar function: the neutral's evaluation demonstrates to one or more of the constituent groups that its position is unlikely to prevail; hence, the settlement proposed by its representative is reasonable. A neutral who has the authority to evaluate and to mediate can use both techniques to deal with constituency pressures.

LINKAGE TO OTHER DISPUTES

The resolution of one dispute may have an effect on other disputes involving one or both parties. If so, this linkage will enter into their calculations, and may so complicate negotiations as to lead to an impasse. Here again, mediation holds much promise since the mediator can make explicit — and factor into the mediation — the linkage. Indeed, enlarging the agenda in many ways facilitates the mediation process.

For example, an automobile manufacturer in a dispute with one of its dealers concerning the dealer's right to sell autos made by other companies may ultimately be willing — for reasons specific to this dealer — to allow it to do so. But the manufacturer may so fear the effect of such an agreement on similar disputes with other dealers that the parties arrive at an impasse. It is possible that the manufacturer did not make this concern explicit in its negotiations with the dealer because it did not want the dealer to know it was engaged in similar disputes elsewhere. If the manufacturer confidentially discloses its concerns to the mediator, the mediator may be able to devise a settlement formula that meets the dealer's needs, yet preserves the manufacturer's position vis-à-vis other dealers. Alternatively, the mediator and the parties may devise an agreement that the manufacturer is willing to offer to all its dealers. The point is not that such a settlement could not have been reached without mediation but that the dynamic of mediation — in this case, the ability of the parties to make confidential disclosures to the mediator — can facilitate agreement.

This result might also be reached in the other nonbinding processes — the minitrial, the summary jury trial, and neutral evaluation — *if* the neutral in those processes plays a mediatory as well as an evaluative role, which is not always the case.

MULTIPLE PARTIES

When there are multiple parties, with diverse interests, the problems are similar to those raised by diverse constituencies and by issue linkages. Here, too, mediation will sometimes succeed in finding a balance of interests that satisfies all.

DIFFERENT LAWYER/CLIENT INTERESTS

Lawyers and clients often have divergent attitudes and interests concerning settlement. This may be a matter of personality (one may be a fighter, the other a problem solver) or of money. An attorney who is paid on an hourly basis stands to profit handsomely from a trial, and may be less interested in settlement than the client. On the other hand, an attorney paid on a contingent fee basis is interested in a prompt recovery without the expense of preparing for or conducting a trial, and may be more interested in settlement than is the client. It is in part because of this potential conflict of interest that most processes that seek to promote settlement provide for the client's direct involvement.

One way to remove the impediment created by different lawyer-client interests is to make explicit these differences. If a mediator conducts some meetings with clients separate from their lawyers, conflicting interests are likely to emerge. (Since both client and lawyer may, however, be concerned about such separate meetings, they are rarely conducted without the agreement of both.)

Suppose, instead, that the problem is not between lawyer and client on one side, but between opposing lawyers. Both clients are ready to settle the case on a reasonable basis, but the lawyers, for their own reasons, are intent on taking the case to trial. Such cases are often difficult to settle, and the best the mediator can do is to make sure that the costs — financial and otherwise — of the lawyers' kamikaze strategy are apparent to their clients. In fact, some mediators request attorneys to file premediation statements in which they estimate the cost and duration of a trial.

If the neutral plays a mediatory role and if the clients are present, the minitrial, the summary jury trial, and neutral evaluation can also be helpful in these situations.

THE "JACKPOT" SYNDROME

An enormous barrier to settlement often exists in those cases where the plaintiff is confident of obtaining in court a financial recovery far exceeding its damages, and the defendant thinks this is highly unlikely.

For example, the case may be one in which the controlling statute provides for the discretionary award of punitive damages to a successful plaintiff. If the underlying damage claim is for $10 million, and the plaintiff thinks that $50 million in punitive damages is a real possibility while the defendant does not, the vast disparity in case valuation may make settlement close to impossible. To be sure, one of the evaluative processes may affect one or the other party's estimate of the plaintiff's chance of hitting the jackpot, but the size of the jackpot may justify to the plaintiff the costs of litigation even if the odds against it are great. After all, millions of people play the lottery daily, even though their chances of success are infinitesimal; the temptation here is similar.

A RULE OF PRESUMPTIVE MEDIATION

Mediation will most often be the preferred procedure for overcoming the impediments to settlement. It has the greatest likelihood of overcoming all impediments except different views of facts and law, and the jackpot syndrome. Furthermore, a skilled mediator can often obtain a settlement without the necessity of resolving disputed questions of fact or law. Thus, there is much to be said for a rule of "presumptive mediation" — that mediation, if it is a procedure that satisfies the parties' goals, should, absent compelling indications to the contrary, be the first procedure used.

Under this approach, the mediator would first attempt to resolve the dispute by using customary mediation techniques. In doing so, the mediator would gain a clearer sense of the parties' goals and the obstacles to settlement than could be obtained by counsel prior to mediation. If mediation were not successful, the mediator could then make an informed recommendation for a different procedure. For example, if the parties were so far apart in their views of the facts or law that meaningful settlement negotiations could not take place, the mediator might recommend a referral to one of the evaluative procedures to move the parties closer to a common view of the facts and law. Once that had been accomplished, mediated settlement negotiations would recommence.

One of the strengths of this approach is that the mediator's process recommendation might be more readily accepted by both parties than would the suggestion of either of their attorneys, since attorney suggestions are sometimes suspected of being based on tactical considerations. Thus, the approach of "presumptive mediation" seems promising, particularly when the parties are having difficulty in agreeing upon an ADR procedure.

The presumption in favor of mediation would be overcome when the goals of one or both parties could not be satisfied in mediation, or mediation was clearly incapable of overcoming a major impediment to settlement. The most common situation in which this could occur would be when either party has a strong interest in receiving a neutral opinion, obtaining a precedent, or being vindicated, and is unwilling to consider any procedure that forecloses the possibility of accomplishing that objective. . . .

Conclusion

In addressing the problem of "fitting the forum to the fuss," we have suggested two lines of inquiry: What are the disputants' goals in making a forum choice? And, if the disputants are amenable to settlement, what are the obstacles to settlement, and in what forum might they be overcome?

The fact that these inquiries rarely lead to a clear answer to the question of forum selection does not, we think, indicate that the analysis is faulty. Rather, it indicates that the question of forum selection ultimately turns on the extent to which the interests of the disputing parties (and sometimes of the public) will be met in various forums. Thus, the most that analysis can offer is a framework that clarifies the interests involved and promotes a thoughtful weighing and resolution of those interests.

Moreover such an inquiry concerning goals and impediments is often independently helpful in clarifying the dimensions of the basic dispute. When it then comes to exploring the ADR implications of that analysis, a sophisticated ADR user might well ask: "If these are my goals and my impediments, what kinds of third-party help do I need, and how can I design a procedure that provides that kind of help"? But we believe that the approach reflected in Tables 1 and 2 is more helpful for the typical ADR user.

As noted, the difficulties of process selection are substantially eased by a recognition that mediation, where it satisfies the client's goals, is typically the preferred procedure for overcoming the impediments to settlement. It is on this basis that we suggest a rule of presumptive mediation — that mediation, if it satisfies the client's goals, should, absent compelling indications to the contrary, be the first procedure used. If mediation is not successful, the mediator can then make an informed recommendation for a different procedure.

One final word: Although our focus here has been largely on disputes as they arise on their way to court or in court, the analysis is applicable in many other settings. For example, the parties to a long-term relationship, such as joint venturers, may request advice on appropriate processes for dealing with the disputes that may arise in their relationship. A similar request may come from a manufacturer routinely faced with claims by dissatisfied customers, or from a hospital faced with a spate of malpractice actions. In such situations, the focus will not be on an individual dispute but a series of actual or possible disputes. The attorney's task will be to analyze the client's interests in all those disputes, as well as the likely impediments to settlement, and to recommend a procedure or series of procedures that are likely to deal with those disputes efficiently and effectively.

[For a later, more comprehensive version of the Sander and Goldberg article, see Sander and Rozdeiczer (2006), where the authors examine three other attempts to match disputes to processes and come up with a simplified conclusion: Because of the predominant applicability of mediation in most situations, the dispute-process matcher should begin with a presumption of mediation, unless the case falls into the narrow category of cases *not* suitable for mediation (see section 3B of the article), in which case the matching approach outlined in section 2 of the article should be used. If the case does *not* fall into the exceptions-to-mediation category, then one must consider what type of mediation would be most suitable (see section 3C of the article).]

A subsequent empirical study of nearly 500 cases administered by four providers of mediation services (Brett, Barsness, and Goldberg, 1996) supports the Sander-Goldberg preference for mediation in two respects:

- When disputing parties had no prior contractual obligation specifying the procedure to be used in the event of a dispute, but were free to select a dispute resolution procedure, 83 percent chose mediation (11 percent chose arbitration, and 6 percent chose other procedures).
- Mediation was successful in overcoming the barriers to settlement in 78 percent of a wide variety of cases—contract, construction, personal injury, property damage, environmental.

The same study also supports the Sander-Goldberg hypothesis that the "jackpot" syndrome constitutes a major barrier to settlement. Those cases that did not settle were characterized either by the potential of a very large recovery for one party or by the fact that it was not in the financial interest of one of the parties to settle. (The latter was described by Sander and Goldberg as a situation in which a party should not seek settlement.)

2. *Courts*

As pointed out by Sander and Goldberg (p. 337), if the attorneys for the disputing parties cannot agree on an ADR process, and the dispute is taken to court, it is increasingly likely that the court itself will consider whether the dispute is suitable for resolution by some means other than litigation. For either a judge or a court employee responsible for recommending an ADR procedure, the question regarding barriers to settlement and how they can be overcome is the same as it is for individual disputants. The other question concerning goals is similar, but with a broader perspective. In lieu of asking what are the objectives one party wishes to achieve, as would counsel, the question is what both parties want to achieve.

When a process selection is made from a public perspective, the public interest must also be considered. If the dispute is one in which a trial is likely to be lengthy, and so consume precious court time, there may be a public interest in referring the dispute to *some* form of ADR. Beyond that, one must ask if there is a public interest in having the dispute resolved pursuant to a *particular* procedure. For example, the referral of child custody disputes to mediation is required by law in several jurisdictions. The disputing parents may believe that they have no interest in a better relationship, but only in vindication, and hence prefer court to mediation. However, many states believe that a better relationship between the parents serves the public interest by improving the life of the child, and so mandate that child custody disputes go first to mediation.

The final question that must be asked in the public context is whether the public interest will be better served by a court decision than by a private settlement. If, for example, the dispute raises a significant question of statutory or constitutional interpretation, a court resolution might be preferable to a private settlement.

While a court normally has no power to prevent parties from settling their own dispute, it does not follow that the court, as a public agency, should encourage or assist settlement in such a case.

Litigation may also serve the public interest better than mediation in cases of consumer fraud, which are often handled by the consumer protection division of an attorney general's office. Here not only the issue of *precedent,* but also the related issue of *recurring violations,* is key. The establishment of a general principle or a class remedy, by means of a class action, is clearly preferable to a series of repetitive and inconsistent mediations.

Another situation in which public adjudication is called for is when there is a *need for sanctioning.* If the defendant's conduct constitutes a public danger (assault with a deadly weapon, say, or maintaining a building in a grossly unsafe condition), ADR is inappropriate.

Finally, two more situations may militate against any use of ADR. First, *one or more of the parties may be incapable of negotiating effectively.* An unsophisticated pro se litigant, for example, may be vulnerable to exploitation in an ADR process. (On the other hand, such an individual, if not represented by a lawyer, may not fare better in court.) Second, court process may be required for some other reason: for example, *when serious issues of compliance or discovery are anticipated.*

Process recommendations in the public sector are regularly made by screening officers in a multidoor courthouse (MDC). Originally proposed by Professor Frank Sander at the 1976 Pound Conference (the National Conference on the Causes of Popular Dissatisfaction with the Administration of Justice) (Sander, 1976), the MDC is a multifaceted dispute resolution center that is premised on the notion that the modern courthouse should not have only one door leading to the courtroom but many doors leading to different processes. For example, there might be doors leading to mediation, arbitration, case evaluation, and summary jury trial. The task of the screening officer is to recommend (or direct) that cases be assigned to one of these processes, or more than one, in an effort to obtain a settlement without the need for a courtroom trial. In the event that settlement cannot be achieved, the disputants retain the right to insist upon a trial. (For a detailed discussion of diagnosing a case for ADR, see Edward Dauer (2000) *Alternative Dispute Resolution and Practice* ch. 6 (Juris. Publishers); (see pp. 396-400.)

Questions

5.14 You represent National Insurance Co. James Black, who is insured by National, has been sued by Arnold Green, who was struck and injured by Black when Black lost control of his car. Green, an office manager, sustained a serious fracture of his left arm, requiring both surgery and physical therapy. His medical bills are $6,000 and his lost wages are $4,000. His orthopedic surgeon has diagnosed him with a 25 percent permanent partial disability of his arm. Green is demanding $300,000 in damages.

The orthopedic surgeon retained by the insurance company has diagnosed Green with a 5 percent permanent partial disability of his arm. On the basis of that diagnosis, you offered $25,000 in settlement of the claim. Green's attorney, who has just begun practicing law, refused that offer. He also refused to make a counteroffer, stating that his $300,000 claim was entirely justified.

You are in a jurisdiction in which opposing counsel are required to discuss the possible use of ADR to resolve pending claims. Which process should you propose?

5.15* You represent Perfect Packaging Company, a small family-owned business, which has been sued by Acme Printing Company for $27,000 on a breach of contract claim. The ink on printed inserts provided to Perfect by Acme, and used by Perfect in the packaging for broiler chickens, ran, discoloring the chickens. Perfect has refused to pay Acme the $27,000 contract price for the inserts, and has counterclaimed for $45,000, the total of the damages it had to pay the chicken seller and its lost profits on the sale of inserts to the chicken seller (who refused to pay for the packaging provided by Perfect).

This was supposed to be the first of many transactions between Perfect and Acme, but their relationship has now soured. Indeed, your client says that he would rather close down his business than pay Acme. He also says that he wants this matter resolved quickly, inexpensively, and without publicity.

What process would you recommend to your client for a resolution of this matter?

5.16 You represent the parents of a five-year-old girl who died during surgery due to the failure of a new type of anesthetic equipment. You have brought suit against the manufacturer of the equipment, the hospital in which the surgery was performed, and the anesthesiologist, claiming $2 million for wrongful death. You are convinced that you have an excellent case.

Your efforts to focus your clients on a possible settlement have been stymied by the emotional condition of the mother, who had an extremely close relationship with her daughter. You are concerned that a lengthy trial will be emotionally draining for her, but that she needs to tell her "story" in a safe and somewhat formal setting to help her move through the grieving process.

You have had some discussions with defendants' counsel and have learned that they will contest both liability and the amount of damages. They also wish to avoid the negative publicity of a trial.

What process would you recommend to your client for the resolution of this matter? Would there be any difference in your recommendation if you were the screening clerk in a multidoor courthouse?

5.17 You represent a ten-year-old boy who sustained injuries to his right leg while running alongside the defendants' swimming pool. The leg was severely gashed, requiring stitches, and may be permanently scarred, but there were no broken bones. You have claimed damages in the amount of $150,000.

The ten-year-old boy and his parents live in the same neighborhood as the defendants, who allow all the neighborhood children to use their pool. You allege that the pool was inadequately supervised and that dangerous tools were left around. Defendants allege that plaintiff's parents were present when the accident occurred, and

*Questions 5.15 and 5.16 are used with permission of the Mediation Center for Dispute Resolution and the Dispute Resolution Institute of Hamline University School of Law.

that they failed to supervise their son adequately, with the result that he was running recklessly around the pool.

Defendants have sufficient insurance coverage to pay the $150,000 in damages that you are seeking.

What process will you recommend to your client?

5.18 You represent a multinational manufacturing company that has plants throughout the United States and abroad. For many years prior to 1960, your client, at one of its U.S. plants, discharged into the ground a manufacturing by-product, Zitr, that was believed at the time to be entirely benign. Finite traces of the Zitr made their way into portions of the city drinking water system. As a result of extensive clean-up efforts, largely financed by your client, there are no traces of Zitr in the city drinking water system today.

Approximately five years ago, some laboratory research publications began to suggest that Zitr was toxic and had been shown to cause cancer in rats. Not long afterwards, your client was hit with the first of what today amounts to over 100 individual actions brought by residents of the city in which the plant is located. All these suits claim that the plaintiff contracted cancer as a result of the presence of Zitr in the city water system serving the area of the city in which they lived; approximately 20 of them are wrongful death actions. Additionally, a class action has been filed on behalf of all residents in those areas of the city in which there was evidence of tainted drinking water, alleging that they are entitled to damages for the emotional strain under which they are living as a result of the risk that they or their children will contract cancer or suffer birth defects. The total amount of damages claimed in the individual actions is approximately $750 million and in the class action $1 billion.

Your client's top management has a variety of reactions to this situation. Initially, there is a general sentiment that the company did nothing wrong. At the time that it discharged Zitr into the ground, there was no evidence or even allegation that it was toxic. Furthermore, its disposal complied with all existing environmental protection laws at the time. There is also considerable doubt among top management that Zitr, in the trace amounts in which it appeared in the city drinking water, could lead to cancer. This doubt is backed by a considerable body of expert opinion that you have put together.

All this leads to a desire to fight these claims in the courts. At the same time, management realizes that trial time and costs will be enormous, as will the diversion of corporate energies. There is also a finite risk that the scientific evidence will be a draw in the eyes of the jury, and that, under those circumstances, the jury's sympathy for the plaintiffs and its belief that your client has ample resources to compensate them will lead to some very substantial damage awards.

Finally, there is great concern in top management that settlement would leave the company open to future suits by persons who lived in the affected area and who contract cancer in the future. There is also concern that settlement would lead to the company being regarded as an easy target for similar suits in other areas in which it does business.

All things considered, what advice would you give to your client?

5.19 Professor Jeffrey Stempel (1996) has suggested that the recommendation of the multidoor courthouse case screener regarding an appropriate dispute resolution process should be binding on the parties and that there should be a right to appeal this recommendation to the court. Assuming that the case screener's process recommendation is binding (see Chapter 6), do you agree with Stempel's proposal for judicial review? Goldberg and Sander suggest that mediation might be a presumptive process. Why not, instead of using the Stempel approach, just authorize the screener to require mediation except when there are contraindications? If this is a sound approach, what should be the contraindications (see Sander and Rozdeiczer (2006))? What would be the reason, if any, to allow an appeal if mediation is the only process that the screener can require?

5.20 An experienced trial judge who has tried hard to get parties to consider the use of ADR (particularly mediation) has indicated that in screening sessions the common objections to ADR voiced by attorneys are the following:

1. "The case is not ready for ADR because more discovery is needed."
2. "The case is a 'clear winner' [*or* "the other side's case is 'clearly frivolous'] and hence ADR is inappropriate."
3. "*I'd* be in favor of ADR but my client won't let me."
4. "There are dispositive motions pending (e.g., a motion to dismiss for failure to state a valid legal claim) and ADR is inappropriate until these are disposed of."
5. "The case involves a matter of principle."

In light of these objections, a sizable number of cases do not go to ADR and proceed instead to trial.

The judge turns to you as an ADR expert and asks you how she should evaluate these objections.

5.21 Is the Sander and Goldberg approach in "Fitting the Forum to the Fuss" deficient in its failure to focus on fitting the neutral to the fuss?

5.22 The Administrative Dispute Resolution Act of 1996, which sought to facilitate greater use of ADR within federal administrative agencies, contains the following provision (5 U.S.C. §572(b)):

> An agency shall consider not using a dispute resolution proceeding if—
>
> (1) a definitive or authoritative resolution of the matter is required for precedential value, and such a proceeding is not likely to be accepted generally as an authoritative precedent;
>
> (2) the matter involves or may bear upon significant questions of Government policy that require additional procedures before a final resolution may be made, and such a proceeding would not likely serve to develop a recommended policy for the agency;
>
> (3) maintaining established policies is of special importance, so that variations among individual decisions are not increased and such a proceeding would not likely reach consistent results among individual decisions;
>
> (4) the matter significantly affects persons or organizations who are not parties to the proceeding;
>
> (5) a full public record of the proceeding is important and a dispute resolution proceeding cannot provide such a record; and
>
> (6) the agency must maintain continuing jurisdiction over the matter with authority to alter the disposition of the matter in the light of changed circumstances, and a dispute resolution proceeding would interfere with the agency's fulfilling that requirement.

How would you evaluate these suggested contraindications for the use of ADR? Which of them have validity in other contexts (e.g., the multidoor courthouse)?

EXERCISE 5.3: THE DAILY BUGLE*

Two weeks ago, the *Daily Bugle,* its editor, and reporter Terry Ives were sued for defamation by John Roark, M.D. The article that was the basis of the suit described the latest in a series of fires in slum housing, pointing out that the building in which the fire took place was so poorly managed that some tenants lacked heat. It contained the following statements that Roark alleges to be false and defamatory:

> The destroyed building is owned by slum landlord Dr. John Roark, county property records reveal. Dr. Roark is a prominent orthopedic surgeon. . . . A source in the Fire Marshall's office indicated that the office is not ruling out the possibility of arson because it is not uncommon for owners of tenements to intentionally burn them to collect insurance.

Roark alleges that the reporter was negligent—property records show that he was only a limited partner in the group owning the property—and that the reporter acted with malice. He states that the newspaper refused his request for a retraction. He seeks $250,000 in actual damages for harm to his reputation, lost income in his medical practice, aggravation of a serious health problem, and mental anguish. He also seeks $1 million in punitive damages.

Defamation is a communication to a third person that harms a person's reputation or causes harm in that person's business. Truth is a defense. Public figures must show that the defendant acted with actual malice in order to recover. In this jurisdiction, private individuals need only show negligence in order to recover actual damages. Actual malice must be shown in order to recover punitive damages.

In this jurisdiction, the reporter has a privilege to refuse disclosure of a source who has been promised confidentiality. However, under the privilege statute, the judge decides in each instance whether the need for disclosure outweighs the harm caused by disclosure, specifically the harm to the public interest in promoting dissemination of news by assuring the anonymity of sources.

Counsel for the *Daily Bugle* is to meet with the editor of the *Daily Bugle,* explain the options for resolving the dispute, and decide which option(s) should be promoted in meeting with counsel for Dr. Roark.

(Confidential information for both parties is contained in the Teacher's Manual.)

*Exercise 5.3 is reprinted from Nancy H. Rogers, "The Daily Bugle: A Counseling and Process Selection Exercise," in Leonard Riskin, Instructor's Manual for Videotape IV. An Overview of ADR: The Roark v. Daily Bugle Libel Claim, Dispute Resolution and Lawyers Videotape Series (West 1992). Copyright © 1992 by the Curators of the University of Missouri. Reprinted with permission. The exercise is based upon Videotape IV, which was based upon Nanette Laughrey and Sandra Scott, The Doctor and the Daily Bugle in the above Instructor's Manual.

E. REPRESENTING A CLIENT IN MEDIATION

1. *Discovery and Appropriate Timing for Dispute Resolution Processes*

After weighing whether to use dispute resolution processes and assessing settlement options, the lawyer needs to consider timing. With only 2 percent of civil cases in state and federal courts being tried (Gross and Syverud, 1996), mediation and other nonbinding processes are more often a means to move up the time of settlement than a replacement for trial. Clients may value the potential role of dispute resolution in shortening the time to resolution, particularly if settlement can be achieved before or early on in the formal discovery process. Businesses engaged in commercial litigation report major savings when they shorten the average number of months of formal discovery (Cole et al., 2001; CPR, 1989, update 1994). In some cases, clients want to retain personal or business relationships with other parties and fear that discovery battles will sour future dealings. Also, people caught up in disputes may believe that the less time in litigation, like less time with an ulcer, represents an improvement in the quality of life (Williams, 1996).

Lawyers who participate in mediation recognize its potential to reduce the time to resolution. They also comment that setting a case for mediation tends to spur case preparation by their counterparts, thus contributing to earlier settlement (McEwen et al., 1995). They believe that mediation can change the "no compromises" outlook their clients are likely to have early in a dispute (cf. Merry and Silbey, 1984; Williams, 1996), because the mediator encourages the angry client to vent, facilitates an information exchange, and promotes a realization that other parties have a valid point of view and one that the judge or jury may find persuasive (McEwen et al., 1995). Research seems to substantiate the lawyers' intuition. Parties referred to mediation before completion of formal discovery settle almost as often (Kakalik et al., 1996) or as often as those referred after completion of discovery (Wissler, 1997).

All of this would seem to counsel scheduling dispute resolution processes, particularly mediation, before or early in the discovery process. Nonetheless, lawyers infrequently recommend the use of dispute resolution processes before the courts schedule them (Wissler, 1996). When courts set cases for mediation and the mediation is unsuccessful, counsel often complain to researchers that the cases were not yet ready (Daniel, 1995; Kakalik et al., 1996).

What are the factors that weigh against early scheduling for a settlement process? One litigator suggests that lawyers accustomed to traditional discovery schedules resist providing free discovery to opponents and recommending settlement before they have eliminated the possibility of uncovering a key piece of evidence that may change the trial outlook (Siemer, 1991). Corporate in-house counsel suggest that outside litigators may see their economic self-interests disserved by early settlement (CPR 1989, update 1994). "The traditional model of dispute resolution," said one corporate lawyer, "has been a source of great riches for both plaintiff and defense counsel" (10 *Alternatives to the High Cost Litig.* 29, 32, (1992)). It is also possible that lawyers do not understand or give high priority to their clients' concern about time to disposition. For example, a recent federal court study found that litigants were seven times more likely than their lawyers to believe that the case took too long to resolve (Kakalik et al., 1996).

The standard for malpractice liability may also be a factor in whether lawyers will encourage the use of settlement processes prior to completion of formal discovery. In scattered cases, predominately medical malpractice cases, lawyers have been held liable for failing to investigate sufficiently prior to recommending settlement. See, e.g., *Collins ex rel. Collins v. Perrine,* 108 N.M. 714, 778 P.2d 912 (Ct. App. 1989), cert. denied, 108 N.M. 681, 777 P.2d 1325 (1990).

Questions

5.23 Should the standards for lawyer malpractice be changed to encourage lawyers to recommend early settlement? If so, how?

5.24 In light of the significance of litigation costs, burdens for the clients, and lawyers' self-interest, what ethics rules or laws should be put in place to overcome lawyers' reluctance to use dispute resolution processes early in the case? Should courts require lawyers to appear early in the case to canvass dispute resolution possibilities? Would any of these changes decrease the quality of legal advice regarding settlement?

5.25 One company has adopted a policy of trying all cases not settled before the conclusion of formal discovery. Why shouldn't all clients follow the lead of this company?

2. *Premediation*

A case may wind up in mediation in essentially two ways—by direction of the court or as a result of the initiative of either side. In those jurisdictions where the court may order the case to go to mediation, statutes may give parties the option of filing a motion to opt out of mediation for cause shown, thus raising some of the issues canvassed earlier in Section D.1. Even if there is no basis for objecting to the use of mediation—which will be the common situation—you may still have a role in selecting the mediator, either from a court list or, by agreement with the other side, from a larger pool of potential mediators. This necessitates a careful analysis of the kind of skills needed (substantive and process) as pointed out earlier (pp. 115-116). Some situations may call for a mediator having a narrow, evaluative approach. Others may dictate a mediator who paints with a broader brush or who acts in a more facilitative manner.

Suppose the other side suggests a mediator who is known to operate primarily through separate sessions. If you strongly believe that your main goal is to have a good shot at persuading the other side of the reasonableness of your position, would it make sense to veto this mediator, unless you are persuaded that she is so skilled that she would do at least as well as you in achieving your objective?

Alternatively the case may come into mediation through your own suggestion or that of the other side. In the latter case, half the battle is already won, for persuading the other side to agree to mediate can be difficult. To accomplish that objective where there is resistance, some lawyers, in addition to emphasizing the nonbinding, nonprejudicial nature of mediation, let the other side name the mediator, subject only to possible veto. Some lawyers are concerned that actively seeking mediation may make them appear weak and so compromise their negotiating position. ("He must be afraid to go to trial; that's why he's pushing so hard for mediation.") To avoid that risk, a lawyer may try to get a judge to suggest mediation. Alternatively, a lawyer might engage a neutral provider of dispute resolution services to "sell" mediation to a reluctant opponent.

In any event, regardless of whether the initiative comes from you or the other side, there are essentially two issues that need to be addressed: (1) whether mediation is appropriate for this case, and (2) if so, what are the possible benefits and costs of mediating. The first question was discussed at length in Section D.1. As regards the second question, the upside should be relatively obvious by now: the addition of a new head with possibly new ideas for reconciling the interests of the parties or evaluating their respective rights, as well as the injection of a new format (that is, the separate sessions of the neutral with each side that sometimes bring to the surface concerns that did not get clearly identified in the bilateral negotiation). The downsides are less obvious and are thoughtfully canvassed in Siemer, 1991.

A critical question as you prepare for mediation is whether your client will be present at the mediation. As Professor Riskin explains in the ensuing piece, this turns out to be a complex decision.

L. RISKIN, THE REPRESENTED CLIENT IN A SETTLEMENT CONFERENCE: THE LESSONS OF *G. HEILEMAN BREWING CO. v. JOSEPH OAT CORP.*

69 Wash. U. L.Q. 1059, 1099-1103 (1991)

Several years ago, I mediated two personal injury insurance claims on the same day. In the first case, the clients participated along with their lawyers; in the second, they did not. The clients' presence made for vast differences in the content and style of the mediation and in my own experience.

The first case involved an automobile accident in which the victim (I will call her "Alice May") suffered serious injuries and her automobile sustained great damage. Ms. May sat beside her lawyer. For the defense, the claims adjuster (I will call her "Grace Green") assumed the client role, and a local attorney hired by the insurance company represented the insured.

The room crackled with emotion as we discussed the case. In earlier negotiations Grace Green had demanded documentation of Ms. May's damage claims. Alice May was hurt and angry because she felt that Grace Green had "called [her] a liar." Ms. Green also was entangled emotionally. She feared being duped, and although she did not express this until late in the session, she did not want Alice to dislike her.

A highly-charged exchange between the clients consumed a major portion of the mediation; raw feelings spilled over the mahogany conference table. The clients' conduct in the mediation, and their comments afterward, suggest that this conversation was essential to the settlement. Each client felt she had earned the other's respect, and each seemed to think that achieving this kind of "balance" was valuable in itself. Moreover, participation helped them conclude that the resulting monetary agreement was fair. Stated simply, the presence and direct participation of both clients focused attention on the parties' relationship. Achieving mutual respect became an important goal of the mediation.

The clients' conversation could not have taken place unless lawyers and the mediator — the "professionals" — allowed it. During this conversation, the professionals did almost nothing, and I felt extremely tense and uncertain about my role. I think the lawyers may have had similar reactions. I had relinquished control, and had little idea where the conversation would lead. Worse, I was a professional mediator and a lawyer; I was being paid for this. Surely there was *something* I should do.

The second mediation arose out of a claim of police brutality in connection with an allegedly invalid arrest. Only lawyers attended. The defendant's lawyer, a local practitioner, had been hired by the defendant's out-of-state insurance company.

This session felt drastically different from the other. Although the claimant alleged intentional, racially motivated, abusive police conduct, the session was entirely cordial. Each participant wore a "professional mask," which limited the personal aspects of our involvement. A clubby cordiality replaced the tension and uncertainty of the other mediation, and this polite interaction continued even after it became clear that settlement was impossible. . . .

[Riskin comments on his own greater comfort at negotiating without the client's presence and then considers the extent to which client participation in settlement discussions serves the client's interests, pointing out that for each potential advantage, there is a corresponding risk or potential disadvantage.]

- The client's presence increases the likelihood that her lawyer will be well prepared. (But: the client's presence may incline some lawyers to posture, to "show off." In addition, the client may become a great bother, interfering with the lawyer's ability to accomplish her or his work.)
- The client's presence can reduce the risk that interests of the lawyer will prevail over those of the client. For instance, a lawyer might recommend for or against a particular settlement because of the lawyer's own financial or professional needs, which could be related to excessive pressure from the judge. (But: the client's presence may remove tactical advantages. For example, often a lawyer will falsely attribute a stubbornness to the client to give the lawyer negotiating strength. In addition, it may be strategically useful to delay consideration of an offer from the other side; this is easier to do with an absent client.)
- The client may be better able to appreciate the value of alternate dispute resolution processes if he hears about them directly from a settlement judge, rather than from his lawyer, who might be unfamiliar with or biased against such processes. (But: the client may too readily succumb to the allure of a "quick fix," thereby giving up the chance of a better result through trial. In addition, the other side may perceive as weakness the client's expression of willingness to try an alternative process.)
- The client could gain respect for the judicial process. (But: if the client is exposed to the realities of settlement conferences he could lose respect for the process and for the impartiality of the judge.)
- The client will feel he has had a chance to tell his story, in his own words, by participating in a settlement conference. (But: to the extent that such a feeling makes it easier for the client to settle, he loses his real day in court.)

- The client can learn much about the strengths and weaknesses of both sides of the case by observing the conduct of the other parties, the lawyers, and the judge; this can soften his attitudes or positions. (But: exposure to the other side's behavior will anger or harden some clients, making settlement more difficult.)
- If the client actually observes the exchange of monetary offers, he can better assess the strength of the other side's commitment to a position; he may notice things the lawyer misses. Although there may be some lawyers who can fully appreciate and convey the nuances of a settlement negotiation, many are vulnerable to misreading, to oversimplifying, and to embracing too warmly the virtues of their own side's case. (But: the client may misinterpret the events and affect the lawyer's judgment in an erroneous direction or become more difficult to "control.")
- The client's presence permits more rounds of offers and counter-offers. It permits him to act on new information and allows cooperation and momentum to build. In addition, attendance requires the client to pay attention to the case, which, in itself, makes settlement more likely. (But: the client may lose his resolve because of the "crucible effect.")
- The client can clear up miscommunications about facts and interests between lawyers. (But: the client may be too emotionally involved to see the facts clearly.)
- Direct communication between clients can lead to better understanding of each other or of the events that transpired, perhaps even allow a healing of the rift between them. (But: direct communication may cause a flare-up and loss of objectivity. Parties may harden their resolve.)
- The client, because he is more familiar with his situation, may be more able to spot opportunities for problem-solving solutions, which could lead to quicker and more satisfying agreements. (But: the client may give away information about his underlying interests that could leave him vulnerable to exploitation. Moreover, the client will not be sufficiently objective. A lawyer knowledgeable about the client's situation might do a better job of developing problem-solving solutions.)
- Because the client's presence increases the likelihood of a settlement, and a settlement that will be satisfactory to the client, participation likely will result in a savings of time and money for the client. (But: if some of the risks described above materialize, his presence will have caused him to lose time and money.)
- The client would not consider an order to attend a settlement conference as coercive, but rather as an opportunity to participate. (But: the client might react negatively to the coercive nature of the order and be uncooperative.)

These arguments bear two important implications. First, the assertions of both risk and benefit gain strength as the client's actual participation increases. Thus, the client who not only observes the settlement conference, but also talks, may enhance his or her opportunities for developing a problem-solving solution, while simultaneously increasing his or her risks of being exploited, of angering the opponent, or of revealing potentially damaging information. Clearly, this was the situation in the personal injury claim mediation described in the beginning of this Article; the session could have ended explosively at any moment. However, in the police brutality claim mediation, also described in the beginning of this Article, if both the plaintiff and a member of the police department had been present, opportunities would have arisen to discuss more than a financial settlement based upon the probable outcome in court. The clients could have focused on exactly what happened, and on how and why, and looked toward changing police practices. There might even have been a place for an apology. On the other hand, the plaintiff might have revealed damaging information or succumbed to the apology and therefore reduced his demand.

Second, all the arguments in favor of including the client presume that the client is a competent, reasonably intelligent person with good judgment who will not be pushed into making an agreement. Conversely, the arguments against including the client assume he lacks one or more of these qualities, and that the lawyer has them. . . .

Whether or not the client is present at the mediation, the most important thing the lawyer needs to do prior to the mediation is to explain to the client what mediation is all about and what is likely to happen at the mediation session — something akin to the mediator's opening statement at the beginning of a mediation. At a minimum, this discussion should touch on the three p's: purpose, process, and product. Purpose covers the goal of mediation (that is, to reach a mutually acceptable settlement, as distinguished from an imposed decision by a court). Process covers such matters as confidentiality and separate sessions. And under the heading of product comes the likely outcome (that is, an agreement that will be enforceable like a contract).

Beyond this orientation to the landscape, the lawyer needs to cover some general issues applicable to any negotiation, as well as a number of specific matters that are particularly germane to the anticipated mediation.

The general questions are those discussed in Chapter 2:

- Interests of each side (notably, what are *they* likely to need or want?)
- Possible options for settlement
- Criteria that might aid in the settlement of the dispute
- Each party's best alternative to a negotiated agreement (BATNA) and worst alternative to a negotiated agreement (WATNA).

Among the specific issues that need to be addressed are the following:

a. In situations where the mediator requests a premediation statement, what should be said in such a statement? How does it differ from a brief submitted to the court? What kind of information would be useful to a mediator in her attempt to settle the dispute?

b. Who, aside from lawyer and client, should attend the mediation sessions? This requires reference to such issues as knowledge of the subject of the dispute, authority to settle, and the likelihood that the potential attendee will handle herself well in the mediation sessions. When the disputant is a large organization, the task of selection becomes more complex. As mediator Lewis (1995) puts it:

> There are times when a company might want to have most involved in the mediation the person who best knows the aspect of the business in dispute. In others, the person with the most personal and direct knowledge about a dispute might not be the best company

representative. Employment disputes are a good example of the latter. In those disputes, the person from the company with the most thorough knowledge of the dispute often is the person most complained about by the employee. In that situation, involvement of that particular representative might doom the mediation to a series of charges and counter-charges generating a great deal of heat and very little light.

c. Who should play what role (That is, who should make the opening statement, and exactly what should it contain)?

d. What questions is the mediator likely to ask your client or other individuals who are present at the mediation? What answers should be put forward? It is well to remember that mediation is an informal procedure, and any person sitting at the mediation table — and perhaps even others who have no direct stake in the litigation (for example, family members or fellow employees) — may be asked questions by the mediator if particular issues with respect to which they have direct knowledge become critical.

e. How might effective visuals (that is, charts or videos) help your case? Linda Singer, a well-known mediator, recently described the artful use by an advocate of a series of videotaped excerpts from depositions of the other side's managers to help persuade their supervisor who had not been party to the depositions, and who had been assured that they had gone well. The videotape turned out to be a powerful convincer (Lewis, 1995).

f. Who in the opposing camp should be involved in a dialogue? How could the mediator be helpful in bringing this about?

g. If the opposing client is present, might an apology or at least an expression of sympathy play an important role in defusing the dispute and helping to come to an agreement? (See pp. 137-139.)

3. *Advocacy During Mediation*

If you and your client have carefully prepared for the mediation session, there should be few surprises. Still, mediations often take unpredictable turns, and it is impossible to envision all eventualities. Therefore, you and your client will have to constantly think of ways in which you can use the mediator to communicate more effectively with the other side or otherwise work towards a resolution of the dispute, for example by:

- using special roles for the mediator (for example, as evaluator or decision analysis expert, (see pp. 120, 363);
- using separate session(s);
- using the mediator to persuade your own client or the client on the other side.

Of course, the mediator is not the be-all and end-all to the solution of the dispute. Oftentimes, particularly in the final stages of the mediation, it is through additional ideas of one or the other of the parties that the dispute gets resolved. Are there other ways of bridging the remaining gap? Could some other process (such as arbitration) be utilized to deal with the intractable tenth issue if the parties can agree on the other nine?

Questions

5.26 You represent the plaintiff in a personal injury case. At a pretrial conference, the court orders that the case go to mediation. Court rules require you to file "a brief premediation statement" but give the parties the option of filing a confidential statement or, as with a brief, sending a copy to the other side. Which option will you choose and why?

5.27 You represent the defendant doctor in a bitterly fought malpractice action, involving a claim by the plaintiff that your client botched a difficult operation on the plaintiff's hand, resulting in some residual incapacity and intermittent pain. Your client essentially agrees with the plaintiff's claims as to his impaired condition but feels strongly that it is the result of unpredictable conditions, rather than his own negligence. The case has been referred to mediation. In your preparation session with your client, one scenario you consider is that the plaintiff will begin by poignantly describing his present condition. Suppose the mediator then turns to your client and says "What is your response, Dr. Smith?" How might your client best respond?

5.28 Does your role as a lawyer representing a party in mediation vary depending on whether the mediation was mandatory or voluntary? If so, how and why?

5.29 "If parties have reached an impasse after extensive and skillful negotiation efforts, there is little point to bringing in a mediator."

As a lawyer for plaintiff in just such a situation, do you agree with the advice? Why or why not?

5.30 You represent the plaintiff in a personal injury case growing out of an automobile accident. The defendant, in addition to denying any negligence on his part, has alleged contributory negligence by your client. The jurisdiction has a comparative negligence statute. In discussions with your client about the likely outcome of trial, you have tried — so far unsuccessfully — to persuade him of the risk of the jury finding him contributorily negligent, which, if it occurs, might cut down any award by as much as 50 percent. In the midst of these discussions, the defendant's lawyer proposes mediation. You believe that that might be particularly helpful in persuading your client of the litigation risks he faces, but you are reluctant to be quite so explicit in recommending mediation to him for fear that he will think you are not zealously representing him. Does this course of conduct raise any ethical questions for you?

4. Ethical Issues

What ethical constraints should apply to lawyers representing clients in a mediation? Compare Comment [5] under ABA Rule of Professional Conduct 2.4:

> [5] Lawyers who represent clients in alternative dispute-resolution processes are governed by the Rules of Professional Conduct. When the dispute-resolution process takes place before a tribunal, as in binding arbitration (see Rule 1.0(m)) the lawyer's duty of candor is governed by Rule 3.3. Otherwise, the lawyer's duty of candor toward both the third-party neutral and other parties is governed by Rule 4.1.

with Kimberlee Kovach (2001) "New Wine Requires New Wineskins: Transforming Lawyer Ethics for Effective Representation in a Non-Adversarial Approach to

Problem Solving: Mediation," 28 *Fordham Urb. L.J.* 935, proposing a "more collaborative and cooperative" set of rules, involving such obligations as good faith or minimum meaningful participation and "an ethic of care." Who has the better approach here? If Professor Kovach, how might you concretely flesh out her goal? What difficulties do you see with her approach?

5. Making the Decision to Settle: Decision Analysis

The purpose of most ADR procedures is to encourage settlement. But how do lawyers and clients know when to settle? The classic answer is this: accept a settlement offer if it is better than your BATNA. But suppose that you have filed a complaint seeking $5 million in damages, and you receive a settlement offer of $1.5 million. Is that offer better than your BATNA? That depends, at least in part, on how you view the likelihood of success in litigation. That is where decision analysis (sometimes referred to as litigation risk analysis) comes in.

M. AARON AND D. HOFFER, "DECISION ANALYSIS AS A METHOD OF EVALUATING THE TRIAL ALTERNATIVE" IN D. GOLANN, MEDIATING LEGAL DISPUTES

307-334 (1997)

Decision analysis provides quantitative evaluation of decisions under conditions of uncertainty. Long used by business people to model business decisions, decision analysis has more recently gained recognition within the legal community as a tool for decision making in complex litigation. The term "decision analysis" was originally used to refer specifically to the analysis of *decision trees*— tree-shaped models of the decision to be made and the uncertainties it encompasses. While sometimes used more broadly to describe any number of techniques for thinking systematically about decisions, *decision analysis* is used here to connote the traditional use of decision trees. . . .

Many legal (and business) decisions . . . can be materially improved through the design of even a relatively simple decision tree. To model a choice between litigation and settlement, a lawyer can estimate ranges of damage awards and legal fees with some confidence, and she can approximate probabilities of different rulings or judgments based on previous experience with similar cases. Furthermore, most legal decisions are characterized by multiple uncertainties; decision analysis can be extremely helpful in disaggregating the various states of the litigation process as a means to assess the relative importance of different issues and stages in a case.

For example, a plaintiff in a complex environmental liability case may have to win several important discovery rulings, survive motions to dismiss and for summary judgment, and succeed in coaching its fact and expert witnesses to testify credibly— all before the case reaches a jury. In cases where victory is contingent on such multiple uncertainties, case value is very hard to assess analytically without the aid of decision analysis. While experienced lawyers can sometimes develop an intuitive sense of what a case is worth, their intuition is usually much less accurate in assessing the impact of a midstream change in strategy or particular ruling. Furthermore, intuitive "seat-of-the-pants" valuations are hard to support or explain to clients, and even more so when they are proved wrong. It is for these reasons—accuracy, flexibility, and transparency—that decision analysis can offer significant advantages over traditional "back-of-the-envelope" valuations of cases. . . .

In order to construct a decision tree modeling the settlement decision in a typical litigation, it is helpful to understand the structure and terminology associated with decision trees.

Decision trees are organized chronologically, from left to right. Events are depicted in the tree in the order they are likely to occur. Decision trees contain three different types of branch points or "nodes": decision, chance, and terminal.

- A *decision node* denotes the point at which the decision maker has to choose between two or more options.
- A *chance node* denotes a point at which various possible outcomes may occur, which the decision maker does not control. Each possible outcome after the chance node is reflected on a *branch,* which is assigned a *probability* reflecting how likely it is to occur.
- A *terminal node* denotes a final outcome, after which no events are considered. Each terminal node is assigned a *payoff* value (negative or positive) which reflects the net dollar cost or gain associated with that outcome.

For legal disputes, decision analysis is used to value the parties' litigation alternatives—what will happen in litigation if the case does not settle. A decision tree used in litigation typically has two branches: *litigate* and *settle.* The settle branch may reflect the other side's most recent offer, or it may reflect the lawyer's estimate of what the adverse party might accept in settlement. The litigate branch is generally an extended chance tree, whose branches represent the different events that may transpire during litigation.

The following decision tree represents a situation in which a plaintiff must decide whether to accept a settlement offer of $30,000 or proceed to trial with a chance of recovering $100,000. Assume that you represent the plaintiff, with whom you have a contingent fee arrangement in this lawsuit.

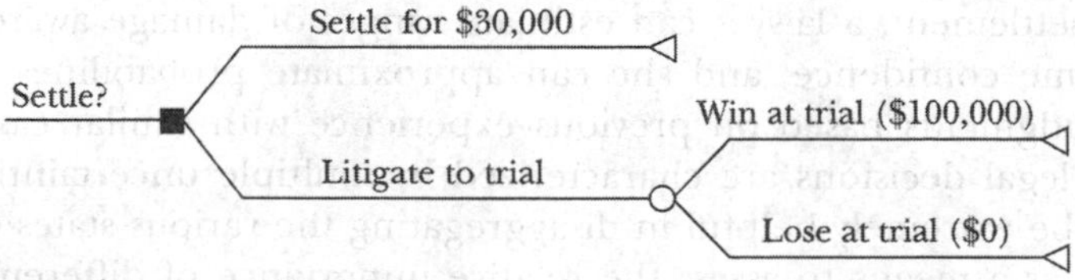

The plaintiff faces two choices—litigate or settle—which are represented by branches emanating from the decision node (solid box) at the left. If the plaintiff settles, the inquiry is complete: He will get $30,000 and the dispute will be over. If he chooses to litigate, there are two possible outcomes: win (a payoff of $100,000) and lose (a payoff of $0). For the purposes of this example, all other uncertainties associated with litigation have been ignored.

To make this decision intelligently, the plaintiff must assess how likely he is to win if litigation is pursued. The $30,000 settlement offer may be inadequate if the plaintiff has an excellent chance of winning $100,000. However, the offer may be attractive if the chance is low.

Assume that, in the attorney's professional judgment, the plaintiff has a 60 percent (.6) chance of winning at trial. This probability would be displayed beneath the chance node labeled "win." Accordingly, it follows that a probability of 40 percent (.4) would be displayed beneath the node labeled "lose."[3]

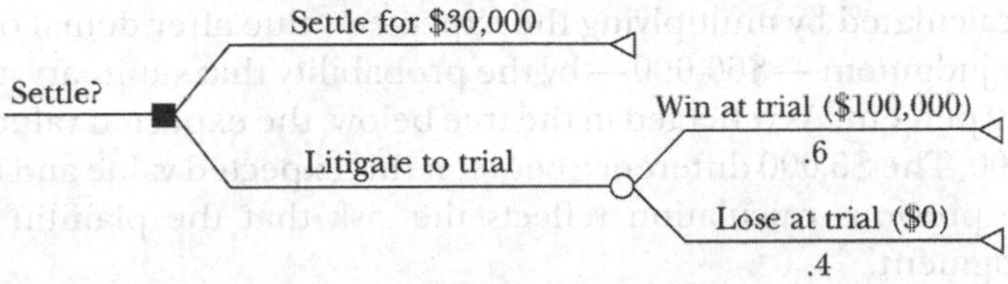

Litigation is apparently preferable to settlement (at least given the current settlement offer) in this case because the probability of winning is more than high enough to warrant gambling at trial. This evaluation is based on the concept of *expected value* or *expected monetary value.* The *expected value of a node* is defined as the sum of the products of the probabilities and the payoffs of its branches. . . .

In this example, the plaintiff should not accept the settlement offer unless other issues such as the need for immediate cash make immediate settlement especially attractive, or unless the plaintiff simply cannot tolerate the risk of losing. However, the plaintiff should accept any settlement over $60,000. In reality, tolerance for risk and the value of current instead of future dollars would undoubtedly operate to make settlement a wise decision if the offer were "within range of" $60,000, albeit a bit lower. . . .

In more complex cases, there will be more than one layer (or *generation*) of chance nodes. Before the case goes to trial, for example, it may be heard on summary judgment. Thus, there would be a chance node for summary judgment (granted or denied). Assume a 10 percent chance that the summary judgment motion will be granted. On the branch of the tree that represents "summary judgment denied," one would find the chance node for liability at trial. The tree below illustrates how a motion for summary judgment would be interposed between the decision to litigate and the outcome of trial.

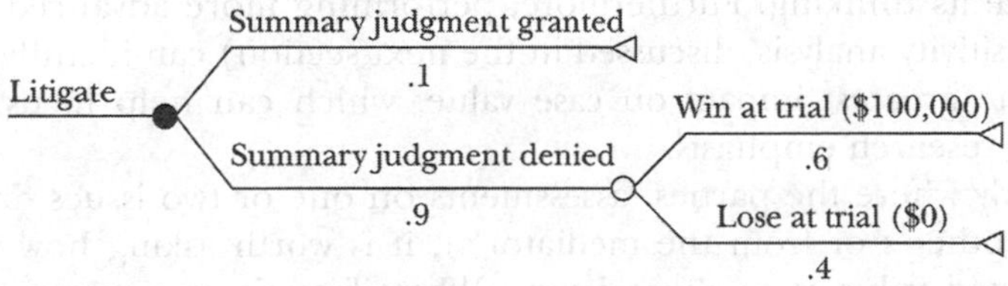

3. There is just one more rule, often overlooked by the novice when building his or her first decision tree of any complexity: *The sum of the probabilities assigned to the branches coming from each chance node must equal 100 percent.* This reads like an impenetrably technical formula, but it is not. If you describe a set of two possibilities — the case could end in a verdict of liability or no liability — but the sum of the probabilities assigned to these probabilities does not equal 100 percent, there must be some other unaccounted-for possibility.

As in all decision trees, the calculations start at the right side. On the far right, the "payoff" is the value anticipated at the end of the process, or the terminal node of the decision tree, represented by a triangular marker. By multiplying the probability of defeat at trial by the payoff, and adding the two figures together, an expected value of $60,000 is calculated (or "rolled back") and displayed next to the branch "summary judgment denied." Thus, the expected value of the case upon denial of summary judgment is $60,000.

In this case, the plaintiff's expected value of litigation must also take into account the possibility of losing on summary judgment. Thus, the expected value of the litigation is calculated by multiplying the expected value after denial of the motion for summary judgment — $60,000 — by the probability that summary judgment will be denied, 90 percent. As reflected in the tree below, the expected value of litigation is thus $54,000. The $6,000 difference between this expected value and the expected value in the previous calculation reflects the risk that the plaintiff will lose on summary judgment.

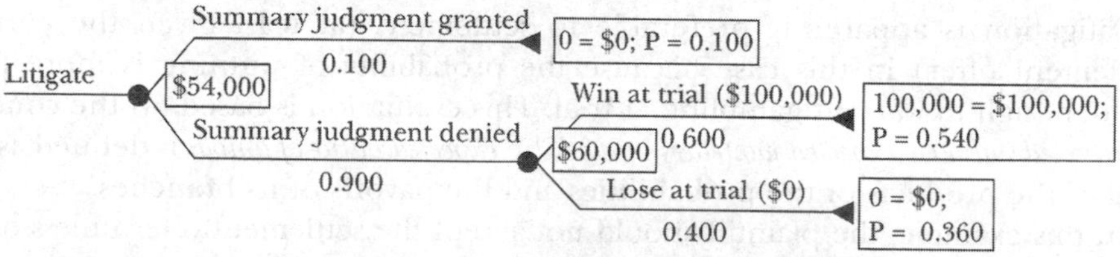

It is important to remember that the outcome of any analysis is only as valuable as the input. One must consider carefully the numbers assigned to the range of predicted awards and associated costs at each terminal node. For example, when a party is paying for its attorney's time (not on a contingency fee), lower legal costs should be factored in at the terminal node where summary judgment is granted than at either of the terminal nodes that follow trial. Depending on the level of precision required, one may design a rough-cut model, limiting the range of possibilities and making bold assumptions about damages. Or, one may develop a more refined tree, taking into account numerous possibilities (even if some have low probabilities) and assigning probabilities to different levels of damage awards.

Notwithstanding the inherent imprecision in assigning probabilities to events at trial, the process of designing a decision tree can itself assist in valuing litigation. Thinking through the hurdles to be surmounted in order to prevail can help each side organize its thinking. Furthermore, performing more advanced calculations (such as sensitivity analysis, discussed in the next section) can identify those issues that have the greatest impact on case value, which can help focus negotiation strategy and research emphasis.

Particularly where the parties' assessments on one or two issues diverge widely (from each other's or from the mediator's), it is worth asking how sensitive the case's expected value is to those issues. What if one's assessment of that issue were to change? How much difference would alteration of the assessment make? Sensitivity analysis answers such questions, whether done with formal computer-generated graphs or the ubiquitous legal pad and hand calculator.

Before turning to the method, a further explanation of sensitivity analysis is in order. The expected value of a case is derived from its many components, as delineated above. However, not all components are equally important; they have different degrees of influence on the expected value. For example, the parties may disagree strenuously on two issues, such as whether a particular witness's testimony would be admitted and whether lost profits would be the appropriate measure of damages in a business case. Both are uncertainties in the case, and sensitivity analysis could determine how much they matter to the end result. In other words, if one were 100 percent certain (or 90 percent, or 70 percent, or 50 percent, etc.) that the witness's testimony would be admitted or that the lost profits measure would be applied, how would that change the expected value? If the expected value is highly sensitive to a given issue, a small change in the probabilities assigned to possible resolutions of that issue would lead to a large swing in the expected value.

Sensitivity analysis is particularly important when using decision trees in a litigation context because of the difficulty and artificiality inherent in assigning probability estimates. . . .

There are two basic and related ways to perform a sensitivity analysis. The first is simply to recalculate the tree, answering the "What if . . . ?" question. Assume that the defendant in the example described earlier disagrees strongly with the assessment of a mere 10 percent likelihood that the summary judgment motion will be successful. The defendant agrees that summary judgment is a "long shot," but more on the order of 25 percent. (After all, 10 percent makes it hard to justify the fees for the summary judgment motion.) [One] might then recalculate the tree, substituting a 25 percent probability of summary judgment for the original 10 percent. The resulting change in the expected value would demonstrate its "sensitivity" to the summary judgment issue. While a recalculation is quicker when the decision tree has been built using computer software, it can certainly be done by hand — using a calculator or "longhand" math — in the same way the tree was calculated originally. . . .

Whether you simply recalculate the tree multiple times using a range of probability or damage estimates or plot graphically the sensitivity of expected value to single issues will depend upon your and the participants' facility with computer software and graphical interpretation. . . .

[The authors go on to discuss the value of decision analysis in mediation, noting that decision analysis reduces the risks inherent in evaluative mediation (discussed at pp. 120-121). They state:]

The greatest potential [risk of a mediator's evaluation of the likely litigation outcome] is that recipients of the more negative evaluation will thereafter view the mediator as an adversary — as an advocate for the other side or for the evaluation itself. The mediator may come to be identified with his or her evaluation; the term "neutral feedback" loses all meaning. The mediator is no longer perceived as a credible neutral and thus cannot function effectively in a mediator's role.

Decision analysis creates a perception of distance between the mediator and the evaluation and, thus, avoids or mitigates this key risk. . . . When calculation of the tree leads to an expected value in a vastly different range than the party's previous settlement position, general mathematical principles seem as much to blame as the mediator. By stepping forward to assess probabilities and payoffs but stepping away from the calculated expected value, the mediator reinforces his or her distance from the evaluation. While acknowledging his or her input, the mediator can sincerely empathize with any disappointed parties, noting that the logic of the analysis leads to the outcome. These dynamics render it less likely that a negative evaluation will be closely identified with the mediator. Indeed, the transparency of the analytic process makes it more difficult to suspect the mediator of manipulation or unholy alliance. Thus, despite the evaluation, the mediator's perceived neutrality may remain intact, as is essential in any mediation process. . . .

[Finally, the authors point out that decision analysis can be performed with or without a computer, depending on the sophistication of the disputants.]

The computer is often effective in business disputes because business people tend to have confidence in the computer's ability to generate valuable information. Many learned the principles of decision analysis for business strategy choices in business school. Thus, decision analysis software for evaluating legal or business disputes applies a familiar method in a technology they trust.

For other people, who may have had difficulty embracing the decision analytic approach or who view computers as alien and suspicious, the pad and the calculator may be the best choice, despite or even because of the slower pace. In many instances, it is best to begin with the handwritten tree and to replicate its structure on the computer if that will help to perform a sensitivity analysis, to alter the tree in response to participant requests, or to generate a written report for review by other decision makers. When the shift is made to software, the participants should be able to recognize the computer-generated structure as essentially identical to the handwritten version presented earlier. . . .

Some Questions About Decision Analysis

If decision analysis is such a useful technique, why is it not used more widely? Undoubtedly some of the explanation lies in the complexity of the process and the fact that many negotiators and mediators are unfamiliar with it. But surely there is more to it than that.

A primary problem is the delusive sense of precision that is conveyed by the specific numbers that are used in the process. At first glance it seems very persuasive when one concludes, as one moves from right to left on the decision tree, that the plaintiff's case is worth $622,100. But is this a somewhat refined and attenuated example of "garbage in, garbage out"? If the basic numbers that make up the decision tree are essentially the result of educated guesswork, how much confidence can we have in the final number?

There is another problem. Not only do the precise numbers provide a false sense of security; they also omit altogether nonquantifiable factors that may prove to be critical in specific cases. The most obvious of these is risk aversion. Since decision analysis is premised on applying the law of averages to various transactions, a plaintiff who would rather have $800 in hand than a 20 percent chance of getting $5,000 might be easily misled. One way to avoid this result is to stop the decision analysis before taking the final step of creating an "expected value" by summing across the product of each potential outcome multiplied by its likelihood of occurrence. If instead the lawyer presents the various potential outcomes with their accompanying likelihoods (e.g., telling the client she has a 20 percent chance of

$5,000 and an 80 percent chance of $0 rather than merely an expected value of $1,000) and allows the client to assess which approach she prefers, the client can take into account her risk aversion in selecting the appropriate approach.

While decision analysis does not purport to evaluate the impact of intangible factors (like fear and anger), those factors may be critical in negotiations or mediations. Consider a medical malpractice case against a pediatric surgeon for negligently causing the death of a musically gifted child. After futile efforts to bridge the monetary gap between the plaintiff and defendant, the mediator sensed that there was more at stake here than money and began to explore ways in which the defendant doctor might address the parents' primary concerns. A solution was worked out involving an expression of sympathy and regret by the doctor, along with an offer to set up a small prize, named after the deceased child, to help other musically gifted children advance their musical training. To avoid situations like this, parties using decision analysis to assist them in negotiations or mediations should remain cognizant that the process may result in positional entrenchment and that efforts should be made to overcome this entrenchment through consideration of nonmonetary factors.

So what are the conclusions that can be drawn from this brief examination of the inherent limitations of decision analysis?

1. Don't be deluded by the apparent precision of the technique. Indeed it may be the *process* of constructing a decision tree, and the resulting dialogue that it usually generates between opposing parties, that is more valuable than any end figure, because that discussion often highlights the key differences between plaintiff and defendant. Once those are identified, additional tools (such as expert opinions) can be utilized.

2. Decision analysis is not a substitute for probing for interests, because, as in the cited medical example, there may be nonmonetary factors that are critical in any specific case.

3. Decision analysis is one flawed but useful tool that must be used with caution and discretion, along with other more traditional dispute resolution techniques.

Questions

5.31 You represent John Robinson, a 15-year-old boy who was employed in a restaurant operated by Barry's Burgers. Your client was badly burned when hot oil overflowed from a fryer in which french fried potatoes were cooking.

You have brought suit against Barry's on the theory that the fryer was improperly positioned, causing the hot oil to overflow. Damages have been stipulated to be $1 million, and you have demanded $1 million in punitive damages.

The positioning of the fryer in the Barry's restaurant in which your client was injured is the same as in all other Barry's restaurants and has been the subject of five prior suits arising out of injuries sustained as the result of oil overflows. Plaintiff prevailed in three of those cases, including the two most recent. In the last case, the jury also awarded punitive damages against Barry's. You estimate the likelihood of recovering punitive damages in this case at 50 percent.

You have a contingency agreement with the plaintiff pursuant to which you will receive one-third of any recovery resulting from a trial and 20 percent of any recovery resulting from settlement.

Barry's has made a settlement offer of $800,000. Should you recommend to your client that he accept that offer?

5.32 You did such a good job representing the plaintiff in his suit against Barry's Burgers that you are engaged by Barry's to represent it in a subsequent matter. In this case, Barry's has been sued by a customer who ate part of a live cockroach that was inside a Barry Burger. Plaintiff's complaint alleges no physical injury but seeks $250,000 in damages for the mental anguish caused her by eating a portion of the roach.

You have concluded that plaintiff has a 10 percent probability of recovering $250,000; a 15 percent chance of recovering $100,000-249,000; a 20 percent chance of recovering $50,000-99,000; a 50 percent chance of recovering $25,000-49,000; and a 5 percent chance of recovering $10,000-24,000. (You think there is no reasonable likelihood that a jury will find no liability or award less than $10,000 to the plaintiff.) In addition, anticipated trial costs are $25,000.

Plaintiff has made a demand of $150,000 to settle the matter. What advice will you give Barry's?

5.33 Now suppose that Barry's has been sued by Jane Jones, a former area manager who was discharged by Barry's and who alleges that her discharge was based on sex discrimination. Jones seeks back pay in the amount of $100,000 and front pay (compensation for future lost earnings) in the amount of $500,000.

Under the applicable law, Jones must first establish a prima facie case of sex discrimination. Then, if Barry's offers a legitimate business justification for her discharge, Jones must prove that the alleged justification is but a pretext for discrimination. If she does so, she is entitled to back pay, but she must still prove the amount of front pay to which she is entitled.

You estimate that Jones has an 80 percent chance of establishing a prima facie case of sex discrimination and a 50 percent chance of establishing that Barry's "legitimate business reason" for the dismissal was a pretext for sex discrimination. Back pay, if awarded, would be $100,000. There is a 5 percent likelihood that plaintiff would receive front pay in the amount of $500,000, a 20 percent likelihood that she would receive $250,000, a 30 percent likelihood that she would receive $100,000, and a 45 percent likelihood that she would not be awarded front pay. Your estimated fee for trying this case is $30,000.

Plaintiff has demanded $150,000 to settle this case. What advice should you give to Barry's?

5.34 Suppose that in the circumstances of question 5.33, you were uncertain about your estimate that plaintiff's chances of prevailing on the pretext issue were 50 percent and thought that they might be as high as 67 percent. Would that affect your advice to Barry's?

5.35 Now suppose that in the circumstances of question 5.33, you and plaintiff's counsel, in an effort to settle the case, jointly construct a decision tree. In the course of doing so, you discover that you agree on all the probabilities, except that relating to plaintiff's likelihood of prevailing on the pretext issue. As in question 5.34, you view that probability as between 50 and 70 percent, but plaintiff's counsel views it as 90 percent. Doing a sensitivity analysis demonstrates that if plaintiff's counsel is correct, the expected value (cost) to Barry's of litigating is substantially greater than plaintiff's settlement offer; if you are correct, the expected value (cost) to Barry's of litigating is substantially less than plaintiff's settlement offer. What might you do under these circumstances?

6. *Postmediation*

If the dispute is resolved, there is often a tendency to exult and relax in the good feeling that comes with a satisfactory outcome. But this is precisely the point where additional effort is needed. The agreement needs to be at least memorialized, if not reduced to a binding legal document, as discussed in Chapter 7, particularly if reached during a privileged mediation session. And it is important that all parties—particularly the disputants—understand the precise terms of what they have agreed to.

Sometimes, too, the agreement calls for future action. This requires some attention to the method by which compliance will be monitored. Conceivably, the agreement may provide that the parties will return to mediation if either party feels that the agreement is not being carried out as stated or if future problems connected with the present dispute arise.

F. APPLICATIONS

At times, commentators have published discussions regarding dispute system design issues. The applications of dispute system design in this section are current favorites for these discussions and are particularly germane to the lessons of this chapter.

1. *E-ADR*

Just as the Internet has revolutionized the transmission of information generally, so it has had a potentially far-reaching impact on the practice of ADR (Katsh and Rifkin, 2001).

There are two types of disputes that are amenable to electronic ADR: (1) disputes that are created by the existence of the Internet (e.g., controversies over domain names or disputes resulting from Internet transactions); and (2) disputes arising out of non-Internet dealings (e.g., a traditional commercial transaction using the Internet to provide dispute resolution services).

Question

5.36 As an example of the former category, assume that your client, Internet Commerce (IC), acts as an agent for cyberspace buyers and sellers of merchandise of all kinds who are located all over the world. For a 3 percent commission from the seller on completed sales, IC monitors the quality of merchandise, thus giving the buyer, who generally has no opportunity to inspect the merchandise, some assurance of reliability. This in turn leads buyers to prefer IC-covered products.

IC now comes to you and tells you that it envisions a variety of disputes that may arise from these transactions (e.g., disputes about quality, damaged merchandise, missing items, etc.). It asks you to set up an electronic scheme for effectively handling the envisioned disputes, using the schema set forth on pp. 321-330 of the casebook. What will be the key features of such a scheme? What differences in the electronic climate will require special treatment as compared with in-person DR schemes?

2. *Streams of Cases**

In a number of situations the legal system is presented by a large number of claims (a stream of cases) requiring efficient, low-transaction-cost resolution (Shaw and Cohn, 1999).

Streams of cases can arise in a variety of contexts: class actions, mass tort situations, and when there are a number of similar claims against a single defendant, as arises often in workplace settings. The subject of streams is often linked with a discussion of hybrids because streams are often dealt with through multi-step procedures or procedures which combine elements of mediation and arbitration.

The need to address streams of cases can arise both pre- and post-dispute.

Pre-dispute: In-house dispute resolution programs
Cases expected to arise out of a natural disaster (e.g., World Trade Center disaster, Hurricane Andrew, Oakland Landslide)
Construction projects

Post-dispute: Class actions (pre- and post-class certification)
Mass torts (e.g., asbestos, Dalkon shield, breast implant litigation)
Bankruptcy (e.g., Drexel Burnham and Milken, Bradlees Stores)

Well-articulated principles of system design are often applied in handling pre-dispute streams (see Goldberg, Brett, and Ury, pp. 321-330).

There are some special and unique pressures in designing processes for handling post-dispute streams:

- tension between efficiency/low transaction costs and giving fair consideration to individual claims (i.e., when is "rough justice" not enough justice);
- people designing the system or who must be consulted about the system design are often self-interested; often there are others whose interests must be taken into account (e.g., class members who are pro se or represented by independent counsel);
- in some situations (e.g., class actions) the system must be designed without knowing the number of claims;
- in other types of cases (e.g., asbestos) the question is how future claims will be addressed (how much, if anything, should be reserved for future claims);
- claimants and/or counsel may be geographically dispersed;
- repeat player issues (between attorneys, between neutrals and attorneys); and
- the extent to which individual settlements and awards should be consistent.

*We are indebted to Margaret Shaw of ADR Associates in New York City for this material and the two Questions that follow.

Questions

5.37 The EEOC brought suit against Astra USA, Inc., a pharmaceutical company, alleging, inter alia, claims of hostile work environment and retaliation under Title VII of the Civil Rights Act. The suit alleged widespread sexual harassment throughout the company, including by the company's top management. Individual claims varied, and included a range of behavior from repetitive incidents of touching to offensive statements to pressure to sign a letter disavowing knowledge of harassment at the company.

The suit was settled, and the Consent Decree provided for the establishment of a Claim Fund in the amount of $9.9 million to be distributed by a special master appointed by the court pursuant to Rule 53 of the Federal Rules of Civil Procedure.

One hundred eighty-three claim forms detailing each claimant's allegations and damages were received by the special master. How should she go about distributing the Claim Fund?

5.38 Your law firm is contemplating filing a class action against Investment Advisers (IA), a large company with offices all around the country. The conduct complained of includes a variety of race discrimination claims (e.g., failure to promote, salary differentials and hostile environment). The parties decided to mediate at the pre-class-certification stage. There are six named plaintiffs, who have raised both state and federal claims.

The potential class could involve current as well as former employees; the parties' estimates of the class size vary wildly from about 100 on the one hand to as many as 550 on the other. All plaintiffs will be represented by the same law firm.

While the parties, in theory, are all interested in an expeditious process, the plaintiffs are concerned about the company's perceived power; they want to make sure the company "gets it" in terms of race issues in their workplace, and they also want current employees to have the opportunity to resolve their claims quickly if they so desire and be able to move on. The company is very concerned about discouraging unmeritorious claims, and also wants to protect their local managers from being pilloried in the press.

What kind of claims resolution process would you recommend for handling this case? Would you recommend a fixed fund or no fixed fund? A cap on the amount of settlement or award for any individual claimant or no cap? An adversarial or settlement-oriented process? Any aggregation of claims? What type of relief would be recoverable? Who would pay attorneys' fees? How would the process you recommend be administered? What would be the bases for your recommendation? What would be the major objections to your recommendation that would likely be raised? How would you respond?

3. *Collaborative Lawyering*

As a dispute systems designer, suppose that your job is to suggest ways to improve negotiations in a given arena without adding any third-party processes. Lax and Sebenius (pp. 50-53) point out that results for clients as a group improve if negotiators are "value-creators," using the candid, interest-based approach suggested by Fisher and others. Mnookin and Gilson (1994) argue that lawyers can contribute to improved negotiations by counseling a cooperative approach to negotiation. Riskin (pp. 357-360) and McEwen and Rogers (pp. 494-498) suggest a number of benefits for clients when both lawyers and clients participate in negotiations, including the prospect of earlier settlement, greater satisfaction and commitment to the results, preservation of relationships, and less hostility.

Lawyers in a number of cities have created a negotiating structure they call "collaborative lawyering" that has the aim of improving negotiation in the ways suggested by these commentators. The key components of the collaborative law structure include:

- Training for the lawyers in interest-based negotiation;
- An agreement to negotiate with other collaborative lawyers and their clients in a candid and constructive manner; and
- An understanding that the collaborative lawyers will withdraw as counsel if no settlement is reached and any party wants to litigate.

Clients and their collaborative lawyers sign an agreement on these approaches. Clients are told that the switch in counsel, should the case not settle, may mean that they must pay both the old and new lawyers to learn about the case. In fact, the latter disclosure has been crucial to bar ethics counsel asked to approve the collaborative lawyering approach.

As Mnookin and Gilson predicted, domestic relations lawyers have dominated the collaborative lawyering efforts. These lawyers know each other's negotiating reputations because they typically practice locally in a specialized bar with repeated dealings. In addition, domestic lawyers may understand that improved domestic negotiation has special payoffs in divorce cases. Clients and their offspring gain if settlement occurs prior to litigation in a manner that is satisfying, likely to lead to higher compliance, and leads to future constructive communications (see Wallerstein and Blakeslee, 1990). Also, savings in attorney's fees are especially important, as divorce creates economic stress for many parents (id.).

So far, the collaborative lawyering projects reach only a small portion of domestic relations cases. The projects themselves are small — 12 to 60 attorneys typically. Also, most lawyers who belong to such projects take only a portion of their cases on a collaborative lawyering basis. Domestic lawyers advise excluding cases in which court orders will be needed, such as those involving abuse or efforts to hide assets. They also suggest exclusion of cases in which clients, because of personality, anger, or desire to "win" the divorce, are likely to resist a cooperative approach. Another factor that reduces case numbers is that one party will often resist retaining a collaborative lawyer.

Though few cases are affected, individual collaborative lawyers are enthusiastic about the success in these cases. A Minneapolis lawyer estimates that fewer than a tenth of his collaborative lawyering clients have hired litigation counsel. The Columbus, Ohio, project reports 100 percent settlement prior to litigation in its first 15 collaborative lawyering domestic cases. These lawyers believe that they have crafted agreements for collaborative clients that suit their interests more closely than settlement agreements reached in the midst of litigation. For example, they cite more frequent inclusion of clauses to handle future disputes and greater attention to counseling for the family. Stuart G. Webb of Minneapolis notes improvements in tone (a father expressing concern that the mother may have underestimated the financial help she needs for the children, for instance) and joint gains (in one case, agreement that the parents take turns in the only housing that suits the children's needs, when two such housing spots are beyond the parties' means, so that both can retain parenting contact).

The collaborative lawyering groups have only about a decade of experience, so it is not surprising that many questions remain unresolved (see Rack, 1998). What are the prospects that the culture of negotiation among lawyers will move toward the collaborative model? What are the barriers to expansion of collaborative lawyering? What should the collaborative lawyering groups do if one lawyer complains that the other has hidden key facts? If no settlement is reached, should the collaborative lawyer pass on notes and mental impressions to litigation counsel? Should collaborative lawyers also shun arbitration?

The National Conference of Commissioners on Uniform State Laws, which created the Uniform Mediation Act, has convened a drafting committee for a uniform law regarding collaborative lawyering. Already, Texas has such a statute and some courts have local rules. To what degree would laws or ethics provisions help or hurt (see Fairman (2002) and Lande (2003))?

4. *Single Complex Case*

F. McGOVERN, TOWARD A FUNCTIONAL APPROACH FOR MANAGING COMPLEX LITIGATION

53 U. Chi. L. Rev. 440, 456-468 (1986)

II. Allocation of Scarce Resources: Who Owns the Great Lakes?

A. Problem

In 1979 Judge Fox of the Eastern District of Michigan ruled that the Treaty of 1836 between the United States and the Ottawa and Chippewa peoples reserved to the tribes the right to fish in the treaty waters of the Great Lakes unfettered by regulation by the State of Michigan. The U.S. Department of the Interior subsequently ceased regulating Great Lakes fishing, leaving two independent sovereigns to govern a common natural resource. The tribal commercial fishers and other Michigan commercial and sport fishers competed for fish in most of the Michigan waters of Lakes Superior, Huron, and Michigan.

This competition triggered significant resource depletion and violence among the competitors. In an attempt to save the basic stocks of fish, the tribes, the state, and the United States agreed to close the fishery each year as soon as a certain amount of fish had been caught. As the competition increased, closure occurred earlier and earlier each year, and the tribes took a smaller and smaller percentage of the catch. The tribes could not compete technologically with the state commercial fishers, nor were they numerous enough to compete with the burgeoning state sport fishers.

As a result of the reduced catch and threats of violence, the tribes moved Judge Fox's successor, Judge Enslen, to allocate the treaty waters between the tribes and the state. A literal reading of Judge Fox's original opinion supported the tribes' view that they had a primary right to the resource and thus should be able to take whatever fish were necessary to maintain reasonable tribal living standards. Given the tribes' depressed economic state, they might obtain a virtual monopoly on Great Lakes fish stocks. The State of Michigan countered that any allocation should be made on equitable grounds, taking into account not only the tribes' subsistence needs but also how best to maximize the fishery's potential economic benefits to all Michigan citizens. Because sports fishing generated far more direct and indirect income than tribal fishing, an economic analysis would tilt the scales toward control of the fishery by Michigan sports fishers. The United States argued for a 50-50 split between the tribes and the state. The treaty itself contained little guidance for resolving the allocation issue.

Given the paucity of precedent for any allocation scheme, the parties' wildly differing approaches, the extreme volatility of the situation, the complexity of any allocation process, and institutional weaknesses associated with continuing judicial management, Judge Enslen decided that if allocation was appropriate, the parties preferably should do it. He also believed that an expeditious decision was necessary to minimize the potential for violence in the uncertain situation. Judge Enslen appointed a special master to prepare the case for trial within eight months and explore the possibilities for settlement. The master's duties did not include ruling on substantive issues, and all his decisions were subject to de novo review by the judge.

B. DIAGNOSIS

United States v. Michigan was relatively complex litigation; the five named parties represented virtually all Michigan citizens. The issues and information involved every conceivable problem associated with managing the largest lakes in the world. From one perspective the case was a generic conflict—a distributional dispute to divide a common pool among competing users. Large numbers of equally situated parties, the fishers, had similar incentives to use a common asset, the Great Lakes, as much as possible. Without intervention, the cumulative use would destroy the resource through massive overfishing. The essential problem was to determine what kind of intervention would help to resolve the dispute.

Under this view of the lawsuit, its big issues were polycentric, not susceptible to the yes-or-no answers or mutually exclusive inquiries typical of special interrogatories posed to juries. The solution to any given question concerning resource division was dependent upon the solutions reached on the other questions: no issues were independent. This complex interrelationship of issues created difficulties which were compounded by the lack of any—much less clear—legal standards. The court was being asked to make extremely complex management decisions by using policy differences unreflected in the substantive law—"reasonable living standards," "subsistence," "maximizing value," and "equal distribution." Because of the continuing relationship among the parties, any court-imposed solution would probably generate future conflict. Even under optimal conditions, changes in the resource itself would breed future controversies.

Judge Enslen concluded that these characteristics begged for an allocation plan developed by the parties themselves. It was a classic case for integrative bargaining. The parties could identify their respective interests, share information concerning how they valued those interests, and reach for a combination of trade-offs that would maximize each side's use of the resource. Under an economic analysis of integrative bargains, they could seek superior allocations, reduce conflicts of interest, and possibly achieve an optimal solution. Given constraints on a court's ability to gather and evaluate this type of information, the parties would be in a superior position to locate an optimal allocation plan. A party-developed plan would also eliminate any dislocation that could accompany a court-ordered resolution.

However, this diagnosis posed two major problems. First, the parties asserted that the case involved fundamental political values not subject to compromise. Leaders on both sides had invested substantial political capital in their incompatible positions and had constructed arguments slicing to the core of the relationship between two sovereigns in the United States. Second, these political leaders had attempted to achieve a negotiated resolution on numerous occasions over the years. Thus major behavioral impediments had arisen from personal animosities and low expectations of reaching satisfactory agreement. The tribal leaders, in particular, had witnessed a long history of negotiation that had not brought prosperity to their peoples. If the behavioral and value-laden components of the lawsuit predominated, judicial resolution was almost inevitable.

C. PRESCRIPTION

Given the apparently great likelihood of a litigated resolution but also significant potential benefits from negotiation, the master implemented both prongs of the judge's order: preparing the case for trial and assisting settlement efforts. Primary importance was given to pretrial development. An expedited discovery schedule was issued to ready the case for trial in four months. Because massive amounts of information needed to be gathered, the schedule included several abbreviated forms of discovery and substantial sharing of information.

The negotiation prong was more difficult—insuring that the parties could reach agreement if they chose, without coercing them into a settlement. The initial negotiation strategy borrowed from final offer arbitration. It contemplated that each party would prepare an allocation scheme for the court. Since the special master would meet ex parte to explore negotiation possibilities with the parties and would thus discover their real interests (as opposed to their litigation-generated positions), he would also recommend an allocation plan. Presumably his plan would be more acceptable to all sides, and could be used either for negotiations or as a mandated resolution to the dispute. Upon further analysis, however, this strategy was fundamentally flawed: because the parties themselves would not develop the plan, its implementation would have the same weaknesses as any court-ordered result. The strategy was changed, therefore, to focus on assisting the parties to develop their own allocation plans in accordance with classic integrative bargaining. This was a higher-risk strategy but, if successful, would have substantially more potential for legitimacy and longevity.

The first task was to determine the likelihood of success for any bargain at all. In conjunction with the Program on Negotiation at Harvard, the master attempted to develop a scorable game that would mimic the actual dispute. The task involved identifying each party's interests, selecting all feasible elements to any allocation plan, stating the parties' priorities, and determining the variety of systems that could be used to organize those interests and elements. Each priority was then quantified in regard to each issue. The negotiation theory applied to the game was so-called differences orientation. For example, each party might value the same portion of Lake Michigan differently. The tribes living in the northern Michigan peninsula would probably prefer unlimited access to waters close to their homes. In contrast, the sports fishers generally lived in southern Michigan and would value the southern waters more highly. Differences orientation was particularly valuable here because of the economic and cultural disparities among the parties: what appeared in the litigation context to be a major problem of fundamental value differences was actually an asset in developing a mutually acceptable allocation plan. Once relative differences had been identified, they were entered into a computer.

A program was run to determine if any scenario would satisfy each party's minimum priorities. When the game was limited to the case's legal issues, no negotiated outcome seemed possible. If, however, the issues were expanded to include other items that might be subject to negotiation, some solutions might satisfy the hypothetical minimum interests of the parties. A court, for example, was limited to interpreting the treaty in perpetuity; an agreement by the parties could be for a term of years. A negotiated disposition, unlike a typical court decision, could also include provisions for plantings of fish, monetary payments, and market development. When these and other issues were added to the computer, there emerged combinations of components which indicated different possible solutions where agreement was feasible.

As originally designed, the scorable game had another, more important function. Its primary purpose was as an educational tool, not just to provide specific answers, but to teach the parties how to negotiate. If all of the key decisionmakers could play the game, typically separately, they might better appreciate their own and their adversaries' positions. Moreover, they might develop more confidence in their own abilities and power as negotiators. The negotiation prong thus became an educational and behavioral task, aimed at educating the parties concerning the potential for maximizing their own interests, developing their strategic negotiating capacity, expanding the roster of issues subject to bargaining, and softening communication and behavioral barriers to face-to-face negotiation.

1. Parties

The plaintiffs consisted of three Indian tribes and the United States; the defendant was the State of Michigan. The tribes had extremely varying interests: one tribe desired to perpetuate the traditional cultural values of Indian fishing, another desired to maximize the tribes' overall economic benefit, and the third valued accommodation consistent with limited tribal fishing in one area of Lake Michigan. The United States represented the tribal interests and the concerns of the Fish and Wildlife Service in restoring the Great Lakes to their earlier economic prosperity—goals that were not always consistent.

The State of Michigan also represented competing interests: those of state commercial fishers, the developing sports fishing and tourist industry, Indian citizens of Michigan living outside the reservations, and the public peace. The state's prime mover was its Department of Natural Resources, but the organized commercial and sports fishers were independent, politically powerful constituents. Judge Enslen decided, therefore, to bring these groups of state fishers into the litigation, but without full party status. He named them litigating amici: they had a participatory role in discovery and at trial, but could not veto a potential settlement. This innovative organization of parties ensured that all the key decisionmakers were present in the litigation.

The court then assigned the special master to mediate among the named parties and the litigating amici. Because the case would eventually be tried to the judge, his ability to facilitate negotiation was limited by his strong ethical constraints against prejudging the outcome of the case. Therefore, the master performed this role while insulating the judge from the details of any bargaining. As a part of the mediation role, the master also kept the parties' critical decisionmakers aware of the progress of the litigation and the negotiations. He met with the leaders and sometimes virtually all the members of the tribes, officials of the U.S. Department of the Interior, and Michigan's Governor, Attorney General, and the Director of its Department of Natural Resources.

2. *Issues*

The issues were both simplified and expanded. The resource allocation was narrowed to involve five major variables: species of fish, quantity of fish, fishing gear, geography, and time. Even with this gross simplification, a virtually infinite number of combinations of variables and numerous measuring criteria still remained. The parties were asked to narrow these issues further by proposing management plans that they would support at trial. Timing became important in setting the deadlines for identifying plans, because a party might lock itself into a given negotiating posture by solidifying behind a single management plan.

While the parties were narrowing issues, an intensive educational effort was undertaken to broaden the horizons to include additional issues suitable for negotiation. All the parties were questioned in great detail concerning their interests — some totally unrelated to the case — to see if they might be interested in placing them on the bargaining table.

3. *Information*

Normal discovery had been expedited somewhat by the parties' agreement to pool data concerning Great Lakes fishing. A tripartite group of biologists from the tribes, the state, and the United States had cooperated in developing consensus recommendations based upon shared information. In addition, the tribes turned over all of their fish catch reports to the state so that the data could be computerized and made available to everyone.

Early in the lawsuit it had appeared that disagreements among the biologists would constitute a major portion of the evidence during trial. Some thought was given to appointing an expert to assist in resolving scientific issues. Because the biologists were cooperating in some areas, however, they were asked if they could develop a joint computer model of the five critical variables. If this could be done, computer runs could be made for each suggested management plan to determine the effects of that plan on these variables. A neutral expert in modeling was asked to assist the biologists and the special master in creating the computer model.

This process has been called computer-assisted negotiation. Experts attempt to create a consensus model of a complex phenomenon that will, in effect, constitute a negotiated dispute resolution or enable the policymakers to negotiate a result. The created model then scrutinizes hypothetical solutions to verify that any chosen solution can meet parties' expectations.

In this situation the computer-assisted negotiation was enormously successful, but for a different reason. Negotiations over the model soon revealed that the biologists were generally in agreement, except in areas of massive uncertainty or where basic policy choices were involved. Thus the major by-product of developing this model was to resolve most of the case's biological issues.

Finally, information was added to the lawsuit concerning parallel litigation over Indian salmon fishing rights in the Pacific Northwest. In *United States v. Washington,* various tribes won a share of the Washington salmon catch. The parties had declined to negotiate a solution to their allocation dilemma, and years of intense litigation ensued. Representatives of several parties to that case were invited to speak to the participants in *United States v. Michigan* concerning the court's management of their resource. They reported in detail how the court made decisions — even on a fish-by-fish basis — and how fishery managers and fishers coped with these decisions. They also recounted some of the spillovers to tribal relations that had developed out of the case. They generally recommended that a negotiated management plan — if feasible — was preferable to a litigated one.

D. RESULTS

After three days of negotiations the parties reached a settlement on March 28, four weeks before the scheduled trial. The settlement agreement closely paralleled one of the scorable game solutions that indicated possible areas of compromise. The court approved the settlement, but one of the tribes overruled its leaders on a subsequent 31-29 vote and decided to proceed with the litigation. All the other parties ratified the negotiated agreement. The judge severed the two alternative management plans for trial, conducted a trial, and ruled on the merits in favor of the negotiated plan.

Insufficient time has passed to evaluate the success or failure of the negotiated plan. No one appealed the judge's ruling, no subsequent violence has occurred in the lakes, and the policymakers of each of the parties are jointly managing the resource. Most remarkable of all is the agreement's longevity even though one of three tribes rejected it. Given a long history of solidarity among the tribes in this lawsuit, it was almost inconceivable that an alliance among two tribes, the state, and the United States could withstand the pressures of one tribe's dissent.

But significant problems still remain in implementing the agreement. The lines of authority for managing the fish are not clear, there are dislocation problems in certain geographical areas, and the funds provided by the agreement have not been allocated among the tribes. The parties agreed upon an ADR process, so that the court can resolve any outstanding issues without full trial. No disputes have yet risen to a level requiring judicial intervention.

1. *Economy*

The court has requested the special master to evaluate the trial preparation and settlement process, and a report should issue after the next fishing season. Any evaluation will be extremely difficult to accomplish. An economic analysis suggests that the direct expenses were significant — approximately $200,000 for master, experts, and expenses. Attorneys for the parties worked almost full-time on the case from January to March and during May of 1985. Policy leaders and support personnel were also substantially involved during this time. Yet most of these expenses would have been incurred in traditional litigation. The cost to the court in time and money was minimal: only four conferences and a four-day trial. None of the master's rulings was appealed to the court. On balance there was a trade-off between identifiable additional expenses associated with the master's work and unidentifiable savings because of the expedited trial preparation process and the abbreviated trial.

Error and opportunity costs are also difficult to ascertain. All of the parties except for the dissident tribe apparently felt that the outcome minimized their perceived concerns about errors in a court-ordered allocation plan. Given the litigation's twelve-year history and expectations that it would continue indefinitely, settlement was greatly beneficial in that it allowed the parties to devote their energies to other productive endeavors. But the dissenting tribe felt that they failed to achieve their expectations and that their treaty rights had been reduced. Some concern was expressed that the trial's posture had benefited the majority at the expense of the lone dissenter. As the court's opinion indicates, however, strong support existed for the merits of the negotiated agreement as opposed to the dissenters' management plan.

2. *Fairness*

The fairness criteria seemed generally satisfied for all except the dissident tribe, but their concerns seemed to relate more to internal leadership policies than to the trial preparation and settlement process. The parties had negotiated the discovery schedule, which was memorialized in a pretrial order. The negotiation dates had been determined far in advance, and all parties seemed well prepared to present their positions. On the other hand, the attorneys' time resources had been spread extremely thin during trial and negotiation. Arguably, the state suffered some disadvantage because of the critical role played by one attorney and the short time it had to respond to the final tribal allocation plan.

3. *Other Values*

The negotiations themselves afforded significant opportunity for maximizing the values of dignity, autonomy, and participation. They took place in Sault Ste. Marie, near the homes of most tribal members; over fifty people were invited to participate. Media representatives were present for virtually the entire three-day period, although they did not attend the actual negotiations.

Because of the multiplicity of issues that would be contained in any allocation plan and the numerous individuals present in Sault Ste. Marie, negotiations were bifurcated into two separate efforts. Although everyone who desired to participate could do so, the smaller negotiating session was reserved for the named parties, and it coped with the more critical issues.

There was a conscious effort to avoid coercing the parties. The judge attended the opening negotiation session but left soon thereafter. The special master coordinated and facilitated the discussions but never suggested that one outcome was preferable to another. The master's most active intervention was to remind the policy leaders that they had a limited time to determine whether they wanted settlement or trial.

Were the deviations from the traditional trial method—the special master, scorable game, abbreviated discovery schedule, computer-assisted negotiations, and presentation from *United States v. Washington*—justified? Would the parties have settled anyway? Was the settlement "better" than an adjudicated outcome? Given the stated criteria, an ex post analysis suggests that the intervention was worthwhile. Ex ante, however, with the extremely high risk of no settlement, the answers are less clear.

References

AARON, Marjorie Corman, and David P. HOFFER (1997) "Decision Analysis as a Method of Evaluating the Trial Alternative," in D. Golann, *Mediating Legal Disputes: Effective Strategies for Lawyers and Mediators.* New York: Aspen Publishers.

ALTERNATIVES TO THE HIGH COST LITIG. (1992) "Motorola Tries Moving ADR to Next Steps," 29, 32.

ALFINI, James (1989) "Summary Jury Trials in State and Federal Courts: A Comparative Analysis of the Perceptions of Participating Lawyers," 4 *Ohio St. J. Disp. Resol.* 213.

BINGHAM, Lisa B. (2002) "Self-Determination in Dispute System Design and Employment Arbitration," 56 *U. Miami L. Rev.* 873.

BREGER, Marshall (2000) "Should an Attorney Be Required to Advise a Client of ADR Options?," 13 *Geo. J. Legal Ethics* 427.

BRETT, Jeanne M., Zoe I. BARSNESS, and Stephen B. GOLDBERG (1996) "The Effectiveness of Mediation: An Independent Analysis of Cases Handled By Four Major Service Providers," 12 *Neg. J.* 259.

BRETT, Jeanne M., Stephen B. GOLDBERG, and William L. URY (1994) "Managing Conflict: The Strategy of Dispute Systems Design," 6 Bus. Wk. Executive Briefing Service.

BRETT, Jeanne M., Deborah SHAPIRO, and Rita DRIEGHE (1985) "Mediator Behavior and the Outcome of Mediation," 41 *J. Social Issues* 101.

BUEHRING-UHLE, Christian (1990) *"Co-Med-Arb": A Comprehensive Model for Third Party Intervention with Divided Roles in Complex Disputes.* Cambridge, Mass.: Program on Negotiation at Harvard Law School, Working Paper Series 90-12. Reprinted in 3 *World Arbitration and Mediation Report* 21 (January 1992).

——— (1991) "The IBM-Fujitsu Arbitration: A Landmark in Innovative Dispute Resolution," 2 *Am. Rev. Intl. Arb.* 113.

CENTER FOR PUBLIC RESOURCES (1989, update 1994) *ADR Cost-Savings Benefits.* New York: Center for Public Resources.

COCHRAN, Robert F., Jr. (1993) "Must Lawyers Tell Clients About ADR?," *Arb. J.* 8 (June).

——— (1999) "ADR, the ABA and Client Control: A Proposal That the Model Rule Require Lawyers to Present ADR Options to Clients," 41 *S. Tex. L. Rev.* 183.

COLE, Sarah R., Craig A. McEWEN, and Nancy H. ROGERS (2003) *Mediation: Law, Policy, Practice* (2d ed. & 2006 Supp.). Rochester, N.Y.: Lawyers Co-operative and Clark Boardman Callaghan.

COOLEY, John W. (1996) *Mediation Advocacy.* South Bend, Ind.: National Institute Trial Advocacy.

COSTANTINO, C., and C. MERCHANT (1996) *Designing Conflict Management Systems.* San Francisco: Jossey-Bass.

CPR INSTITUTE FOR DISPUTE RESOLUTION (2001) *ADR Suitability Guide.* New York: CPR.

DANIEL, Johnnie (1995) *Assessment of the Mediation Program of the U.S. District Court for the District of Columbia.* Washington, D.C.: Administrative Conference of the United States.

DAUER, Edward (2000) *Alternative Dispute Resolution and Practice.* Juris. Publishers.

DRAKE, William R. (1989) "Statewide Office of Mediation," 5 *Neg. J.* 359.

FAIRMAN, Christopher M. (2003) "Ethics and Collaborative Lawyering: Why Put Old Hats on New Heads?" 18 *Ohio St. J. on Disp. Resol.* 505.

FISHER, Roger, William URY, and Bruce PATTON (1991) *Getting to Yes: Negotiating Agreement Without Giving In* (2d ed.). New York: Penguin.

FULLER, Lon (1962) "Collective Bargaining and the Arbitrator," *Proceedings, Fifteenth Annual Meeting, National Academy of Arbitrators.* Washington, D.C.: Bureau of National Affairs.

GALTON, Eric (1994) *Representing Clients in Mediation.* Dallas: Texas Lawyer Press.

GOLDBERG, Stephen B. (1989) "Grievance Mediation: A Successful Alternative to Labor Arbitration," 5 *Neg. J.* 9.

——— (1990) "The Case of the Squabbling Authors: A 'Med-Arb' Response," 6 *Neg. J.* 391.

——— (2006) "Getting the Best Possible Deal in Mediation," 9 *Negotiation* 1-4 (November).

GOLDBERG, Stephen B., Jeanne BRETT, and William URY (1991) "Designing an Effective Dispute Resolution System," in J. Wilkinson ed., *Donovan Leisure Newton and Irvine ADR Practice Book* 38-47.

GRAY, E. (1992) "One Approach to Diagnostic Assessment of Civil Cases: The Individual Case-Screening Conference," *The Court Manager* 21.

GREEN, Eric D. (1982a) "The CPR Mini-Trial Handbook," 1982 *Corporate Dispute Management.* New York: Matthew Bender.

——— (1982b) "Growth of the Mini-Trial," 9 *Litigation* 12 (Fall).

GREEN, Eric D., Jonathan M. MARKS, and Ronald OLSON (1978) "Settling Large Case Litigation: An Alternative Approach," 11 *Loy. L.A. L. Rev.* 493.

GROSS, Samuel R., and Kent D. SYVERUD (1996) "Don't Try: Civil Jury Verdicts in a System Geared to Settlement," 44 *UCLA L. Rev.* 1.

HARTER, Philip J. (2005) "Ombuds: A Voice for the People," *Disp. Resol. Mag.* 5 (Winter).

JUDICIAL CONFERENCE OF THE UNITED STATES (1991) *Report of the Judicial Conference Ad Hoc Committee on Asbestos Litigation.*

KAKALIK, James S., Terence DUNWORTH, Laural A. HILL, Daniel McCAFFREY, Marian OSHIRO, Nicholas M. PACE, and Mary E. VAIANA (1996) *An Evaluation of Mediation and Early Neutral Evaluation Under the Civil Justice Reform Act.* Santa Monica: RAND Corp.

KATSH, Ethan, and Janet RIFKIN (2001) *Online Dispute Resolution.* San Francisco: Jossey-Bass.

KELLY, Joan B. (1989) "Dispute Systems Design: A Family Case Study," 4 *Neg. J.* 373.

KOCHAN, Thomas A. (1980) *Collective Bargaining and Industrial Relations.* Homewood, Ill.: Richard D. Irwin.

KOVACH, Kimberlee (2001) "New Wine Requires New Wineskins: Transforming Lawyer Ethics for Effective Representation in a Non-Adversarial Approach to Problem Solving: Mediation," 28 *Fordham Urb. L.J.* 935.

LANDE, John (2002) "Using Dispute Systems Design in Court-Connected Mediation Programs," 50 *UCLA L. Rev.* 69.

——— (2003) "Possibilities for Collaborative Law: Ethics and Practice of Lawyer Disqualification and Process Control in a New Model of Lawyering," 64 *Ohio St. L.J.* 1315.
LAX, David A., and James K. SEBENIUS (1986) *The Manager as Negotiator.* New York: Free Press.
LEWIS, Michael (1995) "Advocacy in Mediation: One Mediator's View," *Disp. Resol. Mag.* 7 (Fall).
McEWEN, Craig A., Nancy H. ROGERS, and Richard J. MAIMAN (1995) "Bring in the Lawyers: Challenging the Dominant Approaches to Ensuring Fairness in Divorce Mediation," 79 *Minn. L. Rev.* 1319.
McGOVERN, Francis (1986) "Toward a Functional Approach for Managing Complex Litigation," 53 *U. Chi. L. Rev.* 440.
MERRY, Sally, and Susan SILBEY (1984) "What Do Plaintiffs Want? Reexamining the Concept of Dispute," 9 *Just. Sys. J.* 151.
MNOOKIN, Robert H., and Ronald J. GILSON (1994) "Disputing Through Agents: Cooperation and Conflict Between Lawyers in Litigation," 94 *Colum. L. Rev.* 509.
NIEMIC, Robert J., Donna STIENSTRA, and Randall E. RAVITZ (2001) *Guide to Judicial Management of Cases in ADR.* Washington, D.C.: Fedl. Judicial Center.
PLAPINGER, Elizabeth, and Donna STIENSTRA (1996) *ADR and Settlement in the Federal District Courts.* Washington, D.C.: The Federal Judicial Center. New York: The CPR Institute for Dispute Resolution.
RACK, Robert W., Jr. (1998) "Settle or Withdraw: Collaborative Lawyering Provides Incentive to Avoid Costly Litigation," *Disp. Resol. Mag.* 8 (Summer).
RISKIN, Leonard (1991) "The Represented Client in a Settlement Conference: The Lessons of *G. Heileman Brewing Co. v. Joseph Oat Corp.*," 69 *Wash. U. L.Q.* 1059.
ROGERS, Nancy H., and Craig McEWEN (1998) "Employing the Law to Increase the Use of Mediation and to Encourage Direct and Early Negotiations," 13 *Ohio St. J. Disp. Resol.* 831.
ROGERS, Stephen C. (2001) "Can Tripartite Arbitration Panels Reach Fair Results?," 8 *Disp. Resol. Mag.* 27 (Fall).
ROWE, Mary P. (1991) "The Ombudsman's Role in a Dispute Resolution System," 7 *Neg. J.* 353.
SANDER, Frank E. A. (1976) "Varieties of Dispute Processing," 70 F.R.D. 111.
SANDER, Frank E. A., and Stephen GOLDBERG (1994) "Fitting the Forum to the Fuss: A User-Friendly Guide to Selecting an ADR Procedure," 10 *Neg. J.* 49.
SANDER, Frank E. A., and Michael PRIGOFF (1990) "Professional Responsibility: Should There Be a Duty to Advise of ADR Options?," 76 *A.B.A. J.* 50 (Nov.).
SANDER, Frank E. A., and Christopher M. THORNE (1995) "Dispute Resolution in the Construction Industry: The Role of Dispute Review Boards," 19 *Construction L. Rep.* 194.
SANDER, Frank E. A., and Lukasz ROZDEICZER (2006) "Matching Cases and Dispute Resolution Procedures: Detailed Analysis Leading to a Mediation-Centered Approach," 11 *Harv. Negot. L. Rev.* 1.
SHAW, Margaret, and Lynn COHN (1999) "Employment Class Action Settlements Provide Unique Context for ADR," *Disp. Resol. Mag.* 10 (Summer).
SIEMER, Deanne C. (1991) "Perspectives of Advocates and Clients on Court-Sponsored ADR," in *Emerging ADR Issues in State and Federal Courts.* Chicago: ABA Litig. Sect.
SINGER, Linda R. (1994) *Settling Disputes* (2d ed.). Boulder, Colo.: Westview Press.
SLAIKEU, Karl A. (1989) "Designing Dispute Resolution Systems in the Health Care Industry," 4 *Neg. J.* 395.
STEMPEL, Jeffrey (1996) "Reflections on Judicial ADR and the Multi-Door Courthouse at Twenty: Fait Accompli, Failed Overture, or Fledgling Adulthood?," 11 *Ohio St. J. Disp. Resol.* 297.
SYMPOSIUM (2000) "ADR in Cyberspace," 15 *Ohio St. J. Disp. Resol.*, No. 3.
TESLER, Pauline H. (2001) *Collaborative Law.* Chicago: ABA Section on Family Law.

URY, William, Jeanne M. BRETT, and Stephen B. GOLDBERG (1988) *Getting Disputes Resolved: Designing Systems to Cut the Costs of Conflict.* San Francisco: Jossey-Bass.

WALLERSTEIN, Judith S., and Sandra BLAKESLEE (1990) *Second Chances: Men, Women, and Children a Decade After Divorce.* New York: Houghton Mifflin.

WEISE, Richard H. (1989) "The ADR Program at Motorola," 4 *Neg. J.* 381.

WISSLER, Roselle L. (1996) *Ohio Attorneys' Experience with and Views of Alternative Dispute Resolution Procedures.* Columbus: Supreme Court of Ohio.

——— (1997) *Evaluation of Settlement Week Mediation.* Columbus: Supreme Court of Ohio.

PART III

DISPUTE RESOLUTION AND THE JUSTICE SYSTEM

Chapter 6
Courts and ADR

Much of the burgeoning use of dispute resolution processes stems from court and public agency sponsorship of the programs, as well as from the heavy hand of the judge in steering disputants to the processes. This dispute resolution role is a novel one for courts. Until fairly recently it was generally assumed that the primary function of judges was to decide cases. The public justice system provided disputing parties little assistance in negotiating their differences.

The new role for courts has generated substantial criticism. Professor Judith Resnik (1982) suggests the "managerial judge" will neglect adjudicative roles. The article by Professor Owen Fiss (p. 390) argues forcefully that the parties and public lose under a pro-settlement regime. Professor Carrie Menkel-Meadow (1991) warns that involvement with the justice system will make the mediation process more rigid and directed toward legal issues. And Professor Nancy Welsh (2001) points out that as mediation becomes more pervasive there is a real danger of loss of quality services. The courts themselves are concerned that support for settlement may compromise their effectiveness in setting precedent and have made clear that settlement support must yield to that more primary function.

Despite misgivings by some, public opinion now backs an alternative dispute resolution function for the courts and for public agencies in their administrative adjudication. The federal Alternative Dispute Resolution Act of 1998 requires every federal district court to implement a dispute resolution program; the federal appellate courts already offer mediation. In 1996 Congress renewed the Administrative Dispute Resolution Act and in 1998 earmarked $13 million of the Equal Employment Opportunity Commission's budget for expansion of mediation. A number of states have also moved to offer ADR in their courts.*

This chapter begins with a section on the court's role in settlement, followed by a review of the processes typically used by courts and the information available on their effectiveness. The third section examines the use and possible limitations on the justice system's use of its coercive powers to compel participation and the concerns about pressures to settle. The chapter concludes with an exploration of the interplay between the public justice system and the expanding group of private providers who look to the courts and public agencies for referrals and credibility. When the court requires the parties to participate in mediation, should the court provide that mediation through staff or volunteer mediators? Or should the court instead order the parties to use private providers from an approved list and to pay

*Florida and Texas have longstanding pervasive programs. Major initiatives were recently undertaken in Minnesota, New Hampshire, Ohio, and Wisconsin.

them for their services? Should private providers be authorized to issue rulings that carry the force of a court judgment?

A. THE ROLE OF COURTS

As just discussed, current law in many jurisdictions encourages the courts to help the parties settle as well as adjudicate their disputes. In the first article, law professor Owen Fiss argues against this dual role. The Second Circuit, in the case following the Fiss article, faces a situation in which the court's role in establishing precedent seems to clash with its role in encouraging settlement.

O. FISS, AGAINST SETTLEMENT

93 Yale L.J. 1073, 1075-1078, 1082, 1085-1090 (1984)

. . . I do not believe that settlement as a generic practice is preferable to judgment or should be institutionalized on a wholesale and indiscriminate basis. It should be treated instead as a highly problematic technique for streamlining dockets. Settlement is for me the civil analogue of plea bargaining: Consent is often coerced; the bargain may be struck by someone without authority; the absence of a trial and judgment renders subsequent judicial involvement troublesome; and although dockets are trimmed, justice may not be done. Like plea bargaining, settlement is a capitulation to the conditions of mass society and should be neither encouraged nor praised.

The Imbalance of Power

By viewing the lawsuit as a quarrel between two neighbors, the dispute-resolution story that underlies ADR [alternative dispute resolution] implicitly asks us to assume a rough equality between the contending parties. It treats settlement as the anticipation of the outcome of trial and assumes that the terms of settlement are simply a product of the parties' predictions of that outcome. In truth, however, settlement is also a function of the resources available to each party to finance the litigation, and those resources are frequently distributed unequally. Many lawsuits do not involve a property dispute between two neighbors, or between AT&T and the government (to update the story), but rather concern a struggle between a member of a racial minority and a municipal police department over alleged brutality, or a claim by a worker against a large corporation over work-related injuries. In these cases, the distribution of financial resources, or the ability of one party to pass along its costs, will invariably infect the bargaining process, and the settlement will be at odds with a conception of justice that seeks to make the wealth of the parties irrelevant.

The disparities in resources between the parties can influence the settlement in three ways. First, the poorer party may be less able to amass and analyze the information needed to predict the outcome of the litigation, and thus be disadvantaged in the bargaining process. Second, he may need the damages he seeks immediately and thus be induced to settle as a way of accelerating payment, even though he realizes he would get less now than he might if he awaited judgment. All plaintiffs want their damages immediately, but an indigent plaintiff may be exploited by a rich defendant because his need is so great that the defendant can force him to accept a sum that is less than the ordinary present value of the judgment. Third, the poorer party might be forced to settle because he does not have the resources to finance the litigation, to cover either his own projected expenses, such as his lawyer's time, or the expenses his opponent can impose through the manipulation of procedural mechanisms such as discovery. It might seem that settlement benefits the plaintiff by allowing him to avoid the costs of litigation, but this is not so. The defendant can anticipate the plaintiff's costs if the case were to be tried fully and decrease his offer by that amount. The indigent plaintiff is a victim of the costs of litigation even if he settles.[12] . . .

Of course, imbalances of power can distort judgment as well: Resources influence the quality of presentation, which in turn has an important bearing on who wins and the terms of victory. We count, however, on the guiding presence of the judge, who can employ a number of measures to lessen the impact of distributional inequalities. He can, for example, supplement the parties' presentations by asking questions, calling his own witnesses, and inviting other persons and institutions to participate as amici. These measures are likely to make only a small contribution toward moderating the influence of distributional inequalities, but should not be ignored for that reason. Not even these small steps are possible with settlement. There is, moreover, a critical difference between a process like settlement, which is based on bargaining and accepts inequalities of wealth as an integral and legitimate component of the process, and a process like judgment, which knowingly struggles against those inequalities. Judgment aspires to an autonomy from distributional inequalities, and it gathers much of its appeal from this aspiration.

The Absence of Authoritative Consent

The argument for settlement presupposes that the contestants are individuals. These individuals speak for themselves and should be bound by the rules they generate. In many situations, however, individuals are ensnared in contractual relationships that impair their autonomy: Lawyers or insurance companies might, for example, agree to settlements that are in their interests but are not in the best interests of their clients, and to which their clients would not agree if the choice were still theirs. But a deeper and more intractable problem arises from the fact that many parties are not individuals but rather organizations or groups. We do not know who is entitled to speak for these entities and to give the consent upon which so much of the appeal of settlement depends. . . .

12. The offer-of-settlement rule of the proposed Rule 68 would only aggravate the influence of distributional inequalities. It would make the poorer party liable for the attorney's fees of his adversary, which are likely to be greater than the plaintiff's own legal fees when the defendant retains higher-priced counsel. Thus, fee shifting presents a greater risk to plaintiffs than to defendants. . . .

The Lack of a Foundation for Continuing Judicial Involvement

The dispute-resolution story trivializes the remedial dimensions of lawsuits and mistakenly assumes judgment to be the end of the process. It supposes that the judge's duty is to declare which neighbor is right and which wrong, and that this declaration will end the judge's involvement (save in that most exceptional situation where it is also necessary for him to issue a writ directing the sheriff to execute the declaration). Under these assumptions, settlement appears as an almost perfect substitute for judgment, for it too can declare the parties' rights. Often, however, judgment is not the end of a lawsuit but only the beginning. The involvement of the court may continue almost indefinitely. In these cases, settlement cannot provide an adequate basis for that necessary continuing involvement, and thus is no substitute for judgment. . . .

Justice Rather Than Peace

The dispute-resolution story makes settlement appear as a perfect substitute for judgment, as we just saw, by trivializing the remedial dimensions of a lawsuit, and also by reducing the social function of the lawsuit to one of resolving private disputes: In that story, settlement appears to achieve exactly the same purpose as judgment — peace between the parties — but at considerably less expense to society. The two quarreling neighbors turn to a court in order to resolve their dispute, and society makes courts available because it wants to aid in the achievement of their private ends or to secure the peace.

In my view, however, the purpose of adjudication should be understood in broader terms. Adjudication uses public resources, and employs not strangers chosen by the parties but public officials chosen by a process in which the public participates. These officials, like members of the legislative and executive branches, possess a power that has been defined and conferred by public law, not by private agreement. Their job is not to maximize the ends of private parties, nor simply to secure the peace, but to explicate and give force to the values embodied in authoritative texts such as the Constitution and statutes: to interpret those values and to bring reality into accord with them. This duty is not discharged when the parties settle.

In our political system, courts are reactive institutions. They do not search out interpretive occasions, but instead wait for others to bring matters to their attention. They also rely for the most part on others to investigate and present the law and facts. A settlement will thereby deprive a court of the occasion, and perhaps even the ability, to render an interpretation. A court cannot proceed (or not proceed very far) in the face of a settlement. To be against settlement is not to urge that parties be "forced" to litigate, since that would interfere with their autonomy and distort the adjudicative process; the parties will be inclined to make the court believe that their bargain is justice. To be against settlement is only to suggest that when the parties settle, society gets less than what appears, and for a price it does not know it is paying. Parties might settle while leaving justice undone. The settlement of a school suit might secure the peace, but not racial equality. Although the parties are prepared to live under the terms they bargained for, and although such peaceful coexistence may be a necessary precondition of justice, and itself a state of affairs to be valued, it is not justice itself. To settle for something means to accept less than some ideal. . . .

The Real Divide

To all this, one can readily imagine a simple response by way of confession and avoidance: We are not talking about *those* lawsuits. Advocates of ADR might insist that my account of adjudication, in contrast to the one implied by the dispute-resolution story, focuses on a rather narrow category of lawsuits. They could argue that while settlement may have only the most limited appeal with respect to those cases, I have not spoken to the "typical" case. My response is twofold.

First, even as a purely quantitative matter, I doubt that the number of cases I am referring to is trivial. My universe includes those cases in which there are significant distributional inequalities; those in which it is difficult to generate authoritative consent because organizations or social groups are parties or because the power to settle is vested in autonomous agents; those in which the court must continue to supervise the parties after judgment; and those in which justice needs to be done, or to put it more modestly, where there is a genuine social need for an authoritative interpretation of law. I imagine that the number of cases that satisfy one of these four criteria is considerable; in contrast to the kind of case portrayed in the dispute-resolution story, they probably dominate the docket of a modern court system.

Second, it demands a certain kind of myopia to be concerned only with the number of cases, as though all cases are equal simply because the clerk of the court assigns each a single docket number. All cases are not equal. The Los Angeles desegregation case, to take one example, is not equal to the allegedly more typical suit involving a property dispute or an automobile accident. The desegregation suit consumes more resources, affects more people, and provokes far greater challenges to the judicial power. The settlement movement must introduce a qualitative perspective; it must speak to these more "significant" cases, and demonstrate the propriety of settling them. Otherwise it will soon be seen as an irrelevance, dealing with trivia rather than responding to the very conditions that give the movement its greatest sway and saliency.

Nor would sorting cases into "two tracks," one for settlement, and another for judgment, avoid my objections. Settling automobile cases and leaving discrimination or antitrust cases for judgment might remove a large number of cases from the dockets, but the dockets will nevertheless remain burdened with the cases that consume the most judicial resources and represent the most controversial exercises of the judicial power. A "two track" strategy would drain the argument for settlement of much of its appeal. I also doubt whether the "two track" strategy can be sensibly implemented. It is impossible to formulate adequate criteria for prospectively sorting cases. The problems of settlement are not tied to the subject matter of the suit, but instead stem from factors that are harder to identify, such as the wealth of the parties, the likely post-judgment history of the suit, or the need for an authoritative interpretation of law. . . .

[W]hat divides me from the partisans of ADR is not that we are concerned with different universes of cases, that Derek Bok, for example, focuses on boundary quarrels while I see only desegregation suits. I suspect instead that what divides us is much deeper and stems from our understanding of the purpose of the civil law suit and its place in society. It is a difference in outlook.

Someone like Bok sees adjudication in essentially private terms: The purpose of lawsuits and the civil courts is to resolve disputes, and the amount of litigation we encounter is evidence of the needlessly combative and quarrelsome character of Americans. Or as Bok put it, using a more diplomatic idiom: "At bottom, ours is a society built on individualism, competition, and success." I, on the other hand, see adjudication in more public terms: Civil litigation is an institutional arrangement for using state power to bring a recalcitrant reality closer to our chosen ideals. We turn to the courts because we need to, not because of some quirk in our personalities. We train our students in the tougher arts so that they may help secure all that the law promises, not because we want them to become gladiators or because we take a special pleasure in combat.

To conceive of the civil lawsuit in public terms as America does might be unique. I am willing to assume that no other country . . . has a case like *Brown v. Board of Education* in which the judicial power is used to eradicate the caste structure. I am willing to assume that no other country conceives of law and uses law in quite the way we do. But this should be a source of pride rather than shame. What is unique is not the problem, that we live short of our ideals, but that we alone among the nations of the world seem willing to do something about it. Adjudication American-style is not a reflection of our combativeness but rather a tribute to our inventiveness and perhaps even more to our commitment.

MANUFACTURERS HANOVER TRUST CO. v. NICHOLAS YANAKAS

11 F.3d 381 (2d Cir. 1993)

KEARSE, Circuit Judge:

The appeal in this matter, in which defendant Nicholas Yanakas challenged the granting of summary judgment to plaintiff Manufacturers Hanover Trust Co. (the "Bank") on its claim to enforce certain guarantees, was decided in an opinion filed on October 18, 1993, see *Manufacturers Hanover Trust Co. v. Yanakas,* 7 F.3d 310 (2d Cir. 1993) ("October judgment"). We affirmed in part, reversed in part, and remanded for trial as to certain defenses and counterclaims asserted by Yanakas. On October 27, 1993, after the filing of our opinion but before the issuance of the mandate, Yanakas and the Bank jointly moved for vacatur of the October judgment on the ground that they have conditionally reached an agreement to settle all of the claims in the suit if this Court will vacate its decision. For the reasons below, we deny the motion. . . .

None of the Supreme Court cases indicates that the appellate court has a duty to vacate the district court judgment when the parties have agreed on a settlement of the claims between them, that is, where the mootness is neither happenstance, nor attributable to one party but not the other. Nonetheless, the appellate court has discretion to order such a vacatur. . . .

Nor do we view the granting of such a motion as a wise exercise of discretion, for vacatur of the appellate court's judgment would facilitate two abuses. First, it would allow the parties to obtain an advisory opinion of the court of appeals in a case in which there may not be, or may no longer be, any genuine case or controversy; the federal courts of course have no jurisdiction to render such opinions. Second, even where there was a genuine case or controversy, it would allow a party with a deep pocket to eliminate an unreviewable precedent it dislikes simply by agreeing to a sufficiently lucrative settlement to obtain its adversary's cooperation in a motion to vacate. We do not consider this a proper use of the judicial system. Indeed, for this reason some of our sister Circuits refuse to vacate even a district court judgment upon the parties' settlement. See, e.g., *In re Memorial Hospital of Iowa County, Inc.*, 862 F.2d 1299, 1301-02 (7th Cir. 1988). Although this Circuit's refusal to vacate is limited to judgments as to which there is no right of review, we agree with the Seventh Circuit that

> [w]hen a clash between genuine adversaries produces a precedent, . . . the judicial system ought not allow the social value of that precedent, created at cost to the public and other litigants, to be a bargaining chip in the process of settlement. The precedent, a public act of a public official, is not the parties' property.

In re Memorial Hospital of Iowa County, Inc., 862 F.2d at 1302. The Tenth Circuit in *Oklahoma Radio Associates*, after surveying cases from the Supreme Court and all of the Circuits, see 3 F.3d at 1437-44, similarly concluded that

> The furthering of settlement of controversies is important and desirable, but there are significant countervailing considerations which we must also weigh. A policy permitting litigants to use the settlement process as a means of obtaining the withdrawal of unfavorable precedents is fraught with the potential for abuse. . . .

Oklahoma Radio Associates, 3 F.3d at 1444 (quoting *In re Memorial Hospital of Iowa County, Inc.*, 862 F.2d at 1300 and 1303).

In sum, while this Court has encouraged the parties to settle cases before the filing of a decision that is not reviewable as of right, once such a decision has been rendered we decline to allow them to dictate, by purchase and sale, whether the precedent it sets will remain in existence.

Finally, we reject the parties' argument that we should grant their motion in the interest of judicial economy because vacatur would avoid the need for further proceedings on remand. There are some indications that the promise of greater judicial economy may be illusory. More importantly, when the proposed savings can be realized only at the cost of increasing the vulnerability of the judicial system to manipulation, we view the investment as unsound. . . .

Subsequent to this ruling, the U.S. Supreme Court in *U.S. Bancorp Mortgage Co. v. Bonner Mall Partnership*, 513 U.S. 18 (1994), expressed similar views in dicta — that a judgment should not be vacated solely on the ground that a settlement agreement provides for it. What should the courts weigh in determining whether to grant the parties' joint motion to vacate judgment? Some suggest that the courts should consider the stage at which vacatur is raised (for example, before or after argument), the importance of the decision for third parties, and the correctness of the ruling (see Resnik, 1994; Anstaett, 1991; Fisch, 1991).

Question

6.1 A federal district court sanctions an attorney and then, for other reasons, dismisses the complaint. While the appeal is pending, the parties, with the help of the appellate court's mediator, settle the underlying dispute on the condition that the district court rescind the sanctions against the attorney. Should the district court grant the parties' joint motion to vacate the sanctions in order to facilitate the settlement? Should federal appellate court mediators assist in the negotiation of a settlement conditioned on vacatur? Cf. *Keller v. Mobil Corp.*, 55 F.3d 94 (2d Cir. 1995).

B. COURT-RELATED PROCESSES

There are many ways in which cases in court can get into ADR. Some statutes require that certain types of cases must go to a designated ADR process.* Other statutes or court rules give the court (or a designated court official) discretion to send a specific case to an appropriate form of alternative dispute resolution.† Or counsel and a magistrate or judge may agree at a pretrial conference to use a particular ADR process.

There are also many dispute resolution processes to which—singly or in combination—cases may be referred. Depending upon local availability, the choice usually comes down to mediation, arbitration, early neutral evaluation, minitrial, or summary jury trial. See pp. 303-321 for a fuller description of these options.

Perhaps the most encompassing mechanism for institutionalizing systematic ADR referral in the public sector is the multidoor courthouse (MDC) (see generally Stempel, 1996). The MDC is a multifaceted dispute resolution center that is premised on the notion that there are advantages and disadvantages in any specific case to using one or another dispute resolution process. Hence instead of just one "door" leading to the courtroom, such a comprehensive justice center has many doors through which individuals can get to an appropriate process. Among the doors may be ones labeled "arbitration," "mediation," "minitrial," "summary jury trial," and "case evaluation." Provision can also be made for channeling disputes into specialized tribunals, such as medical malpractice screening boards.

The key feature of the multidoor courthouse is the initial procedure: intake screening and referral. Here disputes are analyzed according to various criteria to determine what mechanism or sequence of mechanisms would be appropriate for the resolution of the problem. (The criteria are more fully examined at pp. 337-348) For example, if the intake staff is dealing with a typical landlord-tenant case involving a dispute over inadequate services by the landlord, then the case might be initially referred to mediation because that process may be particularly helpful in restructuring a frayed relationship between parties who have an ongoing

*See, e.g., Cal. Fam. Code §3170(a) (all contested custody cases must go to mediation); Hawaii Arb. Rules, Rules 6, 8(a) (all money claim tort actions below $150,000, with specified exceptions, must go to court-annexed arbitration).

†Tex. Code Ann., Civ. Prac. & Remedies Code §154.021; Fla. Stat. Ann. §44.102.

relationship. On the other hand, if the staff is dealing with a one-time simple tort case, then it might be referred to court-annexed arbitration or early neutral evaluation. Of course, if a case presented a novel question of statutory interpretation, then, most likely, it would be directly referred to court because courts are the agencies that are charged with the task of giving meaning to statutes, thus providing guidance to others as well as an answer to the immediate disputants.

Three issues that arise in the multidoor courthouse deserve brief mention. First, intelligent diagnosis and referral by the intake official assumes that he or she is completely aware of all the relevant facts. However, disputants are often notoriously inarticulate in voicing their real grievances, or lawyers may transmute that grievance into legal language that obscures the client's real concerns. The true complaint may not surface until much later in the proceeding. Hence the referral process must be viewed as a tentative and dynamic one, subject to modification as particular mechanisms prove to be ineffective or as additional facts develop that suggest the desirability of other choices.

A related concern centers around the sometimes-voiced objection that disputes must be viewed in their specific contexts and that it is therefore not possible to develop generic dispute processing principles. On this question, too, more experimentation is needed. Meanwhile, as was just noted, the dispute taxonomy that is envisioned must be seen as a tentative guide rather than a rigid formula.

A final question is whether the referral process should be optional or compulsory. This question is considered in Section C.*

A description of case screening in practice is contained in Ericka Gray's article on the Middlesex (Massachusetts) multidoor courthouse.

E. GRAY, ONE APPROACH TO DIAGNOSTIC ASSESSMENT OF CIVIL CASES: THE INDIVIDUAL CASE-SCREENING CONFERENCE

The Court Manager 21-25 (Summer 1992)

The Middlesex Multi-door Courthouse (MMDC) is a pilot project of the civil division of the Cambridge, Massachusetts, Superior Court. MMDC provides a coordinated approach to dispute resolution within the administrative structure of the trial court. It designs, implements, and manages dispute resolution programs to meet the varied needs of the court system and its users. Since case processing began in March 1990, more than 1,200 individual case-screening conferences have been held.

Dispute resolution offered through the program includes case evaluation, mediation, arbitration, and complex case management, with summary jury trials and minitrials available as required. MMDC staff developed and managed a pool of professional dispute resolution providers. Cases handled by MMDC include all types of civil litigation, including torts, contract, commercial, general equity, and real estate, usually with damages claimed ranging from $25,000 to millions of dollars.

*Needless to say, the multidoor idea has applications far beyond courts. Any large organization (whether corporation, university, or hospital) can use this concept to develop a systematic framework for handling disputes within the organization as well as those between it and outsiders. See Chapter 5C.

The individual case-screening conference is a unique feature of MMDC because few systematic methods currently exist for determining what dispute resolution process is likely to be most appropriate for a case. MMDC developed the screening conference as a diagnostic tool to provide the best match of process and provider. . . .

Mechanics of the Case-Assessment Process

MMDC's professional staff conducts the screening conferences. One hour is allotted for each case, but actual screening time varies depending on type of case, number of parties, counsels' previous experience with MMDC-screening conferences, and other pertinent factors. A judicial order mandates attendance of all parties. Although litigants are encouraged to attend, one or more litigants are present in fewer than 10 percent of case-screening conferences.

Since the implementation of these screening conferences, the process has developed to include at least three major components. After an introductory statement reiterates the confidentiality, purpose, and informality of the conference, the following areas are covered: (1) review of case facts and procedural history, including discussion of disputed factual, legal, and procedural issues; (2) determination of subjective factors; and (3) education about dispute resolution and what each process can offer each case.

Case facts and procedural history. Because the case facts and procedural history are easy to elicit from counsel, this part of the screening conference generally takes only a few minutes. The intent of obtaining a case history is not to get a detailed, play-by-play account of the entire case, but, rather, to get an overview of the cause of action; the disputed legal, factual, and liability issues; the estimated damages or equitable relief sought; the status of discovery; scheduled court dates; and previous attempts at settlement.

Subjective case factors. The subjective case factors usually are the most difficult to elicit from the attorneys, but they are often the key to matching the case to the most appropriate dispute resolution option and to settling the case. The people issues cannot be separated from the legal, factual, and procedural issues if appropriate and timely case resolution is to occur. Who are the people involved— the clients, the lawyers, the claims adjusters? Indeed, who are the principals in the case, whether named or unnamed parties? What are the relationships among these people? What are their needs in terms of control of the outcome of the case? Do the litigants have a need to tell their story? What are the emotional, financial, and legal needs and resources of each party? What are the personal styles of the people involved—cooperative, contentious, meticulous, quiet, loud, passive, intimidating? What are the risks and benefits for all in resolving the case weighed against the risks and benefits of continuing down the traditional adjudication track? Is a judgment of settlement likely to be collectable? These and other factors provide greater knowledge about the case and about the driving forces behind the conflict. MMDC staff use this knowledge to explore ways to address the conflict most appropriately. . . .

. . . The following are specific examples of the types of information MMDC screeners elicit. An attorney was acting on behalf of his brother in an area of law in which he had limited knowledge and experience. The brother was attempting to avoid bankruptcy and could not afford to hire a litigator experienced in this area. In the screening conference, this issue was identified, as were certain discovery needs. A follow-up screening conference was scheduled with an agreement between the lawyers that certain information would be exchanged at that session. At the second conference, all information was available, and a settlement was reached.

Another case involved two attorneys who, after being asked about the people involved, exchanged glances and admitted that both of their clients were extremely angry, making what the attorneys considered to be unreasonable demands for settlement. The attorneys told the MMDC screener that, had they known what they were getting into, they would have considered refusing the case. Counsel did not believe that a trial would resolve the conflict and that further litigation was likely to occur despite the verdict. The attorneys had little hope of a mediated settlement but were willing to try to convince their clients to participate in this process. They were successful. A mediation was held, and an agreement was reached within three hours. All involved, including the judge who was scheduled to try the case, were delighted.

Yet another case involved an attorney who was representing a relative of her employer. The attorney's performance was being closely scrutinized, and she believed that a promotion hinged on obtaining a good settlement. The attorney believed her client's assessment of the value of the case to be too high, however, and was having difficulty convincing her client of a more realistic value. Initially, opposing counsel was unwilling to consider dispute resolution and believed the attorney to be making unreasonable demands. When the attorney's position was identified in the screening conference, opposing counsel agreed to enter into a case evaluation to establish a more realistic dollar value which could be reported to the client. Settlement occurred at this case evaluation with the client present, and both the client and the attorneys involved were highly satisfied with the entire process. . . .

Screening as Dispute Resolution

The screening conference is, in itself, a dispute resolution process. It sets the tone for what is to come in whatever dispute resolution process is selected. Settlements have occurred at or shortly after a screening conference. Often, the conference is the first time all counsel and, at times, the litigants themselves, have been together in the same room.

Matching a Neutral to the Case

Using such an individual case diagnostic process, the MMDC screener cannot only determine the most appropriate dispute resolution process for the case but also make a good match between the case and the neutral who will conduct the dispute resolution process. The screener can often ferret out special litigant and attorney needs in terms of style as well as case content, area knowledge, and other pertinent factors. For example, an attorney identified her client as a law student who had read everything possible on the law concerning his contract dispute. He was characterized as being very meticulous and wanting to prove his case before a judge. His attorney referred to difficulties she was having making her client aware of the realities of litigation, the strengths and weaknesses of his case, and all possible outcomes if the case were tried. This attorney also indicated that the litigant's wife needed a very supportive approach and that the wife's participation was a key to resolving the case. In selecting the neutral for this case, the screener was able to assign a law professor who possessed knowledge of the case content area and whose style was appropriate for the spouse. This match was extremely successful, and a settlement was reached. . . .

Summary of Results

The Middlesex Multi-door Courthouse disposes, through settlement, of almost 30 percent of the cases that are noticed for a screening conference. One-third of the cases that come through the screening process use some form of dispute resolution, most often the case-evaluation process, with mediation the second most frequently used process. Settlements occur in 63 percent of all cases entering either case evaluation or mediation.

Process recommendations (or case screening, as it is often called) may be categorical rather than individual. Categorical screening typically occurs according to predefined groups of disputes. For example, in the Comprehensive Justice Center (Burlington, New Jersey), all small claims cases are referred to mediation on the day of trial. Another example of categorical screening is the common practice of referring all contested child custody and visitation issues to mediation.

Some courts, in lieu of selecting a dispute resolution procedure, impose an obligation on the parties to do so. The nature of that obligation varies substantially:

- In Minnesota medical malpractice cases, the parties are required to meet and discuss the feasibility of using ADR to resolve the dispute. Minn. Stat. §604.11, subdivision 2.
- In Oregon, the court selects a process, but any party can escape by filing a written objection. Or. Rev. Stat. §36.185.
- In New Hampshire, each party must select an ADR process; if they do not agree, they must participate in a mediation. However, upon request of one party and a showing of good cause, the court can also schedule the case for nonbinding evaluation. N.H. Super. Ct. Rule 170(b) (2003).

One of the most difficult questions raised by judicial efforts at process selection is whether the court's selection should be binding on the parties. That question is discussed in Chapter 6C.

Question

6.2 What are the pros and cons of various methods of case referral (e.g., individualized screening as explained by Gray, categorical screening, or judicial discretion—with or without party participation)? Compare pp. 428-434.

Note: Empirical Research

The parties respond positively to court dispute resolution programs (Keilitz, 1993). At the same time, savings in time and money for the parties and courts does not always occur. Some suggest that the structure of the program is key to its success, while others point to the manner in which lawyers use the process (McEwen and Plapinger, 1997). Political scientist and law professor Deborah Hensler notes the varying findings regarding court-ordered arbitration (Sander et al., 1996:890):

> [W]hat arbitration does in these kinds of court-annexed arbitration programs is provide people with a way of getting a quasi-adjudicative hearing in situations where they would not otherwise get such a hearing. It does that, in many cases, without appreciably reducing the cost of litigation, either for the private parties or the courts. It appears to give lay litigants something they value greatly—a chance for a hearing before a neutral. It frequently does not speed the process of litigation. The data suggests the reason for that is that people value going to these arbitration hearings enough so they delay settling their cases until they can get before an arbitrator to get that neutral judgment.

Research on some programs documents more positive results in terms of the reduction of trial rates (Clarke et al., 1989:40) and of discovery time and therefore lower attorney's fees for parties paying by the hour (Barkai and Kassebaum, 1989).

Time and cost results vary in court mediation programs as well (see Cole et al., 2002). A Federal Judicial Center study of one federal district court indicated that the cases settled earlier and the attorneys reported costs savings (Snapp, 1997). At the same time, RAND Corporation researchers conducting a study of four federal court mediation and two federal court neutral evaluation programs concluded that the programs had little effect on time and costs for the parties or the court (Kakalik et al., 1996).

For mediation, time is a key variable in determining whether the parties' costs are reduced. Earlier referral to mediation, regardless of how much formal discovery has been done, is more likely to produce settlement than later referral, according to research on about 1,700 mediated civil cases in nine Ohio courts (Wissler, 2002). And, of course, one would expect lower costs for the parties with settlement reached earlier in the litigation process.

How do court dispute resolution programs affect the use of dispute resolution outside the court context? Many hope that the courts will send a message about appropriate ways to resolve disputes by placing their imprimatur on dispute resolution processes. A recent study of Ohio attorneys suggests that attendance at court mediation programs does more to encourage lawyers to refer clients to mediation than their undergoing mediation training or attending educational programs about mediation (Wissler, 1996).

Other touted benefits of court-connected dispute resolution do not lend themselves to empirical research, including better outcomes, increased access to justice, reconciliation or preservation of relationships, and public confidence in the judicial system. Law professor Francis McGovern (1997) suggests, partially for this reason, that courts may adopt the dispute resolution program to save time and costs, but then sometimes maintain the program even when researchers cannot demonstrate that these goals were met.

C. MANDATORY PARTICIPATION AND PRESSURE TO SETTLE

SPIDR, MANDATED PARTICIPATION AND SETTLEMENT COERCION: DISPUTE RESOLUTION AS IT RELATES TO THE COURTS

Report 1 of the Law and Public Policy Committee of the Society of Professionals in Dispute Resolution (1990)

Growth of Mandates to Participate and Coercion to Settle

The use of mandates to participate in dispute resolution processes has grown rapidly during the last decade. At present, courts in many states operate under a statutory requirement or authorization to mandate participation by the parties in a variety of dispute resolution processes in specified types of cases. In many other jurisdictions, the courts are authorized by rule of procedure or court rule to compel participation. A similar expansion in mandated participation has occurred in the federal courts. . . .

Mandated participation at times is framed as a prerequisite to initiating litigation, as in some farm-credit mediation and medical malpractice screening panels. In other instances, categories of cases in litigation are sent wholesale to a mandated process, such as in some domestic relations mediation programs and some court-annexed non-binding arbitration programs. In still other instances, the court is authorized to select cases for mandatory referral or to require participation by one party when the other requests it. . . .

When participation is mandated, the level of required participation is defined in a variety of ways. In some jurisdictions, the disputing parties are only required to attend a mediation "orientation." In others, they may be required variously to attend a full dispute resolution session, to bring information, to stay a period of time if not excused by the third-party neutral, to bring settlement authority, to negotiate in good faith, or to participate in a meaningful way.

In some programs, public officials pressure the parties to participate in dispute resolution processes even though the referrals are formally termed "voluntary." . . . When participation by the parties is not mandated by law, the Committee believes that the parties should not be induced to participate under the guise of a "strong referral" by court personnel who do not clearly inform them that they could refuse to participate.

In contrast to the rapid increase in mandatory participation programs, there has been a more sporadic appearance of procedures that have the effect of coercing settlement. For example, a California statute permits local courts to order transmission of a mediator's report to the child custody referee in cases not settling through compulsory mediation.[17] However, only a portion of California's domestic relations courts have authorized the mediator's report. Several other states have specifically forbidden transmission of a mediator's report.

States have also experimented with a variety of financial disincentives to trial in connection with mandatory court-annexed arbitration programs. Some required payments are tied to a request for a full trial, and others are imposed only when the party rejecting the arbitrator's award fails to improve upon it by a certain percentage at trial. They vary from low fixed fees, such as $75, to a shifting in costs and attorney's fees that may amount to tens of thousands of dollars.

Recommendations

1. Mandating participation in non-binding dispute resolution processes often is appropriate. However, compulsory programs should be carefully designed to reflect a variety of important concerns. These concerns include the monetary and emotional costs for the parties, as well as the interests of the parties in achieving results that suit their needs and will last; the justice system's ability to deliver results that do not harm the interests of those groups that have historically operated at a disadvantage in this society; the need to have courts that function efficiently and effectively; the importance of the public's trust in the justice system; the interests of non-parties whose lives are affected and sometimes disrupted by litigation; the importance of the courts' development of legal precedent; and the general interest in maximizing party choice. In weighing these valid and sometimes competing concerns, policymakers should be cautious not to give undue emphasis to the desire to facilitate the efficient administration of court business and thereby subordinate other interests. Participation should be mandated only when the compulsory program is more likely to serve these broad interests of the parties, the justice system, and the public than would procedures that would be used absent mandatory dispute resolution.

POSSIBLE POSITIVE EFFECTS OF MANDATED PARTICIPATION . . .

a. The parties frequently respond favorably to mandated dispute resolution. . . . In some instances, this is preferable to placing control in the hands of an opponent, who may be forcing them to spend thousands of dollars in litigation while refusing a "face to face" discussion.

17. . . . But see *McLaughlin v. Superior Court*, 140 Cal. App. 3d 473, 189 Cal. Rptr. 479 (1st Dist. 1983) (legislation permitting report to trier of fact would deny due process unless cross-examination of the mediator allowed).

b. Rates of voluntary usage are often low, perhaps because parties or their lawyers may be more accustomed to the litigation process or do not want to signal to their adversary a desire for compromise. Mandating use of dispute resolution processes often increases substantially the total number of cases settled through their use. As a result, more parties arrive at solutions that they prefer to an adjudicated result and that better suit their needs and preferences than would a court-imposed judgment. Moreover, the settlements may reduce disruption caused by protracted litigation in the lives of affected non-parties, such as the children of a divorcing couple. These settlements, particularly those that avert trials and post-judgment motions, may also free court resources for other cases.

c. Effective dispute resolution programs require adequate administrative support. By increasing the caseload, mandated participation allows the administration to be provided on a cost-effective basis.

d. The expanded use of these processes as a result of mandating participation will serve to educate the parties and their lawyers, perhaps resulting in an increased voluntary use of dispute resolution programs outside the court processes.

POSSIBLE NEGATIVE EFFECTS OF MANDATED PARTICIPATION . . .

a. If not designed and administered well, mandated processes may simply pose an unnecessary and costly hurdle for parties who will resolve their case by trial or settlement in any event.

b. There is a risk that the flexibility and high quality of dispute resolution programs will fall prey to the deadly routinizing influence of bureaucracy. In mediation programs particularly, narrowly focused procedures and briefer, more formulaic sessions seem likely to resolve a narrower range of issues and thus not meet the broader needs of the parties. The short, rigid sessions may result in lower party involvement, poor resolution, and thus lower voluntary compliance with the resolution.

c. Broadly mandated participation may sweep cases into an inappropriate process, resulting in wasted time and effort, unfair settlements, and other possible harm.

d. The parties may have preferences for particular procedures. For example, the more structured presentation of the case at trial or arbitration may be more comfortable than negotiation processes for parties who are fearful of each other.

THE EFFECTS OF COERCION TO SETTLE

If there is coercion to settle within the process, this shifts the weights and counterweights relevant to determining whether participation should be mandated. A party's option to decline settlement provides the primary protection for the fairness of the process. In addition, the freely obtained consent by the parties makes it more likely that their interests will be served by the settlement and that they will voluntarily comply with it. Coercion to settle within mandatory processes may remove, as a practical matter, this option to forego settlement. Further, the coercion may affect the procedural fairness by increasing the degree to which access to trial depends on wealth.

BALANCING COMPETING POSSIBILITIES

Mandatory dispute resolution could either improve or impede the administration of justice. This uncertainty counsels for careful consideration before a compulsory program is instituted and careful monitoring as it is administered. At a minimum, participation should be compulsory only when Recommendations 2, 3, and 4 regarding funding, coercion to settle, and quality, are met.

2. Funding for mandatory dispute resolution programs should be provided on a basis comparable to funding for trials.

Mandatory dispute resolution has the same compulsory character as hearings and trials, so the public commitment to provide litigation facilities without charging the users except through the imposition of a filing fee and allocation of court costs should be expanded to provide access to mandatory dispute resolution processes on a comparable basis.

User fees imposed only on those referred to mandatory processes pose particular problems. If not properly regulated, dispute resolution user fees can result in undesirable coercion to settle for the parties who cannot afford them and in unseemly practices through which the court provides lucrative employment to private providers.

Under current practices, in exceptional cases the parties must pay substantial litigation user fees which greatly exceed the filing fee. For example, the court may appoint a special master to hold an evidentiary hearing and impose the expense on the parties. In these exceptional cases, the courts may also properly impose substantial dispute resolution fees on the parties. However, the court should first determine that the burden is not unreasonable given the amount at stake and financial abilities of the parties.

Except in these unusual cases, parties who are ordered to use a process should not also be ordered to pay the cost. User fees should never be charged in criminal cases, where access to justice is particularly important. . . .

3. Coercion to settle in the form of reports to the trier of fact and of financial disincentives to trial should not be used in connection with mandated mediation. In connection with court-annexed arbitration, the financial disincentives should be clear, commensurate with the interests at stake, and used only when the parties could afford to risk their imposition and proceed to trial.

Financial disincentives to trial and reports on substantive issues to the trier of fact are sometimes imposed to make the parties take the process more seriously and to "think twice" before proceeding to trial. In essence, these pressures are designed to avoid the problem of parties who refuse to participate meaningfully in the process. The pressures may be applied ad hoc, such as when the settlement evaluation is given by the judge who will later hear the case without a jury.

MEDIATION

Settlement coercion tied to a neutral's evaluation has a significant negative impact on mediation. The coercion results in strategic argument by the parties, who accurately view the mediator as having an effect on an adjudicated outcome. Thus, the coercion destroys the environment of frank communication necessary for the negotiation process. Further, the mediator's recommendation seems unlikely to provide the proper basis for judicial resolution or cost shifting, because mediators hold separate meetings with the parties and do not hear evidentiary presentations. For these reasons, financial disincentives to trial and reports to the trier of fact should not be used in connection with mediation.

HEARING PROCESSES

The policy issues regarding pressures to settle are different for hearing processes, such as court-annexed arbitration. The parties already act strategically within the hearing. Moreover, they have the right to present evidence and question adverse witnesses. Ex parte conferences with the arbitrators are not permitted. Thus, the prime concerns with financial disincentives following court-annexed arbitration are the effective denial of trial and the disparate effect these disincentives have on those who cannot afford the payments, or even the risk of the payments, and are thus forced to settle. . . .

4. Mandatory participation should be used only when a high quality program (i) is readily accessible, (ii) permits party participation, (iii) permits lawyer participation when the parties wish it, and (iv) provides clarity about the precise procedures that are being required. . . .

5. Plans for mandated dispute resolution programs should be formed in consultation with judges, other court officials, lawyers, and other dispute resolution professionals as well as representatives of the public. Mandatory programs should be monitored to insure that they constitute an improvement over existing procedures, using criteria listed in Recommendation 1. The programs should be altered or discontinued when appropriate. . . .

6. Procedures for compulsory referrals should include, to the extent feasible, case assessment by a person knowledgeable about dispute resolution procedures and should provide for timely consideration of motions for exclusion. . . .

The choice of appropriate cases and processes is not easily defined and applied by category. Thus, large categorical referrals to a particular process seem likely to result in many parties simply going through the motions, adding to party and court costs. Blanket referrals also seem to result in use of one process rather than a range of processes, so that courts may refer all cases involving, for example, claims below $25,000 to court-annexed arbitration. . . .

As a result, there should be means to mitigate the consequences of over-broad, especially categorical, mandatory referrals. Any compulsory program should include procedures for exempting cases that are demonstrably inappropriate for the mandatory program, such as when the parties are seeking emergency court relief in cases of spousal abuse. The court should quickly hear motions to be excused which are made on the grounds that the interests of justice would not be served by a mandatory referral. . . .

7. Requirements for participation and sanctions for noncompliance should be clearly defined.

Most parties seem to participate actively in mandated dispute resolution processes even when the statute or rule appears to require no more than mere attendance. . . . It may not, therefore, be very important to add regulation of participation or strengthen sanctions for those not complying.

Nonetheless, additional clear requirements might be added without being unduly burdensome. Thus, for example, it may be helpful to require attendance by the party as well as the lawyer. When the party is a business entity, it may be useful to require attendance by a party representative with decision-making authority. If attendance is burdensome, such a party may be required to be available by telephone. . . . Where the compliance standards are clear and the sanctions are specified and not unreasonable, the risk of litigation over compliance seems small. . . .

[For a later assessment of the pros and cons of mandatory mediation, see Reuben (2007) and Sander (2007).]

F. SANDER, H. ALLEN, AND D. HENSLER, JUDICIAL (MIS)USE OF ADR? A DEBATE

27 U. Tol. L. Rev. 885, 887-889, 892 (1996)

[Excerpts from a debate between Mr. H. William Allen, Professor Frank Sander and Professor Deborah Hensler:]

Mr. Allen: Let me make four points. [F]irst of all, my position is that ADR, while a laudable and commendable adjunct to the system of justice, is an inferior brand of justice compared to our traditional trial. Second, courts and lawyers have already been disposing of all but a small amount of cases by settlement and dispositive motions without ADR. Third, there is no caseload crisis in the federal courts justifying any effort to further cut down the cases actually tried. And fourth, what little empirical research there is on the experimental programs does not establish their goals of cost saving in the justice system. . . .

Charles Allen Wright . . . said, "[I have] spent my entire career on the principle that the best way to achieve justice is by an adversary presentation of law and facts to an impartial tribunal, presided over by a judge with life tenure. Perhaps the day will come when the most prosperous society the world has ever known will feel it can no longer afford this luxury, and some citizens will have to settle for second class justice." Are we in such a crisis today? I say we are not. A Rand Corporation report states: "Almost ninety-five percent of all private civil cases filed in the federal courts never reach trial, ending instead in settlements or other pretrial dispositions." So, we are only trying five percent of the cases that are filed. So let us keep our goal in mind. Are we trying to get that five percent down to two or three percent?

Let's look at the statistics for case filings in the federal courts over the past ten years. These are civil and criminal cases. You see that beginning with the almost 300,000 cases filed in 1985, each year filings progressively declined to 264,038 in 1993. That is total filings, criminal and civil, in our district courts. We are not awash in cases, we are not over-burdened now anymore than we were in 1985.

The decline in filings per federal judgeship is even more dramatic: from 476 in 1985 to 354 in 1993. Criminal filings (felonies) have gone up some, from 44 in 1985 to 53 in 1993, but there is plenty of room for them since civil filings are down by 122 cases per judgeship for the same period.

What about delay? The average time from filing to disposition was nine months in 1985. In 1993 it's down to eight months. Time between issue and trial (issue ordinarily means when the answer is filed) was fourteen months in 1985 and was still only fourteen months in 1992, the most recent figures available to me.

What type of justice do you get with these mandatory arbitration programs? The following Western District of Oklahoma rule was thought so well of by the Federal Judicial Center that they put it in the Manual for Litigation Management and Cost of Delay Reduction: "The hearing shall be conducted informally. All evidence shall be presented through counsel who may incorporate argument on such evidence in his or her presentation. The Federal Rules of Evidence shall be a guide, but shall not be binding." How easily we drift away from the federal rules of evidence! "Counsel may present factual representations . . . by a professional representation that counsel personally spoke with the witness and is repeating what the witness stated. Statements, reports, and depositions may be read from, but not at undue length. Physical evidence, including documents, may be exhibited during a presentation."

I am sure no one in this room would take advantage of that rule, but if you think about the advocate who has to zealously represent his client, if he can go in there and quote witnesses, I mean the temptation to stretch things may be too much.

The reason we have federal district judges appointed for life is because we want to put them in the position to be independent of any public pressure and be able to make decisions, to decide our cases impartially. We should not turn them into court room administrators that just direct traffic to different doors of the courthouse. Our concept is that these men and women are elevated to try cases, and I submit to you they are not over-burdened. We were talking before about cases by federal judgeship — these are trials by federal judgeships in our 96 districts. In the 1970s, we had in the high 40s, trying somewhere between 47, 48, 49 cases a year. It dropped to 35 in 1985-89. In 1991 and 1992, they were down to 31 trials per federal judge. . . .

. . . So who has the right to make that decision to arbitrate? I submit to you that the litigants have the right to make that decision. . . . If the ADR option is so attractive, people will voluntarily go to it.

Questions

6.3 Does the SPIDR Report adequately answer Allen's concerns? If not, how would you? If you were a member of a state ADR task force considering the institution of mandatory mediation for all contested child custody cases as well as mandatory arbitration for all money claim cases under $50,000, how would you vote? What additional data, if any, would you want?

One consideration that might be relevant in this connection is whether mandatory mediation programs have achieved a lower settlement rate than their voluntary counterparts. One might assume that if individuals are forced to mediate they will be less prone to settle than if they have chosen the process. But the evidence seems to be otherwise (Goldberg and Brett, 1990; McEwen and Maiman, 1989; Pearson and Thoennes, 1989). Compare Wissler (2002) (empirical research suggests that in court systems where the mediators were attorneys with considerable mediation experience, cases were more likely to settle if parties entered mediation at a judge's or a party's request than if the mediation was randomly assigned, but that with less experienced attorney mediators, settlement was not related to how the cases entered mediation). Perhaps this is because although many disputants are unfamiliar with the process and hence do not use it voluntarily, when they get into it they find it to their liking. Of course the cited research does not tell us whether the settlements arrived at in mandatory mediation were as uncoerced as those in voluntary mediation. But coercion *into* mediation does not necessarily mean coercion *in* mediation.

What about mandatory arbitration? Although there is a relatively high resort to trial de novo in some mandatory arbitration programs, most of these "appeals" are taken primarily for bargaining purposes and the vast preponderance of these cases settle before trial. Moreover, as pointed out earlier (p. 401), the satisfaction rates among attorneys and litigants in these programs are very high.

6.4 Are there special concerns where cases are mandatorily referred to outside providers (for example, to a retired judge now doing ADR work, or to an attorney who also mediates cases on referral from the court)? How might these concerns best be addressed? (See pp. 428-434 below.)

6.5 So far we have considered primarily the *desirability* of mandatory referrals. Are there any legal constraints? By and large, attempts at facial challenges to such programs have been unsuccessful (see Harvard Law Review, 1990; Golann, 1989). The case that follows is a notable exception.

STRANDELL v. JACKSON COUNTY, ILL.

838 F.2d 884 (7th Cir. 1987)

RIPPLE, CIRCUIT JUDGE.

In this appeal, we must decide whether a federal district court can *require* litigants to participate in a nonbinding summary jury trial. . . . Thomas Tobin, Esquire, appeals from a judgment of criminal contempt for refusing to participate in such a procedure. . . .

I. FACTS

Mr. Tobin represents the parents of Alex Strandell in a civil rights action against Jackson County, Illinois. The case involves the arrest, strip search, imprisonment, and suicidal death of Mr. Strandell. . . . At the pretrial conference, the district court suggested that the parties consent to a summary jury trial. . . . Mr. Tobin informed the district court that the plaintiffs would not consent to a summary jury trial, and filed a motion to advance the case for trial. The district court ordered that discovery be closed on January 15, 1987, and set the case for trial.

During discovery, the plaintiffs had obtained statements from 21 witnesses. The plaintiffs learned the identity of many of these witnesses from information provided by the defendants. After discovery closed, the defendants filed a motion to compel production of the witnesses' statements. The plaintiffs responded that these statements constituted privileged work-product; they argued that the defendants could have obtained the information contained in them through ordinary discovery. The district court denied the motion to compel production; it concluded that the defendants had failed to establish "substantial need" and "undue hardship," as required by Rule 26(b)(3) of the Federal Rules of Civil Procedure.

On March 23, 1987, the district court again discussed settlement prospects with counsel. . . . On March 26, 1987, Mr. Tobin advised the district court that he would not be willing to submit his client's case to a summary jury trial, but that he was ready to proceed to trial immediately. He claimed that a summary jury trial would require disclosure of the privileged statements. The district court rejected this argument, and ordered the parties to participate in a summary jury trial.

On March 31, 1987, the parties and counsel appeared, as ordered, for selection of a jury for the summary jury trial. . . . Mr. Tobin then respectfully declined to proceed with the selection of the jury. . . . The court then held Mr. Tobin in criminal contempt for refusing to proceed with the summary jury trial. . . .

III. Analysis

A

In turning to the narrow question before us—the legality of *compelled* participation in a summary jury trial—we must also acknowledge, at the very onset, that a district court no doubt has substantial inherent power to control and to manage its docket. . . . That power must, of course, be exercised in a manner that is in harmony with the Federal Rules of Civil Procedure. . . .

In this case, the district court quite properly acknowledged, at least as a theoretical matter, this limitation on its power to devise a new method to encourage settlement. Consequently, the court turned to Rule 16 of the Federal Rules of Civil Procedure in search of authority for the use of a mandatory summary jury trial. In the district court's view, two subsections of Rule 16(c) authorized such a procedure. As amended in 1983, those subsections read:

> The participants at any conference under this rule may consider and take action with respect to . . .
>
> (7) the possibility of settlement or the use of extrajudicial procedures to resolve the dispute; . . .
>
> (11) such other matters as may aid in the disposition of the action.

. . . We do not believe that these provisions can be read as authorizing a *mandatory* summary jury trial. In our view, while the pretrial conference of Rule 16 was intended to foster settlement through the use of extra-judicial procedures, it was not intended to require that an unwilling litigant be sidetracked from the normal course of litigation. The drafters of Rule 16 certainly intended to provide, in the pretrial conference, "a neutral forum" for discussing the matter of settlement. However, it is also clear that they did not foresee that the conference would be used "to impose settlement negotiations on unwilling litigants. . . ." . . . As the Second Circuit, commenting on the 1983 version of Rule 16, wrote: "Rule 16 . . . was not designed as a means for clubbing the parties — or one of them — into an involuntary compromise." . . .

The use of a mandatory summary jury trial as a pretrial settlement device would also affect seriously the well-established rules concerning discovery and work-product privilege. These rules reflect a carefully crafted balance between the needs for pretrial disclosure and party confidentiality. Yet, a compelled summary jury trial could easily upset that balance by requiring disclosure of information obtainable, if at all, through the mandated discovery process. . . .

CONCLUSION

Because we conclude that the parameters of Rule 16 do not permit courts to compel parties to participate in summary jury trials, the contempt judgment of the district court is vacated. . . .

Note

In 1993 the Sixth Circuit followed the Seventh in banning mandatory reference to summary jury trials, *In re NLO,* 5 F.3d 1154 (6th Cir. 1993), though a 1993 amendment to Federal Rule of Civil Procedure 16 left the continuing validity of these rulings in doubt (see Tenerowicz, 1998). In 1998 Congress in the Alternative Dispute Resolution Act adopted the position of the Sixth and Seventh Circuits by omitting summary jury trials from a list of dispute resolution processes for which compulsory reference was appropriate (28 U.S.C. §652(a)):

> Any district court that elects to require the use of alternative dispute resolution in certain cases may do so only with respect to mediation, early neutral evaluation, and, if the parties consent, arbitration.*

Question

6.6 Should state legislatures authorize mandatory summary jury trials? In a recent study of summary jury trials in North Carolina, a majority of the participating

*U.S. Justice Department Special Counsel Peter Steenland reports that summary jury trials were omitted at the insistence of representatives of several federal agencies who found the process to be burdensome.

attorneys, although generally favorable to the process, opposed permitting courts to mandate summary jury trials. This, along with other considerations, led the authors of the study to recommend against mandatory summary jury trials, at least in state court, where courts are generally less familiar with case management and hence less likely to be able adequately to select the most appropriate cases (Metzloff et al., 1991).

IN RE ATLANTIC PIPE CORP.

304 F.3d 136 (1st Cir. 2002)

Selya, Circuit Judge.

This mandamus proceeding requires us to resolve an issue of importance to judges and practitioners alike: Does a district court possess the authority to compel an unwilling party to participate in, and share the costs of, non-binding mediation conducted by a private mediator? We hold that a court may order mandatory mediation pursuant to an explicit statutory provision or local rule. We further hold that where, as here, no such authorizing medium exists, a court nonetheless may order mandatory mediation through the use of its inherent powers as long as the case is an appropriate one and the order contains adequate safeguards. Because the mediation order here at issue lacks such safeguards (although it does not fall far short), we vacate it and remand the matter for further proceedings.

I. Background

In January 1996, Thames-Dick Superaqueduct Partners (Thames-Dick) entered into a master agreement with the Puerto Rico Aqueduct and Sewer Authority (PRASA) to construct, operate, and maintain the North Coast Superaqueduct Project (the Project). Thames-Dick granted subcontracts for various portions of the work, including a subcontract for construction management to Dick Corp. of Puerto Rico (Dick-PR), a subcontract for the operation and maintenance of the Project to Thames Water International, Ltd. (Thames Water), and a subcontract for the fabrication of pipe to Atlantic Pipe Corp. (APC). After the Project had been built, a segment of the pipeline burst. Thames-Dick incurred significant costs in repairing the damage. Not surprisingly, it sought to recover those costs from other parties. In response, one of PRASA's insurers filed a declaratory judgment action in a local court to determine whether Thames-Dick's claims were covered under its policy. The litigation ballooned, soon involving a number of parties and a myriad of issues above and beyond insurance coverage.

On April 25, 2001, the hostilities spilled over into federal court. Two entities beneficially interested in the master agreement — CPA Group International and Chiang, Patel & Yerby, Inc. (collectively CPA) — sued Thames-Dick, Dick-PR, Thames Water, and various insurers in the United States District Court for the District of Puerto Rico, seeking remuneration for consulting services rendered in connection with repairs to the Project. A googol of claims, counterclaims, cross-claims, and third-party complaints followed. Some of these were brought against APC (the petitioner here). To complicate matters, one of the defendants moved to dismiss on grounds that, inter alia, (1) CPA had failed to join an indispensable party whose presence would destroy diversity jurisdiction, and (2) the existence of the parallel proceeding in the local court counseled in favor of abstention.

While this motion was pending before the district court, Thames-Dick asked that the case be referred to mediation and suggested Professor Eric Green as a suitable mediator. The district court granted the motion over APC's objection and ordered non-binding mediation to proceed before Professor Green. The court pronounced mediation likely to conserve judicial resources; directed all parties to undertake mediation in good faith; stayed discovery pending completion of the mediation; and declared that participation in the mediation would not prejudice the parties' positions vis-à-vis the pending motion or the litigation as a whole. The court also stated that if mediation failed to produce a global settlement, the case would proceed to trial.

After moving unsuccessfully for reconsideration of the mediation order, APC sought relief by way of mandamus. . . .

Prior to argument in this court, two notable developments occurred. First, the district court considered and rejected the challenges to its exercise of jurisdiction. Second, APC rejected an offer by Thames-Dick to pay its share of the mediator's fees.

II. Jurisdiction

[The court first concluded that the case was appropriate for advisory mandamus.]

III. The Merits

There are four potential sources of judicial authority for ordering mandatory non-binding mediation of pending cases, namely, (a) the court's local rules, (b) an applicable statute, (c) the Federal Rules of Civil Procedure, and (d) the court's inherent powers. Because the district court did not identify the basis of its assumed authority, we consider each of these sources.

A. The Local Rules

A district court's local rules may provide an appropriate source of authority for ordering parties to participate in mediation. *See Rhea v. Massey-Ferguson, Inc.*, 767 F.2d 266, 268-69 (6th Cir. 1985) (per curiam). In Puerto Rico, however, the local rules contain only a single reference to any form of alternative dispute resolution (ADR). That reference is embodied in the district court's Amended Civil Justice Expense and Delay Reduction Plan (CJR Plan). See D.P.R. R. app. III.

The district court adopted the CJR Plan on June 14, 1993, in response to the directive contained in the Civil Justice Reform Act of 1990 (CJRA), 28 U.S.C. §§471-482. Rule V of the CJR Plan states:

> Pursuant to 28 U.S.C. §473(b)(4), this Court shall adopt a method of Alternative Dispute Resolution ("ADR") through mediation by a judicial officer.

> Such a program would allow litigants to obtain from an impartial third party—the judicial officer as mediator—a flexible non-binding, dispute resolution process to facilitate negotiations among the parties to help them reach settlement.

D.P.R. R. app. III (R. V.). In addition to specifying who may act as a mediator, Rule V also limns the proper procedure for mediation sessions and assures confidentiality. *See id.*

The respondents concede that the mediation order in this case falls outside the boundaries of the mediation program envisioned by Rule V. It does so most noticeably because it involves mediation before a private mediator, not a judicial officer. Seizing upon this discrepancy, APC argues that the local rules limit the district court in this respect, and that the court exceeded its authority thereunder by issuing a non-conforming mediation order (i.e., one that contemplates the intervention of a private mediator). The respondents counter by arguing that the rule does not bind the district court because, notwithstanding the unambiguous promise of the CJR Plan (which declares that the district court "shall adopt a method of Alternative Dispute Resolution"), no such program has been adopted to date.

This is a powerful argument. APC does not contradict the respondents' assurance that the relevant portion of the CJR Plan has remained unimplemented, and we take judicial notice that there is no formal, ongoing ADR program in the Puerto Rico federal district court. Because that is so, we conclude that the District of Puerto Rico has no local rule in force that dictates the permissible characteristics of mediation orders. Consequently, APC's argument founders.

B. THE ADR ACT

There is only one potential source of statutory authority for ordering mandatory non-binding mediation here: the Alternative Dispute Resolution Act of 1998 (ADR Act), 28 U.S.C. §§651-658. Congress passed the ADR Act to promote the utilization of alternative dispute resolution methods in the federal courts and to set appropriate guidelines for their use. The Act lists mediation as an appropriate ADR process. *Id.* §651(a). Moreover, it sanctions the participation of "professional neutrals from the private sector" as mediators. *Id.* §653(b). Finally, the Act requires district courts to obtain litigants' consent only when they order arbitration, *id.* §652(a), not when they order the use of other ADR mechanisms (such as non-binding mediation).

Despite the broad sweep of these provisions, the Act is quite clear that some form of the ADR procedures it endorses must be adopted in each judicial district by local rule. *See id.* §651(b) (directing each district court to "devise and implement its own alternative dispute resolution program, by local rule adopted under [28 U.S.C.] section 2071(a), to encourage and promote the use of alternative dispute resolution in its district"). In the absence of such local rules, the ADR Act itself does not authorize any specific court to use a particular ADR mechanism. Because the District of Puerto Rico has not yet complied with the Act's mandate, the mediation order here at issue cannot be justified under the ADR Act. . . .

Although the ADR Act was designed to promote the use of ADR techniques, Congress chose a very well-defined path: it granted each judicial district, rather than each individual judge, the authority to craft an appropriate ADR program. In other words, Congress permitted experimentation, but only within the disciplining format of district-wide local rules adopted with notice and a full opportunity for public comment. *See* 28 U.S.C. §2071(b). To say that the Act authorized each district judge to disregard a district-wide ADR plan (or the absence of one) and fashion innovative procedures for use in specific cases is simply too much of a stretch.

We add, however, that although the respondents cannot use the ADR Act as a justification, neither can APC use it as a nullification. Noting that the Act requires the adoption of local rules establishing a formal ADR program, APC equates the absence of such rules with the absence of power to employ an ADR procedure (say, mediation) in a specific case. But that is wishful thinking: if one assumes that district judges possessed the power to require mediation prior to the passage of the ADR Act, there is nothing in the Act that strips them of that power. After all, even the adoption of a federal procedural rule does not implicitly abrogate a district court's inherent power to act merely because the rule touches upon the same subject matter. [Citations omitted.] . . . [W]e know of nothing in either the ADR Act or the policies that undergird it that can be said to restrict the district courts' authority to engage in the case-by-case deployment of ADR procedures. Hence, we conclude that where, as here, there are no implementing local rules, the ADR Act neither authorizes nor prohibits the entry of a mandatory mediation order.

C. THE CIVIL RULES

The respondents next argue that the district court possessed the authority to require mediation by virtue of the Federal Rules of Civil Procedure. They concentrate their attention on Fed.R.Civ.P. 16, which states in pertinent part that "the court may take appropriate action [ ] with respect to . . . (9) settlement and the use of special procedures to assist in resolving the dispute when authorized by statute or local rule. . . ." Fed.R.Civ.P. 16(c)(9). But the words "when authorized by statute or local rule" are a frank limitation on the district courts' authority to order mediation thereunder,[3] and we must adhere to that circumscription. . . .

D. INHERENT POWERS

Even apart from positive law, district courts have substantial inherent power to manage and control their calendars. . . .

3. We think it is pertinent here to quote the advisory committee's note:

> The rule acknowledges the presence of statutes and local rules or plans that may authorize use of some [ADR] procedures even when not agreed to by the parties. The rule does not attempt to resolve questions as to the extent a court would be authorized to require such proceedings as an exercise of its inherent powers.

Fed.R.Civ.P. 16, advisory committee's note (1993 Amendment) (citations omitted).

Of course, a district court's inherent powers are not infinite. There are at least four limiting principles. First, inherent powers must be used in a way reasonably suited to the enhancement of the court's processes, including the orderly and expeditious disposition of pending cases. . . . Second, inherent powers cannot be exercised in a manner that contradicts an applicable statute or rule. . . . Third, the use of inherent powers must comport with procedural fairness. . . . And, finally, inherent powers "must be exercised with restraint and discretion." . . .

At one time, the inherent power of judges to compel unwilling parties to participate in ADR procedures was a hot-button issue for legal scholars. . . . Although many federal district courts have forestalled further debate by adopting local rules that authorize specific ADR procedures and outlaw others, *e.g.*, D.N.H.R. 53.1 (permitting mandatory mediation); D. Me. R. 83.11 (permitting only voluntary mediation); D. Mass. R. 16.4 (permitting mandatory summary jury trials but only voluntary mediation), the District of Puerto Rico is not among them. Thus, we have no choice but to address the question head-on.

We begin our inquiry by examining the case law. In *Strandell v. Jackson County*, 838 F.2d 884 (7th Cir. 1987), the Seventh Circuit held that a district court does not possess inherent power to compel participation in a summary jury trial. In the court's view, Fed.R.Civ.P. 16 occupied the field and prevented a district court from forcing "an unwilling litigant [to] be sidetracked from the normal course of litigation." *Id.* at 887. But the group that spearheaded the subsequent revision of Rule 16 explicitly rejected that interpretation. *See* Fed.R.Civ.P. 16, advisory committee's note (1993 Amendment) ("The [amended] rule does not attempt to resolve questions as to the extent a court would be authorized to require [ADR] proceedings as an exercise of its inherent powers."). Thus, we do not find *Strandell* persuasive on this point.

The *Strandell* court also expressed concern that summary jury trials would undermine traditional discovery and privilege rules by requiring certain disclosures prior to an actual trial. 838 F.2d at 888. We find this concern unwarranted. . . .

Relying on policy arguments, the Sixth Circuit also has found that district courts do not possess inherent power to compel participation in summary jury trials. . . .

The concerns articulated by these two respected courts plainly apply to mandatory mediation orders. When mediation is forced upon unwilling litigants, it stands to reason that the likelihood of settlement is diminished. Requiring parties to invest substantial amounts of time and money in mediation under such circumstances may well be inefficient. *Cf.* Richard A. Posner, *The Summary Jury Trial and Other Methods of Alternative Dispute Resolution: Some Cautionary Observations,* 53 U. Chi. L. Rev. 366, 369-72 (1986) (offering a model to evaluate ADR techniques in terms of their capacity to encourage settlements).

The fact remains, however, that none of these considerations establishes that mandatory mediation is always inappropriate. There may well be specific cases in which such a protocol is likely to conserve judicial resources without significantly burdening the objectors' rights to a full, fair, and speedy trial. Much depends on the idiosyncracies of the particular case and the details of the mediation order.

In some cases, a court may be warranted in believing that compulsory mediation could yield significant benefits even if one or more parties object. After all, a party may resist mediation simply out of unfamiliarity with the process or out of fear that a willingness to submit would be perceived as a lack of confidence in her legal position. *See* Campbell C. Hutchinson, *The Case for Mandatory Mediation*, 42 Loy. L. Rev. 85, 89-90 (1996). In such an instance, the party's initial reservations are likely to evaporate as the mediation progresses, and negotiations could well produce a beneficial outcome, at reduced cost and greater speed, than would a trial. While the possibility that parties will fail to reach agreement remains ever present, the boon of settlement can be worth the risk.

This is particularly true in complex cases involving multiple claims and parties. The fair and expeditious resolution of such cases often is helped along by creative solutions—solutions that simply are not available in the binary framework of traditional adversarial litigation. Mediation with the assistance of a skilled facilitator gives parties an opportunity to explore a much wider range of options, including those that go beyond conventional zero-sum resolutions. Mindful of these potential advantages, we hold that it is within a district court's inherent power to order non-consensual mediation in those cases in which that step seems reasonably likely to serve the interests of justice. . . .

E. THE MEDIATION ORDER

Our determination that the district courts have inherent power to refer cases to non-binding mediation is made with a recognition that any such order must be crafted in a manner that preserves procedural fairness and shields objecting parties from undue burdens. We thus turn to the specifics of the mediation order entered in this case. As with any exercise of a district court's inherent powers, we review the entry of that order for abuse of discretion. . . .

As an initial matter, we agree with the lower court that the complexity of this case militates in favor of ordering mediation. At last count, the suit involves twelve parties, asserting a welter of claims, counterclaims, cross-claims, and third-party claims predicated on a wide variety of theories. The pendency of nearly parallel litigation in the Puerto Rican courts, which features a slightly different cast of characters and claims that are related to but not completely congruent with those asserted here, further complicates the matter. Untangling the intricate web of relationships among the parties, along with the difficult and fact-intensive arguments made by each, will be time-consuming and will impose significant costs on the parties and the court. Against this backdrop, mediation holds out the dual prospect of advantaging the litigants and conserving scarce judicial resources.

In an effort to parry this thrust, APC raises a series of objections. Its threshold claim is that the district court erred in ordering mediation before resolving a pending motion to dismiss for lack of subject-matter jurisdiction (or, alternatively, to abstain). . . .

Given what has transpired, this argument is fruitless. While this proceeding was pending, the district court denied the motion in question and confirmed the existence of its subject-matter jurisdiction. . . . Thus, even if it were error to enter the mediation order before passing upon the motion to dismiss, the error was harmless: it would be an empty exercise to vacate the mediation order on this ground when the lower court has already rejected the challenges to its exercise of jurisdiction. . . .

Next, APC posits that the appointment of a private mediator proposed by one of the parties is per se improper (and, thus, invalidates the order). We do not agree. The district court has inherent power to "appoint persons unconnected with the court to aid judges in the performance of specific judicial duties." *Ex parte Peterson*, 253 U.S. 300, 312, 40 S. Ct. 543, 64 L. Ed. 919 (1920). In the context of non-binding mediation, the mediator does not decide the merits of the case and has no authority to coerce settlement. Thus, in the absence of a contrary statute or rule, it is perfectly acceptable for the district court to appoint a qualified and neutral private party as a mediator. The mere fact that the mediator was proposed by one of the parties is insufficient to establish bias in favor of that party. . . .

We hasten to add that the litigants are free to challenge the qualifications or neutrality of any suggested mediator (whether or not nominated by a party to the case). APC, for example, had a full opportunity to present its views about the suggested mediator both in its opposition to the motion for mediation and in its motion for reconsideration of the mediation order. Despite these opportunities, APC offered no convincing reason to spark a belief that Professor Green, a nationally recognized mediator with significant experience in sprawling cases, is an unacceptable choice. When a court enters a mediation order, it necessarily makes an independent determination that the mediator it appoints is both qualified and neutral. Because the court made that implicit determination here in a manner that was procedurally fair (if not ideal), we find no abuse of discretion in its selection of Professor Green.[7]

APC also grouses that it should not be forced to share the costs of an unwanted mediation. We have held, however, that courts have the power under Fed.R.Civ.P. 26(f) to issue pretrial cost-sharing orders in complex litigation. *See In re San Juan Dupont Plaza Hotel Fire Litig.*, 994 F.2d 956, 965 (1st Cir. 1993). Given the difficulties facing trial courts in cases involving multiple parties and multiple claims, we are hesitant to limit that power to the traditional discovery context. *See id.* This is especially true in complicated cases, where the potential value of mediation lies not only in promoting settlement but also in clarifying the issues remaining for trial.

The short of the matter is that, without default cost-sharing rules, the use of valuable ADR techniques (like mediation) becomes hostage to the parties' ability to agree on the concomitant financial arrangements. This means that the district court's inherent power to order private mediation in appropriate cases would be rendered nugatory absent the corollary power to order the sharing of reasonable mediation costs. To avoid this pitfall, we hold that the district court, in an appropriate case, is empowered to order the sharing of reasonable costs and expenses associated with mandatory non-binding mediation.

The remainder of APC's arguments are not so easily dispatched. Even when generically appropriate, a mediation order must contain procedural and substantive safeguards to ensure fairness to all parties involved. The mediation order in this case does not quite meet that test. In particular, the order does not set limits on the duration of the mediation or the expense associated therewith.[8]

7. We say "not ideal" because, in an ideal world, it would be preferable for the district court, before naming a mediator, to solicit the names of potential nominees from all parties and to provide an opportunity for the parties to comment upon each others' proposed nominees.

8. We do not assign significant weight to Thames-Dick's belated offer to pay APC's share of the mediator's fee. There are other expenses involved, and there is too much of a risk that "free rider" status will itself breed problems.

We need not wax longiloquent. As entered, the order simply requires the parties to mediate; it does not set forth either a timetable for the mediation or a cap on the fees that the mediator may charge. The figures that have been bandied about in the briefs—$900 per hour or $9,000 per mediation day—are quite large and should not be left to the mediator's whim. Relatedly, because the mediator is to be paid an hourly rate, the court should have set an outside limit on the number of hours to be devoted to mediation. Equally as important, it is trite but often true that justice delayed is justice denied. An unsuccessful mediation will postpone the ultimate resolution of the case—indeed, the district court has stayed all discovery pending the completion of the mediation—and, thus, prolong the litigation. For these reasons, the district court should have set a definite time frame for the mediation.

The respondents suggest that the district court did not need to articulate any limitations in its mediation order because the mediation process will remain under the district court's ultimate supervision; the court retains the ability to curtail any excessive expenditures of time or money; and a dissatisfied party can easily return to the court at any time. While this might be enough of a safeguard in many instances, the instant litigation is sufficiently complicated and the mediation efforts are likely to be sufficiently expensive that, here, reasonable time limits and fee constraints, set in advance, are appropriate.

A court intent on ordering non-consensual mediation should take other precautions as well. For example, the court should make it clear (as did the able district court in this case) that participation in mediation will not be taken as a waiver of any litigation position. The important point is that the protections we have mentioned are not intended to comprise an exhaustive list, but, rather, to illustrate that when a district court orders a party to participate in mediation, it should take care to assuage legitimate concerns about the possible negative consequences of such an order. . . .

IV. Conclusion

We admire the district court's pragmatic and innovative approach to this massive litigation. Our core holding—that ordering mandatory mediation is a proper exercise of a district court's inherent power, subject, however, to a variety of terms and conditions—validates that approach. We are mindful that this holding is in tension with the opinions of the Sixth and Seventh Circuits in *NLO* and *Strandell,* respectively, but we believe it is justified by the important goal of promoting flexibility and creative problem-solving in the handling of complex litigation.

That said, the need of the district judge in this case to construct his own mediation regime ad hoc underscores the greater need of the district court as an institution to adopt an ADR program and memorialize it in its local rules. In the ADR Act, Congress directed that "[e]ach United States district court shall authorize, by local rule under section 2071(a), the use of alternative dispute resolution processes in all civil actions. . . ." 28 U.S.C. §651(b). While Congress did not set a firm deadline for compliance with this directive, the statute was enacted four years ago. This omission having been noted, we are confident that the district court will move expediently to bring the District of Puerto Rico into compliance.

We need go no further. For the reasons set forth above, we vacate the district court's mediation order and remand for further proceedings consistent with this opinion. The district court is free to order mediation if it continues to believe that such a course is advisable or, in the alternative, to proceed with discovery and trial.

Note

1. On the potential utility of mediation, even in a case where the objector to such a referral ultimately turned out to win on the merits, compare *Dunnett v. Railtrack*, 2 All. E.R. 850, 853 (2002), where Brooke L.J. of the British Court of Appeal opined as follows:

> [Defendant's attorney] when asked by the court why his clients were not willing to contemplate alternative dispute resolution, said that this would necessarily involve the payment of money, which his clients were not willing to contemplate, over and above what they had already offered. This appears to be a misunderstanding of the purpose of alternative dispute resolution. Skilled mediators are now able to achieve results satisfactory to both parties in many cases which are quite beyond the power of lawyers and courts to achieve. This court has knowledge of cases where intense feelings have arisen, for instance in relation to clinical negligence claims. But when the parties are brought together on neutral soil with a skilled mediator to help them resolve their differences, it may very well be that the mediator is able to achieve a result by which the parties shake hands at the end and feel that they have gone away having settled the dispute on terms with which they are happy to live. A mediator may be able to provide solutions which are beyond the powers of the court to provide. Occasions are known to the court in claims against the police, which can give rise to as much passion as a claim of this kind where a claimant's precious horses are killed on a railway line, by which an apology from a very senior police officer is all that the claimant is really seeking and the money side of the matter falls away.

Accordingly, the court refused to award the winner Railtrack the usual costs, and added:

> It is to be hoped that any publicity given to this . . . judgment of the court will draw the attention of lawyers . . . to the possibility that, if they turn down out of hand the chance of alternative dispute resolution when suggested by the court . . . they may have to face uncomfortable costs consequences.

Compare *Halsey v. Milton Keynes*, 4 All. E.R. 920 (2004), in which the English Court of Appeal elaborated on the *Dunnett* case, reminding counsel that the Civil Procedure Rules include a provision for "encouraging the parties to use an alternative dispute resolution procedure if the Court considers that appropriate," but that they cannot be compelled to do so. This conclusion raises the question of the consequences if one side refuses the other side's suggestion that ADR be used. The court pointed out that such a refusal, even by the party that ultimately prevails on the merits, can be sanctioned with a denial of costs only if the refusal was "unreasonable."

It then discusses six factors that should be used (but not by way of a limitation) in determining whether the refusal to use ADR was "unreasonable":

a. the nature of the dispute;
b. the merits of the case;
c. the extent to which other settlement methods have been attempted;
d. whether the costs of the ADR would be disapportionately high;
e. whether any delay in setting up and attending the ADR would have been prejudicial; and
f. whether the ADR had a reasonable prospect of success.

What, if any, application might these decisions have in the United States, where normally each party bears its own costs?

2. What accounts for the different result in *Strandell* and *Atlantic Pipe* (APC)? That one case involved summary jury trial and the other involved mediation? The 1993 Rule 16 amendment discussed in the APC case? Section 652(a) of the ADR Act of 1998, quoted at p. 398? The specific facts of *Strandell* (i.e., the court's view that a summary jury trial would impair "the well-established rules concerning discovery and work product privilege")?

3. Was the APC court correct in its statement: "when mediation is forced upon unwilling litigants, it stands to reason that the likelihood of settlement is diminished"?

4. How likely is it for other cases to raise the issue involved in APC? Not only would the jurisdiction have to have a similar absence of a local rule authorizing mandatory referral to mediation; one of the parties would also have to be willing to stand up to the judge's recommendation.

5. Suppose a local federal rule provided that all non-indigent parties must pay for mediation services whenever a judge, pursuant to a local rule mandating mediation in all civil cases, ordered a case to mediation. Would such a rule be valid under *Atlantic Pipe* and the Federal Rules of Civil Procedure? Would it be desirable? See pp. 428-434.

Note: Compulsory Attendance of Parties

As noted earlier (pp. 357-360), one of the issues that has come into prominence as a result of the increased focus on settlement efforts is the participation of the litigants themselves in these proceedings. The issue came to a legal head in *G. Heileman Brewing Co. v. Joseph Oat Corp.*, 871 F.2d 648 (7th Cir. 1989). A federal magistrate in Madison, Wisconsin, ordered "a corporate representative with authority to settle [of the defendant corporation, located in New Jersey]" to come to a pretrial conference. Although the defendant's attorney appeared, no corporate official came. This resulted in the imposition of a $5,860 sanction under Rule 16, representing the opposing parties' costs and attorney's fees for attendance at the pretrial conference. On appeal to the U.S. Court of Appeals for the Seventh Circuit, the decision was reversed by a 2-1 vote, but the Court of Appeals sitting en banc, by a 6-5 vote, with six different opinions, reversed the panel and affirmed the trial court.

In the course of its consideration of the Civil Justice Reform Act of 1990, Congress specifically addressed the *Heileman* issue. Section 473(b)(5) provides that in formulating its litigation management plan, each district court, in consultation with its Advisory Committee,

> shall consider adopting the following litigation management and cost and delay reduction techniques: . . .
>
> (5) a requirement that, upon notice by the court, representatives of the parties with authority to bind them in settlement discussions be present or available by telephone during any settlement conference. . . .

How do you read this provision? If you were a district judge faced with the *Heileman* issue would you take comfort from §473(b)(5)?

Quite aside from the authority issue, there continues to be considerable controversy over whether principals should be required to be present.

The case for was stated succinctly by Judge Posner (871 F.2d at 657):

> The only possible reason for wanting a represented party to be present is to enable the judge or magistrate to explore settlement with the principals rather than with just their agents. Some district judges and magistrates distrust the willingness or ability of attorneys to convey to their clients adequate information bearing on the desirability and terms of settling a case in lieu of pressing forward to trial. . . . Although few attorneys will defy a district court's request to produce the client, those few cases may be the very ones where the client's presence would be most conducive to settlement.

But, Judge Posner added, "power corrupts," noting an instance where the Acting Secretary of Labor was ordered to appear before a judge on the very day of his Senate confirmation hearing:

> The broader concern illustrated by the Brock episode is that in their zeal to settle cases judges may ignore the value of other people's time. One reason people hire lawyers is to economize on their own investment of time in resolving disputes.

This point was underscored by Judge Manion (whose opinion was joined by several other judges) (871 F.2d at 667):

> Litigants hire attorneys to take advantage of the attorneys' training and skill. . . . Part of an attorney's expertise includes evaluating cases, advising litigants whether or not to settle, and conducting negotiations. I realize that attorneys may sometimes convey inadequate information to their clients regarding settlement. But an attorney has a strong self interest in realistically conveying to the client relevant information necessary for the client to make an informed settlement decision, and in accurately conveying the client's settlement position to the court and opposing litigants. The attorney also has an ethical duty to convey that information. The threat of malpractice suits and disciplinary proceedings should be sufficient to make any attorney think twice before trying to mislead his client or the court. Attorneys play an important role in our adversary system, and we should not denigrate that role by presuming that attorneys will be incompetent to perform one of the most important functions for which their clients hire them.

Judge Coffey, in his opinion joined in by several other judges, stressed the other side of the coin — the client's inability to make the necessary judgments under these circumstances (871 F.2d at 662):

> I am convinced that if the attorney does not wish to have the litigant personally appear before the court at the pretrial conference, he [should not be] bound to do so, lest, among other problems, the litigant make an admission of some type which would be damaging to the case and which had not previously been elicited in discovery proceedings. I believe we are all aware of the fact that the appearance of fairness, impartiality and justice is all imperative, and based upon logic I fail to understand how a litigant sitting at a *command appearance before a judge* who injects himself into an adversarial role for either of the parties' positions during settlement negotiations can feel that he or she (the litigant) will have a fair trial before the judge if he or she fails to agree with the judge's reasoning or direction regarding a recommended settlement. We may express in grandiose terms all sorts of theory and postulation about being careful not to influence, intimidate and/or coerce a settlement, but under the pressure that our trial judges experience today from their ever-burgeoning caseloads, we would be foolhardy not to anticipate an undesirable and unnecessary psychological impact upon the litigant in circumstances of this nature. The difficulties associated with active judicial participation in settlement negotiations is expressly exacerbated when the trial is scheduled before the court rather than a jury of one's peers. The appearance of partiality and impropriety must be avoided at all lengths if our nation is to continue to show respect for its judicial judgments. Since litigants are neither trained in the law nor have the basic understanding of the nuances of legal proceedings that we as lawyers have gained through years of education, professional training and experience, they could well be confused and dismayed with judicial participation in settlement negotiations.

How do you evaluate these arguments? It is interesting to note that four of the six members voting to affirm the trial court's authority, but none of the five dissenters, had been trial judges.

If you were a magistrate or district judge faced with this issue would you require the principals to be present? What factors might you look to in exercising this judgment? Cf. pp. 357-360.

Nick v. Morgan's Foods, 270 F.3d 590 (8th Cir. 2001), involved a sexual harassment action under Title VII. The district court, in accordance with a local rule and pursuant to the consent of both parties, issued an order for mediation with a court-appointed mediator, requiring, inter alia, each side to (1) file a pre-mediation memorandum at least seven days before the mediation session; (2) participate in such session in good faith, as required by the local rule; and (3) send a representative with full settlement authority. Defendant failed to file the requisite memo and sent only its outside counsel, plus a company representative whose settlement authority was limited to $500. (Any higher settlement figure had to be cleared with defendant's General Counsel, who was available by phone.) At the mediation session, plaintiff made two offers which were both rejected by the defendant without making a counteroffer.

Following the conclusion of the mediation session, the court mediator reported these events to the court which, following a motion by plaintiff, issued an order to the defendant company to show cause why it should not be sanctioned for failure to participate in good faith. Following a hearing, the defendant company, as well as its outside counsel, were each ordered to pay $1,390 covering plaintiff's ADR fees and attorneys' fees for the abortive mediation session. In addition, defendant was fined $1,500 for failure to file the pre-mediation statement. Defendant filed a motion to reconsider, which resulted in an additional fine of $1,250 for the defendant and $1,250 for its outside counsel "for vexatiously increasing the costs of litigation by filing a frivolous motion." On appeal, the order was affirmed in all respects, including a rejection of defendant's argument that any fine should be imposed solely on its outside counsel.

E. SHERMAN, COURT-MANDATED ALTERNATIVE DISPUTE RESOLUTION: WHAT FORM OF PARTICIPATION SHOULD BE REQUIRED?

46 SMU L. Rev. 2079, 2089-2111 (1993)

A. Good Faith Participation

Over the past several years some judges in ordering parties to participate in ADR proceedings have included a provision that they must participate in good faith. A number of states have also adopted, by statute or rule, a good faith participation requirement for mediation or ADR. . . .

1. INADEQUACY OF CASE PRECEDENTS FOR POLICY GUIDANCE

. . . The recent court-annexation of ADR processes has resulted in few decisions in either federal or state courts concerning required participation in ADR, and such decisions provide little policy guidance as to what kind of participation is required. In most cases courts have relied on Rule 16 (or an equivalent in state courts) or on inherent judicial authority for their power to sanction for nonparticipation. The decisions that have addressed the issue tend to rely on narrow questions of a court's authority to make such an order or on the appropriateness of the sanctions imposed for noncompliance. . . .

Other cases have determined that the applicable statute did not, in fact, require "good faith participation." . . .

Some cases have simply found that the conduct did not amount to an absence of good faith. . . .

2. INADEQUACY OF THE COLLECTIVE BARGAINING ANALOGY

A possible source for policy guidance in applying the "good faith participation" requirement is collective bargaining. Under the labor laws, unions and management that are required to engage in collective bargaining must bargain in good faith. Is that an apt analogy for ADR? Both ADR and collective bargaining would undoubtedly benefit from the parties' good faith participation. But there are differences in ADR which suggest that such participation is not as critical to the process as in collective bargaining and that the content of "good faith participation" is more difficult to determine. . . .

. . . Negotiators are not obligated to demonstrate an intent to find a basis for agreement, or to display a sincere desire to reach common ground, or to respond to and counter meaningfully the offers of the other side. ADR offers a process of assisted negotiation where the parties should be able to choose to be forthcoming and make concessions or not. To deny them the right to take strong, or even extreme, positions (for example, that there is no liability or that a certain sum is the only basis on which a settlement is possible) would deprive them of litigant autonomy and the legitimate right to hold out and have those issues determined in a trial. The level of accommodation to the other side required in collective bargaining is clearly unsuitable for ADR.

One further consideration operating against the use of the good faith participation standard in ADR is its inherent ambiguity. Phrased in terms of subjective intent, it seems to require an examination into a party's motives rather than its objective conduct. Its subjectivity raises the spectre of courts having to make complex investigations into the bargaining process of an ADR proceeding upon any party's claim of bad faith participation by another. The possibility of satellite litigation seeking sanctions for bad faith participation could severely undermine its claim to economy and efficiency.

Sanction motions also raise difficult issues of confidentiality. Many jurisdictions accord confidentiality to ADR. Proper determination of a sanction motion for bad faith participation could require the parties and the third party neutral to testify concerning communications made during the ADR proceeding. Courts would thus be faced with either rejecting confidentiality in bad faith participation cases (thereby undermining the need to encourage candor in ADR), or upholding confidentiality (thereby denying the parties access to crucial evidence on the participation issue). . . .

B. Exchange of Position and Objective Information

If a "good faith participation" requirement is undesirable in ADR, there are forms of participation that would enhance the likelihood of success that rely on objective conduct and therefore are more easily enforced by courts. For any form of ADR to succeed, there must be some indication of the parties' positions on the relevant issues and some exchange of basic factual information. Requiring the parties to provide each other and the third-party neutral with position papers and other relevant information lays a basis for meaningful consideration of the case without mandating specific forms of presentation or interaction with the other party. It encourages further oral participation and interaction without having to specify its form, since once having submitted a position paper, parties and counsel are less likely to refuse to discuss their positions at the ADR proceeding.

A reasonable order would be that the parties provide a position paper in advance of the ADR proceeding which would include a plain and concise statement of: (1) the legal and factual issues in dispute, (2) the party's position on those issues, (3) the relief sought (including a particularized itemization of all elements of damage claimed), and (4) any offers and counter-offers previously made. This is a shortened list of the kinds of items that are routinely required by federal courts in proposed pretrial orders under the authority of the Rule 16 pretrial conference rule.

The order might also require the parties to provide to the other side in advance, or to bring to the ADR proceeding, certain documents, such as current medical reports or specific business records. It would thus also serve as a discovery or subpoena order. . . .

Questions

6.7 The State of Arkabama has a statute requiring all parties in cases involving "a long-term relationship between the parties" to attempt "to mediate the issues in good faith" with a state-provided mediator before a complaint can be filed in court. Under the applicable court rules, a certificate of compliance must be obtained from the mediator before the complaint can be filed.

You are a trial judge in Arkabama faced with the following case. James Martin has been a tenant in Robert Nelson's house. Recently Martin gave notice that he wished to terminate his lease effective in 60 days, as the lease permitted. Nelson is angered by this development and refuses to return Martin's $2,000 security deposit. Nelson claims that various items of damage had occurred, which Martin denies. Martin now is bringing suit to obtain the return of the deposit. In opposition to Martin's claim, Nelson alleges that Martin did not file the requisite certificate of compliance with mediation; he also asserts that the two parties did have a 30-minute session with the assigned mediator but that Martin merely "went through the motions" rather than attempting to mediate in good faith. According to Nelson, Martin simply kept saying that he wanted his money back.

How will you decide this case? Suppose the mediation session was covered by a privilege (see pp. 443-444). Can the judge consider any evidence as to what occurred during the mediation session?

Suppose you had been in the legislature when the mediation statute was passed. Would you have favored its enactment in its present or some alternate form? Why? Why not?

6.8 Robert Damon was involved in an automobile collision with James Friar. Damon believes it was Friar's fault. Pursuant to an applicable court-annexed mandatory arbitration statute, Damon files for arbitration. Friar's lawyer does not show up at the arbitration hearing. Friar himself tells the arbitrator he believes the accident was Damon's fault, but he does not put on any witnesses or cross-examine Damon's two witnesses. He also tells the arbitrator that it is too expensive for him in a small case like this to have his lawyer present at both arbitration and trial. At the conclusion of the proceeding, the arbitrator renders an award in Damon's favor.

Friar's attorney has now filed for a de novo trial in court. Damon contends that the case should be dismissed on the ground that Friar did not participate "meaningfully," as required in the local court rule, and therefore has forfeited his right to trial. The local rule provides that where a party has not participated "meaningfully" in the arbitration the judge may "impose any appropriate sanction, including dismissal of the case."

How would you as trial judge rule in this case?

6.9 As an alternative to the typical court-ordered arbitration programs, it has been suggested that states adopt the following remedy for court congestion: Every civil plaintiff may propose arbitration of his case. If the defendant refuses, the court, if it finds for the plaintiff, may award costs, including attorney's fees, to the plaintiff. If plaintiff does not propose arbitration, defendant may do so in his answer, subject to similar conditions. The arbitration award can be "appealed" to court on any ground applicable to the appeal of trial court decisions.

Would you recommend the adoption of this proposal? Why? Why not?

6.10 Some courts permit the mediator to make a recommendation to the judge if the parties do not settle. Law professor Trina Grillo (1991:1594) relates an incident from a child custody mediation conducted under these procedures:

> [The mediator] said Jerry was entitled to have his son half the time; the only question was which half. Although the mediator recognized the difficulty of arranging for frequent long-distance travel for Kenny, she nonetheless recommended that Kenny spend alternative months with each parent. When Linda protested that, because of Jerry's work schedule, Kenny would have frequent and continuing contact with neither parent when he was staying with Jerry, the mediator made it clear that if Linda did not agree to sharing custody on the terms she suggested, she would recommend to the court that Jerry get sole custody.

Assume that mandatory mediation programs experience substantially higher settlement rates if the mediators make custody recommendations following unsuccessful mediation. Moreover, judges rely heavily on such recommendations because the mediator is a neutral expert. Do you agree with the SPIDR Report stance against such recommendations?

6.11 As an alternative to mandatory mediation, the following statute has been proposed.

> In any case where any party requests mediation, the court shall order all parties to participate.

How do you evaluate this proposal? Would you favor it in this or an amended form? Why? Why not?

6.12 An English commentator on the SPIDR Report (Marshall, 1991:8) wrote as follows:

> I think the Committee has accepted the existence of mandated mediation much too readily. In fact, I see only one real justification for it. That is an economic one. The costliest process of the law cannot be applied to every single case, without some consideration of the importance of the issues. Most dispute resolution must of necessity be informal and "cheap" (but not necessarily poor in quality). While I cannot see a good reason for ever denying right to trial in cases involving human rights issues, discrimination, or the use of violence, I think one must allow that some property disputes and regulatory matters can be diverted from the full legal processes. However, if one is to exercise diversionary discretion in an acceptable and undiscriminating way, I can see no way of accepting the recommendation that such decisions should be made on a case by case basis. There must be clear definitions of what will fall within the remit of the courts and what will

not. . . . The proper answer to the issues to which mandatory schemes give rise does not lie in pseudo-legalese of the Committee's recommendations. The solution is in the promotion of a grassroots community capacity for resolving problems at the lowest (and best) level, and public education in the pros and cons of different styles of handling conflicts. Once this capacity is in place, individuals will be able to make informed decisions about the procedure that will suit their own best interests, without the need of others making them on their behalf by mandate.

Do you agree? If not, how would you respond?

D. THE ROLE OF PRIVATE PROVIDERS

Should the courts encourage settlement by requiring the parties to use private neutrals? U.S. Magistrate Judge Wayne Brazil in the next article grapples with the complex issues raised by that question, not only in terms of the quality of the dispute resolution services, but also in terms of the values implicit in the justice system. What about the converse situation—should the court encourage use of private neutrals by reviewing the decisions rendered by them? The second piece examines this issue in the context of a process that has been dubbed "private judging" or "rent-a-judge." Unlike voluntary arbitration, private judging involves a selection of a "referee" who is empowered by statute to enter a judgment having the finality, precedent value, and appealability of a regular trial court decree (Chernick, 1989; *Harvard Law Review,* 1981). California's statute, like those in a number of other states, dates back to frontier days when public judges might not be nearby, but Ohio recently enacted such a statute to meet the current need created by public judges whose dockets are too backlogged to hold prompt hearings.

W. BRAZIL, COMPARING STRUCTURES FOR THE DELIVERY OF ADR SERVICES BY COURTS: CRITICAL VALUES AND CONCERNS

14 Ohio St. J. Disp. Resol. 715 (1999)*

I. INTRODUCTION

This essay is about the main chance. It is presumptuous and risky. Presumptuous because it purports to identify the values and concerns that should occupy center stage when we decide how to structure court-connected ADR programs. Risky because it will be irrelevant to policy makers who do not agree (either as a matter of philosophic election or fiscal necessity) that the values and concerns I identify should or can play ascendant roles in this comparative analysis. . . .

What is important to acknowledge at this point is that how a court defines the primary purpose of its program, and how that court prioritizes the values and

*Based on pre-publication manuscript.

interests its program could serve, could dramatically affect that court's thinking about which model or system for delivering ADR services is most attractive. . . .

II. The Values That Should Dominate the Choices We Make

There are scores of different considerations, interests, values, and concerns that decision-makers could take into account when they compare different ways of structuring court-connected ADR programs. That fact creates a risk that when we make the comparisons we will lose track of the main chance — that confusion or want of focus will lead us to make choices that we would not make if we kept firmly in mind what is most important to us. We also must acknowledge that, at least in some settings, some of the values and interests that are at play here are mutually exclusive. So we must make choices. Before we choose, we should have a clear idea of what our priorities are, which values we can least afford to compromise or place in jeopardy. . . .

These facts of life mean that there likely will always be real limits on the resources that courts will be able to commit to their ADR programs. If those real limits force courts to choose between volume and quality, I believe the former always must be sacrificed for the latter. We should refuse to operate a program that is any larger or more ambitious than we can support at a high quality level — especially in programs where the court either requires participation in an ADR process or generates considerable momentum in that direction. Stated differently, if we are forced to choose, we should concentrate our resources in smaller, higher quality programs — rather than strain our resources to offer thin support for services in whose quality our confidence is substantially compromised. . . .

The goal of an ADR program that is sponsored by a public court cannot be simply to have the disputing be over. The business of the courts is not business. It is justice. And the dimension of justice for which courts are primarily responsible is process fairness — which includes, among many other things, assuring that all people stand equal before the law and are greeted by the judicial system with the same presumption of respect. It follows that the primary concern of any court that sponsors an ADR program must be with the process fairness of the services that are provided in that court's name. Those processes must be fully respect-worthy. . . .

These notions — that the process should be fully respect-worthy and should be something of value in itself — are the centerpieces of my contention that courts which sponsor ADR processes should resolve program design issues in favor of maximizing the likelihood that the neutrals will be of the highest character and that the services they provide will be of the highest quality. An ADR program that delivers less jeopardizes public confidence in and respect for the courts. In sharp contrast, an ADR program that provides only high quality service by neutrals increases the public's confidence in and respect for our system of justice and, by giving the parties a service they really value, increases their sense of gratitude toward the government and their sense of connection to our society. The more respect for and gratitude toward the courts the people feel, the more likely they are to respect the whole notion of law, to feel the importance and to acknowledge the legitimacy of having democratically developed norms govern relations within our country.

We can approach this same conclusion from a slightly different vantage point. Courts are charged with performing what is probably the most important function of government: peacefully resolving disputes and thus giving order and stability to relationships that do not order and stabilize themselves. Courts cannot perform this essential function unless the vast majority of people in our society will comply peacefully with the courts' decisions. Over time, in a democracy, the people will comply only if they trust and respect the courts as institutions. It follows that we must take great care to do nothing that jeopardizes that trust and respect. This is the main chance — so when we design court-sponsored ADR programs our greatest concern should be to preserve, at least, and to increase, if possible, the people's respect for, confidence in, and gratitude toward our system of justice. . . .

What are the attributes of court-sponsored programs that are likely to be most important to encouraging public respect and trust? Stated succinctly, the attributes are: the public's perception of the motives and purposes that inspire and drive the program, the extent to which fairness permeates it, and the quality of the work performed and the value of the service delivered by the neutrals.

[A] considerable number of program variables can affect the public's perception in each of these areas — but I contend that the single factor of greatest significance is the quality of the neutrals. More than anything else, it is their integrity, their commitment, their sensitivity, their substantive knowledge, their process skill, their energy and their performance that will determine the level of respect and trust that the program enjoys.

IV. The Models

We have been asked to compare the following five[39] "models" that courts might use for delivering ADR services.

1. FULL-TIME IN-HOUSE NEUTRALS

In this model, the court hires and pays with public funds the people who serve as the mediators. The mediators are full-time employees of the court. Mediation services in the court's program are not provided from any other source.

2. COURT CONTRACTS WITH A NON-PROFIT ORGANIZATION THAT PROVIDES THE NEUTRALS AND ADMINISTERS THE PROGRAM

This model could be implemented in either of two ways. Under one variation, the parties are charged either nothing or only a nominal fee for the services performed by the neutrals, and the neutrals either are not paid at all or are paid

39. Other authors may describe the models somewhat differently and may identify six (or more) models for discussion. The models are conceptual constructs which we use primarily to explicate the issues we have been asked to address. They do not purport to exhaust the universe of possibilities or to reflect all the variations that have been adopted.

far below market rates with money that is provided by the court through the contract with the non-profit organization.

Under the other variation, the parties are charged more substantial fees (approaching market rates) for the neutral's services—while neither the court nor the non-profit organization that orchestrates the service by the neutrals makes any significant contribution to the income received by the neutrals.

3. COURT DIRECTLY PAYS PRIVATE INDIVIDUALS OR FIRMS TO SERVE AS NEUTRALS

Under this model, the contractual relationship that underlies provision of the neutral services is between the court and the neutral, not between the parties and the neutral. The court, not the parties, pays the neutral's fees. While the fees often are not as high as pure market rates would dictate (at least for some of the neutrals), they are not nominal and could constitute a significant portion of some neutrals' income. But the neutrals are not full-time employees of the court. In most courts that operate under this model, the fees are fixed on a per case basis, not per hour.

4. COURT ORCHESTRATES SERVICES BY PRIVATE INDIVIDUALS WHO SERVE AS THE NEUTRALS WITHOUT PAY

Under this model, the court recruits, trains, monitors, and disciplines the neutrals, who are private citizens who serve without pay and who generally devote only a small percentage of their work life to service in this capacity. Because the neutrals work on what is essentially a pro bono basis, there is little or no charge to the parties for participation in the ADR program.

5. COURT REFERS PARTIES TO PRIVATE NEUTRALS, WHO CHARGE THE PARTIES MARKET RATES FOR THEIR SERVICES

Under this model, there is no contractual or financial relationship between the neutrals and the court. The court might establish some minimum criteria for serving, and might set up a clearing house list of people eligible to serve—but the court's involvement in quality control is either non-existent or modest.

The principal variations of the model include: (1) the court ordering the parties to use a neutral that the court names, (2) the court ordering the parties to select a neutral from an approved list, (3) the court simply ordering the parties to go into the private market and find a neutral on their own, or (4) the court accepting a stipulation by the parties that they will participate with a neutral of their choice in an ADR session during a defined period—during which, usually, the court suspends the case development obligations the parties might otherwise have. Under all of the variations of this model, the parties end up paying, usually on a 50-50 basis, the market rate fees of the neutral. In some programs, if an impecunious party is ordered to participate in a mediation, either the neutral will waive her fee or the court will pay it. . . .

The Mobile and Multiple "Bottom Lines"

Like some parties who attend mediations without understanding the principles of the process, readers who are looking for crisp directives and an uncomplicated argument for the superiority of a single model for delivering ADR services will be disappointed by this essay. It is quite likely that no one model is superior in all settings—even for those who are willing to limit their vision to the values on which I have focused. The "bottom line" of our inquiry is mobile—likely changing with a host of assumptions and variables, as well as with the specific context in which that "bottom line" is sought. Among the many pertinent factors, it is especially important that we attend to the prioritized purposes of the particular ADR program, to the kinds of cases and parties to be served, whether participation is mandatory or voluntary, whether the parties are represented by counsel, the volume of cases the system will be asked to accommodate, and the role the court wants the neutrals to play. . . .

Bearing all these cautions in mind, I suggest that the staff neutral model is most likely to inspire confidence in the motives that drive the court to establish an ADR program, most likely to signal that the court values ADR processes, least likely to inspire feelings that ADR processes are second rate and that litigants whose cases proceed through an ADR program are second class, most likely to communicate that the court defines itself as a service-oriented institution, and most likely to inspire a sense of gratitude toward the court and a feeling of connection to our society.

Two models seem likely to inspire the most confidence in the motives of the neutrals—the staff neutral model and the model that relies on service by unpaid volunteers. The neutrals may enjoy the greatest presumption of respect under the staff neutral model. The model that could be next most attractive from this perspective is the model in which an outside organization orchestrates the delivery of the services by the neutrals—as long as the particular outside organization enjoys widespread respect in the affected parts of the community.

Comparing the models with respect to various dimensions of "democratization" yields a more complex picture. The economic and procedural barriers to participation are likely to be lowest under the staff neutral model. Barriers to participation based on fear, ignorance, or distrust of the process and its purposes also probably are lowest under this model. Similarly, this model probably is least likely to provoke concerns about conflicts of interest or biases in the neutrals.

On the other hand, the staff neutral model is clearly inferior to the extent that a visibly diverse panel of neutrals is important to inspiring confidence in the political or moral integrity of a program, or confidence in the capacity of the neutrals to understand and appropriately empathize with the litigants' real-world circumstances. Models that use large pools of neutrals offer obvious advantages from these perspectives. These models also offer courts a substantially greater capacity to provide parties with neutrals who have subject matter expertise—at least if the goal is to provide such expertise to a wide range of cases.

Models that rely on large pools of neutrals also are superior with respect to two additional aspects of "democratization"—both potentially important. First, these models equip courts to offer ADR services to much larger numbers of cases than courts that rely on small cadres of professionals—on staff or otherwise. This would be a consideration of great significance to a court that believed deeply in the value (to litigants, as well perhaps to itself) of its ADR processes *and* that believed that it could maintain an appropriate level of quality control over a large pool of neutrals.

Second, models that use large and diverse pools of neutrals are superior vehicles for extending the reach and influence of ADR into more segments of our society. This is accomplished in two ways. One is by having the court's program directly serve a larger, more diverse group of cases—so more litigants, in a wider range of circumstances, are exposed to the value and the philosophy of ADR. The second way these models extend the influence of ADR is by the effect that training and service has on the way the neutrals in the program conduct themselves even when they are not serving as neutrals. The theory is that, once trained in ADR service, the neutrals will approach their other professional work (e.g., for lawyers, the other cases they litigate) with both the tools and the spirit of the ADR process in which they have been "indoctrinated."

We also confront something of a mixed picture when we examine the models' relative capacity to attract neutrals who have the appropriate set of attributes. While I am inclined to give a slight edge to the staff neutral model, there are so many factors at play here that I have little confidence in this feeling. Models that rely on essentially pro bono service by experienced professionals have attracted very high quality neutrals—at least when the court asks them to serve only a few times a year. And it is not clear why high quality people could not be recruited by a court that pays neutrals (or firms of neutrals) at approximately market rates. The model that inspires the least confidence from this perspective is the model in which the court requires litigants to find and pay a neutral from the private sector.

It is not clear which model promises the greatest ability to retain the services of high quality neutrals. The risk of "burn out" among staff neutrals may be real, but also may lend itself to exaggeration. The risk that volunteers who serve only occasionally will drift away from a program also is real—but its magnitude remains unclear. And while one would expect occasional volunteers to bring considerable enthusiasm and energy to their neutraling work, there is some risk that they will be distracted or pulled away by their "real" jobs before the ADR process has exhausted its capacity to benefit the parties. Courts that can sustain the flow of payment at market rates to professional service providers might be best able to retain the services of high quality neutrals over time—but it is not clear that there are many such courts, or, at least, that ADR programs so funded could afford to service significant numbers of cases.

The neutrals' motivation to give a lot of themselves to their work, and the influence of performance-enhancing incentives, appear greatest under the staff neutral model—and, perhaps, under the model in which the court pays the neutrals at or near market rates. On the other hand, potentially role distorting pressures also may be greatest under these models. The model in which the neutrals would appear to be least vulnerable to such pressures is the model in which the court arranges to have an outside organization orchestrate the delivery of the ADR services. The staff neutral model probably creates the greatest risk that the parties will equate the neutral with the court—an equation that could either enhance or distort how the parties behave in the ADR process.

The staff neutral model is clearly superior to most others in the two remaining arenas I have considered. This model promises to develop more sophisticated neutrals (people with more refined and sensitive process skills, and a wider range of neutraling tools) faster than any other model—save, perhaps, a model under which a court pays market rates to professionals who work regularly in the ADR field. Neutrals working in these two models also are most likely, over time, to retain and to use appropriately their process skills and techniques.

The staff neutral model offers far and away the most reliable and least expensive performance quality control. It is under that system that courts can have the most confidence that the way their neutrals carry out their work conforms to the procedural protocols and rules the courts have established. Finally, adopting the staff neutral model also enables courts to avoid having to develop and administer potentially burdensome and intrusive systems for regulating service by providers from the private sector.

I close by re-acknowledging that I have not addressed a good many practical and other considerations that courts that are trying to choose between these models need to take into account. I hope, however, that this essay will prove useful—by helping policy makers identify for themselves the values that they want to play the dominant roles when they decide how to structure the delivery of ADR services in their court or court system.

Question

6.13 Judge Brazil argues, "No responsible court can place its imprimatur on, and send parties off to participate in, proceedings whose elements and basic character are unknown or out of control." He adds that courts can supervise their own staff mediators but not large lists of private neutrals. "It would only be by expending considerable resources monitoring and regulating the neutrals on an approved list that a court using this model could be reasonably confident that the neutrals were adhering closely to prescribed protocols and rules." (Brazil, 1999). Do you agree? Review the materials on regulating mediation (pp. 158-183). Which aspects of regulation could be eliminated for a court using solely staff mediators?

R. CHERNICK, H. BENDIX, AND R. BARRETT, PRIVATE JUDGING: PRIVATIZING CIVIL JUSTICE

2-4, 33 (1997)

CRITICISM OF PRIVATE JUDGING

Critics urge that private judging inhibits reform of the public system by providing alternative *fora* to the wealthy and to corporations. Its very existence (and growing popularity) thus harms the public and the courts. The easy availability of lucrative careers in private judging, combined with the drawing-off of some of the more interesting civil disputes into the private sector, are said to induce experienced judges to retire prematurely.

The availability of a convenient, albeit costly, alternative to the courts is thus seen as creating a two-tiered justice system, a private one for the wealthy and the public courts for the rest of society, much like public and private education (with all of the negative connotations for the public alternative).

Critics also suggest that private judges may tend to skew their decisions in favor of litigants and lawyers who are more likely to hire them in future cases, e.g., large corporations and law firms.

Sensitive ethical and disclosure issues are raised by repeated or simultaneous use in different cases of the same judges by a particular lawyer or firm. Perhaps the most troublesome criticism of true private judging is that the promise of high compensation encourages early retirement of the most talented sitting judges.

Support for Private Judging

Contrary to popular opinion, private judging is not only for the rich. About 30 percent of the privately-judged proceedings involved personal injury or domestic relations disputes. Many "consumer" lawyers cite the availability of private alternatives as an advantage to their less than wealthy clients because of the economy and efficiency of those processes.

Although it is argued that many California litigants have abandoned the public court system in favor of private justice, California enjoys a most vibrant "court reform" movement.

The [Institute for Social Analysis (ISA)] Study concluded that there is "no support to the idea that more judges are retiring early to do private judging and that there was no statistically significant difference between the average age at retirement by those who do private judging and those who do not." The Rand [Corporation] Study reached similar conclusions. . . . Since the parties choose the private judge and control the kind of procedures that will apply in the hearing, it is unsurprising that they are more likely to perceive the outcome as fair, and indeed the ISA study concluded that litigants had "extremely high perceptions of fairness and satisfaction with private judging on both sides of the case." Invariably, private judge proceedings are more civil and efficient than court trials. . . .

A fundamental tenet of our justice system is that it be open to public scrutiny. Although private judging is criticized for limiting public access to civil cases and for making judges less accountable to the public, California has changed private judging procedures to deal effectively with these issues. [. . . In California, Rule of Court 244 makes private judge proceedings public to the same degree they would be if conducted in a public courthouse. Nonetheless, such a proceeding—usually conducted in a lawyer's office or rented facilities such as a hotel meeting room—is inherently more private than a trial conducted in the county courthouse. . . .]

Private judging has also been criticized for enabling litigants to "leapfrog" up to five years of court congestion and thereby get into the appellate courts ahead of public litigants whose disputes arose at the same time. The effect of privately judged cases on our appellate courts is extraordinarily small given the modest number of true private-judged cases, according to ISA. . . .

To the extent the public system needs to be improved by appointing more judges, updating procedures or technology or building new courtrooms, the bar, the bench, court administrators and public officials should provide courts with the tools and resources they need. Nothing about private judging undermines these efforts. . . .

Questions

6.14 How persuasive do you find this defense of private judging? Compare the following statement by another California lawyer, Robert Raven (1988), former president of the ABA:

> True, private judging has the laudable goals of reducing delay and increasing the public's access to justice. However, the potential dangers of providing one system of justice for the affluent, and another for everyone else, should stimulate us all to improve our system of public justice. This 200-year-old system with vital safeguards cannot simply be replaced by private judging.

Is there a way to have one's cake and eat it too (that is, to have a high-quality system of public justice existing side by side with a private justice regime)?

6.15 In a survey of Los Angeles litigators, respondents criticized the courts' routine reference of discovery disputes to private judges. The private judges charged the parties from $250 to $500 per hour to resolve the discovery disputes (Chernick et al., 1997:48). Should there be more concern that private judges are used for discovery disputes than for rendering judgments? How much difference should it make that the courts, rather than the parties, decide that private providers should be used? Is there an inherent danger of cronyism? How could this be prevented?

References

ANSTAETT, Elizabeth (1991) "Is Settlement Conditioned on Vacatur an Option? Should It Be?," 1991 *J. Disp. Resol.* 87.

BARKAI, John, and Gene KASSEBAUM (1989) "Using Court-Annexed Arbitration to Reduce Litigant Costs and to Increase the Pace of Litigation," 16 *Pepp. L. Rev.* 543.

BERNSTEIN, Lisa (1993) "Understanding the Limits of Court-Connected ADR: A Critique of Federal Court-Annexed ADR Programs," 141 *U. Pa. L. Rev.* 2169.

BRAZIL, Wayne D. (1988) *Effective Approaches to Settlement: A Handbook for Lawyers and Judges.* Clifton, N.J.: Prentice-Hall Law & Bus.

——— (1990) "A Close Look at Three Court-Sponsored ADR Programs: Why They Exist, How They Operate, What They Deliver, and Whether They Threaten Important Values," *U. Chi. Legal F.* 303.

——— (1999) "Comparing Structures for the Delivery of ADR Services by Courts: Critical Values and Concerns," 14 *Ohio St. J. Disp. Resol.* 715.

CENTER FOR DISPUTE SETTLEMENT (1992) *National Standards for Court-Connected Mediation Programs.* Washington, D.C.: CDS.

CENTER FOR PUBLIC RESOURCES (1991) *Special Issue: ADR in the Courts,* 9 *Alternatives* (July).

CHERNICK, Richard (1989) "The Rent-a-Judge Option," *Los Angeles Lawyer,* Oct., p. 18, Nov., p. 19.

CHERNICK, Richard, Helen J. BENDIX, and Robert C. BARRETT (1997) *Private Judging: Privatizing Civil Justice.* Washington, D.C.: National Legal Center for the Public Interest.

CLARKE, Stevens, Laura DONNELLY, and Sara GROVE (1989) *Court-Ordered Arbitration in North Carolina: An Evaluation of Its Effects.* Chapel Hill: University of North Carolina Institute of Government.

COLE, Sarah, Craig McEWEN, and Nancy H. ROGERS (2003 & 2006 Supp.) *Mediation: Law, Policy, Practice* (2d ed.). St. Paul: West.

CPR LEGAL PROGRAM (1987) *ADR and the Courts: A Manual for Judges and Lawyers.* New York: Butterworth.

EDWARDS, Harry T. (1986) "Alternative Dispute Resolution: Panacea or Anathema," 99 *Harv. L. Rev.* 668.

FISCH, Jill E. (1991) "Rewriting History: The Propriety of Eradicating Prior Decisional Law Through Settlement and Vacatur," 76 *Cornell L. Rev.* 589.

FISS, Owen (1984) "Against Settlement," 93 *Yale L.J.* 1073.

GALANTER, Marc, and Mia CAHILL (1994) " 'Most Cases Settle': Judicial Promotion and Regulation of Settlements," 46 *Stan. L. Rev.* 1339.

GOLANN, Dwight (1989) "Making Alternative Dispute Resolution Mandatory: The Constitutional Issues," 68 *Or. L. Rev.* 487.

GOLDBERG, Stephen B., and Jeanne M. BRETT (1990) "Disputants' Perspectives on the Differences Between Mediation and Arbitration," 6 *Neg. J.* 249.

GRILLO, Trina (1991) "The Mediation Alternative: Process Dangers for Women," 100 *Yale L.J.* 1545.

HARVARD LAW REVIEW (1981) "The California Rent-a-Judge Experiment: Constitutional and Policy Considerations of Pay as You Go Courts," 94 *Harv. L. Rev.* 1592.

——— (1990) "Mandatory Mediation and Summary Jury Trial: Guidelines for Ensuring Fair and Effective Processes," 103 *Harv. L. Rev.* 1086.

HENSLER, Deborah R. (1990) "Court-Annexed ADR." In John H. Wilkinson, ed., *Donovan Leisure Newton & Irvine ADR Practice Book.* New York: Wiley.

KAKALIK, James S., et al. (1996) *An Evaluation of Mediation and Early Neutral Evaluation Under the Civil Justice Reform Act.* Santa Monica, CA: RAND Corp.

KATZ, Lucy (1993) "Compulsory Alternative Dispute Resolution and Volunteerism: Two-Headed Monster or Two Sides of the Coin?" 1993 *J. Disp. Resol.* 1.

KEILITZ, Susan, ed. (1993) *National Symposium on Court-Connected Dispute Resolution Research: A Report on Recent Research Findings—Implications for Courts and Future Research Needs.* Williamsburg, VA: National Center for State Courts.

KRITZER, Herbert M. (1991) *Let's Make a Deal.* Madison: University of Wisconsin Press.

LANDE, John (2002) "Using Dispute System Design Methods to Promote Good-Faith Participation in Court-Connected Mediation Programs," 50 *UCLA L. Rev.* 69.

MARSHALL, T. F. (1991) "Mandatory Mediation: Commentary from England," *Conflict Resol. Notes* (June): 8.

MAX, Eric (1990) *Bench Manual for the Appointment of a Mediator,* reproduced in 136 F.R.D. 499.

McEWEN, Craig A., and Richard J. MAIMAN (1989) "Mediation in Small Claims Court: Consensual Processes and Outcomes." In Kenneth Kressel, Dean G. Pruitt, and Associates, *Mediation Research.* San Francisco: Jossey-Bass.

McEWEN, Craig, and Elizabeth PLAPINGER (1997) "RAND Report Points Way to Next Generation of ADR Research," 3 *Disp. Resol. Mag.* 8 (Summer).

McGOVERN, Francis (1986) "Toward a Functional Approach for Managing Complex Litigation," 53 *U. Chi. L. Rev.* 440.

——— (1997) "Beyond Efficiency: A Bevy of ADR Justifications," 3 *Disp. Resol. Mag.* 12 (Summer).

MENKEL-MEADOW, Carrie (1991) "Pursuing Settlement in an Adversary Culture: A Tale of Innovation Co-Opted, or 'The Law of ADR,' " 19 *Fla. L. Rev.* 1.

METZLOFF, Thomas B., Don R. WILLETT, Jeffrey J. RICE, and Thom H. PETERS (1991) *Summary Juries in the North Carolina State Court System.* Durham: Duke Law School Private Adjudication Center.

NELLE, Andreas (1992) "Making Mediation Mandatory: A Proposed Framework," 7 *Ohio St. J. Disp. Resol.* 287.

PEARSON, Jessica, and Nancy THOENNES (1989) "Divorce Mediation: Reflections on a Decade of Research." In Kenneth Kressel, Dean G. Pruitt, and Associates, *Mediation Research.* San Francisco: Jossey-Bass.

PLAPINGER, Elizabeth, and Margaret SHAW (1992) *Court ADR: Elements for Program Design.* New York: Center for Public Resources Institute for Dispute Resolution.

PLAPINGER, Elizabeth, and Donna STIENSTRA (1996) *ADR and Settlement in the Federal District Courts.* Washington, D.C.: The Federal Judicial Center. New York: The CPR Institute for Dispute Resolution.

PROVINE, D. Marie (1986) *Settlement Strategies for Federal District Court Judges.* Washington, D.C.: Federal Judicial Center.

RAVEN, Robert D. (1988) "Private Judging: A Challenge to Public Justice," 74 *Am. B. A. J.* 8 (Sept.).

RESNIK, Judith (1982) "Managerial Judges," 96 *Harv. L. Rev.* 376.

——— (1994) "Whose Judgment? Vacating Judgments, References for Settlement, and the Role of Adjudication at the Close of the Twentieth Century," 41 *UCLA L. Rev.* 1471.

——— (1995) "Many Doors? Closing Doors? Alternative Dispute Resolution and Adjudication," 10 *Ohio J. Disp. Resol.* 211.

REUBEN, Richard C. (2007) "Tort Reform Renews Debate over Mandatory Mediation," 13 *Disp. Resol. Mag.* 13 (Winter).

RISKIN, Leonard L. (1991) "The Represented Client in a Settlement Conference: Lessons of *G. Heileman Brewing Co. v. Joseph Oat Corp.*," 69 *Wash. U. L.Q.* 1059.

ROLPH, Elizabeth, Eric MOLLER, and Laura PETERSON (1994) *Escaping the Courthouse: Private Alternative Dispute Resolution in Los Angeles.* Santa Monica: Rand Institute for Civil Justice.

SANDER, Frank E. A., ed. (1991) *Emerging ADR Issues in State and Federal Courts.* Chicago: ABA Section on Litigation.

——— (2007) "Another View of Mandatory Mediation," 13 *Disp. Resol. Mag.* 16 (Winter).

SANDER, Frank E. A., H. William ALLEN, and Deborah HENSLER (1996) "Judicial (Mis)Use of ADR? A Debate," 27 *U. Tol. L. Rev.* 885.

SHERMAN, Edward (1993) "Court-Mandated Alternative Dispute Resolution: What Form of Participation Should Be Required?" 46 *SMU L. Rev.* 2079.

SNAPP, Kent (1997) "Five Years of Random Testing Shows Early ADR Successful," 3 *Disp. Resol. Mag.* 16 (Summer).

SOCIETY OF PROFESSIONALS IN DISPUTE RESOLUTION (1990) *Mandated Participation and Settlement Coercion: Dispute Resolution as It Relates to the Courts.* Report 1 of the Law and Public Policy Committee of SPIDR.

STEMPEL, Jeffrey W. (1996) "Reflections on Judicial ADR and the Multi-Door Courthouse at Twenty: Fait Accompli, Failed Overture, or Fledgling Adulthood?" 11 *Ohio St. J. Disp. Resol.* 297.

TENEROWICZ, Matthew A. (1998) "'Case Dismissed'—or Is It? Sanctions for Failure to Participate in Court Mandated ADR," 13 *Ohio St. J. Disp. Resol.* 975.

WEINSTEIN, Jack B. (1996) "Some Benefits and Risks of Privatization of Justice Through ADR," 11 *Ohio St. J. Disp. Resol.* 241.

WELSH, Nancy A. (2001a) "The Thinning Vision of Self-Determination in Court-Connected Mediation," 6 *Harv. Neg. L. Rev.* 1.

——— (2001b) "Making Deals in Court-Connected Mediation: What's Justice Got to Do with It," 79 *Wash. U. L.Q.* 787.

WIEHL, Lis (1989) "Private Justice for a Fee: Profits and Problems," *N.Y. Times*, Feb. 17, p. B5.
WILKINSON, John H., ed. (1990) *Donovan Leisure Newton & Irvine ADR Practice Book.* New York: Wiley.
WISSLER, Roselle (1996) *Ohio Attorneys' Experience with and Views of Alternative Dispute Resolution Procedures.* Supreme Court of Ohio.
——— (2002) "Court-Connected Mediation in General Civil Cases: What We Know from Empirical Research," 17 *Ohio St. J. Disp. Resol.* 641.

Chapter 7

Confidentiality

A. INTRODUCTION

The defendant in an attempted murder trial claims that evidence from a mediation session will substantiate a claim of self-defense by showing that the defendant had reason to fear the victim. The outcome of the trial may hinge on whether the court excludes the evidence. At the same time, the outcome of future mediation may hinge on whether the parties are relaxed and candid as they negotiate. This, in turn, may be more likely if they are confident that what is said in mediation will not be used in a court or administrative process. Further, a lack of confidentiality may thin the ranks of those mediators who are wary of subpoenas. Absent confidentiality, a court-wise party may use mediation as an informal deposition of the unwary party. Can the courts and legislatures draw a line on confidentiality to promote candor while making evidence available to the courts and administrative agencies when the need is greatest (Section B)?

Use of mediation information in court or agency proceedings is only one aspect of confidentiality. Another is disclosure of this information in other contexts (Section C). In this situation, no one is being compelled to disclose or testify. Rather, a mediator or party wants to disclose, perhaps to talk with a friend, to teach a class on mediation, to contact the media, or to advise a judge who will rule on the case. Often the mediator and parties enter into an agreement to keep all communications confidential. Of course, at the time of the agreement none of them sees any reason not to maintain the agreement. Then, occasionally, something unforeseen occurs. Suppose that harm to nonparties could be avoided by reporting to a public official or alerting the affected person about what the parties said during the dispute resolution process. For example, one of the parties admits failing to maintain basic sanitation for a small child. Or the parties' discussion reveals that the automobile defect causing injury to the plaintiff may occur as well in other cars produced at this factory. Is the greater good served by maintaining the parties' expectations of secrecy or disclosing to others what was revealed at the dispute resolution session (Section D)?

Public access to dispute resolution sessions and records is another aspect of confidentiality (Section E). In an era of televised trials and legislative debates, laws that allow exclusion of all but the parties and neutrals from some dispute resolution sessions seem like a startling departure. This greater protection from the public eye may make dispute resolution especially attractive today and even a prerequisite to the frank exchanges needed to reach consensus. What is lost when discussion moves out of the public arena? For example, public officials and citizen groups argue openly for several years about the location of a freeway. Then they meet with a mediator in sessions closed to the news media and resolve their differences within a few days. Work on the freeway begins. Has the public gained or lost?

These are only a few of the competing values that ride on the decision concerning how much confidentiality should be afforded dispute resolution processes. In fact, the processes themselves are affected. Aspects of legal policy already discussed above, such as mandatory mediation, enforceability of mediated agreements, and conflict of interest, will be affected by decisions related to confidentiality. These provisions depend for their effectiveness on production of evidence from the mediation session. Sanctions for failing to negotiate in good faith, for example, will be imposed only when evidence of a lack of good faith has been put before the court.

The effort to achieve the appropriate balance between, on the one hand, policies favoring confidentiality and, on the other hand, policies favoring disclosure has created a complex labyrinth of confidentiality rights and obligations, riddled with exceptions. To get a full picture of the law regarding confidentiality, one must examine: contract law regarding secrecy agreements; court and agency rules and orders regarding nondisclosure of information from their mediation programs; statutory and common law privileges; statutes regarding duties to maintain confidentiality, duties to report or disclose, and duties to maintain public access; rules of procedure regarding discovery; rules of evidence; and common law doctrines regarding public access and limits on the enforceability of secrecy agreements. To keep it simple, we have divided these ethics provisions, rules, orders, statutes, and common law doctrines into parts:

- Rights to resist disclosure within legal proceedings (Part B);
- Obligations to maintain confidentiality (Part C); and
- Limits on confidentiality because of policies favoring
  - reporting or disclosing (Part D), or
  - public access (Part E).

B. RIGHTS TO RESIST DISCLOSURE WITHIN LEGAL PROCEEDINGS

The courts and other legal authorities with subpoena power are not bound by a confidentiality agreement among participants in a dispute resolution process. The key question in terms of whether statements made during a dispute resolution process can be disclosed later during legal proceedings is whether the communications are protected by a privilege. The focus of this section is on mediation. Absent a mediation privilege, the parties also might argue that disclosure of the mediation communications cannot be compelled during formal discovery under rules of procedure and would be excluded from evidence as compromise discussions under rules of evidence. But, they will often lose. The evidentiary exclusion for compromise discussions typically offers less protection than the privilege, as discussed below. And discovery is not limited to admissible evidence.

Evidentiary exclusions for compromise discussions. In most jurisdictions, negotiations concerning a disputed legal claim are not admissible in evidence to prove the claim or its amount (see Fed. R. Evid. 408 or comparable state rules). The "compromise discussion" exclusion is based on the policy of promoting settlement and a concern that the jury will give undue weight to an offer "motivated by a desire for peace rather than from any concession of weakness of position."* This rule applies to negotiations conducted with or without a mediator.

The rule results in exclusion of such negotiations under most, but not all, circumstances. The courts have commonly found the following outside the purview of the rule: information requested through the discovery process; negotiations not involving legal claims, such as those regarding family tranquility; negotiations of undisputed claims, such as when the parties agree on the amount owed but not the payment schedule; and evidence offered to prove something other than the claim or the amount, such as evidence to prove the bias of a witness or perhaps the guilt of a criminal defendant.

Privileges. A mediation privilege is often broader than an evidentiary exclusion and typically may be asserted to block compelled disclosure, not merely admission into evidence. Thus, it often applies in pretrial, discovery, and administrative proceedings not governed by the rules of evidence. Privilege statutes and rulings differ in several respects: who may assert or waive the privilege (the "holders" of the privilege); exceptions to the privilege; what programs or mediators are covered; and whether a court may order disclosure despite the privilege where the need for the evidence outweighs the purpose served by nondisclosure (whether the privilege is "qualified" as opposed to "absolute").

In deciding whether to recognize a mediation privilege, legislatures and courts weigh the need for the evidence against the importance of effective mediation and the utility of confidentiality in promoting the effectiveness of mediation.

Lawmakers have little evidence to guide them in assessing whether assurance of confidentiality is necessary to promote the frank discussion necessary to achieve settlement. Nor are there studies to buttress other arguments given for mediation confidentiality—that frequent subpoenas will thin the ranks of volunteer mediators; that otherwise parties will use mediation as a form of informal discovery, to the detriment of the legally naive party; and that the public will perceive testifying mediators as biased. In fact, mediation programs not covered by a privilege attract volunteer mediators and users and settle cases. It is possible that participants are largely unaware that their discussion may be disclosed or admissible at trial. Disclosures may be rare events because mediation programs commonly seek to preserve confidentiality through a variety of informal practices, such as discarding documentation that might later serve to refresh the mediator's recollection. In addition, they may resist subpoenas to their mediators, using the arguments discussed above.

Legislatures have been persuaded by the arguments in favor of a mediation privilege, without awaiting research, and about half have enacted mediation privileges covering a wide variety of mediation contexts. In 2002, the National Conference of Commissioners of Uniform State Laws approved the Uniform

*Fed. Rule Evid. 408 Advisory Committee Note.

Mediation Act, which provides for a mediation privilege that can be adopted by states (Appendix E). As of February 1, 2007, eight states (Vermont, Utah, Illinois, Iowa, Nebraska, New Jersey, Ohio, and Washington) and the District of Columbia have enacted the Uniform Mediation Act. The National Conference of Commissioners on Uniform State Laws amended the Act in 2003 to provide for a privilege in international commercial mediation (Appendix E). Absent a statutory mediation privilege, the courts sometimes recognize a common law mediation privilege. In the case that follows, the communications were not protected by a statutory privilege. The opinion demonstrates the balancing of interests that is at the basis of a decision to recognize a mediation privilege.

FOLB v. MOTION PICTURE INDUSTRY PENSION & HEALTH PLANS

16 F. Supp. 2d 1164 (C.D. Cal. 1998), aff'd, 216 F.3d 1082 (9th Cir. 2000)

PAEZ, United States District Judge.

Plaintiff Scott Folb contends that defendants discriminated against him on the basis of gender and retaliated against him because he objected when Directors of the Motion Picture Industry Pension & Health Plans (the "Plans") violated fiduciary duties under the Employee Retirement Income Security Act of 1974. . . . Defendants allegedly relied on a complaint that Folb had sexually harassed another employee, Vivian Vasquez, as a pretext to discharge him for his whistle-blowing activities. . . .

In approximately February 1997, Vasquez and the Plans attended a formal mediation with a neutral in an attempt to settle Vasquez' potential claims against defendants arising out of the alleged sexual harassment. Vasquez and the Plans signed a contract agreeing to maintain the confidentiality of the mediation and all statements made in it. Vasquez' counsel prepared a mediation brief and provided copies to opposing counsel and to the mediator. The parties apparently did not reach an agreement during the mediation. After the mediation, counsel presumably engaged in further settlement negotiations and the parties ultimately settled Vasquez' potential claims against the Plans. At some point, counsel for the Plans, Lawrence Michaels of Mitchell, Silberberg & Knupp, provided Saxe [, the attorney retained by the Plans to investigate Vasquez' sexual harassment claim,] with a copy of the mediation brief. Neither Vasquez nor her attorneys, Hadsell & Stormer, authorized the Plans to provide a copy of the mediation brief to Saxe.

Saxe refused to produce the mediation brief in response to Folb's subpoena, asserting that the confidentiality of the brief is protected under Fed. R. Evid. 408 and Cal. Evid. Code §1119. Likewise, Hadsell & Stormer refused to produce either the mediation brief or documents relating to settlement negotiations with the Plans on behalf of Vasquez. Folb sought to compel production of (1) Vasquez' mediation brief; (2) correspondence between Vasquez' counsel and counsel for the Plans regarding mediation or other settlement discussions; and (3) notes to the file prepared by Vasquez' counsel regarding settlement communications. Folb argues that the Plans are trying to take a position in this litigation that is inconsistent with the position he believes they took in settlement negotiations with Vasquez. Folb suggests that the Plans will argue that he was properly terminated for sexually harassing Vasquez, despite the fact that they may have argued in mediation or settlement negotiations with Vasquez that she was never sexually harassed at all. Magistrate Judge Woehrle denied Folb's motion to compel production, and Folb filed the pending Objections. . . .

While the Court concludes that the magistrate judge did not err in ruling that the motion to compel production of the mediation brief should be denied, the legal foundation for that ruling must comport with the analysis set forth in the Supreme Court's decision in *Jaffee v. Redmond,* 581 U.S. 1 . . . (1996). . . . In addition, the Court finds that Folb is entitled to discover information relating to any settlement negotiations conducted after the conclusion of the formal mediation session. . . .

2. Applicable Law

. . . Because the mediation brief and the communications relating to settlement negotiations between the Plans and Vasquez are arguably relevant to both plaintiff's federal and state law claims, the Court must determine whether state or federal law controls disclosure. Federal Rule of Evidence 501 provides:

> Except as otherwise required by the Constitution of the United States or provided by Act of Congress or in rules prescribed by the Supreme Court pursuant to statutory authority, the privilege of a witness, person, government, State, or political subdivision thereof shall be governed by the principles of the common law as they may be interpreted by the courts of the United States in the light of reason and experience. However, in civil actions and proceedings, with respect to an element of a claim or defense as to which State law applies the rule of decision, the privilege of a witness, person, government, State, or political subdivision thereof shall be determined in accordance with State law. . . .

Because [, under rulings in the Ninth Circuit,] the federal common law of privileges governs both federal and pendent state law claims in federal question cases, the Court must decide whether to adopt a federal mediation privilege under Fed. R. Evid. 501.

3. Federal Mediation Privilege

The federal courts are authorized to define new privileges based on interpretation of "common law principles . . . in the light of reason and experience." *Jaffee,* 518 U.S. at 8. . . . The general mandate of Rule 501 was substituted by the Congress for a set of privilege rules drafted by the Judicial Conference Advisory Committee on Rules of Evidence and approved by the Judicial Conference of the United States and by [the Supreme] Court. . . . In rejecting the proposed Rules and enacting Rule 501, Congress manifested an affirmative intention not to freeze the law of privilege. Its purpose rather was to provide the courts with the flexibility to develop rules of privilege on a case-by-case basis . . . and to leave the door open to change. . . . Nonetheless, that authority must be exercised with caution because the creation of a new privilege is based upon considerations of public policy. In general, the appropriate question is not whether a federal mediation privilege should exist in the abstract, but whether "(1) the need for that privilege is so clear, and (2) the desirable contours of that privilege are so evident, that it is appropriate for this [c]ourt to craft it in common law fashion, under Rule 501." . . .

The general rule is that the public is entitled to every person's evidence and that testimonial privileges are disfavored. . . . To determine whether an asserted privilege constitutes such a public good, in light of reason and experience, the Court must consider (1) whether the asserted privilege is "rooted in the imperative need for confidence and trust[;]" (2) whether the privilege would serve public ends; (3) whether the evidentiary detriment caused by exercise of the privilege is modest; and (4) whether denial of the federal privilege would frustrate a parallel privilege adopted by the states.

A. NEED FOR CONFIDENCE AND TRUST

. . . Rule 408 provides that "[e]vidence of conduct or statements made in compromise negotiations is [ ] not admissible." Viewed in combination with Fed. R. Civ. P. 26(b), Rule 408 only protects disputants from disclosure of information to the trier of fact, not from discovery by a third party. Consequently, without a federal mediation privilege under Rule 501, information exchanged in a confidential mediation, like any other information, is subject to the liberal discovery rules of the Federal Rules of Civil Procedure, at least where jurisdiction is premised on a federal question and the material sought in discovery is relevant to the federal claims presented.

To determine whether there is a need for confidentiality in mediation proceedings, the Court looks first to judicial and Congressional pronouncements on the issue. No federal court has definitively adopted a mediation privilege as federal common law under Rule 501. In one of the leading cases on the treatment of confidential communications in mediation, however, the Ninth Circuit approved revocation of a subpoena that would have required a Federal Mediation and Conciliation Service ("FMCS") mediator to testify in a National Labor Relations Board ("NLRB") enforcement proceeding. *National Labor Relations Board v. Joseph Macaluso,* 618 F.2d 51, 52 (9th Cir. 1980). Relying on United States policy favoring resolution of labor disputes through collective bargaining and on Congress' creation of government facilities for mediation, the Ninth Circuit in *Macaluso* concluded that "the public interest in maintaining the perceived and actual impartiality of federal mediators does [] out-weigh the benefits derivable from [the mediator's] testimony." . . .

The Ninth Circuit's conclusion that requiring a federal mediator to disclose information about the mediation proceedings would inevitably impair or destroy the usefulness of the FMCS in future proceedings is equally applicable in the context of private mediation. Admittedly, the express federal interest in preserving a labor mediation system establishes a stronger basis for a mediator privilege in the context of NLRB proceedings. Nonetheless, mediation in other contexts has clearly become a critical alternative to full-blown litigation, providing the parties a more cost-effective method of resolving disputes and allowing the courts to keep up with ever more unmanageable dockets.

Focusing on the role of the mediator, the *Macaluso* court emphasized that "the purpose of excluding mediator testimony . . . is to avoid a breach of impartiality, not a breach of confidentiality." *Macaluso,* 618 F.2d at 56 n.3. Nevertheless, rules protecting the confidentiality of mediation proceedings and rules protecting the actual or perceived impartiality of mediators serve the same ultimate purpose: encouraging parties to attend mediation and communicate openly and honestly in order to facilitate successful alternative dispute resolution. . . .

Given the facts presented by the parties before the Court, we need only consider whether communications between parties who agreed in writing to participate in a confidential mediation with a neutral third party should be privileged and whether that privilege should extend to communications between the parties after they have concluded their formal mediation with the neutral. . . .

Legal authority on the necessity of protecting confidential communications between the parties to a mediation is sparse. . . . Taking the foregoing authorities en masse, the majority of courts to consider the issue appear to have concluded that the need for confidentiality and trust between participants in a mediation proceeding is sufficiently imperative to necessitate the creation of some form of privilege. This conclusion takes on added significance when considered in conjunction with the fact that many federal district courts rely on the success of ADR proceedings to minimize the size of their dockets. . . . [The pending federal ADR bill] provides additional evidence of the important federal and public interest in protecting confidential communications in court-ordered mediation*. . . . The proliferation of federal district court rules purporting to protect the confidentiality of mediation and the ADR Bill now pending before the United States Senate indicate a commitment to encouraging confidential mediation as an alternative means of resolving disputes that would otherwise result in protracted litigation. . . .

B. PUBLIC ENDS

A new privilege must serve a public good sufficiently important to justify creating an exception to the "general rule disfavoring testimonial privileges." . . . The proposed blanket mediation privilege would serve public ends by encouraging prompt, consensual resolution of disputes, minimizing the social and individual costs of litigation, and markedly reducing the size of state and federal court dockets. . . . Idealism aside, a mediation privilege would serve important public ends by promoting conciliatory relationships among parties to a dispute, by reducing litigation costs and by decreasing the size of state and federal court dockets, thereby increasing the quality of justice in those cases that do not settle voluntarily.

C. EVIDENTIARY DETRIMENT

In assessing the necessity of adopting a new privilege, the courts must consider whether "the likely evidentiary benefit that would result from the denial of the privilege is modest." *Jaffee,* 581 U.S. at 11-12. In *Jaffee,* the Supreme Court reasoned that in the absence of psychotherapist-patient privilege, "much of the desirable

*The bill referenced in this opinion was subsequently enacted. 28 U.S.C. §651 et seq.

evidence to which litigants . . . seek access — for example, admissions against interest by a party — is unlikely to come into being. This unspoken 'evidence' will therefore serve no greater truth-seeking function than if it had been spoken and privileged." *Id.* at 12. The same rationale applies with respect to party admissions in mediation proceedings.

[T]here is very little *evidentiary* benefit to be gained by refusing to recognize a mediation privilege.

First, evidence disclosed in mediation may be obtained directly from the parties to the mediation by using normal discovery channels. For example, a person's admission in mediation proceedings may, at least theoretically, be elicited in response to a request for admission or to questions in a deposition or in written interrogatories. In addition, to the extent a party takes advantage of the opportunity to use the cloak of confidentiality to take inconsistent positions in related litigation, evidence of that inconsistent position only comes into being as a result of the party's willingness to attend mediation. Absent a privilege protecting the confidentiality of mediation, the inconsistent position would presumably never come to light.

Although the Court need not, and indeed may not, address the outer limits of a federal mediation privilege, it seems appropriate to note one potential limitation here. A federal mediation privilege may be attenuated of necessity in criminal or quasi-criminal cases where the defendant's constitutional rights are at stake. . . .

D. MEDIATION PRIVILEGE IN THE 50 STATES

In assessing a proposed privilege, a federal court should look to a consistent body of state legislative and judicial decisions adopting such a privilege as an important indicator of both reason and experience. *Jaffee,* 518 U.S. at 12-13. . . . At the forefront of the inquiry, however, is the fact that every state in the Union, with the exception of Delaware, has adopted a mediation privilege of one type or another. . . . [T]his Court finds it is appropriate, in light of reason and experience, to adopt a federal mediation privilege applicable to all communications made in conjunction with a formal mediation.

E. CONTOURS OF THE PRIVILEGE

[T]he mediation privilege adopted today applies only to information disclosed in conjunction with mediation proceedings with a neutral. . . . On the facts presented here, the Court concludes that communications to the mediator and communications between parties during the mediation are protected. In addition, communications in preparation for and during the course of a mediation with a neutral must be protected. Subsequent negotiations between the parties, however, are not protected even if they include information initially disclosed in the mediation. To protect additional communications, the parties are required to return to mediation. A contrary rule would permit a party to claim the privilege with respect to any settlement negotiations so long as the communications took place following an attempt to mediate the dispute. . . .

Questions

7.1 The Court assumes that candor and therefore the effectiveness of mediation depend on assurance that mediation communications will not be disclosed through the discovery process and, presumably, the rest of the litigation process. Suppose a researcher could document that mediation settlement rates are the same in jurisdictions that recognize a mediation privilege and those that do not. Could a mediation privilege then be justified?

7.2 The Court stops short of protecting communications after mediation concludes. Why shouldn't negotiations without a mediator also be protected from disclosure? What about letters sent between counsel while the mediation is still pending? Would it matter what the letters said? What about videotapes or witness statements prepared for mediation?

Note: The "Holder" of the Privilege

As legislatures have enacted statutory privileges, they have designated different "holders" of the privilege (those who can raise or waive it): the parties, the mediator, the parties and the mediator; or each participant as to statements made in mediation by that participant. In *Folb,* attorneys for the parties raised the privilege. In *Joseph Macaluso,* cited in the *Folb* opinion, representatives of both parties already had testified about what had transpired during the mediation session when the mediator asserted a privilege. If the privilege had been intended solely to protect the parties' expectations of confidentiality, the privilege should have been waived by the testimony presented by the parties. For example, in the analogous attorney-client privilege, the client's testimony waives the privilege and the attorney can also be forced to testify. In contrast, the *Joseph Macaluso* court, cited in *Folb,* held that the mediator had an independent right to assert the privilege, at least with respect to his own testimony. By making the mediator a "holder" of the privilege, the court recognized that the federal mediation agency, or the process of mediation itself, might be furthered by protecting against disclosure, even when the parties sought it. The Uniform Mediation Act makes the mediator, the parties, and nonparty participants all holders to some extent (Section 5, Appendix E).

The more persons deemed to be holders of the privilege, the greater is the likelihood that disclosure will not be compelled.

Questions

7.3 The issue of whether to recognize a common law mediation privilege was also raised in the U.S. District Court for the District of Columbia in *Mack Truck v. United Auto Workers.* The collective bargaining negotiations had been conducted by private attorneys acting as mediators, William Hobgood and Bill Usery. Lawyers for the company issued a subpoena duces tecum to the mediators for depositions, in preparation for a preliminary injunction hearing scheduled just two weeks later in another federal district. At the hearing, key issues would include whether the parties had reached agreement during mediation and the terms of any agreement reached.

The mediators balked. Judge Thomas F. Hogan held an expedited hearing in response to motions by lawyers for the company and the mediators and he ruled from the bench.

Read the excerpts from the oral arguments and be prepared to rule on the mediators' motion for a protective order. Keep in mind that you may need to decide who "holds" the privilege and whether there should be an exception to the privilege for oral settlements.

The court began with a question concerning assurances of confidentiality.

*Counsel for the Mediators:** [T]he standard in the industry . . . is so clear that confidentiality is assumed. . . . I'm sure if Mr. Usery had picked up the phone and broadcast what went on in those mediation sessions, we would see Mack Truck in this court but in a completely different role and deservedly so, too. . . .

Plaintiff's Counsel: [T]o the extent the discussion concerning Mr. Usery's engagement covered the matter of confidentiality, it was clearly in the context that . . . matters which each of the parties discussed with Mr. Usery or with his associate, Mr. Hobgood, . . . would be kept in confidence from the other party. There was no discussion or, indeed, no understanding . . . that the entire process—and particularly the results of that process—would be forever confidential.

The Court: You agree you don't have any prior decisions extending this "privilege" to private mediators in the Federal labor law sector?

Counsel for the Mediators: Where private mediators were specifically before the court? Not in a Federal law sector, [but the federal courts are] free to look to the tradition of the common law for that, or as the court in *Macaluso* did, develop a federal common law privilege. . . .

Plaintiff's Counsel: The issue that we are here to seek testimony on is the ultimate question of whether agreement was reached between the parties. We are not looking for any testimony on the deliberative process or on the bargaining position of the U.A.W. . . .

The Court: . . . As I understand, reading the material submitted to me, . . . what [the Union] submitted to their locals and was ratified was different than that which *Mack* thinks the agreement consisted of, and that these are essential items that go to the heart of any agreement [and] that you would have to question Usery whether or not those are covered and what he thought was covered or not by the agreement. That's my concern. How do you handle it?

. . . It's easy to say "Mr. Usery, was there an agreement?" He says "Yes." The next question is "What did it consist of?" And then the debate starts.

[W]hy is it [important] that we allow the deposition of Mr. Usery and Mr. Hobgood? . . .

Plaintiff's Counsel: [D]espite the fact that the deponent's testimony or briefs describe what we seek as basically a tie-breaker, . . . it's a tie-breaker in the most critical sense. All of our testimony would be that of our own parties and all of the U.A.W.'s testimony would be that of its parties. . . .

Defense Counsel: . . . Our view of the problem that we have is that Mr. Usery's testimony would certainly impede the possibility of a settlement in this case

*The arguments have been reordered in this excerpt.

because his knowledge of the dispute, his testimony, is going to impact upon the perceived impartiality that he might have, and it really will preclude him from continuing to serve as a mediator in a position where he certainly is knowledgeable and can be of great assistance to the parties in an attempt to settle this dispute.

The Court: Where do you go if you have a scenario where there is an announced public agreement? The mediator announces it to the press. They have an agreement. It's made public and then one side says "Oh, no, we don't have an agreement," and one of their principal evidentiary matters would be calling the person who announced there was an agreement. . . . How can that be privileged?

Counsel for the Mediators: [T]hat defeats the entire purpose of mediation. [I]f a dispute arose over what are the terms of that agreement, that calls for the mediation to continue rather than try to shift the mediator from his neutral position into a position where he becomes an adjudicator or an arbitrator.

Plaintiff's Counsel: Here we have a situation of an employer with over 8,000 members of the U.A.W. whose futures are very much dependent upon the outcome of this dispute, as is the future of Mack Trucks. It's clear [that] the public and the employees and the company want to know the answer and that Mr. Usery and Mr. Hobgood can provide critical testimony in that regard.

7.4 What is the rationale for extending a privilege to mediators who are not employed by a public agency and who are selected by the parties? Is that rationale applicable to the mediation of all disputes or only to the mediation of collective bargaining disputes?

7.5 Suppose, as suggested in the argument, having promised confidentiality, Mr. Usery broadcast what went on in the mediation sessions. Rulings regarding doctors and other professionals suggest that the mediator might be liable for breaching the promised confidentiality. What different interests must be weighed in determining, on the one hand, whether to hold the mediator liable and, on the other hand, whether a subpoena is enforceable against the mediator?

7.6 Suppose that the union and the company both sought to have the mediator testify, but the mediator invoked the privilege. Would that make any difference in the result?

7.7 Absent exceptions, statutes that make mediation confidential may make it impossible to introduce evidence necessary to enforce oral agreements, the issue raised in *Mack Truck,* or to secure sanctions for violations of mediation-related rules or statutes. Would exceptions for each of the situations listed below allow admission of so much evidence from the mediation session that they would render the mediation privilege useless? For each, is it more important to maintain the confidentiality of mediation or facilitate enforcement of these laws?

a. Duties to negotiate in good faith during the mediation session;

b. A grievance against a mediator alleging violation of an established standard of conduct;

c. Defense to enforcement of an agreement reached in mediation alleging that the mediator failed to make certain disclosures or gave erroneous information to one of the parties.

Courts recognize the potential for injustice whenever a privilege is recognized. What would have been the cost of recognizing a privilege in the case below?

STATE v. CASTELLANO

460 So. 2d 480 (Fla. App. 1984)

GRIMES, ACTING CHIEF JUDGE.

The state seeks to appeal an order denying its motion to quash respondent's deposition subpoena of Roger Mallory.

The respondent was charged with attempted first degree murder. In responding to a demand for discovery, the state listed Mallory as a person having information about the case. The respondent subpoenaed Mallory for the taking of his deposition. Mallory is a mediator in the Citizens Dispute Settlement Program (CDSP) in the Tenth Judicial Circuit. The respondent asserts that Mallory will be able to testify that during the course of mediation the person who became the victim of the alleged attempted murder made life-threatening statements to the respondent. He maintains such testimony will support his contention of self-defense. The state filed a motion to quash the deposition subpoena urging that statements made to CDSP mediators were privileged. The court denied the motion to quash. [P]rivileges in Florida are no longer creatures of judicial decision. . . .

In this case, the state argues for privilege on two grounds. First, the state contends that communications made by parties in the CDSP are privileged as being in the nature of offers of compromise. However, the rule protecting offers of compromise appears to be one more of admissibility than privilege. . . .

Alternatively, the state asserts that since the CDSP is an investigatory arm of the state attorney, the privilege accorded to statements made to a prosecuting attorney should be extended to those made to a CDSP mediator. We know of no rationale to make such an extension. The parties to a CDSP program are simply attempting to resolve a dispute so that a criminal prosecution will be unnecessary. All statements are made voluntarily by persons under no legal compulsion to attend. The record reflects no authority for the mediator's statement that the parties' communications were confidential. The fact that he may have advised the parties that their communications would be held confidential does not now excuse him from being compelled by respondent to testify concerning what was said.

There is no legal basis for a privilege which would prevent the respondent from obtaining Mallory's testimony. If confidentiality is essential to the success of the CDSP program, the legislature is the proper branch of government from which to obtain the necessary protection. . . .

Questions

7.8 Would the *Folb* court have recognized a common law mediation privilege if faced with these facts? What additional interests must be weighed in this case?

7.9 Subsequent to the *Castellano* trial, Florida enacted a statute (Fla. Stat. Ann. §44.201(5)) providing in part:

> Any information relating to a dispute obtained by any person while performing any duties for the [Citizen Dispute Settlement Center] from the files, reports, case summaries, mediator's notes, or other communications or materials is exempt from the provisions of [the State Public Records Act].

A subsequent provision defines mediation communications as confidential and prohibits a mediation participant (i.e., party) from disclosing mediation communications. A mediation party may also "refuse to testify and to prevent any other person from testifying in a subsequent proceeding regarding mediation communications." Fla. Stat. Ann. §44.405. What suggestions do you have to improve the statute, with respect to:

1. Who holds the privilege?
2. Whether the privilege should apply in criminal cases?
3. Whether the privilege should be "qualified" (as opposed to "absolute"), authorizing the courts to order disclosure if the potential for injustice is great and outweighs the purpose served by preventing disclosure?

Compare your suggested statute with the Uniform Mediation Act (Appendix E). Why did the drafters take a different approach?

1. *Accommodating the Interests of Justice: Predictability Versus Fine Tuning*

If the *Castellano* mediation took place today, the pertinent Florida mediation privilege statute would not authorize the court to enforce the subpoena. Defense counsel would be left with the argument that the criminal defendant's constitutional rights require the privilege to yield (see *Davis v. Alaska,* 415 U.S. 308 (1974) (confidentiality of juvenile record must yield to a criminal defendant's rights to confront witnesses)).

Of course, a state could deal with the compelling need for evidence in criminal cases like *Castellano* by enacting a mediation privilege that is applicable only to civil proceedings. California did just that. In the case below, U.S. Magistrate Judge Wayne Brazil (a supporter of mediation and author of the article on p. 428) considers whether a statutory mediation privilege should yield to a strong need for evidence even in a civil case.

OLAM v. CONGRESS MORTGAGE COMPANY

68 F. Supp. 2d 1110 (N.D. Cal. 1999)

Wayne D. Brazil, United States Magistrate Judge.

The court addresses in this opinion several difficult issues about the relationship between a court-sponsored voluntary mediation and subsequent proceedings whose purpose is to determine whether the parties entered an enforceable agreement at the close of the mediation session.

As we explain below, . . . the parties participated in a lengthy mediation [of a case involving the federal Truth in Lending Act and related state and federal claims] that was hosted by this court's ADR Program Counsel [, Mr. Herman] — an employee of the court who is both a lawyer and an ADR professional. At the end of the mediation (after midnight), the parties signed a "Memorandum of Understanding" (MOU) that states that it is "intended as a binding document itself. . . ." Contending that the consent she apparently gave was not legally valid, plaintiff [, Mrs. Olam,] has taken the position that the MOU is not enforceable. She has not complied with its terms. Defendants have filed a motion to enforce the MOU as a binding contract.

One of the principal issues with which the court wrestles, below, is whether evidence about what occurred during the mediation proceedings, including testimony from the mediator, may be used to help resolve this dispute. . . .

[What Law Applies to the Use of Evidence from the Mediation]

Counsel for plaintiff [, Mrs. Olam,] contended that the parties must be presumed . . . to have entered the mediation process expecting federal law to serve as the source of the protection of the confidentiality of the mediation proceedings. Plaintiff further argued that such expectations were reasonable and that it would be unfair not to honor them.

In support of that contention, plaintiff emphasized that the mediation took place expressly under the auspices of this court's ADR program — and that there has been in effect in this court for a good many years a local rule that purports to fix the terms under which mediation confidences will be protected. . . .

The core problem in plaintiff's approach is that it ignores the express provision of Federal Rule of Evidence 501 that appears to be applicable here. That provision . . . directs that "in civil actions and proceedings, with respect to an element of a claim or defense as to which State law supplies the rule of decision, the privilege of a witness . . . shall be determined in accordance with State law." Defendants' motion to enforce the settlement agreement is a civil proceeding in which state law, and only state law, provides the rule of decision. The only question that motion raises is whether the parties entered an enforceable contract at the conclusion of the mediation — and the rule of decision for resolving this one substantive question will have only one source — the substantive law of the state of California.

Given these undisputed and foreseeable circumstances, the parties should have understood, before their mediation, that if, later, one party initiated proceedings designed to secure a determination that the mediation produced an enforceable settlement contract disputes about the confidentiality of mediation communications would be resolved in those proceedings by applying the law of the state of California. . . .

[Who Holds the Privilege]

California law confers on mediators a privilege that is independent of the privilege conferred on parties to a mediation. By declaring that, subject to exceptions not applicable here, mediators are incompetent to testify "as to any statement, conduct, decision, or ruling, occurring at or in conjunction with [the mediation]," section 703.5 of the Evidence Code has the effect of making a mediator the holder of an independent privilege. Section 1119 of the Evidence Code appears to have the same effect—as it prohibits courts from compelling disclosure of evidence about mediation communications and directs that all such communications "shall remain confidential." As the California Court of Appeal recently pointed out, "the Legislature intended that the confidentiality provision of section 1119 may be asserted by the mediator as well as by the participants in the mediation." It follows that, under California law, a waiver of the mediation privilege by the parties is not a sufficient basis for a court to permit or order a mediator to testify. Rather, an independent determination must be made before testimony from a mediator should be permitted or ordered. . . .

[T]he court announced that it would proceed on the assumption that Mr. Herman [, the mediator,] was respectfully and appropriately asserting the mediator's privilege and was formally objecting to being called to testify about anything said or done during the mediation. . . .

[Weighing the Need for Evidence and the Interest in Protecting Confidentiality]

In [*Rinaker v. Superior Court*, 62 Cal. App. 4th 155 (3d Dist. 1998),] the Court of Appeal held that there may be circumstances in which a trial court, over vigorous objection by a party and by the mediator, could compel testimony from the mediator in a juvenile delinquency proceeding [deemed a "civil" matter under California law]. The defendant in the delinquency proceeding wanted to call the mediator to try to impeach testimony that was expected from a prosecution witness. That witness and the delinquency defendant had earlier participated in a mediation—and the delinquency defendant believed that the complaining witness had made admissions to the mediator that would substantially undermine the credibility of the complaining witnesses' testimony—and thus would materially strengthen the defense. In these circumstances, the *Rinaker* court held that the mediator could be compelled to testify if, after in camera consideration of what her testimony would be, the trial judge determined that her testimony might well promote significantly the public interest in preventing perjury and the defendant's fundamental right to a fair judicial process. . . .

[T]he court is to weigh and comparatively assess (1) the importance of the values and interests that would be harmed if the mediator was compelled to testify (perhaps subject to a sealing or protective order, if appropriate), (2) the magnitude of the harm that compelling the testimony would cause to those values and interests, (3) the importance of the rights or interests that would be jeopardized if the mediator's testimony was not accessible in the specific proceedings in question, and (4) how much the testimony would contribute toward protecting those rights or advancing those interests—an inquiry that includes, among other things, an assessment of whether there are alternative sources of evidence of comparable probative value. . . .

Like many other variables in this kind of analysis, however, the magnitude of these risks can vary with the circumstances. Here, for instance, all parties to the mediation want the mediator to testify about things that occurred during the mediation—so ordering the testimony would do less harm to the actual relationships developed than it would in a case where one of the parties to the mediation objected. . . .

We acknowledge, however, that the possibility that a mediator might be forced to testify over objection could harm the capacity of mediators in general to create the environment of trust that they feel maximized the likelihood that constructive communication will occur during the mediation session. But the level of harm to that interest likely varies, at least in some measure, with the perception within the community of mediators and litigants about how likely it is that any given mediation will be followed at some point by an order compelling the neutral to offer evidence about what occurred during the session. . . . [T]his case represents the first time that I have been called upon to address these kinds of questions in the more than fifteen years that I have been responsible for ADR programs in this court. Nor am I aware of the issue arising before other judges here. Based on that experience, my partially educated guess is that the likelihood that a mediator or the parties in any given case need fear that the mediator would later be constrained to testify is extraordinarily small.

That conviction is reinforced by another consideration. As we pointed out above, under California law, and this court's view of sound public policy, there should be no occasion to consider whether to seek testimony from a mediator for [the] purpose of determining whether the parties entered an enforceable settlement contract unless the mediation produced a writing (or competent record) that appears on its face to constitute an enforceable contract, signed or formally assented to by all the parties. Thus, it is only when there is such a writing or record, and when a party nonetheless seeks to escape its apparent effect, that courts applying California law would even consider calling for evidence from a mediator for purposes of determining whether the parties settled the case. Surely these circumstances will arise after only a tiny fraction of mediations.

The magnitude of the risk to values underlying the mediation privilege . . . that can be created by ordering a mediator to testify also can vary with the nature of the testimony that is sought. . . .

[T]he kind of testimony sought from the mediator in this case poses less of a threat to fairness and reliability values than the kind of testimony that was sought from the mediator in *Rinaker*. During the first stage balancing analysis in the case at bar, the parties and I assumed that the testimony from the mediator that would be most consequential would focus not primarily on what Ms. Olam said during the mediation, but on how she acted and the mediator's perceptions of her physical, emotional, and mental condition. The purpose would not be to nail down and dissect her specific words, but to assess at a more general and impressionistic level her condition and capacities. That purpose might be achieved with relatively little disclosure of the content of her confidential communications. . . .

The interests that are likely to be advanced by compelling the mediator to testify in this case are of considerable importance. . . .

The first interest we identify is the interest in doing justice. For reasons described below, the mediator is positioned in this case to offer what could be crucial, certainly very probative, evidence about the central factual issues in this matter. . . .

In sharp contrast, refusing to compel the mediator to testify might well deprive the court of the evidence it needs to rule reliably on the plaintiff's contentions—and thus might either cause the court to impose an unjust outcome on the plaintiff or disable the court from enforcing the settlement. In this setting, refusing to compel testimony from the mediator that may address its condition and capacities might end up being tantamount to denying the motion to enforce the agreement—because a crucial source of evidence about the plaintiff's condition and capacities would be missing. Following that course, defendants suggest, would do considerable harm not only to the court's mediation program but also to fundamental fairness. If parties believed that courts routinely would refuse to compel mediators to testify, and that the absence of evidence from mediators would enhance the viability of a contention that apparent consent to a settlement contract was not legally viable, cynical parties would be encouraged either to try to escape commitments they made during mediations or to use threats of such escapes to try to renegotiate, after the mediation, more favorable terms—terms that they never would have been able to secure without this artificial and unfair leverage. . . .

[ENFORCEABILITY OF THE MEMORANDUM OF UNDERSTANDING]

[The court reviews the evidence, including the mediator's testimony, and concludes:] Because plaintiff has failed to prove either of the necessary elements of undue influence, and because she has established no other grounds to escape the contract she signed on September 10, 1998, the court grants defendants' Motion to Enforce the settlement contract that is memorialized in the MOU.

Note on "Qualified" vs. "Categorical" Privilege

If one likes Judge Brazil's balancing approach, a logical statutory approach would be to propose a "qualified" mediation privilege statute that specifically authorizes the court to do what Judge Brazil did in *Olam*—to weigh the need for evidence in the individual case against the purposes served by the privilege (see La Rev. Stat. §9:4112(B)). A disadvantage of a qualified privilege is the parties' inability, at the time of mediation, to predict the need for evidence, and therefore whether their statements at the mediation will be admitted into evidence. Another statutory option is a "categorical" approach in which the privilege is stated in absolute terms but the statute sets out a series of exceptions that reflect an a priori weighing of confidentiality versus the likely need for evidence of this type. The categorical approach permits the parties to gauge the breadth of confidentiality at the time of the mediation, at least to the extent that the exceptions yield clear results. Even these exceptions do not improve predictability, however, if they depend on the use made later of the evidence, such as whether it is offered in a child protection proceeding, or if they depend in part on the need for the evidence. In 2001 the National Conference of Commissioners on Uniform State Laws approved a Uniform Mediation Act (Appendix E), which takes a "categorical" approach for the most part. The Act contains nine exceptions. However, the drafters could not resist introducing a balancing test for two of the exceptions. In addition, some exceptions apply only in some kinds of proceedings. Had the Act been applicable to the mediation in *Olam*, the pertinent provisions would have been the following:

UNIFORM MEDIATION ACT

SECTION 6. EXCEPTIONS TO PRIVILEGE.

(b) There is no privilege under Section 4 if a court, administrative agency, or arbitrator finds, after a hearing in camera, that the party seeking discovery or the proponent of the evidence has shown that the evidence is not otherwise available, that there is a need for the evidence that substantially outweighs the interest in protecting confidentiality, and that the mediation communication is sought or offered in: . . .

(2) except as otherwise provided in subsection (c), a proceeding to prove a claim to rescind or reform or a defense to avoid liability on a contract arising out of the mediation.

(c) A mediator may not be compelled to provide evidence of a mediation communication referred to in subsection . . . (b)(2). . . .

Were the Uniform Law Commissioners right to exempt the mediator from testifying?

2. *Conflict of Laws*

The Uniform Mediation Act also responds to another issue raised by the *Olam* case: certainty at the time of the mediation about what jurisdiction's privilege law will apply to mediation. In *Olam,* one party claimed surprise that the privilege for a federal court mediation would be governed by California law, especially when some of the substantive claims in the case were based in federal law. Ellen Deason terms these "vertical" conflicts (Deason, 2002). The Uniform Mediation Act (see Appendix E), if widely adopted by the states, deals with a comparable "horizontal" problem across state jurisdictions. The Reporter's Notes explain:

> Uniformity of the law helps bring order and understanding across state lines, and encourages effective use of mediation in a number of ways. First, uniformity is a necessary predicate to predictability if there is any potential that a statement made in mediation in one State may be sought in litigation or other legal processes in another State. Without uniformity, there can be no firm assurance in any State that a mediation is privileged.
>
> A second benefit of uniformity relates to cross-jurisdictional mediation. Mediation sessions are increasingly conducted by conference calls between mediators and parties in different States and even over the Internet. Because it is unclear which State's laws apply, the parties cannot be assured of the reach of their home state's confidentiality protections.
>
> A third benefit of uniformity is that a party trying to decide whether to sign an agreement to mediate may not know where the mediation will occur and therefore whether the law will provide a privilege or the right to bring counsel or support person.

Uniformity will add certainty on these issues, and thus allows for more informed party self-determination.

Finally, uniformity contributes to simplicity. Mediators and parties who do not have meaningful familiarity with the law or legal research currently face a more formidable task in understanding multiple confidentiality statutes that vary by and within relevant States than they would in understanding a Uniform Act. Mediators and parties often travel to different States for the mediation sessions. If they do not understand these legal protections, participants may react in a guarded way, thus reducing the candor that these provisions are designed to promote, or they may unnecessarily expend resources to have the legal research conducted.

Questions

7.10 What is gained by the Uniform Mediation Act (Appendix E) in terms of the parties' ability to predict whether their mediation discussions will be used in legal proceedings? How would you suggest changing the Act to enhance predictability? Would it be better if the Act just authorized the courts to weigh the interests (confidentiality versus need for evidence) in each case, as Judge Brazil did in *Olam*?

7.11 Judge Brazil has referred your client's federal claim to mediation before the federal district court mediator. The federal court local rule simply prohibits use of mediation communications in any court proceeding. If California has enacted the Uniform Mediation Act (Appendix E), what advice should you give to your client about the extent of confidentiality for that session? Should it make any difference if there are pendent state claims (see *Folb*, p. 444)? If there are uncertainties at the time of mediation about what mediation privilege law will govern whether communications must be disclosed, how can those uncertainties be reduced?

7.12 A bill containing the Uniform Mediation Act (Appendix E) has been introduced in your state legislature. What would be gained or lost if your state modified the Act to make the parties the only holders of the privilege?

7.13 Under the Uniform Mediation Act (Appendix E), what protection does a mediation party have if another participant makes important false statements?

7.14 Are there constitutional issues that need to be kept in mind when drafting a mediation privilege statute? See, e.g., *Davis v. Alaska*, 415 U.S. 308 (1974) (confidentiality of juvenile records must yield to a criminal defendant's right to confront witnesses).

7.15 Under the law in state *A*, statements made during mediation are privileged only if the mediator has completed 30 hours of "training in mediation." If Joan Mowry takes a law school dispute resolution course of 32 class hours before mediating her first case, is it accurate for her to begin the session with the statement, "This mediation is confidential"? Would it matter whether the case might be tried in federal court if no settlement results? Compare, e.g., *United States v. Gullo*, 672 F. Supp. 99 (W.D.N.Y. 1987) (federal court applying New York mediation privilege in criminal case), with *Matter of International Horizons, Inc.*, 689 F.2d 996 (11th Cir. 1982) (federal bankruptcy court refusing to apply state accountant-client privilege). What exactly *should* Mowry say to the parties about confidentiality?

C. THE NEUTRAL'S OBLIGATION TO MAINTAIN CONFIDENTIALITY

The hardest fought battles regarding a neutral's obligation to maintain confidentiality have occurred in the context of mediation. Throughout the four-year drafting process for the Uniform Mediation Act, some argued that mediators should have a statutory obligation to maintain the confidentiality of mediation communications. Of course, even without such a statute, some mediators must maintain confidentiality because they have promised to do so or because they are governed by ethics or court rules requiring them to keep the communications secret. Other mediators must keep mum because of a court order. The argument was that mediators who had never promised and were operating outside of ethics rules or court programs should also have that responsibility. For example, two neighbors agree in writing that a third neighbor should mediate their driveway dispute, stating that they want the mediation to be privileged but saying nothing about keeping it secret. A statutory confidentiality provision might make the third neighbor liable for disclosures to a fourth neighbor. Should casual mediators be required to know the obligations imposed by law on them?

A sizeable group urged the drafters to impose a similar secrecy obligation on all participants in the mediation process, even if they had not agreed to maintain the confidentiality of the process and had not been ordered by a court to keep the discussions secret. The result might be that a person attending a community mediation and then telling a friend about what was said could be held responsible for that disclosure's adverse consequences on others.

Ultimately, the drafters were hesitant to impose general confidentiality obligations through statute (see Section 8, Uniform Mediation Act, Appendix E), noting that such a statute might penalize those who were unaware of it and that existing contractual, ethical, or legal obligations provided adequate protection (see Sections 7 and 8 and Reporter's Notes, Uniform Mediation Act, Appendix E). They made one exception. The Uniform Mediation Act prohibits mediators from reporting to judges who will rule in the dispute if it is not settled (Section 7).

At heart, the arguments in favor of confidentiality obligations rest on a desire of parties, mediators, and policymakers to assure the parties that there will be no serious repercussions if they speak candidly during mediation. This "off the record" discussion, many think, will lead to a settlement that eluded the parties during their more guarded discussions. Translating the goal of protecting the parties' expectations into law has proved difficult. What are the advantages and disadvantages of letting the parties "opt in" to confidentiality through an agreement rather than providing by statute that the mediator and parties must maintain confidentiality unless they "opt out"? Does it matter whether the source of the disclosure is the mediator or one of the parties? When should the parties' secrecy agreement be unenforceable (see Reporter's Note to Section 8, Uniform Mediation Act, Appendix E)?

1. *Confidentiality Agreements and Protective Orders*

Mediation confidentiality agreements provide an avenue for increasing confidentiality. Rulings in other settings (see *Cohen v. Cowles Media Co.*, 501 U.S. 663 (1991)) indicate that breaching such a confidentiality agreement may result in liability. In the event of a subpoena, the situation is uncertain. If construed by the court to be an agreement to suppress evidence, the mediation confidentiality agreement would be against public policy and unenforceable against the subpoena. Further, as a contract, it is unenforceable against nonparties to the agreement.

As a result of uncertain enforcement by courts, parties often try to increase the certainty of protection against a subpoena by incorporating the confidentiality agreement into a joint request for a protective order. Once the agreement is issued as a court order, the party seeking the information must convince the court to set aside the protective order as either lacking in justification or serving a purpose outweighed by the need for the information.

If only one party seeks a protective order against a discovery request regarding statements made in a mediation session, Rule 26(c) of the Federal Rules of Civil Procedure and comparable state discovery rules provide the framework for the court to balance the burdensome nature of the request against the need of the party seeking disclosure.

2. *Ethical and Legal Obligations*

Ethical codes for mediators typically require them to maintain the parties' reasonable expectations regarding confidentiality (see, e.g., Model Standards of Practice for Family and Divorce Mediation VII, Appendix G; Model Standards of Conduct for Mediators V, Appendix H). The codes are relatively new, but some carry serious consequences for mediators. A mediator may lose certification to mediate in certain contexts. In addition, as the codes gain acceptance as standards for sound practice, one can expect that the parties will seek damages when the mediator harms them through actions that violate the code.

When mediation is court-annexed, the courts often do not leave it up to the parties to contract not to disclose. Courts, acting either by court rule or court order, also often require the mediators, and sometimes even the parties, to be mum about what was said in mediation. Consequences of violating that order can be severe. In a Florida case, the court, citing its rule as well as the parties' agreement and a statute, dismissed the complaint of a plaintiff who told the media about an offer made by the defendant during mediation (*Paranzino v. Barnett Bank of South Florida*, 690 So. 2d 725 (Fla. Dist. Ct. App. 1997)). Perhaps surprisingly, then, many parties and some mediators violate state statutes or local court rules protecting the confidentiality of mediation communications (Coben & Thompson, 2006) (reporting that between 1998 and 2003, 22 reported cases involved party challenges to testimony offered by mediators).

Sometimes the statutes or rules prohibit the mediator from disclosing to those persons within the same organization who might prosecute or rule on the case. This prohibition promotes candor and keeps the mediator from threatening disclosure in order to pressure settlement (see pp. 405-406). For example, the U.S. Justice Department mediators for civil rights cases are prohibited by statute from disclosing mediation information, even to other units of the Justice Department, and their violation of this statute carries criminal penalties (42 U.S.C. §2000g-2(b)). As a result, the parties can be candid without fear that the disclosures will be used for prosecution. The Uniform Mediation Act prohibits a mediator from disclosing mediation communications to a judge or other authority who may rule in the dispute that is being mediated (Section 7, Uniform Mediation Act, Appendix E). In these two examples, the wall between mediation and legal consequences could not be achieved simply by agreement of the parties. Absent a statute, the prosecutors and courts might require the mediators to disclose.

D. LIMITS ON CONFIDENTIALITY BECAUSE OF POLICIES FAVORING REPORTING OR WARNING

Communications in dispute resolution processes are susceptible not only to subpoena but also to reporting laws. For example, state statutes often require social workers or other professionals to notify specified authorities when they learn about harm to children, the elderly, or others. Neutrals may have a common law duty to prevent harm, sometimes requiring them to warn potential victims. See, e.g., *Tarasoff v. Regents of University of California,* 17 Cal. 3d 425, 131 Cal. Rptr. 14, 551 P.2d 334 (1976).

Parties or mediators may want to disclose information either that is protected by privilege or that they previously agreed to keep secret. A Florida appellate court facing both a confidentiality agreement and a desire to warn others opted to enforce the confidentiality agreement. The dissenting appellate judge sets out the arguments favoring disclosure.

C. R. & S. R. v. E.

573 So. 2d 1088 (Fla. Dist. Ct. App. 1991)

Cobb, Judge, dissenting.

The issue posed by this appeal is whether the trial court erred in refusing to dissolve a temporary injunction entered against the appellants, the parents of a minor child. They were enjoined from communicating with the press or other third parties regarding the facts and findings of an arbitration proceeding administered by the Christian Conciliation Service of Central Florida, Inc. (CCS).

In 1983, the parents alleged that a Catholic priest had fondled or molested their minor daughter. The parties agreed to resolve the matter through the mediation/arbitration forum offered by CCS. [The CCS rules provide for confidentiality.] . . .

Following an unsuccessful mediation, the parties submitted to binding arbitration. Thereafter, on August 25, 1986, the CCS arbitrators reached a final decision with various findings of fact and conclusions of law. Generally, it was held that the priest had touched the daughter in an inappropriate manner on several occasions and that the Church was negligent in retaining and supervising him. Additionally, the arbitration panel found against the priest and the Church, jointly and severally, in the amount of $250,000.00. This amount was subsequently paid by the local Diocese to the parents within thirty days of the arbitration decision.

On April 18, 1988, counsel for the parents informed church counsel that they considered any confidentiality agreement to be null and void, and that they would maintain confidentiality only upon condition that they could meet with parish counsel in the priest's new assignment and with the Bishop of that area to discuss the underlying facts and findings of the arbitration panel as well as the possibility of a public apology.

On May 12, 1988, the priest filed an amended petition for a temporary and permanent injunction. . . .

I can agree with the trial judge that the priest may have established the threat of irreparable injury for which there would be no adequate remedy at law based upon the documents and evidence submitted below. It is the third requirement [that he has a clear legal right to the relief requested] that causes the difficulty: can the priest have a clear legal right to "confidentiality"—i.e., suppression of the facts—surrounding the criminality involved in child molestation? I think not. The requirement of confidentiality herein at issue is void as a matter of public policy. Section 415.504, Florida Statutes (1989) provides that "any person . . . who knows, or has reasonable cause to suspect, that a child is . . . abused . . . shall report such knowledge or suspicion to the (Department of Health and Rehabilitative Services). . . ." Moreover, a person who takes money on an agreement to conceal a felony is guilty of a third degree felony. See §843.14, Fla. Stat. (1989).

I believe it was error to grant the temporary injunction to the priest, and it should have been dissolved. It would seem to follow that the payment of the $250,000.00 award pursuant to a void arbitration proceeding predicated upon confidentiality cannot stand, unless it could be shown that such payment was the product of a settlement agreement between the parties that was not dependent upon the element of confidentiality, an issue not before us at this time. The order denying the motion to dissolve the temporary injunction should be reversed.

Questions

7.16 An attorney mediating a medical malpractice case asked plaintiff's counsel why he had sued the hospital but not the surgeon. Plaintiff's counsel replied that he "was the surgeon's attorney." The mediator then asked plaintiff's counsel to tell the court of his conflict of interest. When the lawyer failed to report the conflict, the mediator informed the court himself, despite the fact that the mediation was conducted under a confidentiality order. Plaintiff's counsel was found to have violated ethical duties and was suspended from the practice of law for 60 days. *In re Waller*, 573 A.2d 780 (D.C. App. 1990). Would the majority in *C. R. & S. R. v. E.* have ruled that the mediator should have been sanctioned for violating the order of confidentiality? How can this case be distinguished from *C. R. & S. R. v. E.*? Should confidentiality orders or agreements exempt statements evidencing a violation of ethical provisions or criminal laws? What would the mediator be permitted to report under the Uniform Mediation Act (Appendix E)?

7.17 The plaintiff was quoted in a magazine as saying that she had turned down the defendant's offer of $25,000 made during a mediation and cited the offer as evidence that the defendant bank felt that its case was "shaky." The court found that the plaintiff had deliberately violated the statute and rule regarding confidentiality in mediation, as well as a confidentiality agreement. The trial court struck her pleadings, and the appellate court affirmed. *Paranzino v. Barnett Bank of South Florida,* 690 So. 2d 725 (Fla. Dist. Ct. App. 1997). How would you distinguish the plaintiff's disclosure in this case from the disclosure by the mediator in the *Waller* case reported in question 7.16?

E. LIMITS ON CONFIDENTIALITY BECAUSE OF PUBLIC ACCESS RIGHTS

BANK OF AMERICA NATIONAL TRUST & SAVINGS ASSOCIATION v. HOTEL RITTENHOUSE ASSOCIATES

800 F.2d 339 (3d Cir. 1986)

SLOVITER, CIRCUIT JUDGE.

In this appeal, we are faced with an issue that this court has confronted with increasing frequency in recent years: under what circumstances documents filed in the district court may be sealed from public access.

I. FACTS AND PROCEDURAL HISTORY

The dispute that forms the basis for this case arose out of the construction of the Hotel Rittenhouse in Philadelphia. . . .

In 1981, the Bank of America (the Bank), contracted with Hotel Rittenhouse Associates (HRA) and other developers to finance the construction of the hotel. FAB III, the appellant here, was the concrete contractor on the project.

In June 1983, the Bank filed suit against HRA, its partners and some involved individuals (referred to collectively as HRA) in the United States District Court for the Eastern District of Pennsylvania to foreclose on the Hotel Rittenhouse property and to collect on a loan. . . .

In April 1984, FAB III filed suit in federal court against the Bank, but not against HRA, seeking over $800,000 on the basis of an alleged assurance by the Bank of direct payment for FAB III's HRA work. . . .

The Bank-HRA action proceeded to trial in January 1985. Before the case was sent to the jury, the parties reached a settlement and the jury was discharged. At the parties' request, the settlement agreement was filed under seal in the district court. Prior to this time, all proceedings in the litigation had been open to the public. . . .

On July 1, 1985, FAB III filed a complaint in state court against the Bank and HRA charging them with a continuing conspiracy to deny it money owed for its work on the Hotel Rittenhouse project. In that complaint, FAB III charges that as part of the conspiracy "the Bank and the Wolgin Group [HRA] agreed to seal certain portions of the otherwise public proceedings in the federal court action."

Shortly thereafter, FAB III filed a formal motion with the district court to unseal the settlement documents. . . . In a one-paragraph order, the court stated that it had weighed "the public interest in access to judicial records," as well as FAB III's interest in access to the settlement, against the "public and private interests in settling disputes" and found that the latter interest was paramount. FAB III appeals the denial of its motion to unseal. . . .

III. Discussion

FAB III bases its claim for access to the documents filed in the district court on the common law right of access, rather than on the First Amendment. The right of the public to inspect and copy judicial records antedates the Constitution. . . . Just as the right of access is firmly entrenched, so also is the correlative principle that the right of access, whether grounded on the common law or the First Amendment, is not absolute. . . . The burden is on the party who seeks to overcome the presumption of access to show that the interest in secrecy outweighs the presumption. . . .

The district court was cognizant that its decision required it to balance the factors favoring secrecy against the common law presumption of access. In denying FAB III's motion for access to the settlement documents, the court held that the "public and private interests in settling disputes" outweighed the "public interest in access to judicial records" and FAB III's private interest in knowing the terms of the settlement.

The balancing of the factors for and against access is a decision committed to the discretion of the district court. Thus, the issue before us is whether the district court abused its discretion in holding that the judicial policy of promoting the settlement of litigation justifies the denial of public access to records and proceedings to enforce such settlements.

We acknowledge the strong public interest in encouraging settlement of private litigation. Settlements save the parties the substantial cost of litigation and conserve the limited resources of the judiciary. In order to encourage the compromise and settlement of disputes, evidence of settlements or offers of settlement are ordinarily not admissible in federal proceedings. Thus, it is likely that had HRA and the Bank chosen to settle and file a voluntary stipulation of dismissal, as provided in Rule 41(a)(1) of the Federal Rules of Civil Procedure, they would have been able to prevent public, and even FAB III's, access to these papers. That is not the course the parties chose.

Instead, HRA and the Bank filed their settlement agreement in the district court, because, as they frankly concede, they anticipated that they would disagree on the terms, and would want recourse to the court. That, of course, is precisely what occurred. . . .

Having undertaken to utilize the judicial process to interpret the settlement and to enforce it, the parties are no longer entitled to invoke the confidentiality ordinarily accorded settlement agreements. Once a settlement is filed in the district court, it becomes a judicial record, and subject to the access accorded such records.

Such public access serves several of the important interests we identified in our earlier cases. First, it promotes "informed discussion of governmental affairs by providing the public with [a] more complete understanding of the judicial system" and the "public perception of fairness which can be achieved only by permitting full public view of the proceedings." Disclosure of settlement documents serves as a check on the integrity of the judicial process. . . . Even if we were to assume that some settlements would not be effectuated if their confidentiality was not assured, the generalized interest in encouraging settlements does not rise to the level of interests that we have recognized may outweigh the public's common law right of access. . . .

IV. Conclusion

We conclude that the district court abused its discretion in denying FAB III's motion to unseal the motions and settlement agreement papers. . . .

Garth, Circuit Judge, dissenting. . . .

II

As the majority recognizes, in deciding whether the common law right of access compels disclosure of materials before the court, the district court must "weigh[] the interests advanced by the parties in light of the public interest and the duty of the courts." This court has held that the common law right of access creates a presumption of access to all judicial records and documents. I therefore agree that, as a general matter, the common law right of access applies to settlement agreements when such agreements are filed with the court and become a part of the public record.

However, a settlement agreement that has never been disclosed to the public, but which was only entered into the record by the parties with the understanding that it would remain secret, presents a situation different from any situation that this court has addressed before. Although a presumption of access certainly arises when a court seals the transcript of a sidebar conference that has already taken place on the record in open court, or when a party seeks access to material already entered into evidence and provided to the jury, this case involves material and information that was *never* public, giving rise to a new and different factor: the reliance of the parties on the initial and continuing secrecy of the settlement agreement. . . .

I would . . . hold that where, as here, a settlement agreement has been filed with the court in reliance upon its being sealed, a third party who comes along after the fact bears the burden of establishing a "compelling need" or other "extraordinary circumstance" justifying access to the sealed agreement. I would further hold that because no such need or circumstance has been demonstrated, the burden has not been carried in this case, and the order of the district court should therefore be affirmed.

III

Even if I were to accept (which I do not) the majority's holding that the presumption in favor of access to judicial records still applies when a third party seeks to unseal a settlement agreement entered under seal and in reliance upon secrecy, I still could not agree to the majority's rule of law that the interest in settling cases cannot serve to rebut the presumption of access and therefore cannot justify the sealing of a settlement agreement. I believe that such a rule is completely out of touch with the reality of running a trial court docket—a reality with which our district court judges must wrestle every day—and if permitted to remain as the law of our circuit will wreak havoc with judicial efforts to encourage settlement of appropriate cases. . . .

A . . .

Although arbitration, mediation, mini-trials, and other forms of alternative dispute resolution have gained prominence in recent years as potent weapons in the war against litigation glut, the key component of every rational approach to reducing the burden on our clogged court dockets has been and remains settlement. With very rare exceptions, see Fiss, Against Settlement, commentators and judges who may concur on little else, agree on the value and necessity of a vigorous policy of encouraging fair and reasonable settlement of civil claims whenever possible. Indeed, the literature on the settlement of civil suits focuses not on whether settlement is desirable, but on how best to achieve it and how far a judge should go to encourage it. . . .

As any trial judge knows, the settlement of civil cases is not just a permissible and desirable goal, but a practical necessity. In one study of cases filed in ten courts, fully *88 percent* were settled; only nine percent went to trial.

B

While the importance of settlement would seem to be self-evident, I believe it is equally obvious that confidentiality is often a key ingredient in a settlement agreement—and that many settlements would not be reached if the secrecy of their terms could not be safeguarded. . . .

While few cases address the question of the sealing of settlement agreements, I suspect that this is because many trial judges regard it as self-evident that secrecy is often necessary and they therefore order settlement agreements filed under seal as a matter of course. . . .

Parties may have many reasons for desiring secrecy for the terms of their settlements.[4] Settlement agreements may include trade secrets or information that threaten the privacy of the parties. While this kind of information would itself justify a seal order, parties may in good faith be concerned about releasing a far wider range of information, including information which would not itself entitle the parties to a protective order, but which might stand in the way of settlement if required to be disclosed.

4. The majority suggests that parties seeking to keep their settlement terms secret should simply stipulate on the record to dismiss the case while negotiating a private settlement. However, this approach is not always practicable, since the parties may, as in the present case, require the further involvement of the court in enforcing the terms of the settlement: a more efficient mechanism than bringing an entirely new suit. Moreover, the court may require terms of settlement to be submitted for its approval as to their fairness and reasonableness. In addition, many settlements, particularly in the mass tort and other contexts may not be implemented without the court's assistance. This is especially so when payments and document exchanges are deferred over extended periods of time.

The necessity for confidentiality may be particularly acute in the mass tort area, where a defendant must look beyond the parameters of a settlement with a single plaintiff and anticipate the impact of its settlement on innumerable future cases. . . .

For example, if a defendant facing multiple plaintiffs seeks to settle a meritorious claim for a certain sum of money, it may be deterred from doing so if it knows that the terms of such a settlement would have to be made public. The defendant may reasonably assume that disclosure of the comparatively favorable settlement terms would interfere with its ability to settle other cases for smaller amounts. I have no doubt that if all such settlement details were by rule of law always public, many settlements would never take place at all. Many defendants would almost certainly proceed to trial rather than broadcast to all potential plaintiffs how much they might be willing to pay.

Moreover, it is precisely in the context of mass torts with multiple plaintiffs—such matters as air disasters, toxic injuries, and product liability claims—that the interest in settlement is particularly strong. Such cases are characteristically long, complex, and costly to try, and the savings in public and private resources achieved by settling them are immense. . . .

Under the majority's rule, a district court judge faced with the prospect of a six month, 12 month or longer trial, who is told by the parties that they would settle the case if the terms of settlement could be filed with the court under seal, would have only one choice—to reject the settlement and proceed to trial. The judge would have no discretion to accept the settlement under seal even if the proposed settlement contained little information of public interest and the interests of both sides of the dispute would be furthered by the settlement.

With all due respect to my colleagues in the majority, theirs is an illogical and impractical result. We are dealing here not with a constitutional right, but with a flexible common-law rule that has historically been applied subject to the discretion of the district court. Moreover, decisions regarding the management of its docket and the expediting of case resolutions would seem to lie at the core of the district court's discretionary powers. Therefore, assuming that a district court judge correctly weighs the public and private interests involved in deciding whether to order a settlement admitted under seal, I can see no reason why (contrary to the majority rule) the interest in encouraging settlement should not be entitled to due weight. Indeed, any other rule would improperly abridge the traditional discretion of the district judge and seriously impair the ability of judges to expedite settlement.

CINCINNATI GAS & ELECTRIC GAS CO. v. GENERAL ELECTRIC CO.

854 F.2d 900 (6th Cir. 1988)

KEITH, CIRCUIT JUDGE.

I

This appeal arises out of a lawsuit involving the design and construction of the William H. Zimmer Nuclear Power Plant ("Plant"). The plaintiffs below . . . were three Ohio electric utility companies that undertook jointly to build the Plant. In July of 1984, plaintiffs filed a lawsuit against the General Electric Company and Sargent & Lundy Engineers (defendants-appellees), an architectural and engineering firm, alleging breach of contractual duties and common law concerning the modification of the Plant. . . .

From the outset of this litigation, the parties recognized the need for confidential treatment of much of the material that would be produced in discovery. As a result, the parties negotiated a comprehensive protective order, which the magistrate approved on December 6, 1984. . . .

On June 26, 1987, the district court issued an order requiring the parties to participate in a summary jury trial scheduled to commence on September 8, 1987. The order included a provision closing the proceeding to the press and public. . . .

On September 4, 1987, appellants [*The Cincinnati Post*] moved to intervene in the underlying action for the limited purpose of challenging the order closing the summary trial. On September 14, 1987, the district court denied appellants' motion to intervene, holding that they had no right to attend the summary jury trial. The court observed that "[t]he summary jury trial, for all it may appear like a trial, is a settlement technique." . . .

II

The precise issue before us is whether the first amendment right of access attaches to the summary jury proceeding in this case. Appellants argue that the district court erred in refusing to allow them to intervene for the purpose of attending the summary jury trial proceeding. Appellants specifically argue that: (1) the summary jury proceeding is analogous in form and function to a civil or criminal trial on the merits, and therefore, the first amendment right of access which encompasses civil and criminal trial and pre-trial proceedings also encompasses the summary jury proceedings; and (2) public access would play a significant positive role in the functioning of the judicial system and summary jury trials. . . .

The Supreme Court has in recent years decided a number of cases dealing with the right of access.

In *Press-Enterprise II* the Court held that a qualified right of access applied in criminal proceedings to a preliminary hearing which was conducted before a magistrate in the absence of a jury. The Court held that the analysis of a first amendment claim of access involves two "complementary considerations." First, the proceeding must be one for which there has been a "tradition of accessibility." . . . Second, public access must play a "significant positive role in the functioning of the particular process in question." Moreover, even if these elements are satisfied, the right of access is a qualified one and must be outweighed by a strong countervailing interest in maintaining the confidentiality of the proceedings.

With regard to the first part of the test, we concur with the district court that "there is no historically recognized right of access to summary jury trials in that this mechanism has been in existence for less than a decade." The summary jury trial is a device that is designed to settle disputes. Settlement techniques have historically been closed to the press and public. Thus, we find that "while the history of the summary jury trial is limited, there is general agreement that historically settlement techniques are closed procedures rather than open."

Appellants argue that summary jury trials are structurally similar to ordinary civil jury trials, which have historically been open to the public. However, it is clear that while the summary jury trial is a highly reliable predictor of the likely trial outcome, there are manifold differences between it and a real trial.

At every turn the summary jury trial is designed to facilitate pretrial settlement of the litigation, much like a settlement conference. It is important to note that the summary jury trial does not present any matter for adjudication by the court. Thus, we find appellants' argument to be unpersuasive and therefore hold that the "tradition of accessibility" element has not been met.

The second criterion in the Court's public access analysis is whether access "plays a significant positive role in the functioning of the particular process in question." Appellants contend that public access would have community therapeutic value because of the importance of the nuclear power and utility rate issues raised. We disagree. [W]here a party has a legitimate interest in confidentiality, public access would be detrimental to the effectiveness of the summary jury trial in facilitating settlement. Thus, public access to summary jury trials over the parties' objections would have significant adverse effects on the utility of the procedure as a settlement device. Therefore, allowing access would undermine the substantial governmental interest in promoting settlements, and would not play a "significant positive role in the functioning of the particular process in question."

Appellants' claim of a public "right to know" has no validity with regard to summary jury trials. As the lower court correctly noted, the public would have no entitlement to observe any negotiations leading to a traditional settlement of the case, and the parties would be under no constitutional obligation to reveal the content of the negotiations. Thus, the public has no first amendment right to access to the summary jury trial.

Appellants also argue that the summary jury trial should be open to the public because the facilitation of a settlement between the parties has a final and decisive effect on the outcome of the litigation. To support their argument, appellants rely on the Court's language in *Press-Enterprise II,* that preliminary criminal hearings must be open to the public because of their decisive effect on criminal cases. We disagree.

In contrast to the summary proceedings in this case, the proceeding at issue in *Press-Enterprise II* resulted in a binding judicial determination which directly affected the rights of the parties. Summary jury trials do not present any matters for adjudication by the court. Thus, it is the presence of the exercise of a court's coercive powers that is the touchstone of the recognized right to access, not the presence of a procedure that might lead the parties to voluntarily terminate the litigation. Therefore, we find appellant's argument to be meritless.

Accordingly, for the reasons set forth above, we affirm the judgment. . . .

George Clifton Edwards, Jr., Senior Circuit Judge, concurring in part and dissenting in part.

The proceeding conducted in this case resulted in a settlement and a court decree. It resembled both settlement negotiations and a bench trial. While I join the majority in holding that the negotiations which led to the settlement of this case could properly be conducted in camera, I do not agree that the record can appropriately continue to be sealed after a settlement has been effected. . . .

Note

Given the growing attempts by the press and others to gain access to court proceedings and records (Miller, 1991), it is not surprising to see the same issues arising with respect to court-connected ADR processes. The cases pose the same tension between the parties' need for privacy (either to encourage settlement or for some other reason such as the protection of trade secrets) and the public's right to know. The answers in particular cases will depend on a complex interplay of a number of factors:

1. *Type of process.* In the *Cincinnati Gas* case, the court stressed that the summary jury trial was not an adjudicative process but a settlement process. There is less need to hold a third party accountable when that individual has no power to impose a decision on the disputants. With mediation, there is the additional concern that the power of the process depends on the ability of the mediator to explore in confidence with each party their real interests and concerns. Thus subjecting the process to public scrutiny may seriously impair its effectiveness.

A related issue concerns the connection between the dispute process and the court system. The case for openness is strongest in court-connected processes because they are publicly funded and directed, although *Cincinnati Gas* showed that that fact in itself is not dispositive. On the other hand, party negotiations before any case is filed in court are usually immune to public access, as most likely are purely private mediation and arbitration proceedings. Note in that connection the *Rittenhouse* majority's reliance on the fact that the settlement resulted in a court decree that was subsequently the basis of enforcement proceedings. But the presence of a decree was not deemed dispositive by the majority in *Cincinnati Gas.*

2. *Type of access sought.* As indicated above, permitting an outsider to attend a mediation proceeding may be very undesirable. But suppose the outsider wants only to look at the terms of the resulting settlement. That would represent much less of an intrusion into the mediation process, while perhaps still satisfying the public's "need to know." Still, even such limited access would be likely to lead to publicizing the settlement—usually the precise purpose of seeking access—and hence might preclude settlement in the first place, as Judge Garth points out in his *Rittenhouse* dissent.

Similar issues are presented in the resolution of public disputes outside of court.

After two years of public hearings and controversy over the location of the John Rolfe Parkway near Richmond, the Virginia Department of Transportation hired the Community Mediation Center to mediate. The Mediation Center convened a meeting of government and neighborhood representatives and asked them to try to agree on a joint recommendation to the state transportation agency. The group decided to exclude others, including the press, from the sessions and authorized the mediators to issue periodic public reports about their progress.

When excluded from the mediation session, the Richmond Newspapers filed suit in state court, asking that all persons attending the mediation session be enjoined from holding closed sessions. The newspaper argued that the Virginia Freedom of Information Act required open meetings when entities supported wholly or principally by public funds are created to advise a public body. The Department of Transportation countered, inter alia, that Virginia's mediation privilege created an exception from access requirements. While the trial court's refusal to grant the injunction was on appeal, the parties participated in a sixth private mediation session and reached agreement on recommendations for the siting and design of the John Rolfe Parkway. *Richmond Newspapers v. Robert P. Morris,* Record No. 90136 (Va. 1990).

If the resulting agreement is released to the public, is there any public interest served in promoting access to the mediation sessions themselves? If so, would periodic reports to the media by the mediator suffice?

3. *Nature of case.* The claim of public access is obviously much stronger if the dispute is a waste siting controversy affecting the entire community than if it is an ordinary divorce proceeding.

A related issue concerns the identity of the parties. If a government entity is one of the parties, then the case for public scrutiny becomes much stronger. In addition, as indicated above, open meeting laws sometimes come into play in these cases.

4. *Why access is sought.* In *Cincinnati Gas,* a newspaper was attempting to gain access to the summary jury trial. Suppose instead it had been a competitor of GE? Or a prosecutor who sought to gain evidence for presentation to a grand jury?

If a settlement has some of the indicia of a court decree (for example, because it is approved, interpreted, or enforced by a court), does that justify access? Consider the decision of a private judge in California (see pp. 436-437) whose decision has precedential value. Should that require that the proceedings be open?

5. *Importance of settlement.* As Judge Garth forcefully points out, given the congested state of the courts, the facilitation of settlement is always an important concern. But are there some cases where this is more so (for example, in a divorce case, because a consensual resolution may produce a "better" result for the children of a divorcing couple than an adjudicated one)?

Questions

7.18 Following the Sixth Circuit's ruling in *Cincinnati Gas & Electric,* a federal district court within that circuit orders a summary jury trial of the civil cases arising out of a prison riot in which ten persons were killed. The local newspaper seeks access, arguing that the public importance of this highly publicized event should be weighed in determining press access. How should the court rule? See *In re Cincinnati Enquirer,* 85 F.3d 255, vacated, 94 F.3d 198 (6th Cir. 1996).

7.19 A state ADR task force recently makes the following proposal regarding openness of ADR records and proceedings. Assume you are the chair of the State Bar ADR Committee that is asked to comment on this proposal. What changes would you suggest?

For court-connected proceedings:

- Adjudicative proceedings (e.g., court-annexed arbitration) should be presumptively open, and the outcome should normally be part of the publicly available record.

- Settlement procedures (for example, court-connected mediation and summary jury trial) should normally be private. Any resulting settlement should also normally be confidential, unless the court, for good cause shown, orders otherwise.

For private proceedings:

- Dispute proceeding and outcomes should normally not be open to the public.
- Where a court is called on to enforce the outcome of such proceeding, courts may review the proceeding to be sure it complied with procedural standards (for example, the parties were apprised of the desirability of recourse to an attorney).

7.20 Suppose you represent a company in a lawsuit against a competitor involving highly confidential trade information. Following preliminary settlement discussions, you see an acceptable settlement in the making. But it is extremely important to your client that the terms of the settlement not be disclosed. What would you do to facilitate such a result?

7.21 The Uniform Mediation Act makes an exception to the mediation privilege for mediation communications available under open records and meetings laws or made during a mediation session that is open to the public (Section 6(a)(2), Appendix E). Why should these mediation communications be available for legal proceedings?

7.22 A school superintendent and school board execute an agreement in which the superintendent agrees to resign on the condition that the school board keep confidential its investigation of the superintendent for sexual harassment. Under state law, an agreement regarding the resignation of a public official is a public record. After school board employees are quoted by the local newspaper as speaking about the sexual harassment allegations, the superintendent sues the school board. How should the court rule on the school board's motion for summary judgment?

References

ASSEY, James M., Jr. (1996) "Mum's the Word on Mediation: Confidentiality and *Snyder Falkinham v. Stockburger*," 9 *Geo. J. Legal Ethics* 991.

BERNARD, Phyllis E. (2001) "Only Nixon Could Go to China: Third Thoughts on the Uniform Mediation Act," 85 *Marq. L. Rev.* 113.

COBEN, James R., and Peter N. THOMPSON (2006) "Disputing Irony: A Systematic Look at Litigation about Mediation," 11 *Harv. Negot L. Rev.* 43.

COLE, Sarah, ROGERS, Nancy H., and Craig A. McEWEN (2003 & 2006 Supp.) *Mediation: Law, Policy, Practice* (2d ed.), Ch. 9. St. Paul: West.

CONFIDENTIALITY IN MEDIATION (1999) 5 *ABA Disp. Resol. Mag.* 4 (Winter).

DEASON, Ellen E. (2001) "Enforcing Mediated Settlement Agreements: Contract Law Collides with Confidentiality," 35 *U. Davis L. Rev.* 33.

——— (2001) "The Quest for Uniformity in Mediation Confidentiality, Foolish Consistency or Crucial Predictability?" 85 *Marq. L. Rev.* 79.

——— (2002) "Predictable Mediation Confidentiality in the U.S. Federal System," 17 *Ohio St. J. Disp. Resol.* 239.

DEITERS, Cynthia A., Note (1988) "A Setback for the Public Policy of Encouraging Settlements," *J. Disp. Resol.* 219.

FREEDMAN, Lawrence R., and Michael L. PRIGOFF (1986) "Confidentiality in Mediation: The Need for Protection," 2 *Ohio St. J. Disp. Resol.* 37.

FRIEDMAN, Eileen D. (1981) "Protection of Confidentiality in the Mediation of Minor Disputes," 11 *Cap. U. L. Rev.* 181.

GIBSON, Kent (1992) "Confidentiality in Mediation: A Moral Reassessment," 1992 *J. Disp. Resol.* 25.

GREEN, Eric (1986) "A Heretical View of Mediation Privilege," 2 *Ohio St. J. Disp. Resol.* 1.

HUGHES, Scott H. (2001) "The Uniform Mediation Act: To the Spoiled Go the Privileges," 85 *Marq. L. Rev.* 9.

KENTRA, Pamela A. (1997) "Hear No Evil, See No Evil, Speak No Evil: The Intolerable Conflict for Attorney-Mediators Between the Duty to Maintain Confidentiality and the Duty to Report Fellow Attorney Misconduct," 1997 *B.Y.U. L. Rev.* 715.

KIRTLEY, Alan (1995) "The Mediation Privilege's Transition from Theory to Implementation: Designing a Mediation Privilege Standard to Protect Mediation Participants, the Process and the Public Interest," *J. Disp. Resol.* 1.

KUESTER, Erin L., Comment (1995) "Confidentiality in Mediation: A Trail of Broken Promises," 16 *Hamline J. Pub. L. & Pol'y* 573.

LEATHERBURY, Thomas A., and Mark A. COVER (1993) "Keeping Public Mediation Public: Exploring the Conflict between Confidential Mediation and Open Government," 46 *SMU L. Rev.* 2221.

McCRORY, John P. (1988) "Confidentiality in Mediation of Matrimonial Disputes," 51 *Mod. L. Rev.* 442.

McISAAC, Hugh (2001) "Mediation Developments: Confidentiality Revisited: Californian Style," 39 *Fam. Ct. Rev.* 405.

MENKEL-MEADOW, Carrie (1993) "Public Access to Private Settlements: Conflicting Legal Policies," 11 *Alternatives High Cost Litig.* 85.

MILLER, Arthur R. (1991) "Confidentiality, Protective Orders, and Public Access to the Courts," 105 *Harv. L. Rev.* 427.

PRIGOFF, Michael L. (1988) "Toward Candor or Chaos: The Case of Confidentiality in Mediation," 12 *Seton Hall Legis. J.* 1.

PRYOR, Will, and Robert M. O'BOYLE (1993) "Public Policy ADR: Confidentiality in Conflict," 46 *SMU L. Rev.* 2207.

REICH, J. Brad (2001) "A Call for Intellectual Honesty: A Response to the Uniform Mediation Act's Privilege Against Disclosure," *J. Disp. Resol.* 197.

ROSENBERG, Joshua P. (1994) "Keeping the Lid on Confidentiality: Mediation Privilege and Conflict of Laws," 10 *Ohio St. J. Disp. Resol.* 157.

RUFENACHT, Mindy D. (2000) "Comment, The Concern Over Confidentiality in Mediation—An In-Depth Look at the Protection Provided by the Proposed Uniform Mediation Act," 85 *J. Disp. Resol.* 113.

SAID, Irene Stanley, Comment (1995) "The Mediator's Dilemma: The Legal Requirements Exception to Confidentiality Under the Texas ADR Statute," 36 *S. Tex. L. Rev.* 579.

SCHNEIDER, Andrea K. (2001) "Introduction: Which Means to an End Under the Uniform Mediation Act," 86 *Marq. L. Rev.* 1.

SUN, Jeffrey C. (1999) "University Officials as Administrator and Mediators: The Dual Role Conflict and Confidentiality Problems," *BYU Educ. & L.J.* 19.

SYKES, Andrew, Comment (1989) "*Cincinnati Gas & Electric v. General Electric:* Extinguishing the Light on Summary Jury Trials," 49 *Ohio St. L.J.* 1453.

TAYLOR, Garrett S. (2001) "Be Careful What You Say in Mediation," *J. Disp. Resol.* 375.

THOMPSON, Peter N. (1997) "Confidentiality Competency and Confusion: The Uncertain Promise of the Mediation Privilege in Minnesota," 18 *Hamline J. Pub. L. & Pol'y* 329.

WESTON, Maureen A. (2001) "Checks on Participant Conduct in Compulsory ADR: Reconciling the Tension in the Need for Good-Faith Participation, Autonomy, and Confidentiality," 76 *Ind. L.J.* 591.

ZYLSTRA, Alexandria (2001) "Privacy: The Road from Voluntary Mediation to Mandatory Good Faith Requirements: A Road Best Left Untraveled," 17 *J. Am. Acad. Matrimonial Law* 69.

PART IV

SELECTED APPLICATIONS

Chapter 8

Family Disputes

Most family disputes are resolved within the family, and without third-party involvement, by negotiation, mediation, and sometimes private adjudication (or more aptly parental fiat). Principles of family autonomy vis-à-vis the state underscore the desirability of such indigenous procedures, unless the protection of family members from serious harm warrants outside intervention.

In many situations, however, the family itself seeks outside help because family members are unable to resolve their own disputes. It is these disputes — between parents or between parents and children — that are our primary concern here.

Family disputes have a number of features that make them prime candidates for alternative dispute resolution methods. For instance, in family relations we are usually dealing with continuing and interdependent relationships. Hence, it is important that any dispute settlement system help to facilitate constructive relationships in the future, rather than lead to the exacerbation of existing problems. This is true even where the family is seeking to dissolve itself (that is, in the case of divorce). Even in such cases there will be continuing relations between the parties concerning financial and child-rearing questions. Lon Fuller (1971) observed that this continuing-relationship aspect of family controversies often necessitates "person-oriented" rather than "act-oriented" interventions.

Family disputes are also well suited to alternative forums because the conflicts often involve a complex interplay of emotional and legal complaints. It is sometimes difficult to discover the "real" issue in dispute. Thus, there may be a great need for an open-ended, unstructured process that permits the disputants to air their true sentiments. In addition, disputants often have such intense feelings that a question arises about whether the formal legal processes will be effective. Not infrequently disputants take the law into their own hands if they are dissatisfied with the results of adjudication. This suggests the desirability of maximizing the use of consensual processes that reflect the greatest commitment by the parties to the undertaking.

Given these dominant characteristics, it is not surprising that mediation has assumed particular importance in family cases as an alternative to the adjudicatory process. One reason is that mediation, as we have seen, looks to the future and has as a major goal the repair of the frayed relationship. Second, mediated solutions are more flexible than those brought about by adjudication because they are crafted by the parties themselves, albeit with the help of the mediator. Third, mediation avoids the winner-loser syndrome, a consideration that assumes special importance where an ongoing relationship is involved. Fourth, the mediation process involves a wide-ranging inquiry into what the interested parties want to talk about; it is not dominated by what the judge wants to hear about. Although mediation is not therapy, it can certainly be a therapeutic experience. It can also be an important learning experience. People who go through mediation appear to learn something about how better to handle conflicts that may arise in the future. Obviously this dispute-prevention aspect is critically important if one is dealing with continuing relationships. Finally, mediation gives an enhancing sense of participation to the disputants. Thus, they have a stronger commitment to the result that is reached. It is not surprising, therefore, to learn that compliance with mediated solutions is as good as with adjudicated ones (p. 156).

Our emphasis here will be on divorce mediation since that is where most of the recent developments have taken place. We begin with a brief description of an actual case, which is designed to give the reader a "feel" for the divorce mediation process in action. The case demonstrates the special role of mediation for the divorcing parents' children. Public concern for these children has led domestic courts in most states to refer contested parenting issues to mediation. The case is followed by an overview of policy issues. Research psychologist Jessica Pearson next summarizes studies regarding the effectiveness of these court mediation programs. This is followed by an article challenging the dominant approach of discouraging lawyers from attending divorce mediation sessions.

Mediation is also useful for disputes within the ongoing family. Students of family law will recall the famous case in which an older wife who had become tired of living a frugal lifestyle sued her penny-pinching husband for adequate support. The court threw out the case on the ground that it was not competent to adjudicate this kind of controversy (*McGuire v. McGuire,* 157 Neb. 226, 59 N.W.2d 336 (1953)). From a jurisprudential point of view, this may be a plausible result, given the limited ability of a court to investigate, resolve, and monitor this type of controversy. But what about poor Mrs. McGuire? Where should she take her entirely legitimate grievance? Perhaps if at that time Nebraska had had an institution like the Jewish Conciliation Board that mediates (or if necessary adjudicates) various kinds of family controversies, an effective remedy could have been provided (Yaffee, 1972). Similar issues frequently come up between parents and children. In Cambridge, Massachusetts, the Children's Hearings Project recruited and trained volunteers from the community to sit on panels to mediate parentchild disputes involving truancy, curfews, and other behavioral issues (Merry, 1987). The proceeding was patterned after a somewhat similar institution in Scotland (ABA, 1982:483). Mediation also is used as a preventive measure when marriages result in "blended" families (Mosten, 1996).

Arbitration is becoming a more common method of resolving domestic relations disputes. A number of jurisdictions enforce agreements to arbitrate spousal and child support issues. See, for example, *Kelm v. Kelm,* 623 N.E.2d 39 (Ohio 1993) (citing jurisdictions). Concerned primarily about the ability of the arbitration process to protect the best interests of the child, however, courts are more reluctant to enforce agreements to arbitrate child custody disputes. See *Glauber v. Glauber,* 600 N.Y.S.2d 740 (App. Div. N.Y. 1993). Among the reasons parties select arbitration to resolve their domestic relations disputes are that they wish to control decision-maker selection, ensure confidentiality, and limit judicial review. Ironically, limited judicial review is also perceived as a disadvantage of matrimonial arbitration. With limited judicial review, an arbitrator's failure to follow the law will go uncorrected. Another disadvantage of matrimonial arbitration is that courts may ignore arbitral finality by reviewing arbitral awards, particularly if the arbitration involved child custody issues. Despite these disadvantages, parties are increasingly interested in drafting pre-dispute arbitration clauses in their pre-nuptial and post-nuptial agreements. In what situations would the balance of competing interests lead you to recommend an arbitration agreement to an engaged or divorcing couple?

Not all types of family disputes are amenable to dispute resolution. Section C includes discussion of the appropriateness of using mediation to resolve cases involving spouse abuse.

Finally, family members, like other disputants (see pp. 405-406), hesitate to use dispute resolution in the midst of a dispute. For this reason, most domestic relations court mediation programs involve compulsory participation by the parties (Pearson, 1994). Here, as elsewhere, parties can anticipate their own intransigence by agreeing to mediate in advance of the dispute. We conclude this chapter with a discussion of mediation clauses.

A. DIVORCE MEDIATION PRACTICE

J. HAYNES, DIVORCE MEDIATION

102-109 (1981)

Bea and Ben: Why the Children Cannot Be Left Out

Bea and Ben have been married for seventeen years. They have two children, a daughter, Alice (age sixteen) and a son, Sam (age fourteen). They live in the same house, although they have had separate living arrangements for the past three years. The decision to separate and divorce was apparently initiated by Bea, who wants to move out of the house.

Ben said that he had already developed most of the budget material but that Bea probably had not. My case notes record

> Bea said that she was in business for herself and had been for a number of years and thought she could get the material together. She indicated that she had been reluctant to move on the divorce until she was sure what she would need and fully understood the details of alimony and child support. Ben said that this was the first time he had heard about alimony, and he thought that the broad outlines of a settlement were already set.

The mediator often finds that an issue which has been carefully avoided by the couple is raised in mediation. This occurs when one partner cannot deal directly with the other on the issue. The mediator, however, provides a protection from an immediate emotional or physical response to the idea. Once the couple have discussed the issue openly, it no longer holds the threat to either party. The mediator notes the issue, who raised it, and how, and incorporates that material into the marital power analysis.

The couple apparently had agreed that the son would live with the father and the daughter with the mother, but no details had been developed on how this would work. That the children would fit into the arrangement was taken for granted from the beginning, an idea that was reinforced during the negotiations by information shared with me, indicating that the children related better with the proposed custody parent than with the other parent. As it turned out, this was not necessarily correct and it reinforced my belief that children, particularly teenagers, must be involved in the mediation as arrangements affecting their lives are being made.

This case provided me with some new challenges. First, the wife was perpetually late, often arriving as much as an hour late and once trying to cancel the appointment about thirty minutes after it was supposed to start. I established clear ground rules. The couple paid for the time scheduled, whether they used it or not.

In addition, the wife spent long periods of time on the telephone with me, clarifying goals and questions. I permitted this because I determined that, although she had initiated the divorce, she had little outside support and needed to be able to talk things through. However, it did add considerably to the time spent on the case.

The major areas of disagreement appeared to be over the amount of support, the date Bea would move out of the jointly owned house, and the manner in which the house would be disposed of and the proceeds divided after its sale.

These areas were further complicated by the difficulty of getting any hard data. Ben provided six copies of his W-2 form since all of his income came from salary. Bea, however, was very reluctant to state the specific income derived from her business. Up until the previous year, Ben had managed the books of the business and claimed she netted about $12,000 a year. Bea said business had declined since he stopped handling the books and that she actually only made about $3,000 net this year. The $3,000 figure was slowly increased during the negotiations to "about $5,000." But Ben had secretly opened her bank statements and copied them, showing a gross of approximately $27,500 over the year. He shared these figures with me but did not use them in the actual negotiations.

Unfortunately, the mediator cannot subpoena the records of either party. However, in all the cases in which there is other than salary income, the hard data are impossible to get immediately and slowly change upward as more information is revealed during the negotiations.

Bea and Ben had filed joint income tax returns, but these showed Bea's income at less than $2,000 for tax purposes. No matter how I pressed, I was unable to determine the real income derived from the business, and without that figure on the table, negotiations about the amount of support were very difficult. In order to assist me in my thinking, I assumed that her real income was somewhere between the $5,000 to which she had admitted and the $12,000 Ben had estimated. So I functioned as if it were about $8,000.

I began by dealing with the easiest item of dispute first: the house. Bea had agreed to move out and Ben was to live in it with the son. I then suggested the standard procedure for splitting the equity. However, Ben wanted the right to buy out Bea's share, and she wanted protection in the way in which the value was appraised. She came back with a proposal for each of them to appoint an appraiser, with the two appraisers selecting a third and the actual value to be determined from the average of the three figures. I pointed out that this would be expensive, since appraising was not a charity.

She then came back and suggested that Ben have the house appraised, and that she have the option to buy him out if the price was to her liking. They hassled over this for some time until I suggested that we write into the agreement a clause that I would appoint the appraiser, who would be unknown to either of the parties. They found this acceptable, and we were able to move to another item.

When there is little trust between the parties, they will often suggest complicated and expensive ways of settling an issue. The mediator can save the couple money and build increased confidence in him/her by suggesting more direct and less expensive ways of solving differences.

The issue of financial support was tied up with the true incomes of each party and the date at which the house would actually be sold. Ben wanted to settle for $25-a-week child support. Bea felt she could not live on less than $150 a week. As I tried to move Ben up, he revealed that the price for increasing his payments would be that he could live in the house for as long as he was making child-support payments. His reasoning was that he could not afford to pay child support and live in an apartment.

Alice was almost seventeen; therefore, child support would be required for another year but Ben would be willing to pay until she was twenty-one. On the other hand, I felt that Bea's interests were best served by maximizing support in the immediate future as she found her feet and concentrated on building the business. I therefore went back and forth between them, suggesting $100 a week for child support for a period of two years. Ben would continue to live in the house for those two years, and it would be sold concurrently with the ending of child support. At this point Ben also pressed for establishing a date when Bea would actually move out. He had resolved his earlier reluctance about the separation and now wanted to make the move as quickly as possible. The agreement was reached in a final session that took about three hours. Ben and Bea were very suspicious of each other, which made it difficult for either of them to negotiate directly with the other. At no time did they place any proposal on the table in a joint session. Each new idea or proposal was made to me. I then took it to the other party and described it, taking the answer back to the proposer. I spent most of the time shuttling back and forth between the two parties. I drafted the agreement and sent them each a copy. Ben called to say it was substantially correct, except for a clarification regarding, his liability for Alice's college expenses. I suggested he talk to Bea, get her concurrence with the change, and I would then modify the agreement.

Bea did not call. Since we were approaching the Christmas holidays, I did not press her for a response. However, early in January I talked to her, and she said she had some additions to the agreement. She described them to me on the phone, and I identified two as being economic and the rest noneconomic.

I suggested she talk to Ben and ask him if he was ready to reopen talks. I also said that I would be prepared to reopen talks only if both parties would agree on what items were to be added before we reopened the negotiations. She agreed with that, as did Ben, and we set a date for the reopener.

When we met I put the new items in writing and had each party initial the list, agreeing that it was what we would be negotiating about. At this point Ben also added two items. The initial list showed:

1. Revise date for Bea to vacate the house.
2. Make a separate list of the division of property.
3. Provide that if part of the house is rented, each party shares equally in the income.
4. Make the clause "Major Decisions Affecting Alice and Sam" subject to arbitration.

5. Indicate that medical-dental coverage be maintained at present level, regardless of employment.
6. Provide for tuition for Alice after age nineteen and remove the stipulation that child support will be paid directly to Alice if she is enrolled as a full-time student.
7. Negotiate terms of filing joint tax returns.
8. Incorporate into the agreement the current status of life insurance held by each party.
9. Provide that the children of this marriage shall be the prime beneficiaries of each other's estate. In the event that either parent remarries, the children of this marriage shall remain beneficiaries of not less than 50 percent of the estate.
10. Provide protection of co-signer of the loan.

Item 2 was added because, although both had agreed that there was no problem regarding the division of property, there were disagreements that needed negotiating.

Item 3 was added when Bea learned that Ben intended to rent a room to a friend.

Item 5 was added because the first draft identified the medical-dental insurance as being employer-provided.

Item 6 was added to reflect more accurately what the parties were willing to do for Alice and to provide that the support would continue to go to Bea.

Item 7 proved to be a particularly difficult one. Ben had arranged to be deliberately overdeducted on his income tax. Therefore the couple each year received a refund of approximately $1,500. Bea wanted to guarantee that she shared in one-half of the refund if she agreed to file a joint return.

Item 8 was designed to reduce the cost to both parties of providing life insurance coverage for the children and to recognize the fact that Bea could not carry as much coverage for them as Ben could.

Item 10 was included by Ben. He had co-signed a loan for $5,000 for Bea to expand her business. He wanted an assurance that if she defaulted on the loan, he would not be held responsible for it.

The parties quickly agreed on items 2, 4, 5, 6, 8, 9, and 10, although, in keeping with all other sessions, never directly but always through me. That left three items to be decided. I determined to focus on items 3 and 7 because these had provoked the most emotion from both parties. Ben took the position that if he rented part of the house that was his decision, and since this reduced the attractiveness of the house to him, he felt that he should derive the benefits of the rental income. On the tax item he also argued that Bea's contribution to the taxable income was only $2,000; therefore she should not share equally in the refunds.

Bea argued that the house was jointly owned, and therefore the income belonged to both of them. In addition she questioned now whether she should be the one to move out—why shouldn't he be the one to move? On the tax returns she also felt that if they were filed jointly, the refunds should be shared jointly.

With these two economic items outstanding, I tried to see whether a trade could be made between the parties. I suggested that they share the rental income equally, and share the tax refund in proportion to the amount each paid in. This was done in an exploratory way in private sessions with each of them.

Ben indicated that he might make some movement; I could not get Bea to move on either of the items. At the end of three hours I brought them together and suggested that we were at an impasse that called my usefulness into question. I suggested that Bea think about the pros and cons of the two outstanding economic items. She asked to see me again privately. We caucused again.

In this meeting she expressed her concern as to whether she could make it alone. We explored this concern and the dangers of early remarriage. She said that she had thought about it a great deal and was not ready to get remarried. I then pointed out that she had now been married for almost eighteen years. In two more years she would be covered under Ben's Social Security provisions. I suggested that we explore the idea of his agreeing not to convert any separation agreement [into a divorce] until the twenty-year date had passed.* This seemed to ease some concern for the future. However, she was still unable to compromise on any of the outstanding items.

I met with Ben and explored the idea of limiting his right to convert the agreement, and he concurred, so I added that to my list of items.

We then met again as a triad, and I said that I thought we should have one more session with a strict time limit. I said I was willing to meet once more for no more than two hours—starting from the scheduled hour. If we had not reached an agreement within that time, I would terminate the process and recommend that they each retain an attorney and fight it out.

At that point Ben asked me what I thought was fair. He said he would like to know what I would recommend. I said I normally did not reveal my ideas since that placed me more in the role of an arbitrator. However, Bea also asked me to suggest what I thought was fair.

I then told them that since the house was jointly owned, I had sympathy with Bea's position that the income should be shared. On the other hand, I did not sympathize with her position on the tax returns. I said that I thought each party should share in that portion of the returns for which they contributed to the taxable income.

Ben said that he thought that was fair, and he could live with it. Bea smiled and said that she thought it was fair, and she could live with it. They both looked at one another, surprised that they had reached an agreement. I then introduced the last item, the date Bea would vacate the house. She said that she would need at least until June—six months—to vacate. Ben said he thought she should move out by January 31. I said I thought that a slightly later date would be more appropriate and suggested February 28, aware that any deadline would be difficult for Bea to meet.

I drafted the revised settlement. The second round of negotiations reinforced two beliefs I had held: the advisability of having the final agreement reviewed by an attorney, since a review by a third party allows for identification of special items that may have been overlooked, and the advantage of intervention in order to assist the parties to (1) set goals, (2) identify areas of disagreement, and (3) identify solutions to those areas. This case helped me to understand the importance of intervention at the appropriate time to assist the parties in reaching an agreement instead of making the agreement for them.

*This provision was reduced by Congress to 10 years.—Eds.

About a week after I had mailed the revised agreements to the parties, I got a call from Bea. She said she did not know whether she could sign the agreement because Alice had announced that she wanted to stay with her father through the end of this school year. If Alice stayed with the father, Bea would not get the child support, and without that $100 a week she did not think she could survive alone.

Bea related that Alice had told her she did not want to leave her school right now, and that Alice had suggested that Bea come up to the house a couple of times a week to cook for her, because Alice and Bea ate health foods, while Ben and Sam ate junk food.

I spent a long time on the telephone with Bea, trying to help her identify whether the reluctance to make the move was hers or Alice's. I pointed out that it was only natural for Alice to be reluctant to change schools in mid-year. However, Alice had to understand the consequences of the separation and be prepared to accept her share of the dislocations.

On the other hand, if it was Bea who really did not want to go through with the move, she needed to think through what to do. At this point, Ben seemed reconciled to the separation and if Bea wanted to change her mind, some form of counseling would have to take place to redefine their relationship. Bea ended the phone consultation with the thought that she had to deal with Alice so as to be able to make the move.

A few days later Bea arranged for a session for herself and Alice with me. I also suggested that Ben and Sam meet with me and added that I wanted to meet with Alice and Sam alone. The time was set. I began with Bea and Alice. At this meeting, Alice made her case that she did not want to move because of her friends. We talked about the need for the separation and Bea's relationship with Alice. I helped Bea establish the fact that she was indeed going to move out and go through with the separation and ended the session with the comment that if Alice wanted to stay with the father, I would simply help them all to renegotiate the financial arrangements to permit Bea to leave and Alice to stay.

I then met privately with Alice and explored her feelings regarding each of the parents. She clearly did not relate well to the father and wanted to stay with the mother. However, she did not want to leave her school friends at that moment and thought that if she could delay the separation, she might also prevent the divorce. I tried to clarify for Alice the fact that (1) Bea was moving out and that I would help negotiate a different arrangement to make that possible for Bea, and (2) there was nothing she could do to stop the divorce, just as there had been nothing she had done to cause the divorce. I then suggested that she think about different plans, such as being able to spend weekends at the house so that she could visit her friends after she and Bea had moved.

My discussion with Ben and Sam convinced me that the living arrangement for them was what both wanted. It also appeared that Sam would be just as happy to have his sister move out, so that he would be the only child.

I then met again with Bea and Alice. After a lot of tears and assurances that arrangements could be made for Alice to return to the house for visits whenever she wanted, and after assuring Alice that Bea really intended to move out, Alice agreed to go with her mother. All five of us came together for one final session to clarify for each party exactly what would happen. Ben agreed that Alice could come up for weekends whenever she wanted. I then went around the group explaining what each would be doing, their rights and responsibilities. Bea and Ben signed the agreement the following week, and the household divided within the agreed-upon time. In six months Alice spent one weekend with her father and brother.

This case demonstrates the importance of involving the children in the decisions that affect them. Such an involvement limits the fantasizing about the possibility of the children reconciling the parents. It also limits the children's sense of responsibility for the end of the marriage. Finally, it gives the children an opportunity to make their own needs part of the final agreement, thus making it easier for them to live with the inevitable parental decision.

J. FOLBERG, DIVORCE MEDIATION: PROMISES AND PROBLEMS

Paper prepared for Midwinter Meeting of ABA Section on Family Law, St. Thomas (Jan. 1983)

. . . The very elements that make divorce mediation so appealing compared to the adversarial model also create its dangers and raise substantial issues. Because mediation distinguishes itself as an approach that recognizes divorce and family disputes as both matters of the heart and of the law, there exist issues of how emotional feelings are to be weighed against and blended with legal rights and obligations and what are appropriate subjects for mediation. Because mediation is conducted in private and is less hemmed-in by rules of procedure, substantive law, and precedent, there will remain the question of whether the process is fair and the terms of a mediated agreement are just. This concern for a fair and just result has particular applicability to custody and child support provisions because mediated bargaining occurs between parents, and children are rarely present or independently represented during mediation.

Because mediation represents an "alternative" to the adversarial system, it lacks the precise and perfected checks and balances that are the principal benefit of the adversary process. The purposeful "a-legal" character of mediation creates a constant risk of overreaching and dominance by the more knowledgeable, powerful, or less emotional party. Some argue that the "a-legal" character of divorce mediation requires all the more careful court scrutiny before mediated agreements are approved and incorporated into a decree. Others argue against court review of mediated agreements. They reason that if the parties have utilized mediation to reach agreement, there is no need for the expense, delay, and imposition of a judge's values — all features of the judicial review process. Questions about the enforceability of agreements to mediate as well as the enforceability of mediated agreements cannot long be avoided.

Because family mediation is a new practice which crosses traditional professional boundaries and recognizes divorce as a family process within a legal context, there are likely to be questions about interdisciplinary cooperation and struggles for turf and assertions of professional dominance through claims of right, experience, or unique expertise. Lawyers are concerned about their continuing role in divorce. Mental health professionals and attorneys may not eagerly cooperate in creating joint roles nor in relinquishing their traditional domain. They may, however, become strange bedfellows in checking the emergence of a new "profession" of family mediators. Tight economic times may draw marginal practitioners of all stripes to what is viewed as a growth industry. Questions of certification, licensure and standards have yet to be answered. Because family mediation does involve professionals in a new or hybrid role where few rules are established and where fairness is a central concern, delicate issues of professional restraint and ethics will persist for some time without refined and tested answers.

Because there is wide public dissatisfaction with the present application of the adversary process to divorce cases and no clear direction from the legal profession for the improvement or replacement of that process, there will surely be exaggerated claims and expectations for mediation. Some will herald mediation as a panacea rather than a promising and rational alternative with its own set of problems and no magic answers. Some will insist that it be mandated in all divorce cases, others will argue that it must always be voluntary. Naive, if not zealous, enthusiasm may create disappointment and frustration that could thwart long-term innovations and improvements. . . .

Fairness

In considering whether mediated settlements will be fair and just, we must ask "compared to what"? We know that the great majority of divorce cases currently go by default. The default may be a result of ignorance, guilt, or a total sense of powerlessness. The default may also be a result of an agreement between the parties on the distributional questions eliminating the need for an appearance. The question persists in our present dispute resolution system of whether such agreements are the result of unequal bargaining power due to different levels of experience, patterns of dominance, the greater emotional need of one divorcing party to get out of the marriage or a greater desire on the part of one of the parties to avoid the expense and uncertainty of litigation. The present "adversarial" approach does not require the adverse parties to be represented nor does it impose a mediator or "audience" to point out these imbalances and assure that they are recognized by the parties, as mediation should attempt to do. Pro se divorce is increasingly popular and sanctioned by our present system in which there need be no professional intervention prior to court review. Mediation, at least, provides a knowledgeable third party to help the couple evaluate their relative positions so that they may make reasoned decisions with minimal judicial intrusion.

The most common pattern of legal representation in divorce is for one party to retain an attorney for advice and preparation of the documents. The other party will often negotiate directly with the moving party's attorney or retain an attorney to do so without filing an appearance. If a second attorney has not been retained by the non-moving party prior to preparation of the settlement agreement or proposed decree containing settlement terms, the unrepresented party will often consult with an attorney to determine whether the proposed settlement is "fair enough" not to contest and if all necessary items have been covered or discussed. The reviewing attorney serves as a check to assure that all major items have been considered by the parties and that the proposed agreement accurately states the client's understanding. The reviewing attorney usually informs the client of any other options to the suggested terms and whether the points of agreement fall within acceptable legal norms. These norms are often raised in the context of what would be the likely range of court resolution if agreement was not reached. The likelihood of a different court outcome than the proposed agreement is weighed against the financial, time, and emotional expenses of further negotiation or litigation.

A similar pattern of independent legal consultation could, and should, be utilized for review of mediated agreements. Current mediation practice, influenced by ethical restraints, is to urge or require that each divorcing party seek independent legal counsel to review the proposed agreement before it is signed. Though the criteria for independent attorney review of the proposed mediated agreement are not clear, the purpose of the review is no less clear than it is under the present "fair enough" practice. The initial mediated agreement is formed in a cooperative environment with the assistance of a neutral person who serves as a check against intimidation and overreaching. Independent legal review by an attorney for one spouse pursuant to a "fair enough" standard should assure at least as great a fairness safeguard as the common reality of our present adversary system. When both parties to the mediation obtain independent legal review, as they should be encouraged to do, there is a double-check of what is fair enough. In some complex cases, other professional review, such as that of a CPA, may be necessary for still another opinion and double-check. . . .

Protection of Children

When divorce involves minor children, some argue that the state has a responsibility for the children beyond encouraging the speedy, private settlement of disputes between parents. The state, however, under the well-developed doctrine of parens patriae has a responsibility for the welfare of children only when *parents cannot agree or cannot adequately provide for them.* Divorce mediation begins with the premise that parents love their children and are best able to decide how, within their resources, they will care for them. . . .

A mediated agreement is much more likely than a judicial decision to match the parents' capacity and desires with the child's needs. Whether the parents' decision is the result of reasoned analysis or is influenced by depression, guilt, spite, or selfishness, it is preferable to an imposed decision that is more likely to impede cooperation and stability for the child. In any event, a resolution negotiated by attorneys, reviewed by a court, or litigated before a court, is no more likely than a mediated settlement to disclose which outcomes are the result of depression, spite, guilt, or selfishness. . . .

The principal protection that the mediator can offer the child is to ensure that the parents consider all factors that can be developed between them relative to the child's needs and their abilities to meet those needs. The mediator should be prepared to ask probing and difficult questions and to help inform the parents of available alternatives. The mediator's ethical commitment, however, is to the process of parental self-determination and not to any given outcome. . . .

Financial Issues

If divorce mediation is a good idea whose time has come, its benefits may be needlessly restricted by focusing the mediation process on only child custody issues and leaving resolution of the financial issues to a different process. Division between these aspects of divorce is only superficially separable because they are inextricably intertwined. . . .

The Continuing Role of Courts and Attorneys

Increased use of divorce mediation would not remove the courts from the divorce process and would not entirely eliminate adversarial proceedings. We know that some cases cannot be settled or mediated. There must be a fair and credible forum with procedural safeguards and rules to assure the peaceful resolution of disputes for parties who are unwilling or unable to make cooperative decisions or to recognize the benefits that may come from a less coercive process. The threat of court litigation, with all of the human and material expense that it requires, may be the very element that will help some parties cut through their egocentric near-sightedness to see that their self-interests, as well as the interest of the family, may be promoted through mediation rather than a court fight. . . .

Who Should Serve as Mediators

As with the exploration and establishment of any new territory, there are grave risks that there will be struggles for turf and assertions of professional dominance by both attorneys and mental health professionals. Divorce is a legitimate concern of several helping professions. Divorce involves a myriad of emotional issues and legal questions. Clinicians working in the area of divorce are concerned with family processes, personal insight into divorce adjustment, and the psychological barriers inhibiting rational problem solving. Lawyers focus on the more tangible issues of property division, support, taxes, custody arrangements, and divorce procedures. Marital and divorce therapists are accustomed to working with multiple parties and looking at individuals in relation to each other as members of a family. A lawyer, on the other hand, by training and ethical constraints, traditionally offers services to one family member and champions the legal interests of that individual, rather than the well-being of the entire family constellation. Neither professional approach is perfectly suited to divorce mediation without adaptations.

Lawyers need not flatter themselves by thinking that intelligent counselors dedicating their professional careers to the subject cannot adequately understand the basic legal principles necessary to mediate family disputes, subject to review and formal memorialization by the attorneys for each party. Non-lawyers may not advise on how the law would be applied to the facts and issues presented in mediation. There will be cases in which the tax, real estate, or business planning aspects are sufficiently complex to require early consultation with or referral to a lawyer, but this is no different than dozens of other similar situations faced by counselors and other non-lawyer professionals. Those who choose divorce mediation should be encouraged, as previously discussed, to have any settlement agreement reviewed by legal counsel.

Mental health professionals are no less possessive in guarding their turf than are attorneys. Clinicians see themselves as uniquely qualified to move the parties through the psychological barriers inhibiting their openness and communication toward reaching agreement. Many therapists believe that only they can help the parties adequately understand the underlying and even unconscious reasons for the marital breakdown in order to deal with the issues surrounding divorce; that they alone can help deal with the ambivalence or non-mutuality around the decision to part. Some will claim that a clinician is necessary to help resolve the feelings of personal loss and grief as parties resolve the feelings of emotional attachment to one another. Attorneys, it is claimed, are self-selected by aptitude and training to deal with cold, hard facts and logic rather than feelings, which are a necessary part of every divorce dispute.

It is submitted that lawyers can and should be offering their services as divorce mediators. Lawyers, by aptitude and training, are problem solvers who deal daily in their practices with the creative exploration of compromise alternatives. They are skilled at sorting through issues to isolate points of agreement from disagreement for purposes of suggesting settlement solutions. Attorneys regularly help clients predict the consequences of various choices as well as interpret legal guidelines derived from cases and statutes so that clients can make informed decisions. One of the principal roles of a mediator is to help balance power by equalizing information concerning the law and financial issues. Lawyers are in a unique position to equalize bargaining positions by providing nonpartisan legal information and advice to the parties jointly, since the less informed spouse is more vulnerable to intimidation, or may perceive him or herself to be disadvantaged. . . .

Divorce mediation may represent a new role for attorneys, requiring qualities of sensitivity and skills of facilitation that they can, with some effort, master. If attorneys don't provide mediation services, the void will be filled by others and the public will have fewer meaningful choices. The bar should concentrate its energy and resources on improving the services offered by lawyers rather than thwarting consumer options. . . .

Conclusion

Divorce mediation has been touted as a replacement for the adversary system and a way of making divorce less painful. Though it should be available as an alternative for those who choose to use it, it is not a panacea that will create love where there is hate, nor will it totally eliminate the role of the adversary system in divorce. It may, however, reduce acrimony and post-divorce litigation by promoting cooperation. It may also lessen the burden of the courts in deciding many cases that can be diverted to less hostile and less costly procedures. . . .

Divorce mediation does appear to be a rational alternative attracting considerable interest. It is still in its infancy and, therefore, along with its promises, it raises substantial issues. The resolution of these issues will require additional empirical research, experience, and dialogue. Premature and categorical rejection of mediation by the bar will only preclude meaningful lawyer involvement in the development of divorce mediation and fan exaggerated claims for its benefits in all cases. This paper is offered to help the bar explore the promise of family mediation, frame the initial issues and stimulate the dialogue.

Questions

8.1 Professor Folberg suggests that, if mediation is effective for resolution of child custody issues, it might also be useful for resolution of financial issues. Do you agree? An American Academy of Matrimonial Lawyers survey of its lawyer-members suggested that lawyers believe that court-ordered mediation is helpful for resolving custody and support issues but is less useful for resolving financial issues. (Kisthardt, 1997:358.) Why do you think lawyers are reluctant to utilize court-ordered mediation for the resolution of financial issues? Do you think lawyer attitudes would be different if the mediation process were voluntary? If lawyers participated?

8.2 Professor Folberg also suggests that lawyers, acting as divorce mediators, can help level the playing field between the parties by providing "nonpartisan legal information and advice to the parties jointly." Would it be ethical for the mediator to provide legal advice to both parties if that advice were nonpartisan? Is Folberg's view consistent with current opinion regarding mediator provision of legal advice? What exactly is "nonpartisan legal advice"? How does it differ from legal information? See Chapter 3 at pp. 183-184.

J. PEARSON, FAMILY MEDIATION

In National Symposium on Court-Connected Dispute Resolution Research, A Report on Current Research Findings—Implications for Courts and Future Research Needs 51-77 (1994)

[Dr. Pearson, a sociologist, summarizes the results of 15 empirical studies of divorce mediation conducted by a variety of researchers over a 15-year period.]

Settlement rates: There is little doubt that mediation is effective in disposing of a substantial proportion of contested custody and visitation cases for courts. Across studies, settlement rates stand in the 50-75 percent range. . . .

In addition to producing agreements during the sessions, several evaluations also find that mediation has various "spillover" effects that translate into more voluntary agreement-making and less judicial decision-making. . . .

Court costs and processing times: Despite the impressive agreement rates produced in most divorce mediation programs, they appear to have little impact on the courts' overall workload. Contested custody and visitation cases comprise a small proportion of the domestic relations calendar. . . .

Another reason for the modest effects of mediation programs on court costs and workload is that many courts require that the parties appear in court before being referred to mediation and after mediation to present agreements to the court. . . .

Mediation programs may actually increase the number of post-divorce court appearances that occur in such cases. This was the conclusion reached by researchers at the NCSC who assessed samples of couples who mediated and used traditional court procedures in four different states and observed higher numbers of hearings among the mediation samples at some sites. They speculate that this is because mediators often sensitize parents to the need to revise visiting plans periodically to reflect the changing needs of children and as a result, mediating couples return to court to make periodic adjustments. . . . Evaluators of Washington D.C.'s Multi-Door Court House conclude that mediation increases resources expended by the court per case if mediator time and program administration costs are taken into account. . . .

Litigant cost savings: There is much less ambivalence in the research literature on the impact of mediation on savings to the parties in attorneys' fees. Virtually all studies that examine this issue find evidence of cost savings. . . .

User satisfaction: Another strong area of consensus in the evaluation literature is the high level of user satisfaction with both the mediation process and the outcomes it generates. With few exceptions, study after study concludes that mediation is consistently favored as compared with adversarial interventions. Most assessments find that user satisfaction falls in the 70-90 percent range. These patterns do not differ for users of mandatory versus voluntary mediation programs, challenging the notion that mediation cannot be effective and liked unless participation is voluntary. . . .

Some common themes that run through many of the client satisfaction evaluations are an appreciation of the opportunity to express a point of view without interruption; the professionalism, control, and neutrality displayed by the mediator; the understandability of the process and the outcomes generated in it; and the opportunity to focus on the children and the issues pertaining to their care. . . .

Overall, the mediation research literature finds few differences in the reactions of men versus women to the mediation experience. Where gender differences appear, they tend to favor women. . . .

User dissatisfaction: Not everyone reacts to mediation with enthusiasm: all evaluations reveal at least some level of client disaffection; a few evaluations reveal high incidences of disappointment. . . .

Types of agreements: . . . While some studies find evidence of generosity in mediation agreements and others reveal the opposite, the general consensus across the studies is that agreements produced in different forums resemble one another in many important ways. Moreover, other legal changes, such as child support guidelines, have had the effect of reducing variation in divorce agreements.

Thus, while early evaluations revealed a tendency for mediating couples to opt for joint legal custody arrangements as compared with sole maternal custody arrangements in adversarial samples, more recent evaluations fail to find distinct custody outcomes among those who mediate. . .

Assessments of property division and alimony awards in mediated and nonmediated agreements reveal that they are comparable and reflect prevailing legal norms, with wives receiving just over half the property and alimony being awarded about 20 to 25 percent of the time, mainly in lengthy marriages and high paternal income situations.

Finally, direct questioning about the incidence of custody blackmail in mediation reveals that it is a relatively rare phenomenon. . . .

Compliance and relitigation: Although the evidence regarding the compliance and relitigation patterns associated with mediated and adjudicated agreements is somewhat mixed, several longitudinal studies find short-term improvements in compliance and relitigation for those who mediate. . . .

Given . . . contradictory findings, it may be safest to conclude that while mediation is not more effective than adjudication in promoting long-term compliance and preventing relitigation, mediated agreements are no more unstable than those originating from judicial forums or lawyer-conducted negotiations.

Relationships with ex-spouses and adjustment of children and adults: Research results on spousal relationships and the psychological adjustment of children and adults following divorce underscore that mediation is a brief intervention that essentially produces short-term effects. While several studies find that mediation produces impressive short-term reductions in conflict and higher levels of cooperation among mediation participants, these advantages do not appear to last. . . .

Mandatory vs. voluntary: As to mandatory approaches, several studies comparing mandatory mediation clients with their voluntary counterparts find that agreement rates are comparable, as are satisfaction levels, willingness to recommend the process to others, and support for mandatory formats. . . .

Mediator characteristics and training: . . . Comparisons of lawyer-trained versus social worker-trained mediators in the [Denver Custody Mediation Project] also failed to reveal consistent differences. Indeed, the only background characteristic that was associated with more favorable outcomes was the experience level of the mediator. For both lawyers and social workers, agreement rates and approval ratings improved significantly after they had mediated five cases. A recent evaluation of mandatory, comprehensive mediation in Maine finds support for the use of volunteer lay people who present little threat to the role of lawyers in the divorce process. . . .

B. MEDIATION AND LAWYERS

C. McEWEN AND N. ROGERS, BRING THE LAWYERS INTO DIVORCE MEDIATION

Disp. Resol. Mag. 8-10 (Summer 1994)*

Critics of divorce mediation paint a picture of divorcing parties who enter mediation with bargaining imbalances and encounter a mediator who exacerbates the inequality. The solution, according to prominent critics such as Professors Trina Grillo and Penelope Bryant, is to let the parties choose whether to participate in mediation. In other words, to preserve fairness in divorce mediation, critics advocate eliminating the mandatory mediation programs now operating in about ten percent of the nation's domestic relations courts.

Those supporting mandatory mediation either do not accept the unfairness charges or, taking a middle ground, contend that mandatory mediation can be regulated to assure that any bargaining imbalances are redressed. This middle-ground approach has produced considerable regulation: a few statutory provisions directed toward preserving fairness in 34 states and a substantial number of provisions in 17 states. For example, without any evidence of their effectiveness in safeguarding fairness, legislatures have variously imposed duties on mediators to assure fairness, required case-by-case selection to eliminate cases with predictable bargaining imbalances, limited issues covered by the mediation to custody and visitation, and set up strict mediator qualifications including requirements for advanced academic degrees. Not only does it seem unlikely that these recent statutes will

*See also McEwen, Craig A., Nancy H. Rogers, and Richard J. Maiman (1995) "Bring in the Lawyers: Challenging the Dominant Approaches to Ensuring Fairness in Divorce Mediation," 79 *Minn. L. Rev.* 1317.

promote fairness, but they also threaten to undermine one of mediation's defining advantages: spontaneity and flexibility in responding to the parties' needs and circumstances.

There is another possible solution to fairness concerns in divorce mediation: encourage the parties to bring their lawyers to the mediation session. Commentators rarely discuss this option, however, because of their assumptions about divorce mediation and attorneys. In essence, all sides in the debate about fairness in divorce mediation imagine lawyers who are strenuous advocates in court but absent from mediation because they would "spoil" the process by their domineering and aggressive approach. Further, they assume that divorcing parties will resolve their cases in court if not in mediation. Although these assumptions may be correct some of the time, they are not always so. Take Maine's experience, for example.

Since 1984, Maine has mandated mediation in contested divorce cases involving minor children. Mediation is not confined to questions of custody and visitation, but may include financial matters as well. Maine lawyers have counseled thousands of clients going through this mandatory process. The results of interviews with 88 Maine divorce lawyers lead us to believe that mandatory mediation can be fair if it includes all divorce-related issues, and if lawyers are encouraged to participate with their clients. The interviews also reveal that the assumptions leading mediation proponents and critics to ignore our approach are in fact myths.

The *first myth* that critics and advocates of mandatory mediation share is that lawyers disappear when mediation begins. For advocates the disappearance of lawyers is often a goal because presumably it diminishes adversary conduct, empowers parties, and reduces costs. For critics it is a central problem because lawyers are seen as guardians of client rights, and their absence disadvantages weaker parties especially.

In Maine, however, divorce lawyers do not vanish when mediation starts. Indeed, 95 percent of those attorneys interviewed reported that they always or usually attend mediation sessions with their clients. Not only do lawyers attend, but they participate actively, though selectively, on behalf of their clients. Their presence and participation are premised on concerns about fairness because they recognize, as one lawyer said, that "mediation is like a crucible and bad decisions can be made." That is, even the best and most balanced mediation can create a momentum toward settlement that may lead parties to disregard their interests. But lawyers are also concerned about unfairness resulting from pressures from the other party and from the mediator. One lawyer reflected a common view among those interviewed: "I'm there to protect [my client] if I think things are not being run fairly and to watch out for his or her interests, but primarily it's up to him or her, the mediator, and the other spouse." Lawyers also recognize that some clients may need support in articulating their interests and concerns if fair results are to be achieved. As one lawyer said, "It depends on the client, but I'll tell them, 'If you want to talk, feel free to talk. The mediator would rather have you talk, but if you prefer me to talk, that's fine.'"

Thus, unlike the common picture of a lawyerless process, Maine divorce mediation involves lawyers actively, and they participate with an eye toward fairness.

A *second myth* about divorce mediation is that lawyer participation would spoil the mediation process for parties by permitting attorneys to take over the process. Further, it is supposed, lawyers will argue the law and pursue aggressive adversarial tactics in mediation, ruining efforts at settlement. This view is shared by many advocates of mediation and has produced statutes or court rules in five states prohibiting lawyer participation in custody mediation altogether or limiting the attorney role to observer. Opponents of mandatory mediation, on the other hand, assume that lawyers, by providing the vigorous advocacy necessary to assert and protect client rights, would thwart a mediation process that "steamrolls" the parties.

The view of lawyers as habitual spoilers proves erroneous in Maine. That state reports settlement rates of about 50 percent in its fairly short, single-session mediations, a figure comparable to those in many other divorce mediation programs where lawyers do not participate. Settlements even with lawyers present seem to happen because the mediator's demeanor and the mediation setting encourage lawyers to behave in accord with the professional norm of the "reasonable lawyer," who discourages unrealistic client expectations, refrains from identifying with the client emotionally, resists inflating demands, understands the likely legal outcome, and engages straightforwardly in the settlement process. In fact, lawyers sometimes report that the usual structure of mediation sessions discourages antagonistic conduct by lawyers: "It's easy to be Tarzan over the telephone, it really is. It's real hard to pull that garbage when the client [is right there]."

Even with their lawyers present, clients participate because that is the expectation of the mediator. Thus, one lawyer's description of her relationship to her client in mediation was typical of Maine lawyers: "I want to sit back and listen, and I'm not going to interrupt unless I feel that you've misstated something or you're misinformed on an area or need some counseling."

This client involvement allows parties to voice their feelings and to identify and deal with intensely important emotional issues that may block settlement. Said one lawyer: "I'm much more inclined to let the client talk in the mediation room. [I]t's one of the few times [the parties] have the opportunity to be face-to-face, and they need to get some stuff off their chest, and it can be done in that setting safely and usefully." The chance for parties to talk is prized and encouraged by most lawyers. "This is the only opportunity I have," said another lawyer, "to have [the other spouse] sitting there listening to my client's point of view. He's probably never done it before in his life. Now he's got someone who's describing what her life is going to be like, going through her budget."

Parties in Maine engage actively in most mediation sessions, express their feelings, and participate in settlement discussions. Their chances of achieving a fair result are increased both by the support of legal counsel and by their opportunity to take a leading role in crafting a divorce settlement for themselves.

The *third myth* about mandatory mediation is that it supplants trial. For mediation advocates this is its advantage because it gives the parties rather than a judge control over process and outcomes. For mediation critics this is mediation's weakness because it substitutes an informal process for one that presumably protects the rights of parties, especially weaker parties. But both advocates and critics are mistaken; most often mandated divorce mediation replaces or supplements *negotiation* rather than substitutes for trials. Trials, even in initially contested divorces, are relatively uncommon. Our research in Maine confirms that where mediation is mandated in contested cases, most parties who enter the process would have settled on their own in any event. However, mediation moves settlement to an earlier point.

Maine lawyers appreciate the advantages of mediation because it facilitates communication with clients and makes the negotiation process more efficient. By participating in mediation, lawyers can work more effectively with clients whose demands are perceived as unreasonable. As one lawyer pointed out: "Sometimes the mediator . . . will help me in my role with a client, if I have a hard sell with my client." That can happen because mediators can help "reality test" with parties in ways that lawyers find hard to do. Lawyers understandably worry about being too blunt in challenging their clients' demands and expectations, for fear of undermining the clients' confidence in them as resolute advocates. Mediation can help lawyers in such circumstances, as noted by most Maine lawyers. One lawyer said, for example, "At mediation, it's an opportunity for my client to kind of expose his or her case to reality, and the mediator many times is going to say, 'Wait, is that what you really mean?'" According to another attorney, "You can say, 'You can't get that.' You go to mediation, the mediation takes place and this and that, and it shows that it's not only my ideas. Then I can come out and say, 'Well I told you.' [Mediation] gives them almost a second opinion."

With such openings provided by a mediation process in which they participate, attorneys can more effectively advise clients about reasonable expectations for their divorces.

Lawyers also find that they can reduce some of the delay, cost, and frustration of negotiation by phone, letter, and fax — what one lawyer described as "months of diddling back and forth between lawyers." Instead, as another Maine lawyer described the mediation process, "Everybody's there. You don't have to say, 'Well, I've got to ask my client.' If there's any confusion, they're both there to talk about it." Not only is this four-way meeting more efficient, it also reduces confusion and miscommunication, as may happen in the negotiation process when client tells lawyer who summarizes for the other lawyer who then translates for her client. "It gets them face-to-face with the other side," one lawyer said. "It eliminates all the rumors. [Often] clients tell me what their spouse said their lawyer said. All that smoke is gone when we sit down in mediation."

Mediation also introduces each attorney to the other party, so that they can see with their own eyes and hear with their own ears what he or she is like. With that better understanding negotiation can be more effective because a good attorney can better gauge the other parties' interests and needs.

The *final myth* is that all mediation is alike, either like the ideal mediation program the advocate envisions or the problematic one the critic abhors. Instead, as the Maine experience suggests and a wider comparison of mediation programs would show, mediation differs substantially from jurisdiction to jurisdiction. This variation provides the opportunity to assess various approaches in order to maximize the likelihood of fairness in mediation, while preserving its other values such as flexibility and low cost.

With these myths aside, we can entertain another approach to assuring fairness: including the lawyers as active participants in mandatory divorce mediation sessions. To do so would require repeal of the statutes proscribing such participation in a few jurisdictions. Lawyer participation is more likely, the Maine research indicates, if mandatory mediation extends to the economic issues that divorce attorneys view as strategically important. Broadening the issues covered by mediation would also necessitate statutory amendment in some states.

Certainly, we need to know more before advocating that divorce mediation everywhere be broadened to include economic issues and to encourage active participation by the parties' lawyers in the give and take of mediation sessions. However, our research into the effectiveness of the Maine approach leads us to think that the lawyered approach is superior, for several reasons:

- Statutes regulating divorce mediation provide little hope that fairness problems are eased by regulation;
- Regulation in other fields tends to be costly, and early analysis indicates that mediation is no exception;
- Adding lawyers to the mediation process may not increase the cost; with all parties present the efficiency of negotiation can be improved, it takes fewer sessions to complete mediation, additional issues can be included, and mediators need not be as expert and, thus, as expensive.

In short, the critics of mandatory divorce mediation may be on target with their concerns about fairness, but are taking too narrow a view of possible solutions. By looking beyond the rhetoric and examining evidence of the operation of divorce mediation that includes lawyers, we can see new possibilities for resolving the fairness issue in divorce mediation. The alternatives to examining this fresh approach are to limit mediation to circumstances in which the parties agree to the mediation, to wink at unfairness, or to risk a heavily regulated mandatory mediation that will be less fair than the traditional system, yet equally rigid and bureaucratic.

Question

8.3 For a warning that lawyers may not negotiate effectively during mediation, see Bryan (1994). Would it help to train lawyers to represent clients effectively in mediation? What should such training consist of?

C. MEDIATION AND SPOUSAL ABUSE

The piece that follows addresses domestic violence issues in court-ordered mediation. Both the article and the Note that follows the article focus on how the dynamics of this mediation may change when one party has abused the other.

R. RIMELSPACH, MEDIATING FAMILY DISPUTES IN A WORLD WITH DOMESTIC VIOLENCE: HOW TO DEVISE A SAFE AND EFFECTIVE COURT-CONNECTED MEDIATION PROGRAM

17 Ohio St. J. Disp. Resol. 95 (2001)

. . . [T]he appropriateness of family mediation in cases involving domestic violence has been a point of contention between those who favor the use of mediation in the family arena and those who contend that mediation can be both unfair and potentially dangerous. It is important to carefully consider both sides of this division, and recognize that persuasive arguments emanate from each side in this dispute. . . .

II. The Arguments Weighing Against Court-Connected Mediation Programs in Light of the Prevalence of Domestic Violence

The arguments against utilizing mediation where there is evidence of domestic violence raise significant public policy concerns. Power issues are of a major concern to those who disfavor mediation in situations where there is evidence of domestic violence. . . . Critics of mediation argue that effective mediation is premised on a relatively equal balance of power, and that where domestic violence is present, even the most skilled mediator will likely not be able to compensate for the disparity of power.

Those not in favor of mediating where there has been domestic violence also argue that the methodology and ideology of mediation make it ill-equipped to deal with domestic violence. Mediation requires that parties engage in joint decision making that is premised on honesty, that they have a desire to settle the dispute, and that they have the capacity to compromise; all characteristics that may be lacking in a relationship plagued with domestic violence. As one commentator stated, "It is difficult to imagine a batterer coming to a mutually agreeable outcome with his partner in mediation; it is equally difficult to imagine that he will comply with an agreement he believes is unfair to him."

Another range of arguments against using mediation in situations of domestic violence challenges the presumption that women who have been victims are able to articulate and/or discern their own interests and needs. Advocates note that women who have been conditioned to always consider their spouse's needs ahead of their own will be unable to break out of this habit in a mediation setting. As one outspoken mediation critic has stated,

> The reality is that the battered woman is not free to choose. She is not free to elect or reject mediation if the batterer prefers it, not free to identify and advocate for components essential for her autonomy and safety and that of her children, not free to terminate mediation when she concludes it is not working. She is ultimately not free to agree or disagree with the language of the agreement. Her apparent consent is under duress. . . .

Another reason marshaled against using mediation where there has been violence is the belief that mediation places victims at increased risk for future violence. As most commentators will agree, "the most dangerous time for a battered woman is when she separates from her partner." But if mediation is used, even mandated, then the mediation conference may allow a batterer access to a spouse who has successfully evaded contact since the separation. As a result of those mediated conversations, the batterer may have the opportunity to discover his spouse's location, or even harass her at the mediation. Of even more concern than the potential danger from face-to-face contact is the possibility that mediated agreements will give the batterer more access to the victim overall, because of the alleged pressure in mediation to agree to generous visitation provisions.

Critics have also argued that court-connected mediation of cases presenting allegations of domestic abuse is just another example of the court failing to treat domestic violence as a crime. The mere fact that the court allows mediation of cases where family violence is present sends a message to both the abuser and the victim that "violence is not so serious as to compromise the parties' ability to negotiate as relative equals;" additionally, "the message of offender accountability for his use of violence becomes blurred." . . . Critics fear that relegating cases of domestic violence to mediation programs rather than criminal prosecution or public civil divorce trials will take violence out of the public eye, and reinforce the old adage that domestic violence is a "family problem."

These are only some of the criticisms that have been leveled against mediation in the context of domestic violence; while they may represent some of the most persuasive arguments, this is far from an exhaustive list. Other fears include the following: that mediators will not be aware of violence because it is typically well-hidden; that mediation agreements have few enforceability mechanisms, and therefore fewer noncompliance consequences; that without discovery powers, mediation cannot ensure full disclosure; that mediators utilize coercive tactics to force agreements; that the future-oriented nature of the process ignores the reality of the past abuse and many others. It is undeniable that critics of mediating when domestic violence is present have relevant, forceful arguments, not easily discounted.

III. The Arguments Supporting Court-Connected Mediation Programs Despite the Prevalence of Domestic Violence

It has been argued that the question of whether or not to mediate in light of domestic violence should be evaluated based upon a utilitarian analysis: does mediation provide more benefits than harms? . . .

Most mediation proponents agree that there are some cases where mediation is simply inappropriate, a fact that many opponents of mediation seem oftentimes to ignore. Those who argue emphatically against mediation tend to assume that the couple is involved in a pervasive "culture of battering," whereby the woman has been so brutalized and demoralized by her abusive partner that she is rendered a passive shadow of her former self, unable to bargain in any meaningful way. However, this ignores the reality of a "continuum" of family violence, ranging from pervasive abuse to occasional violence.

Another assumption by opponents of mediation in cases of domestic violence is that in order to mediate effectively, the parties must have relatively equal power— something that can never happen in a battering relationship. . . .

[P]ower imbalances are not unique to families where domestic violence is a factor; many divorcing relationships can be characterized as exhibiting an unequal balance of power. If mediation is only effective where there is relatively equal power between the parties, then certainly more than just families with violence would have to be excluded from the process.

It can also be argued that despite the drawbacks, mediation is more appropriate and effective than the adversarial process, even in cases of domestic violence.

Experts have argued that "the overwhelming view by both social science professionals and judicial observers is that the adversarial system is simply inappropriate" as an approach to divorce or custody. More specifically, the nature of the adversarial process can actually exacerbate the relationship between abusive partners. As some commentators have observed, "[t]he adversarial approach escalates the conflict, encourages scapegoating and victim behaviors, and reinforces just those factors that contribute to abuse in the first place." It can also be argued that mediation is superior to the adversarial process when domestic violence is present, because mediators themselves are more likely than attorneys to identify abuse and be in a better position to deal with intimidation and violence.

In response to the argument that the mediation process protects batterers from legal sanctions and in turn fails to treat battering as a crime, it can be argued that mediation actually encourages participants to seek outside help. As one commentator has asserted, "[m]ediation can be an effective forum for getting people to commit to treatment." In the traditional adversarial process, litigants lack incentives to admit to past abuse (and, in fact, actually have incentives to litigate and deny the abuse) for fear that a fact-finder will take abuse into account in a decision. Mediation, on the other hand, provides batterers and their spouses the opportunity to address the violence in a way that enables them to devise safety mechanisms. The mediation process, unlike traditional litigation, encourages the participants to create guidelines governing future relations. Finally, eliminating the systematic forces encouraging batterers to deny abuse can further the victim's healing process.

Another benefit to the mediation process is the sense of empowerment it can provide to the victims of domestic violence. . . .

Finally, and perhaps most importantly, there is evidence to support the argument that mediation in cases of domestic violence can actually have an impact on lessening the incidents of abuse. "A study conducted in Ontario by Professor Desmond Ellis (Family Mediation Pilot Project Final Report, Ministry of the Attorney General, Toronto, Ontario, July 1994) found that mediation was associated with a greater reduction in physical, verbal, and emotional abuse than lawyer-assisted settlement." . . .

In addition to these arguments for expanding and encouraging divorce and custody mediation despite the prevalence of domestic violence, there are numerous other arguments that have not been explored in depth here. Other arguments include the fact that mediators, unlike judges, can customize the process; that mediation, unlike the adversarial system, provides a model of future interaction; that mediation can address issues the court typically would not include; and the general advantages of mediation, such as being more efficient and less expensive than the adversarial process.

IV. If We Ultimately Decide That Mediation Is More Beneficial Than Not, How Do We Devise a Court-Connected Program that Serves and Protects?

A. Pre-Mediation Safeguards

Cases entering a domestic relations court mediation program will fit into one of the following three categories: appropriate for standard mediation; appropriate for mediation but necessitating some modification in form; or inappropriate for mediation. . . .

To begin, it is important that screening be detailed enough to elicit the many types of violence that can be present in a marital relationship. For instance, simply asking, "Has your spouse ever struck you?," would not uncover the many forms of psychological abuse that may be present, such as threats of violence. It is also somewhat intuitively obvious that the screening needs to be private, as many victims will not reveal abuse in the presence of their spouse. Having the screening done by an individual other than the person assigned to mediate the case is also an important safeguard, so that any incidence of mediator bias can be avoided. Screening should also involve at least some verbal component in addition to written questionnaires, as some parties may not be literate. This could involve either a face-to-face interview at the time of the mediation or a prior telephone interview. . . .

The screener must distinguish between a relationship where the parties still are able to mediate on relatively equal terms, and where there has been a "culture" of battering. At a minimum, it would seem that mediation is inappropriate if the abuse is ongoing, there have been threats with or use of weapons, and/or the victim appears unable to place her needs ahead of the batterer's.

B. SAFEGUARDS THROUGHOUT THE MEDIATION PROCESS

[The author states that, "[n]ot only is it important for court-connected programs to establish protocols for the pre-mediation stage, but it is also important to have various safeguards in place during the actual mediation conference. . . ." Courts can institute a variety of precautionary measures for use during mediation, including:

- Creating male/female mediation teams;
- Allowing victim advocates or attorneys into the mediation;
- Utilizing caucusing procedures;
- Advising all participants of their right to terminate the mediation at any stage during the process;
- Providing or making available to participants information about other community resources;
- Implementing safety measures to ensure the protection of all mediation participants.]

C. POST-MEDIATION PROCESS SAFEGUARDS

It is extremely important to the mediation process that courts not only facilitate mediation agreements, but assure their fairness on at least some level. . . . Agreements that are so unjust as to offend basic sensibilities should be disallowed in the interest of court and mediation program legitimacy. It is the recommendation of this Article that mediation agreements be read into the record in the presence of a judge, so there is at least some amount of judicial review available.

It is also important for courts to consider the feasibility of some sort of follow-up services when mediation has been successfully completed. . . .

Finally, the role of the lawyer in any court-connected mediation program is too essential to be overlooked. Lawyers have a role throughout the process, including the following: educating their clients about the mediation process; helping clients assess whether or not mediation is appropriate for them; assisting their clients in obtaining civil protection orders, if necessary; preparing their clients to be good advocates; attending the mediation, if it would be in the best interests of their client; and finally, reviewing any mediated agreement before the client signs it. It must be stressed that "[t]he mediation process does not eliminate the need for independent legal counsel." . . .

V. Conclusion

There does not seem to be a clear case to reject mediation for family disputes, despite the prevalence of domestic violence. One of the key factors in the area of dispute resolution is to offer as many alternatives to parties as possible, so that the most appropriate method can be chosen for each case. Considering the numerous benefits that mediation can offer over the adversary system, it would seem a senseless loss to exclude all court mediation programs as an option for individuals whose interpersonal relationships contain elements of domestic violence.

However, this is not to say that court-connected mediation programs can be unmindful of the special difficulties that the prevalence of domestic violence in our society presents. In fact, because court-connected programs are under the auspices of the court system, court-connected programs have an even higher duty to protect those members of society who need it the most. With proper planning, thorough training, and special safeguards, court-connected mediation programs can provide high quality, safe service to their constituents.

Note: Domestic Violence and Mediation

Rimelspach discusses mediation between abuser and victim where the alternative to settlement is adjudicating parental rights issues. Some programs offer mediation where the alternative to settlement is prosecution (Lerman, 1984: 71-72, 98-99, 101-113). Ann Yellott, the administrator of a community program that mediates domestic violence cases, contends that mediation can play a useful role, even in a community with a mandatory arrest policy regarding domestic violence complaints and adequate prosecutorial assistance for victims. She argues that victims should be permitted to choose mediation over continued prosecution if they want to work out the terms of separation or the need for counseling. Yellott suggests that those opposing all domestic violence mediation fail to recognize that "[a]n elderly couple arrested after throwing coffee at each other requires different options than a couple where the man has systematically beaten and emotionally brutalized the woman over a number of years" (1990:44).

Yellott focuses on the use of mediation in place of prosecution in certain kinds of domestic violence cases. Different issues are presented by divorce mediation cases involving allegations of spousal violence. In the latter, criminal justice issues of punishment and deterrence are less important while another issue assumes more significance—whether the power imbalance will impede a solution that is in the children's and victim's best interest.

Psychologist Robert Geffner and sociologist Mildred Pagelow paint a bleak picture of what might occur in a court-ordered child custody mediation between a batterer and victim. They suggest that because of a power relationship, a batterer can use custody mediation to maintain dominance over the spouse and to secure control of children, who then are at risk themselves (1990:152-153):

> [W]omen in general, and battered women in particular, are typically the primary caretakers of the children before and after divorce, and they have great fear of losing custody, while the batterer has nothing to lose by requesting custody as a bargaining and power tactic. Batterers have already demonstrated their willingness to use violence as a response to anger, stress, or frustration, and to control the behavior of others. . . . Thus, the children in these cases are at risk for being abused after divorce even if they have not been abused before.

Sociologist David Chandler studied a Honolulu child custody mediation program and concluded that negotiations with the help of a mediator may offer advantages, even for victims of domestic violence. Twenty-three percent of the mediated cases had a history of violence. However, the patterns among these cases differed significantly (1990:344):

> One stereotype of violent relationships is that abusive males isolate their wives to keep and control them, that spouses are ambivalent about leaving them, and victims are confused and unassertive about their interests. [T]he women in the forty-nine violent relationships in this study could not be so uniformly described. . . . Most were living separately, most had attorneys, and the average time since the last abuse was six months. [O]nly the small number [nine] who reported being currently afraid and unable to communicate matched accounts of serious spouse abuse closely. . . . This group had the fewest agreements, and the agreements seemed to meet the interests of the women. None seemed obviously unfair. . . . The specific structuring of visitation, controls on conduct, and the control of communication seem to meet the victim's interests in achieving an orderly and complete separation, with any communication conducted on a structured and businesslike basis.

Is there a continuum of violence as Rimelspach and Chandler seem to suggest so that a spouse who engages in "occasional violence" should be allowed to mediate while a more violent spouse should not? Given disagreement on these points, it is not surprising that courts have taken widely disparate approaches to mediation for child custody and visitation cases involving alleged spousal violence. Some courts refer these cases to mediation. In Wisconsin, a pilot project was created to mediate cases involving children in need of protection or services whose parents were simultaneously facing criminal child abuse charges (Martin and Weller, 2002.) The project suggested that situations involving family violence can be mediated if the proper infrastructure is in place, but did not consider whether the dispute "should" be mediated. Others are prohibited by statute from doing so (for example, Minn. Stat. Ann. §518.619; N.D. Cent. Code §14-09.1-02). Those courts referring violence cases to mediation at times impose restrictions. In California, for example, the courts mandate mediation of child custody cases involving domestic violence allegations, but the parties are not permitted to attend sessions together if the spouse alleging abuse so requests and the alleged victim can bring a support person of their choice (Family Code §§10012, 6303).

These statutory schemes depend on the abused spouse to raise abuse in the pleadings or by motion. What if the abused person is afraid to speak publicly? To protect the reticent victims, the Maine courts require domestic mediators to conduct a premediation conference with each party and that party's attorney to screen for violence. The mediators use a protocol of suggested questions that are designed to surface abuse, even from a reticent victim. In an effort to keep from contributing to the victim's problems, the mediators' instructions state, "It is important to try to start with the abuser so that he or she will not think you are asking the questions based on what the other person told you; this procedure will decrease the risk of retaliation" (State of Maine Judicial Branch, 1997). For the same reason, the instructions warn the mediator who terminates the mediation not to disclose the reason for doing so (id.). If the mediator uncovers violence, mediation can be conducted only if both parties agree and if the mediator thinks that both parties will be safe during mediation; the "levels of power and control" are "balanced enough so that each party can participate in discussion and negotiation, even if it is in separate rooms," and the "parties appear able to express their wishes freely without fear of reprisal and to make decisions autonomously" (id.). Should the mediator assigned to the case also conduct the screening? Rimelspach suggests not.

D. MEDIATION CLAUSES

Research on mediation paints a picture of human nature that suggests the importance of including mediation clauses in divorce agreements:

- People are unlikely to agree to mediation in the midst of a dispute (see p. 148);
- If disputants are compelled to participate in mediation, either by court order or by prior agreement, they are as likely to settle and feel pleased as those who agreed to mediate in the midst of a dispute (see pp. 156, 405-406, 481).

This research has suggested to some lawyers and legislators that divorcing parents, who tend to return to court frequently after divorces are final, are strong candidates for predispute agreements to mediate. Perhaps for this reason, the Washington legislature has required that all parties settling their custody or visitation differences include a dispute resolution clause in their agreement. The statute also authorizes sanctions for any party who does not comply with the clause (Wash. Rev. Code §26.09.184).

The key to drafting an effective mediation clause is to anticipate the kinds of disputes that are likely to arise and then to specify some aspects of the mediation that should be the same regardless of the dispute. It is particularly important to resolve issues in the clause if the issues will be more difficult to resolve in the heat of a dispute (see form clauses, Appendix A). These issues often include:

- How will the mediator be selected;
- What issues are covered by the clause;
- Who will pay for the mediation;
- What constitutes compliance; and
- What the parties cannot do, such as file postdecree motions except for emergencies, until the mediation has been completed.

Among these issues, defining compliance with the requirement to mediate presents the most difficulty for the drafter. To avoid future litigation over interpretation of the clause, some drafters prefer objective standards, such as attendance for a specified time period, exchanges of information, and payment of the mediator's fees. Others opt for vague requirements such as good faith negotiation that may open the door to litigation on compliance issues (Cole, Rogers, and McEwen, 2003 & 2006 Supp.).

More recently, institutional repeat players have begun to insert mediation clauses into the contracts of one-shot players, such as employees and consumers. Repeat players who will not have to negotiate the terms of the mediation clause may attempt to skew the clause in their favor by, for example, locating the mediation in a place that is convenient to the repeat player but not the one-shot player. In the arbitration context, courts have rejected as unconscionable repeat player efforts to garner too many benefits from the implementation of an arbitration clause (casebook pp. 272-278). Although one would expect fewer unconscionability challenges to agreements to mediate because mediation is nonbinding, a recent case suggests that such a finding is possible. In *Garrett v. Hooters-Toledo,* 295 F. Supp. 2d 774 (N.D. Ohio 2003), the court considered whether an agreement that required a claimant in Toledo, Ohio, to mediate in Kentucky in front of a mediator of her choice and a mediator of the defendant's choice, selected from a list of mediators provided by the company, was conscionable. Emphasizing the short time frame for filing for mediation and selecting a mediator — the claimant had only 10 days from the last date of the triggering incident to file for mediation — and other factors, including that the claimant was not permitted to bring a representative to the mediation and the take-it-or-leave-it nature of the mediated agreement, the court concluded that the provision was unconscionable.

Absent a sanctions statute, such as the one in Washington, the courts have generally enforced nonbinding dispute resolution clauses. Some courts reason that statutes providing for summary enforcement of arbitration clauses can be extended to authorize summary enforcement of nonbinding dispute resolution clauses as well (see *Fisher v. GE Medical Systems,* 276 F. Supp. 891 (M.D. Tenn. 2003); *AMF, Inc. v. Brunswick Corp.,* 621 F. Supp. 456 (E.D.N.Y. 1985); *Kelly v. Benchmark Homes,* 250 Neb. 367, 550 N.W.2d 640 (1996); but see *Harrison v. Nissan Motor,* 111 F.3d 343 (3d Cir. 1997) (declining to apply Federal Arbitration Act to informal automobile sale dispute resolution processes). Absent provisions for summary enforcement, courts use contract law as a basis to dismiss litigation filed by recalcitrant parties or to provide specific enforcement (see *DeValk Lincoln Mercury v. Ford Motor Co.,* 811 F.2d 326 (7th Cir. 1987); *Haertl Wolff Parker, Inc. v. Howard S. Wright Constr. Co.,* 1989 U.S. Dist.

LEXIS 14756 (D. Or. 1989); Katz, 1988; Cole, Rogers, and McEwen, 2003 & 2006 Supp.).

Mediation clauses in divorce and dissolution agreements may be only one aspect of the attorney's strategy to avoid unnecessary adjudication of family matters. Should mediation clauses be placed in prenuptial agreements? Should arbitration clauses be included to resolve economic issues? Should the parties agree to non-binding arbitration of child custody issues? Should the parties agree in advance to use "collaborative law" attorneys who will negotiate using an interest-based approach whenever they have serious disputes (see pp. 373-375)? What issues are important to preserve for court action? The research suggests that these questions should be resolved while relations are cordial between the parties.

Questions

8.4 In Maine, attorneys typically attend mediation sessions with their clients (see pp. 494-498). Should the domestic violence guidelines used in Maine (p. 505) be different for a state in which lawyers typically do not attend mediation sessions? If so, how? Given the high incidence of domestic violence in the contested cases that are candidates for mediation (see p. 504), should courts exclude from mediation all cases in which any party will attend the sessions unaccompanied by an attorney?

8.5 *A request for advice.* A close friend telephones you from a distant community to tell you that he and his wife are having serious marital problems and have begun to consider the possibility of divorce. They both think that they need assistance in dealing with their problems and deciding on a course of action, but they do not know where to turn for such assistance. They ask your advice, both as to the type of assistance you think they need and as to how to find a competent person to provide that assistance. How would you respond?

8.6 *Ethical dilemmas for the mediator.*

a. You are mediating the divorce between a financially experienced man (age 45) and his inexperienced wife (age 38). She has compelling personal reasons for desiring a quick resolution of the divorce, and the husband is aware of this. To avoid the threat of prolonged litigation and conflict, she is willing to agree to a very unfavorable settlement, waiving all rights to custody of their only child as well as support for herself. She is also willing to accept only 15 percent of their approximately $300,000 worth of marital assets, which is about half of what a court would be likely to award. The wife is reluctant to get her own lawyer since she fears that this would precipitate a prolonged adversarial battle. Should you go along with the proposed settlement? If you do, should you tell the parties that you feel the proposed settlement is unfair to the wife? Should you tell the wife only? Does it matter what the wife's compelling personal reasons are? What effect is this likely to have on your future usefulness as a mediator, both in this case and in future cases? Alternatively, should you withdraw, even though this would probably preclude any speedy settlement? What difference would it make to your actions if the wife was an experienced businesswoman?

b. After considerable bargaining between a couple, you manage to mediate what seems to you to be an eminently fair agreement. In going over the agreement with them, you suddenly realize that both parties have a misconception of the husband's chances of winning custody in court—a misconception based on which both have been bargaining. Assuming the misconception did not arise from your legal advice to them, what should you do?

c. In the course of a divorce mediation, you begin to suspect that the husband has not made full disclosure of his assets, but that given full discovery in an adversary situation the assets would come to light. What should you do? Can you behave differently depending on your evaluation of the fairness of the proposed settlement? Should an agreement of full disclosure by both disputants be one of the conditions of every mediation?

d. You are mediating for a couple contemplating divorce. In a separate caucus, the wife tells you confidentially that her husband is the father of only one of the two children born during their marriage. Later the parties ask you to recommend an amount of child support to be paid by the husband. What should you do?

e. You are a divorce mediator, and a sophisticated couple comes to you with the broad outline of an agreement already worked out between them. On reviewing the proposed settlement you become convinced that the couple have subordinated the best interests of their two young children to their own best interests. On being questioned about this, they deny it, maintaining that they know best what is best for their children. Bearing in mind the known tendency of judges to "rubber-stamp" divorce agreements, what should you do?

8.7 *Divorce mediation and conventional representation.* You are a traditional family lawyer and are somewhat dismayed when an old client of yours comes to you with a proposed divorce agreement that has been mediated, asking you to "look it over" before he signs. You have never had any prior dealings with divorce mediation but are reluctant to turn away an old client. The client tells you that he and his wife worked the agreement out in four two-hour sessions with Dr. Smith, a psychologist divorce mediator. At the conclusion of the mediation, Dr. Smith suggested that each spouse take the agreement to a separate lawyer for approval. What issues should you be worried about if you accept the assignment? The client is both unsophisticated and still clearly distraught about the divorce, while his wife, as you recall, is an experienced negotiator.

8.8 *Institutionalization of divorce mediation.* What are the pros and cons of providing divorce mediation through private individuals rather than as a public service connected with a family court? Are the ethical issues that are presented identical in the two contexts?

8.9 *Practice and policy issues.* One of the touted advantages of mediation between divorcing parties in lieu of negotiation between their attorneys is its tendency to help the divorcing parties deal with their anger. Indeed, psychologists Karen Somary and Robert Emery state that "assistance in dealing with anger during mediation improves post-divorce communication, cooperation, and satisfaction" (1991:186). However, law professor Trina Grillo contends that child custody mediators in mandatory programs are so focused on settlement rates that they discourage expressions of anger. She quotes California court mediators who would "never let any hostile feelings be expressed because the parties would blow up and the chance for an agreement would be lost" (1991:1575). Are the psychologists or the California mediators right? If legislators want to encourage the type of mediation suggested by Somary and Emery, should they require mediators to have training in dealing with anger? Make mediation voluntary? Change the laws in other ways?

8.10 *Referral.* Helen and George were divorced three years ago. Custody of their nine-year-old daughter Lisa was awarded to Helen. George has now petitioned for a change of custody, because of (1) Helen's unfitness as a result of occasional bouts of drunkenness and (2) his recent remarriage to Mary, a more suitable custodian for Lisa.

In the ensuing litigation, Helen's attorney takes a deposition of Mary and asks her about alleged sexual misconduct by her two years ago while she was still married to her prior husband, John. On advice of counsel, Mary refuses to answer on account of self-incrimination (adultery is still a crime in the jurisdiction) and relevancy.

You are the judge assigned to hear Helen's motion to compel Mary to answer the question. You have read a lot about custody mediation and note that a recent state statute authorizes the referral of cases to "appropriate ADR procedures." Would you refer this case to mediation? Why? If so, what type of mediator would you select? How might the case play out in mediation as compared to the pending court proceeding?

8.11 See question 5.13, p. 336.

References

AMERICAN BAR ASSOCIATION (1982) *Family Dispute Resolution: Options for All Ages.* Washington, D.C.: ABA.

BRYAN, Penelope E. (1992) "Killing Us Softly: Divorce Mediation and the Politics of Power," 40 *Buff. L. Rev.* 441.

——— (1994) "Reclaiming Professionalism: The Lawyer's Role in Divorce Mediation," 28 *Fam. L.Q.* 177.

BUSH, Robert A. Baruch (1992) *The Dilemmas of Mediation Practice.* Washington, D.C.: National Institute for Dispute Resolution.

CHANDLER, David (1990) "Violence, Fear, and Communication: The Variable Impact of Domestic Violence on Mediation," 7 *Mediation Q.* 331.

COLE, Sarah, Nancy ROGERS, and Craig A. McEWEN (2003 & 2006 Supp.) *Mediation: Law, Policy, Practice* (2d ed.). St. Paul: West.

COULSON, Robert (1996) *Family Mediation: Managing Conflict, Resolving Disputes.* San Francisco: Jossey-Bass.

DINGWALL, Robert, and John EEKELAAR, eds. (1988) *Divorce Mediation and the Legal Process.* New York: Oxford University Press.

ELLIS, Desmond (1996) *Mediating and Negotiating Marital Conflicts.* Thousand Oaks, CA: Sage.

EMERY, Robert E. (1994) *Renegotiating Family Relationships: Divorce, Child Custody, and Mediation.* New York: Guilford.

FISCHER, Karla, Neil VIDMAR, and Rene ELLIS (1993) "The Culture of Battering and the Role of Mediation in Domestic Violence Cases" 46 *S.M.U. L. Rev.* 2117.

FOLBERG, Jay (1983) "Divorce Mediation: Promises and Problems." Paper prepared for Midwinter Meeting of ABA Section on Family Law, St. Thomas (Jan.).

FOLBERG, Jay, and Ann MILNE, eds. (1988) *Divorce Mediation: Theory and Practice.* New York: Guilford.

FOLBERG, Jay, and Alison TAYLOR (1984) *Mediation: A Comprehensive Guide to Resolving Conflicts Without Litigation.* San Francisco: Jossey-Bass.

FOLBERG, Jay, Ann MILNE, and Peter SALEM, eds. (2004) *Divorce and Family Mediation — Models, Techniques, and Applications.* New York: Guilford.

FRIEDMAN, Gary, and Jack HIMMELSTEIN (1993) *A Guide to Divorce Mediation: How to Reach a Fair, Legal Settlement at a Fraction of the Cost.* New York: Workman.

FULLER, Lon (1971) "Mediation: Its Forms and Functions," 44 *S. Cal. L. Rev.* 305.

GAGNON, Andre G. (1992) "Ending Mandatory Divorce Mediation for Battered Women," 15 *Harv. Women's L.J.* 272.

GEFFNER, Robert, and Mildred PAGELOW (1990) "Mediation and Child Custody Abusive Relationships," 8 *Behav. Sci. & L.* 151.

GRILLO, Trina (1991) "The Mediation Alternative: Process Dangers for Women," 100 *Yale L.J.* 1545.

HAYNES, John (1981) *Divorce Mediation: A Practical Guide for Therapists and Counselors.* New York: Springer.

——— (1994) *The Fundamentals of Family Mediation.* Albany: State University of New York.

HAYNES, John M., Thelma FISHER, and Dick GREENSLADE (1993) *Alternative Dispute Resolution: Fundamentals of Family Mediation.* Kent, Eng.: Old Bailey Press.

KATZ, Lucy V. (1988) "Enforcing an ADR Clause — Are Good Intentions All You Have?," 26 *Am. Bus. L.J.* 575.

KELLY, Joan B., and Lynn L. GIGY (1989) "Divorce Mediation: Characteristics of Clients and Outcomes." In Kenneth Kressel and Dean C. Pruitt, eds. (1989) *Mediation Research: The Process and Effectiveness of Third-Party Intervention* 263. San Francisco: Jossey-Bass.

KISTHARDT, Mary Kay (1997) "The Use of Mediation and Arbitration for Resolving Family Conflicts: What Lawyers Think About Them," 14 *J. Am. Acad. Matrimonial L.* 353.

MARLOW, Lenard (1997) *Divorce Mediation: A Practice in Search of a Theory.* Garden City, N.Y.: Harlan Press.

MARLOW, Lenard, and S. Richard SAUBER (1990) *The Handbook of Divorce Mediation.* New York: Plenum.

MARTIN, John A., and Steven WELLER (2002) "Mediated Child Protection Conferencing: Lessons from the Wisconsin Unified Family Court Project," *Judge's J.* 5 (Spring).

MAUTE, Judith (1991) "Public Values and Private Justice: A Case for Mediator Accountability," 4 *Geo. J. Legal Ethics* 503.

McEWEN, Craig A., Richard MAIMAN, and Lynn MATHER (1994) "Lawyers, Mediation, and the Management of Divorce Practice," 28 *Law & Soc'y Rev.* 149.

Mcewen, Craig A., and Nancy H. ROGERS (1994) "Bring the Lawyers into Divorce Mediation," *Disp. Resol. Mag.* 8-10 (Summer).

MEDIATION QUARTERLY (1990) *Special Issue: Mediation and Spouse Abuse,* vol. 7, no. 4.

MERRY, Sally (1987) "The Culture and Practice of Mediation in Parent-Child Conflicts," 3 *Neg. J.* 411.

MNOOKIN, Robert, and Lewis KORNHAUSER (1979) "Bargaining in the Shadow of the Law: The Case of Divorce," 88 *Yale L.J.* 950.

MOSTEN, Forrest S. (1996) "Preventive Mediation in Blended Families," 3 *Disp. Resol. Mag.* No. 1, at 16.

——— (1997) *The Complete Guide to Mediation: The Cutting-Edge Approach to Family Law Practice.* Chicago: ABA.

PEARSON, Jessica (1994) "Family Mediation." In *National Symposium on Court-Connected Dispute Resolution Research, A Report on Current Research Findings — Implications for Courts and Future Research Needs,* 51-77. Washington, D.C.: State Justice Institute.

PEARSON, Jessica, and Nancy THOENNES (1989) "Divorce Mediation: Reflections on a Decade of Research in Mediation Research." In Kenneth Kressel and Dean C. Pruitt, eds. (1989) *Mediation Research: The Process and Effectiveness of Third-Party Intervention.* San Francisco: Jossey-Bass.

PORTLAND MEDIATION SERVICE (1992) *Mediation in Cases of Domestic Abuse: Helpful Option or Unacceptable Risks? The Final Report of the Domestic Abuse and Mediation Project.* Portland, Me.: Portland Mediation Service.

RIMELSPACH, René L. (2002) "Mediation Family Disputes in a World with Domestic Violence: How to Devise a Safe and Effective Court-Connected Mediation Program," 17 *Ohio St. J. Disp. Resol.* 95.

RISKIN, Leonard L. (1984) "Toward New Standards for the Neutral Lawyer in Mediation," 26 *Ariz. L. Rev.* 329.

———, ed. (1985) *Divorce Mediation: Readings.* Washington D.C.: ABA.

ROSENBERG, Joshua (1991) "In Defense of Mediation," 33 *Ariz. L. Rev.* 467.

SAPOSNEK, Donald T. (1998) *Mediating Child Custody Disputes: A Strategic Approach.* San Francisco: Jossey-Bass.

SCHWEBEL, Andrew I., and Milton SCHWEBEL (1996) "Mediating with Children: Two Psychologists' Views," 3 *Disp. Resol. Mag.* No. 1, at 3.

SILBERMAN, Linda (1982) "Professional Responsibility Problems of Divorce Mediation," 16 *Fam. L.Q.* 107.

SINGER, Linda (1994) *Settling Disputes: Conflict Resolution in Business, Families, and the Legal System* (2d ed.). Boulder: Westview Press.

SOMARY, Karen, and Robert EMERY (1991) "Emotional Anger and Grief in Divorce Mediation," 8 *Mediation Q.* 185.

SPENCER, Janet M., and Joseph P. ZAMMIT (1976) "Mediation-Arbitration: A Proposal for Private Resolution of Disputes Between Divorced or Separated Parents," 1976 *Duke L.J.* 911.

STATE OF MAINE JUDICIAL BRANCH (1997) *Domestic Abuse Screening and Assessment Guidelines.* West Bath, Me.: Court Alternative Dispute Resolution Service.

TREUTHART, Mary Pat (1993) "In Harm's Way? Family Mediation and the Role of the Attorney Advocate," 23 *Golden Gate U. L. Rev.* 717.

U.S. COMMISSION ON CIVIL RIGHTS (1982) *Under Rule of Thumb: Battered Women and the Administration of Justice.* Washington, D.C.: Government Printing Office.

VERMONT LAW SCHOOL DISPUTE RESOLUTION PROJECT (1987) *The Role of Mediation in Divorce Proceedings: A Comparative Perspective (United States, Canada, and Great Britain).* South Royalton: Vermont Law School.

YAFFEE, James (1972) *So Sue Me! The Story of a Community Court.* New York: Saturday Review Press.

YELLOTT, Ann (1990) "Mediation and Domestic Violence: A Call for Collaboration," 8 *Mediation Q.* 39.

Chapter 9
Public Disputes

The use of ADR methods to resolve disputes of public importance is an intriguing concept. Instead of the eternally frustrating political and judicial stalemate that often accompanies decisions involving siting of waste-disposal facilities or low-income housing, might it not be more productive to seek negotiated agreement of such disputes? In the first excerpt in this chapter, Lawrence Susskind and Jeffrey Cruikshank address some of the questions presented by efforts to seek negotiated agreement on public issues.

The chapter then turns to the use of negotiation as a means of developing federal agency regulations, a concept described in an excerpt from a seminal article by Philip Harter. This is followed by a summary of a recent study by Professor Coglianese that suggests that the benefits of negotiated rulemaking have been substantially overstated. Finally, a response by Harter takes issue with Coglianese and suggests that it is not the process of negotiated rulemaking that is flawed but the current administration of that process.

L. SUSSKIND AND J. CRUIKSHANK, BREAKING THE IMPASSE

4-11, 93-94, 101-105, 200-201, 241-243 (1987)

. . . Almost everyone in Middletown agreed that something needed to be done to help the homeless. The rapid rise in housing costs (as well as cutbacks in spending for public housing) had increased the number of families without shelter, as well as those living in terribly overcrowded conditions. In addition, the deinstitutionalization of mental patients and cutbacks in funds for mental health care dramatically increased the number of people with severe disabilities on the street. Crime levels had risen, both public and private social service agencies were overburdened, and a great many groups were clamoring for the city to take action.

A task force appointed by the mayor completed a quick survey that confirmed the scope of the problem. The task force report called on the city to make additional community development funds available to build and operate temporary shelters for the homeless. Next, the city's housing department identified fifteen possible sites for such shelters. The city welfare department then proposed an innovative design for inexpensive communal shelters. The local press supported the findings and recommendations of the task force, and editorialized in favor of quick action.

Nevertheless, as soon as the housing department's suggested list of sites was published, the city council was overwhelmed with calls from community groups and business organizations opposed to the construction of temporary shelters in their own neighborhoods. A new organization—Real Help for the Homeless (RHH)—began a media blitz against the idea of temporary shelters. They claimed that the people on the street were in need of permanent housing, as well as a wide range of support services—job training, better nutrition, family counseling, day care, and help in dealing with a range of alcohol and drug-related abuse problems. Moreover, RHH criticized the mayor for failing to appoint one of its members to the task force, and charged that the whole idea of temporary communal shelters was simply window dressing, designed to keep costs to a minimum and to salve the consciences of middle-class do-gooders.

A third group, the Coalition for the Homeless (CFH)—spearheaded by church groups and well-established social service organizations—went to court to press the city to act on the recommendations of the mayor's task force. CFH charged that the city was in violation of its own laws, as well as regulations governing the use of federal and state community development grants. These grants, they pointed out, were intended to benefit *all* citizens, especially the poor and the homeless.

Meanwhile, the city buildings department issued a statement indicating that the proposed temporary shelters would have to meet regular city building codes for residences or they would not be allowed to open. The state social service agency informed the mayor and the local welfare department that federal and state housing assistance funds had to be used to provide real housing, not simply temporary communal shelter. Without access to these funds, the city was going to have insufficient resources to tackle the problem of the homeless. Moreover, the social service agency expressed its opposition to temporary communal shelters as a solution to the problems of the homeless. . . . In one neighborhood, a group of residents drew up a referendum designed to exempt their community from consideration as a shelter site. They already had a jail, they argued; why should they also be stuck with a shelter?

In the first eighteen months after the task force issued its report, nothing was done. CFH's legal challenge was rejected by the court; it promptly filed an appeal. . . .

The mayor and the governor—who each represented different political parties—transformed the question of whether state housing assistance funds could be used for temporary shelter into a battle over local versus state control. Concurrently, bills introduced by Middletown's legislative delegation were bottled up in a subcommittee headed by a rural legislator, who cast the problem of homelessness as something each city should handle on its own. In various public forums and on talk shows, RHH and CFH engaged in increasingly acrimonious debates about the elusive distinction between the types of public assistance that would solve the problems of the homeless and those that would create dependency.

Winter came and went. Newspaper accounts of families suffering from exposure began to dwindle. As the public gradually lost interest, the city council and the mayor turned their attention to other issues. The municipal and state agencies involved with the problems of the homeless continued to meet and discuss alternative courses of action. The RHH members staged several dramatic confrontations, occupying an abandoned building that they claimed should be turned over to advocates for the homeless. The city council decided to hold still another round of hearings, but nothing came of them. During the summer and early fall, the city threatened police action to evict the squatters from the abandoned building, but again, nothing happened.

As the next Thanksgiving approached, the mayor announced that the city was about to begin construction of two temporary shelters. As soon as that announcement was made, angry residents in the two targeted neighborhoods went to court, charging that the proposed temporary structures would violate the city's zoning code and also that the city had failed to complete the necessary environmental impact studies. The RHH organized a demonstration by "street people" who announced that they would refuse to live in temporary communal shelters. Then, RHH insisted that it should be given funds to build real housing and provide social services for the homeless.

The Middletown Chamber of Commerce announced that it had identified a team of experienced business executives prepared to work with the city to find ways of operating the two existing shelters more effectively. This turn of events suggested that the problems of the homeless had once again percolated to the top of the city's agenda. This time, though, there were differences. In general, the key players had a lot less patience. The mayor was rebuffed when he sought further support from the business community. Several neighborhood leaders who were energetic and respected participants the previous winter now dropped out of sight. On other fronts, people who could have been helpful apparently decided to throw in the towel. . . .

Though our representative democracy—with its separate levels and branches of government—is the foundation of our political system, we need to improve the ways in which we use it to resolve public disputes. We must achieve better results at lower cost. In particular, we need to find ways of dealing with differences that will restore public confidence in government, and improve relationships among the various segments of our society.

Fortunately, new approaches to resolving public disputes have been developed and tested over the past few years. . . . Those tools are *negotiated approaches to consensus building* and they have worked effectively in many situations.

Consensus building requires informal, face-to-face interaction among specially chosen representatives of all "stakeholding" groups; a voluntary effort to seek "all-gain" rather than "win-lose" solutions or watered-down political compromise; and, often, the assistance of a neutral facilitator or mediator. Such approaches must be treated as supplements—and not alternatives—to conventional decision making. Officials with statutory power must retain their authority in order to ensure accountability.

Negotiated approaches to consensus building are both deceptively simple and extraordinarily complex. What could possibly be simpler than the idea of getting everyone in a dispute together to talk things out? Yet consider the challenging questions that must be answered before anyone is likely to come to the negotiation table.

- How should the appropriate participants be identified?
- How can informal negotiations avoid violating "sunshine" (e.g., open meeting) laws and other regulations that guarantee government accountability?
- Why would those with formal authority or substantial political power agree to meet with less powerful groups?

- Do people have to give up their right to litigate if they participate in a consensus-building effort?
- How can ad hoc groups be bound by the promises they make?
- What sort of technical help must be provided to less experienced participants?

Successful negotiations are difficult to manage, and when more than two parties are involved, they are especially complicated. Because distributional disputes typically involve quite a few groups (each made up of numerous members) who may have little or no experience working together, they are among the most difficult to resolve through face-to-face negotiation.

Based on our experience in the field of public dispute resolution, and given the daunting list of obstacles cited earlier, we have concluded that most distributional disputes — and certainly the most complex ones — can only be resolved with the aid of a professional intermediary, whose job it is to offer nonpartisan assistance at key steps in the negotiation process. . . .

[Among the "key steps in the negotiation process" at which Susskind and Cruikshank suggest a mediator can be helpful is the following:]

Representation

. . . Productive negotiations cannot begin until two problems are solved: figuring out which groups should be represented, and choosing representatives empowered to speak for the groups they claim to represent.

On the first point, our experience suggests that it is always better to include too many people or groups than too few — especially at the outset. There is a logistical advantage, of course, in limiting the number of voices directly involved in consensus-building discussions. That advantage is far outweighed, however, by the problems that arise if someone decides they have been unfairly excluded.

It is possible to begin with a large number of potential stakeholders and reduce the size of the group through the election or designation of selected representatives. This can be achieved by shifting the focus from the number of parties to the categories of people who want (and ought) to participate. . . .

In some situations, it may prove impossible to put together an effective group in time. Some groups may need time to select representatives. Other groups (typically those representing the poor, people without political connections, or groups such as illegal aliens with dubious or no legal standing) may need financial assistance. Even when members of such groups perceive themselves to be a coherent interest group, they may be unable to present their views effectively. These unempowered groups often need organizational support to ensure fair representation.

There is no simple generalization to be made about the resolution of these problems. Nevertheless, the parties to a public dispute must agree that it is necessary to involve all legitimate stakeholding interests in whatever negotiations are planned. If they leave out a key group, even unintentionally, the credibility of ad hoc consensus building may be irretrievably damaged. . . .

When the representatives arrive at the table, another challenge to effective negotiations presents itself. How can negotiators be sure that those at the table can actually commit the groups they purport to represent? This is a terribly important point. There is nothing more frustrating than discovering at the last minute that a designated spokesperson was not empowered to speak for his or her group.

One way of avoiding such letdowns is to clarify at the outset what representation means. Unlike elected officials with statutory authority, ad hoc representatives are rarely empowered to commit their members to anything. They should, however, be in a good position to shuttle back and forth between the negotiating group and the people they represent. Their task is not to speak for their constituents, but to speak with them. Representatives in ad hoc negotiations of the sort we advocate serve primarily to amplify the concerns of larger groups, to carry messages and information to them, and to return with a sense of the group's willingness to commit to whatever consensus emerges.

[Other tasks with which the mediator in consensus building negotiation can assist (discussed by the authors at pp. 105-129) are drafting protocols and setting an agenda, dealing with the media, organizing joint fact-finding, inventing options for mutual gain, producing a written agreement, binding the parties to their commitments, and obtaining ratification. The latter is a crucial step, since it is at this point that a splinter group may come forward to challenge the agreement that has been reached. How should this problem be dealt with?]

. . . The emergence of a splinter group cannot be fully guarded against. Your best insurance is to pay a great deal of attention to the representation issues throughout the negotiating process. Be sure to confirm, as often as you can, that the representatives are in close contact with their respective groups. When agreement is reached, be sure each representative takes it back to his or her constituents for ratification. . . .

What happens when a splinter group does emerge? This question can be broken into two parts. First, how do you interact with such a group? And second, what happens if that group resorts to litigation — the very outcome you have worked long and hard to avoid?

The first question is relatively easy to answer. You should adopt the following stance: "Look — here is what we did. Here's how the process worked; it was open and thorough. Here's the agreement we reached; it attends to the interests of all those who chose to participate. I'm sorry, but this issue is not currently open to further discussion. . . . Of course, if you can come up with an amendment to the agreement that everyone involved will accept, that's another story." In other words, use your commitment to the process to deflect the splinter group. . . .

The second question is somewhat more troublesome. Perhaps if we phrase it differently — "Does litigation invalidate all that has gone before?" — the answer comes more easily: No. If you have kept an adequate record of your process (such as minutes of meetings), and if you have produced a public document that the interested parties have all signed, these facts may well be considered favorably by the courts. You certainly cannot prevent a group from litigating, but given a sound process and an outcome that all the participants support, you may be able to blunt a court's willingness to hear the complaint, or at least minimize the court's sympathy for the complainant. . . .

[The next crucial step, if agreement is reached, is linking the informal agreement to the formal process for government decision-making.]

After the agreement is ratified, the negotiating parties must find a way to link the ad hoc, informal agreement they have fashioned to the formal decision-making processes of government. Up to this point, typically, the negotiating process has been kept "unofficial." (It may have been this very ad hoc quality, in fact, which persuaded some of the key players to participate.) An unofficial process has produced an informal result, which probably could not have been reached by other means; the challenge now is to formalize that result. It seems paradoxical: How can an informal agreement be formalized?

The answer to this question varies, of course, depending on individual circumstances. In some instances, the negotiated agreement can be converted into a statute or a bylaw by a legislative vote. In others, it may be converted into a legally enforceable contract with city, state, or federal agencies. In still others, an executive order or administrative action may put an agency of the government on record as the enforcer of the agreement. Each of these approaches presents its own advantages and perils. (A statute, for example, is only as permanent as the legislative and judicial branches allow it to be.) Nevertheless, the negotiating parties must seek and employ the most effective means for linking the formal and the informal processes of decision making. . . .

Limits on Consensual Approaches to Dispute Resolution

Why are the techniques described in this book still underutilized?

The most important reason seems to be a concern on the part of public officials that participating in consensual negotiations may constitute an abdication of legal responsibility. Such assumptions are misplaced. . . . As long as the consensus-building process is conducted openly and all interested parties are invited to participate, there is no reason to worry about abdication of responsibility. Moreover, if the product of such negotiations is an informal written agreement that must still be ratified, all due process and equal protection requirements can be met.

Some public officials presume that consensus building means giving up power. This is not true. Because informally negotiated agreements must be formally ratified by those in positions of authority, the status quo with regard to decision making will not change. Moreover, consensus means that all key participants — including the elected and appointed officials involved — must agree that an agreement serves their interests. Thus, no official who initiates or agrees to participate in a consensus-building process is giving up his or her power to veto an outcome. . . .

From citizens and public interest advocates, we often encounter concerns about entering negotiations when resources and political power are unequally distributed. "Won't less powerful and less well-endowed parties be coopted or overwhelmed by more powerful adversaries?" they ask, "Isn't court the only place that the parties with less political power can be sure of getting fair treatment?"

In fact, conventional approaches to resolving distributional disputes place a heavy emphasis on political power and legal rights. Legislatures are particularly sensitive to the "clout" of lobbyists and interest groups. The courts, for their part, are primarily concerned with determining past facts rather than shaping future possibilities. This favors the innocent, not the less powerful. Moreover, the courts are singularly unconcerned about future relationships. The distributional cases that wind up in court are handled pretty much like criminal cases — winners and losers are identified — because that is what the courts are equipped to do.

Less powerful groups may have legitimate concerns about entering into consensus-building negotiations, but they should be wary as well about engaging in expensive court battles when distributional issues, rather than legal rights, are at stake.

Power and politics are essential ingredients in all public disputes, and they cannot be ignored. But consensus-building approaches to dispute resolution place a premium on problem solving rather than "settling" disputes. When the outcomes could be life-threatening, even the most politically powerful groups should be worried about the wisdom of the agreements reached. Indeed, in many public disputes a wise outcome is much more urgent than winning. When a powerful group commits to work for consensus, it tacitly agrees that raw political power is not a sufficient basis for resolving public disputes. This empowers those who are less politically powerful. On the other hand, it takes nothing away from those with more political power because all groups retain a veto. . . .

Questions

9.1 Suppose that the mayor of Middletown contacts you and asks you to organize a consensus-building negotiation to resolve the problem of shelter for the homeless. What steps would you take? What problems might you encounter, and how might you deal with them?

9.2 Suppose that the groups involved in the Middletown dispute conducted lengthy and open negotiations that involved a mediator, the state housing agency, and all interested parties and reached an agreement regarding the location of shelters. A member of one of the participating organizations then brought suit to enjoin construction of the shelters, alleging that the location of the shelters provided for in the agreement violated the city zoning law.

You are the judge before whom the matter is pending. You conclude that the agreement's compliance with the zoning law is a very close question but that, on balance, it probably does not comply. What should you do? Why?

9.3 Suppose that in the course of the litigation referred to in question 9.2 the supporters of the agreement seek to introduce into evidence the minutes of the consensus-building session at which a lengthy discussion of Middletown's zoning law took place. Plaintiff objects, fearing that these minutes may weaken his case. What arguments should plaintiff make in support of his objection? How would you rule on plaintiff's objection? Why?

9.4 Despite the importance that Susskind and Cruikshank place on the aid of a mediator in the resolution of public disputes, public officials rarely seek such assistance. To some extent this reflects a lack of knowledge that such resources exist and may be useful. Additionally, public officials may fear a loss of their authority to an outside manager of the dispute resolution process. Thus a formidable problem for the would-be mediator of public disputes is often that of achieving entry into the dispute (Murray, 1984).

Successful entry is sometimes achieved through the intervention of the judge before whom litigation relating to the dispute is pending. The judge may perceive the value of mediation more clearly than the parties, and it may require his encouragement for the parties to accept mediation. At times, as discussed in Chapter 6, a judge will seek to demonstrate his commitment to the mediation effort by appointing the mediator as a special master of the court (Fine, 1987:207-244).

Such an appointment encourages the parties to take the process seriously. It also strengthens the mediator's ability to assure the participants that he cannot be called to testify about the negotiations (see Chapter 7). Still another advantage may lie in the ability of the mediator to communicate with the judge. For example, the mediator might advise the judge whether ruling on a pending motion would interfere with the negotiations. Or the mediator might find out from the judge whether a draft agreement would be acceptable to the judge and, if not, what changes would be necessary to make it acceptable. What, if any, objections are there to this form of communication between the judge and the mediator? Are these objections sufficiently powerful to preclude such communication?

9.5 Consensus-building negotiation has been extensively used to resolve public disputes affecting the environment. Judge Harry Edwards (1986:677-678), however, finds such negotiations troubling:

> . . . When Congress or a government agency has enacted strict environmental protection standards, negotiations that compromise these strict standards with weaker standards result in the application of values that are simply inconsistent with the rule of law. Furthermore, environmental mediation and negotiation present the danger that environmental standards will be set by private groups without the democratic checks of governmental institutions. Professor Schoenbrod recently has written of an impressive environmental mediation involving the settlement of disputes concerning the Hudson River. According to Schoenbrod, in that case private parties bypassed federal and state agencies, reached an accommodation on environmental issues, and then presented the settlement to governmental regulators. The alternative to approval of the settlement was continued litigation, which was already in its seventeenth year, with no end in sight.
>
> The resulting agreement may have been laudable in bringing an end to protracted litigation. But surely the mere resolution of a dispute is not proof that the public interest has been served. This is not to say that private settlements can never produce results that are consistent with the public interest; rather, it is to say that private settlements are troubling when we have no assurance that the legislative- or agency-mandated standards have been followed, and when we have no satisfactory explanation as to why there may have been a variance from the rule of law. . . .

Do you share Judge Edwards's concerns? Why?

9.6 The negotiated resolution of a public dispute is often embodied in a consent decree. This provides an opportunity for broad public comment on the negotiated resolution before it becomes final, court approval of the resolution, and greater certainty of compliance thereafter. An interesting question is the extent to which changed circumstances subsequent to the entry of a consent decree should permit a court to modify that decree. In one case, for example, jail inmates brought an action against the county sheriff, alleging that the conditions under which pretrial detainees were held, particularly the placing of two persons in a single cell ("double-celling") violated the Constitution. After a judgment in the inmates' favor, the district court enjoined the sheriff from housing detainees in the jail after a certain date. State and county officials were unable to provide an acceptable plan for a new jail by that date, and the court held that if they failed to do so within six months, it would order the old jail closed. The parties then entered into an agreement, embodied in a consent decree, that established standards for a new jail and provided that the old jail could be used, beyond the six-month pending period, pending completion of the new one.

Subsequently, the Supreme Court held that double-celling of pretrial detainees in another jail did not violate the Constitution. The sheriff now contends that the Supreme Court's ruling, as well as a substantial increase in the number of pretrial detainees, justifies modifying the consent decree to authorize double-celling. How should the court rule?

9.7 What are the principal differences between the mediation of public policy disputes and mediation of more traditional private disputes?

9.8 What are the special qualifications needed for public policy mediators? Subject matter expertise? Special process skills?

Note: Consensus Building

The necessary major steps in a consensus building effort are more systematically examined in the Consensus Building Handbook (1999:20-35):

1. Convening (including the preparation of a conflict assessment);
2. Identification of appropriate representatives;
3. Location of necessary funding;
4. Clarification of roles of facilitators, mediators and recorders;
5. Setting an agenda and ground rules;
6. Encouraging constructive deliberations (e.g., separate inventing from deciding, use of single negotiating text);
7. Use of subcommittees;
8. Ways of obtaining expert advice;
9. Seeking ratification by constituencies; and
10. Addressing issues of implementation.*

The Handbook contains 17 chapters, some of which elaborate the various steps listed above, while others address particular issues (e.g., chapter 12 "Dealing With Deep Value Differences," and chapter 13 "Legal Issues in Consensus Building").

The volume concludes with 17 case studies of consensus building at work in a variety of settings ranging from a superfund cleanup on Cape Cod (Case 7) to negotiating AIDS Policies in Colorado (Case 14).** Each case description is "annotated" by one or more dispute resolution scholars. An unusual case (No. 2) involving a four-town area in Maine that had elevated cancer rates is summarily described below; the various steps are more fully analyzed at pp. 713-741 of the Handbook.

*For an alternative description of the necessary steps, see Best Practices, 1997.

**For application of consensus building to environmental disputes, see Susskind et al., 2000; to land use disputes, see Susskind and van der Wansem, 1999.

An effort to create a U.S. Consensus Council is pending in Congress (Gross, 2002).

S. McKEARNAN AND P. FIELD, THE NORTHERN OXFORD COUNTY COALITION: FOUR MAINE TOWNS TACKLE A PUBLIC HEALTH MYSTERY*

Consensus Building Handbook (1999)

In February 1991, a popular New England television news show ran a segment called "Cancer Valley." The story depicted a rural American community's worst nightmare. It suggested that the people living in Northern Oxford County, Maine were experiencing extraordinarily high rates of cancer, and it implied that air emissions from a local paper mill might be responsible. Images of local residents walking through cemeteries, with the mill's billowing smokestacks looming in the distance, struck an alarmist tone.

The television show amplified a debate that had been under way for some time in four rural towns surrounding, and economically dependent on, the mill: Rumford, Mexico, Peru, and Dixfield (hereafter referred to as the four-town area). For many residents of the towns, the television show lent credence to suspicions that an abnormally high percentage of their family members, friends, and neighbors had contracted cancer. Others were angry, opposing the claim that there was a health problem in their community. These residents warned that the label "Cancer Valley" could unjustly tarnish the community's reputation and hinder economic development for a long time to come. Still others were equally concerned that the controversy over cancer rates would force the mill to close, breaking the valley's economic backbone.

In the midst of the controversy, the mill was indignant about the charges leveled against it. Mill managers pointed out that they were in compliance with all existing federal and state regulations concerning air quality. They were quick to note that the mill had recently invested more than $50 million in technologies designed to reduce both the odor and the toxicity of the wastes emitted through the mill's stacks.

Although many residents had very real fears of high cancer rates, few data were available to substantiate or alleviate those fears. Likewise, data on the quality of the air in the four towns were limited. In the absence of credible information, the controversy seemed sure to produce an extended series of attacks and counterattacks. In a set of communities small enough that people recognize each other at crosswalks or in the supermarket, this kind of protracted debate was sure to be painful. But what could any one person do? What, if anything, could the community do collectively?

With leadership from the Maine Department of Environmental Protection (DEP) and the U.S. Environmental Protection Agency (EPA), town residents on different sides of the debate came together in 1994 to initiate a community-based consensus building process. They called their group the Northern Oxford County Coalition (NOCC).

The 25-member coalition met over two years, with support from the Consensus Building Institute (CBI), a nonprofit provider of nonpartisan facilitation assistance. Many stakeholder groups participated, including concerned residents of the towns (including some employed by the mill), health care providers, small businesses, the mill management, local and state elected officials (including members of the Maine

*Written by Sarah McKearnan and Patrick Field.

legislature), and state and federal agencies responsible for protecting human health and the environment.

Over two years, the coalition gradually overcame distrust and recriminations to complete several fact-finding and action-oriented projects. The members

- jointly designed a study to investigate cancer rates in the valley,
- initiated a community-wide radon-testing program through which 400 homeowners tested their homes for the cancer-causing gas,
- worked with agencies to evaluate recent air-monitoring data and to design a continuing air-monitoring program,
- held a public forum on dioxin and pollution prevention,
- wrote and distributed an action plan with numerous recommendations in the form of a community newsletter, and
- organized a new "Health Communities" coalition to continue the work of the NOCC.

In addition to conducting studies and organizing forums, the NOCC allowed residents with differing viewpoints, incomes, and interests to build more trusting and collaborative working relationships. This case study does not seek to retell the complete story of the NOCC. Rather, it explores in depth several aspects of the work undertaken by the NOCC, including getting started, investigating cancer rates jointly, and taking actions to ensure that the coalition's recommendations would be implemented. The case study also identifies key lessons about the process of building consensus in a community setting.

Question

9.9 What do you suppose will be the main obstacles encountered by NOCC? Suppose the data gathered had shown that the emissions by the mill were toxic, and that there was a high likelihood — but no certainty — that this toxicity contributed to the elevated cancer rates. Would that be likely to torpedo the consensus building efforts and lead to more adversary procedures?

Note: Negotiated Rulemaking

Among the uses of consensus-building negotiations to resolve public policy disputes has been the negotiation of regulations by federal agencies. Traditionally, federal regulations are developed under procedures established by the Administrative Procedure Act of 1946. Using in-house expertise and informal meetings with parties who will be affected by the rule, an agency will issue a proposed regulation. This is followed by an opportunity for public comment, usually in writing, and then agency promulgation of a final rule. This traditional notice and comment approach to rulemaking has been criticized as both slow and adversarial, leading to high levels of judicial review, sometimes quite lengthy (Susskind and McMahon, 1985:134).

Philip Harter, in a seminal article published in 1982, suggested that the failure of the traditional rulemaking model to result in final rules in a timely fashion was primarily due to the adversarial nature of that model. Harter wrote (19-20):

> The agencies and the private parties tend to take extreme positions, expecting that they may be pushed toward the middle. For example, an agency may propose a far more stringent regulation than it expects to issue ultimately because it expects the adversarial process to create considerable pressure for it to moderate its position. Moreover, if the agency tempers its original proposal, the agency appears reasonable and responsive.
>
> The private participants tend to take extreme positions because they also expect to be drawn toward the middle as part of the adversarial process. Participants that oppose any regulation or that hope to obtain a minimally intrusive regulation may argue that no regulation is needed or that at most a weak one is required, and will tailor their evidence accordingly. Because the parties advocate the extreme, they may be reluctant to provide data to the agency and to each other because they fear the data may be misused or reveal weaknesses in the extreme position. Thus, it is frequently difficult for parties to join forces, and frontally address the factual and policy questions. Instead, the parties dig in and defend their extreme positions.
>
> In addition, the adversarial process affects the presentation of proposals when people deal with each other as adversaries. A party is likely to encounter difficulty in expressing its true concerns because it may fear losing on issues of minor interest without gaining concessions on those it cares about a great deal. Moreover, a party may feel compelled to advocate a position it may not actually favor at the time to preserve the option of advocating that position in the future. Thus, the parties' presentations appear flat; they raise every issue to nearly equal prominence and place far more issues in contention than may be necessary.
>
> The parties in an adversarial process do not deal directly with one another; rather, each makes its presentation to the decisionmaker. Because of this presentation, the issues in controversy may be limited to those within the jurisdiction of the forum. These issues, however, may not be the ones actually separating the parties. For example, one wonders whether the challenge to the Tellico Dam in *Tennessee Valley Authority v. Hill* was prompted by a grave concern for the endangered snail darter or by a broader opposition to the adverse effect on the environment and human life. If the parties are unable to define the true issues of concern, the decisionmaker and the other parties will have difficulty in addressing the parties' positions and in making informed tradeoffs when developing the factual basis of a rule and striking the inherently political choice embodied therein.

In response to these concerns Harter suggested that federal agencies experiment with negotiated rulemaking (sometimes referred to as regulatory negotiation or "reg-neg"). In this process, the agency and the private parties with a significant stake in the proposed rule participate in facilitated face-to-face negotiations designed to produce a consensus. In these negotiations, they have the opportunity, lacking in the adversarial process, to explore shared interests and differences of opinion, collaborate in gathering and analyzing technical information, generate options, and bargain and trade across those options according to their different priorities. If agreement is reached, it is published as the agency's notice of proposed rulemaking, and then the conventional review and comment process takes over. Because, however, most or all of the interested parties have participated in framing the proposed rule, there should be little critical comment, and few judicial challenges (Susskind and McMahon, 1985:136-137).

In 1990, Congress passed the Negotiated Rulemaking Act, establishing a framework for negotiated rulemaking similar to that proposed by Harter (1982) and used by most federal agencies. In 1996, Congress amended certain confidentiality provisions of the Act and repealed those provisions that had called for the Act to expire after five years.

In its statement of findings supporting the passage of the 1990 Act, Congress found that "[a]gencies currently use rulemaking procedures that may . . . cause parties with different interests to assume conflicting and antagonistic positions and to engage in expensive and time-consuming litigation over agency rules." Negotiated rulemaking, on the other hand, "can increase the acceptability and improve the substance of rules, making it less likely that the affected parties will resist enforcement or challenge such rules in court. It may also shorten the amount of time needed to issue final rules."

So much for the theory. In 1997, Professor Cary Coglianese of the Kennedy School of Government challenged the claims of the reg-neg proponents. He asserted that: (1) the procedure was used in only 68 cases between 1993 and 1996, whereas 47,603 regulations were adopted by the traditional method; (2) reg-neg was not faster; (3) its use did not reduce the frequency of litigation challenging agency rules; and (4) reg-neg is a costly process for the participating organizations.

The reaction to Coglianese's critique raises interesting questions of empirical methodology. Specifically, respondents pointed out that the cases examined by Coglianese were not selected at random and hence were not representative of the typical rule promulgation. Thus, if the selected cases presented unusual difficulties, that would obviously affect the time and cost involved. Similarly, one would have to compare closely the quality of the reg-neg rules with that of the notice-and-comment-promulgated rules. Costs, too, would have to be carefully compared.

Harter (2000) concludes as follows:

> If "better rules" were the aspiration of negotiated rulemaking, the question remains as to whether the process has lived up to that expectation. From my own personal experience, the rules that emerge from negotiated rulemaking tend to be both more stringent and yet more cost-effective to implement. That somewhat paradoxical result comes precisely from the practical orientation of the committee because it can determine what information is needed to make a reasonable, responsible decision and what actions will best achieve the goal. It can, therefore, avoid common regulatory mistakes that are costly but do not contribute substantially to accomplishing the task.
>
> The only formal evaluation of negotiated rulemaking that has been conducted supports these observations. . . .
>
> The benefits envisioned by the proponents of negotiated rulemaking have indeed been realized. That is demonstrated both by Coglianese's own methodology when properly applied and by Kerwin and Langbein's work, the only careful and comprehensive study of reg-neg. Reg-neg has proven to be an enormously powerful tool in addressing highly complex, politicized rules, the very kind that stall agencies when traditional or conventional procedures are used. Properly understood and appropriately used, negotiated rulemaking does indeed fulfill its proponents' expectations.

Questions

9.10 Assume that Coglianese and Harter both accurately characterize the advantages and disadvantages. For what types of proposed rulemaking should an agency use negotiated rulemaking?

9.11 The Negotiated Rulemaking Act of 1990 provides that "a rule which is the product of negotiated rulemaking shall not be accorded any greater deference by a court than a rule which is the product of other rulemaking procedures." Is this an appropriate standard of judicial review for rules developed by negotiated rulemaking? What other standard might be used? Compare Wald (1985) with Harter (1986).

9.12 EPA is contemplating convening a negotiated rulemaking procedure to develop a rule governing disposal of low-level radioactive waste. The industry has indicated a willingness to agree to a rule that would bar all but a de minimis level of radioactivity at disposal sites, and several environmental groups have informally indicated a willingness to accept such a standard, though they would expect to negotiate just what level would be regarded as de minimis, as well as other related issues. Two important environmental groups, however, have told EPA that while they will certainly participate in a negotiated rulemaking if EPA convenes it, their position is that the de minimis level must be zero. Should EPA convene the contemplated rulemaking procedure? Why?

9.13 In early 1994, the Federal Communications Commission (FCC) convened a negotiated rulemaking committee for the purpose of negotiating rules relating to mobile telephone satellite services. The procedures used by the FCC in this negotiated rulemaking were described by one participant (Goldberg, 1994) as follows:

> The agency selected participants to represent all interests affected by the proposed rules, convened representatives of those interests to serve as a negotiated rulemaking advisory committee, and nominated a facilitator for the committee. The facilitator had technical expertise on the issues under consideration, as well as experience in chairing committees, but no dispute resolution experience as mediator or arbitrator.
>
> Most of the industry participants were represented by a team of lawyers and technical experts. The agency was represented by a senior technical expert, who was assisted by agency attorneys and members of the agency technical staff. All the industry participants believed that if no consensus was reached on proposed rules, the agency representative would play a significant role in the agency's internal deliberations regarding proposed rules. The agency representative was not, however, authorized to communicate the agency's views on the merits of the proposals made by industry representatives or the agency's likely action in the event no consensus was reached. Accordingly, he did not do so.

The negotiated rulemaking committee reached consensus on some issues, but did not do so on the central issue — a rule regarding the sharing of available spectrum by providers of mobile satellite services. Which, if any, aspects of the procedures used in the rulemaking may have contributed to the failure to reach consensus?

EXERCISE 9.1: THE HALFWAY HOUSE*

Northampton is a decaying manufacturing center in the Midwest, with a population of 150,000. The city recently has begun to attract new business and to

*This exercise is based on a simulation developed by Linda Singer and Michael Lewis, Washington, D.C.

undertake modest urban renewal. Due to declining enrollment and budgetary restraints, the city has had to close several elementary schools. All but one of the vacant schools have been torn down or auctioned off to private developers at a price well below the market value of the land. The one remaining school, Larchmont, is now vacant. Larchmont School is located on a relatively quiet residential street in a middle-class neighborhood.

Recently, the director of the State Department of Rehabilitation approached the mayor of Northampton and asked whether the city would consider renting Larchmont School to the Center for Community Living, a private, nonprofit corporation that would operate a halfway house for former patients of the State Mental Hospital. The Department of Rehabilitation would contract with Community Living to house 60 residents in the school, after it had been renovated at the department's expense.

The department must find community placements for as many patients of the State Mental Hospital as possible, since it is under court order to reduce overcrowding in the hospital within 60 days. Since the department failed to comply with a previous order concerning conditions at the State Mental Hospital, it faces a real possibility of being held in contempt of court if it fails to meet this deadline. The department is seeking to set up halfway houses in a number of communities.

The mayor has the authority to rent Larchmont School to the Center for Community Living if she decides that is the best use of the property. Making that decision, however, may not be easy. Word of the proposed halfway house has leaked out, and the neighborhood is in an uproar. Last week the school was vandalized.

In order to provide a forum for discussion about the proposed halfway house, the mayor has scheduled a meeting between her representatives, the State Department of Rehabilitation, the Center for Community Living, and representatives of the groups opposing the halfway house. The groups opposing the halfway house are the Larchmont Property Owners' Association, the Grey Panthers, and the Larchmont PTA.

(Confidential facts are provided in the Teacher's Manual.)

EXERCISE 9.2 CAROLINE'S DONUT SHOP*

Pleasantown is a comfortably affluent suburb of wide, tree-lined streets and graceful gardens. It sits on the outskirts of Metropolis, one of the major cities of the state. During the past two years, and particularly in the last several months, Metropolis has become home to a growing number of refugees from the nation of Libertad, where civil war has threatened lives and has led to a breakdown in the market system for their crops and products.

The city planners of Pleasantown placed the town's "main drag" of charming shops, trees, and restaurants on High Street, a road leading directly into Metropolis. A bus regularly travels between the two communities, taking city workers into town and bringing back shoppers. Caroline's Donut Shop is located on High Street near a bus stop. Like most of Pleasantown's shops, Caroline's provides parking for only one

*This exercise was written by Cheryl B. McDonald, Pepperdine University School of Law, and Nancy Rogers and is reprinted with their permission.

or two cars; most of Caroline's business comes from people waiting for the bus or enjoying a shopping stroll.

Over the past few months large numbers of Libertadan men have been hanging around Caroline's Donut Shop. They arrive early in the morning and usually lean against the walls outside Caroline's and neighboring businesses, drinking coffee, talking to one another, and waiting.

Every weekday morning, just as the commuter traffic begins to build, gardeners and construction contractors, among others, come cruising slowly along High Street searching for day workers from among the gathered Libertadans. Because there is no place to park, workers rush out to cars and trucks in the street in order to guarantee their selection for one job or another. Some of the potential employers have hired particular men in the past, and they wait with their motors running until others have cleared a path for their favorites to get close enough to jump into the truck. The frenzy is usually over in an hour or two—most contractors get an early start. But with lowered demands in recent weeks, more and more of the Libertadans are left on the sidewalk.

Most of the workers have bus fare for only one round trip per day. Many are illiterate or speak only Spanish. Some are in the country illegally. As a result, they have little prospect for other work; they stay at Caroline's just in case someone has a late job. Some drink coffee or soda, leaving the empty containers on the curb or sidewalk. Some step out into the street to wave at passing vehicles. One or two follow women with their eyes as they pass by, sometimes making comments or laughing behind their backs. Some have used nearby lawns and bushes as toilets.

The homeowners and merchants of Pleasantown have become more and more upset over the last few months by the men gathering in front of Caroline's. The merchants feel that having the men hanging around makes potential customers (most of whom are women, out in the middle of the day) uneasy and that their businesses are suffering as a result. They have expressed concern that someone will be killed as people run out and have conversations in the street. The residents also complain about the disruption of early morning traffic. They have requested increased police patrols around the area, but that does not seem to have helped.

Last month some of the unhappy residents of Pleasantown put pressure on the town council to pass an ordinance prohibiting any person from standing on the street or highway to solicit employment from anyone in a motor vehicle and prohibiting any occupant of a stopped or parked motor vehicle from hiring a person from the vehicle. Although the owner of Caroline's tried to argue that the Libertadans were not hurting anyone (in fact, their labor was making Pleasantown an *affordable,* beautiful place to live) and were nice people, the ordinance passed unanimously.

As soon as the Libertadans found out about the ordinance, they realized what a threat it was to their ability to make a living. The gathering place at Pleasantown is conveniently accessible by cheap transportation and offers the only steady work to be found. The men feel that what little bread they can feed their families is being snatched from their mouths. Even though they have no money, they must fight back. They have enlisted the support of a group in the local parish. One of the church members has been asked to be their spokesperson and to accompany them as they come to you for help.

You are aware that a case involving a similar situation was filed in another jurisdiction. The complaint raised first and fourteenth amendment issues. Unfortunately, the court in that case refused to enjoin enforcement of the ordinance.

You will be assigned to a small group. Working together, prepare one member to advise your clients, the Libertad day workers, on the following questions:

1. Assume that no action has been taken since the passage of the ordinance. What are the advantages or disadvantages for the clients of trying mediation in this case?

2. If a mediation will be arranged for this case, what is the best timing in relation to litigation (that is, filing the action, conducting formal or informal discovery, filing motions, and so forth)?

3. Assume for questions 3 through 6 that the parties have agreed in principle to mediate the case. Who should attend? Parties only? Lawyers only? Both? Who should participate?

4. If representatives of the laborers, the merchants, the homeowners, and the town council will attend the mediation, should there be ground rules about disclosures to others, including the press? What ground rules do you propose?

5. How should the mediator(s) be selected? What qualifications should the mediator(s) have?

6. If the clients will attend the mediation session, how will you prepare them for the mediation session? How do you anticipate that your role as counsel in the mediation will differ from your role representing the clients at trial?

References

BACOW, Lawrence S., and Michael WHEELER (1984) *Environmental Dispute Resolution.* New York: Plenum.

BEST PRACTICES FOR GOVERNMENT AGENCIES—Guidelines for Using Collaborative Agreement-Seeking Processes (1997). http:/www.acresolution.org/research.nsf/key/EPPbestpractices.

CARPENTER, Susan, and W. J. D. KENNEDY (1988) *Managing Public Disputes.* San Francisco: Jossey-Bass.

COGLIANESE, Cary (1997) "Assessing Consensus: The Promise and Performance of Negotiated Rulemaking," 46 *Duke L.J.* 1255.

CROWFOOT, James E., and Julia M. WONDOLLECK (1991) *Environmental Disputes: Community Involvement in Conflict Resolution.* Washington, D.C.: Island Press.

EDWARDS, Harry T. (1986) "Alternative Dispute Resolution: Panacea or Anathema," 99 *Harv. L. Rev.* 668.

FINE, Erika S., ed. (1987) *ADR and the Courts: A Manual for Judges and Lawyers.* New York: Butterworth.

FREEMAN, Jody (1997) "Collaborative Governance in the Administrative State," 45 *UCLA L. Rev.* 1.

FUNK, William (1997) "Bargaining Towards the New Millennium: Regulatory Negotiation and the Subversion of the Public Interest," 46 *Duke L.J.* 1351.

GOLDBERG, Stephen B. (1994) "Reflections on Negotiated Rulemaking," 9 *Wash. Law.* 42 (Sept./Oct.).

GOLDMANN, Robert, ed. (1980) *Roundtable Justice.* Boulder: Westview Press.

GRAY, Barbara (1989) *Collaborating.* San Francisco: Jossey-Bass.

GRING, Pamela (1990) "The Special Master's Role as Mediator," 6 *Ohio St. J. Disp. Resol.* 21.

GROSS, Dick (2002) "A U.S. Consensus Council," *Disp. Resol. Mag.* 15 (Winter).

HARTER, Philip J. (1982) "Negotiating Regulations: A Cure for Malaise," 71 *Geo. L.J.* 1.

——— (1986) "The Role of the Courts in Reg-Neg: A Response to Judge Wald," 11 *Colum. J. Envtl. L.* 51.

——— (1997) "Negotiating Rules and Other Policies: Pay Close Heed to Structure for Success," *Disp. Resol. Mag.* 15 (Fall).

——— (2000) "Assessing the Assessors," 9 *N.Y.U. Envtl. L.J.* 32.

LOVE, Lela P., and Cheryl B. McDONALD (1997) "A Tale of Two Cities: Day Labor and Conflict Resolution for Communities in Crisis," *Disp. Resol. Mag.* 8 (Fall).

MURRAY, John S. (1984) "Third-Party Intervention: Successful Entry for the Uninvited," 48 *Albany L. Rev.* 573.

NATIONAL LAW JOURNAL (1991) "EPA Calls Off Sessions on Rules," July 8.

PRITZKER, David M., and Deborah S. DALTON, eds. (1990) *Negotiated Rulemaking Sourcebook.* Washington, D.C.: U.S. Government Printing Office.

SENGER, Jeffrey M. (2004) *Federal Dispute Resolution.* San Francisco: Jossey-Bass.

SUSSKIND, Lawrence (1981) "Environmental Mediation and the Accountability Problem," 6 *Vt. L. Rev.* 1.

——— (1991) "Public Policy Disputes in the Courts: The Promise of Mediation." In *Emerging ADR Issues in State and Federal Courts.* Chicago: ABA Section of Litigation.

——— (1995) "Environmental Mediation: Theory and Practice Reconsidered," Workshop on Environmental Mediation and Negotiation, Nov. 13 (unpublished).

——— (2000) "Confessions of a Public Dispute Mediator," 16 *Neg. J.* 129.

SUSSKIND, Lawrence, and Jeffrey CRUIKSHANK (1987) *Breaking the Impasse.* New York: Basic Books.

——— (2006) *Breaking Robert's Rules.* New York: Oxford University Press.

SUSSKIND, Lawrence E., and Patrick FIELD (1996) *Dealing with an Angry Public: The Mutual Gains Approach to Resolving Disputes.* New York: Free Press.

SUSSKIND, Lawrence, and Gerald McMAHON (1985) "The Theory and Practice of Negotiated Rulemaking," 3 *Yale J. Reg.* 133.

SUSSKIND, Lawrence, and Mieke van der WANSEM (1999) *Using Assisted Negotiation to Settle Land Use Disputes.* Cambridge, Mass.: Lincoln Institute of Land Policy.

SUSSKIND, Lawrence, Paul F. LEVY, and Jennifer THOMAS-LARMER (2000) *Negotiating Environmental Agreements.* Cambridge, Mass.: MIT Harvard Public Disputes Program.

SUSSKIND, Lawrence, Sarah McKEARNAN, and Jennifer THOMAS-LARMER, eds. (1999) *The Consensus Building Handbook.* Thousand Oaks, Cal.: Sage.

UNIVERSITY OF CHICAGO LEGAL FORUM (1987) *Consent Decrees: Practical Problems and Legal Dilemmas.*

WALD, Patricia W. (1985) "Negotiation of Environmental Disputes: A New Role for the Courts?," 10 *Colum. J. Envtl. L.* 1.

Chapter 10

International Disputes

International disputes may present even thornier obstacles to resolution than the public policy disputes discussed in the last chapter. International disputes fall into two categories presenting problems that are quite different though they have some similarities. There are disputes in the realm of public international law involving differences between states as well as disputes between private parties that fall under private international law. Negotiations between states stem from a long tradition; diplomacy is a special field with its own principles and its own literature. Diplomatic practice includes mediation and the provision of "good offices" by third parties which may include other nations or international organizations such as the United Nations. In the excerpt in Section A, former President Jimmy Carter describes his efforts to mediate a settlement of the long-standing conflict between Egypt and Israel. Unlike domestic disputes, diplomatic issues do not function in the shadow of law since there is often no court to resort to for settlement of differences the parties cannot resolve. Although the International Court of Justice in the Hague has limited jurisdiction based on the consent of the parties, it nevertheless has more cases on its docket now than at any time in its history. The United Nations Charter provides for Security Council enforcement of the court's rulings, but in practice enforcement usually depends on the cooperation of the nations that are parties to the dispute. Other fora for specialized conflicts include those provided by the Law of the Sea Tribunal, the World Trade Organization, and the North American Free Trade Agreement. Another forum, the European Court of Justice, which resolves European Union disputes, is now more like the top court of a federal system rather than an international tribunal. In the absence of effective jurisdiction, states unable to resolve their differences may resort to economic sanctions or other penalties including, in extreme cases, military actions.

Courts are more commonly available to resolve private international disputes—disputes between individuals, corporate, commercial, and non-profit interests in more than one country. Even so, litigation may be less useful in the international setting than the national setting for resolving disputes.

Concerned about bias in the other party's courts or laws, international parties may disagree on a forum and applicable law. Except for disputes falling under certain treaties,* litigation may proceed simultaneously in two or more countries because of the absence of international procedures for resolving jurisdictional

*Exceptions include the North American Free Trade Agreement (NAFTA) for the United States, Canada, and Mexico, and the 1968 Brussels Convention on Jurisdiction and Enforcement of Judgments in Civil and Commercial Matters for European Community Nations. The Lugano Convention extends the

disputes. The courts may apply different laws. The courts in one nation often will not enforce a judgment rendered by another nation's courts.

To overcome the jurisdictional, choice of law, and enforcement problems, parties to international commercial contracts commonly include an arbitration clause in their business agreements. International commercial arbitration has replaced litigation as the means to adjudicate private international disputes. Professor William Park comments, "In an international sale or investment dispute, arbitration and mediation commend themselves not so much by virtue of their alleged efficiency, as by their utility in reducing both political and procedural bias" (Bühring-Uhle, 1996: vii).

As of August 2002, 132 nation-states had become parties to the 1958 United Nations Convention on the Recognition and Enforcement of Foreign Arbitral Awards, known as the New York Convention. In these nations, the courts will enforce an agreement to arbitrate, stay concurrent litigation, and enforce the arbitration award. The United States is a signatory to the New York Convention and, as demonstrated by *Mitsubishi Motors v. Soler Chrysler-Plymouth*, 473 U.S. 614 (1985), has a strong public policy in favor of international arbitration.

Cultural differences among the parties constitute an important barrier to the resolution of both private and public international disputes. (See generally Chapter 11, Section A.) President Carter worked hard to overcome cultural obstacles to settlement in the Camp David negotiations. Culture presents obstacles to settlement of private disputes as well; in fact, settlement of cases in international commercial arbitration tends to occur late in the arbitration process and in only about 40 percent of the cases (see pp. 558-560).

Logistical problems also complicate the work of international dispute resolvers. The parties may speak different languages, and translators may miss the language nuances that are key to negotiation. Currency exchange rates change in the midst of negotiations.

The distinction between private and public disputes is increasingly blurred; mixed disputes involving public and private parties are now commonplace. The International Centre for the Settlement of Investment Disputes regularly arbitrates such disputes and oversees award enforcement. Under NAFTA, a private party may institute an arbitration proceeding against a nation-state even when the parties have not signed an arbitration clause, and multinational private tribunals sometimes review the judgments of courts. The Internet is plainly making communication across national boundaries easier, increasing contacts among nation-states. International disputes are now arising at a rate and in situations not seriously contemplated as late as the 1980s.

The impact of the Internet and other forces of globalization have driven new developments in dispute resolution. Means for resolving Internet disputes, as well as intellectual property disputes, are in place. More methods for resolving disputes are developing, especially new uses of mediation. The field of international dispute resolution is one of the oldest in international law, and the practice of diplomacy and conflict resolution pre-dates the study of international relations. After centuries of steady growth, both the law and practice of international dispute resolution are growing exponentially in the Internet era. Despite the changing context, courts are

Brussels Convention rules to members of the European Free Trade Association. The proposed Hague Convention on International and Foreign Judgments in Civil and Commercial Matters, www.hcch.net, will address conflicts in jurisdiction and judgments. It will also preclude parallel litigation.

unlikely to dominate these fields. Rather, the methods will remain negotiation, good offices, mediation, conciliation, arbitration, and variations on these means. This chapter introduces international dispute resolution and provides references for further study at the end.

A. NEGOTIATING AND MEDIATING PUBLIC DISPUTES

J. CARTER, KEEPING FAITH

319-322, 324-325, 327-351, 355-357, 359-373, 375-380, 382-397, 401, 403 (1982)

Thirteen Days

It was an especially beautiful evening in one of the loveliest places on earth. . . . But . . . my thoughts were not on . . . the beauties of nature. . . . I was studying a thick volume, written especially for me, about two men — Menachem Begin and Anwar el-Sadat. In a few days, on September 5, I would welcome them to Camp David. I was already familiar with the issues we would be discussing, because we had debated them privately and through the news media for months — without success. Ours would be a new approach, perhaps unprecedented in history. Three leaders of nations would be isolated from the outside world. An intensely personal effort would be required of us. I had to understand these men!

I was poring over psychological analyses of two of the protagonists which had been prepared by a team of experts within our intelligence community. This team could write definitive biographies of any important world leader, using information derived from a detailed scrutiny of events, public statements, writings, known medical histories, and interviews with personal acquaintances of the leaders under study. I wanted to know all about Begin and Sadat. What had made them national leaders? What was the root of their ambition? What were their most important goals in life? What events during past years had helped to shape their characters? What were their religious beliefs? Family relations? State of their health? Political beliefs and constraints? Relations with other leaders? Likely reaction to intense pressure in a time of crisis? Strengths and weaknesses? Commitments to political constituencies? Attitudes toward me and the United States? Whom did they *really* trust? What was their attitude toward one another? I was certain they were preparing for our summit conference in a similar manner.

From time to time I paused to consider the negotiating strategy I would follow at Camp David; I made careful detailed notes. These few quiet evenings away from Washington were an ideal time for me to concentrate almost exclusively on a single major challenge — peace in the Middle East. During the coming days at Camp David, my studies at the foot of the Grand Tetons were to pay rich dividends. . . .

I directed our negotiating group to assume as our immediate ambition a written agreement for peace between Egypt and Israel, with an agenda for implementation of its terms during the succeeding months. I was convinced that if we three leaders could not resolve the very difficult issues, some of which had never before been addressed forthrightly, then no group of foreign ministers or diplomats could succeed. Both President Sadat and Prime Minister Begin were courageous men, well-liked and trusted in their own countries, who could make tough decisions with relative political impunity. If the *overall* settlement proved to be popular, then some of the unpopular details would be acceptable.

I had no idea whether we would succeed. I only knew that we were at a turning point and that the stakes were very high. We were prepared to stay as long as necessary to explore all the potential agreements. Our plans called for three days, but we were willing to stay as long as a week if we were making good progress and success seemed attainable. We never dreamed we would be there through thirteen intense and discouraging days, with success in prospect only during the final hours. . . .

Despite my efforts to the contrary, expectations had built up to a fever pitch. My only hope was that, in the quiet and peaceful atmosphere of our temporary home, both Begin and Sadat would come to know and understand each other better, and that they would trust me to be honest and fair in my role as mediator and active negotiator. It was soon to be obvious that Sadat seemed to trust me too much, and Begin not enough. . . .

. . . Because of the space restrictions, each of us had to limit our aides to a minimum number. President Sadat had on his team Mohamed Ibrahim Kamel, Minister of Foreign Affairs; Boutros Ghali, Minister of State for Foreign Affairs; and Osama el-Baz, Under Secretary of Foreign Affairs. Prime Minister Begin's key assistants were Foreign Minister Moshe Dayan, Defense Minister Ezer Weizman, and Attorney General Aharon Barak. Secretary of State Vance stayed with me most of the time, and National Security Adviser Brzezinski and Assistant Secretary of State Harold Saunders worked closely with us. . . .

During the days ahead, the members of the negotiating teams were to become much more involved in the outcome of our deliberations than I had originally anticipated. Two of them whom I had never met, Barak and el-Baz, would be spending many hours in private sessions with me, going over the detailed language of the various proposals and searching for compromises that might be acceptable to Begin and Sadat, who would not be participating in these discussions.

Before the negotiations could begin, however, all of us tried to understand the issues involved and to search out some acceptable solutions to the questions. My own list included these items as having already been decided:

Jerusalem will be an undivided city, with free access to holy places.
Egypt will end its economic boycott against Israel.
Israeli access to the Suez Canal and other international waterways will be guaranteed.
Israel must have security, including some presence on the West Bank.
There will be an end to the state of war and a declaration of peace.
Egypt will have undisputed sovereignty over the Sinai.
Jordan and the Palestinians will be given a major negotiating role. There will be phased implementation of any agreements (implementation in sequential steps).
Future negotiations are to be continuous and in good faith.

Though there was partial agreement on such issues as the following, the minor differences could be very significant.

UN Resolution 242 would be the basis for any peace agreement. (Begin did not accept some of the terms as applicable to the West Bank.)
There should be normal relations between the two countries. (Sadat was not at all ready for full diplomatic recognition of Israel.)
None of us preferred an independent Palestinian state. (But Sadat wanted Palestinian self-determination, while Begin supported a limited form of autonomy.)
Israelis should terminate their military rule in the West Bank–Gaza. (No one was sure what Begin meant by his promise to do so.)

I also listed some of the certain problems, such as:

Dismantling of all Israeli settlements on Egyptian soil.
No new settlements to be built in any occupied territory.
All parts of Resolution 242 to apply to the West Bank.
Free participation of Palestinians in all future negotiations.
What the permanent status of the West Bank would be.
Israel's perceived threat from Egyptian military forces in the Sinai.
Arab role in Jerusalem.
Nature of any final agreement.

Because of the historic importance of the negotiations and the unique personal interrelationships at play within Camp David, I kept meticulous notes, recording verbatim some of the more significant statements made in my presence. . . .

Here is my account, based on what I recorded during the thirteen days, in much more detail than other days or events of my administration.

TUESDAY, DAY ONE (SEPTEMBER 5, 1978)

Rosalynn had come to Camp David in time to help me greet President Sadat in the early afternoon. . . . I had particularly wanted the three wives to be with us, so they could ease some of the tension and create a more congenial atmosphere. There was no compatibility at all between Begin and Sadat on which to base any progress. This warmer relationship would have to be created from scratch. . . .

About 2:30 P.M., Rosalynn and I received word that Sadat would soon be arriving. We walked up to the helicopter landing pad to welcome him. . . .

When he and I sat behind my cabin — Aspen — on the terrace, he did not waste any time expressing his thoughts and plans. He emphasized that he was eager to conclude a total settlement of the issues, and not merely establish procedures for future negotiations. He was convinced that Begin did not want an agreement and would try to delay progress as much as possible. Sadat stated that he would back me in all things, and that he had a comprehensive settlement plan "here in my pocket." He let me know that he was prepared to be flexible on all issues except two: land and sovereignty.

For instance, he concurred with me that if Begin would negotiate in good faith, the agreement should include the establishment of diplomatic relations and the end of the economic boycott against Israel. He predicted that it would be very difficult to hold Prime Minister Begin to the main issues. Sadat told me that as far back as 1971 he had offered to conclude a comprehensive settlement with Israel and had discussed this offer with Secretary of State William Rogers, but without success. He said that all Israelis must leave Egyptian territory and that any agreement had to provide for the Palestinians, for the West Bank, and for future agreements between Israel and her other neighbors. The details could be worked out by me. . . .

About two hours later, Prime Minister Begin landed on the mountaintop, and we went down to Aspen for a brief conversation. . . .

He pointed out to me that there had not been an agreement between a Jewish nation and Egypt for more than two thousand years, and that our meeting was historically unprecedented. However, unlike Sadat, Begin was clearly planning for an agreement at Camp David only on general principles, which might then serve as a basis for future meetings, when the specifics and remaining differences could be resolved by the Ministers of Foreign Affairs and Defense. I objected strongly to this plan, and told the Prime Minister that we three principals could not expect others to settle major issues later if we could not do so now, and that all the controversial questions should be addressed among us directly. . . .

Through their leaders, we urged everyone not to relay to the outside world any information about negotiating positions or successes and failures as the talks progressed. On the few occasions when an indiscreet statement was made to someone outside, it became known instantly through the resulting news stories. As we all came to believe that the same restrictions were being observed by everyone, it was easier to enforce the necessary discipline. There is no doubt in my mind that success would have been impossible if we had explained our own opinions or goals to the press each day. It would have been difficult to be flexible, with every necessary change in position being interpreted as a defeat for one or more of the negotiating parties. . . .

After supper that first night, Begin and I met alone in my cabin. . . .

. . . My first goal that evening was to put him at ease and assure him there would be no surprises. I described my understanding of Israel's special problems and positions, and emphasized again the importance of our meeting. I told him we had plenty of time. We were isolated at Camp David and could remain so as long as necessary to reach agreement. We should not depend on referring problems to our subordinates to solve at a later time. I assured him that we would have no bilateral secrets, and that I would not give to Sadat nor to him any official United States proposals without discussing the unofficial drafts first with both sides.

Where we could not reach a final agreement on an issue at Camp David, I said, we should carefully define what differences remained, so that we would not later have to start at the beginning of the debate. I reserved the right, and had the duty, to put forward compromise proposals, and might on occasion merely adopt either the Egyptian or the Israeli position if I believed it to be best. I would not be timid, but would not deal in surprises, I assured him again. . . .

I spelled out to Begin the advantages of a good rapport between him and Sadat during the days ahead. I believed that as they got to know each other, it would be easier for them to exchange ideas without rancor or distrust. Yet in fact, for the last ten days of negotiation leading up to our final agreement, the two men never spoke to one another, although their cottages were only about a hundred yards apart.

This first evening I was determined to accentuate the positive. I emphasized our awareness that Israel's security was paramount and that Begin's team could not be satisfied with hazy guarantees on this crucial issue. I also told him that his self-government proposal for the Palestinians was bold and gratifying in its basic concept, and that his willingness to recognize Egyptian sovereignty over the entire Sinai was a constructive development which had not been adequately acknowledged. . . .

Begin interjected that on the security issue, which Israel considered vital, the Egyptians had taken just the opposite view. This was the most crucial point for the Israelis. If they were to withdraw from the West Bank or allow the Arabs there to have enhanced political status, they wanted to be certain that no successful military attack could be launched against them. With total withdrawal from the West Bank, their security problems would be very serious. I described the Egyptian position, admitting that there were some differences, with the reminder that it was the differences that had brought us together at Camp David.

Begin then outlined without modification his previous position on the Sinai, emphasizing his most disturbing point—that the Israeli settlements on Egyptian soil were a necessary buffer between Gaza and Egypt. He said he wanted a complete agreement with Egypt, but first would need an agreement with the United States. He had tabulated that the total time of negotiation between their two countries had been only thirty-two hours, and that this was obviously inadequate. We would all need patience, he said, and could not hope to reach an early settlement. He was talking not about years, but about a matter of a few months to work out the remaining differences. He knew that Sadat suspected the Israelis of deliberate delay, but he added that this was not true. . . .

Begin proposed that the question of sovereignty over the West Bank–Gaza area be left open, and reiterated that some Israeli military forces would have to be kept there. He was convinced that if Israel pulled out completely, the PLO terrorists would take over within twenty-four hours. But he stated emphatically that he was willing for the West Bank Palestinians to have autonomy—Begin always said, "*full* autonomy." (We were destined to spend several hours one evening seeking a common understanding of what "autonomy" meant—unsuccessfully.) . . .

Begin was concerned about the permanence of any peace accord, even if he and Sadat could come to a complete understanding. I reminded him that any agreement would last as long as it appeared to be advantageous to the people as well as the leaders involved. In this case, I was convinced that the benefits of peace would be so obvious that the commitments would be honored. The direct interest and influence of the United States would help ensure it, no matter who might lead our nations in future years. I pointed out that our three nations and we three leaders were strong enough to prevail, even if other more radical leaders disagreed with certain aspects of our settlement and tried to disrupt what we had done. . . .

We then addressed the really tough issues. I told the Prime Minister that Sadat would never yield on the question of leaving Israeli settlements anywhere in the Sinai region. For him, complete sovereignty over the Sinai meant a total absence of Israeli dwellers. Begin did not respond, but it was my impression that he thought I was mistaken about this, and that with proper inducements through other Israeli concessions, Sadat might change his mind.

Another potentially serious difference was the phrase from United Nations Resolution 242, "inadmissibility of acquisition of territory by war." The Arabs would all insist that Israel acknowledge the applicability of this principle in any treaties signed, because it would recognize that lands occupied by Israel after the Six Day War had not legally changed hands. Begin understood this well, and said that the principle was good, but he would agree only if the word "belligerent" was inserted before the word "war." He said Israel had been attacked by its Arab neighbors, and the war was a defensive act by his country; therefore, Israel had a right to occupy the lands taken in its own defense. This interpretation of 242 was to become a very difficult problem, on which the discussions almost foundered. . . .

In general, the conversation was discouraging. I had hoped that Begin would bring some new proposals to Camp David, but the Prime Minister simply repeated almost verbatim the old Israeli negotiating positions. There were few indications of flexibility, but at least I made it clear that we wanted final decisions at Camp David and that we were going to put forward our positions forcefully. He agreed with this—without apparent enthusiasm. We said good night at about 11:00 P.M., about two and a half hours after he had come to my cabin. . . .

WEDNESDAY, DAY TWO (SEPTEMBER 6, 1978)

. . . Sadat was always punctual, calm, and self-assured; he was brief and to the point in all his discussions. . . .

When he arrived at my cottage, . . . I first gave him a brief report of my meeting with Prime Minister Begin. I told him that it had been basically nonproductive and that Israel's previously known positions had been reiterated, but that this in itself was necessary as a first step for progress among us. It was very important, we agreed, not to put Begin on the defensive at this early stage of the discussions, but to let him spell out Israel's position for the record.

I emphasized to Sadat that unless the proposals were patently fair to Israel, Begin's government and the Israeli people would not support them. I also reminded Sadat of the importance of public opinion in the United States and the intense interest that the American Congress and public would have in the terms of an agreement as it related to the security of Israel.

Sadat responded that the Prime Minister was a very formal man, difficult to approach or to understand. He believed Begin was bitter, inclined to look back into ancient history rather than to deal with the present and the future. He promised to go to extremes in being flexible, in order to uncover the full meaning of Begin's positions, and stated that if our efforts at Camp David should be unsuccessful, then when the equitable Egyptian proposals were made known, they would bring the condemnation of the world on the Israeli leader.

I pointed out that Begin was a man of integrity and honor, with very deep and long-held opinions. It was difficult for him to change. He had spent a lifetime in public affairs developing his ideas, expounding them, and defending them, even at great personal danger. When he was elected to his present office, his campaign statements were quite clear on some of the issues we would be negotiating, and any change in his position made necessary through compromises would be the object of criticism in the open, aggressive, and free political environment existing in Israel. I did not want anyone to be embarrassed by either success or failure at

Camp David, but a positive attitude during our discussions was essential, to build up mutual confidence and to improve our chances for success.

I sat at my desk, taking notes as I had the night before. Now it was Sadat's time to spell out Egypt's position. He sat erect and spoke calmly, referring to a few notes he had brought with him. Sadat said there were two points on which he could not be flexible. One was land, and the other was sovereignty. These were closely related, but I needed to know exactly what he meant. He explained that Egypt must have every inch of her land returned, with unequivocal sovereignty over it, and that other Arab nations must be treated the same. I interrupted to ask how he assessed the difference between sovereignty on the Golan Heights and in the Sinai versus the West Bank and Gaza. He said there was a great difference. There were recognized international boundaries for Sinai, all of which belonged to Egypt, and for the Golan, all of which belonged to Syria. I asked him where he ascribed sovereignty in the West Bank and Gaza, and he replied, "Sovereignty rests among the people who live there — not in either Jordan or Israel." He would not yield any of the occupied land to Israel, at least in this early session. All of it should go back to Egypt, Syria, or the Palestinians, he said. . . .

Sadat next handed me the plan he had mentioned when he first arrived, spelling out the opening proposal of the Egyptians. As I read it my heart sank; it was extremely harsh and filled with all the unacceptable Arab rhetoric. It blamed all previous wars on Israel, and demanded that Israelis offer indemnities for their use of the occupied land, pay for all the oil they had pumped out of Egyptian wells, permit the refugees free entry to the West Bank, withdraw all their forces entirely to the original pre-1967 boundaries, allow the Palestinians to form their own nation, and relinquish control over East Jerusalem. Sadat let me read it through without comment, and when I had finished, he said he would like to offer me some modifications which could later be adopted as acceptable to him. He cautioned me not to reveal these to anyone, because it would destroy his negotiating strength if his final positions were to be placed on the table at this early time. He had carefully studied the points I had been making during the past few months, he said, and he found them reasonable. He recalled the first time we had met, and his conviction then that some of my dreams would never be realized in his lifetime. Now he was prepared to make those dreams come true, because he was convinced that the people of the two countries and most of the world wanted peace.

As President Sadat delineated for me what he would accept in a final agreement, I saw for the first time that we might possibly achieve substantial success. With a few notable exceptions, his positions had a good chance of being satisfactory to the Israelis. It would certainly not be an easy task to convince both parties, but a basis for peace now existed. Under certain circumstances, Sadat might even agree to my frequent request to him that full diplomatic relations be established between Egypt and Israel, including open borders and an exchange of ambassadors. . . .

Sadat's plan was to present his written proposals to me and Begin at the afternoon meeting. I knew they were certain to be rejected — with feeling — and my assessment was that he thought Begin would not agree to any settlement. Sadat wanted a strong initial proposal on the record, to appease his fellow Egyptians and the Arab world, but during the negotiations he would be willing to make major concessions (within carefully prescribed limits), so that his final proposal would prove to everyone the reasonableness of his approach. The first part of this strategy was a waste of time, but the latter part suited me perfectly, because if the Egyptian proposals were indeed reasonable, there was at least a fighting chance that the Israelis would accept them. . . .

Begin came first to the afternoon meeting. I told him quickly that Sadat would present a very aggressive proposal and cautioned him not to overreact. . . .

I decided to play a minimal role during these first sessions, so that the other two leaders could become better acquainted and have a more fruitful exchange. I knew what they had to say—I could have recited some of the more pertinent passages in my sleep. I asked Sadat to begin, but he used his higher rank and requested that Begin do so. Begin said that many differences between the two nations were not yet resolved, and that the basic disagreements were so broad as to require a few months of negotiation by technicians working full time five days a week. . . .

I then asked Sadat to respond to Begin's remarks. He said there was already a fundamental difference of opinion, even in these preliminary comments, about what we were to accomplish at Camp David. He stated that his peace initiative to Jerusalem had brought forth a new era. The era of war was coming to an end, he said. Sadat reiterated what he and I had agreed, that we ourselves must produce a comprehensive framework for peace, not avoiding any of the controversial issues, and then give the technicians three months of drafting time merely to put our agreement into final form. . . .

On this question, I sided with Sadat, of course, and stated that the principals must address all the controversial issues directly. The United States would reserve the right to put forward its own ideas on an equal basis with the other two, because there might be times when either one of them might accept, albeit reluctantly, a proposal originating with me which they would be unwilling to accept from one another. Begin said these concepts were all right with him.

It was time for the discussion of specific issues; I nodded to Begin to start. He said that he had made a proposal in December concerning self-rule in the West Bank-Gaza areas, had not received an adequate response, and was looking forward to hearing Sadat's counterproposal.

I asked Sadat specifically, "Are you willing to act in the administration of the West Bank and to conclude an Arab-Israeli treaty if Jordan is not willing to participate?" He replied, "Yes, we are." I then asked if he was willing to negotiate a Sinai agreement at the same time that a West Bank-Palestinian treaty was being concluded, and he replied affirmatively but added, "I will not sign a Sinai agreement before an agreement is also reached on the West Bank." Sadat was to prove adamant on this point.

He then began to read his extremely tough and unacceptable proposal, after requesting that Begin not respond to it until he had discussed it with his aides. When Begin agreed, they both seemed relieved.

During the reading of the paper, Begin sat without changing his expression, but I could feel the tension building. When it was over, no one spoke for a while, and I tried to break the tension by telling Begin that if he would sign the document as written, it would save all of us a lot of time.

I was surprised when everyone broke into gales of genuine laughter. After a few moments Begin asked, "Would you advise me to do so?" I said no, we had better consult with our aides. All of a sudden both men seemed happy, friendly. Begin made a very nice statement about how glad he was to get the document, how hard he knew the Egyptians had worked on it, and how much he appreciated the thoroughness of their preparation. Listening to it had been very interesting to him, he said, but reading it would be much more informative.

We agreed to meet again the following day, and I invited them to go for a walk with Rosalynn and me. Sadat declined, saying that he had already had his exercise for the day, but the Prime Minister decided to go find his wife and join us. We parted in good spirits, everyone patting each other on the back. It was the high point in feeling until the final hours, many days later. . . .

Half an hour later, when we were walking through the woods, Prime Minister Begin became very excited about Sadat's proposals being so drastic and unacceptable. After reading the document over, he was convinced that it was either an opening gambit or would be an obvious impediment to progress. I tried to convince him it was the former. . . .

After supper, I brought the entire American group together in my cottage to discuss the apparent damage Sadat's proposal had done. Begin was treating it as an insurmountable obstacle, and the other members of the Israeli delegation were also deeply troubled. We knew that Sadat was ready to make immediate modifications, but it seemed advisable for me to meet with all the Israelis before Begin and Sadat met again with each other, so that I could ease their concern.

THURSDAY, DAY THREE (SEPTEMBER 7, 1978)

Beginning at 8:30 A.M., I met for two hours with Begin, Dayan, and Weizman. Vance and Brzezinski were with me. . . .

Prime Minister Begin was now even more excited and irate about the tone and substance of the document than he had been during our walk the previous evening. He said, "This smacks of a victorious state dictating peace to the defeated!" Begin reviewed the text in detail, and finally concluded, "This document is not a proper basis for negotiations."

I tried to calm the group without denigrating Sadat's efforts. I wanted to file Sadat's paper and go on to more realistic options for our discussions, but it soon became obvious that such a course would not be possible. Begin insisted that we analyze the Egyptian proposals in detail.

The discussions were of benefit to me, however, because in the presence of Dayan and Weizman, the Prime Minister outlined much more clearly than before the basic Israeli attitude toward the more controversial issues. He focused on words and their meaning. . . .

"Sinai settlements! There is a national consensus in Israel that the settlements *must* stay!" This claim was to become the most serious problem of all. Sadat was absolutely insistent that all Israelis must move out of his territory, and Begin was equally insistent that no Israeli settlements in the Sinai would *ever* be "dismantled."

We had a heated discussion about borders. How much the 1967 borders would be modified was a constant argument. The official Arab position was that the borders should be restored to their exact locations as they had been prior to the Six Day War. The Israelis wanted maximum flexibility in the final borders, with some leaders, though not Begin, calling for partition of the disputed West Bank territory.

I told the Israeli delegation that the key question was: "Are you willing to withdraw from the occupied territories and honor Palestinian rights, in exchange for adequate assurances for your security, including an internationally recognized treaty of peace? If not," I said, "Egypt will eventually turn away from the peace process, and the full power of the Arabs, and perhaps world opinion, will be marshaled against you."

The expanding settlements under Begin's government were creating doubt that the Israelis were bargaining in good faith concerning any reduction in Israeli influence on the West Bank. This was the root of Sadat's distrust of Begin's motives, and I must admit that I shared the belief that the Israeli leader would do almost anything concerning the Sinai and other issues in order to protect Israel's presence in "Judea and Samaria." I expressed this concern as forcefully as possible. Begin's response was evasive. . . .

I replied that an Israeli commitment to withdraw was imperative, but that I was not trying to specify how much. I insisted that the interim proposal to let the Palestinians have full autonomy be as forthcoming as possible, with maximum authority for the people who lived on the West Bank and in Gaza. A continuing military occupation and deprivation of basic citizenship rights among the Arabs was unacceptable to the world, and contrary to the principles which had always been such an integral part of Jewish teachings and religious beliefs about freedom from persecution of others and personal liberty for all human beings.

Dayan asked, "What does withdrawal mean? Troops, settlements? Will I be a foreigner on the West Bank? Will I have to get a visa to go to Jericho? With autonomy, can the Arabs there create a Palestinian state? Can they resettle the refugees from Lebanon to the West Bank? Who will protect us from Jordan? Who will be responsible for controlling terrorists?"

I asked for Israel's answers to Dayan's questions, but Begin shifted back to Sadat's proposal and began to analyze it again in minute detail. It was obvious that we were wasting time.

I became angry, and almost shouted, "What do you actually want for Israel if peace is signed? How many refugees and what kind can come back? I need to know whether you need to monitor the border, what military outposts are necessary to guard your security. What else do you want? If I know the facts, then I can take them to Sadat and try to satisfy both you and him. I must have your frank assessment. My greatest strength here is your confidence — but I don't feel that I have your trust. What do you really need for your defense? It is ridiculous to speak of Jordan overrunning Israel! I believe I can get from Sadat what you *really* need, but I just do not have your confidence."

Weizman replied, "We wouldn't be here if we didn't have confidence in you."

I repeated my point. "You are as evasive with me as with the Arabs. The time has come to throw away reticence. Tell us what you really need. My belief is that Sadat is strong enough to make an agreement here — and impose it on other nations. I believe I can get Sadat to agree to your home-rule proposal if you convince him and me that you are not planning to keep large parts of the West Bank under your permanent control."

I accused Begin of wanting to hold onto the West Bank, and said that his home-rule or autonomy proposal was a subterfuge. He resented this word very much and brought it up many times in our subsequent discussions.

While Begin and I cooled off, Weizman outlined some of the changes that had taken place during the last eleven years—differences on the West Bank, in Jerusalem, with the Egyptians, and new possibilities such as a joint police force to control terrorism. He stated flatly that a complete withdrawal of Israeli settlers was not possible but that real home rule was.

I stressed again Sadat's courage and his personal sacrifice in making the peace initiative. A demilitarized Sinai and Egypt's signed agreement with Israel would serve to protect Israel's security in the world community, and even within the Arab world, after Sadat and we were gone as leaders. I emphasized that, in Begin, the Israelis had a prime minister with a demonstrated willingness to give his life for Israel's security. Thus, if we wasted this opportunity we would never have it again. . . .

It was now time for Begin and me to go to our 10:30 A.M. meeting with Sadat, and I asked the four who would remain to continue their discussion of the specific issues that had been raised. This had been an unpleasant and heated argument, but it was necessary and understandable because of the one-sided nature of Sadat's proposals.

Begin and I walked together from Holly to Aspen, arriving at the front door of my cottage just in time to greet President Sadat. I led the way down the hall to the study and sat behind the desk. They took the other two chairs, facing each other across the desk as before. At the very beginning, I decided to withdraw from the discussion between Begin and Sadat. I wanted them to address each other directly. While they talked, I took notes without looking up, and they soon refrained from talking to me or attempting to seek my opinion.

Begin was well prepared, and he did not waste any time. He was brutally frank as he discussed each issue in Sadat's paper.

Sadat remained silent and impassive until Begin derided the idea of Israel's paying reparations for the use of the occupied lands. Then he interrupted, and a hot argument took place. . . .

All restraint was now gone. Their faces were flushed, and the niceties of diplomatic language and protocol were stripped away. They had almost forgotten that I was there, and there was nothing to distract me from recording this fascinating debate.

Begin repeated that no Israeli leader could possibly advocate the dismantling of the Sinai settlements, and he added that four other conditions would have to be met before the Sinai could be returned to Egypt.

Begin had touched a raw nerve, and I thought Sadat would explode. He pounded the table, shouting that land was not negotiable, especially land in the Sinai and Golan Heights. Those borders were internationally recognized. He pointed out that for thirty years the Israelis had desired full recognition, no Arab boycott, and guaranteed security. He was giving them all of that. He wanted them to be secure. "Security, yes! Land, no!" he shouted. . . .

Begin was calmer than Sadat. He responded that he had already demonstrated his good will by changing a long-standing policy of his government concerning the Sinai land between Eilat and Sharm el-Sheyk. His predecessors had been determined to keep this land, and he was offering it back to Egypt, which was very difficult for him. He added that the continued presence in the Sinai of a few homes of Israeli settlers was not an infringement on Egyptian sovereignty. . . .

We adjourned under considerable strain. Begin expressed his complete confidence in Sadat, and it was quite conspicuous that Sadat did not make a similar statement in response.

I did not know where to go from there. We had accomplished little so far except to name the difficult issues. There was no compatibility between the two men, and almost every discussion of any subject deteriorated into an unproductive argument, reopening the old wounds of past political or military battles. Under intense pressure, the Egyptian leader moved away from details and words and into the realm of general principles and broad strategic concepts. When he was feeling pressed, the Israeli leader invariably shifted to a discussion of minutiae or semantics, with a recurrent inclination to recapitulate ancient history or to resurrect an old argument. Sadat had immediately outlined to me the two or three points on which he would not yield and had, in effect, given me a free hand to negotiate with great flexibility on almost all the other issues — full diplomatic recognition of Israel being one exception. The Israeli delegation was very reluctant to trust us with any revelation of its real ultimate desires or areas of possible compromise.

These differences shaped the negotiating technique I developed in the days ahead, and eventually opened up the road to an agreement. I would draft a proposal I considered reasonable, take it to Sadat for quick approval or slight modification, and then spend hours or days working on the same point with the Israeli delegation. Sometimes, in the end, the change of a word or phrase would satisfy Begin, and I would merely inform Sadat. I was never far from a good dictionary and thesaurus, and on occasion the American and Israeli delegations would all be clustered around one of these books, eagerly searching for acceptable synonyms. Would the Israelis withdraw "out of" certain areas or "into" military encampments? What was meant by "autonomy," "self-rule," "devolution," "insure, ensure, or guarantee," and so forth? The Egyptians were never involved in these kinds of discussions with me.

On any controversial issue, I never consulted Sadat's aides, but always went directly to their leader. It soon became obvious to all of us, however, that Dayan, Weizman, or Attorney General Barak could be convinced on an issue more quickly than the Prime Minister, and they were certainly more effective in changing Begin's mind than I ever was. The contrasting attitudes of the two leaders in dealing with details dovetailed very well, allowing me to plan our approach with increasing effectiveness whenever we reached one of the frequent crises. Had both men been preoccupied with semantics or details, my job would have been much more difficult.

More important was the bottom line: all three of us wanted peace; the people of Israel and Egypt wanted peace. Our efforts at Camp David were now prominent in the eyes of the world, and we did not want to fail — both leaders looked on themselves as men of destiny, holding the future of their nations in their hands.

When we agreed to meet again in the afternoon, none of us had any idea it would be our last meeting together for the duration of the negotiations. Paradoxically, it was the profound differences between them that allowed us to find a way to save the day. But these very differences would make things much worse before they could improve.

At the beginning, the afternoon meeting reflected the strain of the earlier arguments. . . .

Begin said that Sadat would get the Sinai back, but we had to remember that Israel had suffered repeatedly when King Farouk, President Nasser, and President Sadat had all sent Egyptian forces to attack Israel from that area. . . .

Now, Begin went on, it was important that the few Israeli settlers in the Sinai be accepted by the Egyptian people as no threat to them and as no encroachment on their sovereignty. There were little more than two thousand Israelis in the thirteen Sinai settlements. The removal of these settlements would not be acceptable to Israel. Sadat could, if he wished, convince his people to accept them as permanent residents.

There seemed an absolute deadlock on the Sinai settlements. Within a few minutes Sadat announced angrily that a stalemate had been reached. He saw no reason for the discussions to continue. As far as he was concerned, they were over. Sadat then ignored Begin, stood up, and looked at me.

I was desperate, and quickly outlined the areas of agreement and the adverse consequences to both men if the peace effort foundered at this point because of the differences we had just discussed. I emphasized the United States' role in the Middle East, and reminded them that a new war in this troubled region under present conditions could easily escalate into another world war. I asked them to give me at least one more day to understand as best I could the positions of the two delegations, to devise my own compromise proposals, and to present my views to both of them. I pointed out to Prime Minister Begin that if the only cause for his rejection of the peace effort was the Sinai settlers, I did not believe the people of his nation or the Knesset would agree with him. It was my belief that he could sell this action to his people if he would let the settlers leave Egyptian territory.

He disputed this, saying that there was *no way* he could sell a dismantling of the Israeli settlements to his government or to his people. (He always said "dismantling," although we pointed out to him that the buildings need not be destroyed but could continue in use, after the Israelis left, if that was his preference.) To move the settlers would mean the downfall of his government — an outcome he was willing to accept if he believed in the cause. But he did *not* believe in it.

They were moving toward the door, but I got in front of them to partially block the way. I urged them not to break off their talks, to give me another chance to use my influence and analysis, to have confidence in me. Begin agreed readily. I looked straight at Sadat; finally, he nodded his head. They left without speaking to each other. . . .

During a brief reception for . . . other visitors, I asked Sadat to let me meet that evening with the Egyptian delegation. [Walter] Mondale and [Harold] Brown joined me, Vance, and Brzezinski. . . .

I opened the discussion. "I know you are all very discouraged right now. The issue we addressed today was the Israeli settlements in the Sinai, which may be the most difficult one of all. Our position is that they are illegal and should be removed. On this, your views and ours are the same. President Sadat and Prime Minister Begin both have very deep and adamant feelings about this matter, and I do not yet know how it can be resolved. All of us will explore every possibility with the Israeli delegation, in hopes that we might uncover some route to progress. I ask that you give me some more time before you leave."

Sadat replied, "My good friend Jimmy, we have already had three long sessions. You know that on two issues I cannot compromise — land and sovereignty. I cannot yield conquered land to Israel, and if sovereignty is to mean anything to Egyptians, all the Israelis must leave our territory. . . ."

Then Mondale spoke. "One of the most powerful arguments is that the Sinai is yours, and the world and Israel acknowledge that it is yours. There should be no Israeli settlements on it. But what about the other issues — can they be resolved?

Sadat said, "I must have also a resolution of the West Bank and Gaza. I cannot do the Sinai alone. I am ready to be flexible, but not on the Sinai."

I replied, "Sovereignty issues are different in the Sinai and Golan Heights from the West Bank. Begin cannot now accept foreign sovereignty over the West Bank, and I agree with him. For the time being, we must permit the Jews and Arabs to live together. We should be able to work out something on self-rule."

Sadat said, "I am willing to give them two years to phase out the Sinai settlements."

I replied, "You must be more flexible on the exact time — two or three years."

Sadat: "Okay." . . .

I suggested to Sadat that he let me develop a paper based on some of his own positions with which I agreed, Begin's proposal on home rule for the West Bank and Gaza, plus my own proposals which might be acceptable compromises. I would have to count on him for maximum flexibility to accommodate the Israeli position. . . .

I had been worrying about how to handle some remaining differences between Egypt and Israel, and now thought of a precedent which might be applied. "On a few unresolved issues there can also be different Egyptian and Israeli interpretations. This is what was done in the Shanghai communiqué between my country and China. We both agreed that there was one China, but we did not destroy the agreement by trying to define 'one China' too specifically." The wording had been precise, but the meaning deliberately obscure, permitting each nation to interpret it as desired. . . .

As we prepared to adjourn, I said, "Stalemate here would just provide an opportunity for the most radical elements to take over in the Middle East. A trial period for the West Bank can work, if we agree on it. If we don't, then Moscow and the radicals will rejoice. All of you must understand our special commitment to Israel, and the fact that the Israelis do indeed want peace. They have not yet responded adequately to the Sadat peace initiative — but they have offered to leave the Sinai and to give autonomy or self-government to the West Bank Arabs; and our hope is that they will stop building settlements in the West Bank and remove them from the Sinai. All of this should be acknowledged. We simply must find a formula that both Egypt and Israel can accept. If you give me a chance, I don't intend to fail." . . .

FRIDAY, DAY FOUR (SEPTEMBER 8, 1978)

. . . I arranged to see Begin at 2:30 P.M. and Sadat two hours later. When the Israeli leader arrived, there was very little I could say. My only option was to outline again the areas of agreement and request flexibility on his part. He complained that the United States negotiators were all agreeing with the Egyptian demand that the Sinai settlements be removed, and that this was no way for a mediating team to act. Then he pulled from his pocket the dog-eared copy of Sadat's demands and began once again to delineate its unacceptable portions. I tried to convince him that this was not the final Egyptian position, and that the Egyptians were willing to be accommodating within the limits previously explained to him. . . .

Begin said he did not see how honorable men could put forward one thing publicly and a different thing privately.

I explained that there were some things the Egyptians could not propose as their own preference, but might be willing to accept if they knew it was my desire and if in the general negotiation the totality of an agreement was considered to be in Egypt's interest. There were different degrees of intensity in Sadat's beliefs; he had told all of us that he would not yield on sovereignty or land, but would try to compromise on other issues. I said that this attitude toward the negotiations was the reason Sadat strongly desired the United States to be a full partner in the talks — to probe for acceptable modifications in the original proposals of both nations.

Prime Minister Begin ignored this comment completely, and listed in detail the elements of the original Sadat demands, even though many of them had never been pursued by the Egyptians and others had almost immediately been abandoned. . . .

He stated emphatically, "I will never personally recommend that the settlements in the Sinai be dismantled!" He added, "Please, Mr. President, do not make this a United States demand."

I noted with great interest, but without comment, the change in his words and was heartened by it. "Never personally recommend" did not mean that he would never permit the settlements to be removed. The change was subtle but extremely significant. If others in Israel could be made to assume the onus for the decision, then finally there was at least a possibility for resolving this vital issue.

I reiterated that Sadat was flexible, and that the Egyptians' written position was not their final one. (Once Sadat made up his mind on an issue, he was immutable. The challenge was to avoid a final decision by him until after I had a chance to give him all my arguments, and to let him know how strongly I was going to pursue the particular point.) I also stated to Begin that I absolutely disagreed with him about the settlements, now that Sadat had agreed there would be no attack forces in the Sinai. Instead, there would be 130 kilometers of demilitarized desert between Egypt and Israel, with buffer zones and monitoring stations to insure that this commitment would be honored. I emphasized that there were no reasons for the settlements to exist after a peace agreement, and that they would be a source more of aggravation and dissension than of peace and security.

Once more Begin implored, "Mr. President, do not put this in a proposal to us."

I responded, "Mr. Prime Minister, we cannot avoid addressing the most contentious issues, and this is the one on which the entire Camp David talks have foundered so far. I cannot let Sadat tell me not to discuss Israeli security on the West Bank. I cannot let you tell me not to discuss the Israeli presence on Egyptian territory." . . .

I reminded him that for months Sadat had urged me to play an active role, to be a full partner, and that I saw no possibility of progress if the United States should withdraw and simply leave the negotiations to the Egyptians and Israelis, who honestly did not trust each other and often admitted an absence of even mutual respect. I noted that when Sadat had arrived at Camp David, the first analysis he had made was that Begin did not want a peace agreement and only wanted land.

Begin replied, "Both of those claims are false."

I said, "I realize that, but that is the way the Egyptians feel. This atmosphere between the two of you is not conducive to any agreement. We are going to present a comprehensive proposal for peace. It will not surprise either you or Sadat. When it is finished tomorrow, I will present it to you first, and then to the Egyptians. I can see no other possibility for progress." . . .

When I arrived at Sadat's cabin, he welcomed me warmly. He had prepared some heavily flavored mint tea, which I always enjoyed. I told him that we faced some serious problems and asked him to be patient. It would be very embarrassing to me if both nations were to reject the proposals on which I had been working. My impression after meeting with Prime Minister Begin this afternoon was that the Israelis were sure to reject them.

Sadat promised that he would be totally patient and would under no circumstances put me in a difficult position. He wanted to know my plans for the coming days at Camp David.

I told him that Begin did not want me to present an official United States proposal, but that I had already informed him the paper would be completed tomorrow and presented first to the Israelis and then to Sadat. I would spend the Jewish Sabbath concluding my work on the draft, preparing a summary of the agreements and differences, and having the texts typed for distribution. After study, each group should present its views to me, and I would relay them to the other. The time for the three of us to meet together was over. I would continue to meet individually with the two leaders, back and forth, until the best possible compromise had been evolved, at which point the three of us, along with our key advisers, would all meet. . . .

We ended our meeting with a mutual pledge of friendship and fair settlement of the Middle East peace talks. Sadat said that he had no animosity toward Begin or the Israelis, did not wish to put them in an awkward position, and wanted mutual success rather than a victory over anyone. . . .

SATURDAY, DAY FIVE (SEPTEMBER 9, 1978)

. . . Now we were having to look to the future and devise an agreement that might resolve the apparent deadlock between Begin and Sadat. I knew that Sadat and I could come up with a reasonable agreement which a majority of Israelis would gladly accept. My major task was to convince Prime Minister Begin. In a way, I understood his dilemma. He was the one who was being pressured to change the private and public commitments of a lifetime. Although he had my sympathy, I was not reluctant to do all I could to persuade him.

The only thing that would succeed was a proposal that was patently fair, that did not violate Sadat's broad principles, and that—hopefully—we could sell to the other members of the Israeli delegation. From daybreak and throughout Saturday, the entire American delegation bent to this task, and shortly after midnight the document was ready to be put into final form.

Our proposal incorporated all the attractive items. Among these were: an end to war; permanent peace; free transit by Israel through all international waterways; secure and recognized borders; a full range of normal relations between nations; phased withdrawal by Israel from the Sinai; demilitarization of that area; monitoring stations to insure compliance with this agreement; termination of blockades and boycotts; a procedure for settling future disputes; the extension of the principles of future agreements between Israel and its other neighbors; rapid granting of full autonomy to the Palestinians, followed by a five-year transition period for determining the permanent status of the West Bank and Gaza; withdrawal of Israeli armed forces from the West Bank into specified security locations; a prompt settlement of the refugee problem; and a three-month period to complete a peace treaty between Egypt and Israel.

It also included American judgments on the most controversial issues: inclusion of the phrase "inadmissibility of acquisition of territory by war"; the possibility of full diplomatic recognition of Israel by Egypt; the participation of Jordan and the Palestinians as equal partners with Israel and Egypt in all future negotiations concerning the West Bank, including control of returning refugees; recognition of the legitimate rights of the Palestinian people and their participation in determining their own future; linking of the West Bank and Gaza to Jordan; authority in these areas to be developed jointly from Egypt, Israel, and Jordan; a strong local police force with Jordanian participation; and the application of United Nations Resolution 242 in determining the permanent status of the West Bank. In addition, there was a paragraph defining the status of Jerusalem. We had decided to call for the removal of all Israeli settlements from the Sinai, and a freeze on settlements in other occupied territory until all negotiations were complete, but we would not include this request in the first draft. Otherwise, Prime Minister Begin would have concentrated on it almost to the exclusion of the other issues.

SUNDAY, DAY SIX (SEPTEMBER 10, 1978)

. . . Late in the afternoon, after returning from Gettysburg, we had our meeting with the Israelis. Mondale, Vance, Brzezinski, Dayan, Weizman, and Barak joined Begin and me. I knew this would be a crucial session, in which I would have to secure the Israelis' confidence and give them a positive preview of the kind of peace settlement I thought would be acceptable in Israel when its terms were revealed.

I began by stressing that the meeting was the culmination of months of work and years of planning in the hope of bringing peace; the consequences of failure were clear. I tried to assure them that the document was a balanced one, but had to acknowledge that the final decisions would not be easy for either side.

"There are phrases in it which both you and Sadat will find difficult to accept—not because they would hurt your countries, but because they are different from positions you have taken and statements you have made in the past. My task will now be hopeless if either of you rejects the language of United Nations Resolution 242. . . .

"This document which I am about to hand you will be given tonight to Sadat. I hope you will be flexible and minimize any proposed changes.

"We are holding back on three issues: sovereignty of the West Bank and Gaza—not to be resolved here at Camp David; Israeli settlements—they will need to be treated separately; and specific agreements on the Sinai withdrawal. I would like to resolve the last two issues during our negotiations here." . . .

Begin began. "Parts of the document are deeply appreciated and positive—a beautiful number [paragraph] on Jerusalem. We appreciate your efforts, but we have a proposal for some changes. Tomorrow we will have a response to the Egyptian document. Tonight we have responses to your proposal, number by number." . . .

A serious problem developed when we got to the part about autonomy for the Palestinians (or "full autonomy," to use Begin's frequently repeated phrase). As the Israelis proposed alternate language, it became clear that they did not want to give the residents of the West Bank and Gaza any appreciable control over their own affairs. Although they had already agreed to withdraw their military government, to confine their forces to prescribed security points, and to cut their military presence by more than half, they now wanted to plant Israelis throughout the region, in order to maintain "public order." Additionally, they wanted a veto right over decisions made by the local citizens on any subject. . . .

I said, "No self-respecting Arab would accept this. It looks like a subterfuge. We are talking about full autonomy — self-control. You are not giving them autonomy if you have to approve their laws, exercise a veto over their decisions, and maintain a military governor."

Begin insisted, "Autonomy doesn't mean sovereignty." . . .

We then spent a lot of time with dictionaries, looking up the meaning of "autonomy," "sovereignty," and "rights."

Dayan finally said, "We shall reconsider our objections — we will look into it. If we accept your language, it is because we understand that Sadat cannot negotiate such details. We are not after political control. If it seems that way to you, we will look at it again." . . .

We finally adjourned, and I asked Dayan to walk back with me to my cottage.

I told Dayan that I considered Begin to be unreasonable and an obstacle to progress, and was beginning to have doubts about his genuine commitment to an agreement and to a subsequent peace treaty. I outlined the moves Sadat had made to be forthcoming, and his private assurances to me concerning additional flexibility — provided a few crucial points were honored. I asked Dayan to help me within the Israeli delegation with these few issues.

Dayan understood my problem but was convinced that Begin did want an agreement. He said that the issue of the settlements was the most difficult for Begin, especially as it concerned those in the Sinai. He asked me to try to induce Sadat to let the title to the settlements be transferred to Egypt but allow the Israelis to continue to live there for a limited time, just as they would be permitted to live in Cairo or Alexandria. This request seemed reasonable to him, and might satisfy both Begin and Sadat, he said.

I promised to bring this matter up with Sadat, but did not think there was any chance for success, because he would consider it a violation of Egyptian sovereignty. The subject had been almost exhausted as far as I was concerned. Since arriving at Camp David, more than half my time with Begin, whether or not Sadat was present, had been spent in discussing the Sinai settlements. . . .

MONDAY, DAY SEVEN (SEPTEMBER 11, 1978)

Although I got up early to incorporate into our proposal the Israeli changes with which we agreed, a final typed version was not ready when Sadat arrived at

Aspen. He came alone, and we discussed the prospective Sinai negotiations while we waited.

Though I was not well prepared, I outlined the kind of agreement I had in mind, including Dayan's proposals. Sadat . . . immediately rejected the idea of Egyptian title to the Sinai settlements while Israelis continued to live in them.

When I asked him if he would permit Jews from any nation, including Israel, to live in Cairo or in Aswan, he replied, "Of course." I pointed out to him that in that case it was not logical to exclude them from the Sinai settlements.

Sadat said, "Some things in the Middle East are not logical or reasonable. For Egypt, this is one of them."

He was firm — they would have to leave. . . .

The documents arrived, and Sadat read the entire proposal aloud, pausing occasionally to comment or to suggest a change. The first difficulty came as a surprise; he made a new demand that Egyptian and Jordanian armed forces be allowed in the West Bank–Gaza areas. I objected strongly, but he replied that otherwise he would be agreeing to exclusive Israeli military occupation in those territories. . . .

Sadat said that he and his legal advisers would go over the paper in detail, and after supper tonight we could get together for another session.

I was pleased. With the exception of the very serious question of Arab armed forces in the occupied territories, the changes he had suggested were quite modest. However, we were certain that his advisers would have many technical proposals. Secretary Vance told me that they had a reputation of being the most contentious of all Arabs in international negotiations. . . .

Later that evening, I met for about two hours with Dayan and Barak. . . .

Attorney General Aharon Barak was outstanding, and later became a real hero in the Camp David discussions. . . . This evening he said quite clearly that the settlements were extremely important, and typically explained the reason. He said that if Sadat, or later his successor, should violate the Egyptian commitment and move strike forces beyond the passes as a threat to Israel, it should be justifiable and inevitable to move Israeli forces into the Sinai west of Gaza, ostensibly to protect the settlers, but actually to protect the nation of Israel. He added that the removal of settlers from the Sinai would also set an unfortunate precedent for Israeli settlements on the West Bank and the Golan Heights. I suspected that the latter was the more important issue. His frankness was encouraging because it indicated that he trusted me enough to tell me about the Israelis' real concerns. . . .

. . . I told him I was becoming increasingly concerned about the entire Middle East and Persian Gulf regions, with the threat of the Soviet Union in South Yemen, Afghanistan, Ethiopia, Libya, Iraq, Syria, and possibly Sudan. It was imperative that he and I begin to shift our influence toward resolving those more serious border issues rather than continuing to be almost exclusively focused on the Israeli-Egyptian dispute. A successful resolution at Camp David was necessary for this purpose — to release a large portion of the Egyptian armed forces now marshaled along the Suez looking toward Israel, and to give a new impetus to a general search for peace. I pointed out that Sadat had five divisions lined up facing Israel; a peace treaty would let his friends in Sudan and Saudi Arabia, as well as his potential enemies in Libya and Ethiopia, know of this new Egyptian capability to act militarily, if necessary.

TUESDAY, DAY EIGHT (SEPTEMBER 12, 1978)

. . . Sadat arrived for our visit five minutes late. He seemed very troubled and was somewhat evasive in his greetings. . . . I immediately felt that he had come to tell me the Camp David negotiations were over, and I decided to delay any such announcement by discussing for a while the strategic implication of a peace agreement on regional and global issues. . . .

My comments seemed effective, and Sadat soon departed, still very troubled but without having delivered to me the fatal message of failure and departure.

Vance and Brzezinski came to report that, like Sadat, the other Egyptians were extremely anxious about our draft proposal and about possible adverse reactions throughout the Arab world if it should become public. However, the Israelis had been surprisingly cooperative during the morning meetings, with Barak and Dayan coming forward with some beneficial and generous suggestions for improving the draft text. I decided to work that afternoon on the terms of an Egyptian-Israeli treaty, and spread the Sinai maps out on the dining table to begin this task, writing the proposed agreement on a yellow scratch pad.

Within three hours I had finished, and walked over to Sadat's cottage to go over the draft with him. I began to read it aloud, but he reached out for the pad, read it carefully, made two changes which would make it more pleasing to Israel, and handed it back to me. "It's all right," he said. I promised to bring him a typed copy before going over it with the Israelis. Our meeting had lasted less than twenty minutes.

I ate supper with the Israeli delegation in the dining hall, and during the meal Begin said he wanted to see me as soon as possible for the most serious talk we had ever had. . . .

. . . He claimed that he sincerely wished he could sign my proposal, but the will of the Israeli people must be represented by him as their Prime Minister.

I pointed out that I had seen public-opinion polls every two or three weeks in which a substantial majority of the Israeli people were willing to accept a peace treaty with an end to the settlements, the removal of Israeli settlers from the Sinai, and the yielding of substantial portions of the territory in the West Bank now under Israeli military government. I was distressed by his attitude and, perhaps ill-advisedly, said that my position represented the Israeli people better than his. . . .

It was a heated discussion, unpleasant and repetitive. I stood for him to leave, and accused him of being willing to give up peace with his only formidable enemy, free trade and diplomatic recognition from Egypt, unimpeded access to international waterways, Arab acceptance of an undivided Jerusalem, permanent security for Israel, and the approbation of the world — all this, just to keep a few illegal settlers on Egyptian land.

As he left he said, interestingly, that Israel did not want any territory in the Sinai, and none in the West Bank *for the first five years.*

WEDNESDAY, DAY NINE (SEPTEMBER 13, 1978)

After this meeting with Begin, I decided to concentrate on a new Framework draft, and to work directly with Aharon Barak and Osama el-Baz. Barak seemed to have Begin's trust, and el-Baz, the most militant of the Egyptians, could speak accurately for the Arab position. If el-Baz agreed to something, the other Egyptian aides would go along, and I could always override him, if necessary, by going directly to Sadat. At the same time, I could depend on Barak to influence Begin. Both these men were brilliant draftsmen, fluent in English, and they understood the nuances of the difficult phrases with which we had to work. . . .

Some differences could not be resolved. Barak refused to discuss the Israeli settlements at all, saying that it was a subject only Begin could address. El-Baz, backed by Sadat, refused to include a commitment to open borders and full diplomatic recognition. . . .

I went to bed late, tired but pleased. Sadat was staying, the Israelis were being more helpful, and we had a good new plan for a Sinai agreement leading to a peace treaty. . . .

THURSDAY, DAY TEN (SEPTEMBER 14, 1978)

I was waiting for Sadat when he emerged from his cabin, and I joined him for about an hour during his regular morning walk. . . .

When I returned from the walk, Barak was waiting for me. He was still encouraged about the positive attitude prevailing among Begin and the other Israelis. He suggested that I discuss the Sinai questions with Dayan, who was more knowledgeable than he about the subject. Dayan and Weizman came to see me, and soon it all boiled down to the settlements. In desperation, I promised to draft language allowing this issue to be left open for future resolution, without preconditions, for at least three months. Thus, the question might be finessed with Sadat.

No luck. When I showed my new draft to Sadat, he immediately stated that there *were* preconditions — one being the airfields, and the other being the settlements, and that he would negotiate on *when* they would be withdrawn, not *if* they would be withdrawn.

I asked, "What procedure do you suggest if the Israelis will not agree to move the settlements?"

He replied, "I will sign the American document anyway, because it will describe my position."

This impasse would be the end of our effort for peace. I could not think of any way to resolve this fundamental difference between the Israelis and the Egyptians. On the Sinai settlements, Begin did not stand alone among his delegation. So far as I could tell, the Israelis were united in their belief that the settlers could not be moved. . . .

That evening I began to list the differences between the two nations, and was heartbroken to see how relatively insignificant they really were, compared to the great advantages of peace. I sat on the back terrace late into the night, but could think of no way to make further progress. My only decision was that all of us should work together to leave Camp David in as positive a mood as possible, taking credit for what we had done and resolved to continue our common search for an elusive accord.

FRIDAY, DAY ELEVEN (SEPTEMBER 15, 1978)

. . . I instructed staff members to begin drafting an outline of a speech for me to make to Congress, explaining what we had attempted during the two weeks at Camp David and why we had not been successful. They also took the private notes I had compiled the previous evening to put them into more formal words, listing the unresolved differences between Egypt and Israel and enumerating the benefits that would accrue to both nations if a peace agreement could be reached in the future. . . .

As I was getting ready to meet with Vance and Brown, Dayan reported that he and Sadat had just concluded an unsatisfactory meeting. It had been arranged by Weizman in hopes that the two men might find some basis for continuing the talks. Then Vance told me that Sadat had just sent for him.

After Harold and I had been at work for about twenty minutes, Vance burst into the room. His face was white, and he announced, "Sadat is leaving. He and his aides are already packed. He asked me to order him a helicopter!"

It was a terrible moment. Now, even my hopes for a harmonious departure were gone. I sat quietly and assessed the significance of this development—a rupture between Sadat and me, and its consequences for my country and for the Middle East power balance. I envisioned the ultimate alliance of most of the Arab nations to the Soviet Union, perhaps joined by Egypt after a few months had passed. I told Vance that the best thing for us to do now, to salvage what we could, would be to refuse to sign any document with either country—just to terminate the talks and announce that we had all done our best and failed. . . .

Then, for some reason, I changed into more formal clothes before going to see Sadat. He was on his porch with five or six of his ministers, and Vance and Brown were there to tell them all good-bye.

I nodded to them, and walked into the cabin. Sadat followed me. I explained to him the extremely serious consequences of his unilaterally breaking off the negotiations: that his action would harm the relationship between Egypt and the United States, he would be violating his personal promise to me, and the onus for failure would be on him. I described the possible future progress of Egypt's friendships and alliances—from us to the moderate and then radical Arabs, thence to the Soviet Union. I told him it would damage one of my most precious possessions—his friendship and our mutual trust.

He was adamant, but I was dead serious, and he knew it. I had never been more serious in my life. I repeated some of the more telling arguments I had previously used at our meeting by the swimming pool. He would be publicly repudiating some of his own commitments, damaging his reputation as the world's foremost peacemaker, and admitting the fruitlessness of his celebrated visit to Jerusalem. His worst enemies in the Arab world would be proven right in their claims that he had made a foolish mistake.

I told Sadat that he simply had to stick with me for another day or two—after which, if circumstances did not improve, all of us simultaneously would take the action he was now planning.

He explained the reason for his decision to leave. Dayan had told him the Israelis would not sign any agreements. This made Sadat furious. He had accused Dayan of wasting time by coming to Camp David in the first place. His own advisers had pointed out the danger in his signing an agreement with the United States alone. Later, if direct discussions were ever resumed with the Israelis, they could say, "The Egyptians have already agreed to all these points. Now we will use what they have signed as the original basis for all future negotiations." It was a telling argument. I thought very rapidly and told him that we would have a complete understanding that if any nation rejected *any* part of the agreements, *none* of the proposals would stay in effect.

Sadat stood silently for a long time. Then he looked at me and said, "If you give me this statement, I will stick with you to the end." (He kept his promise, but it never proved necessary to give him any such statement.)

Those were sweet words to hear. I went back to Aspen and told Rosalynn, Fritz, Cy, Harold, and Zbig that everything was all right. I described my conversation with Sadat, and we pledged ourselves to silence and went back to work. It had been a bad time. . . .

SATURDAY, DAY TWELVE (SEPTEMBER 16, 1978)

I got up earlier than usual and wrote down all the items in the Sinai document with which the Israelis could possibly disagree. I simply listed them, and then went for another long walk with President Sadat. . . .

I . . . probed very hard for some opening on the Sinai settlements issue, but without success. Sadat was willing . . . to wait three years after the peace treaty was signed for the people to leave. But they had to leave — that was it.

Later I walked over to Holly, where the Americans and Israelis were talking, and discussed the same issue with Dayan. The best I could get out of him was his personal willingness to have the settlers leave after twenty years. He said that Begin would not agree even to such an extended time period if there had to be an ultimate commitment for them to leave. On the West Bank, Dayan was willing to agree to no *new* settlements — to be specified in an exchange of letters between me and the Prime Minister. . . .

At this point, as far as the settlements were concerned, we had . . . three levels of opposition in the Israeli delegation: Begin wanted no commitment to withdrawal; Dayan was willing to promise withdrawal after an extended period of time; and Weizman believed that the settlers should leave if the Knesset would agree.

When Sadat and el-Baz came to meet with me and Cy in the afternoon, . . . I listed all the advantages that might come to Egypt with a peace agreement.

We then reviewed the more specific Sinai proposal, and found no significant disagreement except over the Israeli settlements — and no disagreement at all between myself and Sadat.

On the more comprehensive Framework, we were also very close. In referring to the Palestinians' authority on the West Bank, I agreed to find a synonym for "self-government." (Sadat thought the word sounded too much like Begin's "self-rule.") . . .

I told him that there was no alternative to my handling the question of the settlements directly and personally with Prime Minister Begin, who would be arriving in just a few minutes. Sadat left, having been in an exceptionally sober but nevertheless constructive mood. . . .

Begin came with Dayan and Barak, for which we were thankful. If anyone at Camp David had influence on Begin, it was these two men.

Cy and I ate some crackers and cheese as I listed the benefits of the proposed agreement to Israel. Immediately Begin began talking about the blessed settlements, but I insisted that we go through both documents in an orderly fashion, paragraph by paragraph. I wanted the Israelis to realize how few differences remained. In an hour we were finished with the Sinai document, and it was obvious to me that Sadat would be willing to accept almost all the Israeli demands for change. The few others were not very important to Begin, and I felt sure that he would not insist on them.

We then moved to the settlements again, and Begin insisted that he would negotiate with Sadat on all other items for three months in search of a final peace treaty and the resolution of all remaining differences. If this effort was completely successful, he would submit the settlement withdrawal question to the Knesset. I told him again and again that this proposal was totally unacceptable to Sadat, who insisted on a commitment to remove all Israeli settlers from his territory *before* any other negotiations could be conducted.

I thought the discussion would never end. It was obviously very painful for Prime Minister Begin, who was shouting words like "ultimatum," "excessive demands," and "political suicide." However, he finally promised to submit to the Knesset within two weeks the question: "If agreement is reached on all other Sinai issues, will the settlers be withdrawn?"

I believed this concession would be enough for Sadat. Breakthrough!

I asked Begin if he would maintain a neutral position as the Knesset debated the issue, but he would not promise. He did agree, however, to remove the requirements of party loyalty and let each member of the Knesset vote as an individual. He assured me that the same would apply to cabinet members. I questioned Dayan, but he would not give me a firm commitment of support.

We all agreed that what we had just decided represented a great step forward.

We then had a surprisingly amicable discussion about the Framework for Peace. Barak was a tremendous help as we went over the entire proposed text. Dayan was quite forthcoming on the Palestinian question, and said with some enthusiasm, "We'll let the Palestinians join the Jordanians during the negotiation of the peace treaty with Israel." To accommodate Sadat's request, we searched for a synonym for "self-government for the Palestinians," and came up with "how the Palestinians shall govern themselves." There was no apparent difference, so no harm was done. By this time I had become a master at making insignificant editorial changes to overcome significant objections.

I had a lot of latitude in dealing with the West Bank–Gaza questions. Fortunately, Sadat was not particularly interested in the detailed language of the Framework for Peace, and with the exception of the settlements, Begin was not very interested in the details of the Sinai agreement. . . .

On the West Bank settlements, we finally worked out language that was satisfactory: that no new Israeli settlements would be established after the signing of this Framework for Peace, and that the issue of additional settlements would be resolved by the parties during the negotiations. This would be stated in a letter, to be made public, from Begin to me. (Begin later denied that he had agreed to this, and claimed that he had promised to stop building settlements only for a three-month period. My notes are clear — that the settlement freeze would continue until all negotiations were completed — and Cy Vance confirms my interpretation of what we decided. This was the only serious post-Camp David disagreement about our decisions, so our batting average was good.)

After the Israelis left, Vance and I agreed that we had a settlement, at least for Camp David. There was no doubt that Sadat would accept my recommendations on the issues we had just discussed with Begin. What the Knesset might decide was uncertain, but I was convinced that the people of Israel would be in favor of the overall agreement, including the withdrawal of the settlers from the Sinai. Weizman would be a big help. I intended to try in every way possible to shape world opinion and to get the American Jewish community to support this effort.

SUNDAY, DAY THIRTEEN (SEPTEMBER 17, 1978)

I was eager to meet with President Sadat, and he and I quickly went over the proposals for the final language. The few predictable changes that he advocated would, I was sure, be acceptable to the Israelis. . . .

Only then did I fully realize we had succeeded. I called Rosalynn first. . . . Then I called the Democratic and Republican congressional leaders to give them a brief report. In the meantime, Sadat was paying a courtesy call on Begin, and later they met in front of Aspen. We embraced enthusiastically, went to the helicopter, and flew to the White House together. . . .

The Framework for Peace in the Middle East and the Framework for the Conclusion of a Peace Treaty Between Egypt and Israel were two major steps forward. For a few hours, all three of us were flushed with pride and good will toward one another because of our unexpected success. We had no idea at that time how far we still had to go.*

Note

Despite former President Carter's imaginative and persistent mediation efforts at Camp David, subsequent events have shown the continued volatility of the region and the failure to achieve a lasting peace between Israel and its Arab neighbors. Perhaps the most interesting recent development was the attempt to bring about a comprehensive settlement between the Israelis and the Palestinians, beginning with the secret back channel negotiations at Oslo early in 1993, leading to the Oslo Accord in September 1993, featuring Israeli Prime Minister Yitzak Rabin and PLO Chairman Yassar Arafat shaking hands on the White House lawn (Watkins and Lundberg, 1998).† Alas, once again the seesaw nature of events in the Mideast, beginning with the 1995 assassination of Yitzak Rabin, threatens to derail the peace efforts so promisingly heralded in 1993.

*For another interesting view of the Camp David negotiations, see Quandt (1988).

†See also The Oslo Channel: Getting to the Negotiating Table, Kennedy School of Government, Harvard University, Case No. C113-98-1333.0. For other interesting first-hand accounts of international efforts to negotiate or mediate peace, see Mitchell (1999) and Princen (1992).

The international mediation lessons of Camp David nonetheless continue to influence attempts to bring peace elsewhere. Richard Holbrooke, the Assistant Secretary of State for European and Canadian Affairs and the U.S. chief negotiator among parties to the Balkan armed conflicts in 1995, reports giving Carter's book on Camp David, as well as other memoirs of that negotiation, to every member of his team as they prepared for the historic peace talks in Dayton. Holbrooke then contacted Carter to ask about details not covered in *Keeping Faith* (1998:204-205):

> Had the Americans been able to create any sort of personal rapport between Sadat and Begin? Could we do so at Dayton? Do people become more malleable after being cooped up for days? Will sheer fatigue make tempers flare?
>
> I . . . listened in fascination as [Carter] described how he had tried without success to get Sadat and Begin to talk directly to each other. He had then reverted to "proximity talks," a diplomatic technique originating in Mideast negotiations held in the 1940s at the U.N., in which the mediator moves between the two parties, who rarely meet face-to-face — a sort of "shuttle diplomacy by foot." . . . Carter recounted his constant efforts to reduce the personal distaste between the two men. His most memorable effort was a field trip to the Gettysburg battlefield, where, he hoped, being at a site of wasted sacrifice would produce a breakthrough. No such thing happened, of course, and Carter sat in the car between Sadat and Begin for hours, their knees touching, while they ignored each other.

Questions

10.1 What elements of good mediation practice are illustrated by Carter's activities at Camp David?

10.2 Confidentiality is often considered the key to ensuring party candor. Is this likely to be the case for negotiations among world leaders? What impact might Carter's disclosures in the above excerpt have on his ability to act as a mediator in future international disputes or on the future behavior of negotiators in international disputes?

B. ARBITRATING PRIVATE DISPUTES

The private justice of international commercial arbitration strikes U.S. litigators as a markedly different approach to adjudication. Christian Bühring-Uhle (1996:89) quotes an international lawyer as follows:

> International arbitration is at once serious business and great fun, but it isn't everyone's cup of tea. You may have to structure your arguments under a substantive law you have never considered before, appear in a hearing in a remote country before arbitrators trained in three different legal systems who have worked out some weird, fish-and-fowl rules of procedure which are revealed to you as you go along. If you are truly lucky, your case will depend on your skill in cross-examining a brilliant rogue who insists he can express himself only in Greek or Danish or Thai, and who lengthily answers the question he thinks you ought to have asked, through a befuddled interpreter, all while the

jet-lagged chairman's concentration seems exclusively focused upon his watch. Many litigators who perform superbly in their home courts are unable to function in this kind of environment.

In the first excerpt, Bühring-Uhle describes the development and current practices in international commercial arbitration. Yves Dezalay and Bryant Garth, in the second excerpt, focus on the increasing involvement of governments in influencing dispute resolution in private cases. This conclusion is borne out in the final excerpt, which describes the elaborate dispute resolution procedures of the World Trade Organization (WTO).

C. BÜHRING-UHLE, ARBITRATION AND MEDIATION IN INTERNATIONAL BUSINESS

39-40, 49-52, 144, 163-164, 293 (1996)

Commercial arbitration is probably as old as commerce itself. In the Anglo-American world, mercantile dispute resolution through merchants can be traced back to the 13th century where merchants sat as private judges in "piepowder courts," staple courts and on tribunals of the merchant guilds and trading companies. In the 18th and 19th centur[ies] commercial and maritime arbitration was developed under the auspices of trade associations, mercantile, shipping and stock exchanges, chambers of commerce, and toward the end of the 19th century, specialized arbitration institutions. The first international arbitration institution with a global reach was the Court of Arbitration of the International Chamber of Commerce (ICC).* The ICC is a non-governmental "world business organization," founded after World War I in 1919. . . . The Court of Arbitration was established in 1923 at the seat of the headquarters of the ICC in Paris.

Since the foundation of the ICC Court of Arbitration ("ICC Court"), the history of arbitration has been characterized by a dramatic expansion of the caseload, by rising stakes and increasing complexity of the disputes, by growing participation of governments and of parties from non-European countries, and perhaps most importantly by a change in the nature of the procedures away from an informal "merchant's justice" towards professionalism, legalism and proceduralization. During the first 20 years of its existence, the great majority of cases administered by the ICC were disposed of by conciliation. In 1991, the proportion of conciliation cases had sunk to 3%. And whereas traditionally commercial arbitration was handled by "commercial men," and today still is in certain specialized types of arbitrations . . . , in ICC arbitration nowadays the proportion of lawyers among arbitrators has been estimated at 97%.

[Parties with different nationalities have different procedural traditions. A key difference is the preference of American litigators for formal discovery.]

[Some parties use ad hoc arbitration, in which they specify their own rules for the process, rather than institutional arbitration, where rules and most aspects of the process are pre-determined by the organization administering the arbitration.

*While the ICC was one of the earliest arbitration institutions, there are now many others.

The dilemma for the arbitration clause drafter — for international, as in domestic, agreements — is this:] [B]efore the dispute arises the parties lack the necessary information about the dispute to really cover all aspects that might become relevant — unless they want to cover every contingency which, if it is not impossible, will be too expensive to do. And once the dispute has materialized, the parties are often too much at odds with each other . . . to reach agreement about the many issues that have to be covered.

Institutional arbitration comes a long way in solving this dilemma in that it provides a set of rules that can be easily incorporated by reference, and are detailed enough to cover the most important contingencies but sufficiently general to give the parties and the tribunal the flexibility to adapt the proceedings to the particularities of the dispute. And, most importantly, it provides for a neutral authority that warrants the establishment of the tribunal and resolves deadlocks and disputes about the procedures. . . .

A compromise solution sometimes chosen when the parties do not want to or cannot agree to employ the services of an arbitration institution has been made available through the promulgation in 1976 of the [United Nations Commission on International Trade Laws (UNCITRAL)] Arbitration Rules. Sponsored by the United Nations, . . . they offer a detailed, culturally and ideologically neutral set of rules that has found widespread acceptance all over the world. Many arbitration institutions have adopted them in whole or in large part . . . , and through the practice of the Iran-United States Claims Tribunal which has been operating under these rules for almost 10 years, there exists a solid body of published arbitral precedents dealing . . . with the application of the UNCITRAL Rules. . . .

Unless otherwise specified, arbitration will be held according to rules of law. According to ICC statistics, the parties fail to specify applicable law only in about one sixth of the cases. In that case, the arbitrators either choose the applicable law they deem appropriate or proceed on the basis of choice of law rules. Most national laws and many arbitration rules, however, accept the possibility for the parties to grant the arbitrators the powers to decide as *amiable compositeurs* [who may sometimes ignore laws the parties have specified by contract when their application would lead to an inequitable result] or according to principles of equity, i.e. *ex aequo et bono*.

[The author's research indicates that] arbitration was seen as faster but not less expensive than litigation. . . . On average, the settlement rate came to 40.6%. . . . The settlement rate in international commercial arbitration seems to be markedly lower than in domestic litigation where settlement rates approach 90%.* . . . Although a substantial number of arbitrations end with a settlement, this tends to happen at a fairly advanced stage of the procedure and mainly as a result of the parties becoming more realistic and more aware of the costs as the procedure unfolds. . . .

*Although at first glance it may seem inappropriate to compare international arbitration rates with domestic litigation rates, the comparison may be apt since, as pointed out in the introduction, the alternative to international arbitration is often domestic litigation.

Y. DEZALAY AND B. GARTH, DEALING IN VIRTUE: INTERNATIONAL COMMERCIAL ARBITRATION AND THE CONSTRUCTION OF A TRANSNATIONAL LEGAL ORDER

313-315 (1996)

[The International Chamber of Commerce (ICC) approach] studiously put aside the regulations of the nation-state. The approach employed a private institutional platform — the ICC, which is after all an organization of private business — that has no formal ties with states. The ICC could persuasively argue that the arbitration of disputes with third-world or Communist states was simply a matter of private, commercial arbitration. . . . The academic world of learned law was able to provide the neutral authority through the *lex mercatoria* [customary merchant law developed by the arbitrators over time]. . . .

[T]he legal picture has been transformed by the increasing dominance of the political and economic model of Western liberal democracies. No longer do we face fundamental opposition between communism and capitalism, or between various models of authoritarianism and relatively democratic entities. . . . The states . . . concede certain of their prerogatives to supranational entities, such as [the World Trade Organization (WTO)] or the United Nations, or to courts, exemplified by the European Court of Justice; or quasi courts, exemplified by [NAFTA] and WTO panels.

A. GUZMAN AND B. SIMMONS, TO SETTLE OR EMPANEL? AN EMPIRICAL ANALYSIS OF LITIGATION AND SETTLEMENT AT THE WORLD TRADE ORGANIZATION

31 J. Legal Stud. 205 (2002)

I. Introduction

The World Trade Organization (WTO) came into being on January 1, 1995, to replace the General Agreement on Tariffs and Trade (GATT). Of the changes to international trade brought about through the establishment of the WTO, one of the most important — and almost certainly the most discussed — is the dispute resolution procedure. The new procedure was developed in an attempt to improve on what existed under GATT, most notably by shortening the duration of cases and eliminating the veto power states previously had over the adoption of panel rulings. . . .

II. Dispute Settlement at the World Trade Organization

The dispute settlement procedures of the WTO . . . include[ ] several phases: consultation, panel investigation and report, appellate review, decision adoption, and implementation. When a dispute arises between WTO member states, either party may call for consultation. Members are required to enter into consultation within 30 days of such a request; if a member refuses to do so, the complaining party may ask for the establishment of a panel. If consultation fails to yield a settlement 60 days after the request is made, the complaining party may request the establishment of a panel, which must be established no later than at the meeting of the Dispute Settlement Body (DSB) that follows the request. Panels typically consist of three people from countries not party to the dispute. If the parties fail to agree on the composition of the panel within 20 days of its establishment, the director-general is authorized to decide the issue upon the request of either party.

Once issued, panel reports are considered for adoption by the DSB. Unless the DSB decides by consensus not to adopt the report or one of the parties notifies the DSB of its intention to appeal, it is automatically adopted within 60 days of issuance. If one or both parties request an appeal, a three-person appellate panel is established. Appeals are intended to be limited to issues of law covered in the panel report and legal interpretations developed by the panel. The entire process, from establishment of a panel to the adoption of the panel or appellate body report by the DSB, is to take place within 9 months if there is no appeal and 12 months if there is an appeal.

If the offending party fails to implement a panel recommendation or ruling within a reasonable period of time, it must enter into negotiations with the aggrieved party to develop a satisfactory scheme of compensation. If there is no agreement on compensation within 20 days, a party to the dispute may request authorization of the DSB to suspend concessions or other obligations to the other party. The DSB will grant such a request within 30 days of the expiry of the agreed time frame for implementation unless it decides by consensus not to do so. The party subject to retaliation may object, in which case the issue goes to arbitration.

In summary, then, the full dispute settlement provisions of the WTO provide for the filing of a grievance by the complainant, a period of consultation, a panel investigation and report, an appellate panel and report, implementation, negotiation regarding compensation, and retaliation. The parties are able to settle the case through mutual consent at any point in the process. For the purposes of this paper, it is settlement prior to the panel stage that is of interest. This is the stage most analogous to the question of settlement before "trial" in the existing litigation and settlement literature. In any event, virtually all cases for which a panel decision is announced are appealed, making the prepanel stage the one time, prior to final adjudication, at which the parties truly enter into negotiations. . . .

[The authors conducted an empirical study of WTO disputes to test their hypothesis that negotiated settlement is more likely when the subject matter of the dispute allows more flexible resolution (such as tariff rate disputes), but less likely when the subject matter of the dispute has "an all-or-nothing" character (such as health or safety regulations) where it would be difficult to expand the resources available for settlement. After studying all the cases filed at the WTO between 1995 and 2000, the authors made the following conclusions.]

The major findings of this paper center on the nature of the disputed issue in influencing the settlement of trade disputes. Our central hypothesis was that continuous, easily divisible problems would tend to be resolved in the consultation phase, while issues that have an all-or-nothing quality—lumpy issues—are more likely to escalate to the panel phase. Our findings suggest this is especially likely to be the case when two democracies disagree over trade. After all, highly democratic disputants are likely to face even greater domestic political consequences for making concessions than are relatively autocratic governments. Certainly, it might be possible to make an inherently lumpy issue more continuous by making side payments or attempting to engage in issue linkage. Our argument, however, is that democracies find it much harder to pull off these more complicated deals, since they are likely to affect the interests of other groups who might oppose the strategy of such linkage.

The evidence seems to suggest this is the case. When nondemocratic pairs dispute noncontinuous issues, they were no more likely (and are possibly less likely) to resort to panels. Democracies, on the other hand, were shown to resort to panels at a significantly higher rate conditional on the nature of the issue. They tend to take lumpy problems to panels. Note that our findings indicate that there is nothing inherent in democracy alone that suggests they prefer to resolve their cases before a panel. On the contrary, democratic pairs dealing with continuous issues usually settle in the consultation phase. This suggests that transaction costs, rather than legal culture or a high comfort level with "the rule of law," better account for these patterns of escalation in cases that have been submitted to the WTO's dispute settlement process.*

Question

10.3 Several U.S. states have enacted a version of the UNCITRAL Model Laws that authorizes enforcement of agreements to conciliate international disputes. (See Appendix E.) (Conciliation is essentially the same process as mediation and is a term often used in the international context in lieu of mediation.) Do these statutes raise the same policy issues as those debated in Chapter 3 in connection with public encouragement of mediation?

EXERCISE 10.1: THE MOUSE EXERCISE**

Background Information

GENERAL INFORMATION

The setting is Marne-la-Vallee, a short distance outside of Paris, France. Eighteen months ago, Mouse, the world's largest entertainment conglomerate, and the French government, signed a Master Agreement to create the EuroMouse development in Marne-la-Vallee. This agreement was quite controversial within France at the time, and since its signing a major debate has been playing out in the court of public opinion. Although there are many problems surrounding the project, one of

*For another interesting perspective on the role of alternative dispute resolution in international disputes, see Joost Paulwelyn, "The limits of Litigation: 'Americanization' and Negotiation in the Settlement of WTO Disputes," 19 *Ohio St. J. Disp. Resol.* 121 (2002).

**This exercise has been adapted by Professors Jeanne M. Brett and Stephen B. Goldberg from an exercise of the same name created by Geoffrey D. Fink and Maria Baute Stewart. It is used with their permission.

the most difficult involves the poor relationship between Mouse and the four towns within which the development is occurring. These towns, called "communes," are Bailly, Coupvray, Magny, and Chessy. In a bid to ease the tensions and to work out some form of agreement, the government has called for a meeting between one of its representatives, the four mayors, and Mouse.

The elected representatives of the communes had no role in the Master Agreement's negotiation. The national government acquired almost 5,000 hectares (1 hectare = 10,000 square meters) of farmland by eminent domain at the agricultural price of FF 4.00 per square meter. It then resold the land to Mouse at the commercially zoned rate of FF 11.90. Local farmers are very upset at what they see as government profiteering at their expense.

Construction began almost as soon as Mouse took ownership of the property. The construction has fundamentally altered the nature of Marne-la-Vallee. This quiet, rural farming area was transformed almost overnight into Europe's biggest worksite. The entire area is suffering from noise, dirt, and congestion due to the construction. EuroMouse has employed 10,000 temporary workers, many of whom commute to the worksite daily, entering either through Bailly or Magny, whose roads were not designed to handle such traffic, much less the heavy equipment and loads of construction material that enter the site daily.

Residents are extremely annoyed with the disturbance to their lifestyle. Highway signs directing people to the village have been spray painted and are unintelligible. Posters of Uncle Scrooge rampaging through the countryside have appeared in the area. EuroMouse is almost always the headline story in the local paper. A recent story speculated on whether local farmers might block access to the site with their tractors and haywagons. When the Master Agreement was announced, the national press ballyhooed American cultural imperialism. Now the national press is covering the "Destruction of Traditional Life in Marne-la-Vallee."

The construction has caused a huge administrative burden for the towns that must issue licenses and permits and carry out inspections. EuroMouse is behind schedule and has been pressuring the mayors to expedite EuroMouse's permits. At the same time, the towns are being overwhelmed by demands for permits for secondary construction by independent developers trying to capitalize on the EuroMouse project.

EuroMouse has a master plan for the development of the park and the provision of services. Electricity, water, and waste removal are all contracted for directly, without the involvement of the towns. There is no master plan, however, for the secondary construction, and the towns are concerned that they will not be able to cope with the demands for services resulting from it. EuroMouse, realizing that the mayors lacked an overall vision of the park and its surroundings, recently took all four mayors and their families to visit MouseWorld in Florida.

EuroMouse should eventually bring considerable tax revenues to the towns. Property values have already increased as independent developers have been buying land adjacent to the park and Mouse employees have begun buying houses. Some local residents, however, are extremely disturbed about the projected increase in property taxes associated with increased property values. Increased property taxes are a double bind for the mayors. They desperately need the increased revenue, but the political reality is that the mayors must work with the local Ministry of Economy officials to keep local property taxes down.

A different source of revenue would be a *tax professionnelle* or payroll-based tax that the national government could levy on EuroMouse and distribute to the communes. This tax is commonly paid by large French employers; however, no provision for it was included in the Master Agreement.

THE PARTIES

The Communes: Represented by their mayors, the communes believe that they are in the center of a storm that is not of their own making. Mouse and the French government worked out an agreement without soliciting their participation, and then presented it to them as a fait accompli.

Mouse Representative: Mouse will be represented at the meeting by its manager of government and public relations. This manager is a California native, has an MBA, has been at corporate headquarters in strategic planning for five years, and was recently transferred to EuroMouse.

National Government: The French government will be represented by an official who participated in the Master Agreement negotiations for the French government. This official is a graduate of the prestigious Ecole Nationale d'Administration and has been active in formulating the government's strategy to encourage international investment and to make France better attuned to the realities of international business.

The government has asked all of the above parties to attend a meeting to discuss their various concerns and seek some sort of resolution to the increasingly acrimonious conflict that has been developing. Given that the EuroMouse project is certain to go forward, the purpose of this meeting is not to discuss whether the park should be there in the first place, but to deal with some of the problems associated with the park.

THE AGENDA

The following issues are to be discussed during the meeting.

Press Release: The press has been giving the Mouse project and the communes' problems with it a great deal of publicity. The press knows that this meeting is scheduled to take place and will be seeking to interview its participants. The parties may use this opportunity either to express their goodwill or their animosity towards each other.

Payroll Tax: The parties will consider whether a payroll tax should be levied on Mouse. They will also discuss the amount of the tax to be imposed, which could range from one-half to 2 percent of total payroll. (By French law, the tax *must* be a multiple of .5, i.e., .5, 1.0, 1.5, or 2.0.) Total payroll has been estimated to vary between 700 million francs and 1,300 million francs annually, depending on EuroMouse's success. The expected average payroll is approximately 1,000 million francs annually. While all parties' input will be relevant to this issue, the final decisions as to both the imposition and the amount of this tax rest solely with the national government.

Absent any separate agreement between the towns, the payroll tax would be divided almost equally between Chessy and Coupvray, the towns in which nearly all of the park's employees will work.

Annual Payments to the Towns: All of the towns have experienced tremendous upheaval since the construction of EuroMouse began. Additional administrative demands (i.e., the countless licenses, permits, notices, and the like that must be issued before the project can proceed) have strained the resources of the communes. Therefore, some of the mayors have called for reimbursement by Mouse or the national government for the increased costs of governing. At the meeting, the parties must decide whether such compensation is warranted, and, if so, in what amount and under what terms annual payments will be made. How payments are to be divided among the towns is also likely to be an issue.

Expediting Permits: Mouse has expressed its concern that the EuroMouse project is seriously behind schedule, and its view is that this delay is attributable in substantial part to the towns' failure to deal promptly with permit applications. Mouse is almost certain to demand that the process of granting permits be expedited.

Other Issues: Other issues may also arise during the negotiations, and each party is free to discuss those issues and may enter into any agreement not precluded by its Confidential Instructions, which are in the Teacher's Manual.

C. NEGOTIATING PRIVATE DISPUTES

International negotiation is often said to present particular difficulties because of cultural differences between the negotiators. In an experiment regarding intra- and cross-cultural negotiations, Professors Jeanne Brett and Tetsushi Okumura noted that Japanese and American negotiators achieved joint gains less frequently when negotiating across nationalities than when negotiating with others of the same nationality (Brett and Okumura, 1998). A multinational group of social scientists also identified some negotiating cultures as less likely to encourage the generation of joint gains, even when both negotiators shared the culture (Brett et al., 1998). This research suggests that negotiating effectiveness may be lost because of two effects of culture: the inability of negotiating approaches to work as well across cultures and the fact that the other negotiator may come from a negotiating culture not suited to the creation of joint gains.

In the excerpt below, the authors offer advice to persons approaching negotiation of an international dispute.

EXERCISE 10.2: ALPHA-BETA ROBOTICS NEGOTIATION*

Profile of Alpha, Inc. Alpha, Inc. is a large and broadly diversified electrical company based in the nation of Alpha. The company plans to become a leader in equipping the "factory of the future" and is already one of the leading makers of numerical control equipment. It has recently spent hundreds of millions of dollars developing a factory automation capability, including robotics and

*This exercise is adapted from a simulation created by Professor Thomas Gladwin, Stern School of Business, New York University.

computer-aided design and manufacturing. Alpha, Inc. has been acquiring companies, investing heavily in new plant, and spending considerable sums on product development. It has innovative robots, some equipped with vision, under development, but they have been a bit slow in making their way out of the company's R&D labs. To meet its objective of quickly becoming a major worldwide and full-service supplier of automation systems, Alpha Inc. has found it necessary to link up, in various ways, with foreign firms that are further down the robotics learning curve.

Robotics in the nation of Alpha. There are 30 robotics manufacturers in Alpha. Alphan computer and auto firms have also recently been entering the business. Use and production of robots in Alpha is only about a third of what it is in the nation of Beta. One survey reported that 1,269 robots were produced in Alpha in 1997; the survey also revealed that 4,370 robots were in use in Alpha in 1997, mainly in the auto and foundry industries. Robot sales in that year were estimated to be $92 million, with a significant share accounted for by imports. The industrial automation market in Alpha is growing at well over 20 percent a year. The robotics portion of it is expected to become a $2 billion a year domestic market within five years.

Profile of Beta, Inc. Beta, Inc. is the leading manufacturer of integrated electrical machinery in the nation of Beta. The company has been run by scientists since its founding and is Beta's most research-oriented corporation. It employs more than 9,000 researchers, and its R&D spending equals 5.9 percent of corporate sales. Beta, Inc.'s aim is to become the world's largest producer of robotics in the next few years. To meet this goal, Beta, Inc. will have to double its manufacturing capacity and develop a strong export market. To date nearly all of Beta, Inc.'s robotics production has been sold domestically. The company's deep commitment to robotics is reflected in the recent formation of a large task force to develop a universal assembly robot with both visual and tactile sensors.

Robotics in the nation of Beta. There are 150 companies making or selling robots in Beta. The nation has "robot fever" and a government that has declared automation to be a national goal. An estimated 12,000 to 14,000 programmable robots are already on the job in Beta, representing 59 percent of those in use worldwide. Betan firms churned out nearly $400 million worth of robots in 1997 (approximately 3,200 units or one-half of world production). The nation exported only 2.5 percent of its production and imported less than 5 percent of its robots. Industry analysts see robot production in Beta rising to $2 billion in the next five years and $5 billion in the next 10 years.

(Confidential information is contained in the Teacher's Manual.)

References

ABA DISPUTE RESOLUTION MAGAZINE (1998) Symposium: Focus on International ADR (Spring).

BERCOVITCH, Jacob, and Jeffrey RUBIN (1992) *Mediation in International Relations.* New York: St. Martin's.

———, eds. (1992) *Mediation in International Relations: Multiple Approaches to Conflict Management.* New York: St. Martin's Press.

BILDER, Richard (1989) "International Third Party Dispute Settlement," 17 *Denv. J. Int'l L. & Pol'y* 471.

BRETT, Jeanne M., et al. (1998) "Culture and Joint Gains in Negotiation," 14 *Neg. J.* 61.
BRETT, Jeanne M., and Tetsushi OKUMURA (1998) "Inter- and Intra-Cultural Negotiation: U.S. and Japanese Negotiators," 4 *Acad. Mgmt. J.* 495 (Oct.).
BROWN, Frederick, and Catherine A. ROGERS (1997) "The Role of Arbitration in Resolving Transnational Disputes: A Survey of Trends in the People's Republic of China," 15 *Berkeley J. Int'l L.* 329.
BÜHRING-UHLE, Christian (1996) *Arbitration and Mediation in International Business.* The Hague: Kluwer Law International. Boston: Kluwer Law International.
CARBONNEAU, Thomas E., ed. (1990) *Lex Mercatoria and Arbitration: A Discussion of the New Law Merchant.* New York: Transnational Juris Publications.
CARTER, Jimmy (1982) *Keeping Faith: Memoirs of a President.* New York: Bantam Books.
CARTER, James H. (1998) "NAFTA: How It Has Transformed Dispute Resolution in Canada, Mexico and the United States," *ABA Disp. Resol. Mag.* 19 (Spring).
COLLIER, John G., and Vaughan LOWE (1999) *The Settlement of Disputes in International Law: Institutions and Procedures.* Oxford: Oxford University Press.
COT, Jean Pierre (1972) *International Conciliation.* London: Europa Publications.
DEZALAY, Yves, and Bryant G. GARTH (1996) *Dealing in Virtue: International Commercial Arbitration and the Construction of a Transnational Legal Order.* Chicago: University of Chicago Press.
DONELAN, M.D., and F.S. NORTHEDGE (1971) *International Disputes: The Political Aspects.* New York: St. Martin's Press.
FAURE, Guy, and Jeffrey RUBIN (1993) *Culture and Negotiation.* Newbury Park, CA: Sage.
FISHER, Roger, et al. (1994) *Beyond Machiavelli: Tools for Coping with Conflict.* Cambridge, MA: Harvard University Press.
FOX, William F., Jr. (1992) *International Commercial Agreements, Second Edition.* Boston: Kluwer Law and Taxation Publishers.
GREENBERG, Melanie, et al., eds. (2000) *Words over War: Mediation and Arbitration to Prevent Deadly Conflict.* Lanham, MD: Rowman & Littlefield Publishers.
GUZMAN, Andrew, and Beth A. SIMMONS (2002) "To Settle or Empanel? An Empirical Analysis of Litigation and Settlement at the World Trade Organization," 31 *J. Legal Stud.* 205.
HANDBOOK ON THE PEACEFUL SETTLEMENT OF DISPUTES BETWEEN STATES (1992). New York: United Nations.
HOLBROOKE, Richard (1998) *To End a War.* New York: Random House.
KREMENIUK, Victor A., ed. (1991) *International Negotiation.* San Francisco: Jossey-Bass.
LEDERACH, John P., and Janice M. JENNER, eds. (2002) *A Handbook of International Peacebuilding: Into the Eye of the Storm.* San Francisco: Jossey-Bass.
LEWICKI, Roy J., et al. (1997) *Essentials of Negotiation.* Chicago: Irwin.
MERRILLS, J.G. (1999) *International Dispute Settlement* (3d ed.). Cambridge: Cambridge University Press.
MITCHELL, George J. (1999) *Principles of Peace: Northern Ireland and the Middle East.* Jerusalem: The Hebrew University.
O'CONNELL, Mary Ellen, ed. (2003) *International Dispute Settlement.* Burlington, VT: Ashgate.
——— (2006) *International Dispute Resolution — Cases and Materials.* Durham: Caroline Academic Press.
PARK, William W. (1995) *International Forum Selection.* Boston: Kluwer Law and Taxation Publishers.
PRINCEN, Thomas (1987) "International Mediation — The View from the Vatican; Lessons from Mediating the Beagle Channel Dispute," 3 *Neg. J.* 347 (Oct.).
——— (1992) *Intermediaries in International Conflict.* Princeton: Princeton University Press.
QUANDT, William (1988) *The Middle East.* Washington, D.C.: Brookings.

RIVKIN, David (1991) "International Arbitration." In Richard Medalie, ed., *Commercial Arbitration for the 1990s.* Chicago: American Bar Association, Litigation Section.

RUBIN, Jeffrey, and Jeswald SALACUSE (1993) "Culture and International Negotiation: Lessons for Business," *Alternatives to the High Cost Litig.* 95 (July).

RUBIN, Jeffrey Z., and Frank E. A. SANDER (1991) "Culture, Negotiation, and the Eye of the Beholder," 7 *Neg. J.* 249.

SALACUSE, Jeswald (1998) "Ten Ways That Culture Affects Negotiating Style: Some Survey Results," 14 *Neg. J.* 221.

——— (2006) *International Dispute Resolution Cases and Materials.* Durham, N.C.: Carolina Academic Press.

SWIRE, Peter (1998) "Of Elephants, Mice, and Privacy: International Choice of Law and the Internet," 32 *Int'l Law.* 991.

TOUVAL, Sadia, and I. William ZARTMAN, eds. (1985) *International Mediation in Theory and Practice.* Boulder: Westview.

VAGTS, Detlev (1987) *Dispute Resolution Mechanisms in International Business.* Boston: Martinus Nijhoff.

VARADY, Tibor, John J. BARCELO, and Arthur T. VON MEHREN (2006) *International Commercial Arbitration* (3d ed.). St. Paul: West.

VERZIJL, J. H. W., VIII, vol. 8 (1976) *International Law in Historical Perspective: Inter-State Disputes and Their Settlement.* Leyden: A.W. Sitjthoff.

WALDOCK, M., ed. (1972) *International Disputes: The Legal Aspects.* London: Europa Publications.

WATKINS, Michael, and Kirsten LUNDBERG (1998) "Getting to the Table in Oslo: Driving Forces and Channel Factors," 14 *Neg. J.* 115.

WATKINS, Michael, and Susan ROSEGRANT (2001) *Breakthrough International Negotiations.* San Francisco: Jossey-Bass.

ZARTMAN, I. William (1976) *The 50% Solution.* Garden City, N.Y.: Anchor.

——— (1989) *Ripe for Resolution: Conflict and Intervention in Africa.* New York: Oxford University Press.

ZARTMAN, I. William, and Maureen K. BERMAN (1982) *The Practical Negotiator.* New Haven: Yale University Press.

ZARTMAN, I. William, and J. Lewis RASMUSSEN, eds. (1997) *Peacemaking in International Conflict: Methods & Techniques.* Washington, D.C.: United States Institute of Peace Press.

Chapter 11

Learning from Other Cultures

Much of this book focuses on people who approach dispute resolution from a shared perspective. Suppose instead that the disputing parties come from cultures that vary significantly in their negotiating approaches. One can imagine the missteps that might occur in cross-cultural negotiation, the subject of Section A. One negotiator, for example, might ask questions about the counterpart's interests related to resolving the dispute. The counterpart, however, may choose to resolve the dispute in the same way that similar disputes have been resolved for generations in his community, with the parties' interests of little importance to that negotiator. Further, it may be seen as insulting in that negotiator's culture to be on the receiving end of direct questions. Anticipating such differences may help the negotiators reach agreement.

Learning about cultural differences can also help resolve many persistent dispute resolution problems in the United States. Section B focuses on situations in which there are no court-based alternatives to reaching agreement. For example, suppose police shoot an Arab-American suspect after a traffic stop. In response, members of the Arab-American community stage protests against ethnic profiling and police practices in general, and rioting breaks out. The courts may punish those who break the law, whether they are the rioters or the police, but the community remains divided over the police practices and perhaps other instances of perceived unequal treatment. The festering anger and community division may not provide the basis for a legal claim, so the courts will not resolve the conflict. Scholars quoted in Section B examine dispute resolution institutions that have had success in resolving what might be termed "identity group–based conflicts" in other parts of the world.

A. CROSS-CULTURAL NEGOTIATION

Lawyers are increasingly engaging in cross-cultural negotiation and mediation. One U.S. executive estimates that his company negotiated $40 billion in purchases across national borders in 2005 (Movius et al., 2006:n.1). Not only are people interacting globally more frequently (Friedman, 2005), but the present diversity within the United States means that lawyers sometimes encounter cross-cultural negotiations even in domestic matters. Consequently, lawyers may long for formulaic advice on deal-making and dispute-resolving negotiations that could be applied to any culture. Despite a great deal of fascinating research (see, e.g., Avruch, 1998; Brett, 2001; Gelfand and Brett, 2004; Lederach, 1995), there is no five-step solution for the challenges of cross-cultural negotiation.

Scholars in the cross-cultural negotiation field warn about two potential pitfalls. First, we may be tempted to overgeneralize. Rubin and Sander (1991) explain that negotiating differences might have a noncultural explanation, and that culture itself is far more complex than we might assume. Second, we might underestimate the effects of culture. The authors of a new book, excerpted in the second series below, draw from research on cross-cultural negotiation to point out the deep differences in negotiation as taught to U.S. law students compared with those employed in other cultures.

Imagine, for example, that your university received a grant to provide technical assistance in the rural area of a developing nation. You flew to the site yesterday, replacing your dispute resolution professor, who canceled at the last minute because of illness. The professor asked you to negotiate with the owner of the only hotel about providing housing, food, and communications for the delegation of 20 professors scheduled to arrive in a month. Your professor said that she made a morning appointment with the hotel owner, which you are to keep, and left a message that you will be arriving instead of her. When you reach the hotel, the desk clerk tells you that the owner cannot see you until dinner that evening. The desk clerk offers to discuss tentative arrangements, subject to the owner's approval, when you explain that you are scheduled to depart tomorrow. As you read the following essay by Rubin and Sander, make a list of possible explanations for the hotel owner's behavior.

J. RUBIN AND F. SANDER, CULTURE, NEGOTIATION, AND THE EYE OF THE BEHOLDER

7 Neg. J. 249 (1991)

. . . Our thesis is that, although differences in culture clearly *do* exist and have a bearing on the style of negotiation that emerges, some of the most important effects of culture are felt even before the negotiators sit down across from one another and begin to exchange offers. Culture, we believe, is a profoundly powerful organizing prism, through which we tend to view and integrate all kinds of disparate interpersonal information.

Consider, by way of broad illustration, the following situation: You are seated across from a male negotiator from a culture very different than your own. In the course of the negotiations, he makes an unexpectedly large concession. While you are pleased by this behavior, you probably also wish to explain and understand it. There are several distinct possibilities.

First, the other negotiator may have made his concession because of the kind of person he is. That is, something about his personality led him to do what he did, in which case he might be expected to behave this way under lots of other circumstances. Second, it may be something about the particular conflict that the two of you are engaged in; thus, the problem over which you are negotiating may be one that invites or tolerates large concessions. Third, the explanation may have to do with the unique interaction created by the two of you working together; thus, had your opposite number been seated across from someone else, perhaps his negotiating behavior would have been very different. Finally, in this listing of explanations for the other side's negotiation behavior, is the possibility of culture. Perhaps people from his culture tend to be rather conciliatory in negotiation.

Each of these possible reasons—and others, no doubt—could explain why another negotiator behaves in particular ways. We suspect, however, that culture is far more likely than other possibilities (at least in international settings) to be invoked as the dominant explanation. When in doubt, we tend to begin with the assumption that culture or nationality is *the* source of behavior, when, in reality, all of the above sources may be implicated. Moreover, rare is the individual who sits down to ponder the exact reason why his or her counterpart has made a particular negotiating move. . . .

The label of culture may have an effect very similar to that of gender . . . ; it is a "hook" that makes it easy for one negotiator (the perceiver) to organize what he or she sees emanating from that "different person" seated at the other side of the table. To understand how culture may function as a label, consider the following teaching exercise, used during a two-week session on negotiation conducted with a multinational, multicultural gathering. During one class session, the fifty or so participants were formed into rough national groups, and were asked to characterize their national negotiating style—as seen by others. That is, the task was *not* to describe true differences that may be attributable to culture or nationality, but to characterize the stereotypic perceptions that others typically carry around in their heads.

This exercise yielded a set of very powerful, albeit contradictory, stereotypic descriptions of different nationalities. To give a couple of examples, British participants characterized others' stereotypic characterization of the British as "reserved, arrogant, old-fashioned, eccentric, fair, and self-deprecating." A cluster of Arab participants from several Middle East nations characterized a "Levantine" negotiating style as "inclined to violence, aggressive, incohesive, indecisive, irrational, temperamental, emotional, impulsive, and romantic." The Irish self-characterization included such adjectives as "good social grease, people-oriented, fast-talking, good for a laugh, passionate but not serious, provincial, inefficient and undisciplined, unreliable, and simple but shrewd." And a cluster of Central Americans listed others' stereotypes of them as negotiators as "idealistic, impractical, disorganized, unprepared, stubborn in arguments, and flowery in style."

Now imagine that you have begun to negotiate with someone from another culture, who at some point in the proceedings simply insists that he or she can go no further, and is prepared to conclude without an agreement if necessary; in effect, says this individual, his BATNA* has been reached, and he can do just as well by walking away from the table. How should you interpret such an assertion? If you share the general cluster of stereotypes described by the students, your interpretation will probably depend on the other person's culture or nationality. Thus, if the other negotiator is British, and (among other things) you regard the British as

*Best alternative to a negotiated agreement. See p. 33.

"fair," you may interpret this person's refusal to concede further as an honest statement of principle. The same behavior issuing from a Central American, however (someone you suspect of being "stubborn in arguments"), may lead you to suspect your counterpart of being stubborn and perhaps deceitful. Wouldn't you therefore be more likely to strike an agreement with a British than a Central American negotiator—despite the fact that each has behaved in the identical way?

If there is any truth to our surmise, you can see how powerful the effects of culture may prove to be, leading us (even before we have had a chance to gather information about our counterpart) to hold a set of expectations that guide and inform our judgments. Moreover, once our "hypotheses" about others are in place, it becomes very difficult to disprove them. We tend to gather impersonal information in such a way that we pay attention only to the "facts" that support our preconceived ideas, ignoring or dismissing disconfirming data. . . .

What, then, are some implications of this brief essay for more effective negotiation across cultural/national boundaries? First, while cultural/national differences clearly *do* exist, much of what passes for such differences may well be the result of expectations and perceptions which, when acted upon, help to bring about a form of self-fulfilling prophecy. Perhaps the best way to combat such expectations is to go out of one's way to acquire as much information as one can beforehand about the way people in other cultures view the kind of problem under consideration. Thus, if we are negotiating with a German about a health care contract, we should try to find out whatever we can about how Germans tend to view health care. Of course, in large countries, there may be regional variations that also need to be taken into account.

Second, it is important to enter into such negotiations with self-conscious awareness of the powerful tendency we share toward stereotyping; this kind of consciousness-raising may, in its own right, help make it a bit less likely that we will slip into a set of perceptual biases that over-determine what transpires in the negotiations proper.

Third, it is important to enter into negotiations across cultural/national lines by trying to give your counterpart the (cultural) benefit of the doubt. Just as you would not wish others to assume that you are nothing more than an exemplar of people from your culture, try similarly to avoid making the same mistaken assumption about the other person. Few of us, if asked to characterize an American negotiation style, would be able to do so, arguing that the differences between Texans and Bostonians, Hawaiians and Tennesseans are so vast that it makes no sense whatever to attempt a single characterization. Yet we are often willing to seek information about the Japanese negotiating style, the French way of conducting international business, etc. Unless and until proven otherwise, it is wise to begin by assuming that differences within a culture or national group are as profound as the differences between various groups. In short, we should be continually open to treating what we learned about the foreign culture as simply a hypothesis, to be constantly tested against the data that we are in fact continually receiving. . . .

One final thought: Although our focus has been primarily on cultural issues, we believe that similar considerations apply to other differences that come into play in negotiation, such as gender, race, and age. Here, too, we can become more effective negotiators by acknowledging the possible effects of labeling on the negotiating process, while remaining open to information about our counterpart as an individual.

Note

Returning to the hypothetical about the negotiations with the hotel owner (see p. 572), assume that one of your explanations for the events is that the hotel owner's behavior stems primarily from the local negotiating culture. Based on that assumption, develop a tentative approach to the possible cultural differences, using the suggestions below from a book for U.S. negotiators (Blankley, ed., 2006).

- **Should the U.S. negotiator begin by discussing the parties' interests?**

Beginning with substance may be problematic. A U.S. negotiator may believe that "time is money," and one should move to substance immediately after the opening pleasantries. "[A] U.S. negotiator is often goal-based and believes that there can exist a short-term, mutually acceptable agreement that does not include a promise of further dealings. . . . [Yet, i]n some cultures, a negotiator may feel that in order to reach any agreement, there needs to be a long-term relationship in place. . . . The relationship-based counterpart will often ask extensive personal questions about the negotiator and try to establish a relationship. A negotiator may find himself being invited to participate in social events and recreational activities" (Cooper, 2006:12, 16).

Interest-based negotiation may seem foreign to the counterpart. "Kevin Avruch of the Institute for Conflict Analysis and Resolution at George Mason University contends that the entire field of conflict resolution literature in the United States, including interest-based negotiation, is 'culturally situated within a North American, male, white, and middle-class world.' . . . A negotiator using the interest-based model may become baffled when confronted with a counterpart who insists on . . . haggling. . . . In some cultures, it may be considered insulting to ask about interests. . . . Indeed, there exist times when changing styles and attempting to introduce an interest-based model of negotiation may beget more distrust than simply reciprocating the counterpart's negotiation style" (Roach, 2006:36, 39 (quoting Avruch, 1998)).

The counterpart may not be swayed by the parties' interests. "[P]eople in some cultures place greater weight on the needs of the community than people in other cultures. In Bengal, for example, a poor woman became impregnated by a rich man belonging to a different faith. The community outcry was quick, and the woman's community demanded reparation when the man refused to marry the woman. In the ensuing negotiations, the man's family offered the woman's family more than adequate financial compensation; however, the woman's family refused. The woman's family preferred to seek a criminal "trial," but ultimately the parties employed the help of a mediator, who fined the young man and ordered reparations. Often, the U.S. negotiator will be faced with a counterpart, [who], appearing and acting autonomously, must bow to the needs of the community." (Wang, 2006:26 (quoting Madaripur Legal Aid Association)).

- **Should the U.S. negotiator in a cross-cultural negotiation try to set the agenda, looking for trade-offs on various issues?**

Separating issues may seem strange in some negotiating cultures. "Some negotiators may feel that nothing is settled until everything is settled. They either may not want to separate issues from one another or may not want to commit to any issues without commitment on the whole proposal" (Cooper, 2006:14). "Instead of insisting upon discussing issues separately, it may be beneficial for a U.S. negotiator to agree to reciprocate the full proposal approach" (Worthing, 2006:140).

One might consider reciprocating the approach of the counterpart. "[A] reason to reciprocate, especially when representing the United States, is because it may symbolize a gesture of politeness and a willingness to cooperate. Greeting someone in the native language or manner can immediately place a counterpart at ease" (Wang, 2006:23).

- **Should the U.S. negotiator discuss the parties' differences candidly?**

It may be important not to directly contradict or criticize in some cultures. "A negotiating counterpart may never actually say 'no' or directly reject an issue, but that does not mean the counterpart agrees with the U.S. negotiator's formulation of the issues. Therefore, a U.S. negotiator should tread lightly when proceeding with issues that his negotiating counterpart seems quiet or only lukewarm about discussing" (Worthing, 2006:141).

- **Should the U.S. negotiator depart from the usual assumptions about the importance of trust?**

An agreement may not be enforceable in all nations, so trust may be of paramount importance. In the United States, "enforcement mechanisms ensured through an independent judiciary enable the effectiveness of dispute resolution processes. [This may lead the U.S. negotiator to the false assumption that the counterpart's experience is the same, but many nations lack the same ready access to independent courts]" (Reddy, 2006:98).

Trust may be of even more importance to resolving issues following an agreement, as an agreement may mean something different in other nations or cultures. "Up until the late 1990's, China did not have a universal contract law similar to the Uniform Commercial Code of the United States. Why did Chinese law [omit] . . . what is [considered] a vital piece of law in the United States? The simple answer is that some Chinese have a different concept of what constitutes a contract than an American does. For some Chinese, it is understood that once an agreement is reached, it is generally an understanding by the parties to start a relationship." (Wang, 2006:27-28)

Even a low level of trust may be difficult to achieve. "Most research indicates that trust is usually hard to establish in everyday relationships, more difficult across a negotiation table, and most complex in a cross-cultural negotiation setting. This is so because as opposed to the former two situations, there is seldom any actual or comparable prior relationship from which the negotiators can gauge the trustworthiness of the counterpart. . . . Taking that into account, while relationships are arguably important to all negotiators, the U.S. negotiator should acknowledge that people in some cultures may expect to develop and emphasize close-knit associations before negotiations begin — even in the most routine of negotiations. Similarly, because 'each culture's "collective programming" results from different norms and values, the processes trustors use to decide whether and whom to trust may be heavily dependent upon a society's culture' and thus, it can be hard to bridge the trust gap." (Lennane and Weidner, 2006: 48 (quoting Doney, 1998))

The negotiation counterpart's view of the United States may exacerbate the trust problem. "[J]ust as U.S. negotiators may have preconceived notions about other cultures, their counterparts also may rely on assumptions and stereotypes about the United States that they may have heard, seen, read, or even experienced in the past. . . . [The media, American products and marketing, history, and politics may lead the counterpart to view any U.S. person as an "ugly American"], a loud, obnoxious, rude, and ill-mannered person who offers an opinion about everything, despite allegedly knowing nothing about anything [or a sexually immoral person, or a person who cannot be trusted, or a wealthy and materialistic individual, or one who is violent and aggressive. Further, certain sub-stereotypes may relate to subgroups of the U.S. population]." (Petroff and Siegel, 2006:72, 77).

- **Should the U.S. negotiator assume that negotiating power derives primarily from having a better alternative to an agreement than the counterpart has and from knowledge about the counterpart's situation?**

Sometimes the key source of power is status. "Those in hierarchical cultures, . . . tend to view power in terms of status (i.e., rank, age, history) and influence. . . . [A] negotiator's willingness to reach an agreement can sometimes hinge on his counterpart's rank within the culture's hierarchy" (Johnson, 2006:107).

- **In cross-cultural negotiations, do values transcend culture?**

Experts suggest that U.S. negotiators be prepared for culture-based value clashes, not just differences in negotiation approaches. "It is suggested that negotiators 'who are not prepared to grapple with moral ambiguity and tension should pack their bags and come home' because values in tension are the rule rather than the exception" (Hammond and McCarty, 2006:129 (quoting Donaldson, 1996)).

Distrust may arise because the counterpart whose values differ from the U.S. negotiator's values may believe that the U.S. negotiator has less integrity. "Is it ethically impermissible for the seller to tell [the] buyer: "our fittings are the best in the world"? "Probably not," says William F. Fox, a law professor at Catholic University. U.S. negotiators often participate in the act of puffing, which may also be characterized as a "little white lie." "This type of behavior . . . is age old business conduct," according to Fox and is generally not condemned in the United States . . . [but] may not be respectable or permissible in all countries." (Hammond and McCarty, 2006:119 (quoting Fox, 1998))

"Governments in Islamic countries often specifically insist upon incorporation of the Shari'ah into contracts. . . . [T]he Shari'ah . . . insists on a "literalist approach to the contract," which may forbid "cancellation or revision of a contract on the basis of impossibility or frustration." Two sources of the Shari'ah. . . . reinforce these obligations by requiring Muslims to "abide by their promises and obligations." . . . Thus, a negotiating counterpart from a country ruled by an Islamic legal system will likely have a strong ethical preference toward carrying out the promises made in a contract, both by himself and by the U.S. negotiator. In contrast, the U.S. negotiator may find it acceptable to break a contract if she is prepared to reimburse her counterpart for the damages suffered." (Hammond and McCarty, 2006:125).

U.S. negotiators may face a counterpart who considers it perfectly moral to bribe public officials. "While the U.S. legal system and general moral tenor of the nation have declared corruption to be unethical and intolerable, other cultures do not find it as deplorable and see it as a necessary method of doing business" (Hammond and McCarty, 2006:120).

Applying this advice: If you had a few weeks to prepare for the hotel negotiation mentioned at the start of this note, what inquiries would you make? Certainly, one would want to learn all that is possible about language and communication practices and be certain to use an excellent interpreter (see Johnson, 2006; Cronmiller, 2006). Consider as well what kind of research would help you with possible different approaches to negotiation and values and the greater need to establish trust.

Question

11.1 The authors of the book excerpted above (Blankley, ed., 2006) suggest that a U.S. negotiator might consider reciprocating the negotiating approach used by a counterpart from a different culture. What are the advantages of this approach? When might reciprocation be counterproductive?

B. LISTENING TO THE WORLD* ON THE DESIGN OF DISPUTE RESOLUTION SYSTEMS FOR IDENTITY GROUP–BASED CONFLICTS

Rioting followed the police beating of Rodney King in Los Angeles in 1992, alarming a nation that had not seen race riots on this scale since the 1960s. So, too, the public reactions to the relief efforts in New Orleans following Hurricane Katrina served as a reminder that race and economic status continue to divide communities. And in a nation proud of its religious tolerance, the perceptions of religious and ethnic profiling following the terrorist attacks of September 11, 2001, revealed vulnerability to new kinds of identity-based conflict.

This section focuses on a positive aspect of studying other cultures — the possible importing of ideas that have been successful in those settings for resolving similar "identity group–based" disputes. Excerpts analyzing dispute systems from Northern Ireland and South Africa follow. Mindful of the caveats that the comparisons might be confounded by differing goals, cultures, and political systems, what can we learn by listening to these and other nations in the development of our own approach?

*"Listening to the World" was the title of a symposium published by the Ohio State Journal on Dispute Resolution (2006).

1. *Identity Group–Based Conflict Resolution in Other Nations*

M. HAMILTON AND D. BRYAN, DEEPENING DEMOCRACY? DISPUTE SYSTEM DESIGN AND THE MEDIATION OF CONTESTED PARADES IN NORTHERN IRELAND

22 Ohio St. J. Disp. Resol. 133 (2006)

Northern Ireland is a complex modern industrial society with large disparities in class and wealth. It suffers from many of the same social and economic problems as other Western European and North American countries. It is, however, a transitional society emerging from years of violent conflict. Of the 1.7 million populace, approximately 46% regard themselves as belonging to the Protestant community (and, for the most, are ascribed as "Unionist" or "Loyalist" as they wish to remain part of the United Kingdom) and 40% to the Catholic community (who, for the most, wish to be part of a politically united Ireland, and hence are ascribed as "Nationalist" or "Republican"). These divisions have been manifested in many different contexts, including employment and education. Divisions have also resulted in territorial separation along communal lines. In both urban and rural areas, public space and housing is often defined as "Protestant" or "Catholic." In Belfast, sporadic violence and the fear of attacks from the other community has led to the building of "peace walls" between "interface" areas. Towns and villages are also often viewed as being "Protestant" or "Catholic," with objects like war memorials or churches becoming ethnic markers.

[R]itual practices (including commemorations, parades, and demonstrations) have played an important performative role in defining communal identities. Within the Protestant community, local marching bands and organizations . . . organize a wide range of parades. . . . Parades sustain a sense of locality and territory. In this sense, parade routes can become determinants of spatial inclusion and exclusion, and residents of the areas through which they pass sometimes feel threatened. Processions, demonstrations, commemorations, feast days, and even funerals have long provided the context for public disorder in Northern Ireland, and parades were described as the "distinguishing public order challenges" in Northern Ireland at the close of the twentieth century. . . .

When parade disputes escalated in the mid-1990s, a number of mediative interventions occurred (sometimes concurrently) outside of the legal framework. On occasion, these involved local church leaders, representatives of the business community, local politicians, and sometimes also the police. . . . In July 1996, Orangemen were initially prevented from marching to Portadown town center from Drumcree Parish Church along the Garvaghy Road by a decision by then Chief Constable, Sir Hugh Annesley. This decision precipitated widespread public disorder on a scale rarely witnessed before in Northern Ireland. Orangemen and their supporters blocked major roads and hijacked vehicles. Despite marathon attempts to reach an accommodation, the decision was reversed on public order grounds following the murder of Michael McGoldrick, a Catholic taxi driver, and the parade was allowed to proceed. This decision did nothing to reduce tensions. Nationalists and Republicans were outraged by the u-turn, and in the rioting and destruction of property which ensued, another civilian, Dermot McShane, was crushed to death by a police vehicle in Derry/Londonderry. As David Feldman states, "[t]he way in which these matters were handled gave rise to further polarisation of the already divided community in Northern Ireland, and intensified suspicion of the motives of the RUC [Royal Ulster Constabulary] and unhappiness about the apparent vacillation of its Chief Constable." . . .

[T]he RUC increasingly made efforts to engage with both parties to disputes. In August 1996, for example, Ronnie Flanagan, then Deputy Chief Constable, initially acted as an intermediary. . . . These meetings (each side meeting separately with the RUC) did not lead to agreement. . . .

By having to make decisions about parade routes, and then enforce those same decisions, the RUC's role was inevitably politicized. As long ago as 1985, then Chief Constable Jack Hermon stated that too much was expected of the police in effecting political and community reconciliation. He argued that "it may perhaps be worth considering if responsibility for decisions on the holding and routing of parades should rest with an independent public tribunal." . . . Yet, it was not until 1998 that similar proposals were brought forward by the government following the recommendations of the Independent Review of Parades and Marches (the North Review). . . .

The North Review represented an attempt to address the systemic failures highlighted by the partisan regulation of public processions in Northern Ireland. . . . The review team's key recommendation was the establishment of a five member independent body whose members would "have a geographical spread, and both cross-community and gender balance." This body, to be called the "Parades Commission," would [hear the parties' views,] encourage them to settle difficulties locally, [and if needed, impose conditions on the parades.]

The Commission was established on March 27, 1997. . . . The Commissioners had no adjudicatory powers until February 1998, when the newly elected Labour Government enacted the Public Processions (NI) Act 1998 (the PPA). This placed the Commission on a legislative footing and transferred to it the adjudicatory powers previously held by the police — a move described by David Feldman as a "constitutional innovation." In 1998, it was therefore the Parades Commission — not the police — that re-routed the Drumcree parade. A massive security operation was put in place to enforce the Commission's determination, and a protest involving thousands of people supporting the Orangemen ensued. It only reduced after three young boys were burnt to death in Ballymoney after a petrol bomb was thrown at a house. Many moderate Orangemen withdrew from the protest, but an Orange protest at Drumcree has been continued up until the present day (September 2006). . . .

The Commission is a hybrid body performing a dual function — issuing determinations in respect of particular proposed public processions (the adjudication function) carried out by state-appointed commissioners and "facilitating mediation" (the mediation function) undertaken by contracted Authorized Officers (AOs). . . . There is nothing in the PPA which prescribes how the relationship between the adjudicatory and mediative functions of the Parades Commission should work in practice, and there has long been a tension between these two elements. . . .

While the creation of the Parades Commission has undoubtedly extended the means for building mediative capacity, opportunities to stimulate greater consensus around the underlying interests, values and norms at stake have been missed. Two factors in particular have inhibited the Commission's contribution to deepening democracy. First, the Parades Commission has not done enough to stimulate the background consensus. . . . Without this consensus, the vocabularies of community relations and human rights remain contested. We argue that this framing, or clarifying, of the public interest is an essential strand in deepening Northern Ireland's post-conflict democracy. . . . [Second,] [w]hile the AOs have become very skilled in engaging with different individuals and groups, and have been able to play a key role in deescalating tensions and reducing the likelihood of violence, greater attention must be devoted to devising structures which ensure both the neutrality of mediators and the confidentiality of the process. . . .

Note

The Parades Commission mediative branch, discussed above, refrains from determining fault. In the article that follows, Richard Goldstone, a justice on the South African Constitutional Court during the transition from apartheid and afterward, suggests a role for a more fault-based approach as part of building consensus going forward.

R. GOLDSTONE, THE SOUTH AFRICAN TRUTH AND RECONCILIATION COMMISSION

12 Disp. Resol. Mag. 19-21 (Spring 2006)

Accountability for war crimes and other serious human rights violations is invariably the result of a complex mix of calls from victims for justice and acknowledgement, on the one hand — and political resistance from perpetrators to be held accountable, on the other.

In South Africa, there was a political compromise between Nuremberg-style trials from the leaders of the apartheid government and the grant of blanket amnesties. The compromise was embodied a decade ago in the legislation establishing the Truth and Reconciliation Commission (TRC). Victims were encouraged to tell their stories in public, and discrete amnesties were granted only in return for full and complete confessions by the perpetrators who sought them. . . .

Initially, there was ambivalence with regard to a truth and reconciliation commission. There was no agreement within the [African National Congress (ANC)] and strong opposition from the apartheid leaders. Then there was an unexpected development. During the transition that began in February 1990, charges emerged of serious human rights abuses having been committed by the ANC in its own army camps in Angola, Malawi and Tanzania.

In 1992 and 1993, the ANC established two internal commissions of inquiry — the Skweyiya and Motesuenyane Commissions — that found serious abuses and irregularities. The commissions recommended that the names of those responsible should be made public. However, the ANC leaders said that they felt that it was inappropriate to take action against their own members as long as the ruling National Party and security forces had engaged in no similar exercise.

At the same time, the ANC National Executive Committee called in 1993 for:

> the establishment of a Commission of Truth, similar to bodies established in a number of countries in recent years to deal with the past. The purpose of such a Commission will be to investigate all abuses of human rights and their perpetrators, to propose a future code of conduct for all public servants, to ensure appropriate compensation to the victims and to work out the best basis for reconciliation. In addition, it will provide the moral basis for justice and for preventing any repetition of abuses in the future.

After wide consultation and much debate, parliament passed the Promotion of National Unity and Reconciliation Act 34 of 1995, commonly referred to as the Truth and Reconciliation Act. The object of the Act, as stated in section 3, is to "promote national unity and reconciliation in a spirit of understanding which transcends the conflicts and divisions of the past." It directed "establishing as complete a picture as possible of the causes, nature and extent of the gross violations of human rights" committed during the period commencing March 1, 1960 to the cutoff date that was later agreed to be the day prior to the 1994 elections.

The statute urged regard for "the perspectives of the victims and the motives and perspectives of the persons responsible for the commission of the violations." It also required "the granting of amnesty to persons who make full disclosure of all the relevant facts relating to acts with a political objective." Among the factors to be taken into account were "the relationship between the act, omission or offence and the political objective pursued, and in particular the directness and proximity of the relationship and the proportionality of the act, omission or offence to the objective pursued."

Three committees were established to achieve these objectives:

- The Committee on Human Rights Violations — to conduct inquiries pertaining to gross violations of human rights with extensive powers to gather and receive evidence and information.
- The Committee of Reparations and Rehabilitation — which was given similar powers to gather information and receive evidence for the purpose of ultimately recommending to the president suitable reparations for victims of gross violations of human rights, and
- The Committee on Amnesties — to consider applications for amnesty. . . .

The Constitutional Court also found the denial of a civil remedy to be constitutional. One of the main reasons for that conclusion was the statutory promise of reparations for the victims.

The response to the TRC exceeded the optimistic hopes of its most enthusiastic supporters: testimony from more than 22,000 victims and amnesty applications from some 7,000. The outpouring of information had several important consequences, including:

- ending the denials and fabrications that accompanied the most serious human rights abuses
- recording one history in perpetuity of those most serious consequences of the apartheid regime, and
- facilitating programs of the new democratic government to begin removing some of the imbalances that were a consequence of over three centuries of oppression and discrimination.

There was also a cost. Some victims went away from the TRC angry and frustrated. Like all good compromises, none of the parties was completely satisfied by it. But looking back on the first decade of democracy, I have no doubt at all that South Africa is immeasurably better off than it would have been but for the TRC.

I turn now to the United States.

I have had the privilege of teaching classes at some middle and high schools in Boston, Los Angeles, Memphis and New York. That came about through the programs of Facing History and Ourselves, a Boston-based nonprofit organization that has school programs teaching understanding of, and tolerance for, "others." It attempts to teach the prevention of violence and an end to racism. I have spoken of the TRC, and invariably, young school students ask me whether there should be a truth and reconciliation [commission] in their own country. The question clearly and visibly finds empathy in black students.

When I have discussed this reaction with white Americans, the answer I usually receive is that the history of slavery and racial discrimination in the United States is amply recorded and that there is thus no point in considering a truth and reconciliation commission. I would suggest that this simplistic response misses the point. Much of the evidence that emerged before the TRC was known to the majority of South Africans and certainly black South Africans. The victims always know the truth regarding their victimization. . . .

That problems with regard to race and discrimination continue in the United States cannot be denied and even less wished away. In this context, the extent to which the TRC is relevant to the United States is for the people of this country to determine. A serious examination of this possibility would certainly be a useful learning experience at all levels of American society.

Questions

11.2 Hamilton and Bryan, the authors of the first of the two excerpts, suggest that the Parades Commission should consider building consensus about the basic values and norms that divide the groups. Would that be a good component of the system designed for identity group–based disputes in the United States?

11.3 Taking into account the pertinent ways in which the U.S. situation differs from that of South Africa, what would be the advantages and disadvantages of creating a Truth and Reconciliation Commission in the United States? What other institutions in other nations might have relevance for the United States (see the bibliography on other such institutions at http://moritzlaw.osu.edu/bridge_initiative/)?

2. *The Community Relations Service*

One U.S. institution that promotes discussions aimed at reconciliation or resolution of identity group–based conflict is the Community Relations Service (CRS). In 1964, in the midst of civil rights strife, Congress created the CRS to assist "in resolving disputes . . . relating to the discriminatory practices based on race, color or national origin." 42 U.S.C. §2000g-1. The statute placed the new dispute resolution agency within the U.S. Justice Department, which also had civil rights enforcement obligations, but prohibited the CRS staff from sharing the information they collected with other parts of the Department. 42 U.S.C. §2000g-2(b).

Over the years, the CRS has intervened to reduce the likelihood of violence in marches, including the march from Selma to Montgomery, Alabama, in 1965 and the planned 1978 march by a neo-Nazi group through Skokie, Illinois, where many Holocaust survivors lived. They sent a mediator when a Native American group took over the Village of Wounded Knee in 1973, and in 1977 when Kent State University planned to build a gymnasium at the site of the National Guard's deadly shooting of students who were demonstrating against the Vietnam War (Rogers and Salem, 1987: 34-37). In 2005 the CRS intervened in over 600 disputes concerning police-community relations, race-based violence in schools, hate crimes, demonstrations, and other incidents within its statutory charge. CRS staff have suggested ways to conduct marches that would avoid violence, they have shuttled among parties, they have held open forums, they have assembled diverse commissions to negotiate more effectively with public officials, and they have mediated (U.S. Department of Justice, 2005:5, 14).

Is this the best dispute system design (see Chapter 5) for identity group–based conflict in the United States?

Questions

11.4 What would be the advantages of the CRS adopting a normative approach such as that used by the Truth and Reconciliation Commission in South Africa? In what ways could this hurt the effectiveness of the CRS?

11.5 Some would argue that the Truth and Reconciliation Commission, even with its inquiry into who is at fault, does not go far enough. An alternative approach would be to hold trials of those who have abused human rights, such as the recent trials of Saddam Hussein and other officials in his regime or the Nuremberg trials following World War II (see Crocker, 2002). Justice Albie Sachs of the South African Constitutional Court defended the reconciliation approach of the Commission:

> We had to take stern action in relation to ending Apartheid. It did not just happen because some people decided they were giving up. Many of you will recall the international economic boycott and the divestment campaigns. Many people died in South Africa fighting physically for freedom. . . . There were trade union actions, actions on cultural fronts everywhere. It was a very, very active, very, very forceful response that in the end frustrated Apartheid and compelled the leaders to negotiate. But the fact was that, in the end, we focused on changing the system, transforming the society, finding people on the other side willing to talk to us and finding people on our side willing to talk to them, to bring about that kind of transformation. Our country has huge difficulties today . . . but we have a country. We have a wonderful constitution. We have the institutions of democracy. Our economy is ready for take-off. Human dignity is respected in a way that seemed absolutely impossible before. . . . We broke the cycle of violence (Sachs, 2002:1047).

What situations in the United States might be inappropriate for a reconciliation approach like that of the Truth and Reconciliation Commission?

11.6 Professors Amy J. Cohen and Ellen E. Deason (2006) suggest that the comparative dispute designer ask a series of key questions when developing a system for identity group–based disputes. The answers to each of the following questions fall on a continuum rather than in one category or the other.

a. The goals: Settling or "fostering social change"? Blaming or simply moving on?
b. The structure: Public or private? Local or international?
c. The decision-making: Individual parties only or community involvement? Agreement among parties or decision by an agency?
d. Methods used, including how a third party intervenes, seeks participation, facilitates/mediates/decides, and treats information (e.g., is it confidential?), and how the resolution is enforced.

What dispute resolution system would you propose to deal with identity group–based conflicts in your state? How would the system you propose deal with each of Cohen and Deason's design considerations? How and why does your proposed system differ from the CRS, the Parades Commission, and the Truth and Reconciliation Commission?

11.7 What would be the advantages and disadvantages of providing the CRS with the enforcement authority that the Parades Commission had? What would be the legal impediments to giving the CRS enforcement authority? Alternatively, could the same advantages be achieved by removing the statutory confidentiality provided the CRS? What would be lost with that change?

11.8 With the capacity to intervene in only 600 disputes a year, the CRS cannot reach all identity-based conflict in the United States. What should be the criteria for prioritizing among interventions? Should the CRS be expanded? Alternatively, should each state create a similar agency?

11.9 What are the advantages of placing the CRS within an enforcement agency such as the U.S. Justice Department? In what ways does this placement inhibit its effectiveness? If states created similar agencies, would the state attorney general's office be the best location? What alternative placement would you suggest?

NEGOTIATION EXERCISES

Each of the problem descriptions below is for a person who will play one of the negotiators. Confidential instructions for each role player are provided to the instructor in the Teacher's Manual.*

EXERCISE 11.1: A JOINT MILITARY EXERCISE

The air forces of the United States and Sololia have reached a high-level agreement to conduct a three-week joint military exercise next fall in Sololia. About 500 military personnel will be involved from each nation. There is no "status of forces" or other existing agreement between the two parties, so their lawyers agreed to meet to discuss with respect to the U.S. Air Force personnel:

1. Conduct of religious ceremonies
2. Use of alcoholic beverages by off-duty personnel
3. Jurisdiction over U.S. personnel for civil damages or criminal charges
4. Documentation needed to enter Sololia

Each lawyer will bring an interpreter; neither lawyer is bilingual.

EXERCISE 11.2: FACTORY EXPLOSION

Acme Corporation manufactures fireworks in Mona, Mantaglo. A few months ago, an explosion in a factory warehouse flattened the nearby home of Gi and Lila Som and their three children. Lila's face was burned, but no others were injured. Gi Som has filed a complaint against Acme in a Mantagloan court, seeking the equivalent of $10 million. Mr. Som will meet with a lawyer for Acme to discuss a possible settlement. Assume that there are no language differences.

EXERCISE 11.3: BOTTLED WATER

Acme Corporation, a U.S. company, entered an agreement with an Italian company to build a clothing factory in a small town in Mornalia. An Acme lawyer has been sent to arrange accommodations for the Acme employees, who will be arriving next week. The last remaining task is to arrange the delivery of 200 bottles of water per week for the next year. The Jo Company is the only bottled water company in the region. The owner of Jo Company has agreed to meet with the Acme lawyer to discuss the purchase. Both speak English.

*Other appropriate exercises for this chapter include Alpha-Beta Robotics Negotiation (p. 566), the Mouse Exercise (p. 571), and Paternal Visitation (p. 206).

References

AVRUCH, Kevin (1998) *Culture and Conflict Resolution.* Washington, D.C.: United States Institute of Peace Press.

BLANKLEY, Kristen, ed. (2006) *Cross Cultural Negotiation for U.S. Negotiators.* Montgomery, Ala.: U.S. Air Force.

BRETT, Jeanne M. (2001) *Negotiating Globally: How to Negotiate Deals, Resolve Disputes, and Make Decisions across Cultural Boundaries.* San Francisco: Jossey-Bass.

BRETT, Jeanne M., et al. (1998) "Culture and Joint Gains in Negotiation," 14 *Neg. J.* 61.

BRETT, Jeanne M., and Tetsushi OKUMURA (1998) "Inter- and Intra-Cultural Negotiation: U.S. and Japanese Negotiators," 4 *Acad. Mgmt. J.* 495 (Oct.).

CHEW, Pat K., ed. (2001) *The Conflict and Culture Reader.* New York: New York University Press.

COBEN, James R. (2006) "Dispute Resolution Institute Symposium: Intentional Conversations about the Globalization of ADR," 27 *Hamline J. Pub. L. & Pol'y* 217.

COHEN, Amy J. (2006) "Debating the Globalization of U.S. Mediation: Politics, Power, and Practice in Nepal," 11 *Harv. Neg. L. Rev.* 295.

COHEN, Amy J., and Ellen E. DEASON (2006) "Comparative Considerations Toward the Global Transfer of Ideas About Dispute System Design," 12 *Disp. Resol. Mag.* 23.

COOPER, Carrie Luria (2006) "Varied Negotiation Approaches," in Kristen Blankley (ed.), *Cross Cultural Negotiation for U.S. Negotiators* 11-19. Montgomery, Ala.: U.S. Air Force.

CROCKER, David A. (2002) "Punishment, Reconciliation, and Democratic Deliberation," 5 *Buff. Crim. L. Rev.* 509.

CRONMILLER, Cherish L. (2006) "Using an Interpreter During Negotiations: Ensuring that Everyone Has the Chance to Hear and Be Heard," in Kristen Blankley (ed.), *Cross Cultural Negotiation for U.S. Negotiators* 153-162. Montgomery, Ala.: U.S. Air Force.

DONALDSON, Thomas (1996) "Values in Tension: Ethics Away from Home," *Harv. Bus. Rev.* 48, 49 (Sept.-Oct.).

DONEY, Patricia M. (1998) "Understanding the Influence of National Culture on the Development of Trust," 23 *Acad. Mgmt. Rev.* 601.

ERBE, Nancy D. (2006) "Appreciating Mediation's Global Role in Promoting Good Governance," 11 *Harv. Neg. L. Rev.* 335.

FAURE, Guy, and Jeffrey RUBIN (1993) *Culture and Negotiation.* Newbury Park, CA: Sage.

FOX, William F., Jr. (1998) *International Commercial Agreements: A Primer on Drafting, Negotiating and Resolving Disputes* (3d ed.). Boston: Kluwer Law International

FRIEDMAN, Thomas (2005) *The World is Flat: A Brief History of the Twenty-first Century.* New York: Farrar, Straus and Giroux.

GELFAND, Michele J., and Jeanne M. BRETT, eds. (2004) *The Handbook of Negotiation and Culture.* Stanford, Calif.: Stanford Business Books.

GOLDSTONE, Richard J. (2006) "The South African Truth and Reconciliation Commission: Is It Relevant to the United States?" 12 *Disp. Resol. Mag.* 19 (Spring).

HAMILTON, Michael, and Dominic BRYAN (2006) "Deepening Democracy? Dispute System Design and the Mediation of Contested Parades in Northern Ireland," 22 *Ohio St. J. Disp. Resol.* 133.

HAMMOND, Carly A., and Sarah C. McCARTY (2006) "Ethics in Cross-Cultural Negotiations," in Kristen Blankley (ed.), *Cross Cultural Negotiation for U.S. Negotiators* 117-134. Montgomery, Ala.: U.S. Air Force.

JOHNSON, Tamara (2006) "Power and Authority," in Kristen Blankley (ed.), *Cross Cultural Negotiation for U.S. Negotiators.* Montgomery, Ala.: U.S. Air Force.

LeBARON, Michelle (2003) *Bridging Cultural Conflicts: A New Approach for a Changing World.* San Francisco: Jossey-Bass.

LeBARON, Michelle, and Venashri PILLAY (2006) *Conflict across Cultures: A Unique Experience of Bridging Differences.* Boston: Intercultural Press.

LEDERACH, John Paul (1995) *Preparing for Peace: Conflict Transformation across Cultures.* Syracuse, N.Y.: Syracuse University Press.

LENNANE, Michael T., and Laura E. WEIDNER (2006) "In Each Other We Trust: The Importance of Relationship Building in Cross-Cultural Negotiation," in Kristen Blankley (ed.), *Cross Cultural Negotiation for U.S. Negotiators* 47-68. Montgomery, Ala.: U.S. Air Force.

MADARIPUR LEGAL AID ASSOCIATION (1996) *Nabing and Nasima: A Clash of Hindu and Muslim Communities in Constructive Conflict Management, Asian-Pacific Cases* (Fred E. Jandt and Paul B. Pedersen, eds.) 76-81. London: Sage.

McGILL, William J. (1979) "Peacemaking in an Adversary Society," in *The Pound Conference: Perspectives on Justice in the Future.* St. Paul, Minn.: West.

MINOW, Martha (1998) *Between Vengeance and Forgiveness.* Boston: Beacon Press.

MOVIUS, Hal, Masa MATSUURA, Jin YAN, and Dong-Young KIM (2006) "Tailoring the Mutual Gains Approach for Negotiations with Partners in Japan, China, and Korea," 22 *Neg. J.* 389.

PETROFF, Ronald R., and Leslie E. SIEGEL (2006) "The View from Abroad: How the International Community Perceives Americans," in Kristen Blankley (ed.), *Cross Cultural Negotiation for U.S. Negotiators* 71-92. Montgomery, Ala.: U.S. Air Force.

REDDY, Vinay (2006) "Managing Assumptions about the Negotiation Process," in Kristen Blankley (ed.), *Cross Cultural Negotiation for U.S. Negotiators* 95-103. Montgomery, Ala.: U.S. Air Force.

ROACH, Steven Robert (2006) "Effectively Using Interest-Based Negotiation in the Cross-Cultural Context," in Kristen Blankley (ed.), *Cross Cultural Negotiation for U.S. Negotiators* 35-45. Montgomery, Ala.: U.S. Air Force.

ROGERS, Nancy H., and Richard A. SALEM (1987) *A Student's Guide to Mediation and The Law.* New York: Matthew Bender.

RUBIN, Jeffrey, and Jeswald SALACUSE (1993) "Culture and International Negotiation: Lessons for Business," *Alternatives High Cost Litig.* 95 (July).

RUBIN, Jeffrey Z., and Frank E. A. SANDER (1991) "Culture, Negotiation, and the Eye of the Beholder," 7 *Neg. J.* 249.

SACHS, Albie (2002) "South African's Truth and Reconciliation Commission," 34 *Conn. L. Rev.* 1037.

SALACUSE, Jeswald (1998) "Ten Ways that Culture Affects Negotiating Style: Some Survey Results," 14 *Neg. J.* 221.

SALEM, Paul, ed. (1997) *Conflict Resolution in the Arab World: Selected Essays.* Beirut: American University of Beirut.

SALEM, Richard A. (1985) "Mediation as an Alternative to Civil Rights Litigation," in Carl F. Pinkele and William C. Louthan (eds.), *Discretion, Justice, and Democracy* (90-101. Ames: Iowa State University Press.

U.S. DEPARTMENT OF JUSTICE (2005) *Community Relations Service Annual Report,* available at www.justice.gov/crs/pubs/fy2005/annualreport2005.pdf.

WANG, Xi Scott (2006) "Tit for Tat in the Global Perspective," in Kristen Blankley (ed.), *Cross Cultural Negotiation for U.S. Negotiators* 21-45. Montgomery, Ala.: U.S. Air Force.

WEAVER, Gary, ed. (2000) *Culture, Communication and Conflict: Readings in Intercultural Relations.* Upper Saddle River, NJ: Pearson Custom Press.

WORTHING, Elizabeth M. (2006) "Collision Course: Avoiding Clashes on Agenda in Cross-Cultural Negotiations," in Kristen Blankley (ed.), *Cross Cultural Negotiation for U.S. Negotiators* 137-142. Montgomery, Ala.: U.S. Air Force.

PART V

THE FUTURE OF ADR

Chapter 12

The Future of ADR

A. THE SOCIETAL-PUBLIC PERSPECTIVE

As we try to assess the future of ADR three decades plus after the Pound Conference (p. 7), a mixed picture emerges. On the one hand, there is evidence that much progress has been made:

- Dispute resolution clauses (sometimes quite sophisticated) are being used increasingly in contracts of all kinds (see Appendix A for sample clauses).
- The federal Dispute Resolution Act of 1998 directs each federal district court to establish an ADR program by local rule; there is also comparable state legislation, sometimes mandating referral of specific kinds of cases to ADR or authorizing judges in their discretion to do so, in a large number of states.
- Some businesses and law firms systematically canvass cases for ADR potential (Weise, 1989: 385); relatedly, some law firms have set up ADR Practice Groups.
- The CPR International Institute for Dispute Prevention and Resolution, an organization of representatives from 800 leading businesses and law firms, is dedicated to the goal of educating its members and others concerning better ways of resolving disputes; its "CPR pledge" commits signers to explore ADR before resorting to court.
- Some state ethics rules (p. 336) require attorneys to discuss ADR options with clients or to certify on the pleading that they have done so.*
- For disputes in the public sector, the Administrative Dispute Resolution Act of 1996 requires federal agencies to consider the use of ADR and to appoint an ADR specialist.
- About half the states now have state offices of dispute resolution that seek to facilitate the resolution of public disputes by providing technical assistance or recommending competent dispute resolvers.
- Virtually every law school, as well as many schools of business and planning, now offer ADR courses.
- 25,000 persons, mostly volunteers, mediate in 600 community mediation centers.†

*See, e.g., Federal Rule of Procedure 16.1 for the Massachusetts District.

† Telephone interview with Irvin P. Foster, National Association of Community Mediation, Washington, D.C., October, 19, 2006.

These, then, are a few of the encouraging signs that ADR has come of age. Still, if we look at the potential, the glass seems not even half full. Disputants often do not use ADR where it would be clearly beneficial to do so. Nor do all lawyers systematically discuss with disputants appropriate forms of ADR that might be employed. Why is this so?

The reason most frequently given for the failure of disputants to make greater use of mediation and other alternatives to the courts is that they do not know about their existence. Despite increasing publicity given to alternatives, we suspect that if a Gallup poll were taken today asking what an individual should do if he had a dispute with his neighbor that they could not resolve, most citizens would say "go to court" or "see your lawyer," rather than "visit your local neighborhood justice center." The emphasis given to courts and lawyers as the ideal dispute resolvers in American society is simply too pervasive to be easily disturbed. One need only consider, by way of example, the consistent message conveyed by television — "People's Court," "Judge Judy," and "Perry Mason." We have no television programs entitled "Perry Mediator," "Judy's Neighborhood Justice Center," or "People's Ombudsman."

Even when potential disputants are aware of alternatives to the court and live in a community where they are available, it is often difficult to locate such mechanisms because they have not gained status as public institutions. The frequent segregation of alternatives from the judicial process has other adverse consequences, such as the common absence of public funding, which sometimes requires disputants to pay for alternative dispute resolution services even as the judicial ones are provided free. More subtle discouragements derive from the distrust that often accompanies processes that are new and unfamiliar and that appear to be unaccompanied by the legal protections that disputants have been taught over the years to value so highly. A related deterrent may be the absence of mechanisms for ensuring high quality in the provision of alternatives.

Psychological factors may also play a part in the gravitational pull of disputants toward the courts. Over a hundred years ago, de Tocqueville commented on the tendency of most social problems in the United States to devolve eventually into legal problems. Many disputants go to court because they want to challenge their adversaries rather than come to terms with them. According to one study of disputing in a small American city, once disputants have failed to reach a negotiated solution of interpersonal problems with the help of family and friends, they look not for "uninvolved" outsiders to mediate their cases but for a third party who will make a definitive decision about right and wrong (Merry and Silbey, 1984). In twentieth-century United States, lawsuits are a socially acceptable form of fighting.

In addition to these general explanations, special considerations may come into play in particular sectors of the disputing universe. For example, large institutional litigants may want a binding precedent to guide future disputes, which they can only get from a court. In bureaucratic organizations, such as the government, there is also the tendency toward following the path of least resistance and minimal risk. This means taking the tried-and-true route of dumping the problem into the court's lap, rather than risking possible criticism for what some superior views as an unwise settlement.

Sometimes well-intended substantive statutes have unanticipated anti-settlement consequences. An example is the Health Care Quality Improvement Act of 1986, which required all court judgments of medical malpractice, as well as voluntary settlements, to be reported to a federal registry. The fear that a settlement would be interpreted as an admission of fault has tended to deter doctors and their lawyers from settling any case that they believe they might be able to win in court.

The reluctance of lawyers to use ADR stems from many of the same considerations applicable to clients. Although lawyers are more likely than their clients to be aware of the existence of alternatives, a surprising number of lawyers know very little about them, frequently confusing mediation and arbitration; hence, they are reluctant to suggest their use. The path of least resistance is still to litigate. Lawyer and client are apt to agree that adversary combat in a judicial arena is the normal, socially acceptable, and psychologically satisfying method of resolving disputes. Indeed, most legal education is still premised on an adversarial approach to dispute resolution (Riskin, 1982).

Economic considerations may also constitute a significant impediment to the greater use of alternatives. Over the past decade, law firms have built up immense litigation departments. Even though some of the leading litigation practitioners are prominent in the alternatives movement because they see the advantages of accommodative problem-solving in many situations, the very existence of these expanding litigation empires constitutes a self-reinforcing movement toward litigation. Consider, too, the disincentive to early settlement that exists where an organization or governmental entity charges the unit involved in the dispute for damages paid but not for litigation costs (Rogers and McEwen, 1998).

Finally, public policy considerations play a part in explaining the limited use of ADR. Because of the difficulty and expense of doing effective cost-benefit research in this area,* many of the questions that we posed at the end of Chapter 1 (pp. 11-12) still remain unanswered and perhaps unanswerable. When legislatures demand proof of demonstrable savings from instituting ADR programs, their demands often cannot be satisfied.

What can be done about these forces supporting the status quo? A provocative recent book, *The Tipping Point* (2000), by Malcolm Gladwell, may provide a promising prospect for change. The subtitle of the book is "How Little Things Can Make a Difference." Gladwell's thesis is that the cumulative impact of many small changes at some point may lead to a "tipping point," when social policy shifts dramatically, as recently happened, for example, with respect to smoking and seat belts.

What are the implications of this thesis for ADR? How can we achieve a paradigm shift from a court-based system of dispute resolution to one that sees the court as a last resort, except in cases that involve novel issues of legal interpretation and hence call for a judicial ruling?

- We must recognize that even small changes can make a difference if they come in sufficient quantity and at the right times so that their cumulative impact leads to a tipping point;
- We should focus on ideas that have leverage potential (i.e., a multiplier effect). An example is the duty to apprise disputants about ADR options (pp. 336-337) because these duties not only inform clients but compel lawyers to learn

*How, for example, would one do a sophisticated study comparing the costs and benefits of court adjudication and mediation?

enough to fulfill this obligation. Another example is peer mediation in schools (NIDR, 1991; ABA, 1988) which benefits not only the students, but also the schools and sometimes even the parents.

Yet another illustration of a change with leverage potential builds on the research (Wissler, 1996) showing that lawyers who *experience* ADR are more likely to make future use of it than lawyers who are merely told about it in CLE courses. This suggests use of carrots (cf. *Dunnett,* p. 420) or sticks (see chapter 6C re mandatory ADR) to provide lawyers with direct ADR experience.

- We should focus on ideas that seek to change accepted ways of resolving disputes, as is true for example, of collaborative lawyering (pp. 373-375).
- We should try to build new institutions into the existing dispute resolution structure, rather than create exogenous mechanisms. An example: the Multi-door Courthouse (pp. 396-397).

Aside from these structural changes, there are many specific ideas and actions that may help us to reach a tipping point towards ADR. Here are a few further examples:

1. Continue to promote state and federal ADR legislation and court rules, particularly ones that increase use without increasing costs or limiting the flexibility of the processes.
2. Continue to promote ADR clauses in contracts.
3. Encourage the role of settlement counsel (a lawyer whose sole task is to explore settlement for his client).
4. Help to overcome ADR funding problems (e.g., by providing seed money for ADR experiments, with a provision for permanent funding — e.g., by add-on filing fees — if the experiment proves successful).
5. Identify key movers and shakers and work with them.
6. Work with other key players (such as CPR and the ABA Section of Dispute Resolution).
7. Develop and disseminate ADR success stories, as, for example, one involving an effective mediation of a specific complex problem or the systematic canvassing of business disputes for ADR potential (e.g., by GE or Motorola).
8. Find better ways of spreading the word to potential users, such as business school students and/or insurance adjusters.
9. More generally, do more to teach and use ADR in schools of all levels so as to inculcate in future citizens different ways of resolving disputes.

What additional suggestions do you have for reaching the tipping point?

Another approach for encouraging the further use of mediation and other forms of ADR was recently proposed by Professor Frank Sander (Sander, 2007). After noting the disparate use of mediation in various jurisdictions, he proposed the development of a metric — The Mediation Receptivity Index (MRI) — to measure the extent of mediation activity in particular jurisdictions. If such a tool could be validly formulated, it would permit all kinds of insights about how to enhance mediation utilization in a particular jurisdiction. For example, by closely studying the evolution over time in a high-MRI jurisdiction, one might learn much about what factors facilitate enhanced utilization as well as what barriers impede it.

Similar insights might be gained by comparing state X, which has a high MRI, with state Y, with a low MRI; such a comparison might be very useful in helping state Y enhance its use of mediation. This approach might be called "Follow the Leader(s)."

Questions

12.1 How might the MRI be determined? What problems do you foresee? How might they be addressed?

12.2 You are asked by the senior partner of your law firm to chair a committee charged with recommending how the firm can improve its understanding, use, and marketing of alternative dispute resolution skills. Some members of your committee advocate setting up an "ADR and Settlement Department." They argue that alternative dispute resolution settlement is a specialty, like tax, domestic relations, and litigation; particularly skilled individuals (mostly from the corporate department), who are experts in putting together deals rather than in fighting over who did what to whom, and will stay abreast of an expanding field, can provide the highest quality service to clients and other lawyers in the firm. Second, they argue that fighting hard and settling are incompatible functions: to get the best of both, they should be pursued single-mindedly by different people.

Others on the committee argue that clients rightfully expect that each lawyer who handles disputes will litigate effectively when necessary but will also look for dispute resolution opportunities and negotiate good settlements. They argue that dispute resolution expertise is part of every lawyer's standard equipment rather than a distinct skill for specialists. They also argue that splitting the litigating function from the settling function will increase costs to clients and be perceived as a "huckstering" attempt to appear up to date. What do you recommend?

12.3 The President's Council on Competitiveness proposed in 1991 that

> In most cases, the right to sue should be conditioned on a showing that the parties have attempted, and failed, to resolve their dispute. The party alleging harm would be required to prove that it gave timely notice of the grievance prior to filing the suit, except where emergency or other circumstances require immediate resort to the courts without prior notice to the opposing party.

Another proposal of the council urges that a party who refused a settlement offer before trial and ultimately did not do better at trial be required to pay the opposing party's trial costs.

How do you evaluate these proposals?

12.4 How do you evaluate the following institutionalization proposal?

> The National Institute for Dispute Resolution should establish a counter-part of the Good Housekeeping seal of approval to designate whether a dispute resolution mechanism offered by a particular provider meets requisite characteristics such as accessibility, fairness, and finality. Such a designation would guide potential users and might act as an incentive to the creator of the mechanism to build in the requisite features.

12.5 As noted (p. 592), the absence of adequate funding remains a major impediment to the growth of ADR. There are presently four ways of funding ADR processes in the courts (Sander, 1992):

1. Disputants pay;
2. Use of volunteers;
3. The general court budget; and
4. A special filing fee added to all civil cases to create a fund to cover ADR costs.

What approach would you favor and why? Does it depend on the nature of the case (for example, neighborhood dispute versus large commercial case)? See pp. 428-434.

12.6 "It seems fairly clear that there are significant impediments to the proliferation of ADR practices in law firms. At least five jump off the page: law firm pricing, products, compensation, staffing and training" (Zeughauser, 1997).

The author proposes that a high and low litigation budget be established for each case. The litigators would pursue litigation strategies, charging by the hour, as usual; settlement specialists would pursue settlement, keeping track of hours spent but not billing the client unless settlement was achieved. If it was, the firm's fee would equal the difference between the total budget (perhaps taken at a midpoint between the high and low budget estimate) and the amount actually paid to date by the client (that is, the unspent litigation budget).* "This pricing structure would provide an incentive to use ADR to resolve the dispute as early as possible." In addition, the compensation of attorneys would be adjusted to reflect the fees earned.

How would you evaluate this proposal? Would it be likely to create adequate incentives for lawyers to use ADR techniques? For clients to push their lawyer towards ADR resolutions?

12.7 One corporate litigator recently said:

> I have never settled a case in mediation. This is so because these [large business] cases involve a great deal of discovery and once discovery is complete people just want to go to trial. People are unwilling to resolve cases without all the facts and thus extensive discovery (Rogers and McEwen, 1998:42).

If you were consulted by the company president concerning ways of remedying this situation, what suggestions might you have?

12.8 Mnookin and Gilson (1994) suggested commercial law as another likely arena for cooperative negotiation, but this area of practice presents special sources of resistance for the collaborative lawyering approach. Corporate law firms seem more hesitant to withdraw as counsel for a client if their efforts do not culminate in settlement (Rack, 1998). How important is that aspect of collaborative law?

*For example, if the litigation budget was set at $90,000 (high) or $60,000 (low), and the case was settled after $35,000 had been billed by the litigators, then the amount due would be $40,000 ($75,000 (midpoint of litigation budget) less $35,000 (amount paid to date)).

B. THE STUDENT PERSPECTIVE: "CAN I EARN A LIVING IN ADR?"

Both students and practicing attorneys frequently ask us whether it is possible to earn a living as a neutral provider of dispute resolution services. In 1985, when the first edition of this book was published, our answer was that the only way to do so was by serving as a labor arbitrator or divorce mediator. By 1992, when the second edition was published, the list had expanded to include a small number of full-time neutrals mediating commercial and environmental disputes, as well as a few full-time ombudsmen. Today, the number of full-time neutrals has grown substantially. The spread of court-connected mandatory mediation and arbitration has played a major role in this growth, as has the explosion of employment litigation, which has proven to be fertile territory for ADR. The number of organizational ombudsmen has also multiplied. Though no accurate statistics exist, some observers speculate that, apart from labor arbitration, there may be over 3,000 full-time providers of ADR services in the United States today.

There are also many full-time administrators of ADR programs in federal and state government offices, federal and state courts, private sector users of ADR services (such as the insurance industry), and ADR providers (such as the American Arbitration Association). In the federal government alone, there are probably close to 1,000 coordinators of ADR programs. Finally, dwarfing all other categories in numerical terms, are the part-time providers of ADR services. The *1996 Martindale-Hubbell Dispute Resolution Directory* lists approximately 15,000 lawyers offering dispute resolution services, nearly all of whom are primarily engaged in the practice of law. There are also many family therapists who do some mediation, as well as many college and university professors who mediate disputes related to their area of expertise. In sum, there are many thousands of people who today earn part or all of their living through the provision or administration of ADR services.

Nonetheless, as the following profiles show, carving out a career as a provider of ADR services remains a daunting task, requiring a high degree of commitment, a willingness to take financial risks, and a capacity to survive lean times in the early days of one's career. The central reason for these difficulties is clear. The law firm model, in which the firm engages young lawyers, assigning them to research and writing tasks while they learn their trade and develop a client base, does not exist in the ADR world. The vast majority of neutrals practice either alone or in small groups, with no apprenticeship program. This appears due to a variety of factors. Initially, the provision of mediation, by far the most common ADR service, typically requires neither research nor document drafting, tasks typically assigned to law firm associates. Additionally, mediation, even more than lawyering, tends to be viewed as a hands-on skill, so that work is not easily transferred from a senior mediator to a junior mediator, as it might be from a senior law firm partner to a junior partner.

To be sure, there are a few large groups offering ADR services. Among these are JAMS, the American Arbitration Association, and the CPR International Institute for Dispute Prevention and Resolution. With rare exceptions, however, these organizations do not hire neutrals as employees. Rather, they market and administer the services of established neutrals who are known to the consumers of ADR services.

They offer little aid to the beginning neutral, who is thus faced with a Catch 22. If you can't get work as a neutral, how are people going to have confidence in you as a neutral?

While there are no easy answers to this question, we have set out below the profiles of three mediators, Dana Curtis, William Baten, and David Hoffman, who describe how they were able to establish themselves in the ADR field. None of them followed exactly the same path, but there are some common themes, suggesting a variety of steps that you might take if you want a career in ADR:*

- **If you are a practicing attorney, conduct yourself so that those with whom you deal respect you for your fairness, integrity, and ability.** Stated otherwise, practice law in such a way that others will observe in you the qualities they would want in a neutral.
- **Take at least a basic course in mediation**. Ideally, you should take more than one such course in order to obtain different perspectives on mediation. Mediation courses are offered in nearly every part of the country.
- **Obtain a degree in dispute resolution**. Degree-granting programs in dispute resolution are offered by, among others, the University of Missouri Law School, Columbia, Missouri; Nova Southeastern University, Ft. Lauderdale, Florida; George Mason University, Fairfax, Virginia; The University of Massachusetts, Boston; Pepperdine University School of Law, Malibu, California; and Antioch College, Yellow Springs, Ohio. Certificate programs are offered by Ohio State University Moritz College of Law, Columbus, Ohio; and Willamette University, Salem, Oregon. (An alternative is to obtain a general master's degree at a leading school that offers outstanding courses in dispute resolution.)
- **Serve as a volunteer unpaid mediator**. Many cities have court-related programs that will provide free mediation training in exchange for a commitment to mediate a certain number of disputes each year.
- **Search for part-time paid mediation work**. Some mediation programs, particularly those that deal with a high volume of cases, will engage comparatively inexperienced mediators on a part-time basis. If you can spend part of your time mediating, and part of your time practicing law, you can gain both mediation experience and a reputation as a paid mediator without the financial risk of cutting your law firm ties completely.
- **Find a mentor, someone who knows her way around the ADR world, and who will give you advice**. Ideally, this person will allow you to observe her at work, and discuss ADR tactics and strategy as they unfold before you. Recently a number of well-established mediators have taken on paid interns, akin to law clerks for judges.
- **Market your services**. Among the ways in which you might do so, in addition to advertising, are by speaking and writing on ADR, as well as by participating in the ADR activities of your local bar association. If ADR is not currently being

*What follows focuses on mediation, both because it is the fastest growing form of ADR, and because it is an essential element of most ADR processes other than arbitration. Many of the steps that might be taken by an aspiring arbitrator would be similar to those taken by an aspiring mediator, though for the arbitrator there would be less emphasis on process skills and more emphasis on acquiring substantive knowledge in the area in which she sought to arbitrate.

used in your area of substantive expertise, promote its use and your capacity to provide it.

- **Meet and share experiences (and support) with other aspiring and successful ADR practitioners**. This can best be done by joining ACR (the Association for Conflict Resolution, formerly SPIDR, in Washington, D.C.), as well as your local ACR chapter. Also consider joining the Section on Dispute Resolution of the American Bar Association, and the ADR Committee of your local Bar Association.
- **Keep up with developments in the ADR field** by reading such publications as *Dispute Resolution Magazine* (ABA Section of Dispute Resolution); *Dispute Resolution Journal* (American Arbitration Association); *World Arbitration and Mediation Report* (Transnational Juris Publications); *Alternatives* (CPR Institute); *Negotiation Journal* (Blackwell); *Ohio State Journal on Dispute Resolution; Harvard Negotiation Law Review; Journal of Dispute Resolution* (Univ. of Missouri-Columbia); *ACR Quarterly* (Jossey-Bass).*

The profiles that follow are those of three successful mediators, each of whom arrived at where he or she is by a slightly different route. Dana Curtis knew she wanted to be a mediator when she was still in law school, and, except for a short stint in a San Francisco law firm, has been mediating ever since. William Baten went from large-firm law practice to opening a two-person dispute resolution firm, and, until recently, David Hoffman practiced mediation as a partner in a large law firm.

J. ALFINI AND E. GALTON, ADR PERSONALITIES AND PRACTICE TIPS

1-9, 49-52, 85-94 (1998)

Dana Curtis

I knew I wanted to be a mediator when I was introduced to mediation in a second-year law school course. My other courses, though interesting intellectually, minimized the role of the human being behind the legal claims. Mediation focused on the individuals involved and on the meaning they attached to the dispute. The parties' priorities could be the most important reference point for resolution. In addition to, or instead of, the rule of law, their concerns, needs, fears, hopes and desires all mattered. As well as seeing how mediation could better meet the needs of the parties than a litigated resolution, I realized that mediation better utilized my strengths. As a mediator, I could use relationship and communication skills I had developed in my first career as a teacher.

Full of enthusiasm for mediation, I asked my professor where to learn about mediating as a career. He referred me to Gary Friedman, a pioneer lawyer mediator and Director of the Center for Mediation in Law in Mill Valley, California. I sought Gary's advice about mediating employment and other commercial disputes. He encouraged me, but warned that such a career would be difficult to forge, as the application of mediation in civil disputes was uncommon at that time. He also noted that I seemed to have what it would take — the commitment to mediation and an

*See Appendix I for a more complete list of ADR resources, including online services.

entrepreneurial spirit, evidenced by the fact that I had entered law school as a single mother after moving to California from Idaho with my three children.

Gary advised me to remain committed, to be patient and to get litigation experience to enhance my credibility with lawyers and my understanding of the legal process. Following his advice, after law school I clerked for a California Supreme Court associate justice and thereafter joined a large San Francisco law firm, practicing commercial and employment litigation in San Jose and San Francisco. I began as an enthusiastic associate and during much of my first year of practice seriously considered a long-term litigation career. Before long, my enthusiasm abated. The enormity of financial and human resources spent on litigation astounded me. The inefficiency of the discovery process (where the object, it seemed to me, was to provide the other side with as little information as possible), the lack of predictability and fairness of jury trials, and the failure of litigation to address the clients' true needs all left me disaffected.

In addition, the demands of big firm practice, the often sixty and sometimes eighty hour work weeks, and the isolation I experienced among 200 other big firm lawyers convinced me that I was not willing to sacrifice more years of "being" for "becoming." The idea of partnership became unthinkable. As one of my law school friends put it, partnership is like a pie eating contest where the prize is more pie.

I dreamed of mediating. Although I had trained as a mediator and had been teaching mediation for several years, I was unable to see a way to make the transition.

A few days later, I ran into Gary Friedman on the street in San Francisco. When he discovered I was leaving my law practice, he invited me to meet with him. Over a series of meetings, I learned that he was becoming increasingly interested in mediation of civil disputes and would like to work closely with lawyers who were pursuing commercial mediation. Within a few months, I hung out my mediation shingle (literally!) at Gary's office in Mill Valley. There, I practiced mediation for two years with Laura Farrow, another lawyer who left the firm at the same time I did. It was an exciting time — the invigoration of moving from a high-rise Financial District office to a renovated house with rose bushes, even an apple tree, in the yard, where at last my whole heart was in my work, as well as the uncertainty of whether a mediation practice could actually support my family. . . .

After two years at Mediation Law Offices, I had the opportunity to become a Circuit Court Mediator for the U.S. Court of Appeals for the Ninth Circuit in San Francisco. I was persuaded to leave private practice by the promise of an endless array of Federal cases to mediate and a steady paycheck. In the Ninth Circuit Mediation Program, I worked with five other full-time mediators to resolve cases on appeal. It was a mediator's dream come true. We selected our caseload from hundreds of diverse civil appeals. On any day, we might conduct a telephone mediation in a securities case, an employment discrimination dispute, a products liability matter, an IRS appeal, a bankruptcy case or an insurance coverage dispute. Several times a month, I would mediate in person, often in complex multi-party disputes. It was a time of applying my experience and knowledge of a face-to-face mediation model, where the parties could reach understanding in order to craft a resolution that addressed their priorities, not just their assessment of their legal positions. I sought to provide more than a settlement conference. In fact, when I began to speak of legal argument in mediation as an *option*, not a *given*, I was surprised by how frequently the parties, and even their lawyers, agreed that discussing the law would not be productive. The first time I suggested that we may not want to discuss the law, the plaintiff (in an employment discrimination case) said, "Thank God! If I had to listen for five more minutes to the company's lawyer telling me what a rotten case I have, I'd leave!" . . .

A year ago, I left the Ninth Circuit to return to private mediation practice and to join the Negotiation and Mediation Program at Stanford Law School, where I am a lecturer teaching two mediation courses a year. . . . I have found the perfect career: teaching makes me a better mediator and mediation makes me a better teacher.

William A. Baten

In the early stages of my legal career, I thought I was on the right track. After several years as a corporate paralegal and law clerk at Gibson, Dunn & Crutcher's D.C. office, I felt certain that I wanted to pursue a transactional corporate practice. I had attended Georgetown Law School, become an editor of the law review, graduated among the top in my class, and accepted a position at a prestigious Wall Street law firm. At Cleary, Gottlieb, Steen & Hamilton, I had a chance to work with the best and the brightest on the most interesting deals. Life was good. In fact, I had just returned to my office in D.C. from two weeks in New York to close a tricky international bank merger when the call came. It appeared that a longstanding Japanese client of the firm was about to become embroiled in product liability litigation of mass-tort proportions in the U.S., and I was asked pinch hit as a litigator until our office could properly staff up to deal with the onslaught of cases. . . .

It quickly became apparent that our client was destined to be involved in more lawsuits than anyone could try in a lifetime. This fact, coupled with the potential for significant exposure, caused us to place emphasis on settlement rather than a "scorched earth" defense strategy. Despite this, it did not take long for settlement discussions to break down in several significant cases staring at imminent trial dates. Two weeks before the first of these trials, and still seven figures apart after numerous, lengthy settlement discussions, someone suggested that I turn to what he labeled a "last resort" method to attempt settlement—mediation. Opposing counsel agreed to mediation and we chose a mediator. During the course of this nine-hour mediation, the gap astonishingly narrowed from seven figures to six, and then to five, all the way down to discussing terms of the settlement release. What could not be accomplished during several months of "hand-to-hand combat" settlement negotiations with opposing counsel was accomplished in one day through mediation.

With one successful mediation under my belt, I tried it with another case on the verge of trial. Different opposing counsel, different state, different mediator, but the same result—a successful settlement accomplished in one day. As I began to resolve more tough cases through mediation, I began to see the process in a different light. Rather than a "last resort" on the eve of trial, I started to use it earlier in the litigation spectrum, before we deposed every expert and turned over every stone (which in most cases did not materially affect either side's valuation of the matter). The cases continued to settle, and my clients reaped the benefits of that old saying, "a penny saved on attorneys' fees and expenses is a penny earned."

Pushing the envelope still farther, I started to engage in "pre-suit" mediation for less serious cases, with equally successful results. Don't get me wrong — there was, and continues to be, a need for attorney analyzation and evaluation — but I found that part of my job as counsel to my clients was to determine how soon in the litigation process I had enough information to evaluate a claim effectively, and at that point move toward mediation or some other ADR process. For smaller cases (i.e., valued less than $50,000) I would continue to at least attempt direct negotiation with opposing counsel, but for any significant case, I began to realize that mediation was the perfect forum to present an initial offer, and the rationale behind it, directly to the opposing counsel *and* her client in order for the offer and subsequent negotiations to have the most impact.

THE TRANSFORMATION

As I began to participate in close to one hundred mediations as an advocate, not only did my appreciation grow for the process of mediation, but it grew for the mediators as well. As I came to recognize that the skill set of the mediator was just as important as the mediation process itself, I narrowed the group of mediators I worked with down to the most effective in each part of the country where I litigated. . . .

While I was generally pleased with my select group of mediators, as I sat through more mediations as an advocate I became increasingly discerning with respect to their skills and techniques, and felt that my people skills, even temperament, negotiation skills and knowledge of the law would make me a formidable mediator. In addition, I was already known for my never-say-die approach to handling tough problems. I also became envious of the relatively low stress level of a mediator's practice compared to a trial lawyer's, and their uniform ability to have some control over their calendars and lead a fulfilling life outside the office. Further, I had a strong sense that ADR in general, and mediation in particular, would see the most growth and provide the most opportunities for lawyers during the remainder of my legal career. With all these thoughts in mind, I planned a path to a career in mediation.

First, I thought it would be a good idea to make certain that I enjoyed mediation and that I, in fact, could do it well. I took a 40-hour training course and signed up to do pro bono mediations in the courts in Washington D.C. and in Arlington and Fairfax, Virginia. When I got the notice of my first mediation, I was tremendously excited, and after I settled the case and enjoyed every second and aspect of the mediation from the mediator's perspective, I was hooked.

After several subsequent positive experiences as a mediator, the next part of my plan was to determine if I could make a living out of performing ADR services. To my dismay, every ADR organization I spoke with in the D.C. area about a career in mediation had the same general response — "Don't quit your day job!" Evidently, the number of people in the D.C.-metropolitan area wanting to mediate far exceeded the number of mediations in which parties were engaged. On top of that, there were so many pro bono mediators serving on court programs that (1) the mediators in each program would rarely get to serve and (2) there developed long waiting lists even to serve as a volunteer mediator. This situation did not surprise me — the D.C. legal community is the largest in the country and certainly has its share of overworked, disillusioned lawyers looking for other outlets for their talents. The bottom line of my D.C. based search for a mediator position was that supply far outweighed demand, and that even folks who set out years earlier to mediate full time were having a rough go of it to develop successful practices and keep busy.

Not being one to give up easily, I then researched whether I could create a market for my services and strike out on my own to establish a solo mediation practice. I started to call around to insurance companies, businesses, and plaintiff and defense firms to survey their level of ADR use. To my shock and amazement, not only was mediation rarely used by these sectors, it was often confused with arbitration or not understood at all. Further, those who did have some familiarity with the process only had experience with the free, court-based programs, which produced two distinct camps — those that had a good experience and therefore had no desire to *pay* for a mediator, and those that had a bad experience (often due to the time limitations or limited experience of the mediators) and vowed never to mediate again. It appeared from all indications that to quit my job and try to jumpstart a full-time mediation practice in D.C. would be financial suicide.

AN ADR SABBATICAL

Though dismayed with what appeared to be an endless array of obstacles standing between me and my ADR career, I continued to try to figure out how to get past them. I thought to myself, "Surely the many successful mediators that I have hired in the past must have faced similar obstacles — how did they get started?" I then decided to do some in-depth research to find out. My firm offered a sabbatical policy, and I was eligible to take two months off for whatever purpose I chose. I decided to take a two month sabbatical to meet for two or three days each with many of the top mediators throughout the country.

During my sabbatical, I found a marked difference in the use of mediation (and a consequent demand for mediators) in states that had in place either court rules or legislation that either made mediation mandatory in certain cases or gave judges the authority to compel parties to mediation before trial. What was most interesting about this observation, however, was that these rules had their primary effect in the period shortly after their promulgation, as a means of getting a reluctant bar to try mediation to efficiently resolve their clients' disputes. Over time, say two to four years, as the plaintiff and defense bars came to understand the benefits of mediation, they unilaterally would seek to mediate matters earlier in the litigation spectrum, long before it became mandatory through court or legislative edicts.

One of the best examples of the impact of court rules on mediation was seen in Indiana, one of the first stops on my sabbatical. In 1992, the Indiana Supreme Court enacted rules which gave authority to state judges to order parties to mediation. In conjunction with these rules, Indiana instituted a 40-hour certification program in order to create a pool of trained mediators within the state. At the same time, each of Indiana's ninety-two counties began creating a roster of these "certified" mediators from which a judge would choose three names to accompany his order to mediate. This entire program differed from my experience in D.C. not only in terms of voluntary v. mandatory, but in terms of pro bono v. fee-based mediators as well.

Early in the life of these rules, while the concept of mediation was still in its incubacy for many in Indiana, judges regularly ordered parties to mediation and the mediator chosen was typically one of the three candidates provided by the court. After three years, the Indiana Bar was regularly opting to go to mediation long before the court would order it. Likewise, they were selecting mediators not from the courts' rosters, but from their own experience or after getting recommendations from colleagues. Further, because mediators were getting to mediate a lot of cases and refine their expertise and techniques, they were able to settle tougher and tougher cases, thereby fostering even more confidence in the mediation process. This confidence translated into the expanded use of mediation through the years to more types of disputes and earlier in the litigation process. . . .

Because of the fee-based nature of Indiana mediation and a consistent flow of cases to good mediators based upon reputation and track record, I concluded that Indiana would provide a much better chance for me to establish a practice than I could ever hope for in D.C. At the same time I was concluding this, and perhaps as my reward for enduring all the naysayers, false starts and dead ends along my multi-year quest to become a full-time mediator, I finally got my big break. While in Indianapolis during the middle of my sabbatical, I had scheduled two days with John Van Winkle, who at that time was Chairman of the ABA's newly-formed Section of Dispute Resolution. . . .

During our dinner, I was surprised to learn that John intended to leave his firm at which he had been a partner for twenty years, and where he was solidly recognized for his mediation work, to create his own mediation firm. . . . [A few weeks later, I] placed a call to John Van Winkle in Indiana to see if he would be interested in my joining him in his new venture. His level of interest was high, and a few months later we opened Van Winkle Dispute Resolution, the Indianapolis office of the national ADR organization JAMS/Endispute.

ESTABLISHING A PRACTICE

By early 1995 I had done it—I had hung my shingle as a mediator. Only one minor thing was missing, however, which was a clientele. Don't get me wrong, I knew that the idea of starting a new practice in a new field in a new city would not be easy, but I never envisioned just how painstakingly slow it would be. My first miscalculation was the thought that clients of John's would be likely to utilize me as their mediator if John was booked during the time they needed to mediate. Even though when I practiced and chose mediators I was highly selective and never would even consider my favorite mediators' partner as a substitute, however highly recommended, I failed to anticipate that most lawyers were just like me and were reluctant to choose a mediator either they or their colleagues had not worked with before. My second miscalculation was in failing to recognize that in picking a mediator, it takes two to tango. In other words, even though all my friends and former colleagues vowed that they would utilize my services, I failed to recognize that the ultimate decision was not theirs alone to make, and that in many cases the sheer mention of a preferred mediator by one side automatically caused that person to be struck from consideration by the other side. . . .

When I was fortunate enough to be selected for a mediation, I would analyze and reanalyze my performance. . . . I would follow up with each attorney after the mediation to get their reactions and feedback, preferably over lunch to give me an opportunity to know them better. Little by little, the cases began to flow. . . .

MY PRACTICE, AND LIFE, TODAY

Fast forward to today. Now in my fourth year since becoming a full-time mediator, my practice has increased exponentially, and has many advantages over trial practice. Gone are the days when one particular type or series of cases would consume my practice for years. My mediation practice is a general one, and I would not have it any other way. In the past two weeks, for example, I have mediated the following types of disputes: construction/surveyor malpractice, products liability, will contest, claims/counterclaims between an automaker and a multi-point dealer, serious injury from an auto accident, a legal malpractice claim stemming from a multi-million dollar construction trial gone bad, and a business dispute arising from an oral contract. . . .

My mediation practice also allows me to avoid that sinking feeling at the end of each day that all I have accomplished was to push the ball incrementally farther on four or five cases out of two hundred. Today, my typical mediation lasts only one day, and usually ends with a settlement. Because I am in the middle of the action and essentially thinking on my feet all day, each day provides a host of new challenges and stimulation, and the time I spend in mediation rushes by. And when the day is over, the only thing I have to take home is the "high" from seeing opposing sides shaking hands over their settlement agreement and feeling a tremendous sense of accomplishment that I have helped resolve in a matter of hours or days a dispute that has gone on for years.

David Hoffman

"The truth shall make ye free," they say, "but first it shall make ye miserable." The truth was that in the late 1980's, after devoting my full attention to becoming a trial lawyer, civil litigation had lost much of its luster for me. There may be some lawyers, I concluded, who thrive on a steady diet of litigation, but I was not one of them. I had just returned to my law practice at Hill & Barlow, after a year as staff attorney at the ACLU of Massachusetts, and I found myself agreeing (for once) with Chief Justice Warren Burger, who described our litigation system as "too costly, too painful, too destructive, too inefficient for a truly civilized people." Although a trial might be what is needed in some cases, I wanted to use my knowledge of the law to help clients avoid litigation.

GETTING STARTED

I called Prof. Frank Sander, my former law school advisor, for advice about converting my litigation practice into an ADR practice. I did not realize at the time how many calls of this kind Frank was receiving each year from disgruntled litigators and burned-out corporate attorneys. With enormous patience, however, Frank outlined some useful steps for developing an ADR group at Hill & Barlow and getting the training I needed to begin mediating and arbitrating. . . . Much to my surprise, I encountered no resistance at Hill & Barlow. In fact, unbeknownst to me, a small committee of very senior partners in the firm had begun meeting to discuss setting up an ADR practice of some kind, because they wanted to hire a very prominent Massachusetts judge who was about to retire. One of the firm's senior partners, Carl Sapers (a long-time member of the AAA National Board) and I decided to co-chair Hill & Barlow's fledgling ADR Practice Group. Carl's experience as an arbitrator in high-stakes construction cases for many years gave us instant credibility, while I went about getting training and looking for the unfortunate souls who would be my first ADR clients.

My strategy for developing an ADR practice was to knock, rather indiscriminately, on the door of every organization that might have cases to refer. My first stop, after taking training programs in mediation and arbitration, was a community program, the Cambridge Dispute Settlement Center, which provides mediation services for low- and moderate-income individuals in a working-class section of Cambridge. CDSC maintains a roster of approximately 40 volunteer mediators handling landlord-tenant, divorce, small claims, employment and neighborhood disputes. I thought that, with my law background and the experience of working in a 100-lawyer downtown firm where I had handled all of those kinds of cases and more, I would be welcomed with open arms. I discovered, to my surprise, that even after submitting a detailed application and being interviewed, I was put on a waiting list along with a number of highly qualified people. Welcome to the crowded ADR marketplace where, in Boston (as in some other cities), there are more would-be mediators than cases!

Although I was one of many seeking to enter the profession, I found that the experienced mediators and arbitrators who ran the programs welcomed newcomers. I think they cast a somewhat skeptical eye in the direction of recovering litigators like me, waiting to see whether we had truly changed our ways. I guess I passed muster in that regard, because after continued and persistent door knocking, I eventually found myself on the panels of a number of organizations — the AAA, the Middlesex Multi-Door Courthouse, the Massachusetts Office of Dispute Resolution, The Center for Public Resources, The Private Adjudication Center, The Mediation Group, JAMS/Endispute, among others — and I started getting cases. . . .

WHY PRACTICE LAW?

Some of my colleagues in the dispute resolution community have asked me why I do not abandon the practice of law altogether, and I have come to the following conclusion: as fascinating as the practice of dispute resolution is, I also enjoy the relationship I have with my clients in a law practice. Each type of work has different rewards — and costs.

When I represent clients, I am sometimes uncomfortable with the harshness of the positions they wish me to take, the one-sidedness of their view of the case, and the difficulty they have in seeing and understanding the other party's point of view. On the other hand, I value the close relationships I have with my clients, the ability to stand entirely by their side, to be their friend, their ally, their confidante. In arbitration work I must, of course, stand completely apart from the parties, my communications with them structured by the formalities of adjudication (no ex parte communications, little if any expression of my own point of view until the end of the case, etc.).

However, even in my work as a mediator, in which I can meet in confidential, private sessions with each side, there are limits to everyone's candor. For example, the parties seldom share with me the true bottom line they bring to the negotiation (although, to be sure, sometimes they do not know it themselves), and I must keep a certain distance emotionally in order to maintain both the appearance and reality of impartiality. . . .

ADR IN THE LAW FIRM SETTING

My colleagues at Hill & Barlow sometimes ask me why I continue to do this work in the high-overhead setting of a downtown law firm. They point out—correctly, as far as I can tell—that my costs would be lower and I would probably make more money in an office of my own where I could get by with a half-time secretary and a few pieces of office equipment. I would also be able to serve in cases from which I am currently precluded by conflicts created by my colleagues, both past and present. In a law firm which has been in existence for over 100 years and has 100+ lawyers, the list of individuals and companies that have been clients or adverse parties is formidable.

I respond to these inquiries as follows.

Conflicts. The conflicts are not an enormous problem. The Hill & Barlow computer prints out a list of the cases in which one or more of the parties has dealt with the firm. After making appropriate disclosures to the parties in the mediation or arbitration and telling them that I believe I can be impartial, they almost invariably tell me that they have no objection.

Administrative burdens. Although the costs of a solo-practice might be lower, I would have to devote time and attention to managing the financial and administrative aspects of my practice. . . . I am . . . quite grateful for the staff at Hill & Barlow who handles billing, insurance, bookkeeping, taxes, employee benefits (including my own), facilities management, relations with vendors, mailing and copying, and—perhaps most importantly in this day and age—maintaining and improving my computer equipment. . . .

A vantage point on the legal world. Working in a law firm gives me an inside view of the world of legal disputes. I have access to information about the practice of law—from internal memos and attending in-house workshops and meetings—that would be otherwise unobtainable. . . . Thus, when I mediate, I bring to the table first-hand experience of the legal, financial, and practical constraints under which the lawyers in the case operate.

Information resources. Most of my ADR cases reach me in the form of legal disputes, and law is, at least in part, a knowledge industry. The firm is a rich environment in that regard. Hill & Barlow's library circulates to me and the other lawyers daily and weekly advance sheets with information about developments in the areas of law in which we practice. . . . Could I practice as mediator or arbitrator without such information? Absolutely. Is there a benefit from keeping abreast of changes in the law? I think so.

Physical and technological resources. Any mediator or arbitrator needs offices, conference rooms, and reception areas in which to practice. These are easily obtainable in any city, but the firm provides me with the ability to use several conference rooms at once, in a highly complicated multi-party case, or a single compact room, depending on my needs. . . .

Referrals. One of the benefits of law firm life is the referral network—one of the principal reasons for organizing a professional services firm. Naturally, I cannot provide mediation or arbitration services in a current case for a current client. But if one of my colleagues at Hill & Barlow is asked if they know of a good mediator or arbitrator, there is a good chance that my colleague will mention my name or the name of some other member of our ADR Practice Group.

Visibility and credibility. Perhaps most importantly, practicing in a well-respected law firm has provided me with visibility and credibility which, as a relatively junior member of the bar (law school class of 1984), ordinarily take much longer to acquire. My ADR clients make certain assumptions about me, my integrity, and my ability—whether deserved or undeserved—based solely on the fact that a reputable law firm has kept me on board for thirteen years and even promoted me to membership in the firm. What are those assumptions? I can think of a few: (a) that I know how to maintain confidences and adhere to ethical standards; (b) that I am comfortable handling cases in which the stakes are high and the legal issues complex; and (3) that I have a strong work ethic. In the crowded ADR marketplace of today, even such assumptions are not enough to attract business, but they might be helpful in a close contest between or among other providers.

Advantages for the firm. The advantages of ADR practice in a law firm setting are not a one-way street. I would like to think—and I have often been told—that my ADR work brings with it a number of benefits for the firm. First, I know a lot of mediators and arbitrators. I attend professional meetings with them. I hear them lecture and lead seminars about their approaches to dispute resolution. . . . That kind of personal knowledge of the people in the field makes me a useful resource for the lawyers at Hill & Barlow who are trying to evaluate a list of potential ADR providers in a particular case. I receive such inquiries from lawyers in the firm on a more or less weekly basis. Second, when my colleagues at Hill & Barlow are drafting agreements, there is usually some type of dispute resolution mechanism built into the agreement, and I am frequently called upon for advice about such clauses. Finally, our clients occasionally wish to implement a far-reaching dispute resolution system of some kind, and I am the lawyer who is usually called upon for advice.

Challenges for law firm providers of ADR services. While the advantages of ADR practice in a large firm have—for me, at least—outweighed the disadvantages, some challenges lie ahead. Law firms are under continuing economic pressure. Costs continue to rise, with continuing increases in the price of office space, high-tech phones, faxes and computers, and higher staff costs. Billing rates for lawyers in large firms have increased to the point where a significant gap exists between very able ADR providers working inside such firms and those practicing on their own. I have to keep my own hourly rate, which is set by the firm, in a reasonable relationship to the market set by other providers.

In addition, court-based ADR programs have generally set up fee structures which cap the hourly rate that a mediator or arbitrator can charge. Unless they are modified, such structures will force many experienced providers to drop out of court-connected programs or leave their firms. At present, these programs provide the majority of referrals in some cities, and probably will continue to do so for the foreseeable future. Because many of my cases come from such programs, this is an issue I am currently discussing with program administrators.

Finally, even in those cases where I am billing at my full hourly rate, my value to the firm depends in part on my ability to generate business (i.e., rainmaking) and supervise the work of associates and paralegals, thus creating profitable leverage for this firm. An ADR provider who does nothing more than fill his or her plate with work is a less profitable member than one who generates work for him/herself and others. Thus the challenge for those of us who practice ADR inside a firm is either to generate work for others (and it is not an easy task to generate ADR referrals for others, because the parties are usually looking for a specific individual, not a firm) or to persuade firm management that we provide a valuable service to the firm and its clients wholly apart from any rain we may make for our colleagues.

[Note: In 2002, David Hoffman left Hill & Barlow to join the New Law Center in Boston, a firm specializing in collaborative law. Six months later, Hill & Barlow voted to go out of business. Compare Bickerman, 1998, explaining why the author left his law firm in order to better perform his ADR work.]

References

ALFINI, James J., and Eric R. GALTON, eds. (1998) *ADR Personalities and Practice Tips.* Washington, D.C.: ABA, Section of Dispute Resolution.

AMERICAN BAR ASSOCIATION (1988) *Education and Mediation: Explaining the Alternatives.* Washington, D.C.: ABA.

BICKERMAN, John (1998) "Practitioner's Notebook: Why ADR Providers May Want to Leave the Firm," *Disp. Resol. Mag.* 24 (Winter).

CENTER FOR PUBLIC RESOURCES (1989) *Mainstreaming: Corporate Strategies for Systematic ADR Use* (CPR Practice Guide). New York: CPR.

CPR INSTITUTE FOR DISPUTE RESOLUTION (1994) "Dispute Resolution Clauses: A Guide for Drafters of Business Agreements," 12 *Alternatives* 66.

DRAKE, William R. (1988) "Statewide Offices of Mediation," 5 *Neg. J.* 359.

GLADWELL, Malcolm (2000) *The Tipping Point—How Little Things Can Make a Difference.* Boston: Little Brown.

MERRY, Sally E., and Susan S. SILBEY (1984) "What Do Plaintiffs Want? Reexamining the Concept of Dispute," 9 *Just. Sys. J.* 151.

MILLHAUSER, Marguerite (1987) "The Unspoken Resistance to Alternative Dispute Resolution," 3 *Neg. J.* 29.

——— (1988) "Gladiators and Conciliators: ADR—A Law Firm Staple," 14 *Bar Leader* 20 (Sept.-Oct.).

MNOOKIN, Robert H., and Ronald J. GILSON (1994) "Disputing Through Agents: Cooperation and Conflict Between Lawyers in Litigation," 94 *Colum. L. Rev.* 509.

NATIONAL INSTITUTE FOR DISPUTE RESOLUTION (1991) "Dispute Resolution in Education," *Forum* (Spring).

RACK, Robert W., Jr. (1998) "Settle or Withdraw: Collaborative Lawyering Provides Incentive to Avoid Costly Litigation," *Disp. Resol. Mag.* 8 (Summer).

RISKIN, LEONARD (1982) "Mediation and Lawyers," 43 *Ohio St. L.J.* 29.

ROGERS, Nancy H., and Craig A. McEWEN (1998) "Employing the Law to Increase the Use of Mediation and to Encourage Direct and Early Negotiations," 13 *Ohio St. J. Disp. Resol.* 831.

SANDER, Frank E. A. (1992) "Paying for ADR," *A.B.A. J.* 105 (Feb.).

——— (2000) "The Future of ADR," 2000 *J. Disp. Resol.* 1.

——— (2007) "Developing the Mediation Receptivity Index (MRI)," 22 *Chio St. J. Disp. Resol.* —.

SYMPOSIUM ON STATE ADR (2001) *Disp. Resol. Mag.* (Summer).

VAN WINKLE, John (2000) *Mediation — A Path Back for the Lost Lawyer.* Washington, D.C.: ABA.

WALLERSTEIN, Judith S., and Sandra BLAKESLEE (1990) *Second Chances: Men, Women, and Children a Decade After Divorce.* New York: Houghton Mifflin.

WEISE, Richard H. (1989) "The ADR Program at Motorola," 5 *Neg. J.* 381.

WISSLER, Roselle (1996) *Ohio Attorneys' Experience with and Views of Alternative Dispute Resolution Procedures.* Columbus: Ohio Supreme Court.

ZEUGHAUSER, Peter R. (1997) "Price and Product: A Proposal for a Focused ADR Structure," *Alternatives* 1 (Nov.).

PART VI

DISPUTE RESOLUTION PROBLEMS

Chapter 13

Dispute Resolution Problems

PROBLEM 13.1: IRVING WESTON v. LAWYER'S PRESS, INC.,

In April 1995, Lawyer's Press, the second-largest U.S. publisher of legal books, entered into an agreement with Irving Weston to publish the session laws of various states and territories. Weston had previously acquired these rights. The Weston-Lawyer's agreement assigned them to Lawyer's in exchange for a royalty of 15 percent of sales. The agreement obligated Lawyer's to use "reasonable efforts" to promote the publication and to provide quarterly royalty reports and payments.

Sales of this publication did not meet expectations. In August 1998, Weston sued Lawyer's Press in federal court in the Southern District of New York. Weston alleged that Lawyer's failed to use reasonable efforts to promote the property and did not provide royalty reports and payments as agreed. Specifically, Weston alleged that Lawyer's did not expend sufficient promotional and sales efforts on the publication, failed to respond in a timely fashion to inquiries, failed to fill orders in a timely manner, and failed to respond to complaints about incomplete shipments. Weston alleged further that the publisher's royalty reports were inaccurate and incomplete and regularly understated sales and royalties due him. The complaint also charged loss of revenue of $40,000 to $50,000 yearly and damage to Weston's reputation of an unspecified amount. Separate counts alleged fraud and misrepresentation on the part of Lawyer's and sought punitive damages.

A second cause of action alleged that Lawyer's misappropriated another Weston idea—an annotated edition of the complete works of Felix Frankfurter. Weston alleged that he disclosed this idea to the publisher's management in 1995 when he negotiated the session laws deal. In 1997, Lawyer's did publish *The Complete Works of Felix Frankfurter*, annotated but with commentary by leading scholars. The publisher's serials editor contends that Lawyer's had this idea independent of and prior to Weston's alleged disclosure of the "annotated Frankfurter" idea (which the editor does not recall) and that, in any event, the "complete Frankfurter" with scholarly commentary is different from an "annotated Frankfurter."

With regard to the session laws publication, the publisher's marketing vice president contends that Lawyer's did use reasonable efforts to promote the publication but that it was "just a loser." The vice president contends that company documents show that annual promotional mailings were sent to those on the publishing house's standard mailing list, that its salespeople promoted the publication while visiting libraries, and that the books were displayed at law library conventions. However, in mid-1996 the Lawyer's Press salesforce went through a major reorganization and very few of the sales personnel from 1995 are still with the company. There is also a problem with respect to the royalties. In June 1997, the company's computer inadvertently erased all sales data on the session laws to that date, so sales and royalty figures had to be reconstructed from poorly organized hard-copy records. There is some possibility that the sales and royalty figures provided to Weston are off.

Weston is represented by a small New York City law firm that specializes in literary law. Lawyer's is represented by outside counsel from a large New York law firm and a member of its in-house staff. So far, no discovery has been taken and no motions have been filed. But emotional feelings run strong on both sides of the dispute, and all efforts to settle the case by traditional negotiations have failed.

As counsel for Lawyer's, what process would you suggest for resolving this dispute? Why?

PROBLEM 13.2: THE MATTER OF CASEY'S FEE

A class action suit filed under Title VII of the Civil Rights Act of 1964 charging an Ironworkers' Union local with racial discrimination in admitting members has been partially settled after six years of litigation on procedural issues and a year of mediated negotiations. The mediation consumed over 150 hours of meetings, some joint but most of them separate. Most of this time was devoted to the union's admissions procedure. Ultimately, a tentative settlement, quite intricate but satisfactory to both parties, was reached on this issue. The parties then turned to the issues of (1) the amount of damages due to 10 individual plaintiffs alleged to have been discriminatorily denied admission and (2) the amount of attorney's fees due to John Casey, plaintiffs' attorney. While defendant agreed to damages for the individual plaintiffs totaling $500,000 (contingent on a resolution of the attorney's fee issue), and while defendant agreed in principle to payment of a fee to Casey, since he would be entitled to a fee if plaintiffs prevailed in court, negotiations on the amount of Casey's fee quickly reached impasse.

Casey asserts that he has worked 3,000 hours on the case, and demands payment at his current rate of $200 per hour, plus a multiplier of 1.5 because of the difficulty of the case — a total of $900,000. Defendant doubts that Casey has actually worked 3,000 hours and contends that he should be paid at the rates he was charging at the time the work was done without any multiplier since the case was settled, not won. Thus, defendant has countered with an offer of $250,000 (2,500 hours at $100 per hour, which it calculates as the average rate charged by Casey over the course of the litigation).

Casey has offered to submit the fee issue to the federal district judge to whom the case is currently assigned (the fourth judge on this case in its seven-year history) for his resolution. The defendant has refused to agree to such a submission. Its position is that it does not want to litigate an issue on which the only question is how much more it will pay than the amount it has already agreed to, and that if it must litigate, it will insist on litigating all issues in the case, not just the fee issue.

If you were the mediator in this case, what suggestions might you make to break the impasse?

PROBLEM 13.3: AMERICAN CAN CO. v. WISCONSIN ELECTRIC POWER CO.

During the early 1990s American Can Company (ACC) established its Americology Division to exploit a process it had developed for turning municipal waste into supplemental boiler fuel (SBF). In January 1995, Americology reached an agreement with the City of Milwaukee to take that city's waste and to process it. Americology subsequently worked out an agreement by which Wisconsin Electric Power Co. (WEPCO) would take that refuse-derived fuel and burn it at two of its generating units. The ACC-WEPCO agreement called for an extensive testing program during which WEPCO would determine the maximum amount of SBF it could burn. The economic risk was to be all ACC's: the agreement was on a no-profit, no-loss basis for WEPCO. The value of this agreement to WEPCO was that if SBF proved to be a feasible fuel, WEPCO would have available a locally generated fuel to supplement coal. This would both reduce its dependence on coal and, by making productive use of municipal garbage, generate local goodwill.

Under the ACC-WEPCO agreement, the cost to WEPCO of burning the fuel (including, for example, all the cost of facility modifications) was to be no more than the cost of an equivalent number of BTUs of coal. Further, WEPCO was to maintain complete operating control of the burning process.

Paragraph 4 of the agreement provided in part as follows:

> On completion of the evaluation and start-up phases, the parties shall review the utilization and burning of SBF in the units. Should the parties agree that it is economically and technically feasible to burn SBF in the units, this agreement shall continue as provided. Should the parties disagree as to such feasibility, they will make every effort to reconcile their differences, employing if necessary at their shared expense, a mutually acceptable independent expert to review, evaluate, and render a nonbinding advisory opinion as to such feasibility. If after receiving such advisory opinion, the parties are in good faith still unable to agree as to such feasibility, this agreement shall terminate in accordance with its provisions.

As time went on, WEPCO encountered considerable difficulties in burning the fuel (including an EPA air pollution citation) and ultimately decided that it was not "technically and economically feasible" to continue the effort. Consistent with its view of the contract, WEPCO ceased burning the fuel. Subsequent negotiations between the parties at the technical and managerial level on what to do next were fruitless. After an escalating exchange of threatening letters, ACC commenced suit against WEPCO alleging breach of contract and claiming damages of $40 million. In essence, ACC contended that WEPCO breached the agreement by:

1. Not burning to the maximum capability of the units;
2. Not making all the modifications necessary to burn SBF (as required by paragraph 3 of the agreement) despite ACC's willingness to pay for the modifications;
3. Not fairly conducting all the tests required to reach a proper evaluation of SBF burning; and

4. Not completing the evaluation period required by the contract or submitting the issue of technical and economic feasibility to an independent expert as required by paragraph 4.

WEPCO has responded with a counterclaim for $20 million, alleging that its actual costs attributable to burning fuel—including the damage allegedly done to a turbine shaft—exceeded the amount of previous billings to Americology by that amount. Meanwhile, the Americology recycling facility and the two WEPCO boilers that were modified to burn SBF stand idle.

According to the general counsel for both ACC and WEPCO, the lawsuit bristles with factual and contract interpretation issues. The technical issues are particularly intricate, potentially necessitating, among numerous other things, an hour-by-hour review and evaluation of the operating history of two large electric generating units over a period of several years. The technical issues will also require close analysis of the state of the art in the developing refuse utilization industry. The factual complexities of the case will undoubtedly result in an extremely lengthy discovery process and trial. The parties estimate that legal and expert fees and costs to trial will run to several million dollars and that the trial will take 75 days. Initial discovery has validated these estimates.

ACC estimates its chances of winning $40 million at trial to be 75 percent. Thus, it values the case at $30 million, less transaction costs (estimated at $2 million), or $28 million, discounted to present value. WEPCO also estimates its chances of winning at 75 percent. Thus, it values ACC's claim at a maximum of $10 million plus its transaction costs (also estimated at $2 million), or $12 million, discounted to present value. The parties hold similarly disparate views regarding the likelihood that each will prevail on WEPCO's counterclaim; WEPCO views the claim as worth $16 million, ACC views it as worth $4 million. The difference between the parties' expected values of the case is thus $28 million.

As a neutral ADR consultant, what process would you suggest for resolving this dispute? Why?

PROBLEM 13.4: THE MATTER OF THE HAL 2001 COMPUTER

In August 1997, Leasco, a computer leasing company, bought 150 HAL 2001 Information Processors from the HAL Corporation, fully equipped and with software included, for a purchase price of $5 million. The purchase was made on a standard HAL sales contract having a payment schedule of $90,000 per month covering principal and interest. Shortly after the end of the warranty period, Leasco stopped paying. Collection efforts by HAL failed.

In March 1998, HAL Corp. filed a lawsuit against Leasco in federal district court in Chicago, where Leasco has its principal place of business. HAL's complaint alleges that Leasco owes $320,000 in overdue installments and is in default in the amount of $4,680,000, which represents the total balance due under an acceleration clause.

Leasco's answer and counterclaim alleges that HAL breached its delivery and maintenance obligations and misrepresented the performance capabilities of the 2001. Specifically, Leasco alleges that various system components and software packages were delivered late, that there were many difficulties with the equipment that was delivered, that HAL service was slow and inadequate, causing considerable downtime for end-users, and that the systems could not perform many of the functions that HAL salespersons claimed they could. In a second counterclaim, Leasco alleges that HAL's actions were part of an attempt to drive Leasco out of the leasing business, in violation of the antitrust laws. HAL has a subsidiary in the computer leasing business, and Leasco contends that HAL sought to drive it out of business to aid the HAL subsidiary. Leasco seeks $10 million in actual damages on the fraud claim and $50 million (before trebling) on the antitrust claim.

HAL's internal investigation indicates that there were some delays in delivery but nothing beyond the usual delays that can be expected with a new product of this sort. The HAL service record is mixed, but HAL maintenance personnel contend that any deficiencies were caused by Leasco's own delays in calling for service in order to avoid extra charges for "after work" hours.

As Counsel for Leasco, what process would you suggest for resolving this dispute? Why?

PROBLEM 13.5: CINCINNATI FOODS

Cincinnati Foods, a large food processing company, has asked your law firm to write a dispute resolution clause for its form contracts with about 50 farm operators providing potatoes for Cincinnati Foods' frozen fried potatoes. Disputes between Cincinnati Foods and its potato suppliers are frequent, growing out of such matters as the quality of the potatoes and the appropriate price for them. These disputes have led to substantial turnover in suppliers, interruption in potato supplies, and temporary curtailments in production of frozen fries. Still, there has been no litigation arising out of these disputes, since the farm operators lack the resources to sue.

What dispute resolution clause will you recommend?

PROBLEM 13.6: DYNA-MO CO.

Dyna-Mo Co., a computer software manufacturer, has a workforce of 500 employees. None of these employees are represented by a union, and Dyna-Mo would like that situation to continue. In recent months, top management has become concerned that some lower-level supervisory personnel may be treating employees unfairly. In order to provide a means for such employees to present claims to management in an orderly fashion, Dyna-Mo institutes a mediation procedure. The first three grievances presented under the procedure involve claims of unfair discharge.

Dyna-Mo has asked you to serve as the mediator for these and all subsequent claims. Would you agree to do so? Why?

PROBLEM 13.7: THE CASE OF NEIGHBORHOOD CARE, INC.

You have been asked by a friend who lives on the east side of town if you have any suggestions for heading off what he believes may become an ugly confrontation between his church and some of its neighbors over a church proposal to lease space to a mental health organization.

Your friend has given you the following position papers drawn up by church leaders and the neighborhood association.

EAST SIDE CHURCH
Expanding Needed Services

We have, after careful consideration, decided to rent space in our building to Neighborhood Care, Inc. This is a highly regarded, not-for-profit mental health organization that provides recreational counseling services to residents of our general area. They are certified by the state department of mental health. They operate three facilities in neighboring towns. We've checked with officials in those towns and heard only good things about them.

Neighborhood Care, Inc. proposes to operate its program from 9 A.M. to 9 P.M. six days a week, although it may take them a year or two to reach that scale of operation. They will provide one-on-one counseling during the 9 to 3 hours, by appointment only. They expect to provide counseling for 10 to 12 clients a day. They will also offer recreational activities for 20 to 30 clients each day from 3 to 9 P.M.

Our church feels strongly that mentally retarded teenagers and adults who have been deinstitutionalized deserve a comfortable setting in which to meet and play. Neighborhood Care, Inc. will be serving clients from our own community and nearby towns.

Our church has lost many of its members over the past 10 to 15 years. Our congregation has dispersed. To maintain our physical plant we must generate new income. Neighborhood Care's request came to us at just the right time. From what we've heard, they have no other place available to them at the reasonable price we have offered. While our building may not be exactly what they wanted, it will serve their needs in the short term. In the future, they may be willing to pay to renovate the lower floor of the church.

Neighborhood Care assures us that they will always have a trained counselor on hand and a trained psychiatric nurse on call.

Residents of almost every community oppose halfway houses and other facilities designed to serve the mentally disadvantaged. We expect opposition, and we see no reason to sit down and talk with selfish people who care only about themselves. We are prepared to withstand any abuse. This important service to the community must be provided.

The residents of the abutting neighborhood have complained in the past about everything. The problem, in our view, is that they are of a different faith.

EAST SIDE NEIGHBORHOOD ASSOCIATION, INC.
Preserving Neighborhood Values

We have heard rumors that the church on the corner is going to lease space in its building to an organization that provides services to the mentally retarded, some of whom have recently been released from mental hospitals. We are angry and frightened. As far as we are concerned, this kind of activity has no place in our quiet residential neighborhood. We have every intention of turning out in force at the upcoming Zoning Board hearing to protest the granting of a permit for this facility.

At a recent meeting of neighbors opposed to the facility, the following demands were drawn up:

1. The church should not be allowed to rent its space for any use that will disturb the neighborhood. Many of us have lived here for more than 25 years, and we've paid our taxes and kept up our homes. We deserve peace and quiet.

2. If mentally disturbed people are attracted to this area in large numbers, there is bound to be trouble. Some of our neighbors are elderly and have no ability to defend themselves. This facility will cause some of us to become shut-ins.
3. There have been break-ins in the area. This facility is likely to increase the crime rate. It will be impossible to walk outside in front of our homes.
4. We are opposed to any new activity in the neighborhood that will increase parking and traffic hazards, increase noise levels, and diminish the value of our property.
5. In the past the church has expanded its activity (i.e., Sunday school and day care) without consulting us. The results have been completely unacceptable—cars parking on our lawns, strangers coming and going at all hours. We demand that no additional activity be allowed.
6. We've heard that the group that the church proposes to rent to—Neighborhood Care, Inc.—will not be able to provide full-time supervision for the disturbed patients it hopes to serve. We are convinced that the church is not an appropriate setting in which to provide health services. Moreover, we are concerned that neither the church nor Neighborhood Care, Inc. will be able to deal with the disturbed people who will wander in off the streets once they hear that a place to stay is available.
7. If the Zoning Board is not empowered to stop this intrusion into our community, we insist that very strict conditions be imposed: (a) hours of operation must be limited to 10 A.M. to 2 P.M. four days a week with no activity on Fridays or weekends; (b) no more than 10 people in the church at any time; (c) parking only in the church parking lot; (d) the church must accept responsibility for any and all damage caused by strangers in the neighborhood; and (e) no noise or trash.
8. Our group is prepared to go to court if necessary. We have contacted our representative to demand that the Board of Aldermen undertake an investigation to be certain that Neighborhood Care, Inc. is qualified to run such a facility. If this kind of facility is so important, why doesn't the city government offer space (at no cost) in one of our public buildings?

What suggestions do you have for resolving this dispute? What problems do you anticipate? How would you attempt to deal with these problems?

PROBLEM 13.8: WHITTAMORE v. FAIRVIEW CLINIC*

Three years ago, Dr. Richard Singson, director of the Fairview Medical Clinic, the only medical service provider in a small rural town, was seeking two physicians to fill open positions on his staff. After several months of extensive and difficult recruiting, he hired two doctors, Andrew and Jane Whittamore, to fill the respective positions of pediatrician and gynecologist. The fact that the doctors were married did not seem to be a problem at the time they were hired.

Fairview Clinic liked to keep its doctors and generally paid them well for their work with patients. The clinic was also concerned about maintaining its patient load and income and required each doctor joining the practice to sign a five-year contract detailing what he or she was to be paid and what conditions would apply should the contract be broken by either party. One of these conditions was a

*This exercise has been adapted from Moore, 1996.

no-competition clause stating that should a doctor choose to leave the clinic prior to the expiration of the contract, he or she could not practice medicine in the town or county in which the Fairview Clinic was located without paying a penalty. This clause was designed to protect the clinic from competition and to prohibit a doctor from joining the staff, building up a practice, and then leaving with his or her patients to start a private competitive practice before the term of the contract had expired.

When Andrew and Jane joined the Fairview Clinic staff, they both signed the contract and initialed all the clauses. Both doctors performed well in their jobs at the clinic and were respected by their colleagues and patients. Unfortunately, their personal life did not fare so well. The Whittamores' marriage went into a steady decline almost as soon as they began working at Fairview. Their arguments increased, and the amount of tension between them mounted to the point that they decided to divorce. Since both doctors wanted to be near their two young children, they agreed to continue living in the same town.

Since each physician at the clinic has a specialty, they all relied on consultations with their colleagues. Thus, some interaction between the estranged couple was inevitable. Over time the hostility between the couple grew to such a point that the Whittamores decided one of them should leave the clinic for their own good and that of other clinic staff. Since they believed Andrew, as a pediatrician, would have an easier time finding patients, they agreed that he was the one who should go.

Andrew explained his situation to Singson and noted that because he would be leaving for the benefit of the clinic, he expected that no penalty would be assessed for breaking the contract two-and-a-half years early and that the no-competition clause would not be applied to him.

Singson was surprised and upset that his finely tuned staff was going to lose one of its most respected members. And he was shocked by Whittamore's announcement that he planned to stay in town and open a medical practice. Singson visualized the long-range impact of Whittamore's decision: the doctor would leave and set up a competing practice, and many of his patients would leave the clinic, and follow him. The clinic would lose revenue from the doctor's fees, lose patients, incur the cost of recruiting a new doctor, and, if the no-competition clause was not enforced, establish a bad precedent for managing doctors in the clinic. Singson responded that the no-competition clause would be enforced if Whittamore wanted to practice within the county, and the clinic would have to arrive at a penalty for violating the contract. He estimated that the penalty could be as much as 100 percent of the revenues that Whittamore might earn in the two-and-a-half years remaining on his contract (or approximately $125,000).

Whittamore was irate at Singson's response. He considered it unreasonable and irresponsible. If that was the way the game was to be played, he threatened, he would leave and set up a practice, and Singson could take him to court to try to get his money. Singson responded that he would get an injunction against the practice if necessary and would demand the full amount if pushed into a corner. Whittamore left Singson's office mumbling that he was going to "get that son of a gun" as he went down the hall.

What are the major impediments to a negotiated settlement of this dispute? What kinds of ADR methods might be useful in this case? Why? What outcomes might they develop that a court could not? If you had been consulted by Singson and Whittamore at the time they signed their initial contract, what advice would you have given them?

PROBLEM 13.9: UNIVERSITY HOUSING DISPUTES

Disputes between university area landlords and tenants, as well as among roommates, have begun to interfere with the quality of life for students and have caused some of the landlords for the best managed properties to threaten to sell. University officials have hired you to set up a nonbinding dispute resolution program for complaints between university area landlords and student tenants and among roommates, and have indicated that they will budget $50,000 per year for the program.

Most area landlords will agree to include a clause in their form lease that requires resort to the university program for all disputes with their tenants, as long as the process will not delay a court filing by more than two weeks. Local tenants' groups also agree that they will urge tenants to agree to the clause, if the program is fair.

Draft the clause and design the university program. Be certain to address the following issues: How will you respond to different levels of access to legal expertise between landlords and tenants? Do you propose that the university seek enactment of a statute to assist the operation of the program? What will be included in the clause and what will be the program rules about confidentiality? What will be the qualifications for the third-party neutrals?

PROBLEM 13.10: GRISWOLD v. LANGDELL

The City of Langdell is seriously in need of a site for a new solid waste landfill. Its existing site is under closure orders from the State Department of Natural Resources (DNR) because the landfill has reached capacity and is threatening to pollute ground water and a nearby trout stream. Langdell's preferred location is outside its boundary, and it annexes 150 acres in the adjacent town of Griswold and proceeds with site development and permitting procedures. A manufacturing company in Langdell vigorously supports this decision because it will be a principal user of the landfill and will profit from its proximity. The company is joined by the union of its employees and other members of Langdell's economic community in lobbying for this site.

Unwilling to be the neighbors of the new "dump," certain residents of Griswold, already resentful of Langdell's encroachments, wage an active campaign against Langdell's chosen site. Eventually they succeed in winning the support of Griswold officials. These officials first use informal political means to try to pressure Langdell into reconsidering its decision. However, Griswold stands virtually alone when nearby towns, fearing they might be considered as alternative sites, offer only nominal support to Griswold.

Griswold resolves to take all available legal means to stop the project. It files an appeal to DNR and a court action challenging the annexation and the environmental impact assessment for the landfill. It also passes an ordinance limiting the use of town roads needed for access to the site.

Just as landfill construction is getting under way, Griswold succeeds in winning a three-day restraining order to halt development. The judge indicates, however, that he would hesitate to give favorable consideration to an injunction. Meanwhile, Langdell moves to invalidate Griswold's road ordinance.

Langdell has invested two years in studying various sites and developing this particular one. It faces a major setback if Griswold succeeds in having this site rejected. The weather is also a factor. It is the end of summer, and Langdell planned to complete construction by winter.

Griswold has already spent more than originally appropriated to fight the landfill. While it has succeeded in delaying the project, it has no assurance of eventual victory. Town residents who live a distance from the site are beginning to criticize the amount of money being spent on litigation. Some residents are also dissatisfied that more effort is not being exerted to solve Griswold's own solid waste problems.

Another party to the dispute is Environmentalists in the Public Interest (EPI), a statewide citizen organization dedicated to acting as a watchdog of the DNR's regulatory activities. EPI believes that the DNR may have violated the State Environmental Policy Act in its handling of this case and is contesting the adequacy of the agency's review of alternative sites and the required documentation of that review. Although EPI has joined Griswold in petitioning the Circuit Court for an order to have DNR amend its documentation, the group has been reluctant to commit its limited resources to a full-scale legal battle. It does not have reason to believe the landfill itself will cause environmental harm, and it is aware of the harm threatened by the continued use of the old facility.

The DNR, too, is anxious, both because of the pollution threatened by Langdell's overloaded existing landfill and because the DNR procedures and decisions are the subject of legal challenge by Griswold and EPI.

You are director of the State Office of Dispute Resolution and are considering becoming involved in this controversy. Should you do so? If so, how would you proceed? What obstacles would you anticipate? How would you deal with those obstacles?

PROBLEM 13.11: CITIZENS v. WESTERN NUCLEAR CORP.

Western Nuclear Corporation has been engaged for approximately 15 years in the generation of electricity at its nuclear plant in central Michiana. It is one of the largest nuclear facilities in the United States, with an average net annual profit of $300 million and a net worth of approximately $3 billion.

Approximately a year ago, state environmental officials discovered that Western was discharging small amounts of radioactively contaminated water into the ground and had been doing so for approximately 10 years. Horrified by this news, a group of citizens consisting of all persons living within a three-mile radius of the Western plant (the area that the Michiana Environmental Commission determined had been reached by the contaminated ground water) filed a class action suit against Western, seeking $500 million in damages.

Western concedes its negligence in allowing the contaminated water to escape into the ground but contends that the amounts involved were so small as to cause no injury to any of the plaintiffs. The plaintiffs concede that none of them have yet become ill, but they contend that their lives have been ruined because they live in constant fear of the potential long-term effects on their health and that of any children they may have resulting from 10 years of exposure to radioactive water.

Although no case raising the damages issues here presented has previously been decided, plaintiffs' attorneys are certain that a jury from this area will understand and sympathize with the plaintiffs' fears and issue a huge verdict in their favor. Defendant's attorneys, on the other hand, are equally sure that they will prevail in their contention that after 10 years there is absolutely no evidence of any harm to any plaintiff and that plaintiffs are entitled to no recovery whatsoever. Negotiations aimed at settling the suit have reached an impasse.

As a neutral ADR consultant, what process would you suggest to resolve this dispute. Why?

PROBLEM 13.12: SATCOM, INC. v. TELECOM

Worldsat, a joint venture company, was established to seek a license for, and, if successful, to operate, a worldwide satellite communications system intended to increase the range and the reliability of portable cellular phones. One of the two joint venturers, Satcom, Inc., had primary responsibility for satellite construction; the other, Telecom, which was composed of three corporations acting as equal partners, had primary responsibility for satellite operations.

Both joint venturers knew that they would have to invest substantial amounts of money in this project and that there was no guarantee that they would receive a license. (The Federal Communications Commission (FCC) had announced that only one applicant would be granted a license.) The bulk of the up-front investment was to consist of designing and building a prototype satellite. After lengthy negotiations with Telecom's general counsel, Satcom's president agreed to undertake that task, at Satcom's expense, on the condition that if the license were awarded to another applicant, Satcom would be reimbursed for 50 percent of its expenses, plus interest, by Telecom. The contract also contained a force majeure clause, which provided that if the joint venture could not be carried out for reasons beyond the control of either party, neither party would be liable to the other.

After Satcom had completed its work, at a cost of $400 million, the FCC announced that, because of limited world spectrum availability, it would not grant a license to any of the applicants. Satcom demanded $200 million, plus interest, from Telecom on the basis of the reimbursement clause. Telecom refused, arguing that the reimbursement clause applied only if a license were granted to another applicant, not if *no* license were granted. The latter situation, Telecom argued, was controlled by the force majeure clause, under which no recovery was available. Satcom responded that Telecom ignored the purpose of the cost allocation provision, which was to share the loss if the joint venture failed because it did not receive a license. This provision, designed specifically for this contingency, argued Satcom, ought to prevail over the general force majeure clause.

Satcom brought suit against Telecom seeking $200 million in damages. After three years of discovery and motions, nothing has been resolved. Each party has incurred approximately $2 million in attorney's fees and expenses to date, and each anticipates spending at least another $2 million in fees and expenses if the case goes to trial. Demands on executives' time have been and will continue to be great.

Settlement negotiations, carried on by Satcom's and Telecom's general counsel, have been desultory and marked by frequent accusations of bad faith. Telecom's general counsel insists that he negotiated only a limited reimbursement provision with Satcom and has let it be known that he regards Satcom's contention to the contrary as frivolous and motivated by the desire of Satcom's president to keep his job. Telecom's most recent settlement offer, which it characterizes as a "nuisance payment," was $4 million; Satcom's most recent demand was $160 million. No trial date has yet been set, and the judge estimates that it will be at least two years to trial.

If you were Satcom's outside counsel, what advice might you give Satcom regarding an appropriate dispute resolution procedure?

PROBLEM 13.13: A NEIGHBORHOOD DISPUTE

Smith and Jones are neighbors who share a driveway. In the past year, there have been numerous instances in which one of them has blocked the other's car, leading to angry exchanges and threats of physical harm. Last week, things finally reached a boiling point. When Smith once again blocked Jones's car, Jones came out of his house and socked Smith on the jaw. Smith called the local police and said he wanted to file an assault charge against Jones.

If you were the prosecutor, would you refer this case to the Neighborhood Justice Center for mediation?

PROBLEM 13.14: THOMAS v. EAGLE RIFLE CO.

You represent the parents of Roger Thomas, a 15-year-old boy who accidentally shot and killed himself while playing with an air rifle manufactured by Eagle Rifle Co. Shortly after Roger's death, his parents brought suit against Eagle for negligence in manufacturing the rifle involved, as well as for breach of warranty in manufacturing a product not reasonably safe for purchasers in the age-group for which the product was intended. The suit seeks $5 million in damages.

According to Mr. and Mrs. Thomas, they intend to use whatever amount they recover from Eagle to warn other parents about the dangers of air rifles. If they receive any amount close to the $5 million they have demanded, they plan to establish a charitable foundation to carry out this publicity campaign. They do not, however, want this case to go to trial, as reliving the events leading to their son's death would be extremely painful for them.

You are aware of three similar suits against Eagle which have gone to trial in the last two years. In each of those suits, Eagle received a jury verdict in its favor. In two other suits, Eagle prevailed on motions for summary judgment. In each case its defense has been the same: Eagle takes all precautions to manufacture air rifles that are as safe as possible. Additionally, Eagle has spent substantial sums to publicize the inherent risks associated with air rifles. Under these circumstances, neither negligence nor breach of warranty claims are well-founded. Additionally, Eagle typically asserts that the purchaser has assumed whatever risks are inherent in the use of its air rifles.

What dispute resolution procedure would best serve your clients' interests in this matter? How would you estimate your chances of reaching agreement with counsel for Eagle on a dispute resolution procedure?

PROBLEM 13.15: THE VIRGINIA MEDICAL GROUP

The Virginia Medical Group (VMG) is an Independent Physician's Association (IPA), founded in 1985 by three physicians (Tom Lane, Diane Shawn, and Hal Ross) who thought that by joining with other physicians they could achieve two objectives: (1) negotiate better contracts with HMOs and insurance companies for the provision of medical services; (2) reduce their overhead costs by having a single office deal with the paperwork involved in their performing services pursuant to HMO and insurance company contracts. Lane and Shawn contributed $250 each and Ross contributed $500 to cover the costs of incorporating VMG and printing letterhead and brochures. Each of them received stock in proportion to the contribution made, with Lane and Shawn each receiving 25 percent of the VMG stock and Ross receiving 50 percent.

Over the next decade, VMG became quite successful. By 1997, it was composed of 35 physicians, each of whom had successful practices composed in substantial part of patients who were covered by HMO and insurance company contracts negotiated by VMG. The total number of such patients exceeded 30,000. Much of this growth was due to the energy, vision, and efforts of Ross, who had succeeded in negotiating profitable contracts with HMOs and insurance companies and in efficiently managing the administration of those contracts. Ross also maintained a busy medical practice as part of the VMG group. Over the same period of time, Lane and Shawn had less and less to do with VMG. By 1997, neither was practicing with VMG or had any relationship with VMG other than stock ownership.

In July 1997, a local hospital indicated interest in purchasing a controlling interest in VMG and offered $4 million for 51 percent of the VMG stock. Lane and Shawn were willing to sell their 50 percent, but Ross did not want to turn over control of VMG to a hospital. When the 35 physician members of VMG learned of the hospital's offer, and the possibility that it would be accepted, they were furious. First, they, like Ross, did not want VMG controlled by a hospital, which, they feared, would have interests quite different from those of the physicians. Second, they took the view that the value of VMG was the result of their skill as physicians, and that it was unthinkable that someone else, particularly Lane and Shawn, who had nothing to do with VMG other than a miniscule investment many years ago, should profit from their labor. Many of the physicians began talking about leaving VMG. As a result, the hospital withdrew its offer.

The termination of negotiations with the hospital calmed the situation temporarily, but the physicians, in discussions among themselves, expressed the fear that even though this sale had not taken place, they had no guarantee that a future sale would not take place, regardless of their opposition. To prevent that from happening, the physicians formed a group whose objective was to purchase the 50 percent stock ownership in VMG that was held by Lane and Shawn. The physicians' view was that if they held 50 percent of the stock, they could effectively block a sale, since they would never consent to a sale, and no purchaser who wanted control would have any interest in purchasing the remaining 50 percent held by Ross.

Efforts by the physicians to purchase the stock held by Lane and Shawn have, to date, been fruitless. The physicians offered $500,000 to each of them, a total of $1 million, but Lane and Shawn have said they want $1 million each and have refused to budge from that figure. Their view is that some day Ross will also be interested in selling his stock, and when that happens, the three of them can sell a controlling interest in VMG for at least the $4 million that the hospital offered.

Faced with this stalemate, many of the physicians are talking openly of abandoning VMG and starting another IPA. They have pointed out to Lane and Shawn that if enough of them do leave VMG, it will be worth nothing, as will Lane's and Shawn's investment. Lane and Shawn have responded that they doubt many physicians will leave VMG, which has contributed substantially to the success of their practices.

Lane's and Shawn's refusal to accept the physicians' offer, or to move at all off their $2 million demand, have further antagonized the physicians. From their perspective, Lane and Shawn are greedy profiteers, who invested a pittance, were lucky in their investment, and are now seeking to take unfair advantage of the very physicians who have been responsible for the success of their investment.

You are counsel for Ross, who has asked for your advice in this matter. In your conversations with Ross, the doctor has expressed genuine concern at the possibility that those doctors with the largest practices will leave VMG if the physicians are unable to obtain 50 percent of the stock, and so block all possibility of a sale. Ross is as opposed to a sale of VMG as are the other physicians, both because he believes in the principle of physicians controlling their own practices and because VMG has been his "baby" for so many years. For this reason, too, he would be desolate if VMG were to founder because the key physicians left.

Ross has spoken to Lane and Shawn in an effort to persuade them to accept the physicians' $1 million offer, but they have refused to do so or to reduce their asking price below $2 million. Ross sees his "baby" on the verge of collapse and has asked for your advice. What will you tell him?

PROBLEM 13.16: DUE PROCESS FOR MEDIATION CASES?

A student of mediation who is also an experienced litigator recently expressed surprise that mediation is so devoid of many of the basic procedural protections used in litigation, such as (1) pleadings, (2) discovery, (3) res judicata, (4) evidentiary rules, (5) use of transcripts, and (6) sanctions for perjury. She also wonders why we do not have (7) a compilation of past mediation agreements, similar to the reports of court decisions, or (8) court review (akin to an appellate review) of mediated agreements. Lastly she is puzzled why (9) mediators are not required to follow the law applicable to a particular situation.

She is thinking of proposing that some or all of these devices be incorporated into mediation. To help her in this undertaking, she asks you as an ADR expert to advise her whether her concern is justified, and, if so, what, if any, aspects of litigation could and should usefully be incorporated into mediation.

APPENDICES

Appendix A

Dispute Resolution Clauses

CPR INSTITUTE FOR DISPUTE RESOLUTION, DRAFTER'S DESKBOOK—DISPUTE RESOLUTION CLAUSES

Appendix A (2002)*

CPR MODEL CLAUSES AND SAMPLE LANGUAGE

PREAMBLE

Any dispute arising out of or relating to this Agreement shall be resolved in accordance with the procedures specified in this Article 00, which shall be the sole and exclusive procedures for the resolution of any such disputes.

CPR MODEL MULTI-STEP DISPUTE RESOLUTION CLAUSE

Negotiation Between Executives

(A) The parties shall attempt in good faith to resolve any dispute arising out of or relating to this [Agreement] [Contract] promptly by negotiation between executives who have authority to settle the controversy and who are at a higher level of management than the persons with direct responsibility for administration of this contract. Any party may give the other party written notice of any dispute not resolved in the normal course of business. Within [15] days after delivery of the notice, the receiving party shall submit to the other a written response. The notice and the response shall include (a) a statement of that party's position and a summary of arguments supporting that position, and (b) the name and title of the executive who will represent that party and of any other person who will accompany the executive. Within [30] days after delivery of the initial notice, the executives of both parties shall meet at a mutually acceptable time and place, and thereafter as

*The cited booklet, though focusing solely on business to business disputes, contains a large variety of alternative or supplemental clauses (e.g., for a minitrial or stand-alone mediation or arbitration proceeding, as well as for hybrid processes, such as med-arb). It also includes a valuable discussion of negotiationg various DR clauses and a compilation of clauses utilized by some major companies.

For another source, see American Arbitration Association, Drafting Dispute Resolution Clauses—A Practical Guide (2000).

often as they reasonably deem necessary, to attempt to resolve the dispute. All reasonable requests for information made by one party to the other will be honored.

All negotiations pursuant to this clause are confidential and shall be treated as compromise and settlement negotiations for purposes of applicable rules of evidence.

Mediation

(B) If the dispute has not been resolved by negotiation as provided herein within [45] days after delivery of the initial notice of negotiation, [or if the parties failed to meet within [20] days,] the parties shall endeavor to settle the dispute by mediation under the CPR Mediation Procedure [currently in effect OR in effect on the date of this Agreement], [provided, however, that if one party fails to participate in the negotiation as provided herein, the other party can initiate mediation prior to the expiration of the [45] days.] Unless otherwise agreed, the parties will select a mediator from the CPR Panels of Distinguished Neutrals.

Arbitration

(C) Any dispute arising out of or relating to this [Agreement] [Contract], including the breach, termination or validity thereof, which has not been resolved by mediation as provided herein [within [45] days after initiation of the mediation procedure] [within [30] days after appointment of a mediator], shall be finally resolved by arbitration in accordance with the CPR Rules of Non-Administered Arbitration [currently in effect OR in effect on the date of this Agreement], by [a sole arbitrator] [three independent and impartial arbitrators, of whom each party shall designate one] [three arbitrators of whom each party shall appoint one in accordance with the 'screened' appointment procedure provided in Rule 5.4] [three independent and impartial arbitrators, none of whom shall be appointed by either party]; [provided, however, that if one party fails to participate in either the negotiation or mediation as agreed herein, the other party can commence arbitration prior to the expiration of the time periods set forth above.] The arbitration shall be governed by the Federal Arbitration Act, 9 U.S.C. §§1-16, and judgment upon the award rendered by the arbitrator(s) may be entered by any court having jurisdiction thereof. The place of arbitration shall be (city, state).

Or Litigation

(C) If the dispute has not been resolved by mediation as provided herein [within [45] days after initiation of the mediation procedure] [within 30 days after appointment of a mediator], this Agreement does not preclude either party from initiating litigation [upon 00 days written notice to the other party]; [provided, however, that if one party fails to participate in either the negotiation or mediation as agreed herein, the other party can initiate litigation prior to the expiration of the time periods set forth above.]

[See also CPR Model Master Dispute Resolution Agreements at www.cpradr.org (OnLine Form Book).]

Appendix B

Federal Arbitration Act

FEDERAL ARBITRATION ACT

9 U.S.C. §§1 et seq.

§1. "Maritime Transactions" and "Commerce" Defined; Exceptions to Operation of Title

"Maritime transactions," as herein defined, means charter parties, bills of lading of water carriers, agreements relating to wharfage, supplies furnished vessels or repairs to vessels, collisions, or any other matters in foreign commerce which, if the subject of controversy, would be embraced within admiralty jurisdiction; "commerce," as herein defined, means commerce among the several States or with foreign nations, or in any Territory of the United States or in the District of Columbia, or between any such Territory and another, or between any such Territory and any State or foreign nation, or between the District of Columbia and any State or Territory or foreign nation, but nothing herein contained shall apply to contracts of employment of seamen, railroad employees, or any other class of workers engaged in foreign or interstate commerce.

§2. Validity, Irrevocability and Enforcement of Agreements to Arbitrate

A written provision in any maritime transaction or a contract evidencing a transaction involving commerce to settle by arbitration a controversy thereafter arising out of such contract or transaction, or the refusal to perform the whole or any part thereof, or an agreement in writing to submit to arbitration an existing controversy arising out of such a contract, transaction, or refusal, shall be valid, irrevocable, and enforceable, save upon such grounds as exist at law or in equity for the revocation of any contract.

§3. Stay of Proceedings Where Issue Therein Referable to Arbitration

If any suit or proceeding be brought in any of the courts of the United States upon any issue referable to arbitration under an agreement in writing for such arbitration, the court in which such suit is pending, upon being satisfied that the issue involved in such suit or proceeding is referable to arbitration under such an agreement, shall on application of one of the parties stay the trial of the action until such arbitration has been had in accordance with the terms of the agreement, providing the applicant for the stay is not in default in proceeding with such arbitration.

§4. Failure to Arbitrate Under Agreement; Petition to United States Court Having Jurisdiction for Order to Compel Arbitration; Notice and Service Thereof; Hearing and Determination

A party aggrieved by the alleged failure, neglect, or refusal of another to arbitrate under a written agreement for arbitration may petition any United States district court which, save for such agreement, would have jurisdiction under Title 28, in a civil action or in admiralty of the subject matter of a suit arising out of the controversy between the parties, for an order directing that such arbitration proceed in the manner provided for in such agreement. Five days' notice in writing of such application shall be served upon the party in default. Service thereof shall be made in the manner provided by the Federal Rules of Civil Procedure. The court shall hear the parties, and upon being satisfied that the making of the agreement for arbitration or the failure to comply therewith is not in issue, the court shall make an order directing the parties to proceed to arbitration in accordance with the terms of the agreement. The hearing and proceedings, under such agreement, shall be within the district in which the petition for an order directing such arbitration is filed. If the making of the arbitration agreement or the failure, neglect, or refusal to perform the same be in issue, the court shall proceed summarily to the trial thereof. If no jury trial be demanded by the party alleged to be in default, or if the matter in dispute is within admiralty jurisdiction, the court shall hear and determine such issue. Where such an issue is raised, the party alleged to be in default may, except in cases of admiralty, on or before the return day of the notice of application, demand a jury trial of such issue, and upon such demand the court shall make an order referring the issue or issues to a jury in the manner provided by the Federal Rules of Civil Procedure, or may specially call a jury for that purpose. If the jury find that no agreement in writing for arbitration was made or that there is no default in proceeding thereunder, the proceeding shall be dismissed. If the jury find that an agreement for arbitration was made in writing and that there is a default in proceeding thereunder, the court shall make an order summarily directing the parties to proceed with the arbitration in accordance with the terms thereof.

§5. Appointment of Arbitrators or Umpire

If in the agreement provision be made for a method of naming or appointing an arbitrator or arbitrators or an umpire, such method shall be followed; but if no method be provided therein, or if a method be provided and any party thereto shall fail to avail himself of such method, or if for any other reason there shall be a lapse in the naming of an arbitrator or arbitrators or umpire, or in filling a vacancy, then upon the application of either party to the controversy the court shall designate and appoint an arbitrator or arbitrators or umpire, as the case may require, who shall act under the said agreement with the same force and effect as if he or they had been specifically named therein; and unless otherwise provided in the agreement the arbitration shall be by a single arbitrator.

§6. Application Heard as Motion

Any application to the court hereunder shall be made and heard in the manner provided by law for the making and hearing of motions, except as otherwise herein expressly provided.

§7. Witnesses Before Arbitrators; Fees; Compelling Attendance

The arbitrators selected either as prescribed in this title or otherwise, or a majority of them, may summon in writing any person to attend before them or any of them as a witness and in a proper case to bring with him or them any book, record, document, or paper which may be deemed material as evidence in the case. The fees for such attendance shall be the same as the fees of witnesses before masters of the United States courts. Said summons shall issue in the name of the arbitrator or arbitrators, or a majority of them, and shall be signed by the arbitrators, or a majority of them, and shall be directed to the said person and shall be served in the same manner as subpoenas to appear and testify before the court; if any person or persons so summoned to testify shall refuse or neglect to obey said summons, upon petition the United States district court for the district in which such arbitrators, or a majority of them, are sitting may compel the attendance of such person or persons before said arbitrator or arbitrators, or punish said person or persons for contempt in the same manner provided by law for securing the attendance of witnesses or their punishment for neglect or refusal to attend in the courts of the United States.

§8. Proceedings Begun by Libel in Admiralty and Seizure of Vessel or Property

If the basis of jurisdiction be a cause of action otherwise justiciable in admiralty, then, notwithstanding anything herein to the contrary, the party claiming to be aggrieved may begin his proceeding hereunder by libel and seizure of the vessel or other property of the other party according to the usual course of admiralty proceedings, and the court shall then have jurisdiction to direct the parties to proceed with the arbitration and shall retain jurisdiction to enter its decree upon the award.

§9. Award of Arbitrators; Confirmation; Jurisdiction; Procedure

If the parties in their agreement have agreed that a judgment of the court shall be entered upon the award made pursuant to the arbitration, and shall specify the court, then at any time within one year after the award is made any party to the arbitration may apply to the court so specified for an order confirming the award, and thereupon the court must grant such an order unless the award is vacated, modified, or corrected as prescribed in sections 10 and 11 of this title. If no court is specified in the agreement of the parties, then such application may be made to the United States court in and for the district within which such award was made. Notice of the application shall be served upon the adverse party, and thereupon the court shall have jurisdiction of such party as though he had appeared generally in the proceeding. If the adverse party is a resident of the district within which the award was made, such service shall be made upon the adverse party or his attorney as prescribed by law for service of notice of motion in an action in the same court. If the adverse party shall be a nonresident, then the notice of the application shall be served by the marshal of any district within which the adverse party may be found in like manner as other process of the court.

§10. Same; Vacation; Grounds; Rehearing

(a) In any of the following cases the United States court in and for the district wherein the award was made may make an order vacating the award upon the application of any party to the arbitration—

(1) Where the award was procured by corruption, fraud, or undue means.

(2) Where there was evident partiality or corruption in the arbitrators, or either of them.

(3) Where the arbitrators were guilty of misconduct in refusing to postpone the hearing, upon sufficient cause shown, or in refusing to hear evidence pertinent and material to the controversy; or of any other misbehavior by which the rights of any party have been prejudiced.

(4) Where the arbitrators exceeded their powers, or so imperfectly executed them that a mutual, final, and definite award upon the subject matter submitted was not made.

(5) Where an award is vacated and the time within which the agreement required the award to be made has not expired the court may, in its discretion, direct a rehearing by the arbitrators.

(b) The United States district court for the district wherein an award was made that was issued pursuant to section 580 of title 5 may make an order vacating the award upon the application of a person, other than a party to the arbitration, who is adversely affected or aggrieved by the award, if the use of arbitration or the award is clearly inconsistent with the factors set forth in section 572 of title 5.

§11. Same; Modification or Correction; Grounds; Order

In either of the following cases the United States court in and for the district wherein the award was made may make an order modifying or correcting the award upon the application of any party to the arbitration —

(a) Where there was an evident material miscalculation of figures or an evident material mistake in the description of any person, thing, or property referred to in the award.

(b) Where the arbitrators have awarded upon a matter not submitted to them, unless it is a matter not affecting the merits of the decision upon the matter submitted.

(c) Where the award is imperfect in matter of form not affecting the merits of the controversy.

The order may modify and correct the award, so as to effect the intent thereof and promote justice between the parties.

§12. Notice of Motions to Vacate or Modify; Service; Stay of Proceedings

Notice of a motion to vacate, modify, or correct an award must be served upon the adverse party or his attorney within three months after the award is filed or delivered. If the adverse party is a resident of the district within which the award was made, such service shall be made upon the adverse party or his attorney as prescribed by law for service of notice of motion in an action in the same court. If the adverse party shall be a nonresident then the notice of the application shall be served by the marshal of any district within which the adverse party may be found in like manner as other process of the court. For the purposes of the motion any judge who might make an order to stay the proceedings in an action brought in the same court may make an order, to be served with the notice of motion, staying the proceedings of the adverse party to enforce the award.

§13. Papers Filed with Order on Motions; Judgment; Docketing; Force and Effect; Enforcement

The party moving for an order confirming, modifying, or correcting an award shall, at the time such order is filed with the clerk for the entry of judgment thereon, also file the following papers with the clerk:

(a) The agreement; the selection or appointment, if any, of an additional arbitrator or umpire; and each written extension of the time, if any, within which to make the award.

(b) The award.

(c) Each notice, affidavit, or other paper used upon an application to confirm, modify, or correct the award, and a copy of each order of the court upon such an application.

The judgment shall be docketed as if it was rendered in an action.

The judgment so entered shall have the same force and effect, in all respects, as, and be subject to all the provisions of law relating to, a judgment in an action; and it may be enforced as if it had been rendered in an action in the court in which it is entered.

§14. Contracts Not Affected

This title shall not apply to contracts made prior to January 1, 1926.

§15. Inapplicability of the Act of State Doctrine

Enforcement of arbitral agreements, confirmation of arbitral awards, and execution upon judgments based on orders confirming such awards shall not be refused on the basis of the Act of State doctrine.

§16. Appeals

(a) An appeal may be taken from—

(1) an order—

(A) refusing a stay of any action under section 3 of this title,

(B) denying a petition under section 4 of this title to order arbitration to proceed,

(C) denying an application under section 206 of this title to compel arbitration,

(D) confirming or denying confirmation of an award or partial award, or

(E) modifying, correcting, or vacating an award;

(2) an interlocutory order granting, continuing, or modifying an injunction against an arbitration that is subject to this title; or

(3) a final decision with respect to an arbitration that is subject to this title.

(b) Except as otherwise provided in section 1292(b) of title 28, an appeal may not be taken from an interlocutory order—

(1) granting a stay of any action under section 3 of this title;

(2) directing arbitration to proceed under section 4 of this title;

(3) compelling arbitration under section 206 of this title; or

(4) refusing to enjoin an arbitration that is subject to this title.

Appendix C

Uniform Arbitration Act*

1. Validity of Arbitration Agreement

A written agreement to submit any existing controversy to arbitration or a provision in a written contract to submit to arbitration any controversy thereafter arising between the parties is valid, enforceable and irrevocable, save upon such grounds as exist at law or in equity for the revocation of any contract. This act also applies to arbitration agreements between employers and employees or between their respective representatives [unless otherwise provided in the agreement].

2. Proceedings to Compel or Stay Arbitration

(a) On application of a party showing an agreement described in Section 1, and the opposing party's refusal to arbitrate, the Court shall order the parties to proceed with arbitration, but if the opposing party denies the existence of the agreement to arbitrate, the Court shall proceed summarily to the determination of the issue so raised and shall order arbitration if found for the moving party, otherwise, the application shall be denied.

(b) On application, the court may stay an arbitration proceeding commenced or threatened on a showing that there is no agreement to arbitrate. Such an issue, when in substantial and bona fide dispute, shall be forthwith and summarily tried and the stay ordered if found for the moving party. If found for the opposing party, the court shall order the parties to proceed to arbitration.

(c) If an issue referable to arbitration under the alleged agreement is involved in an action or proceeding pending in a court having jurisdiction to hear applications under subdivision (a) of this Section, the application shall be made therein. Otherwise and subject to Section 18, the application may be made in any court of competent jurisdiction.

(d) Any action or proceeding involving an issue subject to arbitration shall be stayed if an order for arbitration or an application therefor has been made under

*The National Conference of Commissioners on Uniform State Laws enacted the Revised Uniform Arbitration Act in 2000. It is contained in Appendix D. The Uniform Arbitration Act of 1954 remains the law in the vast majority of states. See www.nccusl.org. Compilation of The National Conference of Commissioners on Uniform State Laws, Chicago, IL.

this section or, if the issue is severable, the stay may be with respect thereto only. When the application is made in such action or proceeding, the order for arbitration shall include such stay.

(e) An order for arbitration shall not be refused on the ground that the claim in issue lacks merit or bona fides or because any fault or grounds for the claim sought to be arbitrated have not been shown.

3. Appointment of Arbitrators by Court

If the arbitration agreement provides a method of appointment of arbitrators, this method shall be followed. In the absence thereof, or if the agreed method fails or for any reason cannot be followed, or when an arbitrator appointed fails or is unable to act and his successor has not been duly appointed, the court on application of a party shall appoint one or more arbitrators. An arbitrator so appointed has all the powers of one specifically named in the agreement.

4. Majority Action by Arbitrators

The powers of the arbitrators may be exercised by a majority unless otherwise provided by the agreement or by this act.

5. Hearing

Unless otherwise provided by the agreement:

(a) The arbitrators shall appoint a time and place for the hearing and cause notification to the parties to be served personally or by registered mail not less than five days before the hearing. Appearance at the hearing waives such notice. The arbitrators may adjourn the hearing from time to time as necessary and, on request of a party and for good cause, or upon their own motion may postpone the hearing to a time not later than the date fixed by the agreement for making the award unless the parties consent to a later date. The arbitrators may hear and determine the controversy upon the evidence produced notwithstanding the failure of a party duly notified to appear. The court on application may direct the arbitrators to proceed promptly with the hearing and determination of the controversy.

(b) The parties are entitled to be heard, to present evidence material to the controversy and to cross-examine witnesses appearing at the hearing.

(c) The hearing shall be conducted by all the arbitrators but a majority may determine any question and render a final award. If, during the course of the hearing, an arbitrator for any reason ceases to act, the remaining arbitrator or arbitrators appointed to act as neutrals may continue with the hearing and determination of the controversy.

6. Representation by Attorney

A party has the right to be represented by an attorney at any proceeding or hearing under this act. A waiver thereof prior to the proceeding or hearing is ineffective.

7. Witnesses, Subpoenas, Depositions

(a) The arbitrators may issue (cause to be issued) subpoenas for the attendance of witnesses and for the production of books, records, documents and other evidence, and shall have the power to administer oaths. Subpoenas so issued shall be served, and upon application to the Court by a party or the arbitrators, enforced, in the manner provided by law for the service and enforcement of subpoenas in a civil action.

(b) On application of a party and for use as evidence, the arbitrators may permit a deposition to be taken, in the manner and upon the terms designated by the arbitrators, of a witness who cannot be subpoenaed or is unable to attend the hearing.

(c) All provisions of law compelling a person under subpoena to testify are applicable.

(d) Fees for attendance as a witness shall be the same as for a witness in the ______________ Court.

8. Award

(a) The award shall be in writing and signed by the arbitrators joining in the award. The arbitrators shall deliver a copy to each party personally or by registered mail, or as provided in the agreement.

(b) An award shall be made within the time fixed therefor by the agreement or, if not so fixed, within such time as the court orders on application of a party. The parties may extend the time in writing either before or after the expiration thereof. A party waives the objection that an award was not made within the time required unless he notifies the arbitrators of his objection prior to the delivery of the award to him.

9. Change of Award by Arbitrators

On application of a party or, if an application to the court is pending under Sections 11, 12 or 13, on submission to the arbitrators by the court under such conditions as the court may order, the arbitrators may modify or correct the award upon the grounds stated in paragraphs (1) and (3) of subdivision (a) of Section 13, or for the purpose of clarifying the award. The application shall be made within twenty days after delivery of the award to the applicant. Written notice thereof shall be given forthwith to the opposing party, stating he must serve his objections thereto, if any, within ten days from the notice. The award so modified or corrected is subject to the provisions of Sections 11, 12 and 13.

10. Fees and Expenses of Arbitration

Unless otherwise provided in the agreement to arbitrate, the arbitrators' expenses and fees, together with other expenses, not including counsel fees, incurred in the conduct of the arbitration, shall be paid as provided in the award.

11. Confirmation of an Award

Upon application of a party, the Court shall confirm an award, unless within the time limits hereinafter imposed grounds are urged for vacating or modifying or correcting the award, in which case the court shall proceed as provided in Sections 12 and 13.

12. Vacating an Award

(a) Upon application of a party, the court shall vacate an award where:

(1) The award was procured by corruption, fraud or other undue means;

(2) There was evident partiality by an arbitrator appointed as a neutral or corruption in any of the arbitrators or misconduct prejudicing the rights of any party;

(3) The arbitrators exceeded their powers;

(4) The arbitrators refused to postpone the hearing upon sufficient cause being shown therefor or refused to hear evidence material to the controversy or otherwise so conducted the hearing, contrary to the provisions of Section 5, as to prejudice substantially the rights of a party; or

(5) There was no arbitration agreement and the issue was not adversely determined in proceedings under Section 2 and the party did not participate in the arbitration hearing without raising the objection; but the fact that the relief was such that it could not or would not be granted by a court of law or equity is not ground for vacating or refusing to confirm the award.

(b) An application under this Section shall be made within ninety days after delivery of a copy of the award to the applicant, except that, if predicated upon corruption, fraud or other undue means, it shall be made within ninety days after such grounds are known or should have been known.

(c) In vacating the award on grounds other than stated in clause (5) of Subsection (a) the court may order a rehearing before new arbitrators chosen as provided in the agreement, or in the absence thereof, by the court in accordance with Section 3, or if the award is vacated on grounds set forth in clauses (3) and (4) of Subsection (a) the court may order a rehearing before the arbitrators who made the award or their successors appointed in accordance with Section 3. The time within which the agreement requires the award to be made is applicable to the rehearing and commences from the date of the order.

(d) If the application to vacate is denied and no motion to modify or correct the award is pending, the court shall confirm the award. [As amended Aug. 1956.]

13. Modification or Correction of Award

(a) Upon application made within ninety days after delivery of a copy of the award to the applicant, the court shall modify or correct the award where:

(1) There was an evident miscalculation of figures or an evident mistake in the description of any person, thing or property referred to in the award;

(2) The arbitrators have awarded upon a matter not submitted to them and the award may be corrected without affecting the merits of the decision upon the issues submitted; or

(3) The award is imperfect in a matter of form, not affecting the merits of the controversy.

(b) If the application is granted, the court shall modify and correct the award so as to effect its intent and shall confirm the award as so modified and corrected. Otherwise, the court shall confirm the award as made.

(c) An application to modify or correct an award may be joined in the alternative with an application to vacate the award.

14. Judgment or Decree on award

Upon the granting of an order confirming, modifying or correcting an award, judgment or decree shall be entered in conformity therewith and be enforced as any other judgment or decree. Costs of the application and of the proceedings subsequent thereto, and disbursements may be awarded by the court.

15. Judgment Roll, Docketing

(a) On entry of judgment or decree, the clerk shall prepare the judgment roll consisting, to the extent filed, of the following:

(1) The agreement and each written extension of the time within which to make the award;

(2) The award;

(3) A copy of the order confirming, modifying or correcting the award; and

(4) A copy of the judgment or decree.

(b) The judgment or decree may be docketed as if rendered in an action.

16. Applications to Court

Except as otherwise provided, an application to the court under this act shall be by motion and shall be heard in the manner and upon the notice provided by law or rule of court for the making and hearing of motions. Unless the parties have agreed otherwise, notice of an initial application for an order shall be served in the manner provided by law for the service of a summons in an action.

17. Court, Jurisdiction

The term "court" means any court of competent jurisdiction of this State. The making of an agreement described in Section 1 providing for arbitration in this State confers jurisdiction on the court to enforce the agreement under this Act and to enter judgment on an award thereunder.

18. Venue

An initial application shall be made to the court of the [county] in which the agreement provides the arbitration hearing shall be held or, if the hearing has been held, in the county in which it was held. Otherwise the application shall be made in the [county] where the adverse party resides or has a place of business or, if he has no residence or place of business in this State, to the court of any [county]. All subsequent applications shall be made to the court hearing the initial application unless the court otherwise directs.

19. Appeals

(a) An appeal may be taken from:

(1) An order denying an application to compel arbitration made under Section 2;

(2) An order granting an application to stay arbitration made under Section 2(b);

(3) An order confirming or denying confirmation of an award;

(4) An order modifying or correcting an award;

(5) An order vacating an award without directing a rehearing; or

(6) A judgment or decree entered pursuant to the provisions of this act.

(b) The appeal shall be taken in the manner and to the same extent as from orders or judgments in a civil action.

20. Act Not Retroactive

This act applies only to agreements made subsequent to the taking effect of this act.

21. Uniformity of Interpretation

This act shall be so construed as to effectuate its general purpose to make uniform the law of those states which enact it.

22. Constitutionality

If any provision of this act or the application thereof to any person or circumstance is held invalid, the invalidity shall not affect other provisions or applications of the act which can be given effect without the invalid provision or application, and to this end the provisions of this act are severable.

23. Short Title

This act may be cited as the Uniform Arbitration Act.

24. Repeal

All acts or parts of acts which are inconsistent with the provisions of this act are hereby repealed.

25. Time of Taking Effect

This act shall take effect ________________________.

Appendix D
Revised Uniform Arbitration Act (2000)*

[The blackletter text and explanatory notes for the RUAA may be found by entering the following URL: *http://www.law.upenn.edu/bll/ulc/ulc_frame.htm* and clicking on the appropriate links at the site.]

PREFATORY NOTE

The Uniform Arbitration Act (UAA), promulgated in 1955, has been one of the most successful Acts of the National Conference of Commissioners on Uniform State Laws. Forty-nine jurisdictions have arbitration statutes; 35 of these have adopted the UAA and 14 have adopted substantially similar legislation. A primary purpose of the 1955 Act was to insure the enforceability of agreements to arbitrate in the face of oftentimes hostile state law. That goal has been accomplished. Today arbitration is a primary mechanism favored by courts and parties to resolve disputes in many areas of the law. This growth in arbitration caused the Conference to appoint a Drafting Committee to consider revising the Act in light of the increasing use of arbitration, the greater complexity of many disputes resolved by arbitration, and the developments of the law in this area.

The UAA did not address many issues which arise in modern arbitration cases. The statute provided no guidance as to (1) who decides the arbitrability of a dispute and by what criteria; (2) whether a court or arbitrators may issue provisional remedies; (3) how a party can initiate an arbitration proceeding; (4) whether arbitration proceedings may be consolidated; (5) whether arbitrators are required to disclose facts reasonably likely to affect impartiality; (6) what extent arbitrators or an arbitration organization are immune from civil actions; (7) whether arbitrators or representatives of arbitration organizations may be required to testify in another proceeding; (8) whether arbitrators have the discretion to order discovery, issue protective orders, decide motions for summary dispositions, hold prehearing conferences and otherwise manage the arbitration process; (9) when a court may enforce a preaward ruling by an arbitrator;

 Twelve states have adopted the RUAA.

(10) what remedies an arbitrator may award, especially in regard to attorney's fees, punitive damages or other exemplary relief; (11) when a court can award attorney's fees and costs to arbitrators and arbitration organizations; (12) when a court can award attorney's fees and costs to a prevailing party in an appeal of an arbitrator's award; and (13) which sections of the UAA would not be waivable, an important matter to insure fundamental fairness to the parties will be preserved, particularly in those instances where one party may have significantly less bargaining power than another; and (14) the use of electronic information and other modern means of technology in the arbitration process. The Revised Uniform Arbitration Act (RUAA) examines all of these issues and provides state legislatures with a more up-to-date statute to resolve disputes through arbitration.

There are a number of principles that the Drafting Committee agreed upon at the outset of its consideration of a revision to the UAA. First, arbitration is a consensual process in which autonomy of the parties who enter into arbitration agreements should be given primary consideration, so long as their agreements conform to notions of fundamental fairness. This approach provides parties with the opportunity in most instances to shape the arbitration process to their own particular needs. In most instances the RUAA provides a default mechanism if the parties do not have a specific agreement on a particular issue. Second, the underlying reason many parties choose arbitration is the relative speed, lower cost, and greater efficiency of the process. The law should take these factors, where applicable, into account. For example, Section 10 allows consolidation of issues involving multiple parties. Such a provision can be of special importance in adhesion situations where there are numerous persons with essentially the same claims against a party to the arbitration agreement. Finally, in most cases parties intend the decisions of arbitrators to be final with minimal court involvement unless there is clear unfairness or a denial of justice. This contractual nature of arbitration means that the provision to vacate awards in Section 23 is limited. This is so even where an arbitrator may award attorney's fees, punitive damages or other exemplary relief under Section 21. Section 14 insulates arbitrators from unwarranted litigation to insure their independence by providing them with immunity.

Other new provisions are intended to reflect developments in arbitration law and to insure that the process is a fair one. Section 12 requires arbitrators to make important disclosures to the parties. Section 8 allows courts to grant provisional remedies in certain circumstances to protect the integrity of the arbitration process. Section 17 includes limited rights to discovery while recognizing the importance of expeditious arbitration proceedings.

In light of a number of decisions by the United States Supreme Court concerning the Federal Arbitration Act (FAA), any revision of the UAA must take into account the doctrine of preemption. The rule of preemption, whereby FAA standards and the emphatically pro-arbitration perspective of the FAA control, applies in both the federal courts and the state courts. To date, the preemption-related opinions of the Supreme Court have centered in large part on the two key issues that arise at the front end of the arbitration process — enforcement of the agreement to arbitrate and issues of substantive arbitrability. *Prima Paint Corp. v. Flood & Conklin Mfg. Co.*, 388 U.S. 35 (1967); *Moses H. Cone Mem'l Hosp. v. Mercury Constr. Corp.*, 460 U.S. 1 (1983); *Southland Corp. v. Keating*, 465 U.S. 2 (1984); *Perry v. Thomas*, 482 U.S.

483 (1987); *Allied-Bruce Terminix Cos. v. Dobson*, 513 U.S. 265 (1995); *Doctor's Assocs. v. Cassarotto,* 517 U.S. 681 (1996). That body of case law establishes that state law of any ilk, including adaptations of the RUAA, mooting or limiting contractual agreements to arbitrate must yield to the pro-arbitration public policy voiced in Sections 2, 3, and 4 of the FAA.

The other issues to which the FAA speaks definitively lie at the back end of the arbitration process. The standards and procedure for vacatur, confirmation and modification of arbitration awards are the subject of Sections 9, 10, 11, and 12 of the FAA. In contrast to the "front end" issues of enforceability and substantive arbitrability, there is no definitive Supreme Court case law speaking to the preemptive effect, if any, of the FAA with regard to these "back end" issues. This dimension of FAA preemption of state arbitration law is further complicated by the strong majority view among the United States Circuit Courts of Appeals that the Section 10(a) standards are not the exclusive grounds for vacatur.

Nevertheless, the Supreme Court's unequivocal stand to date as to the preemptive effect of the FAA provides strong reason to believe that a similar result will obtain with regard to Section 10(a) grounds for vacatur. If it does, and if the Supreme Court eventually determines that the Section 10(a) standards are the sole grounds for vacatur of commercial arbitration awards, FAA preemption of conflicting state law with regard to the "back end" issues of vacatur (and confirmation and modification) would be certain. If the Court takes the opposite tack and holds that the Section 10(a) grounds are not the exclusive criteria for vacatur, the preemptive effect of Section 10(a) would most likely be limited to the rule that state arbitration acts cannot eliminate, limit or modify any of the four grounds of party and arbitrator misconduct set out in Section 10(a). Any definitive federal "common law," pertaining to the nonstatutory grounds for vacatur other than those set out in Section 10(a), articulated by the Supreme Court or established as a clear majority rule by the United States Courts of Appeals, likely would preempt contrary state law. A holding by the Supreme Court that the Section 10(a) grounds are not exclusive would also free the States to codify other grounds for vacatur beyond those set out in Section 10(a). These various, currently nonstatutory grounds for vacatur are discussed at length in Section C to the Comment to Section 23.

An important caveat to the general rule of FAA preemption is found in *Volt Information Sciences, Inc. v. Stanford University*, 489 U.S. 468 (1989) and *Mastrobuono v. Shearson Lehman Hutton, Inc.*, 514 U.S. 52 (1995). The focus in these cases is on the effect of FAA preemption on choice-of-law provisions routinely included in commercial contracts. *Volt* and *Mastrobuono* establish that a clearly expressed contractual agreement by the parties to an arbitration contract to conduct their arbitration under state law rules effectively trumps the preemptive effect of the FAA. If the parties elect to govern their contractual arbitration mechanism by the law of a particular State and thereby limit the issues that they will arbitrate or the procedures under which the arbitration will be conducted, their bargain will be honored — as long as the state law principles invoked by the choice-of-law provision do not conflict with the FAA's prime directive that agreements to arbitrate be enforced. *See, e.g., ASW Allstate Painting & Constr. Co. v. Lexington Ins. Co.*, 188 F.3d 307 (5th Cir. 1999); *Russ Berrie & Co. v. Gantt,* 988 S.W.2d 713 (Tex. Ct. App. 1999). It is in these situations that the RUAA will have most impact. Section 4(a) of the RUAA also explicitly provides that the parties to an arbitration agreement may waive or vary the terms of the Act to the extent otherwise permitted by law. Thus, when parties choose to contractually specify the procedures to be followed under their arbitration agreement, the RUAA contemplates that the contractually-established procedures will control over contrary state law, except with regard to issues designated as "nonwaivable" in Section 4(b) and (c) of the RUAA.

The contractual election to proceed under state law instead of the FAA will be honored presuming that the state law is not antithetical to the pro-arbitration public policy of the FAA. *Southland* and *Terminix* leave no doubt that anti-arbitration state law provisions will be struck down because preempted by the federal arbitration statute.

Besides arbitration contracts where the parties choose to be governed by state law, there are other areas of arbitration law where the FAA does not preempt state law, in the absence of definitive federal law set out in the FAA or determined by the federal courts. First, the Supreme Court has made clear its belief that ascertaining when a particular contractual agreement to arbitrate is enforceable is a matter to be decided under the general contract law principles of each State. The sole limitation on state law in that regard is the Court's assertion that the enforceability of arbitration agreements must be determined by the same standards as are used for all other contracts. *Terminix,* 513 U.S. at 281 (1995) (quoting *Volt,* 489 U.S. at 474 (1989)) and quoted in *Cassarotto,* 517 U.S. 681, 685 (1996); and *Cassarotto,* 517 U.S. at 688 (quoting *Scherk v. Alberto-Culver Co.,* 417 U.S. 506, 511 (1974)). Arbitration agreements may not be invalidated under state laws applicable only to arbitration provisions. *Id.* The FAA will preempt state law that does not place arbitration agreements on an "equal footing" with other contracts.

During the course of its deliberations the Drafting Committee considered at length another issue with strong preemption undertones — the question of whether the RUAA should explicitly sanction contractual provisions for "opt-in" review of challenged arbitration awards beyond that presently contemplated by the FAA and current state arbitration acts. "Opt-in" provisions of two types are in limited use today. The first variant permits a party who is dissatisfied with the arbitral result to petition directly to a designated state court and stipulates that the court may vacate challenged awards, typically for errors of law or fact. The second type of "opt-in" contractual provision establishes an appellate arbitral mechanism to which challenged arbitration awards can be submitted for review, again most typically for errors of law or fact.

As explained in detail in Section B of the Comment to Section 23, there were a number of reasons that resulted in the decision not to include statutory sanction of the "opt-in" device for expanded judicial review in the RUAA: (1) the current uncertainty as to the legality of a state statutory sanction of the "opt-in" device, (2) the "disconnect" between the Act's purpose of fostering the use of arbitration as a final and binding alternative to traditional litigation in a court of law, and (3) the inclusion of a statutory provision that would permit the parties to contractually render arbitration decidedly non-final and non-binding. Simply stated, the potential gain to be realized by codifying a right to opt-into expanded judicial review that has not yet been definitively confirmed to exist does not outweigh the potential threat that adoption of an opt-in statutory provision would create for the integrity and viability of the RUAA as a template for state arbitration acts.

Unlike the "opt-in" judicial review mechanism, there are few, if any, legal concerns raised by statutory sanction of "opt-in" provisions for appellate arbitral review. Nevertheless, as explained in the Section B of the Comments to Section 23, because the current, contract-based view of arbitration establishes that the parties are free to design the inner workings of their arbitration procedures in any manner they see fit, the Drafting Committee determined that codification of that right in the RUAA would add nothing of substance to the existing law of arbitration.

The decision not to statutorily sanction either form of the "opt-in" device in the RUAA leaves the issue of the legal propriety of this means for securing review of awards to the developing case law under the FAA and state arbitration statutes. Parties remain free, within the constraints imposed by the existing and developing law, to agree to contractual provisions for arbitral or judicial review of challenged awards.

It is likely that matters not addressed in the FAA are also open to regulation by the States. State law provisions regulating purely procedural dimensions of the arbitration process (*e.g.*, discovery [RUAA Section 17], consolidation of claims [RUAA Section 10], and arbitrator immunity [RUAA Section 14]) likely will not be subject to preemption. Less certain is the effect of FAA preemption with regard to substantive issues like the authority of arbitrators to award punitive damages (RUAA Section 21) and the standards for arbitrator disclosure of potential conflicts of interest (RUAA Section 12) that have a significant impact on the integrity and/or the adequacy of the arbitration process. These "borderline" issues are not purely procedural in nature but unlike the "front end" and "back end" issues they do not go to the essence of the agreement to arbitrate or effectuation of the arbitral result. Although there is no concrete guidance in the case law, preemption of state law dealing with such matters seems unlikely as long as it cannot be characterized as anti-arbitration or as intended to limit the enforceability or viability of agreements to arbitrate. . . .

SECTION 1. DEFINITIONS.

In This [Act]:

(1) "Arbitration organization" means an association, agency, board, commission, or other entity that is neutral and initiates, sponsors, or administers an arbitration proceeding or is involved in the appointment of an arbitrator.

(2) "Arbitrator" means an individual appointed to render an award, alone or with others, in a controversy that is subject to an agreement to arbitrate.

(3) "Court" means [a court of competent jurisdiction in this State].

(4) "Knowledge" means actual knowledge.

(5) "Person" means an individual, corporation, business trust, estate, trust, partnership, limited liability company, association, joint venture, government; governmental subdivision, agency, or instrumentality; public corporation; or any other legal or commercial entity.

(6) "Record" means information that is inscribed on a tangible medium or that is stored in an electronic or other medium and is retrievable in perceivable form.

Section 2. Notice.

(a) Except as otherwise provided in this [Act], a person gives notice to another person by taking action that is reasonably necessary to inform the other person in ordinary course, whether or not the other person acquires knowledge of the notice.

(b) A person has notice if the person has knowledge of the notice or has received notice.

(c) A person receives notice when it comes to the person's attention or the notice is delivered at the person's place of residence or place of business, or at another location held out by the person as a place of delivery of such communications.

Section 3. When [Act] Applies.

(a) This [Act] governs an agreement to arbitrate made on or after [the effective date of this [Act]].

(b) This [Act] governs an agreement to arbitrate made before [the effective date of this [Act]] if all the parties to the agreement or to the arbitration proceeding so agree in a record.

(c) On or after [a delayed date], this [Act] governs an agreement to arbitrate whenever made.

Section 4. Effect of Agreement to Arbitrate; Nonwaivable Provisions.

(a) Except as otherwise provided in subsections (b) and (c), a party to an agreement to arbitrate or to an arbitration proceeding may waive, or the parties may vary the effect of, the requirements of this [Act] to the extent permitted by law.

(b) Before a controversy arises that is subject to an agreement to arbitrate, a party to the agreement may not:

(1) waive or agree to vary the effect of the requirements of Section 5(a), 6(a), 8, 17(a), 17(b), 26, or 28;

(2) agree to unreasonably restrict the right under Section 9 to notice of the initiation of an arbitration proceeding;

(3) agree to unreasonably restrict the right under Section 12 to disclosure of any facts by a neutral arbitrator; or

(4) waive the right under Section 16 of a party to an agreement to arbitrate to be represented by a lawyer at any proceeding or hearing under this [Act], but an employer and a labor organization may waive the right to representation by a lawyer in a labor arbitration.

(c) A party to an agreement to arbitrate or arbitration proceeding may not waive, or the parties may not vary the effect of, the requirements of this section or Section 3(a), (c), 7, 14, 18, 20(c) or (d), 22, 23, 24, 25(a) or (b), 29, 30, 31, or 32.

SECTION 5. [APPLICATION] FOR JUDICIAL RELIEF.

(a) Except as otherwise provided in Section 28, an [application] for judicial relief under this [Act] must be made by [motion] to the court and heard in the manner provided by law or rule of court for making and hearing [motions].

(b) Unless a civil action involving the agreement to arbitrate is pending, notice of an initial [motion] to the court under this [Act] must be served in the manner provided by law for the service of a summons in a civil action. Otherwise, notice of the motion must be given in the manner provided by law or rule of court for serving [motions] in pending cases.

SECTION 6. VALIDITY OF AGREEMENT TO ARBITRATE.

(a) An agreement contained in a record to submit to arbitration any existing or subsequent controversy arising between the parties to the agreement is valid, enforceable, and irrevocable except upon a ground that exists at law or in equity for the revocation of a contract.

(b) The court shall decide whether an agreement to arbitrate exists or a controversy is subject to an agreement to arbitrate.

(c) An arbitrator shall decide whether a condition precedent to arbitrability has been fulfilled and whether a contract containing a valid agreement to arbitrate is enforceable.

(d) If a party to a judicial proceeding challenges the existence of, or claims that a controversy is not subject to, an agreement to arbitrate, the arbitration proceeding may continue pending final resolution of the issue by the court, unless the court otherwise orders.

SECTION 7. [MOTION] TO COMPEL OR STAY ARBITRATION.

(a) On [motion] of a person showing an agreement to arbitrate and alleging another person's refusal to arbitrate pursuant to the agreement:

(1) if the refusing party does not appear or does not oppose the [motion], the court shall order the parties to arbitrate; and

(2) if the refusing party opposes the [motion], the court shall proceed summarily to decide the issue and order the parties to arbitrate unless it finds that there is no enforceable agreement to arbitrate.

(b) On [motion] of a person alleging that an arbitration proceeding has been initiated or threatened but that there is no agreement to arbitrate, the court shall proceed summarily to decide the issue. If the court finds that there is an enforceable agreement to arbitrate, it shall order the parties to arbitrate.

(c) If the court finds that there is no enforceable agreement, it may not pursuant to subsection (a) or (b) order the parties to arbitrate.

(d) The court may not refuse to order arbitration because the claim subject to arbitration lacks merit or grounds for the claim have not been established.

(e) If a proceeding involving a claim referable to arbitration under an alleged agreement to arbitrate is pending in court, a [motion] under this section must be made in that court. Otherwise a [motion] under this section may be made in any court as provided in Section 27.

(f) If a party makes a [motion] to the court to order arbitration, the court on just terms shall stay any judicial proceeding that involves a claim alleged to be subject to the arbitration until the court renders a final decision under this section.

(g) If the court orders arbitration, the court on just terms shall stay any judicial proceeding that involves a claim subject to the arbitration. If a claim subject to the arbitration is severable, the court may limit the stay to that claim.

SECTION 8. PROVISIONAL REMEDIES.

(a) Before an arbitrator is appointed and is authorized and able to act, the court, upon [motion] of a party to an arbitration proceeding and for good cause shown, may enter an order for provisional remedies to protect the effectiveness of the arbitration proceeding to the same extent and under the same conditions as if the controversy were the subject of a civil action.

(b) After an arbitrator is appointed and is authorized and able to act:

(1) the arbitrator may issue such orders for provisional remedies, including interim awards, as the arbitrator finds necessary to protect the effectiveness of the arbitration proceeding and to promote the fair and expeditious resolution of the controversy, to the same extent and under the same conditions as if the controversy were the subject of a civil action and

(2) a party to an arbitration proceeding may move the court for a provisional remedy only if the matter is urgent and the arbitrator is not able to act timely or the arbitrator cannot provide an adequate remedy.

(c) A party does not waive a right of arbitration by making a [motion] under subsection (a) or (b).

SECTION 9. INITIATION OF ARBITRATION.

(a) A person initiates an arbitration proceeding by giving notice in a record to the other parties to the agreement to arbitrate in the agreed manner between the parties or, in the absence of agreement, by certified or registered mail, return receipt requested and obtained, or by service as authorized for the commencement of a civil action. The notice must describe the nature of the controversy and the remedy sought.

(b) Unless a person objects for lack or insufficiency of notice under Section 15(c) not later than the beginning of the arbitration hearing, the person by appearing at the hearing waives any objection to lack of or insufficiency of notice.

SECTION 10. CONSOLIDATION OF SEPARATE ARBITRATION PROCEEDINGS.

(a) Except as otherwise provided in subsection (c), upon [motion] of a party to an agreement to arbitrate or to an arbitration proceeding, the court may order consolidation of separate arbitration proceedings as to all or some of the claims if:

(1) there are separate agreements to arbitrate or separate arbitration proceedings between the same persons or one of them is a party to a separate agreement to arbitrate or a separate arbitration proceeding with a third person;

(2) the claims subject to the agreements to arbitrate arise in substantial part from the same transaction or series of related transactions;

(3) the existence of a common issue of law or fact creates the possibility of conflicting decisions in the separate arbitration proceedings; and

(4) prejudice resulting from a failure to consolidate is not outweighed by the risk of undue delay or prejudice to the rights of or hardship to parties opposing consolidation.

(b) The court may order consolidation of separate arbitration proceedings as to some claims and allow other claims to be resolved in separate arbitration proceedings.

(c) The court may not order consolidation of the claims of a party to an agreement to arbitrate if the agreement prohibits consolidation.

SECTION 11. APPOINTMENT OF ARBITRATOR; SERVICE AS A NEUTRAL ARBITRATOR.

(a) If the parties to an agreement to arbitrate agree on a method for appointing an arbitrator, that method must be followed, unless the method fails. If the parties have not agreed on a method, the agreed method fails, or an arbitrator appointed fails or is unable to act and a successor has not been appointed, the court, on [motion] of a party to the arbitration proceeding, shall appoint the arbitrator. An arbitrator so appointed has all the powers of an arbitrator designated in the agreement to arbitrate or appointed pursuant to the agreed method.

(b) An individual who has a known, direct, and material interest in the outcome of the arbitration proceeding or a known, existing, and substantial relationship with a party may not serve as an arbitrator required by an agreement to be neutral.

SECTION 12. DISCLOSURE BY ARBITRATOR.

(a) Before accepting appointment, an individual who is requested to serve as an arbitrator, after making a reasonable inquiry, shall disclose to all parties to the agreement to arbitrate and arbitration proceeding and to any other arbitrators any known facts that a reasonable person would consider likely to affect the impartiality of the arbitrator in the arbitration proceeding, including:

(1) a financial or personal interest in the outcome of the arbitration proceeding; and

(2) an existing or past relationship with any of the parties to the agreement to arbitrate or the arbitration proceeding, their counsel or representatives, a witness, or another arbitrators.

(b) An arbitrator has a continuing obligation to disclose to all parties to the agreement to arbitrate and arbitration proceeding and to any other arbitrators any facts that the arbitrator learns after accepting appointment which a reasonable person would consider likely to affect the impartiality of the arbitrator.

(c) If an arbitrator discloses a fact required by subsection (a) or (b) to be disclosed and a party timely objects to the appointment or continued service of the arbitrator based upon the fact disclosed, the objection may be a ground under Section 23(a)(2) for vacating an award made by the arbitrator.

(d) If the arbitrator did not disclose a fact as required by subsection (a) or (b), upon timely objection by a party, the court under Section 23(a)(2) may vacate an award.

(e) An arbitrator appointed as a neutral arbitrator who does not disclose a known, direct, and material interest in the outcome of the arbitration proceeding or a known, existing, and substantial relationship with a party is presumed to act with evident partiality under Section 23(a)(2).

(f) If the parties to an arbitration proceeding agree to the procedures of an arbitration organization or any other procedures for challenges to arbitrators before an award is made, substantial compliance with those procedures is a condition precedent to a [motion] to vacate an award on that ground under Section 23(a)(2).

SECTION 13. ACTION BY MAJORITY.

If there is more than one arbitrator, the powers of an arbitrator must be exercised by a majority of the arbitrators, but all of them shall conduct the hearing under Section 15(c).

SECTION 14. IMMUNITY OF ARBITRATOR; COMPETENCY TO TESTIFY; ATTORNEY'S FEES AND COSTS.

(a) An arbitrator or an arbitration organization acting in that capacity is immune from civil liability to the same extent as a judge of a court of this State acting in a judicial capacity.

(b) The immunity afforded by this section supplements any immunity under other law.

(c) The failure of an arbitrator to make a disclosure required by Section 12 does not cause any loss of immunity under this section.

(d) In a judicial, administrative, or similar proceeding, an arbitrator or representative of an arbitration organization is not competent to testify, and may not be required to produce records as to any statement, conduct, decision, or ruling occurring during the arbitration proceeding, to the same extent as a judge of a court of this State acting in a judicial capacity. This subsection does not apply:

(1) to the extent necessary to determine the claim of an arbitrator, arbitration organization, or representative of the arbitration organization against a party to the arbitration proceeding; or

(2) to a hearing on a [motion] to vacate an award under Section 23(a)(1) or (2) if the [movant] establishes prima facie that a ground for vacating the award exists.

(e) If a person commences a civil action against an arbitrator, arbitration organization, or representative of an arbitration organization arising from the services of the arbitrator, organization, or representative or if a person seeks to compel an arbitrator or a representative of an arbitration organization to testify or produce records in violation of subsection (d), and the court decides that the arbitrator, arbitration organization, or representative of an arbitration organization is immune from civil liability or that the arbitrator or representative of the organization is not competent to testify, the court shall award to the arbitrator, organization, or representative reasonable attorney's fees and other reasonable expenses of litigation.

SECTION 15. ARBITRATION PROCESS.

(a) An arbitrator may conduct an arbitration in such manner as the arbitrator considers appropriate for a fair and expeditious disposition of the proceeding. The authority conferred upon the arbitrator includes the power to hold conferences with the parties to the arbitration proceeding before the hearing and, among other matters, determine the admissibility, relevance, materiality and weight of any evidence.

(b) An arbitrator may decide a request for summary disposition of a claim or particular issue:

(1) if all interested parties agree; or

(2) upon request of one party to the arbitration proceeding if that party gives notice to all other parties to the proceeding, and the other parties have a reasonable opportunity to respond.

(c) If an arbitrator orders a hearing, the arbitrator shall set a time and place and give notice of the hearing not less than five days before the hearing begins. Unless a party to the arbitration proceeding makes an objection to lack or insufficiency of notice not later than the beginning of the hearing, the party's appearance at the hearing waives the objection. Upon request of a party to the arbitration proceeding and for good cause shown, or upon the arbitrator's own initiative, the arbitrator may adjourn the hearing from time to time as necessary but may not postpone the hearing to a time later than that fixed by the agreement to arbitrate for making the award unless the parties to the arbitration proceeding consent to a later date. The arbitrator may hear and decide the controversy upon the evidence produced although a party who was duly notified of the arbitration proceeding did not appear. The court, on request, may direct the arbitrator to conduct the hearing promptly and render a timely decision.

(d) At a hearing under subsection (c), a party to the arbitration proceeding has a right to be heard, to present evidence material to the controversy, and to cross-examine witnesses appearing at the hearing.

(e) If an arbitrator ceases or is unable to act during the arbitration proceeding, a replacement arbitrator must be appointed in accordance with Section 11 to continue the proceeding and to resolve the controversy.

SECTION 16. REPRESENTATION BY LAWYER.

A party to an arbitration proceeding may be represented by a lawyer.

SECTION 17. WITNESSES; SUBPOENAS; DEPOSITIONS; DISCOVERY.

(a) An arbitrator may issue a subpoena for the attendance of a witness and for the production of records and other evidence at any hearing and may administer oaths. A subpoena must be served in the manner for service of subpoenas in a civil action and, upon [motion] to the court by a party to the arbitration proceeding or the arbitrator, enforced in the manner for enforcement of subpoenas in a civil action.

(b) In order to make the proceedings fair, expeditious, and cost effective, upon request of a party to or a witness in an arbitration proceeding, an arbitrator may permit a deposition of any witness to be taken for use as evidence at the hearing, including a witness who cannot be subpoenaed for or is unable to attend a hearing. The arbitrator shall determine the conditions under which the deposition is taken.

(c) An arbitrator may permit such discovery as the arbitrator decides is appropriate in the circumstances, taking into account the needs of the parties to the arbitration proceeding and other affected persons and the desirability of making the proceeding fair, expeditious, and cost effective.

(d) If an arbitrator permits discovery under subsection (c), the arbitrator may order a party to the arbitration proceeding to comply with the arbitrator's discovery-related orders, issue subpoenas for the attendance of a witness and for the production of records and other evidence at a discovery proceeding, and take action against a noncomplying party to the extent a court could if the controversy were the subject of a civil action in this State.

(e) An arbitrator may issue a protective order to prevent the disclosure of privileged information, confidential information, trade secrets, and other information protected from disclosure to the extent a court could if the controversy were the subject of a civil action in this State.

(f) All laws compelling a person under subpoena to testify and all fees for attending a judicial proceeding, a deposition, or a discovery proceeding as a witness apply to an arbitration proceeding as if the controversy were the subject of a civil action in this State.

(g) The court may enforce a subpoena or discovery-related order for the attendance of a witness within this State and for the production of records and other evidence issued by an arbitrator in connection with an arbitration proceeding in another State upon conditions determined by the court so as to make the arbitration proceeding fair, expeditious, and cost effective. A subpoena or discovery-related order issued by an arbitrator in another State must be served in the manner provided by law for service of subpoenas in a civil action in this State and, upon [motion] to the court by a party to the arbitration proceeding or the arbitrator, enforced in the manner provided by law for enforcement of subpoenas in a civil action in this State.

SECTION 18. JUDICIAL ENFORCEMENT OF PREAWARD RULING BY ARBITRATOR.

If an arbitrator makes a preaward ruling in favor of a party to the arbitration proceeding, the party may request the arbitrator to incorporate the ruling into an award under Section 19. A prevailing party may make a [motion] to the court for an expedited order to confirm the award under Section 22, in which case the court shall summarily decide the [motion]. The court shall issue an order to confirm the award unless the court vacates, modifies, or corrects the award under Section 23 or 24.

SECTION 19. AWARD.

(a) An arbitrator shall make a record of an award. The record must be signed or otherwise authenticated by any arbitrator who concurs with the award. The arbitrator or the arbitration organization shall give notice of the award, including a copy of the award, to each party to the arbitration proceeding.

(b) An award must be made within the time specified by the agreement to arbitrate or, if not specified therein, within the time ordered by the court. The court may extend or the parties to the arbitration proceeding may agree in a record to extend the time. The court or the parties may do so within or after the time specified or ordered. A party waives any objection that an award was not timely made unless the party gives notice of the objection to the arbitrator before receiving notice of the award.

SECTION 20. CHANGE OF AWARD BY ARBITRATOR.

(a) On [motion] to an arbitrator by a party to an arbitration proceeding, the arbitrator may modify or correct an award:

(1) upon a ground stated in Section 24(a)(1) or (3);

(2) because the arbitrator has not made a final and definite award upon a claim submitted by the parties to the arbitration proceeding; or

(3) to clarify the award.

(b) A [motion] under subsection (a) must be made and notice given to all parties within 20 days after the movant receives notice of the award.

(c) A party to the arbitration proceeding must give notice of any objection to the [motion] within 10 days after receipt of the notice.

(d) If a [motion] to the court is pending under Sections 22, 23, or 24, the court may submit the claim to the arbitrator to consider whether to modify or correct the award:

(1) upon a ground stated in Section 24(a)(1) or (3);

(2) because the arbitrator has not made a final and definite award upon a claim submitted by the parties to the arbitration proceeding; or

(3) to clarify the award.

(e) An award modified or corrected pursuant to this section is subject to Sections 19(a), 22, 23, and 24.

Section 21. Remedies; Fees and Expenses of Arbitration Proceeding.

(a) An arbitrator may award punitive damages or other exemplary relief if such an award is authorized by law in a civil action involving the same claim and the evidence produced at the hearing justifies the award under the legal standards otherwise applicable to the claim.

(b) An arbitrator may award reasonable attorney's fees and other reasonable expenses of arbitration if such an award is authorized by law in a civil action involving the same claim or by the agreement of the parties to the arbitration proceeding.

(c) As to all remedies other than those authorized by subsections (a) and (b), an arbitrator may order such remedies as the arbitrator considers just and appropriate under the circumstances of the arbitration proceeding. The fact that such a remedy could not or would not be granted by the court is not a ground for refusing to confirm an award under Section 22 or for vacating an award under Section 23.

(d) An arbitrator's expenses and fees, together with other expenses, must be paid as provided in the award.

(e) If an arbitrator awards punitive damages or other exemplary relief under subsection (a), the arbitrator shall specify in the award the basis in fact justifying and the basis in law authorizing the award and state separately the amount of the punitive damages or other exemplary relief.

Section 22. Confirmation of Award.

After a party to an arbitration proceeding receives notice of an award, the party may make a [motion] to the court for an order confirming the award at which time the court shall issue a confirming order unless the award is modified or corrected pursuant to Section 20 or 24 or is vacated pursuant to Section 23.

Section 23. Vacating Award.

(a) Upon [motion] to the court by a party to an arbitration proceeding, the court shall vacate an award made in the arbitration proceeding if:

(1) the award was procured by corruption, fraud, or other undue means;

(2) there was:

(A) evident partiality by an arbitrator appointed as a neutral arbitrator;

(B) corruption by an arbitrator; or

(C) misconduct by an arbitrator prejudicing the rights of a party to the arbitration proceeding;

(3) an arbitrator refused to postpone the hearing upon showing of sufficient cause for postponement, refused to consider evidence material to the controversy, or otherwise conducted the hearing contrary to Section 15, so as to prejudice substantially the rights of a party to the arbitration proceeding;

(4) an arbitrator exceeded the arbitrator's powers;

(5) there was no agreement to arbitrate, unless the person participated in the arbitration proceeding without raising the objection under Section 15(c) not later than the beginning of the arbitration hearing; or

(6) the arbitration was conducted without proper notice of the initiation of an arbitration as required in Section 9 so as to prejudice substantially the rights of a party to the arbitration proceeding.

(b) A [motion] under this section must be filed within 90 days after the [movant] receives notice of the award pursuant to Section 19 or within 90 days after the [movant] receives notice of a modified or corrected award pursuant to Section 20, unless the [movant] alleges that the award was procured by corruption, fraud, or other undue means, in which case the [motion] must be made within 90 days after the ground is known or by the exercise of reasonable care would have been known by the [movant].

(c) If the court vacates an award on a ground other than that set forth in subsection (a)(5), it may order a rehearing. If the award is vacated on a ground stated in subsection (a)(1) or (2), the rehearing must be before a new arbitrator. If the award is vacated on a ground stated in subsection (a)(3), (4), or (6), the rehearing may be before the arbitrator who made the award or the arbitrator's successor. The arbitrator must render the decision in the rehearing within the same time as that provided in Section 19(b) for an award.

(d) If the court denies a [motion] to vacate an award, it shall confirm the award unless a [motion] to modify or correct the award is pending.

SECTION 24. MODIFICATION OR CORRECTION OF AWARD.

(a) Upon [motion] made within 90 days after the [movant] receives notice of the award pursuant to Section 19 or within 90 days after the [movant] receives notice of a modified or corrected award pursuant to Section 20, the court shall modify or correct the award if:

(1) there was an evident mathematical miscalculation or an evident mistake in the description of a person, thing, or property referred to in the award;

(2) the arbitrator has made an award on a claim not submitted to the arbitrator and the award may be corrected without affecting the merits of the decision upon the claims submitted; or

(3) the award is imperfect in a matter of form not affecting the merits of the decision on the claims submitted.

(b) If a [motion] made under subsection (a) is granted, the court shall modify or correct and confirm the award as modified or corrected. Otherwise, unless a motion to vacate is pending, the court shall confirm the award.

(c) A [motion] to modify or correct an award pursuant to this section may be joined with a [motion] to vacate the award.

SECTION 25. JUDGMENT ON AWARD; ATTORNEY'S FEES AND LITIGATION EXPENSES.

(a) Upon granting an order confirming, vacating without directing a rehearing, modifying, or correcting an award, the court shall enter a judgment in conformity therewith. The judgment may be recorded, docketed, and enforced as any other judgment in a civil action.

(b) A court may allow reasonable costs of the [motion] and subsequent judicial proceedings.

(c) On [application] of a prevailing party to a contested judicial proceeding under Section 22, 23, or 24, the court may add reasonable attorney's fees and other reasonable expenses of litigation incurred in a judicial proceeding after the award is made to a judgment confirming, vacating without directing a rehearing, modifying, or correcting an award.

SECTION 26. JURISDICTION.

(a) A court of this State having jurisdiction over the controversy and the parties may enforce an agreement to arbitrate.

(b) An agreement to arbitrate providing for arbitration in this State confers exclusive jurisdiction on the court to enter judgment on an award under this [Act].

SECTION 27. VENUE.

A [motion] pursuant to Section 5 must be made in the court of the [county] in which the agreement to arbitrate specifies the arbitration hearing is to be held or, if the hearing has been held, in the court of the [county] in which it was held. Otherwise, the [motion] may be made in the court of any [county] in which an adverse party resides or has a place of business or, if no adverse party has a residence or place of business in this State, in the court of any [county] in this State. All subsequent [motions] must be made in the court hearing the initial [motion] unless the court otherwise directs.

SECTION 28. APPEALS.

(a) An appeal may be taken from:

(1) an order denying a [motion] to compel arbitration;

(2) an order granting a [motion] to stay arbitration;

(3) an order confirming or denying confirmation of an award;

(4) an order modifying or correcting an award;

(5) an order vacating an award without directing a rehearing; or

(6) a final judgment entered pursuant to this [Act].

(b) An appeal under this section must be taken as from an order or a judgment in a civil action.

Section 29. Uniformity of Application and Construction.

In applying and construing this uniform act, consideration must be given to the need to promote uniformity of the law with respect to its subject matter among States that enact it.

Section 30. Electronic Signatures in Global and National Commerce Act.

The provisions of this [Act] governing the legal effect, validity, or enforceability of electronic records or signatures, and of contracts formed or performed with the use of such records or signatures conform to the requirements of Section 102 of the Electronic Signatures in Global and National Commerce Act, Pub. L. No. 106-229, 114 Stat. 464 (2000), and supersede, modify, and limit the Electronic Signatures in Global and National Commerce Act.

Section 31. Effective Date.

This [Act] takes effect on [effective date].

Section 32. Repeal.

Effective on [delayed date should be the same as that in Section 3(c)], the [Uniform Arbitration Act] is repealed.

Section 33. Savings Clause.

This [Act] does not affect an action or proceeding commenced or right accrued before this [Act] takes effect. Subject to Section 3 of this [Act], an arbitration agreement made before the effective date of this [Act] is governed by the [Uniform Arbitration Act].

Appendix E

Uniform Mediation Act (2002)*

PREFATORY NOTE

. . . [L]aws play a limited but important role in encouraging the effective use of mediation and maintaining its integrity, as well as the appropriate relationship of mediation with the justice system. In particular, the law has the unique capacity to assure that the reasonable expectations of participants regarding the confidentiality of the mediation process are met, rather than frustrated. For this reason, a central thrust of the Act is to provide a privilege that assures confidentiality in legal proceedings (*see* Sections 4-6). Because the privilege makes it more difficult to offer evidence to challenge the settlement agreement, the Drafters viewed the issue of confidentiality as tied to provisions that will help increase the likelihood that the mediation process will be fair. Fairness is enhanced if it will be conducted with integrity and the parties' knowing consent will be preserved. The Act protects integrity and knowing consent through provisions that provide exceptions to the privilege (Section 6), limit disclosures by the mediator to judges and others who may rule on the case (Section 7), require mediators to disclose conflicts of interest (Section 9), and assure that parties may bring a lawyer or other support person to the mediation session (Section 10). In some limited ways, the law can also encourage the use of mediation as part of the policy to promote the private resolution of disputes through informed self-determination. A uniform act that promotes predictability and simplicity may encourage greater use of mediation. . . .

At the same time, it is important to avoid laws that diminish the creative and diverse use of mediation. The Act promotes the autonomy of the parties by leaving to them those matters that can be set by agreement and need not be set inflexibly by

*Editor's Note: The National Conference of Comissioners on Uniform State Law consists of lawyers appointed by the official designated by statute in each state, often the governor, to represent that state in the development, drafting, and adoption of uniform and model legislation. The Conference has approved many other uniform acts, including the Uniform Commercial Code and the Revised Uniform Arbitration Act. The Uniform Mediation Act was drafted in cooperation with a similar committee representing the American Bar Associaton Section on Dispute Resolution. Most citations in the comments have been omitted here. The full text including comments is posted at *www.law.upenn.edu/bll/ulc/ulc_frame.htm.*

statute. In addition, some provisions in the Act may be varied by party agreement, as specified in the comments to the sections. . . .

1. PROMOTING CANDOR

Candor during mediation is encouraged by maintaining the parties' and mediators' expectations regarding confidentiality of mediation communications. *See* Sections 4-6. Virtually all state legislatures have recognized the necessity of protecting mediation confidentiality to encourage the effective use of mediation to resolve disputes. Indeed, state legislatures have enacted more than 250 mediation privilege statutes. Approximately half of the States have enacted privilege statutes that apply generally to mediations in the State, while the other half include privileges within the provisions of statutes establishing mediation programs for specific substantive legal issues, such as employment or human rights.

The Drafters recognize that mediators typically promote a candid and informal exchange regarding events in the past, as well as the parties' perceptions of and attitudes toward these events, and that mediators encourage parties to think constructively and creatively about ways in which their differences might be resolved. This frank exchange can be achieved only if the participants know that what is said in the mediation will not be used to their detriment through later court proceedings and other adjudicatory processes. . . . This rationale has sometimes been extended to mediators to encourage mediators to be candid with the parties by allowing the mediator to block evidence of the mediator's notes and other statements by the mediator. *See, e.g.,* Ohio Rev. Code Ann. §2317.023 (West 1996).

Similarly, public confidence in and the voluntary use of mediation can be expected to expand if people have confidence that the mediator will not take sides or disclose their statements, particularly in the context of other investigations or judicial processes. The public confidence rationale has been extended to permit the mediator to object to testifying, so that the mediator will not be viewed as biased in future mediation sessions that involve comparable parties. *See, e.g., NLRB v. Macaluso,* 618 F.2d 51 (9th Cir. 1980) (public interest in maintaining the perceived and actual impartiality of mediators outweighs the benefits derivable from a given mediator's testimony). To maintain public confidence in the fairness of mediation, a number of States prohibit a mediator from disclosing mediation communications to a judge or other officials in a position to affect the decision in a case. This justification also is reflected in standards [that prohibit] the use of a threat of disclosure or recommendation to pressure the parties to accept a particular settlement.

A statute is required only to assure that aspect of confidentiality that relates to evidence compelled in a judicial and other legal proceeding. The parties can rely on the mediator's assurance of confidentiality in terms of mediator disclosures outside the proceedings, as the mediator would be liable for a breach of such an assurance. Also, the parties can expect enforcement of their agreement to keep things confidential through contract damages and sometimes specific enforcement. The courts have also enforced court orders or rules regarding nondisclosure through orders striking pleadings and fining lawyers. Promises, contracts, and court rules or orders are unavailing, however, with respect to discovery, trial, and otherwise compelled or subpoenaed evidence. Assurance with respect to this aspect of confidentiality has rarely been accorded by common law. Thus, the major contribution of the Act is to provide a privilege in legal proceedings, where it would otherwise either not be available or would not be available in a uniform way across the States.

As with other privileges, the mediation privilege must have limits, and nearly all existing state mediation statutes provide them. Definitions and exceptions primarily are necessary to give appropriate weight to other valid justice system values, in addition to those already discussed in this Section. They often apply to situations that arise only rarely, but might produce grave injustice in that unusual case if not excepted from the privilege.

Finally . . . [a] uniform and generic privilege makes it easier for the parties and mediators to understand what law will apply and therefore to understand the coverage and limits of the Act, so that they can conduct themselves in a mediation accordingly.

2. ENCOURAGING RESOLUTION IN ACCORDANCE WITH OTHER PRINCIPLES

. . . The primary guarantees of fairness within mediation are the integrity of the process and informed self-determination. Self-determination also contributes to party satisfaction. Consensual dispute resolution allows parties to tailor not only the result but also the process to their needs, with minimal intervention by the State. . . .

Self-determination is encouraged by provisions that limit the potential for coercion of the parties to accept settlements, *see* Section 9(a), and that allow parties to have counsel or other support persons present during the mediation session. *See* Section 10. The Act promotes the integrity of the mediation process by requiring the mediator to disclose conflicts of interest, and to be candid about qualifications. *See* Section 9.

3. IMPORTANCE OF UNIFORMITY

This Act is designed to simplify a complex area of the law. Currently, legal rules affecting mediation can be found in more than 2500 statutes. Many of these statutes can be replaced by the Act, which applies a generic approach to topics that are covered in varying ways by a number of specific statutes currently scattered within substantive provisions. . . .

6. DRAFTING PHILOSOPHY

Mediation often involves both parties and mediators from a variety of professions and backgrounds, many of who are not attorneys or represented by counsel. With this in mind, the Drafters sought to make the provisions accessible and understandable to readers from a variety of backgrounds, sometimes keeping the Act shorter by leaving some discretion in the courts to apply the provisions in accordance with the general purposes of the Act, delineated and expanded upon in Section 1 of this Prefatory Note. These policies include fostering prompt, economical, and amicable resolution, integrity in the process, self-determination by parties, candor in negotiations, societal needs for information, and uniformity of law.

The Drafters sought to avoid including in the Act those types of provisions that should vary by type of program or legal context and that were therefore more appropriately left to program-specific statutes or rules. Mediator qualifications, for example, are not prescribed by this Act. The Drafters also recognized that some general standards are often better applied through those who administer ethical standards or local rules, where an advisory opinion might be sought to guide persons faced with immediate uncertainty. Where individual choice or notice was important to allow for self-determination or avoid a trap for the unwary, such as for nondisclosure by the parties outside the context of proceedings, the Drafters left the matter largely to local rule or contract among the participants. As the result, the Act largely governs those narrow circumstances in which the mediation process comes into contact with formal legal processes.

Section 1. Title.

This [Act] may be cited as the Uniform Mediation Act.

Section 2. Definitions.

In this [Act]:

(1) "Mediation" means a process in which a mediator facilitates communication and negotiation between parties to assist them in reaching a voluntary agreement regarding their dispute.

(2) "Mediation communication" means a statement, whether oral or in a record or verbal or nonverbal, that occurs during a mediation or is made for purposes of considering, conducting, participating in, initiating, continuing, or reconvening a mediation or retaining a mediator.

(3) "Mediator" means an individual who conducts a mediation.

(4) "Nonparty participant" means a person, other than a party or mediator, that participates in a mediation.

(5) "Mediation party" means a person that participates in a mediation and whose agreement is necessary to resolve the dispute.

(6) "Person" means an individual, corporation, business trust, estate, trust, partnership, limited liability company, association, joint venture, government; governmental subdivision, agency, or instrumentality; public corporation, or any other legal or commercial entity.

(7) "Proceeding" means:

(A) a judicial, administrative, arbitral, or other adjudicative process, including related pre-hearing and post-hearing motions, conferences, and discovery; or

(B) a legislative hearing or similar process.

(8) "Record" means information that is inscribed on a tangible medium or that is stored in an electronic or other medium and is retrievable in perceivable form.

(9) "Sign" means:

(A) to execute or adopt a tangible symbol with the present intent to authenticate a record; or

(B) to attach or logically associate an electronic symbol, sound, or process to or with a record with the present intent to authenticate a record.

Reporter's Notes

2. *Section 2(2). "Mediation Communication."*

Mediation communications are statements that are made orally, through conduct, or in writing or other recorded activity. This definition is aimed primarily at the privilege provisions of Sections 4-6. It is similar to the general rule, as reflected in Uniform Rule of Evidence 801, which defines a "statement" as "an oral or written assertion or nonverbal conduct of an individual who intends it as an assertion." Most generic mediation privileges cover communications but do not cover conduct that is not intended as an assertion. The mere fact that a person attended the mediation—in other words, the physical presence of a person—is not a communication. By contrast, nonverbal conduct such as nodding in response to a question would be a "communication" because it is meant as an assertion; however nonverbal conduct such as smoking a cigarette during the mediation session typically would not be a "communication" because it was not meant by the actor as an assertion.

A mediator's mental impressions and observations about the mediation present a more complicated question, with important practical implications. *See Olam v. Congress Mortgage Co.*, 68 F.Supp. 2d 1110 (N.D. Cal. 1999). As discussed below, the mediation privilege is modeled after, and draws heavily upon, the attorney-client privilege, a strong privilege that is supported by well-developed case law. Courts are to be expected to look to that well developed body of law in construing this Act. In this regard, mental impressions that are based even in part on mediation communications would generally be protected by privilege.

More specifically, communications include both statements and conduct meant to inform, because the purpose of the privilege is to promote candid mediation communications. By analogy to the attorney-client privilege, silence in response to a question may be a communication, if it is meant to inform. Further, conduct meant to explain or communicate a fact, such as the re-enactment of an accident, is a communication. Similarly, a client's revelation of a hidden scar to an attorney in response to a question is a communication if meant to inform. In contrast, a purely physical phenomenon, such as a tattoo or the color of a suit of clothes, observable by all, is not a communication.

If evidence of mental impressions would reveal, even indirectly, mediation communications, then that evidence would be blocked by the privilege. For example, a mediator's mental impressions of the capacity of a mediation participant to enter into a binding mediated settlement agreement would be privileged if that impression was in part based on the statements that the party made during the mediation, because the testimony might reveal the content or character of the mediation communications upon which the impression is based. In contrast, the mental impression would not be privileged if it was based exclusively on the mediator's observation of that party wearing heavy clothes and an overcoat on a hot summer day because the choice of clothing was not meant to inform.

There is no justification for making readily observable conduct privileged, certainly not more privileged than it is under the attorney-client privilege. If the conduct is seen in the mediation room, it can also be observed, even photographed, outside of the mediation room, as well as in other contexts. One of the primary reasons for making mediation communications privileged is to promote candor, and excluding evidence of a readily observable characteristic is not necessary to promote candor. . . .

SECTION 3. SCOPE.

(a) Except as otherwise provided in subsection (b) or (c), this [Act] applies to a mediation in which:

(1) the mediation parties are required to mediate by statute or court or administrative agency rule or referred to mediation by a court, administrative agency, or arbitrator;

(2) the mediation parties and the mediator agree to mediate in a record that demonstrates an expectation that mediation communications will be privileged against disclosure; or

(3) the mediation parties use as a mediator an individual who holds himself or herself out as a mediator or the mediation is provided by a person that holds itself out as providing mediation.

(b) The [Act] does not apply to a mediation:

(1) relating to the establishment, negotiation, administration, or termination of a collective bargaining relationship;

(2) relating to a dispute that is pending under or is part of the processes established by a collective bargaining agreement, except that the [Act] applies to a mediation arising out of a dispute that has been filed with an administrative agency or court;

(3) conducted by a judge who might make a ruling on the case; or

(4) conducted under the auspices of:

(A) a primary or secondary school if all the parties are students or

(B) a correctional institution for youths if all the parties are residents of that institution.

(c) If the parties agree in advance in a signed record, or a record of proceeding reflects agreement by the parties, that all or part of a mediation is not privileged, the privileges under Sections 4 through 6 do not apply to the mediation or part agreed upon. However, Sections 4 through 6 apply to a mediation communication made by a person that has not received actual notice of the agreement before the communication is made.

Reporter's Notes

1. In general.

The Act is broad in its coverage of mediation, a departure from the common state statutes that apply to mediation in particular contexts, such as court-connected mediation or community mediation, or to the mediation of particular types of disputes, such as worker's compensation or civil rights. Moreover, unlike many mediation privileges, it also applies in some contexts in which the Rules of Evidence are not consistently followed, such as administrative hearings and arbitration.

Whether the Act in fact applies is a crucial issue because it determines not only the application of the mediation privilege but also whether the mediator has the obligations regarding the disclosure of conflicts of interest and, if asked, qualifications in Section 9; is prohibited from making disclosures about the mediation to courts, agencies and investigative authorities in Section 7; and must accommodate requirements regarding accompanying individuals in Section 10. . . .

2. Section 3(a). Mediations covered by Act; triggering mechanisms.

Section 3(a) sets forth three conditions, the satisfaction of any one of which will trigger the application of the Act. This triggering requirement is necessary because the many different forms, contexts, and practices of mediation and other methods of dispute resolution make it sometimes difficult to know with certainty whether one is engaged in a mediation or some other dispute resolution or prevention process that employs mediation and related principles. This problem is exacerbated by the fact that unlike other professionals — such as doctors, lawyers, and social workers — mediators are not licensed and the process they conduct is informal. If the intent to mediate is not clear, even a casual discussion over a backyard fence might later be deemed to have been a mediation, unfairly surprising those involved and frustrating the reasonable expectations of the parties.

[T]he Drafting Committees discussed whether it should cover the many cultural and religious practices that are similar to mediation and that use a person similar to the mediator, as defined in this Act. On the one hand, many of these cultural and religious practices, like more traditional mediation, streamline and resolve conflicts, while solving problems and restoring relationships. Some examples of these practices are Ho'oponopono, circle ceremonies, family conferencing, and pastoral or marital counseling. These cultural and religious practices bring richness to the quality of life and contribute to traditional mediation. On the other hand, there are instances in which the application of the Act to these practices would be disruptive of the practices and therefore undesirable. On balance, furthering the principle of self-determination, the Drafting Committees decided that those involved should make the choice to be covered by the Act in those instances in which other definitional requirements of Section 2 are met by entering into an agreement to mediate reflected by a record or securing a court or agency referral pursuant to Section 3(a)(1). At the same time, these persons could opt out the Act's coverage by not using this triggering mechanism. This leaves a great deal of leeway, appropriately, with those involved in the practices. . . .

7. *Section 3(c). Alternative of non-privileged mediation.*

This Section allows the parties to opt for a non-privileged mediation or mediation session by mutual agreement, and furthers the Act's policy of party self-determination. If the parties so agree, the privilege sections of the Act do not apply, thus fulfilling the parties' reasonable expectations regarding the confidentiality of that mediation or session. For example, parties in a sophisticated commercial mediation, who are represented by counsel, may see no need for a privilege to attach to a mediation or session, and may by express written agreement "opt out" of the Act's privilege provisions. Similarly, parties may also use this option if they wish to rely on, and therefore use in evidence, statements made during the mediation. It is the parties rather than the mediator who make this choice, although a mediator could presumably refuse to mediate a mediation or session that is not covered by this Act. Even if the parties do not agree in advance, the parties, mediator, and all nonparty participants can waive the privilege pursuant to Section 5. In this instance, however, the mediator and other participants can block the waiver in some respects.

If the parties want to opt out, they should inform the mediators or nonparty participants of this agreement, because without actual notice, the privileges of the Act still apply to the mediation communications of the persons who have not been so informed until such notice is actually received. . . .

Section 4. Privilege Against Disclosure; Admissibility; Discovery.

(a) Except as otherwise provided in Section 6, a mediation communication is privileged as provided in subsection (b) and is not subject to discovery or admissible in evidence in a proceeding unless waived or precluded as provided by Section 5.

(b) In a proceeding, the following privileges apply:

(1) A mediation party may refuse to disclose, and may prevent any other person from disclosing, a mediation communication.

(2) A mediator may refuse to disclose a mediation communication, and may prevent any other person from disclosing a mediation communication of the mediator.

(3) A nonparty participant may refuse to disclose, and may prevent any other person from disclosing, a mediation communication of the nonparty participant.

(c) Evidence or information that is otherwise admissible or subject to discovery does not become inadmissible or protected from discovery solely by reason of its disclosure or use in a mediation.

Reporter's Notes

4. Section 4(b). Operation of privilege. . . .

a. The holders of the privilege.

1. In general.

A critical component of the Act's general rule is its designation of the holder—i.e., the person who is eligible to raise and waive the privilege. . . . Those statutes that designate a holder tend to be split between those that make the parties the only holders of the privilege, and those that also make the mediator a holder. The Act adopts an approach that provides that both the parties and the mediators may assert the privilege regarding certain matters, thus giving weight to the primary concern of each rationale.

2. Parties as holders.

The mediation privilege of the parties draws upon the purpose, rationale, and traditions of the attorney-client privilege, in that its paramount justification is to encourage candor by the mediation parties, just as encouraging the client's candor is the central justification for the attorney-client privilege. . . . It should be noted that even if the mediator loses the privilege to block or assert a privilege, the parties may still come forward and assert their privilege, thus blocking the mediator who has lost the privilege from providing testimony about the affected mediation. . . .

3. Mediators as holders.

Mediators are made holders with respect to their own mediation communications, so that they may participate candidly, and with respect to their own testimony, so that they will not be viewed as biased in future mediations. . . .

4. Nonparty participants as holders.

In addition, the Act adds a privilege for the nonparty participant, though limited to the communications by that individual in the mediation. The purpose is to encourage the candid participation of experts and others who may have information that would facilitate resolution of the case. . . .

SECTION 5. WAIVER AND PRECLUSION OF PRIVILEGE.

(a) A privilege under Section 4 may be waived in a record or orally during a proceeding if it is expressly waived by all parties to the mediation and:

(1) in the case of the privilege of a mediator, it is expressly waived by the mediator; and

(2) in the case of the privilege of a nonparty participant, it is expressly waived by the nonparty participant.

(b) A person that discloses or makes a representation about a mediation communication which prejudices another person in a proceeding is precluded from asserting a privilege under Section 4, but only to the extent necessary for the person prejudiced to respond to the representation or disclosure.

(c) A person that intentionally uses a mediation to plan, attempt to commit or commit a crime, or to conceal an ongoing crime or ongoing criminal activity is precluded from asserting a privilege under Section 4.

Reporter's Notes

1. *Section 5(a) and (b). Waiver and preclusion.*

[T]hese provisions differ from the attorney-client privilege in that the mediation privilege does not permit waiver to be implied by conduct. The rationale for requiring explicit waiver is to safeguard against the possibility of inadvertent waiver, such as through the often salutary practice of parties discussing their dispute and mediation with friends and relatives. In contrast to these settings, there is a sense of formality and awareness of legal rights in all of the proceedings to which the privilege may be waived if the waiver is oral. They generally are conducted on the record, easing the difficulties of establishing what was said.

[Requiring explicit waiver] created the anomalous situation of permitting the opportunity for one party to blurt out potentially damaging information in the midst of a trial and then use the privilege to block the other party from contesting the truth. To address this anomaly, the Drafters added Section 5(b), a preclusion provision to cover situations in which the parties do not expressly waive the privilege but engage in conduct inconsistent with the assertions of the privilege, and that cause prejudice. As under existing interpretations for other communications privileges, waiver through preclusion would not typically constitute a waiver with respect to all mediation communications, only those related in subject matter. . . .

2. *Section 5(c). Preclusion for use of mediation to plan or commit crime.*

. . . This Section should be read together with Section 6(a)(4), which applies to particular communications within a mediation which are used for the same purposes. The two differ on the purpose of the mediation: Section 5(c) applies when the mediation itself is used to further a crime, while Section 6(a)(4) applies to matters that are being mediated for other purposes but which include discussion of acts or statements that may be deemed criminal in nature. Under Section 5(c), the preclusion applies to all mediation communications because the purpose of the mediation frustrates public policy. Under Section 6(a)(4), the preclusion only applies to those mediation communications that have a criminal character; the privilege may still be asserted to block the introduction of other communications made during the mediation. . . .

SECTION 6. EXCEPTIONS TO PRIVILEGE.

(a) There is no privilege under Section 4 for a mediation communication that is:

(1) in an agreement evidenced by a record signed by all parties to the agreement;

(2) available to the public under [insert statutory reference to open records act] or made during a session of a mediation which is open, or is required by law to be open, to the public;

(3) a threat or statement of a plan to inflict bodily injury or commit a crime of violence;

(4) intentionally used to plan a crime, attempt to commit or commit a crime, or to conceal an ongoing crime or ongoing criminal activity;

(5) sought or offered to prove or disprove a claim or complaint of professional misconduct or malpractice filed against a mediator;

(6) except as otherwise provided in subsection (c), sought or offered to prove or disprove a claim or complaint of professional misconduct or malpractice filed against a mediation party, nonparty participant, or representative of a party based on conduct occurring during a mediation; or

(7) sought or offered to prove or disprove abuse, neglect, abandonment, or exploitation in a proceeding in which a child or adult protective services agency is a party, unless the

[Alternative A: [State to insert, for example, child or adult protection] case is referred by a court to mediation and a public agency participates.]

[Alternative B: public agency participates in the [State to insert, for example, child or adult protection] mediation].

(b) There is no privilege under Section 4 if a court, administrative agency, or arbitrator finds, after a hearing in camera, that the party seeking discovery or the proponent of the evidence has shown that the evidence is not otherwise available, that there is a need for the evidence that substantially outweighs the interest in protecting confidentiality, and that the mediation communication is sought or offered in:

(1) a court proceeding involving a felony [or misdemeanor]; or

(2) except as otherwise provided in subsection (c), a proceeding to prove a claim to rescind or reform or a defense to avoid liability on a contract arising out of the mediation.

(c) A mediator may not be compelled to provide evidence of a mediation communication referred to in subsection (a)(6) or (b)(2).

(d) If a mediation communication is not privileged under subsection (a) or (b), only the portion of the communication necessary for the application of the exception from nondisclosure may be admitted. Admission of evidence under subsection (a) or (b) does not render the evidence, or any other mediation communication, discoverable or admissible for any other purpose.

Reporter's Notes

1. In general.

The exceptions in Section 6(a) apply regardless of the need for the evidence because society's interest in the information contained in the mediation communications may be said to categorically outweigh its interest in the confidentiality of mediation communications. In contrast, the exceptions under Section 6(b) would apply only in situations where the relative strengths of society's interest in a mediation communication and mediation participant interest in confidentiality can only be measured under the facts and circumstances of the particular case. . . .

2. *Section 6(a)(1). Record of an agreement.*

. . . This exception is noteworthy only for what is not included: oral agreements. The disadvantage of exempting oral settlements is that nearly everything said during a mediation session could bear on either whether the parties came to an agreement or the content of the agreement. In other words, an exception for oral agreements has the potential to swallow the rule of privilege. As a result, mediation participants might be less candid, not knowing whether a controversy later would erupt over an oral agreement. Unfortunately, excluding evidence of oral settlements reached during a mediation session would operate to the disadvantage of a less legally sophisticated party who is accustomed to the enforcement of oral settlements reached in negotiations. Such a person might also mistakenly assume the admissibility of evidence of oral settlements reached in mediation as well. However, because the majority of courts and statutes limit the confidentiality exception to signed written agreements, one would expect that mediators and others will soon incorporate knowledge of a writing requirement into their practices. Despite the limitation on oral agreements, the Act leaves parties other means to preserve the agreement quickly. For example, parties can agree that the mediation has ended, state their oral agreement into the tape recorder and record their assent. . . .

3. *Section 6(a)(2). Mediations open to the public; meetings and records made open by law.*

Section 6(a)(2) makes clear that the privileges in Section 4 do not preempt state open meetings and open records laws, thus deferring to the policies of the individual States regarding the types of meetings that will be subject to these laws. In addition, it provides an exception when the mediation is opened to the public, such as a televised mediation. . . .

5. *Section 6(a)(4). Communications used to plan or commit a crime.*

[T]his exception does not cover mediation communications constituting admissions of past crimes, or past potential crimes, which remain privileged. Thus, for example, discussions of past aggressive positions with regard to taxation or other matters of regulatory compliance in commercial mediations remain privileged against possible use in subsequent or simultaneous civil proceedings. The Drafting Committees discussed the possibility of creating an exception for the related circumstance in which a party makes an admission of past conduct that portends future bad conduct. However, they decided against such an expansion of this exception because such past conduct can already be disclosed in other important ways. The other parties can warn others, because parties are not prohibited from disclosing by the Act. . . .

7. *Section 6(a)(6). Evidence of professional misconduct or malpractice by a party or representative of a party.*

Sometimes the issue arises whether anyone may provide evidence of professional misconduct or malpractice occurring during the mediation. The failure to provide an exception for such evidence would mean that lawyers and fiduciaries could act unethically or in violation of standards without concern that evidence of the misconduct would later be admissible in a proceeding brought for recourse. This exception makes it possible to use testimony of anyone except the mediator in proceedings at which such a claim is made or defended. Because of the potential adverse impact on a mediator's appearance of impartiality, the use of mediator testimony is more guarded, and therefore protected by Section 6(c). . . . Mediators and others are not precluded by the Act from reporting misconduct to an agency or tribunal other than one that might make a ruling on the dispute being mediated, which is precluded by Section 8(a) and (b).

8. *Section 6(a)(7). Evidence of abuse or neglect.*

An exception for child abuse and neglect is common in domestic mediation confidentiality statutes, and the Act reaffirms these important policy choices States have made to protect their citizens. By referring to "child and adult protective services agency," the exception broadens the coverage to include the elderly and disabled if that State has protected them by statute and has created an agency enforcement process. It should be stressed that this exception applies only to permit disclosures in public agency proceedings in which the agency is a party or nonparty participant. The exception does not apply in private actions, such as divorce, because the need for the evidence is not as great as in proceedings brought to protect against abuse and neglect so that the harm can be stopped, and is outweighed by the policy of promoting candor during mediation. For example, in a mediation between Husband and Wife who are seeking a divorce, Husband admits to sexually abusing a child. Husband's admission would not be privileged in an action brought by the public agency to protect the child, but would be privileged in the divorce hearings. The last bracketed phrases make an exception to the exception to privilege of mediation communications in certain mediations involving such public agencies. . . . These alternatives are bracketed and offered to the states as recommended model provisons because of concerns raised by some mediators of such cases that mediator testimony sometimes can be necessary and appropriate to secure the safety of a vulnerable party in a situation of abuse.

9. *Section 6(b). Exceptions requiring demonstration of need.*

The exceptions under this Section constitute less common fact patterns that may sometimes justify carving an exception, but only when the unique facts and circumstances of the case demonstrate that the evidence is otherwise unavailable, and the need for the evidence outweighs the policies underlying the privilege. Thus, Section 6(b) effectively places the burden on the proponent to persuade the court on these points. The evidence will not be disclosed absent a finding on these points after an in camera hearing. Further, under Section 6(d) the evidence will be admitted only for that limited purpose.

10. Section 6(b)(1). Felony [and misdemeanors].

[T]he Act affords more specialized treatment for the use of mediation communications in subsequent felony proceedings, which reflects the unique character, considerations, and concerns that attend the need for evidence in the criminal process. States may also wish to extend this specialized treatment to misdemeanors, and the Drafters offer appropriate model language for states in that event.

Existing privilege statutes are silent or split as to whether they apply only to civil proceedings, apply also to some juvenile or misdemeanor proceedings, or apply as well to all criminal proceedings. The split among the States reflects clashing policy interests. On the one hand, mediation participants operating under the benefit of a privilege might reasonably expect that statements made in mediation would not be available for use in a later felony prosecution. The candor this expectation promotes is precisely that which the mediation privilege seeks to protect. It is also the basis upon which many criminal courts throughout the country have established victim-offender mediation programs, which have enjoyed great success in misdemeanor, and, increasingly, felony cases. Public policy specifically supports the mediation of gang disputes, for example, and these programs may be less successful if the parties cannot discuss the criminal acts underlying the disputes.

On the other hand, society's need for evidence to avoid an inaccurate decision is greatest in the criminal context — both for evidence that might convict the guilty and exonerate the innocent — because the stakes of human liberty and public safety are at their zenith. For this reason, even without this exception, the courts can be expected to weigh heavily the need for the evidence in a particular case, and sometimes will rule that the defendant's constitutional rights require disclosure.

After great consideration and public comment, the Drafting Committees decided to leave the critical balancing of these competing interests to the sound discretion of the courts to determine under the facts and circumstances of each case. Critically, it is drafted in a manner to ensure the same right to evidence introduced by the prosecution, thus assuring a level playing field. In addition, it puts the parties on notice of this limitation on confidentiality.

11. Section 6(b)(2). Validity and enforceability of settlement agreement.

This exception is designed to preserve traditional contract defenses to the enforcement of the mediated settlement agreement that relate to the integrity of the mediation process, which otherwise would be unavailable if based on mediation communications. A recent Texas case provides an example. An action was brought to enforce a mediated settlement. The defendant raised the defense of duress and sought to introduce evidence that he had asked the mediator to permit him to leave because of chest pains and a history of heart trouble, and that the mediator had refused to let him leave the mediation session. *See Randle v. Mid Gulf, Inc.*, No. 14-95-01292, 1996 WL 447954 (Tex. App. 1996) (unpublished). The exception might also allow party testimony in a personal injury case that the driver denied having insurance, causing the plaintiff to rely and settle on that basis, where such a misstatement would be a basis for reforming or avoiding liability under the settlement. Under this exception the evidence will not be privileged if the weighing requirements are met. This exception differs from the exception for a record of an agreement in Section 6(a)(1) in that Section 6(a)(1) only exempts the admissibility of the record of the agreement itself, while the exception in Section 6(b)(2) is broader in that it would permit the admissibility of other mediation communications that are necessary to establish or refute a defense to the validity of a mediated settlement agreement. . . .

SECTION 7. PROHIBITED MEDIATOR REPORTS.

(a) Except as required in subsection (b), a mediator may not make a report, assessment, evaluation, recommendation, finding, or other communication regarding a mediation to a court, administrative agency, or other authority that may make a ruling on the dispute that is the subject of the mediation.

(b) A mediator may disclose:

(1) whether the mediation occurred or has terminated, whether a settlement was reached, and attendance;

(2) a mediation communication as permitted under Section 6; or

(3) a mediation communication evidencing abuse, neglect, abandonment, or exploitation of an individual to a public agency responsible for protecting individuals against such mistreatment.

(c) A communication made in violation of subsection (a) may not be considered by a court, administrative agency, or arbitrator.

Reporter's Notes

. . . In contrast to the privilege, which gives a right to refuse to provide evidence in a subsequent legal proceeding, this Section creates a prohibition against disclosure. . . . The purpose of this Section is consistent with the conclusions of seminal reports in the mediation field [that] condemn the use of such reports as permitting coercion by the mediator and destroying confidence in the neutrality of the mediator and in the mediation process.

Importantly, the prohibition is limited to reports or other listed communications to those who may rule on the dispute being mediated. While the mediators are thus constrained in terms of reports to courts and others that may make rulings on the case, they are not prohibited from reporting threatened harm to appropriate authorities, for example, if learned during a mediation to settle a civil dispute. In this regard, Section 7(b)(3) responds to public concerns about clarity and makes explicit what is otherwise implied in the Act, that mediators are not constrained by this Section in their ability to disclose threats to the safety and well being of vulnerable parties to appropriate public authorities, and is consistent with the exception for disclosure in proceedings in Section 6(a)(7). Similarly, while the provision prohibits mediators from making these reports, it does not constrain the parties.

The communications by the mediator to the court or other authority are broadly defined. The provisions would not permit a mediator to communicate, for example, on whether a particular party engaged in "good faith" negotiation, or to state whether a party had been "the problem" in reaching a settlement. Section 7(b)(1), however, does permit disclosure of particular facts, including attendance and whether a settlement was reached. For example, a mediator may report that one party did not attend and another attended only for the first five minutes. States with "good faith" mediation laws or court rules may want to consider the interplay between such laws and this Section of the Act.

Section 8. Confidentiality.

Unless subject to the [insert statutory references to open meetings act and open records act], mediation communications are confidential to the extent agreed by the parties or provided by other law or rule of this State.

Reporter's Notes

This Section restates the general rule in the states regarding the confidentiality of mediation communications outside the context of proceedings. Typically, confidentiality agreements are enforceable against a signatory under state contract law, through damages and sometimes specific enforcement. . . .

Early drafts were criticized by some in the mediation community for failing to impose an affirmative duty on mediation participants not to disclose mediation communications to third persons outside of the context of the proceedings at which the Section 4 privilege applies. In several subsequent drafts, the Drafters attempted to establish a rule that would prohibit such disclosures, but found it impracticable to do so without imposing a severe risk of civil liability on the many unknowing mediation participants who might discuss their mediations with friends and family members, for example, for any number of salutary reasons. In addition, the Drafters were deeply concerned about their capacity to develop a truly comprehensive list of legitimate and appropriate exceptions — such as for the education and training of mediators, for the monitoring evaluation and improvement of court-related mediation programs, and for the reporting of threats to police and abuse to public agencies — as each draft drew forth more calls for legitimate and appropriate exceptions. Similarly, efforts to create a simpler rule with fewer exceptions but with greater judicial discretion to act as appropriate on a case-by-case basis to prevent "manifest injustice" also met severe resistance from many different sectors of the mediation community, as well as a number of state bar ADR committees. Finally, recognizing the important role of non-lawyer mediators and the many people who participate in mediations without counsel or knowledge of the law, the Drafters were concerned about the intelligibility and accessibility of the provisions. In the end, the Drafters ultimately chose to draw a clear line, and to follow the general practice in the states of leaving the disclosure of mediation communications outside of proceedings to the good judgment of the parties to determine in light of the unique characteristics and circumstances of their dispute. . . .

SECTION 9. MEDIATOR'S DISCLOSURE OF CONFLICTS OF INTEREST; BACKGROUND.

(a) Before accepting a mediation, an individual who is requested to serve as a mediator shall:

(1) make an inquiry that is reasonable under the circumstances to determine whether there are any known facts that a reasonable individual would consider likely to affect the impartiality of the mediator, including a financial or personal interest in the outcome of the mediation and an existing or past relationship with a mediation party or foreseeable participant in the mediation; and

(2) disclose any such known fact to the mediation parties as soon as is practical before accepting a mediation.

(b) If a mediator learns any fact described in subsection (a)(1) after accepting a mediation, the mediator shall disclose it as soon as is practicable.

(c) At the request of a mediation party, an individual who is requested to serve as a mediator shall disclose the mediator's qualifications to mediate a dispute.

(d) A person that violates subsection [(a) or (b)][(a), (b), or (g)] is precluded by the violation from asserting a privilege under Section 4.

(e) Subsections (a), (b), [and] (c), [and] [(g)] do not apply to an individual acting as a judge.

(f) This [Act] does not require that a mediator have a special qualification by background or profession.

[(g) A mediator must be impartial, unless after disclosure of the facts required in subsections (a) and (b) to be disclosed, the parties agree otherwise.]

Reporter's Notes

1. *Sections 9(a) and 9(b). Disclosure of mediator's conflicts of interest. . . .*

b. Reasonable duty of inquiry

. . . The reasonable inquiry . . . depends on the circumstances. For example, if a small claims court refers parties to a mediator who has a volunteer attorney standing in court, the parties would not expect that mediator to check on conflicts with all lawyers in the mediator's firm in the five minutes between referral and mediation. Presumably, only conflicts known by the mediator would affect that mediation in any event.

2. *Section 9(c) and (f). Disclosure of mediator's qualifications.*

It must be stressed that the Act does not establish mediator qualifications. No consensus has emerged in the law, research, or commentary as to those mediator qualifications that will best produce effectiveness or fairness. As clarified by Section 9(f), mediators need not be lawyers. In fact, the American Bar Association Section on Dispute Resolution has issued a statement that "dispute resolution programs should permit all individuals who have appropriate training and qualifications to serve as neutrals, regardless of whether they are lawyers." ABA Section of Dispute Resolution Council Res., April 28, 1999.

At the same time, the law and commentary recognize that the quality of the mediator is important and that the courts and public agencies referring cases to mediation have a heightened responsibility to assure it. The decision of the Drafting Committees against prescribing qualifications should not be interpreted as a disregard for the importance of qualifications. Rather, respecting the unique characteristics that may qualify a particular mediator for a particular mediation, the silence of the Act reflects the difficulty of addressing the topic in a uniform statute that applies to mediation in a variety of contexts. Qualifications may be important, but they need not be uniform. It is not the intent of the Act to preclude a statute, court or administrative agency rule, arbitrator or contract between the parties from requiring that a mediator have a particular background or profession; those decisions are best made by individual states, courts, governmental entities, and parties.

5. *[Section 9(g). Mediator impartiality.]*

This provision is bracketed to signal that it is suggested as a model provision and need not be part of a Uniform Act. . . . While few would argue that it is almost always best for mediators to be impartial as a matter of practice, including such a requirement into a uniform law drew considerable controversy. Some mediators, reflecting a deeply and sincerely felt value within the mediation community that a mediator not be predisposed to favor or disfavor parties in dispute, persistently urged the Drafters to enshrine this value in the Act; for these, the failure to include the notion of impartiality in the Act would be a distortion of the mediation process. Other mediators, service providers, judges, mediation scholars, however, urged the Drafters not to include the term "impartiality" for a variety of reasons. At least three are worth stressing. One pressing concern was that including such a statutory requirement would subject mediators to an unwarranted exposure to civil lawsuits by disgruntled parties. In this regard, mediators with a more evaluative style expressed concerns that the common practice of so-called "reality checking" would be used as a basis for such actions against the mediator. A second major concern was over the workability of such a statutory requirement. Scholarly research in cognitive psychology has confirmed many hidden but common biases that affect judgment, such as attributional distortions of judgment and inclinations that are the product of social learning and professional culturation. Similarly, mediators in certain contexts sometimes have an ethical or felt duty to advocate on behalf of a party, such as long-term care ombuds in the health care context. Third, some parties seek to use a mediator who has a duty to be partial in some respects — such as a domestic mediator who is charged by law to protect the interests of the children. It has been argued that such mediations should still be privileged. . . .

SECTION 10. PARTICIPATION IN MEDIATION.

An attorney or other individual designated by a party may accompany the party to and participate in a mediation. A waiver of participation given before the mediation may be rescinded.

Reporter's Notes

The fairness of mediation is premised upon the informed consent of the parties to any agreement reached. Some statutes permit the mediator to exclude lawyers from mediation, resting fairness guarantees on the lawyer's later review of the draft settlement agreement. At least one bar authority has expressed doubts about the ability of a lawyer to review an agreement effectively when that lawyer did not participate in the give and take of negotiation. Boston Bar Ass'n, Op. 78-1 (1979). . . . Some parties may prefer not to bring counsel. However, because of the capacity of attorneys to help mitigate power imbalances, and in the absence of other procedural protections for less powerful parties, the Drafting Committees elected to let the parties, not the mediator, decide. Also, their agreement to exclude counsel should be made after the dispute arises, so that they can weigh the importance in the context of the stakes involved. . . .

As a practical matter, this provision has application only when the parties are compelled to participate in the mediation by contract, law, or order from a court or agency. In other instances, any party or mediator unhappy with the decision of a party to be accompanied by an individual can simply leave the mediation. In some instances, a party may seek to bring an individual whose presence will interfere with effective discussion. In divorce mediation, for example, a new friend of one of the parties may spark new arguments. In these instances, the mediator can make that observation to the parties and, if the mediation flounders because of the presence of the nonparty, the parties or the mediator can terminate the mediation. The pre-mediation waiver of this right of accompaniment can be rescinded, because the party may not have understood the implication at that point in the process. However, this provision can be waived once the mediation begins.

Editor's Note

The National Conference of Commissioners on Uniform State Laws amended the Uniform Mediation Act in 2003. The purpose of the amendment was to encourage state adoption of the United Nations Commission on International Trade Law's Model Law on International Commercial Conciliation and to make the confidentiality provisions of that law consistent with the Uniform Mediation Act. The UN Commission urged member nations to vary the wording of the Commission's law as little as possible to facilitate international understanding and thereby encourage the use of mediation for international commercial matters. To accommodate this desire, the UMA drafters incorporated the Model Law by reference in a new section 11. The original UMA sections 11-16 were renumbered as sections 12-17, and the Model Law was attached as an appendix to the UMA.

The definition of international commercial mediation encompasses some types of mediation that might be considered normal fare in this country. For example, the mediation of a dispute between a European car manufacturer and a local dealer would be an international commercial mediation. Thus, the drafters faced a notice problem in adopting the UN Commission's Model Law. Unless they added material to change the confidentiality provisions of the Model Law, some mediation participants would be surprised to learn that their communications fell under the Model Law's privilege rather than the broader privilege of the UMA. To prevent this surprise, the drafters made the UMA's privilege applicable to international commercial mediations as well, unless the parties agree otherwise. This eliminates the possibility of a surprise while preserving the international group's concept for those who prefer it.

Section 11. International Commercial Mediation

(a) In this section, "Model Law" means the Model Law on International Commercial Conciliation adopted by the United Nations Commission on International Trade Law on 28 June 2002 and recommended by the United Nations General Assembly in a resolution (A/RES/57/18) dated 19 November 2002, and "international commercial mediation" means an international commercial conciliation as defined in Article 1 of the Model Law.

(b) Except as otherwise provided in subsections (c) and (d), if a mediation is an international commercial mediation, the mediation is governed by the Model Law.

(c) Unless the parties agree in accordance with Section 3(c) of this [Act] that all or part of an international commercial mediation is not privileged, Sections 4, 5, and 6 and any applicable definitions in Section 2 of this [Act] also apply to the mediation and nothing in Article 10 of the Model Law derogates from Sections 4, 5, and 6.

(d) If the parties to an international commercial mediation agree under Article 1, subsection (7), of the Model Law that the Model Law does not apply, this [Act] applies.

Legislative Note. The UNCITRAL Model Law on International Commercial Conciliation may be found at www.uncitral.org/en-index.htm. Important comments on interpretation are included in the Draft Guide to Enactment and Use of UNCITRAL Model Law on International Commercial Conciliation. The states should note the Draft Guide in a Legislative Note to the Act. This is especially important with respect to interpretation of Article 9 of the Model Law.

COMMENT

1. Varying by Agreement/Choice of Law

This Amendment allows parties to international commercial mediation to take advantage of the privilege protections of the Uniform Mediation Act, which typically are broader than the evidentiary exclusions of the UNCITRAL Model Law. A number of choices are available to the mediation participants:

(1) *If the participants prefer to have the mediation covered by the privilege protections of the Uniform Mediation Law,* which are typically broader than the evidentiary exclusions of the UNCITRAL Model Law: This is the default situation under this Amendment to the Uniform Mediation Act. This result is reached by reading subsections (a) and (c) together. No additional agreement is necessary.

(2) *If the participants prefer not to have the mediation covered by the provisions of the UNCITRAL Model Act but want the mediation covered by the Uniform Mediation Act*: The parties should agree, pursuant to Article 1, subsection (7) of the UNCITRAL Model Law, to exclude the applicability of the Model Law. In this situation, subsection (d) of the Amendment provides that the default is that the mediation is covered by the Uniform Mediation Act.

(3) *If the participants prefer the narrower protections for the use of mediation communications provided by the UNCITRAL Model Law and do not want to be covered by the privilege provisions of the Uniform Mediation Act*: The participants should agree, in a record (written or other electronic form), that the privileges under Sections 4 through 6 of the Uniform Mediation Act do not apply to the mediation or part agreed upon. It is important to note that this agreement does not preclude the raising of the privilege by a participant who does not know of the agreement before making the statement that is the subject of the privilege. Section 3(c) provides:

> If the parties agree in advance in a signed record, or a record of proceeding reflects agreement by the parties, that all or part of a mediation is not privileged, the privileges under Sections 4 through 6 do not apply to the mediation or part agreed upon. However, Sections 4 through 6 apply to a mediation communication made by a person that has not received actual notice of the agreement before the communication is made.

If the participants so agree, the UNCITRAL Model Law provision on the use of mediation communications, Article 10, will be the default position.

(4) *If the parties would like to have an open mediation, with mediation communications being available for later proceedings*: The parties should enter the agreement described in point (3) and also agree that they exclude the applicability of Articles 9 and 10 of the UNCITRAL Model Law.

(5) *If the parties would like to have the mediation covered by another law*: They should designate in their agreement to mediate what law that will cover the international commercial mediation, in addition to taking the steps listed in point (4). They should realize, however, that a court may be unwilling to import a law of privilege because the court might deem privilege to be an aspect of procedure governed by the forum state's law. In addition, if the parties seek to import a mediation privilege law that is broader than that of the forum state, the court might view the agreement as an attempt to keep evidence from the tribunal and against public policy and therefore unenforceable.

2. *Confidentiality*

Article 9 of the UNCITRAL Model Law is consistent with Section 8 of the Uniform Mediation Act, which indicates that mediation communications are confidential to the extent agreed upon by the parties or provided in state law, when Article 9 is read together with the notes on interpretation in the Draft Guide to Enactment and Use of UNCITRAL Model Law on International Commercial Conciliation. The Draft Guide makes clear that the violation of Article 9 should not be a basis for sanctions unless the party disclosing understood that the mediation was governed by the confidentiality rule. The Draft Guide also makes clear that a participant may warn or disclose in the public interest despite the prohibitions. This is the current state of U.S. contract law regarding secrecy agreements as discussed in the Reporter's Notes to Section 8. The pertinent portion of the Draft Guide states:

> The Working Group agreed that an illustrative and non-exhaustive list of possible exceptions to the general rule on confidentiality would more appropriately be provided in the Guide to Enactment. Examples of such laws may include laws requiring the conciliator or parties to reveal information if there is a reasonable threat that a person will suffer death or substantial bodily harm if the information is not disclosed and laws requiring disclosure if it is in the public interest (for example, to alert the public about a health or environmental or safety risk). It is the intent of the drafters that, in the event a court or other tribunal is considering an allegation that a person did not comply with Article 9, it should include in its consideration any evidence of conduct of the parties that shows whether they had, or did not have, an understanding that a conciliation existed and consequently an expectation of confidentiality. When enacting the Model Law, certain states may wish to clarify Article 9 to reflect that interpretation. . . .

3. *Conflict of Laws*

The drafters intend the privilege provisions to be widely applied by courts so that the mediation participants will know the breadth of the mediation communications privilege when they are engaged in the mediation, even though they may not anticipate all of the nations or states where the mediation communications might be sought or introduced. Nonetheless, the mediation participants should realize that choice of law rules in other nations and states vary and those rules may result in application of law other than that of the state where the mediation took place. *See, e.g., Asten, Inc. v. Wagner Systems Corp.,* No. C.A. 15617, 1999 WL 803965 (Del. Ch. Sept 23, 1999) (applying South Carolina law to dispute arising out of Florida mediation of South Carolina court litigation between parties incorporated in Delaware because South Carolina had the most significant relationship to the transaction). In addition, courts in other nations and states may consider mediation privilege provisions to be procedural in nature, rather than substantive, and therefore apply the forum's privilege law rather than the law where the mediation occurred. Even within the United States, the courts have acted inconsistently with respect to mediation privileges that apply where the mediation was held. *See, e.g., United States v. Gullo,* 672 F. Supp. 99 (W.D.N.Y. 1987) (applying a state privilege in a federal grand jury proceeding concerning communications made during mediation in state program); *In re March, 1995—Special Grand Jury,* 897 F. Supp. 1170 (S.D. Ind. 1995) (refusing to apply state court mediation privilege in a federal grand jury proceeding concerning communications made during mediation in state court mediation program); *In re Grand Jury Subpoena Dated Dec. 17, 1996*, 148 F.3d 487 (5th Cir. 1998) (refusing to apply state privilege in a federal grand jury proceeding concerning mediation conducted in federally funded mediation program operated by state).

The choice of law rules in many jurisdictions in the United States recognize party autonomy to select the law that will govern their transactions. For this reason, the drafters believe that courts in the United States will be most likely to apply this law to international commercial mediations occurring in other nations or states that later become the subject of a suit in the United States if the parties to the mediation have specified that it will be governed by the Uniform Mediation Act. . . .

5. *Reports to the Court*

Whenever mediation occurs as part of a legal proceeding, the parties would be especially aggrieved if, in absence of full settlement, the mediator could make reports to the judge who will rule on the dispute being mediated. Such reports are specifically prohibited by Section 7 of the Uniform Mediation Act.

The drafters believe that Articles 9 and 10 of the UNCITRAL Model Law achieve the same result as Section 7 of the Uniform Mediation Act. Article 10(1) prohibits disclosures by a mediator and Article 10(3) prohibits a court or arbitral tribunal from ordering disclosures. When Article 9, which broadly requires confidentiality for all mediation information, is read in conjunction with these prohibitions, it should be interpreted to include a narrower confidentiality requirement that prohibits mediator reports, including recommendations of a specific outcome, to a judge or arbitrator. This interpretation maintains the reasonable expectations of the parties regarding confidentiality and avoids a situation in which the mediator could pressure settlement by threatening to make an unwelcome report to the person who will rule in the event that the mediation does not result in settlement.

6. *Derogation from the Uniform Mediation Act*

The Amendment, subsection (c), provides that "nothing in Article 10 of the Model Law *derogates* from Section 4, 5, or 6." *Black's Law Dictionary* indicates that one law derogates another law if it "limits the scope or impairs its utility and force." The drafters intend that the Uniform Mediation Act purposes should be achieved. For example, under the Uniform Mediation Act, a mediation communication includes any mediator statement whereas the Model Law protects only mediator proposals. This provision directs the court to protect mediator statements that were not proposals so that the protections of the Uniform Mediation Act are given full force. As a further example, the Uniform Mediation Act applies to the discovery process, while the Model Law does not mention discovery. Under this provision, the court should accord a privilege during the discovery phase in order to avoid limiting the force of the Uniform Mediation Act.

The provision that the Model Law does not derogate also would apply to exceptions to the Uniform Mediation Act that are not recognized in the Model Act. For example, the Uniform Mediation Act excepts from the privilege a mediation communication that is a threat to commit a crime of violence, but the Model Law does not. The derogation provision makes clear that the court should give effect to the exception for the threat, because to do otherwise would frustrate the purposes of the Uniform Mediation Act.

7. *Interpretation of the Model Law*

The Model Law was drafted jointly by an international group. Therefore, the courts should use the interpretation guide referenced in the Legislative Note rather than drafting conventions of U.S. law as they interpret the Model Law.

8. *Incorporation by Reference*

It is important to note that the Amendment incorporates by reference a specific version of the Model Law, that adopted on June 22, 2002. An amendment of the Model Law will not change this Section.

Some state legislatures may hesitate to incorporate by reference and may prefer to enact the Model Law. In that situation, the state can achieve uniformity by enacting this amendment as well as the Model Law, changing the internal references accordingly.

APPENDIX TO UMA SECTION 11

(Model Law as adopted by the United Nations Commission on International Trade Law — UNCITRAL — at its 35th session in New York on 28 June 2002 and approved by the United Nations General Assembly on November 19, 2002).

UNCITRAL Model Law on International Commercial Conciliation: Article 1. Scope of Application and Definitions

(1) This Law applies to international commercial conciliation.

(2) For the purposes of this Law, "conciliator" means a sole conciliator or two or more conciliators, as the case may be.

(3) For the purposes of this Law, "conciliation" means a process, whether referred to by the expression conciliation, mediation or an expression of similar import, whereby parties request a third person or persons ("the conciliator") to assist them in their attempt to reach an amicable settlement of their dispute arising out of or relating to a contractual or other legal relationship. The conciliator does not have the authority to impose upon the parties a solution to the dispute.

(4) A conciliation is international if:

(a) The parties to an agreement to conciliate have, at the time of the conclusion of that agreement, their places of business in different States; or

(b) The State in which the parties have their places of business is different from either:

(i) The State in which a substantial part of the obligations of the commercial relationship is to be performed; or

(ii) The State with which the subject matter of the dispute is most closely connected.

(5) For the purposes of this article:

(a) If a party has more than one place of business, the place of business is that which has the closest relationship to the agreement to conciliate;

(b) If a party does not have a place of business, reference is to be made to the party's habitual residence.

(6) This Law also applies to a commercial conciliation when the parties agree that the conciliation is international or agree to the applicability of this Law.

(7) The parties are free to agree to exclude the applicability of this Law.

(8) Subject to the provisions of paragraph (9) of this article, this Law applies irrespective of the basis upon which the conciliation is carried out, including agreement between the parties whether reached before or after a dispute has arisen, an obligation established by law, or a direction or suggestion of a court, arbitral tribunal, or competent governmental entity.

(9) This Law does not apply to:

(a) Cases where a judge or an arbitrator, in the course of judicial or arbitral proceedings, attempts to facilitate a settlement. . . .

Article 2. Interpretation

(1) In the interpretation of this Law, regard is to be had to its international origin and to the need to promote uniformity in its application and the observance of good faith.

(2) Questions concerning matters governed by this Law which are not expressly settled in it are to be settled in conformity with the general principles on which this Law is based.

Article 3. Variation by Agreement

Except for the provisions of Article 2 and Article 6, paragraph (3), the parties may agree to exclude or vary any of the provisions of this Law.

Article 4. Commencement of Conciliation Proceedings

(1) Conciliation proceedings in respect of a dispute that has arisen commence on the day on which the parties to that dispute agree to engage in conciliation proceedings.

(2) If a party that invited another party to conciliate does not receive an acceptance of the invitation within thirty days from the day on which the invitation was sent, or within such other period of time as specified in the invitation, the party may elect to treat this as a rejection of the invitation to conciliate.

Article 5. Number and Appointment of Conciliators

(1) There shall be one conciliator, unless the parties agree that there shall be two or more conciliators.

(2) The parties shall endeavour to reach agreement on a conciliator or conciliators, unless a different procedure for their appointment has been agreed upon.

(3) Parties may seek the assistance of an institution or person in connection with the appointment of conciliators. In particular:

(a) A party may request such an institution or person to recommend suitable persons to act as conciliator; or

(b) The parties may agree that the appointment of one or more conciliators be made directly by such an institution or person.

(4) In recommending or appointing individuals to act as conciliator, the institution or person shall have regard to such considerations as are likely to secure the appointment of an independent and impartial conciliator and, where appropriate, shall take into account the advisability of appointing a conciliator of a nationality other than the nationalities of the parties.

(5) When a person is approached in connection with his or her possible appointment as conciliator, he or she shall disclose any circumstances likely to give rise to justifiable doubts as to his or her impartiality or independence. A conciliator, from the time of his or her appointment and throughout the conciliation proceedings, shall without delay disclose any such circumstances to the parties unless they have already been informed of them by him or her.

Article 6. Conduct of Conciliation

(1) The parties are free to agree, by reference to a set of rules or otherwise, on the manner in which the conciliation is to be conducted.

(2) Failing agreement on the manner in which the conciliation is to be conducted, the conciliator may conduct the conciliation proceedings in such a manner as the conciliator considers appropriate, taking into account the circumstances of the case, any wishes that the parties may express, and the need for a speedy settlement of the dispute.

(3) In any case, in conducting the proceedings, the conciliator shall seek to maintain fair treatment of the parties and, in so doing, shall take into account the circumstances of the case.

(4) The conciliator may, at any stage of the conciliation proceedings, make proposals for a settlement of the dispute.

Article 7. Communication between Conciliator and Parties

The conciliator may meet or communicate with the parties together or with each of them separately.

Article 8. Disclosure of Information

When the conciliator receives information concerning the dispute from a party, the conciliator may disclose the substance of that information to any other party to the conciliation. However, when a party gives any information to the conciliator, subject to a specific condition that it be kept confidential, that information shall not be disclosed to any other party to the conciliation.

Article 9. Confidentiality

Unless otherwise agreed by the parties, all information relating to the conciliation proceedings shall be kept confidential, except where disclosure is required under the law or for the purposes of implementation or enforcement of a settlement agreement.

Article 10. Admissibility of Evidence in Other Proceedings

(1) A party to the conciliation proceedings, the conciliator, and any third person, including those involved in the administration of the conciliation proceedings, shall not in arbitral, judicial, or similar proceedings rely on, introduce as evidence, or give testimony or evidence regarding any of the following:

(a) An invitation by a party to engage in conciliation proceedings or the fact that a party was willing to participate in conciliation proceedings;

(b) Views expressed or suggestions made by a party in the conciliation in respect of a possible settlement of the dispute;

(c) Statements or admissions made by a party in the course of the conciliation proceedings;

(d) Proposals made by the conciliator;

(e) The fact that a party had indicated its willingness to accept a proposal for settlement made by the conciliator;

(f) A document prepared solely for purposes of the conciliation proceedings.

(2) Paragraph (1) of this article applies irrespective of the form of the information or evidence referred to therein.

(3) The disclosure of the information referred to in paragraph (1) of this article shall not be ordered by an arbitral tribunal, court, or other competent governmental authority and, if such information is offered as evidence in contravention of paragraph (1) of this article, that evidence shall be treated as inadmissible. Nevertheless, such information may be disclosed or admitted in evidence to the extent required under the law or for the purposes of implementation or enforcement of a settlement agreement.

(4) The provisions of paragraphs (1), (2), and (3) of this article apply whether or not the arbitral, judicial, or similar proceedings relate to the dispute that is or was the subject matter of the conciliation proceedings.

(5) Subject to the limitations of paragraph (1) of this article, evidence that is otherwise admissible in arbitral or judicial or similar proceedings does not become inadmissible as a consequence of having been used in a conciliation.

Article 11. Termination of Conciliation Proceedings

The conciliation proceedings are terminated:

(a) By the conclusion of a settlement agreement by the parties, on the date of the agreement;

(b) By a declaration of the conciliator, after consultation with the parties, to the effect that further efforts at conciliation are no longer justified, on the date of the declaration;

(c) By a declaration of the parties addressed to the conciliator to the effect that the conciliation proceedings are terminated, on the date of the declaration; or

(d) By a declaration of a party to the other party or parties and the conciliator, if appointed, to the effect that the conciliation proceedings are terminated, on the date of the declaration.

Article 12. Conciliator Acting as Arbitrator

Unless otherwise agreed by the parties, the conciliator shall not act as an arbitrator in respect of a dispute that was or is the subject of the conciliation proceedings or in respect of another dispute that has arisen from the same contract or legal relationship or any related contract or legal relationship.

Article 13. Resort to Arbitral or Judicial Proceedings

Where the parties have agreed to conciliate and have expressly undertaken not to initiate during a specified period of time or until a specified event has occurred arbitral or judicial proceedings with respect to an existing or future dispute, such an undertaking shall be given effect by the arbitral tribunal or the court until the terms of the undertaking have been complied with, except to the extent necessary for a party, in its opinion, to preserve its rights. Initiation of such proceedings is not of itself to be regarded as a waiver of the agreement to conciliate or as a termination of the conciliation proceedings.

Article 14. Enforceability of Settlement Agreement

If the parties conclude an agreement settling a dispute, that settlement agreement is binding and enforceable . . . *[the enacting State may insert a description of the method of enforcing settlement agreements or refer to provisions governing such enforcement].*

SECTION 12. RELATION TO ELECTRONIC SIGNATURES IN GLOBAL AND NATIONAL COMMERCE ACT.

This [Act] modifies, limits, or supersedes the federal Electronic Signatures in Global and National Commerce Act, 15 U.S.C. Section 7001 et seq., but this [Act] does not modify, limit, or supersede Section 101(c) of that Act or authorize electronic delivery of any of the notices described in Section 103(b) of that Act.

SECTION 13. UNIFORMITY OF APPLICATION AND CONSTRUCTION.

In applying and construing this [Act], consideration should be given to the need to promote uniformity of the law with respect to its subject matter among States that enact it.

SECTION 14. SEVERABILITY CLAUSE.

If any provision of this [Act] or its application to any person or circumstance is held invalid, the invalidity does not affect other provisions or applications of this [Act] which can be given effect without the invalid provision or application, and to this end the provisions of this [Act] are severable.

Section 15. Effective Date.

This [Act] takes effect ________________________ .

Section 16. Repeals.

The following acts and parts of acts are hereby repealed:
(1)
(2)
(3)

Section 17. Application to Existing Agreements or Referrals.

(a) This [Act] governs a mediation pursuant to a referral or an agreement to mediate made on or after [the effective date of this [Act]].

(b) On or after [a delayed date], this [Act] governs an agreement to mediate whenever made.

Appendix F

National Standards for Court-Connected Mediation Programs

NATIONAL STANDARDS FOR COURT-CONNECTED MEDIATION PROGRAMS

Center for Dispute Settlement and The Institute of Judicial Administration, 1992

EXECUTIVE SUMMARY

1.0 ACCESS TO MEDIATION

1.1 Mediation services should be available on the same basis as are other services of the court.

1.2 Each court should develop policies and procedures that take into consideration the language and cultural diversity of its community at all stages of development, operation and evaluation of court-connected mediation services and programs.

1.3 To ensure that parties have equal access to mediation, non-judicial screeners should have clearly stated written policies, procedures and criteria to guide their discretion in referring cases to mediation.

1.4 Courts should take steps to ensure that pro se litigants make informed choices about mediation.

1.5 Courts should ensure that information about the availability of mediation services is widely disseminated in the languages used by the consumers of court services.

1.6 a. Courts should provide orientation and training for attorneys, court personnel and others regarding the availability, nature and use of mediation services.

b. Prior to and at the filing of a case, courts should provide to the parties and their attorneys information regarding the availability of mediation.

1.7 In choosing the location and hours of operation of mediation services, courts should consider the effect on the ability of parties to use mediation effectively and the safety of mediators and parties.

2.0 COURTS' RESPONSIBILITY FOR MEDIATION

2.1 The degree of a court's responsibility for mediators or mediation programs depends on whether a mediator or program is employed or operated by the court, receives referrals from the court, or is chosen by the parties themselves.

a. The court is fully responsible for mediators it employs and programs it operates.

b. The court has the same responsibility for monitoring the quality of mediators and/or mediation programs outside the court to which it refers cases as it has for its own programs.

c. The court has no responsibility for the quality or operation of outside programs chosen by the parties without guidance from the court.

2.2 The court should specify its goals in establishing a mediation program or in referring cases to mediation programs or services outside the court and provide a means of evaluating whether or not these goals are being met.

2.3 Program Management

a. Information provided by the court to the mediator

(1) When parties choose to go to mediation outside the court, the court should have no responsibility to provide any information to the mediator.

(2) When a court makes a mandatory referral of parties to mediation, whether inside or outside the court, it should be responsible for providing the mediator or mediation program sufficient information to permit the mediator to deal with the case effectively.

b. Information provided by the mediator or the parties to the court

(1) If the program is court-operated, or if the case is referred to an outside program or mediator by the court, the program or individual mediator should have the responsibility to report information to the court, in order to permit monitoring and evaluation.

(2) If the mediator or program is chosen by the parties without guidance from the court, the provider should have no responsibility to report to the court.

2.4 Aggregate Information

Court-operated mediation programs and programs to which the court refers cases should be required to provide periodic information to the court. The information required should be related to:

a. The court's objectives in establishing the program; and

b. The court's responsibility for ensuring the quality of the services provided.

2.5 The court should designate a particular individual to be responsible for supervision, monitoring and administration of court-connected mediation programs.

2.6 Complaint Mechanism

Parties referred by the court to a mediation program, whether or not it is operated by the court, should have access to a complaint mechanism to address any grievances about the process.

3.0 INFORMATION FOR JUDGES, COURT PERSONNEL AND USERS

3.1 Courts, in collaboration with the bar and professional mediation organizations, are responsible for providing information to the public, the bar, judges and court personnel regarding the mediation process; the availability of programs; the differences between mediation, adjudication and other dispute resolution processes; the possibility of savings in cost and time; and the consequences of participation.

3.2 Courts should provide the following information:

a. To judges, court personnel and the bar:

(1) the goals and limitations of the jurisdiction's program(s)

(2) the basis for selecting cases

(3) the way in which the program operates

(4) the information to be provided to lawyers and litigants in individual cases

(5) the way in which the legal and mediation processes interact

(6) the enforcement of agreements

(7) applicable laws and rules concerning mediation

b. To users (parties and attorneys) in addition to the information in (a):

General information:

(1) issues appropriate for mediation

(2) the possible mediators and how they will be selected

(3) party choice, if any, of mediators

(4) any fees

(5) program operation, including location, times of operation, intake procedures, contact person

(6) the availability of special services for non-English speakers, and persons who have communication, mobility or other disabilities

(7) the possibility of savings or additional expenditures of money or time

Information on process:

(1) the nature and purpose of mediation

(2) confidentiality of process and records

(3) role of the parties and/or attorneys in mediation

(4) role of the mediator, including lack of authority to impose a solution

(5) voluntary acceptance of any resolution or agreement

(6) the advantages and disadvantages of participating in determining solutions

(7) enforcement of agreements

(8) availability of formal adjudication if a formal resolution or agreement is not achieved and implemented

(9) the way in which the legal and mediation processes interact, including permissible communications between mediators and the court

(10) the advantages and disadvantages of a lack of formal record

3.3 The court should encourage attorneys to inform their clients of the availability of court-connected mediation programs.

4.0 SELECTION OF CASES AND TIMING OF REFERRAL

4.1 When courts must choose between cases or categories of cases for which mediation is offered because of a shortage of resources, such choices should be made on the basis of clearly articulated criteria. Such criteria might include the following:

a. There is a high probability that mediation will be successful in the particular cases or category of case, in terms of both the number and quality of settlements.

b. Even if there is not a high probability that mediation will be successful in the particular case or category of cases, continuing litigation would harm non-parties, the dispute involves important continuing relationships, or the case, if not mediated, is likely to require continuing involvement by the court.

4.2 The following considerations may militate against the suitability of referring cases to mediation:

a. when there is a need for public sanctioning of conduct;

b. when repetitive violations of statutes or regulations need to be dealt with collectively and uniformly; and

c. when a party or parties are not able to negotiate effectively themselves or with assistance of counsel.

4.3 Courts should make available or encourage the availability of mediation to disputants before they file their cases in court as well as after judgment to address problems that otherwise might require relitigation.

4.4 While the timing of a referral to mediation may vary depending upon the type of case involved and the needs of the particular case, referral should be made at the earliest possible time that the parties are able to make an informed choice about their participation in mediation.

4.5 Courts should provide the opportunity on a continuing basis for both the parties and the court to determine the timing of a referral to mediation.

4.6 If a referral to mediation is mandated, parties should have input on the question of when the case should be referred to mediation, but the court itself should determine timing.

4.7 Courts should establish presumptive deadlines for the mediation process, which may be extended by the court upon a showing by the parties that continuation of the process will assist in reaching resolution.

5.0 MANDATORY ATTENDANCE

5.1 Mandatory attendance at an initial mediation session may be appropriate, but only when a mandate is more likely to serve the interests of parties (including those not represented by counsel), the justice system and the public than would voluntary attendance. Courts should impose mandatory attendance only when:

a. the cost of mediation is publicly funded, consistent with Standard 13.0 on Funding;

b. there is no inappropriate pressure to settle, in the form of reports to the trier of fact or financial disincentives to trial; and

c. mediators or mediation programs of high quality (i) are easily accessible; (ii) permit party participation; (iii) permit lawyer participation when the parties wish it; and (iv) provide clear and complete information about the precise process and procedures that are being required.

5.2 Courts may use a variety of mechanisms to select cases for mandatory referral to mediation. Any mechanism chosen should provide for an assessment of each case to determine its appropriateness for mediation, which takes into account the parties' relative knowledge, experience and resources.

5.3 Any system of mandatory referral to mediation should be evaluated on a periodic basis, through surveys of parties and through other mechanisms, in order to correct deficiencies in the particular implementation mechanism selected and to determine whether the mandate is more likely to serve the interests of parties, the justice system and the public than would voluntary referral.

6.0 QUALIFICATIONS OF MEDIATORS

6.1 Courts have a continuing responsibility to ensure the quality of the mediators to whom they refer cases. Qualifications of mediators to whom the courts refer cases should be based on their skills. Different categories of cases may require different types and levels of skills. Skills can be acquired through training and/or experience. No particular academic degree should be considered a prerequisite for service as a mediator in cases referred by the court.

6.2 Courts need not certify training programs but should ensure that the training received by the mediators to whom they refer cases includes role-playing with feedback.

6.3 Courts are responsible for determining that the mediators to whom they refer cases are qualified. The level of screening needed to determine qualifications will vary depending upon the type of case involved.

6.4 Courts should orient qualified mediators to court procedures.

6.5 Courts should continue to monitor the performance of mediators to whom they refer cases and ensure that their performance is of consistently high quality.

6.6 Courts should adopt procedures for removing from their roster of mediators those mediators who do not meet their performance expectations and/or ensuring that they do not receive further court referrals.

7.0 SELECTION OF MEDIATORS

7.1 To enhance party satisfaction and investment in the process of mediation, courts should maximize parties' choice of mediator, unless there are reasons why party choice may not be appropriate. Such reasons might include:

a. there is significant inequality in the knowledge or experience of the parties.

b. the court has a particular public policy it is trying to achieve through mediation, which requires selection of a particular mediator or group of mediators.

c. party choice would cause significant and undesirable delay.

7.2 When a court determines that it should refer the parties to a private mediator who will receive a fee, the court should permit the parties to choose from among a number of providers.

8.0 ETHICAL STANDARDS FOR MEDIATORS

8.1 Courts should adopt a code of ethical standards for mediators, together with procedures to handle violations of the code.

Any set of standards should include provisions that address the following concerns:

a. Impartiality
b. Conflict of Interest
c. Advertising by Mediators
d. Disclosure of Fees
e. Confidentiality
f. Role of Mediators in Settlement

9.0 CONFIDENTIALITY

9.1 Courts should have clear written policies relating to the confidentiality of both written and oral communications in mediation consistent with the laws of the jurisdiction. Among the issues such a policy should address specifically are:

a. the mediators and cases protected by confidentiality;
b. the extent of the protection;
c. who may assert or waive the protection; and
d. exceptions to the protection.

9.2 Courts should ensure that their policies relating to confidentiality in mediation are communicated to and understood by the mediators to whom they refer cases.

9.3 Courts should develop clear written policies concerning the way in which confidentiality protections and limitations are communicated to parties they refer to mediation.

9.4 Mediators should not make recommendations regarding the substance or recommended outcome of a case to the court.

9.5 Policies relating to confidentiality should not be construed to prohibit or limit effective monitoring, research or program evaluation.

10.0 THE ROLE OF LAWYERS IN MEDIATION

10.1 Courts should encourage attorneys to advise their clients on the advantages, disadvantages, and strategies for using mediation.

10.2 Parties, in consultation with their attorneys, should have the right to decide whether their attorneys should be present at mediation sessions.

10.3 Courts and mediators should work with the bar to educate lawyers about:

a. the difference in the lawyer's role in mediation as compared with traditional representation; and

b. the advantages and disadvantages of active participation by the parties and lawyers in mediation sessions.

11.0 INAPPROPRIATE PRESSURE TO SETTLE

11.1 Courts should institute appropriate provisions to permit parties to opt out of mediation. Courts also should consider modifying mediation procedures in certain types of cases to accommodate special needs, such as cases involving domestic violence. Special protocols should be developed to deal with domestic violence cases.

11.2 Courts should provide parties who are required to participate in mediation with full and accurate information about the process to which they are being referred, including the fact that they are not required to make offers and concessions or to settle.

11.3 Courts should not systematically exclude anyone from the mediation process. Lawyers never should be excluded if the parties want them to be present.

11.4 Settlement rates should not be the sole criterion for mediation program funding, mediator advancement, or program evaluation.

12.0 COMMUNICATIONS BETWEEN MEDIATORS AND THE COURT

12.1 During a mediation the judge or other trier of fact should be informed only of the following:

a. the failure of a party to comply with the order to attend mediation;

b. any request by the parties for additional time to complete the mediation;

c. if all parties agree, any procedural action by the court that would facilitate the mediation; and

d. the mediator's assessment that the case is inappropriate for mediation.

12.2 When the mediation has been concluded, the court should be informed of the following:

a. If the parties do not reach an agreement on any matter, the mediator should report the lack of an agreement to the court without comment or recommendation.

b. If agreement is reached, any requirement that its terms be reported to the court should be consistent with the jurisdiction's policies governing settlements in general.

c. With the consent of the parties, the mediators' report also may identify any pending motions or outstanding legal issues, discovery process, or other action by any party which, if resolved or completed, would facilitate the possibility of a settlement.

12.3 Whenever possible, all communications with the judge who will try the case should be made by the parties. Where the mediator must communicate with the trial judge, it is preferable for such communications to be made in writing or through administrative personnel.

13.0 FUNDING OF PROGRAMS AND COMPENSATION OF MEDIATORS

13.1 Courts should make mediation available to parties regardless of the parties' ability to pay.

a. Where a court suggests (rather than orders) mediation, it should take steps to make mediation available to indigent litigants, through state funding or through encouraging mediators who receive referrals from the court to provide a portion of their services on a free or reduced fee basis.

b. When parties are required to participate in mediation, the costs of mediation should be publicly funded unless the amount at stake or the nature of the parties makes participants' payments appropriate.

13.2 In allocating public funds to mediation, a court may give priority for funding to certain types of cases, such as family and minor criminal matters.

13.3 Where public funds are used, they may either: (a) support mediators employed by the court or (b) compensate private mediators. Where public funds are used to compensate private mediators, fee schedules should be set by the court.

13.4 a. Where courts offer publicly funded mediation services, courts should permit parties to substitute a private mediator of their own choosing except in those circumstances under which the court has decided that party choice is inappropriate. Parties should have the widest possible latitude in selecting mediators, consistent with public policy.

b. Where parties elect to pay a private mediator, they should be permitted to agree with the mediator on the appropriate fee.

14.0 LIABILITY OF MEDIATORS

14.1 Courts should not develop rules for mediators to whom they refer cases that are designed to protect these mediators from liability. Legislatures and courts should provide the same indemnity or insurance for those mediators who volunteer their services or are employed by the court that they provide for non-judicial court employees.

15.0 THE ENFORCEABILITY OF MEDIATED AGREEMENTS

15.1 Agreements that are reached through court-connected mediation should be enforceable to the same extent as agreements reached without a mediator.

16.0 EVALUATION

16.1 Courts should ensure that the mediation programs to which they refer cases are monitored adequately on an ongoing basis, evaluated on a periodic basis, and that sufficient resources are earmarked for these purposes.

16.2 Programs should be required to collect sufficient, accurate information to permit adequate monitoring on an ongoing basis and evaluation on a periodic basis.

16.3 Courts should ensure that program evaluation is widely distributed and linked to decision-making about the program's policies and procedures.

Appendix G

Model Standards of Practice for Family and Divorce Mediation (2001)*

OVERVIEW AND DEFINITIONS

Family and divorce mediation ("family mediation" or "mediation") is a process in which a mediator, an impartial third party, facilitates the resolution of family disputes by promoting the participants' voluntary agreement. The family mediator assists communication, encourages understanding and focuses the participants on their individual and common interests. The family mediator works with the participants to explore options, make decisions and reach their own agreements.

Family mediation is not a substitute for the need for family members to obtain independent legal advice or counseling or therapy. Nor is it appropriate for all families. However, experience has established that family mediation is a valuable option for many families because it can:

- increase the self-determination of participants and their ability to communicate;
- promote the best interests of children; and
- reduce the economic and emotional costs associated with the resolution of family disputes.

Effective mediation requires that the family mediator be qualified by training, experience and temperament; that the mediator be impartial; that the participants reach their decisions voluntarily; that their decisions be based on sufficient factual data; that the mediator be aware of the impact of culture and diversity; and that the best interests of children be taken into account. Further, the mediator should also be prepared to identify families whose history includes domestic abuse or child abuse.

*A copy of the Model Standards of Practice for Family and Divorce Mediation, adopted by the ABA House of Delegates in February 2001, may be found in 35 Fam. L.Q. 27 (2001). The model standards have been adopted by several groups, including the ACR, ABA, and AFCC.

These Model Standards of Practice for Family and Divorce Mediation ("Model Standards") aim to perform three major functions:

1. to serve as a guide for the conduct of family mediators;
2. to inform the mediating participants of what they can expect; and
3. to promote public confidence in mediation as a process for resolving family disputes.

The Model Standards are aspirational in character. They describe good practices for family mediators. They are not intended to create legal rules or standards of liability.

The Model Standards include different levels of guidance:

- Use of the term "may" in a Standard is the lowest strength of guidance and indicates a practice that the family mediator should consider adopting but which can be deviated from in the exercise of good professional judgment.
- Most of the Standards employ the term "should" which indicates that the practice described in the Standard is highly desirable and should be departed from only with very strong reason.
- The rarer use of the term "shall" in a Standard is a higher level of guidance to the family mediator, indicating that the mediator should not have discretion to depart from the practice described.

STANDARD I

A family mediator shall recognize that mediation is based on the principle of self-determination by the participants.

A. Self-determination is the fundamental principle of family mediation. The mediation process relies upon the ability of participants to make their own voluntary and informed decisions.

B. The primary role of a family mediator is to assist the participants to gain a better understanding of their own needs and interests and the needs and interests of others and to facilitate agreement among the participants.

C. A family mediator should inform the participants that they may seek information and advice from a variety of sources during the mediation process.

D. A family mediator shall inform the participants that they may withdraw from family mediation at any time and are not required to reach an agreement in mediation.

E. The family mediator's commitment shall be to the participants and the process. Pressure from outside of the mediation process shall never influence the mediator to coerce participants to settle.

STANDARD II

A family mediator shall be qualified by education and training to undertake the mediation.

A. To perform the family mediator's role, a mediator should:

1. have knowledge of family law;

2. have knowledge of and training in the impact of family conflict on parents, children and other participants, including knowledge of child development, domestic abuse and child abuse and neglect;

3. have education and training specific to the process of mediation;

4. be able to recognize the impact of culture and diversity.

B. Family mediators should provide information to the participants about the mediator's relevant training, education and expertise.

STANDARD III

A family mediator shall facilitate the participants' understanding of what mediation is and assess their capacity to mediate before the participants reach an agreement to mediate.

A. Before family mediation begins, a mediator should provide the participants with an overview of the process and its purposes, including:

1. informing the participants that reaching an agreement in family mediation is consensual in nature, that a mediator is an impartial facilitator, and that a mediator may not impose or force any settlement on the parties;

2. distinguishing family mediation from other processes designed to address family issues and disputes;

3. informing the participants that any agreements reached will be reviewed by the court when court approval is required;

4. informing the participants that they may obtain independent advice from attorneys, counsel, advocates, accountants, therapists or other professionals during the mediation process;

5. advising the participants, in appropriate cases, that they can seek the advice of religious figures, elders or other significant persons in their community whose opinions they value;

6. discussing, if applicable, the issue of separate sessions with the participants, a description of the circumstances in which the mediator may meet alone with any of the participants, or with any third party and the conditions of confidentiality concerning these separate sessions;

7. informing the participants that the presence or absence of other persons at a mediation, including attorneys, counselors or advocates, depends on the agreement of the participants and the mediator, unless a statute or regulation otherwise requires or the mediator believes that the presence of another person is required or may be beneficial because of a history or threat of violence or other serious coercive activity by a participant;

8. describing the obligations of the mediator to maintain the confidentiality of the mediation process and its results as well as any exceptions to confidentiality;

9. advising the participants of the circumstances under which the mediator may suspend or terminate the mediation process and that a participant has a right to suspend or terminate mediation at any time.

B. The participants should sign a written agreement to mediate their dispute and the terms and conditions thereof within a reasonable time after first consulting the family mediator.

C. The family mediator should be alert to the capacity and willingness of the participants to mediate before proceeding with the mediation and throughout the process. A mediator should not agree to conduct the mediation if the mediator reasonably believes one or more of the participants is unable or unwilling to participate;

D. Family mediators should not accept a dispute for mediation if they cannot satisfy the expectations of the participants concerning the timing of the process.

STANDARD IV

A family mediator shall conduct the mediation process in an impartial manner. A family mediator shall disclose all actual and potential grounds of bias and conflicts of interest reasonably known to the mediator. The participants shall be free to retain the mediator by an informed, written waiver of the conflict of interest. However, if a bias or conflict of interest clearly impairs a mediator's impartiality, the mediator shall withdraw regardless of the express agreement of the participants.

A. Impartiality means freedom from favoritism or bias in word, action or appearance, and includes a commitment to assist all participants as opposed to any one individual.

B. Conflict of interest means any relationship between the mediator, any participant or the subject matter of the dispute, that compromises or appears to compromise the mediator's impartiality.

C. A family mediator should not accept a dispute for mediation if the family mediator cannot be impartial.

D. A family mediator should identify and disclose potential grounds of bias or conflict of interest upon which a mediator's impartiality might reasonably be questioned. Such disclosure should be made prior to the start of a mediation and in time to allow the participants to select an alternate mediator.

E. A family mediator should resolve all doubts in favor of disclosure. All disclosures should be made as soon as practical after the mediator becomes aware of the bias or potential conflict of interest. The duty to disclose is a continuing duty.

F. A family mediator should guard against bias or partiality based on the participants' personal characteristics, background or performance at the mediation.

G. A family mediator should avoid conflicts of interest in recommending the services of other professionals.

H. A family mediator shall not use information about participants obtained in a mediation for personal gain or advantage.

I. A family mediator should withdraw pursuant to Standard IX if the mediator believes the mediator's impartiality has been compromised or a conflict of interest has been identified and has not been waived by the participants.

STANDARD V

A family mediator shall fully disclose and explain the basis of any compensation, fees and charges to the participants.

A. The participants should be provided with sufficient information about fees at the outset of mediation to determine if they wish to retain the services of the mediator.

B. The participants' written agreement to mediate their dispute should include a description of their fee arrangement with the mediator.

C. A mediator should not enter into a fee agreement that is contingent upon the results of the mediation or the amount of the settlement.

D. A mediator should not accept a fee for referral of a matter to another mediator or to any other person.

E. Upon termination of mediation a mediator should return any unearned fee to the participants.

STANDARD VI

A family mediator shall structure the mediation process so that the participants make decisions based on sufficient information and knowledge.

A. The mediator should facilitate full and accurate disclosure and the acquisition and development of information during mediation so that the participants can make informed decisions. This may be accomplished by encouraging participants to consult appropriate experts.

B. Consistent with standards of impartiality and preserving participant self-determination, a mediator may provide the participants with information that the mediator is qualified by training or experience to provide. The mediator shall not provide therapy or legal advice.

C. The mediator should recommend that the participants obtain independent legal representation before concluding an agreement.

D. If the participants so desire, the mediator should allow attorneys, counsel or advocates for the participants to be present at the mediation sessions.

E. With the agreement of the participants, the mediator may document the participants' resolution of their dispute. The mediator should inform the participants that any agreement should be reviewed by an independent attorney before it is signed.

STANDARD VII

A family mediator shall maintain the confidentiality of all information acquired in the mediation process, unless the mediator is permitted or required to reveal the information by law or agreement of the participants.

A. The mediator should discuss the participants' expectations of confidentiality with them prior to undertaking the mediation. The written agreement to mediate should include provisions concerning confidentiality.

B. Prior to undertaking the mediation, the mediator should inform the participants of the limitations of confidentiality such as statutory, judicially or ethically mandated reporting.

C. As permitted by law, the mediator shall disclose a participant's threat of suicide or violence against any person to the threatened person and the appropriate authorities if the mediator believes such threat is likely to be acted upon.

D. If the mediator holds private sessions with a participant, the obligations of confidentiality concerning those sessions should be discussed and agreed upon prior to the sessions.

E. If subpoenaed or otherwise noticed to testify or to produce documents, the mediator should inform the participants immediately. The mediator should not testify or provide documents in response to a subpoena without an order of the court if the mediator reasonably believes doing so would violate an obligation of confidentiality to the participants.

STANDARD VIII

A family mediator shall assist participants in determining how to promote the best interests of children.

A. The mediator should encourage the participants to explore the range of options available for separation or post-divorce parenting arrangements and their respective costs and benefits. Referral to a specialist in child development may be appropriate for these purposes. The topics for discussion may include, among others:

1. information about community resources and programs that can help the participants and their children cope with the consequences of family reorganization and family violence;
2. problems that continuing conflict creates for children's development and what steps might be taken to ameliorate the effects of conflict on the children;
3. development of a parenting plan that covers the children's physical residence and decision-making responsibilities for the children, with appropriate levels of detail as agreed to by the participants;
4. the possible need to revise parenting plans as the developmental needs of the children evolve over time; and
5. encouragement to the participants to develop appropriate dispute resolution mechanisms to facilitate future revisions of the parenting plan.

B. The mediator should be sensitive to the impact of culture and religion on parenting philosophy and other decisions.

C. The mediator shall inform any court-appointed representative for the children of the mediation. If a representative for the children participates, the mediator should, at the outset, discuss the effect of that participation on the mediation process and the confidentiality of the mediation with the participants. Whether the representative of the children participates or not, the mediator shall provide the representative with the resulting agreements insofar as they relate to the children.

D. Except in extraordinary circumstances, the children should not participate in the mediation process without the consent of both parents and the children's court-appointed representative.

E. Prior to including the children in the mediation process, the mediator should consult with the parents and the children's court-appointed representative about whether the children should participate in the mediation process and the form of that participation.

F. The mediator should inform all concerned about the available options for the children's participation (which may include personal participation, an interview with a mental health professional, the mediator interviewing the child and reporting to the parents, or a videotaped statement by the child) and discuss the costs and benefits of each with the participants.

STANDARD IX

A family mediator shall recognize a family situation involving child abuse or neglect and take appropriate steps to shape the mediation process accordingly.

A. As used in these Standards, child abuse or neglect is defined by applicable state law.

B. A mediator shall not undertake a mediation in which the family situation has been assessed to involve child abuse or neglect without appropriate and adequate training.

C. If the mediator has reasonable grounds to believe that a child of the participants is abused or neglected within the meaning of the jurisdiction's child abuse and neglect laws, the mediator shall comply with applicable child protection laws.

1. The mediator should encourage the participants to explore approriate services for the family.
2. The mediator should consider the appropriateness of suspending or terminating the mediation process in light of the allegations.

STANDARD X

A family mediator shall recognize a family situation involving domestic abuse and take appropriate steps to shape the mediation process accordingly.

A. As used in these Standards, domestic abuse includes domestic violence as defined by applicable state law and issues of control and intimidation.

B. A mediator shall not undertake a mediation in which the family situation has been assessed to involve domestic abuse without appropriate and adequate training.

C. Some cases are not suitable for mediation because of safety, control or intimidation issues. A mediator should make a reasonable effort to screen for the existence of domestic abuse prior to entering into an agreement to mediate. The mediator should continue to assess for domestic abuse throughout the mediation process.

D. If domestic abuse appears to be present the mediator shall consider taking measures to insure the safety of participants and the mediator including, among others:

1. establishing appropriate security arrangements;

2. holding separate sessions with the participants even without the agreement of all participants;

3. allowing a friend, representative, advocate, counsel or attorney to attend the mediation sessions;

4. encouraging the participants to be represented by an attorney, counsel or an advocate throughout the mediation process;

5. referring the participants to appropriate community resources;

6. suspending or terminating the mediation sessions, with appropriate steps to protect the safety of the participants.

E. The mediator should facilitate the participants' formulation of parenting plans that protect the physical safety and psychological well-being of themselves and their children.

STANDARD XI

A family mediator shall suspend or terminate the mediation process when the mediator reasonably believes that a participant is unable to effectively participate or for other compelling reason.

A. Circumstances under which a mediator should consider suspending or terminating the mediation, may include, among others:

1. the safety of a participant or well-being of a child is threatened;

2. a participant has or is threatening to abduct a child;

3. a participant is unable to participate due to the influence of drugs, alcohol, or physical or mental condition;

4. the participants are about to enter into an agreement that the mediator reasonably believes to be unconscionable;

5. a participant is using the mediation to further illegal conduct;

6. a participant is using the mediation process to gain an unfair advantage;

7. if the mediator believes the mediator's impartiality has been compromised in accordance with Standard IV.

B. If the mediator does suspend or terminate the mediation, the mediator should take all reasonable steps to minimize prejudice or inconvenience to the participants which may result.

STANDARD XII

A family mediator shall be truthful in the advertisement and solicitation for mediation.

A. Mediators should refrain from promises and guarantees of results. A mediator should not advertise statistical settlement data or settlement rates.

B. Mediators should accurately represent their qualifications. In an advertisement or other communication, a mediator may make reference to meeting state, national or private organizational qualifications only if the entity referred to has a procedure for qualifying mediators and the mediator has been duly granted the requisite status.

STANDARD XIII

A family mediator shall acquire and maintain professional competence in mediation.

A. Mediators should continuously improve their professional skills and abilities by, among other activities, participating in relevant continuing education programs and should regularly engage in self-assessment.

B. Mediators should participate in programs of peer consultation and should help train and mentor the work of less experienced mediators.

C. Mediators should continuously strive to understand the impact of culture and diversity on the mediator's practice.

Appendix H
Model Standards of Conduct for Mediators (September 2005)*

The *Model Standards of Conduct for Mediators* was prepared in 1994 by the American Arbitration Association, the American Bar Association Section of Dispute Resolution, and the Association for Conflict Resolution.[a] A joint committee consisting of representatives from the same successor organizations revised the Model Standards in 2005.[b] Both the original 1994 version and the 2005 revision have been approved by each participating organization.[c]

PREAMBLE

Mediation is used to resolve a broad range of conflicts within a variety of settings. These Standards are designed to serve as fundamental ethical guidelines for persons mediating in all practice contexts. They serve three primary goals: to guide the conduct of mediators; to inform the mediating parties; and to promote public confidence in mediation as a process for resolving disputes.

Mediation is a process in which an impartial third party facilitates communication and negotiation and promotes voluntary decision making by the parties to the dispute.

Mediation serves various purposes, including providing the opportunity for parties to define and clarify issues, understand different perspectives, identify interests, explore and assess possible solutions, and reach mutually satisfactory agreements, when desired.

*Reporter's notes accompanying the model standards are omitted and can be found at www.moritzlaw.osu.edu/programs/adr/msoc/.

a. The Association for Conflict Resolution is a merger of the Academy of Family Mediators, the Conflict Resolution Education Network, and the Society of Professionals in Dispute Resolution (SPIDR). SPIDR was the third participating organization in the development of the 1994 Standards.

b. Reporter's Notes, which are not part of these Standards and therefore have not been specifically approved by any of the organizations, provide commentary regarding these revisions.

c. The 2005 version to [sic] the Model Standards were approved by the American Bar Association's House of Delegates on August 9, 2005, the Board of the Association of Conflict Resolution on August 22, 2005, and the Executive Committee of the American Arbitration Association on September 8, 2005.

Note on Construction

These Standards are to be read and construed in their entirety. There is no priority significance attached to the sequence in which the Standards appear.

The use of the term "shall" in a Standard indicates that the mediator must follow the practice described. The use of the term "should" indicates that the practice described in the Standard is highly desirable, but not required, and is to be departed from only for very strong reasons and requires careful use of judgment and discretion.

The use of the term "mediator" is understood to be inclusive so that it applies to co-mediator models.

These Standards do not include specific temporal parameters when referencing a mediation, and therefore, do not define the exact beginning or ending of a mediation.

Various aspects of a mediation, including some matters covered by these Standards, may also be affected by applicable law, court rules, regulations, other applicable professional rules, mediation rules to which the parties have agreed, and other agreements of the parties. These sources may create conflicts with, and may take precedence over, these Standards. However, a mediator should make every effort to comply with the spirit and intent of these Standards in resolving such conflicts. This effort should include honoring all remaining Standards not in conflict with these other sources.

These Standards, unless and until adopted by a court or other regulatory authority, do not have the force of law. Nonetheless, the fact that these Standards have been adopted by the respective sponsoring entities should alert mediators to the fact that the Standards might be viewed as establishing a standard of care for mediators.

Standard I. Self-Determination

A. A mediator shall conduct a mediation based on the principle of party self-determination. Self-determination is the act of coming to a voluntary, uncoerced decision in which each party makes free and informed choices as to process and outcome. Parties may exercise self-determination at any stage of a mediation, including mediator selection, process design, participation in or withdrawal from the process, and outcomes.

1. Although party self-determination for process design is a fundamental principle of mediation practice, a mediator may need to balance such party self-determination with a mediator's duty to conduct a quality process in accordance with these Standards.

2. A mediator cannot personally ensure that each party has made free and informed choices to reach particular decisions, but, where appropriate, a mediator should make the parties aware of the importance of consulting other professionals to help them make informed choices.

B. A mediator shall not undermine party self-determination by any party for reasons such as higher settlement rates, egos, increased fees, or outside pressures from court personnel, program administrators, provider organizations, the media, or others.

STANDARD II. IMPARTIALITY

A. A mediator shall decline a mediation if the mediator cannot conduct it in an impartial manner. Impartiality means freedom from favoritism, bias, or prejudice.

B. A mediator shall conduct a mediation in an impartial manner and avoid conduct that gives the appearance of partiality.

1. A mediator should not act with partiality or prejudice based on any participant's personal characteristics, background, values and beliefs, or performance at a mediation, or any other reason.
2. A mediator should neither give nor accept a gift, favor, loan, or other item of value that raises a question as to the mediator's actual or perceived impartiality.
3. A mediator may accept or give de minimis gifts or incidental items or services that are provided to facilitate a mediation or respect cultural norms so long as such practices do not raise questions as to a mediator's actual or perceived impartiality.

C. If at any time a mediator is unable to conduct a mediation in an impartial manner, the mediator shall withdraw.

STANDARD III. CONFLICTS OF INTEREST

A. A mediator shall avoid a conflict of interest or the appearance of a conflict of interest during and after a mediation. A conflict of interest can arise from involvement by a mediator with the subject matter of the dispute or from any relationship between a mediator and any mediation participant, whether past or present, personal or professional, that reasonably raises a question of a mediator's impartiality.

B. A mediator shall make a reasonable inquiry to determine whether there are any facts that a reasonable individual would consider likely to create a potential or actual conflict of interest for a mediator. A mediator's actions necessary to accomplish a reasonable inquiry into potential conflicts of interest may vary based on practice context.

C. A mediator shall disclose, as soon as practicable, all actual and potential conflicts of interest that are reasonably known to the mediator and could reasonably be seen as raising a question about the mediator's impartiality. After disclosure, if all parties agree, the mediator may proceed with the mediation.

D. If a mediator learns any fact after accepting a mediation that raises a question with respect to that mediator's service creating a potential or actual conflict of interest, the mediator shall disclose it as quickly as practicable. After disclosure, if all parties agree, the mediator may proceed with the mediation.

E. If a mediator's conflict of interest might reasonably be viewed as undermining the integrity of the mediation, a mediator shall withdraw from or decline to proceed with the mediation regardless of the expressed desire or agreement of the parties to the contrary.

F. Subsequent to a mediation, a mediator shall not establish another relationship with any of the participants in any matter that would raise questions about the integrity of the mediation. When a mediator develops personal or professional relationships with parties, other individuals, or organizations following a mediation in which they were involved, the mediator should consider factors such as time elapsed following the mediation, the nature of the relationships established, and services offered when determining whether the relationships might create a perceived or actual conflict of interest.

STANDARD IV. COMPETENCE

A. A mediator shall mediate only when the mediator has the necessary competence to satisfy the reasonable expectations of the parties.

1. Any person may be selected as a mediator, provided that the parties are satisfied with the mediator's competence and qualifications. Training, experience in mediation, skills, cultural understandings, and other qualities are often necessary for mediator competence. A person who offers to serve as a mediator creates the expectation that the person is competent to mediate effectively.

2. A mediator should attend educational programs and related activities to maintain and enhance the mediator's knowledge and skills related to mediation.

3. A mediator should have available for the parties information relevant to the mediator's training, education, experience, and approach to conducting a mediation.

B. If a mediator, during the course of a mediation, determines that the mediator cannot conduct the mediation competently, the mediator shall discuss that determination with the parties as soon as is practicable and take appropriate steps to address the situation, including, but not limited to, withdrawing or requesting appropriate assistance.

C. If a mediator's ability to conduct a mediation is impaired by drugs, alcohol, medication, or otherwise, the mediator shall not conduct the mediation.

STANDARD V. CONFIDENTIALITY

A. A mediator shall maintain the confidentiality of all information obtained by the mediator in mediation, unless otherwise agreed to by the parties or required by applicable law.

1. If the parties to a mediation agree that the mediator may disclose information obtained during the mediation, the mediator may do so.

2. A mediator should not communicate to any non-participant information about how the parties acted in the mediation. A mediator may report, if required, whether parties appeared at a scheduled mediation and whether or not the parties reached a resolution.

3. If a mediator participates in teaching, research, or evaluation of mediation, the mediator should protect the anonymity of the parties and abide by their reasonable expectations regarding confidentiality.

B. A mediator who meets with any persons in private session during a mediation shall not convey directly or indirectly to any other person, any information that was obtained during that private session without the consent of the disclosing person.

C. A mediator shall promote understanding among the parties of the extent to which the parties will maintain confidentiality of information they obtain in a mediation.

D. Depending on the circumstance of a mediation, the parties may have varying expectations regarding confidentiality that a mediator should address. The parties may make their own rules with respect to confidentiality, or the accepted practice of an individual mediator or institution may dictate a particular set of expectations.

Standard VI. Quality of the Process

A. A mediator shall conduct a mediation in accordance with these Standards and in a manner that promotes diligence, timeliness, safety, presence of the appropriate participants, party participation, procedural fairness, party competency, and mutual respect among all participants.

1. A mediator should agree to mediate only when the mediator is prepared to commit the attention essential to an effective mediation.
2. A mediator should only accept cases when the mediator can satisfy the reasonable expectation of the parties concerning the timing of a mediation.
3. The presence or absence of persons at a mediation depends on the agreement of the parties and the mediator. The parties and mediator may agree that others may be excluded from particular sessions or from all sessions.
4. A mediator should promote honesty and candor between and among all participants, and a mediator shall not knowingly misrepresent any material fact or circumstance in the course of a mediation.
5. The role of a mediator differs substantially from other professional roles. Mixing the role of a mediator and the role of another profession is problematic and thus, a mediator should distinguish between the roles. A mediator may provide information that the mediator is qualified by training or experience to provide, only if the mediator can do so consistent with these Standards.
6. A mediator shall not conduct a dispute resolution procedure other than mediation but label it mediation in an effort to gain the protection of rules, statutes, or other governing authorities pertaining to mediation.
7. A mediator may recommend, when appropriate, that parties consider resolving their dispute through arbitration, counseling, neutral evaluation, or other processes.
8. A mediator shall not undertake an additional dispute resolution role in the same matter without the consent of the parties. Before providing such service, a mediator shall inform the parties of the implications of the change in process and obtain their consent to the change. A mediator who undertakes such role assumes different duties and responsibilities that may be governed by other standards.
9. If a mediation is being used to further criminal conduct, a mediator should take appropriate steps including, if necessary, postponing, withdrawing from, or terminating the mediation.
10. If a party appears to have difficulty comprehending the process, issues, or settlement options, or difficulty participating in a mediation, the mediator should explore the circumstances and potential accommodations, modifications,

or adjustments that would make possible the party's capacity to comprehend, participate, and exercise self-determination.

B. If a mediator is made aware of domestic abuse or violence among the parties, the mediator shall take appropriate steps including, if necessary, postponing, withdrawing from, or terminating the mediation.

C. If a mediator believes that participant conduct, including that of the mediator, jeopardizes conducting a mediation consistent with these Standards, a mediator shall take appropriate steps including, if necessary, postponing, withdrawing from, or terminating the mediation.

Standard VII. Advertising and Solicitation

A. A mediator shall be truthful and not misleading when advertising, soliciting, or otherwise communicating the mediator's qualifications, experience, services, and fees.

1. A mediator should not include any promises as to outcome in communications, including business cards, stationery, or computer-based communications.

2. A mediator should only claim to meet the mediator qualifications of a governmental entity or private organization if that entity or organization has a recognized procedure for qualifying mediators and it grants such status to the mediator.

B. A mediator shall not solicit in a manner that gives an appearance of partiality for or against a party or otherwise undermines the integrity of the process.

C. A mediator shall not communicate to others, in promotional materials or through other forms of communication, the names of persons served without their permission.

Standard VIII. Fees and Other Charges

A. A mediator shall provide each party or each party's representative true and complete information about mediation fees, expenses, and any other actual or potential charges that may be incurred in connection with a mediation.

1. If a mediator charges fees, the mediator should develop them in light of all relevant factors, including the type and complexity of the matter, the qualifications of the mediator, the time required, and the rates customary for such mediation services.

2. A mediator's fee arrangement should be in writing unless the parties request otherwise.

B. A mediator shall not charge fees in a manner that impairs a mediator's impartiality.

1. A mediator should not enter into a fee agreement which is contingent upon the result of the mediation or the amount of the settlement.

2. While a mediator may accept unequal fee payments from the parties, a mediator should not use fee arrangements that adversely impact the mediator's ability to conduct a mediation in an impartial manner.

Standard IX. Advancement of Mediation Practice

A. A mediator should act in a manner that advances the practice of mediation. A mediator promotes this Standard by engaging in some or all of the following:

1. Fostering diversity within the field of mediation.
2. Striving to make mediation accessible to those who elect to use it, including providing services at a reduced rate or on a pro bono basis as appropriate.
3. Participating in research when given the opportunity, including obtaining participant feedback when appropriate.
4. Participating in outreach and education efforts to assist the public in developing an improved understanding of, and appreciation for, mediation.
5. Assisting newer mediators through training, mentoring, and networking.

B. A mediator should demonstrate respect for differing points of view within the field, seek to learn from other mediators, and work together with other mediators to improve the profession and better serve people in conflict.

Appendix I

Dispute Resolution: An Annotated Guide to Selected Resources*

CONTENTS

*This guide was written by Carole L. Hinchcliff, Associate Director, The Ohio State University Moritz Law Library and Associate Professor, Clinical, Mediation Practicum, Moritz College of Law. Carole L. Hinchcliff can be reached at hinchcliff.1@osu.edu.

PURPOSE OF GUIDE

This research guide provides a snapshot of the dispute resolution literature thirty-one years after the seminal Pound Conference in 1976, in which Harvard Law Professor Frank E.A. Sander presented his concept of the "multi-door courthouse."[1] Established dispute resolution processes such as mediation, arbitration,

1. See Frank E.A. Sander, "Varieties of Dispute Processing," in *The Pound Conference: Perspectives on Justice in the Future* (A. Leo Levin & Russell R. Wheeler eds.), Proceedings of the National Conference on the Causes of Popular Dissatisfaction with the Administration of Justice (Sponsored by the American Bar

fact finding, and the use of ombudspersons featured prominently in Frank Sander's proposal for reducing judicial caseloads. As the use of these dispute resolution processes has expanded since the late 1970s, so has the literature. As a leading scholar in dispute resolution, Frank Sander brought to our attention the legal literature in this developing field as it existed during the early 1980s by way of his two bibliographies, which are cited in this guide.

This research guide assists the dispute resolution researcher to quickly locate materials such as relevant books, bibliographies, periodicals, directories, legislation, and arbitration awards. The sources range from those that provide general overviews of dispute resolution to those that offer current awareness services used by sophisticated dispute resolution researchers. The major organizations providing dispute resolution services and publications are highlighted, as are various online and Internet services. Due to the multidisciplinary nature of dispute resolution, books and articles can be found in the literature of fields as diverse as anthropology, business, criminology, education, environmental planning, political science, international relations, psychology, social work, sociology, workplace relations, the building and construction industry, healthcare, and law.

While there are a number of periodicals specifically covering areas of dispute resolution, many of these titles are not included in the periodical indexes traditionally consulted by legal researchers. This guide notes periodicals listed in *Index to Legal Periodicals and Books* and *Current Law Index* and its online counterpart, *LegalTrac,* and lists online databases, including *LexisNexis* and *Westlaw,* which offer dispute resolution periodical articles in full text. A striking feature of this survey of dispute resolution literature is the small number of periodical articles that are currently available in full text on *LexisNexis* or *Westlaw,* or otherwise available via the Internet. Despite the widely held belief that researchers can find everything they need on the Internet or the information universes of *LexisNexis* or *Westlaw,* this research guide shows that a thorough search of the literature requires searchinga combination of print and online sources. Titles of indexes for finding older articles are given, since few articles published prior to 1980 are found online. Print and electronic periodicals are listed alphabetically by title under the following broad subject headings: Arbitration — International, Business/Corporations/Employment, Family, General, International, and Negotiation. Newsletters are listed separately. The last section provides contact information for dispute resolution organizations and information about general dispute resolution web sites and listservs.

There is no set procedure for researching dispute resolution materials, or in fact for tackling most other legal research problems. The approach taken will depend on the nature of the research task, the information sought, and the knowledge of the researcher. This guide informs the reader of the wide range of sources available, indicates if the information is available online, and gives some helpful research advice. If using a URL listed in this guide results in an error message, try truncating the URL at the "/" symbol, which separates the domain name, path, and file name; or alternatively, try using more than one search engine, such as Google

Association, the Conference of Chief Justices, and the Judicial Conference of the United States), St. Paul, MN: West (1979) at pp. 65-67; and *Addresses Delivered at the National Conference on the Causes of Popular Dissatisfaction with the Administration of Justice* (Apr. 7-9, 1976), in 70 F.R.D. at pp. 111-134 (1976).

(*http://www.google.com*), alltheweb.com (*www.alltheweb.com*), Vivisimo.com (*www.Vivisimo.com*), or Yahoo (*www.yahoo.com*), to find the site you need.

Glossaries

Many books and web sites about dispute resolution include glossaries to familiarize readers with commonly used terms used in the dispute resolution literature. For researchers who are unfamiliar with the area, glossaries and dictionaries are useful in defining the language of dispute resolution as used in various disciplines that address conflict. They are especially helpful for finding words and synonyms to include in search queries for searching the Internet or online sources. Since good search results depend largely on the terms used in the search request, familiarity with the language of dispute resolution is essential.

Dictionary of Conflict Resolution, compiled and edited by Douglas H. Yarn, San Francisco: Jossey-Bass (1999).

Authored by a law professor in consultation with the former organization Society of Professionals in Dispute Resolution (SPIDR), this dictionary provides brief explanations for approximately 1,400 terms and definitions that are used in the conflict resolution literature. See also the references and suggestions for further reading that are listed at the end of many entries.

Catherine Morris, *What Is "Alternative Dispute Resolution" (ADR)?: Some Ways of Processing Disputes and Addressing Conflict* (revised May 2002).
http://www.peacemakers.ca/publications/ADRdefinitions.html

Hosted at the web site of Peacemakers Trust, "a Canadian non-profit organization dedicated to research, education and consultation on conflict resolution and peacebuilding," this article describes methods of processing disputes and dispute processing alternatives. This source provides descriptions of each process, refers to important works in dispute resolution literature, and includes links to relevant bibliographies compiled by the author and to other web sites.

General Encyclopedia

Encyclopedias provide concise, general overviews of a subject and how it relates to other areas. The following example acknowledges the interdisciplinary nature of dispute resolution and is written by scholars in the field.

Encyclopedia of Conflict Resolution, by Heidi Burgess & Guy M. Burgess, Santa Barbara, CA: ABC-CLIO (1997).

Provides over 340 short entries relating to aspects of conflict as broadly defined by the authors. Intended readers of this glossary-style work range from consumers of dispute resolution services to dispute resolution professionals. This source provides entries relating to types of conflicts, including long-running conflicts, short-term disputes, two-party relationships, the context of conflicts, international conflicts, labor management, environmental and public policy, business negotiations, victim-offender reconciliation, and tensions between social groups. Alternative dispute resolution processes, concepts and techniques for conflict resolution, ethical issues, significant events, and case studies also have entries. "See also" references and "References and Further Reading" recommendations accompany each entry.

Legal Encyclopedias

Both of the major United States legal encyclopedias provide very general overviews of dispute resolution processes under headings such as those mentioned below. These legal encyclopedias, now both published by West Group, have preserved their differences in style and emphasis: *Am. Jur. 2d* focuses more on federal law and cites to cases more selectively than *C.J.S.,* which tends to have many more references to state case law. Although either encyclopedia can provide useful background information to a researcher unfamiliar with the subject of dispute resolution, their best use is as a tool for locating citations to cases, federal statutes, and other secondary sources. Many *C.J.S.* and more recent *Am. Jur. 2d* volumes suggest West topic and key numbers to use on *Westlaw* or in West Digests to find cases addressing particular legal issues. For a more authoritative analysis of laws relating to dispute resolution, and for commentary on subtle changes in the law and trends in developing areas, a treatise or law review article by a legal scholar will provide more information.

Corpus Juris Secundum (*C.J.S.*). Available on *Westlaw.*
See titles such as "Arbitration" and "Compromise and Settlement."

American Jurisprudence 2d (*Am. Jur. 2d*). Available on *LexisNexis* and *Westlaw.*
See topics such as "Alternative Dispute Resolution," "Pretrial Conference and Procedure," and "Compromise and Settlement."

Neither encyclopedia has a separate "Mediation" heading. For more suggested headings to use in *Am. Jur. 2d* and *C.J.S.*, see *Alternative Dispute Resolution in a Nutshell,* listed below. *C.J.S.* includes table-of-cases volumes. This enables the researcher to see if an important dispute resolution case has been mentioned in a general discussion of a legal issue in dispute resolution. Keep in mind that even if you use the online versions of these encyclopedias on *LexisNexis* and *Westlaw,* they may be no more current than the hardbound volumes and annual pocket parts or paper supplements of the current print sets. The cases and references to federal statutes that you find in *C.J.S.* and *Am. Jur. 2d* may not be the most recent ones available; therefore remember to update your cases and statutes using *Shepards* (available via *LexisNexis*) and/or *KeyCite* (available via *Westlaw*).

American Law Reports

American Law Reports (ALR), which is available in print and on *LexisNexis* and *Westlaw,* offers "annotations." These articles provide an overview of selected legal topics in more depth than legal encyclopedias. ALR annotations are useful finding

aids because they survey how selected legal topics are treated in different U.S. jurisdictions. Finding a relevant ALR annotation is a good way to begin researching a dispute resolution topic, because a relevant annotation is most useful for its lists of citations to cases, statutes, and secondary sources.
LexisNexis—LEDALR
Westlaw—ALR

Finding Cases

This section suggests some case-finding techniques that can be used on *LexisNexis* and *Westlaw.* Free, although less comprehensive, sources of cases on the Internet include Findlaw.com and lexisONE, described below in the section "Other Selected Internet Resources."

There are a number of important cases in this casebook. By looking at a case in a print reporter published by West Group, or on *Westlaw,* the researcher can quickly identify the legal issues in the case by looking at the headnotes and their associated topics and key numbers. If viewing a case on *LexisNexis,* the researcher can do this by reading the headnotes prepared by the *LexisNexis* editors.

WEST DIGEST TOPICS AND KEY NUMBERS

The best-known printed indexes to United States case law are the various titles making up the West Digest System of federal, state, and subject digests. There are currently 414 West topics and approximately 100,000 individual key numbers comprising the West topic and key number system, which is used to provide subject access to cases printed in reporters by West Group. The book *West's Analysis of American Law,* West Group (2006), sets out the complete scheme and can be used along with the Descriptive Word Index volumes for the particular digest title used. In dispute resolution research, some helpful topics and key numbers are "Arbitration," key numbers 1-89; "Labor Relations," key numbers 411-486; "Pre-trial Procedure," key numbers 741-753; and "Compromise and Settlement," key numbers 51-72.

The easiest way to use any printed West Digest, or to search any of *Westlaw*'s case databases, is to use the "known case" method, by which the researcher identifies the on-point headnotes and topics and key numbers of a relevant case in a West reporter or on *Westlaw,* and uses them to find more cases with the same topic and key number. If you are using a print digest, look for the jurisdiction you are researching, and check the annual pocket part of the digest and any interim paper-bound supplements included in the set.

If instead of using print digests you prefer to use *Westlaw* to find cases about dispute resolution issues, you can browse the West topics and key numbers by selecting the custom digest option appearing at the top of every search screen for searching case databases on *Westlaw.* Searching for cases with a particular headnote gives more pertinent results than searching the full text of all the cases in the database. Another alternative to full-text searching is to use the *Westlaw* field searching capability. For example, you can find cases about mediation in a particular database by searching the headnote field for forms of the word "mediation." This type of search can be further narrowed by adding more terms to the search.

For example, to search the headnotes for cases addressing confidentiality in mediation, you would type the following in the search box:

He(mediat! /p confident!)

KeySearch, another *Westlaw* service, can help you find reported and unpublished cases in *Westlaw* case databases. After you identify a topic under "Alternative Dispute Resolution" from the pull-down KeySearch window, you can select whether you wish to search cases with or without West headnotes and whether you would like to run your search in encyclopedias and treatises or in journals and law reviews on *Westlaw*. KeySearch automatically generates a search using relevant West topics and key numbers and their concepts. By clicking on View/Edit at the bottom of the search screen, you can see the search request used and edit it as necessary to find more relevant results.

LEXISNEXIS SEARCH ADVISOR

LexisNexis's counterpart product to the West key number system is called Search Advisor and was introduced in 1999. Search Advisor allows the novice user to select a topic to research. While there is no initial legal topic designated "alternative dispute resolution," there is an ADR subtopic listing under "Civil Procedure" that is further subdivided into "Mandatory ADR," "Judicial Review," "Validity of ADR Methods," and "Mediations." Also, the initial topic "International Trade" has a subtopic called "Dispute Resolution." Another approach to using Search Advisor is to enter search terms such as "mediation" and "dispute resolution," which gives you a list of possible sources to search.

LexisNexis now prefaces many of its cases with a case summary, core terms, and core concepts. This means that the researcher can find a "known case" on *LexisNexis* and click on the hypertext links of the core concepts to find other material in *LexisNexis* on that legal issue. Another technique is to use the core terms identified in the "known case" to construct a search in an appropriate source of cases.

FINDING BOOKS

For a list of the books and articles referred to in this casebook, refer to the "Collected References" section (pp. 761-000). The authors of this casebook have brought to your attention the work of many important scholars and writers in the dispute resolution area.

Most academic and other large law libraries in the United States use the Library of Congress classification system to arrange books and most other materials in their libraries. While there is a concentration of general dispute resolution titles relating to United States law at the call number KF 9084, dispute resolution titles can also be found shelved with titles relating to their pertinent jurisdictions and with other legal and nonlegal subjects. The following suggestions can be used to assist you in finding helpful books covering dispute resolution methods and issues, since libraries do not usually keep materials about dispute resolution in a discrete location.

LIBRARY OF CONGRESS CALL NUMBERS

For researchers who like to browse the shelves or the call numbers of their library's online catalog, titles about dispute resolution can be found at the following selected call numbers:

Psychology

BF 637	Conflict management

Industries, Land Use, Labor

HD 42	Conflict management
HD 58.6	Negotiation, Negotiation in business
HD 5574	Sit-down strikes, Factory occupation, Arbitration and conciliation
HD 6972.5	Grievance procedures

Sociology

HM 1126	Conflict management

General Legal Jurisdictions

K 2390	Negotiated settlement, Compromise
K 2400	General works — titles covering arbitration and award, commercial arbitration in more than one jurisdiction

United States Law

KF 9084	Negotiated settlement, Compromise
KF 9085	Arbitration and award, Commercial arbitration
KF 9086	American Arbitration Association

LIBRARY OF CONGRESS SUBJECT HEADINGS

If you have found a helpful book, check the copyright page to see if subject headings are included in the "Library of Congress Cataloging-in-Publication Data." Although Library of Congress subject headings tend to be broad, they can be used to find more books in an area of dispute resolution and will usually yield more specific results than performing a key word search in an online catalog. Some commonly assigned subject headings are:

Arbitration
Arbitration and Award
Arbitration, Industrial
Arbitration, International

Collective Bargaining
Compromise (Law)
Conflict Management
Consensus (Social Sciences)
Dispute Resolution (Law)
Grievance Arbitration
Grievance Procedures
Mediation
Mediation and Conciliation, Industrial
Negotiation

LIBRARY CATALOGS

Harvard Law School Library, The Ohio State University Moritz Law Library, and Pepperdine Law School Library have extensive collections of dispute resolution titles in various formats to support their dispute resolution programs. This bibliography largely covers titles reflected in The Ohio State University Moritz Law Library collection. The Ohio State, Harvard, and Pepperdine online catalogs may be browsed via the Internet:

Harvard Law School Library Hollis Catalog
URL: *http://lib.harvard.edu/library*

The Ohio State University Libraries Library Catalog
URL: *http://library.ohio-state.edu*

Pepperdine Law School Library Catalog
URL: *http://law.pepperdine.edu/library/*

ONLINE UNION CATALOG

WorldCat
An online subscription service available at many libraries, allowing users to access over 69 million cataloging records for titles of library materials in all formats owned by thousands of libraries in the United States and other countries. Users perform searches through user-friendly search templates to find records for library materials and the names of libraries owning each title. The information uncovered by searching *WorldCat* can be used to initiate inter-library loan requests. A major library cooperative, Online Computer Library Center, Inc. (OCLC), is responsible for this database.

OTHER CATALOGS

Bowker's Global Books in Print
A subscription-based Internet service available at many academic libraries, allowing one to search for in-print, out-of-print, and forthcoming book, audio, and video

titles from Canada, the United States, Great Britain, Australia, and New Zealand. Key word, author, title, and ISBN searching options available.

Bowker's Law Books & Serials in Print: A Multimedia Sourcebook, New York: R.R. Bowker (2006)

A three-volume set indexing over 131,700 law titles by author, title, and subject using Library of Congress subject headings. Books are drawn from Bowker's *Books in Print* database and serials from *Ulrich's Periodical Directory,* 44th edition. Non-print titles include audiocassettes, videocassettes, and software.

INDEXMASTER

Indexmaster is a service that provides tables of contents and index information in PDF format for thousands of titles by a number of large and small legal publishers, including bar associations. While you may not find a whole book devoted to a narrow area or issue in dispute resolution, you may be able to search Indexmaster to locate a relevant chapter or section of a book. Indexmaster is an Internet-based subscription service available at many law libraries.
URL: *http://www.indexmaster.com*

COMMERCIAL PUBLISHERS

There are a number of commercial publishers of dispute resolution titles. In this section, the offerings of a selection of important publishers are briefly described. For information about the publications produced by dispute resolution organizations, see the section "Selected Dispute Resolution Organizations — Internet and E-mail Resources."

Jossey-Bass

Jossey-Bass is a major publisher of a wide range of conflict resolution books, usually found in the social sciences, by respected authors.
URL: *http://www.josseybass.com*

Juris Publishing, Inc.

Juris Publishing, Inc. publishes journals, newsletters, and books, including loose-leaf services, covering international commercial arbitration, litigation, and dispute resolution. All the Juris arbitration and dispute resolution titles are available in print or electronic format, via ArbitrationLaw Online, the company's fully searchable electronic database, which is updated daily. Primary sources such as arbitration legislation, rules, case law, international treaties, and conventions are included in this subscription web site.
URL: *http://www.arbitrationlaw.com*

Kluwer

Kluwer Law International, a publisher of a variety of titles in the field of international arbitration, including those of the International Council for Commercial Arbitration,

is now offering these titles online. Although access to full-text documents is available only to subscribers to the web site, anyone can search and browse the web site at no charge. Conventions, legislation, rules, model clauses case law, commentary from relevant Kluwer titles, links to web sites, and a calendar of events are available. There is also a bibliography of over 12,000 books and reviews on arbitration and dispute resolution selected from a database compiled by the Documentation Center on Arbitration of the Chamber of National and International Arbitration of Milan, Italy. In addition, the current issue of InternationalADR.com newsletter, which is published in affiliation with the Permanent Court of Arbitration and the Institute for Transnational Arbitration, is available to everyone visiting the site.
URL: *http://www.KluwerArbitration.com*

CD-ROM: Resources on International Commercial Arbitration
Kluwer's semi-annually updated CD-ROM, similar in coverage to their web-based title above, offers books and journals in this area along with arbitration treaties, legislation, and case law.

Overviews of Dispute Resolution

For more titles providing an overview of dispute resolution processes or treatises, consult the bibliographies mentioned below or search your library catalog.

NUTSHELL

Jacqueline Nolan-Haley, *Alternative Dispute Resolution in a Nutshell*, St. Paul, MN: West Group, 2d ed. (2001).

An overview and explanation of negotiation, mediation, arbitration, dispute resolution processes used in the court system, and hybrid dispute resolution procedures, including references to important statutes and cases. A "Research References" section prepared by the publisher's staff lists dispute resolution topics and key numbers used in the print West digests and on *Westlaw*; topics and section numbers used in *American Jurisprudence 2d*; and titles and section numbers used in *Corpus Juris Secundum, ALR Index, ALR Digest, Am. Jur. Legal Forms 2d, Am. Jur. Pleading & Practice, American Jurisprudence Trials, Proof of Facts 3d,* and *Proof of Facts 2d.* The appendices include relevant Federal Rules of Evidence, standards of practice or conduct, ethical standards, and legislation.

HORNBOOK

Stephen J. Ware, *Alternative Dispute Resolution*, St. Paul, MN: West Group (2001).

A comprehensive yet concise survey of the law that affects alternative dispute resolution processes used in the United States. This hornbook describes arbitration, negotiation, and mediation, and the legal issues that affect the practice of these major and other, related dispute resolution processes. The useful appendix, "Researching Alternative Dispute Resolution on *Westlaw*," provides a chart of relevant *Westlaw* databases and a review of basic *Westlaw* strategies using dispute resolution examples.

Treatises

ARBITRATION

Frank Elkouri, *How Arbitration Works,* co-edited by Edna Asper Elkouri and Alan Miles Ruben, Washington, D.C.: BNA, 6th ed. (2003).

This most recent edition of this well-known labor arbitration treatise consists of contributions from members of the Committee on ADR in Labor and Employment Law of the ABA Section of Labor and Employment Law. Twenty-two chapters cover aspects of labor arbitration such as grievances, arbitration and techniques, evidence in arbitrations, standards for interpreting contract language, use of substantive rules of law, precedent value of awards, custom and practice, management rights, seniority, discipline and discharge, safety and health, standards in arbitration of interest disputes, and employee rights and benefits.

World Arbitration Reporter, edited by Hans Smit and Vratislav Pechota (1986) (ISBN 0880630956)

A looseleaf publication of the Parker School of Foreign and Comparative Law. "A multi-volume work that endeavors to deal exhaustively and comprehensively with all aspects of international commercial arbitration." For information, including tables of contents for volumes 1-4a, see *http://www.jurispub.com/*.

MEDIATION

Sarah R. Cole, Craig A. McEwen & Nancy H. Rogers, *Mediation: Law, Policy, Practice,* St. Paul, MN: West Group, 2d ed. (1994).

The major, comprehensive mediation treatise that addresses important issues in mediation from the legal perspective. Chapters cover topics including the dilemmas presented by the institutionalization of mediation, practices in mediation, advising clients about mediation, policy objectives of mediation, planning court and other public mediation programs, mandatory mediation and settlement pressure, mediation clauses in contracts, confidentiality, the provision of legal services by mediators, and regulating for quality, fairness, effectiveness, and access issues related to specific types of disputes and "toward a simple code of mediation procedure." Appendices include state and federal mediation legislation and codes of ethics and standards of conduct for mediators. This three-volume, looseleaf set is updated annually.

Available on *Westlaw: MEDIATION*

NEGOTIATION

Charles B. Craver, *Effective Legal Negotiation and Settlement,* Newark, N.J.: LexisNexis, 5th ed. (2005).

A book that provides theoretical and practical information about negotiation, including how psychological, sociological, communicational, and game theory factors affect the process. Issues in negotiation, international negotiations, mediation as assisted negotiation, and negotiation ethics are some of the topics examined.

Available on *LexisNexis: EFFLNS*

BIBLIOGRAPHIES

The following are print and online bibliographies listed in reverse chronological order.

SELECTED GENERAL DISPUTE RESOLUTION BIBLIOGRAPHIES

Bibliographies can be found by searching in a library catalog using subject headings such as Dispute Resolution (Law) — Bibliography, Conflict Management — Bibliography, and Mediation — Bibliography.

Legal Newsletters in Print 2007: Including Electronic and Fax Newsletters, compiled and edited by Arlene L. Eis, Teaneck, N.J.: Infosources.

An annual publication listing dispute resolution newsletters under the headings "Arbitration" and "Dispute Resolution." The title listings provide brief bibliographical information and publisher contact information, including frequency and cost, brief annotations, and notes on whether the newsletter is available on *LexisNexis, Westlaw,* and/or the Internet.

Legal Looseleafs in Print, compiled and edited by Arlene L. Eis, Teaneck, N.J.: Infosources (2006).

An annual publication with a subject index, which lists dispute resolution titles in looseleaf format under the headings "Arbitration" and "Dispute Resolution." The title listings offer brief bibliographical information, including publisher, frequency of supplementation, and cost, and also indicate whether the title is available via CD-ROM, diskette, *LexisNexis, Westlaw,* or the Internet.

Kendall F. Svengalis, *The Legal Information Buyer's Guide & Reference Manual,* Providence, RI: LawPress (2006), pp. 185-187.

Considered an essential tool for law librarians with acquisitions and collection development responsibilities, this book is also helpful for legal researchers who wish to find books covering different legal topics. Under the "Arbitration and Alternative Dispute Resolution" heading in the chapter covering treatises and subject specialty titles, a selection of thirteen titles ranging from treatises to nutshells published by major U.S. legal publishers is listed with annotations.

Catherine Morris, *Conflict Resolution and Peacebuilding: A Selected Bibliography* (2002).

A regularly updated, web-based bibliography that lists print and web-based resources in over thirty-five topic areas related to conflict resolution, dispute processing, and peacebuilding. Begun in 1997, when it was known as *Readings in Dispute Resolution: A Selected Bibliography,* this bibliography has been expanded to encompass

English-language titles from instructors, researchers, and practitioners from Canada, Australia, New Zealand, and South Africa, as well as the United States. URL: *http://www.peacemakers.ca/bibliography/indx.html*

Francis R. Doyle, *Searching the Law: The States—A Selective Bibliography of State Practice Materials in the 50 States,* Ardley, N.Y.: Transnational, 3d ed. (2003).

Supplementing the second edition of this work, dispute resolution practice titles for each state are listed under the headings "Arbitration" or "Arbitration, Mediation and Negotiation." Under the subject, the titles are arranged by author and/or title. Titles include books, looseleaf services, periodicals, CLE materials, audiotapes, CD-ROM titles, computer disks, and videos.

Searching the Law, compiled by Francis R. Doyle, Frank S. Bae, Joel Fishman, and Leverett L. Preble, III, Ardsley, N.Y.: Transnational, 3d ed. (2000), pp. 14-19.

Under the subject "Arbitration, Negotiation and Mediation" are a list of treatises and texts, a short list of periodicals, and a brief entry under "Bibliographies and Finding Tools." Titles are published by United States legal publishers.

Dispute Resolution: A Selected Bibliography 1987-1988, A Cooperative Project of The Ohio State University College of Law, Harvard Program on Negotiation, and the American Bar Association's Standing Committee on Dispute Resolution. Compiled by Carole L. Hinchcliff and published by the American Bar Association (1991).

Over 1,600 annotated entries for books and periodical articles from law literature and other disciplines. Each entry is assigned the appropriate number of subject headings drawn from a detailed subject heading list.

The bibliography is updated with entries for books and articles in the following issues of the *Ohio State Journal on Dispute Resolution*:

Vol. 7: 1989 Edition: A Selected Bibliography, 1 (no. 3) (1989).
Vol. 8: 1990 Edition: A Selected Bibliography, 1 (no. 1) (1990)
1991 Edition: A Selected Bibliography, 493 (no. 3) (1991).
Vol. 9: 1992 Edition: A Selected Bibliography, 433 (no. 3) (1992).
—available on *Westlaw: OHSJDR*
Vol. 10: 1993 Edition: A Selected Bibliography, 509 (no. 3) (1993).
—available on *Westlaw: OHSJDR*
Vol. 11: 1994 Edition: A Selected Bibliography, 549 (no. 3) (1994).
—available on *Westlaw: OHSJDR*
Vol. 12: 1995/1996 Edition: A Selected Bibliography, 831 (no. 4) (1995/6).
—available on *Westlaw: OHSJDR*
Vol. 13: 1997 Edition: A Selected Bibliography, 1095 (no. 4) (1997).
Vol. 14: 1998/9 Edition: A Selected Bibliography, 967 (no. 4) (1988/9).
—available on *LexisNexis: OHSJDR*
Vol. 15: 1999 Edition: A Selected Bibliography, 913 (no. 4) (2000).
Vol. 16: 2000 Edition: A Selected Bibliography, 855 (no. 4) (2001).
Vol. 17: 2001 Edition: A Selected Bibliography, 711 (no. 4) (2002).
Vol. 18: 2002/2003 Edition: A Selected Bibliography, 1013 (no. 4) (2003).

Vol. 19: 2003 Edition: A Selected Bibliography, 1137 (no. 4) (2004).
—available on *LexisNexis: OHSJDR & Westlaw: OHSJDR*
Vol. 20: 2004 Edition: A Selected Bibliography, 1063 (no. 4) (2005).
—available on *LexisNexis: OHSJDR*
N.B. Only selected bibliography issues are available on *LexisNexis* and *Westlaw*.

Encyclopedia of Legal Information Sources, edited by Brian L. Baker and Patrick J. Petit, Detroit: Gale Research (1993).
Legal materials are listed under topics and categorized by a total of twenty different types of sources. "Arbitration and Award," "Compromise and Settlement," "Dispute Resolution," "International Arbitration," and "Labor Arbitration" are useful headings for the dispute resolution researcher to find resources such as handbooks, manuals, hornbooks, textbooks, general works, periodicals, databases, and organizations pertaining to dispute resolution.

Frank E. A. Sander, *Mediation: A Selected Annotated Bibliography*, Washington, D.C.: American Bar Association Special Committee on Dispute Resolution (1984).
Over 200 entries with annotations indexed under the following headings: Anthropological Approaches, Bibliographies, Case Studies, Civil Rights, Collected Works, Community Courts, Comparative, Criminal, Education, Environmental, Ethics, Family-Divorce, General, Historical, International Labor, Mediation/Arbitration, Practical Guides, Prisons, Psychological, Schools, and Small Claims.

Alternative Methods of Dispute Settlement: A Selected Bibliography (updated May 1982), compiled by Frank E. A. Sander and Frederick E. Snyder, Washington, D.C., ABA Committee on Resolution of Minor Disputes (1982).
Based on their 1979 publication and with a 1982 update, this seminal dispute resolution bibliography with over two hundred entries presents dispute resolution literature at a time when interest in the field was developing.

SELECTED ARBITRATION BIBLIOGRAPHIES

Arbitration — General

Rosabel E. Goodman-Everard, *Directory of Arbitration Websites and Information on Arbitration Available Online*
URL: *http://www.arbitration-icca.org/directory_of_arbitration_website.htm* (last visited January 3, 2007)
An extensive list of links concerning commercial arbitration at the International Council for Commercial Arbitration web site. Links include those to relevant resources such as treaties and conventions, national arbitration laws, international institutions, national institutions, and online journals.

Paul Felix Warburg Union Catalog of Arbitration: A Selective Bibliography and Subject Index of Peaceful Dispute Settlement Procedures, compiled and edited by Katherine Seide, published for the Eastman Library of The American Arbitration Association, Totowa, N.J.: Rowman & Littlefield (1974).

A three-volume listing of arbitration materials through early 1972 from nineteen libraries. Materials including periodical articles are listed alphabetically and under the subjects Commercial Arbitration, International Commercial Arbitration, International Public Arbitration, Labor Arbitration, and Special Procedures.

Commercial Arbitration

International Council for Commercial Arbitration (ICCA., Albert Jan Van Den Berg (General Editor), *Yearbook: Commercial Arbitration,* Deventer, The Netherlands: Kluwer (1976-).

Annual volumes include an annotated bibliography listing titles under the headings Register of Texts, Congresses, Bibliographies and Dictionaries, and Books. Books are listed by country as are the journal titles. Book annotations indicate if the title offers a bibliography.

Jean M. Wenger, *Update to International Commercial Arbitration: Locating the Resources,* at: *http://www.llrx.com/features/arbitration2.htm* (published May 24, 2004).

This source is a selective, annotated guide covering print and electronic primary and secondary resources for anyone interested in researching aspects of international commercial arbitration. Previous versions of the guide are also available at the highly regarded *llrx.com* web site.

Gloria Miccioli, *ASIL Guide to Electronic Resources for International Law — International Commercial Arbitration* at *www.asil.org/resource/arb1.htm* (last updated October 15, 2006).

A brief overview of international commercial arbitration precedes research advice for locating international agreements, conventions and treaties, documents from both international and regional institutions, information about Internet domain name disputes, links to national arbitration statutes, and the offerings of online commercial sources such as Kluwer Arbitration Online, Arbitration Law Online, *Westlaw, LexisNexis,* WorldTradeLaw.net, and selected free web sites.

Gloria Miccioli, *A Selective Guide to Online Arbitration Resources* (published June 21, 2004) at *www.llrx.com/features/interarbitration.htm.*

Provides guidance to finding arbitration treaties and conventions, and information and decisions from institutions such as the International Chamber of Commerce, ICC International Court of Arbitration, International Center for the Settlement of Investment Disputes, Permanent Court of Arbitration, WIPO Arbitration and Mediation Center, and the World Trade Organization. In addition, it compares the international arbitration offerings of *LexisNexis, Westlaw,* Kluwer Arbitration Online, and Arbitration LawOnline from Juris Publishing.

Lyonette Louis-Jacques, *International Commercial Arbitration: Resources in Print and Electronic Format,* at *http://www.lib.uchicago.edu/~llou/intlarb.html* (last updated October 15, 2003).

An extensive, regularly updated list of titles, both print and electronic, for anyone interested in researching aspects of international commercial arbitration.

Hans Smit and Vratislav Pechota, *Commercial Arbitration: An International Bibliography*, Huntington, N.Y.: Juris, 2d ed. (1998).

The eighth volume in the Parker School of Foreign and Comparative Law series of guides covering different aspects of international arbitration. This looseleaf bibliography updated biannually, in its first part, lists entries by subject, usually following UNCITRAL categorization, and in the second part, lists entries by 161 regions and countries. Some materials in languages other than English are included. To further update this title, the compilers recommend that readers consult the section "Recent Books and Articles on International Commercial Arbitration," which appears in the Parker School's quarterly law journal, *American Review of International Arbitration*.

Labor Arbitration

Suzanne Thorpe and Laura J. Cooper, *Researching Labor Arbitration & Alternative Dispute Resolution in Employment*, at *www.llrx.com/features/arbitration2.htm* (published October 24, 2004) and in Laura J. Cooper, Dennis R. Nolan, and Richard A. Bales, *ADR in the Workplace*, 2d ed., Appendix A (2005).

An annotated bibliography of print and electronic sources listed under the headings Bibliographies, Major Texts, Arbitration Awards, Information about Dispute Resolution Professionals, Procedural and Ethical Rules, and Other Resources on Workplace Dispute Resolution—Books, Periodicals and Web Sites. An earlier version of this research guide is at 91 *Law Library Journal* 367 (1999).

Charles J. Coleman, Theodora T. Haynes, and Marie T. Gibson McGraw, eds., *Labor and Employment Arbitration: An Annotated Bibliography 1991-1996*, Ithaca, N.Y.: ILR Press (1997).

Updating the 1994 bibliography by Coleman and Haynes, this bibliography has 536 entries including books, monographs, journal articles, proceedings of professional meetings, and some doctoral dissertations and master's theses. The revised title reflects over 100 entries from 1991-1996 relating to issues in employment arbitration. Articles on alternative dispute resolution and the Americans with Disabilities Act are included, as are entries covering arbitration outside Canada and the United States. Author and subject indexes are included.

Charles J. Coleman and Theodora T. Haynes, eds., *Labor Arbitration: An Annotated Bibliography*, Ithaca, N.Y.: ILR Press (1994).

This work includes almost every one of the 590 entries in the 1985 annotated bibliography on labor arbitration edited by Howard Foster and Mario Bognanno and prepared under the auspices of the Committee on Research of the National Academy of Arbitrators. Also, this source contains titles of books and monographs on arbitration and related topics published since 1950, journal articles in non-legal periodicals published since 1970, and articles in law journals published since 1980. This compilation of references to Canadian and United States literature has a books and monographs division comprising 154 entries and an articles and proceedings division comprising 1,182 entries. Entries are arranged chronologically by date of publication within each subject area. Separate author and subject indexes are included.

Annual Reports and Yearbooks

ADR & the Law: A Report of the American Arbitration Association, the Fordham International Law Journal and the Fordham Urban Law Journal (1981-1994, 1997) (ISSN 1535-4326).

Known as *Arbitration & the Law: AAA General Counsel's Report* until 1994, this annual publication from the Office of the General Counsel of the American Arbitration Association, beginning with the 1997 edition, which covered developments from 1994-1997, is now published in conjunction with the Fordham International Law Journal and the Fordham Urban Law Journal. This report provides commentary on important cases in general commercial and international alternative dispute resolution, new legislation, rules, and procedures.

International Ombudsman Yearbook, Kluwer (1997) (ISSN 1387-1846).

Formerly known as the *International Ombudsman Journal*, this annual publication of the International Ombudsman Institute publishes the papers presented at the organization's conferences.

Proceedings of the Annual Meeting National Academy of Arbitrators, Washington, D.C.: BNA (1955-) (ISSN 0148-4176).

Annual volumes present papers delivered at each year's meeting of the National Academy of Arbitrators.

International Council for Commercial Arbitration (ICCA), Albert Jan Van Den Berg (General Editor), *Yearbook: Commercial Arbitration*, Deventer, The Netherlands: Kluwer (1976-).

Annual volumes containing national reports, recent developments in arbitration law and practice, Iran-U.S. Claims Tribunal, arbitral awards, court decisions on arbitration, court decisions applying the UNCITRAL Model Law, arbitration rules, court decisions on the New York Convention of 1958, the European Convention of 1961, the Washington Convention of 1965 and the Panama Convention of 1975. Further, some volumes include articles on arbitration, and each volume concludes with a bibliography of "the important publications in arbitration."

Directories and Biographical Information About Dispute Resolution Professionals

In addition to consulting the sources below, background information about a dispute resolution professional can be found through, in the case of an arbitrator, searches of the person's name in applicable databases of arbitration awards,[2] and in the case of dispute resolution professionals in general, searches of the person's web site (if one exists), searches of the person's name in *LexisNexis*, *Westlaw*, and other databases of cases, verdicts, law reviews, law journals, trade journals, newspapers,

2. See below under other headings in this section.

magazine articles, and pending law suits. General searches of the Web for material such as postings to discussion groups may also elicit useful material.[3]

GENERAL

American Arbitration Association
URL: *http://www.adr.org*

Provides biographies of AAA mediators, searchable by keyword, last name, and area of expertise.

Martindale-Hubbell Dispute Resolution Directory, New Providence, N.J.: Martindale-Hubbell (1996).

A directory that includes contact information for dispute resolution practitioners and organizations, relevant statutes and rules, professional standards, and ethical codes.
LexisNexis: DRD

Martindale-Hubbell International Arbitration and Dispute Resolution Directory, New Providence, N.J.: Martindale-Hubbell (2000).

Extensive listings of neutrals from around the globe along with general materials and articles including a worldwide survey of developments in dispute resolution. The text of the relevant rules, codes, conventions, and codes of ethics and listings for national and international dispute resolution organizations are also provided.

LexisNexis: IDRD — International Dispute Resolution Directory

A file, updated each spring, that contains a listing of international (other than U.S.) organizations and individuals who practice in the areas of adjudication, arbitration, case evaluation, conciliation, facilitation, mediation, negotiation, and training.

MIRC — Mediation and Information and Resource Center

URL: *http://www.mediate.com/*

A popular site about mediation that allows users to search for mediators by practice area or state, and which consists of information submitted by mediators.

West Legal Directory — Alternative Dispute Resolution
Westlaw *WLD-ADR*

A database, updated daily, of profiles submitted by attorneys, law firms, and government or corporate law offices that provide dispute resolution services, or that otherwise practice in the area.

West Legal Directory — ADR Professionals
Westlaw *WLD-ADRP*

A database of profiles of ADR professionals compiled from *Findlaw*.

3. See Zimmerman's Research Guide, URL: *http://www.llrx.com/guide-gen/0/80.html*, which provides general search tips and advice on finding information about securities and labor arbitrators.

ARBITRATORS

BNA Labor Arbitration and Dispute Settlement (1946-)

The looseleaf volume "Labor Arbitration & Dispute Settlements," includes arbitrator biographies. This set is described below in more detail under "Arbitration Decisions."

LexisNexis: ARBBIO — BNA Labor Relations Reporter Selected Arbitrator's Biographies

Biographies supplied by practicing labor arbitrators who are registered with the Federal Mediation and Conciliation Service or who have their awards published in BNA's *Labor Arbitration Reports.*

Westlaw: LRR-DIR — BNA Labor Relations Reporter: Directory of Arbitrators

Biographical information about arbitrators who have their awards published in *BNA's Labor Arbitration Reports.*

Hans Smit and Vratislav Pechota, *Roster of International Arbitrators,* Huntington, N.Y.: Juris (1999).

One of the eight volumes of Smit's Guides to International Arbitration, this looseleaf volume, updated annually, provides an alphabetical listing of biographies of almost 1,000 eligible international arbitrators. The arbitrators are also listed by nationality, language, and area of specialization. This volume also includes the Code of Ethics for International Arbitrators, IBA Rules of Ethics for International Arbitrators, and AAA and ABA Code of Ethics for Arbitrators in Commercial Disputes.

Labor Arbitration Awards (CCH) (1961-)

A one-volume looseleaf of arbitration awards that includes biographies of arbitrators.

Arbitration Decisions — United States

LABOR AND EMPLOYMENT

AAA Labor Arbitration Awards
LexisNexis: AAALAB

American Arbitration Association Awards from January 2003 through February 2006.

Arbsearch.com
URL: *http://arbsearch.com*

A subscription-based web site from LRP Publications that allows you to search over 75,000 federal, private-, and public-sector arbitration awards published since 1950 from over 4,400 arbitrators. Summaries of cases matching search requests include citations to the full text of the award and are available from arbitration award publishers such as AAA, BNA, CCH, and LRP. Arbitrator biographies, decision statistics, and individual arbitrator's rulings (management, union, or split) are also available.

BNA Labor Relations Reporter (1937-)

Bound volumes and twenty looseleaf binders updated weekly with current information including state and federal labor legislation, analysis, news, and background on topical issues. The binder "Labor Arbitration and Dispute Settlements" contains the full text of the latest awards and settlements in every type of labor dispute plus information about individual arbitrators. Cases and awards are compiled into six accompanying sets of bound volumes. *Labor Relations Reference Manual* contains decisions of the National Labor Relations Board (NLRB) and the courts from the Labor Management Relations binders. *Labor Arbitration Reports* (formerly known as *War Labor Reports* from 1942 to 1945) contains "significant decisions and reports of arbitrators and agencies." Other case reporters in the set are Wages & Hours Cases, Fair Employment Practice Cases, Individual Employment Rights Cases, and Americans with Disabilities Cases. Also available in CD-ROM format updated monthly, and an Internet subscription service, which is regularly updated.

LexisNexis: LRRLA — BNA Labor Relations Reporter Labor Arbitration Reports

Contains the full text of decisions and rulings of arbitrators, fact-finding bodies, and other agencies concerned with settling labor disputes. Includes decisions from 1979, volume 73 to current. Updated weekly.

BNA files are available via law school *LexisNexis* contracts under separate subscription arrangements.

Westlaw: BNA Combined Labor Arbitration Decisions (LA-COMB)

Decisions from *Westlaw's LLRR-LA* and *LA-UNP* databases.

BNA Labor Relations Reporter: Labor Arbitration Reports (LRR-LA) (1979-)

Decisions and recommendations of labor arbitrators, fact-finding bodies, and other agencies along with editorial information as found in volume 73 to date of *Labor Arbitration Reports.*

BNA Unpublished Arbitration Decisions (LA-UNP) (1988-)

Full text of decisions and recommendations of arbitrators, fact-finding bodies, and other agencies submitted to BNA but not published in *BNA's Labor Arbitration Reports.*

Labor Arbitration Awards (CCH) (1961-)

Bound volumes and a one-volume looseleaf with a monthly summary newsletter reporting news from the field and summaries of recent, selected awards, which appear in full text in the publication along with a glossary of labor terms, a topical index, and tables of awards by party and arbitrator. Includes arbitrator biographies.

Arbsearch.com

Telephone to request a search of over 75,000 arbitration awards rendered since 1950 by more than 4,400 arbitrators in the public, private, and federal sectors. Database includes biographical data about the arbitrator and covers every published award from LRP, BNA, CCH (up until 2004), and AAA.

Labor Arbitration Information System, LRP Publications (ISSN 0744-5253) (1982-)
Summaries of all reported private and public-sector labor arbitration awards. Includes full-text citations from the reporting services of AAA, BNA, CCH, and LRP. Full text of selected awards. Two looseleaf binders updated monthly.

Westlaw: LAIS (1960-)
Selected summaries of arbitrations from LRP Publications and biographical records of labor arbitrators. Information is drawn from (1) American Arbitration Association (AAA) publications such as *Arbitration in the Schools, Labor Arbitration in Government,* and *Summary of Labor Arbitration Awards;* (2) Labor Relations Press (LRP) publications such as *Federal Labor Relations Reporter,* and (3) arbitration awards from the Labor Agreement Information Retrieval System (LAIRS) and Labor Arbitration Information System (LAIS), Bureau of National Affairs (BNA), *Government Employee Relations Reporter* and *Labor Arbitration Reports,* and Commerce Clearing House's (CCH) *Labor Arbitration Awards.*

Labor Arbitration Index (1970/72-) (ISSN 0195-0762)
Annual publication by LRP indexing over 2,500 arbitration awards published each year by the American Arbitration Association, BNA, CCH, and LRP. Awards can be found by arbitrator, subject (using detailed key classification numbers), employer, and union. From 1982, this title contains the same information as found in volume 1 of *Labor Arbitration Information System.*

LRP's Arbitration Database on CD-ROM (1978-)
CD-ROM includes private-and public-sector published arbitration decisions. Information offered includes arbitrator's background, statistics, how the arbitrator ruled, case summaries, and cites to full-text awards. Updated biannually.

Westlaw: ARBIT Private Database: ARBIT (1963-)
Unpublished awards are included in this database of arbitration documents from attorney Gregory J. Kamer.

Summary of Labor Arbitration Awards (1959-) (ISSN 0039-5005)
A monthly newsletter published by LRP Publications for the American Arbitration Association. Provides summaries of significant private-sector labor arbitration cases with biannual subject indexes. Full text of awards can be purchased from AAA.

SECURITIES

SCAN (SAC-CCH Awards Network) (1989-)
URL: *http://scan.cch.com*
An Internet-based subscription database of over 26,000 securities arbitration awards from various exchanges such as National Association of Securities Dealers and Regulators (NASDR), New York Stock Exchange (NYSE), Pacific Exchange (PCX), and American Arbitration Association (AAA). Also, this source includes state and federal cases pertaining to broker-dealer arbitrations. Subscribers can retrieve award summary reports and copies of the awards.

Westlaw: Federal Securities — Arbitration Awards (*FSEC-ARB*) (1989-)

Summaries of arbitrations between investors and broker-dealers released by securities exchanges such as the New York Stock Exchange (NYSE), the American Stock Exchange (ASE), and the National Association of Securities Dealers (NASD).

National Association of Securities Dealers — Arbitration Awards (*NASD-ARB*) (1989-)

Summaries of arbitrations between investors and broker-dealers released by NASD Regulation, Inc.

Arbitration Decisions — International Arbitration

Mealey's International Arbitration Report (1996-) (ISSN 1089-2397)

Monthly issues have provided arbitration and related decisions from courts around the globe, including the Iran-U.S. Claims Tribunal and the United Nations Compensation Commission. From 1986 to 1996, the title was known as *International Arbitration Report.* In addition, issues provide commentary and announcements about arbitration news and events.

Model Arbitration Law Quarterly Reports (1995-) (ISSN 1358-6904)

Reports translated into English from countries that have adopted the UNCITRAL Model Arbitration Law. Cases include commentary, headnotes, and UNCITRAL's CLOUT abstract, if available. Issues may include articles, materials from UNCITRAL national law commissions and similar reports, statutes from countries that have adopted UNCITRAL, and comparative analyses.

Reports of International Arbitral Awards (*Recueil Des Sentences Arbitrales*) (1948-) (ISSN 0251-7833)

Prepared by the Codification Division of the Office of Legal Affairs at the United Nations, each volume prints awards in their original language, which is usually English or French. Headnotes may appear in both languages.

Stockholm Arbitration Report (2001-) (ISSN 1404-1075)

A biannual publication from the Stockholm Chamber of Commerce (SCC) Institute, to replace its former yearbook, *Arbitration in Sweden: Yearbook of the Arbitration Institute of the Stockholm Chamber of Commerce.* Includes articles on topical issues in international arbitration and extracts of arbitral awards and judicial decisions. Electronic subscription available from Juris Publishing, Inc.

Hans Smit and Vratislav Pechota, *World Arbitration Reporter,* Juris Publishing, Inc. (1998).

Eight-volume looseleaf service presenting international conventions and agreements, national legislation, arbitration institutions and their rules, court decisions, and arbitral awards along with commentary and analysis and references to scholarly literature relating to aspects of international arbitration. Appears to be updated once or twice a year.

Legislation

FEDERAL LEGISLATION

Internet sites providing federal dispute resolution legislation invariably link to the official text of the United States Code at the House of Representatives' web site at *http://uscode.house.gov/search/criteria.shtml,* or the unofficial (but easier to search) version offered by Cornell Law School's Legal Information Institute at *http://www4.law.cornell.edu/uscode/.*

Sarah R. Cole, Craig A. McEwen, and Nancy H. Rogers, *Mediation: Law, Policy, Practice,* St. Paul, MN: West Group, 2d ed. (1994).

Mediation treatise in a three-volume looseleaf title that is updated annually and includes an appendix with selected confidentiality legislation by scope and jurisdiction, significant mediation legislation by topic and jurisdiction, and the text of selected mediation legislation by jurisdiction.

STATE LEGISLATION

Legal Information Institute
URL: *http://www.law.cornell.edu/topics/state_statutes.html#alternative_dispute_resolution*
Cornell's Legal Information Institute includes alternative dispute resolution in its topical index with links to free versions of unannotated state statutes on the Web.

Cheryl Rae Nyberg, *Subject Compilations of State Laws 2004-2005: An Annotated Bibliography,* Twin Falls, Ida: Cheryl Boast & Cheryl Rae Nyberg (2006).

Cumulative volumes beginning in 1960 list over 13,000 law review and other periodical articles, books, federal and state government publications, looseleaf services, appellate court opinions, and web sites including citations to state laws. Titles with citations to dispute resolution session laws, codes, and court rules are found under the headings "Arbitration and Arbitrators" and "Mediators and Mediation." Beginning with the 2001 volume, annual volumes now include citations to briefs submitted to the United States Supreme Court.

ADRWorld.com
URL: *http://www.adrworld.com*
ADRWorld is a subscription web site that lists links to free versions of unannotated statutes on the Web.

STATUTES AND LEGISLATIVE MATERIALS ON *LEXISNEXIS*

Some sources to search on *LexisNexis* for dispute resolution legislation are:

State Codes, Constitutions, Court Rules & ALS (Advanced Legislative Services) from the *ALLCDE* file.
United States Code Service — Titles 5 and 9

Federal Arbitration Act *FAACT* (United States Code Service version)

Martindale-Hubbell—Uniform Arbitration Act (annually updated version of the Uniform Arbitration Act as published by Martindale-Hubbell and appearing in *Martindale-Hubbell Dispute Resolution Directory*)

STATUTES AND LEGISLATIVE MATERIALS ON *WESTLAW*

Under "Topical Practice Areas" *Westlaw* offers the topic "Alternative Dispute Resolution," where there are databases covering international commercial arbitration.

International Commercial Arbitration—Legislation (ICA LEGIS)

Legislation from Australia, China, France, Germany, The Netherlands, Singapore, Switzerland, and the United Kingdom.

International Commercial Arbitration—Model Laws (ICA-MODL)

Model laws relating to international commercial arbitration drawn from the publications of various organizations and institutions.

International Commercial Arbitration—Uniform Laws Annotated (ICA-ULA)

The Uniform Arbitration Act as it appears in *Uniform Laws Annotated.*

United Nations Commission on International Trade Law—Model Laws (UNCITRAL-MODL)

UNCITRAL model laws drawn from *International Legal Materials* and the *International Economic Law Documents Database (IEL)*

United States International Commercial Arbitration—State Annotated Statutes (USAICA-STANN)

U.S. state statutes covering international commercial arbitration.

United States of America International Commercial Arbitration—United States Code Annotated (USAICA-USCA)

Statutes covering international commercial arbitration drawn from USCA.

To search for other federal statutes about dispute resolution processes, select a database such as *United States Code Annotated (USCA)*; and to search for state legislation, select the relevant state annotated code from the *Westlaw* Directory or search all state statutes together by selecting *All States—ST-ANN-ALL.*

UNIFORM ACTS

The National Conference of Commissioners on Uniform State Laws is responsible for preparing statutes on a variety of topics that can be adopted by states. Print copies of the Uniform Arbitration Act (UAA) or Uniform Mediation Act (UMA) are found in an annotated, code-like set, which also provides such features as official comments by commissioners on uniform state laws, annotations to relevant cases, and tables of adopting jurisdictions.

Uniform Laws Annotated Master Edition, St. Paul, MN: West (1968).
A compilation of uniform laws updated by annual pocket parts.

Westlaw: ULA
Both the UMA and UAA can also be found at the web site of the National Conference of Commissioners on Uniform State Laws at *http://www.nccusl.org/update/DesktopDefault.aspx?tabindex=2&tabid=60*
See also *Guide to the Uniform Mediation Act* at the web site *Mediation Law Project of the American Bar Association and Section of Dispute Resolution and the National Conference of Commissioners on Uniform State Laws, http://www.pon.harvard.edu/guests/uma/*

ETHICS

Phyllis Bernard and Bryant Garth, eds., *Dispute Resolution Ethics: A Comprehensive Guide,* Washington, D.C.: American Bar Association Section of Dispute Resolution (2002).
A collection of essays addressing ethical issues in dispute resolution relating to the settlement process, engaging a mediator, aspects of mediator and lawyer ethics, unauthorized practice of law in dispute resolution, enforcement of ethics in mediation, ethical issues arising in negotiation, provider organizations, arbitration and ombuds practice, and online dispute resolution. Appendices include standards, model standards, codes of ethics, guidelines, principles, and rules that may apply to various types of dispute resolution professionals and types of disputes.

Sarah R. Cole, Craig A. McEwen, and Nancy H. Rogers, *Mediation: Law, Policy, Practice,* St. Paul, MN: West Group, 2d ed. (1994).
Includes an annually updated appendix that offers codes of ethics and standards of conduct for mediators.

Hans Smit and Vratislav Pechota, *Roster of International Arbitrators,* Huntington, N.Y.: Juris (1999).
A volume of Smit's Guides to International Arbitration, which contains biographical information about arbitrators and includes the Code of Ethics for International Arbitrators, IBA Rules of Ethics for International Arbitrators, and AAA & ABA Code of Ethics for Arbitrators in Commercial Disputes.

American Arbitration Association
URL: *www.adr.org/*
The American Arbitration Association's web site provides the Code of Ethics for Arbitrators in Commercial Disputes, Model Standards of Conduct for Mediators, and Statement of Ethical Principles for the American Arbitration Association.

National Academy of Arbitrators, *Code of Professional Responsibility for Arbitrators of Labor-Management Disputes*
URL: *http://www.naarb.org/code.html*
A code applying largely to the voluntary arbitration of labor disputes by members of the American Arbitration Association, Federal Mediation & Conciliation Service, and the National Association of Arbitrators.

DISPUTE RESOLUTION MATERIALS ON *LEXISNEXIS* AND *WESTLAW*

LEXISNEXIS

One of the subjects under Area of Law — By Topic on the opening screen after signing on to *LexisNexis* is Alternative Dispute Resolution, which offers various categories of materials, some of which are mentioned below.

Remember to check the "i" symbol next to each file description to check coverage of materials described and to examine the segments available for searching in each file. Segment searching used in conjunction with terms and connectors searching can improve the efficiency of searching *LexisNexis.*

Cases

Cases are divided into *Combined Federal and State Cases* (cases drawn from the *MEGA* file of all available state and federal cases) and *Arbitration Related Labor Cases, Federal and State Courts* (cases drawn from the *ADRCAS* file).

Law Reviews and Journals

The table on pp. 754-777 indicates which periodicals and newsletters are presently found on *LexisNexis.*

Treatises and Analytical Materials

Materials under this heading presently include three looseleaf service titles from Matthew Bender Co., Inc., and five practical handbooks published by the National Institute of Trial Advocacy (NITA).

General News and Information

The most notable file under this heading is the *New York Times* file, *NYTADR,* which allows you to search articles from June 1, 1980, about alternative dispute resolution.

Legal News

Includes a file, *IBAAAN,* which offers selected articles about arbitration and alternative dispute resolution from various International Bar Association newsletters and publications.

Model ADR Practices and Procedures

Under this heading are over twenty-five publications from the Center for Public Resources (CPR) Institute for Dispute Resolution, including their newsletter, *Alternatives to the High Cost of Litigation.* There are also a number of older CPR titles under the heading Archived Materials.

WESTLAW

One approach to finding dispute resolution material on *Westlaw* is to search for a desired title or words in a title by using the "*Westlaw* Wizard," a search box that is available in the left column next to any display of the *Westlaw* directory. Under "Topical Materials by Area of Practice," there is the category "Alternative Dispute Resolution," which has a diverse collection of materials under various subheadings. Some *Westlaw* offerings under those headings are briefly described.

International Centre for Settlement of Investment Disputes ALL (ICSID-ALL)

Offers arbitration awards, model clauses, and historical arbitration rules from the international organization ICSID, which is charged with mediating and conciliating investment disputes between governments and private foreign investors.

International Chamber of Commerce ALL (ICC-ALL)

Rules from this world business organization that provides arbitration services.

International Commercial Arbitration ALL (ICA-ALL)

A database of all international commercial arbitration material found on *Westlaw,* including cases, legislation, rules, model laws, guidelines, treaties, commentaries, journal and law review articles from various countries, and dispute resolution institutions.

Personnet Arbitration Multibase (PNET-ARB)

Provides the full text of arbitration decisions covering human resources matters involving federal government employees, arbitrators' biographies, statistics and court cases from 1973, and related court cases from 1979.

United States of America International Commercial Arbitration ALL (USAICA-ALL)

A database offering both United States federal and state international commercial arbitration case law and international commercial arbitration statutes.

Administrative Materials

Arbitration awards from Bureau of National Affairs (BNA), Labor Arbitration Information System, National Mediation Board, Federal Arbitration Awards, ICSID Awards, treaties, Iran-U.S. Claims Tribunal decisions, Uniform Domain Name Dispute Resolution Policy Project arbitration decisions, and WTO and GATT panel decisions. Coverage varies for the different sources of information.

Journals and Law Reviews

The table on pp. 754-777 indicates which periodicals and newsletters are presently found on *Westlaw.*

Forms, Treatises, and Other Practice Materials

A diverse array of databases falls under this heading, which include books; looseleaf services published by Thomson; practice guides from California, Georgia, and Texas; labor and employment forms from West's Legal Forms; publications such as guides, journal articles, rules, and model clauses from the American Arbitration Center for Dispute Resolution; Commercial Arbitration and Mediation Center for the Americas; CPR Institute for Dispute Resolution; International Bar Association; International Centre for Settlement of Investment Disputes; International Chamber of Commerce; Permanent Court of Arbitration; Society of Maritime Arbitrators; and World Intellectual Property Organization. For each database under this heading, check the information symbol for details of the types of publication and years offered.

Legal Newspapers, Newsletters, and Current Materials

Includes database with news items about international arbitration from the International Law Office and Ellis Publications.

FINDING FULL-TEXT ARTICLES ON *LEXISNEXIS*, *WESTLAW*, *HEIN ONLINE*, AND *GOOGLE SCHOLAR*

Probably the most often used method to quickly find law review articles on a topic is to search the full-text periodical databases on *LexisNexis* or *Westlaw*. This method works well for finding articles about dispute resolution appearing in general law reviews published in the United States; however, as the list of some fifty periodicals below shows, few dispute resolution periodicals are included in either *LexisNexis* or *Westlaw*. Searching the full text of all the articles in the database may uncover discussion of an issue that may not otherwise be indexed by the broad subject headings used by periodical indexes. Another advantage is that the search query may find footnotes to other relevant sources available in print or online. If the results are overwhelming from searching the full text of the articles, using segment searching in *LexisNexis* or field searching in *Westlaw* is a method to find articles with particular words in the heading, by a particular author, or in a particular publication. Researchers who need to find more articles about dispute resolution should consider searching both *LexisNexis* and *Westlaw*, since the titles selected vary between the databases, and the extent of coverage can be different for the same law review.

LexisNexis: Legal Publications Group File (*LGLPUB*)

According to the "content-summary" information, this source comprises over 900 secondary source titles including law reviews, bar journals, ABA journals, legal newspapers, legal newsletters, specialty legal publications, and continuing legal education (CLE) materials. Search results appear following this order.

Westlaw: Texts and Periodicals — All Law Reviews, Texts, and Bar Journals (*TP-ALL*)

TP-ALL offers law reviews, bar journals, other legal periodicals, treatise-like materials from selected texts, *American Law Reports* (*ALR 3d, ALR 4th, ALR 5th,* and *ALR*

Federal), *American Jurisprudence 2d,* and *Corpus Juris Secundum,* and continuing legal education (CLE) course materials. Full coverage for some law reviews is from 1994. To check the coverage of a law review or journal title, click on the "i" symbol next to its database abbreviation for the scope summary and contents information.

Hein Online
URL: *http://heinonline.org*

Legal publisher William S. Hein Co. provides a full-text, searchable database of predominantly pre-1980, indexed law journal articles in PDF format. *Hein Online* is a work-in-progress with the aim to provide electronic access to all issues of indexed law reviews. This Internet subscription service is available at many academic and other law libraries and is helpful for finding older legal periodical articles not available on *LexisNexis* or *Westlaw.*

Google Scholar
URL: *www.scholar.google.com*

Search *Google Scholar* to find scholarly literature about dispute resolution, including articles, abstracts of articles, research reports, and book reviews. Before paying to access an article from a publisher's web site, search the journal title in your library catalog, because your library may provide free access to the articles you need. Searching *Google Scholar* is a convenient method for finding periodical articles about dispute resolution that are in non-law journals.

Using Periodical Indexes

Index to Legal Periodicals (Jones and Chipman, eds.), pre-1887 to 1937

This six-volume index, now available in an online version to libraries that subscribe to Nineteenth Century Masterfile, includes the heading "Arbitration" and variations thereof, which is useful for researchers interested in finding older legal periodical literature on this topic. Articles from over 158 legal journals from the United States, England, Scotland, Ireland, and the English colonies and various publications from the American Bar Association (ABA) and state bar associations are included, along with selected articles from "principal literary reviews and magazines." This legal periodicals index is the only title that indexes United States legal periodical articles prior to 1908.

Index to Legal Periodicals & Books, 1908-
LexisNexis: LRI 1981-
Westlaw: LGLIND 1981-

Until September 1994, this title was known as *Index to Legal Periodicals.* Over 925 sources including legal journals, yearbooks, institutes, bar association publications, law reviews, and government publications from the United States, Canada, Great Britain, Ireland, Australia, and New Zealand are found on the online subscription or in the print versions.

It is interesting to note that "Mediation" first appeared as a subject heading in the September 1964-August 1967 *Index to Legal Periodicals* cumulative volume;

however, no articles appeared under that heading. Instead, researchers are referred to the headings "Arbitration and Award," "Industrial Arbitration," and "International Arbitration." Entries under "Mediation" began appearing in the September 1993-August 1994 volume. "Dispute Resolution" first appeared as a subject heading in the September 1985-August 1986 cumulation; however, entries did not appear under that heading until the September 1987-August 1988 volume.

The online version is available via an Internet subscription or *LexisNexis* and *Westlaw* from 1981 to present. Some law schools subscribe to the online database, *Index to Legal Periodicals Retrospective: 1908-1981.*

Index to Foreign Legal Periodicals: A Subject Index to Selected International and Comparative Law Periodicals and Collections of Essays (1960-) (ISSN 0019-400X)
LexisNexis:
Westlaw: IFLP (available to *Westlaw* subscribers other than law schools)

Under the auspices of the American Association of Law Libraries, this print title (also available via Internet subscription) indexes legal periodicals covering international law (public and private), comparative law, and municipal law. This title covers legal periodicals from countries other than the United States and British Commonwealth countries such as Australia, Canada, and the United Kingdom. Many law schools subscribe to an online version of *IFLP* from the publisher.

Current Index to Legal Periodicals
URL: *http://lib.law.washington.edu/pubs/pubs.html#cilp*

A weekly current awareness service from the University of Washington's Marian Gould Gallagher Library. This source indexes articles from recent issues of over 475 law reviews under 100 subject headings, including "Dispute Resolution," and provides tables of contents. SmartCILP subscribers may receive customized versions of the service via e-mail.

Current Law Index & LegalTrac (1980-)
LexisNexis: LGLND
Westlaw: LRI

The print version of this index is called *Current Law Index.* The Internet subscription version, *LegalTrac,* and versions available via *LexisNexis* and *Westlaw* also index prominent U.S. legal newspapers. Searches for relevant articles may be done using Library of Congress subject headings.

PAIS International (Public Affairs International Service) (1972-)

A subscription database that indexes articles, books, and documents from the United States and other countries covering political, economic, and social sciences.

PsycINFO (1967-) (Historic PsycINFO, 1872-1966)

Indexes and provides summaries of some journal articles, book chapters, books, dissertations and technical reports on psychology, and psychology materials from disciplines such as medicine, psychiatry, nursing, sociology, education, pharmacology, physiology, linguistics, anthropology, business, and law. Academic libraries often subscribe to the Internet version.

Sociological Abstracts (1963-)

A subscription database that "indexes the international literature in sociology and related disciplines in the social and behavioral sciences." Provides abstracts of journal articles (added to the database after 1974), books, book chapters, dissertations, and conference papers. Academic libraries often subscribe to the Internet version.

Social Science Citation Index (SSCI) (1983-)
Westlaw: SS-ABS (not available via law school subscriptions)

Indexes articles in over 350 English-language journals covering disciplines such as addiction studies, anthropology, area studies, community health and medical care, corrections, criminal justice, criminology, economics, environmental studies, ethics, family studies, gender studies, geography, gerontology, international relations, law, minority studies, planning and public administration, policy studies, political science, psychiatry, psychology, public welfare, social work, sociology, and urban studies. Academic libraries often subscribe to the Internet version.

Finding Leading Articles in Dispute Resolution

COLLECTIONS OF ARTICLES

Michael Freeman, ed., *Alternative Dispute Resolution,* New York: NYU Press (1995).

One book in the first series, *The International Library of Essays in Law and Legal Theory,* is devoted to dispute resolution. A selection of fourteen of the best articles about dispute resolution topics by leading scholars in the area are reprinted in this volume under the headings "The Courts and Dispute Resolution," "Alternative Dispute Resolution," "The Critics," "Legal Scholarship and Alternative Dispute Resolution," and "The Quality of Dispute Resolution."

Carrie Menkel-Meadow, ed., *Mediation: Theory, Policy & Practice,* Aldershot, England/Burlington, VT: Ashgate/Dartmouth (2001).

One volume in the second series of *The International Library of Essays in Law and Legal Theory* is devoted to "exciting and controversial issues" in mediation. Twenty-five essays are reprinted and categorized under the headings "Theory, Purposes and Goals of Mediation," "Definitions, Origins, Ideologies and Controversies," "Practice and Policy Issues," "Applications and the Future Hope," and "Promise of Mediation."

Selected Periodicals and Newsletters

The following table of selected periodicals and newsletters comprises titles focused on areas of dispute resolution under the headings "Arbitration—International," "Business/Corporate/Employment," "Family," "General," "International," and "Negotiation." Most of the titles are from the United States. As the table shows, a number of titles are not indexed by readily available legal periodical or other indexes, nor are they available either free or via subscription on the Internet or from *LexisNexis* or *Westlaw.* If you identify a title that looks relevant, you may need to check the publisher's web site to find out if tables of contents or full-text versions of the articles are available, or you may need to resort to browsing print issues of a journal title to find pertinent articles.

Selected Periodicals and Newsletters

Arbitration — International

Periodical	*ISSN*	*Annotation*	*LegalTrac*	*Index to Legal Periodicals & Books*	*LexisNexis*	*Westlaw*	*Hein Online*
American Review of International Arbitration	1050-4109	1990- : A quarterly publication of the Center for International Arbitration and Litigation Law, Columbia University, that publishes articles, summaries, and commentary on significant arbitral and judicial decisions, practice notes, book reviews, and bibliographies. Available to online subscribers from Juris Publishing, Inc.	Indexing begins in 2004 with vol. 15	Indexing begins in 1996 with vol. 7	*AMRVIA* From 1996 with vol. 7, issue 3-4	*AMRIARB* From 1997 with vol. 7	
Arbitration International	0957-0411	1985- : This journal of the London Court of International Arbitration is published quarterly. Its purpose is to serve as "[a] forum for the rigorous examination of the international arbitral process, whether public or private; to publish not information or news, but contributions to a deeper understanding of the subject." Available to online subscribers from Kluwer Law International.		Indexing begins in 1997 with vol. 13			

Arbitration Law Monthly	1472-9822	2001- : Formerly known as *Arbitration & Dispute Resolution Law Journal* and published ten times per year. Edited by Robert Merkin, this publication strives to analyze leading decisions and legislative developments in arbitration law with an emphasis on jurisdictions that have adopted the UNCITRAL Model Law.
ASA Bulletin	1010-9153	2002- : Formerly known as *Bulletin*, 1983-2001, this official quarterly of the Swiss Arbitration Association (ASA) provides articles, leading cases of the Swiss Federal Tribunal, leading cases from other Swiss courts, selected landmark cases from jurisdictions worldwide, arbitral awards and acts from various international dispute resolution institutions, announcements about forthcoming conferences, publications, and reviews. Accompanying each article and case, which is published in its original language, is a headnote in English, French, and German. Available to online subscribers from Kluwer Law International and Academic Search Premier.

Selected Periodicals and Newsletters *(continued)*

Periodical	*ISSN*	*Annotation*	*LegalTrac*	*Index to Legal Periodicals & Books*	*LexisNexis*	*Westlaw*	*Hein Online*
Asian International Arbitration Journal	1574-3330	Published in collaboration with the Singapore International Arbitration Centre, this journal publishes practical articles about international commercial arbitration in the Asia-Pacific region. Available to online subscribers from Kluwer Law International.					
Global Arbitration Review	1749-611X	Features law firm news and items about international arbitrators, brief case reports, and developments in arbitration from various jurisdictions.					
ICC International Court of Arbitration Bulletin	1017-284X	1990- : A semiannual periodical that often publishes extracts from recent International Chamber of Commerce arbitral awards and articles about the work of the International Court of Arbitration and other current information about international commercial arbitration. For descriptive information and tables of contents for all volumes and issues, see:					

		URL: *http://www.iccbooks.com/ Product/ProductInfo. aspx?id=446&cid=117*			
ICSID Review: Foreign Investment Law Journal	0258-3690	1986- : Published twice a year by the International Centre for Settlement of Investment Disputes, this journal includes articles relating to the law and practice of foreign investments, including the resolution of investment disputes.	Indexing begins Spring 1991 with vol. 6, issue 1, and ceases in 1994 with vol. 9, issue 1.	Indexing begins with Spring 1997, vol. 12, and ceases with Fall 2001, vol. 16, no. 2.	
International Arbitration Law Review	1367-8272	1997- : Extensive coverage of the field of international arbitration is provided by Sweet & Maxwell's journal, which is published seven times per year. This law review includes news, case summaries, legislative developments, analysis, and commentary about arbitration issues in all major jurisdictions.			*INTALR* From 1998 with vol. 1
Journal of International Arbitration	0255-8106	1984- : A quarterly journal featuring articles, discussion of arbitral awards, court decisions, international conventions, arbitration rules, profiles of arbitrators, and reports on the activities of arbitration associations.	Indexing begins in 1989 with vol. 6, issue 1.	Indexing begins in 1985 with vol. 2.	

Selected Periodicals and Newsletters *(continued)*

Periodical	*ISSN*	*Annotation*	*LegalTrac*	*Index to Legal Periodicals & Books*	*LexisNexis*	*Westlaw*	*Hein Online*
		Available to online subscribers from Kluwer Law International, Business Source Complete and SPORTDISCUS.					
Mealey's International Arbitration Quarterly Law Review	1530-7484	2000- : A quarterly that publishes articles that first appeared as commentary in *Mealey's International Arbitration Report*, "a monthly monitor of commercial dispute resolution and related litigation in courts worldwide."					
Mealey's International Arbitration Report	1089-2397	1986- : Monthly report, formerly known as *International Arbitration Report*, offers selected cases, awards and other documents, news items, commentary, and articles.					
Model Law Materials	1358-6904	2005- : Known as *Model Arbitration Law Quarterly Reports* from 1995 to 2004, this title offers statutes, case reports, articles, book reviews, and other materials on the					

		UNCITRAL Model Law on International Commercial Arbitration. English-language translations appear alongside documents in their original languages.	
Transnational Dispute Management		Published every two months, *TDM* is an Internet newsletter available to subscribers. It is "a combination of newsletter, review-journal, Internet service and primary materials database which goes across disciplines — law, psychology-psychoanalysis, international business management, economics, arbitration, WTO, international investment law, and across various areas of 'dispute management.' "	
World Arbitration & Mediation Report	0960-0949	1990- : Formerly called *Alternative Dispute Resolution Report*, this monthly newsletter, now published by Juris Publications, Inc., has expanded its international coverage. Available to online subscribers from Juris Publishing, Inc.	*WAMREP* Full coverage from vol. 6, no. 4 (1995)

Selected Periodicals and Newsletters *(continued)*

Business/Corporate/Employment

Periodical	*ISSN*	*Annotation*	*LegalTrac*	*Index to Legal Periodicals & Books*	*LexisNexis*	*Westlaw*	*Hein Online*
ACCA Docket: The Journal of the Association of Corporate Counsel Association	1546-4776	2003- : From the 1980s to 2003, this journal was known as *ACCA Docket: The Journal of the American Corporate Counsel Association.* This publication often includes articles about dispute resolution.				*ACCADKT* Selected coverage from vol. 6, no. 1, 1988; full coverage from 1992, vol. 10, no. 3	
Alternatives to the High Cost of Litigation	0736-3613	1983- : A monthly newsletter from CPR International Institute for Conflict Prevention and Resolution that includes articles and reports on news and events concerning dispute resolution. Available online from Wiley and Business Source Complete.			*ALTERN* From January 1993	*ALTHCL* Selected coverage from vol. 2, 1984; full coverage begins with vol. 9, 1991	

Securities Arbitration Commentator	1041-3057	A newsletter reporting the latest news in securities and commodities arbitration. It features information about legislative and regulatory developments, case law, arbitration awards, and award surveys. A free weekly e-mail service called *Arbitration Alert Service* is also available to subscribers. URL: *http://www.sacarbitration.com/framecomm.htm*				
Family						
Family Court Review: An Interdisciplinary Journal	1531-2445	2001- : *Family Court Review*, known as *Family and Conciliation Courts Review* from 1989 to 2000, is published by "AFCC, an association of family, court and community professionals," established in 1963, in conjunction with the Center for Children, Families and the Law, Hofstra University School of Law. Family court dispute resolution is the focus of the published articles.	Indexing begins in 2001 with vol. 39.		*FCCR* From vol. 37, no. 2, 1999	*FAMLR* From vol. 36, no. 2, 1998

Selected Periodicals and Newsletters *(continued)*

Periodical	*ISSN*	*Annotation*	*LegalTrac*	*Index to Legal Periodicals & Books*	*LexisNexis*	*Westlaw*	*Hein Online*
Journal of Divorce and Remarriage	1050-2556	1977- : Publishes research and clinical studies in family theory, family law, family mediation, and family therapy. The purpose of the journal is to further interdisciplinary understanding of the divorce process and theory to improve therapeutic, legal, and community services for those who are divorcing and their families. For information, see: URL: *http://www.haworthpressinc.-com/store/product.asp?sku=J087*		Indexed from 1990		*JDIVREMAR* Coverage begins 1997 See inside front cover of a recent issue for extensive list of indexing and abstracting services covering this title (e.g., PsycINFO: Indexing from 1990, vol. 14, issue 1).	
Mediation Quarterly	0739-4098	1983-2001: Published by the former Academy of Family				*PsycINFO* Indexed	

		Mediators, the journal aimed at advancing professional understanding of mediation from an interpersonal perspective by publishing articles about mediation theory, research, and practice. Volume 1-vol. 18, no. 4, Summer 2001. Continued as *Conflict Resolution Quarterly*. For information, see *Conflict Resolution Quarterly* below.		from 1983, vol. 1, issue 1 Sociological Abstracts: Indexed from 1983, vol. 1, issue 1 to 2000, vol. 18, issue 3

General

ACResolution	1537-6648	2001- : The quarterly magazine of the Association for Conflict Resolution. Its issues provide feature articles on a theme usually written by practitioners, offering practical advice. For a list of theme issues, see: URL: *www.acresolution.org/*		
Australasian Dispute Resolution Journal	1034-3059	1999- : A quarterly journal, formerly known as *Australian Dispute Resolution Journal* from 1990 to 1998, which was previously published in association with the Australian Dispute Resolution Association.	Indexing begins in 2000 with vol. 11.	

Selected Periodicals and Newsletters *(continued)*

Periodical	*ISSN*	*Annotation*	*LegalTrac*	*Index to Legal Periodicals & Books*	*LexisNexis*	*Westlaw*	*Hein Online*
Cardozo Journal of Conflict Resolution (COJCR)		1999- : Formerly known as *Cardozo Online Journal of Conflict Resolution*, this biannually published journal "aims to explore all aspects of this burgeoning field of law and its relationship to legal practice, scholarship and jurisprudence."			*COJCR* From vol. 1, 1999/ 2000	*CDZJCR* From vol. 1, 1999	
Conflict Resolution Quarterly	1536-5581	2001- : Sponsored by the Association for Conflict Resolution and formerly known as *Mediation Quarterly*. "The mission of *Conflict Resolution Quarterly* is to publish scholarship on relationships between theory, research, and practice in the conflict management and dispute resolution field to promote more effective professional applications." New features to be added to each colloquoy issue include "Book Reviews and Reader Responses" and "Research Matters." Available to online subscribers from Wiley, and the previous				*PsycINFO* Indexed from 2000, vol. 19, issue 1	

		title, *Mediation Quarterly*, is available from Business Source Complete.			
Dispute Resolution Journal	0003-7893	1993- : From the American Arbitration Association, a quarterly magazine formerly known as *Arbitration Journal*, from 1937 to 1993, which includes articles, a review of court decisions, and book reviews. Available to subscribers to Business Source Complete and SportDiscus select.	Indexing begins in 1994 with vol. 49, issue 2.	Indexing begins in 1995 with vol. 50.	*DRJ*. *Arbitration Journal*, vol. 48, nos. 1-3 (1993) *Dispute Resolution Journal*, vol. 48, no. 4
Dispute Resolution Magazine	1077-3582	1994- : This quarterly magazine by the American Bar Association Section of Dispute Resolution covers news and developments in dispute resolution.			*DISPRES* From vol. 3, no. 1 (1996)
Journal of American Arbitration	1050-4109	2001- : Now based at Dickinson School of Law, the journal is published twice per year and offers information and practical commentary on developments in domestic U.S. arbitration law.			*JAMARB* From vol. 1, no. 1
Journal of International Dispute Resolution: IDR		2004- : A quarterly periodical published in cooperation with Gesellschaft fur Wirtschaftsmediation und Konfliktmanagement. Each issue contains short articles, some in English and			

Selected Periodicals and Newsletters *(continued)*

Periodical	*ISSN*	*Annotation*	*LegalTrac*	*Index to Legal Periodicals & Books*	*LexisNexis*	*Westlaw*	*Hein Online*
		some in German, about dispute resolution developments and decisions.					
Journal of Dispute Resolution	1025-2566	1996- : Formerly called *Missouri Journal of Dispute Resolution*, from 1984 to 1987, the *Journal of Dispute Resolution* "is an inter-disciplinary, academic journal published on a bi-annual basis. The journal features writings of special relevance to lawyers, other practitioners of dispute resolution, and scholars from many disciplines who are concerned with how to prevent and resolve disputes through various methods, including mediation, negotiations, con-sensus building, arbitration and litigation."	Indexing begins with vol. 1984.	Indexing begins with vol. 1984.	*JDISPR* From vol. 1, 1995	*JDR* Selected coverage from vol. 1991; full coverage from vol. 1993, no. 2	1984-
Journal of Mediation, Negotiation and Ar-bitration		A forthcoming print and online periodical. See: URL: *http://www.jmna.org/*					
Mayhew-Hite Report on Dispute Resolu-tion and the Courts		A quarterly online newsletter produced by the students on the *Ohio State Journal on Dispute*					

		Resolution, who report on "ADR Developments across the nation."					
Mediation News & Updates		2005- : Mediator and arbitrator Keith L. Seat's free monthly mediation newsletter available to e-mail subscribers informs the reader of recent cases and resolutions, news, and initiatives with links to news sources. All issues of the newsletter are available at: URL: *http://keithseat.com/publications.htm*					
Ohio State Journal on Dispute Resolution	1046-4344	1985- : This official journal of the American Bar Association's Section of Dispute Resolution annually publishes three article issues and a bibliography issue. The mission of the journal is to "serve as an exchange of information between scholars, who develop and comment upon theoretical models of dispute resolution, and practitioners, who are involved in implementing models as actual arbitrators, mediators and judges."	Indexing begins with vol. 1, 1985.	Indexing begins with vol. 2, 1986.	*OHSJDR* Full text of articles from 1995, vol. 10, issue no. 2	*OHSJDR* Full text of selected articles from 1985, vols. 1-8; full text of all articles from 1993, vol. 9	1985-
Online Journal of Peace & Conflict Resolution	1522-211X	1998- : This free online journal hosted at the Tabula Rasa Institute web site is "intended as a resource for students, teachers					

Selected Periodicals and Newsletters *(continued)*

Periodical	*ISSN*	*Annotation*	*LegalTrac*	*Index to Legal Periodicals & Books*	*LexisNexis*	*Westlaw*	*Hein Online*
		and practitioners in fields relating to the reduction and elimination of conflict." Editorial board members and contributors from around the world have written the articles. For information and full text articles, see: URL: *http://www.trinstitute.org/ojper/*					
Pepperdine Dispute Resolution Journal	1536-3090	2000- : This dispute resolution law review with some theme issues now publishes three issues per year, dedicated to the scholarly review of issues in alternative dispute resolution.	Indexing begins in 2000 with vol. 1.		*PEPPDR* Coverage begins in 2000 with vol. 1.	*PEPDRLJ* Coverage begins in 2000 with vol. 1.	
Rutgers Conflict Resolution Law Journal		2002- : The Rutgers State University School of Law–Newark publishes an interdisciplinary, online journal. RCRLJ was founded by students of the university's Conflict Management Certificate Program. "The RCRLJ is dedicated to the exploration of alternative dispute resolution, such as negotiations,					

		mediations, arbitration, consensus building and alternative forms of litigation such as mini-trials." URL: *http://pegasus.rutgers.edu/rcrlj/*

International

African Journal on Conflict Resolution	1562-6997	1999- : This is a journal with articles "focusing on conflict transformation in Africa" and published by the African Center for Constructive Resolution of Disputes (ACCORD), "a South-African based non-governmental conflicts management organization." Full text of articles available at: URL: *http://www.accord.org.za/ajcr/intro.htm*
Conflict Trends		1998- : A quarterly magazine from the African Center for Constructive Resolution of Disputes (ACCORD) that "focuses on reporting and analyzing trends in current and emerging conflicts on the continent of Africa." For online versions of articles, see: URL: *http://www.accord.org.za/web.nsf*

Selected Periodicals and Newsletters *(continued)*

Periodical	*ISSN*	*Annotation*	*LegalTrac*	*Index to Legal Periodicals & Books*	*LexisNexis*	*Westlaw*	*Hein Online*
International Journal of Conflict Management	1044-4068	1990- : A journal of the Center for Advanced Studies in Management that "publishes original empirical and conceptual articles, case studies simulations and book reviews on conflict." Available online for subscribers to services such as Academic Search Premier, Business Source Complete, and Sociological Collection.				*INTLJCONFLICT* From vol. 11, 2000	
Journal of Conflict and Security Law	1467-7954	2000- : Formerly known as *Journal of Armed Conflict Law*, this title provides peer-reviewed articles for academics, government officials, military lawyers, and lawyers working in all phases of armed conflict from the pre-conflict stage to post-conflict resolution phases.				*JCSECL* From vol. 7, no. 1, 2002	
Journal of Conflict Resolution	0022-0027	1957- : "The *Journal of Conflict Resolution* is an interdisciplinary journal of social scientific theory and research on human conflict. It focuses especially on		From 1970s Indexing begins in 1998 with vol. 32		*JCONFLRES* From April 1, 1997	

		international conflict, but its pages are open to a variety of contributions about intergroup conflict, within as well as between nations, that may help in understanding problems of war and peace. Reports about innovative applications, as well as about basic research, are welcomed, especially when the results are of interest to scholars in several disciplines." This journal of the Peace Society (International) is published six times per year and continues *Conflict Resolution.* Available to online subscribers to JSTOR and Sage Publications.	
Journal of Peace Research	0022-3433	1964- : An interdisciplinary, international quarterly of scholarly work in peace research, published under the auspices of the International Peace Research Association, Oslo, Norway. Available to online subscribers from Sage Publications.	*JPEACER* From February 1989
Lebanese Review of Arab & International Arbitration		1996- : A quarterly periodical with contributions usually appearing in Arabic. Issues may include articles, arbitration awards and	

Selected Periodicals and Newsletters *(continued)*

Periodical	*ISSN*	*Annotation*	*LegalTrac*	*Index to Legal Periodicals & Books*	*LexisNexis*	*Westlaw*	*Hein Online*
		cases, relevant legislation and rules, and news about arbitration. For contents information, including a summary foreword in English from each issue, see: URL: *http://www.dm.net.lb/rla*					
Vindobona Journal of International Commercial Law and Arbitration	1439-9741	1997- : Published by the Moot Alumni Association in Vienna, Austria, this biannual law journal publishes articles from authors around the world about international commercial law and arbitration. *Vindobona* is included in the journal's name because it was the name of the settlement on the Danube River from which Vienna grew and where the Moot Association is based. Also, the name recognizes Vienna's prominence in events associated with developments in international law and the law of arbitration. For information, see: URL: *http://www.maa.net/vindobonajournal/about.htm*				VJ Begins 1999	

Willamette Journal of International Law & Dispute Resolution	1521-0235	1993- : Formerly known as *Willamette Bulletin of International Law & Policy* for volumes 1-4, this journal publishes articles covering international law and international dispute resolution.	Indexing begins in 1998 with vol. 6, issue 1, to vol. 9, issue 1, 2000	*WJILDR* Indexing begins in 1997 with vol. 5	*WMTJILDR* Indexing begins in 1997 with vol. 5	1997-
World Trade & Arbitration Materials	1022-6538	1994- : This quarterly journal resulted from the merger of the journals *World Trade Materials* and *Arbitration Materials*. It focuses on arbitration in international business disputes and includes lists and information about arbitrators, arbitration organizations, arbitral awards, international conventions, court decisions, statutes, and arbitration rules. Available to online subscribers from Kluwer Law International.				

Negotiation

Group Decision and Negotiation	0926-2644	1992- : A bimonthly journal published by Kluwer Academic Publishers in cooperation with the Institute for Operations Research and the Management				

Selected Periodicals and Newsletters *(continued)*

Periodical	*ISSN*	*Annotation*	*LegalTrac*	*Index to Legal Periodicals & Books*	*LexisNexis*	*Westlaw*	*Hein Online*
		Sciences and its section on group decision and negotiation. This journal presents theoretical and empirical research, practical applications, and case studies about group decision and negotiation processes. It includes articles about applied game theory and areas of application such as labor-management negotiations, inter-organizational negotiations, environmental negotiations, and development of software for group decision and negotiation. Available to online subscribers from Kluwer Academic.					
Harvard Negotiation Law Review		1996- : A quarterly "multidisciplinary journal on dispute resolution" that covers "legal negotiation" (i.e., negotiation with lawyers in the middle and legal institutions in the background). The law review publishes interdisciplinary legal	Indexing begins in March 2004.		*HRVNLR* Indexing begins in 1997 with vol. 2.	*HVNLR* Indexing begins in 1996 with vol. 1.	1996-

		perspectives on topics such as multi-party bargaining, litigation settlement, mediation, the legislative process, and negotiated rule-making.
International Negotiation: A Journal of Theory & Practice	1382-340X	1996- : A journal focusing on interdisciplinary theories and models of the negotiation process and mediation and how these processes can result in meaningful outcomes. Contributors include scholars from fields such as political science, history, law, sociology, psychology, anthropology, economics, public policy, mathematics, business administration, negotiation, and mediation. Each issue has a theme and presents articles ranging from original research papers, traditional historical and case studies, to conceptual articles that contribute to the field and that identify future directions for study. For information including tables of contents and abstracts of articles, see: URL: *http://interneg.org/in.* Available online from Ingenta/Brill Academic Press.

Selected Periodicals and Newsletters *(continued)*

Periodical	*ISSN*	*Annotation*	*LegalTrac*	*Index to Legal Periodicals & Books*	*LexisNexis*	*Westlaw*	*Hein Online*
Journal of Collective Negotiations	0047-2301	1972- : Formerly known as the *Journal of Collective Negotiations in the Public Sector,* this title "[s]erves as a forum for the interchange of ideas and information for those in the international community concerned with the negotiations process." Available online from Baywood Publishing Company and Business Source Complete.	Indexing begins in 1980 with vol. 9, no. 1 and ceases in Fall 2005			*JCNEGP-SECT* From January 1989	
Negotiation Journal	0748-4526	1985- : An international journal devoted to the publication of works that advance the theory, analysis, and practice of negotiation and dispute resolution that is published quarterly by the Harvard Program on Negotiation. Available online from Blackwell Publishing Inc.					
Negotiation Newsletter	0897-0718	1983- : Harvard Law School's Program on Negotiation publishes this monthly newsletter,					

which offers short, practical articles and reports on research in the field. For the topic index to newsletter articles, see:

URL: *www.pon.harvard.edu/publications/newsletter/topic_index.php*

Selected Dispute Resolution Organizations—Internet and E-Mail Resources

Many of the dispute resolution organizations below offer bibliographies and searchable databases of dispute resolution materials.

If you need to find Web pages that are no longer available, a site called the Internet Archive Wayback Machine allows you to search by URL for archived copies of Web pages collected since 1996. Go to *http://www.archive.org/web/web.php* and simply type in the URL, and click on the "Take Me Back" button. Please note that you are unlikely to find pages from subscription web sites, and the number of archived copies of a site will vary from a few to many for each year.

American Arbitration Association

URL: *http://www.adr.org/*

Includes an overview of the association and offers a wide range of dispute resolution information, including AAA rules and procedures, forms, guides, fact sheets, and other educational and training information. A variety of materials appear under the heading for each subject or "focus area." News stories from ADRWorld.com are provided.

Westlaw: AAA-PUBS—American Arbitration Association Publications

American Bar Association Section of Dispute Resolution

URL: *http://www.abanet.org/dispute/home.html*

This Web page highlights information about the section and its activities in promoting dispute resolution, including its publications.

Westlaw: AMBAR-TP—American Bar Association Journals

Association for Conflict Resolution

URL: *http://www.acrnet.org/*

ACR was formed in 2001 as the result of the merging of the former Academy of Family Mediators, CREnet (Conflict Resolution Education Network), and SPIDR (Society for Professionals in Dispute Resolution). ACR's mission is "promoting peaceful, effective conflict resolution." Information about the various sections of the organization appears at the site and may include copies of newsletters, articles, and bibliographies. The sections include Commercial, Community, Consumer, Court, Criminal Justice, Crisis Intervention, Education, Environmental/Public Policy, Family, Health Care, International, Ombuds/Ombudsman, Online Dispute Resolution, Organizational Conflict Management, Research Section, Restorative & Criminal Justice, Spirituality, Training, and Workplace.

Association of Family and Conciliation Courts

URL: *http://www.afccnet.org*

AFCC is an international and interdisciplinary association dedicated to the constructive resolution of family disputes. The site provides information and links for family mediators.

Center for Analysis of Alternative Dispute Resolution Systems (CAADRS)

URL: *http://www.caadrs.org/*

Established in 1995, CAADRS provides information, research, and analysis of court-related alternative dispute resolution in Illinois. The site offers an annotated, searchable database of books, articles, studies, and other programs about court-related dispute resolution and annotated lists of links to web sites of organizations, bar associations, listservs, e-mail notification services, court sites, online publications, bibliographies, and other sites providing information about dispute resolution.

CPR Institute for International Conflict Prevention & Resolution

URL: *http://www.cpadr.org*

"CPR Institute is a membership-based non-profit organization that promotes excellence and innovation in public and private dispute resolution, serving as a primary multinational resource for avoidance, management, and resolution of business-related disputes." The web site includes suggested ADR clauses, rules, codes, and procedures for business agreements, information about finding a mediator or arbitrator, and a listing of CPR publications such as *CPR Practice Guides* and *Model ADR Procedures.*

LexisNexis: Model ADR Practices and Procedures

This source includes over twenty-five publications from CPR.

Westlaw: CPR-ALL—CPR Institute for Dispute Resolution—All

CPR-MAPP—CPR Model ADR Procedures and Practice Series

CPR-MODC—CPR Institute for Public Resolution—Model Clauses

CPR-RULES—CPR Institute for Dispute Resolution—Rules

CRInfo: A Comprehensive Gateway to Conflict Resolution Resources

URL: *http://www.crinfo.org*

A project co-directed by Guy and Heidi Burgess, CRInfo is an extensive searchable database of over 25,000 links to dispute resolution information sources from a range of disciplines. This resource includes the Beyond Intractability Project, browsable summaries of over 300 books and articles, browsable lists of materials by conflict type and ADR process, and links to recent news items about conflict from Google News. Other features include conflict resolution educational, training, and networking resources.

Federal Mediation & Conciliation Service (FMCS)

URL: *http://www.fmcs.gov/*

FMCS was established by the U.S. Congress in 1947 "as an independent agency to promote sound and stable labor-management relations." The web site outlines the services it offers in the form of dispute resolution and conflict management, relationship development and training, arbitration services, online mediation, administering a labor-management grants program, and International Dispute Resolution Services.

Harvard Law School Program on Negotiation

URL: *http://www.pon.harvard.edu/main/home/*

Provides information about the Program on Negotiation, "a consortium of faculty, students and staff at Harvard University, Massachusetts Institute and Tufts University," and its clearinghouse for books and teaching materials, training and other educational opportunities, research fellowships, and affiliated research projects.

INCORE: An International Center of Excellence for the Study of Peace and Conflict

URL: *www.incore.ulst.ac.uk/*

Established in 1993, INCORE is a joint project of the United Nations and the University of Ulster. This site provides information about research projects and publishes occasional papers, conference papers, research updates, and research reports. Reviews of the relevant literature appear in the searchable database, *Ethnic Conflict Research Digest* (ECDR), and *Conflict Data Services* (CDS) offers a database of conflicts from around the globe. Includes a link to *Conflict Archive on the Internet* (CAIN), which covers information about the conflict in Northern Ireland from 1969 to the present.

Institute for Conflict Analysis & Resolution (ICAR)

URL: *http://www.gmu.edu/departments/ICAR/ICAR_About.html*

Based at George Mason University, ICAR's major research interests are the connection between globalization and conflict, religion and conflict, dynamics of change in conflict, identity issues in conflict, and reflective practice.

Institute on Conflict Resolution (ICR)

URL: *http://www.ilr.cornell.edu/depts/ICR*

Based at Cornell University's School of Industrial and Labor Relations, ICR is a research organization that offers conflict resolution services and focuses on conflict in the workplace.

Indiana Conflict Resolution Institute

URL: *http://www.spea.indianu.edu/icri/*

Based in the Indiana School of Public and Environmental Affairs (SPEA), the Indiana Conflict Resolution Institute (ICRI) was established in 1997 and "is dedicated to the understanding and expansion of conflict and dispute resolution in public and private arenas." The web site offers a bibliography database with entries reflecting empirical field studies and program evaluation on conflict resolution. Many of the entries include annotations, which are searchable. A list of Indiana ADR providers is also offered.

International Academy of Mediators

URL: *www.iamed.org*

This membership site includes a number of full-text articles on various topics of dispute resolution.

International Association of Facilitators (IAF)

URL: *http://www.iaf-world.org*

"The IAF promotes, supports and advances the art and practice of professional facilitation through methods exchange, professional growth, practical research, collegial networking and support services." The site includes information about the association's publication, *Group Facilitation: A Research and Applications Journal*, and an extensive list of links of interest to facilitators.

JAMS

URL: *http://www.jams.adr.com/*

A web site from a provider of mediation and arbitration services, which offers an archive of the *JAMS Dispute Resolution Alert Newsletter*, and a searchable database of articles by JAMS arbitrators and mediators.

Mediate.com (MIRC)

URL: *http://www.mediate.com*

MIRC provides a wide range of resources of interest to mediators, including the e-mail newsletters *The Mediate.com Newsletter* and *Keith Seat's Mediation News*. The site features a large, searchable database of short, full-text articles on conflict and the practice of mediation and negotiation. Other popular offerings are the listings of mediators, information about mediation training programs, and marketing services for mediators.

National Arbitration Forum

URL: *www.adrforum.com*

A provider of dispute resolution services provides this site, which offers a free weekly e-mail newsletter called *ADR Law & Policy Update*; the quarterly *ADR Reporter*

Newsletter, *Domain News*, covering domain name dispute decisions; and white papers on various topics.

National Association for Community Mediation (NAFCM)

URL: *http://www.nafcm.org/*

NAFCM "supports the maintenance and growth of community-based mediation programs and processes." The site provides basic information and resources about community mediation, links to other mediation organizations, and features such as a directory of community mediation centers and access to some issues of NAFCM's newsletter, *The Community Mediator*.

Ohio State Journal on Dispute Resolution

URL: *http://mortizlaw.osu.edu/jdr/index.html*

This site contains a list of the tables of contents for all issues of the *Ohio State Journal on Dispute Resolution*, which is the official law journal of the ABA Section of Dispute Resolution. This site also offers the *Mayhew-Hite Report on Dispute Resolution and the Courts*, a quarterly e-mail newsletter that highlights developments in dispute resolution from around the country.

Ombudsman Association

URL: *http://www.ombudsassociation.org/*

Established in July 2005, after the merger of the University and College Ombudsman Association (UCOA) and the Ombudsman Association. This international association's web site includes ombudsman standards of practice.

Permanent Court of Arbitration

URL: *http://www.pca-cpa.org/*

The Permanent Court of Arbitration, located in The Hague, is an independent international organization established in 1899 for the settlement of disputes between states (or organizations of states) and disputes between states and private parties. Services provided include mediation, commissions of inquiry (fact finding), conciliation, and arbitration. This site includes a helpful guide, "Directory of Arbitration Websites and Information on Arbitration Available Online" by Rosabel E. Goodman-Everard.

Policy Consensus Initiative (PCI) and National Policy Consensus Center (NPCC)

URL: *http://www.policyconsensus.org/*

The Policy Consensus Initiative and National Policy Consensus Center "play a catalytic role in helping state leaders develop a collaborative system of governance." PCI offers services including consultation and technical assistance; information resources, such as the database of public policy case studies and the directory of state programs, collaborative problem-solving and dispute resolution services; workshops and training; and materials on consensus building and conflict resolution.

The monthly e-mail newsletter, *EPolicy News*, "features information and updates on state dispute resolution programs and initiatives."

RAND

URL: *http://www.rand.org/icj/*

This site provides key information about the RAND Institute for Civil Justice (ICJ), which "is committed to a program of research that will provide accurate information about the use of ADR," including its activities, research agenda, and publications.

United States Department of Justice Office of Dispute Resolution

URL: *http://www.usdoj.gov/odr/documents.htm*

This site offers links to Department of Justice documents relating to dispute resolution, ADR-related presidential documents, Federal Judicial Center Publications and the home page of the federal government's Interagency Alternative Dispute Resolution Working Group.

Other Selected Internet Resources

ADRWorld.com

URL: *http://www.ADRWorld.com/*

Established in 1999, this subscription web site offers news about arbitration, mediation, and other forms of alternative dispute resolution. Since early 2000, ADRWorld.com has been a subsidiary of the American Arbitration Association. E-mail updates highlighting news about cases and state and federal legislative and regulatory developments on the site are available free to subscribers and non-subscribers. The searchable ADR library provides searching of federal statutes, state statutes, state regulatory updates, court rules, private-sector and international ADR rules, policy documents and reports, an archive of news articles, recent court decisions, state legislation, and Federal Register documents.

CataLaw

URL: *http://www.catalaw.com/topics/ADR.shtml*

This site provides access to worldwide Internet resources about dispute resolution categorized by jurisdiction.

FindLaw

URL: *http://findlaw.com*

Provides access to sites generally covering dispute resolution as well as sites focused on specific aspects of dispute resolution, such as educational programs, providers of conflict resolution services, and dispute resolution in the international arena. Look under the practice area "Dispute Resolution and Arbitration."

Guide to ADR Links, Arranged by Deborah S. Laufer, Esq., Executive Director, Federal ADR Network

URL: *http://www.adr.af.mil/general/RecommendedADRLinks.doc* (last updated January 2002)

An extensive list of links arranged under the following headings: Bibliographies and Search Tools, Codes, Model Rules and Guidelines, Federal Agencies, Federal Documentation, International Resources, Job Listings and Openings, Journals, Newsletters, Publishers, Listservs, National Organizations, Online Dispute Resolution (ODR), Online Documents, Professional Resources and References and Consulting Organizations, Rosters of Neutrals, State Resources, and University Programs — University Courses of Study on ADR and ADR Institutes and Programs Located at Universities.

lexisONE

URL: *http://www.lexisone.com*

Describing itself as "The Resource for Small Law Firms," lexisONE provides low-cost searching options to a variety of *LexisNexis* sources and links to free law and law-related information on the Internet. "ADR, Arbitration & Mediation," listed as one of the practice areas, provides links to the web sites of dispute resolution organizations and service providers, online articles on various dispute resolution topics, and free sources of codes and statutes relating to dispute resolution.

WEX — Cornell Law School

URL: *http://www.law.cornell.edu/wex/index.php/ADR*

Cornell's well-known site provides links to relevant federal legislation appearing in Title 9 of the *United States Code,* recent decisions on arbitration by the U.S. Supreme Court and the U.S. Circuit Courts of Appeals, state statutes covering dispute resolution, the Uniform Arbitration Act, state appellate judicial decisions, conventions and treaties, and other well-known web sites.

World Legal Information Institute (WorldLII) — Free Global Law

URL: *http://www.worldlii.org/*

"A free, independent and non-profit global legal research facility" formed by Australasian Legal Information Institute (AustLII), British and Irish Legal Information Institute (BAILII), Canadian Legal Information Institute (CanLII), Hong Kong Legal Information Institute (HKLII), Legal Information Institute (LII-Cornell), Pacific Islands Legal Information Institute (PacLII), and Wits University School of Law. From the main page, click on "Subjects" under the heading "Catalogs" to see a page that gives links to arbitration, mediation, conciliation, and other forms of alternative dispute resolution sources from around the globe. The links are arranged by the following designations: country, commentary, law journals, legislation, and other indexes. Links to the full text of treaties and international agreements are provided as well as a list of domain names for dispute resolution bodies.

WWW Virtual Library: Arbitration Database

URL: *http://www.interarb.com/ul/*

In addition to its free electronic newsletter, *European Arbitration*, and journal, *Model Arbitration Law Quarterly Reports*, interarb, an information provider in the fields of arbitration and dispute resolution, provides a database of full-text materials and links to web sites covering arbitration and dispute resolution.

Zimmerman's Research Guide

URL: *http://www.lexisnexis.com/infopro/zimmerman/*

"Arbitration, Mediation and Alternative Dispute Resolution" is one of the many topics mentioned. This concise guide provides links to relevant information services and information such as various arbitration and mediation rules and sources for treaties and conventions relating to international arbitration.

LISTSERVS AND ADR BLOG FINDER

Listservs, or e-mail discussion groups, allow subscribers to communicate ideas and to seek feedback and post announcements about position vacancies, publications, and professional meetings to interested persons via e-mail.

ADR List

URL: *http://www.abanet.org/dispute/discuss.html*

The American Bar Association Section of Dispute Resolution sponsors a discussion group open to the public to promote wider understanding of dispute resolution. The list provides information sharing, updates on events, and discussions on issues related to dispute resolution. Subscribers may elect to receive postings in a digest format.

DISPUTE-RES Listserv

A listserv for persons who teach or who are interested in dispute resolution. Subscribe to *DISPUTE-RES@listerv.law.cornell.edu* by writing in the text of your message:

subscribe dispute-res [Your Name].

Legal Scholarship Network (LSN)

URL: *http://www.ssrn.com/lsn/index.html*

Many law schools subscribe to the Social Science Research Network, primarily to offer access to its Legal Scholarship Network. "The goal of LSN is to facilitate the distribution of scholarly information related to law to legal, economics, and business scholars and practitioners throughout the world." Subscribers can elect to receive electronic journals in the form of e-mail messages covering various legal topics such as "Negotiation and Dispute Resolution," which provides abstracts of articles accepted for publication, and working papers and weekly professional announcements publicizing conferences, calls for papers, special issues of journals, and professional job listings. Law school working papers can be downloaded from the LSN web site.

Negotiations Research Network (NEG)

URL: *http://www.ssrn.com/update/neg/index.html*

A network from Social Science Research Network (SSRN) launched in Spring 2002 providing access to working papers, conference materials, and professional announcements for scholars in the dispute resolution area. NEG offers the following twelve abstracting journals: *Conflict & Dispute Resolution; Culture, Conflict & Negotiation; Decision Making & Negotiation; Justice & Negotiations; Multiple Party, Conflict, Decision and Negotiation; Negotiation Applications; Negotiation Processes & Communications; Third-Party Intervention;* and *Two-Party Negotiations.*

Willamette University Center for Dispute Resolution

URL: *http://www.willamette.edu/wucl/wlo/dis-res/index.htm*

DIS-RES (Recent Developments in Dispute Resolution)

Offers a free e-mail distribution list for biweekly updates on court decisions (predominantly those from the Pacific Northwest region), legislation, regulations, and articles and books covering alternative dispute resolution. The site also offers a searchable archive of newsletters from the service's inception in June 1997.

World Directory of Alternative Dispute Resolution Blogs

URL: *http://www.adrblogs.com/index.html*

Diane Levin, a mediator, trainer, consultant, attorney, and blogger from the Greater Boston area, presents an alphabetical list of ADR blogs, a list by country, and a list by category. Categories include ADR, ADR-Friendly, ADR Marketing, Arbitration, Conflict Resolution, Innovations in the Practice of Law, Ombuds and Peacemaking, Mediation, Negotiation, Online Dispute Resolution, Restorative Justice, Video Blogs, and Podcasts.

Table of Cases*

*Principal cases are in italics.

Collected References*

AARON, Benjamin, Beatrice BURGOON, Donald CULLEN, Dana EISCHEN, Mark KAHN, Charles REHMUS, and Jacob SEIDENBERG, eds. (1977) *The Railway Labor Act at Fifty.* Washington, D.C.: National Mediation Board.

AARON, Marjorie Corman (1995) "The Value of Decision Analysis in Mediation Practice," 11 *Neg. J.* 123.

AARON, Marjorie Corman, and David P. HOFFER (1997) "Decision Analysis as a Method of Evaluating the Trial Alternative," in Dwight Golann, *Mediating Legal Disputes: Effective Strategies for Lawyers and Mediators.* New York: Aspen Publishers.

ABA DISPUTE RESOLUTION MAGAZINE (1998) Symposium: Focus on International ADR (Spring).

ABA SECTION OF DISPUTE RESOLUTION (2002) *Report on Mediator Credentialing and Quality Assurance: Discussion Draft.* Available at www.abanet.org/dispute/home.html.

ABEL, Richard (1985) "Informalism: A Tactical Equivalent to Law," 19 *Clearinghouse Rev.* 375.

ACR TASK FORCE ON MEDIATOR CERTIFICATION (2004) *Report to ACR Board of Directors.* Available at www.ACRnet.org.

ADLER, Robert S., and Elliot M. SILVERSTEIN (2000) "When David Meets Goliath: Dealing with Power Differentials in Negotiations," 5 *Harv. Neg. L. Rev.* 1.

AIKEN, Jane (1992) "Settlement of AIDS Cases" (Unpublished manuscript available at Arizona State University College of Law).

ALFINI, James J. (1999) "Settlement Ethics and Lawyering in ADR Proceedings: A Proposal to Revise Rule 4.1," 19 *N. Ill. U. L. Rev.* 225.

——— (1989) "Summary Jury Trials in State and Federal Courts: A Comparative Analysis of the Perceptions of Participating Lawyers," 4 *Ohio St. J. Disp. Resol.* 213.

ALFINI, James J., and Eric R. GALTON, eds. (1998) *ADR Personalities and Practice Tips.* Washington, D.C.: ABA Section of Dispute Resolution.

ALFINI, James J., Sharon B. PRESS, Jean R. STERNLIGHT, and Joseph B. STULBERG (2001) *Mediation Theory and Practice.* New York: Lexis Publishing Co.

ALLEYNE, Reginald (1996) "Statutory Discrimination Claims: Rights 'Waived' and Lost in the Arbitration Forum," 13 *Hofstra Lab. L.J.* 381.

AMERICAN BAR ASSOCIATION (2001) "Symposium on State ADR," *Disp. Resol. Mag.* (Summer).

——— (1990) *Family Dispute Resolution: Options for All Ages.* Washington, D.C.: ABA.

——— (1988) *Education and Mediation: Explaining the Alternatives.* Washington, D.C.: ABA.

——— (1983) *Model Rules of Professional Conduct.* Washington, D.C.: ABA.

AMERICAN BAR ASSOCIATION SECTION OF DISPUTE RESOLUTION (2000) *ABA Directory of Law School Alternative Dispute Resolution Courses and Programs.* Washington, D.C.: ABA.

——— (1982) *Family Dispute Resolution: Options for All Ages.* Washington, D.C.: ABA.

*This alphabetical compilation includes all books and articles from which excerpts have been taken, as well as all works cited in the references that appear at the end of chapters.

ANSTAETT, Elizabeth (1991) "Is Settlement Conditioned on Vacatur an Option: Should It Be?," 1991 *J. Disp. Resol.* 87.

ASSEY, James M., Jr. (1996) "Mum's the Word on Mediation: Confidentiality and *Snyder Falkinham v. Stockburger*," 9 *Geo. J. Legal Ethics* 991.

AXELROD, Robert (1984) *The Evolution of Cooperation.* New York: Basic Books.

AUERBACH, Jerold S. (1983) *Justice Without Law?* New York: Oxford University Press.

AVRUCH, Kevin (1998) *Culture and Conflict Resolution.* Washington, D.C.: United States Institute of Peace Press.

BABCOCK, Linda, and Sara LASCHEVER (2003) *Women Don't Ask: Negotiation and the Gender Divide.* Princeton, N.J.: Princeton University Press.

BACOW, Lawrence S., and Michael WHEELER (1984) *Environmental Dispute Resolution.* New York: Plenum.

BARKAI, John, and Gene KASSEBAUM (1989) "Using Court-Annexed Arbitration to Reduce Litigant Costs and to Increase the Pace of Litigation," 16 *Pepperdine L. Rev.* 543.

BASTRESS, Robert F., and Joseph D. HARBAUGH (1990) *Interviewing, Counselling, and Negotiating.* Boston: Little, Brown.

BEER, Jennifer (1986) *Peacemaking in Your Neighborhood.* Philadelphia: New Society Publishers.

BEER, Jennifer, Eileen STIEF, and Charles WALKER (1982) *Peacemaking in Your Neighborhood.* Concordville, PA: Friends Suburban Project.

BERCOVITCH, Jacob, and Jeffrey Z. RUBIN (1992) *Mediation in International Relations.* New York: St. Martin's.

BERNARD, Phyllis E. (2001) "Only Nixon Could Go to China: Third Thoughts on the Uniform Mediation Act," 85 *Marq. L. Rev.* 113.

BERNSTEIN, Lisa (1993) "Understanding the Limits of Court-Connected ADR: A Critique of Federal Court-Annexed ADR Programs," 141 *U. Pa. L. Rev.* 2169.

BICKERMAN, John (1998) "Practitioner's Notebook: Why ADR Providers May Want to Leave the Firm," *Disp. Resol. Mag.* 24 (Winter).

BICKNER, Mei L., Christine VER PLOEG, and Charles FEIGENBAUM (1997) "Developments in Employment Arbitration," 52 *Disp. Resol. J.* 8.

BILDER, Richard (1989) "International Third Party Dispute Settlement," 17 *Denv. J. Int'l L. & Pol'y* 471.

BINGHAM, Lisa B. (1998) "On Repeat Players, Adhesive Contracts, and the Use of Statistics in Judicial Review of Employment Arbitration," 29 *McGeorge L. Rev.* 223.

———(1997) "Employment Arbitration: The Repeat Player Effect," 1 *Employee Rts. & Employment Pol'y J.* 189.

BOK, Derek C. (1983) "A Flawed System of Law Practice and Training," 33 *J. Legal Educ.* 530.

BOLLER, Harvey R., and Donald J. PETERSON (1998) "Job Discrimination Claims Under Collective Bargaining," *Disp. Resol. J.* 38 (August).

BRAZIL, Wayne D. (1999) "Comparing Structures for the Delivery of ADR Services by Courts: Critical Values and Concerns," 14 *Ohio St. J. Disp. Resol.* 715.

———(1990) "A Close Look at Three Court-Sponsored ADR Programs: Why They Exist, How They Operate, What They Deliver, and Whether They Threaten Important Values," *U. Chi. Legal F.* 303.

———(1988) *Effective Approaches to Settlement: A Handbook for Lawyers and Judges.* Clifton, N.J.: Prentice-Hall Law & Business.

BREGER, Marshall (2000) "Should an Attorney Be Required to Advise a Client of ADR Options?," 13 *Geo. J. Legal Ethics* 427.
BRESLIN, J. William, and Jeffrey Z. RUBIN, eds. (1991) *Negotiation Theory and Practice.* Cambridge, Mass.: Program on Negotiation.
BRETT, Jeanne M. (2001) *Negotiating Globally: How to Negotiate Deals, Resolve Disputes, and Make Decisions Across Cultural Boundaries.* San Francisco: Jossey-Bass.
———(1991) "Negotiating Group Decisions," 7 *Neg. J.* 291.
BRETT, Jeanne M., et al. (1998) "Culture and Joint Gains in Negotiation," 14 *Neg. J.* 61.
BRETT, Jeanne M., Zoe I. BARSNESS, and Stephen B. GOLDBERG (1996) "The Effectiveness of Mediation: An Independent Analysis of Cases Handled by Four Major Service Providers," 12 *Neg. J.* 259.
BRETT, Jeanne M., Stephen B. GOLDBERG, and William L. URY (1994) "Managing Conflict: The Strategy of Dispute Systems Design," 6 *Bus. Wk. Executive Briefing Service.*
BRETT, Jeanne M., Deborah SHAPIRO, and Rita DRIEGHE (1985) "Mediator Behavior and the Outcome of Mediation," 41 *J. Social Issues* 101.
BRETT, Jeanne M., and Tetsushi OKUMURA (1998) "Inter- and Intra-Cultural Negotiation: U.S. and Japanese Negotiators," 41 *Acad. Mgmt. J.* 495 (October).
BROOME, Stephen A. (2006) "An Unconscionable Application of the Unconscionability Doctrine: How the California Judiciary Is Circumventing the Federal Arbitration Act," 3 *Hastings Bus. L.J.* 39.
BROWN, Frederick, and Catherine A. ROGERS (1997) "The Role of Arbitration in Resolving Transnational Disputes: A Survey of Trends in the People's Republic of China," 15 *Berkeley J. Int'l L.* 329.
BRUNET, Edward, and Charles B. CRAVER (2006) *Alternative Dispute Resolution: An Advocate's Perspective* (3d ed.). Newark, N.J.: LexisNexis.
BRUNET, Edward, Richard E. SPEIDEL, Jean R. STERNLICHT, and Stephen J. WARE (2006) *Arbitration Law in America: A Critical Assessment.* New York: Cambridge University Press.
BRYAN, Penelope E. (1994) "Reclaiming Professionalism: The Lawyer's Role in Divorce Mediation," 28 *Fam. L.Q.* 177.
———(1992) "Killing Us Softly: Divorce Mediation and the Politics of Power," 40 *Buff. L. Rev.* 441.
BÜHRING-UHLE, Christian (1996) *Arbitration and Mediation in International Business.* The Hague: Kluwer Law International. Boston: Kluwer Law International.
———(1991) "The IBM-Fujitsu Arbitration: A Landmark in Innovative Dispute Resolution," 2 *Am. Rev. Int'l Arb.* 113.
———(1990) *"Co-Med-Arb": A Comprehensive Model for Third Party Intervention with Divided Roles in Complex Disputes.* Cambridge, Mass.: Program on Negotiation at Harvard Law School, Working Paper Series.
BURTON, Lloyd, Larry FARMER, Elizabeth GEE, Lorie JOHNSON, and Gerald WILLIAMS (1991) "Feminist Theory, Professional Ethics, and Gender-Related Distinctions in Attorney Negotiating Styles," *J. Disp. Resol.* 199.
BUSH, Robert A. Baruch (1996a) "The Unexplored Possibilities of Community Mediation: A Comment on Merry and Milner, 21 *Law & Soc. Inquiry* 715.
———(1996b) "What Do We Need a Mediator For?: Mediation's 'Value-Added' for Negotiators," 12 *Ohio St. J. Disp. Resol.* 1.
———(1994) "Symposium: Dilemmas of Mediation Practice," *J. Disp. Resol.* 1.
———(1992) *The Dilemmas of Mediation Practice.* Washington, D.C.: National Institute for Dispute Resolution.
———(1989) "Efficiency and Protection, or Empowerment and Recognition? The Mediator's Role and Ethical Standards in Mediation," 41 *Fla. L. Rev.* 253.

BUSH, Robert A. Baruch, and Joseph P. FOLGER (2005) *The Promise of Mediation.* (2d ed.) San Francisco: Jossey-Bass.

CAPELLETTI, Mauro, ed. (1978) *Access to Justice.* 4 vols. Alphen aan den Rijn: Sijthoff and Nordhoff.
CARBONNEAU, Thomas E. (1997) *Cases and Materials on Commercial Arbitration.* New York: Juris Publishers.
———, ed. (1990) *Lex Mercatoria and Arbitration: A Discussion of the New Law Merchant.* New York: Transnational Juris Publications.
CARPENTER, Susan, and W.J.D. KENNEDY (1988) *Managing Public Disputes.* San Francisco: Jossey-Bass.
CARTER, James H. (1998) "NAFTA: How It Has Transformed Dispute Resolution in Canada, Mexico and the United States," *ABA Disp. Resol. Mag.* 19 (Spring).
CARTER, Jimmy (1982) *Keeping Faith: Memoirs of a President.* New York: Bantam Books.
CENTER FOR DISPUTE SETTLEMENT (1992) *National Standards for Court-Connected Mediation Programs.* Washington, D.C.: Center for Dispute Settlement.
———(1991) *Mediation for the Professional: Training Manual.* Washington, D.C.: Center for Dispute Settlement.
CENTER FOR PUBLIC RESOURCES (1989, update 1994) *ADR Cost-Savings Benefits.* New York: Center for Public Resources.
———(1992) "Motorola Tries Moving ADR to the Next Stage," *Alternatives* 29, 32 (March).
———(1991) "Special Issue: ADR in the Courts," 9 *Alternatives* (July).
———(1989) *Mainstreaming: Corporate Strategies for Systematic ADR Use* (CPR Practice Guide). New York: CPR.
CHANDLER, David (1990) "Violence, Fear, and Communication: The Variable Impact of Domestic Violence on Mediation," 7 *Mediation Q.* 331.
CHERNICK, Richard (1989) "The Rent-a-Judge Option," *Los Angeles Law.*, October, p. 18, November, p. 19.
CHERNICK, Richard, Helen J. BENDIX, and Robert C. BARRETT (1997) *Private Judging: Privatizing Civil Justice.* Washington, D.C.: National Legal Center for the Public Interest.
CHEW, Pat K., ed. (2001) *The Conflict and Culture Reader.* New York and London: New York University Press.
CLARKE, Stevens, Laura DONNELLY, and Sara GROVE (1989) *Court-Ordered Arbitration in North Carolina: An Evaluation of Its Effects.* Chapel Hill: University of North Carolina Institute of Government.
CLOKE, Kenneth (2000) *Mediating Dangerously.* San Francisco: Jossey-Bass.
———(1990) *Mediation: Revenge and the Magic of Forgiveness.* Santa Monica: Center for Dispute Resolution.
COBB, Sara, and Janet RIFKIN (1991) "Practice and Paradox: Deconstructing Neutrality in Mediation," 16 *Law & Soc. Inquiry* 35 (Winter).
COBEN, James R. (2006) "Dispute Resolution Institute Symposium: Intentional Conversations About the Globalization of ADR," 27 *Hamline J. Pub. L. & Pol'y* 217.
COBEN, James R., and Peter N. THOMPSON (2006) "Disputing Irony: A Systematic Look at Litigation About Mediation," 11 *Harv. Negot. L. Rev.* 43.
COCHRAN, Robert F., Jr. (1999) "ADR, The ABA and Client Control: A Proposal that the Model Rules Require Lawyers to Present ADR Options to Clients," 41 *S. Tex. L. Rev.* 183.
———(1993) "Must Lawyers Tell Clients About ADR?," *Arb. J.* 8 (June).

COGLIANESE, Cary (1997) "Assessing Consensus: The Promise and Performance of Negotiated Rulemaking," 46 *Duke L.J.* 1255.
COHEN, Amy J. (2006) "Debating the Globalization of U.S. Mediation: Politics, Power, and Practice in Nepal," 11 *Harv. Negot. L. Rev.* 295.
COHEN, Amy J., and Ellen E. DEASON (2006) "Comparative Considerations Toward the Global Transfer of Ideas About Dispute System Design," 12 *Disp. Resol. Mag.* 23.
COLE, Sarah R. (2006) "Unauthorized Practice of Law Charges: A Risk for Lawyers Representing Clients in Mediation and Arbitration in a Multijurisdictional Practice Environment," 13 *Disp. Resol. Mag.* 26.
———(2005) "Mediator Certification: Has the Time Come?," 11 *Disp. Resol. Mag.* 7
———(2004) "Updating Arbitrator Ethics," 10 *Disp. Resol. Mag.* 24 (Summer).
———(2001) "Uniform Arbitration: 'One Size Fits All' Does Not Fit," 16 *Ohio St. J. Disp. Resol.* 759.
———(2000) "Managerial Litigants? The Overlooked Problem of Party Autonomy in Dispute Resolution," 51 *Hastings L.J.* 1199.
———(1997) "A Funny Thing Happened on the Way to the (Alternative) Forum: Reexamining *Alexander v. Gardner-Denver* in the Wake of *Gilmer v. Interstate/Jonhson Lane Corp.*, 1997 *B.Y.U. L. Rev.* 591.
———(1996) "Incentives and Arbitration: The Case Against Enforcement of Executory Arbitration Agreements Between Employers and Employees, 64 *UMKC L. Rev.* 449.
COLE, Sarah R., Nancy H. ROGERS, and Craig A. McEWEN (2003 & 2006 Supp.) *Mediation: Law, Policy, Practice* (2d ed.). St. Paul: West.
COLLIER, John G., and Vaughan LOWE (1999) *The Settlement of Disputes in International Law: Institutions and Procedures.* Oxford: Oxford University Press.
COLOSI, Thomas (1984) Foreword, *SPIDR, Ethical Issues in Dispute Resolution,* 1983 Annual Proceedings.
COMMISSION ON THE FUTURE OF WORKER-MANAGEMENT RELATIONS (DUNLOP COMMISSION) (1994) *Report and Recommendations.* Washington, D.C.
CONDLIN, Robert J. (1992) "Bargaining in the Dark: The Normative Incoherence of Lawyer Dispute Bargaining Role," 51 *Md. L. Rev.* 1.
COOK, Royer, Janice ROEHL, and David SHEPPARD (1980) *Neighborhood Justice Centers Field Test.* Washington, D.C.: U.S. Department of Justice, National Institute of Justice.
COOLEY, John W. (1996) *Mediation Advocacy.* South Bend: National Institute of Trial Advocacy.
COOPER, Carrie Luria (2006) "Varied Negotiation Approaches," in Kristen Blankley ed. *Cross Cultural Negotiation for U.S. Negotiators* 11-19. Montgomery, Ala.: U.S. Air Force.
COSTANTINO, C., and C. MERCHANT (1996) *Designing Conflict Management Systems.* San Francisco: Jossey-Bass.
COT, Jean Pierre (1972) *International Conciliation.* London: Europa Publications.
COULSON, Robert (1996) *Family Mediation: Managing Conflict, Resolving Disputes.* San Francisco: Jossey-Bass.
———(1982) *Business Arbitration: What You Need to Know.* New York: American Arbitration Association.
CPR INSTITUTE FOR DISPUTE RESOLUTION (2001) *ADR Suitability Guide.* New York: CPR.
———(1994) "Dispute Resolution Clauses: A Guide for Drafters of Business Agreements," 12 *Alternatives* 66.
CPR LEGAL PROGRAM (1987) *ADR and the Courts: A Manual for Judges and Lawyers.* New York: Butterworth.
CRAVER, Charles (1990) "The Impact of Gender on Clinical Negotiating Achievement," 6 *Ohio St. J. Disp. Resol.* 1.

CROCKER, David A. (2002) "Punishment, Reconciliation, and Democratic Deliberation," 5 *Buff. Crim. L. Rev.* 509.

CRONMILLER, Cherish L. (2006) "Varied Negotiation Approaches," in Kristen Blankley, ed. *Cross Cultural Negotiation for U.S. Negotiators* 153-162. Montgomery, Ala.: U.S. Air Force.

CROUCH, Richard (1982) "The Dark Side of Mediation: Still Unexplored," in Alternative Means of Family Dispute Resolution. Washington, D.C.: ABA.

CROWFOOT, James E., and Julia M. WONDOLLECK (1991) *Environmental Disputes: Community Involvement in Conflict Resolution.* Washington, D.C.: Island Press.

DANIEL, Johnnie (1995) *Assessment of the Mediation Program of the U.S. District Court for the District of Columbia.* Washington, D.C.: Administrative Conference of the United States.

DANIELS, Stephen (1984) "Ladders and Bushes: The Problem of Caseloads and Studying Court Activities Over Time," *Am. B. Found. Res. J.* 751.

DANZIG, Richard (1973) "Towards the Creation of a Complementary, Decentralized System of Criminal Justice," 26 *Stan. L. Rev.* 1.

DAUER, Edward (2000) *Alternative Dispute Resolution and Practice.* Yonkers, N.Y.: Juris Publishing.

DAVIS, Albie (1986) "Dispute Resolution at an Early Age," 2 *Neg. J.* 287.

DEASON, Ellen E. (2002) "Predictable Mediation Confidentiality in the U.S. Federal System," 17 *Ohio St. J. Disp. Resol.* 239.

———(2001) "The Quest for Uniformity in Mediation Confidentiality, Foolish Consistency or Crucial Predictibility?" 85 *Marq L. Rev.* 79.

———(1992) "Confidentiality in Mediation: A Moral Reassessment," *J. Disp. Resol.* 25.

DEITERS, Cynthia A. (1988) Note, "A Setback for the Public Policy of Encouraging Settlements," *J. Disp. Resol.* 219.

DELGADO, Richard (1988) "ADR and the Dispossessed: Recent Books About the Deformalization Movement," 13 *Law & Soc. Inquiry* 145.

DEZALAY, Yves, and Bryant G. GARTH (1996) *Dealing in Virtue: International Commercial Arbitration and the Construction of a Transnational Legal Order.* Chicago: University of Chicago Press.

DINGWALL, Robert, and John EEKELAAR, eds. (1988) *Divorce Mediation and the Legal Process.* New York: Oxford University Press.

DOMINGUEZ, David (1994) "Beyond Zero-Sum Games: Multiculturalism as Enriched Law Training for All Students," 44 *J. Legal Educ.* 175.

DONALDSON, Thomas (1996) "Values in Tension: Ethics Away from Home," *Harv. Bus. Rev.* 48, 49 (Sept.-Oct.).

DONELAN, M.D., and F.S. NORTHEDGE (1971) *International Disputes: The Political Aspects.* New York: St. Martin's Press.

DONEY, Patricia M. (1998) "Understanding the Influence of National Culture on the Development of Trust," 23 *Acad. Mgmt. Rev.* 601.

DRAKE, William R. (1989) "Statewide Offices of Mediation," 5 *Neg. J.* 359.

DUNLOP, John T., and Arnold M. ZACK (1997) *Mediation and Arbitration of Employment Disputes.* San Francisco: Jossey-Bass.

EDWARDS, Harry T. (1986) "Alternative Dispute Resolution: Panacea or Anathema," 99 *Harv. L. Rev.* 668.

———(1985) "Hopes and Fears for Alternative Dispute Resolution," 21 *Willamette L. Rev.* 425.
EFFRON, Jack (1989) "Alternatives to Litigation: Factors in Choosing," 52 *Mod. L. Rev.* 480.
EISENBERG, Melvin (1976) "Private Ordering Through Negotiation: Dispute Settlement and Rulemaking," 89 *Harv. L. Rev.* 637.
EISENBERG, Theodore, and Elizabeth HILL (2003-2004) "Employment Arbitration and Litigation: An Empirical Comparison," 58 *Disp. Resol. J.* 44, 51 (Nov.-Jan.).
ELLIS, Desmond, and Noreen STUCKLESS (1996) *Mediating and Negotiating Marital Conflicts.* Thousand Oaks: Sage Publications.
EMERY, Robert (1994) *Renegotiating Family Relationships: Divorce, Child Custody, and Mediation.* New York: Guilford.
EMERY, Robert, and Joanne JACKSON (1989) "The Charlottesville Mediation Project: Mediated and Litigated Child Custody Disputes," 3 *Mediation Quarterly* (Summer).
ENGEL, David M. (1983) "Cases, Conflict and Accommodation: Patterns of Interaction in a Small Community," *Am. B. Found. Research J.* 803.
EQUAL EMPLOYMENT OPPORTUNITY COMMISSION (1997) "Policy Statement on Mandatory Binding Arbitration of Employment Discrimination Disputes as a Condition of Employment," 52 *Disp. Resol. J.* 11 (Fall).
ERBE, Nancy D. (2006) "Appreciating Mediation's Global Role in Promoting Good Governance," 11 *Harv. Negot. L. Rev.* 335.
ESSER, John P. (1989) "Evaluations of Dispute Processing: We Do Not Know What We Think and We Do Not Think What We Know," 66 *Denv. U. L. Rev.* 499.

FAURE, Guy Olivier, and Jeffrey Z. RUBIN (1993) "Lessons for Theory and Research," in *Culture and Negotiation* 209-231, in Guy Olivier Faure and Jeffrey Z. Rubin, eds. Newbury Park, Cal.: Sage Publications.
———(1993) *Culture and Negotiation.* Newbury Park, Cal.: Sage Publications.
FELSTINER, William F. (1974) "Influences of Social Organization on Dispute Processing," 9 *Law & Soc'y Rev.* 63.
FELSTINER, William F., Richard L. ABEL, and Austin SARAT (1980-1981) "The Emergence and Transformation of Disputes: Naming, Blaming, Claiming," 15 *Law & Soc'y Rev.* 631.
FINE, Erika S., ed. (1987) *ADR and the Courts: A Manual for Judges and Lawyers.* New York: Butterworth.
FISCH, Jill E. (1991) "Rewriting History: The Propriety of Eradicating Prior Decisional Law Through Settlement and Vacatur," 76 *Cornell L. Rev.* 589.
FISCHER, Karla, Neil VIDMAR, and Rene ELLIS (1993) "The Culture of Battering and the Role of Mediation in Domestic Violence Cases," 46 *S.M.U. L. Rev.* 2117.
FISHER, Roger, et al. (1994) *Beyond Machiavelli: Tools for Coping with Conflict.* Cambridge, Mass.: Harvard University Press.
FISHER, Roger, and William URY (1981) *Getting to Yes: Negotiating Agreement Without Giving In.* Boston: Houghton Mifflin
FISHER, Roger, William URY, and Bruce PATTON (1991) *Getting to Yes: Negotiating Agreement Without Giving In* (2d ed.). New York: Penguin.
———(1991) *Getting to Yes: Negotiating Agreement Without Giving In* (2d ed.). Boston: Houghton Mifflin.
FISS, Owen (1984) "Against Settlement," 93 *Yale L.J.* 1073.
FITZGIBBON, Susan A. (2000) "Teaching Unconscionability Through Agreements to Arbitrate Employment Claims," 44 *St. Louis U. L.J.* 1401.

FLORIDA LAW REVIEW (1998) Symposium Issue, Vol. 50 (September).
FLORIDA STATE LAW REVIEW (1991) Symposium Issue, Vol. 19 (Summer).
FOLBERG, Jay (1983) "Divorce Mediation: Promises and Problems." Paper prepared for Midwinter Meeting of ABA Section of Family Law, St. Thomas (January).
FOLBERG, Jay, Dwight GOLANN, Lisa KLOPPENBERG, and Thomas STIPANOWICH (2005) *Resolving Disputes: Theory, Practice and Law.* New York: Aspen.
FOLBERG, Jay, and Joshua KADISH (1987) "Family Law Mediation," in *Arbitration and Mediation.* Lake Oswego: Oregon State Bar Committee on Continuing Legal Education.
FOLBERG, Jay, and Ann MILNE, eds. (1988) *Divorce Mediation: Theory and Practice.* New York: Guilford Press.
FOLBERG, Jay, Ann MILNE, and Peter SALEM, eds. (2004) *Divorce and Family Mediation—Models, Techniques, and Applications.* New York: Guilford.
FOLBERG, Jay, and Alison TAYLOR (1984) *Mediation.* San Francisco: Jossey-Bass.
FOLGER, Joseph (1991) "Assessing Community Dispute Resolution Needs," in Karen Grover Duffy, James Grosch, Paul Olczak, eds. *Community Mediation.* New York: Guilford Press.
FOX, William F., Jr. (1998) *International Commercial Agreements: A Primer on Drafting, Negotiating and Resolving Disputes* (3d ed.). Boston: Kluwer Law International.
———(1992) *International Commercial Agreements* (2d ed.). Boston: Kluwer Law and Taxation Publishers.
FREEDMAN, Larry, and Michael PRIGOFF (1986) "Confidentiality in Mediation: The Need for Protection," 2 *Ohio St. J. Disp. Resol.* 37.
FREEMAN, Jody (1997) "Collaborative Governance in the Administrative State," 45 *UCLA L. Rev.* 1.
FRIEDMAN, Eileen D. (1981) "Protection of Confidentiality in the Mediation of Minor Disputes," 11 *Cap. U. L. Rev.* 181.
FRIEDMAN, Gary (1993) *A Guide to Divorce Mediation.* New York: Workman.
FRIEDMAN, Thomas (2005) *The World Is Flat: A Brief History of the Twenty-first Century.* New York: Farrar, Straus and Giroux.
FULLER, Lon (1978) "The Forms and Limits of Adjudication," 92 *Harv. L. Rev.* 353.
———(1971) "Mediation: Its Forms and Functions," 44 *S. Cal. L. Rev.* 305.
———(1963) "Collective Bargaining and the Arbitrator," 1963 *Wis. L. Rev.* 1.
———(1962) "Collective Bargaining and the Arbitrator," *Proceedings, Fifteenth Annual Meeting, National Academy of Arbitrators.* Washington, D.C.: Bureau of National Affairs.
FUNK, William (1997) "Bargaining Towards the New Millennium: Regulatory Negotiation and the Subversion of the Public Interest," 46 *Duke L.J.* 1351.

GAGNON, Andre G. (1992) "Ending Mandatory Divorce Mediation for Battered Women," 15 *Harv. Women's L.J.* 272.
GALENTER, Marc (2004) "The Vanishing Trial: An Examination of Trials and Related Matters in Federal and State Courts," 1 *J. Empirical Legal Stud.* 459.
———(1988) "The Quality of Settlements," *Mo. J. Disp. Resol.* 55.
———(1986) "The Emergence of the Judge as a Mediator in Civil Cases," 69 *Judicature* 257.
———(1983) "Reading the Landscape of Disputes: What We Know and Don't Know (and Think We Know) About Our Allegedly Contentious and Litigious Society," 31 *UCLA L. Rev.* 4.
GALENTER, Marc, and Mia CAHILL (1994) " 'Most Cases Settle': Judicial Promotion and Regulation of Settlements," 46 *Stan. L. Rev.* 1339.

———(1974) "Why the 'Haves' Come Out Ahead: Speculations on the Limits of Legal Change," 9 *Law & Soc'y Rev.* 95.

GALTON, Eric (1994) *Representing Clients in Mediation.* Dallas: Texas Lawyer Press.

GANGEL-JACOB, Phyllis (1995) "Some Words of Caution About Divorce Mediation," 23 *Hofstra L. Rev.* 825.

GEFFNER, Robert, and Mildred PAGELOW (1990) "Mediation and Child Custody in Abusive Relationships," 8 *Behav. Sci. & L.* 151.

GELFAND, Michele J., and Jeanne M. BRETT, eds. (2004) *The Handbook of Negotiation and Culture.* Stanford, Calif.: Stanford Business Books.

GENN, Hazel (1987) *Hard Bargaining: Out of Court Settlement in Personal Injury Actions.* Oxford: Clarendon Press.

GIBSON, Kevin (1992) "Confidentiality in Mediation: A Moral Reassessment," *J. Disp. Resol.* 25.

GIFFORD, Courtney D., and William P. HOBGOOD (1985) *Directory of U.S. Labor Arbitrators.* Washington, D.C.: Bureau of National Affairs.

GIFFORD, Donald G. (1989) *Legal Negotiation.* St. Paul, Minn.: West.

GLADWELL, Malcolm (2000) *The Tipping Point—How Little Things Can Make a Difference.* Boston: Little, Brown.

GOLANN, Dwight (1997) *Mediating Legal Disputes: Effective Strategies for Lawyers and Mediators.* New York: Aspen Publishers.

———(1989) "Making Alternative Dispute Resolution Mandatory: The Constitutional Issues," 68 *Or. L. Rev.* 487.

GOLDBERG, Stephen B. (1994) "Reflections on Negotiated Rulemaking," 9 *Wash. Law.* 42 (Sept./Oct.).

———(1990) "The Case of the Squabbling Authors: A 'Med-Arb' Response," 6 *Neg. J.* 391.

———(1989) "Grievance Mediation: A Successful Alternative to Labor Arbitration," 5 *Neg. J.* 9.

———(1986) "Meditations of a Mediator," 2 *Neg. J.* 245.

GOLDBERG, Stephen B., and Jeanne M. BRETT (1990) "Disputants' Perspectives on the Differences Between Mediation and Arbitration," 6 *Neg. J.* 249.

GOLDBERG, Stephen B., Jeanne M. BRETT, and William L. URY (1991) "Designing an Effective Dispute Resolution System," in J. Wilkinson, ed., *Donovan Leisure Newton and Irvine ADR Practice Book* 38-47.

GOLDBERG, Stephen B., Eric D. GREEN, and Frank E. A. SANDER (1989) "Litigation, Arbitration or Mediation: A Dialogue," *ABA Journal* 70 (June).

GOLDMANN, Robert, ed. (1980) *Roundtable Justice.* Boulder: Westview Press.

GOLDSTONE, Richard J. (2006) "The South African Truth and Reconciliation Commission: Is It Relevant to the United States?," 12 *Disp. Resol. Mag.* 19.

GORMAN, Robert A. (1995) "The *Gilmer* Decision and the Private Arbitration of Public Law Disputes," 1995 *U. Ill. L. Rev.* 635.

GRAY, Barbara (1989) *Collaborating.* San Francisco: Jossey-Bass.

GRAY, Erika (1992) "One Approach to Diagnostic Assessment of Civil Cases: The Individual Case-Screening Conference," *The Court Manager* 21.

GREATBATCH, David, and Robert DINGWALL (1989) "Selective Facilitation: Some Preliminary Observations on a Strategy Used by Divorce Mediators," 23 *Law & Soc'y Rev.* 613.

GREBE, Sarah Childs (1988) "Structured Mediation and Its Variants: What Makes It Unique," in J. Folberg and A. Milne, eds. *Divorce Mediation: Theory and Practice.* New York: Guilford Press.

GREEN, Eric D. (1986) "A Heretical View of Mediation Privilege," 2 *Ohio St. J. Disp. Resol.* 1.

———(1982a) "The CPR Mini-Trial Handbook," *Corporate Dispute Management.* New York: Matthew Bender.

———(1982b) "Growth of the Mini-Trial," 9 *Litigation* 12 (Fall).

GREEN, Eric D., Jonathan M. MARKS, and Ronald OLSON (1978) "Settling Large Case Litigation: An Alternative Approach," 11 *Loy. L.A. L. Rev.* 493.

GREENBERG, John H., et al., eds. (2000) *Words Over War: Mediation and Arbitration to Prevent Deadly Conflict.* Lanham, MD: Rowman & Littlefield Publishers.

GRILLO, Trina (1991) "The Mediation Alternative: Process Dangers for Women," 100 *Yale L.J.* 1545.

GRING, Pamela (1990) "The Special Master's Role as Mediator," 6 *Ohio St. J. Disp. Resol.* 21.

GROSS, Dick (2002) "A U.S. Consensus Council," *Disp Resol. Mag.* 15 (Winter).

GROSS, Samuel R., and Kent D. SYVERUD (1996) "Don't Try: Civil Jury Verdicts in a System Geared to Settlement," 44 *UCLA L. Rev.* 1.

GUTHRIE, Chris, and James LEVIN (1998) "A 'Party Satisfaction' Perspective on a Comprehensive Mediation Statute," 13 *Ohio St. J. Disp. Resol.* 885.

GUZMAN, Andrew, and Beth A. SIMMONS (2002) "To Settle or Empanel? An Empirical Analysis of Litigation and Settlement at the World Trade Organization," 31 *J. Legal Stud.* 205.

HAMILTON, Michael, and Dominic BRYAN (forthcoming 2007) "Deepening Democracy? Dispute System Design and the Mediation of Contested Parades in Northern Ireland," 22 *Ohio St. J. Disp. Resol.* 1.

HAMMOND, Carly A., and Sarah C. McCARTY (2006) "Ethics in Cross-Cultural Negotiations," in Kristen Blankley, ed. *Cross Cultural Negotiation for U.S. Negotiators* 117-134. Montgomery, Ala.: U.S. Air Force.

HARTER, Philip J. (1997) "Assessing the Assessors," 9 *N.Y.U. Envtl. L.J.* 32.

———(1997) "Negotiating Rules and Other Policies: Pay Close Heed to Structure for Success," *Disp. Resol. Mag.* 15 (Fall).

———(1986) "The Role of the Courts in Reg-Neg: A Response to Judge Wald," 11 *Colum. J. Envtl. L.* 51.

———(1982) "Negotiating Regulations: A Cure for Malaise," 71 *Geo. L.J.* 1.

HARVARD LAW REVIEW (1996) "Developments in the Law—Employment Discrimination," 109 *Harv. L. Rev.* 1568.

———(1990) "Mandatory Mediation and Summary Jury Trial: Guidelines for Ensuring Fair and Effective Processes," 103 *Harv. L. Rev.* 1086.

———(1981) "The California Rent-a-Judge Experiment: Constitutional and Policy Considerations of Pay As You Go Courts," 94 *Harv. L. Rev.* 1592.

HAYFORD, Stephen L. (1996) "Law in Disarray: Judicial Standards for Bacatur of Commercial Arbitration Awards," 20 *Ga. L. Rev.* 731.

HAYFORD, Stephen L., and Alan R. PALMITER (2002) "Arbitration Federalism: A State Role in Commercial Arbitration," 54 *Fla. L. Rev.* 175.

HAYNES, John (1994) *The Fundamentals of Family Mediation.* Albany: State University of New York Press.

———(1984) "Mediated Negotiations—The Function of the Intake," *Mediation Q.* 3 (December).

———(1981) *Divorce Mediation: A Practical Guide for Therapists and Counselors.* New York: Springer.

HAYNES, John M., and Gretchen HAYNES (1993) *Alternative Dispute Resolution: Fundamentals of Family Mediation.* Kent, England: Old Bailey Press.

HEGLAND, Kenny (1982) "Why Teach Trial Advocacy? An Essay on Never Ask Why," in J. Himmelstein and H. Lesnick, eds. *Humanistic Education in Law.* New York: Columbia University School of Law.

HEINSZ, Timothy J. (2001) "The Revised Uniform Arbitration Act: Modernizing, Revising, and Clarifying Arbitration Law," *J. Disp. Resol.* 1.

HENSLER, Deborah R. (1990) "Court-Annexed ADR," in John H. Wilkinson, ed., *Donovan Leisure Newton & Irvine ADR Practice Book.* New York: Wiley.

HERRMAN, Margaret, ed. (2006) *The Blackwell Handbook of Mediation—Bridging Theory, Practice and Research.* Malden, Mass: Blackwell.

HERMANN, Michele (1994) "New Mexico Research Examines Impact of Gender and Ethnicity in Mediation," *Disp. Resol. Mag.* 10 (Fall).

HERMANN, Michele, Gary LAFREE, Christine RACK, and Mary Beth WEST (1993) *The Metrocourt Project Final Report.* Albuquerque: University of New Mexico Center for the Study and Resolution of Disputes.

HINCHCLIFF, Carole (1991) *Dispute Resolution: A Selective Bibliography.* Washington, D.C.: ABA.

HOLBROOKE, Richard (1998) *To End a War.* New York: Random House.

HONEYMAN, Christopher (1990) "On Evaluating Mediators," 6 *Neg. J.* 23.

HOUCK, Stephen D. (1988) "Complex Commercial Arbitration: Designing a Process to Suit the Case," 43 *Arb. J.* 3.

HUBER, Peter (1984) "Competition, Conglomerates, and the Evolution of Cooperation," 93 *Yale L.J.* 1147.

JOHNSON, Tamara (2006) "Power and Authority," in Kristen Blankley, ed. *Cross Cultural Negotiation for U.S. Negotiators.* Montgomery, Ala.: U.S. Air Force.

JUDICIAL CONFERENCE OF THE UNITED STATES (1991) *Report of the Judicial Conference Ad Hoc Committee on Asbestos Litigation.*

KAGEL, Sam, and Kathy KELLY (1989) *The Anatomy of Mediation.* Washington, D.C.: Bureau of National Affairs.

KAKALIK, James S., Terrence DUNWORTH, Laural A. HILL, Daniel McCAFFREY, Marian OSHIRO, Nicholas M. PACE, and Mary A. VAIANA (1996) *An Evaluation of Mediation and Early Neutral Evaluation Under the Civil Justice Reform Act.* Santa Monica: RAND Corp.

———(1996) *Implementation of the Civil Justice Reform Act in Pilot and Comparison Districts.* Santa Monica: Rand Institute for Civil Justice.

KANOWITZ, Leo (1985) *Cases and Materials on Alternative Dispute Resolution.* St. Paul, Minn.: West.

KATSH, Ethan, and Janet RIFKIN (2001) *Online Dispute Resolution.* San Francisco: Jossey-Bass.

KATZ, Lucy V. (1993) "Compulsory Alternative Dispute Resolution and Volunteerism: Two Headed Monster or Two Sides of the Coin?," 1993 *J. Disp. Resol.* 1.

———(1988) Enforcing an ADR Clause—Are Good Intentions All You Have?," 26 *Am. Bus. L.J.* 575.

KEILITZ, Susan, ed. (1993) *National Symposium on Court-Connected Dispute Resolution Research: A Report on Recent Research Findings—Implications for Courts and Future Research Needs.* Williamsburg, Va: National Center for State Courts.

KELLY, Joan B. (1996) "A Decade of Divorce Mediation Research: Some Answers and Questions," 34 *Fam. & Conciliation Cts. Rev.* 373.

———(1995) "Power Imbalance in Divorce and Interpersonal Mediation: Assessment and Intervention," 13 *Mediation Q.* 85.

———(1989) "Dispute Systems Design: A Family Case Study," 4 *Neg. J.* 373.

KELLY, Joan, and Lynn GIGY (1989) "Divorce Mediation: Characteristics of Clients and Outcomes," in Kenneth Kressel and Dean Pruitt, eds. *Mediation Research.* San Francisco: Jossey-Bass.

KENTRA, Pamela A. (1997) "Hear No Evil, See No Evil, Speak No Evil: The Intolerable Conflict for Attorney-Mediators Between the Duty to Maintain Confidentiality and the Duty to Report Fellow Attorney Misconduct," 1997 *B.Y.U. L. Rev.* 715.

KIRTLEY, Alan (1995) "The Mediation Privilege's Transition from Theory to Implementation: Designing a Mediation Privilege Standard to Protect Mediation Participants, the Process and the Public Interest," *J. Disp. Resol.* 1.

KISTHARDT, Mary Kay (1997) "The Use of Mediation and Arbitration for Resolving Family Conflicts: What Lawyers Think About Them," 17 *Am. Acad. of Matrimonial Law* 353.

KNEBEL, Fletcher, and Gerald CLAY (1987) *Before You Sue.* New York: Morrow.

KOCHAN, Thomas A. (1980) *Collective Bargaining and Industrial Relations.* Homewood, Ill.: Richard D. Irwin.

KOLB, Deborah M., and Associates (1994) *When Talk Works: Profiles of Mediators.* San Francisco: Jossey-Bass.

KOLB, Deborah M., and Judith WILLIAMS (2000) *The Shadow Negotiation: How Women Can Master the Hidden Agendas That Determine Bargaining Success.* New York: Simon & Schuster.

KOROBKIN, Russell (2002) *Negotiation Theory and Strategy.* New York: Aspen.

KOVACH, Kimberlee (2001) "New Wine Requires New Wineskins: Transforming Lawyer Ethics for Effective Representation in a Non-Adversarial Approach to Problem Solving: Mediation," 28 *Fordham Urb. L.J.* 935.

———(2000) *Mediation: Principles and Practice.* St. Paul: West.

KREMENIUK, Victor A., ed. (1991) *International Negotiation.* San Francisco: Jossey-Bass.

KRESSEL, Kenneth, and Dean G. PRUITT (1989) *Conclusion: A Research Perspective on the Mediation of Social Conflict,* in Kenneth Kressel, Dean G. Pruitt and Associates, *Mediation Research: The Process and Effectiveness of Third-Party Intervention.* San Francisco: Jossey-Bass.

KRITZER, Herbert M. (1991) *Let's Make a Deal.* Madison: University of Wisconsin Press.

———(1986) "Adjudication to Settlement: Shading in the Gray," 70 *Judicature* 161.

KRIVIS, Jeffrey (2006) *Improvisational Negotiation.* San Francisco: Jossey-Bass.

KUESTER, Erin L. (1995) Comment, "Confidentiality in Mediation: A Trail of Broken Promises," 16 *Hamline J. Pub. L. & Pol'y* 573.

LAX, David A., and James K. SEBENIUS (2006) *3-D Negotiation.* Boston: Harvard Business School Press.

———(1986) *The Manager as Negotiator.* New York: Free Press.

LEATHERBURY, Thomas A., and Mark A. COVER (1993) "Keeping Public Mediation Public: Exploring the Conflict between Confidential Mediation and Open Government," 46 *S.M.U. L. Rev.* 2221.

LeBARON, Michelle (2003) *Bridging Cultural Conflicts: A New Approach for a Changing World.* San Francisco: Jossey-Bass.

LEDERACH, John Paul (1995) *Preparing for Peace: Conflict Transformation Across Cultures.* Syracuse, N.Y.: Syracuse University Press.

LEDERACH, John P., and Janice M. JENNER, eds. (2002) *A Handbook of International Peacemaking: Into the Eye of the Storm.* San Francisco: Jossey-Bass.

LENNANE, Michael T., and Laura E. WEIDNER (2006) "In Each Other We Trust: The Importance of Relationship Building in Cross-Cultural Negotiation," in Kristen Blankley, ed. *Cross Cultural Negotiation for U.S. Negotiators* 47-68. Montgomery, Ala.: U.S. Air Force.

LERMAN, Lisa (1984) "Mediation of Wife Abuse Cases: The Adverse Impact of Informal Dispute Resolution on Women," 7 *Harv. Women's L.J.* 57.

LEVI, Deborah L. (1997) "The Role of Apology in Mediation," 72 *N.Y.U. L. Rev.* 1165.

LEVIN, A. Leo, and Russell WHEELER, eds. (1979) *The Pound Conference: Perspectives on Justice in the Future.* St. Paul: West.

LEVINE, Matthew (1984) "Power Imbalances in Dispute Resolution," in Vermont Law School Dispute Resolution Project, *A Study of Barriers to the Use of Alternative Methods of Dispute Resolution.* South Royalton: Vermont Law School.

LEWICKI, Roy J., et al. (1997) *Essentials of Negotiation.* Chicago: Irwin.

LEWICKI, Roy J., Joseph LITTERER, David M. SAUNDERS, and John W. MINTON (1994) *Negotiation* (2d ed.). Homewood, Ill.: Irwin.

LEWIS, Michael (1995) "Advocacy in Mediation: One Mediator's View," *Disp. Resol. Mag.* 7 (Fall).

LIND, E. Allen, Robert MACCOUN, Patricia EBENER, William FELSTINER, Deborah HENSLER, Judith RESNIK, and Tom TYLER (1990) "In the Eye of the Beholder: Tort Litigants' Evaluations of Their Experiences in the Civil Justice System," 24 *Law & Soc'y Rev.* 953.

LIND, E. Allen, and Tom R. TYLER (1988) *The Social Psychology of Procedural Justice.* New York: Plenum.

LOVE, Lela P. (1997) "The Top Ten Reasons Why Mediators Should Not Evaluate," 24 *Fla. St. U. L. Rev.* 937.

LOVE, Lela P., and Cheryl B. McDONALD (1997) "A Tale of Two Cities: Day Labor and Conflict Resolution for Communities in Crisis," *Disp. Resol. Mag.* 8 (Fall).

LOWENTHAL, Gary T. (1988) "The Bar's Failure to Require Truthful Bargaining by Lawyers," 2 *Geo. J. Legal Ethics* 411.

MACNEIL, Ian R., Richard E. SPEIDEL, and Thomas J. STIPANOWICH (1994) *Federal Arbitration Law—Agreements, Awards, and Remedies Under the Federal Arbitration Act.* Boston: Little, Brown.

Madaripur Legal Aid Association (1996) "Nabin and Nasima: A Clash of Hindu and Muslim Communities," in Fred E. Jandt and Paul B. Pedersen, eds. *Constructive Conflict Management: Asian-Pacific Cases* 76-81. London and New Delhi: Thousand Oaks and Sage Publications.

MAGGIOLO, Walter (1985) *Techniques of Mediation.* New York: Oceana Publications.

MARKS, Jonathan M., Earl JOHNSON, Jr., and Peter L. SZANTON (1984) *Dispute Resolution in America: Processes in Evolution.* Washington, D.C.: National Institute for Dispute Resolution.

MARLOW, Lenard (1997) *Divorce Mediation: A Practice in Search of a Theory.* Garden City, NY: Harlan Press.

MARLOW, Lenard, and S. Richard SAUBER (1990) *The Handbook of Divorce Mediation.* New York: Plenum.

MARSHALL, T. F. (1991) "Mandatory Mediation: Commentary from England," 8 *Conflict Resol. Notes* (June).

MARTIN, John A., and Steven WELLER (2002) "Mediated Child Protection Conferencing: Lessons from the Wisconsin Unified Family Court Project," 41 *Judges' Journal* 5 (Spring).

MAUTE, Judith (1991) "Public Values and Private Justice: A Case for Mediator Accountability," 4 *Geo. J. Legal Ethics* 503.

———(1990) "Mediator Accountability: Responding to Fairness Concerns," *J. Disp. Resol.* 347.

MAX, Eric (1990) *Bench Manual for the Appointment of a Mediator,* reproduced in 136 F.R.D. 499.

MAYER, Bernard (2004) *Beyond Neutrality: Confronting the Crisis in Conflict Resolution.* San Francisco: Jossey-Bass.

McCRORY, John P. (1988) "Confidentiality in Mediation of Matrimonial Disputes," 51 *Mod. L. Rev.* 442.

McEWEN, Craig A., and Richard J. MAIMAN (1989) "Mediation in Small Claims Court: Consensual Processes and Outcomes," in Kenneth Kressel, Dean G. Pruitt and Associates *Mediation Research.* San Francisco: Jossey-Bass.

McEWEN, Craig A., Richard MAIMAN, and Lynn MATHER (1994) "Lawyers, Mediation, and the Management of Divorce Practice," 28 *Law & Soc'y Rev.* 249.

McEWEN, Craig A., and Elizabeth PLAPINGER (1997) "RAND Report Points Way to Next Generation of ADR Research," *Disp. Resol. Mag.* 8 (Summer).

McEWEN, Craig A., and Nancy H. ROGERS (1994) "Bring the Lawyers into Divorce Mediation," *Disp. Resol. Mag.* 8-10 (Summer).

McEWEN, Craig A., Nancy H. ROGERS, and Richard J. MAIMAN (1995) "Bring in the Lawyers: Challenging the Dominant Approaches to Ensuring Fairness in Divorce Mediation," 79 *Minn. L. Rev.* 1319.

McEWEN, Craig A., and Laura C. WILLIAMS (1998) "Legal Policy and Access to Justice Through Courts and Mediation," 13 *Ohio St. J. Disp. Resol.* 865.

McGILL, William J. (1979) "Peacemaking in an Adversary Society," in *The Pound Conference: Perspectives on Justice in the Future.* St. Paul, Minn.: West.

McGILLIS, Daniel (1997) *Community Mediation Programs: Developments and Challenges.* Washington, D.C.: U.S. Department of Justice, National Institute of Justice.

McGOVERN, Francis (1997) "Beyond Efficiency: A Bevy of ADR Justifications," *Disp. Resol. Mag.* 12 (Summer).

———(1986) "Toward a Functional Approach for Managing Complex Litigation," 53 *U. Chi. L. Rev.* 440.

McISAAC, Hugh (2001) "Mediation Developments: Confidentiality Revisited: California Style," 39 *Fam. Ct. Rev.* 405.

MEDIATION QUARTERLY, *Special Issue: Mediation and Spouse Abuse,* vol. 7, no. 4.

MELTSNER, Michael, and Philip G. SCHRAG (1973) "Negotiating Tactics for Legal Services Lawyers," 7 *Clearinghouse Rev.* 259.

MENKEL-MEADOW, Carrie (2001) "Ethics in ADR: The Many 'Cs' of Professional Responsibility and Dispute Resolution," 28 *Fordham Urb. L.J.* 979.

———, ed. (2000) *Mediation—Theory, Policy and Practice.* Burlington, Vt.: Ashgate.

———(1997) "The Silences of the Law Governing Lawyers: Lawyering as Only Adversary Practice," 10 *Geo. J. Legal Ethics* 631.

———(1993) "Public Access to Private Settlements: Conflicting Legal Policies," 11 *Alternatives High Cost Litig.* 85.

———(1991) "Pursuing Settlement in an Adversary Culture: A Tale of Innovation Co-Opted, or 'The Law of ADR,'" 19 *Fla. L. Rev.* 1.

MENKEL-MEADOW, Carrie J., Lela P. LOVE, Andrea K. SCHNEIDER, and Jean R. STERNLIGHT (2005) *Dispute Resolution: Beyond the Adversarial Model.* New York: Aspen.

MENKEL-MEADOW, Carrie, and Michael WHEELER (2004) *What's Fair—Ethics for Negotiators.* San Francisco: Jossey-Bass.

MERRILLS, J.G. (1999) *International Dispute Settlement* (3d ed.). Cambridge: Cambridge University Press.

MERRY, Sally (1990) *Getting Justice and Getting Even: Legal Consciousness of Working-Class Americans.* Chicago: University of Chicago Press.

———(1987) "The Culture and Practice of Mediation in Parent-Child Conflicts," 3 *Neg. J.* 411.

MERRY, Sally, and Neil MILNER (1993) *Popular Justice, Social Transformation and the Ideology of Community: Perspectives on Community Mediation.* Ann Arbor: University of Michigan Press.

MERRY, Sally, and Susan SILBEY (1984) "What Do Plaintiffs Want? Reexamining the Concept of Dispute," 9 *Just. Sys. J.* 151.

METZLOFF, Thomas B., Don R. WILLETT, Jeffrey J. RICE, and Thom H. PETERS (1991) *Summary Juries in the North Carolina State Court System.* Durham: Duke Law School Private Adjudication Center.

MILLER, Arthur R. (1991) "Confidentiality, Protective Orders, and Public Access to the Courts," 105 *Harv. L. Rev.* 427.

MILLER, Richard E., and Austin SARAT (1980-1981) "Grievances, Claims, and Disputes: Assessing the Adversary Culture," 15 *Law & Soc'y Rev.* 525.

MILLHAUSER, Marguerite (1988) "Gladiators and Conciliators: ADR—A Law Firm Staple," 14 *Bar Leader* 20 (Sept.-Oct.).

———(1987) "The Unspoken Resistance to Alternative Dispute Resolution," 3 *Neg. J.* 29.

MINOW, Martha (1998) *Between Vengeance and Forgiveness.* Boston: Beacon Press.

MITCHELL, George J. (1999) *Principles of Peace: Northern Ireland and the Middle East.* Jerusalem: The Hebrew University.

MNOOKIN, Robert H. (1993) "Why Negotiations Fail: An Exploration of Barriers to the Resolution of Conflict," 8 *Ohio St. J. Disp. Resol.* 235.

MNOOKIN, Robert H., and Ronald J. GILSON (1994) "Disputing Through Agents: Cooperation and Conflict Between Lawyers in Litigation," 94 *Colum. L. Rev.* 509.

———(1994) "Cooperation and Conflict Between Litigators," 12 *Alternatives* 125.

MNOOKIN, Robert, and Lewis KORNHAUSER (1979) "Bargaining in the Shadow of the Law: The Case of Divorce," 88 *Yale L.J.* 950.

MNOOKIN, Robert H., Scott PEPPET, and Andrew TULUMELLO (2000) *Beyond Winning: Negotiating to Create Value in Deals and Disputes.* Cambridge, Mass.: Harvard University Press.

———(1996) "The Tension Between Empathy and Assertiveness," 12 *Neg. J.* 217.

MNOOKIN, Robert H., and Lawrence SUSSKIND, eds. (1999) *Negotiating on Behalf of Others.* Thousand Oaks: Sage.

MOFFITT, Michael L., and Robert C. BORDONE, eds. (2005) *Handbook of Dispute Resolution.* San Francisco: Jossey-Bass.

MOORE, Christopher W. (1996) *The Mediation Process* (2d ed.). San Francisco: Jossey-Bass.

———(1988) *Techniques to Break Impasse,* in Jay Folberg and Anne Milne, eds., *Divorce Mediation: Theory and Practice.* New York: Guilford Press.

MORROW, Duncan, and Derick WILSON (1993) "Three into Two Won't Go? From Mediation to New Relationships in Northern Ireland," *NIDR Forum* 13 (Winter).

MOSTEN, Forrest S. (1997) *The Complete Guide to Mediation: The Cutting-Edge Approach to Family Law Practice.* Chicago: ABA.

———(1996) "Preventive Mediation in Blended Families," 3 *Disp. Resol. Mag.* No. 1, at 16.

MOTTEK, Jacqueline E. (2000) "The Impact of Mandatory Arbitration Clauses on Class Certification," 69 *USLW* 2307.

MOVIUS, Hal, Masa MASUURA, Jin YAN, and Dong-Young KIM (2006) "Tailoring the Mutual Gains Approach for Negotiations with Partners in Japan, China, and Korea," 22 *Negot. J.* 389.

MURNIGHAN, J. Keith (1991) *The Dynamics of Bargaining Games.* Englewood Cliffs, N.J.: Prentice-Hall.

MURRAY, John (1984) "Third-Party Intervention: Successful Entry for the Uninvited," 48 *Albany L. Rev.* 573.

MURRAY, John, Alan RAU, and Edward SHERMAN (1991) *Dispute Resolution: Materials for Continuing Legal Education.* Washington, D.C.: Nat. Inst. Disp. Res.

NADER, Laura (1993) "Controlling Processes in the Practice of Law: Hierarchy and Pacification in the Movement to Re-Form Dispute Ideology," 9 *Ohio St. J. Disp. Resol.* 1.

———(1979) "Disputing Without the Force of Law," 88 *Yale L.J.* 998.

NADER, Laura, and Harry TODD (1978) *The Disputing Process: Law in Ten Societies.* New York: Columbia University Press.

NATIONAL INSTITUTE FOR DISPUTE RESOLUTION (1991) "Dispute Resolution in Education," *Forum* (Spring).

———(1987) "Statewide Offices of Mediation: Experiments in Public Policy," *Forum* (December).

NATIONAL LAW JOURNAL (1991) "EPA Calls Off Sessions on Rule," July 8.

NEALE, Margaret A., and Max H. BAZERMAN (1991) *Cognition and Rationality in Negotiation.* New York: Free Press.

NEGOTIATION JOURNAL (1993) "Who Really Is a Mediator? A Special Section on the Interim Guidelines," Vol. 9, p. 290.

NELLE, Andreas (1992) "Making Mediation Mandatory: A Proposed Framework," 7 *Ohio St. J. Disp. Resol.* 287.

NIEMIC, Robert J. (1997) *Mediation and Conference Programs in the Federal Courts of Appeals.* Washington, D.C.: Federal Judicial Center.

NIEMIC, Robert J., Donna STIENSTRA, and Randall E. RAVITZ (2001) *Guide to Judicial Management of Cases in ADR.* Washington, D.C.: Federal Judicial Center.

O'CONNELL, Mary Ellen (2006) *International Dispute Resolution—Cases and Materials.* Durham, N.C.: Carolina Academic Press.

———, ed. (2002) *International Dispute Settlement.* Burlington, VT: Ashgate.

OH, Heidi M. (1996) Note, "Look Before You Leap: The Failed Promises of Child Custody Mediation," 13 *Prob. L.J.* 157.

OHIO STATE JOURNAL ON DISPUTE RESOLUTION (1986) *Symposium on Critical Issues in Mediation Legislation,* Vol. 2, No. 1.

PALEFSKY, Cliff (2001) "Only a Start: ADR Provider Ethics Principles Don't Go Far Enough," *Disp. Resol. Mag.* 19 (Spring).

PARK, William W. (1995) *International Forum Selection.* Boston: Kluwer Law and Taxation Publishers.

PEARSON, Jessica (1994) "Family Mediation," in *National Symposium on Court-Connected Dispute Resolution Research, A Report on Current Research Findings—Implications for Courts and Future Research Needs* 51-77. Washington, D.C.: State Justice Institute.

———(1991) "The Equity of Mediated Divorce Agreements," 9 *Mediation Q.* 179.

PEARSON, Jessica, and Nancy THOENNES (1989) "Divorce Mediation: Reflections on a Decade of Research," in Kenneth Kressel, Dean G. Pruitt, and Associates, *Mediation Research.* San Francisco: Jossey-Bass.

———(1988) "Divorce Mediation Results," in Jay Folberg and Ann Milne, eds. *Divorce Mediation: Theory and Practice,* 429. New York: Guilford Press.

PETROFF, Ronald R., and Leslie E. SIEGEL (2006) "The View from Abroad: How the International Community Perceives Americans," in Kristen Blankley, ed. *Cross Cultural Negotiation for U.S. Negotiators* 95-103. Montgomery, Ala.: U.S. Air Force.

PIOR, Anne (1993) "What Do the Parties Think? A Follow-Up Study of the Marriage Guidance South Australia (MGSA) Family Mediation Project," 4 *Australian Disp. Resol. J.* 99.

PIPER, Christine (1993) *The Responsible Parent: A Study in Divorce Mediation.* New York: Harvester Wheatsheat.

PLAPINGER, Elizabeth, and Margaret SHAW (1992) *Court ADR: Elements for Program Design.* New York: Center for Public Resources Institute for Dispute Resolution.

PLAPINGER, Elizabeth, and Donna STIENSTRA (1996) *ADR and Settlement in the Federal District Courts.* Washington, D.C.: The Federal Judicial Center. New York: The CPR Institute for Dispute Resolution.

PORTLAND MEDIATION SERVICE (1992) *Mediation in Cases of Domestic Abuse: Helpful Option or Unacceptable Risks? The Final Report of the Domestic Abuse and Mediation Project.* Portland, Me.: Portland Mediation Service.

POSNER, Richard (1986) "The Summary Jury Trial and Other Methods of Alternative Dispute Resolution: Some Cautionary Observations," 53 *U. Chi. L. Rev.* 366.

PRIGOFF, Michael L. (1988) "Toward Candor or Chaos: The Case of Confidentiality in Mediation," 12 *Seton Hall Legis. J.* 1.

PRINCEN, Thomas (1992) *Intermediaries in International Conflict.* Princeton: Princeton University Press.

———(1987) "International Mediation—The View from the Vatican; Lessons from Mediating the Beagle Channel Dispute," 3 *Neg. J.* 347 (Oct.).

PRITZKER, David M., and Deborah S. DALTON, eds. (1990) *Negotiated Rulemaking Sourcebook.* Washington, D.C.: U.S. Government Printing Office.

PROVINE, D. Marie (1986) *Settlement Strategies for Federal District Court Judges.* Washington, D.C.: Federal Judicial Center.

PRYOR, Will, and Robert M. O'BOYLE (1993) "Public Policy ADR: Confidentiality in Conflict," 46 *S.M.U. L. Rev.* 2207.

QUANDT, William (1988) *The Middle East.* Washington, D.C.: Brookings Institution.

RACK, Robert W., Jr., (1998) "Settle or Withdraw: Collaborative Lawyering Provides Incentive to Avoid Costly Litigation," *Disp. Resol. Mag.* 8 (Summer).

RAIFFA, Howard (1982) *The Art and Science of Negotiation.* Cambridge, Mass.: Harvard University Press.

RAIFFA, Howard, John RICHARDSON, and David Metcalfe (2003) *Negotiation Analysis: The Science and Art of Collaborative Decision Making.* Cambridge, Mass.: Harvard University Press.

RAU, Alan, Edward F. SHERMAN, and Scott R. PEPPET (2002) *Processes of Dispute Resolution: The Role of Lawyers* (3d ed.). New York: Foundation Press.

RAVEN, Robert D. (1988) "Private Judging: A Challenge to Public Justice," 74 *A.B.A. J.* 8 (September).

RAY, Larry (1985) "The Multi-Door Courthouse Idea: Building the Courthouse of the Future . . . Today," 1 *Ohio St. J. Disp. Resol.* 7.

REDDY, Vinay (2006) "Managing Assumptions About the Negotiation Process," in Kristen Blankley, ed. *Cross Cultural Negotiation for U.S. Negotiators* 95-103. Montgomery, Ala.: U.S. Air Force.

REICH, J. Brad (2001) "A Call for Intellectual Honesty: A Response to the Uniform Mediation Act's Privilege Against Disclosure," *J. Disp. Resol.* 197.

RESNIK, Judith (1995) "Many Doors? Closing Doors? Alternative Dispute Resolution and Adjudication," 10 *Ohio St. J. Disp. Resol.* 211.

———(1994) "Whose Judgment? Vacating Judgments, References for Settlement, and the Role of Adjudication at the Close of the Twentieth Century," 41 *UCLA L. Rev.* 1471.

———(1982) "Managerial Judges," 96 *Harv. L. Rev.* 376.

REUBEN, Richard C. (2007) "Tort Reform Renews Debate over Mandatory Mediation," 13 *Disp. Resol. Mag.* 2 (Winter).

———(2002) "*Howsam, First Options,* and the Demise of Separability: Restoring Access to Justice for Contracts with Arbitration Provisions," 56 *SMU L. Rev.* 000.

REUBEN, Richard C., and Nancy H. ROGERS (1999) "Choppy Waters: Movement Toward a Uniform Confidentiality Privilege Faces Cross Currents," 5 *Disp. Resol. Mag.* 4 (Winter).

RIFKIN, Janet, and Joanne SAWYER (1982) "Alternative Dispute Resolution: From a Legal Services Perspective," *NLADA Briefcase* 20 (Fall).

RIMELSPACH, René L. (2002) "Mediating Family Disputes in a World with Domestic Violence: How to Devise a Safe and Effective Court-Connected Mediation Program," 17 *Ohio St. J. Disp. Resol.* 95.

RISKIN, Leonard L. (1996) "Understanding Mediators' Orientations, Strategies, and Techniques: A Grid for the Perplexed," *Harv. Neg. L. Rev.* 7.

———(1993) "Mediator Orientations, Strategies and Techniques," *Alternatives* 111 (Sept.).

———(1991) "The Represented Client in a Settlement Conference: The Lessons of *G. Heileman Brewing Co. v. Joseph Oat Corp.*, 69 *Wash. U. L. Q.* 1059.

———, ed. (1985) *Divorce Mediation: Readings.* Washington, D.C.: ABA.

———(1984) "Toward New Standards for the Neutral Lawyer in Mediation," 26 *Ariz. L. Rev.* 329.

———(1982) "Mediation and Lawyers," 43 *Ohio St. L.J.* 29.

RISKIN, Leonard L., James E. WESTBROOK, Chris GUTHRIE, Timothy J. HEINSZ, Richard C. REUBEN, and Jennifer K. ROBBENNHOLT (2005) *Dispute Resolution and Lawyers* (3d ed.). St. Paul, Minn.: West.

RIVKIN, David (1991) "International Arbitration," in Richard Medalie, ed. *Commercial Arbitration for the 1990s.* Chicago: American Bar Association, Litigation Section.

ROACH, Steven Robert (2006) "Effectively Using Interested-Based Negotiation in the Cross-Cultural Context," in Kristen Blankley, ed. *Cross Cultural Negotiation for U.S. Negotiators* 95-103. Montgomery, Ala.: U.S. Air Force.

ROGERS, Nancy H., and Craig A. McEWEN (1998) "Employing the Law to Increase the Use of Mediation and to Encourage Direct and Early Negotiations," 13 *Ohio St. J. Disp. Resol.* 831.

———(1989 & 1991 Supp.) *Mediation: Law, Policy, Practice.* Rochester, N.Y.: Lawyers Co-operative & Clark Boardman Callaghan.

ROGERS, Nancy, and Richard SALEM (1987) *A Student's Guide to Mediation and the Law.* New York: Matthew Bender.

ROGERS, Stephen C. (2001) "Can Tripartite Arbitration Panels Reach Fair Results?" 8 *Disp. Resol. Mag.* 27 (Fall).

ROLPH, Elizabeth, Eric MOLLER, and Laura PETERSON (1994) *Escaping the Courthouse: Private Alternative Dispute Resolution in Los Angeles.* Santa Monica: Rand Institute for Civil Justice.

ROSENBERG, Joshua P. (1994) "Keeping the Lid on Confidentiality: Mediation Privilege and Conflict of Laws," 10 *Ohio St. J. Disp. Resol.* 157.

———(1991) "In Defense of Mediation," 33 *Ariz. L. Rev.* 467.

ROSENTHAL, Douglas (1974) *Lawyer and Client: Who's in Charge.* New York: Russell Sage.

ROSS, Jerome (1984) "Should the Mediator Raise Public Interest Considerations During Negotiations," *SPIDR, Ethical Issues in Dispute Resolution,* 1983 Annual Proceedings 50.

ROTHMAN, Jay (1997) *Resolving Identity-Based Conflict in Nations, Organizations, and Communities.* San Francisco: Josscy-Bass.

ROWE, Mary P. (1991) "The Ombudsman's Role in a Dispute Resolution System," 7 *Neg. J.* 353.

RUBIN, Alvin B. (1975) "A Causerie on Lawyers' Ethics in Negotiation," 35 *La. L. Rev.* 577.

RUBIN, Jeffrey Z., and Jeswald SALACUSE (1993) "Culture and International Negotiation: Lessons for Business," *Alternatives to the High Cost Litig.* 95 (July).

RUBIN, Jeffrey Z., and Frank E. A. SANDER (1991) "Culture, Negotiation, and the Eye of the Beholder," 7 *Neg. J.* 249.

———(1988) "When Should We Use Agents? Direct vs. Representative Negotiation," 4 *Neg. J.* 395.

RUFENACHT, Mindy D. (2000) "Comment, The Concern Over Confidentiality in Mediation—An In-Depth Look at the Protection Provided by the Proposed Uniform Mediation Act," 86 *Marq. L. Rev.* 1.

SACHS, Albie (2002) "South African's Truth and Reconciliation Commission," 34 *Conn. L. Rev.* 1037.

SAID, Irene Stanley (1995) Comment, "The Mediator's Dilemma: The Legal Requirements Exception to Confidentiality under the Texas ADR Statute," 36 *S. Tex. L. Rev.* 579.

St. ANTOINE, Theodore J. (2001) "The Changing Role of Labor Arbitration," 76 *Ind. L.J.* 83.

SALACUSE, Jeswald W. (1998) "Ten Ways That Culture Affects Negotiating Style: Some Survey Results," 14 *Neg. J.* 249.

———(1993) "Implications for Practitioners," in Guy Olivier Faure and Jeffrey Z. Rubin, eds. *Culture and Negotiation* 199-208. Newbury Park, Cal.: Sage Publications.

SALEM, Paul, ed. (1997) *Conflict Resolution in the Arab World: Selected Essays.* Beirut: American University of Beirut.

SALEM, Richard A. (1985a) "The Alternative Dispute Resolution Movement: An Overview," 40 *Arb. J.* 3 (September).

———(1985b) "Mediation as an Alternative to Civil Rights Litigation," in Carl F. Pinkele and William C. Louthan, eds. *Discretion, Justice, and Democracy* 90-101. Ames: Iowa State University Press.

SANDER, Frank E.A. (2007) "Another View of Mandatory Mediation," 13 *Disp. Resol. Mag.* 13 (Winter).

———(2000) "The Future of ADR," 2000 *J. Disp. Resol.* 1

———(1992) "Paying for ADR," *A.B.A. J.* 105 (February).

———, ed. (1991) *Emerging ADR Issues in State and Federal Courts.* Chicago: ABA Section on Litigation.

———(1985) "Alternative Methods of Dispute Resolution: An Overview," 37 *U. Fla. L. Rev.* 1.

———(1984) *Mediation: A Selected Annotated Bibliography.* Washington, D.C.: American Bar Association.

———(1976) "Varieties of Dispute Processing," 70 F.R.D. 111.

SANDER, Frank E. A., H. William ALLEN, and Deborah HENSLER (1996) "Judicial (Mis)Use of ADR? A Debate," 27 *U. Tol. L. Rev.* 885.

SANDER, Frank E. A., and Mark C. FLEMING (1996) "Arbitration of Employment Disputes Under Federal Protective Statutes: How Safe Are Employment Rights?," *Disp. Resol. Mag.* 13 (Spring).

SANDER, Frank E. A., and Stephen B. GOLDBERG (1994) "Fitting the Forum to the Fuss: A User-Friendly Guide to Selecting an ADR Procedure," 10 *Neg. J.* 49.

SANDER, Frank E. A., and Michael PRIGOFF (1990) "Professional Responsibility: Should There Be a Duty to Advise of ADR Options?," 76 *A.B.A. J.* 50 (November).

SANDER, Frank E. A., and Jeffrey Z. RUBIN (1988) "The Janus Quality of Negotiations: Dealmaking and Dispute Settlement," 4 *Neg. J.* 109.

SANDER, Frank E. A., and Frederick E. SYNDER (1979) *Alternative Methods of Dispute Settlement—A Selected Bibliography.* Washington, D.C.: ABA.

SAPOSNEK, Donald T. (1998) *Mediating Child Custody Disputes.* San Francisco: Jossey-Bass.

———(1983) *Mediating Child Custody Disputes.* San Francisco: Jossey-Bass.

SAVAGE, Cynthia A. (1996) "Culture and Mediation: A Red Herring," 5 *Am. U. J. Gender & L.* 269.

SCHELLING, Thomas C. (1984) *Choice and Consequence.* Cambridge, Mass.: Harvard University Press.

SCHNEIDER, Andrea K. (2002) "Shattering Negotiation Myths: Empirical Evidence on the Effectiveness of Negotiation Style," 7 *Harv. Neg. L. Rev.* 143.

———(2001) "Introduction: Which Means to an End Under the Uniform Mediation Act," 86 *Marq. L. Rev.* 1.

SCHNEIDER, A.K., and Christopher HONEYMAN, eds. (2006) *Negotiator's Fieldbook.* Washington, D.C.: ABA Section of Dispute Resolution.

SCHWEBEL, Andrew I., and Milton SCHWEBEL (1996) "Mediating with Children: Two Psychologists' Views," 3 *Disp. Resol. Mag.* No.1, at 3.

SELMI, Michael (1996) "The Value of the EEOC: Reexamining the Agency's Role in Employment Discrimination Law," 57 *Ohio St. L.J.* 1.

SENGER, Jeffrey M. (2004) *Federal Dispute Resolution.* San Francisco: Jossey-Bass.

SHAW, Margaret L., and Lynn COHN (1999) "Employment Class Action Settlements Provide Unique Context for ADR," *Disp. Resol. Mag.* 10 (Summer).

SHAW, Margaret L., and Elizabeth PLAPINGER (2001) "Ethical Guidelines—ADR Provider Organizations Should Increase Transparency, Disclosure," *Disp. Resol. Mag.* 14. (Spring).

SHELL, G. Richard (1999) *Bargaining for Advantage.* New York: Viking.

———(1991) "When Is It Legal to Lie in Negotiations?" *Sloan Mgmt. Rev.* 93 (Spring).

SHERMAN, Edward (1993) "Court-Mandated Alternative Dispute Resolution: What Form of Participation Should Be Required?," 46 *SMU L. Rev.* 2079.

SHONHOLTZ, Ray (1984) "Neighborhood Justice Systems: Work, Structure, and Guiding Principles." 5 *Mediation Q.* (September).

SIEMER, Deanne C. (1991) "Perspectives of Advocates and Clients on Court-Sponsored ADR," in *Emerging ADR Issues in State and Federal Courts.* Chicago: ABA Litigation Section.

SILBERMAN, Linda (1982) "Professional Responsibility Problems of Divorce Meditation," 16 *Fam. L.Q.* 107.

SIMKIN, William E., and Nicholas A. FIDANDIS (1986) *Mediation and the Dynamics of Collective Bargaining* (2d ed.). Washington, D.C.: Bureau of National Affairs.

SIMON, William (1985) "Legal Informality and Redistributive Politics," 19 *Clearinghouse Rev.* 385.

SINGER, Linda R. (1994) *Settling Disputes: Conflict Resolution in Business, Families, and the Legal System* (2d ed.). Boulder: Westview Press.

———(1990) *Settling Disputes.* Boulder: Westview Press.

SLAIKEU, Karl A. (1996) *When Push Comes to Shove: A Practical Guide to Mediating Disputes.* San Francisco: Jossey-Bass.

———(1989) "Designing Dispute Resolution Systems in the Health Care Industry," 4 *Neg. J.* 395.

SMITH, David (1978) "A Warmer Way of Disputing: Mediation and Conciliation," 26 *Am. J. Comp. L.* 365.

SMITH, William (1985) "Effectiveness of the Biased Mediator," 1 *Neg. J.* 363.

SNAPP, Kent (1997) "Five Years of Random Testing Shows Early ADR Successful," *Disp. Resol. Mag.* 16 (Summer).

SOCIETY OF PROFESSIONALS IN DISPUTE RESOLUTION (1998) *Guidelines for Voluntary Mediation Programs Instituted by Agencies Charged with Enforcing Workplace Rights, Report of the Law and Public Policy Committee.*

———(1997) *Best Practices for Government Agencies—Guidelines for Using Collaborative Agreement-Seeking Processes. Report of the Environment/Public Dispute Sector.* http://www.acresolution.org/research.nsf/key/EPPbestpractices.

———(1995) *Ensuring Competence and Quality in Dispute Resolution Practice, Report #2 of the SPIDR Commission on Qualifications.*

———(1990) *Mandated Participation and Settlement Coercion: Dispute Resolution as It Relates to the Courts. Report 1 of the Law and Public Policy Committee of SPIDR.*

———(1989) *Report of The SPIDR Commission on Qualifications.*

SOHN, Louis B. (1983) "The Future of Dispute Settlement," in R. St. J. McDonald and D. M. Johnston, eds. *The Structure and Process of International Law: Essays in Legal Philosophy, Doctrines & Theory.* Hingham, Mass.: Martinus Nijhoff.

SOMARY, Karen, and Robert EMERY (1991) "Emotional Anger and Grief in Divorce Mediation, 8 *Mediation Q.* 185.

SPEIDEL, Richard E. (1989) "Arbitration of Statutory Rights Under the Federal Arbitration Act: The Case for Reform," 4 *Ohio St. J. Disp. Resol.* 157.

SPENCER, Janet M., and Joseph P. ZAMMIT (1976) "Mediation-Arbitration: A Proposal for Private Resolution of Disputes Between Divorced or Separated Parents," 1976 *Duke L.J.* 911.

STARK, James H. (1997) "The Ethics of Mediation Evaluation: Some Troublesome Questions and Tentative Proposals From an Evaluative Lawyer Mediator," 38 *S. Tex. L. Rev.* 769.

STATE OF MAINE JUDICIAL BRANCH (1997) *Domestic Abuse Screening and Assessment Guidelines.* West Bath, Me.: Court Alternative Dispute Resolution Service.

STEMPEL, Jeffrey W. (1996) "Reflections on Judicial ADR and the Multi-Door Courthouse at Twenty: Fait Accompli, Failed Overture, or Fledgling Adulthood?," 11 *Ohio St. J. Disp. Resol.* 297.

STERNLIGHT, Jean R. (2000) "As Mandatory Binding Arbitration Meets the Class Action, Will the Class Action Survive," 42 *Wm. & Mary L. Rev.* 1.

STONE, Douglas, Bruce PATTON, and Sheila HEEN (1999) *Difficult Conversations.* New York: Viking.

STONE, Katherine V.W. (2000) *Private Justice: The Law of Alternative Dispute Resolution.* New York: Foundation Press.

STULBERG, Joseph (2005) "Mediation and Justice: What Standards Govern?," 6 *Cardozo J. Conflict Resol.* 213.

———(1990) "Tactics of the Mediator," in John H. Wilkinson, ed. *Donovan Leisure Newton & Irvine ADR Practice Book* 137. New York: Wiley.

———(1987) *Taking Charge/Managing Conflict.* Lexington, Mass.: Lexington Books.

———(1981) "The Theory and Practice of Mediation: A Reply to Professor Susskind," 6 *Vt. L. Rev.* 85.

SUN, Jeffrey C. (1999) "University Officials as Administrators and Mediators: The Dual Role Conflict and Confidentiality Problems," *BYU Educ. & L.J.* 19.

SUPERIOR COURT OF THE DISTRICT OF COLUMBIA (1990) *ADR Case Classification System.*

SUSSKIND, Lawrence E. (2000) "Confessions of a Public Dispute Mediator," 16 *Neg. J.* 129.

———(1995) "Environmental Mediation: Theory and Practice Reconsidered," Workshop on Environmental Mediation and Negotiation," Int. Acad. of the Environment.

———(1991) "Public Policy Disputes in the Courts: The Promise of Mediation" in *Emerging ADR Issues in State and Federal Courts.* ABA Section of Litigation.

———(1981) "Environmental Mediation and the Accountability Problem," 6 *Vt. L. Rev.* 1.

SUSSKIND, Lawrence, and Jeffrey CRUIKSHANK (2006) *Breaking Robert's Rules.* New York: Oxford University Press.

———(1987) *Breaking The Impasse.* New York: Basic Books.

SUSSKIND, Lawrence E., and Patrick FIELD (1996) *Dealing with an Angry Public: The Mutual Gains Approach to Resolving Disputes.* New York: Free Press.

SUSSKIND, Lawrence, Paul F. LEVY, and Jennifer THOMAS-LARMER, eds. (2000) *Negotiating Environmental Agreements: How to Avoid Escalating Confrontation, Needless Costs, and Unnecessary Litigation.* Washington, D.C.: Island Press.

SUSSKIND, Lawrence, and Gerald McMAHON (1985) "The Theory and Practice of Negotiated Rulemaking," 3 *Yale J. Reg.* 133.

SUSSKIND, Lawrence, Sarah McKEARNAN, and Jennifer THOMAS-LARMER, eds. (1999) *The Consensus Building Handbook: A Comprehensive Guide to Reaching Agreement.* Thousand Oaks: Sage Publications.

SUSSKIND, Lawrence, Mieke van der WANSEM, and Armand CICCARELLI (2000) *Mediating Land Use Disputes: Pros and Cons.* Cambridge, Mass.: Lincoln Institute of Land Policy.

SWIRE, Peter (1998) "Of Elephants, Mice, and Privacy: International Choice of Law and the Internet," 32 *Int'l Law.* 991.

SYKES, Andrew (1989) Comment, "*Cincinnati Gas & Electric v. General Electric*—Extinguishing the Light on Summary Jury Trials," 49 *Ohio St. L.J.* 1453.

SYMPOSIUM (2000) "ADR in Cyberspace," 15 *Ohio St. J. Disp. Resol.* No. 3.

SYMPOSIUM ON ARBITRATION (1998) *Disp. Resol. Mag.* (Fall).

SYMPOSIUM ON VANISHING TRIAL (2006) *J. Disp. Resol.* 1.

TAYLOR, Garrett S. (2001) "Be Careful What You Say in Mediation," *J. Disp. Resol.* 375.

TENEROWICZ, Matthew A. (1998) "Case Dismissed—or Is It? Sanctions for Failure to Participate in Court Mandated ADR," 13 *Ohio St. J. Disp. Resol.* 975.

TERRELL, Timothy (1987) "Rights and Wrongs in the Rush to Repose: On Jurisprudential Dangers of Alternative Dispute Resolution," 36 *Emory L.J.* 541.

TESLER, Pauline H. (2001) *Collaborative Law.* Chicago: ABA Section on Family Law.

THOENNES, Nancy, Jessica PEARSON, and Julie BELL (1991) *Evaluation of the Use of Mandatory Divorce Mediation.* Denver: Center for Policy Research.

THOMPSON, Leigh (1998) *The Mind and Heart of the Negotiator.* Upper Saddle River, N.J.: Prentice-Hall.

THOMPSON, Peter N. (1997) "Confidentiality Competency and Confusion: The Uncertain Promise of the Mediation Privilege in Minnesota," 18 *Hamline J. Pub. L. & Pol'y* 329.

TOMASIC, Roman (1983) "Mediation as an Alternative to Adjudication: Rhetoric and Reality in the Neighborhood Justice Movement." In Roman Tomasic and Malcolm Feeley (eds.) *Neighborhood Justice: Assessment of an Emerging Idea.* New York: Longman.

TOUVAL, Sadia, and I. William ZARTMAN, eds. (1985) *International Mediation in Theory and Practice.* Boulder: Westview.

TRACHTE-HUBER, E. Wendy, and Steven P. HUBER (1996) *Alternative Dispute Resolution.* Cincinnati: Anderson.

TREUTHART, Mary Pat (1993) "In Harm's Way? Family Mediation and the Role of the Attorney Advocate," 32 *Golden Gate U. L. Rev.* 717.

TYLER, Tom R. (1989) "The Quality of Dispute Resolution Processes and Outcome: Measurement Problems and Possibilities," 66 *U. Denv. L. Rev.* 419.

UNITED NATIONS CODIFICATION DIVISION (1992) *Handbook on the Peaceful Settlement of Disputes Between States.* New York: United Nations.

UNIVERSITY OF CHICAGO LEGAL FORUM (1987) *Consent Decrees: Practical Problems and Legal Dilemmas.*

URY, William (1991) *Getting Past No: Negotiating with Difficult People.* New York: Bantam Books.

URY, William, Jeanne M. BRETT, and Stephen B. GOLDBERG (1988) *Getting Disputes Resolved: Designing Systems to Cut the Costs of Conflict.* San Francisco: Jossey-Bass.

U.S. COMMISSION ON CIVIL RIGHTS (1982) *Under Rule of Thumb: Battered Women and the Administration of Justice.* Washington, D.C.: Government Printing Office.

U.S. DEPARTMENT OF JUSTICE (2005) *Community Relations Service Annual Report.* Available at www.justice.gov/crs/pubs/fy2005/annualreport2005.pdf.

VAGTS, Detlev (1987) *Dispute Resolution Mechanisms in International Business.* Boston: Martinus Nijhoff.

VAN WINKLE, John (2000) *Mediation—A Path Back for the Lost Lawyer.* Washington, D.C.: ABA.

VARADY, Tibor, John J. BARCELO, and Arthur T. VON MEHREN (2006) *International Commercial Arbitration* (3d ed.). St. Paul: West.

VERMONT LAW SCHOOL DISPUTE RESOLUTION PROJECT (1987) *The Role of Mediation in Divorce Proceedings: A Comparative Perspective (United States, Canada, and Great Britain).* South Royalton, Vt.: Vermont Law School.

VERZIJL, J.H.W., VIII (1976) *International Law in Historical Perspective: Inter-State Disputes and Their Settlement* (vol. 8). Leyden: A.W. Sitjthoff.

WAGATSUMA, Hiroshi, and Arthur ROSETT (1986) "The Implications of Apology: Law and Culture in Japan and the United States," 20 *Law & Soc'y Rev.* 461.

WALD, Patricia W. (1985) "Negotiation of Environmental Disputes: A New Role for the Courts?," 10 *Colum. J. Envtl. L.* 1.

WALDOCK, M., ed. (1972) *International Disputes: The Legal Aspects.* London: Europa Publications.

WALL, James, Lawrence SCHILLER, and Ronald EBERT (1984) "Should Judges Grease the Slow Wheels of Justice? A Survey on the Effectiveness of Judicial Mediary Techniques," 8 *Am. J. Trial Advoc.* 83.

WALL, Victor D., Jr., and Marcia L. DEWHURST (1991) "Mediator Gender: Communication Differences in Resolved and Unresolved Mediations," 9 *Mediation Q.* 63.

WALLERSTEIN, Judith S., and Sandra BLAKESLEE (1990) *Second Chances: Men, Women, and Children a Decade After Divorce.* New York: Houghton Mifflin.

WANG, Xi Scott (2006) "Tit for Tat in the Global Perspective," in Kristen Blankley, ed. *Cross Cultural Negotiation for U.S. Negotiators* 25-45. Montgomery, Ala.: U.S. Air Force.

WARE, Stephen J. (2001) *Alternative Dispute Resolution.* St. Paul: West.

WATKINS, Michael, and Kirsten LUNDBERG (1998) "Getting to the Table in Oslo: Driving Forces and Channel Factors," 14 *Neg. J.* 115.

WATKINS, Michael, and Susan ROSENGRANT (2001) *Breakthrough International Negotiations.* San Francisco: Jossey-Bass.

WEAVER, Gary, ed. (2000) *Culture, Communication and Conflict: Readings in Intercultural Relations.* Upper Saddle River, N.J.: Pearson Custom Press.

WECKSTEIN, Donald T. (1996) "Mediation Certification: Why and How?," 30 *U.S.F. L. Rev.* 757.

WEINSTEIN, Jack B. (1996) "Some Benefits and Risks of Privatization of Justice Through ADR," 11 *Ohio St. J. Disp. Resol.* 241.

WEISE, Richard H. (1989) "The ADR Program at Motorola," 4 *Neg. J.* 381.

WELSH, Nancy A. (2001a) "The Thinning Vision of Self-Determination in Court-Connected Mediation," 6 *Harv. Neg. L. Rev.* 1.

———(2001b) "Making Deals in Court-Connected Mediation: What's Justice Got to Do With It?," 79 *Wash. U. L.Q.* 787.

WESTON, Maureen A. (2001) "Checks on Participant Conduct in Compulsory ADR: Reconciling the Tension in the Need for Good-Faith Participation, Autonomy, and Confidentiality," 76 *Ind. L.J.* 591.

WETLAUFER, Gerald B. (1990) "The Ethics of Lying in Negotiations," 75 *Iowa L. Rev.* 1219.

WHITE, James (1984) "The Pros and Cons of 'Getting to Yes,' " 34 *J. Legal Educ.* 115.

———(1980) "Machiavelli and the Bar: Ethical Limitations on Lying in Negotiation," *Am. B. Found. Res. J.* 926.

WIEHL, Lis (1989) "Private Justice for a Fee: Profits and Problems," N.Y. Times, Feb. 17, p. B5.

WILLNER, Gabriel M. (2005 & Supps.) *Domke on Commercial Arbitration.* Deerfield, Ill.: Callaghan.

WILLIAMS, Gerald (1996) "Negotiation as a Healing Process," *J. Disp. Resol.* 1.

———(1983) *Legal Negotiation and Settlement.* St. Paul: West.

WISSLER, Roselle L. (2002) "Court-Connected Mediation in General Civil Cases: What We Know from Empirical Research," 17 *Ohio St. J. Disp. Resol.* 641.

———(1997) *Evaluation of Settlement Week Mediation.* Columbus: Supreme Court of Ohio.

———(1996) *Ohio Attorneys' Experience with and Views of Alternative Dispute Resolution Procedures.* Columbus: Supreme Court of Ohio.

WOODS, Laurie (1985) "Mediation: A Backlash to Women's Progress on Domestic Violence Issues," 19 *Clearinghouse Rev.* 431.

WORTHING, Elizabeth M. (2006) "Collision Course: Avoiding Clashes on Agenda in Cross-Cultural Negotiations," in Kristen Blankley, ed. *Cross Cultural Negotiation for U.S. Negotiators* 137-142. Montgomery, Ala.: U.S. Air Force.

WRIGHT, Martin, and Burt GALAWAY, eds. (1989) *Mediation and Criminal Justice.* London: Sage Publications.

YAFFE, James (1972) *So Sue Me! The Story of a Community Court.* New York: Saturday Review Press.

YELLOTT, Ann (1990) "Mediation and Domestic Violence: A Call for Collaboration," 8 *Mediation Q.* 39.

ZARTMAN, I. William (1989) *Ripe for Resolution: Conflict and Intervention in Africa.* New York: Oxford University Press.

———(1976) *The 50% Solution.* Garden City, N.Y.: Anchor.

ZARTMAN, I. William, and Maureen K. BERMAN (1982) *The Practical Negotiator.* New Haven: Yale University Press.

ZARTMAN, I. William, and J. Lewis RASMUSSEN, eds. (1997) *Peacemaking in International Conflict: Methods and Techniques.* Washington, D.C.: United States Institute of Peace Press.

ZEUGHAUSER, Peter R. (1997) "Price and Product: A Proposal for a Focused ADR Structure," *Alternatives* 1 (November).

ZYLSTRA, Alexandria (2001) "Privacy: The Road from Voluntary Mediation to Mandatory Good Faith Requirements: A Road Best Left Untraveled," 17 *J. Am. Acad. Matrimonial Law* 69.

Index

References are to page numbers.